Invitation to PSYCHOLOGY

Invitation to PSYCHOLOGY

SECOND CANADIAN EDITION

CAROLE WADE
Dominican University of California

CAROL TAVRIS

GARY POOLE
University of British Columbia

Toronto

Library and Archives Canada Cataloguing in Publication

Wade, Carole
    Invitation to psychology / Carole Wade, Carol Tavris, Gary Poole.—2nd Canadian ed.

Includes bibliographical references and index.
ISBN 0-13-127557-7

1. Psychology—Textbooks. I. Tavris, Carol II. Poole, Gary, 1950– III. Title.

BF121.W24 2006 fol.   150   C2005-906477-3

ISBN 0-13-127557-7

Vice-President, Editorial Director: Michael J. Young
Senior Acquisitions Editor: Ky Pruesse
Executive Marketing Manager: Judith Allen
Senior Developmental Editor: John Polanszky
Production Editor: Charlotte Morrison-Reed
Substantive Editor: Karen Alliston
Copy Editor: Lenore Latta
Proofreaders: Tally Morgan, Claudia Forgas
Production Manager: Wendy Moran
Composition: Christine Velakis
Photo and Permissions Research: Terri Rothman
Art Director: Julia Hall
Cover and Interior Design: Julia Hall
Cover Images: Photonica/Pete Starman

 2 3 4 5   10 09 08 07 06

Printed and bound in the United States of America.

CONTENTS AT A GLANCE

Part One   Your Self

At the heart of psychology lies a question: What is a person? This section shows how psychologists from five schools of thought address this question. What traits define personality, and where do they come from? What milestones occur on the way to becoming a person?

Part Two   Your Body

We cannot understand our psychological selves without understanding our physical selves. These chapters describe how brain activity, neurons, and hormones affect your psychological functioning, and how you are able to sense and perceive the world around you.

Part Three   Your Mind

"I think, therefore I am," said the philosopher René Descartes. This section discusses the impressive ways in which human beings think—and why they so often fail to think and reason well—and explores the puzzles and paradoxes of memory.

Part Four   Your Environment

Even unsociable hermits are influenced by their surroundings and by other people. In these chapters you will learn how physical and social environments—from the immediate situation to the larger cultural context—affect your actions and attitudes.

Part Five   Your Mental Health

At some point, many of us struggle with psychological problems, which range from everyday difficulties to incapacitating conditions. This part describes the major mental and emotional disorders and evaluates the therapies that have been designed to treat them.

Part Six   Your Life

A satisfying life depends on having healthy emotions, coping well with stress, and knowing how to reach your goals. In these closing chapters, we see how the influences discussed in the previous units—personality, body, mind, and environment—affect your emotions, well-being, and four of life's fundamental motives: love, sex, eating, and work.

CONTENTS

TO THE INSTRUCTOR

Psychology textbooks have always had a little problem with length. William James's two-volume classic, *Principles of Psychology* (1890), took him twelve long years to write and weighed in at a hefty 1,393 pages. (And today's students think *they* have it hard!) Just two years after it was published, James followed it with *Psychology, Briefer Course*, which was much shorter, under 500 pages. But James was not happy with his briefer book; in a letter to his publishers, he complained that he had left out "all bibliography and experimental details, all metaphysical subtleties and digressions, all quotations, all humor and pathos, all *interest* in short...." (quoted in Weiten & Wight, 1992).

The great James was probably too hard on himself; he was entirely incapable of writing anything dull or uninteresting. Nevertheless, we kept his words in mind as we were working on our own "briefer" introduction to psychology. From the outset, we were guided by a philosophy that we hoped would help us avoid some of the pitfalls of the genre:

1. A brief book should have not only fewer chapters than a longer book but also its own meaningful organization.

2. Students at all levels need critical-thinking tools for evaluating psychological issues intelligently.

3. Brief or long, a textbook needs to use examples, analogies, lively writing, and a strong narrative sense to pull students into the material and make it relevant to their lives.

4. Students remember more if they learn actively.

5. Research on culture, gender, and ethnicity is as integral to psychology as is research on the brain, genetics, and hormones.

In the rest of this preface, we describe how we have tried to translate our philosophy about writing this book into reality, and what is new in this second edition.

1. BREVITY AND ORGANIZATION

We know that instructors often feel hard pressed to cover all of the material of a 17- or 18-chapter introductory text in a semester or quarter. The

14 chapters in this book cover all the major topics in introductory psychology. We wanted to do two things: engage students quickly and provide a logical "scaffolding" for the diverse topics in psychology. The first chapter, which introduces students to the field and to the fundamentals of critical and scientific thinking, is followed by six sections, each consisting of two chapters (or in one case, three). The title of each section invites the reader to consider how the discipline of psychology can illuminate aspects of his or her own life and provides the reader with a personal frame of reference for assimilating the information:

- **PART ONE: YOUR SELF** examines major theories of personality (Chapter 2) and development (Chapter 3). These are extremely high-interest topics for students, and will draw them into the course right away. Moreover, starting off with these chapters allows us to avoid redundancy in coverage of the major schools of psychology—biological, learning, cognitive, sociocultural, and psychodynamic. Instead of introducing these perspectives in the first chapter and then having to explain them again in a much later personality chapter, we cover them once, in this section.

- **PART TWO: YOUR BODY** explores the many ways in which the brain, neurons, and hormones affect psychological functioning (Chapter 4), body rhythms and states of consciousness (Chapter 5), and the neurological and psychological underpinnings of sensation and perception (Chapter 6).

- **PART THREE: YOUR MIND** discusses the impressive ways in which human beings think and reason—and why they so often fail to think and reason well (Chapter 7)—and explores the puzzles and paradoxes of memory (Chapter 8).

- **PART FOUR: YOUR ENVIRONMENT** covers basic principles of learning (Chapter 9) and the impact of social and cultural contexts on behaviour (Chapter 10). Combining learning and social psychology in the same part is a break from convention, but we think it makes wonderful sense, for these two fields share an emphasis on external influences on behaviour.

- **PART FIVE: YOUR MENTAL HEALTH** reviews the major mental and emotional disorders (Chapter 11) and evaluates the therapies designed to treat them (Chapter 12).
- **PART SIX: YOUR LIFE** shows how mind, body, and environment influence emotions, stress, and health (Chapter 13) and the fundamental motives that drive people: Eating and appetite, love and sex, and work and achievement (Chapter 14).

Naturally, we could not include every topic that might be found in a longer book, but we have retained those that are truly essential in an introductory course. In most cases, you will find these topics in the chapters where you expect them to be, but there are a few exceptions. For example, eating disorders are not discussed in the chapter on psychological disorders; instead, we discuss them in the context of psychological, genetic, and cultural factors in eating, overweight, and dieting (Chapter 14). If at first you do not see a topic that interests you, we urge you to look for it in the table of contents or the index.

2. CRITICAL AND CREATIVE THINKING

The importance of critical thinking in the study of psychology has been growing steadily in recent years. Without critical-thinking skills, learning ends at the classroom door.

In this book, too, our goal is to get students to reflect on what they learn, resist leaping to conclusions on the basis of personal experience alone (so tempting in psychological matters), apply rigorous standards of evidence, and listen to competing views. We introduce eight basic guidelines to critical and creative thinking right away, in the first chapter, and then teach and model these guidelines throughout the book.

We use a critical-thinking icon—like the one in the sample on this page—to draw the reader's attention to some (but not all) of the critical-thinking discussions in the text. The icon is meant to say to students, "Listen up! As you read about this topic, you will need to be especially careful about assumptions, evidence, and conclusions."

True critical thinking, we have always maintained, cannot be reduced to a set of rhetorical questions or to a formula for analyzing studies. It is a *process of evaluating claims and ideas, and thus it must be woven into a book's narrative.* We try to

model critical thinking for students in our evaluations not only of popular but unsupported ideas in the popular culture, for example about ESP and "PMS," but also in our evaluations of unsupported academic beliefs, such as the notion that the sexes differ in moral reasoning (they don't), that projective tests like the Rorschach and anatomically detailed dolls are reliable and valid ways of assessing personality and emotional disorders (they aren't), or that the effective ingredient of the popular therapy EMDR is the finger-waving by the therapist (it isn't). Likewise, we try to convey the importance of critical thinking and empirical evidence in our coverage of psychological issues that have evoked emotional debate, such as children's eyewitness testimony, multiple personality disorder, "recovered" memories, parental versus peer influence on children, the role of biology in addiction, definitions of racism and sexism, and many others.

Thinking Critically About...

3. LIVELINESS AND RELEVANCE

Virginia Woolf once said that fiction is not dropped like a pebble upon the ground, but, like a spider's web, is attached to life at all four corners. The same principle applies to good textbook writing. Authors of texts at all levels have a unique opportunity to combine scholarly rigor and authority with warmth and compassion in conveying what psychologists know (and still seek to know) about the predicaments and puzzles of life.

Right from the outset, we want students to see that psychology can deepen our understanding of those predicaments and puzzles. Its lessons apply to the world, and to us all as individuals. Each chapter therefore begins with a feature called **Psychology in the News**, real news items taken from headlines in Canada and around the world—for example, about a 63-year-old woman giving birth, a man being sentenced to just 5 years in prison after brutally stabbing his wife to death, a shop in Vancouver being closed down for selling marijuana, a Supreme Court decision on the legality of spanking, an Internet dating site visited by over 250,000 people in Toronto alone.

We use these stories to raise issues that will be addressed in the chapter. Then, at the end of the chapter, we revisit the opening story, using concepts and findings that the reader has been studying, to show how they illuminate the issues

Psychology In The News

BUSINESS IS BRISK AT MARIJUANA SHOP

VANCOUVER, BC, September 11, 2004. A shop on Commercial Drive in Vancouver has been defying the law and operating a thriving business selling marijuana to its customers, a business that drew considerable public attention after a police raid resulting in the arrest of the shop's owner and seven employees.

The Da Kine Food and Beverage Shop has been dubbed "pot café" after four months of having marijuana on its menu. When a Crime Stoppers call brought it to the attention of the police, they raided the establishment, confiscating 20 pounds of pot, 1 pound of hashish, and $63 000 in cash.

The manager of the Da Kine vowed to reopen each time it was closed, criticizing the police for "terror tactics" that were out of touch with the lives of the people they are supposed to serve.

For their part, the police claim that the Da Kine is not a "compassion club" selling marijuana to people with government-approved medical reasons for using the drug. Rather, they estimate that the Da Kine brings in about $500 000 a month for its not-for-profit society. Police counted 230 visitors to the Da Kine during a one-hour surveillance.

raised. We think this device helps promote critical thinking and also helps students appreciate that psychology is indeed "attached to life at all four corners."

At the end of each chapter, another feature, called **Taking Psychology With You**, draws on research reported in the chapter to tackle practical topics, such as living with chronic pain (Chapter 6), eliminating bad habits (Chapter 9), getting along with people of other cultures (Chapter 10), and evaluating self-help programs and books (Chapter 12).

Taking Psychology With You   Travels Across the Cultural Divide

A French salesman worked for a company that was bought by Americans. When the new American manager ordered him to step up his sales within the next three months, the employee quit in a huff, taking his customers with him. Why? In France, it takes years to develop customers; in family-owned businesses, relationships with customers may span generations. The American wanted instant results, as Americans often do, but the French salesman knew this was impossible and quit. The American view was "He wasn't up to the job; he's lazy and disloyal, so he stole my customers." The French view was "There is no point in explaining anything to a person who is so stupid as to think you can

rules of a culture, look, listen, and observe. What is the pace of life like? Do people regard brash individuality and loud speech as admirable or embarrassing? When customers enter a shop, do they greet and chat with the shopkeeper or ignore the person as they browse?

Remember, though, that even when you know the rules, you may find it difficult to carry them out. In the Middle East, two men will look directly at one another as they talk, but such direct gazes would be deeply uncomfortable to most Japanese and a sign of insult or confrontation to some African-Americans

4. ACTIVE LEARNING

One of the soundest findings about learning is that you can't just sit there like a sack of potatoes while it happens. You have to be actively involved, whether practicing the new skill or encoding new material. Our textbook includes several pedagogical features that encourage students to become actively involved in what they are reading.

What's Ahead introduces each major section within a chapter with a set of brief questions. These are not merely rhetorical but are intended to be provocative or intriguing enough to arouse students' curiosity and draw them into the material: Why do some people get depressed even though they "have it all"? Why are people who are chronically angry and mistrustful their own worst enemy? What is the "Big Lie," and why does it influence so many people?

Looking Back, at the end of each chapter, lists all of the *What's Ahead* questions along with page numbers to show where the material for each question was covered. By using this feature, students can check their retention and can easily review if they find that they can't answer a question. Some instructors may want to turn some of these questions into essay or short-answer test items or written assignments.

Quick Quizzes are periodic self-tests that encourage students to check their progress while they are reading and to go back and review if necessary. The quizzes do more than test for memorization of definitions; they tell students whether they comprehend the issues. Mindful of the common tendency to skip quizzes or to peek at the answers, we have used various formats and have included entertaining examples in order to motivate students to test themselves.

Many of the quizzes also include critical-thinking questions. They invite the student to reflect on the implications of findings and to consider how psychological principles might illuminate real-life issues. For example: What kinds of questions should a critical thinker ask about a new drug for depression? If a woman's job performance is declining, what else besides low achievement might be the reason? Why should consumers be cautious about accepting the success of a therapy, self-help program, or drug on the basis of some individual's enthusiastic testimonial?

Get Involved exercises provide an entertaining approach to active learning. Some consist of quick demonstrations (e.g., swing a flashlight in a dark closet to see how briefly images remain in sensory memory); some are simple mini-studies (e.g., violate a social norm and see what happens); and some help students relate course material to their own lives (e.g., if you drink, list the motives you have for doing so). Instructors may want to assign some of these exercises to the entire class and then discuss the results and what they mean.

Other pedagogical features include **graphic illustrations** of complex concepts; a **running glossary** that defines boldfaced technical terms

---

Quick Quiz

Is all this information about eating making you hungry for knowledge?

1. *True or false?*: Emotional problems explain why fat people are heavy.
2. Falling and rising levels of leptin help the brain regulate appetite and _____ and play a role in maintaining a person's genetically influenced _____.
3. Rising rates of obesity can best be explained by (a) genetic changes over the past few decades, (b) a lack of willpower, (c) an abundance of high-calorie food and sedentary lifestyles, (d) the increase in eating disorders.
4. Bill, who is thin, reads in the newspaper that genes set the range of body weight and shape. "Oh, good," he exclaims, "now I can eat all the junk food I want; I was born to be skinny." What's wrong with Bill's conclusion?

Answers:

1. false   2. metabolism, set point   3. c

4. Bill is right to recognize that there may be limits to how heavy he can become. But he may also be oversimplifying and jumping to conclusions. Many people who have a set point for leanness will gain considerable weight on fatty foods and excess calories, especially if they don't exercise. Also, rich junk food is unhealthy for reasons that have nothing to do with becoming overweight.

on the pages where they occur for handy reference and study; a **cumulative glossary** at the back of the book; a list of **key terms** at the end of each chapter with page numbers so that students can find the sections where the terms are covered; **chapter outlines**; and **chapter summaries** in paragraph form to help students review major concepts.

5. MAINSTREAMING CULTURE, GENDER, AND BIOLOGY

Of course, all introductory textbooks are divided into chapters that cover particular topics or subfields, such as the brain, emotion, developmental psychology, and social psychology. Increasingly, however, some areas of investigation can no longer be squeezed into a single chapter, because they are relevant to topics throughout the course. This is especially true of findings from the "bookends" of human behaviour, culture and biology, as well as research on gender, that little subject of immense interest!

Where possible, therefore, we have tried to integrate research in these areas wherever it applies, rather than relegating studies on gender, culture, or biology to an intellectual ghetto of separate chapters or boxed features.

GENDER For examples of how we treat gender issues, see our discussions of:

- Male-female similarities in moral reasoning (p. 86)
- Sex differences in the brain (pp. 133–135)
- Gender and emotion (pp. 424–425)
- Evolutionary theories of sexual behaviour (pp. 457–459)
- Weight and eating disorders in women and men (pp. 466–467)

For example, we cover many gender differences in this book—in pain, sexual attitudes and motives, sexual coercion, body satisfaction, depression, antisocial personality disorder, children's play preferences, and ways of expressing love, intimacy, and emotion, to mention just a few. (You will find many other topics in the index.) We do not equate "gender" with "women," either! We have been particularly attentive to research on the psychology of men, for example by considering the underdiagnosis of male depression and the rise of eating disorders and distorted body images in young men. In many cases, we have tried to go beyond mere description of differences, by examining competing explanations for them: Biological influences, biological and evolutionary influences, social roles, gender socialization, gender schemas, and the power of current situations and experiences to shape people's choices and lives.

Nor do we focus exclusively on gender *differences*. Many differences, though reliable, are

---

Get Involved   Turn on Your Right Hemisphere

These faces have expressions of happiness on one side and sadness on the other. Look at the nose of each face; which face looks happier? Which face looks sadder?

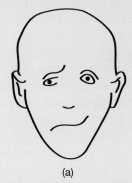
(a)

(b)

You are likely to see face b as the happier one and face a as the sadder one. The likely reason is that in most people the left side of a picture is processed by the right side of the brain, where recognition of emotional expression primarily occurs (see Chapter 4; Oatley & Jenkins, 1996).

trivial in terms of real-life importance. And gender *similarities*, though they are often overlooked, are every bit as important and interesting as the eternal search for differences. We therefore include findings on similarities, too—for example, that men and women do not, overall, differ in moral reasoning (Chapter 3), mood swings in the course of an average month (Chapter 5), or obedience to authority (Chapter 10).

CULTURE For examples of how we treat culture, see our discussions of:

- Attitudes toward achievement (p. 59)
- Cultural influences on personality (pp. 60–62)
- Ethnic identity and acculturation (p. 338)
- Ethnocentrism (pp. 337)
- Addiction rates and drug abuse (pp. 372–374)

In recent years, most psychologists have come to appreciate the profound influence of culture on all aspects of life, from nonverbal behaviour to the deepest attitudes about how the world should be. Thus we raise empirical findings about culture and ethnicity, as topics warrant, throughout the book: For example, in our discussions of addiction, mental disorders, social norms (e.g., for cleanliness, risk, and conversational distance), emotional expression, group differences in IQ scores and academic achievement, motivational conflicts, personality, psychotherapy, rules about time, attitudes toward weight and the ideal body, and the effectiveness of medication. (Again, we refer you to the index for a complete listing of topics.) In addition, Chapter 2 highlights cultural factors in personality and Chapter 10 contains extended discussions of ethnocentrism, prejudice, and cross-cultural relations.

For us, the scientific study of cultural diversity is not synonymous with the popular movement called multiculturalism. The study of culture, in our view, should increase students' understanding of what culture means, and of how and why ethnic and national groups differ, and why no group is inherently better, kinder, or more moral than another. Thus we try to apply critical thinking to our own coverage of culture, avoiding the twin temptations of ethnocentrism and stereotyping.

BIOLOGY For examples of how we cover biological research, see our discussions of:

- Genetics and personality (pp. 51–54)
- Stem cells and the production of new neurons (pp. 115–116)
- Schizophrenia (pp. 379–381)
- Sexual desire and behaviour (pp. 4562–454)
- Weight and body shape (pp. 466–467)

Anyone who is awake and conscious knows that we are in the midst of a biomedical revolution that is transforming science and psychology. Findings from the Human Genome Project, studies of behavioural genetics, astonishing discoveries about the brain, technologies such as PET scans and fMRIs, the proliferation of medications for psychological disorders—all have had a profound influence on our understanding of human behaviour and on interventions to help people with chronic problems. This work, too, can no longer be confined to a single chapter; accordingly, we report new findings from the biological front wherever they are relevant throughout the book: In our discussions of the brain, memory, emotion, stress, child development, aging, mental illness, personality, and many other topics. But just as we do with culture and gender, we apply principles of critical thinking to this domain of research, too. Thus we caution students about the dangers of reducing complex behaviours solely to biology, overgeneralizing from limited data, failing to consider other explanations, and oversimplifying solutions (e.g., as promises of "miracle" drugs often do).

WHAT'S NEW IN THIS EDITION?

In this second Canadian edition of *Invitation to Psychology*, we have retained the text's basic approach, organization, and pedagogy. We have made no changes just for the sake of making changes! Many of the book's features have been tested by time and student reaction; students and instructors like them. However, in response to requests from many instructors, we did make one major change: We added a chapter on states of consciousness (Body Rhythms and Mental States, Chapter 5), a topic that is hugely popular with students. In the first Canadian edition, much of this chapter's material—on body rhythms, sleep and dreams, psychotropic drugs, and hypnosis—was distributed throughout the book, but many teachers wanted them to be all in one place.

On Being a Canadian Edition

A number of the concepts in this book manifest themselves in Canada in ways that differ from other parts of the world. Cultural diversity, interpersonal violence, mental health services, and elements of our health care and judicial systems are uniquely ours. The stories we use as authors and teachers of psychology in Canada need to reflect this uniqueness, and in this Canadian edition we have attempted to do just that. Yet, in other ways, placing a nationality on a field of study is an unwise thing to do. In writing this book, we have been told that, in science, the country of origin isn't important; rather, the quality of the idea is. We agree. So why point out, as we do in this book from time to time, that a given study was conducted at a particular Canadian university or other Canadian location? Not because we think it makes it "better knowledge." Instead, we want to communicate to students that fine psychological research is conducted in this country and that, should they choose to do so, they can become part of that research community.

Here are just some of the examples of the Canadian research we present in this text:

- French immersion early schooling has a positive effect in first language development (p. 80)

- Increased exposure to light is a useful treatment for seasonal affective disorder (p. 148)

- Memory theory can be a useful tool for helping to find children who get lost on their way home (p. 267)

- A comparison of the rates of suicide and cancer deaths in Canada (p. 382)

- A look at what predicts Canadian males' drives to become muscular (p. 467)

Of course, this second Canadian edition contains many new chapter-opening stories. And throughout the book we have added the latest research on cutting-edge issues and controversies, from findings on stem cells and neuronal growth throughout life to research showing why well-meaning interventions in the aftermath of trauma so often fail or even backfire.

INSTRUCTOR AND STUDENT SUPPLEMENTS TO ACCOMPANY *INVITATION TO PSYCHOLOGY*

This edition's supplements package has been created to provide you and your students with the best teaching and learning materials, both in print and media formats.

Media Supplements

NEW OneKey Adapted by Rodney Schmaltz of the University of Alberta, OneKey is Pearson Education Canada's inclusive online resource for *Invitation to Psychology, Second Canadian Edition*, offering instructors and students all of their resources—all in one place—all organized to accompany this text. OneKey provides a wealth of valuable online material including access to ResearchNavigator™, a collection of three exclusive databases of relevant and reliable source material, and an interactive e-book version of the text with rich multimedia content including *Live!Psych* experiments and simulations. Designed to get students to interact with the material and to appeal to different learning styles, these experiments and simulations were created in consultation with psychology instructors and carefully reviewed by a board of experts to ensure accuracy and pedagogical effectiveness. Students can also build a customized study plan through a series of diagnostic tests designed to help them prepare for and perform better on exams.

The OneKey media content is linked to the text by the numbered OneKey icons found throughout the margins of the book. These icons make for a thoroughly integrated learning package by indicating when further relevant multimedia content is available online. See the list below for details.

Instructors can access OneKey by going to *www.pearsoned.ca/onekey* and following the instructions on the page. Students get OneKey with the access code that is bundled with this text. Instructors can also contact their Pearson Education Canada representative for further information.

OneKey Icons

The following is a list of the media content connected to the OneKey icons found throughout the text. This media is available through both OneKey and the Companion Website that accompanies *Invitation to Psychology, Second Canadian Edition* (www.pearsoned.ca/wade).

1.1 Live!Psych: Observational Studies, p. 17

1.2 Live!Psych: Correlational Studies, p. 21

1.3 HandsOnPsych: Correlation, p. 22

1.4 Live!Psych: The Experimental Method, p. 24

13.4 Live!Psych: Stress and the Immune System, p. 427

14.1 HandsOnPsych: Motivation, p. 452

Live!Psych **Experiments and Simulations on CD-ROM** A CD-ROM containing all the *Live!Psych* experiments and simulations, including all those listed above, can be purchased alone or packaged with the text at no additional charge on request by an adopter. (ISBN: 0131947745.)

Supplements for the Instructor

Instructor's Resource Manual Available both on the Instructor's Resource Centre on CD-ROM and online at http://vig.pearsoned.ca, this manual includes the following resources for each text chapter: Introducing the chapter; learning objectives; lecture suggestions and discussion topics; classroom activities, demonstrations, and exercises; out-of-class assignments and projects; multimedia resources; video resources; transparency masters; and handouts. Designed to make your lectures more effective and to save you preparation time, this extensive resource gathers together the most effective activities and strategies for teaching your Introductory Psychology course.

Test Item File Adapted by Luigi Pasto of John Abbott College, the Test Item File is available on the Instructor's Resource Centre on CD-ROM, this test bank contains over 2,250 multiple choice, true/false, and short-answer essay questions. Every question references the relevant section and page number in the text; while multiple choice questions also provide a key for level of difficulty; and list the question type—factual, conceptual, or applied.

NEW **TestGen** Available on both the Instructor's Resource Centre on CD-ROM and online at http://vig.pearsoned.ca, this dual-platform test-generator program provides instructors with "best in class" features in an easy-to-use program. You will be able to create tests using the TestGen Wizard and easily select questions with drag-and-drop or point-and-click functionality. You can also add or modify test questions using the built-in Question Editor. TestGen also offers algorithmic functionality, which allows for the creation of unlimited versions of a single test. The Quiz Master feature allows for online test delivery. TestGen comes complete with an instructor's gradebook and full technical support.

PowerPoint Slides Adapted by Rena Borovilos of the Humber College Institute of Technology and Advanced Learning, each chapter's presentations highlight the key points covered in the text. Available on the Instructor's Resource Centre on CD-ROM or on online at http://vig.pearsoned.ca.

Image Library Available on the Instructor's Resource Centre on CD-ROM, this library includes all of the artwork from the text. Instructors can make use of these images in their handouts and in-class presentations.

NEW **Instructor's Resource Centre on CD-ROM** This valuable, time-saving resource provides you with electronic versions of all of the instructor supplements including, PowerPoint slides, media presentations, the artwork from the text, the Overhead Transparencies, the Instructor's Resource Manual, and the Test Item File. Instructors can search and export all of these resources to create customized presentations and assignments.

Pearson Prentice Hall's Introductory Psychology Transparencies Designed for use in large lecture settings, this set of over 130 full-colour transparencies includes illustrations from the text as well as images from a variety of other sources. Available in acetate form, and on the Instructor's Resource Centre on CD-ROM.

Online Course Management with Customized WebCT, BlackBoard, or CourseCompass Instructors interested in using online course management have several options, all free upon adoption of the text. Each course comes preloaded with text-specific tests and can be fully customized for your course. Contact your Pearson Education Canada representative or visit our Technology Solutions page on our online catalogue at http://vig.pearsoned.ca.

Additional Resources for Instructors

Pearson Education Canada has an exciting, extensive video and media library that is available to qualified adopters of *Invitation to Psychology, Second Canadian Edition*. For more details about the video supplements that are available with adoptions of the textbook, contact your local Pearson Education Canada sales representative or e-mail us at *soc-sci.marketing@pearsoned.com*.

NEW Lecture Launcher Video for Introductory Psychology This new video consists of short clips covering all major topics in introductory psychology. The clips have been selected from *Films for Humanities and Sciences* and edited to provide brief and compelling images and stories to enhance your lectures.

Films for Humanities and Sciences* and the *PBS Video Library This is an extensive collection of films and documentaries on a wide array of topics in the humanities and sciences.

Movies as Illustrations for Introductory Psychology by Steven V. Rouse. This guide is full of wonderful suggestions on how to use videos in class to illustrate psychological topics and issues (ISBN: 0131455109).

Supplements for the Student

Study Guide Adapted by Jackie Cohen of Dawson College, this student study guide helps students master the core concepts presented. For each text chapter, there are learning objectives, a brief chapter summary, a preview outline, and three different practice tests.

Companion Web Site at *www.pearsoned. ca/wade* This online study guide allows students to review each chapter's material, take practice tests, research topics for course projects, and more. The *Invitation to Psychology,* Second Canadian Edition Companion Web site includes the following resources for each chapter: chapter objectives, interactive lectures, five different types of quizzes that provide immediate, text-specific feedback and coaching comments, WebEssays, WebDestinations, NetSearch, new FlashCards, and new Live!Psych Activities and Experiments (read the section on OneKey in this Preface for

further details). Access to the Web site is free and unrestricted to all students.

ACKNOWLEDGMENTS

Like any other cooperative effort, writing a book requires a support team. We are indebted to the many instructors who reviewed the text for their many insightful and substantive suggestions during the development of this and previous editions of *Invitation to Psychology*, including Peter R. Bender, Ph.D., John Abbott College; Barry Cull, Conestoga College; Meagan Daley, CÉGEP Champlain-St. Lawrence; Robin Gagnon, Tom Hanrahan, Canadore College; Dawson College; Louise Jarrold, Dawson College; Luigi Pasto, John Abbott College; Clayton Rhodes, Durham College; V. Gordon Rose, Simon Fraser University; Sue Smiley, Nova Scotia Community College; Crystal Kotow-Sullivan, St. Clair College.

We would also like to thank all the people at Pearson Education Canada who worked on this book. From editorial, to production, to marketing and sales, their efforts are truly appreciated.

We hope that you will enjoy reading and using Invitation to Psychology, and that your students will find it a true invitation to the field we love. We welcome your reactions, experiences using it, and suggestions for improvements or for teaching from it.

CAROLE WADE

CAROL TAVRIS

GARY POOLE

TO THE STUDENT

If you are reading this introduction, you are starting your introductory psychology course on the right foot. It always helps to get a general picture of what you are about to read before charging forward.

Our goal in this book is to guide you to think critically and imaginatively about psychological issues, and to help you apply what you learn to your own life and the world around you. We ourselves have never gotten over our initial excitement about psychology, and we have done everything we can think of to make the field as absorbing for you as it is for us. However, what you bring to this book is as important as what we have written—we can pitch ideas at you, but you have to step up to the plate to connect with them. This text will remain only a collection of pages with ink on them unless you choose to read actively. The more involved you are in your own learning, the more successful the book and your course will be, and the more enjoyable, too.

GETTING INVOLVED

To encourage you to read and study actively, we have included some special features:

- Every chapter opens with **Psychology in the News**, an actual story from the media related to issues that will be discussed in the chapter. *Do not skip these stories!* We return to them at the end of the chapter, to show you how findings from psychology might help you understand each story in particular and others like it that you will encounter. How do you feel about a 63-year-old woman who gives birth to a baby? What explains the attraction of Internet dating to hundreds of thousands of people in Toronto alone? How can a man who murdered his six children be considered sane? As you read the chapter, try to link its findings and ideas to the opening story and come up with your own insights.

- Each chapter contains several **Get Involved** exercises, entertaining little experiments or explorations you can do that demonstrate what you are reading about. In Chapter 2, for instance, you get to see where you fall on an inventory of basic personality traits, and in Chapter 12, we will show you how your own thoughts affect your moods. Some Get Involved exercises take only a minute; others are "mini-studies" that you can do by observing or interviewing others.

- Before each major section, a feature called **What's Ahead** lists some preview questions to stir your curiosity and indicate what that section will cover. For example: Why does paying children for good grades sometimes backfire? Do people remember better when they're hypnotized? Do men and women differ in the ability to love? When you finish the chapter, you will encounter these questions again, under the heading **Looking Back**. Use this list as a self-test; if you can't answer a question, go to the page indicated after the question and review the material.

- In Chapter 1, we will introduce you to the basic guidelines of **critical and creative thinking**—the principles we hope will help you distinguish unsupported claims or "psychobabble" from good, scientific reasoning. A special icon identifies areas with a particular emphasis on critical thinking. Throughout the book, some (but not all) of our critical-thinking discussions are signaled in the text by the icon, like the one shown here. We will be telling you about many lively and passionate debates in psychology—about sex and gender differences, therapy, memory, "multiple personality disorder," and many other topics—and we hope our coverage of these debates will increase your involvement with the ongoing discoveries of psychology.

  Thinking Critically About...

- Every chapter contains several **Quick Quizzes** that test your understanding, retention, and ability to apply what you have read to examples. Do not let the word "quiz" give you a sinking feeling. These quizzes are for your practical use and even, we hope, for your enjoyment. When you have trouble with a question, do not go on; pause right then and there, review what you have read, and then try again.

- Some of the Quick Quizzes also contain critical-thinking items. The answers we give for these items are only suggestions; feel free to come up with different ones. Quick Quizzes containing critical-thinking items are not really so quick, because they ask you to reflect on what you have read and to apply the critical-thinking guidelines described in Chapter 1. But if you take the time to respond thoughtfully to them, we think you will become more engaged with the material, learn more, and become a more sophisticated user of psychology.

- At the end of each chapter, a feature called **Taking Psychology with You** draws on research to suggest ways you can apply what you have learned to everyday problems and concerns (such as how to boost your motivation or improve your memory) as well as more serious ones, such as how to live with chronic pain or help a friend who seems suicidal.

HOW TO STUDY

In our years of teaching, we have found that certain study strategies can vastly improve learning, and so we offer the following suggestions. (Reading Chapter 8, on memory, and Chapter 9, on learning, will also be helpful.)

- Before starting a chapter, read the chapter title and major headings to get an idea of what is in store. Browse through the chapter, looking at the pictures and reading the headings.

- Do not read the text as you might read a novel, taking in large chunks at a sitting. To get the most from your studying, we recommend that you read only a part of each chapter at a time.

- Instead of simply reading silently, nodding along saying "hmmmmm" to yourself, try to restate what you have read in your own words at the end of each major section. Some people find it helpful to write down main points. Others prefer to recite main points aloud to someone else—or even into a tape recorder. Do not count on getting by with just one reading of a chapter. Most people need to go through the material at least twice, and then review the main points several times before an exam.

- When you have finished a chapter, read the **Summary**. Some students tell us they find it useful to write down their own summaries first, then compare them with the book's. Use the list of **Key Terms** at the end of each chapter as a checklist. Try to define and discuss each term in the list to see how well you understand and remember it. If you need to review a term, a page number is given to tell you where it is first mentioned in the chapter. Finally, review the **Looking Back** questions to be sure you can answer them.

- Important new terms in this textbook are printed in **boldface** and are defined in the margin of the page on which they appear or on the facing page. The **marginal glossary** permits you to find these terms and concepts easily, and will help you when you study for exams. A complete glossary also appears at the end of the book.

- The **Study Guide** for this book, available at your bookstore, is an excellent learning resource. It contains review materials, exercises, and practice tests to help you understand and apply the concepts in the book.

- If you are assigned a term project or a report, you may need to track down some references or do further reading. Throughout the book, discussions of studies and theories include *citations* in parentheses that look like this: (Aardvark & Zebra, 2001). A citation tells you who the authors of a book or paper are and when their work was published. The full reference can then be looked up in the alphabetical **Bibliography** at the end of the book. At the back of the book you will also find a *Name Index* and a *Subject Index*. The name index lists the name of every author cited and the pages where each person's work is discussed. If you remember the name of a psychologist but not where he or she was mentioned, look up the name in the index. The subject index lists all the major topics mentioned in the book. If you want to review material on, say, depression, you can look up "depression" in the subject index and find each place it is mentioned.

We have done our utmost to convey our own enthusiasm about psychology, but, in the end, it is your efforts as much as ours that will determine whether you find psychology to be exciting or boring, and whether the field will make a difference in your own life. This book is our way of inviting you into the world of psychology. Our warmest welcome!

CAROLE WADE

CAROL TAVRIS

GARY POOLE

ABOUT THE AUTHORS

Carole Wade earned her Ph.D. in cognitive psychology at Stanford University. She began her academic career at the University of New Mexico, where she taught courses in psycholinguistics and developed the first course at the university on the psychology of gender. She was professor of psychology for ten years at San Diego Mesa College, then taught at College of Marin, and is now affiliated with Dominican University of California. She is coauthor, with Carol Tavris, of *Invitation to Psychology*, *Psychology in Perspective*, and *The Longest War*: *Sex differences in perspective*. Dr. Wade has a long-standing interest in making psychology accessible to students and the general public. For many years she has focused her efforts on the teaching and promotion of critical-thinking skills, diversity issues, and the enhancement of undergraduate education in psychology. She chaired the APA Board of Educational Affairs's Task Force on Diversity Issues at the Precollege and Undergraduate Levels of Education in Psychology, as well as the APA's Public Information Committee; has been a G. Stanley Hall lecturer at the APA convention; and served on the steering committee for the National Institute on the Teaching of Psychology. Dr. Wade is a Fellow of the American Psychological Association and a charter member of the American Psychological Society. When she isn't busy with her professional activities, she can be found riding the trails of northern California on her Arabian horse, Condé, or his stablemate, Ricochet.

Carol Tavris earned her Ph.D. in the interdisciplinary program in social psychology at the University of Michigan, and as a writer and lecturer she has sought to educate the public about the importance of critical and scientific thinking in psychology. She is author of *The Mismeasure of Woman*; *Anger: The misunderstood emotion*; and, with Carole Wade, *Invitation to Psychology*, *Psychology in Perspective*, and *The Longest War: Sex differences in perspective*. She has written on psychological topics for a wide variety of magazines, journals, edited books, and newspapers. Many of her book reviews and opinion essays for *The Los Angeles Times, The New York Times Book Review, Scientific American*, and other publications have been collected in *Psychobabble and Biobunk: Using psychology to think critically about issues in the news*. Dr. Tavris lectures widely on, among other topics, pseudoscience in psychology and psychiatry, anger, and the science and politics of research on gender. She has taught in the psychology department at UCLA and at the Human Relations Center of the New School for Social Research in New York. She is a Fellow of the American Psychological Association and a charter Fellow of the American Psychological Society; a member of the board of the Council for Scientific Clinical Psychology and Psychiatry; and a member of the editorial board of the APS journal *Psychological Science in the Public Interest*. When she is not writing or lecturing, she can be found walking the trails of the Hollywood Hills with her border collie, Sophie.

Gary Poole earned his Ph.D in social psychology from Simon Fraser University. For 10 years, he was the director of SFU's Centre for University Teaching as well as a member of the Psychology Department, where he taught Introductory Psychology, Social Psychology, and Health Psychology. His teaching has been recognized nationally, with a prestigious 3M Fellowship for Excellence in Teaching, and at Simon Fraser, where he won an Excellence in Teaching Award. He is a co-author of *The Psychology of Health and Health Care: A Canadian Perspective*, and he has published journal articles in health psychology. Dr. Poole has dedicated many hours to making psychology accessible to people both inside and outside the university community. For more than two years, he hosted *Human Nature*, a weekly segment on the Discovery Channel dedicated to the science of psychology. Dr. Poole is currently an Associate Professor in the Department of Health Care and Epidemiology and the Director of the Centre for Teaching and Academic Growth at the University of British Columbia.

Psychology In The News

MAN SUES ONTARIO LOTTERY AND GAMING CORPORATION FOR LETTING HIM GAMBLE

MARKHAM, ON, December 7, 2002. After losing $250 000 to his gambling addiction, Constantin Digalakis sued the Ontario Lottery and Gaming Corporation for letting him gamble. Digalakis knew he was addicted to gambling—so much so that he signed voluntary exclusion orders that allowed casinos to bar him from entering. But so strong was his addiction that he wore disguises to gain entry. In his lawsuit, Digalakis is

Terry Fox was unable to complete his Marathon of Hope. Still, his courage and commitment have inspired thousands, and he is considered by many to be Canada's Greatest Hero.

headlights revealed a severely beaten and naked body in Stanley Park in the early hours of Saturday morning, it turned out to be the most horrific of discoveries. Aaron Webster died after being beaten by a group of men and youths wielding baseball bats and pool cues. And Webster had been Chisholm's best friend. Aaron Webster had been attacked in a section of Stanley Park frequented by members of Vancouver's gay community, and members of that community called for the murder to be classified as a hate crime. This could have resulted in harsher sentences for those found guilty. However, the judge presiding

Should people who are addicted to roulette be able to sue the casinos who spin the wheel?

claiming that the casinos did not guard their doors well enough or inspect their clientele with sufficient vigilance.

MAN BEATEN TO DEATH IN APPARENT ANTI-GAY HATE CRIME

VANCOUVER, BC, November 19, 2001. When Tim Chisholm's car

chose not to declare the murder a hate crime.

TERRY FOX HONOURED AS CANADA'S GREATEST HERO

ST. JOHN'S, NL, April 12, 2004. In April of 1980, Terry Fox began his Marathon of Hope. After losing a leg to cancer, he decided to run across

Canada to raise funds for cancer research. He began his trek in St. John's, but never made it to the west coast. It ended in Thunder Bay, 143 days and 3330 miles from St. John's, having raised $2 million. On June 28, 1981, Terry Fox succumbed to cancer. He was not yet 23 years old. The annual Terry Fox runs held across Canada have since raised over $300 million for cancer research. In June of 1999, Terry Fox was voted Canada's Greatest Hero in a national survey.

ZANINESS ON PARADE IN EDMONTON

EDMONTON, AB, August 19, 1995. Anything goes at Edmonton's Fringe

Living on the edge. The Fringe Parade draws a crowd in Edmonton.

MISSISSAUGA, ON, December 15, 2003. Maybe there's something about being a truck driver that encourages one to develop empathy for one's fellow drivers. Maybe Charles Carriere is just the sort of person who was destined to save a life someday. Whatever the reason, a 21-year-old woman from Mississauga is alive today because Carriere was driving his truck down Highway 401 when her Mazda left the road at 100 km/h and burst into flames. Working quickly with another man who arrived on the scene, Carriere was able to open the

A firefighter hoses down what is left of a burning car from which Charles Carriere pulled a 21-year-old woman, saving her life.

vehicle, fight the flames and chemical smoke, search for other passengers, and eventually release the driver, who had been pinned in the car by the collision.

Parade. This year, sword fights, Scots with green hair, flashers, bagpipes, and a Russian band were all part of the procession. Over 500 onlookers were treated to previews of some of the 815 performances that will be part of the Fringe Festival, a time when this Alberta prairie city goes just a bit loony. Over 11 000 tickets had been sold before the first show hit the stage.

1 What Is Psychology?

THE SCIENCE OF PSYCHOLOGY

WHAT PSYCHOLOGISTS DO

CRITICAL AND SCIENTIFIC THINKING IN PSYCHOLOGY

DESCRIPTIVE STUDIES: ESTABLISHING THE FACTS

CORRELATIONAL STUDIES: LOOKING FOR RELATIONSHIPS

THE EXPERIMENT: HUNTING FOR CAUSES

EVALUATING THE FINDINGS

PSYCHOLOGY IN THE NEWS, REVISITED

TAKING PSYCHOLOGY WITH YOU: WHAT PSYCHOLOGY CAN DO FOR YOU—AND WHAT IT CAN'T

If you are in the habit of reading the newspaper, you may have come across the five stories shown here. Newspapers and magazines are full of tales of heroism and courage, murder and mayhem, personal accomplishment, and emotional controversies. But why, you may be wondering, are we starting this book with these stories? What on earth do they have to do with psychology?

The answer: everything.

People usually associate psychology with mental and emotional disorders, personal problems, and psychotherapy. But psychologists take as their subject the entire spectrum of beautiful and brutish things that human beings do—the kinds of things you read and hear about every day. Psychologists reading these particular stories would want to know why gambling addiction has become a problem in North America. Is it because of people's lack of willpower, or do the temptations of a big payoff from casinos have something to do with it? They would want to find out why some individuals, although perfectly pleasant to friends and relatives, burn with hatred for people of different sexual orientations, ethnicities, religions, or nationalities, and why others are willing to put their lives in jeopardy to help others, without a thought about ethnic or other differences. They would be curious to know why some people, like the jovial marchers in the Fringe Parade, are extroverts, whereas others find comfort in quiet conformity. And they would want to know what motivates someone facing the challenge of cancer to take on even more challenges, like running across a vast country.

If you want to know what psychology is about, then a newspaper is a pretty good place to start! Indeed, in this book we will be discussing all the issues raised by these stories and many others in the news. But psychology is not just about behaviour that is newsworthy. Psychologists are also interested in how ordinary human beings—and other animals, too—learn, remember, solve problems, perceive, feel, and get along (or fail to get along) with others. They are therefore as likely to study commonplace experiences—rearing children, gossiping, remembering a shopping list, daydreaming, making love, and making a living—as exceptional ones.

If you have ever wondered what makes people tick, or if you want to gain some insight into your own behaviour, then you are in the right course. We invite you now to step into the world of psychology, the discipline that dares to explore the most complex topic on earth: you.

psychology The discipline concerned with behaviour and mental processes and how they are affected by an organism's physical state, mental state, and external environment; often represented by Ψ, the Greek letter psi (usually pronounced "sy").

empirical Relying on or derived from observation, experimentation, and measurement.

WHAT'S AHEAD

- What's the difference between psychology and plain old common sense?
- How old is the science of psychology?
- Was Sigmund Freud the official founder of scientific psychology?
- What are the five major perspectives in psychology?

THE SCIENCE OF PSYCHOLOGY

Psychology can be defined as *the discipline concerned with behaviour and mental processes and how they are affected by an organism's physical state, mental state, and external environment.* This definition, however, is a little like defining a car as a vehicle for transporting people from one place to another, without explaining how a car differs from a train or a bus, how a Ford differs from a Ferrari, or how a catalytic converter works. To get a clear picture of what psychology is, you are going to need to know more about its methods, its findings, and its ways of interpreting information.

Psychology, Pseudoscience, and Common Sense

Let's begin by considering what psychology is *not.* First, the psychology that you are about to study bears little relation to the popular psychology ("pop psych") often found in self-help books or on talk shows. In recent years, the public's appetite for psychological information has created a huge market for "psychobabble": pseudoscience and quackery covered by a veneer of psychological language. Pseudoscience (*pseudo* means "false") promises quick fixes to life's problems, such as "reliving" the supposed trauma of birth to resolve your current unhappiness, playing Mozart to your 2-month-old child so she'll have a high IQ at age 10, or "reprogramming" your brain to make it more creative. Serious psychology is more complex, more informative, and, we think, far more helpful than psychobabble because it is based on rigorous research and **empirical** evidence—evidence gathered by careful observation, experimentation, and measurement.

Second, serious psychology differs radically from such nonscientific competitors as graphology (handwriting analysis), fortune-telling, numerology, and, the most popular, astrology. Like psychologists, promoters of these competing systems try to explain people's problems and predict their behaviour. If you are having romantic problems, for example, an astrologer may advise you to choose an Aries instead of an Aquarius as your next love, and a "past-lives channeller" may say it's because you were jilted in a former life. Across North America, belief in these nonscientific approaches is widespread (De Robertis & Delaney, 2000; National Science Board, 2000). Yet whenever the predictions of psychics, astrologers, and the like are put to the test, they turn out to be so vague that they're meaningless—or just plain wrong (Park, 2000; Rowe, 1993; Shermer, 1997). What should have been the fatal blow to astrological and psychic claims occurred on September 11, 2001, when the World Trade Center was destroyed. Not one psychic or astrologer had predicted that devastating event.

"I see you being less gullible in the future."

Third, psychology is not just a fancy name for common sense. Often, psychological research produces findings that directly contradict prevailing beliefs, and throughout this book you will be discovering many of them. For example, are unhappy memories "repressed" and then accurately recalled years later, as if they had been recorded on videotape? Are most abused children destined to become abusive parents themselves? Do policies of abstinence from alcohol reduce rates of alcoholism? All of these common beliefs and many

others have been refuted by empirical evidence.

Psychological findings do not have to be surprising, however, to be important. Psychological researchers, like scientists in other fields, strive not only to discover new phenomena, but also to deepen our understanding of an already familiar world—by identifying the varieties of love, the origins of violence, or the reasons that a great song can lift our hearts.

The Birth of Modern Psychology

Most of the great thinkers of history, from Aristotle to Zoroaster, raised questions that today would be called psychological. They wanted to know how people take in information through their senses, use information to solve problems, and become motivated to act in brave or villainous ways. They wondered about the elusive nature of emotion, and whether it controls us or is something we can control. Like today's psychologists, they wanted to *describe, predict, understand,* and *modify* behaviour in order to add to human knowledge and increase human happiness. But unlike modern psychologists, scholars of the past did not rely heavily on empirical evidence. Often, their observations were based simply on anecdotes or descriptions of individual cases.

This does not mean that the forerunners of modern psychology were always wrong. On the contrary, they often had insights and made observations that were verified by later work. Hippocrates (460 B.C.E.–377 B.C.E.), the Greek physician known as the founder of modern medicine, observed patients with head injuries and inferred that the brain must be the ultimate source of "our pleasures, joys, laughter, and jests as well as our sorrows, pains, griefs, and tears." And so it is. In the first century C.E., the Stoic philosophers observed that people do not become angry or sad or anxious because of actual events but because of their explanations of those events. And so they do.

But without empirical methods, the forerunners of psychology also committed terrible blunders. A good example comes from the early 1800s, when

---

Get Involved   Read All About It

To get an idea of just how broad a discipline psychology is, take any newspaper and circle the headlines of stories about which psychology might be able to offer insights. Don't skip the sports, business, and "people" sections! How many headlines did you mark?

functionalism An early psychological approach that emphasized the function or purpose of behaviour and consciousness.

Bumpy logic? Phrenology, a nineteenth-century pseudoscientific fad, linked bumps on the skull with character traits. On this phrenology "map," notice the tiny space allocated to self-esteem and the large one devoted to cautiousness!

the theory of *phrenology* (Greek for "study of the mind") became wildly popular. Inspired by the writings and lectures of Austrian physician Joseph Gall (1758–1828), phrenologists argued that different brain areas accounted for specific character and personality traits, such as "stinginess" and "religiosity," and that such traits could be "read" from bumps on the skull. Thieves, for example, supposedly had large bumps above the ears. When phrenologists examined people who had "stealing bumps" but were not thieves, they explained away this counterevidence by saying that other brain bumps represented positive traits that were holding the person's thieving impulses in check. Parents, teachers, and employers flocked to phrenologists for advice (Benjamin, 1998). But phrenology was a classic pseudoscience—sheer nonsense.

At about the time that phrenology was peaking in popularity, several pioneering men and women in Europe and America were starting to study psychological issues using scientific methods. In 1879, the first psychological laboratory was officially established, in Leipzig, Germany, by Wilhelm Wundt (VIL-helm Voont). Wundt (1832–1920), who was trained in medicine and

psychoanalysis A theory of personality and a method of psychotherapy that was developed by Sigmund Freud; it emphasizes unconscious motives and conflicts.

philosophy, promoted a method called *trained introspection*, in which volunteers were taught to carefully observe, analyze, and describe their own sensations, mental images, and emotional reactions. Wundt's introspectors might take as long as 20 minutes to report their inner experiences during a 1.5-second experiment. The goal was to break behaviour down into its most basic elements, much as a chemist might analyze water into hydrogen plus oxygen. Most psychologists eventually rejected trained introspection as too subjective, but Wundt still is usually credited for formally initiating the movement to make psychology a science. Many early psychologists in North America were trained in Wundt's laboratory.

Another early approach to scientific psychology, called **functionalism**, emphasized the function of behaviour, instead of its analysis and description. One of functionalism's leaders was William James (1842–1910), an American philosopher, physician, and psychologist. Attempting to grasp the nature of the mind through introspection, wrote James (1890/1950), is "like seizing a spinning top to catch its motion, or trying to turn up the gas quickly enough to see how the darkness looks." Inspired in part by the evolutionary theories of British naturalist Charles Darwin (1809–1882), James and other functionalists instead asked how various actions help a person or animal adapt to the environment. This emphasis on the causes and consequences of behaviour was to set the course of psychological science.

Psychology also has roots in Vienna, Austria, where it first developed as a method of psychotherapy. While researchers were at work in their laboratories, struggling to establish psychology as a science, Sigmund Freud (1856–1939), an obscure neurologist, was in his office listening to his patients' reports of depression, nervousness, and obsessive habits. Freud became convinced that their symptoms had mental, not bodily, causes. His patients' distress was due, he concluded, to conflicts, memories, and emotional traumas that originated in early childhood and were too threatening to be remembered consciously. Freud's ideas eventually evolved into a broad theory of personality, and both his theory and his methods of treating people with emotional problems became known as **psychoanalysis**.

From its early beginnings in philosophy, natural science, and medicine, psychology eventually grew into a complex discipline encompassing many different specialties, perspectives, and methods. (In other chapters, you will be learning more about the history of psychology and the people who played a prominent role in its development.) Today the field is like a large, sprawling family. The members of this family share common great-grandparents, but some of the cousins have formed alliances, some are quarrelling, and a few are barely speaking to one another.

Psychology's Present

The various approaches to psychology eventually evolved into five major theoretical perspectives, which now predominate. These approaches reflect different questions that psychologists ask about human behaviour, different assumptions about how the mind works, and, most important, different ways of explaining why people do what they do.

1   The **biological perspective** focuses on how bodily events affect behaviour, feelings, and thoughts. Researchers such as Donald Hebb at McGill University have argued that the physical activity within the brain gives rise to all behavioural and mental phenomena (Hebb, 1949). Electrical impulses shoot along the intricate pathways of the nervous system. Hormones course through the bloodstream, signalling internal organs to slow down or speed up. Chemical substances flow across the tiny gaps that separate one microscopic brain cell from another. Biological psychologists study how these physical events interact with events in the external environment to produce perceptions, memories, emotions, and many other features of human behaviour. They also investigate the contribution of genes and other biological factors to the development of abilities and personality traits. A popular new biological specialty, **evolutionary psychology**, follows in the tradition of functionalism by focusing on how genetically influenced behaviour that was functional or adaptive during our evolutionary past may be reflected in many of our present behaviours, mental processes, and traits.

2   The **learning perspective** is concerned with how the environment and experience affect a person's (or a nonhuman animal's) actions. Within this perspective, *behaviourists* focus on the environmental rewards and punishments that maintain or discourage specific behaviours. Behaviourists do not invoke the mind to explain behaviour; they prefer to stick to what they can observe and measure directly: acts and events taking place in the

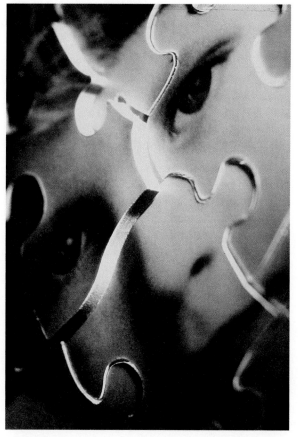

What makes us who we are? Psychologists approach questions about human behaviour from five major perspectives: biological, learning, cognitive, sociocultural, and psychodynamic.

environment. For example, do you have trouble sticking to a schedule? Lots of people do. A behaviourist would analyze the environmental distractions that could help account for this common problem. *Social–cognitive learning theorists*, on the other hand, combine elements of behaviourism with research on thoughts, values, and intentions. They believe that people learn not only by adapting their behaviour to the environment, but also by imitating others and by thinking about the events happening around them. As we will see in other chapters, the learning perspective has many practical applications.

3   The **cognitive perspective** emphasizes what goes on in people's heads—how people reason, remember, understand language, solve problems, explain experiences, acquire moral standards, and form beliefs. (The word *cognitive* comes from the Latin for "to know.") Using clever methods, cognitive psychologists infer mental processes from observable behaviour. One of the most important contributions of this perspective has been to show

biological perspective A psychological approach that emphasizes bodily events and changes associated with actions, feelings, and thoughts.

evolutionary psychology A field of psychology emphasizing evolutionary mechanisms that may help explain human commonalities in cognition, development, emotion, social practices, and other areas of behaviour.

learning perspective A psychological approach that emphasizes how the environment and experience affect a person's or animal's actions; it includes *behaviourism* and *social–cognitive learning theories*.

cognitive perspective A psychological approach that emphasizes mental processes in perception, memory, language, problem solving, and other areas of behaviour.

how our thoughts and explanations of events affect what we feel and do. All of us are constantly seeking to make sense of the world and of our own physical and mental states. Our ideas may not always be realistic or sensible, but they continually influence our actions and choices. The cognitive approach is one of the strongest forces in psychology, and it has inspired an explosion of research on the intricate workings of the mind.

4 The **sociocultural perspective** focuses on social and cultural forces outside the individual forces that shape every aspect of behaviour, from how we kiss to what and where we eat. Most of us underestimate the impact of other people (the social context) and of cultural rules on nearly everything we do: how we perceive the world, express joy or grief, manage our households, and treat our friends and enemies. We are like fish that are unaware they live in water, so obvious is water in their lives. Sociocultural psychologists study the water—the social and cultural environments that people "swim" in every day.

5 The **psychodynamic perspective** deals with unconscious dynamics within the individual, such as inner forces, conflicts, or instinctual energy. It has its origins in Freud's theory of psychoanalysis, but many other psychodynamic theories now

exist. Psychodynamic psychologists try to dig below the surface of a person's behaviour to get to the roots of personality; they think of themselves as archaeologists of the mind. As we will see in Chapter 2, psychodynamic psychology is the thumb on the hand of psychology—connected to the other fingers, but also set apart from them because it differs radically from the others in its language, methods, and standards of acceptable evidence. Many psychological scientists believe that psychodynamic approaches belong in philosophy or literature rather than in academic psychology. But psychotherapists and laypeople are often attracted to the psychodynamic perspective's emphasis on such grand psychological issues as the power of sexuality and the universal fear of death.

We will be encountering the major findings and methods of these five approaches in the rest of this book. The differences among these schools of thought are very real; a psychoanalyst's explanation of your personality will not be the same as a cognitive psychologist's, and neither account will be the same as a biological, learning, or sociocultural psychologist's. However, not all psychologists feel they must swear allegiance to one approach or another. Many draw on what they take to be the best features of diverse schools of thought.

sociocultural perspective A psychological approach that emphasizes social and cultural influences on behaviour.

psychodynamic perspective A psychological approach that emphasizes unconscious dynamics within the individual, such as inner forces, conflicts, or the movement of instinctual energy.

Quick Quiz

Here is your first Quick Quiz. Try it; you won't be graded!

A. See whether psychology's past is still present in your memory.

1. *True or false*?: Psychology's forerunners relied heavily on empirical evidence.
2. Credit for founding modern scientific psychology usually goes to _____.
3. Early psychologists who emphasized how behaviour helps an organism adapt to its environment were known as _____.

B. To find out whether you understand the five major perspectives in psychology, match each possible explanation of anxiety on the left with a perspective on the right.

1. Anxious people often think about the future in distorted ways.
2. Anxiety is due to forbidden, unconscious desires.
3. Anxiety symptoms often bring hidden rewards, such as being excused from exams.
4. Excessive anxiety can be caused by a chemical imbalance.
5. A national emphasis on competition and success promotes anxiety about failure.

a. learning
b. psychodynamic
c. sociocultural
d. biological
e. cognitive

Answers:

A. 1. false   2. Wilhelm Wundt   3. functionalists   B. 1. e   2. b   3. a   4. d   5. c

Further, many psychologists have been affected by psychological movements and intellectual trends that do not fit neatly into any of the major perspectives. One such movement, **humanist psychology**, which gained force in the 1960s, emphasizes free will, personal growth, resilience, and the achievement of human potential and self-fulfillment. Humanists argue that psychology should focus on what really matters to most people—their uniquely human hopes and aspirations. Although many researchers regard humanism as a philosophy of life rather than a systematic or scientific approach to psychology, this movement has had considerable influence both inside and outside the field. A contemporary research specialty known as "positive psychology" follows in the footsteps of humanism by focusing on the qualities that enable people to be happy, optimistic, and resilient in times of stress (Fredrickson, 2001; Taylor, 2001; Seligman & Csikszentmihalyi, 2000). And humanism has had a direct influence on psychotherapy and the human potential and on self-help movements.

Despite the diversity of psychological approaches, however, most psychological scientists agree on certain basic guidelines about what is and what is not acceptable in their discipline. Nearly all reject supernatural explanations of events—evil spirits, psychic forces, miracles, and so forth. Most believe in the importance of gathering empirical evidence and not relying on hunches or personal belief. This insistence on rigorous standards of proof is what sets psychology apart from other, nonscientific explanations of human experience.

WHAT'S AHEAD

- If someone tells you that he or she is a psychologist, why can't you assume the person is a therapist?
- If you decided to call yourself a "psychotherapist," would you be breaking the law?
- What's the difference between a clinical psychologist and a psychiatrist?

WHAT PSYCHOLOGISTS DO

Now you know the main viewpoints that guide psychologists in their work. But what do psychologists actually do with their time between breakfast and dinner?

The professional activities of psychologists generally fall into three broad categories: (1) teaching and doing research in colleges and universities; (2) providing health or mental-health services, often referred to as *psychological practice*; and (3) conducting research or applying its findings in nonacademic settings such as business, sports, government, law, and the military (see Table 1.1). Some psychologists move flexibly across these areas. A researcher might also provide counselling services in a mental-health setting, such as a clinic or a hospital; a university professor might teach, do research, and serve as a consultant in legal cases.

Psychological Research

Most psychologists who do research have doctoral degrees (Ph.D.s or Ed.D.s, doctorates in education). Some, seeking knowledge for its own sake, work in **basic psychology**; others, concerned with the practical uses of knowledge, work in **applied psychology**. A psychologist doing basic research might ask, "How does peer pressure influence people's attitudes and behaviour?" An applied psychologist might ask, "How can knowledge about peer pressure be used to reduce binge drinking in colleges?"

Psychologists doing basic and applied research have made important contributions in areas as diverse as health, education, child development, testing, conflict resolution, marketing, industrial design, worker productivity, and urban planning.

Psychological Practice

Psychological practitioners, whose goal is to understand and improve physical and mental health, work in mental hospitals, general hospitals, clinics, schools, counselling centres, the criminal justice system, and private practice. Since the late 1970s, the proportion of psychologists who are practitioners has steadily increased: Practitioners now account for over half of new psychologists in Canada (Lefton, Boyes, & Ogden, 2000).

Some practitioners are *counselling psychologists*, who generally help people deal with problems of everyday life, such as test anxiety, family conflicts, or low job motivation. Others are *school psychologists*, who work with parents, teachers, and students to enhance students' performance and resolve emotional difficulties. The majority, however, are *clinical psychologists*, who diagnose, treat, and study mental or emotional problems. Clinical psychologists are trained to do psychotherapy with

humanist psychology A psychological approach that emphasizes free will, personal growth, resilience, and the achievement of human potential.

basic psychology The study of psychological issues in order to seek knowledge for its own sake rather than for its practical application.

applied psychology The study of psychological issues that have direct practical significance; also, the application of psychological findings.

TABLE 1.1 What Is a Psychologist?		
Not all psychologists do clinical work. Many do research, teach, work in business, or consult. The professional activities of psychologists with doctorates fall into three general categories.		
Academic/Research Psychologists	**Clinical Psychologists**	**Psychologists in Industry, Law, or Other Settings**
Specialize in areas of pure or applied research, such as:	Do psychotherapy and sometimes research; may work in any of these settings:	Do research or serve as consultants to institutions on, for example:
Human development	Private practice	Sports
Psychometrics (testing)	Mental-health clinics	Consumer issues
Health	General hospitals	Advertising
Education	Mental hospitals	Organizational problems
Industrial/organizational psychology	Research laboratories	Environmental issues
Physiological psychology	Colleges and universities	Public policy
Sensation and perception		Opinion polls
Design and use of technology		Military training
		Animal behaviour
		Legal issues

severely disturbed people, as well as with those who are simply troubled or unhappy and want to learn to handle their problems better.

In Canada, four provinces (British Columbia, Manitoba, Ontario, and Prince Edward Island) require a doctorate in order to get a licence to practice clinical psychology. Other provinces require a master's degree (CPA, 2005). Most clinical psychologists have a Ph.D., some have an Ed.D., and a smaller but growing number have a Psy.D. (doctorate in psychology, pronounced "sy-dee"). Clinical psychologists typically do four or five years of graduate work in psychology, plus at least a year's internship under the direction of a practising psychologist. Clinical programs leading to a Ph.D. or Ed.D. are usually designed to prepare a person both as a scientist and as a practitioner; they require completion of a dissertation, a major scholarly project (usually involving research) that contributes to knowledge in the field. There are currently no programs in Canada that lead to a Psy.D. In the United States, programs leading to a Psy.D. focus on professional practice and do not usually require a dissertation, although they typically require the student to complete a study, theoretical paper, or literature review.

People often confuse clinical psychologist with three other terms: *psychotherapist, psychoanalyst,* and *psychiatrist.* But these terms mean different things. A psychotherapist is simply someone who does any kind of psychotherapy. The term is not legally regulated. A psychoanalyst is a person who practises one particular form of therapy, psychoanalysis. To call yourself a psychoanalyst, you must have an advanced degree, get specialized training at a psychoanalytic institute, and undergo extensive psychoanalysis yourself. A psychiatrist is a medical doctor (M.D.) who has done a five-year residency in psychiatry under the supervision of more experienced physicians to learn to diagnose and treat mental disorders. Like some clinical psychologists, some psychiatrists do research on mental problems, such as depression or schizophrenia, instead of, or in addition to, working with patients.

Psychiatrists and clinical psychologists do similar work, but psychiatrists, because of their medical training, are more likely to focus on possible biological causes of mental disorders and often treat these problems with medication. They can write prescriptions, whereas most clinical psychologists cannot. The exception is clinical psychologists who receive specialized training in using drugs to treat psychological disorders, called psychopharmacology (Litman, 2005). This special training is designed in part to remedy a situation in which over 80 percent of all medications prescribed for psychological conditions are written by physicians with no expertise in mental health (Litman, 2005).

Licensed clinical social workers, counsellors with various specialties, and marriage, family, and child counsellors (MFCCs) also do mental-health work. These professionals ordinarily treat general

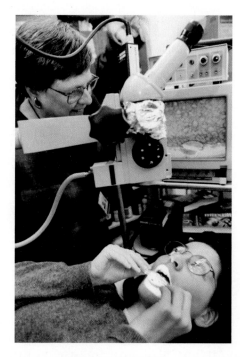

Psychological researchers and practitioners work in all sorts of settings, from classrooms to courtrooms. Here, Linda Bartoshuk (top) uses technology to study how the anatomy of the tongue influences the way we experience different tastes. A clinical psychologist (lower right) helps a couple in therapy. And Louis Herman (upper right) studies a dolphin's ability to understand an artificial language comprising hand signals; in response to the gestural sequence "person" and "over," the dolphin will leap over the person in the pool.

problems rather than serious mental disturbances, although their work may bring them into contact with people with serious problems—violent delinquents, sex offenders, and individuals involved in domestic violence or child abuse. Licensing requirements vary by jurisdiction, but usually include a master's degree in psychology or social work and one or two years of supervised experi-

ence. (For a summary of the types of psychotherapists and the training they receive, see Table 1.2.)

Psychology in the Community

During the second half of the twentieth century, psychology expanded rapidly in terms of scholars, publications, and specialties. The Canadian Psychological Association (2005) now has

TABLE 1.2   Types of Psychotherapists

Just as not all psychologists are psychotherapists, not all psychotherapists are clinical psychologists. Here are the major terms used to refer to mental-health professionals:

Psychotherapist	Practises psychotherapy; may have anything from no degree to an advanced professional degree; the term is unregulated.
Clinical psychologist	Diagnoses, treats, and/or studies mental and emotional problems, both mild and severe; has a Ph.D. or an Ed.D.
Psychoanalyst	Practises psychoanalysis; has specific training in this approach after an advanced degree (usually, but not always, an M.D. or a Ph.D.); may treat any kind of emotional disorder or pathology.
Psychiatrist	Does work similar to that of a clinical psychologist but is likely to take a more biological approach; has a medical degree (M.D.) with a specialty in psychiatry.
Licensed clinical social worker (LCSW); marriage, family, and child counsellor (MFCC)	Typically treats common individual and family problems, but may also deal with more serious problems such as addiction or abuse. Licensing requirements vary, but generally has at least an M.A. in psychology or social work.

26 divisions. Some represent major fields such as developmental psychology or physiological psychology. Others represent specific research or professional interests, such as the psychology of women, the psychology of men, ethnic minority issues, sports, the arts, environmental problems, gay and lesbian issues, peace, psychology and the law, and health.

As psychology has grown, psychologists have found ways to contribute to their communities in many different fields. They consult with companies to improve worker satisfaction and productivity. They establish programs to improve race relations and reduce ethnic tensions. They advise commissions on how pollution and noise affect mental health. They do rehabilitation training for people who are physically or mentally disabled. They educate judges and juries about eyewitness testimony. They assist the police in emergencies involving hostages or disturbed persons. They conduct public-opinion surveys. They run suicide-prevention hot lines. They advise zoos on the care and training of animals. They help coaches improve the athletic performances of their teams. And on and on.

Is it any wonder that people are a little fuzzy about what a psychologist is?

critical thinking The ability and willingness to assess claims and make objective judgments on the basis of well-supported reasoning and evidence, rather than emotion and anecdote.

WHAT'S AHEAD

- Can you be too open-minded?
- What guidelines can help you evaluate psychological claims?
- What's the secret of a good scientific definition?
- Why is a psychological theory nonscientific if it explains anything that could conceivably happen?
- What's wrong with drawing conclusions about behaviour from a collection of anecdotes?

CRITICAL AND SCIENTIFIC THINKING IN PSYCHOLOGY

One of the greatest benefits of studying psychology is that you learn not only how the brain works in general but also how to use yours in particular—by thinking critically. **Critical thinking** is the ability and willingness to assess claims and make objective judgments on the basis of well-supported reasoning and evidence, rather than emotion and anecdote. Critical thinkers are able to look for flaws in arguments and to resist claims that have no supporting evidence. They realize that criticizing an argument is not the same as criticizing the person making it, and they are willing to engage in vigorous debate about the validity of an idea. Critical thinking, however, is not merely negative thinking. It includes the ability to be creative and constructive—to come up with alternative explanations for events, think of implications of research findings, and apply new knowledge to social and personal problems.

Most people know that you have to exercise the body to keep it in shape, but they may not realize that clear thinking also requires effort and practice. All around us we can see examples of flabby thinking. Sometimes people justify their mental laziness by proudly telling you they are open-minded. It's good to be open-minded, many scientists have observed, but not so open that your brains fall out!

Critical thinking is not only indispensable in ordinary life; it is also fundamental to all science, including psychological science. By exercising critical thinking, you will be able to distinguish serious psychology from the psychobabble that clutters the airwaves and bookstores. Critical thinking requires logical skills, but other skills and dispositions are also important (Anderson, in press; Halpern, 1995; Levy, 1997; Paul, 1984; Ruggiero, 1997). Here are eight essential critical-thinking guidelines that we will be emphasizing throughout this book.

Ask Questions; Be Willing to Wonder What is the one kind of question that most exasperates parents of young children? "Why is the sky blue, Mommy?" "Why doesn't the plane fall?" "Why don't pigs have wings?" Unfortunately, as children grow up, they tend to stop asking "why" questions like these. (Why do you think this is?)

"The trigger mechanism for creative thinking is the disposition to be curious, to wonder, to inquire," observed Vincent Ruggiero (1988). "Asking 'What's wrong here?' and/or 'Why is this the way it is, and how did it come to be that way?' leads to the identification of problems and challenges." We hope that you will not approach psychology as received wisdom but will ask many questions about the theories and findings we present in this book.

Define Your Terms Once you have raised a general question, the next step is to frame it in clear and concrete terms. Vague or poorly defined terms in a question can lead to misleading or incomplete answers. For example, have you ever wondered whether animals can use language? The answer depends on how you define "language." If you mean "a system of communication," then birds do it, bees do it, and even worms do it. But if you mean "a system of communication that combines sounds or gestures into an infinite number of structured utterances that convey meaning" (which is how linguists define it), then, as far as anyone can tell, only people use language, though some animals are able to acquire some aspects of language in special settings (see Chapter 7).

For scientists, defining terms means being precise about just what it is that they're studying. Researchers often start out with a **hypothesis**, a statement that attempts to describe or explain a given behaviour. Initially, this hypothesis may be stated quite generally, as in, say, "Misery loves company." But before any research can be done, the hypothesis must be made more precise. For example, "Misery loves company" might be rephrased as "People who are anxious about a threatening situation tend to seek out others facing the same threat."

A hypothesis, in turn, leads to explicit predictions about what will happen in a particular

"I still don't have all the answers, but I'm beginning to ask the right questions."

situation. In a prediction, terms such as *anxiety* or *threatening situation* are given **operational definitions**, which specify how the phenomena in question are to be observed and measured. "Anxiety" might be defined operationally as a score on an anxiety questionnaire; "threatening situation" might be defined as the threat of an electric shock. The prediction might be, "If you raise people's anxiety scores by telling them they are going to receive electric shocks, and then you give them the choice of waiting alone or with others in the same situation, they will be more likely to choose to wait with others than they would be if they were not anxious." The prediction can then be tested, using systematic methods.

Examine the Evidence Have you ever heard someone in the heat of an argument exclaim, "I just know it's true, no matter what you say" or "That's my opinion; nothing's going to change it"? Have you ever made such statements yourself? Accepting a conclusion without evidence, or expecting others to do so, is a sure sign of lazy thinking. A critical thinker asks, "What evidence supports or refutes this argument and its opposition? How reliable is the evidence?" If checking the reliability of the evidence directly is not possible, the person considers whether it came from a reliable source.

In scientific research, an idea may initially generate excitement because it is plausible, imaginative, or appealing, but, as we have seen,

operational definition A precise definition of a term in a hypothesis; specifies the operations for observing and measuring the process or phenomenon being defined.

hypothesis A statement that attempts to predict or to account for a set of phenomena; scientific hypotheses specify relationships among events or variables and are empirically tested.

eventually it must be backed by empirical evidence if it is to be taken seriously. A collection of anecdotes or an appeal to authority will not do.

Here's an example involving childhood autism, a serious mental disorder. Autistic children often live in a silent world of their own, cut off from normal social interaction. They may rock back and forth for hours, and sometimes they do self-destructive things, such as poking pencils in their ears. At one time, many clinicians thought that autism was caused by rejecting, cold "refrigerator mothers." Their belief was influenced by the writings of the eminent psychoanalyst Bruno Bettelheim. Bettelheim drew his conclusions from just a few case studies of autistic children whose mothers had psychological problems—and he exaggerated the number of cases he had examined (Pollak, 1997). Yet Bettelheim's authority was so great that many people accepted his claims despite his meagre data.

When proper studies were finally done, however, using objective testing procedures and a larger, representative group of autistic children and their parents, scientists learned that parents of autistic children are as psychologically healthy as any other parents. Today we know that autism stems from a neurological problem rather than from any psychological problems of the mothers, and that certain genes probably increase susceptibility to the disorder (Ingram et al., 2000). But because so many people uncritically accepted Bettelheim's claims, thousands of women blamed themselves for their children's disorder and suffered needless guilt and remorse.

Analyze Assumptions and Biases *Assumptions* are beliefs that are taken for granted, and *biases* are assumptions that keep us from considering the evidence fairly or that cause us to ignore the evidence entirely. Critical thinkers try to identify and evaluate the unspoken assumptions on which claims and arguments may rest—in the books they read, the political speeches they hear, and the advertisements that bombard them every day. In science, as in other fields, a questioning attitude toward assumptions is what drives progress. Some of the greatest scientific advances have been made by those who dared to doubt what everyone else assumed to be true: that the sun revolves around the earth, that illness can be cured by applying leeches to the skin, that madness is a sign of demonic possession.

principle of falsifiability The principle that a scientific theory must make predictions that are specific enough to expose the theory to the possibility of disconfirmation.

When demonstrating "levitation" and other supposedly magical phenomena, illusionists such as André Kole exploit people's tendency to trust the evidence of their own eyes even when such evidence is misleading. Critical thinkers ask questions about the nature and reliability of the evidence for a phenomenon.

Critical thinkers are willing to analyze and test not only other people's assumptions, but also their own (which is much more difficult). Researchers put their own assumptions to the test by stating a hypothesis in such a way that it can be *refuted*, or disproved by counterevidence. This principle, known as the **principle of falsifiability**, does not mean that the hypothesis *will* be disproved, only that it *could be* if contrary evidence were to be discovered.

Another way of saying this is that a scientist must risk disconfirmation by predicting not only what will happen, but also what will *not* happen if the hypothesis is correct. In the "misery loves company" study, the hypothesis would be supported if most anxious people sought each other out, but disconfirmed if most anxious people went off alone to sulk and worry, or if anxiety had no effect on their behaviour (see Figure 1.1). A willingness to risk disconfirmation forces the scientist to take negative evidence seriously and to abandon mistaken assumptions. Any researcher who refuses to do this is not a true scientist.

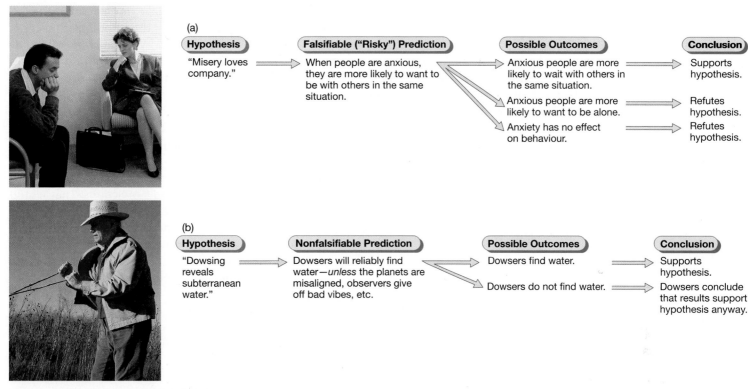

FIGURE 1.1 The Principle of Falsifiability

The scientific method requires researchers to expose their ideas to the possibility of counterevidence, as in row (a). In contrast, people claiming psychic powers, such as dowsers (who say they can find underground water with a "dowsing rod" that bends when water is present), typically interpret all possible outcomes as support for their assertions, as in row (b). Their claims are therefore untestable.

If you keep your eyes open, you will find many violations of the principle of falsifiability in everyday life. When police officers believe a suspect is guilty, they may take even the person's protestations of innocence as evidence of guilt ("the skunk is just covering up"). Of course, many guilty people claim they are innocent, but so do innocent people! An interviewer in such situations must therefore be open to disconfirming evidence. Similarly, people who believe in alien abductions, when faced with evidence that "alien spaceships" are merely natural phenomena or weather balloons, will reply that the government must be engaged in a cover-up or that aliens must have clever, sneaky ways of disguising their spacecraft. By simply explaining away all counterevidence, they avoid ever putting their beliefs to the test.

Avoid Emotional Reasoning Emotion has a place in critical thinking and in science, too. Passionate commitment to a view motivates people to think boldly, to defend unpopular ideas, and to seek evidence for creative new theories. But emotional conviction alone cannot settle arguments.

You probably already hold strong beliefs about child rearing, drugs, the causes of crime, racism, the origins of intelligence, gender differences, homosexuality, and many other issues of concern to psychologists. As you read this book, you may find yourself quarrelling with findings that you dislike. Disagreement is fine; it means that you are reading actively and are engaged with the material. All we ask is that you think about why you are disagreeing: Is it because the evidence is unpersuasive or because the results make you feel anxious or annoyed?

Don't Oversimplify A critical thinker looks beyond the obvious, resists easy generalizations, and rejects either–or thinking. For example, is it better to feel you have control over what happens to you or to accept with tranquility whatever life serves up? Either answer oversimplifies. As we will see in Chapter 13, control has many important benefits, but sometimes it's best to "go with the flow."

One common form of oversimplification is *argument by anecdote*—generalizing from a personal experience or a few examples to everyone: One crime committed by a paroled ex-convict means that parole should be abolished; one friend who hates his or her school means that everybody who goes there hates it. Anecdotes are often the source of stereotyping, as well: One dishonest welfare mother means they are all dishonest; one encounter with a fun-loving Newfoundlander means they are all wild and crazy. Critical and scientific thinkers want more evidence than one or two stories before drawing such sweeping conclusions.

Consider Other Interpretations A critical thinker creatively formulates hypotheses that offer reasonable explanations of the topic at hand. In science, the goal is to arrive at a **theory**, an organized system of assumptions and principles that purports to explain certain phenomena and how they are related. A scientific theory is not just someone's personal opinion, as people imply when they say, "It's only a theory." Theories that come to be accepted by the scientific community make as few assumptions as possible and account for many empirical findings.

Before settling on an explanation of some behaviour, however, critical thinkers are careful not to shut out alternative possibilities. They generate as many interpretations of the evidence as they can before choosing the most likely one. For example, suppose a news magazine reports that people who are chronically depressed are more likely than nondepressed people to develop cancer. Before concluding that depression causes cancer, you would need to consider some other possibilities. Perhaps depressed people are more likely to smoke and to drink excessively, and it is these unhealthful habits that increase their cancer risk. Or perhaps, in studies of depression and cancer, early, undetected cancers were responsible for the patients' feelings of depression.

Tolerate Uncertainty Ultimately, learning to think critically teaches us one of the hardest lessons of life: how to live with uncertainty. Sometimes there is little or no evidence available to examine. Sometimes the evidence permits only tentative conclusions. Sometimes the evidence seems strong enough to permit strong conclusions . . . until, exasperatingly, new evidence throws our beliefs into disarray. Critical thinkers are willing to accept this state of uncertainty. They are not afraid to say, "I don't know" or "I'm not sure."

In science, tolerating uncertainty means that researchers must avoid drawing firm conclusions until other researchers have repeated, or *replicated*, their studies and verified their findings. Secrecy is a big "no-no" in science; you must be willing to tell others where you got your ideas and how you tested them so that others can challenge the findings if they think the findings are wrong. Replication is an essential part of the scientific process because sometimes what seems to be a fabulous phenomenon turns out to be only a fluke.

The need to accept a certain amount of uncertainty does not mean that we must abandon all assumptions, beliefs, and convictions. That would be impossible, in any case: We all need values and principles to guide our actions. As Vincent Ruggiero (1988) wrote, "It is not the embracing of an idea that causes problems—it is the refusal to relax that embrace when good sense dictates doing so."

As you read this book, you will have many opportunities to think critically about psychological theories and about the personal and social issues that affect us all. From time to time, a blue tab with a light bulb symbol (like the one shown here) will highlight a discussion to which one or more of our critical-thinking guidelines are especially relevant. Also, in Quick Quizzes, the light bulb will indicate questions that give you practice in applying the guidelines. Keep in mind,

Thinking Critically About . . .

theory An organized system of assumptions and principles that purports to explain a specified set of phenomena and their interrelationships.

Many questions currently have no firm answers. For example, several explanations of sexual orientation have been offered, but no one theory can account for the many variations of both homosexuality and heterosexuality, as we will see in Chapter 14.

however, that critical thinking is important throughout the book, not only where the light bulb appears.

Critical thinking is a tool to guide us on a lifelong quest for understanding—a tool that we must keep sharpening. And it is as much an attitude as it is a set of skills. True critical thinking, in the words of philosopher Richard W. Paul (1984), is "fair-mindedness brought into the heart of everyday life."

WHAT'S AHEAD

- When are psychological case studies informative, and when are they useless?
- Why do psychologists often observe people in laboratories instead of simply watching them in everyday situations?
- What's the test of a good test?
- Why should you be skeptical about psychological tests that appear in magazines and newspapers?
- What's the difference between a psychological survey and a poll of listeners conducted by a radio talk-show host?

DESCRIPTIVE STUDIES: ESTABLISHING THE FACTS

Psychologists gather evidence to support their hypotheses by using different methods, depending on the kinds of questions they want to answer. These methods are not mutually exclusive, however. Just as a police detective may rely on DNA samples, fingerprints, and interviews of suspects to figure out "who done it," psychological sleuths often draw on different techniques at different stages of an investigation. As you read about these methods, you may want to list their advantages and disadvantages, to help you remember them better, then check your list against the one in Table 1.3 on page 28.

We will begin with **descriptive methods**, which allow researchers to describe and predict behaviour but not necessarily to choose one explanation over competing ones.

descriptive methods Methods that yield descriptions of behaviour but not necessarily causal explanations.

Case Studies

A **case study** (or *case history*) is a detailed description of a particular individual, based on careful observation or on formal psychological testing. It may include information about a person's childhood, dreams, fantasies, experiences, relationships, and hopes—anything that will provide insight into the person's behaviour. Case studies are most commonly used by clinicians, but sometimes academic researchers use them as well, especially when they are just beginning to study a topic or when practical or ethical considerations prevent them from gathering information in other ways.

For example, suppose you want to know whether the first few years of life are critical for

case study A detailed description of a particular individual being studied or treated.

Quick Quiz

Can you identify how the guidelines to critical thinking were violated in each of the following cases?

1. For years, writer Norman Cousins told how he had cured himself of a rare, life-threatening disease through a combination of humour and vitamins. In a best-selling book, he recommended the same approach to others.

2. Benjamin Rush, an eighteenth-century physician, believed that yellow fever should be treated by bloodletting. Many of his patients died, but Rush did not lose faith in his approach; he attributed each recovery to his treatment and each death to the severity of the disease (Stanovich, 1996).

Answers:

1. Cousins oversimplified, arguing by anecdote instead of examining evidence from controlled studies that included people who were not helped by humour and vitamins; he may also have been reasoning emotionally because of his own dramatic recovery.

2. Rush failed to analyze and test his assumptions; he violated the principle of falsifiability, interpreting a patient's survival as support for his hypothesis and explaining away each death by saying that the person had been too ill for the treatment to work. Thus, there was no possible counterevidence that could refute the theory (which, by the way, was dead wrong—the "treatment" was actually as dangerous as the disease).

observational study A study in which the researcher carefully and systematically observes and records behaviour without interfering with the behaviour; it may involve either naturalistic or laboratory observation.

acquiring a first language. Can children who have missed out on hearing speech (or, in the case of deaf children, seeing signs) "catch up" later? Obviously, psychologists cannot answer this question by isolating children and seeing what happens! So instead they have studied unusual cases of language deprivation.

Case studies illustrate psychological principles in a way that abstract generalizations and cold statistics never can, and they produce a more detailed picture of an individual than other methods do. In biological research, cases of patients with brain damage have yielded important clues to how the brain is organized (see Chapter 4). But in most instances, case studies have serious drawbacks. Information is often missing or is hard to interpret. The observer may have biases that cause him or her to notice some facts and overlook others. The person who is the focus of the study may report selective or inaccurate memories. And that person may be *unrepresentative* of the group that the researcher is interested in. For example, it is possible that Genie was born with mental deficits that made her unlike most other children. For all these reasons, case studies are usually only sources, rather than tests, of hypotheses. You should be extremely cautious about pop-psych books and TV programs that present only testimonials and vivid case histories as evidence.

This picture, drawn by Genie, a young girl who endured years of isolation and mistreatment, shows one of her favourite pastimes: listening to researcher Susan Curtiss playing the piano. Genie's drawings were used along with other case material to study her mental and social development.

Observational Studies

In **observational studies**, the researcher observes, measures, and records behaviour while taking care to avoid intruding on the people (or animals) being observed. The primary purpose of *naturalistic observation* is to find out how people or other animals act in their normal social environments. Psychologists use naturalistic observation wherever people happen to be—at home, on playgrounds or streets, in schoolrooms, or in offices. Often, however, researchers prefer to make their observations in a laboratory setting. In *laboratory observation*, they have more control. They can use sophisticated equipment, determine how many people will be observed at once, maintain a clear line of vision, and so forth.

Suppose that you wanted to know how infants of different ages respond when left with a stranger. The most efficient approach might be to have parents and their infants come to your laboratory, observe them playing together for a while through a one-way window, then have a stranger enter the room and, a few minutes later, have the parent leave. You could record signs of distress, interactions with the stranger, and other behaviour, checking your observations against those of others to ensure accuracy. If you did this, you would find that very young infants carry on cheerfully with whatever they are doing when the parent leaves. However, by the age of about eight months, children will often burst into tears or show other signs of what child psychologists call "separation anxiety" (see Chapter 3).

One shortcoming of laboratory observation is that the presence of researchers and special equipment may cause participants to behave differently

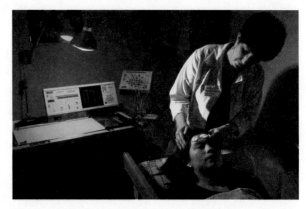

This woman is slumbering for science. By sleeping in the laboratory instead of in the natural environment of their own homes, volunteers can provide researchers with valuable information about brain and muscle activity during sleep.

than they would in their usual surroundings. Further, observational studies, like other descriptive studies, are more useful for describing behaviour than for explaining it. If we observe infants protesting whenever a parent leaves the room, we cannot be sure why they are protesting. Is it because they have become attached to their parents and want them nearby, or have they learned from experience that crying brings an adult with a cookie and a cuddle? Observational studies alone cannot answer such questions.

Tests

Psychological tests, sometimes called *assessment instruments*, are procedures for measuring and evaluating personality traits, emotional states, aptitudes, interests, abilities, and values. Typically, tests require people to answer a series of written or oral questions. The answers may then be totalled to yield a single numerical score or a set of scores. *Objective tests*, also called *inventories*, measure beliefs, feelings, or behaviours of which an individual is aware; *projective tests* are designed to tap unconscious feelings or motives (see Chapter 11).

At one time or another, you no doubt have taken a personality test, an achievement test, or a vocational-aptitude test. Hundreds of psychological tests are used in industry, education, the military, and the helping professions. Some are given to individuals, others to large groups. These measures help clarify differences among individuals as well as differences in the reactions of the same person on different occasions or at different stages of life. Tests may be used to promote self-understanding, to evaluate treatments and programs, or, in scientific research, to draw generalizations about human behaviour. Well-constructed psychological tests are a great improvement over simple self-evaluation because many people have a distorted view of their own abilities and traits.

One measure of a good test is whether it is **standardized**—that is, whether uniform procedures exist for giving and scoring the test. It would hardly be fair to give some people detailed instructions and plenty of time and others only vague instructions and limited time. Those who administer the test must know exactly how to explain the tasks involved, how much time to allow, and what materials to use. Scoring is usually done by referring to **norms**, or established standards of performance. The usual procedure for developing norms is to give the test to a large group of people who resemble those for whom the test is intended. Norms determine which scores can be considered high, low, or average.

Test construction presents many challenges. For one thing, the test must have **reliability**—that is, it must produce the same results from one time and place to the next. A vocational-aptitude test is not reliable if it tells Tom that he would make a wonderful engineer but a poor journalist, but then gives different results when Tom retakes the test a week later. Nor is it reliable if alternative forms of the test, intended to be comparable, yield different results.

To be useful, a test must also have **validity**; that is, it must measure what it is designed to measure. A creativity test is not valid if what it actually measures is verbal sophistication. The validity of a test is often measured by its ability to predict other, independent measures, or *criteria*, of the trait in question. The criterion for a scholastic aptitude test might be college grades; the criterion for a test of shyness might be behaviour in social situations. Among psychologists, controversy exists about the validity of even some widely used tests, such as IQ tests and the Scholastic Assessment Test (SAT).

Criticisms and re-evaluations of psychological tests keep psychological assessment honest and

standardize In test construction, to develop uniform procedures for giving and scoring a test.

norms In test construction, established standards of performance.

psychological tests Procedures used to measure and evaluate personality traits, emotional states, aptitudes, interests, abilities, and values.

reliability In test construction, the consistency of test scores from one time and place to another.

validity The ability of a test to measure what it was designed to measure.

Get Involved   A Study of Personal Space

Try a little naturalistic observation of your own. Go to a public place where people seat themselves, such as a movie theatre or a cafeteria with large tables. You might recruit some friends to help you; you can divide the area into sections and assign each observer one section to observe. As individuals and groups sit down, note how many seats they leave between themselves and the next person. On the average, how far do people tend to sit from strangers? Once you have your results, see how many possible explanations you can come up with.

Many people attach a lot of importance to their test scores.

representative sample A group of individuals, selected from a population for study, which matches that population in important characteristics such as age and sex.

scientifically rigorous. In contrast, the pop-psych tests frequently found in magazines and newspapers and on the Internet usually have not been evaluated for either validity or reliability. These questionnaires often have inviting headlines such as "What Breed of Dog Are You Most Like?" or "The Seven Types of Lovers," but they are merely lists of questions that someone thought sounded good.

Surveys

surveys Questionnaires and interviews that ask people directly about their experiences, attitudes, or opinions.

Psychological tests usually generate information about people indirectly. In contrast, **surveys** are questionnaires and interviews that gather information by asking people *directly* about their experiences, attitudes, or opinions. Most of us are familiar with national opinion surveys, such as Ipsos Reid and *Maclean's* Year in Review polls. Surveys have been done on many topics, from Internet use to sexual preferences.

volunteer bias A shortcoming of findings derived from a sample of volunteers instead of a representative sample; the volunteers may differ from those who did not volunteer.

"Are You (a) Contented, (b) Happy, (c) Very Happy, (d) Mildly Happy, (e) Deliriously Happy?"

Surveys produce bushels of data, but they are not easy to do well. The biggest hurdle is getting a **representative sample**, a group of individuals who accurately represent the larger population that the researcher wishes to describe. Suppose you wanted to know about drug use among college students. Questioning every college student in the country would not be practical; instead, you would need to recruit a sample. You could use special selection procedures to ensure that this sample contained the same proportion of women, men, Asians, Central Americans, Muslims, Catholics, Jews, and so on as in the general population of college students. Even then, a sample drawn just from your own school or town might not yield results applicable to the entire country or even the province.

Thinking Critically About Opinion Polls and Surveys

Most people do not realize that a sample's size is less critical than its representativeness. A small but representative sample may yield extremely accurate results, whereas a survey or poll that fails to use proper sampling methods may yield questionable results, no matter how large the sample. For example, when a radio talk-show host surveys listeners about a political issue, or a magazine surveys readers about their sexual habits, the results are not likely to generalize to the population as a whole—even if thousands of people respond. Why? As a group, people who listen to talk radio or read *Chatelaine* are likely to hold different opinions than those who prefer, say, CBC Radio 2 or *Canadian Geographic*. Moreover, such polls suffer from a **volunteer bias**: Those who feel strongly enough to volunteer their opinions may differ from those who stay silent. When you read about a survey (or any other kind of study), always ask who participated. A biased, nonrepresentative sample does not necessarily mean that a survey is worthless or uninteresting, but it does mean that the results may not hold true for other groups.

Another problem with surveys is that people sometimes lie, especially when the survey is about a touchy topic ("What? Me do that disgusting/dishonest/fattening thing? Never!"). The likelihood of lying is reduced when respondents are guaranteed anonymity. Computer technology can help in this regard because people are more likely to feel anonymous when they "talk" to a computer than when they fill out a paper-and-pencil questionnaire (Turner et al., 1998). Also, there are ways to check for lying—for example, by asking a question several times with different wording. But not all surveys use these techniques, and even when people are trying to be truthful, they may misinterpret the survey questions or misremember the past.

When you hear about the results of a survey or opinion poll, you also need to consider which questions were (and were not) asked, and how the questions were phrased. The questions a researcher asks may reflect his or her assumptions about the topic or may be designed to further a particular agenda (Ericksen & Steffen, 1999). Many years ago, famed sex researcher Alfred Kinsey made it his practice always to ask, "How many times have you (masturbated, had nonmarital sex, etc.)?" rather than "Have you ever (masturbated, had nonmarital sex, etc.)?" The first type of question elicits more truthful responses than the second because it decreases the respondent's potential self-consciousness about having done the act in question. The second way of phrasing the question would have permitted embarrassed respondents to reply with a simple but dishonest "No."

As you can see, although surveys can be extremely informative, they must be conducted and interpreted carefully.

Quick Quiz

Be careful how you interpret these questions.

A. Which descriptive method would be most appropriate for studying each of the following topics? (All of them, by the way, have been investigated by psychologists.)

1. Ways in which the games of boys differ from those of girls
2. Changes in attitudes toward nuclear disarmament after a TV movie about the nuclear holocaust
3. The math skills of children in Canada versus those in Japan
4. Physiological changes that occur when people watch violent movies
5. The development of a male infant who was reared as a female after his penis was accidentally burned off during a routine surgery

    a. case study
    b. naturalistic observation
    c. laboratory observation
    d. survey
    e. test

B. Professor Flummox gives her new test of aptitude for studying psychology to her psychology students at the start of the year. At the end of the year, she finds that those who did well on the test averaged only a C in the course. The test lacks _____.

Answers:

A. 1.b 2.d 3.e 4.c 5.a   B. validity

WHAT'S AHEAD

- If two things are "negatively" correlated, such as grades and TV watching, what is the relationship between them?
- If watching TV and behaving aggressively are positively correlated, does that mean TV causes violence?

CORRELATIONAL STUDIES: LOOKING FOR RELATIONSHIPS

In descriptive research, psychologists often want to know whether two or more phenomena are related and, if so, how strongly. For example, are students' grade-point averages related to the number of hours they spend watching television? To find out, a psychologist would do a **correlational study**.

correlational study A descriptive study that looks for a consistent relationship between two phenomena.

Measuring Correlations

correlation A measure of how strongly two variables are related to each other.

variables Characteristics of behaviour or experience that can be measured or described by a numerical scale; variables are manipulated and assessed in scientific studies.

positive correlation An association between increases in one variable and increases in another, or between decreases in one and decreases in another.

coefficient of correlation A measure of correlation that ranges in value from −1.00 to +1.00.

negative correlation An association between increases in one variable and decreases in another.

The word **correlation** is often used as a synonym for "relationship." Technically, however, a correlation is a numerical measure of the *strength* of the relationship between two things. The "things" may be events, scores, or anything else that can be recorded and tallied. In psychological studies, such things are called **variables** because they can vary in quantifiable ways. Height, weight, age, income, IQ scores, number of items recalled on a memory test, number of smiles in a given time period—anything that can be measured, rated, or scored can serve as a variable.

A **positive correlation** means that high values of one variable are associated with high values of the other, and that low values of one variable are associated with low values of the other.

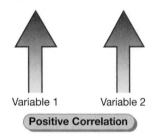

Variable 1   Variable 2

Positive Correlation

Height and weight are positively correlated, for example; so are IQ scores and school grades. Rarely is a correlation perfect, however. Some tall people weigh less than some short ones; some people with average IQs are superstars in the classroom, and some with high IQs get poor grades. Figure 1.2(a) shows a positive correlation between men's educational level and their annual income.

A **negative correlation** means that high values of one variable are associated with low values of the other.

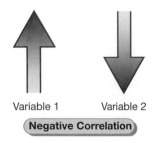

Variable 1   Variable 2

Negative Correlation

Figure 1.2(b) shows a negative correlation between average income and the incidence of den-

tal disease for groups of 100 families; in general, as you can see, the higher the income, the fewer the dental problems. In the automobile business, the older the car, the lower the price, except for antiques and models favoured by collectors. As for human beings, in general, the older adults are, the fewer kilometres they can run, the fewer crimes they are likely to commit, and the fewer hairs they have on their heads. And remember the correlation between hours spent watching TV and grade-point averages? It's a negative one, too: Spending many hours in front of the television is associated with lower grades (Potter, 1987; Ridley-Johnson, Cooper, & Chance, 1983). See whether you can think of other variables that are negatively correlated. Remember, though, a negative correlation means that a certain kind of relationship exists. If there is no relationship between two variables, as in Figure 1.2(c), we say that they are *uncorrelated*. Shoe size and IQ scores are uncorrelated.

The statistic used to express a correlation is called the **coefficient of correlation**. This number conveys both the size of the correlation and its direction. A perfect positive correlation has a coefficient of +1.00, and a perfect negative correlation has a coefficient of −1.00. Suppose you weighed 10 people and listed them in order, from lightest to heaviest, then measured their heights and listed the people in order, from shortest to tallest. If the names on the two lists were in exactly the same order, the correlation between weight and height would be +1.00. If the correlation between two variables is +.80, it means that the two are strongly related. If the correlation is −.80, the relationship is just as strong, but it is negative. When there is no association between two variables, the coefficient is zero or close to zero.

Cautions about Correlations

Correlational studies are common in psychology and are often reported in the news. But beware: correlations can be misleading. The important thing to remember is that *a correlation does not show causation*. It is easy to assume that if A predicts B, then A must be causing B—that is, making B happen—but that is not necessarily so. The number of storks nesting in some European villages is reportedly correlated (positively) with the number of human births in those villages. Therefore, knowing when the storks nest allows you to predict when more births than usual will occur. But that doesn't mean that storks bring

Thinking Critically About Correlation and Causation

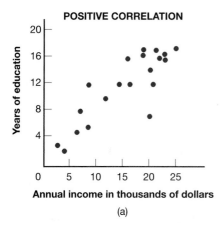

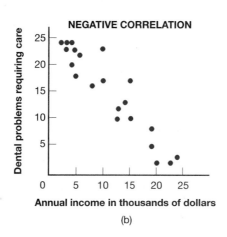

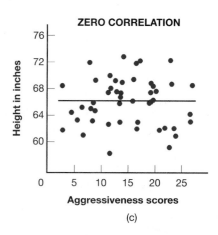

(a)   (b)   (c)

FIGURE 1.2 Correlations

Graph (a) shows a positive correlation: In general, income rises with education. Graph (b) shows a negative correlation: In general, the higher people's incomes are, the fewer dental problems they have. Graph (c) shows a zero correlation between height and aggressiveness.

babies or that babies attract storks! Human births seem to be somewhat more frequent at certain times of the year (you might want to speculate on the reasons), and the peaks just happen to coincide with the storks' nesting periods.

The coincidental nature of the correlation between nesting storks and human births is obvious, but in other cases, unwarranted conclusions about causation are more tempting. For example, children's TV watching is moderately correlated with their aggressiveness. What does this positive correlation mean? Many psychologists have concluded that violent programs make some children more aggressive (Bushman & Anderson, 2001). Another possibility, however, is that aggressive children are drawn to television violence. Or some third factor, such as growing up in a family where physical violence is common, may account for *both* children's aggressiveness and their attraction to violent programs. (We will discuss this issue further in Chapter 9.) Similarly, the negative correlation between TV watching and grades might exist because heavy TV watchers have less time to study, but it is also possible that they have some personality trait that attracts them to TV and makes them dislike studying, or that they use TV as an escape when their grades are low, or that TV is especially appealing to people who are not academically inclined . . . you get the idea.

The moral of the story: When two variables are associated, one variable may or may not be causing the other.

Quick Quiz

Are you clear about correlations?

A. Identify each of the following as a positive or negative correlation:

1. The higher a male monkey's level of the hormone testosterone, the more aggressive he is likely to be.

2. The older people are, the less frequently they tend to have sexual intercourse.

3. The hotter the weather is, the more crimes against persons (such as muggings) tend to occur.

B. Now see whether you can generate two or three possible explanations for each of the preceding findings.

Answers:

A. 1. positive   2. negative   3. positive

B. 1. The hormone may cause aggressiveness, or acting aggressively may stimulate hormone production.

2. Older people may have less interest in sex than younger people, have less energy or more physical ailments, or simply have trouble finding partners.

3. Hot temperatures may make people edgy and cause them to commit crimes; potential victims may be more plentiful in warm weather because more people go outside; criminals may find it more comfortable to be out committing their crimes in warm weather than in cold. (Our explanations for these correlations are not the only ones possible.)

WHAT'S AHEAD

- Why do psychologists rely so heavily on experiments?
- What, exactly, do control groups control for?
- In a double-blind study, what people are "blind," and what are they not supposed to "see"?

THE EXPERIMENT: HUNTING FOR CAUSES

experiment A controlled test of a hypothesis in which the researcher manipulates one variable to discover its effect on another.

independent variable A variable that an experimenter manipulates.

dependent variable A variable that an experimenter predicts will be affected by manipulations of the independent variable.

Researchers gain plenty of information from descriptive studies, but when they want to actually track down the causes of behaviour, they rely heavily on the experimental method. An **experiment** allows the researcher to control or manipulate the situation being studied. Instead of being a passive recorder of what is going on, the researcher actively does something that he or she believes will affect people's behaviour and then observes what happens. These procedures allow the experimenter to draw conclusions about cause and effect—about what causes what.

All psychological studies must conform to certain ethical guidelines, but such guidelines are especially important in experimental research because of this element of manipulation. In most colleges and universities, a review committee must approve all proposed studies. In addition, the Canadian Psychological Association (CPA) has a code of ethics (2000), stating that participants in a study must voluntarily consent to participate and must know enough about the study to make an intelligent decision, a doctrine known as *informed consent*. Investigators must protect participants from physical and mental discomfort or harm and, if any risk exists, must warn them and give them an opportunity to withdraw at any time.

The CPA's code also covers the humane treatment of research animals, which are used in a minority of psychological studies but are crucial to progress in some fields, especially biological psychology and behavioural research. Every experiment involving vertebrates must now be reviewed by a research institution's Research Ethics Board (REB).

Experimental Variables

Imagine that you are a psychologist and you come across reports that cigarette smoking improves reaction time on simple tasks. You have a hunch that nicotine may have the opposite effect, however, when the task is as complex and demanding as driving a car. Therefore you decide to do an experiment to test your hypothesis. In a laboratory, you ask smokers to "drive" using a computerized driving simulator equipped with a stick shift and a gas pedal. The object, you tell them, is to maximize distance by driving as fast as possible on a winding road while avoiding collisions with other cars. At your request, some of the participants smoke a cigarette immediately before climbing into the driver's seat. Others do not. You are interested in comparing how many collisions the two groups have. The basic design of this experiment is illustrated in Figure 1.3, to which you may want to refer as you read the next few pages.

The aspect of an experimental situation manipulated or varied by the researcher is known as the **independent variable**. The reaction of the subjects—the behaviour that the researcher tries to predict—is the **dependent variable**. Every experiment has at least one independent and one dependent variable. In our example, the independent variable is nicotine use: one cigarette versus none. The dependent variable is the number of collisions.

Ideally, everything in the experimental situation except the independent variable is held constant—that is, kept the same for all participants. You would not have some people use a stick shift and others an automatic, unless shift type were an independent variable. Similarly, you would not have some people go through the experiment alone and others perform in front of an audience. Holding everything but the independent variable constant ensures that whatever happens is due to the researcher's manipulation and nothing else. It allows you to rule out other interpretations.

Understandably, students often have trouble keeping independent and dependent variables straight. You might think of it this way: The dependent variable—the outcome of the study—depends on the independent variable. When psychologists set up an experiment, they think, "If I do X, people in my study will do Y." The "X" represents the independent variable; the "Y" represents the dependent variable:

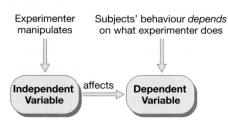

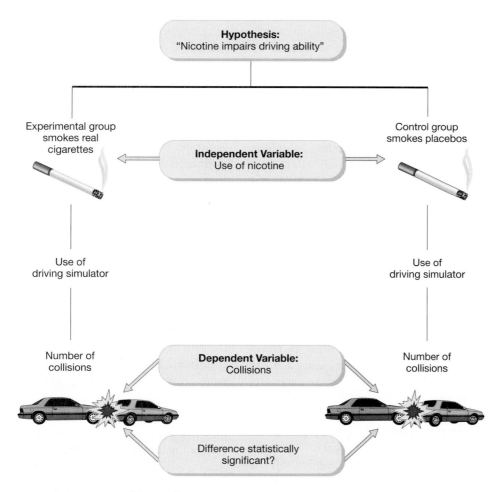

FIGURE 1.3 Do Smoking and Driving Mix?

The text describes this experimental design to test the hypothesis that nicotine in cigarettes impairs driving ability.

Most variables may be either independent or dependent, depending on what the experimenter wishes to find out. If you want to know whether eating chocolate makes people nervous, then the amount of chocolate eaten is the independent variable. If you want to know whether feeling nervous makes people eat chocolate, then the amount of chocolate eaten is the dependent variable.

Experimental and Control Conditions

Experiments usually require both an experimental condition and a comparison, or **control condition**. People in the control condition are treated exactly like those in the experimental condition, except that they are not exposed to the same treatment or manipulation of the independent variable. Without a control condition, you can't be sure if the behaviour you are interested in would have occurred anyway, even

without your manipulation. In some studies, the same subjects can be used in both the control and the experimental condition; they are said to serve as their own controls. In other studies, people are assigned to either an *experimental group* or a *control group*.

In our nicotine experiment, the participants who smoke before driving make up the experimental group, and those who do not smoke make up the control group. We want these two groups to be roughly the same in terms of average driving skill. It would not do to start out with a bunch of reckless roadrunners in the experimental group and a bunch of tired tortoises in the control group. We probably also want the two groups to be similar in average intelligence, education, smoking history, and other characteristics so that none of these variables will affect our results. One way to accomplish this is to use **random assignment** of people to one group or another. If we have enough

control condition In an experiment, a comparison condition in which subjects are not exposed to the same treatment of the independent variable as are those in the experimental condition.

random assignment A procedure for assigning people to experimental and control groups in which each individual has the same probability as any other of being assigned to a given group.

participants in our study, individual characteristics that could possibly affect the results are likely to be roughly balanced in the two groups, so we can ignore the characteristics.

We now have two groups. We also have a problem. In order to smoke, people in the experimental group must light up and inhale. These acts might set off certain expectations—of feeling relaxed, getting nervous, feeling confident, or whatever—and this, in turn, might affect driving performance. It would be better to have the control group do everything the experimental group does except use nicotine. Therefore, let's change our experimental design a bit. Instead of having participants in the control group refrain from smoking, we will give them a **placebo**, a fake treatment.

Placebos, which are critical when testing new drugs, often take the form of pills or injections containing no active ingredients. (For example, to see what placebos revealed in a study of Viagra for women's sexual problems, see Figure 1.4.) In our nicotine study, we will use phony cigarettes that taste and smell like the real thing but contain no active ingredients. Our control subjects will not know their cigarettes are fake and will have no way of distinguishing them from real ones. Now if they have substantially fewer collisions than the experimental group, we will feel safe in concluding that nicotine increases the probability of an auto accident.

placebo An inactive substance or fake treatment used as a control in an experiment.

single-blind study An experiment in which subjects do not know whether they are in an experimental or a control group.

experimenter effects Unintended changes in subjects' behaviour due to cues inadvertently given by the experimenter.

double-blind study An experiment in which neither the participants nor the individuals running the study know which participants are in the control group and which are in the experimental group until after the results are tallied.

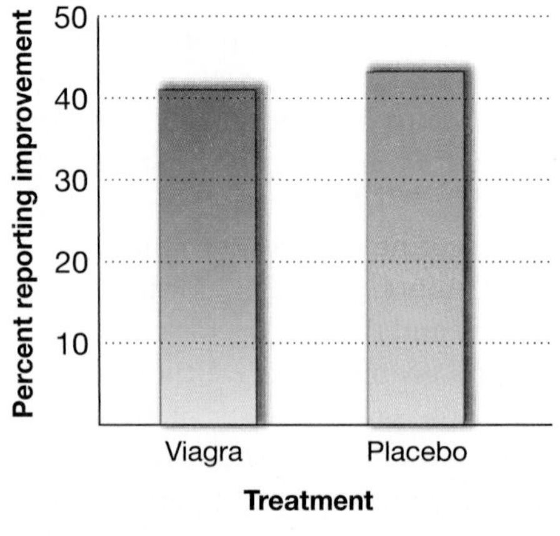

FIGURE 1.4 Does Viagra Work for Women?

Placebos are essential to determine whether people taking a new drug improve because of the drug—or because of their expectations about it. In one study, 41 percent of women taking Viagra said their sex lives had improved. It sounds impressive, but 43 percent taking a placebo pill said their sex lives had also improved (Basson et al., 2002).

Control groups, by the way, are also important in nonexperimental studies. Consider one highly publicized descriptive study of children whose parents divorced when the children were young (Wallerstein, Lewis, & Blakeslee, 2000). In lengthy interviews over many years, the children (who are now adults) revealed many psychological problems, such as low motivation and difficulties in relationships. The clinical researchers who did the study attributed these problems to the parents' divorces. However, the study did not include a control group of children growing up with two parents, or better yet, of children growing up with two unhappy, quarrelling parents. Without a control group, the results cannot tell us much; maybe these young people's problems were due to something else entirely and were no different from the problems of their classmates from intact families. Research that did include a control group of two-parent families found that, although divorce clearly did increase the risk of psychological problems in children, by adulthood, fully 75 to 80 percent had adjusted and were doing fine (Hetherington & Kelly, 2002).

Experimenter Effects

Because expectations can influence the results of a study, participants should not know whether they are in an experimental or a control group. When this is so (as it usually is), the experiment is said to be a **single-blind study**. But participants are not the only ones who bring expectations to the laboratory; so do researchers. And researchers' expectations and hopes for a particular result may cause them to inadvertently influence the participants' responses through facial expressions, posture, tone of voice, or some other cue. Such **experimenter effects** can be powerful; even an experimenter's friendly smile can affect people's responses in a study (Rosenthal, 1994).

One solution to the problem of experimenter effects is to do a **double-blind study**. In such a study, the person running the experiment—the one having actual contact with the participants—also does not know who is in which group until the data have been gathered. Double-blind procedures are standard in drug research. Different doses of a drug are coded in some way, and the person administering the drug is kept in the dark about the code's meaning until after the experiment. To run our nicotine study in a double-blind fashion, we would keep the person dispensing the cigarettes from knowing which ones were real and which were placebos.

Advantages and Limitations of Experiments

Because experiments allow conclusions about cause and effect, and because they permit researchers to distinguish real effects from placebo effects, they have long been the method of choice in psychology.

However, like all methods, the experiment has its limitations. Just as in other kinds of studies, the participants are not always representative of the larger population. Most volunteers in academic experiments are college students, who differ in many ways from people who are not in school. Moreover, in an experiment, the researcher determines which questions are asked and which behaviours are recorded, and the participants try to do as they are told. In their desire to co-operate, advance scientific knowledge, or present themselves in a positive light, they may act in ways

that they ordinarily would not (Kihlstrom, 1995).

Thus, research psychologists confront a dilemma: The more control they exercise over the situation, the more unlike real life it may be. For this reason, many psychologists have called for more **field research**, the careful study of behaviour in natural contexts such as schools and the workplace, using both descriptive and experimental methods. For example, a psychologist interested in ways of reducing prejudice might study that problem not just in the laboratory, but also in offices and schools. Field research on prejudice has led to successful strategies for reducing ethnic conflict (see Chapter 10).

Every research method has both strengths and weaknesses. Did you make a list of each method's advantages and disadvantages, as we suggested earlier? If so, you can compare it now with the one in Table 1.3.

field research Descriptive or experimental research conducted in a natural setting outside the laboratory.

Quick Quiz

A. Name the independent and dependent variables in studies designed to answer the following questions:
   1. Whether sleeping after learning a poem improves memory for the poem
   2. Whether the presence of other people affects a person's willingness to help someone in distress
   3. Whether people get agitated from listening to heavy-metal music

B. On a talk show, Dr. Blitznik announces a fabulous new program: Chocolate Immersion Therapy (CIT). "People who spend one day a week doing nothing but eating chocolate are soon cured of eating disorders, depression, drug abuse, and poor study habits," claims Dr. Blitznik. What should you find out about CIT before signing up?

Answers:

A.
1. Opportunity to sleep after learning is the independent variable; memory for the poem is the dependent variable.
2. The presence of other people is the independent variable; willingness to help others is the dependent variable.
3. Exposure to heavy-metal music is the independent variable; agitation is the dependent variable.
B. Some questions to ask: Is there research showing that people who go through CIT did better than those in a control group who did not have the therapy, or who had a different therapy—say, Broccoli Immersion Therapy? If so, how many people were studied? How were they selected, and how were they assigned to the therapy and no-therapy groups? Did the person running the experiment know who was getting CIT and who was not? How long did the "cures" last? Has the research been replicated?

TABLE 1.3 Research Methods in Psychology: Their Advantages and Disadvantages

Method	Advantages	Disadvantages
Case study	Good source of hypotheses. Provides in-depth information on individuals. Unusual cases can shed light on situations or problems that are unethical or impractical to study in other ways.	Vital information may be missing, making the case hard to interpret. The individual's memories may be selective or inaccurate. The individual may not be representative or typical.
Naturalistic observation	Allows description of behaviour as it occurs in the natural environment. Often useful in first stages of a research program.	Allows researcher little or no control of the situation. Observations may be biased. Does not allow firm conclusions about cause and effect.
Laboratory observation	Allows more control than does naturalistic observation. Allows use of sophisticated equipment.	Allows researcher only limited control of the situation. Observations may be biased. Does not allow firm conclusions about cause and effect. Behaviour may differ from behaviour in the natural environment.
Test	Yields information on personality traits, emotional states, aptitudes, and abilities.	Difficult to construct tests that are reliable and valid.
Survey	Provides a large amount of information on large numbers of people.	If sample is nonrepresentative or biased, it may be impossible to generalize from the results. Responses may be inaccurate or untrue.
Correlational study	Shows whether two or more variables are related. Allows general predictions.	Does not permit identification of cause and effect.
Experiment	Allows researcher to control the situation. Allows researcher to identify cause and effect and to distinguish placebo effects from treatment effects.	Situation is artificial, and results may not generalize well to the real world. Sometimes difficult to avoid experimenter effects.

descriptive statistics Statistics that organize and summarize research data.

arithmetic mean An average that is calculated by adding up a set of quantities and dividing the sum by the total number of quantities in the set.

WHAT'S AHEAD

- In psychological studies, why are averages sometimes misleading?
- How can psychologists tell whether a finding is impressive or trivial?
- Why are some findings statistically significant but unimportant in practical terms?

EVALUATING THE FINDINGS

If you are a psychologist who has just done an observational study, a survey, or an experiment, your work has only just begun. Once you have some results in hand, you must do three things with them: (1) describe them, (2) assess how reliable and meaningful they are, and (3) figure out how to explain them.

Why Psychologists Use Statistics

Let's say that 30 people in the nicotine experiment smoked real cigarettes, and 30 smoked placebos. We have recorded the number of collisions for each person on the driving simulator. Now we have 60 numbers. What can we do with them?

The first step is to summarize the data. The world does not want to hear how many collisions each person had. It wants to know what happened in the nicotine group as a whole compared with what happened in the control group. To provide this information, we need numbers that sum up our data. Such numbers, known as **descriptive statistics**, are often depicted in graphs and charts.

A good way to summarize the data is to compute group averages. The most commonly used type of average is the **arithmetic mean**. (For two

Averages can be misleading if you don't know the extent to which events deviated from the statistical mean and how they were distributed.

other types, see the Appendix.) The mean is calculated by adding up all the individual scores and dividing the result by the number of scores. We can compute a mean for the nicotine group by adding up the 30 collision scores and dividing the sum by 30. Then we can do the same for the control group. Now our 60 numbers have been boiled down to 2. For the sake of our example, let's assume that the nicotine group had an average of 10 collisions, whereas the control group's average was only 7.

We must be careful, however, about how we interpret these averages. It is possible that no one in our nicotine group actually had 10 collisions: Perhaps half the people in the group were motoring maniacs and had 15 collisions, whereas the others were more cautious and had only 5. Perhaps almost all the subjects had 9, 10, or 11 collisions. Perhaps the number of accidents ranged from 0 to 15. The mean does not tell us about such variability in the subjects' responses. For that, we need other descriptive statistics. For example, the **standard deviation** tells us how clustered or spread out the individual scores are around the mean; the more spread out they are, the less "typical" the mean is. (For details, see the Appendix.) Unfortunately, when research is reported in newspapers or on the nightly news, you usually hear only about the mean.

At this point in our nicotine study, we have one group with an average of 10 collisions and another with an average of 7. Should we break out the champagne? Try to get on TV? Call our mothers? Better hold off. Perhaps if one group had an average of 15 collisions and the other an average of 1, we could get excited. But rarely does a psychological study hit you between the eyes with a sensationally clear result. In most cases, there is some possibility that the difference between the two groups was due simply to chance.

Perhaps the people in the nicotine group just happened to be a little more accident-prone, and their behaviour had nothing to do with the nicotine.

To find out how impressive the data are, psychologists use **inferential statistics**. These statistics do not merely describe or summarize the data; they permit a researcher to draw inferences (conclusions based on evidence) about how meaningful the findings are. Like descriptive statistics, inferential statistics involve the application of mathematical formulas to the data (again, see the Appendix for details). The most commonly used inferential statistics are **significance tests**, which tell researchers how likely it is that a result occurred by chance. In our nicotine study, a significance test will tell us how likely it is that the difference between the nicotine group and the placebo group occurred by chance. It is not possible to rule out chance entirely, but if the likelihood that a result occurred by chance is extremely low, we say that the result is *statistically significant*. This means that the probability that the difference is "real" is overwhelming—not certain, mind you, but overwhelming.

By convention, psychologists consider a result to be significant if it would be expected to occur by chance 5 or fewer times in 100 repetitions of the study. Another way of saying this is that the result is significant at the .05 ("point oh five") level. If the difference could be expected to occur by chance in 6 out of 100 studies, we would have to say that the results failed to support the hypothesis—that the difference we obtained might well have occurred merely by chance—although we might still want to do further research to be sure. You can see that psychologists refuse to be impressed by just any old result.

By the way, a nicotine study similar to our hypothetical example has actually been done, using somewhat more complicated procedures

inferential statistics Statistical procedures that allow researchers to draw inferences about how statistically meaningful a study's results are.

significance tests Statistical tests that assess how likely it is that a study's results occurred merely by chance.

standard deviation A commonly used measure of variability that indicates the average difference between scores and their mean.

(Spilich, June, & Renner, 1992). Smokers who lit up before driving got a little farther on the simulated road, but they also had significantly more collisions on average (10.7) than did temporarily abstaining smokers (5.2) or nonsmokers (3.1). After hearing about this research, the head of Federal Express banned smoking on the job among all of the company's drivers.

Quick Quiz

Check your understanding of the descriptive–inferential distinction by mentally placing a check in the appropriate column for each phrase:

	Descriptive Statistics	Inferential Statistics
1. Summarize the data	_____	_____
2. Give likelihood of data occurring by chance	_____	_____
3. Include the mean	_____	_____
4. Give a measure of statistical significance	_____	_____
5. Tell you whether to call your mother about your results	_____	_____

Answers:

1. descriptive 2. inferential 3. descriptive 4. inferential 5. inferential

---

From the Laboratory to the Real World

The last step in any study is to figure out what the findings mean. Trying to understand behaviour from uninterpreted findings is like trying to become fluent in Swedish by reading a Swedish–English dictionary. Just as you need the grammar of Swedish to tell you how the words fit together, the psychologist needs hypotheses and theories to explain how the facts that emerge from research fit together.

Choosing the Best Explanation Sometimes it is hard to choose between competing explanations. Does nicotine disrupt driving by impairing coordination, by increasing a driver's vulnerability to distraction, by interfering with the processing of information, by distorting the perception of danger—or by some combination of these factors? In interpreting any study, we must not go too far beyond the facts. Several explanations may fit those facts equally well, which means that more research will be needed to determine the best one.

Sometimes the best interpretation of a finding does not emerge until a hypothesis has been tested in different ways. If the findings of studies using different methods converge, there is greater reason to be confident about them. On the other hand, if they conflict, researchers will know they must modify their hypotheses or do more research.

Here's an example. When psychologists compare the mental-test scores of young people and old people, they usually find that younger people consistently outscore older ones. This type of study, in which groups are compared at a given time, is called **cross-sectional**:

Cross-sectional Study
Different groups compared at one time:

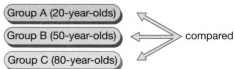

But **longitudinal studies** can also be used to investigate mental abilities across the life span. In a longitudinal study, the same people are followed over a period of time and are reassessed at regular intervals:

Longitudinal Study
Same Group compared at different times:

In contrast to cross-sectional studies, longitudinal studies find that as people age, they sometimes continue to perform as well as they ever did on certain mental tests. A *general* decline in ability may not occur until people reach their 70s or 80s

---

cross-sectional study A study in which individuals of different ages are compared at a given time.

longitudinal study A study in which individuals are followed and periodically reassessed over a period of time.

(Salthouse, 1998; Schaie, 1993). Why do results from the two types of studies conflict? Probably because cross-sectional studies measure generational differences; younger generations tend to outperform older ones because they are better educated or are more familiar with the tests used. Without longitudinal studies, we might falsely conclude that all types of mental ability inevitably decline sharply with age.

Judging the Result's Importance Sometimes psychologists agree on the reliability and meaning of a finding, but not on its ultimate relevance for theory or practice. Statistical significance alone does not provide the answer. A result may be statistically significant at the "point oh five" level yet be small and of little consequence in everyday life because the independent variable does not explain most of the variation in people's behaviour. On the other hand, a result may not quite reach statistical significance yet be worth following up on (Falk & Greenbaum, 1995; Hunter, 1997). Because of these problems, many

Thinking Critically About "Significant" Research Findings

psychologists now prefer other statistical procedures that reveal how powerful the independent variable really is—how much of the variation in the data the variable accounts for.

One popular statistical technique, called **meta-analysis**, combines and analyzes data from many studies, instead of assessing each study's results separately. Meta-analysis tells the researcher how much of the variation in scores across all the studies examined can be explained by a particular variable. For example, a meta-analysis of nearly 50 years of research found that gender accounts for a good deal of the variance in performance on certain spatial–visual tasks, with males doing better than females on the average (Voyer, Voyer, & Bryden, 1995). In contrast, other meta-analyses have shown that gender accounts for only 1 to 5 percent of the variance on tests of verbal ability, math ability, and aggressiveness (Feingold, 1988; Hyde, 2000; Hyde, Fennema, & Lamon, 1990; Hyde & Linn, 1988). Although gender differences on these tests are reliable, they are small, and scores for males and females greatly overlap.

meta-analysis A procedure for combining and analyzing data from many studies; it determines how much of the variance in scores across all studies can be explained by a particular variable.

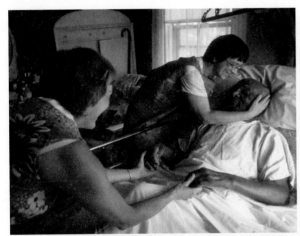

Psychologists use scientific methods to study many puzzles of human behaviour. Why does human touch reduce anxiety and feel so comforting? Why do people strive to become champion athletes in spite of physical disabilities? What causes people to become anorexic, and even starve themselves to death? And what could motivate terrorists to kill themselves and thousands of innocent people?

Psychological Topics

Techniques such as meta-analysis are useful because rarely does one study prove anything, in psychology or any other field. That is why you should be suspicious of headlines that announce a sudden, major scientific breakthrough based on a single study.

Psychology In The News *Revisited*

Now that you have finished the first chapter of this book, you are ready to explore more deeply what psychologists have learned about human behaviour.

At the start of each of the remaining chapters, we will present a real story from the news, one that raises some intriguing psychological questions. Then, at the end of the chapter, we will revisit the story to show how the material you have learned can help answer those questions. If you are ready to share the excitement of studying human behaviour, if you love mysteries and want to know not only who did it but also why they did it, if you are willing to reconsider what you think you think . . . then you are ready to read on.

Taking Psychology With You   What Psychology Can Do for You—and What It Can't

If you intend to become a psychologist or a mental-health professional, you have an obvious reason for taking a course in psychology. But psychology can contribute to your life in many ways, whether you plan to work in the field or not. Here are a few things psychology can do for you:

- **Make you a more informed person.** One purpose of education is to acquaint people with their cultural heritage and with human achievements in literature, the arts, and science. Because psychology plays a large role in contemporary society, being a well-informed person requires knowing something about psychological methods and findings.

- **Satisfy your curiosity about human nature.** When the Greek philosopher Socrates admonished his students, "Know thyself," he was only telling them to do what most people want to do anyway. Psychology—along with the other social sciences, literature, history, and philosophy—can contribute to a better understanding of yourself and others.

- **Help you increase control over your life.** Psychology cannot solve all your problems, but it does offer helpful techniques for handling your emotions, improving your memory, and eliminating unwanted habits. It can also foster an attitude of objectivity that is useful for analyzing your behaviour and your relationships.

- **Help you on the job.** A bachelor's degree in psychology is useful for getting a job in a helping profession, for example as a welfare caseworker or a rehabilitation counsellor. Anyone who works as a nurse, doctor, member of the clergy, police officer, or teacher can also put psychology to work on the job. So can waiters, flight attendants, bank tellers, salespeople, receptionists, and others whose jobs involve customer service. Finally, psychology can be useful to those whose jobs require them to predict people's behaviour—for example, labour negotiators, politicians, advertising copywriters, managers, product designers, buyers, market researchers, magicians. . . .

- **Give you insights into political and social issues.** Crime, drug abuse, discrimination, and war are not only social issues but also psychological ones. Psychological knowledge alone cannot solve the complex political, social, and ethical problems that plague every society, but it can help you make informed judgments about them. For example, if you know how social and cultural practices affect rates of drug use and abuse, this knowledge may affect your views about the war on drugs.

- **Help you become a more critical thinker.** If you master and truly understand the material in this course, you will become less likely to confuse correlation and causation, to be swayed by stereotypes, or to accept glib generalizations that are unsupported by evidence. You will be suspicious when a "scientific survey" in the mail comes with a solicitation for funds from a political organization. You will resist drawing conclusions about "most people" on the basis of casual observations of yourself or your friends. And you will make better decisions about the claims and arguments you hear every day ("Buy this!" "Believe that!").

We are optimistic about psychology's role in the world, but we want to caution you that sometimes people expect things from psychology that it can't deliver. For example, psychology can't tell you the meaning of life. A philosophy about the purpose of life requires not only knowledge but also reflection and a willingness to learn from life's experiences. Nor does psychological understanding relieve people of responsibility for their actions. Knowing that your short temper is a result, in part, of your unhappy childhood does not give you a green light to yell at your family or to mistreat your own kids.

Most important, psychology will not provide you with simple answers to complex questions. You have already learned that psychologists, like other scientists, often disagree among themselves. This disagreement is a normal result of their differing perspectives and methods, and it reflects the fact that most human phenomena do not lend themselves to one-note explanations. Therefore, rather than becoming attached to any one approach ("Medication will one day cure all mental illnesses"; "With the right environment, any child can become a genius"), the critical thinker will try to integrate the best contributions of each.

Despite the complexity of behaviour and the lack of simple answers to human problems, psychologists have made enormous progress in unravelling the secrets of the human brain, mind, and heart. At the end of each chapter, starting with the next one, the "Taking Psychology With You" feature will suggest ways to apply psychological findings to your own life—at school, on the job, or in your relationships.

SUMMARY

THE SCIENCE OF PSYCHOLOGY

- *Psychology* is the discipline concerned with behaviour and mental processes and how they are affected by an organism's external and internal environment. Psychology's methods and reliance on *empirical evidence* distinguish it from pseudoscience and "psychobabble."

- Psychological findings sometimes confirm, but often contradict, "common sense." In any case, a result does not have to be surprising to be scientifically important.

- Psychology's forerunners made some valid observations and had some useful insights, but without rigorous empirical methods, they also made serious errors in the description and explanation of behaviour, as in the case of *phrenology*.

- The official founder of scientific psychology was Wilhelm Wundt, who established the first psychological laboratory in 1879, in Leipzig, Germany. Wundt emphasized the analysis of experience into basic elements, through *trained introspection*. A competing approach, *functionalism*, which was inspired in part by the evolutionary theories of Charles Darwin, emphasized the functions of behaviour. One of its leading proponents was William James. Psychology as a method of psychotherapy was born in Vienna, with the work of Sigmund Freud and the establishment of *psychoanalysis*.

- Five points of view predominate today in psychology. The **biological perspective** emphasizes bodily events associated with actions, thoughts, and feelings, and also genetic contributions to behaviour. Within this perspective, a popular new specialty, *evolutionary psychology*, is following in the footsteps of functionalism. The **learning perspective** emphasizes how the environment and a person's history affect behaviour; within this perspective, *behaviourists* reject mentalistic explanations, and *social–cognitive learning theorists* combine elements of behaviourism with the study of thoughts, values, and intentions. The **cognitive perspective** emphasizes mental processes in perception, problem solving, belief formation, and other human activities. The **sociocultural perspective** explores how social contexts and cultural rules affect an individual's beliefs and behaviour. And the **psychodynamic perspective**, which originated with Freud's theory of psychoanalysis, emphasizes unconscious motives, conflicts, and desires; it differs greatly from the other approaches in its methods and standards of evidence.

- Each approach has made important contributions to psychology, but many, if not most, psychologists draw on more than one school of thought. And many have been influenced by movements, such as humanistic psychology, that do not fall neatly into one of the five perspectives we have discussed.

WHAT PSYCHOLOGISTS DO

- Psychologists conduct research and teach in colleges and universities, provide mental-health services (*psychological practice*), and conduct research and apply findings in a wide variety of nonacademic settings. *Applied psychology* is concerned with the practical uses of psychological knowledge. *Basic psychology* is concerned with knowledge for its own sake.

- *Psychotherapist* is an unregulated term for anyone who does therapy, including persons who have no credentials or training at all. Licensed therapists differ according to their training and approach. *Clinical psychologists* have a Ph.D., an Ed.D., or a Psy.D.; *psychiatrists* have an M.D.; *psychoanalysts* are trained in psychoanalytic institutes; and licensed clinical social workers, counsellors with various specialties, and marriage, family, and child counsellors may have a variety of postgraduate degrees. Many psychologists are concerned about an increase in poorly trained psychotherapists who lack credentials or a firm understanding of research methods and findings.

CRITICAL AND SCIENTIFIC THINKING IN PSYCHOLOGY

- One benefit of studying psychology is the development of *critical-thinking* skills and attitudes. The critical thinker asks questions, defines terms clearly, examines the evidence, analyzes assumptions and biases, avoids emotional reasoning, avoids oversimplification, considers alternative interpretations, and tolerates uncertainty. These activities not only are useful in ordinary life but also are the basis of the scientific method. For example, scientists are required to state hypotheses and predictions precisely and formulate operational definitions ("define your terms"); to gather empirical evidence; to comply with the *principle of falsifiability* ("analyze assumptions"); to be cautious in settling on a theory ("consider other interpretations"); and to resist drawing firm conclusions until results are replicated ("tolerate uncertainty").

DESCRIPTIVE STUDIES: ESTABLISHING THE FACTS

- *Descriptive methods* allow psychologists to describe and predict behaviour but not necessarily to choose one explanation over others. Such methods include case studies, observational studies, psychological tests, and surveys, as well as correlational methods.

- *Case studies* are detailed descriptions of individuals. They are often used by clinicians, and they can be valuable in exploring new research topics and addressing questions that would otherwise be difficult to study. But because information is often missing or hard to interpret, and because the person under study may not be representative of people in general, case studies are typically sources of information rather than tests of hypotheses.

- In *observational studies*, the researcher systematically observes and records behaviour without interfering in any way with the behaviour. *Naturalistic observation* is used to find out how people behave in their natural environments. *Laboratory observation* allows more control and requires the use of special equipment; behaviour in the laboratory, however, may differ in certain ways from behaviour in natural contexts.

- *Psychological tests* are used to measure and evaluate personality traits, emotional states, aptitudes, interests, abilities, and values. A good test is one that has been *standardized*, is scored using established *norms*, and is both *reliable* and *valid*. Critics have questioned the reliability and validity of even some widely used tests.

- *Surveys* are questionnaires or interviews that ask people directly about their experiences, attitudes, and opinions. Researchers must take precautions to obtain a sample that is *representative* of the larger population that the researcher wishes to describe and that yields results that are not skewed by a *volunteer bias*. Findings can also be affected by biased questions, and by the fact that respondents sometimes lie, misremember, or misinterpret the questions.

CORRELATIONAL STUDIES: LOOKING FOR RELATIONSHIPS

- In descriptive research, studies that look for relationships between phenomena are known as *correlational*. A *correlation* is a measure of the strength of a positive or negative relationship between two variables, and is expressed by the *coefficient of correlation*. A correlation does not demonstrate a causal relationship between the variables.

THE EXPERIMENT: HUNTING FOR CAUSES

- *Experiments* allow researchers to control the situation being studied, manipulate an *independent variable*, and assess the effects of the manipulation on a *dependent variable*. Because of the element of manipulation, ethical guidelines are especially important in experimental research. These guidelines govern studies with human beings, who must give *informed consent* before participating, and also with animals, which must be treated humanely.

- Experimental studies usually require a comparison or *control condition*, and often involve *random assignment* of subjects to experimental and control groups. In some studies, people in the control group receive a *placebo*. *Single-blind* and *double-blind studies* can be used to prevent the expectations of the subjects or the experimenter from affecting the results. Because experiments allow conclusions about cause and effect, they have long been the method of choice in psychology. However, like laboratory observations, experiments create a special situation that may elicit behaviour not typical in other environments. Many psychologists, therefore, have called for more *field research*.

EVALUATING THE FINDINGS

- Psychologists use *descriptive statistics*, such as the *arithmetic mean* and *standard deviation*, to summarize data. They use *inferential statistics* to find out how impressive the data are. *Significance tests* tell the researcher how likely it is that the results of a study occurred merely by chance. The results are said to be *statistically significant* if this likelihood is very low.

- Choosing among competing interpretations of a finding can be difficult, and care must be taken to avoid going beyond the facts. Sometimes the best interpretation does not emerge until a hypothesis has been tested in more than one way—for example, by using both *cross-sectional* and *longitudinal studies*.

• Statistical significance does not always imply real-world importance because the amount of variation in the data accounted for by a particular variable may be small. Conversely, a result that does not quite reach significance may be potentially useful. Therefore, many psychologists are now turning to other statistical measures. The technique of *meta-analysis*, for example, reveals how much of the variation in scores across many different studies can be explained by a particular variable.

KEY TERMS

Use this list to check your understanding of terms in this chapter. If you have trouble with a term, you can find it on the page listed.

psychology   4

empirical   4

functionalism   6

psychoanalysis   6

biological perspective   7

evolutionary psychology   7

learning perspective   7

cognitive perspective   7

sociocultural perspective   8

psychodynamic perspective   8

humanist psychology   9

basic psychology   9

applied psychology   9

critical thinking   12

hypothesis   13

operational definition   13

principle of falsifiability   14

theory   16

descriptive methods   17

case study   17

observational studies   18

psychological tests   19

standardize   19

norms   19

reliability   19

validity   19

surveys   20

representative sample   20

volunteer bias   20

correlational study   21

correlation   22

variables   22

positive correlation   22

negative correlation   22

coefficient of correlation   22

experiment   24

independent variable   24

dependent variable   24

control condition   25

random assignment   25

placebo   26

single-blind study   26

experimenter effects   26

double-blind study   26

field research   27

descriptive statistics   28

arithmetic mean   28

standard deviation   29

inferential statistics   29

significance tests   29

cross-sectional study   30

longitudinal study   30

meta-analysis   31

LOOKING BACK

Now that you have read this chapter, see whether you can answer the "What's Ahead" questions that preceded each major section. By using these questions to "look back," you can find out how much you have learned—and what you may need to review.

- What's the difference between psychology and plain old common sense? (p. 5)

- How old is the science of psychology? (p. 6)

- Was Sigmund Freud the official founder of scientific psychology? (p. 6)

- What are the five major perspectives in psychology? (pp. 7–8)

- If someone tells you that he or she is a psychologist, why can't you assume the person is a therapist? (p. 9)

- If you decided to call yourself a "psychotherapist," would you be breaking the law? (p. 10)

- What's the difference between a clinical psychologist and a psychiatrist? (p. 10)

- Can you be too open-minded? (p. 12)

- What guidelines can help you evaluate psychological claims? (pp. 13–16)

- What's the secret of a good scientific definition? (p. 13)

- Why is a psychological theory nonscientific if it explains anything that could conceivably happen? (p. 14)

- What's wrong with drawing conclusions about behaviour from a collection of anecdotes? (pp. 15–16)

- When are psychological case studies informative, and when are they useless? (pp. 17–18)

- Why do psychologists often observe people in laboratories instead of simply watching them in everyday situations? (pp. 18–19)

- What's the test of a good test? (pp. 19–20)

- Why should you be skeptical about psychological tests that appear in magazines and newspapers? (p. 20)

- What's the difference between a psychological survey and a poll of listeners conducted by a radio talk-show host? (pp. 20–21)

- If two things are "negatively" correlated, such as grades and watching TV, what is the relationship between them? (p. 22)

- If watching TV and behaving aggressively are positively correlated, does that mean TV causes violence? (pp. 22–23)

- Why do psychologists rely so heavily on experiments? (p. 24)

- What, exactly, do control groups control for? (pp. 25–26)

- In a double-blind study, what people are "blind," and what are they not supposed to "see"? (p. 26)

- In psychological studies, why are averages sometimes misleading? (p. 29)

- How can psychologists tell whether a finding is impressive or trivial? (p. 29)

- Why are some findings statistically significant but unimportant in practical terms? (p. 31)

Psychology In The News

EX-PRIME MINISTER'S DIARIES REVEAL A REMARKABLE PERSONALITY, FASCINATION WITH MILITARY STRATEGY, AND COMMUNICATING WITH THE DEAD

OTTAWA, ON, June 19, 2002. In addition to being the prime minister of Canada for 22 years, William Lyon Mackenzie King was one of the country's most interesting personalities. Canadians knew him to be a very successful politician, strongly committed to national unity and social programs, and the nation's leader for a number of stints between 1921 and 1948.

In public, Mackenzie King was not a charismatic or engaging figure. He did not seem to possess the outgoing and interesting personality we associate with many of today's high-profile politicians. His private life was quite another matter, however. He was a firm believer in the afterlife and in the ability to communicate with those who had moved on to it. In fact, he regularly took part in séances in order to talk to his dead relatives. All this and more is revealed in Mackenzie King's diaries, which are now available word-for-word on the Internet. Searching through the extensive volumes, you might read the entry for Monday, February 22, 1932. On that day, Mackenzie King commented on battles between the Chinese and Japanese. Then, in the very next paragraph, he wrote:

It was 10:30 when I went downstairs, almost immediately thereafter we had another séance in the small darkened room an account of which I have given elsewhere. It was most remarkable. I went at once to my room after & wrote out all I could recall, and then came luncheon. When we had had coffee, we came again to the darkened room for another séance. It too was most remarkable.

One can only wonder whether, in today's political landscape, Canadians would elect a prime minister who took counsel from the dead.

How many Canadians know that the man who adorns our $50 bill had a private life that included séances and conversations with dead relatives?

2 Theories of Personality

How can someone who is able to win the confidence of the people enough to govern a country for 22 years have a personality that many called bland? Furthermore, how can this same so-called bland personality have a completely different side—one that sits in a darkened room and communicates with dead relatives? Who was the real William Lyon Mackenzie King? Can such a question even be answered?

In this chapter, we will see how psychologists address such questions. In psychology, **personality** refers to a distinctive pattern of behaviour, mannerisms, thoughts, motives, and emotions that characterizes an individual over time. This pattern consists of many distinctive **traits**, which are habitual ways of behaving, thinking, and feeling: shy, reliable, friendly, hostile, gloomy, confident, ambitious, and so on. The schools of psychology described in Chapter 1 differ in their view of the origins and stability of those traits.

For much of the twentieth century, Freudian psychoanalytic theory was the dominant approach to explaining personality differences. Its sweeping view held that a person's conflicts, guilts, defences, and ways of dealing with others could be traced to unconscious dynamics originating in early childhood. By the end of the twentieth century, however, biological research was offering an entirely different view of personality: that about half of the variation in human personality traits is due to genetic variations, and has nothing to do with unconscious motives or how your parents treated you.

In this chapter, we will begin with the oldest theory of personality, the psychodynamic one, so that you will have a sense of how influential it was, why it still appeals to many, and why many of its ideas have become outdated. Next we will consider evidence for the newest theory, the genetic view. Most scientists no longer think that babies are tiny lumps of clay, shaped entirely by their experiences, or that parents alone determine whether their infant becomes an adventurer, a sourpuss, a rap star, . . . or William Lyon Mackenzie King. On the other hand, if only half of the human variation in personality traits is due to genetics, what is responsible for the other half?

To answer that question, we will then examine some of the leading approaches to personality that are neither psychodynamic nor biological: the environmental view, which emphasizes the role of social learning, situations, parents, and peers; the cultural view, which emphasizes cultural influences on traits and behaviour; and the humanist view, which emphasizes self-determination and free will.

2.1

personality A distinctive and relatively stable pattern of behaviour, mannerisms, thoughts, motives, and emotions that characterizes an individual.

trait A characteristic of an individual, describing a habitual way of behaving, thinking, or feeling.

When we are done, we will return to the puzzle of William Lyon Mackenzie King. As you read, ask yourself: Is personality set in childhood, or can adult experiences shape and even transform our traits? Which aspects of our personalities seem to be inborn and which learned? Which has more influence on our behaviour: our personality or the situation we are in?

WHAT'S AHEAD

- In Freud's theory of personality, why are the id and the superego always at war?
- When people say you're being "defensive," what defences might they be thinking of?
- How do psychologists regard Freud today—as a genius or a fraud?
- What would Carl Jung have had to say about Darth Vader?
- What are the "objects" in the object-relations approach to personality?

PSYCHODYNAMIC THEORIES OF PERSONALITY

A man apologizes for "displacing" his frustrations at work onto his family. A woman suspects that she is "repressing" a childhood trauma. An alcoholic reveals that he is no longer "in denial" about his drinking. A teacher informs a divorcing couple that their eight-year-old child is "regressing" to immature behaviour. All of this language—about displacing, repressing, denying, and regressing—can be traced to the first psychodynamic theory of personality, Sigmund Freud's theory of **psychoanalysis**.

Freud's theory is called **psychodynamic** because it emphasizes the movement of psychological energy within the person, in the form of attachments, conflicts, and motivations. Today's psychodynamic theories differ from Freudian theory and from one another, but they all share an emphasis on unconscious processes going on within the mind. They also share an assumption that adult personality and ongoing problems are formed primarily by experiences in early childhood. These experiences produce unconscious thoughts and feelings which later form characteristic habits, conflicts, and often self-defeating behaviour.

No one disputes the profound influence that Sigmund Freud had on the twentieth century. But there is enormous dispute about the lasting value

psychoanalysis A theory of personality and a method of psychotherapy developed by Sigmund Freud; it emphasizes unconscious motives and conflicts.

psychodynamic theories Theories that explain behaviour and personality in terms of unconscious dynamics within the individual.

of his work. Freud saw himself as one of the great geniuses of history, and many people agree with that assessment. But many modern scientists think he was a flat-out fraud whose ideas have not stood the test of time—a "dinosaur in the history of ideas" (Medawar, 1982). In this section, we will introduce you to Freud's ideas, and then to two modern psychodynamic approaches. We will also try to show you why attitudes toward Freud today range from reverence to contempt, and why he evokes such controversy.

Freud and Psychoanalysis

To enter the world of Sigmund Freud is to enter a realm of unconscious motives, guilty secrets, unspeakable yearnings, and conflicts between desire and duty. These unseen forces, Freud believed, have far more power over our personalities than our conscious intentions do. The unconscious reveals itself, said Freud, in art, dreams, jokes, apparent accidents, and slips of the tongue (which came to be called "Freudian slips"). The British member of Parliament who referred to the "honourable member from Hell" when he meant to say "from Hull," according to Freud (1920/1960), was revealing his actual, unconscious appraisal of his colleague.

The Structure of Personality In Freud's theory, personality consists of three major systems: the id, the ego, and the superego (see Table 2.1). Any action we take or problem we have results from the interaction and degree of balance among these systems (Freud, 1905, 1920/1960, 1923/1962).

Sigmund Freud (1856–1939).

The **id**, which is present at birth, is the reservoir of unconscious psychological energies and the motives to avoid pain and obtain pleasure. The id contains two competing instincts: the life, or sexual, instinct (fueled by psychic energy called the **libido**) and the death, or aggressive, instinct. As energy builds up in the id, tension results. The id may discharge this tension in the form of reflex actions, physical symptoms, or uncensored mental images and unbidden thoughts.

The **ego**, the second system to emerge, is a referee between the needs of instinct and the demands of society. It bows to the realities of life, putting a rein on the id's desire for sex and aggression until a suitable, socially appropriate outlet for them can be found. The ego, said Freud, is both conscious and unconscious, and it represents "reason and good sense."

The **superego**, the last system of personality to develop, represents morality and parental authority; it includes the conscience, the inner voice that says you did something wrong. The superego, which is partly conscious but largely unconscious, judges the activities of the id, handing out good feelings of pride and satisfaction when you do something well and handing out miserable feelings of guilt and shame when you break the rules.

According to Freud, the healthy personality must keep all three systems in balance. Someone who is too controlled by the id is governed by impulse and selfish desires. Someone who is too controlled by the superego is rigid, moralistic, and bossy. Someone who has a weak ego is unable to balance personal needs and wishes with social duties and realistic limitations.

If a person feels anxious or threatened when the wishes of the id conflict with social rules, the ego has weapons at its command to relieve the tension. These unconscious strategies, called **defence mechanisms**, deny or distort reality, but they also protect us from conflict and anxiety. They become unhealthy only when they cause self-defeating behaviour and emotional problems. Here are some of the primary defences identified by Freud and later analysts (A. Freud, 1967; Vaillant, 1992):

1 *Repression* occurs when a threatening idea, memory, or emotion is blocked from consciousness. A woman who had a frightening childhood experience that she cannot remember, for example, is said to be repressing her memory of it. Freud used the term to mean both *unconscious* expulsion of disturbing material from awareness and *conscious* suppression of such material, but modern analysts tend to think of repression only as an unconscious defence mechanism (McNally, 2003).

2 *Projection* occurs when a person's own unacceptable or threatening feelings are repressed and then attributed to someone else. A person who is embarrassed about having sexual feelings toward members of a different ethnic group, for example, may project this discomfort onto them, saying, "Those people are dirty-minded and oversexed."

id In psychoanalysis, the part of personality containing inherited psychic energy, particularly sexual and aggressive instincts.

libido [li-BEE-do] In psychoanalysis, the psychic energy that fuels the life or sexual instincts of the id.

defence mechanisms Methods used by the ego to prevent unconscious anxiety or threatening thoughts from entering consciousness.

ego In psychoanalysis, the part of personality that represents reason, good sense, and rational self-control.

superego In psychoanalysis, the part of personality that represents conscience, morality, and social standards.

TABLE 2.1 Summary of Freud's Model of the Mind

	Id	**Ego**	**Superego**
What it does	Expresses sexual and aggressive instincts.	Mediates between desires of the id and demands of the superego; uses defence mechanisms to ward off unconscious anxiety.	Represents conscience and the rules of society; follows internalized moral standards.
How conscious it is	Entirely unconscious.	Partly conscious, partly unconscious.	Partly conscious, mostly unconscious.
When it develops	Present at birth.	Emerges after birth, with early formative experiences.	Last system to develop; becomes internalized after the phallic (oedipal) stage (see p. 43).
Example	"I'm so mad I could kill you" (felt unconsciously).	Might make a conscious choice ("Let's talk about this") or resort to an unconscious defence mechanism, such as denial ("What, me angry? Never.").	"Thou shalt not kill."

3 *Displacement* occurs when people direct their emotions toward things, animals, or other people that are not the real object of their feelings. A boy who is forbidden to express anger toward his father, for example, may "take it out" on his toys or his younger sister. When displacement serves a higher cultural or socially useful purpose, as in the creation of art or inventions, it is called *sublimation*. Freud argued that society has a duty to help people sublimate their unacceptable impulses for the sake of civilization. Sexual passion may be sublimated into the creation of art or literature; aggressive impulses may be sublimated into competitive sports.

4 *Reaction formation* occurs when a feeling that produces unconscious anxiety is transformed into its opposite in consciousness. A woman who is afraid to admit to herself that she fears her husband may instead cling to the belief that she loves him deeply. A person who is aroused by erotic images may angrily assert that pornography is disgusting. How does such a transformed emotion differ from a true emotion? In reaction formation the professed feeling is excessive, and the person is extravagant and compulsive about demonstrating it, as when a woman says of an abusive husband: "Of course I love him! I *never* have any bad thoughts about him! He's perfect!"

5 *Regression* occurs when a person reverts to a previous phase of psychological development. An eight-year-old boy who is anxious about his parents' divorce may regress to earlier habits of thumb sucking or clinging. Adults may regress to immature behaviour when they are under pressure—for example, by having temper tantrums when they don't get their way.

6 *Denial* occurs when people refuse to admit that something unpleasant is happening, such as mistreatment by a partner; that they have a problem, such as drinking too much; or that they are feeling a forbidden emotion, such as anger. Denial protects a person's self-image and preserves the illusion of invulnerability: "It can't happen to me."

The Development of Personality Freud argued that personality develops in a series of *psychosexual stages*, in which sexual energy takes different forms as the child matures. Each new stage produces a certain amount of frustration, conflict, and anxiety. If these are not resolved properly, normal development may be interrupted, and the child may remain *fixated*, or stuck, at the current stage.

For example, said Freud, some people remain fixated at the *oral stage*, which occurs during the first year of life, when babies experience the world through their mouths. As adults, they will seek oral gratification in smoking, overeating, nail biting, or chewing on pencils; some may become clinging and dependent, like a nursing child. Others remain fixated at the *anal stage*, at ages two to three, when toilet training and control of bodily wastes are the key issues. They may become "anal retentive," holding everything in, obsessive about neatness and cleanliness. Or they may become just the opposite, "anal expulsive"—messy and disorganized.

For Freud, however, the most crucial stage for the formation of personality was the *phallic (oedipal) stage*, which lasts roughly from age three to age five or six. During this stage, said Freud, the child unconsciously wishes to possess the parent of the other sex and to get rid of the parent

"I'm sorry, I'm not speaking to anyone tonight. My defence mechanisms seem to be out of order."

of the same sex. Children often announce proudly, "I'm going to marry Daddy (or Mommy) when I grow up," and they reject the same-sex "rival." Freud (1924a, 1924b) labelled this phenomenon the **Oedipus complex**, after the Greek legend of King Oedipus, who unwittingly killed his father and married his mother.

Boys and girls, Freud believed, progress through the oedipal stage differently. Boys are discovering the pleasure and pride of having a penis, so when they see a naked girl for the first time, they are horrified. Their unconscious exclaims (in effect), "Her penis has been cut off! Who could have done such a thing to her? Why, it must have been her powerful father. And if he could do it to her, my father could do it to me!" This realization, said Freud, causes the boy to repress his desire for his mother and identify with his father. He accepts his father's authority and the father's standards of conscience and morality; the superego has emerged.

Freud admitted that he did not quite know what to make of girls, who, lacking the penis, could not go through the same steps. He speculated that a girl, upon discovering male anatomy, would panic that she had only a puny clitoris instead of a stately penis. She would conclude that she already had lost her penis. As a result, Freud said, girls do not have the powerful motivating fear that boys do to give up their oedipal feelings and develop a strong superego; they have only a lingering sense of "penis envy."

Freud believed that when the Oedipus complex is resolved, at about age five or six, the child's personality is fundamentally formed. Unconscious conflicts with parents, unresolved fixations and guilts, and attitudes toward the same and the other sex will continue to replay themselves throughout life. The child settles into a supposedly nonsexual *latency stage*, in preparation for the *genital stage*, which begins at puberty and leads to adult sexuality.

In Freud's view, then, your adult personality is shaped by how you progressed through the early psychosexual stages, which defence mechanisms you have developed to reduce anxiety, and whether your ego is strong enough to balance the conflict between the id (what you would like to do) and the superego (your conscience).

As you might imagine, Freud's ideas were not exactly received with yawns. Sexual feelings in five-year-olds! Repressed longings in respectable adults! Unconscious meanings in dreams! Penis envy! This was strong stuff in the early years of the twentieth century, and before long psychoanalysis had captured the public imagination in Europe and America. But it also produced a sharp rift with the emerging schools of empirical psychology.

This rift continues to divide scholars today. Some revere Freud as a hero who battled public censure and ridicule in his unwavering pursuit of truth (Gay, 1988). Others acknowledge that some of Freud's ideas have proved faulty, but they believe that the overall framework of his theory is timeless and brilliant (Westen, 1998). Still others think psychoanalytic theory is nonsense, with little empirical support (Cioffi, 1998). These critics argue that Freud was not the brilliant theoretician, impartial scientist, or even successful clinician that he claimed to be. On the contrary, they note, Freud often bullied his patients into accepting his explanations of their symptoms, and he ignored all evidence disconfirming his ideas (Crews, 1998; Powell & Boer, 1995; Sulloway, 1992; Webster, 1995). In one famous case, he pressured an 18-year-old patient, "Dora" (Ida Bauer), to accept the unwanted sexual advances of one of her father's friends, attributing her "hysterical" refusal to her own supposedly repressed sexual desires. Dora angrily left treatment after three months (Lakoff & Coyne, 1993).

On the positive side, Freud welcomed women into the profession of psychoanalysis, wrote eloquently about the devastating results to women of society's suppression of their sexuality, and argued, ahead of his time, that homosexuality was neither a sin nor a perversion but a "variation of the sexual function" and "nothing to be ashamed of" (Freud, 1961). Freud was thus a mixture of intellectual vision and blindness, sensitivity and arrogance. His provocative ideas left a powerful legacy to psychology—one that others began to tinker with immediately.

Oedipus complex In psychoanalysis, a conflict occurring in the phallic (oedipal) stage, in which a child desires the parent of the other sex and views the same-sex parent as a rival.

Freud believed that during the oedipal stage, little boys fantasize about marrying their mothers and regard their fathers as rivals.

Other Psychodynamic Approaches

archetypes [AR-ki-types] Universal, symbolic images that appear in myths, art, stories, and dreams; to Jungians, they reflect the collective unconscious.

collective unconscious In Jungian theory, the universal memories and experiences of humankind, represented in the symbols, stories, and images (archetypes) that occur across all cultures.

Some of Freud's followers stayed in the psychoanalytic tradition and modified Freud's theories from within. Women, as you might imagine, were not too pleased about "penis envy." Clara Thompson (1943/1973) and Karen Horney [HORN-eye] (1926/1973) argued that it was insulting philosophy and bad science to claim that half the human race is dissatisfied with its anatomy. When women feel inferior to men, they said, we should look for explanations in the disadvantages that women live with and their second-class status. In fact, Horney added, if anyone has an envy problem, it is men. Men have "womb envy": they envy women's ability to bear children.

Others broke away from Freud, or were actively rejected by him, and went off to start their own schools. Today, there are many psychodynamic approaches, but two are especially popular: those of Carl Jung and of the object-relations theorists.

Jungian Theory Carl Jung (1875–1961) was originally one of Freud's closest friends and a member of his inner circle. But the friendship ended with a furious quarrel about the nature of the unconscious. In addition to the individual's own unconscious, said Jung (1967), all human beings share a vast **collective unconscious**, containing universal memories, symbols, images, and themes, which he called **archetypes**.

An archetype can be a picture, such as the "magic circle," called a *mandala* in Eastern religions, which Jung thought symbolizes the unity of life and "the totality of the self." Or it can be a figure found in fairy tales, legends, and popular stories, such as the Hero, the nurturing Earth Mother, the Powerful Father, or the Wicked Witch. It can even be an aspect of the self. For example, the *shadow* archetype reflects the prehistoric fear of wild animals and represents the bestial, evil side of human nature. Scholars have found that some basic archetypes, such as the Hero and the Earth Mother, do appear in the stories and images of virtually every society (Campbell, 1949/1968; Neher, 1996). Jungians would consider Darth Vader, Dracula, the Dark Lord Sauron, and Harry Potter's tormentor Valdemort as expressions of the shadow archetype.

Two of the most important archetypes, in Jung's view, are those of maleness and femaleness. Jung (like Freud) recognized that "masculine" and "feminine" qualities exist in both sexes. The *anima* represents the feminine archetype in men; the *animus* represents the masculine archetype in women. Problems can arise, however, if a person tries to repress his or her internal, opposite archetype—that is, if a man denies his softer feminine side or if a woman denies her masculine side.

Although Jung shared with Freud a fascination with the darker aspects of the personality, he (along with other dissenters from

In *The Wizard of Oz*, the Wicked Witch of the West is a beloved example of the archetype of evil.

Freudian orthodoxy) had confidence in the positive, forward-moving strengths of the ego. He believed that people are motivated not only by past conflicts, but also by their future goals and their desire to fulfill themselves. Jung was also among the first to identify extroversion/introversion as a basic dimension of personality. Nonetheless, many of Jung's ideas were more suited to mysticism and philosophy than to empirical psychology, which may be why so many Jungian ideas became popular with New Age movements.

Jung had a psychotic breakdown after his split with Freud. And he revealed his own "dark side" when he supported the Nazis, writing vicious attacks on Jews and claiming that their collective unconscious differed from that of gentiles. (So much for its "universality.") But he continued to treat patients and attract many worshipful followers by virtue of his charisma (Hayman, 2001). Like Freud, therefore, Jung left a troubling personal legacy along with theories that appealed to legions of believers.

The Object-Relations School Freud essentially regarded the baby as if it were an independent, greedy little organism ruled by its own instinctive desires; other people were relevant only insofar as they gratified the infant's drives or blocked them. But by the 1950s, increased awareness of the importance of human attachments led to the emergence of the **object-relations school**, developed in Great Britain by Melanie Klein, D. W. Winnicott, and others.

To object-relations theorists, the central problem in life is to find a balance between the need for independence and the need for others. This balance requires constant adjustment to separations and losses: small ones that occur during quarrels, moderate ones such as leaving home for the first time, and major ones such as divorce or death. The way we react to these separations, according to object-relations analysts, is largely determined by our experiences in the first year or two of life.

The reason for the clunky word "object" in object-relations, instead of the warmer word "human" or "parent," is that the infant's attachment is not only to a real person (usually the mother) but also to the infant's evolving perception of her. The child creates a *mental representation* of the mother—someone who is kind or fierce, protective or rejecting. The child's representations of important adults, whether realistic or distorted, unconsciously affect personality throughout life,

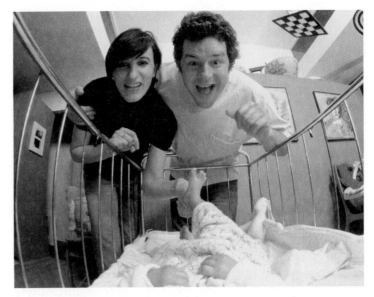

According to object-relations theory, a baby constructs unconscious representations of his or her parents, which will influence the child's relations with others throughout life.

influencing how the person relates to others: with trust or suspicion, acceptance or criticism (Westen, 1998).

The object-relations school also departs from Freudian theory regarding the nature of male and female development (Sagan, 1988; Winnicott, 1957/1990). In the object-relations view, children of both sexes identify first with the mother. Girls, who are the same sex as the mother, do not need to separate from her; the mother treats a daughter as an extension of herself. But boys, to develop a masculine identity, must break away from the mother; the mother encourages a son to be independent and separate. Thus men, in this view, develop more rigid boundaries between themselves and other people than women do.

object-relations school A psychodynamic approach that emphasizes the importance of the infant's first two years of life and the baby's formative relationships, especially with the mother.

Evaluating Psychodynamic Theories

Although modern psychodynamic theorists differ in many ways, they share a general belief that to understand personality we must explore its unconscious dynamics and origins. Many psychologists in other fields, however, regard most psychodynamic ideas as literary metaphors rather than as scientific explanations (Cioffi, 1998; Crews, 1998). Critics argue that psychodynamic theories are guilty of three scientific failings:

Thinking Critically About Psychodynamic Ideas

1 *Violating the principle of falsifiability.* As we saw in Chapter 1, a theory that is impossible to disconfirm in principle is not scientific. Many psychodynamic concepts about unconscious motivations are, in fact, impossible to confirm or disconfirm. Followers often accept an idea because it seems intuitively right or their experience seems to support it. Anyone who doubts the idea or offers disconfirming evidence is then accused of being "defensive" or "in denial." This way of dismissing criticism is neither scientific nor fair!

2 *Drawing universal principles from the experiences of a few atypical patients.* Freud and most of his followers generalized from a few individuals, often patients in therapy, to all human beings. Of course, the problem of overgeneralizing from small samples occurs in other areas of psychology too, and sometimes valid insights about human behaviour can be obtained from case studies. The problem occurs when the observer fails to confirm these observations by studying other samples and incorrectly infers that what applies to some individuals applies to all. For example, some psychodynamically oriented therapists, accepting Freud's notion of a childhood "latency" stage, have assumed that if a child masturbates or takes part in sex play, the child has probably been sexually molested. But masturbation and sexual curiosity are by no means typical only of abused children; these are normal and common behaviours among children in the general population (Friedrich, 1998; Lamb, 2002).

Some psychodynamic ideas can be tested empirically. For example, Freud thought that playing or observing aggressive sports would channel aggressive energy into socially accepted activities, and hence reduce it. But behavioural research finds that aggressive sports actually stimulate increased violence among players and among spectators, like these soccer fans.

3 *Basing theories of personality development on retrospective accounts and the fallible memories of patients.* Most psychodynamic theorists have not observed random samples of children at different ages, as modern child psychologists do, to construct their theories of development. Instead they have worked backward, creating theories based on themes in adults' recollections of childhood. The analysis of memories can be an illuminating way to achieve insights about our lives; in fact, it is the only way we can think about our own lives! But, as we will see in Chapter 8, memory is often inaccurate, influenced as much by what is going on in our lives now as by what happened in the past. If you are currently not getting along with your mother, you may remember all the times when she was hard on you and forget the counter examples of her kindness.

Retrospective analysis has another problem: It creates an *illusion of causality* between events. People often assume that if A came before B, then A must have caused B. For example, if your mother spent three months in the hospital when you were five years old and today you feel shy and insecure in college, an object-relations analyst would probably draw a connection between the two facts. But a lot of other things could be causing your shyness and insecurity, such as being away from home for the first time at a large and impersonal college.

In recent years, some psychologists have been testing psychodynamic ideas empirically. They have identified unconscious processes in thought, memory, and behaviour; and they have found evidence for many of the major defence mechanisms, such as reaction formation, projection, denial, and displacement (Baumeister, Dale, & Sommer, 1998; Cramer, 2000; Marcus-Newhall et al., 2000). More generally, research confirms the psychodynamic idea that we are often unaware of the motives behind our own puzzling or self-defeating actions. However, the modern, empirical study of personality has taken quite a different turn from the all-embracing observations and intuitions of Freud and his descendants.

Quick Quiz

Are you feeling defensive about answering this quiz?

1. An eight-year-old boy is behaving aggressively, hitting classmates and disobeying his teacher. Which of the following explanations of his behaviour might come from a Freudian, Jungian, or object-relations analyst?
   a. The boy is expressing his shadow archetype.
   b. The boy is expressing the aggressive energy of the id and has not developed enough ego control.
   c. The boy has had unusual difficulty separating from his mother and is compensating by behaving aggressively.

2. In the 1950s and 1960s, many psychoanalysts, observing unhappy gay men who had sought therapy, concluded that homosexuality was a mental illness. What violation of the scientific method were they committing?

Answers:

1. a. Jung b. Freu c. object-relations analyst

2. The analysts were drawing inappropriate conclusions from atypical patients in therapy, failing to test these conclusions with gay men who were not in therapy or with heterosexuals. When such research was done, using appropriate control groups, it turned out that gay men were not more mentally disturbed or depressed than were heterosexuals (Hooker, 1957).

WHAT'S AHEAD

• How reliable are those tests that tell you what "personality type" you are?

• How can psychologists tell which personality traits are more central or important than others?

• Which five dimensions of personality seem to describe people the world over?

THE MODERN STUDY OF PERSONALITY

People love to fit themselves and their friends into "types." They have been doing it forever. Early Greek philosophers thought our personalities fell into four fundamental categories depending on mixes of body fluids. For example, if you were an angry, irritable sort of person, you supposedly had an excess of choler, and even now the word *choleric* describes a hothead. And if you were slow-moving and unemotional, you supposedly had an excess of phlegm, making you a "phlegmatic" type.

Popular Personality Tests That particular theory is long gone, but other nonscientific tests of personality types still exist, aimed at predicting how people will do at work, whether they will get along with others, or whether they will succeed as leaders. One such test, the Myers-Briggs Type Indicator, is hugely popular in business and motivational seminars; at least a million people a year take it. The test assigns people to one of 16 different types, depending on how the individual combines various tendencies, such as being introverted or extroverted or being someone who relies on logic or intuition. Unfortunately, the Myers-Briggs is not much more reliable than measuring body fluids; one study found that fewer than half of the respondents scored as the same type a mere five weeks later. And there is little evidence to support the test's key premise that knowledge of a person's type reliably predicts behaviour on the job or in relationships (Barbuto, 1997; Pittenger, 1993).

In addition, the personality-assessment industry has developed more than 2500 personality tests to

Thinking Critically About Personality Tests

THE FAR SIDE® By GARY LARSON

The glass is half full!

The glass is half empty.

Half full... No! Wait! Half empty!... No, half... What was the question?

Hey! I ordered a cheeseburger!

The four basic personality types

factor analysis A statistical method for analyzing the intercorrelations among various measures or test scores; clusters of measures or scores that are highly correlated are assumed to measure the same underlying trait, ability, or aptitude (the factor).

objective tests (inventories) Standardized questionnaires requiring written responses; they typically include scales on which people are asked to rate themselves.

measure specific traits and tendencies that business and government would love to be able to identify: for example, the tendency to steal, take drugs, or be disloyal on the job (Ehrenreich, 2001). But it is important to think critically about these tests, because many of them are nearly useless from a scientific point of view. (In "Taking Psychology With You," we discuss another popular but unreliable effort to measure personality, through "handwriting analysis.")

On the other hand, many measures of personality traits are scientifically valid and useful in research. **Objective tests (inventories)** are standardized questionnaires that require written responses, typically to multiple-choice or true-false items. They provide information about literally hundreds of different aspects of personality, including needs, values, interests, self-esteem, emotional problems, and typical ways of responding to situations. For example, the Minnesota Multiphasic Personality Inventory (MMPI) is used to assess personality disorders (see Chapter 11).

And the Multidimensional Personality Questionnaire (MPQ) is often used to identify key dimensions of personality and the traits that make up each one (Krueger, 2000).

Using well-constructed inventories, psychologists have identified hundreds of traits, ranging from sensation seeking (the enjoyment of risk) to "erotophobia" (the fear of sex). Are some of these traits more important or more central than others? Do some of them overlap or cluster together?

Clustering Traits For Gordon Allport, one of the most influential psychologists in the empirical study of personality, the answer to both questions was yes. Allport (1937, 1961) recognized that not all traits have equal weight and significance in people's lives. Most of us, he said, have 5 to 10 *central traits* that reflect a characteristic way of behaving, dealing with others, and reacting to new situations. For instance, some people see the world as a hostile, dangerous place, whereas others see it as a place for fun and frolic. *Secondary traits*, in contrast, are more changeable aspects of personality, such as music preferences, habits, casual opinions, and the like.

Raymond B. Cattell advanced the study of this issue by applying a statistical method called **factor analysis**. Performing a factor analysis is like adding water to flour: It causes the material to clump up into little balls. When applied to traits, this procedure identifies clusters of correlated items that seem to be measuring some common, underlying factor. For example, the traits of assertiveness, willingness to tell jokes in large groups, and pleasure in meeting new people might share the common factor of extroversion.

Using questionnaires, life descriptions, and observations of thousands of people, Cattell (1965, 1973) measured dozens of personality traits, including humour, intelligence, creativity, dominance, and emotional disorders. Out of these he developed the 16 Personality Factors (PF) Questionnaire. Later in his career, he noted that only 6 of the 16 factors measured by the questionnaire had been repeatedly confirmed, but the 16 PF personality test has nonetheless remained popular (Digman, 1996).

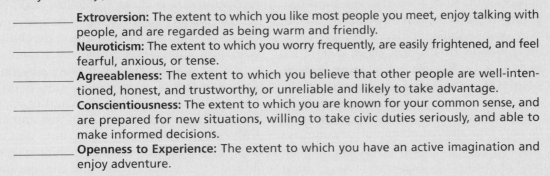

Get Involved Rate Your Traits

For each of the Big Five factors below, indicate on a five-point scale where you think you fall, from 1 = "describes me well" to 5 = "does not describe me at all." (These descriptions are just samples from the full personality inventory.)

_____ **Extroversion:** The extent to which you like most people you meet, enjoy talking with people, and are regarded as being warm and friendly.

_____ **Neuroticism:** The extent to which you worry frequently, are easily frightened, and feel fearful, anxious, or tense.

_____ **Agreeableness:** The extent to which you believe that other people are well-intentioned, honest, and trustworthy, or unreliable and likely to take advantage.

_____ **Conscientiousness:** The extent to which you are known for your common sense, and are prepared for new situations, willing to take civic duties seriously, and able to make informed decisions.

_____ **Openness to Experience:** The extent to which you have an active imagination and enjoy adventure.

Now ask a friend or relative to rate you on each of these dimensions. How closely does this rating match your own? If there is a discrepancy, what might be the reason for it?

Today, hundreds of factor-analytic studies support the existence of a cluster of central personality traits. Although researchers are still debating exactly how many traits belong to this inner core—some say three, others say as many as nine—most personality researchers in Canada and elsewhere agree on the centrality of five "robust factors," known informally as the *Big Five* (Digman, 1996; Jang et al., 1998; McCrae et al., 2000; Paunonen, 2003):

1 *Extroversion versus introversion* describes the extent to which people are outgoing or shy. It includes such traits as being talkative or silent, sociable or reclusive, adventurous or cautious, eager to be in the limelight or inclined to stay in the shadows.

2 *Neuroticism (negative emotionality) versus emotional stability* describes the extent to which a person suffers from such traits as anxiety, an inability to control impulses, and a tendency to feel negative emotions such as anger, guilt, contempt, and resentment. Neurotic individuals are worriers, complainers, and defeatists, even when they have no major problems. They are always ready to see the sour side of life and none of its sweetness.

3 *Agreeableness versus antagonism* describes the extent to which people are good-natured or irritable, co-operative or abrasive, secure or suspicious and jealous. It reflects the tendency to have friendly relationships or hostile ones.

4 *Conscientiousness versus impulsiveness* describes the degree to which people are responsible or undependable, persevering or quick to give up, steadfast or fickle, tidy or careless, self-disciplined or impulsive.

5 *Openness to experience versus resistance to new experience* describes the extent to which people are curious, imaginative, questioning, and creative, or conforming, unimaginative, predictable, and uncomfortable with novelty.

The Big Five have emerged as distinct, central personality dimensions in most places around the world, including Canada, Britain, the Czech

Where do you think this man would score on extroversion?

Republic, China, Turkey, the Netherlands, Japan, Spain, the Philippines, Hawaii, Germany, Portugal, Israel, South Korea, Russia, and Australia (Digman & Shmelyov, 1996; Katigbak et al., 2002; McCrae et al., 2000; Somer & Goldberg, 1999). These five personality factors emerge whether you ask people for self-reports or have people assessed by friends, relatives, or independent observers (Borkenau et al., 2001; Watson, Hubbard, & Wiese, 2000).

Moreover, the Big Five are remarkably stable over a lifetime, especially once a person hits 30 years of age. There is some good news, however, for crabby neurotics, especially young ones. Studies of thousands of people in 10 countries find that young people, ages 16 to 21, are the most neurotic (emotionally negative) and the least agreeable and conscientious. But by age 30, perhaps as a result of the responsibilities of adulthood, people tend to become more agreeable and conscientious and less negative. Unfortunately, in later adulthood people also tend to become less extroverted and less open to new experiences (see Figure 2.1). Because these changes have been found in many different countries, they seem to reflect common maturational changes over the life span (Costa et al., 1999; McCrae et al., 2000).

The Big Five do not provide a complete picture of personality, of course. Clinical psychologists note that important traits involved in mental disorders are missing, such as psychopathy (impulsivity and lack of remorse), self-absorption, and obsessionality (Westen & Shedler, 1999). Personality researchers in Windsor and at the University of Western Ontario note that other important traits are missing, such as religiosity, dishonesty, humorousness, and conventionality (MacDonald, 2000; Paunonen & Ashton, 2001). But the Big Five do seem to lie at the core of personality variations among healthy individuals. Where do these traits, and others, come from?

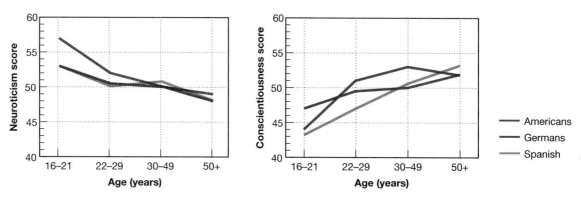

FIGURE 2.1 Consistency and Change in Personality

Although the Big Five traits are fairly stable, changes do occur over the life span. As you can see here, neuroticism (negative emotionality) is highest among young adults and then declines, whereas conscientiousness is lowest among young adults and then steadily increases. These changes probably reflect common experiences that occur as young people leave home and grow up (Costa et al., 1999).

Quick Quiz

Show that you have the trait of conscientiousness by taking this quiz.

1. What is the advantage of inventories over tests of personality "types"?
2. Raymond advanced the study of personality by (a) developing case-study analysis, (b) using factor analysis, (c) devising the Myers-Briggs Type Indicator.
3. Which of the following are not among the Big Five personality factors? (a) introversion, (b) agreeableness, (c) psychoticism, (d) openness to experience, (e) intelligence, (f) neuroticism, (g) conscientiousness.
4. Which one of the Big Five typically decreases by age 30? (a) agreeableness, (b) extroversion, (c) openness to experience, (d) neuroticism.

Answers:

1. They have better reliability and validity. 2. b   3. c, e   4. d

WHAT'S AHEAD

- Is it possible to be born irritable or easygoing?
- To what extent are personality differences among people influenced by their genetic differences?
- Are people who have highly heritable personality traits stuck with them forever?

GENETIC INFLUENCES ON PERSONALITY

A mother we know was describing her two children: "My daughter has always been difficult, intense, and testy," she said, "but my son is the opposite, placid and good-natured. They came out of the womb that way." Was this mother right? Is it possible to be born touchy or good-natured? Or was she treating her two babies differently?

For centuries, efforts to understand why people differ from one another have swung from biological answers ("it's in their nature; they are born that way") to learning and environmental ones ("it's all a matter of nurture—how they are raised and the experiences they have"). The *nature–nurture* debate has been one of the longest-running either–or arguments in philosophy and psychology. Edward L. Thorndike (1903), one of the leading psychologists of the early 1900s, staked out the nature position by claiming that "in the actual race of life . . . the chief determining factor is heredity." But in stirring words that became famous, his contemporary, behaviourist John B. Watson (1925), insisted that experience could write virtually any message on the blank slate of human nature:

> Give me a dozen healthy infants, well-formed, and my own specified world to bring them up in and I'll guarantee to take any one at random and train him to become any type of specialist I might select—doctor, lawyer, artist, merchant-chief and yes, even beggar-man and thief, regardless of his talents, penchants, tendencies, abilities, vocations, and race of his ancestors.

Today, almost all psychologists who study personality regard biology and experience as interacting influences, each shaping the other over time. "The nature–nurture debate is over," says one researcher (Turkheimer, 2000). "The bottom line is that everything is heritable . . . [but the findings] do not show that genes are more fundamental than environments." In this section and

"There's another hereditary disease that runs in the royal family. Your grandfather was a stubborn fool, your father was a stubborn fool, and *you* are a stubborn fool."

the next, we will see what this means, by examining the interlaced influences of nature and nurture on personality.

How can heredity affect personality? **Genes**, the basic units of heredity, are made up of elements of *DNA* (deoxyribonucleic acid). These elements form chemical codes for the synthesis of proteins; proteins, in turn, affect virtually every aspect of the body, from its structure to the chemicals that keep it running. Genes can affect the behaviours we call "personality" through their effects on an infant's developing brain and nervous system.

There are two ways researchers currently measure genetic contributions to personality: by studying the temperaments of infants and children and by doing heritability studies of twins and adopted individuals. These methods permit us only to *infer* the existence of relevant genes—just as, if you find your toddler covered in chocolate, it's pretty safe to infer that candy is somewhere close by. Scientists hope that the actual genes underlying temperaments and key traits will one day be discovered (Plomin et al., 2001). One research team, centred at the University of British Columbia and using data from hundreds of twins in Canada, Germany, and Japan, reported having found a gene that might be involved in both neuroticism and (non)agreeableness (Jang et al.,

genes The functional units of heredity; they are composed of DNA and specify the structure of proteins.

OneKey
2.2

2001). You will be hearing lots more about genetic discoveries in the coming years, so it is important to understand what they mean—and don't mean.

Heredity and Temperament

Even in the first weeks after birth, human babies have tiny personalities. Infants differ in activity level, mood, responsiveness, heart rate, and attention span (Belsky, Hsieh, & Crnic, 1996; Kagan, 1994; Snidman et al., 1995). Some are irritable and cranky; others are placid and sweet-natured. Some will cuddle up in an adult's arms and snuggle; others squirm and fidget, as if they cannot stand being held. Some smile easily; others fuss and cry.

These differences appear even when you control for possible prenatal influences, such as the mother's nutrition, drug use, or problems with the pregnancy. That is why most psychologists believe babies are born with genetically determined **temperaments**, dispositions to respond to the environment in certain ways. Temperaments include *reactivity* (how excitable, arousable, or responsive a baby is), *soothability* (how easy it is to calm an upset baby), and positive and negative emotionality. Temperaments are quite stable over time and may later form the basis of specific personality traits (McCrae et al., 2000; Rothbart, Ahadi, & Evans, 2000).

Jerome Kagan (1997) has spent years studying the temperament of reactivity, following children from infancy to adolescence. About 20 percent of all children are at one extreme (highly reactive) or the other (nonreactive); the other 80 percent fall somewhere in between. Highly reactive infants, even at four months of age, are excitable, nervous, and fearful; they overreact to any little thing, even a colourful picture placed in front of them. As toddlers, they tend to be wary and fearful of new things—toys that make noise, odd-looking robots—even when their moms are right there with them. At five years, many of these children are still timid and uncomfortable in new situations. At seven years, many still have symptoms of anxiety. They are afraid of being kidnapped, they need to sleep with the light on, and they are afraid of sleeping in an unfamiliar house—even if they have never experienced any sort of trauma.

In contrast, nonreactive infants, Kagan (1998a) says, are "California, laid-back babies." They lie there without fussing; they rarely cry;

they babble happily. As toddlers, they are outgoing and curious about new toys and events. They continue to be easygoing and extroverted throughout childhood.

Children at these two extremes differ physiologically, too (Rothbart, Ahadi, & Evans, 2000). During mildly stressful tasks, reactive children are more likely than nonreactive children to have increased heart rates, heightened brain activity, and high levels of stress hormones. Interestingly, the same physiological attributes appear in shy, anxious infant rhesus monkeys (Suomi, 1991). Starting early in life, these "uptight" monkeys respond with anxiety to novelty and challenge, just as highly reactive children do. They too have high heart rates and elevated stress hormones.

Biologically based temperaments, then, influence later personality traits. However, biology is not a blueprint; it is more like a rough sketch. Consistency in a given temperament depends in part on how extreme that trait is in infancy. Kagan put it this way: What proportion of extremely reactive babies remain extremely shy, subdued, and fearful as older children? About 15 percent. What proportion become average, neither extremely shy nor extremely outgoing? The rest. What proportion become vivacious, fearless, and extroverted? Zero. "The environment acts on fearful children to move them toward health, toward the center," Kagan (1998a) explained, "but it's really hard to move them to the other end."

Heredity and Traits

A second way to study genetic contributions to personality is to estimate the **heritability** of specific traits within groups of children or adults. This method is favoured by **behavioural geneticists**, scientists concerned with the genetic bases of behaviour and personality traits. Within any group, individuals will vary in shyness, cheerfulness, impulsiveness, or any other quality. Heritability gives us a statistical estimate of the *proportion of the total variation in a trait that is attributable to genetic variation within a group*. Because the heritability of a trait is expressed as a proportion (such as .60 or 60/100), the maximum value it can have is 1.0 (which would mean that 100 percent of the variation in the trait was due to genetic variation).

We know that heritability is a tough concept to understand at first, so here's an example. Suppose that your entire psychology class takes a test of shyness, and you compute an average

temperaments Physiological dispositions to respond to the environment in certain ways; they are present in infancy and are assumed to be innate.

heritability A statistical estimate of the proportion of the total variance in some trait that is attributable to genetic differences among individuals within a group.

behavioural geneticists Scientists who study an interdisciplinary field of study concerned with the genetic bases of individual differences in behaviour and personality.

Extreme shyness and fear of new situations tend to be biologically based, stable aspects of temperament—both in human beings and in monkeys. On the right, a timid infant rhesus monkey cowers behind a friend in the presence of an outgoing stranger.

shyness score for the group. Some students will have scores close to the average, whereas others will have scores that are much higher or lower than the average. Heritability gives you an estimate of the extent to which your class's variation in shyness is due to genetic differences among the students who took the test. Note, however, that this estimate applies only to the group as a whole. It does not tell you anything about the impact of genetics on any *particular* individual's shyness or extroversion. You might be shy primarily because of your genes, but your friend might be shy because she comes from a culture that values modesty and social reserve in females.

One obvious example of a highly heritable trait is height: Within a group of equally well-nourished individuals, most of the variation among them will be accounted for by their genetic differences. In contrast, table manners have low heritability because most variation among individuals is accounted for by differences in upbringing. Even highly heritable traits, however, can be modified by the environment. For example, although height is highly heritable, malnourished children may not grow up to be as tall as they would have, given sufficient food. Conversely, if children eat an extremely nutritious diet, they may grow up to be taller than anyone thought they could.

Computing Heritability Scientists have no way to estimate the heritability of a trait or behaviour directly, so they must infer it by studying people whose degree of genetic similarity is known. You might think that the simplest approach would be to compare blood relatives within families; everyone knows of families that are famous for some

talent or personality trait. But the fact that a trait "runs" in a family doesn't tell us much, because close relatives usually share environments as well as genes. If Carlo's parents and siblings all love lasagna, that doesn't mean a taste for lasagna is heritable! The same applies if everyone in Carlo's family is shy, neurotic, or moody.

A better approach is to study adopted children (e.g., Loehlin, Horn, & Willerman, 1996; Plomin & DeFries, 1985). Such children share half of their genes with each birth parent, but they grow up in a different environment, apart from

Identical twins Gerald Levey (left) and Mark Newman were separated at birth and raised in different cities. When they were reunited at age 31, they discovered some astounding similarities. Both men were volunteer firefighters, wore moustaches, and were unmarried. Both liked to hunt, watch old John Wayne movies, and eat Chinese food. They drank the same brand of beer and crushed the can when it was empty. The challenge is to figure out which of these traits and behaviours are influenced strongly by heredity, which result mainly from environmental factors such as social class and upbringing, and which are due merely to chance.

their birth parents. On the other hand, they share an environment with their adoptive parents and siblings, but not their genes. Researchers can compare correlations between the children's traits and those of their biological and adoptive relatives and can then use the results to estimate heritability.

Another approach is to compare identical twins with fraternal twins. *Identical twins* develop when a fertilized egg divides into two parts that then become separate embryos. Because the twins come from the same fertilized egg, they share all their genes, barring genetic mutations. (Identical twins may differ slightly at birth, however, because of differences in the blood supply to the two fetuses, or other chance factors.) In contrast, *fraternal twins* develop when a woman's ovaries release two eggs instead of one, and each egg is fertilized by a different sperm. Fraternal twins are wombmates, but they are no more alike genetically than any other two siblings (they share, on average, only half their genes), and they may be of different sexes. Behavioural geneticists can estimate the heritability of a trait by comparing groups of same-sex fraternal twins with groups of identical twins. The assumption is that if identical twins are more alike than fraternal twins, then the increased similarity must be due to genetic influences.

Perhaps, however, people do not treat identical and fraternal twins the same way. People may treat identical twins, well, identically, even dressing them up in the same little outfits. To avoid these problems, investigators have studied identical twins who were separated early in life and were reared apart. (Until recently, adoption policies often permitted such separations to occur.) In theory, separated identical twins share all their genes but not their environments. Any similarities between them should therefore be primarily genetic and should permit a direct estimate of heritability.

How Heritable Are Personality Traits? Findings from adoption and twin studies have provided compelling support for a genetic contribution to personality. Identical twins reared apart will often have unnerving similarities in gestures, mannerisms, and moods; indeed, their personalities often seem as similar as their physical features. If one twin tends to be optimistic, glum, or excitable, the other will probably be that way too (Braungert et al., 1992; Plomin et al., 2001). Philip Vernon at the University of Western Ontario and Kerry Jang at the University of British Columbia also found that twins became more similar as they got older (Jang, Livesley, & Vernon, 1996).

Behavioural-genetic studies have produced remarkably consistent results on the heritability of traits. Whether the trait in question is one of the Big Five, or one of many others from aggressiveness to overall happiness, heritability is typically around .50 (Bouchard, 1997a; Jang et al., 1998; Loehlin, 1992; Lykken & Tellegen, 1996; Waller et al., 1990). This means that within a group of people, about 50 percent of the variation in such traits is attributable to genetic differences among the individuals in the group. These findings have been replicated in many countries.

Some researchers have even reported high heritability for such specific activities as getting divorced (McGue & Lykken, 1992) and watching a lot of television in childhood (Plomin et al., 1990). How on earth can divorce and TV watching be heritable? Our prehistoric ancestors didn't get married, let alone divorced, and they certainly didn't watch TV! Perhaps, though, certain traits or temperaments that *are* heritable could predispose a person to do these things.

Evaluating Genetic Theories

We think you will agree that these behavioural-genetic findings are pretty amazing. Psychologists

Separated at birth, the Mallifert twins meet accidentally.

hope that one intelligent use of such findings will be to help people become more accepting of themselves and their children. Although we can all learn to make improvements and modifications to our personalities, most of us probably will never be able to *transform* our personalities because of our genetic dispositions and temperaments (Efran, Greene, & Gordon, 1998).

On the other hand, it is also important not to oversimplify, by claiming that "genes are everything," and overlook the role of the environment and experience in modifying traits. When people oversimplify, they mistakenly assume that personality problems that have a genetic component

Thinking Critically About Genetic "Inevitability"

are hopeless—that someone is "born to be bad" or a miserable grump forever. Similarly, they may assume that if a problem, such as depression, has "genetic" origins, it will respond only to medication so there is no point trying other interventions (we discuss this fallacy in Chapter 12). But, as we have seen, a genetic *predisposition* does not imply genetic *inevitability*. As Robert Plomin (1989), a leading behavioural geneticist, observed, "The wave of acceptance of genetic influence on behaviour is growing into a tidal wave that threatens to engulf the second message of this research: These same data provide the best available evidence for the importance of environmental influences." Let us now see what some of those influences might be.

Quick Quiz

We hope you have a few quiz-taking genes.

1. What two broad lines of research support the hypothesis that personality differences are due in part to genetic differences?
2. In behavioural-genetic studies, the heritability of personality traits, including the Big Five, is typically about (a) .50, (b) .90, (c) .10 to .20, (d) zero.
3. A newspaper headline announces: "Couch Potatoes Born, Not Made: Kids' TV Habits May Be Hereditary." Why is this headline misleading? What other explanations of the finding are possible? What aspects of TV watching could have a hereditary component?

Answers:

1. Research on temperaments and on heritability of traits
2. a
3. The headline implies that there is a "TV-watching gene," but the writer is failing to consider other explanations. For example, perhaps some temperaments dispose people to be sedentary or passive, and this disposition leads to a tendency to watch a lot of television.

WHAT'S AHEAD

- Are people always consistent across situations?
- How would a social–cognitive theorist explain why Madonna is so different as a performer and as a mom?
- How much can parents shape their children's personalities?
- How do your peers influence your personality?

ENVIRONMENTAL INFLUENCES ON PERSONALITY

The "environment" may account for half of the variation in personality, but what *is* the environment, exactly? In this section, we will consider three crucial aspects of the environment and see how much each contributes to personality: particular situations, parental nurturing, and peer influence.

Situations and Social Learning

The very definition of a trait is that it is consistent across situations. But people often behave one way at home and a different way with their friends. Extroverts don't necessarily behave extrovertedly when they are in church, for example! In a study in which people kept records of their feelings and behaviour five times a day for 13 days, it turned out that almost everyone was extroverted, agreeable, emotionally negative, and so forth, at least to some degree, depending on the situation (Fleeson, 2001).

The reason for people's inconsistency, according to behaviourists in the learning tradition, is that different behaviours are rewarded, punished, or ignored in different contexts. (In Chapter 9, we will examine in greater depth the important principles of behavioural theory.) For example, you are likely to be more extroverted at a "Liberate the Suppressed Self" weekend, where you are rewarded with smiles, praise, and hugs for dancing naked on a tabletop and telling family secrets, than at home, with relatives who would regard such behaviour with alarm and condemnation. Because of such variations in our behaviour across situations, strict behaviourists think it does not even make sense to talk about "personality." In their view, people don't have "traits"; they simply show certain behaviour patterns in some situations and not others.

A major contemporary learning view, **social–cognitive learning theory**, accounts for similarities in traits across situations and also for the inconsistencies that often occur. It holds that personality traits result, in part, from your learning history and your resulting expectations and beliefs. A child who studies hard and gets good grades, attention from teachers, admiration from friends, and praise from parents will come to expect that hard work in other situations will also pay off. That child will become, in terms of personality traits, "ambitious" and "industrious." A child who studies hard and gets poor grades, is ignored by teachers and parents, and is rejected by friends for being a grind will come to expect that working hard isn't worth it. That child will become (in the view of others) "unambitious" or "lazy."

Social–cognitive learning theory also emphasizes the continual interaction between your particular qualities and the situation you are in. Your temperament, habits, and beliefs influence how you respond to others, whom you hang out with, and the situations you seek (Bandura, 2001; Cervone & Shoda, 1999; Mischel & Shoda, 1995). In turn, the situation influences your behaviour and beliefs, rewarding some behaviours and extinguishing others. This process is called **reciprocal (mutual) determinism**.

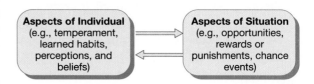

The two-way process of reciprocal determinism (as opposed, say, to the one-way determinism of "genes determine everything" or "everything is learned") helps answer a question asked by everyone who has a sibling: What makes children who grow up in the same family so different, apart from their genes? The answer seems to be: an assortment of experiences that affect each child differently, chance events that cannot be predicted, situations that children find themselves in, and peer groups that the children belong to (Plomin, Asbury, & Dunn, 2001; Rutter et al., 2001). Behavioural geneticists refer to these unique and chance experiences that are not shared with other family members as the **nonshared environment**: for example, being in Mrs. Miller's class in the fourth grade (which might inspire you to become a scientist), winning the lead in the school play (which might push you toward an acting career), or being bullied at school (which

reciprocal (mutual) determinism In social–cognitive theories, the two-way interaction between aspects of the environment and aspects of the individual in the shaping of personality traits.

social–cognitive learning theory A major contemporary learning view of personality, which holds that personality traits result from a person's learning history and his or her expectations, beliefs, perceptions of events, and other cognitions.

nonshared environment Unique aspects of a person's environment and experience that are not shared with family members.

Who is the "real" Madonna—doting mother or flamboyant performer? According to social–cognitive learning theory, our genetic dispositions and personality traits cause us to choose some situations over others, but situations then influence which aspects of our personalities we express.

might have caused you to see yourself as weak and powerless). All these experiences work reciprocally with your own interpretation of them, your temperament, and your perceptions (did Mrs. Miller's class excite or bore you?).

Keeping the concept of reciprocal determinism in mind, let us take a look at two of the most powerful environmental influences in people's lives: their parents and their friends.

The Power of Parents

In April 1999, Dylan Klebold and Eric Harris, two teenagers enraged at the popularity of school jocks and resentful about their own inadequacies, killed 12 classmates and a teacher at Columbine High School in Littleton, Colorado, in a coldly premeditated plan. Then they committed suicide. Months later, a student in Taber, Alberta, shot two students, killing one and seriously injuring the other. In the ensuing atmosphere of panic and blame, many people tried to find reasons for these events. Could the parents have been to blame? The Klebolds should have known, people said. They should have done something to prevent the tragedy. Or they did something wrong in raising their son; maybe they were neglectful or abusive.

These claims reflect an entrenched Western belief that parental child-rearing practices are the strongest influence, maybe even the *sole* influence, on children's personality development. For many decades, few psychologists thought to question this assumption, and many still accept it. Yet the belief that personality is primarily determined by how parents treat their children has begun to crumble under the weight of three lines of evidence (Harris, 1998):

Thinking Critically About the Influence of Parents

1 *The shared environment of the home has little if any influence on personality.* In behavioural-genetic research, the "shared environment" includes the family you grew up with and the experiences and background you shared with your siblings and parents. If these had as powerful an influence as is commonly assumed, then studies should find a strong correlation between the personality traits of adopted children and those of their adoptive parents. In fact, the correlation is weak to nonexistent, indicating that the influence of child-rearing practices and family life is nil compared to the influence of genetics (Cohen, 1999; Plomin, Asbury, & Dunn, 2001). As we just saw, it is only the non-shared environment that has a strong impact.

When teens display violence, those reading about the events in the newspaper often assume the parents are a major part of the problem.

2 *Few parents have a single child-rearing style that is consistent over time and that they use with all their children.* Developmental psychologists have tried for many years to identify the effects of specific child-rearing practices on children's personality traits. The problem is that parents are inconsistent from day to day and over the years. Their child-rearing practices vary, depending on their own stresses, moods, and marital satisfaction (Harris, 1998; Holden & Miller, 1999). As one child we know said to her exasperated mother, "Why are you so mean to me today, Mommy? I'm this naughty every day." Moreover, parents tend to adjust their methods of child rearing according to the temperament of the child; they are often more lenient with easygoing children and more punitive with difficult ones. And researchers at the Universities of Toronto and London have found that parents' differential treatment of their children can also depend on the size of the family and its socioeconomic status (Jenkins & Rasbash, 2003).

3 *Even when parents try to be consistent in the way they treat their children, there may be little relation between what they do and how the children turn out.* Some children of troubled and abusive parents are resilient and do not suffer lasting emotional damage, as we will see in Chapter 3; some children of the kindest and most nurturing parents succumb to drugs, mental illness, or gangs. By all accounts, the parents of Dylan Klebold were loving and involved with their son (Garbarino & Bedard, 2001).

By understanding the parent–child relationship not as a one-way street (parents affect everything about their kids) but as one that runs in both directions, we can see that parents and children continually influence one another. The child's personality is shaped in part by this interaction. For example, we saw in the previous section that *most* infants who are highly reactive and fearful eventually shift away from this extreme (Kagan, 1998a, 1998b). How much they do so depends on how parents and others respond to their reactivity. Imagine a high-strung parent with a baby who is fearful, quick to cry, and slow to be consoled. The parent, feeling desperate or angry, may withdraw from the child or use excessive punishment, which in turn makes the child even more timid and withdrawn. In contrast, a patient parent may have a calming effect on a frightened child, leading the child to become more outgoing. Mothers can also have a reinforcing effect on a child's behaviour. Researchers at McGill, for example, have shown that mothers were more likely to behave in ways that fostered independence when they believed their children were acting competently (Thompson & Zuroff, 1999).

Because of reciprocal determinism, even traits that are highly heritable can be strengthened or diminished by experience. In one important longitudinal study that followed children from age 3 to age 21, those who were impulsive, undercontrolled, and aggressive at age 3 were far more likely than calmer children to grow up to be impulsive, unreliable, and antisocial, and more likely to commit crimes (Caspi, 2000). Early temperament was a strong and consistent predictor of these later personality traits. But not *every* child came out the same way. What protected some of those at risk and helped them move in a healthier direction?

One answer is having parents who made sure they stayed in school (Caspi, 2000). Boys who are at high risk of delinquency and crime are often rescued if they get consistent parental discipline and close supervision, if their parents are affectionate, and if their parents set high standards and expectations (McCord, 1992; Patterson et al., 1998; C. Smith et al., 1997). (In Chapter 3, we will consider further the impact of particular child-rearing practices on children's moral behaviour and aggressiveness.)

United Media / United Feature Syndicate, Inc.

Do parents have total control over how their children turn out, even if they try to keep constant tabs on them?

Keep in mind, too, that parents affect many things about their children other than personality traits. These include religious beliefs, intellectual and occupational interests, feelings of self-esteem or inadequacy, adherence to traditional or modern notions of masculinity and femininity, helpfulness to others, skills, and values (Beer, Arnold, & Loehlin, 1998; Krueger, Hicks, & McGue, 2001; McCrae et al., 2000).

Most of all, what parents do profoundly affects the quality of their relationship with their children—whether their children feel loved, secure, and valued, or humiliated, frightened, and worthless (Harris, 1998). Surely this is the most important influence that parents have! But once children leave home, starting in preschool, parental influence on children's behaviour *outside* the home begins to wane. The nonshared environment—peers, chance events, and circumstances—takes over.

The Power of Peers

Should the parents of Dylan Klebold and Eric Harris have known how angry and resentful their sons felt in their private souls, angry enough to inflict a bloody revenge on their classmates? When two psychologists surveyed 275 first-year students at Cornell University, they found that most of them had "secret lives" and private selves that they never revealed to their parents (Garbarino & Bedard, 2001). Most reported committing crimes, drinking, doing drugs, and having sex without their parents' knowing anything about it. The researchers concluded that Dylan Klebold was just an extreme case of a common adolescent phenomenon: showing only one facet of your personality to your parents and an entirely different one to your peers.

Children, like adults, live in two environments: their homes and their world outside the home. At home, children learn how their parents want them to behave and what they can get away with; as soon as they leave home, however, they conform to the dress, habits, language, and rules of their peers. Children who were law-abiding in the fifth grade may start breaking the law in high school, if that is what it takes—or what they think it takes—to win the respect of their peers (Harris, 1998).

Adolescent culture often consists of many different peer groups, organized by interests (jocks, nerds, musicians, artists), ethnicity, or status and popularity. Unfortunately, children and teenagers who are temperamentally fearful and shy, have few or no friends, or are physically unattractive or weak are more likely than other kids to be bullied, victimized, and rejected by their peers (Hodges & Perry, 1999).

It has been difficult to tease apart the effects of parents and peers because parents usually try to arrange things so that their children's environments duplicate their own values and customs. To see which has the stronger influence on personality and behaviour, therefore, we must look at situations in which these environments clash. For example, when parents value academic achievement and their child's peers do not, who wins? The answer, typically, is peers. This is especially true in North America, but less so in Italy, for example. Michael Claes (1998) at the University of Montreal found that, for adolescents growing up in Italy, family was more influential than close friends. Canadian teens, by comparison, were swayed more by their peers.

Peers, like parents, shape the expression of personality traits, causing us to emphasize some attributes or abilities and downplay others. Of course, as the theory of reciprocal determinism would predict, our temperaments and dispositions also cause us to select particular peer groups (if they are available) instead of others, and our temperaments also influence how we behave within the group. But once we are among peers, most of us go along with them, moulding facets of our personalities to the pressures of the group.

The first day of day care can be a rude awakening for an only child raised at home.

WE'RE HERE AND WE'RE PEERS... GET USED TO IT.

YOU'RE NOT THE CENTER OF THE UNIVERSE, THOUGH YOU ARE A LOT CLOSER THAN I AM.

MICHAEL FRY 5/12

United Media / United Feature Syndicate, Inc.

Quick Quiz

We want to nurture your appreciation of quizzes because it's in our nature to give them to you.

1. What three lines of evidence have disputed the belief that parents are the major influence on their children's personalities?

2. Which contributes most to the variation among siblings in their personality traits: (a) the family environment that all of them share, (b) the way their parents treat them, or (c) the unique experiences they have that are not shared with their families?

Answers:

1. The shared family environment has little if any influence on personality; few parents have a consistent child-rearing style; and even when parents try to be consistent in the way they treat their children, there may be little relation between what they do and how the children turn out. 2. c

individualist cultures Cultures in which the self is regarded as autonomous, and individual goals and wishes are prized above duty and relations with others.

collectivist cultures Cultures in which the self is regarded as embedded in relationships, and harmony with one's group is prized above individual goals and wishes.

culture A program of shared rules that govern the behaviour of members of a community or society, and a set of values, beliefs, and attitudes shared by most members of that community.

WHAT'S AHEAD

- How does belonging to an individualist or collectivist culture influence your personality—and even whether you think you have a stable "self"?
- Why are punctuality and aggressiveness more than just individual personality traits?
- How is male aggressiveness influenced by culture?

CULTURAL INFLUENCES ON PERSONALITY

If you get an invitation to come to a party at 7 p.m., what time are you actually likely to get there? If someone gives you the finger or calls you a rude name, are you likely to become furious in return or to laugh it off?

It might seem that conscientiousness about time and quickness to anger are personality traits that result from genetic dispositions or experience. But culture has a profound effect on these reactions and many others. A **culture** is a program of shared rules that govern the behaviour of members of a community or society, and a set of values and beliefs shared by most members of that community and passed from one generation to another (Lonner, 1995). In this section, we will consider some of the contributions of the cultural approach to understanding personality.

Culture, Values, and Traits

It is not always easy to see how cultural rules affect your own personality, but here's a demonstration. Take as much time as you like to answer this question: "Who are you?" "I am _____."

Your response to "Who am I?" will be influenced by your cultural background, particularly whether your culture emphasizes individualism or community (Hofstede & Bond, 1988; Markus & Kitayama, 1991; Triandis, 1995, 1996). In **individualist cultures**, the independence of the individual takes precedence over the needs of the group, and the self is often defined as a collection of personality traits ("I am outgoing, agreeable, and ambitious") or in occupational terms ("I am a psychologist"). In **collectivist cultures**, group harmony takes precedence over the wishes of the individual, and the self is defined in the context of relationships and the community ("I am the son of a farmer, descended from three generations of story tellers on my mother's side and five generations of farmers on my father's side . . .").

As Table 2.2 shows, individualist and collectivist ways of defining the self influence many aspects of life, including which personality traits we value, how we express emotions, and how much we value having relationships or maintaining freedom (Campbell et al., 1996; Kashima et al., 1995). Individualist and collectivist outlooks even affect how stable we perceive our personalities to be across situations. And in Canada, with our multicultural population, we are able to see both perspectives. Romin Tafarodi and his colleagues at the University of Toronto studied how individualist and collectivist cultural affiliations affect self-esteem. Overall, they found that whether or not we feel good about ourselves stems largely from how our culture defines our role in society—as either individuals competing with others to reach personal goals or as part of a community helping one another to reach common goals (Tafarodi, 1998; Tafarodi, Lang, & Smith, 1999; Tafarodi & Milne, 2002; Tafarodi, Tam, & Milne, 2001).

TABLE 2.2 Some Average Differences Between Individualist and Collectivist Cultures

Members of Individualist Cultures	Members of Collectivist Cultures
Define the self as autonomous, independent of groups.	Define the self as an interdependent part of groups.
Give priority to individual, personal goals.	Give priority to the needs and goals of the group.
Value independence, leadership, achievement, self-fulfillment.	Value group harmony, duty, obligation, security.
Give more weight to an individual's attitudes and preferences than to group norms as explanations of behaviour.	Give more weight to group norms than to individual attitudes as explanations of behaviour.
Attend to the benefits and costs of relationships; if costs exceed advantages, a person is likely to drop a relationship.	Attend to the needs of group members; if a relationship is beneficial to the group but costly to the individual, the individual is likely to stay in the relationship.

Source: Triandis, 1996

Individualist North Americans exercise by running, walking, bicycling, and skating, all in different directions and wearing different clothes. Collectivist Japanese employees at their hiring ceremony exercise in identical fashion.

Culture and Traits When people fail to understand the influence of culture on behaviour, they often attribute another person's mysterious or annoying actions to individual personality traits when they are really due to cultural norms.

Consider the apparently simple matter of *conversational distance:* how close people usually stand to one another when they are speaking (Hall, 1959, 1976). Arabs like to stand close enough to feel your breath, touch your arm, and see the pupils of your eyes—a distance that makes most white North Americans and northern Europeans uneasy, unless they are talking intimately with a lover. The English and the Swedes stand farthest apart when they converse; southern Europeans stand closer; and Latin Americans and Arabs stand the closest (Keating, 1994; Sommer, 1969). One of our students from the Middle East told us he always thought his Anglo classmates were cold and aloof, even prejudiced against him, because they kept moving away from him in conversation. They, in turn, thought he had a "pushy" personality. They were all simply trying to reestablish the conversational distance that made them comfortable.

Or consider tardiness. Individuals differ in whether they try to be "on time" or are always late, but cultural norms affect how individuals regard time in the first place. In northern Europe, Canada, and the United States, time is organized into linear segments in which people do one thing "at a time" (Hall, 1983; Hall & Hall, 1990). The day is divided into appointments, schedules, and routines, and because time is a precious commodity, people don't like to "waste" time or "spend" too much time on any one activity (hence the popularity of multitasking). In such cultures,

therefore, it is considered the height of rudeness (or high status) to keep someone waiting. But in Mexico, southern Europe, the Middle East, South America, and Africa, time is organized along parallel lines. People do many things at once, and the needs of friends and family supersede mere appointments. Latinos and Middle Easterners think nothing of waiting for hours or days to see someone. The idea of having to be somewhere "on time," as if time were more important than a person, is unthinkable.

In culturally diverse North America, the two time systems keep bumping into each other. An Anglo judge in Miami got into hot water when he observed that "Cubans always show up two hours late for weddings"—late in his culture's terms, that is. The judge was accurate in his observation; the problem was his implication that something was wrong with Cubans for being "late." And "late" compared to what, by the way? The Cubans were perfectly on time for Cubans.

Arabs tend to stand much closer to one another than Westerners do. This "personality difference" is due to different cultural norms for conversational distance.

Culture and Male Aggressiveness A good example of how culture "gets into" personality comes from the study of culture and male aggression. Many people assume that male violence is mostly a matter of testosterone, a biologically ordained personality trait. But considerable cross-cultural evidence suggests that it results more from cultural factors than biological ones. After all, men everywhere have testosterone, but rates of male aggressiveness vary enormously across cultures and throughout history.

In cultures in which resources are abundant and there are no serious hazards or enemies to worry about—such as the Ifaluk, the Tahitians, and the people of Sudest Island near New Guinea—men do not feel they have to prove themselves, and they are not raised to be tough and aggressive (Lepowsky, 1994; Levy, 1984). In contrast, in cultures in which competition for resources is fierce and survival is difficult (which has been true of most cultures throughout history), men are "toughened up" and pushed to take risks, even with their lives (Gilmore, 1990).

Evaluating Cultural Approaches

A woman we know, originally from England, married a Lebanese man. They were happy together but had the usual number of marital misunderstandings and squabbles. After a few years, they visited his hometown in Lebanon, where she had never been before. "I was stunned," she told us. "All the things I thought he did because of his *personality* turned out to be because he's *Lebanese*! Everyone there was just like him!"

Our friend's reaction illustrates both the contributions and the limitations of cultural studies of personality. She was right in recognizing that some of her husband's behaviour was attributable to his culture; for example, his Lebanese notions of time were very different from her English notions. But she was wrong to infer that the Lebanese are all "like him": Individuals are affected by their culture, but they vary within it.

Cultural psychologists face the problem of how to describe cultural influences on personality without stereotyping (Church & Lonner, 1998). As one student of ours put it, "How come when we students speak of 'the' Aboriginals or 'the' whites or 'the' blacks it's called stereotyping, and when you do it, it's called 'cross-cultural psychology'?" This question shows excellent critical thinking! The study of culture does not rest on the assumption that all members of a culture behave the same way or have the same personality traits. As we have seen in this chapter, people vary according to their temperaments, beliefs, and learning histories, and this variation occurs within every culture.

Thinking Critically About Culture and Personality

Finally, in spite of their differences, cultures have many human concerns and needs in common—for love, attachment, family, work, and religious or communal tradition. Nonetheless, cultural rules are what, *on average*, make Swedes different from Bedouins and Cambodians different from Italians. The traits that we value, our sense of self versus community, and our notions of the right way to behave—all key aspects of personality—begin with the culture in which we are raised.

Quick Quiz

At the moment, you live in a culture that values the importance of quizzes.

1. Cultures whose members regard the "self" as a collection of stable personality traits are (individualist/collectivist).
2. A Mexican visitor to England wonders why everyone he meets seems to stand too far away from him in conversation. When he moves closer, they move away. Mexico and England have different rules of _____.
3. Why, according to cultural psychologists, do rates of male aggressiveness differ across cultures?

Answers:

1. individualist
2. conversational distance
3. Where there are differences in the availability of resources and prevalence of enemies, men tend to be more aggressive; men are less prone to violence in cultures where they don't feel they have to prove themselves.

WHAT'S AHEAD

- How does the humanist vision of personality differ from psychodynamic and genetic views?
- In the humanist view, what's wrong with saying to a child, "I love you because you've been good"?

THE INNER EXPERIENCE

A final way to look at personality starts with the person's own point of view. Psychologists who take a *humanist* approach to personality emphasize our uniquely human capacity to determine our own actions and futures. Biology may hand us temperamental dispositions that limit us, the environment may deal us some tough experiences, our parents may not treat us as we would have wished, but we have the free will to transcend these forces.

Humanist Approaches

Humanist psychology was launched as a movement in the early 1960s. The movement's chief leaders—Abraham Maslow (1908–1970), Carl Rogers (1902–1987), and Rollo May (1909–1994)—argued that it was time to replace psychoanalysis and behaviourism with a "third force" in psychology, one that would draw a more complete picture of human potential and personality.

Abraham Maslow The trouble with psychology, said Maslow (1970, 1971), was that it had ignored many of the positive aspects of life, such as joy, laughter, love, happiness, and *peak experiences*, rare moments of rapture caused by the attainment of excellence or the experience of beauty. The traits that Maslow thought most important to personality were not the Big Five, but rather the qualities of the *self-actualized person*—the person who strives for a life that is meaningful, challenging, and satisfying.

For Maslow, personality development could be viewed as a gradual progression toward self-actualization. Most psychologists, he argued, had a lopsided view of human nature, a result of their emphasis on studying emotional problems and negative traits such as neuroticism or insecurity. As Maslow (1971) wrote, "When you select out for careful study very fine and healthy people, strong people, creative people . . . then you get a very different view of mankind. You are asking how tall can people grow, what can a human being become?"

Carl Rogers Rogers, like Freud, derived many of his ideas from observing his clients in therapy. As a clinician, Rogers (1951, 1961) was interested not only in why some people cannot function well, but also in what he called the fully functioning individual. How you behave depends on your subjective reality, Rogers said, not on the external reality around you. Fully functioning people experience *congruence*, or harmony, between the image they project to others and their true feelings and wishes. They are trusting, warm, and open, rather than defensive or intolerant. Their beliefs about themselves are realistic.

To become fully functioning people, Rogers maintained, we all need **unconditional positive regard**, love and support for the people we are, without strings (conditions) attached. This doesn't mean that Winifred should be allowed to kick her brother when she is angry with him or that Wilbur may throw his dinner out the window because he doesn't like pot roast. In these cases, a parent can correct the child's behaviour without withdrawing love from the child. The child can learn that the behaviour, not the child, is what is bad. "House rules are 'no violence,' children," is a very different message from "You are horrible children for behaving so badly."

Rogers observed that, unfortunately, many children are raised with conditional positive regard: "I will love you if you behave well, and I won't love you if you behave badly." Adults often treat each other this way, too. People treated with conditional regard begin to suppress or deny feelings or actions that they believe are unacceptable to those they love. The result, said Rogers, is incongruence, a sense of being out of touch with your feelings, of not being true to your "real self," which in turn produces low self-regard, defensiveness, and unhappiness. A person experiencing incongruence scores high on neuroticism, becoming bitter and negative.

Rollo May May shared with the humanists a belief in free will and freedom of choice. But he also emphasized some of the inherently difficult and tragic aspects of the human condition, including loneliness, anxiety, and alienation. In

unconditional positive regard To Carl Rogers, love or support given to another person with no conditions attached.

humanist psychology A psychological approach that emphasizes personal growth, resilience, and the achievement of human potential.

You are never too old for self-actualization. Hulda Crooks, shown here at age 91 climbing Mt. Fuji, took up mountain climbing at 54. "When I come down from the mountain," she said, "I feel like I can battle in the valley again." She died at the age of 101.

existentialism A philosophic approach that emphasizes the inevitable dilemmas and challenges of human existence.

books such as *Love and Will* and *The Meaning of Anxiety*, May brought to North American psychology elements of the European philosophy of **existentialism**. This doctrine emphasizes the inevitable challenges of human existence, such as the search for the meaning of life, the need to confront death, and living with the burden of responsibility for our actions.

Free will, however, carries a price in anxiety and despair, which is why so many people try to escape from freedom into narrow certainties and blame others for their misfortunes. For May, our personalities reflect the ways we cope with the struggles to find meaning in existence, to use our freedom wisely, and to face suffering and death bravely. May popularized the humanist idea that we can choose to make the best of ourselves by drawing on inner resources such as love and courage, but he added that we can never escape the harsh realities of life and loss.

Evaluating Humanist Theories

As with psychodynamic theories, the major criticism of humanist psychology is that many of its assumptions are untestable. Freud looked at humanity and saw destructive drives, selfishness, and lust. Maslow and Rogers looked at humanity and saw co-operation, selflessness, and love. May looked at humanity and saw fear of freedom, loneliness, and the struggle for meaning. These differences, say critics, may tell us more about the observers than about the observed.

Many humanist concepts, although intuitively appealing, are hard to define operationally (see Chapter 1). How can we know whether a person

is self-fulfilled or self-actualized? How can we tell whether a woman's decision to quit her job and become a professional rodeo rider represents an "escape from freedom" or a freely made choice? And what exactly is unconditional positive regard? If it is defined as unquestioned support of a child's efforts at mastering a new skill, or as assurance that the child is loved in spite of his or her mistakes, then it is clearly a good idea. But in the popular culture, unconditional positive regard has often been interpreted as an unwillingness ever to say "no" to a child, or to offer constructive criticism and set limits, which children need.

Thinking Critically About Testing Humanist Ideas

Despite such concerns, humanist psychologists have added balance to the study of personality. A contemporary specialty known as "positive psychology" follows in the footsteps of humanism by focusing on the qualities that enable people to be happy, optimistic, and resilient in times of stress (Fredrickson, 2001; Taylor, 2001; Seligman & Csikszentmihalyi, 2000). Influenced in part by the humanists, psychologists are studying many positive human traits, such as courage, helpfulness to others, the motivation to excel, and self-confidence. Stress researchers have discovered the benefits of humour and hope. Developmental psychologists are studying ways to foster children's empathy and creativity.

Finally, the humanist and existential argument that we have the power to choose our own destinies, even when fate delivers us into tragedy, has fostered a new appreciation of human resilience in the face of adversity.

Quick Quiz

Exercise free will, as a humanist would advise you to, by choosing to take this quiz.

1. According to Carl Rogers, a man who loves his wife only when she is looking her best is giving her positive regard that is (a) conditional or (b) unconditional.

2. The humanist who described the importance of having peak experiences was (a) Abraham Maslow, (b) Rollo May, (c) Carl Rogers.

3. A humanist and a Freudian psychoanalyst are arguing about human nature. What underlying assumptions about psychology and human potential are they likely to bring to their discussion? How can they resolve their differences without either–or thinking?

Answers:

1. a 2. a

3. The Freudian assumes that human nature is basically selfish and destructive; the humanist, that it is basically loving and life-affirming. They can resolve this either–or debate by recognizing that human beings have both capacities; the situation and culture often deter mine which capacity is expressed at a given time.

Together, the approaches to personality discussed in this chapter portray a complex constellation of qualities that make up a human being: unconscious motives and defences, genetic predispositions, habits resulting from life experiences, traits influenced by cultural values and norms, and ways of behaving that develop in the struggle to become our best selves.

One way to integrate these different approaches may lie in recognizing that personality has two "faces." One is the public face, consisting of the traits and temperaments that we present to the world. This is the personality that biological, environmental, and cultural theories address. The other is a private face—our interior sense of self—consisting of our subjective experience of emotions, memories, dreams, wishes, and worries (Singer, 1984). This is the personality that psychodynamic and humanist theories address. Each of us weaves these two dimensions of personality together in the narratives we tell to explain our lives, our inconsistencies, our failures, and our successes—to explain, in short, why we are the way we are.

Psychology In The News *Revisited*

How are the dimensions of personality woven together in the case of William Lyon Mackenzie King, whose multi-sided personality was described in the news item at the start of this chapter?

A psychodynamic theorist would look for unconscious motives in Mackenzie King's apparently anomalous behaviour. Did his interest in the occult spring from his grief at the death of his beloved mother? By speaking with the dead, did he hope somehow to belie the fact of her own death?

Psychologists taking a biological view of personality would emphasize the possible genetic contributions to Mackenzie King's personality traits, such as his conservative exterior. Like his grandfather, William Lyon Mackenzie, he was rebellious as a young man and wanted to help the poor. His mother is said to have been sensitive—and perhaps it is this sensitivity that, in Mackenzie King's case, translated into a rich inner life.

Psychologists who take a learning or environmental perspective would examine situational influences on personality. Mackenzie King was a single man who was never able to find a suitable wife. Despite his great power, he was lonely. When people are in a situation in which they lack companionship, they may be driven toward finding solace through other channels. Mackenzie King spoke not only to the dead, after all—he also talked to his dog, Pat, and considered it "almost human."

Cultural psychologists would want to analyze the specific contributions of Mackenzie King's world in the 1920s through the 1940s. Attitudes toward such things as séances, as well as the mystics Mackenzie King visited and the Ouija boards he used—may well have been very different then.

Finally, humanist psychologists might speculate on the extent to which the private man, the one who lived inside Mackenzie King's skin, could be quite different from any of his public faces. His story teaches us that we should be wary of forming impressions based solely on his public persona or on what we hear others say about him.

Ultimately, we can only guess at who the "real" William Lyon Mackenzie King was. All of us, however, can use the insights of the theorists in this chapter to better understand ourselves and the people we love. Each of us is a mix of genetic influences, learned habits, the pressure of peers, new experiences, cultural norms, unconscious fears and conflicts, and our own private visions of possibility. This mix gives each of us the stamp of our personality, the qualities that make us feel uniquely . . . us.

Taking Psychology With You   How to Avoid the "Barnum Effect"

How well does the following paragraph describe you?

Some of your aspirations tend to be pretty unrealistic. At times you are extroverted, affable, sociable, while at other times you are introverted, wary, and reserved. You pride yourself on being an independent thinker and do not accept others' opinions without satisfactory proof. You prefer a certain amount of change and variety, and you become dissatisfied when hemmed in by restrictions and limitations. At times you have serious doubts as to whether you have made the right decision or done the right thing.

When people believe that this description was written just for them, as the result of a personalized horoscope or handwriting analysis, they all say the same thing: "It describes me *exactly*!" Everyone thinks this description is accurate because it is vague enough to apply to almost everyone and it is flattering (don't we all consider ourselves to be "independent thinkers"?).

This is why many psychologists worry about the "Barnum effect" (Snyder & Shenkel, 1975). P. T. Barnum was the great circus showman who said, "There's a sucker born every minute." He knew that the formula for success was to "have a little something for everybody"—and that is just what unscientific personality profiles, horoscopes, and handwriting analysis (graphology) have in common. They have "a little something for everyone" and hence are nonfalsifiable.

For example, graphologists claim that they can identify your personality traits from the form and distribution of your handwritten letters (Beyerstein, 1996). Wide spacing between words means you feel isolated and lonely. If your lines drift upward, you are an "uplifting" optimist, and if your lines droop downward, you are a pessimist who feels you are being "dragged down." If you make large capital *I*'s, you have a large ego.

Yet whenever graphology has been tested empirically, it has failed. A meta-analysis of 200 published studies found no validity or reliability to graphology in predicting work performance, aptitudes, or personality. No school of graphology fared better than any other, and no graphologist was able to perform better than untrained amateurs making guesses from the same materials (Dean, 1992; Klimoski, 1992).

If handwriting analysis were just an amusing game, no one would worry about it, but graphologists have been hired by companies to predict a person's leadership ability, attention to detail, willingness to be a good team player, honesty, and even criminal tendencies (Beyerstein, 1996). How would you feel if you were turned down for a job because some graphologist branded you a potential thief because you have "desire-for-possession hooks" on your *S*'s?

If you do not want to be taken in by graphology or the many other "personality" assessments that rely on the Barnum effect, research offers this advice:

- **Beware of all-purpose descriptions that could apply to anyone.** Sometimes you doubt your decisions; who among us has not? Sometimes you feel outgoing and sometimes shy; who does not? Do you "have sexual secrets that you are afraid of confessing"? Of course you do. Such secrets are very common.

- **Beware of your own selective perceptions.** Most of us are so impressed when an astrologer, psychic, or graphologist gets something right that we overlook all the descriptions that are plain wrong.

- **Resist flattery.** It is easy to reject a profile that describes you as selfish or stupid. Watch out for the ones that tell you how wonderful and smart you are, what a great leader you will be, or how modest you are about your abilities.

If you keep your critical faculties with you, you won't end up paying hard cash for soft answers, or taking a job you despise because it fits your "personality type." In other words, you'll have proved Barnum wrong.

SUMMARY

- *Personality* refers to an individual's distinctive and relatively stable pattern of behaviour, motives, thoughts, and emotions. Personality is made up of many different *traits*, characteristics that describe a person across situations.

PSYCHODYNAMIC THEORIES OF PERSONALITY

- Sigmund Freud was the founder of *psychoanalysis*, which was the first *psychodynamic* theory. Modern psychodynamic theories share an emphasis on unconscious processes and a belief in the formative role of childhood experiences and early, unconscious conflicts.
- To Freud, the personality consists of the *id* (the source of sexual energy, which he called the *libido*, and the aggressive instinct); the *ego* (the source of reason); and the *superego* (the source of conscience). *Defence mechanisms* protect the ego from unconscious anxiety. They include, among others, repression, projection, displacement (one form of which is sublimation), reaction formation, regression, and denial.
- Freud believed that personality develops in a series of *psychosexual stages*, with the *phallic (oedipal) stage* most crucial. During this stage, Freud believed, the *Oedipus complex* occurs, in which the child desires the parent of the other sex and feels rivalry with the same-sex parent. When the Oedipus complex is resolved, the child identifies with the same-sex parent, but females retain a lingering sense of inferiority and "penis envy"—a notion later contested by female psychoanalysts like Clara Thompson and Karen Horney.
- Carl Jung believed that people share a *collective unconscious* that contains universal memories and images, or *archetypes*. Personality, in this view, includes many archetypes, such as the *shadow* (evil) and the *anima* and *animus*.
- The *object-relations school* emphasizes the importance of the first two years of life, rather than the oedipal phase; the infant's relationships to important figures, especially the mother, rather than sexual needs and drives; and the problem in male development of breaking away from the mother.
- Psychodynamic approaches have been criticized for violating the principle of falsifiability; for overgeneralizing from atypical patients to everyone; and for basing theories on the unreliable memories and retrospective accounts of patients, which can create an *illusion of causality*. However, some psychodynamic ideas have received empirical support, including the existence of unconscious processes and defences.

THE MODERN STUDY OF PERSONALITY

- Most popular tests that divide personality into "types" are not valid or reliable. In research, psychologists typically rely on *objective tests (inventories)*, such as the Minnesota Multiphasic Personality Inventory or the Multidimensional Personality Questionnaire, to identify and study personality traits and disorders.
- Gordon Allport argued that people have a few *central traits* that are key to their personalities, and a greater number of *secondary traits* that are less fundamental. Raymond Cattell used *factor analysis* to identify clusters of traits that he considered the basic components of personality. Today there is strong evidence for the *Big Five* dimensions of personality: extroversion versus introversion, neuroticism (negative emotionality) versus emotional stability, agreeableness versus antagonism, conscientiousness versus impulsiveness, and openness to experience versus resistance to new experience. Although these dimensions are quite stable over time and across circumstances, some of them do change over the life span, reflecting maturational development.

GENETIC INFLUENCES ON PERSONALITY

- The nature–nurture debate is one of the oldest controversies in philosophy and psychology, but it is pretty much over. Today most psychologists recognize that *genes*, the basic units of heredity, account for about half of the variation in human traits, but the environment and experience account for the other half.
- Individual differences in *temperaments*—ways of reacting to the environment—appear to be inborn, emerging early in life and influencing subsequent personality development. Temperamental differences in extremely reactive and nonreactive children may be due to physiological variations in their responses to change and novelty. Experience can help extremely shy children become less shy and timid in new situations, but it cannot make them extroverts.
- *Behavioural-genetic* data from twin and adoption studies suggest that the *heritability* of

many adult personality traits is around .50. Genetic influences create dispositions and set limits on the expression of specific traits. But even traits that are highly heritable are often modified throughout life by circumstances, chance, and learning.

ENVIRONMENTAL INFLUENCES ON PERSONALITY

- People often behave inconsistently in different circumstances because behaviours that are rewarded in one situation may be punished or ignored in another. According to *social–cognitive learning theorists*, personality results from the interaction of aspects of the environment and aspects of the individual, in a pattern of *reciprocal determinism.*

- Behavioural geneticists have found that an important influence on personality is the *non-shared environment*, the unique experiences that each child in a family has.

- Three lines of evidence challenge the popular assumption that parents have the greatest impact on their children's personalities and behaviour: (1) Behavioural-genetic studies find that shared family environment has little if any influence on personality; (2) few parents have a consistent child-rearing style over time and with all their children; and (3) even when parents try to be consistent, there may be little relation between what they do and how the children turn out. However, parents can modify their children's temperaments, prevent children at risk of delinquency and crime from choosing a path of antisocial behaviour, influence many of their children's values and attitudes, and teach them to be kind and helpful. And of course parents profoundly affect the quality of their own relationship with their children.

- One major environmental influence on personality is peer groups, which can be more powerful than parents. Most children and teenagers behave differently with their parents than with their peers.

CULTURAL INFLUENCES ON PERSONALITY

- Many qualities that Western psychologists treat as individual personality traits are heavily influenced by *culture*. People from *individualist cultures* define themselves in different terms than do those from *collectivist cultures*, and they perceive their "selves" as more stable across situations. People vary in their notions of appropriate *conversational distance* and in their attitudes toward time and being "on time."

- Cultural theories of personality face the problem of describing broad cultural differences and their influences on personality without promoting stereotypes or overlooking universal human needs.

THE INNER EXPERIENCE

- *Humanist psychologists* focus on a person's subjective sense of self and the free will to change. They emphasize human potential and the strengths of human nature, as in Abraham Maslow's concepts of *peak experiences* and *self-actualization*. Carl Rogers stressed the importance of *unconditional positive regard* in creating a "fully functioning" person. Rollo May brought *existentialism* into psychology, emphasizing some of the inherent challenges of human existence that result from having free will, such as the search for meaning in life.

- Critics observe that many ideas from humanist psychology are subjective and difficult to measure, but the field has fostered research on many positive aspects of personality, including resilience under adversity.

PSYCHOLOGY IN THE NEWS, REVISITED

- Genetic influences, life experiences and learned habits, the pressure of specific situations, cultural norms, unconscious fears and conflicts, and our private sense of the "inner self" all combine in complex ways to create our distinctive personalities.

KEY TERMS

LOOKING BACK

- In Freud's theory of personality, why are the id and the superego always at war? (p. 41)
- When people say you're being "defensive," what defences might they be thinking of? (pp. 41–42)
- How do psychologists regard Freud today—as a genius or a fraud? (p. 43)
- What would Carl Jung have had to say about Darth Vader? (p. 44)
- What are the "objects" in the object-relations approach to personality? (p. 45)
- How reliable are those tests that tell you what "personality type" you are? (p. 47)
- How can psychologists tell which personality traits are more central or important than others? (p. 48)
- Which five dimensions of personality seem to describe people the world over? (p. 49)
- Is it possible to be born irritable or easygoing? (p. 51)
- To what extent are personality differences among people influenced by their genetic differences? (pp. 52–53)
- Are people who have highly heritable personality traits stuck with them forever? (p. 54)
- Are people always consistent across situations? (p. 56)
- How would a social–cognitive theorist explain why Madonna is so different as a performer and as a mom? (p. 56)
- How much can parents shape their children's personalities? (pp. 57–58)
- How do your peers influence your personality? (p. 59)
- How does belonging to an individualist or collectivist culture influence your personality—and even whether you think you have a stable "self"? (p. 60)
- How is male aggressiveness influenced by culture? (p. 62)
- Why are punctuality and aggressiveness more than just individual personality traits? (pp. 61–62)
- How does the humanist vision of personality differ from psychodynamic and genetic views? (p. 63)
- In the humanist view, what's wrong with saying to a child, "I love you because you've been good"? (p. 64)

Psychology In The News

AGE RECORD BROKEN AS 63-YEAR-OLD WOMAN GIVES BIRTH

LOS ANGELES, CA, April 10, 1997. A fertility specialist at the University of Southern California announced today that a 63-year-old patient, Arceli Keh, has given birth to a healthy baby girl. The child was conceived through in vitro ("test tube") fertilization, with sperm from the woman's 60-year-old husband and an egg donated by a younger woman. Previously, the oldest woman on record to give birth was a 53-year-old Italian woman who had a child in 1994 through the use of similar procedures.

Although the USC infertility program has a policy of rejecting patients over the age of 55, the California woman lied about her age and did not confess the truth until she was 13 weeks pregnant. The woman's own 86-year-old mother, unaware of her daughter's pregnancy until the delivery, is reportedly delighted at becoming a grandparent, and the rest of the close-knit Filipino family has also been supportive. But some fertility experts and ethicists have misgivings about the wisdom of older women giving birth. Dr. Mark Sauer, who pioneered the use of donor eggs in older women, said, "I lose my comfort level after 55 because I have to believe that there are quality-of-life issues involved in raising a child at [the parent's] age. When [the baby] is 5, her mother will be 68. And I have to believe that a 78-year-old dealing with a teenager may have some problems."

One of the oldest women ever to give birth, Arceli Keh, age 63, cuddles her daughter Cynthia.

3 Development over the Life Span

How do you react to the idea of a 63-year-old woman having a baby? Would it make any difference if the mother were "only" 55 years old, or 50, or 45? What if she were older than 63? Do you feel the same about older fathers as you do about older mothers? Is there a "right" time to become a parent? For that matter, is there a "right" time to do anything in life—go to school, get married, retire . . . die?

During the first half of the twentieth century, the answer would have been a resounding "yes." Most people shared a common life trajectory that seemed to divide into distinct stages. Childhood consisted of "formative" years that determined what kind of adult the child would become. Adolescence, the years between the physical changes of puberty and the social markers of adulthood, became longer and longer and was defined by turmoil and turbulence. Adulthood was conceptualized as a series of steps from marriage to parenthood to retirement. Elderly people were increasingly separated from the rest of society on the grounds that they could not keep up with the fast-moving world.

Today, we are undergoing a revolution in the way we think about the universal human journey from birth to death. Because of improvements in health care, a changing economy, a high divorce rate, and advances in reproductive technology, events over the life span are no longer as predictable as they were just a few decades ago. Most college students are still in their late teens or early 20s, but many are older. A person might marry or start a career at 25, and do so again at 45 or 65.

Psychologists are probably no better equipped than anyone else to address the many ethical issues raised by these changes—such as whether a woman should forgo pregnancy if she can't realistically expect to be around until her child grows up. But *developmental psychologists*, who study topics such as these, can help us think critically about the question of "natural" life stages.

Developmental psychologists focus on physiological and cognitive changes across the life span, and on **socialization**, the process by which children learn the attitudes and behaviours expected of them by society. In this chapter, we will explore some of their major findings, starting at the very beginning of human development, with the period from conception to birth, and continuing through adulthood into old age. At the end of the chapter, we will tell you how Arceli Keh and her daughter are doing. As you read, ask yourself what it means, in psychological terms, to be young, middle-aged, or old—and why so many people feel uneasy about the prospect of postmenopausal motherhood.

socialization The process by which children learn the behaviours, attitudes, and expectations required of them by their society or culture.

Developmental psychologists study people of all ages. This six-generation family includes Sara Knauss, age 118 (second from left), her daughter Kitty Sullivan, age 95 (far right), her grandson Bob Butz, age 73 (standing, left), her great-granddaughter Kathy Jacoby, age 49 (standing, right), her great-great-granddaughter Kristina Patton, age 27 (on floor), and her great-great-great-grandson Bradley Patton, age 3 (far left). Bradley doesn't yet know how many family relationships he will be able to remember.

WHAT'S AHEAD

- How can a pregnant woman reduce the risk of damage to the embryo or fetus?

- Given a choice, what do newborns prefer to look at?

- How does culture affect how a baby physically matures?

- Why is cuddling so important for infants (not to mention adults)?

- If you have a one-year-old, why shouldn't you worry if your baby cries when left with a new babysitter?

FROM CONCEPTION THROUGH THE FIRST YEAR

A baby's development, before and after birth, is a marvel of *maturation*, the unfolding of genetically influenced behaviour and physical characteristics. In only nine months of a mother's pregnancy, a cell grows from a dot this big (.) to a squalling bundle of energy that looks just like Aunt Lucy. In another 15 months, that bundle of energy grows into a babbling toddler who is curious about everything. No other time in human development brings so many changes, so fast.

Prenatal Development

Prenatal development is divided into three stages: the germinal, the embryonic, and the fetal. The *germinal stage* begins at conception, when the male sperm unites with the female ovum (egg); the fertilized single-celled egg is called a *zygote*. The zygote soon begins to divide, and in 10 to 14 days it becomes a cluster of cells that attaches itself to the wall of the uterus. The outer portion of this cluster will form part of the placenta and umbilical cord, and the inner portion becomes the embryo. The placenta, connected to the embryo by the umbilical cord, serves as the growing embryo's link for food from the mother. It allows nutrients to enter and wastes to exit, and it screens out some, but not all, harmful substances.

Once implantation is complete, about two weeks after conception, the embryonic stage begins, lasting until the eighth week after conception, at which point the embryo is only four centimetres long. From the fourth to the eighth week, the hormone testosterone is secreted by rudimentary testes in embryos that are genetically male; without this hormone, the embryo will develop to be anatomically female.

After eight weeks, the *fetal stage* begins. The organism, now called a *fetus*, further develops the organs and systems that existed in rudimentary form in the embryonic stage. By 28 weeks, the nervous and respiratory systems are developed enough to allow most fetuses to live if born prematurely. The greatest gains in brain and nervous-system development occur during the last 12 weeks of a full-term pregnancy.

Although the womb is a fairly sturdy protector of the growing embryo or fetus, some harmful influences can cross the placental barrier (O'Rahilly & Müller, 2001). These influences include the following:

1 *German measles* (rubella), especially early in the pregnancy, can affect the fetus's eyes, ears, and heart. The most common consequence is deafness. Rubella is preventable if the mother has been vaccinated, which can be done up to three months before pregnancy.

2 *X-rays or other radiation and toxic chemicals such as lead or mercury* can cause fetal abnormalities and deformities. Exposure to such toxins is also associated with attention problems and lower IQ scores.

3 *Sexually transmitted diseases* can cause mental retardation, blindness, and other physical disorders.

Genital herpes affects the fetus only if the mother has an outbreak at the time of delivery, which exposes the newborn to the virus as the baby passes through the birth canal. (This risk can be avoided by having a Caesarean section.) HIV, the virus that causes AIDS, can also be transmitted to the fetus, especially if the mother has developed AIDS and has not been treated.

4   *Cigarette smoking* during pregnancy increases the likelihood of miscarriage, premature birth, abnormal fetal heartbeat, and an underweight baby. The negative effects may last long after birth, showing up in increased rates of infant sickness, sudden infant death syndrome (SIDS), asthma, and, in later childhood, hyperactivity and learning difficulties.

5   *Having more than two alcoholic drinks every day* significantly increases the risk of a baby's having *fetal alcohol syndrome (FAS)*. FAS infants are smaller than normal and have smaller brains, have facial deformities, are uncoordinated, and are mentally retarded; in fact, FAS is the leading cause of non-hereditary mental retardation. In Canada, FAS is thought to affect 1 to 3 babies in every 1000 live births (Health Canada, 1999). Unfortunately, FAS appears to disproportionately affect ethnic minorities and the poor (Abel, 1995); and researchers at the University of British Columbia have also found that FAS individuals are at increased risk for coming into conflict with the law (Fast, Conry, & Loock, 1999). And even when alcohol does not cause FAS, binge drinking and drinking regularly throughout pregnancy can kill neurons throughout the fetus's developing brain and impair babies' later mental abilities, attention span, and academic achievement (Ikonomidou et al., 2000; Streissguth et al., 1999). In fact, because even small quantities of alcohol can affect many different aspects of fetal brain development, most specialists recommend that a pregnant woman abstain completely.

6   *Drugs other than alcohol* can be harmful to the fetus, whether they are illicit ones such as morphine, cocaine, and heroin, or commonly used legal substances such as antibiotics, antihistamines, tranquilizers, acne medication, and diet pills. Fathers' drug use can also cause fetal defects; cocaine, for example, does so by binding to sperm (Yazigi, Odem, & Polakoski, 1991). Longitudinal studies of children exposed to cocaine in the womb have dispelled the myth of the "crack baby" who

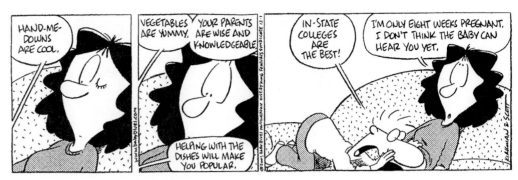

Many parents hope to have a positive influence on their offspring even before their babies are born!

is damaged severely for life (Newman & Buka, 1991). Nonetheless, cocaine can cause small impairments in children's cognitive abilities, attention spans, and impulse control (Lester, LaGasse, & Seifer, 1998).

The lesson is clear. A pregnant woman does well to stop smoking and drinking alcohol, and to take no other drugs of any kind unless they are medically necessary and have been adequately tested for safety—and then to accept the fact that her child will never be properly grateful for all that sacrifice!

The Infant's World

Newborn babies could never survive on their own, but they are far from being passive and inert. As a result of evolution, many abilities, tendencies, and characteristics are universal in human beings and are present at birth or develop very early, given certain experiences.

Newborns begin life with several *motor reflexes*, automatic behaviours that are necessary for survival (see Table 3.1). They will grasp tightly a finger pressed on their palms. They will turn their heads toward a touch on the cheek or corner of the mouth and search for something to suck on, a handy "rooting reflex" that allows them to find the breast or bottle. Many of these reflexes eventually disappear, but others—such as the knee-jerk, eye-blink, and sneeze reflexes—remain.

Babies are also equipped with a set of inborn perceptual abilities. They can see, hear, touch, smell, and taste (bananas and sugar water are in;

The sucking and grasping reflexes at work.

TABLE 3.1 Reflexes of the Newborn Baby

Reflex	Description
Rooting	An infant touched on the cheek or corner of the mouth will turn toward the touch and search for something to suck on.
Sucking	An infant will suck on anything suckable, such as a nipple or finger.
Swallowing	An infant can swallow, though this reflex is not yet well coordinated with breathing.
Moro or "startle"	In response to a loud noise or a physical shock, an infant will throw its arms outward and arch its back.
Babinski	In response to a touch on the bottom of the foot, the infant will splay its toes outward and then curl them in. (In adults, the toes just curl in.)
Grasp	In response to a touch on the palm of the hand, an infant will grasp.
Stepping	If held so the feet just touch the ground, an infant will show "walking" movements, alternating the feet in steps.

rotten eggs are out). A newborn's visual focus range is only about eight inches, the average distance between the baby and the face of the person holding the baby, but visual ability develops rapidly. Newborns can distinguish contrasts, shadows, and edges. They can discriminate their mother or other primary caregiver on the basis of smell, sight, or sound almost immediately. Within a couple of months, they show evidence of depth perception (see Chapter 6).

Infants do not use their perceptual abilities in a random manner. When given a choice, they show a surprising interest in looking at and listening to unfamiliar things—which, of course, includes most of the world. A baby will even stop nursing if someone new enters his or her range of vision. Infants are also primed to gaze at human faces. Babies who are only *nine minutes old* will turn their heads to watch a drawing of a face if it moves in front of them, but they will not turn if the "face" consists of scrambled features or is only the outline of a face (Johnson et al., 1991). A preference for faces over other stimuli in the environment probably has survival value because it helps babies recognize where their next meal is likely to come from.

Despite such commonalities, however, many aspects of infants' maturation depend on cultural customs that govern how their parents hold, touch, feed, and talk to them (Super & Harkness, 1994). For example, in most of North America, babies are expected to sleep for eight uninterrupted hours by the age of four or five months. This milestone is considered a sign of neurological maturity, although many babies wail when the parent puts them in the crib at night and leaves the room. But among Mayan Indians, rural Italians, African villagers, and urban Japanese, this nightly clash of wills never occurs because the infant sleeps with the mother for the first year or two of life, waking and nursing about every four hours. These differences in babies' sleep arrangements reflect cultural and parental values. Mayan and Japanese mothers believe it is important to sleep with the baby in order to forge a close bond; many white North American parents believe it is important to foster the child's independence as soon as possible (Morelli et al., 1992).

Attachment

Emotional attachment is a universal capacity of all primates and is important for health and survival all through life. By becoming attached to a caregiver, children gain a secure base from which they can explore the environment, and a haven of safety to return to when they are afraid (Bowlby, 1982).

Contact Comfort Attachment begins with physical touching and cuddling between infant and parent. Margaret and Harry Harlow first demonstrated the importance of touching, or **contact comfort**, by raising infant rhesus monkeys with two kinds of artificial mothers (Harlow, 1958; Harlow & Harlow, 1966). The first was a forbidding construction of wires and warming lights, with a milk bottle connected to it. The second was constructed of wire and covered in foam rubber and cuddly

contact comfort In primates, the innate pleasure derived from close physical contact; it is the basis of an infant's first attachment.

terry cloth (see Figure 3.1). At the time, many psychologists thought that babies become attached to their mothers simply because mothers provide food (Blum, 2002). But the Harlows' baby monkeys ran to the terry-cloth "mother" when they were frightened or startled, and cuddling up to it calmed them down. Human children, too, often seek contact comfort when they are in an unfamiliar situation, are scared by a nightmare, or fall and hurt themselves.

Separation and Security Once babies are emotionally attached to the mother or other caregiver, separation can be a wrenching experience. Between 6 and 8 months of age, babies become wary or fearful of strangers. They wail if they are put in an unfamiliar setting or are left with an unfamiliar person. And they show **separation anxiety** if the primary caregiver temporarily leaves them. This reaction usually continues until the middle of the second year, but many children show signs of distress at parental separation until they are about three years old (Hrdy, 1999). All children go through this phase, although cultural child-rearing practices influence how strongly the anxiety is felt and how long it lasts. In cultures in which babies are raised with many adults and other children, separation anxiety is not as intense or as long-lasting as it can be in societies like Japan, where babies form attachments primarily or exclusively with the mother (Rothbaum et al., 2000).

To determine the nature of the attachment between mothers and babies, Mary Ainsworth (1973, 1979) devised an experimental method called the *Strange Situation*. A mother brings her baby into an unfamiliar room containing lots of toys. After a while a stranger comes in and attempts to play with the child. The mother leaves the baby with the stranger. She then returns and plays with her child, and the stranger leaves. Finally, the mother leaves the baby alone for three minutes and then returns. In each case, observers carefully note how the baby behaves with the mother, with the stranger, and when alone.

Ainsworth divided children into three categories on the basis of their reactions to the Strange Situation. Some babies are *securely attached*: They cry or protest if the mother leaves the room; they welcome her back and then play happily again; they are clearly more attached to the mother than to the stranger. Other babies are *insecurely attached*, and this insecurity can take two forms. The child may be *avoidant*, not caring if the mother leaves the room, making little effort to seek contact with her on her return, and treating the stranger in approximately the same manner as the mother. Or the child may be *anxious or ambivalent*, resisting contact with the mother at reunion but protesting loudly if she leaves. Anxious or ambivalent babies may cry to be picked up and then demand to be put down, or they may behave as if they are angry with the mother and resist her efforts to comfort them.

separation anxiety The distress that most children develop, at about six to eight months of age, when their primary caregivers temporarily leave them with others.

FIGURE 3.1 The Comfort of Contact

Infants need cuddling as much as they need food. In Margaret and Harry Harlow's studies, infant rhesus monkeys were reared with a cuddly terry-cloth "mother" and with a bare wire "mother" that provided milk (left). The infants would go to the wire "mother" to be fed, (left) but cling to the terry mother when they were not being fed; when they were frightened (as the infant on the right was by a toy spider put in his enclosure), it was the terry mother they ran to.

Insecure attachment is of great concern to psychologists because it is associated with emotional and behavioural problems in childhood and possibly throughout life (Mickelson, Kessler, & Shaver, 1997; Shaw, Keenan, & Vondra, 1994). Psychologists in Wales and Newfoundland, for example, have found that it predicts such problems as difficulties at school (Elgar et al., 2003).

What Causes Insecure Attachment? Ainsworth believed that insecure attachment results primarily from the way mothers treat their babies during the first year. Mothers who are sensitive and responsive to their babies' needs, she said, create securely attached infants; mothers who are uncomfortable with or insensitive to their babies create insecurely attached infants. To many, the assumptions were that babies needed exactly the "right kind" of mothering from the very beginning in order to become securely attached, and that putting a child in daycare would retard this important development—notions that caused insecurity among many mothers!

Thinking Critically About Attachment Theory

These assumptions, however, proved unwarranted. True, there is a modest correlation between a mother's sensitivity and a child's secure attachment, but of course this doesn't tell us which causes what—or whether something else causes both sensitivity and attachment (De Wolff & van IJzendoorn, 1997). Programs designed to help new mothers become less anxious and more attuned to their babies do help some moms become more "sensitive," but they only modestly affect the child's degree of secure attachment (Bakermans-Kranenburg, van IJzendoorn, & Juffer, 2003).

The emphasis on maternal sensitivity, in any event, overlooks the fact that most children form a secure attachment to their mothers in spite of wide variations in child-rearing practices. For example, German babies are frequently left on their own for a few hours at a stretch by mothers who believe that even babies should become self-reliant (Kagan, 1998b). And among the Efe

of Africa, babies spend about half their time away from their mothers, in the care of older children and other adults (Tronick, Morelli, & Ivey, 1992). Yet German and Efe children are not insecure, and they develop as normally as children who spend more time with their mothers. If children like these don't fuss or panic in the Strange Situation when their mothers leave, it is usually because they have learned to be comfortable with strangers.

Likewise, time spent in daycare has no effect on the security of a child's attachment. In a major longitudinal study of more than 1000 children, researchers compared infants who were in child care 30 hours or more a week, from age 3 months to age 15 months, with children who spent less than 10 hours a week in child care. The two groups did not differ on any measure of attachment, and children in high-quality care—with well-trained caregivers and small child–staff ratios—did better on measures of social, language, and cognitive development than did children at home (NICHD Early Child Care Research Network, 1997, 2002).

What factors, then, promote insecure attachment? One is parenting that is truly abusive, neglectful, or erratic. Another is the child's own genetically influenced temperament. Babies who are fearful and prone to crying from birth are more likely than calmer infants to show insecure behaviour in the Strange Situation (Belsky et al., 1996; Seifer et al., 1996). A third factor is stressful circumstances in the child's family. Infants and young children may temporarily shift from secure to insecure attachment—becoming clingy and fearful of being left alone—if their families are undergoing a period of stress, as during parental divorce or a parent's chronic illness (Belsky et al., 1996; Lewis, 1997).

The bottom line is that infants are biologically disposed to become attached to their caregivers, and normal, healthy attachment will occur within a wide range of cultural, family, and individual variations in child-rearing customs.

Quick Quiz

Are you feeling secure, avoidant, or anxious about quizzes?

1. Name as many potentially harmful influences on fetal development as you can.

2. Melanie is playing happily on a jungle gym at her child-care centre when she falls off and scrapes her knee. She runs to her caregiver for a consoling cuddle. Melanie is seeking _____.

3. A baby left in the Strange Situation does not protest when his mother leaves the room, and he seems to ignore her when she returns. What style of attachment does this behaviour reflect?

4. In question 3, what else besides the child's style of attachment could be causing the child's reaction?

Answers:

1. German measles early in pregnancy; exposure to radiation or toxic chemicals; sexually transmitted diseases; the mother's use of cigarettes, alcohol, or other drugs
2. contact comfort
3. insecure (avoidant)
4. the child's own temperament; frequent exposure to and therefore comfort with adults other than the mother; the child's famil-iarity with being left alone temporarily

WHAT'S AHEAD

- Why do so many parents speak "baby talk"?
- Is language an innate ability or an acquired one?
- What important accomplishment are infants revealing when they learn to play "peekaboo"?
- Why will most five-year-olds choose a tall, narrow glass of lemonade over a short, fat glass containing the same amount?

COGNITIVE DEVELOPMENT

Our friend Joel reports how thrilled he was when his 13-month-old daughter Alison looked at him one day and said, for the first time, "Daddy!" His delight was deflated somewhat, though, when the doorbell rang and she ran to the door, calling, "Daddy!" And his delight was completely shattered when the phone rang and Alison ran to it, shouting, "Daddy!" Later Joel learned that there was a two-year-old child in Alison's daycare group whose father would ring the doorbell when he picked her up. Alison had acquired her friend's enthusiasm for doorbells but did not quite get the hang of "Daddy." She will soon enough, though. She will also be able to reason and see the world from Daddy's viewpoint. And soon, too, she will be able to understand what her daddy means when he praises her for being a "good girl"—or scolds her for being a naughty one.

Language

Try to read this sentence aloud:

> Kamaunawezakusomamamanenohayawewe nimtuwamaanasana.

Can you tell where one word begins and another ends? Unless you know Swahili, the syllables of this sentence will sound like gibberish.[1]

Well, to a baby learning its native tongue, *every* sentence must, at first, sound like gibberish. How, then, does an infant pick out discrete syllables and words from the jumble of sounds in its environment, much less figure out what those words mean? And how is it that in only a few short years, children not only understand thousands of words, but can also produce and understand an endless number of new word combinations?

From Cooing to Communicating The process of acquiring language begins in the first months, with crying and cooing. Even at this early stage, babies are highly responsive to the pitch, intensity, and sound of language, and they react to the emotions and rhythms in voices. When most adults speak to babies, their pitch is higher and more varied than usual, and their intonation is exaggerated. Adult use of "baby talk"—researchers call it *parentese*—has been documented all over the world, from

[1] Kama unaweza kusoma maneno haya, wewe ni mtu wa maana sana means, in Swahili, "If you can read these words, you are a remarkable person."

Babies are born with a special delight in looking at faces and imitating expressions.

telegraphic speech A child's first word combinations, which omit (as a telegram did) unnecessary words.

Sweden to Australia to Japan. Parentese helps babies learn the melody and rhythm of their native language (Fernald & Mazzie, 1991; Kuhl et al., 1997). Parentese isn't common to all cultures, however. Some First Nations people in the Atlantic provinces, for example, do not vary their frequency and range when talking to infants (Fee & Shaw, 1998).

By four to six months of age, babies can often recognize their own names and other words that are regularly spoken with emotion, such as "Mommy" and "Daddy." They also know many of the key consonant and vowel sounds of their native language and can distinguish such sounds from those of other languages (Kuhl et al., 1992). Over time, exposure to the baby's native language reduces the child's ability to perceive speech sounds in other languages. Thus, Japanese infants can hear the difference between the English sounds *la* and *ra*, but older Japanese children and Japanese adults cannot. Because this contrast does not exist in their language, they become insensitive to it.

Between six and twelve months of age, infants become increasingly familiar with the sound structure of their native language. They are able to distinguish words from the flow of speech. They will listen longer to nonsense words that violate their expectations of what words should sound like and even to sentences that violate their expectations of how sentences should be structured (Jusczyk, 2002; Jusczyk, Houston, & Newsome, 1999). They start to babble, making many "ba-ba" and "goo-goo" sounds, endlessly repeating sounds and syllables. Then, at about a year of age—though the timing varies considerably—children start to name things. They already have some mental concepts for familiar people and objects, and their first

words represent these concepts ("mama," "doggie," "car").

Starting at about 11 months, babies develop a repertoire of symbolic gestures, another important tool of communication. They gesture to refer to objects (e.g., sniffing to indicate "flower"), to request things (e.g., smacking the lips for "food"), to describe objects (e.g., raising the arms for "big"), and to reply to questions (e.g., opening the palms or shrugging the shoulders for "I don't know"). They clap in response to pictures of things they like, from cartoon characters to baseball games. Children whose parents encourage them to use gestures acquire larger vocabularies, have better comprehension, are better listeners, and are less frustrated in their efforts to communicate than babies who are not encouraged to use gestures (Goodwyn & Acredolo, 1998). When babies begin to speak, they continue to gesture along with their words (just as adults gesture when talking), suggesting that gestures are not a substitute for language but are deeply related to its development (Mayberry & Nicoladis, 2000).

Between the ages of 18 months and 2 years, toddlers begin to produce words in two- or three-word combinations ("Mama here," "go 'way bug," "my toy"). The child's first combinations of words have a common quality: They are **telegraphic**. When people had to pay for every word in a telegram, they quickly learned to drop unnecessary articles (*a, an,* or *the*) and auxiliary verbs (such as *is* or *are*), but they still conveyed the message. Similarly, the two-word "telegrams" of toddlers omit articles, auxiliary verbs, other parts of speech, and word endings, but they are still remarkably accurate in conveying meanings. Children use two-word "telegrams" to locate things ("here toy"), make demands ("more milk"), negate actions ("no want," "all-gone milk"), describe events ("Bambi go," "hit ball"), describe objects ("pretty dress"), show possession ("Mama dress"), and ask questions ("Where Daddy?"). Pretty good for a little kid, don't you think?

At about this age, children develop another impressive talent: the rapid acquisition of new words. By the age of 6, the average child has a vocabulary of between 8000 and 14 000 words, meaning that children acquire up to eight new words *a day* between the ages of one and six. They absorb new words as they hear them, forming a quick impression of a word's likely meaning by using their knowledge of grammatical contexts and the rules for formulating words. The process

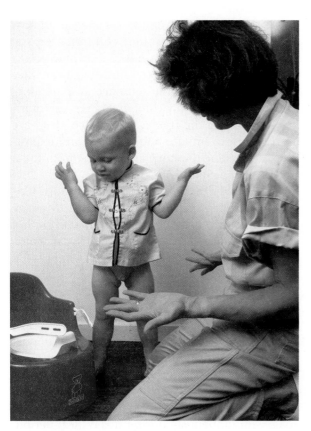

Conversational gestures emerge early!

of absorbing and understanding thousands of new words continues up through adolescence.

How on earth do children do all this?

The Innate Capacity for Language At one time, most psychologists assumed that children acquired language by imitating adults and paying attention when adults corrected the children's mistakes. Then along came linguist Noam Chomsky (1957, 1980), who argued that language was far too complex to be learned bit by bit, as one might learn a list of world capitals.

Language, he noted, is not just any old communication system. It is a system that enables us to combine elements that are themselves meaningless into utterances that convey meaning—and to reject utterances that are not acceptable in our native tongue. It permits us to express and comprehend an infinite number of novel utterances, created on the spot—and this is essential, because except for a few fixed phrases ("How are you?" "Get a life"), most of the utterances we produce or hear over a lifetime are new.

The task facing children, said Chomsky, is far more complicated than merely figuring out which sounds form words. They must also take the *surface*

structure of a sentence—the way the sentence is actually spoken or signed—and apply grammatical rules (*syntax*) in order to infer an underlying *deep structure* that contains meaning. For example, although "Mary kissed John" and "John was kissed by Mary" have different surface structures, any five-year-old knows that the two sentences have essentially the same deep structure, in which Mary is the actor and John gets the kiss.

Because no one actually teaches us grammar when we are toddlers, said Chomsky, the human brain must contain a **language acquisition device**, an innate mental module that allows young children to develop language if they are exposed to an adequate sampling of conversation. Just as a bird is designed to fly, human beings are designed to use language. Children's brains are sensitive to the core features common to all languages, such as nouns and verbs, subjects and objects, and negatives. These common features occur even in languages as seemingly different as Mohawk and English, or Okinawan and Bulgarian (Baker, 2001; Cinque, 1999).

Over the years, linguists and *psycholinguists* (researchers who study the psychology of language) have gathered many types of evidence to support this position:

1 *Children in different cultures go through similar stages of linguistic development.* For example, they will often form their first negatives simply by adding *no* or *not* at the beginning or end of a sentence ("No get dirty"). At a later stage, they will use double negatives ("He don't want no

language acquisition device According to many psycholinguists, an innate mental module that allows young children to develop language if they are exposed to an adequate sampling of conversation.

Human beings appear to have an inborn facility for acquiring language, even when they cannot hear speech. In North America, where many hearing-impaired people use American Sign Language, deaf children learn to sign in ASL as easily as hearing children learn to speak.

milk"; "Nobody don't like me"), even when their language does not allow such constructions (Klima & Bellugi, 1966; McNeill, 1966).

2 *Children combine words in ways that adults never would.* They reduce a parent's sentences ("Let's go to the store!") to their own two-word versions ("Go store!") and make many charming errors that an adult would not ("The alligator goed kerplunk," "Daddy taked me," "Hey, Horton heared a Who") (Ervin-Tripp, 1964; Marcus et al., 1992). Such errors, which psycholinguists call *overregularizations*, are not random; they show that the child has grasped a grammatical rule (add the *t* or *d* sound to make a verb past tense, as in *walked* and *hugged*) and is merely overgeneralizing it (*taked, goed*).

3 *Adults do not consistently correct their children's syntax, yet children learn to speak or sign correctly anyway.* Learning explanations of language acquisition assume that children are rewarded for saying the right words and punished for making errors. But parents do not stop to correct every error in their children's speech, as long as they can understand what the child is trying to say (Brown, Cazden, & Bellugi, 1969). Indeed, parents often *reward* children for incorrect statements! The two-year-old who says "Want milk!" is likely to get it; most parents would not wait for a more grammatical (or polite) request.

4 *Children who are not exposed to adult language may invent a language of their own.* Deaf children who have never learned a standard language, either signed or spoken, have made up their *own* sign languages, and across cultures these languages show similarities in sentence structure (Goldin-Meadow & Mylander, 1998; Senghas & Coppola, 2001).

Chomsky's ideas revolutionized thinking about language development. Most psycholinguists today believe that the capacity for language evolved in human beings because it permitted our ancestors to convey precise information about time, space, objects, and events and to negotiate alliances that were necessary for survival (Pinker, 1994).

The Influence of Learning on Language Of course, anything as complex as language cannot be explained simply as an innate mechanism. Language does not merely unfold biologically; it also depends on what is happening in a child's environment or culture (Gopnik, Choi, & Baumberger, 1996). For example, although parents

may not correct their children's speech all day, neither do they ignore their children's errors. When the child makes a mistake or produces a clumsy sentence, parents almost invariably respond by recasting the sentence or expanding its elements ("Monkey climbing!" "Yes, the monkey is climbing the tree"). In turn, children are more likely to imitate adult recasts and expansions, suggesting that they are learning from them (Bohannon & Stanowicz, 1988).

Language, therefore, depends on both biological readiness and social experience (Marcus, 1999; Pinker, 1999). Abused children who are not exposed to language during their early years (such as Genie, whom we mentioned in Chapter 1), rarely speak normally or catch up grammatically. Such sad evidence suggests a *critical period* in language development during the first few years of life or possibly the first decade. During these years, children need exposure to language and opportunities to practise their emerging linguistic skills in conversation with others.

In Canada and in other parts of the world, children might be exposed to more than one language simultaneously during this critical period. Researchers at McGill University and elsewhere have discovered that children can handle this well, learning each language concurrently and in similar fashion (Holowka, Brosseau-Lapre, & Petitto, 2002). Consistent with this, children enrolled in early French immersion school programs show enhanced learning of English as well as French (Harley, Hart, & Lapkin, 1986).

Thinking

As anyone who has ever observed a young child knows, children do not think the way adults do. At age two, they may call all large animals by one name (say, "horsie") and all small animals by another (say, "bug"). At four, they may protest that a sibling has "more" fruit juice when it is only the shapes of the glasses that differ, not the amount of juice.

In the 1920s, Swiss biologist Jean Piaget [Zhan Pee-ah-ZHAY] (1896–1980) proposed a theory of cognitive development to explain these childish mistakes. Piaget's keen observations of children and his brilliant ideas caused a revolution in thinking about how thinking develops.

Piaget's great insight was that children's errors are as interesting as their correct responses. Children will say things that seem cute or wildly illogical to adults. But the *strategies* that children use to think and solve problems, said Piaget, are not random or meaningless. They reflect a predictable interaction between the child's maturational stage and the child's experience in the world.

Piaget's Theory of Cognitive Stages According to Piaget (1929/1960, 1984), as children develop, they must make constant mental adaptations to new observations and experiences. This adaptation takes two forms: assimilation and accommodation.

Assimilation is what you do when you fit new information into your existing **cognitive schemas** (mental networks of associations, beliefs, and expectations about categories of things and people). Suppose that little Harry learns a schema for *dog* by playing with the family spaniel. If he then sees the neighbour's collie and says "doggie!" he has assimilated the new information about the neighbour's pet into his schema for dogs. **Accommodation** is what you do when, as a result of undeniable new information, you must change or modify your existing schemas. If Harry sees the neighbour's Siamese cat and still says "doggie!" his parents are likely to laugh and correct him. Harry will have to modify his schema for *dogs* to exclude cats, and he will have to create a schema for *cats*. In this way, he accommodates the new information that a Siamese cat is not a dog.

Using these concepts, Piaget proposed that all children go through four stages of cognitive development:

1 *The sensorimotor stage (birth to age 2).* In this stage, the infant learns through concrete actions: looking, touching, hearing, putting things in the mouth, sucking, grasping. "Thinking" consists of coordinating sensory information with bodily movements. Gradually these movements become more purposeful, as the child explores the environment and learns that specific movements will produce specific results. Swatting a cloth away will reveal a hidden toy; letting go of a fuzzy toy duck will cause it to drop out of reach; banging on the table with a spoon will produce dinner (or Mom, taking the spoon away).

A major accomplishment at this stage, said Piaget, is **object permanence**, the understanding that something continues to exist even if you cannot see it or touch it. In the first few months, he observed, infants seem to follow the motto "out of sight, out of mind." They will look intently at a little toy, but if you hide it behind a piece of paper they will not look behind the paper or make an

effort to get the toy. By about six months of age, however, infants begin to grasp the idea that the toy exists whether or not they can see it. If a baby of this age drops a toy from her playpen, she will look for it; she also will look under a cloth for a toy that is hidden. By one year of age, most babies have developed an awareness of the permanence of some objects; even if a toy is covered by a cloth, it must be under there. This is when they love to play peekaboo.

Object permanence, said Piaget, represents the beginning of the child's capacity to use mental imagery and symbols. The child becomes able to hold a concept in mind, to learn that the word "fly" represents an annoying, buzzing creature, and that "Daddy" represents a friendly, playful one.

2 *The preoperational stage (ages 2 to 7).* During this stage, the use of symbols and language accelerates. A two-year-old is able to pretend, for instance, that a large box is a house, table, or train. But Piaget described this stage largely in terms of what the child *cannot* do. Although children can think, said Piaget, they lack the cognitive abilities necessary for understanding abstract principles, cause and effect, and mental "operations" (such as multiplying 2 times 6 to get 12). Piaget also believed—mistakenly, as we will see—that preoperational children cannot take another person's point of view because they use **egocentric thinking**. They see the world only from their own frame of reference and cannot imagine that others see things differently.

Further, said Piaget, preoperational children cannot grasp the concept of **conservation**, the notion that physical properties do not change when their forms or appearances change. Children at this age are unable to understand that an amount of liquid or a number of pennies remains the same even if you pour the liquid from one glass to another or stack the pennies (see Figure 3.2). If you pour liquid from a short, fat glass into a tall, narrow glass, preoperational children will say there is more liquid in the second glass. They attend to the appearance of the liquid (its height in the glass) to judge its quantity, so they are misled.

3 *The concrete operations stage (ages 7 to 12).* In this stage, Piaget said, children's thinking is still grounded in concrete experiences and concepts, rather than in abstractions or logical deductions. However, the nature and quality of their thought processes change significantly. They come to

assimilation In Piaget's theory, the process of absorbing new information into existing cognitive schemas.

cognitive schema An integrated mental network of knowledge, beliefs, and expectations concerning a particular category or concept.

accommodation In Piaget's theory, the process of modifying existing cognitive schemas in response to experience and new information.

egocentric thinking Seeing the world from only your own point of view; the inability to take another person's perspective.

conservation The understanding that the physical properties of objects—such as the number of items in a cluster or the amount of liquid in a glass—can remain the same even when their form or appearance changes.

object permanence The understanding, which develops throughout the first year, that an object continues to exist even when you cannot see it or touch it.

FIGURE 3.2 Piaget's Principle of Conservation

In a typical test for conservation of number (left), the number of blocks is the same in two sets, but those in one set are then spread out and the child must say whether one set has "more" blocks than another. Preoperational children think that the set that takes up more space has more blocks. In a test for conservation of quantity (right), the child is shown two short glasses with equal amounts of liquid. Then the contents of one glass are poured into a tall, narrower glass, and the child is asked whether one container now has more. Most preoperational children do not understand that pouring liquid from a short glass into a taller one leaves the amount of liquid unchanged. They judge only by the height of liquid in the glass.

understand the principles of conservation and cause and effect. They learn mental operations, such as addition, subtraction, and division. They learn to categorize things (e.g., oaks as trees) and to order things serially from smallest to largest, lightest to darkest, and shortest to tallest. And they understand the stability of identity; for example, they know that a girl does not turn into a boy by wearing a boy's hat, and that a brother will always be a brother, even if he grows up.

4 *The formal operations stage (age 12 to adulthood).* In this last stage, teenagers become capable of abstract reasoning. They understand that ideas can be compared and classified, just as objects can. They are able to reason about situations they have not experienced firsthand, and they can think about future possibilities. They are able to search systematically for answers to problems. They are able to draw logical conclusions from premises common to their culture and experience.

Table 3.2 summarizes Piaget's stages of cognitive development.

Current Views of Cognitive Development Piaget was a brilliant observer of children, and his major point has been well supported: New reasoning abilities depend on the emergence of previous ones—you cannot learn algebra before you can count, and you cannot learn philosophy before you under-

Thinking Critically About Piaget's Stages

stand logic. But research has challenged many of Piaget's notions, and today has modified our picture of children's cognitive maturation:

1 *Cognitive abilities develop in continuous, overlapping waves rather than discrete steps or stages.* If you observe children at different ages, as Piaget did, it will seem that they reason differently. But if you study the everyday learning of children at any given age, you will find that a child may use several different strategies to solve a problem, some more complex or accurate than others (Siegler, 2001). Learning occurs gradually, with retreats to former ways of thinking as well as advances to new ones. Children's reasoning ability also depends on the circumstances—who is asking them questions, the specific words used, the materials used, and what they are reasoning about—not just on the stage they are in. In short, cognitive development is *continuous*; new abilities do not simply "pop up" when a child is a certain age (Courage & Howe, 2002).

2 *Preschoolers are not as egocentric as Piaget thought.* Most three- and four-year-olds *can* take another person's perspective (Flavell, 1999). When four-year-olds play with two-year-olds, for example, they modify and simplify their speech so the younger children will understand (Shatz & Gelman, 1973). One preschooler we know showed her teacher a picture she had drawn of a cat and an unidentifiable blob. "The cat is lovely," said the

TABLE 3.2 Summary of Piaget's Stages of Cognitive Development

Stage	Major Accomplishments
Sensorimotor (0–2)	Object permanence Beginning of capacity to use mental images and symbols
Preoperational (2–7)	Accelerated use of symbols and language
Concrete operations (7–12)	Understanding of conservation Understanding of identity Understanding of serial ordering
Formal operations (12–adulthood)	Abstract reasoning Ability to compare and classify ideas

teacher, "but what is this thing here?" "That has nothing to do with you," said the child. "That's what the *cat* is looking at."

3 *Children understand far more than Piaget gave them credit for.* Taking advantage of the fact that infants look longer at novel or surprising stimuli than at familiar ones, psychologists have designed delightfully imaginative methods of testing what babies know. These methods reveal that babies may be born with "mental modules" or "core knowledge systems" for numbers, the spatial relations of objects, some basic categories, and other features of the physical world (Quinn, 2002; Spelke, 2000). For example, at only four months of age, babies will look longer at a ball if it seems to roll through a solid barrier, leap between two platforms, or hang in mid-air than they do when the ball obeys the laws of physics—suggesting that the unusual event is surprising to them (see Figure 3.3). And infants as young as 2 1/2 to 3 1/2 months old are aware that objects continue to exist even when masked by other objects, a form of object permanence that Piaget never imagined possible in babies so young (Baillargeon, 1999).

One team of developmental psychologists calls the infant "the scientist in the crib" (Gopnik, Meltzoff, & Kuhl, 1999). By this they mean that children come into the world ready to form theories about how things work and then test them. When your toddler throws her spoon on the floor for the sixth time as you try to feed her, and you say, "That's enough! I will *not* pick up your spoon again!" the child will immediately test your claim. Are you serious? Are you angry? What will happen if she throws the spoon again? She is not doing this to drive you crazy, though it may feel that way. Rather, she is learning that her desires and yours can differ, and that sometimes those

differences are important and sometimes they are not. Like a good scientist, she will keep testing her hypotheses and revising them with new information.

4 *Cognitive development depends on the child's education and culture.* The Russian psychologist Lev Vygotsky (1896–1934), born in the same year as Piaget, differed from Piaget in emphasizing the sociocultural influences on children's cognitive development. Vygotsky was ahead of his time in making this argument. Today we know that culture—the world of tools, language, rituals, beliefs, games, and social institutions—profoundly shapes and structures children's cognitive development, fostering some abilities and neglecting others (Tomasello, 2000). For example, traditional nomadic hunting peoples, such as Canada's Inuit and the Aborigines of Australia, do not quantify things and do not need to (Dasen, 1994). The Aborigines have number words only up to five; after that, all quantities are described as "many." In such cultures, the conservation of quantity develops late, if at all. But nomadic hunters excel in spatial abilities, because spatial orientation is crucial for finding water holes and successful hunting routes. In contrast, children who live in settled agricultural communities, such as the Baoulé of the Ivory Coast, develop rapidly in the ability to quantify and much more slowly in spatial reasoning. These cultural differences can be altered by education: Many unschooled

Possible event

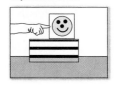
Impossible event

FIGURE 3.3 Testing Infants' Knowledge

In this clever procedure, a baby watches as a box is pushed from left to right along a striped platform. The box is pushed until it reaches the end of the platform (a possible event) or until only a bit of it rests on the platform (an impossible event). Babies look longer at the impossible event, suggesting that it surprises them; somehow they know that an object needs to have physical support and can't just float on air (Baillargeon, 1994).

Experience and culture influence cognitive development. Children who work with clay, wood, and other materials, such as this young potter in India, tend to understand the concept of conservation sooner than children who have not had this hands-on practice.

children of the Wolof, a rural group in Senegal, do not understand conservation, as do their peers who attend school, but brief training can speed the development of their understanding (Greenfield, 1976).

5 *Just as Piaget underestimated the cognitive skills of young children, he overestimated those of many adults.* Not all adolescents and adults develop the ability for formal reasoning and reflective judgment.

Some never develop the capacity for formal operations, and others think concretely unless a specific problem requires abstract thought.

In spite of these corrections to Piaget's theory, Piaget left an enduring legacy by showing that children are not passive vessels into which education and experience are poured. Children actively interpret their worlds, using their developing schemas and abilities to assimilate new information and figure things out.

Quick Quiz

Please use language (and thought) to answer these questions.

1. "More cake!" and "Mommy come" are examples of _____ speech.
2. What did Chomsky mean by a "language acquisition device"?
3. Understanding that two rows of six pennies are equal in number, even if one row is spread out and the other is stacked up, is an example of _____.
4. Understanding that a toy exists even after Mom puts it in her purse is an example of _____, which develops during the _____ stage.
5. List five findings that challenge aspects of Piaget's theory.

Answers:

1. telegraphic speech
2. an innate mental module that permits young children to develop language if they are exposed to it
3. conservation
4. object permanence, sensorimotor
5. The changes from one stage to another are not as clear as Piaget implied; children know more and know it earlier than Piaget thought; they are less egocentric than Piaget thought; their cognitive development is affected by their culture; and not all adolescents and adults achieve the ability for formal operations.

WHAT'S AHEAD

- Is a person who uses sophisticated moral reasoning more likely to behave morally than one who does not?
- When reasoning about moral dilemmas, are women more compassionate and caring than men are?
- What is wrong with "because I say so" as a way of getting children to behave?

MORAL DEVELOPMENT

Piaget (1932) pioneered in the study of another important aspect of cognitive development: moral reasoning, which changes according to a child's cognitive maturity. A young child, he observed, will say that a child who breaks a vase by accident is as naughty as one who breaks it intentionally. Older children, because of their maturing cognitive abilities, are able to evaluate moral behaviour in terms of a person's intentions and motives.

Moral Reasoning

In the 1960s, Lawrence Kohlberg (1964), inspired by Piaget's work, outlined a cognitive-stage theory of moral reasoning that became highly influential. Your moral stage, said Kohlberg, can be determined by the answers you give to hypothetical dilemmas. For example, suppose a man's wife is dying and needs a special drug. The man cannot afford the drug and the druggist refuses to lower his price. Should the man steal the drug for a wife he loves? What if he no longer loves his wife? If the man is caught, should the judge be lenient? To Kohlberg, as to Piaget, the reasoning behind the answers was more important than the decisions themselves.

Kohlberg (1964, 1984) proposed that children progress through three levels of moral development, each consisting of two stages. Very young children obey rules at first because they fear being punished if they disobey and later because they think it is in their best interest to obey. At about age 10 or 11, children shift to the conventional morality of adult society, which is at first based on conformity and loyalty to others and later becomes a "law-and-order" orientation, based on an understanding of law and justice. That is where most people remain, said Kohlberg. But some

According to Kohlberg, Mohandas Gandhi (called the "Mahatma," or wise one) reached the highest level of morality because of his commitment to nonviolence and peaceful change. But people's moral behaviour is not the same in every situation or relationship. Gandhi, for example, was aloof from his family and followers, whom he often treated in a harsh and callous manner.

"postconventional" adults realize that certain laws—such as those that legitimize the mistreatment of minorities—are themselves immoral and must be changed. And a few individuals—such as Martin Luther King Jr., who fought against laws supporting segregation; Mohandas Gandhi, who advocated nonviolent solutions to injustice in India; or Nellie McClung, who fought for women's political rights in Canada—develop a moral standard based on universal human rights. When faced with a conflict between law and conscience, they follow conscience, even at great personal risk.

Kohlberg was right that moral reasoning, like any other cognitive ability, becomes more complex as the child matures. But today, cognitive psychologists recognize that Kohlberg's stage theory, like Piaget's, has significant problems. Here are four of them:

Thinking Critically About Stages of Moral Reasoning

1 *Moral reasoning is influenced by education and culture.* University-educated people tend to give higher-level explanations of moral decisions than people who have not attended university, but all that shows, say Kohlberg's critics, is that university-educated people are more verbally sophisticated and have learned to think in legalistic terms (Eckensberger, 1994). Moreover, Kohlberg greatly underestimated the importance of cultural values (Shweder, Mahapatra, & Miller, 1990). In China, moral decisions and values based on social harmony and devotion to parents often conflict with Kohlberg's notion that "higher" moral reasoning is based on analytic, individualistic thinking (Dien, 1982). A Nigerian psychologist who interviewed

200 teenagers and young adults found that their criteria of moral reasoning involved values of obedience to parents, family interdependence, and the "transcendental authority of divine guidance," concepts not found in Kohlberg's measures (Okonkwo, 1997).

2 *Moral reasoning begins much earlier than previously thought.* Very young children are capable of feeling empathy for others and taking another person's point of view, as we saw. They obey rules not only because they are afraid to disobey, but because they understand right from wrong. Even by age five, they know the difference between doing the right thing and obeying orders; for example, they know it's wrong to hurt someone even if a teacher tells them to (Turiel, 2002).

3 *Moral reasoning is often inconsistent across situations.* The kind of moral reasoning that people do depends on the situation and on the nature of the dilemma (Rest et al., 1999; Wygant, 1997). For example, you might show conventional morality by overlooking a racial slur at a dinner party because you do not want to upset anyone, but reveal postconventional reasoning by protesting a governmental policy you feel harms innocent people. In a Simon Fraser University study that used Kohlberg's dilemmas, most of the participants gave responses spanning three to six stages; only one young man based all his judgments on the same stage (Wark & Krebs, 1996).

4 *Moral reasoning is often unrelated to moral behaviour.* Moral-reasoning ability increases during the school years, but so do cheating, lying, cruelty, and the cognitive ability to rationalize these actions (Kagan, 1993). University students usually draw on lofty principles of justice and fair play to justify moral decisions, yet about one-third of American and Canadian men attending university say they would force a woman into sexual acts if they could get away with it—the lowest form of moral reasoning (Malamuth & Dean, 1990). As Thomas Lickona (1983) wryly summarized, "We can reach high levels of moral reasoning, and still behave like scoundrels."

Another popular approach to moral reasoning was proposed in the early 1980s by Carol Gilligan (1982). Gilligan argued that men tend to base their moral choices on abstract principles of law and justice, asking questions such as "Whose rights should take precedence here?", whereas women tend to base their moral decisions on

principles of compassion and caring, asking questions such as "Who will be hurt least?" This was an appealing theory, especially to women! But a meta-analysis of the many studies that have investigated this argument found no support for Gilligan's view that women predominantly use a "care" orientation and men a "justice" orientation (Jaffee & Hyde, 2000).

The main problem with Gilligan's theory is that it implies that moral reasoning is fixed and consistent, depending primarily on your gender. But both sexes tend to use justice-based reasoning when they are thinking about abstract ethical dilemmas that have no relevance to their lives, and care-based reasoning when they are thinking about personal dilemmas (Clopton & Sorell, 1993; Walker, de Vries, & Trevethan, 1987; Wygant, 1997). And unfortunately, for women as for men, moral reasoning of either kind often has little relation to actual behaviour. Both sexes can talk a good game yet be hurtful, selfish, and uncompassionate toward others.

Moral Behaviour

Today, developmental psychologists recognize that the child's emerging ability to distinguish right from wrong—and to behave accordingly—depends not only on reasoning skills but also on the emergence of conscience and "moral emotions" such as shame, guilt, and empathy (Eisenberg et al., 2002; Hoffman, 1990).

The capacity for moral feeling, like that for language, seems to be inborn. But the desire and willingness to behave well with others can be nurtured or extinguished by experiences in a child's life. For example, when you did something wrong as a child, did the adults in your family spank you, shout at you, punish you, or explain the error of your ways? One of the most common methods used by parents to enforce moral standards and good behaviour is **power assertion**, which includes threats, physical punishment, depriving the child of privileges, and generally taking advantage of being bigger, stronger, and more powerful. Of course, a parent may have no alternative other than "Do it because I say so!" if the child is too young to understand a rule or impishly keeps trying to break it. But when power assertion consists of sheer parental bullying and frequent physical punishment, it is associated with greater aggressiveness and antisocial behaviour in children, reduced empathy, and poorer moral-reasoning ability (Gershoff, 2002; Hoffman, 1994; Lopez,

power assertion A method of child rearing in which the parent uses punishment and authority to correct the child's misbehaviour.

Power Assertion

The parent uses threats, physical force, or other kinds of power to get the child to obey.

Example: "Do it because I say so"; "Stop that right now."

Result: The child obeys, but only when the parent is present; the child often feels resentful.

Induction

The parent appeals to the child's good nature, empathy, love for the parent, and sense of responsibility to others, and offers explanations of rules.

Example: "You're too grown up to behave like that"; "Fighting hurts your little brother."

Result: The child tends to internalize reasons for good behaviour.

Bonenberger, & Schneider, 2001). Verbal abuse and ridicule ("You are so stupid, I wish you had never been born") can be even more devastating to a child than physical punishment (Moore & Pepler, 2004).

This does not mean that power assertion has the same effects on all children, in all environments, in all cultures (Collins et al., 1990). For one thing, the child's own temperament will affect how a parent treats the child, as we noted earlier in discussing attachment. Second, cultures tend to prefer different methods of discipline: Chinese families are often sterner than middle-class white families, but the children generally regard their parents' discipline as evidence of concern, not abusiveness. Third, the *context* in which the discipline occurs makes an enormous difference. Is the parent–child relationship fundamentally loving and trusting, or is it full of hostility and fighting?

Consider spanking. "My parents spanked me and I am fine," some people say—and they may well be. Some psychologists believe that the occasional, moderate use of spanking has no particularly detrimental outcomes for most middle-class children (Baumrind, Larzelere, & Cowan, 2002). The reason is that it typically occurs in an otherwise loving context, as a quick action of last resort when a child is misbehaving. Unsurprisingly, a survey of people in Manitoba, for example, found that only one-third of respondents would support a no-spanking law (Durrant, 1994). (And in

Thinking Critically About Spanking

Chapter 9, you will read about a Supreme Court of Canada decision against legislation that would make spanking illegal.) Physical punishment backfires, however, when it is used inappropriately or harshly, causing anger and resentment in the recipient. If the family atmosphere is one of anger, quarrelling, and constant efforts to subdue the children, the use of physical punishment can easily spiral out of control (Gershoff, 2002).

Researchers have observed how this spiral works, and its devastating consequences, in longitudinal studies of parent–child interactions in the home. The parents of aggressive children are more likely to do a lot of shouting, scolding, and spanking, but they fail to connect the punishment with the child's behaviour. They do not state clear rules, require compliance, consistently punish violations, or praise good behaviour. Instead, they nag and shout, unpredictably tossing in a slap or a loss of privileges. This combination of power assertion with intermittent discipline causes the children's aggressiveness to increase and eventually get out of hand. The child becomes withdrawn, manipulative, and difficult to manage, which causes the parents to assert their power even more forcefully, which makes the child angrier . . . and a vicious cycle escalates (Patterson, Reid, & Dishion, 1992).

A strategy that is more successful than spanking and other forms of power assertion for teaching moral behaviour is **induction**, in which the parent appeals to the child's own resources, helpful nature, affection for others, and sense of

induction A method of child rearing in which the parent appeals to the child's own resources, abilities, sense of responsibility, and feelings for others in correcting misbehaviour.

responsibility. A parent using induction might explain to a misbehaving child that the child's actions could harm or upset another person ("You made Doug cry; it's not nice to bite"; "You must never poke anyone's eyes because that could hurt them seriously"). Or the parent might appeal to the child's own helpful inclinations ("I know you're a person who likes to be good to others"), which is far more effective than citing external reasons to be good ("You'd better be nice or you won't get dessert") (Eisenberg, 1995). Children whose parents use induction tend to feel guilty if they hurt others. They are more likely to internalize standards of right and wrong and be considerate of others (Berkowitz & Grych, 2000; Hoffman, 1994).

Induction is not the same as being overly permissive—letting children do anything they want—or being uninvolved or unconcerned. Parents who use induction tend to be *authoritative* and democratic rather than arbitrarily *authoritarian* or permissive. That is, they give emotional support to the child and listen to the child's concerns and wishes, but they also require good behaviour; they set high but reasonable expectations and teach their children how to meet them (Baumrind, 1989, 1991; Berkowitz & Grych, 2000). When parents are responsive to their children's needs and emotions, the children tend to be more willing and eager to adopt their parents' values and standards of behaviour (Kochanska, 2002).

Quick Quiz

We appeal to your own sense of responsibility to get you to take this quiz.

1. Margo says she pays her taxes because she believes in obeying the law; Manny says he pays because he is afraid of getting caught if he doesn't. What are some problems with concluding that they are at different "stages" of moral development?

2. Which method of disciplining an aggressive child is most likely to teach empathy? (a) induction, (b) authoritarian firmness, (c) power assertion, (d) physical punishment

3. Two psychologists noted that in Kohlberg's system, the cruellest lawyer could get a higher moral-reasoning score than the kindest eight-year-old. Why might that happen?

Answers:

1. Margo and Manny might have had different levels of education; they might be affected by different cultural norms; their reasoning about taxes might differ from how they reason about other issues in other situations; and their reasoning might have nothing to do with whether they are actually honest when filing their tax returns!
2. a
3. The lawyer's score reflects verbal sophistication and education and does not indicate whether he or she actually behaves in a kind and moral way.

WHAT'S AHEAD

- How would a biologically oriented psychologist explain why most little boys and girls are "sexist" in their choice of toys?

- What happens to children's notions about gender once they are able to distinguish males from females?

- How do teachers unintentionally reinforce aggressiveness in boys?

- If a little girl "knows" that girls can't be doctors, does this mean she will never go to medical school?

GENDER DEVELOPMENT

No parent ever excitedly calls a relative to exclaim, "It's a baby! It's a 7 1/2-pound, black-haired baby!" The baby's sex is the first thing everyone notices and announces. Most babies, unless they have rare abnormalities, are born unambiguously male or female—an anatomical distinction. But how do children learn the rules of masculinity and femininity—the things that boys do that are different from what girls do? Why, as one friend of ours observed, do so many preschool children act like the "gender police," insisting, say, that boys can't be nurses and girls can't be doctors?

Many psychologists use the terms *sex* and *gender* to capture the distinction between anatomy and behaviour (Deaux, 1985; Lott, 1997). *Sex* refers to the physiological or anatomical attributes of males and females; there is a sex difference in the frequency of baldness or colour blindness. *Gender* refers to the cultural and psychological attributes that children learn are appropriate for the sexes; there is a gender difference in sexual attitudes, dishwashing, and fondness for romance novels.

Toddlers can label themselves as boys or girls, but it is not until the age of four or five that most children develop a secure **gender identity**, a fundamental sense of maleness or femaleness that exists regardless of what they wear or how they behave. Only then do they understand that what boys and girls do does not necessarily indicate what sex they are: A girl remains a girl even if she can climb a tree, and a boy remains a boy even if he has long hair. In contrast, **gender typing** reflects society's ideas about which abilities, interests, traits, and behaviours are appropriately "masculine" or "feminine." A person can have a strong gender identity and not be gender typed: A man may be confident in his maleness and not feel threatened by doing "unmasculine" things such as needlepointing a pillow; a woman may be confident in her femaleness and not feel threatened by doing "unfeminine" things such as changing a tire.

Influences on Gender Development

Developmental psychologists study the influences of biology, cognition, and learning in the emergence of gender identity, gender differences in behaviour, and gender typing.

Biological Influences Starting in the preschool years, boys and girls congregate primarily with other children of their own sex (Maccoby, 1998). They will play together if required to but, given their druthers, they usually choose to play with same-sex friends. This preference occurs all over the world, almost regardless of how adults treat children—e.g., whether they encourage boys and girls to play together or separate them (Lytton & Romney, 1991; Maccoby, 1998, 2002). Similarly, although many parents lament that they try to give their children of different genders the same toys, often it makes no difference: Their sons want trucks and their daughters want dolls. And according to research conducted in Montreal, these

preferences for gender-typical toys emerge by 18 months of age (Serbin et al., 2001).

Biological researchers believe that these play and toy preferences must have a biological basis, perhaps in prenatal hormones, genes, or brain organization. They point out that girls who were exposed to prenatal androgens (masculinizing hormones) in the womb are later more likely than nonexposed girls to prefer "boys' toys" such as cars, fire engines, and airplanes; they are also more physically aggressive than other girls (Berenbaum & Snyder, 1995; Berenbaum, Duck, & Bryk, 2000). And in all primate species, young males are more likely than females to go in for physical roughhousing, risk taking, and aggressive displays (Maccoby, 1998).

Cognitive Influences Cognitive psychologists explain the mystery of children's gender segregation and toy preferences not in terms of biology but in terms of the child's own unfolding cognitive abilities. As children mature, they develop a **gender schema**, a mental network of knowledge, beliefs, metaphors, and expectations about what it means to be male or female (Bem, 1993; Spence, 1985). And as soon as children have a gender schema, they change their behaviour to conform to it (Martin, Ruble, & Szkrybalo, 2002).

Before you can have a gender schema, of course, you have to be able to recognize that there are two genders. This ability starts to emerge even

gender identity The fundamental sense of being male or female; it is independent of whether the person conforms to the social and cultural rules of gender.

gender typing The process by which children learn the abilities, interests, personality traits, and behaviours associated with being masculine or feminine in their culture.

gender schema A cognitive schema (mental network) of knowledge, beliefs, metaphors, and expectations about what it means to be male or female.

Look familiar? In a scene typical of many nursery schools and homes, the boy builds a gun out of anything he can, and the girl dresses up in any pretty thing she can find. Psychologists (and parents) debate whether such gender typing is biologically based or a result of subtle reinforcements and the emergence of gender schemas.

before children can speak. By the age of 9 to 11 months, most babies can discriminate male from female faces (Fagot & Leinbach, 1993), and they can match female faces with female voices (Poulin-Dubois et al., 1998). But it takes a couple of years before they can label themselves and others consistently as a "boy" or "girl." Once they can do that, they begin to prefer same-sex playmates and sex-traditional toys, without being explicitly taught to do so. They become more gender typed in their toy play, games, aggressiveness, and verbal skills than children who still cannot consistently label males and females. Most notably, girls stop behaving aggressively (Fagot, 1993). It is as if they go along behaving like boys—until they know they are girls. At that moment, but not until that moment, they seem to decide, "Girls don't do this; I'm a girl, so I'd better not either."

One puzzle of gender development is that virtually all over the world, boys' gender schemas are more rigid than girls' are. That is, boys express stronger preferences for "masculine" toys and activities than girls do for "feminine" ones, and boys are harsher on themselves and on other boys when they fail to behave in sex-typed ways (Bussey & Bandura, 1992; Maccoby, 1998). One reason may be that most societies value masculine occupations and traits more than feminine ones, and males have higher status. So when boys behave like (or play with) girls, they lose status, and when girls behave like boys, they gain status (Serbin, Powlishta, & Gulko, 1993).

Gender schemas are most rigid between ages five and seven (Martin, Ruble, & Szkrybalo, 2002). With increasing cognitive ability, however, older children begin to construct their own standards of what boys and girls may or may not do. Eventually, they become aware of the exceptions to their gender schemas; they understand that women can be engineers and men can be cooks. From middle childhood on, many people become more open-minded about gender roles and rules, especially if they have friends of the other sex and if their families, jobs, or cultures encourage such flexibility (Katz & Ksansnak, 1994). Other people retain rigid gender schemas throughout their lives, feeling uncomfortable or angry at the prospect of a male nurse or a female drill sergeant.

Cultures, too, differ in how rigid they are about the roles of women and men. In all

Not long ago, the idea of women serving in the military and men teaching preschoolers would have seemed odd. Today, however, gender roles have become less polarized in Western countries.

industrialized nations, for example, it is now taken for granted that women and men alike should be educated; indeed, laws mandate a minimum education for both sexes. But in Afghanistan, even after the overthrow of the Taliban and its prohibition on female education, many girls who want to go to school have received death threats.

Gender schemas can be very powerful, and events that challenge a person's sense of their legitimacy can be enormously threatening. How flexible are your own gender schemas?

Learning Influences A third influence on gender development is the environment, which is full of subtle and not-so-subtle messages about what girls and boys are supposed to do. Behavioural and social-cognitive learning theorists study how the process of gender socialization instills these messages in children (Bussey & Bandura, 1999). Although many adults say they treat boys and girls equally or that "my little girl was just naturally feminine but my boy was born feisty," research disputes their claims.

Gender socialization begins at the moment of birth. Parents tend to portray their newborn boys as more athletic and strong than newborn girls, and newborn girls as more feminine and delicate than newborn boys—although it is hard to know how athletic a newborn boy could be, and all newborns are pretty delicate (Karraker, Vogel, & Lake, 1995). And many parents are careful to dress their baby in outfits of the "correct" colour and pattern for his or her sex. Clothes don't matter to the infant, of course, but they are signals to adults about how to treat the child. Adults often respond to the same baby differently, depending on whether the child is dressed as a boy or a girl (Stern & Karraker, 1989).

Adults respond to boys and girls differently even when the children are behaving in *exactly the same way*. In one observational study, 12- to 16-month-old boys and girls were equally assertive (as measured by the frequency of their efforts to get an adult's attention) and verbal (as measured by attempts to communicate with others). But teachers responded far more often to assertive boys than to shy ones, and to verbal girls than to nonverbal ones. Subtly, the teachers were reinforcing gender-typed behaviour. When the researchers observed the same children a year later, a gender difference was now apparent, with boys behaving more assertively and girls talking more to teachers (Fagot et al., 1985).

Parents, teachers, and other adults convey their beliefs and expectations about gender even when they are entirely unaware that they are doing so. For example, when parents believe that boys are naturally better at math or sports and that girls are naturally better at English, they unwittingly communicate those beliefs by how they respond to a child's success or failure. They may tell a son who did well in math, "You're a natural math whiz, Johnny!" But if a daughter gets good grades, they may say, "Wow, you really worked hard in math, Jeannie, and it shows!" The implication is that girls have to try hard but boys have a natural gift. Messages like these are not lost on the children, who tend to lose interest in activities that are not "natural" for them—even when they all start out with equal abilities (Frome & Eccles, 1998).

Gender over the Life Span

In today's fast-moving world, gender development has become a lifelong process in which people's gender schemas, attitudes, and behaviour shift as they have new experiences and as society itself changes. In areas of love and sex, gender rules are still being negotiated. On a date, which partner

cathy®   **by Cathy Guisewite**

pays? Who asks whom out? Who makes sexual overtures? In other situations, such as working on an assembly line, gender is usually irrelevant.

Gender differences in personality traits, motivations, and behaviour are greatest in childhood and adolescence, but in North America they often decline significantly in adulthood and the later years (Cohn, 1991). By middle age, many people report a "gender crossover" as they explore aspects of their personalities and interests they had previously suppressed: Women often become more achievement oriented, men more nurturant and family oriented (James & Lewkowicz, 1997; Stewart & Ostrove, 1998).

In sum, young children may behave like sexist piglets while they are trying to figure out what it means to be male or female. Their behaviour is influenced by genes and hormones, cognitive schemas, and parental and social lessons. But their behaviour as three-year-olds often has little to do with how they will behave at 23 or 43. Children can grow up in an extremely gender-typed family and yet, as adults, find themselves in careers or relationships they would never have imagined for themselves (Maccoby, 1998). If three-year-olds are the gender police, many adults end up breaking the law.

Quick Quiz

Quiz-taking is appropriate behaviour for all sexes and genders.

1. Two-year-old Jeremy thinks that if he changed from wearing pants to wearing dresses, he could become a girl. He still lacks a stable _____.

2. A biological psychologist would say that a three-year-old boy's love of going "vroom, vroom" with his truck collection is probably a result of _____; a learning theorist would say that it results from _____ by parents and teachers.

3. Which statement about gender schemas is *false*? (a) They are present in early form by one year of age; (b) they are permanent conceptualizations of what it means to be masculine or feminine; (c) they eventually expand to include many different qualities associated with being male and female; (d) they probably reflect the status of men and women in society.

4. Herb hopes his four-year-old daughter will be a doctor, but she refuses to play with the toy stethoscope he bought her and insists that only boys can be doctors. What conclusions about gender differences can Herb draw?

Answers:

1. gender identity
2. biological factors such as hormones or brain processes; gender socialization
3. b
4. Not many. His daughter's rigid gender-typed behaviour is typical of young children who are acquiring gender schemas, but it does not predict anything about her future attitudes or the career she will choose as an adult.

WHAT'S AHEAD

- What are the advantages and disadvantages of going through puberty earlier than most of your classmates?
- During adolescence, are extreme turmoil and unhappiness the exception or the rule?
- When teenagers and their parents quarrel, what is it typically about?

ADOLESCENCE

Adolescence refers to the period of development between **puberty**, the age at which a person becomes capable of sexual reproduction, and adulthood. In some cultures, the time span between puberty and adulthood is only a few months; a sexually mature boy or girl is expected to marry and assume adult tasks almost immediately. In modern Western societies, however, teenagers are not considered emotionally mature enough to assume the rights, responsibilities, and roles of adulthood.

The Physiology of Adolescence

Until puberty, boys and girls produce roughly the same levels of "male hormones" (androgens) and "female hormones" (estrogens). At puberty, the

puberty The age at which a person becomes capable of sexual reproduction.

brain's pituitary gland begins to stimulate hormone production in the adrenal and reproductive glands. From puberty on, boys have a higher level of androgens than girls do, and girls have a higher level of estrogens than boys do.

In boys, the reproductive glands are the testes (testicles), which produce sperm; in girls, the reproductive glands are the ovaries, which release eggs. During puberty, these sex organs mature and the individual becomes capable of reproduction. In girls, the development of breasts and **menarche**, the onset of menstruation, are signs of sexual maturity. In boys, the signs are the onset of nocturnal emissions and the growth of the testes, scrotum, and penis. Hormones are also responsible for the emergence of *secondary sex characteristics*, such as a deepened voice and facial and chest hair in boys and pubic hair in both sexes.

Researchers used to think that sexual attraction and behaviour followed the onset of puberty; now there is evidence that the age of first sexual attraction—whether heterosexual or homosexual—usually precedes puberty. Adrenal androgens begin to rise in both boys and girls as early as age 6, and the average age of first sexual attraction to another is about age 10, years before a child's reproductive abilities have fully matured (McClintock & Herdt, 1996).

The Timing of Puberty The onset of puberty depends on both genetic and environmental factors. The average age of menarche now occurs at about 12 years and 8 months in white girls and a few months earlier in black girls (Herman-Giddens et al., 1997). Menarche depends on a female's having a critical level of body fat, which is necessary to sustain a pregnancy and which triggers the hormonal changes associated with puberty (Chehab et al., 1997). An increase in body fat among children in developed countries may help explain why the average age of puberty declined in Europe and North America until the mid-twentieth century.

The physical changes of puberty are part of the last "growth spurt" on the child's road to adulthood. For girls, the adolescent growth spurt begins, on average, at age 10, peaks at 12 or 13, and stops at about age 16, by which time most girls are sexually mature. For boys, the average adolescent growth spurt starts at about age 12 and ends at about age 18. This difference in rates of development is often a source of misery to adolescents, because most girls mature sooner than most boys.

Early and Late Puberty The figures we have given you are only averages; individuals vary enormously in the onset and length of puberty. If you entered puberty before most of your classmates, or if you matured much later than they did, you know that your experience of adolescence was different from that of the average teenager (whoever that is). Early-maturing boys generally have a more positive view of their bodies, and their relatively greater size and strength gives them a boost in sports and the prestige that being a good athlete brings young men. But they are also more likely to smoke, drink alcohol, use other drugs, and break the law than later-maturing boys, and to have less self-control and emotional stability (Duncan et al., 1985).

Likewise, some early-maturing girls have the prestige of being socially popular. But, partly because others in their peer group regard them as being sexually precocious, they are also more likely to fight with their parents, drop out of school, have a negative body image, and have emotional problems (Caspi & Moffitt, 1991; Stattin & Magnusson, 1990). Early puberty itself does not cause these problems; rather, it tends to accentuate existing behavioural problems and family conflicts. Girls who go through puberty relatively late, in contrast, have a more difficult time at first, but by the end of adolescence many are happier with

menarche [men-ARR-kee]
The onset of menstruation.

Children typically reach puberty at different times, which can be a source of anxiety for some. These girls are all the same age, but they differ considerably in physical maturity.

their appearance and more popular than their early-maturing classmates (Caspi & Moffitt, 1991; Stattin & Magnusson, 1990).

Brain Development When people think of physical changes in adolescence, they usually think of body maturation and the effects of hormones on mood and sexuality. But the brain undergoes significant developmental changes, too, and these occur at a comparable age in other species. New connections among brain cells are added and others are pruned away (see Chapter 4). One researcher compares what happens to the brain during adolescence with remodelling a house—the basic structure is still there, but it's updated and streamlined. Changes occur primarily in the prefrontal cortex, which is responsible for impulse control and planning, and the limbic system, which is involved in emotional processing (Spear, 2000; Walker, 2002). In Chapter 11 we will see that errors in the "remodelling" process during adolescence may be involved in the onset of schizophrenia and other disorders in vulnerable individuals.

The Psychology of Adolescence

In January 2002, a 15-year-old boy stole a small private plane and crashed it into a building, hoping perhaps to emulate the terrorists who destroyed the World Trade Center the previous September. He succeeded only in committing suicide. His action followed closely upon other dramatic episodes in recent years of teenagers killing classmates and teachers, and sometimes themselves. The media were quick to assert that America was in the midst of an explosion of violence among teenage males: Headlines warned of "Teenage Time Bombs" and "[Teenage] Children Without Souls" (Glassner, 2001). How accurate are these stories? Are growing numbers of teenagers suicidally depressed and murderously angry?

Turmoil and Adjustment In Canada, the rate of violent crimes committed by adolescents has been going down since 1995, and in 2001, teenage homicide rates were the lowest they had been in 30 years (Statistics Canada, 2002). Studies of representative samples of adolescents find that only a small minority are seriously troubled, angry, or unhappy. Most teenagers have supportive families, a sense of purpose and self-confidence, good friends, and the skills to cope with their problems. Extreme turmoil and unhappiness are the exception, not the rule (Steinberg, 1990).

Thinking Critically About "Adolescent Turmoil"

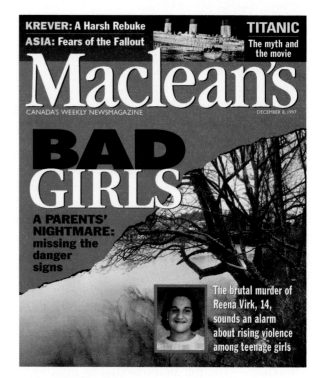

News stories like this one, about troubled, violent, or suicidal teenagers, feed the popular notion that adolescence is a time of misery, anger, and conflict with parents. But is it?

Nevertheless, three kinds of problems are more common during adolescence than during childhood or adulthood: conflict with parents; mood swings and depression; and reckless, rule-breaking behaviour (Arnett, 1999). The years of adolescence can be difficult and challenging because teenagers are developing their own standards and values, often by trying on the styles, actions, and attitudes of their peers in contrast to those of their parents. The peer group represents the values and style of the generation that they identify with, the generation that they will share experiences with as adults. Friends teach each other crucial lessons about getting along, solving personal problems, and making moral choices—lessons that foster greater cognitive complexity (Bukowski, 2001; Hartup, 1999). That is why the peer group becomes especially important during adolescence. Many people report that rejection by peers during adolescence was more devastating than punitive treatment by parents (Ambert, 1997).

Adolescents who are lonely, depressed, worried, or angry tend to express these concerns in ways characteristic of their sex. Boys are more likely than girls to externalize their emotional problems in acts of aggression and other antisocial behaviour. Girls are more likely than boys to internalize their problems, for example by becoming withdrawn or developing eating disorders (Zahn-Waxler, 1996).

Separation and Connection In Western cultures, conflicts between teenagers and adults typically focus on the adolescent's increased desire for autonomy (Eccles et al., 1993). Teenagers are usually trying to *individuate*, to develop their own opinions, values, and style. In one study, adolescents described quarrels over issues like these: "Why my mother manipulates the conversation to get me to hate her"; "How much of a bastard my father is to my sister"; "How ugly my mom's taste is"; "How pig-headed my mom and dad are" (Csikszentmihalyi & Larson, 1984). But most teens do not want to sever the connection with their parents entirely; these fights—over what is important, who should set the rules, differences of opinion and taste, and the like—rarely reflected a true rift between parent and adolescent.

For young men and women in the West, quarrels with parents tend to signify a change from one-sided parental authority to a more reciprocal, adult relationship (Laursen & Collins, 1994). But in the many collectivist and traditionalist cultures around the world, such as in China or India, most adolescents would not dream of rebelling against their parents, to whom they feel they owe allegiance and loyalty, nor would the goal of autonomy be more important than family harmony (Arnett, 1999; Segall et al., 1999). "Adolescent rebellion" is more a matter of generational attitudes and cultural norms than of anything inherent in psychological development, as demonstrated by studies of various cultural groups in Canada (Kwak & Berry, 2001). These studies supported earlier findings showing that rebellion was not a universal phenomenon among adolescents.

ALL parents have unrealistic expectations for their kids

Quick Quiz

If you are not in the midst of adolescent turmoil, try these questions.

1. The onset of menstruation is called _____.
2. *True or false?:* Puberty is the same thing as adolescence.
3. Extreme turmoil and rebellion in adolescence are (a) nearly universal, (b) the exception rather than the rule, (c) rare.
4. In Western societies, conflicts between teenagers and their parents are typically over issues of _____.

Answers:

1. menarche   2. false (can you say why?)   3. b   4. autonomy or individuation

---

WHAT'S AHEAD

- What is wrong with thinking that life occurs in a series of predictable stages?
- What feelings are common during "emerging adulthood," the years from 18 to 25?
- Does menopause make most women depressed and irrational?
- Do men go through a male version of menopause?
- Which mental abilities decline in old age, and which do not?

ADULTHOOD

According to ancient Greek legend, the Sphinx was a monster—half lion, half woman—who terrorized passersby on the road to Thebes. The Sphinx would ask each traveller a question and then murder those who failed to answer correctly. (The Sphinx was a pretty tough grader.) The question was this: What animal walks on four feet in the morning, two feet at noon, and three feet in the evening? Only one traveller, Oedipus, knew the solution to the riddle. The animal, he said, is

Man, who crawls on all fours as a baby, walks upright as an adult, and limps in old age with the aid of a staff.

The Sphinx was the first life-span theorist. Since then, many philosophers, writers, and scientists have speculated on the course of adult development. Are the changes of adulthood predictable, like those of childhood? What are the major psychological issues of adult life? Is mental and physical deterioration in old age inevitable?

Stages and Ages

One of the first modern theorists to propose a life-span approach to psychological development was psychoanalyst Erik H. Erikson (1902–1994). Just as children progress through stages, he said, so do adults. Erikson (1950/1963, 1982) wrote that all individuals go through eight stages in their lives. Each stage is characterized by a "crisis," a particular challenge, which ideally should be resolved before the individual moves on.

1 *Trust versus mistrust* is the challenge that occurs during the baby's first year, when the baby depends on others to provide food, comfort, cuddling, and warmth. If these needs are not met, the child may never develop the essential trust of others necessary to get along in the world.

2 *Autonomy (independence) versus shame and doubt* is the challenge that occurs when the child is a toddler. The young child is learning to be independent and must do so without feeling too ashamed or uncertain about his or her actions.

According to Erik Erikson, children must resolve the crisis of competence and older adults must resolve the crisis of generativity. This child and her grandmother are certainly meeting their respective developmental tasks, but are the needs for competence and generativity confined to a particular stage of life?

3 *Initiative versus guilt* is the challenge that occurs as the preschooler develops. The child is acquiring new physical and mental skills, setting goals, and enjoying newfound talents, but must also learn to control impulses. The danger lies in developing too strong a sense of guilt over his or her wishes and fantasies.

4 *Competence versus inferiority* is the challenge for school-age children, who are learning to make things, use tools, and acquire the skills for adult life. Children who fail these lessons of mastery and competence may come out of this stage feeling inadequate and inferior.

5 *Identity versus role confusion* is the great challenge of adolescence, when teenagers must decide what they are going to be and what they hope to make of their lives. The term *identity crisis* describes what Erikson considered to be the primary conflict of this stage. Those who resolve it will come out of this stage with a strong identity, ready to plan for the future. Those who do not will sink into confusion, unable to make decisions.

6 *Intimacy versus isolation* is the challenge of young adulthood. Once you have decided who you are, said Erikson, you must share yourself with another and learn to make commitments. No matter how successful you are in work, you are not complete until you are capable of intimacy.

7 *Generativity versus stagnation* is the challenge of the middle years. Now that you know who you are and have an intimate relationship, will you sink into stagnation—complacency and selfishness—or will you experience "generativity"—creativity and renewal? Parenthood is the most common means for the successful resolution of this stage, but people can be productive, creative, and nurturant in other ways, in their work or their relationships with the younger generation. Researchers in Montreal, for example, have found that highly generative people that commit to helping the next generation tend to be happier (Ackerman, Zuroff, & Moskowitz, 2000).

8 *Ego integrity versus despair* is the final challenge of old age. As they age, people strive to reach the ultimate goals—wisdom, spiritual tranquility, an acceptance of their lives. Just as the healthy child will not fear life, said Erikson, the healthy adult will not fear death.

Erikson recognized that cultural and economic factors affect people's development through these stages. Some societies, for example, make the passages relatively easy. If you know you are going to be a farmer like your parents and you have no alternative, then moving from adolescence into young adulthood is not a terribly painful step (unless you hate farming). If you have many choices, however, as adolescents in urban societies often do, the transition can become prolonged. Some people put off making choices and never resolve their "identity crisis." Similarly, cultures that place a high premium on independence and individualism will make it difficult for many of their members to resolve Erikson's sixth crisis, that of intimacy versus isolation.

Erikson's work reminds us that development is never finished; it is an ongoing process. His work was important because he placed adult development in the context of family and society, and he specified many of the essential concerns of adulthood: trust, competence, identity, generativity, and the ability to enjoy life and accept death.

Current Approaches to Adult Development

Because Erikson discussed these themes in terms of their relative importance at different ages, many readers of his work assumed that the psychological concerns he identified occur at only one crucial time of life. Erikson was well aware that they can occur "out of order," although that was not his emphasis.

Later researchers, working at a time when people's lives had become less traditional and predictable, discovered just how out of order people's psychological concerns can be. Although in Western societies adolescence *is* often a time of confusion about identity and aspirations, an identity crisis is not limited to the teen years. A man who has worked in one job all his life, and then is laid off and must find an entirely new career, may

have an identity crisis too. Likewise, competence is not mastered once and for all in childhood. People learn new skills and lose old ones throughout their lives, and their sense of competence rises and falls accordingly.

Stage theories, therefore, are no longer considered an adequate way of understanding how adults grow and change (or remain the same) across the life span (Helson & Srivastava, 2001). Psychologists now regard adult development as a process in which many factors interact: biological changes, personality traits, idiosyncratic experiences, historical and cultural events, friends and relations, the particular environment . . . and things that happen by sheer chance (Bronfenbrenner, 1995; Schaie & Willis, 2002). The result of this complex interaction is, as one psychologist summarized, that "there is not one process of aging, but many; there is not one life course followed, but multiple courses. . . . The variety is as rich as the historic conditions people have faced and the current circumstances they experience" (Pearlin, 1982).

The Transitions of Life

Of course, certain events do tend to occur at particular times in life: going to school, learning to drive a car, having a baby, retiring from work. In all societies, people rely on a *social clock* to determine whether they are "on time" for these transitions or "off time." The social clock consists of norms governing what most other people of the same age and historical generation are expected to do (Helson & McCabe, 1993; Moen & Wethington, 1999; Neugarten, 1979).

Cultures have different social clocks. In some, young men and women are supposed to marry and start having children right after puberty, and work responsibilities come later. In others, a man

Doonesbury   BY GARRY TRUDEAU

may not marry until he has shown that he can support a family, which might not be until his 30s. But in all cultures, doing the right thing at the right time, compared to your friends, is reassuring. When nearly everyone your age goes through the same experience or enters a new role at the same time, adjusting to these transitions is relatively easy. Conversely, if you *aren't* doing these things and hardly anyone you know is doing them either, you will not feel out of step.

Today, social clocks are not telling time the way they once did. Most people will face unanticipated transitions—events that happen without warning, such as being fired from a job because of downsizing. And many people have to deal with nontransitions—events that they *expect* to happen that do not: for example, not getting married at the age they expected, not getting promoted, not being able to afford to retire, or not being able to have children (Schlossberg & Robinson, 1996). With this in mind, consider some of the major transitions of life.

Emerging Adulthood In industrialized nations, major demographic changes have postponed the timing of career decisions, marriage or cohabitation, and parenthood until a person's late 20s on the average. The result of these shifts has been the social creation of a new phase of life, between the ages of 18 and 25, that is distinctly different from both adolescence and adulthood. Jeffrey Arnett (2000) calls these years "emerging adulthood." When "emerging adults" are asked whether they feel they have reached adulthood, the majority answer: in some ways yes, in some ways no. As Arnett explains, "They have no name for the period they are in—because the society they live in has no name for it—so they regard themselves as being neither adolescents nor adults."

In certain respects, emerging adults have moved beyond adolescence into maturity, becoming more emotionally controlled, more confident, and less angry and alienated (Roberts, Caspi, & Moffitt, 2001). But they are also the group most likely to live unstable lives, feel unrooted, and take risks. Emerging adults move more often than other demographic groups do—back to their parents' homes and then out again, from one city to another, from living with roommates to living on their own. And their rates of risky behaviour (such as binge drinking, having unprotected sex, and driving at high speeds or while drunk) are higher than those of any other age group, including adolescents.

menopause The cessation of menstruation and of the production of ova; it is usually a gradual process lasting up to several years.

Of course, not all young people in this age group are alike. Some groups within the larger society, such as Mormons, promote early marriage and parenthood. And young people who are poor, who have dropped out of school, who had a child at 16, or who have few opportunities for good jobs will not have the leisure to "explore" many possible options. But Arnett (2000) predicts that the overall shift in all industrialized nations toward a global economy, increased education, and delayed career and family decisions means that emerging adulthood is likely to grow in importance as a distinct phase of prolonged exploration and freedom.

The Middle Years Most people think that the most important issues of the middle years are, for women, the misery of menopause and the "empty nest" (when grown children leave home) and, for men, a corresponding "mid-life crisis."

Actually, according to a large-scale research project that has followed 8000 participants for 10 years, for most women and men the mid-life years—between 35 and 65—are the prime of life (MacArthur Foundation, 1999). These years are often a time of reflection and reassessment: People look back on what they have accomplished, take stock of what they regret not having done, and think about what they want to do with their remaining years (Stewart & Vandewater, 1999). Far from being a time of crisis, mid-life is typically a time of psychological well-being, good health, productivity, and community involvement. When mid-life crises do occur (with equal likelihood for both sexes), it is for reasons related not to aging but to specific life-changing events, such as illness or the loss of a job or spouse (Wethington, 2000).

But doesn't menopause make most mid-life women depressed, irritable, and irrational? **Menopause**, which usually occurs between ages 45 and 55, is the cessation of menstruation and of the production of ova after the ovaries stop producing estrogen and progesterone. Menopause does produce physical symptoms in many women, notably "hot flashes," as the vascular system adjusts to the decrease in estrogen. But only about 10 percent of all women have unusually severe physical symptoms.

The negative view of menopause as a syndrome that causes depression and other negative emotional reactions is based on women who have had an early menopause following a hysterectomy (removal of the uterus) or who have had a lifetime history of

Thinking Critically About Menopause

depression. But these women are not typical. According to many surveys of thousands of healthy, randomly chosen women in the general population, most women view menopause with relief (that they no longer have to worry about pregnancy or menstrual periods) or with no particular feelings at all. The vast majority have only a few, temporarily bothersome symptoms, and do not become depressed; only three percent even report regret at having reached menopause (MacArthur Foundation, 1999; Matthews et al., 1990; McKinlay, McKinlay, & Brambilla, 1987).

Although women lose their fertility after menopause and men theoretically remain fertile throughout their lives, men have a "biological clock" too. Testosterone diminishes, although it never drops as sharply in men as estrogen does in women.

The sperm count may gradually drop, and the sperm that remain are more susceptible to genetic mutations that can increase the risk of certain diseases in children conceived by older fathers. For example, fathers over 50 have three times the risk of conceiving a child who develops schizophrenia as fathers under age 25 (Malaspina, 2001).

Hormone levels decline in the middle years, but the physical changes of mid-life do not by themselves predict how people will feel about aging or how they will respond to it (Moen, 2001; Schaie & Willis, 2002). How a culture views aging is far more important. For example, among the Inuit, successful aging is defined not only by the ability to manage declines in health but also in the passing on of wisdom to younger generations (Collings, 2001).

Get Involved "You're as Old as You Feel"

Ask five people, about a decade apart in age, and one of whom is at least 70, how old they are and how old they feel. (You may include yourself.) What is the gap, if any, between their chronological age and their psychological age? Is the gap larger among the older individuals? If so, ask why they perceive an "age gap" between their actual years and how old they feel.

Old Age

When does old age start? Not long ago you would have been considered old when in your 60s. Today, the number of people over 80 is rapidly growing in Canada. In fact, in 2001, over 400 000 Canadians (1.2 percent) were 85 years of age or older (Statistics Canada, 2002). How will these people fare in a world that is increasingly fast-paced and demanding of cognitive abilities? *Gerontologists*—researchers who study aging and the old—have been providing some answers.

The Bad News and the Good News Various aspects of intelligence, memory, and other forms of mental functioning decline significantly with age; older adults score lower on tests of reasoning, spatial ability, and complex problem solving than do younger adults (Verhaeghen & Salthouse, 1997). It takes older people longer to retrieve names, dates, and other information; the speed of cognitive processing in general slows down significantly (Bashore, Ridderinkhof, & van der Molen, 1997).

But not all cognitive abilities worsen with age. Gerontologists distinguish two kinds of cognitive ability. **Fluid intelligence** is the capacity for deductive reasoning and the ability to use new information to solve problems. It reflects an inherited predisposition, and it parallels other biological capacities in its growth and later decline (Baltes & Graf, 1996; Bosworth & Schaie, 1999).

fluid intelligence The capacity for deductive reasoning and the ability to use new information to solve problems; it is relatively independent of education and tends to decline in old age.

The two images of old age: More and more old people are living healthy, active, mentally stimulating lives, but with increasing longevity; many people are also falling victim to degenerative diseases such as Alzheimer's.

crystallized intelligence Cognitive skills and specific knowledge of information acquired over a lifetime; it is heavily dependent on education and tends to remain stable over the lifetime.

Crystallized intelligence consists of the knowledge and skills that are built up over a lifetime—the kind of intelligence that gives us the ability to do arithmetic, define words, or take political positions. It depends heavily on education and experience, and it tends to remain stable or even improve over the life span (see Figure 3.4). This is why physicians, lawyers, teachers, farmers, musicians, insurance agents, politicians, psychologists, and people in many other occupations can continue working well into old age.

Thinking Critically About "Inevitable" Declines in Old Age

Moreover, researchers have made great strides in showing that many conditions once thought to be an inevitable part of old age are in fact preventable or treatable:

- Apparent senility in the elderly is often caused by prescription medications, harmful combinations of medications, and even by over-the-counter drugs (such as sleeping pills and antihistamines), all of which can be hazardous to older people.

- Depression and passivity often result from the loss of meaningful activity, intellectual stimulation, and control over events (Langer, 1983; Schaie & Zuo, 2001).

- Weakness and frailty are often caused by a sedentary lifestyle. Exercise and moderate levels of weight training can restore strength and flexibility (Rowe & Kahn, 1998).

Gerontologists estimate that only about 30 percent of the physical and mental losses of old age are genetically based. The other 70 percent have to do with behavioural and psychological factors (Rowe & Kahn, 1998). Physical exercise and mental stimulation promote the growth of neural connections in the brain, even well into old age, and improve mental functioning (Colcombe & Kramer, 2003; Hultsch et al., 1999; Kramer & Willis, 2002). Even short-term training programs in memory, solving problems, and concentration for people between 65 and 94 produce significant cognitive gains—improvements that counteract the cognitive decline that would normally have occurred without the training (Ball et al., 2002).

Perhaps the best news is that as people get older, most get happier and their well-being improves; they learn to regulate negative feelings and emphasize the positive (Mroczek & Kolarz, 1998). For example, most are more likely to express happiness and gratitude than anger and frustration, according to research at the University of Manitoba and UCLA (Chipperfield, Perry, & Weiner, 2003). The frequency of intense negative emotions is highest among people aged 18 to 34, then drops sharply until age 65. After 65, it levels off, rising only slightly among old people facing crises of illness and bereavement (Carstensen et al., 2000; Charles, Reynolds, & Gatz, 2001). Apparently, some people do get wiser, or at least more peaceful, with age!

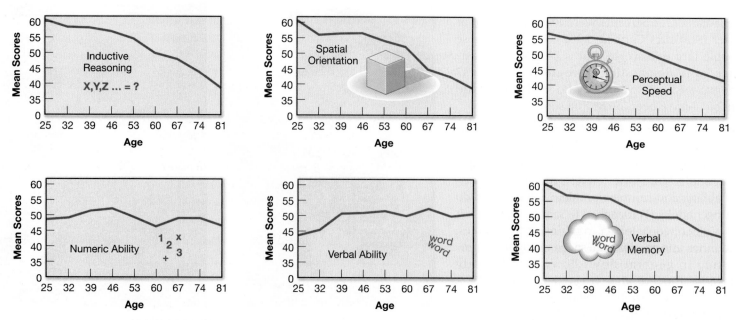

FIGURE 3.4 Changes in Mental Functioning over the Life Span

As these graphs show, some intellectual abilities tend to dwindle with age, but numerical and verbal abilities remain relatively steady over the years.

Some researchers who study aging are therefore optimistic. In their view, people who have challenging occupations and interests, who remain active mentally and physically, and who adapt flexibly to change are likely to maintain their cognitive abilities (Diamond, 1993; Kolb & Whishaw, 1998). "Use it or lose it," they say. Other researchers, however, are less optimistic. "When you've really lost it, you can't use it," they reply. They are worried about the growing numbers of people living into their 90s and 100s, when rates of cognitive impairment and dementia rise dramatically (Thomassen, van Schaick, & Blansjaar, 1998). The challenge for society is to make sure that the many people who will be living beyond 90 can keep using their brains instead of losing them.

Quick Quiz

You are not too old to answer this quiz.

1. The key psychological issue during adolescence, said Erikson, is a(n) _____ crisis.

2. What new phase of life development has been created because of demographic changes, and what years does it include?

3. Most women react to menopause by (a) feeling depressed, (b) regretting the loss of femininity, (c) going a little crazy, (d) feeling relieved or neutral.

4. Which of these statements about the decline of mental abilities in old age is true? (a) It can rarely be lessened with training programs; (b) about 70 percent of the decline is caused by genetic factors; (c) it is often a result of malnutrition or disease rather than aging; (d) it begins to accelerate once people reach age 65.

5. Suddenly, your 80-year-old grandmother has become confused and delusional. Before concluding that old age has made her senile, what other explanations should you rule out?

Answers:

1. identity   2. emerging adulthood, ages 18 to 25   3. d   4. c   5. You should rule out the possibility that she is taking medications, including nonprescription drugs, that can be hazardous in older people, singly or in combination.

WHAT'S AHEAD

- Do traumatic childhood experiences inevitably affect a person forever?
- What makes most children resilient in the face of adversity?

ARE ADULTS PRISONERS OF CHILDHOOD?

Most people take it for granted that the path from childhood to adolescence to adulthood is a fairly straight one. We think of the lasting attitudes, habits, and values our parents taught us. We continue to have deep attachments to our families, even when we are fighting with them. And many people carry with them the scars of emotional wounds they suffered as children. Children who have been beaten, neglected, or constantly subjected to verbal or physical abuse by their parents are more likely than other children to have emotional problems, become delinquent and violent, commit crimes, drop out of school, develop mental disorders such as depression, and develop major chronic illnesses (Emery & Laumann-Billings, 1998; Malinosky-Rummell & Hansen, 1993; Maxfield & Widom, 1996). Children from families characterized by conflict and aggression and by cold, neglectful, unsupportive parents are most at risk of poor mental and physical health as adults (Repetti, Taylor, & Seeman, 2002).

However, when research psychologists began to question the entrenched assumption that early trauma *always* has long-lasting effects and considered the evidence for alternative views, they got quite a different picture. *Most* children are

Thinking Critically About Lifelong Effects of Childhood Trauma

remarkably resilient, eventually overcoming even the devastating effects of war, having abusing or alcoholic parents, or being sexually molested (Cohen, 1999; Kaufman & Zigler, 1987; McNally, 2003; Rathbun, DiVirgilio, & Waldfogel, 1958; Rind & Tromovitch, 1997; Rind, Tromovitch, & Bauserman, 1998; West & Prinz, 1987). One researcher, whose team studied hundreds of biologically vulnerable children from birth to age 32, was surprised by their results: "As we watched these children grow from babyhood to adulthood," she wrote, "we could not help but respect the self-righting tendencies within them that produced normal development under all but the most persistently adverse circumstances" (Werner, 1989).

What are the reasons for such hardiness? Many resilient children have easygoing temperaments or personality traits that allow them to roll with fairly severe punches. Others are rescued by love and attention from their siblings, peers, or caring adults other than their parents (if their parents have been killed or were the source of the trauma). And some have experiences outside the family—in schools, places of worship, or other organizations—that give them a sense of competence, moral support, solace, religious faith, and self-esteem (Cowen et al., 1990; Garmezy, 1991; Masten, 2001; Masten & Coatsworth, 1998).

Perhaps the most powerful reason for the resilience of so many children, and for the changes that adults make throughout life, is that we are all constantly interpreting our experiences. We can decide to repeat the mistakes our parents made or break free of them. We can decide to remain set in our ways or to strike out in new directions at 20, 50, or 70. We can think about our setbacks and victories, our problems and our accomplishments, and decide for ourselves whether we want to remain prisoners of childhood . . . or to be liberated by the possibilities of adulthood.

Psychology In The News *Revisited*

Has our review of events across the life span helped you to clarify your thoughts about Arceli Keh, the woman who gave birth at age 63? A recent article on the family when the child was 7 reported that parents and child were doing fine. But when the girl graduates from high school, her mother will be 81 and her father 78. How do you feel about that?

The concept of the social clock can help us understand why so many people feel queasy about a woman getting pregnant so late in life: She is obviously "off time"! But, as we have also seen, the whole concept of "natural stages" is out of date. Increasingly, age is what we make of it; reaching a certain age has few if any inevitable consequences.

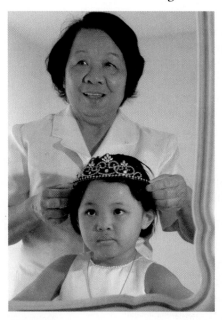

Cynthia Keh at age 6, with her mother, Arceli.

The Kehs say they carefully considered the pros and cons of having a child so late in their lives. They can provide for the child financially, and if one or both of them becomes incapacitated, their large extended family will care for their daughter. But some ethicists and social critics are concerned about the medical, social, and psychological costs of pregnancy and raising a child so late in life. They point out that for every successful pregnancy among older women, there are thousands of failures. They worry that stories about women like Arceli Keh raise women's expectations to unreasonable heights and create false hopes that technology can easily overcome biological limitations.

The older a woman is, the greater her chance of developing medical problems in pregnancy (such as gestational diabetes and high blood pressure). Although plenty of older people, required by unforeseen circumstances to rear their grandchildren, have risen to the challenge, we have seen that age brings a decline in some cognitive and physical abilities. So it seems legitimate to worry about whether elderly parents—of either sex—will have the mental resources and energy to guide their children through the many hurdles of childhood and adolescence.

The Kehs' decision is still highly unusual: Few women over age 50 give birth each year; the birth rate for women in their 40s, however, is much higher (Roan, 2002). Having a child in one's 40s used to seem as weird and "unnatural" as Arceli Keh's decision to have

a baby at 63, but now that it is more common—with celebrities such as Geena Davis having a child at 46—it doesn't seem as "off time" as it once did. Will giving birth after 50 come to be seen the same way?

In the next decades, as the world changes in countless unpredictable ways, the territory of adulthood will continue to expand, providing new frontiers as well as fewer signposts and roadmaps to guide us. In the absence of clear signposts, will people get disoriented and lose their way, or will the result be a more creative and satisfying adventure through life?

Taking Psychology With You   Bringing Up Baby

Every year or so another best-selling book arrives to tell parents they've been doing it all wrong. Years ago the public was warned that the most crucial thing was bonding: The mother had to bond with the baby right away, right after birth, or dire things would happen to the baby's development. Then it turned out that although immediate bonding is certainly nice if you can do it, adopted babies will bond to parents just fine even if they have been adopted several days, months, or years after birth (Eyer, 1992). Throughout the twentieth century and still today, countless books have advised parents to treat their children in very specific, if contradictory ways: Pick them up, don't pick them up; respond when they cry, don't respond when they cry; let them sleep with you, never let them sleep with you; be highly sensitive to their every need so they will securely attach to you, don't overreact to their every mood or complaint or you will spoil them (Hulbert, 2003).

As we have seen in this chapter, babies and young children thrive under a wide variety of child-rearing methods. They bring their own temperaments to the matter, too: Most respond readily to induction; others require stricter discipline. And as children grow up, they are subject to the influences of their peers and generation and to particular experiences that shape their interests and aspirations.

Well, then, how *should* you treat your children? Should you be strict or lenient, powerful or permissive? Should you require your child to stop having tantrums, to clean up his or her room, to be polite? Should you say, "Oh, nothing I do will matter, anyway" or "Children need to express themselves in any way they please"? Even granted the limitations of what parents can do, child-development research does suggest certain overall guidelines to help parents teach children to be confident, considerate, and helpful:

- **Set high expectations that are appropriate to the child's age and temperament, and teach the child how to meet them.** Some parents make few demands on their children, either unintentionally or because they believe a parent should not impose standards. Others make many demands, such as requiring children to be polite, help with chores, control their anger, be thoughtful of others, and do well in school. The children of parents who make few demands tend to be aggressive, impulsive, and immature. The children of parents who have high expectations tend to be helpful and above average in competence and self-confidence (Damon, 1995). But the demands must be appropriate for the child's age. You can't expect two-year-olds to dress themselves, and before you can expect children to get up on time, they have to know how to use an alarm clock.

- **Explain, explain, explain.** Induction—telling a child why you have applied a rule—teaches a child to be responsible. Punitive methods ("Do it or I'll spank you") may result in compliance, but the child will tend to disobey as soon as you are out of sight. Explanations also teach children how to reason and understand; they reward curiosity and open-mindedness. While setting standards for your children, you can also allow them to express disagreements and feelings. This does not mean you have to argue with a four-year-old about the merits of table manners or permit antisocial and destructive behaviour. Once you have explained a rule, you need to enforce it consistently.

- **Encourage empathy.** Call the child's attention to the effects of his or her actions on others, appeal to the child's sense of fair play and desire to be good, and teach the child to take another person's point of view. As we saw, even very young children are capable of empathy and taking another perspective. Vague orders, such as "Don't fight," are less effective than showing the child how fighting disrupts and hurts others. For boys especially, aggression and empathy are strongly and negatively related: the higher the one, the lower the other (Eisenberg et al., 2002).

- **Notice, approve of, and reward good behaviour.** Many parents punish the behaviour they dislike, a form of attention that often is rewarding to the child. It is much more effective to praise the behaviour you do want, which teaches the child how to behave.

Even with the best skills and intentions, you cannot control everything that happens to your child or your child's basic temperamental dispositions. "The idea that we can make our children turn out any way we want is an illusion. Give it up," advises Judith Harris (1998). But, she adds, parents do have the power to make their children's lives miserable or secure, and to affect the quality of the relationship they will have with their child throughout life: one that is filled with conflict and resentment, or one that is close and loving.

SUMMARY

FROM CONCEPTION THROUGH THE FIRST YEAR

- *Developmental psychologists* study people's growth and change over the life span. They study *socialization*, the process by which children learn the rules and behaviour society expects of them, and *maturation*, the unfolding of genetically influenced behaviour and characteristics.

- Prenatal development consists of the *germinal, embryonic,* and *fetal* stages. Harmful influences that can adversely affect the fetus's development include German measles, toxic chemicals, some sexually transmitted diseases, cigarettes, alcohol (which can cause *fetal alcohol syndrome* and cognitive deficits), illegal drugs, and even over-the-counter medications.

- Babies are born with *motor reflexes* and a number of perceptual abilities. Newborns are also naturally attracted to novelty and to human faces. But many aspects of infants' maturation depend on cultural customs that govern how their parents hold, touch, feed, and talk to them.

- Babies' innate need for *contact comfort* gives rise to emotional attachment to their caregivers, and by the age of six to eight months, infants begin to feel *separation anxiety*. Studies of the *Strange Situation* have distinguished *secure* from *insecure* attachment; insecurity can take one of two forms, *avoidant* or *anxious–ambivalent* attachment.

- Styles of attachment are relatively unaffected by the normal range of child-rearing practices, and also by whether or not babies spend time in daycare. Insecure attachment is promoted by parents' rejection, mistreatment, or abandonment of their infants, by the child's own fearful, insecure temperament, or by stressful family situations.

COGNITIVE DEVELOPMENT

- Infants are responsive to the pitch, intensity, and sound of language, which may be why adults in many cultures speak to babies in *parentese*, using higher-pitched words and exaggerated intonation. At four to six months of age, babies begin to recognize the sounds of their own language. They go through a babbling phase from age six months to one year, and at about one year, they start saying single words and using symbolic gestures. At age two, children speak in two- or three-word *telegraphic* sentences that convey a variety of messages.

- Language allows us to express and comprehend an infinite number of novel utterances. Noam Chomsky argued that the ability to take the *surface structure* of any utterance and apply rules of *syntax* to infer its underlying *deep structure* must depend on an innate faculty for language, a *language acquisition device*. Many findings support this view: Children from different cultures go through similar stages of language development; children's language is full of *overregularizations* that reflect grammatical rules; adults do not consistently correct their children's syntax; and children who have never been exposed to adult language often invent their own.

- Nonetheless, parental practices, such as repeating correct sentences verbatim and recasting incorrect ones, aid in language acquisition. Cases of children deprived of exposure to language suggest that a *critical period* exists for acquiring a first language.

- Jean Piaget argued that cognitive development depends on an interaction between maturation and a child's experiences in the world. Children's thinking changes and adapts through *assimilation* and *accommodation*. Piaget proposed four stages of cognitive development: *sensorimotor* (birth to age 2), during which the child learns *object permanence*; *preoperational* (ages 2 to 7), during which language and symbolic thought develop; *concrete operations* (ages 7 to 12), during which the child comes to understand *conservation*, identity, and serial ordering; and *formal operations* (age 12 to adulthood), during which abstract reasoning develops.

- Researchers have found that the changes from one stage to another are not as clear-cut as Piaget implied; that young children have more cognitive abilities, at earlier ages, than Piaget thought; and that young children are not always *egocentric* in their thinking. Cultural practices affect the pace and content of cognitive development, and not all adults develop the ability for formal operations.

MORAL DEVELOPMENT

- Lawrence Kohlberg proposed that as children mature cognitively, they go through three levels of moral reasoning. However, stage theories of moral reasoning have serious limitations. Moral reasoning is affected by education and culture; it begins much earlier than Kohlberg and others thought; it is often inconsistent across situations; and it is often unrelated to moral behaviour.

- Carol Gilligan argued that women's moral reasoning tends to be based on principles of care and compassion, whereas men's is based on abstract principles of justice. Most research, however, finds no gender differences in moral reasoning.

- Parental methods of discipline have different consequences for a child's moral behaviour. *Power assertion* is associated with children who are aggressive and fail to internalize moral standards. However, the effects of physical punishment, such as spanking, depend on the family context and on the severity and frequency of the punishment. *Induction* is associated with children who develop empathy and internalized moral standards and who can resist temptation. In general, *authoritative* parents, who use induction and set limits, have better results with their children than do *authoritarian* or permissive parents.

GENDER DEVELOPMENT

- Gender development includes the emerging awareness of *gender identity*, the cognitive understanding that a person is biologically male or female regardless of what he or she does or wears, and *gender typing*, the process by which boys and girls learn what it means to be masculine or feminine.

- Biological psychologists account for gender differences in behaviour in terms of genetics, hormones, and brain organization, observing that, universally, young boys and girls prefer playing with different toys and games and with other children of their own sex. Cognitive psychologists study how children develop *gender schemas* of "male" and "female" categories and qualities, which in turn shape their gender-typed behaviour. Gender schemas tend to be inflexible at first but often become more flexible as the child cognitively matures and assimilates new information (if the child lives in a culture that promotes flexible gender schemas). Learning theorists study the direct and subtle reinforcers and social messages that foster gender typing.

- Gender development changes over the life span, depending on people's experiences with work and family life and on larger events in society. Gender differences in personality, motivation, and behaviour tend to be greatest in childhood and adolescence, but often decline in adulthood and the later years.

ADOLESCENCE

- *Adolescence* begins with the physical changes of *puberty*. In girls, puberty is signalled by *menarche* and the development of breasts; in boys, it begins with the onset of nocturnal emissions and the development of the testes, scrotum, and penis. Boys and girls who enter puberty early tend to have a more difficult adjustment than do those who enter puberty later than average.

- Most adolescents do not go through extreme emotional turmoil, anger, or rebellion. However, conflict with parents, mood swings and depression, and reckless behaviour do increase in adolescence. The peer group becomes especially important. Boys tend to externalize their emotional problems in acts of aggression and other antisocial behaviour; girls tend to internalize their problems by becoming depressed or developing eating disorders. One challenge of adolescence in Western cultures is *individuation*, breaking away from parents to develop autonomy and a more reciprocal relationship, but this goal is very much influenced by culture and generational values.

ADULTHOOD

- Erik Erikson proposed that life consists of eight stages, each with a unique psychological challenge, or crisis, that must be resolved, such as an *identity crisis* in adolescence. Erikson identified many of the essential concerns of adulthood and showed that development is a lifelong process. However, psychological issues or crises are not confined to particular chronological periods or stages.

- Adults often evaluate their development according to a *social clock* that determines whether they are "on time" or "off time" for a particular event. When most people in an age group go through the same event at about the same time, transitions are easier than when people feel "out of step."

- In industrialized nations, major demographic changes have postponed the timing of career decisions, marriage or commitment to a partner, and parenthood until a person's late 20s on the average. The result is a new life phase between the ages of 18 and 25: "emerging adulthood." For many, this phase is qualitatively different from both adolescence and adulthood.

- The middle years are generally not a time of turmoil or crisis but the prime of most people's lives. In women, *menopause* occurs between 45 and 55. Many women have temporary physical symptoms, but most do not become depressed and irritable or regret the end of

fertility. In middle-aged men, hormone production slows down but fertility continues, although mutations in sperm increase the risk of birth defects in offspring of older fathers.

- *Gerontologists* have revised our ideas about old age, now that people are living longer and healthier lives. The speed of cognitive processing slows down, and *fluid intelligence* parallels other biological capacities in its eventual decline. *Crystallized intelligence*, in contrast, depends heavily on culture, education, and experience, and it tends to remain stable or even improve over the life span.

- Many supposedly inevitable results of aging, such as senility, depression, and physical frailty, are often the result of disease; medication; poor nutrition; and lack of stimulation, control of one's environment, and exercise. Exercise and mental stimulation promote the growth of synapses in the human brain, even well into old age, although some mental losses are inevitable.

ARE ADULTS PRISONERS OF CHILDHOOD?

- Children who experience violence or neglect are at risk of many serious problems later in life. But the majority of children are resilient, able to overcome early traumatic experiences. Psychologists now study not only the sad consequences of neglect, poverty, and violence, but also the origins of resilience under adversity, which they find more common than was once believed.

KEY TERMS

LOOKING BACK

- How can a pregnant woman reduce the risk of damage to the embryo or fetus? (pp. 72–73)
- Given a choice, what do newborns prefer to look at? (p. 74)
- How does culture affect how a baby physically matures? (p. 74)
- Why is cuddling so important for infants (not to mention adults)? (pp. 74–75)
- If you have a one-year-old, why shouldn't you worry if your baby cries when left with a new babysitter? (p. 75)
- Why do so many parents speak "baby talk"? (pp. 77–78)
- Is language an innate ability or an acquired one? (pp. 79–80)
- What important accomplishment are infants revealing when they learn to play "peekaboo"? (p. 81)
- Why will most five-year-olds choose a tall, narrow glass of lemonade over a short, fat glass containing the same amount? (p. 81)
- Is a person who uses sophisticated moral reasoning more likely to behave morally than one who does not? (p. 85)
- When reasoning about moral dilemmas, are women more compassionate and caring than men are? (p. 86)
- What is wrong with "because I say so" as a way of getting children to behave? (p. 86)
- How would a biologically oriented psychologist explain why most little boys and girls are "sexist" in their choice of toys? (p. 89)
- What happens to children's notions about gender once they are able to distinguish males from females? (p. 90)
- How do teachers unintentionally reinforce aggressiveness in boys? (p. 91)
- If a little girl "knows" that girls can't be doctors, does this mean she will never go to medical school? (p. 92)
- What are the advantages and disadvantages of going through puberty earlier than most of your classmates? (p. 93)
- During adolescence, are extreme turmoil and unhappiness the exception or the rule? (p. 94)
- When teenagers and their parents quarrel, what is it typically about? (p. 95)
- What is wrong with thinking that life occurs in a series of predictable stages? (pp. 97–98)
- What feelings are common during "emerging adulthood," the years from 18 to 25? (p. 98)
- Does menopause make most women depressed and irrational? (pp. 98–99)
- Do men go through a male version of menopause? (p. 99)
- Which mental abilities decline in old age, and which do not? (pp. 99–100)
- Do traumatic childhood experiences inevitably affect a person forever? (pp. 101–102)
- What makes most children resilient in the face of adversity? (p. 102)

Psychology In The News

BIRTHDAY BASH FOR HAWKING

LONDON, January 12, 2002. Scientists from around the world, students, and even many celebrities, including members of the band U2, gathered this week at Cambridge University to honour one of the world's great physicists on the occasion of his sixtieth birthday.

Stephen Hawking is known for his groundbreaking work both in physics and in cosmology (the study of the origins and development of the universe) and is author of the international bestseller *A Brief History of Time*. He holds the same professorship at Cambridge University that was once held by Sir Isaac Newton. Among the general public, he is admired for doing his work despite having lived for nearly four decades with a severe neurological disease that typically kills its victims within three to five years after the onset of symptoms. The popular scientist has appeared on many talk shows and has even made guest appearances on *The Simpsons* and *Star Trek*.

Hawking's illness has been diagnosed as amyotrophic lateral sclerosis (ALS), also known as Lou Gehrig's disease. The condition causes motor neurons in the brain and spinal cord to degenerate and die. Ultimately, the brain cannot initiate and control movement of the muscles. Some patients become so completely paralyzed that they are "locked in," unable to communicate even through eye or finger movements. Hawking is confined to a wheelchair, has minimal motor control, and cannot speak. He uses a voice synthesizer to lecture.

Professor Hawking has sometimes made gloomy predictions about the chances for humanity's survival, but gloom was nowhere to be found at his birthday celebration. In an address to his well-wishers, he spoke about experiencing special "eureka moments" of discovery that make a life in science worthwhile. "I won't compare it to sex," he said, "but it lasts longer."

A happy Stephen Hawking gets a birthday kiss from a Marilyn Monroe look-alike.

4 Neurons, Hormones, and the Brain

Millions of people suffer from conditions affecting the brain and nervous system, such as Lou Gehrig's, Alzheimer's, and Parkinson's disease. Some of these diseases harm the brain but leave the rest of the body alone. Others, as in Hawking's case, weaken or deform the body but leave the parts of the brain involved in thought and creativity alone. The brain's effects on our minds and bodies remind us that the three-pound organ inside our skulls provides the bedrock for everything we do and think. *Neuropsychologists*, along with neuroscientists from other disciplines, study the brain and the rest of the nervous system in hopes of gaining a better understanding of consciousness, perception, memory, emotion, stress, mental disorders, and even self-identity.

At this very moment, your own brain, assisted by other parts of your nervous system, is busily taking in these words. Whether you are excited, curious, or bored, your brain is registering some sort of emotional reaction. As you continue reading, your brain will (we hope) store away much of the information in this chapter. Later on, your brain may enable you to smell a flower, climb the stairs, greet a friend, solve a personal problem, or chuckle at a joke. But the brain's most startling accomplishment is its knowledge that it is doing all these things. This self-awareness makes brain research different from the study of anything else in the universe. Scientists must use the cells, biochemistry, and circuitry of their own brains to understand the cells, biochemistry, and circuitry of brains in general.

Because the brain is the site of consciousness, people disagree about what language to use in discussing it. If we say that your brain stores events or registers emotions, we imply a separate "you" that is "using" that brain. But if we leave "you" out of the picture and just say the brain does these things, we risk implying that brain mechanisms alone explain behaviour (which is untrue), and we lose sight of the person. No one has ever resolved this dilemma to everyone's satisfaction.

William Shakespeare called the brain "the soul's frail dwelling house." Actually, this miraculous organ is more like the main room in a house filled with many alcoves and passageways—the "house" being the nervous system as a whole. Before we can understand the windows, walls, and furniture of this house, we need to become acquainted with the overall floor plan. It's a pretty technical plan, which means that you will be learning many new terms, but you will need to know these terms to understand how biological psychologists go about explaining psychological topics.

"THEN IT'S AGREED—YOU CAN'T HAVE A MIND WITHOUT A BRAIN, BUT YOU CAN HAVE A BRAIN WITHOUT A MIND."

central nervous system (CNS) The portion of the nervous system consisting of the brain and spinal cord.

spinal cord A collection of neurons and supportive tissue running from the base of the brain down the centre of the back, protected by a column of bones (the spinal column).

spinal reflexes Automatic behaviours produced by the spinal cord without brain involvement.

peripheral nervous system (PNS) All portions of the nervous system outside the brain and spinal cord; it includes sensory and motor nerves.

As you read, keep Stephen Hawking in mind. Why has he been able not only to survive but to thrive? Will our growing knowledge of the brain lead to cures for disorders such as his? Most important, to what extent can the workings of his brain explain Hawking's amazing resilience and all of his breathtaking "eureka moments" of intellectual discovery and imagination?

WHAT'S AHEAD

- Why do you automatically pull your hand away from something hot, "without thinking"?
- In an emergency, which part of your nervous system whirls into action?

THE NERVOUS SYSTEM: A BASIC BLUEPRINT

The function of a nervous system is to gather and process information, produce responses to stimuli, and coordinate the workings of different cells. Even the lowly jellyfish and the humble worm have the beginnings of such a system. In very simple organisms that do little more than move, eat, and eliminate wastes, the "system" may be no more than one or two nerve cells. In human beings, who do such complex things as dance, cook, and take psychology courses, the nervous system contains billions of cells. Scientists divide

this intricate network into two main parts: the central nervous system and the peripheral (outlying) nervous system (see Figure 4.1).

The Central Nervous System

The **central nervous system (CNS)** receives, processes, interprets, and stores incoming sensory information—information about tastes, sounds, smells, colour, pressure on the skin, the state of internal organs, and so forth. It also sends out messages destined for muscles, glands, and internal organs. The CNS is usually conceptualized as having two components: the brain, which we will consider in detail later, and the **spinal cord**. The spinal cord is actually an extension of the brain. It runs from the base of the brain down the centre of the back, protected by a column of bones (the spinal column), and it acts as a bridge between the brain and the parts of the body below the neck.

The spinal cord produces some behaviours on its own, without any help from the brain. These **spinal reflexes** are automatic, requiring no conscious effort. For example, if you accidentally touch a hot iron, you will immediately pull your hand away, even before your brain has had a chance to register what has happened. Nerve impulses bring a message to the spinal cord (hot!), and the spinal cord immediately sends out a command via other nerve impulses, telling muscles in your arm to contract and pull your hand away from the iron. (Reflexes above the neck, such as sneezing and blinking, involve the lower part of the brain, rather than the spinal cord.)

The neural circuits underlying many spinal reflexes are linked to other neural pathways that run up and down the spinal cord, to and from the brain. Because of these connections, reflexes can sometimes be influenced by thoughts and emotions. An example is erection in men, a spinal reflex that can be inhibited by anxiety or distracting thoughts and initiated by erotic thoughts. And some reflexes can be brought under conscious control. If you concentrate, you may be able to keep your knee from jerking when it is tapped, as it normally would. Similarly, most men can learn to voluntarily delay ejaculation, another spinal reflex. (Yes, they can.)

The Peripheral Nervous System

The **peripheral nervous system (PNS)** handles the central nervous system's input and output. It contains all portions of the nervous system outside the brain and spinal cord, right down to nerves in the tips of the fingers and toes. If your brain

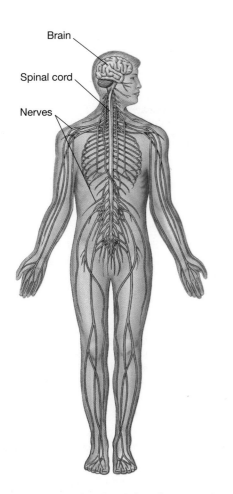

FIGURE 4.1 The Central and Peripheral Nervous Systems

The central nervous system includes the brain and the spinal cord. The peripheral nervous system consists of 43 pairs of nerves that transmit information to and from the central nervous system. Twelve pairs of cranial nerves in the head enter the brain directly; 31 pairs of spinal nerves enter the spinal cord at the spaces between the vertebrae of the spine.

could not collect information about the world by means of a peripheral nervous system, it would be like a radio without a receiver. In the peripheral nervous system, *sensory nerves* carry messages from special receptors in the skin, muscles, and other internal and external sense organs to the spinal cord, which sends them along to the brain. These nerves put us in touch with both the outside world and the activities of our own bodies. *Motor nerves* carry orders from the central nervous system to muscles, glands, and internal organs. They enable us to move, and they cause glands to contract and to secrete substances, including chemical messengers called *hormones.*

Scientists further divide the peripheral nervous system into two parts: the somatic (bodily) nervous system and the autonomic (self-governing)

nervous system. The **somatic nervous system**, sometimes called the *skeletal nervous system*, consists of nerves that are connected to sensory receptors and to the skeletal muscles that permit voluntary action. When you sense the world around you, or when you turn off a light or write your name, your somatic system is active. The **autonomic nervous system** regulates the functioning of blood vessels, glands, and internal (visceral) organs such as the bladder, stomach, and heart. When you see someone you have a crush on, and your heart pounds, your hands get sweaty, and your cheeks feel hot, you can blame your autonomic nervous system.

The autonomic nervous system works more or less automatically, without your conscious control. Some people, however, have learned to heighten or suppress their autonomic responses intentionally, using a technique called *biofeedback* (Miller, 1978). Monitoring devices track the bodily process in question and produce a signal, such as a light or a tone, whenever the desired autonomic response occurs—for example, a change in blood pressure, blood flow, or heart rate. The method for producing the response may be prearranged or left up to the participant. Some clinicians are using biofeedback to treat high blood pressure, asthma, and migraine headaches. It is not clear, though, whether the autonomic responses are being controlled directly or by changing voluntary responses such as breathing, which in turn affect the autonomic nervous system.

The autonomic nervous system is itself divided into two parts: the **sympathetic nervous system** and the **parasympathetic nervous system**. These two parts work together, but in opposing ways, to adjust the body to changing circumstances (see Figure 4.2). The sympathetic system acts like the accelerator of a car, mobilizing the body for action and an output of energy. It makes you blush, sweat, and breathe more deeply, and it pushes up your heart rate and blood pressure. As we will see in Chapter 13, when you are in a situation that requires you to fight, flee, or cope, the sympathetic nervous system whirls into action. The parasympathetic system is more like a brake: It does not stop the body, of course, but it does tend to slow things down or keep them running smoothly. It enables the body to conserve and store energy. If you have to jump out of the way of a speeding motorcyclist, sympathetic nerves increase your heart rate. Afterward, parasympathetic nerves slow it down again and keep its rhythm regular.

somatic nervous system The subdivision of the peripheral nervous system that connects to sensory receptors and to skeletal muscles; sometimes called the *skeletal nervous system.*

autonomic nervous system The subdivision of the peripheral nervous system that regulates the internal organs and glands.

sympathetic nervous system The subdivision of the autonomic nervous system that mobilizes bodily resources and increases the output of energy during emotion and stress.

parasympathetic nervous system The subdivision of the autonomic nervous system that operates during relaxed states and that conserves energy.

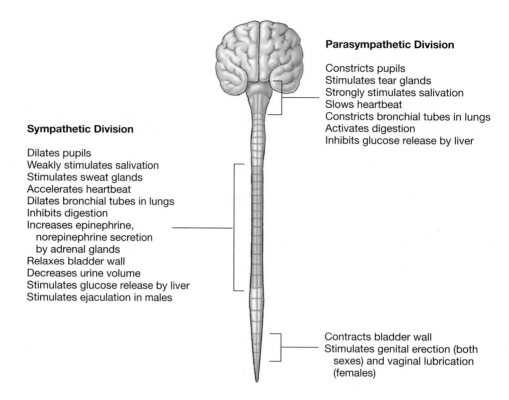

Parasympathetic Division

Constricts pupils
Stimulates tear glands
Strongly stimulates salivation
Slows heartbeat
Constricts bronchial tubes in lungs
Activates digestion
Inhibits glucose release by liver

Sympathetic Division

Dilates pupils
Weakly stimulates salivation
Stimulates sweat glands
Accelerates heartbeat
Dilates bronchial tubes in lungs
Inhibits digestion
Increases epinephrine,
   norepinephrine secretion
   by adrenal glands
Relaxes bladder wall
Decreases urine volume
Stimulates glucose release by liver
Stimulates ejaculation in males

Contracts bladder wall
Stimulates genital erection (both
   sexes) and vaginal lubrication
   (females)

FIGURE 4.2   The Autonomic Nervous System

In general, the sympathetic division of the autonomic nervous system prepares the body to expend energy, and the parasympathetic division restores and conserves energy. Sympathetic nerve fibres exit from areas of the spinal cord shown in red in this illustration; parasympathetic fibres exit from the base of the brain and from spinal cord areas shown in green.

Quick Quiz

Pause now to test your memory by mentally filling in the missing parts of the nervous system "house." Then see whether you can briefly describe what each part of the system does.

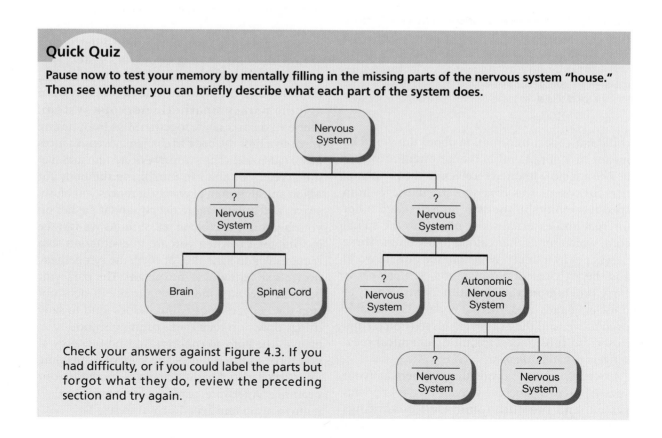

Check your answers against Figure 4.3. If you had difficulty, or if you could label the parts but forgot what they do, review the preceding section and try again.

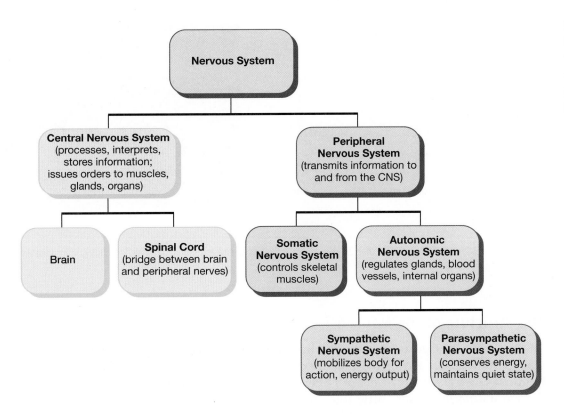

FIGURE 4.3 How the
Nervous System Is
Organized

Use this diagram to check your
answers to the Quick Quiz on
page 112.

WHAT'S AHEAD

- Which cells are the nervous system's "communication specialists," and how do they "talk" to each other?

- Are you born with all the brain cells you'll ever have?

- How do learning and experience alter the brain's circuits?

- What happens when levels of brain chemicals called *neurotransmitters* are too low or too high?

- Which hormones can improve your memory?

COMMUNICATION IN THE NERVOUS SYSTEM

The blueprint we just described provides only a general idea of the nervous system's structure. Now let's turn to the details.

The nervous system is made up in part of **neurons**, or *nerve cells*. Neurons are the brain's communication specialists, transmitting information to, from, and within the central nervous system by way of electrochemical signals. They are held in place by **glia**, or *glial cells* (from the Greek for "glue"), which make up 90 percent of the brain's cells.

For a long time, people thought that glial cells merely provided scaffolding for the more important and exciting neurons. We now know, however, that glial cells also provide neurons with nutrients and insulate them, protect the brain from toxic agents, and remove cellular debris when neurons die. Moreover, glial cells communicate chemically with each other and with neurons, and foster connections between neurons. One type of glial cell seems to give neurons the go-ahead to start "talking" to each other (Ullian et al., 2001). Without glial cells, neurons probably could not function effectively (Gallo & Chittajallu, 2001; Netting, 2001). In coming years, we will be learning much more about the role of glial cells in learning, memory, and other processes.

Although neurons are often called the building blocks of the nervous system, in structure they are more like snowflakes than blocks, exquisitely delicate and differing from one another greatly in size and shape (see Figure 4.4). In the giraffe, a neuron that runs from the spinal cord down the animal's hind leg may be nine feet long! In the human brain, neurons are microscopic. No one is sure how many neurons the human brain contains, but a typical estimate is 100 billion—about the same number as there are stars in our galaxy—and some estimates go much higher.

neuron A cell that conducts electrochemical signals; the basic unit of the nervous system; also called a *nerve cell.*

glia [GLY-uh or GLEE-uh] Cells that support, nurture, and insulate neurons; remove debris when neurons die; and modify neuronal functioning.

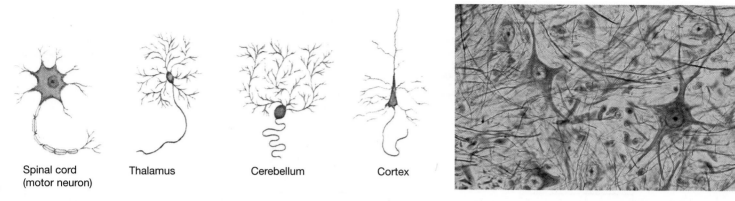

Spinal cord (motor neuron) Thalamus Cerebellum Cortex

FIGURE 4.4 Different Kinds of Neurons

Neurons vary in size and shape, depending on their location and function. More than 200 types of neurons have been identified in mammals. The photograph on the right, taken through a microscope, reveals the delicate fibres of human motor neurons.

The Structure of the Neuron

dendrites A neuron's branches that receive information from other neurons and transmit it toward the cell body.

cell body The part of the neuron that keeps it alive and determines whether it will fire.

nerve A bundle of nerve fibres (axons and sometimes dendrites) in the peripheral nervous system.

axon A neuron's extending fibre that conducts impulses away from the cell body and transmits them to other neurons or to muscle or gland cells.

myelin sheath [My-uh-lin] A fatty insulation that surrounds the axon of some neurons.

As you can see in Figure 4.5, a neuron has three main parts: *dendrites*, a *cell body*, and an *axon*. The **dendrites** look like the branches of a tree; indeed, the word *dendrite* means "little tree" in Greek. Dendrites act like antennas, receiving messages from as many as 10 000 other nerve cells and transmitting these messages toward the cell body. They also do some preliminary processing of those messages. The **cell body**, which is shaped roughly like a sphere or a pyramid, contains the biochemical machinery for keeping the neuron alive. As we will see later, it also determines whether the neuron should "fire"—that is, transmit a message to other neurons—depending on inputs from other neurons. The **axon** (from the Greek for "axle") transmits messages away from the cell body to other neurons or to muscle or gland cells. Axons commonly divide at the end into branches, called *axon terminals*. In adult human beings, axons vary from only four thousandths of an inch to a few feet in length. Dendrites and axons give each neuron a double role: As one researcher put it, a neuron is first a catcher, then a batter (Gazzaniga, 1988).

Many axons, especially the larger ones, are insulated by a surrounding layer of fatty material called the **myelin sheath**, which is made up of glial cells. Constrictions in this covering, called *nodes*, cause it to be divided into segments, which make it look a little like a string of link sausages (see Figure 4.5 again). One purpose of the myelin sheath is to prevent signals in adjacent cells from interfering with each other. Another, as we will see shortly, is to speed up the conduction of neural impulses. In individuals with multiple sclerosis, loss of myelin causes erratic nerve signals, leading to loss of sensation, weakness or paralysis, lack of coordination, or vision problems.

In the peripheral nervous system, the fibres of individual neurons (axons and sometimes dendrites) are collected together in bundles called **nerves**, rather like the lines in a telephone cable. The human body has 43 pairs of peripheral nerves; one nerve from each pair is on the left side of the body, and the other is on the right. Most of these

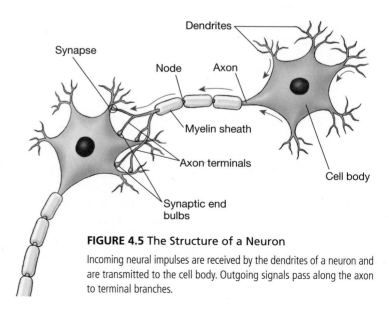

FIGURE 4.5 The Structure of a Neuron

Incoming neural impulses are received by the dendrites of a neuron and are transmitted to the cell body. Outgoing signals pass along the axon to terminal branches.

nerves enter or leave the spinal cord, but the 12 pairs that are in the head, the *cranial nerves*, connect directly to the brain. In Chapter 6, we will discuss the cranial nerves that are involved in the senses of smell, hearing, and vision.

Neurons in the News

Until recently, neuroscientists thought that if neurons in the central nervous system were injured or damaged, they could never regenerate (grow back). But then the conventional wisdom got turned upside down. Animal studies showed that several axons in the spinal cord *can* regrow when treated with certain nervous system chemicals (Schnell & Schwab, 1990). Researchers are now working to fine-tune this process and are hopeful that regenerated axons will someday enable people with spinal cord injuries to use their limbs again.

Scientists have also had to rethink another entrenched assumption, which was accepted for most of the twentieth century, despite some contradictory evidence: that mammals produce no new CNS cells after infancy (Gross, 2000). In the early 1990s, Canadian neuroscientists working with mice immersed immature cells from the animals' brains in a growth-promoting protein and showed that these cells could give birth to new neurons. Even more astonishingly, the new neurons then continued to divide and multiply (Reynolds & Weiss, 1992). One of the researchers, Samuel Weiss at the University of Calgary, said that this result "challenged everything I had read; everything I had learned when I was a student" (quoted in Barinaga, 1992).

Stimulated by landmark research conducted at Princess Margaret Hospital in Toronto in the 1960s by James Till and Ernest McCulloch, scientists have discovered that the human brain and other body organs also contain such cells, which are now usually referred to as **stem cells**. These, too, give rise to new neurons when treated in the laboratory. Stem cells involved in learning and memory seem to divide and mature throughout adulthood—a discovery that holds tremendous promise for human well-being (Eriksson et al., 1998; Gage et al., 1998; Gould et al., 1998; Gould, Reeves, et al., 1999). We may even have some control over that process: In animal studies, physical exercise and mental activity promote the production and survival of these new cells (Gould, Beylin, et al., 1999; Kempermann, Brandon, & Gage, 1998; van Praag, Kempermann, & Gage,

1999). On the other hand, stress can inhibit the production of new cells (Gould et al., 1998), and nicotine can kill them (Berger, Gage, & Vijayaraghavan, 1998).

Stem-cell research is one of the hottest areas in biology and neuroscience, and also one of the most hotly debated. In 1995, when the Canadian government imposed a voluntary moratorium on nine technologies deemed controversial, stem-cell research was among them; groups engaged in these activities would no longer receive federal funding. The controversy arises, in part, from the fact that scientists prefer working with cells from aborted fetuses and from embryos that are a few days old, which consist of just a few cells. (Fertility clinics have countless numbers of these embryos, which they eventually discard, because many "test-tube" fertilizations are created for every patient who hopes to become pregnant.) Embryonic stem cells are especially useful because they can differentiate into any type of cell, from neurons to kidney cells, whereas those from adults are more limited and are also harder to keep alive. Currently, Canadian researchers must get their embryonic cells only from sources that are approved by the Assisted Human Reproduction Agency of Canada, the body that regulates stem-cell research in Canada.

Scientists and patient-advocacy groups feel that this research must continue and expand because transplanted stem cells may eventually help people recover from damage or disease in the brain and spinal cord, as well as other parts of the body. In the meantime, researchers are making progress in prodding stem cells taken from adult organs, such as bone marrow and skin, to transform themselves into brain cells (e.g., Brazelton et al., 2000; Toma et al., 2001). One team has even grown living cells from stem cells taken from the brains of human cadavers (Palmer et al., 2001). It is still unclear, however, whether such cells will be usable for therapeutic purposes.

In an area of the brain associated with learning and memory, new cells develop from immature stem cells, and physical and mental stimulation promotes their production and survival. These mice, who have toys to play with, tunnels to explore, wheels to run on, and other mice to share their cage with, will grow more cells than will mice living alone in standard cages.

stem cells Immature cells that renew themselves and have the potential to develop into mature cells; given encouraging environments, stem cells from early embryos can develop into any cell type.

Each year brings more incredible findings about neurons, findings that only a short time ago would have seemed like science fiction. A long road lies ahead, and many daunting technical hurdles need to be overcome before these findings yield practical benefits. Eventually, however, new treatments for medical and psychological disorders may be among the most stunning contributions of this line of basic biological research.

How Neurons Communicate

Neurons do not directly touch each other, end to end. Instead, they are separated by a tiny space called the *synaptic cleft*, where the axon terminal of one neuron nearly touches a dendrite or the cell body of another. The entire site—the axon terminal, the cleft, and the covering membrane of the receiving dendrite or cell body—is called a **synapse**. Because a neuron's axon may have hundreds or even thousands of terminals, a single neuron may have synaptic connections with a great many others. As a result, the number of communication links in the nervous system runs into the trillions or perhaps even the quadrillions.

When we are born, most of these synapses have not yet formed, but during infancy, new synapses proliferate at a great rate (see Figure 4.6). Axons and dendrites continue to grow, and tiny projections on dendrites, called *spines*, increase in size and in number, producing more complex connections among the brain's nerve cells. Just as new learning and stimulating environments promote the production of new neurons, they also produce the greatest increases in synaptic complexity (Diamond, 1993; Greenough & Anderson, 1991; Greenough & Black, 1992; Rosenzweig, 1984). As the brain integrates and consolidates

synapse The site where transmission of a nerve impulse from one nerve cell to another occurs; it includes the axon terminal, the synaptic cleft, and receptor sites in the membrane of the receiving cell.

action potential A brief change in electrical voltage that occurs when a neuron is stimulated; it serves to produce an electrical impulse.

early experience, unnecessary synapses are pruned away, leaving behind a more efficient neural network (Bruer, 1999).

Some psychologists and popular writers have interpreted these facts to mean that infants need maximum stimulation and crucial experiences in order to develop an optimum number of synapses. But media accounts of research on early brain development have tended to exaggerate and oversimplify the findings, fostering alarm and worry among parents (Thompson & Nelson, 2001). Of course, it's good for parents to nurture and stimulate their babies, but you don't have to read Shakespeare to your child all day and play chess with her all night! What happens after early childhood is important, too. In fact, the process of synapse formation and pruning in different parts of the brain continues all through childhood and again in adolescence, and synapses keep developing even into the later years in response to information, challenges, and changes in the environment (Greenough, Cohen, & Juraska, 1999; Spear, 2000).

This remarkable *plasticity* (flexibility) may help explain why people with brain damage sometimes experience amazing recoveries—why individuals who cannot recall simple words after a stroke may be speaking normally within a matter of months, and why patients who cannot move an arm after a head injury may regain full use of it after physical therapy (Liepert et al., 2000). Their brains have rewired themselves to adapt to the damage! Generally speaking, this rewiring is more easily achieved when we are young. Researchers at the University of Lethbridge have discovered that the optimal time for recovery from injury to the frontal portions of the brain is between one and two years of age. However, the worst time is just before birth and perhaps the first month after birth (Kolb, Gibb, & Gorny, 2000).

Neurons speak to one another, or in some cases to muscles or glands, in an electrical and chemical language. When a nerve cell is stimulated, a brief change in electrical voltage, called an **action potential**, occurs. (The details of this process are beyond the scope of this book.) The action potential produces an electrical current, or impulse. If an axon is unmyelinated, the action potential at each point in the axon gives rise to a new action potential at the next point; thus, the impulse travels down the axon somewhat as fire travels along the fuse of a firecracker. But in myelinated axons, the process is a little different. For

| At birth | 3 months | 6 months | 15 months |

FIGURE 4.6 Getting Connected

Neurons in a newborn's brain are widely spaced, but they immediately begin to form connections. These drawings show the marked increase in the size and number of neurons from birth to age 15 months.

certain reasons having to do with the physics of the process, conduction of a neural impulse beneath the sheath is impossible. Instead, the action potential "hops" from one node to the next. (More precisely, the action potential regenerates at each node.) This arrangement allows the impulse to travel faster than it could if the action potential had to be regenerated at every point along the axon. Nerve impulses travel more slowly in babies than in older children and adults because when babies are born, the myelin sheaths on their axons are not yet fully developed.

When a neural impulse reaches the axon terminal's buttonlike tip, it must get its message across the synaptic cleft to another cell. At this point, *synaptic vesicles*, tiny sacs in the tip of the axon terminal, open and release a few thousand molecules of a chemical substance called a **neurotransmitter**. Like sailors carrying a message from one island to another, these molecules then disperse across the synaptic cleft (see Figure 4.7). When they reach the other side, the neurotransmitter molecules bind briefly with *receptor sites*, special molecules in the membrane of the receiving neuron, fitting these sites much as a key fits a lock. Changes occur in the receiving neuron's membrane, and the ultimate effect is either *excitatory* (a voltage shift in a positive direction) or *inhibitory* (a voltage shift in a negative direction), depending on which receptor sites have been activated. If the effect is excitatory, the probability that the receiving neuron will fire increases; if it is inhibitory, the probability decreases. Inhibition in the nervous system is extremely important. Without it, we could not sleep or coordinate our movements. Excitation of the nervous system would be overwhelming, producing convulsions.

What any given neuron does at any given moment depends on the net effect of all the messages being received from other neurons. Only when the cell's voltage reaches a certain threshold will it fire. Thousands of messages, both excitatory and inhibitory, may be coming into the cell. Essentially, the neuron must average them. The message that reaches a final destination depends on the rate at which individual neurons are firing, how many are firing, what types of neurons are firing, and where the neurons are located. It does not depend on how strongly the neurons are firing, however, because a neuron always either fires or it doesn't. Like the turning on of a light switch, the firing of a neuron is an *all-or-none* event.

Chemical Messengers in the Nervous System

The nervous system "house" would remain forever dark and lifeless without chemical couriers such as the neurotransmitters. Let's look more closely now at these substances, and at two other types of chemical messengers: endorphins and hormones.

Neurotransmitters: Versatile Couriers As we have seen, neurotransmitters make it possible for one neuron to excite or inhibit another. Neurotransmitters exist not only in the brain, but also in the spinal cord, the peripheral nerves, and

neurotransmitter A chemical substance that is released by a transmitting neuron at the synapse and that alters the activity of a receiving neuron.

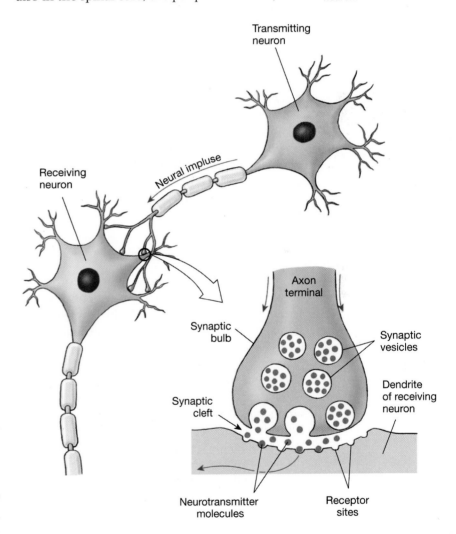

FIGURE 4.7 Neurotransmitter Crossing a Synapse
Neurotransmitter molecules are released into the synaptic cleft between two neurons from vesicles (chambers) in the transmitting neuron's axon terminal. The molecules then bind to receptor sites on the receiving neuron. As a result, the electrical state of the receiving neuron changes and the neuron becomes either more or less likely to fire an impulse, depending on the type of transmitter substance.

certain glands. Through their effects on specific nerve circuits, these substances can affect mood, memory, and well-being. The nature of the effect depends on the type of neurotransmitter, its location, and its level. Hundreds of substances are known or suspected to be neurotransmitters, and the number keeps growing. Here are a few of the better-understood neurotransmitters and some of their known or suspected effects:

- *Serotonin* affects neurons involved in sleep, appetite, sensory perception, temperature regulation, pain suppression, and mood.

- *Dopamine* affects neurons involved in voluntary movement, learning, memory, emotion, and, possibly, response to novelty.

- *Acetylcholine* affects neurons involved in muscle action, cognitive functioning, memory, and emotion.

- *Norepinephrine* affects neurons involved in increased heart rate and the slowing of intestinal activity during stress, and neurons involved in learning, memory, dreaming, waking from sleep, and emotion.

- *GABA (gamma-aminobutyric acid)* functions as the major inhibitory neurotransmitter in the brain.

- *Glutamate* functions as the major excitatory neurotransmitter in the brain.

Harmful effects can occur when neurotransmitter levels are too high or too low. Low levels of serotonin have been associated with severe depression and other mental disorders. Abnormal GABA levels have been implicated in sleep and eating disorders and in convulsive disorders, including epilepsy (Bekenstein & Lothman, 1993). People with Alzheimer's disease lose brain cells responsible for producing acetylcholine, and this deficit may help account for their devastating memory problems. A loss of dopamine is responsible for the tremors and rigidity of Parkinson's disease. In multiple sclerosis, immune cells overproduce glutamate, which damages or kills the glial cells that normally make myelin (Werner, Pitt, & Raine, 2001).

We want to warn you, however, that pinning down the relationship between neurotransmitter abnormalities and behavioural abnormalities is extremely difficult. Each neurotransmitter plays multiple roles, and the functions of different substances often overlap. Further, it is always possible that something about a disorder leads to abnormal neurotransmitter levels, instead of the other

endorphins [en-DOR-fins] Chemical substances in the nervous system that are similar in structure and action to opiates; they are involved in pain reduction, pleasure, and memory, and are known technically as *endogenous opioid peptides.*

way around. Although drugs that boost or decrease levels of particular neurotransmitters are sometimes effective in treating disorders, that does not necessarily mean that abnormal neurotransmitter levels are *causing* the disorders. After all, aspirin can relieve a headache, but headaches are not caused by a lack of aspirin!

Many of us regularly ingest things that affect our own neurotransmitters. For example, most recreational drugs produce their effects by blocking or enhancing the actions of neurotransmitters. So do some herbal remedies. St. John's wort, which many people take for depression, prevents the cells that release serotonin from reabsorbing excess molecules that have remained in the synaptic gap; as a result, serotonin levels rise. Many people do not realize that such remedies, because they affect the nervous system's biochemistry, can interact with other medications and can be harmful in high doses. Even ordinary foods can influence the availability of neurotransmitters in the brain, as we discuss in "Taking Psychology With You."

Endorphins: The Brain's Natural Opiates Another intriguing group of chemical messengers is known collectively as *endogenous opioid peptides,* or more popularly as **endorphins**. Endorphins have effects similar to those of opiate drugs; that is, they reduce pain and promote pleasure. They are also thought to play a role in appetite, sexual activity, blood pressure, mood, learning, and memory. Some endorphins function as neurotransmitters, but most act primarily by altering the effects of

Muhammad Ali and Michael J. Fox both have Parkinson's disease, which involves a loss of dopamine-producing cells. They have used their fame to draw public attention to the disorder.

neurotransmitters—for example, by limiting or prolonging those effects.

Endorphins were identified in the early 1970s. Candace Pert and Solomon Snyder (1973) were doing research on morphine, a pain-relieving and mood-elevating opiate derived from heroin, which is made from poppies. They found that morphine works by binding to receptor sites in the brain. This seemed odd. As Snyder later recalled, "We doubted that animals had evolved opiate receptors just to deal with certain properties of the poppy plant" (quoted in Radetsky, 1991). Pert and Snyder reasoned that if opiate receptors exist, then the body must produce its own internally generated, or *endogenous*, morphine-like substances, which they named "endorphins." Soon they and other researchers confirmed this hypothesis.

Endorphin levels seem to shoot up when an animal or a person is afraid or under stress. This is no accident; by making pain bearable in such situations, endorphins give a species an evolutionary advantage. When an organism is threatened, it needs to do something fast. Pain, however, can interfere with action: A mouse that pauses to lick a wounded paw may become a cat's dinner; a soldier who is overcome by an injury may never get off the battlefield. But, of course, the body's built-in system of counteracting pain is only partly successful, especially when painful stimulation is prolonged.

Hormones: Long-Distance Messengers **Hormones**, which make up the third class of chemical messengers, are produced primarily in **endocrine glands**. They are released directly into the bloodstream, which carries them to organs and cells that may be far from their point of origin. Hormones have dozens of jobs, from promoting bodily growth to aiding digestion to regulating metabolism.

"PSST—ENDORPHINS. AND THEY'RE PERFECTLY LEGAL."

Neurotransmitters and hormones are not always chemically distinct; the two classifications are like clubs that admit some of the same members. A particular chemical, such as norepinephrine, may belong to more than one classification, depending on where it is located and what function it is performing. Nature has been efficient, giving some substances more than one task to perform.

The following hormones, among others, are of particular interest to psychologists:

1   **Melatonin**, which is secreted by the *pineal gland*, deep within the brain, helps to regulate daily biological rhythms and promotes sleep, as we will discuss further in Chapter 5.

2   **Adrenal hormones**, which are produced by the *adrenal glands* (organs that are perched right above the kidneys), are involved in emotion and stress (see Chapter 13). These hormones also rise in response to nonemotional conditions, such as heat, cold, pain, injury, burns, and physical exercise, and in response to some drugs, such as caffeine and nicotine. The outer part of each adrenal gland produces *cortisol*, which increases blood-sugar levels and boosts energy. The inner part produces *epinephrine* (popularly known as adrenaline) and *norepinephrine*. When adrenal hormones are released in your body, activated by the sympathetic nervous system, they increase your arousal level and prepare you for action.

Adrenal hormones also enhance memory. If you give people a drug that prevents their adrenal glands from producing these hormones, they will remember less about emotional stories than a control group will (Cahill et al., 1994). Conversely, if you give epinephrine to animals right after learning, their memories will improve (McGaugh, 1990). The link between emotional arousal and memory makes evolutionary sense: Arousal tells the brain that an event or piece of information is important enough to encode and store for future use. Very high doses of adrenal hormones, however, impair memory for everyday tasks; a moderate level is optimal. For ordinary learning, therefore—the kind you need to do in school—you should aim for an arousal level somewhere between "hyper" and "laid back."

3   **Sex hormones**, which are secreted by tissue in the *gonads* (testes in men, ovaries in women) and also by the adrenal glands, include three main types, all occurring in both sexes but in differing amounts and proportions in males and females after the onset of puberty. *Androgens* (the most

melatonin [mel-a-TOE-nin] A hormone, secreted by the pineal gland, that is involved in the regulation of daily biological rhythms.

adrenal hormones Hormones that are produced by the adrenal glands and that are involved in emotion and stress.

hormones Chemical substances, secreted by organs called glands, that affect the functioning of other organs.

endocrine glands Internal organs that produce hormones and release them into the bloodstream.

sex hormones Hormones that regulate the development and functioning of reproductive organs and that stimulate the development of male and female sexual characteristics; they include androgens, estrogens, and progesterone.

important of which is *testosterone*) are masculinizing hormones produced mainly in the testes but also in the ovaries and the adrenal glands. Androgens set in motion the physical changes males experience at puberty—for example, facial and chest hair and a deepened voice—and cause pubic and underarm hair to develop in both sexes. Testosterone also influences sexual arousal in both sexes. *Estrogens* are feminizing hormones that bring on physical changes in females at puberty, such as breast development and the onset of menstruation, and that influence the course of the menstrual cycle. *Progesterone* contributes to the growth and maintenance of the uterine lining in preparation for a fertilized egg, among other functions. Estrogens and progesterone are produced mainly

in the ovaries but are also produced in the testes and the adrenal glands.

Researchers at McGill University and elsewhere are now studying the possible involvement of sex hormones in behaviour not directly related to sex and reproduction. For example, many researchers believe that the body's natural estrogen may contribute to improved learning and memory by promoting the formation of synapses in certain areas of the brain (Maki & Resnick, 2000; Sherwin, 1998a; Wickelgren, 1997). But the most common belief about the nonsexual effects of sex hormones—that fluctuating levels of estrogen and progesterone make most women "emotional" before menstruation—has not been borne out by research, as we will see in Chapter 5.

Quick Quiz

Get your glutamate going by taking this quiz.

A. Which word in parentheses best fits each of the following definitions?
   1. Basic building blocks of the nervous system (*nerves/neurons*)
   2. Cell parts that receive nerve impulses (*axons/dendrites*)
   3. Site of communication between neurons (*synapse/myelin sheath*)
   4. Opiate-like substance in the brain (*dopamine/endorphin*)
   5. Chemicals that make it possible for neurons to communicate (*neurotransmitters/hormones*)
   6. Hormone closely associated with emotional excitement (*epinephrine/estrogen*)

B. *True or false?*: To remember the material in this chapter well, you should be as relaxed as possible while studying.

C. Imagine that you are depressed, and you hear about a medication for depression that affects the levels of several neurotransmitters thought to be involved in the disorder. Based on what you have learned, what questions would you want to ask before deciding whether to try the treatment?

Answers:

A. 1. neurons 2. dendrites 3. synapse 4. endorphin 5. neurotransmitters 6. epinephrine
B. false (Can you say why?)
C. You might want to ask, among other things, about side effects (each neurotransmitter has several functions, all of which might be affected by the treatment); about evidence that the treatment works; and about whether there is any reason to believe that your own neurotransmitter levels are abnormal or whether there may be other reasons for your depression.

WHAT'S AHEAD

- Why are patterns of electrical activity in the brain called "brainwaves"?
- What scanning techniques reveal changes in brain activity while people listen to music or solve math problems?

MAPPING THE BRAIN

We come now to the main room of the nervous system "house": the brain. A disembodied brain stored in a formaldehyde-filled container is unexciting—a putty-coloured, wrinkled glob of tissue that looks a little like an oversized walnut. It takes an act of imagination to envision this modest-looking organ writing *Hamlet*, discovering radium, or inventing the paper clip.

In a living person, of course, the brain is encased in a thick protective vault of bone. How, then, can scientists study it? One approach is to study patients who have had a part of the brain damaged or removed because of disease or injury. Another involves damaging or removing sections of brain in animals, then observing the effects.

The brain can also be probed with devices called *electrodes*. Some electrodes are coin-shaped and are simply pasted or taped onto the scalp. They detect the electrical activity of millions of neurons in particular regions of the brain and are widely used in research and medical diagnosis. The electrodes are connected by wires to a machine that translates the electrical energy from the brain into wavy lines on a moving piece of paper or a screen. That is why electrical patterns in the brain are known as "brainwaves." Different wave patterns are associated with sleep, relaxation, and mental concentration (see Chapter 5).

A brainwave recording is called an **electroencephalogram (EEG)**. A standard EEG is useful but not very precise because it reflects the activities of many cells at once. "Listening" to the brain with an EEG machine is like standing outside a sports stadium: You know when something is happening, but you can't be sure what it is or who is doing it. Fortunately, computer technology can be combined with EEG technology to get a clearer picture of brain activity patterns associated with specific events and mental processes; the computer suppresses all the background "noise," leaving only the pattern of electrical responses to the event being studied.

For even more precise information, researchers use *needle electrodes*, very thin wires or hollow glass tubes that can be inserted into the brain, either directly in an exposed brain or through tiny holes in the skull. Only the skull and the membranes covering the brain need to be anaesthetized; the brain itself, which processes all sensation and feeling, paradoxically feels nothing when touched. Therefore, a human patient or an animal can be awake and not feel pain during the procedure. Needle electrodes can be used both to record electrical activity from the brain and to stimulate the brain with weak electrical currents. Stimulating a given area often results in a specific sensation or movement. Microelectrodes are so fine that they can be inserted into single cells.

Since the mid-1970s, even more amazing doors to the brain have opened. The **PET (positron-emission tomography) scan** goes beyond anatomy to record biochemical changes in the brain as they are happening. One type of PET scan takes advantage of the fact that nerve cells convert glucose, the body's main fuel, into energy. A researcher can inject a patient with a glucose-like substance that contains a harmless radioactive element. This substance accumulates in brain areas that are particularly active and are consuming glucose rapidly. The substance emits radiation, which in turn is detected by a scanning device, and the result is a computer-processed picture of biochemical activity on a display screen, with different colours indicating different activity levels. Other kinds of PET scans measure blood flow or oxygen consumption, which also reflect brain activity.

PET scans, which were originally designed to diagnose abnormalities, have produced evidence that certain brain areas in people with emotional disorders are either unusually quiet or unusually active. But PET technology can also show which parts of the brain are active during ordinary activities and emotions. It lets researchers see which areas are busiest when a person hears a song, recalls a sad memory, works on a math problem, shifts attention from one task to another, or sees his or her sweetheart enter the room. The PET scans in Figure 4.8 show what an average healthy brain looks like when a person is doing different tasks.

Another technique, **MRI (magnetic resonance imaging)**, allows the exploration of "inner space" without injecting chemicals. Powerful

Electrodes are used to produce an overall picture of electrical activity in different areas of the brain.

electroencephalogram (EEG) A recording of neural activity detected by electrodes.

MRI (magnetic resonance imaging) A method for studying body and brain tissue, using magnetic fields and special radio receivers.

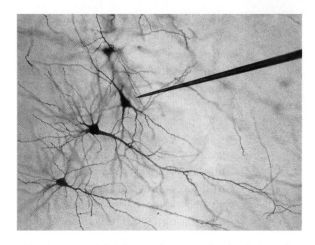

This microelectrode is being used to record the electrical impulses generated by a single cell in the brain of a monkey.

PET (positron-emission tomography) scan A method for analyzing biochemical activity in the brain, using injections of a glucose-like substance containing a radioactive element.

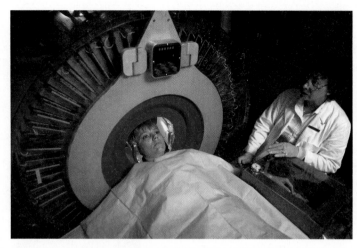

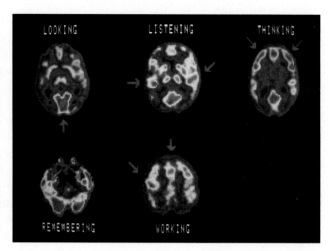

FIGURE 4.8 PET Scans of Metabolic Activity in the Brain

The PET scanner on the left will detect biochemical activity in specific brain areas. In the scans on the right, arrows and the colour red indicate areas of highest activity and violet indicates areas of lowest activity as a person does different things.

magnetic fields and radio frequencies are used to produce vibrations in the nuclei of atoms making up body organs, and the vibrations are then picked up as signals by special receivers. A computer analyzes the signals, taking into account their strength and duration, and converts them into a high-contrast picture of the organ (see Figure 4.9). An ultrafast version of MRI, called *functional MRI,* can capture brain changes many times a second as a person performs a task, such as reading a sentence or solving a puzzle.

Still other scanning methods are becoming available with each passing year. Some even produce a moving picture that shows ongoing changes in the brain as a person writes, solves puzzles, meditates, prays, sings, and so on. Neuroscientists can then identify any heightened activity in specific brain areas that might be associated with these activities. A word of caution, though: Brain scans alone do not tell us precisely what is happening inside a person's head, either mentally or physiologically. They tell us *where* things happen, but not *how* they happen—for example, how different brain circuits connect up to produce behaviour. Enthusiasm for new technology has produced a mountain of findings, but it has also resulted in some unwarranted conclusions about "brain centres" or "critical

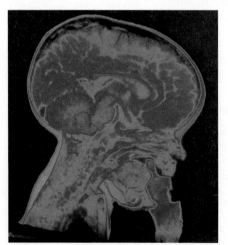

FIGURE 4.9 MRI of a Child's Brain

This MRI shows a child's brain—and the bottle he was drinking from while the image was obtained.

circuits" for this or that behaviour. One scientist (cited in Wheeler, 1998) drew this analogy: A researcher scans the brains of gum-chewing volunteers, finds out which parts of their brains are active, and concludes that he or she has found the brain's "gum-chewing centre"!

Thinking Critically About Brain Scans

Descriptive studies using brain scans, then, are just a first step in understanding brain processes. Nonetheless, they are an exciting first step. We will be reporting many findings from PET scan and MRI research throughout this book. The brain can no longer hide from researchers behind the fortress of the skull. It is now possible to get a clear visual image of our most enigmatic organ without so much as lifting a scalpel.

WHAT'S AHEAD

- Which brain part acts as a "traffic officer" for incoming sensations?
- Which brain part is the "gateway to memory"— and what cognitive catastrophe occurs when it is damaged?
- Why is it a good thing that the outer covering of the human brain is so wrinkled?
- How did a bizarre nineteenth-century accident illuminate the role of the frontal lobes?

A TOUR THROUGH THE BRAIN

Most modern brain theories assume that different brain parts perform different (though overlapping) tasks. This concept, known as **localization of function**, goes back at least to Joseph Gall (1758–1828), the Austrian anatomist who thought that personality traits were reflected in the development of specific areas of the brain (see Chapter 1). Gall's theory of *phrenology* was completely wrongheaded (so to speak), but his general notion of specialization in the brain had merit.

To learn about what the various brain structures do, let's take an imaginary stroll through the brain. Pretend, now, that you have shrunk to a microscopic size and that you are wending your way through the "soul's frail dwelling house," starting at the lower part, just above the spine. Figure 4.10 shows the major structures we will encounter along the tour; you may want to refer to it as we proceed. Keep in mind, though, that in any activity—feeling an emotion, having a thought, performing a task—many different structures are involved. Our description, therefore, is a simplification.

The Brain Stem

We begin at the base of the skull with the **brain stem**, which looks like a stalk rising out of the spinal cord. Pathways to and from upper areas of the brain pass through its two main structures: the medulla and the pons. The **pons** is involved in (among other things) sleeping, waking, and dreaming. The **medulla** is responsible for bodily functions that do not have to be consciously willed, such as breathing and heart rate. Hanging has long been used as a method of execution because when it breaks the neck, nervous pathways from the medulla are severed, stopping respiration.

Extending upward from the core of the brain stem is the **reticular activating system (RAS)**. This dense network of neurons, which extends above the brain stem into the centre of the brain and has connections with higher areas, screens incoming information and arouses the higher centres when something happens that demands their attention. Without the RAS, we could not be alert or perhaps even conscious.

The Cerebellum

Standing atop the brain stem and looking toward the back part of the brain, we see a structure about the size of a small fist. It is the **cerebellum**, or

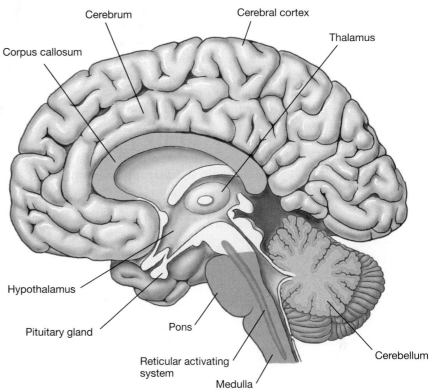

FIGURE 4.10 The Human Brain

This cross section depicts the brain as if it were split in half. The view is of the inside surface of the right half, and shows the structures described in the text.

"lesser brain," which contributes to a sense of balance and coordinates the muscles so that movement is smooth and precise. If your cerebellum were damaged, you would probably become exceedingly clumsy and uncoordinated. You might have trouble using a pencil, threading a needle, or even walking. In addition, this structure is involved in remembering certain simple skills and acquired reflexes (Daum & Schugens, 1996; Krupa, Thompson, & Thompson, 1993). And evidence has accumulated that the cerebellum, which was once considered just a motor centre, is not as

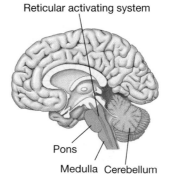

localization of function Specialization of particular brain areas for particular functions.

brain stem The part of the brain at the top of the spinal cord, consisting of the medulla and the pons.

pons A structure in the brain stem involved in, among other things, sleeping, waking, and dreaming.

medulla [muh-DUL-uh] A structure in the brain stem responsible for certain automatic functions, such as breathing and heart rate.

reticular activating system (RAS) A dense network of neurons found in the core of the brain stem; it arouses the cortex and screens incoming information.

cerebellum A brain structure that regulates movement and balance, and that is involved in some kinds of higher cognitive tasks.

4.5

"lesser" as its name implies: It appears to play a part in such complex cognitive tasks as analyzing sensory information, solving problems, and understanding words (Fiez, 1996; Gao et al., 1996; Müller, Courchesne, & Allen, 1998). In fact, Mark Rapoport at the University of Toronto has concluded from a review of the literature that, because of the role the cerebellum plays in cognitive tasks, cerebellar abnormalities are associated with the thought-related symptoms in disorders such as schizophrenia and autism (Rapoport, 2001). (We will discuss schizophrenia in Chapter 11.)

The Thalamus

Deep in the brain's interior, we can see the **thalamus**, the busy traffic officer of the brain. As sensory messages come into the brain, the thalamus directs them to higher centres. For example, the sight of a sunset sends signals that the thalamus directs to a vision area, and the sound of an oboe sends signals that the thalamus sends on to an auditory area. The only sense that completely bypasses the thalamus is the sense of smell, which has its own private switching station, the *olfactory bulb*. The olfactory bulb lies near areas involved in emotion. Perhaps that is why particular odours—the smell of fresh laundry, gardenias, a steak sizzling on the grill—often rekindle memories of important personal experiences.

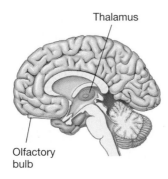

Thalamus

Olfactory bulb

The Hypothalamus and the Pituitary Gland

Beneath the thalamus sits a structure called the **hypothalamus** (*hypo* means "under"). It is involved in drives associated with the survival of both the individual and the species—hunger, thirst, emotion, sex, and reproduction. It regulates body temperature by triggering sweating or shivering, and it controls the complex operations of the autonomic nervous system. It also contains the biological clock that controls the body's daily rhythms (see Chapter 5).

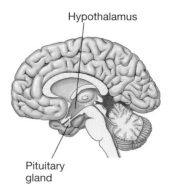

Hypothalamus

Pituitary gland

Hanging down from the hypothalamus, connected to it by a short stalk, is a cherry-sized endocrine gland called the **pituitary gland**. The pituitary is often called the body's "master gland" because the hormones it secretes affect many other endocrine glands. The master, however, is really only a supervisor. The true boss is the hypothalamus, which sends chemicals to the pituitary, telling it when to "talk" to the other endocrine glands. The pituitary, in turn, sends hormonal messages out to these glands.

Many years ago, in a study that became famous, James Olds and Peter Milner, researchers at McGill University, reported finding pleasure centres in the hypothalamus (Olds, 1975; Olds & Milner, 1954). Olds and Milner trained rats to press a lever in order to get a buzz of electricity delivered through tiny electrodes. Some rats would press the bar thousands of times an hour, for 15 or 20 hours at a time, until they collapsed from exhaustion. When they revived, they went right back to the bar. When forced to make a choice, the pleasure-loving little rodents opted for electrical stimulation over such temptations as water, food, and even an attractive rat of the other sex making provocative gestures (provocative to another rat, anyway).

It certainly seemed as though the brain had pleasure centres. However, controversy exists about just how to interpret the rats' responses. Were Olds and Milner's rats really feeling pleasure, or merely some kind of craving or compulsion? And before you go around trying to find your own brain's pleasure centre, we must inform you that when humans' brains are stimulated in the same way, humans don't behave like those little rats. Moreover, today researchers believe that brain stimulation activates complex neural pathways rather than discrete "centres."

The hypothalamus, along with the two structures we will discuss next, has often been considered part of a loosely interconnected set of

pituitary gland [pi-TOO-i-terry] A small endocrine gland at the base of the brain that releases many hormones and regulates other endocrine glands.

thalamus A brain structure that relays sensory messages to the cerebral cortex.

hypothalamus A brain structure involved in emotions and drives vital to survival, such as hunger, thirst, emotion, sex, and reproduction; it regulates the autonomic nervous system.

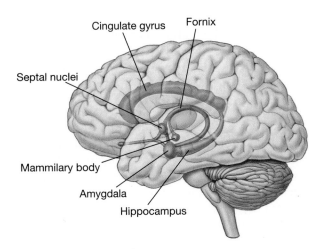

Cingulate gyrus   Fornix

Septal nuclei

Mammilary body

Amygdala

Hippocampus

FIGURE 4.11 The Limbic System

Structures of the limbic system play an important role in memory and emotion. The text describes two of these structures, the amygdala and the hippocampus. The hypothalamus is also often included as part of the limbic system.

structures called the **limbic system**, shown in Figure 4.11. (*Limbic* comes from the Latin for "border": These structures form a sort of border between the higher and lower parts of the brain.) Some anatomists also include parts of the thalamus in this system. Structures in this region are heavily involved in emotions, such as rage and fear, that we share with other animals (MacLean, 1993). The usefulness of speaking of the limbic system as an integrated set of structures is now in dispute, because these structures also have other functions, and because parts of the brain outside of the limbic system are also involved in emotion. However, the term *limbic system* is still in wide use among researchers, so we thought you should know it.

The Amygdala

The **amygdala** (from the ancient Greek word for "almond") appears to be responsible for evaluating sensory information, quickly determining its emotional importance, and contributing to the initial decision to approach or withdraw from a person or situation (see Chapter 13). For example, it instantly assesses danger or threat. The amygdala also plays an important role in mediating anxiety and depression; PET scans find that depressed and anxious patients show increased neural activity in this limbic structure (Davidson et al., 1999; Drevets, 2000).

The Hippocampus

Another important area traditionally classified as limbic is the **hippocampus**, which has a shape

that must have reminded someone of a sea horse, for that is what its name means. This structure compares sensory information with what the brain has learned to expect about the world. When expectations are met, it tells the reticular activating system to "cool it." There's no need for neural alarm bells to go off every time a car goes by, a bird chirps, or you feel your saliva trickling down the back of your throat!

The hippocampus has also been called the "gateway to memory." It enables us to form spatial memories so that we can accurately navigate through our environment (Maguire et al., 2000). And, along with adjacent brain areas, it enables us to form new memories about facts and events—the kinds of information you need to identify a flower, tell a story, or recall a vacation trip. This information is then stored in the cerebral cortex, which we will be discussing shortly. For example, when you recall meeting someone yesterday, various aspects of the memory—information about the person's greeting, tone of voice, appearance, and location—are probably stored in different locations in the cortex (Damasio et al., 1996; Squire, 1987). But without the hippocampus, the information would never get to these destinations (Mishkin et al., 1997; Squire & Zola-Morgan, 1991).

We know about the "gateway" function of the hippocampus in part from research on brain-damaged patients with severe memory problems. The case of one man from Montreal, known to researchers as H. M., is probably the most intensely studied in the annals of medicine (Corkin, 1984; Corkin et al., 1997; Milner, 1970; Ogden & Corkin, 1991). In 1953, when H. M. was 27, surgeons removed most of his hippocampus, along with part of his amygdala. The operation was a last-ditch effort to relieve H. M.'s severe and life-threatening epilepsy. People who have epilepsy, a neurological disorder that has many causes and takes many forms, often have seizures. Usually, the seizures are brief, mild, and controllable by drugs, but in H. M.'s case, they were unrelenting and uncontrollable.

The operation did achieve its goal: Afterward, the young man's seizures were milder and could be managed with medication. His memory, however, had been affected profoundly. Although H. M. continued to recall most events that had occurred before the operation, he could no longer remember new experiences for much longer than 15 minutes; they vanished like water down the drain. With sufficient practice, H. M. could acquire

limbic system A group of brain areas involved in emotional reactions and motivated behaviour.

amygdala [uh-MIG-dul-uh] A brain structure involved in the arousal and regulation of emotion and the initial emotional response to sensory information.

hippocampus A brain structure involved in the storage of new information in memory.

new physical or problem-solving skills, such as playing tennis or solving a puzzle, but he could not remember the training sessions in which he learned these skills. He would read the same magazine over and over without realizing it. He could not recall the day of the week, the year, or even his last meal. Most scientists attribute these deficits to an inability to form new memories for long-term storage.

Today, many years later, H. M., now elderly, will occasionally recall an unusually emotional event, such as the assassination of someone named Kennedy. He sometimes remembers that both his parents are dead, and he knows he has memory problems. But, according to Suzanne Corkin, who studied H. M. extensively, these "islands of remembering" are the exceptions in a vast sea of forgetfulness. This good-natured man still does not know the scientists who have studied him for decades. He thinks he is much younger than he is, and he can no longer recognize a photograph of his own face; he is stuck in a time warp from the past.

Scientists are starting to understand just what happens in the hippocampus and in nearby structures during the formation of a long-term memory. For example, some synaptic pathways become more easily excitable and therefore more receptive to further impulses (Bliss & Collingridge, 1993). Release of the neurotransmitter glutamate may play a critical role in this process (Antonova et al., 2001). But these changes and others take time, which may explain why memories remain vulnerable to disruption for a while after they are stored. Just as concrete takes time to set, memories require a period of *consolidation*, or stabilization, before they solidify.

The Cerebrum

At this point in our tour, the largest part of the brain still looms above us. It is the cauliflower-like **cerebrum**, where the higher forms of thinking take place. The complexity of the human brain's circuitry far exceeds that of any computer in existence, and much of its most complicated wiring is packed into this structure. Compared with many other creatures, we humans may be ungainly, feeble, and thin-skinned, but our well-developed cerebrum enables us to overcome these limitations and creatively control our environment (and, some would say, to mess it up).

The cerebrum is divided into two separate halves, or **cerebral hemispheres**, connected by a large band of fibres called the **corpus callosum**.

In general, the right hemisphere is in charge of the left side of the body and the left hemisphere is in charge of the right side of the body. As we will see shortly, the two hemispheres also have somewhat different tasks and talents, a phenomenon known as **lateralization**.

The Cerebral Cortex Working our way right up through the top of the brain, we find that the cerebrum is covered by several thin layers of densely packed cells known collectively as the **cerebral cortex**. Cell bodies in the cortex, as in many other parts of the brain, produce a grayish tissue; hence the term *gray matter*. In other parts of the brain (and in the rest of the nervous system), long, myelin-covered axons prevail, providing the brain's *white matter*. Although the cortex is only about 3 millimetres (1/8 inch) thick, it contains almost three-fourths of all the cells in the human brain. The cortex has many crevasses and wrinkles, which enable it to contain its billions of neurons without requiring us to have the heads of giants—heads that would be too big to permit us to be born. In other mammals, which have fewer neurons, the cortex is less crumpled; in rats, it is quite smooth.

Lobes of the Cortex In each cerebral hemisphere, deep fissures divide the cortex into four distinct regions, or lobes (see Figure 4.12):

- The **occipital lobes** (from the Latin for "in back of the head") are at the lower back part of the brain. Among other things, they contain the *visual cortex*, where visual signals are processed. Damage to the visual cortex can cause impaired visual recognition or even blindness.

- The **parietal lobes** (from the Latin for "pertaining to walls") are at the top of the brain. They contain the *somatosensory cortex*, which receives information about pressure, pain, touch, and temperature from all over the body. The areas of the somatosensory cortex that receive signals from the hands and the face are disproportionately large because these body parts are particularly sensitive. Parts of the parietal lobes are also involved in attention and various mental operations.

- The **temporal lobes** (from the Latin for "pertaining to the temples") are at the sides of the brain, just above the ears, behind the temples. They are involved in memory, perception, and emotion, and they contain the *auditory cortex*, which processes sounds. An

lateralization Specialization of the two cerebral hemispheres for particular operations.

cerebral cortex A collection of several thin layers of cells covering the cerebrum; it is largely responsible for higher mental functions. *Cortex* is Latin for "bark" or "rind."

occipital [ahk-SIP-uh-tuhl] **lobes** Lobes at the lower back part of the brain's cerebral cortex; they contain areas that receive visual information.

parietal [puh-RYE-uh-tuhl] **lobes** Lobes at the top of the brain's cerebral cortex; they contain areas that receive information on pressure, pain, touch, and temperature.

cerebrum [suh-REE-brum] The largest brain structure, consisting of the upper part of the brain; it is in charge of most sensory, motor, and cognitive processes. From the Latin for "brain."

temporal lobes Lobes at the sides of the brain's cerebral cortex; they contain areas involved in hearing, memory, perception, emotion, and (in the left lobe, typically) language comprehension.

cerebral hemispheres The two halves of the cerebrum.

corpus callosum [CORE-pus ca-LOW-suhm] The bundle of nerve fibres connecting the two cerebral hemispheres.

area of the left temporal lobe known as *Wernicke's area* is involved in language comprehension.

- The **frontal lobes**, as their name indicates, are located toward the front of the brain, just under the skull in the area of the forehead. They contain the *motor cortex*, which issues orders to the 600 muscles of the body that produce voluntary movement. In the left frontal lobe, a region known as *Broca's area* handles speech production. During short-term memory tasks, areas in the frontal lobes are especially active (Goldman-Rakic, 1996). The frontal lobes are also involved in the ability to make plans, think creatively, and take initiative. Researchers at l' Université du Québec à Montréal, for example, have discovered that people whose frontal lobes have been injured have problems with strategic planning for such things as meal preparation (Fortin, Godbout, & Braun, 2003).

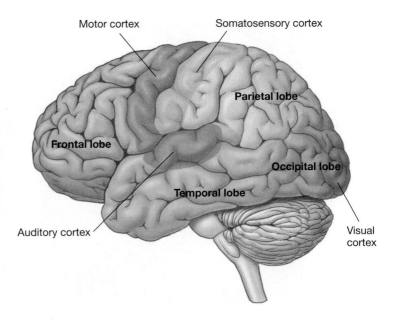

FIGURE 4.12 Lobes of the Cerebral Cortex
Deep fissures divide the cortex of each cerebral hemisphere into four regions.

Because of their different functions, the lobes of the cerebral cortex tend to respond differently when stimulated. If a surgeon applied electrical current to your somatosensory cortex in the parietal lobes, you would probably feel a tingling in your skin or a sense of being gently touched. If your visual cortex in the occipital lobes were electrically stimulated, you might report a flash of light or swirls of colour. But eerily, many areas of your cortex, when stimulated, would do nothing at all. These "silent" areas are sometimes called the *association cortex*, because they are involved in higher mental processes.

Psychologists are especially interested in the forwardmost part of the frontal lobes, the *prefrontal cortex*. This area barely exists in mice and rats and takes up only 3.5 percent of the cerebral cortex in cats and about 7 percent in dogs, but it accounts for fully 29 percent of the cortex in human beings.

Scientists have long known that the frontal lobes, and the prefrontal cortex in particular, must have something to do with personality. The first clue appeared in 1848, when a bizarre accident drove an inch-thick, 3 1/2-foot-long iron rod clear through the head of a young railroad worker named Phineas Gage. As you can see in Figure 4.13, the rod (which is still on display at Harvard University, along with Gage's skull) entered beneath his left eye and exited through the top of his head, destroying much of his prefrontal cortex (H. Damasio et al., 1994). Miraculously, Gage survived this trauma and

retained the ability to speak, think, and remember. But, according to accounts of the accident, his friends complained that he was "no longer Gage." In a sort of Jekyll-and-Hyde transformation, he had changed from a mild-mannered, friendly, efficient worker into a foul-mouthed, ill-tempered, undependable lout who could not hold a steady job or stick to a plan. His employers had to let him go, and he was reduced to exhibiting himself as a circus attraction.

Today, there is some controversy about the exact details of this sad incident. For example, no one is really sure what Gage was like before his accident; his doctors may have exaggerated the extent of his personality transformation (Macmillan, 2000). But many other cases of brain injury support the conclusion that most scientists draw from the Gage case: that parts of the frontal lobes are involved in social judgment, rational decision making, and the ability to set goals and to make and carry out plans (Klein & Kihlstrom, 1998). Like Gage, people with damage in these areas sometimes mismanage their finances, lose their jobs, and abandon their friends.

The frontal lobes also govern the ability to do a series of tasks in the proper sequence and to stop doing them at the proper time. The pioneering Soviet psychologist Alexander Luria (1980) studied many cases in which damage to the frontal lobes disrupted these abilities. One man observed by Luria kept trying to light a match after it was

frontal lobes Lobes at the front of the brain's cerebral cortex; they contain areas involved in short-term memory, higher-order thinking, initiative, social judgment, and (in the left lobe, typically) speech production.

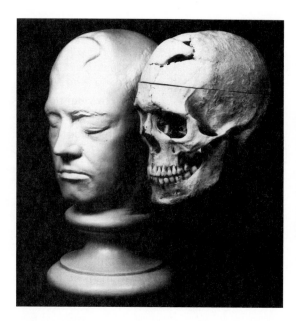
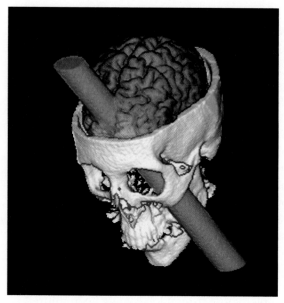

FIGURE 4.13 A Famous Skull

On the left is Phineas Gage's skull and a cast of his head. You can see where an iron rod penetrated his skull, altering his behaviour and personality dramatically. The exact location of the brain damage remained controversial for almost a century and a half, until Hanna and Antonio Damasio and their colleagues (1994) used measurements of Gage's skull and MRIs of normal brains to plot possible trajectories of the rod. The reconstruction on the right shows that the damage occurred in an area of the prefrontal cortex associated with emotional processing and rational decision making.

4.6

already lit. Another planed a piece of wood in the hospital carpentry shop until it was gone, and then went on to plane the workbench! Similarly, researchers at the University of British Columbia have shown that rats with lesions in their pre-frontal lobes will continue to press a bar long after the behaviour has stopped producing food (Thorpe et al., 2002).

Quick Quiz

It's time again to see how your own brain is working.

Match each description on the left with a term on the right.

1. Filters out irrelevant information
2. Known as the "gateway to memory"
3. Controls the autonomic nervous system; involved in drives associated with survival
4. Consists of two hemispheres
5. Wrinkled outer covering of the brain
6. Site of the motor cortex; associated with planning and taking initiative

a. reticular activating system
b. cerebrum
c. hippocampus
d. cerebral cortex
e. frontal lobes
f. hypothalamus

Answers:

1.a 2.c 3.f 4.b 5.d 6.e

WHAT'S AHEAD

- If the two cerebral hemispheres were out of touch, would they feel different emotions and think different thoughts?
- Why do researchers often refer to the left hemisphere as "dominant"?
- Should you sign up for a program that promises to perk up the right side of your brain?

THE TWO HEMISPHERES OF THE BRAIN

We have seen that the cerebrum is divided into two hemispheres that control opposite sides of the body. Although similar in structure, these hemispheres have somewhat separate talents, or areas of specialization.

Split Brains: A House Divided

In a normal brain, the two hemispheres communicate with each other across the corpus callosum, the bundle of fibres that connects them. Whatever happens in one side of the brain is instantly flashed to the other side. What would happen, though, if the two sides were cut off from each other?

In 1953, Ronald E. Myers and Roger W. Sperry took the first step toward answering this question by severing the corpus callosum in cats. Normally, each eye (in cats and in humans) transmits messages to both sides of the brain (see Figure 4.14). After this procedure, a cat's left eye sent information only to the left hemisphere and its right eye sent information only to the right hemisphere.

At first, the cats did not seem to be affected much by this drastic operation. But Myers and Sperry showed that something profound had happened. They trained the cats to perform tasks with one eye blindfolded. For example, a cat might have to push a panel with a square on it to get food but ignore a panel with a circle. Then the researchers switched the blindfold to the cat's other eye and tested the animal again. Now the cats behaved as if they had never learned the trick. Apparently, one side of the brain did not know what the other side was doing. It was as if the animals had two minds in one body. Later studies confirmed this result with other species, including monkeys (Sperry, 1964).

In all the animal studies, ordinary behaviour, such as eating and walking, remained normal.

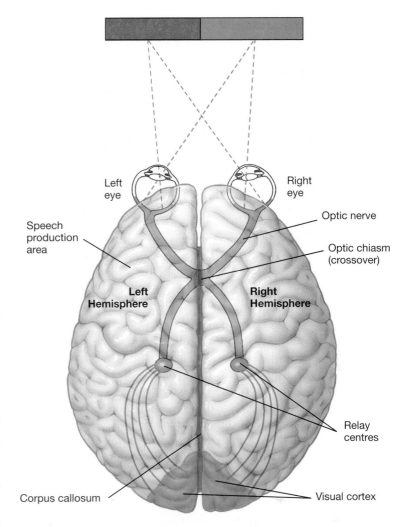

FIGURE 4.14 Visual Pathways

Each cerebral hemisphere receives information from the eyes about the opposite side of the visual field. Thus, if you stare directly at the corner of a room, everything to the left of the juncture is represented in your right hemisphere and vice versa. This is so because half of the axons in each optic nerve cross over (at the optic chiasm) to the opposite side of the brain. Normally, each hemisphere immediately shares its information with the other one, but in split-brain patients, severing the corpus callosum prevents such communication.

Encouraged by this finding, a team of surgeons decided in the early 1960s to try cutting the corpus callosum in patients with debilitating, uncontrollable epilepsy. In severe forms of this disease, disorganized electrical activity spreads from an injured area to other parts of the brain. The surgeons reasoned that cutting the connection between the two halves of the brain might stop the spread of electrical activity from one side to the other. The surgery was done, of course, for the sake of the patients, who were desperate, but as a bonus, scientists would be able to find out what each cerebral hemisphere can do when it is quite literally cut off from the other.

The results of this *split-brain surgery* generally proved successful. Seizures were reduced and sometimes disappeared completely. In their daily lives, split-brain patients did not seem much affected by the fact that the two sides of their brains were incommunicado. Their personalities and intelligence remained intact; they could walk, talk, and in general lead normal lives. Apparently, connections in the undivided deeper parts of the brain kept body movements and other functions normal. But in a series of ingenious studies, Sperry and his colleagues (and later other researchers) showed that perception and memory had been affected, just as they had been in earlier animal research. In 1981, Sperry won a Nobel Prize for his work.

It was already known that the two hemispheres are not mirror images of each other. In most people, language is largely handled by the left hemisphere; thus, a person who suffers brain damage because of a stroke—a blockage in or rupture of a blood vessel in the brain—is much more likely to have language problems if the damage is in the left side than if it is in the right. How would splitting the brain affect language and other abilities?

To understand this research, refer back again to Figure 4.14, which shows how nerves connect the eyes to the brain. (The split-brain patients, unlike Myers and Sperry's cats, did not have these nerves cut.) If you look straight ahead, everything in the left side of the scene before you—the "visual field"—goes to the right half of your brain, and everything in the right side of the scene goes to the left half of your brain. This is true for both eyes.

The procedure was to present information only to one or the other side of the split-brain patients' brains. In one early study (Levy, Trevarthen, & Sperry, 1972), the researchers took photographs of different faces, cut them in two, and pasted different halves together. The reconstructed photographs were then presented on slides. The person was told to stare at a dot on the middle of the screen, so that half the image fell to the left of this point and half to the right. Each image was flashed so quickly that the person had no time to move his or her eyes. When the patients were asked to say what they had seen, they named the person in the right part of the image (which would be the little boy in Figure 4.15). But when they were asked to point with their left hands to the face they had seen, they chose the person in the left side of the image (the moustached man in the figure). Further, they claimed they had noticed nothing unusual about

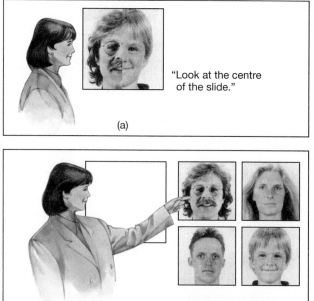

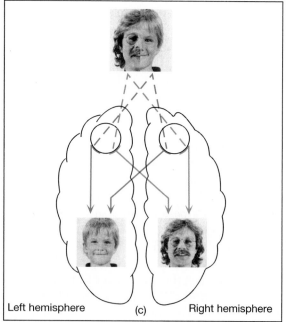

FIGURE 4.15 Divided Brain, Divided View

When split-brain patients were shown composite photographs (a) and were then asked to pick out the face they had seen from a series of intact photographs (b), they said they had seen the face on the right side of the composite—yet they pointed with their left hands to the face that had been on the left. Because the two cerebral hemispheres could not communicate, the verbal left hemisphere was aware of only the right half of the picture, and the relatively mute right hemisphere was aware of only the left half (c).

the original photographs! Each side of the brain saw a different half-image and automatically filled in the missing part. Neither side knew what the other side had seen.

Why did the patients name one side of the picture but point to the other? Speech centres are in the left hemisphere. When the person responded with speech, it was the left side of the brain doing the talking. When the person pointed with the left hand, which is controlled by the right side of the brain, the right hemisphere was giving its version of what the person had seen.

In another study, the researchers presented slides of ordinary objects and then suddenly flashed a slide of a nude woman. Both sides of the brain were amused, but because only the left side has speech, the two sides responded differently. When the picture was flashed to one woman's left hemisphere, she laughed and identified it as a nude. When it was flashed to her right hemisphere, she said nothing but began to chuckle. Asked what she was laughing at, she said, "I don't know . . . nothing . . . oh—that funny machine." The right hemisphere could not describe what it had seen, but it reacted emotionally, just the same (Gazzaniga, 1967).

The Two Hemispheres: Allies or Opposites?

The split-brain operation is still being performed, and split-brain patients continue to be studied. Research on left–right differences is also being done with people whose brains are intact (Springer & Deutsch, 1998). Electrodes and brain scans are used to measure activity in the left and right hemispheres while people perform different tasks. The results confirm that nearly all right-handed people and a majority of left-handers process language mainly in the left hemisphere. The left side is also more active during some logical, symbolic, and sequential tasks, such as solving math problems and understanding technical material.

Because of its cognitive talents, many researchers refer to left-hemisphere *dominance.* They believe that the left hemisphere usually exerts control over the right hemisphere. One well-known split-brain researcher, Michael Gazzaniga (1983), once argued that, without help from the left side, the right side's mental skills would probably be "vastly inferior to the cognitive skills of a chimpanzee." He and others also believe that a mental "module" in the left hemisphere is constantly trying to explain actions and emotions generated by brain parts whose workings are nonverbal and outside of awareness.

You can see in split-brain patients how the left hemisphere concocts such explanations. In one classic example, a picture of a chicken claw was flashed to a patient's left hemisphere, a picture of a snow scene to his right. The task was to point to a related image for each picture from an array, with a chicken being the correct choice for the claw and a shovel for the snow scene. The patient chose the shovel with his left hand and the chicken with his right. When asked to explain why, he responded (with his left hemisphere) that the chicken claw went with the chicken, and the shovel was for cleaning out the chicken shed. The left hemisphere had seen the left hand's response but did not know about the snow scene, so it interpreted the response by using the information it did have (Gazzaniga, 1988).

Get Involved   TAP, TAP, TAP

Have a right-handed friend tap on a paper with a pencil held in the right hand, for one minute. Then have the person do the same with the left hand, using a fresh sheet of paper. Finally, repeat the procedure, having the person talk while tapping. For most people, talking will decrease the rate of tapping—but more for the right hand than for the left, probably because both activities involve the same hemisphere, and there is "competition" between them. (Left-handed people vary more in terms of which hemisphere is dominant for language, so the results for them will be less predictable.)

Other researchers, including Sperry (1982), have rushed to the right hemisphere's defence. The right side, they point out, is no dummy. It is superior in problems requiring spatial–visual abil- ity, the ability you use to read a map or follow a dress pattern, and it excels in facial recognition and the ability to read facial expressions. It is active during the creation and appreciation of art and music. It recognizes nonverbal sounds, such as a dog's barking. The right hemisphere also has some language ability. Typically, it can read a word briefly flashed to it and can understand an experimenter's instructions. In a few split-brain patients, the right hemisphere's language ability has been quite well developed, showing that individual variation exists in brain lateralization.

Thinking Critically About "Right Brain/Left Brain" Theories

Some researchers have credited the right hemisphere with having a cognitive style that is intuitive and holistic (in which things are seen as wholes), in contrast to the left hemisphere's more rational and analytic mode. Over the years, this idea has been oversold by books and programs that promise to make people more creative by making them more "right-brained." But the right hemisphere is not always a "hero": For example, it contains regions that process fear and sadness, emotions that often cause us to withdraw from others (see Chapter 13). Further, the differences between the two hemispheres are relative, not absolute—a matter of degree. In most real-life activities, the two sides co-operate naturally, with each making a valuable contribution. As Sperry (1982) himself once noted, "The left–right dichotomy . . . is an idea with which it is very easy to run wild."

Quick Quiz

Use as many parts of your brain as necessary to answer these questions.

1. Keeping in mind that both sides of the brain are involved in most activities, see whether you can identify which of the following is (are) most closely associated with the left hemisphere: (a) enjoying a musical recording, (b) wiggling the left big toe, (c) giving a speech in class, (d) balancing a chequebook, (e) recognizing a long-lost friend.

2. Thousands of people have taken courses and bought tapes that promise to develop the "creativity" and "intuition" of their right hemispheres. What characteristics of human thought might explain the eagerness of some people to glorify "right-brainedness" and disparage "left-brainedness" (or vice versa)?

Answers:

1. c, d 2. One possible answer: Human beings like to make sense of the world, and one easy way to do that is to divide humanity into opposing categories. This kind of thinking—or either—or thinking can lead to the conclusion that fixing up one brain hemisphere (e.g., making "left-brained" types more "right-brained") will make individuals happier and the world a better place. If only it were that simple!

WHAT'S AHEAD

- Why do some brain researchers think that a unified "self" is only an illusion?
- Do men talk about sports and women about feelings because their brains are different?

TWO STUBBORN ISSUES IN BRAIN RESEARCH

If you have mastered the definitions and descriptions in this chapter, you are prepared to read popular accounts of advances in neuropsychology. But many questions remain about how the brain works, and we will end this chapter with two of them.

Where Is the Self?

When we think about the remarkable blob of tissue in our heads that allows us to remember, to dream, and to think—the blob that can make our existence a hideous nightmare when it is damaged or diseased—we are led, inevitably, to a question that has been pondered for thousands of years: Where, exactly, is the self?

Thinking Critically About the Brain and the Self

When you say, "I am feeling happy," your left hemisphere, your serotonin receptors, your endorphins, and all sorts of other brain parts and processes are active, but who, exactly, is the "I" doing the feeling? When you say, "My mind is playing tricks on me," who is the "me" watching your mind play those tricks, and who is it that's

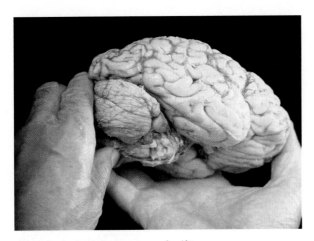

Where in the brain is the sense of self?

being tricked? Isn't the self observing itself a little like a finger pointing at its own tip?

Most religions resolve the problem by teaching that an immortal self or soul exists entirely apart from the mortal brain. But modern brain scientists usually consider mind to be a matter of "matter." They may have personal religious convictions about a soul or a spiritual response to the awesome complexity and interconnectedness of nature, but most assume that what we call "mind," "consciousness," or "self-awareness" can be explained in physical terms as a product of the cerebral cortex.

Our conscious sense of a unified self may even be an illusion. Neurologist Richard Restak (1983, 1994) has noted that many of our actions and choices occur without any direction by a conscious self. He concludes that "the brains of all creatures are probably organized along the lines of multiple centers and various levels." Cognitive scientist Daniel Dennett (1991) suggests that the brain or mind consists of independent brain parts that deal with different aspects of thought and perception, constantly conferring with each other and revising their "drafts" of reality. Likewise, Michael Gazzaniga (1985, 1998) has argued that the brain is organized as a loose confederation of independent modules, or mental systems, all working in parallel, with most of these modules operating outside of conscious awareness. As we saw, Gazzaniga believes that one verbal module, an "interpreter" (usually in the left hemisphere), is constantly explaining the actions, moods, and thoughts produced by the other modules. The result is the sense of a unified self.

Interestingly, the idea that the brain consists of modules and that the self is an illusion is consistent with the teachings of many Eastern spiritual traditions. Buddhism, for example, teaches that the self is not a unified "thing" but rather a collection of thoughts, perceptions, concepts, and feelings that shift from moment to moment. To Buddhists, the unity and the permanence of the self are a mirage. Such notions are contrary, of course, to what most people in the West, including psychologists, have always believed about their "selves."

Over a century ago, William James (1890/1950) described the "self-as-knower," the inner sense we all have of being a distinct person who thinks, feels, and acts. But the mind–brain puzzle continues to plague philosophers and scientists. Even in these days of modern technology, details about the neural circuits responsible for our sense of self remain hazy. Many researchers believe that the frontal lobes play a critical role, but not all accept the idea that cognition can be dissected into mental modules (Uttal, 2001). And no one understands yet how the inner life of the mind or our sense of subjective experience is linked to the physical processes of the brain. Some brain-injured patients who, like H. M., are unable to store new memories about their experiences can nonetheless describe the kind of person they have been since the brain damage occurred (Klein & Kihlstrom, 1998). Where in the brain does this capacity to reflect on one's own personality reside?

Psychologists and cognitive scientists hope eventually to learn more about how our brains and nervous systems give rise to the self-as-knower. In the meantime, what do you think about the existence and location of your own "self" . . . and who, by the way, is doing the thinking? Think about it!

Are There "His" and "Hers" Brains?

A second stubborn issue for brain scientists concerns the existence of sex differences in the brain. Historically, findings on male–female brain differences have often flip-flopped in a most suspicious manner, a result of the biases of the observers rather than the biology of the brain (Shields, 1975). For example, in the 1960s, scientists speculated that women were more "right-brained" and men were more "left-brained," which supposedly explained why men were "rational" and women "intuitive." Then, when the virtues of the right hemisphere were discovered, such as creativity and artistic ability, some researchers decided that men were more right-brained. But it is now clear that the abilities popularly associated with the two sexes do not fall neatly into the two hemispheres of the brain. The left side is more verbal (presumably a "female" trait), but it is also more mathematical (presumably a "male" trait). The right side is more intuitive ("female"), but it is also more spatially talented ("male").

Yet people seem determined to find sex differences in the brain, and when they do, the results make headlines, often prematurely. For example, in 1982, two anthropologists autopsied 14 human brains and reported an average sex difference in the size and shape of the *splenium*, a small section at the end of the corpus callosum, the bundle of fibres dividing the cerebral hemispheres (de Lacoste-Utamsing & Holloway, 1982). This finding quickly made its way into newspapers, magazines, and even textbooks, before anyone had replicated it. Then, a decade later, a thorough review of the literature found that the 1982 results were an exception: 21 later studies found no sex difference at all (Byne, 1993). Further, a Canadian analysis of 49 studies found only trivial differences between the two sexes, differences that paled in comparison with the huge individual variations *within* each sex (Bishop & Wahlsten, 1997). These findings, however, were not widely publicized.

To evaluate the issue of sex differences in the brain intelligently, we need to ask two separate questions: Do male and female brains differ physically? And if they do, what, if anything, does this difference have to do with behaviour?

Let's consider the first question. Many anatomical and biochemical sex differences have been found in animal brains, especially in areas related to reproduction, such as the hypothalamus (McEwen, 1983). Of course, we would expect to find male–female brain differences that are related to the regulation of sex hormones and other aspects of reproduction in human beings, too. But many researchers want to know whether there are also differences that affect how men and women think or behave.

One approach has been to examine the density of neurons in specific areas. In a study of nine autopsied brains, researchers found that the women had an average of 11 percent more cells in areas of the cortex associated with the processing of auditory information; in fact, all of the women had more of these cells than did any of the men (Witelson, Glazer, & Kigar, 1994).

Other researchers have used brain scans to search for average sex differences in brain activity while people do a particular task. In one MRI study, 10 men and 10 women listened to a John Grisham thriller being read aloud. Men and women alike showed activity in the left temporal lobe, but women also showed some activity in the right temporal lobe, as you can see in Figure 4.16 (Phillips et al., 2001). This finding, along with many others, provides evidence for a sex difference in lateralization: For some types of tasks, especially those involving language, men seem to rely more heavily on one side of the brain whereas women tend to use both sides. Such a

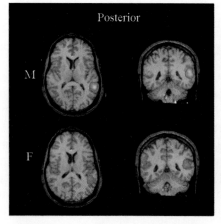 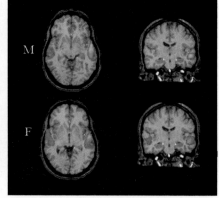

FIGURE 4.16 Gender and the Brain

When women and men listened to a John Grisham thriller read aloud, they showed activity in the left temporal lobe, but women also showed some activity in the right temporal lobe (Phillips et al., 2001). (Because of the orientation of these MRI images, the left hemisphere is seen on the right and vice versa.) Along with other evidence, these results suggest a sex difference in lateralization on tasks involving language.

difference could help explain why left-hemisphere damage is less likely to cause language problems in women than in men after a stroke (Inglis & Lawson, 1981; McGlone, 1978).

Many other intriguing sex differences have been reported—for example, that female brains have a higher proportion of gray matter than men's do (Gur et al., 1999), and that men use the right side of the amygdala while storing memories of an emotionally upsetting film whereas women use the left side (Cahill et al., 2001). In the coming years, research may reveal additional anatomical and information-processing differences in the brains of males and females. But even if average sex differences exist, we are still left with our second question: *What do the differences mean for the behaviour of men and women in real life?*

Some popular writers have been quick to assume that brain differences explain, among other things, women's allegedly superior intuition, women's love of talking about feelings and men's love of talking about sports, women's greater verbal ability, men's greater math ability, and why men won't ask for directions when they're lost. But there are at least three problems with these conclusions:

Thinking Critically About Sex Differences in the Brain

1 *These supposed gender differences are stereotypes.* In each case, the overlap between the sexes is greater than the difference between them. As we saw in Chapter 1, even when differences are statistically, significant they are often quite small in practical terms (Hyde, 2000).

2 *A biological difference does not necessarily have implications for behaviour or performance.* In the study of memories for emotionally upsetting films, for example, the two sexes reported comparable emotional reactions and had similar memories for the films' content. As for how brain differences might be related to more general abilities, speculations are as plentiful as swallows in summer, but at present they remain just that—speculations. As one writer noted, differences between men's and women's brains "are few, they are slight; we don't know what causes them, and in many cases we don't know what they do" (Blum, 1997).

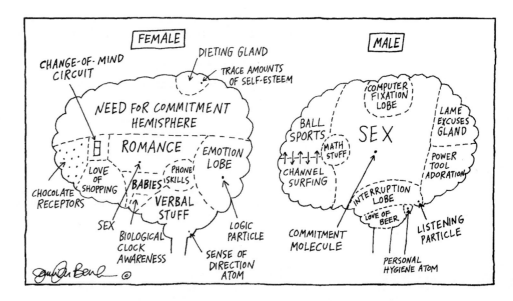

Cartoons like this one make us laugh because we all recognize that men and women often differ in things like "math stuff," "love of shopping," and "power-tool adoration." But this does not mean that all men and women differ in these ways, or that all gender differences are hard-wired in the brain.

3 *Sex differences in the brain could be the result rather than the cause of behavioural differences.* Experiences in life are constantly sculpting the circuitry of the brain, affecting the way brains are organized and how they function. If you are a string musician, the area in your brain associated with music production is likely to be larger than that of nonmusicians (Jancke, Schlaug, & Steinmetz, 1997). If you are a cab driver, the area in your hippocampus responsible for visual representations of the environment is likely to be larger than average (Maguire et al., 2000). Analogously, males and females often have different experiences, which may be literally shaping their brains. That is why, in commenting on the study that had people listen to a John Grisham novel, one of the researchers noted: "We don't know if the difference is because of the way we're raised, or if it's hard-wired in the brain" (quoted in Hotz, 2000).

In sum, the answer to our second question, whether physical differences are linked to behaviour, is "No one really knows." It is important to keep an open mind about new findings on sex differences in the brain. But because the practical significance of these findings (if any) is not clear, it is also important to be cautious and aware of how such results might be exaggerated and misused.

Quick Quiz

Men and women alike have brains that can answer these questions.

1. Many brain researchers and cognitive scientists believe that the self is not a unified "thing" but a collection of _____.

2. Name three reasons we should not assume that sex differences in the brain explain reported gender differences in behaviour or cognition.

Answers:

1. independent modules or mental systems   2. Most of the reported gender differences are stereotypes and are small in practical terms; a biological difference does not necessarily have important behavioural implications; and brain differences could be the result rather than the cause of behavioural differences.

Psychology In The News *Revisited*

Now that you know more about the workings of the brain, let's return to the case of Stephen Hawking.

Amyotrophic lateral sclerosis (ALS) is very different from some of the other brain disorders you may have heard about. Alzheimer's patients can remain physically healthy for years, but their mental abilities inevitably decline and their memories evaporate. Parkinson's patients suffer mainly from weakness, tremors, and rigidity, but when the disease reaches an advanced stage, about a third of all patients show signs of dementia. ALS, in contrast, kills only motor neurons while leaving intact the brain cells responsible for personality and intellect. The body degenerates but the mind does not.

Thus it is not surprising that, despite his illness, which was diagnosed when he was a 22-year-old student, Stephen Hawking has remained Stephen Hawking: an intellectual genius and public figure. What *is* surprising is how long he has survived. Some people suspect that he actually has a different disease, one not as inevitably fatal. Others attribute his longevity to genes, or to the bushels of vitamins he takes. Hawking's case shows us how much we still have to learn about the brain and nervous system, which remain unpredictable and mysterious in so many ways.

At present, the origins of ALS are unknown, and there is no cure. But the research on stem cells and neuronal regeneration that you read about in this chapter may eventually help people like Hawking. In the meantime, some researchers are focusing on the role of the neurotransmitter glutamate in motor neuron degeneration; compared to healthy people, ALS patients have higher levels of glutamate in the bloodstream and spinal fluid. Others are looking at chemicals in the brain and spinal cord that are vital to the development, maintenance, and protection of neurons. And some think that ALS may be an autoimmune disorder or the result of a genetic mutation.

To understand how Stephen Hawking has coped so well with his disabilities, however, we would need to know more than the biological facts about his brain. To understand why some people thrive in spite of dire physical adversity whereas others knuckle under when they get a cold, we must consider not just people's neurons but also their relationships, their cultural traditions, their life histories, and the way they explain and interpret the events that befall them. Neurons alone will not explain the grace and humour Hawking has brought to his battle.

The study of our most miraculous organ, the brain, can help us understand the abilities we all rely on and the memories and emotions that make us human. But analyzing a human being in terms of physiology alone is like analyzing the Taj Mahal solely in terms of the materials that were used to build it. Even if we could monitor every cell and circuit of the brain, we would still need to understand the circumstances, thoughts, and cultural rules that affect whether we are gripped by hatred, consumed by grief, lifted by love, or transported by the transcendent "eureka moments" of life.

Taking Psychology With You   Food for Thought—Diet and Neurotransmitters

"Vitamin improves sex!" "Mineral boosts brain-power!" "Chocolate chases the blues!" Claims like these have long given nutritional theories of behaviour a bad reputation. In the late 1960s, when Nobel laureate Linus Pauling (1901–1994) proposed treating some mental disorders with massive doses of vitamins, few researchers listened. Mainstream medical authorities classified Pauling's vitamin therapy with such infamous cure-alls as snake oil and leeches.

Today, most mental-health professionals remain skeptical of nutritional cures for mental illness. But the underlying premise of nutritional treatments—that diet affects the brain and therefore behaviour—is no longer considered a loony idea. Diet may indeed make a difference in cognitive function and in some types of disorders. In one double-blind study, researchers asked depressed patients to abstain from refined sugar and caffeine. Over a three-month period, these patients showed significantly more improvement in their symptoms than did another group of patients who instead refrained from eating red meat and using artificial sweeteners (Christensen & Burrows, 1990). In another study, older people took a daily supplement containing modest amounts of vitamins, minerals, and trace elements; at the end of a year, they showed improvements in short-term memory, problem-solving ability, abstract thinking, and attention, when compared to participants taking a placebo (Chandra, 2001).

Some of the most exciting work on diet and behaviour has looked at the role played by nutrients in the synthesis of neurotransmitters, the brain's chemical messengers. *Tryptophan*, an amino acid found in protein-rich foods (dairy products, meat, fish, and poultry), is a precursor (building block) of serotonin. *Tyrosine*, another amino acid found in proteins, is a precursor of norepinephrine, epinephrine, and dopamine. *Choline*, a component of the lecithin found in egg yolks, soy products, and liver, is a precursor of acetylcholine.

In the case of tryptophan, the path between the dinner plate and the brain is indirect. Tryptophan leads to the production of serotonin, which reduces alertness, promotes relaxation, and hastens sleep. Because tryptophan is found in protein, you might think that a high-protein meal would make you drowsy and that carbohydrates (sweets, bread, pasta, potatoes) would make you relatively alert. Actually, the opposite is true. High-protein foods contain several amino acids, not just tryptophan, and they all compete for a ride on carrier molecules headed for brain cells. Because tryptophan occurs in foods in small quantities, it doesn't stand much of a chance if all you eat is protein. It is in the position of a tiny child trying to push aside a crowd of adults for a seat on the subway.

Carbohydrates, however, stimulate the production of the hormone insulin, and insulin causes all the other amino acids to be drawn out of the bloodstream while having little effect on tryptophan. So carbohydrates increase the odds that tryptophan will make it to the brain (Wurtman, 1982). Paradoxically, then, a high-carbohydrate, no-protein meal is likely to make you relatively calm or lethargic and a high-protein one is likely to promote alertness, all else being equal (Spring, Chiodo, & Bowen, 1987; Wurtman & Lieberman, 1982–1983). Research with people who tend to become frustrated, angry, or depressed in stressful situations suggests that high-carbohydrate food can actually reduce these responses and help such people cope (Markus et al., 2000).

Keep in mind, though, that many other factors influence mood and behaviour, that the effects of nutrients are subtle, and that some of these effects depend on a person's age, the circumstances, and even the time of day. Further, nutrients interact with each other in complex ways. If you don't eat protein, you won't get enough tryptophan, but if you go without carbohydrates, the tryptophan found in protein will be useless.

In sum, if you're looking for brain food, you are most likely to find it not in a magic pill but in a well-balanced diet.

SUMMARY

- The brain is the bedrock of consciousness, perception, memory, emotion, and self-awareness.

THE NERVOUS SYSTEM: A BASIC BLUEPRINT

- The function of the nervous system is to gather and process information, produce responses to stimuli, and coordinate the workings of different cells. Scientists divide it into the *central nervous system (CNS)* and the *peripheral nervous system (PNS)*. The CNS includes the brain and *spinal cord* (which produces *spinal reflexes* on its own); it receives, processes, interprets, and stores information and sends messages destined for muscles, glands, and organs. The PNS transmits information to and from the CNS by way of *sensory* and *motor nerves*.

- The peripheral nervous system consists of the *somatic nervous system*, which permits sensation and voluntary actions, and the *autonomic nervous system*, which regulates blood vessels, glands, and internal (visceral) organs. The autonomic system usually functions without conscious control.

- The autonomic nervous system is divided into the *sympathetic nervous system*, which mobilizes the body for action, and the *parasympathetic nervous system*, which conserves energy.

COMMUNICATION IN THE NERVOUS SYSTEM

- Neurons are the basic units of the nervous system. They are held in place by *glial cells*, which nourish, insulate, and protect them, and enable them to function properly. Each neuron consists of *dendrites*, a *cell body*, and an *axon*. In the peripheral nervous system, axons (and sometimes dendrites) are collected together in bundles called *nerves*. Many axons are insulated by a *myelin sheath* that speeds up the conduction of neural impulses and prevents signals in adjacent cells from interfering with one another.

- Recent research has challenged two old assumptions about the human central nervous system: that neurons cannot be induced to regenerate, and that no new neurons form after early infancy. In the laboratory, neurons in the CNS have been induced to regenerate. And scientists have learned that *stem cells* in brain areas associated with learning and memory give rise to new neurons and continue to divide and mature throughout adulthood. A stimulating environment seems to enhance this process.

- Communication between two neurons occurs at the *synapse*. Many synapses have not yet formed at birth. During development, axons and dendrites continue to grow as a result of both physical maturation and experience with the world, and throughout life, new learning results in new synaptic connections in the brain. Thus, the brain's circuits are not fixed and immutable but are continually changing in response to information, challenges, and changes in the environment, a phenomenon known as *plasticity*.

- When a wave of electrical voltage *(action potential)* reaches the end of a transmitting axon, *neurotransmitter* molecules are released into the *synaptic cleft*. When these molecules bind to *receptor sites* on the receiving neuron, that neuron becomes either more likely to fire or less so. The message that reaches a final destination depends on how frequently particular neurons are firing, how many are firing, what types are firing, and where they are located.

- Through their effects on neural circuits, neurotransmitters play a critical role in mood, memory, and psychological well-being. Abnormal levels of neurotransmitters have been implicated in several disorders, including depression, Alzheimer's disease, and Parkinson's disease.

- *Endorphins*, which act primarily by modifying the action of neurotransmitters, reduce pain and promote pleasure. Endorphin levels seem to shoot up when an animal or person is afraid or is under stress.

- *Hormones*, produced mainly by the *endocrine glands*, affect and are affected by the nervous system. Psychologists are especially interested in *melatonin*, which promotes sleep and helps regulate bodily rhythms; *adrenal hormones* such as *epinephrine* and *norepinephrine*, which are involved in emotions, memory, and stress; and the *sex hormones*, which are involved in the physical changes of puberty, the menstrual cycle *(estrogens* and *progesterone)*, and sexual arousal *(testosterone)*.

MAPPING THE BRAIN

- Researchers study the brain by observing patients with brain damage; by damaging or removing brain tissue in animals and observing the effects; and by using such techniques as *electroencephalograms (EEGs), positron-emission tomography (PET) scans*, and *magnetic resonance imaging (MRI)*. Brain scans reveal which parts of the brain are active during different tasks but do not tell us precisely what is happening, either physically or mentally, during the task; thus they must be interpreted cautiously.

A TOUR THROUGH THE BRAIN

- All modern brain theories assume *localization of function*. In the lower part of the brain, in the *brain stem*, the *medulla* controls automatic functions such as heartbeat and breathing, and the *pons* is involved in sleeping, waking, and dreaming. The *reticular activating system (RAS)* screens incoming information and is responsible for alertness. The *cerebellum* contributes to balance and muscle coordination, and may also play a role in some higher mental operations.

- The *thalamus* directs sensory messages to appropriate higher centres. The *hypothalamus* is involved in emotion and in drives associated with survival. It also controls the operations of the autonomic nervous system and sends out chemicals that tell the pituitary gland when to "talk" to other endocrine glands. Along with other structures, such as the amygdala and the hippocampus, the hypothalamus has traditionally been considered part of the *limbic system*, which is involved in emotions that we share with other animals. However, the usefulness of speaking of the limbic system as an integrated set of structures is now in dispute.

- The *amygdala* is responsible for evaluating sensory information and quickly determining its emotional importance, and for the initial decision to approach or withdraw from a person or situation. The *hippocampus* has been called the "gateway to memory" because it plays a critical role in the formation of long-term memories for facts and events.

- Much of the brain's circuitry is packed into the *cerebrum*, which is divided into two *cerebral hemispheres* and is covered by thin layers of cells known collectively as the *cerebral cortex*. The *occipital, parietal, temporal*, and *frontal lobes* of the cortex have specialized (but partially overlapping) functions. The *association cortex* appears to be responsible for higher mental processes. The *frontal lobes*, particularly areas in the *prefrontal cortex*, are involved in social judgment, the making and carrying out of plans, and decision making.

THE TWO HEMISPHERES OF THE BRAIN

- Studies of *split-brain* patients, whose *corpus callosum* has been cut, show that the two cerebral hemispheres have somewhat different talents, a phenomenon known as *lateralization*. In most people, language is processed mainly in the left hemisphere, which generally is specialized for logical, symbolic, and sequential tasks. The right hemisphere is associated with spatial–visual tasks, facial recognition, the creation and appreciation of art and music, and the processing of negative emotions. In most mental activities, however, the two hemispheres co-operate as partners, with each making a valuable contribution.

TWO STUBBORN ISSUES IN BRAIN RESEARCH

- An old question in the study of the brain is where the "self" resides. Some brain researchers and cognitive scientists believe that a unified self may be something of an illusion. Some argue that the brain operates as a collection of independent modules or mental systems, perhaps with one of them functioning as an "interpreter." But much remains to be learned about the relationship between the brain and the mind.

- Brain scans have revealed some differences in the brains of males and females, particularly in lateralization during tasks involving language (with females more likely to use both hemispheres). Controversy exists, however, about what these differences mean in real life. Speculation has often focused on behavioural or cognitive sex differences that are small and insignificant. Biological differences do not necessarily explain behavioural ones, and sex differences in experience could affect brain organization rather than the other way around.

PSYCHOLOGY IN THE NEWS, REVISITED

- In evaluating research on the brain and behaviour, it is important to remember that findings about the brain are most illuminating when they are integrated with psychological and cultural ones.

KEY TERMS

LOOKING BACK

- Why do you automatically pull your hand away from something hot, "without thinking"? (p. 110)
- In an emergency, which part of your nervous system whirls into action? (p. 111)
- Which cells are the nervous system's "communication specialists," and how do they "talk" to each other? (p. 113)
- Are you born with all the brain cells you'll ever have? (p. 115)
- How do learning and experience alter the brain's circuits? (p. 116)
- What happens when levels of brain chemicals called *neurotransmitters* are too low or too high? (p. 118)
- Which hormones can improve your memory? (p. 119)
- Why are patterns of electrical activity in the brain called "brainwaves"? (p. 121)
- What scanning techniques reveal changes in brain activity while people listen to music or solve math problems? (pp. 121–122)
- Which brain part acts as a "traffic officer" for incoming sensations? (p. 124)
- Which brain part is the "gateway to memory"—and what cognitive catastrophe occurs when it is damaged? (p. 125)
- Why is it a good thing that the outer covering of the human brain is so wrinkled? (p. 126)
- How did a bizarre nineteenth-century accident illuminate the role of the frontal lobes? (pp. 127–128)
- If the two cerebral hemispheres were out of touch, would they feel different emotions and think different thoughts? (pp. 129–131)
- Why do researchers often refer to the left hemisphere as "dominant"? (p. 131)
- Should you sign up for a program that promises to perk up the right side of your brain? (p. 132)
- Why do some brain researchers think a unified "self" is only an illusion? (p. 133)
- Do men talk about sports and women about feelings because their brains are different? (pp. 133–135)

Psychology In The News

BUSINESS IS BRISK AT MARIJUANA SHOP

VANCOUVER, BC, September 11, 2004. A shop on Commercial Drive in Vancouver has been defying the law and operating a thriving business selling marijuana to its customers, a business that drew considerable public attention after a police raid resulting in the arrest of the shop's owner and seven employees.

The Da Kine Food and Beverage Shop has been dubbed "pot café" after four months of having marijuana on its menu. When a Crime Stoppers call brought it to the attention of the police, they raided the establishment, confiscating 20 pounds of pot, 1 pound of hashish, and $63 000 in cash.

The manager of the Da Kine vowed to reopen each time it was closed, criticizing the police for "terror tactics" that were out of touch with the lives of the people they are supposed to serve.

The manager has said that the Da Kine is part of a not-for-profit society called the Canadian Sanctuary Society, dedicated to providing a secure environment where people can purchase what he referred to as "a product of their choice."

For their part, the police claim that the Da Kine is not a "compassion club" selling marijuana to people with government-approved medical reasons for using the drug. Rather, they estimate that the Da Kine brings in about $500 000 a month for its not-for-profit society. Police counted 230 visitors to the Da Kine during a one-hour surveillance.

Police close Vancouver café for selling marijuana.

5 Consciousness: Body Rhythms and Mental States

Why would a store like the Da Kine Food and Beverage Shop attract so much attention and elicit such polarized attitudes toward its existence? Is it a menace to society, selling marijuana to large numbers of people, some of them alleged to be 18 years of age and younger? Or is it ahead of its time, simply allowing people to pursue personal indulgences as do those who frequent bars and pubs? Certainly, the Da Kine café had no trouble attracting business.

Marijuana is just one of many drugs that people use to alter **consciousness**, the awareness of oneself and the environment. But consciousness also changes in predictable ways without any help from drugs. Each day, we all experience swings in mood, alertness, and efficiency. Each night, we all undergo a dramatic shift in consciousness, when the ordinary rules of logic are suspended in the dream world of sleep. Performance and mood may be subject to much longer cycles as well, stretching over a month's time or even the seasons of the year. Why do these changes occur? And why do some people deliberately try to alter their ordinary states of consciousness?

In this chapter we will see that the mental and physical aspects of consciousness are as intertwined as sunshine and shadow: Fluctuations in subjective experience are accompanied by predictable ups and downs in brain activity and hormone levels. We begin with a discussion of the body's natural rhythms, which ebb and flow over time. Next we will zero in on one particularly fascinating state of consciousness: dreaming. And then we will explore what psychologists have learned about two techniques used to alter consciousness deliberately: the use of hypnosis and the use of recreational drugs. (We will discuss drug *abuse* and addiction in Chapter 11.)

This chapter will give you a better understanding of the human fascination with "altered states of consciousness" and why some people use drugs to achieve them. As you read, ask yourself: Why would the owners of the café sell marijuana illegally? And why would so many people flock to the Da Kine café in spite of the law? Are our current drug policies realistic? We will return to these issues at the end of the chapter.

consciousness Awareness of oneself and the environment.

- Why do you feel "out of sync" when you fly across time zones or change shifts at work?
- If you feel sad in the winter, do you have SAD?
- Does "PMS" cause most women to feel depressed or irritable before their periods?

BIOLOGICAL RHYTHMS: THE TIDES OF EXPERIENCE

At some point you may have come across an ad on the Internet for a "biorhythm chart" that supposedly foretells fluctuations in mood, alertness, and physical performance over your entire lifetime—solely on the basis of when you were born. Well, save your money: Biorhythm charts are pseudo-scientific hogwash. It *is* true, however, that human beings experience dozens of periodic, fairly regular ups and downs in physiological functioning, which is what scientists mean when they speak of **biological rhythms**. A biological clock in our brains governs the waxing and waning of hormone levels, urine volume, blood pressure, and even the responsiveness of brain cells to stimulation. Many of these rhythms continue to occur even in the absence of external time cues; they are **endogenous**, or generated from within.

Some biological rhythms, called **circadian rhythms**, occur approximately every 24 hours. The best-known circadian rhythm is the sleep–wake cycle, but there are hundreds of others. For example, body temperature fluctuates about one degree centigrade each day, peaking, on average, in the late afternoon and hitting a low point, or trough, in the wee hours of the morning. Other rhythms occur less frequently than once a day—for example, the female menstrual cycle, which occurs every 28 days on average. Still others occur more frequently than once a day, many of them on about a 90-minute cycle. Researchers from Dalhousie and elsewhere have found that these shorter cycles include physiological changes during sleep, and (unless social customs intervene) stomach contractions, hormone levels, susceptibility to visual illusions, verbal and spatial performance, brainwave responses during cognitive tasks, alertness, and daydreaming (Escera, Cilveti, & Grau, 1992; Klein & Armitage, 1979; Kripke, 1974; Lavie, 1976).

Biological rhythms influence everything from the effectiveness of medicines taken at different times of the day to alertness and performance on the job. With a better understanding of these internal tempos, we may be able to design our days to take better advantage of our bodies' natural tempos. Let's look more closely at how these cycles operate.

Circadian Rhythms

Circadian rhythms exist in plants, animals, insects, and human beings. They reflect the evolutionary adaptation of organisms to the many changes associated with the rotation of the earth on its axis, such as changes in light, air pressure, and temperature.

In most societies, external time cues abound, and people's bodies become synchronized to them, following a strict 24-hour schedule. To identify endogenous circadian rhythms, therefore, scientists must isolate volunteers from sunlight, clocks, environmental sounds, and all other cues to time. Some hardy souls have spent weeks or even months alone in caves and salt mines, linked to the outside world only by a one-way phone line and a cable transmitting physiological measurements to the surface. More often, volunteers live in specially designed rooms equipped with stereo systems, comfortable furniture, and temperature controls.

When participants in these studies have been allowed to sleep, eat, and work whenever they wished, free of the tyranny of the timepiece, a few have lived a "day" that is much shorter or longer than 24 hours. If they are allowed to take daytime naps, however, most soon settle into a day that averages about 24.3 hours (Moore, 1997). And when people are put on an artificial 28-hour "day," in an environment free of all time cues, their body temperature and certain hormone levels follow a cycle that is very close to 24 hours—24.18 hours to be precise (Czeisler et al., 1999). These rhythms are remarkably similar from one person to the next.

The Body's Clock Circadian rhythms are controlled by a biological clock, or overall coordinator, located in a tiny teardrop-shaped cluster of cells in the hypothalamus called the **suprachiasmatic nucleus (SCN)**. Neural pathways from special receptors in the back of the eye transmit information to the SCN and allow it to respond to changes in light and dark. The SCN then sends out messages that cause the brain and body to adapt to these changes. Other clocks also exist, scattered around the body, and some may operate independently of the SCN, but for most circadian

---

biological rhythm A periodic, more or less regular fluctuation in a biological system; it may or may not have psychological implications.

endogenous Generated from within rather than by external cues.

circadian [sur-CAY-dee-un] rhythm A biological rhythm with a period (from peak to peak or trough to trough) of about 24 hours; from the Latin *circa*, "about," and *dies*, "a day."

suprachiasmatic [soo-pruh-kie-az-MAT-ick] nucleus (SCN) An area of the brain containing a biological clock that governs circadian rhythms.

Stefania Follini (left) spent four months in a New Mexico cave (above), 30 feet underground, as part of an Italian study on biological rhythms. Her only companions were a computer and two friendly mice. In the absence of clocks, natural light, or changes in temperature, she tended to stay awake for 20 to 25 hours and then sleep for 10. Because her days were longer than usual, when she emerged she thought she had been in the cave for only two months.

rhythms, the SCN is regarded as the master pacemaker.

The SCN regulates fluctuating levels of hormones and neurotransmitters, and they in turn provide feedback that affects the SCN's functioning. For example, during the dark hours, one hormone regulated by the SCN, **melatonin**, is secreted by the *pineal gland* deep within the brain. The pineal gland responds to light and dark via complex connections that originate in the back of the eye. When you go to sleep in a darkened room, your melatonin level rises; when you wake up in the morning to a lightened room, it falls. Melatonin, in turn, appears to help keep the biological clock in phase with the light–dark cycle (Haimov & Lavie, 1996; Lewy et al., 1992).

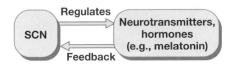

Melatonin treatments have been used to treat insomnia and synchronize the disturbed sleep–wake cycles of blind people who lack light perception and whose melatonin production does not cycle normally (Sack & Lewy, 1997). But efforts to treat the insomnia of *sighted* people by giving them melatonin have had mixed results.

When the Clock Is Out of Sync Under normal conditions, the rhythms governed by the SCN are synchronized, just as wristwatches can be synchronized. Their peaks may occur at different times, but they occur in phase with one another; thus if you know when one rhythm peaks, you can predict when another will do so. But when your normal routine changes, your circadian rhythms may be thrown out of phase with one another. Such **internal desynchronization** often occurs when people take airplane flights across several time zones. Sleep and wake patterns usually adjust quickly, but temperature and hormone cycles can take several days to return to normal. The resulting jet lag affects energy level, mental skills, and motor coordination. A promising preventive strategy for jet lag has been studied by researchers at McGill. Participants who were exposed to six hours of room light early in the day prior to a simulated trip from Montreal to London experienced an adjustment to their melatonin levels and other physiological responses in ways that better prepared them for the schedule at their destination (Boivin & James, 2002). This suggests that flights of this nature taken first thing in the morning, without that preflight exposure to light, make adjustment more difficult when we reach our destination.

Internal desynchronization also occurs when workers must adjust to a new shift. Efficiency

melatonin A hormone secreted by the pineal gland; it is involved in the regulation of circadian rhythms.

internal desynchronization A state in which biological rhythms are not in phase (synchronized) with one another.

Travel can be exhausting, and jet lag makes it worse.

drops, the person feels tired and irritable, accidents become more likely, and sleep disturbances and digestive disorders may occur. For police officers, emergency room personnel, airline pilots, truck drivers, and nuclear power plant operators, the consequences can be a matter of life and death. In the United States, a National Commission on Sleep Disorders concluded that lack of alertness in night-shift equipment operators may have contributed, along with other factors, to the 1989 Exxon *Valdez* oil spill off the coast of Alaska and disastrous accidents during the 1980s at the Three Mile Island and Chernobyl nuclear power plants. Night work itself is not necessarily a problem: With a schedule that always stays the same, even on weekends, people often adapt and do fine. Ideally, a rotating work schedule should follow circadian principles by switching workers as infrequently as possible. However, many swing- and night-shift assignments are made on a rotating basis, so circadian rhythms never have a chance to resynchronize. And even a change to daylight saving time can cause problems. At the University of British Columbia, Stanley Coren discovered that a seven percent increase in traffic accidents occurred in Canada following the shift to daylight saving time (Coren, 1996). When the clock was put back in the fall, the accident rate decreased by about the same amount.

We want to emphasize that circadian rhythms are not perfectly regular and can be affected by illness, stress,

fatigue, excitement, exercise, drugs, mealtimes, and ordinary daily experiences. Further, circadian rhythms differ greatly from individual to individual because of genetic differences (Hur, Bouchard, & Lykken, 1998). Some people are early birds, bouncing out of bed at the crack of dawn, whereas others are night owls who do their best work late at night and can't be pried out of bed until noon. (Schools are not designed to accommodate night owls.) You may be able to learn about your own personal pulses through careful self-observation, and you may want to try putting that information to use when planning your daily schedule.

Moods and Long-Term Rhythms

According to Ecclesiastes, "To every thing there is a season, and a time to every purpose under the heaven." Modern science agrees. Seasonal cycles are common in nonhuman animals: Birds migrate south in the fall, bears hibernate in the winter, and marine animals become active or inactive, depending on bimonthly changes in the tides. In human beings, long-term cycles have been observed in everything from the threshold for tooth pain to conception rates. Folklore holds that our moods follow similar rhythms, particularly in response to seasonal changes and, in women, to menstrual changes. But do they?

"IF WE EVER INTEND TO TAKE OVER THE WORLD, ONE THING WE'LL HAVE TO DO IS SYNCHRONIZE OUR BIOLOGICAL CLOCKS."

Get Involved   Measuring Your Alertness Cycles

For at least two days, except when you are sleeping, keep an hourly record of your mental alertness level, using this five-point scale: 1 = extremely drowsy or mentally lethargic; 2 = somewhat drowsy or mentally lethargic; 3 = moderately alert; 4 = alert and efficient; 5 = extremely alert and efficient. Does your alertness level appear to follow a circadian rhythm, or does it rise and fall more frequently? When does it tend to peak and plummet? Is this cycle the same on weekends as during the week? Most important, how well does your schedule mesh with your natural fluctuations in alertness?

Does the Season Affect Moods? Clinicians report that some people become depressed every winter, when periods of daylight are short, and improve in mood each spring, as daylight increases—a pattern that has come to be known as **seasonal affective disorder (SAD)** (Rosenthal, 1998). During the winter months, such patients report feelings of sadness, lethargy, and drowsiness. To counteract the presumed effects of sunless days, some physicians and therapists have been treating SAD patients with phototherapy, having them sit in front of extremely bright fluorescent lights at specific times of the day.

Evaluating the actual prevalence of SAD is difficult, however. Information comes mainly from clinical case reports rather than controlled studies, and, as we saw in Chapter 1, case studies have serious drawbacks. Many clinicians, extrapolating from patients who believe they suffer from SAD, think the disorder may affect as much as 20 percent of the population. But a telephone survey in Ontario, for example, concluded that the prevalence of SAD severe enough to warrant a clinical diagnosis was about 1.7 percent (Lam, 1998).

These young Norwegian women are receiving light therapy for "seasonal affective disorder" (SAD). This type of treatment is becoming increasingly popular, but far fewer people actually have SAD than is commonly thought.

As for the effectiveness of light treatments, research on this question, too, has been flawed. Most studies have not used control groups, and it has therefore been impossible to rule out placebo effects when SAD patients cheer up. Better research, though, is now being done and may throw some light on the subject, so to speak. In two well-controlled studies, patients had daily sessions of one of four treatments: (a) bright light, (b) exposure to high levels of negative ions, (c) exposure to low levels of negative ions, or (d) placebo sessions in which they sat in front of a machine that they thought was generating negative ions but was not. The light treatments—and also, unexpectedly, the high levels of negative ions—were effective in alleviating the patients' symptoms, but the other two conditions were not (Eastman et al., 1998; Terman, Terman, & Ross, 1998). The effectiveness of the light treatments suggests that true SAD patients have some deficiency in the secretion of melatonin.

Nonetheless, people should be cautious about diagnosing themselves as having SAD or laying out hundreds of dollars for a light-treatment lamp. True cases of SAD may have a biological basis, but the evidence is inconsistent. When people get the winter blues, the reason could be that they hate sleet, ice, and cold weather; that they become less physically active; or that they feel lonely during the winter holidays.

Does the Menstrual Cycle Affect Moods? Controversy has also raged about another long-term rhythm, the monthly female menstrual cycle. During the first half of this cycle, an increase in the hormone estrogen causes the lining of the uterus to thicken in preparation for a possible pregnancy. At midcycle, the ovaries release a mature egg, or ovum. Afterward, the ovarian sac that contained the egg begins to produce progesterone, which helps prepare the uterine lining to receive the egg. Then, if conception does not occur,

Thinking Critically About Seasonal Mood Changes

seasonal affective disorder (SAD) A controversial disorder in which a person experiences depression during the winter and an improvement of mood in the spring.

"PMS" remedies line the shelves of drugstores, and most people think the "syndrome" is common—but is it?

estrogen and progesterone levels fall, the uterine lining sloughs off as the menstrual flow, and the cycle begins again.

The interesting question for psychologists is whether these physical changes are correlated with emotional or intellectual changes, as folklore would have us believe. Most people think so. In the 1970s, a vague cluster of symptoms associated with the days preceding menstruation—including fatigue, headache, irritability, and depression—came to be thought of as an illness and was given a label: "premenstrual syndrome" ("PMS"). Some popular books have asserted, without any evidence whatsoever, that most women suffer from it.

What does the evidence actually show? Many women do have *physical* symptoms associated with menstruation, including cramps, breast tenderness, and water retention, although women vary tremendously in this regard. And of course these physical symptoms can make some women feel grumpy or unhappy, just as pain can make men feel grumpy or unhappy. But *emotional* symptoms specifically associated with menstruation—notably, irritability and depression—are rare, which is why we put "PMS" in quotation marks. In fact, fewer than five percent of all women have such symptoms predictably over their cycles (Brooks-Gunn, 1986; Reid, 1991; Walker, 1994). Just as with SAD, more people claim to have symptoms than actually do.

If true PMS is so uncommon, then why do so many women think they have it? One possibility is that they tend to notice feelings of depression or irritability when these moods happen to occur premenstrually but overlook times when such moods are *absent* premenstrually. Or they may

Thinking Critically About "PMS"

label symptoms that occur before a period as "PMS" and attribute the same symptoms at other times of the month to a stressful day or a low grade on an English paper. A woman's perceptions of her own emotional ups and downs can also be influenced by cultural attitudes and myths about menstruation.

To get around these problems, psychologists have polled women about their psychological and physical well-being without revealing the true purpose of the study (e.g., AuBuchon & Calhoun, 1985; Chrisler, 2000; Englander-Golden, Whitmore, & Dienstbier, 1978; Gallant et al., 1991; Hardie, 1997; Parlee, 1982; Rapkin, Chang, & Reading, 1988; Slade, 1984; Vila & Beech, 1980; Walker, 1994). Using double-blind procedures, they have had women report symptoms for a single day and have then gone back to see what phase of the menstrual cycle the women were in; or they have had women keep daily records for two or three months. Some studies have included a control group that is usually excluded from research on hormones and moods: men! Here are the major findings:

- *No gender differences exist in mood.* Research at the University of British Columbia has shown that, overall, women and men do not differ significantly in the emotional symptoms they report or the number of mood swings they experience over the course of a month, as you can see in Figure 5.1 (McFarlane, Martin, & Williams, 1988).

- *No relation exists between stage of the menstrual cycle and emotional symptoms.* Most women do not have the typical "PMS" symptoms even when they firmly believe they do (Hardie, 1997; McFarlane & Williams, 1994). They may recall their moods as having been more unpleasant before or during menstruation, but, as you can also see in Figure 5.1, their own daily reports fail to bear them out.

- *No connection exists between "PMS" and behaviour.* There is no relationship between stage of the menstrual cycle and work efficiency, problem solving, motor performance, memory, college exam scores, creativity, or any other behaviour that matters in real life (Golub, 1992; Richardson, 1992). In the workplace, men, premenstrual women, postmenstrual women, and nonmenstruating women all report similar levels of stress, wellness, and work performance (Hardie, 1997).

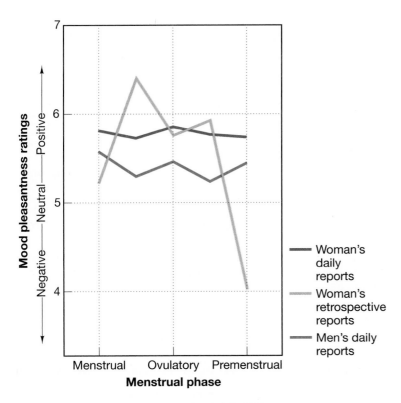

FIGURE 5.1 Mood Changes in Men and Women

In a University of British Columbia study that challenged popular stereotypes about "PMS," university women and men recorded their moods daily for 70 days without knowing the purpose of the study. The women thought their moods had been more negative premenstrually than during the rest of the month (green line), but their daily diaries showed otherwise (purple line). Both sexes experienced only moderate mood changes, and there were no significant differences between women and men at any time of the month (McFarlane, Martin, & Williams, 1988).

These results are unknown to most people and have usually been ignored by doctors, therapists, and the media. As a result, since the 1970s, premenstrual symptoms have come to be defined almost solely in medical and psychiatric terms (Parlee, 1994). In 1994, over the objections of many psychologists, the American Psychiatric Association included "premenstrual dysphoric disorder" (PMDD) in the *Diagnostic and Statistical Manual of Mental Disorders*, the official guide to psychiatric diagnosis. The label is supposed to describe a rare and incapacitating disorder, but its description includes the same hodge-podge of physical and emotional symptoms as "PMS" does. More recently, the antidepressant Prozac™ was repackaged and marketed as Sarafem™, a medication supposedly just for PMDD.

Does Testosterone Affect Moods? Critics believe that the acceptance of "PMS" as a widespread problem and a psychiatric diagnosis has more to do with politics than with facts. The notion that

hormones impair mood and performance, they point out, is rarely extended to men—even though levels of the masculinizing hormone testosterone rise and fall in a cyclical manner, too. Testosterone fluctuates daily in all men, usually reaching a peak in the morning, and it also follows a longer cycle in some men, varying in length from one man to another (Doering et al., 1974). Yet almost no work has been done on the relationship between testosterone cycles and mood or other psychological changes.

Researchers *have*, however, compared men who have relatively high levels of testosterone with those who have relatively low levels. High levels have been linked to a long (and sometimes contradictory) list of behaviours and traits, including criminal violence, delinquency, rambunctiousness, restlessness, elation, sadness, moodiness, sociability, aloofness—and being a trial lawyer (Dabbs et al., 1995; Dabbs, Alford, & Fielden, 1998; Dabbs, Hargrove, & Heusel, 1996; Dabbs, Strong, & Milun, 1997; Mazur & Lamb, 1980; Susman et al., 1987). But researchers have been careful to point out that behaviour affects testosterone levels as well as the reverse. For example, testosterone tends to rise *after* a man behaves aggressively, not before, and it also rises after he watches a favourite sports team win (Bernhardt et al., 1998; Sapolsky, 1997). Moreover, no researcher has suggested that men are victims of hormone fluctuations or that high testosterone levels constitute a syndrome calling for treatment.

We are not suggesting that, either! We raise the issue of testosterone to point out cultural biases in thinking about hormones and behaviour— biases that cause many people to reduce women's behaviour to hormones, but not men's. In reality, few people of either sex are likely to undergo personality

"You've been charged with driving under the influence of testosterone."

shifts solely because of their hormones, except in rare cases of hormonal abnormalities. In most instances, the body only provides the clay for people's symptoms; learning and culture mould that

clay, by teaching us which symptoms are important or worrisome and which are not. The impact of any bodily change depends on how we interpret it and how we respond to it.

Quick Quiz

There are no hormonal excuses for avoiding this quiz.

1. The functioning of the biological clock governing circadian rhythms is affected by the hormone _____.

2. Jet lag occurs because of _____.

3. For most women, the days before menstruation are reliably associated with (a) depression, (b) irritability, (c) elation, (d) creativity, (e) none of these, (f) a and b.

4. A researcher tells male participants in a study that testosterone usually peaks in the morning and that it probably causes hostility. She then asks them to fill out a "Hypertestosterone Syndrome Hostility Survey" in the morning and again at night. Based on menstrual-cycle findings, what results might she get? How could she improve her study?

Answers:

1. melatonin   2. internal desynchronization   3.e

4. Because of the expectations that the men now have about testosterone, they may be biased to report more hostility in the morning. It would be better to keep them in the dark about the hypothesis and to measure their actual hormone levels at different points in the day, because individuals vary in their biological rhythms. Also, a control group of women could be added, to see whether their hostility levels vary in the same way that men's do. Finally, the title on that questionnaire is pretty biased! A more neutral one, say, "Health and Mood Checklist," would be better.

WHAT'S AHEAD

- Why do we sleep?
- What happens when we go too long without enough sleep?
- Why are you likely to be dreaming when the alarm goes off in the morning?

THE RHYTHMS OF SLEEP

Perhaps the most perplexing of all our biological rhythms is the one governing sleep and wakefulness. Sleep, after all, puts us at risk: Muscles that are usually ready to respond to danger relax, and senses grow dull. As the late British psychologist Christopher Evans (1984) once noted, "The behaviour patterns involved in sleep are glaringly, almost insanely, at odds with common sense." Then why is sleep such a profound necessity?

Why We Sleep

Surprisingly, the exact functions of sleep are still uncertain (Maquet, 2001). However, generally speaking, sleep appears to provide a time-out

period, so that the body can eliminate waste products from muscles, repair cells, strengthen the immune system, and recover abilities lost during the day. When we do not get enough sleep, our bodies operate abnormally. For example, levels of hormones that are necessary for normal muscle development and proper immune-system functioning decline (Leproult, Van Reeth, et al., 1997).

Although most people can still get along reasonably well after a day or two of sleeplessness, sleep deprivation that lasts for four days or longer becomes uncomfortable, and soon unbearable. In animals, forced sleeplessness leads to infections and eventually death, and the same seems to be true for people. In one tragic case, a 51-year-old man abruptly began to lose sleep. After sinking deeper and deeper into an exhausted stupor, he developed a lung infection and died. An autopsy showed that he had lost almost all the large neurons in two areas of the thalamus that have been linked to sleep and hormonal circadian rhythms (Lugaresi et al., 1986).

Sleep is also necessary for normal *mental* functioning. After the loss of even a single night's sleep, mental flexibility, attention, and creativity all suffer.

Whatever your age, sometimes the urge to sleep is irresistible—especially because in fast-paced modern societies, many people do not get as much sleep as they need.

For example, at the University of Manitoba, David Koulack (1997) has shown that recognition memory is better for individuals who have had a period of sleep between the time they learned material and were asked to remember it. In chronic sleep deprivation, high levels of cortisol may damage or impair the brain cells that are necessary for learning and memory (Leproult, Copinschi, et al., 1997). After several days of staying awake, people may even begin to have hallucinations and delusions (Dement, 1978).

Of course, sleep deprivation rarely reaches that point, but people frequently suffer from milder versions. Many people are plagued by insomnia—difficulty in falling or staying asleep. Insomnia can result from worry and anxiety, psychological problems, hot flashes during menopause, physical problems such as arthritis, and irregular or overly demanding work and study schedules. (For advice on how to get a better night's sleep, see "Taking Psychology With You.")

Another cause of daytime sleepiness is **sleep apnea**, a disorder in which breathing periodically stops for a few moments, causing the person to

choke and gasp. This disorder affects up to 5 percent of women and 15 percent of men between the ages of 30 and 60 (HealthOntario.com, 2005). Sleep apnea has several causes, from blockage of air passages to failure of the brain to control respiration correctly, and, if chronic, it can cause high blood pressure and an irregular heartbeat. Researchers at the University of Western Ontario have even found that people with untreated sleep apnea are three times as likely as others to have a traffic accident (George, 2001). Successful treatment of the condition returns that risk to normal, however. In **narcolepsy**, another serious disorder, an individual is subject to irresistible and unpredictable daytime attacks of sleepiness or actual sleep, lasting from 5 to 30 minutes. About 27 000 Canadians suffer from this condition, many without knowing it. Genetic factors seem to be involved (Overeem et al., 2001).

The most common cause of sleepiness is probably the most obvious one—staying up late and not allowing yourself to get enough sleep at night. Because sleep is so vital to physical and mental well-being, many researchers are worried about the growing numbers of sleep-deprived people in modern societies. When people are sleepy, traffic and work accidents become far more likely (Coren, 1996; Maas, 1998). In the United States, the National Transportation Safety Board has reported that tired truck drivers who fall asleep at the wheel are responsible for up to 1500 road deaths a year; driver fatigue is a greater safety problem than use of alcohol or other drugs.

According to the 1998 General Social Survey conducted by Statistics Canada, Canadians sleep an average of 8.1 hours per night, though about 15 percent of us sleep less than 6.5 hours per night and almost half say they have cut down on their

narcolepsy A sleep disorder involving sudden and unpredictable daytime attacks of sleepiness or actual sleep.

sleep apnea A disorder in which breathing briefly stops during sleep, causing the person to choke and gasp, and momentarily awaken.

sleep in an attempt to accomplish more in a day. Most people, however, need at least eight or nine hours for optimal performance, and adolescents typically need ten.

The Realms of Sleep

Until the early 1950s, little was known about the physiology of sleep. Then a breakthrough occurred in the laboratory of physiologist Nathaniel Kleitman, who at the time was the only person in the world who had spent his entire career studying sleep. Kleitman had given one of his graduate students, Eugene Aserinsky, the tedious task of finding out whether the slow, rolling eye movements that characterize the onset of sleep continue throughout the night. To both men's surprise, eye movements did indeed occur, but they were rapid, not slow (Aserinsky & Kleitman, 1955). Using the electroencephalograph (EEG) to measure the brain's electrical activity (see Chapter 4), these researchers, along with another of Kleitman's students, William Dement, were able to correlate the rapid eye movements with changes in sleepers' brainwave patterns (Dement, 1992). Adult volunteers were soon spending their nights sleeping in laboratories while scientists measured changes in their brain activity, muscle tension, breathing, and other physiological responses.

As a result of this research, today we know that during sleep, periods of **rapid eye movement (REM)** alternate with periods of fewer eye movements, or *non-REM (NREM) sleep*, in a cycle that recurs about every 90 minutes or so. The REM periods last from a few minutes to as long as an hour, averaging about 20 minutes in length. Whenever they begin, the pattern of electrical activity from the sleeper's brain changes to resemble that of alert wakefulness. Non-REM periods are themselves divided into shorter, distinct stages, each associated with a particular brainwave pattern (see Figure 5.2).

When you first climb into bed, close your eyes, and relax, your brain emits bursts of *alpha waves*. On an EEG recording, alpha waves have a regular, slow rhythm and a high amplitude (height). Gradually, these waves slow down even further, and you drift off into slumber, passing through four stages:

- *Stage 1.* Your brain waves become small and irregular, and you feel yourself drifting on the edge of consciousness, in a state of light sleep. If awakened, you may recall fantasies or a few visual images.

- *Stage 2.* Your brain emits occasional short bursts of rapid, high-peaking waves called *sleep spindles*. Minor noises probably won't disturb you.

- *Stage 3.* In addition to the waves characteristic of Stage 2, your brain occasionally emits *delta waves*, very slow waves with very high peaks. Your breathing and pulse have slowed down, your muscles are relaxed, and you are hard to rouse.

- *Stage 4.* Delta waves have now largely taken over, and you are in deep sleep. It will probably take vigorous shaking or a loud noise to awaken you. Oddly, though, if you talk or walk in your sleep, this is when you are likely to do so. The causes of sleepwalking, which occurs more often in children than adults, are still unknown, but they may involve unusual patterns of brain activity (Bassetti et al., 2000).

This sequence of stages takes about 30 to 45 minutes. Then you move back up the ladder from Stage 4 to 3 to 2 to 1. At that point, about 70 to 90 minutes after the onset of sleep, something peculiar happens. Stage 1 does not turn into drowsy wakefulness, as one might expect. Instead,

rapid eye movement (REM) sleep Sleep periods characterized by eye movement, loss of muscle tone, and dreaming.

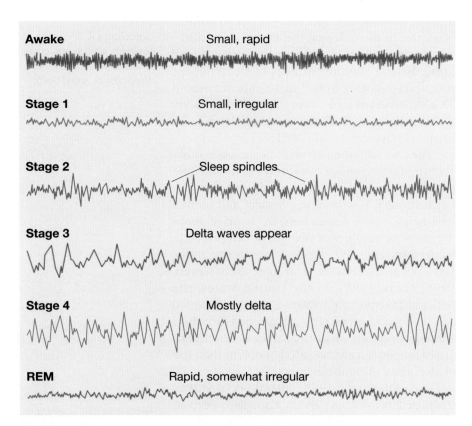

FIGURE 5.2 Brainwave Patterns during Wakefulness and Sleep
Most types of brainwaves are present throughout sleep, but different ones predominate at different stages.

your brain begins to emit long bursts of very rapid, somewhat irregular waves. Your heart rate increases, your blood pressure rises, and your breathing becomes faster and more irregular. Small twitches in your face and fingers may occur. In men, the penis becomes somewhat erect as vascular tissue relaxes and blood fills the genital area faster than it exits. In women, the clitoris enlarges and vaginal lubrication increases. At the same time, most skeletal muscles go limp, preventing your aroused brain from producing physical movement. You have entered the realm of REM.

Because the brain is extremely active while the body is entirely inactive, REM sleep has also been called "paradoxical sleep." It is during these periods that you are most likely to dream. Even people who claim they never dream at all will report dreams if awakened in a sleep laboratory during REM sleep. But dreaming is also often reported during non-REM sleep, though the dreams tend to be shorter, less vivid, and more realistic. In one study, for example, dream reports occurred 82 percent of the time when sleepers were awakened during REM sleep, but they also occurred 51 percent of the time when people were awakened during non-REM sleep (Foulkes, 1962).

REM and non-REM sleep continue to alternate throughout the night, with Stages 3 and 4 tending to become shorter or even to disappear, and REM periods tending to get longer and closer together as the hours pass. This pattern explains why you are likely to be dreaming when the alarm clock goes off in the morning. But the cycles are far

Because cats sleep up to 80 percent of the time, it's easy to catch them in the various stages of slumber. A cat in non-REM sleep (left) remains upright, but during the REM phase (right), its muscles go limp and it flops onto its side.

from regular. An individual may bounce directly from Stage 4 back to Stage 2, or go from REM to Stage 2 and then back to REM. Also, the time between REM and non-REM is highly variable, differing from person to person and also within any given individual.

The purpose of REM sleep is still a matter of debate, but clearly it does have a purpose. If you wake people up every time they lapse into REM sleep, nothing dramatic will happen. When finally allowed to sleep normally, however, they will spend a much longer time than usual in the REM phase, and it will be hard to rouse them. Electrical brain activity associated with REM may burst through into quiet sleep and even into wakefulness, as if the participants are making up for something they were deprived of. Many people think that in adults, at least, this "something" is connected with dreaming, to which we now turn.

Quick Quiz

Wake up and take this quiz!

A. Match each term with the appropriate phrase.

1. REM periods
2. alpha
3. Stage 4 sleep
4. Stage 1 sleep

a. delta waves and talking in one's sleep
b. irregular brainwaves and light sleep
c. relaxed but awake
d. active brain but inactive muscles

B. Sleep is necessary for normal (a) physical and mental functioning, (b) mental functioning but not physical functioning, (c) physical functioning but not mental functioning.

C. *True or false?*: Most people can get by fine with six hours of sleep a night.

Answers:

C. false
B. a
A. 1.d 2.c 3. a 4. b

WHAT'S AHEAD

- Why did Freud call dreams the "royal road to the unconscious"?
- How might your dreams be related to your current problems and concerns?
- How does a disruption of REM sleep affect memory?
- Could dreams be caused by meaningless brain-stem signals?

EXPLORING THE DREAM WORLD

In dreaming, the focus of attention is inward, though occasionally an external event, such as a wailing siren, can influence the dream's content. While a dream is in progress, it may be vivid or vague, terrifying or peaceful. It may also seem to make perfect sense—until you wake up. Then it is often recalled as illogical, bizarre, and disjointed. Although most of us are unaware of our bodies or where we are while we are dreaming, some people report having **lucid dreams**, in which they know they are dreaming and feel as though they are conscious. A few even say that they can control the action in these dreams, much as a scriptwriter decides what will happen in a movie (LaBerge, 1986; LaBerge & Levitan, 1995). Interestingly, researchers at McGill have shown that the ability to have lucid dreams can actually be induced in otherwise non-lucid dreamers (Zadra, Donderi, & Pihl, 1992). There are a number of techniques used for what is called lucid dream induction, including such things as "self-suggestion"—telling yourself just before you fall asleep that you are going to have a lucid dream.

One issue that has bothered sleep researchers for years is whether the eye movements of REM sleep correspond to events and actions in a dream. Are the eyes tracking these images? Some researchers believe that in adult dreamers, eye movements do resemble those of waking life, when the eyes and head move in synchrony as the person moves about and shifts his or her gaze (J. H. Herman, 1992). But others think that eye movements are no more related to dream content than are inner-ear muscle contractions, which also occur during REM sleep. Nearly all mammals, including human fetuses, experience REM sleep (the only known exceptions are the spiny

lucid dream A dream in which the dreamer is aware of dreaming.

anteater, the bottlenose dolphin, and the porpoise), but we might not want to credit mice, opossums, or human fetuses with what we ordinarily call dreams. Moles, which can hardly move their eyes at all, nonetheless show EEG patterns associated with REM sleep.

Why do the images in dreams arise at all? Why doesn't the brain just rest, switching off all thoughts and images and launching us into a coma? Why, instead, do we spend our nights flying through the air, battling monsters, or having weird conversations in the fantasy world of our dreams? We will consider four of the leading explanations and then evaluate them.

Dreams as Unconscious Wishes

One of the first psychological theorists to take dreams seriously was Sigmund Freud, the founder of psychoanalysis. After analyzing many of his patients' dreams and some of his own, Freud concluded that our nighttime fantasies provide insight into desires, motives, and conflicts of which we are unaware—a "royal road to the unconscious." In dreams, said Freud (1900/1953), we are able to express our unconscious wishes and desires, which are often sexual or violent in nature.

According to Freud, every dream is meaningful, no matter how absurd it may seem. But if a dream's message arouses anxiety, the rational part of the mind must disguise and distort it. Otherwise, the dream would intrude into consciousness and waken the dreamer. In dreams, therefore, one person may be represented by another—for example, a father by a brother—or even by several different characters. Similarly, thoughts and objects

are translated into symbolic images. A penis may be disguised as a snake, umbrella, or dagger; a vagina, as a tunnel or cave; and the human body, as a house.

To understand a dream, said Freud, we must distinguish its *manifest content*, the aspects of it that we consciously experience during sleep and may remember upon wakening, from its *latent* (hidden) *content*, the unconscious wishes and thoughts being expressed symbolically. Freud warned against the simple-minded translation of symbols, however. Each dream had to be analyzed in the context of the dreamer's waking life, as well as the person's associations with the dream's contents. Not everything in a dream is symbolic. Sometimes, Freud cautioned, "A cigar is only a cigar."

Dreams as Reflections of Current Concerns

Another explanation holds that dreams reflect the ongoing *conscious* preoccupations of waking life, such as concerns over relationships, work, sex, or health (Siegel, 1991; Webb & Cartwright, 1978). In this *problem-focused approach* to dreaming, the symbols and metaphors in a dream do not disguise its true meaning; they convey it. For example, psychologist Gayle Delaney told of a woman who dreamed she was swimming underwater. The woman's eight-year-old son was on her back, his head above the water. Her husband was supposed to take a picture of them, but for some reason he wasn't doing it, and she was starting to feel as if she were going to drown. To Delaney, the message was obvious: The woman was "drowning" under the responsibilities of child care, and her husband wasn't "getting the picture" (in Dolnick, 1990).

The problem-focused explanation of dreaming is supported by findings that dreams are more likely to contain material related to a person's current concerns than chance would predict. For example, among college students, who are often anxious about grades and tests, "examination dreams" are common: The dreamer is unprepared for or unable to finish an exam, or shows up for the wrong exam, or can't find the room where the exam is being given (Halliday, 1993; Van de Castle, 1994). (Sound familiar?) For their part, instructors often dream that they have forgotten their lecture notes at home, or that their notes contain only blank pages and they have nothing to say!

Men and women, of course, often have different concerns, so we might expect the content of their dreams to differ—and until recently, at least,

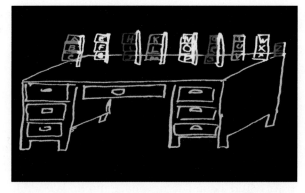

Images in dreams can be either abstract or literal. The desk in this drawing was sketched in 1939 by a scientist to illustrate his dream about a mechanical device for instantly retrieving quotations—a sort of early desktop computer!

that has been true. Typically, women have been more likely than men to dream about children, family members, familiar characters, friendly interactions, household objects, clothes, and indoor events. Men have been more likely than women to dream about strangers, weapons, violence, sexual activity, achievement, and outdoor events (Domhoff, 1996; Hall et al., 1982). But as the lives and concerns of the two sexes have become more similar, so have their dreams. In one study, only two differences showed up: Men were more likely to dream about behaving aggressively, and women were more likely to dream about their anxieties, especially about failing exams (Bursik, 1998).

Some psychologists believe that dreams not only reflect our waking concerns, but also provide us with an opportunity to resolve them. Rosalind Cartwright has been investigating this hypothesis for many years. Among people suffering from the grief of divorce, she finds, recovery is related to a particular pattern of dreaming: The first dream of the night often comes sooner than it ordinarily would, lasts longer, and is more emotional and storylike (Cartwright, 1990, 1996). Depressed people's dreams tend to get less negative and more positive as the night wears on, and this pattern, too, predicts recovery (Cartwright et al., 1998). Cartwright concludes that getting through a crisis or a rough period in life takes "time, good friends, good genes, good luck, and a good dream system." Dreams that keep coming back in similar form, on the other hand, might indicate psychological difficulty. Researchers in Montreal have found that recurring dreams tend to be more negative than positive, and more common to people experiencing poorer psychological well-being (Zadra, O'Brien, & Donderi, 1998).

Dreams as a By-Product of Mental Housekeeping

A third approach explains dreams in physiological and information-processing terms. Dreams, in this view, are a by-product of mental housekeeping, in which unnecessary neural connections in the brain are eliminated and important ones are strengthened (Evans, 1984).

According to this explanation, the brain must periodically shut out sensory input so that it can process and assimilate new data and update what has already been stored. It divides new information into "wanted" and "unwanted" categories, makes new associations, and—to use a computer analogy—revises old "programs" in light of the day's experiences. The data the brain sifts through include not only recent events, but also ideas, obsessions, worries, wishes, and thoughts about the past. What we recall as dreams are really only brief snippets from an ongoing process of scanning and sorting that occurs most intensely during REM sleep but possibly throughout the night. Because these snippets give us only a glimpse of the night's mental activity, they naturally seem odd and nonsensical when recalled.

activation-synthesis theory
The theory that dreaming results from the cortical synthesis and interpretation of neural signals triggered by activity in the lower part of the brain.

Several variations on this theme have been proposed. For example, Francis Crick and Graeme Mitchison (1995) emphasize only the weakening of unused synaptic connections in the brain's vast memory network. In their view, during REM sleep a sort of "reverse learning" occurs, making memory more efficient and accurate and protecting us from becoming obsessed by unwanted thoughts

and images. Dreams are merely mental garbage, and there is no point in trying to remember them or analyze them for their "meanings."

Other researchers emphasize the *strengthening* of synaptic connections associated with recently stored memories. REM sleep seems to be associated with *consolidation*, a process by which the synaptic changes associated with a recently stored memory become durable and stable (see Chapter 4). When people or animals learn a perceptual task and are allowed to get normal REM sleep, their memory for the task is better the next day, even when they have been awakened during non-REM periods; but when they are deprived of REM sleep, their memories are impaired (Karni et al., 1994; Smith, 1995). And when people learn a computerized task (hitting keys when they see a dot in different places on the screen), some of the same brain areas that are active during the task are active later during REM sleep (Maquet et al., 2000). A similar finding has been obtained with rats that learned to run a circular maze (Wilson & Louie, 2001). Were the rats dreaming about the maze?

Dreams as Interpreted Brain Activity

A fourth approach to dreaming, the **activation-synthesis theory**, also draws heavily on physiological research. According to this explanation, first proposed by J. Allan Hobson (1988, 1990), dreams are not "children of an idle brain," as Shakespeare called them. Rather, they are the result of neurons firing spontaneously in the lower part of the brain, in the pons, during REM sleep. These neurons control eye movement, gaze, balance, and posture, and they send messages to sensory and motor areas of the cortex responsible during wakefulness for visual processing and voluntary action.

According to the activation-synthesis theory, the signals originating in the pons have no psychological meaning in themselves. But the cortex tries to make sense of them by *synthesizing*, or integrating, them with existing knowledge and memories to produce some sort of coherent interpretation. This is just what the cortex does when signals come from sense organs during ordinary wakefulness. Indeed, the idea that one part of the brain interprets what has gone on in another is consistent with many modern theories of how the brain works (see Chapter 4).

When neurons fire in the part of the brain that handles balance, for instance, the cortex may generate a dream about falling. When signals occur

"MENTAL HOUSEKEEPING" VIEW OF DREAMS

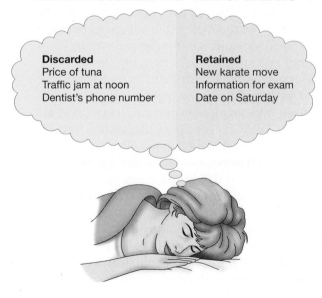

Discarded
Price of tuna
Traffic jam at noon
Dentist's phone number

Retained
New karate move
Information for exam
Date on Saturday

that would ordinarily produce running, the cortex may manufacture a dream about being chased. Because the signals from the pons occur randomly, the cortex's interpretation—the dream—is likely to be incoherent and confusing. And because the cortical neurons that control the initial storage of new memories are turned off during sleep, we typically forget our dreams upon waking unless we write them down or immediately recount them to someone else.

Since Hobson's original formulation, he and his colleagues have added further details and modifications (Hobson, Pace-Schott, & Stickgold, 2000). The brain stem, they say, sets off responses in emotional and visual parts of the brain. At the same time, brain regions that handle logical thought and sensations from the external world shut down. These changes would account for the fact that dreams tend to be emotionally charged, hallucinatory, and illogical.

Wishes, in this view, do not cause dreams; brain mechanisms do. But that does not mean that dreams are meaningless. Hobson (1988) argued that the brain "is so inexorably bent upon the quest for meaning that it attributes and even creates meaning when there is little or none to be found in the data it is asked to process." By studying these attributed meanings, you can learn about your unique perceptions, conflicts, and concerns—not by trying to dig below the surface of the dream, as Freud would, but by examining the surface itself. Or you can relax and enjoy the nightly entertainment that dreams provide.

Evaluating Dream Theories

How are we to evaluate these different attempts to explain dreaming? All four approaches account for some of the evidence, but each one also has its drawbacks.

Most psychologists today accept Freud's notion that dreams are more than incoherent ramblings of the mind—that they have psychological meaning (Fisher & Greenberg, 1996). However, many find Freudian interpretations far-fetched. They point out that no reliable rules exist for interpreting the supposedly latent content of dreams, and there is no objective way to know whether a particular interpretation is correct. Freudian interpretations have crept into popular books and newspaper columns that try to tell you what your dreams mean, but they are only the writers' personal hunches.

ACTIVATION-SYNTHESIS THEORY OF DREAMS

2. Cerebral cortex synthesizes signals, tries to interpret them ("I'm running through the woods")

1. Spontaneous firing of neurons in pons

As for dreams as a way of solving problems, it seems pretty clear that some dreams are focused on current worries and concerns, but skeptics doubt that people can actually solve problems or conflicts while sound asleep (Blagrove, 1996; Squier & Domhoff, 1998). Dreams, they say, merely give expression to our problems. The insights that people seem to gain into those problems could be occurring after they wake up and have a chance to think about what is troubling them.

Thinking Critically About Dream Theories

The mental-housekeeping approach tells us more about the functions of REM sleep than about dreaming per se. Remember those rats who appeared to be "dreaming" about a maze they had run? It is hard to imagine that a rat's "dream," if it has one, is anything like a human being's. The same applies to human babies (not to mention fetuses). Newborns spend about 50 percent of their sleeping hours in REM sleep, versus only 20 percent for adults. Because everything that is happening to them is new, they may have a lot of consolidation of recent learning to do. But it is hard to credit them with actual dreams, because they have not built up the storehouse of images, memories, and experiences that are found in dreams. The notion that dreams are for "mental housekeeping" and the consolidation of memories also fails to explain why some dreams are so storylike, or why some dreams recur periodically for years.

The activation-synthesis theory has also come under criticism (Squier & Domhoff, 1998). Not all dreams are as disjointed or as bizarre as the theory predicts; some tell a coherent, if fanciful, story. Moreover, the activation-synthesis approach does not account well for dreaming that goes on outside of REM sleep. Some neuropsychologists emphasize different brain mechanisms involved in dreams, and many believe that dreams do reflect a person's goals and desires (Solms, 2000).

Perhaps it will turn out that different kinds of dreams have different purposes and origins. We all know from experience that some of our dreams seem to be related to daily problems, some are vague and incoherent, and some are anxiety dreams that occur when we are worried or depressed. For the time being, we are going to have to live with uncertainty about what those fascinating stories and images in our sleeping brains really mean.

Quick Quiz

See if you can dream up an answer to this question.

In his dreams, Andy is an infant crawling through a dark tunnel looking for something he has lost. Which theory of dreams would be most receptive to each of the following explanations?

1. Andy recently misplaced a valuable watch but eventually found it.
2. While Andy was sleeping, neurons in his pons that would ordinarily stimulate parts of the brain involved in leg-muscle movements were active.
3. Andy has repressed an early sexual attraction to his mother; the tunnel symbolizes her vagina.
4. Andy has broken up with his lover and is working through the emotional loss.

Answers:

1. the mental-housekeeping (information-processing) approach (the dreamer is processing information about a recent experience) 2. the activation-synthesis theory 3. psychoanalytic theory 4. the problem-focused approach

WHAT'S AHEAD

- Can a hypnotist force you to do things against your will?
- Can hypnosis help you remember the past more accurately?
- What are the legitimate uses of hypnosis in psychology and medicine?
- Are hypnotized persons merely faking or play-acting?

THE RIDDLE OF HYPNOSIS

For many years, stage hypnotists, "past-lives channellers," and some psychotherapists have been reporting that they can "age regress" hypnotized people to earlier years or even earlier centuries. Some therapists claim that hypnosis helps their patients accurately retrieve long-buried memories, and a few even claim that hypnosis has helped their patients recall alleged abductions by extraterrestrials. What are we to make of all this?

Hypnosis is a procedure in which a practitioner suggests changes in the sensations, perceptions, thoughts, feelings, or behaviour of the subject (Kirsch & Lynn, 1995). The hypnotized person, in turn, tries to alter his or her cognitive processes in accordance with the hypnotist's suggestions (Nash & Nadon, 1997). Hypnotic suggestions typically involve performance of an action ("Your arm will slowly rise"), an inability to perform an act ("You will be unable to bend your arm"), or a distortion of normal perception or memory ("You will feel no pain," "You will forget being hypnotized until I give you a signal"). People usually report that their compliance with these suggestions feels involuntary.

To induce hypnosis, the hypnotist typically suggests that the person being hypnotized feels relaxed, is getting sleepy, and feels the eyelids getting heavier and heavier. In a singsong or monotonous voice, the hypnotist assures the subject that he or she is sinking "deeper and deeper." Sometimes the hypnotist has the person concentrate on a colour or a small object, or on certain bodily sensations. People who have been hypnotized report that the focus of attention turns outward, toward the hypnotist's voice. They sometimes compare the experience to being totally absorbed in a good book, play, or favourite piece of music. The hypnotized person almost always remains fully aware of what is going on and remembers the experience later, unless explicitly instructed to forget it—and even then, the memory can be restored by a prearranged signal.

Because hypnosis has been used for everything from parlour tricks and stage shows to medical and psychological treatments, it is important to understand just what this procedure can and cannot achieve. We will begin with a look at the major findings on hypnosis; then we will consider two leading explanations of hypnotic effects.

The Nature of Hypnosis

Since the late 1960s, thousands of articles on hypnosis have appeared. Based on controlled laboratory and clinical research studies, most researchers agree on the following points (Kirsch & Lynn, 1995; Nash, 2001; Nash & Nadon, 1997):

1 *Hypnotic responsiveness depends more on the efforts and qualities of the person being hypnotized than on the skill of the hypnotist.* Some people are more responsive to hypnosis than others. Surprisingly, however, hypnotic susceptibility is unrelated to

Amazing, right? Or maybe not. This stage hypnotist's audience believes that the man he is standing on can support his weight without flinching because he's hypnotized, but most unhypnotized people can do the same thing. The only way to find out whether hypnosis produces unique results is to do research with control groups.

general personality traits, such as gullibility, trust, submissiveness, or conformity (Nash & Nadon, 1997). People who are easily hypnotized do tend to have the ability to become easily absorbed in their activities and involved in the world of imagination, but this ability is only weakly related to hypnotic susceptibility (Council, Kirsch, & Grant, 1996; Nash & Nadon, 1997).

2 *Hypnotized people cannot be forced to do things against their will.* Like drunkenness, hypnosis can be used to justify letting go of inhibitions ("I know this looks silly, but after all, I'm hypnotized"). Hypnotized individuals may even comply with a suggestion to do something that seems embarrassing or dangerous. But the individual is choosing to turn responsibility over to the hypnotist and to co-operate with the hypnotist's suggestions (Lynn, Rhue, & Weekes, 1990). Some time ago, researchers at Concordia found that there is no evidence that hypnotized people will do anything that actually goes against their morals or that constitutes a real threat to themselves or others (Laurence & Perry, 1988).

3 *Feats performed under hypnosis can be performed by motivated people without hypnosis.* Hypnotic suggestions sometimes lead to feats of great strength or other seemingly surprising abilities,

hypnosis A procedure in which the practitioner suggests changes in the sensations, perceptions, thoughts, feelings, or behaviour of the subject.

"THE WITNESS HAS BARKED, MEOWED AND GIVEN US FIVE MINUTES OF BABY TALK. I'D SAY HYPNOSIS IS NOT THE ANSWER."

but hypnosis does not enable people to transcend their normal physical and mental capacities. Research at Carleton University and elsewhere has shown that suggestion alone, without the special procedures of hypnosis, can produce the same results as long as people are motivated to co-operate, believe they can succeed, and are encouraged to relax, concentrate, and do their best (e.g., Chaves, 1989; Spanos, Stenstrom, & Johnson, 1988).

4 *Hypnosis does not increase the accuracy of memory.* Many people assume that hypnosis can enhance the recall of forgotten experiences. Sometimes hypnosis *can* be used successfully to jog the memories of crime victims. After the 1976 kidnapping of a busload of schoolchildren in Chowchilla, California, a breakthrough in the case occurred when the bus driver, under hypnosis, was able to recall all but one of the licence-plate numbers on the kidnappers' car. But in other cases, hypnotized witnesses have been completely mistaken. Although hypnosis does sometimes boost the amount of information recalled, it also increases *errors*, perhaps because hypnotized people are more willing than others to guess, or because they mistake vividly imagined possibilities for actual memories (Dinges et al., 1992; Kihlstrom, 1994). Nevertheless, when the questioning is over, the hypnotized person is often completely convinced that his or her "memories" are true. Because pseudomemories and errors are so common in hypnotically induced recall, the American Psychological Association and the American Medical Association oppose the use of "hypnotically refreshed" testimony in courts of law.

5 *Hypnosis does not produce a literal re-experiencing of long-ago events.* When Michael Yapko (1994), a clinical psychologist who uses hypnosis in his own practice, surveyed 869 members of the American Association of Marriage and Family Therapists, he discovered that more than half believed that "hypnosis can be used to recover memories from as far back as birth." This belief is just plain wrong. When people are regressed to an earlier age, their mental and moral performance remains adultlike (Nash, 1987). Their brainwave patterns and

reflexes do not become childish; they do not reason as children do or show child-sized IQs. They may use baby talk or report that they feel four years old again, but the reason is not that they *are* four; they are just willing to play the role.

6 *Hypnotic suggestions have been used effectively for many medical and psychological purposes.* Although hypnosis is not of much use for finding out what happened in the past, it can be useful in the treatment of psychological and medical problems. Hypnotic suggestions have been used to reduce stress, anxiety, and severe pain; anaesthetize people undergoing dental work, surgery, or childbirth; eliminate unwanted habits such as smoking or nail biting; improve study skills; reduce nausea in cancer patients undergoing chemotherapy; and pump up the confidence of athletes (Kirsch, Montgomery, & Sapirstein, 1995; Stam, 1989).

Theories of Hypnosis

Over the years, people have proposed many explanations of what hypnosis is and how it produces its effects. One early notion, that hypnosis is a "trance state," was eventually rejected by most researchers. Today, two competing theories predominate, with most scientists taking a position somewhere in the middle.

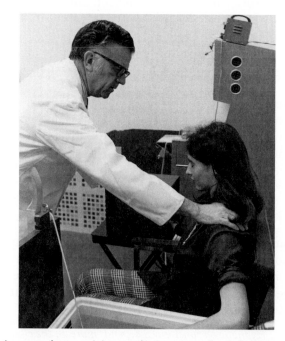

A person whose arm is immersed in ice water ordinarily feels intense pain. But Ernest Hilgard, a pioneer in hypnosis research, found that when hypnotized people are told the pain will be minimal, they report little or no discomfort. Like the young woman shown here in one of Hilgard's studies, they seem to be unperturbed.

Dissociation Theories One leading approach was originally proposed by the late Ernest Hilgard (1977, 1986), who argued that hypnosis, like lucid dreaming and even simple distraction, involves **dissociation**, a split in consciousness in which one part of the mind operates independently of the rest of consciousness. In many hypnotized persons, said Hilgard, while most of the mind is subject to hypnotic suggestion, one part is a *hidden observer*, watching but not participating. Unless given special instructions, the hypnotized part of the mind remains unaware of the observer.

In his research, Hilgard attempted to question the hidden observer directly. In one procedure, hypnotized volunteers had to submerge an arm in ice water for several seconds, an experience that is normally excruciating. They were told that they would feel no pain, but that the nonsubmerged hand would be able to signal the level of any hidden pain by pressing a key. In this situation, many people said they felt little or no pain—yet at the same time, their free hand was busily pressing the key. After the session, these people continued to insist that they had been pain-free, unless the hypnotist asked the hidden observer to issue a separate report.

Similar theories have also been proposed—for example, the late Ken Bowers and his associates at the University of Waterloo held that dissociation occurs between an "executive" system in the frontal lobes and other brain systems involved in thinking and acting, which can then be easily influenced by the hypnotist's suggestions (Woody & Bowers, 1994).

Like the activation-synthesis theory of dreaming, dissociation theories of hypnosis are consistent with modern brain theories, which propose that one part of the brain operates as an interpreter and reporter of activities carried out unconsciously by other brain parts (see Chapter 4). Still, many psychologists believe that there is less to dissociation and the hypnotic state than meets the eye. Some flat-out reject the idea that hypnosis differs from normal consciousness. They point out that when a person follows a hypnotist's instruction to hold out an arm rigidly, all this really tells us is that the person is suggestible and willing to go along (Barber, 1979; Weitzenhoffer, 1996). Moreover, the definition of a hypnotized "state" is circular: How do you know when people are in that state? Because they go along with the suggestions. And why do they go along? Because they are in a hypnotic state!

DISSOCIATION THEORIES OF HYPNOSIS

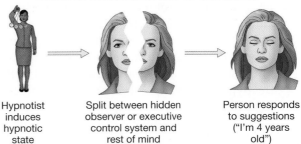

Hypnotist induces hypnotic state

Split between hidden observer or executive control system and rest of mind

Person responds to suggestions ("I'm 4 years old")

The Sociocognitive Approach The second major approach to hypnosis, and one studied extensively at Carleton University, is the *sociocognitive explanation*. This approach holds that the effects of hypnosis result from an interaction between the social influence of the hypnotist (the "socio" part) and the abilities, beliefs, and expectations of the subject (the "cognitive" part) (Kirsch, 1997; Sarbin, 1991; Spanos, 1991). The hypnotized person is basically playing a role, one that has analogies in ordinary life, where we willingly submit to the suggestions of parents, teachers, doctors, therapists, and television commercials. Even the "hidden observer" is simply a reaction to the social demands of the situation and the suggestions of the hypnotist (Kirsch & Lynn, 1998).

The hypnotized person is not merely faking or play-acting, however. A person who has been instructed to fool an observer by faking a hypnotic state will tend to overplay the role and will stop playing it as soon as the observer leaves the room. In contrast, hypnotized subjects continue to follow the hypnotic suggestions even when they think they are not being watched (Kirsch et al., 1989; Spanos et al., 1993). Like many social roles, the role of "hypnotized person" is so engrossing and involving that actions required by the role may occur without the person's conscious intent.

dissociation A split in consciousness in which one part of the mind operates independently of others.

SOCIOCOGNITIVE THEORIES OF HYPNOSIS

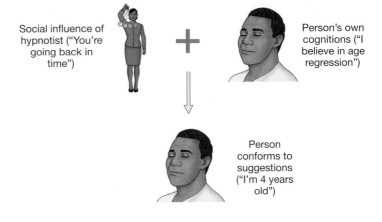

Social influence of hypnotist ("You're going back in time")

Person's own cognitions ("I believe in age regression")

Person conforms to suggestions ("I'm 4 years old")

Sociocognitive views explain why some people under hypnosis report spirit possession or "memories" of alien abductions (Baker, 1992; Spanos, 1996). Such persons may have a need to "escape the self" by turning control over to someone else (Newman & Baumeister, 1996). Often, the hypnotist readily assumes such control, shaping the person's story by giving subtle and not-so-subtle hints about what the person should say.

The sociocognitive view can also explain apparent cases of past-life regression. In a fascinating program of research, Nicholas Spanos and his colleagues directed hypnotized Canadian university students to regress past their own births to previous lives. About a third of the students reported being able to do so.

Thinking Critically About Hypnosis and "Past Lives"

But when they were asked, while supposedly reliving a past life, to name the leader of their country, say whether the country was at peace or at war, or describe the money used in their community, the students could not do it. (One young man, who thought he was Julius Caesar, said the year was 50 C.E. and he was emperor of Rome. But Caesar died in 44 B.C.E. and was never crowned emperor, and dating years as C.E. or B.C.E. did not begin until several centuries later.) Instead, the students tried to fulfill the requirements of the role by weaving events, places, and persons from their present lives into their accounts, and by picking up cues from the experimenter. The researchers concluded that the act of "remembering" another "self" involves the construction of a fantasy that accords with the rememberer's own beliefs and also the beliefs of others—in this case, the authoritative hypnotist (Spanos et al., 1991).

Psychologists who think hypnosis is a special state of consciousness involving dissociation and those who emphasize sociocognitive explanations agree on many issues. They agree, for example, that hypnosis does *not* create a unique state in which people can do extraordinary things, memories become sharper, or early experiences can be replayed with perfect accuracy. And many psychologists feel that both approaches have something to offer (Kihlstrom, 1998; Woody & Sadler, 1998). Whatever hypnosis is, by studying it, psychologists are learning much about human suggestibility, the power of imagination, and the way we perceive the present and remember the past.

Quick Quiz

We'd like to plant a suggestion in your mind—that you'd be wise to take this quiz.

A. *True or false?*:

1. A hypnotized person is usually aware of what is going on and remembers the experience later.
2. Hypnosis gives us special powers that we do not ordinarily have.
3. Hypnosis reduces errors in memory.
4. Hypnotized people play no active part in their behaviour and thoughts.
5. According to Hilgard, hypnosis is a state of consciousness involving a "hidden observer."
6. Sociocognitive theorists view hypnosis as mere faking or conscious play-acting.

B. Some people believe that hypnotic suggestions can bolster the immune system and help a person fight disease. However, support for this belief has so far been modest, and many studies have had methodological flaws (Miller & Cohen, 2001). One therapist dismissed these concerns by saying that a negative result just means that the hypnotist lacks skill or the right personality. As a critical thinker, can you spot what is wrong with his reasoning? (Think back to Chapter 1 and the way a scientific hypothesis must be stated.)

Answers:

A. 1. true 2. false 3. false 4. false 5. true 6. false

B. The therapist's argument violates the principle of falsifiability. If a result is positive, he counts it as evidence. But if a result is negative, he refuses to count it as counterevidence ("Maybe the hypnotist just wasn't good enough"). With this kind of reasoning, there is no way to tell whether the hypothesis is right or wrong.

WHAT'S AHEAD

- In its physiological effects, is alcohol a downer or an upper?
- How do recreational drugs affect the brain?
- Why can a glass of wine make you feel tired at one time but sociable and pepped up at another?

CONSCIOUSNESS-ALTERING DRUGS

In Jerusalem, hundreds of Hasidic men celebrate the completion of the reading of the holy Torah by dancing for hours in the streets; their goal is religious ecstasy. In Ontario, Ojibwe adults sit naked in the darkness and crushing heat of the sweat lodge; their goal is euphoria, the transcendence of pain, and possible connection with the Great Spirit of the Universe. Deep in the Amazon jungle, a young man training to be a shaman, a religious leader, takes a whiff of hallucinogenic snuff made from the bark of the virola tree; his goal is to enter a trance and communicate with animals, spirits, and supernatural forces.

These three rituals, although seemingly quite different, are all aimed at release from the confines of ordinary consciousness. Cultures around the world have devised such practices, often as part of their religions. Because attempts to alter mood and consciousness appear to be universal, some writers believe they reflect a human need, one as basic as the need for food and water (Siegel, 1989).

William James (1902/1936), who was fascinated by alterations in consciousness, would have agreed. After he had experienced the effects of inhaling nitrous oxide ("laughing gas"), he wrote, "Our normal waking consciousness, rational consciousness as we call it, is but one special type of consciousness, whilst all about it, parted from it by the filmiest of screens, there lie potential forms of consciousness entirely different." James hoped that psychologists would study these other forms of consciousness, but for half a century, few took his words seriously. Then, during the 1960s, attitudes changed. During that decade of social upheaval, millions of people began to seek ways of deliberately producing *altered states of consciousness*, especially through the use of psychoactive drugs. Researchers became interested in the psychology, as well as the physiology, of such drugs. The filmy screen described by James finally began to lift.

Classifying Drugs

A **psychoactive drug** is a substance that alters perception, mood, thinking, memory, or behaviour by changing the body's biochemistry. Around the world and throughout history, the most widely used drugs have been tobacco, alcohol, marijuana, opium, cocaine, peyote—and, of course, tea and coffee. The reasons for taking such drugs vary: to alter consciousness, as part of a religious ritual, for recreation, or for psychological escape. But human beings are not the only species that likes to get high on occasion; so do many other animals. Baboons ingest tobacco, elephants love the alcohol in fermented fruit, and reindeer and rabbits seek out intoxicating mushrooms (Siegel, 1989).

In Western societies, a whole pharmacopeia of recreational drugs exists, and each year seems

psychoactive drug A drug capable of influencing perception, mood, thinking, memory, or behaviour.

5.3

All cultures have found ways to alter consciousness. The Maulavis of Turkey (left), the famous whirling dervishes, spin in an energetic but controlled manner in order to achieve religious rapture. People in many cultures meditate (centre) as a way to quiet the mind and achieve spiritual enlightenment. And in some cultures, psychoactive drugs are used for religious or artistic inspiration, as in the case of the Huichol Indians of western Mexico (right), shown here harvesting peyote mushrooms.

to see the introduction of new ones, both natural and synthetic. Most of these drugs can be classified as *stimulants, depressants, opiates,* or *psychedelics,* depending on their effects on the central nervous system and their impact on behaviour and mood (see Table 5.1). Here we describe only their physiological and psychological effects; Chapter 11 covers addiction and Chapter 12 reviews drugs used in the treatment of mental and emotional disorders.

stimulants Drugs that speed up activity in the central nervous system.

opiates Drugs derived from the opium poppy that relieve pain and commonly produce euphoria.

psychedelic drugs Consciousness-altering drugs that produce hallucinations, change thought processes, or disrupt the normal perception of time and space.

depressants Drugs that slow down activity in the central nervous system.

1 **Stimulants** *speed up activity in the central nervous system.* They include, among other drugs, nicotine, caffeine, cocaine, amphetamines ("uppers"), and methamphetamine hydrochloride ("crank," "speed"). In moderate amounts, stimulants produce feelings of excitement, confidence, and well-being or euphoria. In large amounts, they make a person anxious, jittery, and hyperalert. In very large doses, they may cause convulsions, heart failure, and death.

Amphetamines are synthetic drugs taken in pill form, injected, smoked, or inhaled. Cocaine ("coke") is a natural drug, derived from the coca plant. Rural workers in Bolivia and Peru chew coca leaf every day, without apparent ill effects. In North America, the drug is usually inhaled, injected, or smoked in the highly refined form known as crack. These methods of intake give the drug a more immediate, powerful, and dangerous effect than when coca leaf is chewed. Amphetamines and cocaine make users feel peppy but do not actually increase energy reserves. Fatigue, irritability, and depression may occur when the effects of these drugs wear off.

2 **Depressants** *slow down activity in the central nervous system.* They include alcohol, tranquilizers, barbiturates, and most of the common chemicals that some people inhale. Depressants usually make a person feel calm or drowsy, and they may reduce anxiety, guilt, tension, and inhibitions. In large amounts, they may produce insensitivity to pain and other sensations. Like stimulants, in very large doses they can cause irregular heartbeats, convulsions, and death.

People are often surprised to learn that alcohol is a central-nervous-system depressant. In small amounts, alcohol has some of the effects of a stimulant, because it suppresses activity in parts of the brain that normally inhibit impulsive behaviour, such as loud laughter and clowning around. In the long run, however, it slows down nervous-system activity. Like barbiturates and opiates, alcohol can be used as an anaesthetic; if you drink enough, you will eventually pass out. Over time, alcohol consumed in large quantities damages the liver, heart, and brain. Extremely large amounts can kill, by inhibiting the nerve cells in the brain areas that control breathing and heartbeat. Every so often the news reports the death of a college student who had large amounts of alcohol "funnelled" into him as part of an initiation.

On the other hand, *moderate* social drinking—a drink or two of wine or liquor a day—is associated with a variety of health benefits, especially for adults over 40. These benefits include a reduced risk of heart attack and stroke, antidiabetic effects, and increased longevity (Davies et al., 2002; Locher, Suter, & Vetter, 1998; Mukamal et al., 2003; Reynolds et al., 2003; Simons et al., 2000).

3 **Opiates** *relieve pain.* They include opium, derived from the opium poppy; morphine, a derivative of opium; heroin, a derivative of morphine; and synthetic drugs such as methadone. All of these drugs mimic the action of endorphins, and most have a powerful effect on the emotions as well as pain-relieving properties. When injected, they may produce a sudden feeling of euphoria, called a "rush." They may also decrease anxiety and motivation, although the effects vary.

4 **Psychedelic drugs** *disrupt normal thought processes,* such as the perception of time and space. Sometimes, psychedelics produce hallucinations, especially visual ones. Some psychedelics, such as lysergic acid diethylamide (LSD), are made in the laboratory. Others, such as mescaline (from the peyote cactus), *Salvia divinorum* (a plant native to Mexico), and psilocybin (from certain species of mushrooms), are natural substances. Emotional reactions to psychedelics vary from person to person and from one time to another for any individual. A "trip" may be mildly pleasant or unpleasant, a mystical revelation or a nightmare.

Some commonly used drugs fall outside these four classifications, combine elements of more than one category, or have uncertain effects. For example, *marijuana* ("pot," "grass," "weed"), which is smoked or, less commonly, eaten in foods such as brownies, is the most widely used illicit drug in North America and Europe. Some researchers classify it as a mild psychedelic, but others feel that its chemical makeup and its psychological effects place it outside the major classifications. The active ingredient in marijuana is tetrahydrocannabinol (THC), derived from the hemp plant, *Cannabis sativa.* In some respects, THC appears to

TABLE 5.1 Some Psychoactive Drugs and Their Effects

Class of Drug	Type	Common Effects	Results of Abuse/Addiction
Amphetamines	Stimulant	Wakefulness, alertness, raised metabolism, elevated mood	Nervousness, headaches, loss of appetite, high blood pressure, delusions, psychosis, heart damage, convulsions, death
Cocaine	Stimulant	Euphoria, excitation, boost of energy, suppressed appetite	Excitability, sleeplessness, sweating, paranoia, anxiety, panic, depression, heart damage, heart failure, injury to nose if sniffed
Tobacco (nicotine)	Stimulant	Varies from alertness to calmness, depending on mental set, setting, and prior arousal; decreases appetite for carbohydrates	*Nicotine*: heart disease, high blood pressure, impaired circulation, erectile problems in men *Tar*: lung cancer, emphysema, mouth and throat cancer, many other health risks
Caffeine	Stimulant	Wakefulness, alertness, shortened reaction time	Restlessness, insomnia, muscle tension, heartbeat irregularities, high blood pressure
Alcohol (1–2 drinks)	Depressant	Depends on setting, mental set; tends to act like a stimulant because it reduces inhibitions and anxiety	
Alcohol (several/many drinks)	Depressant	Slowed reaction time, tension, depression, reduced ability to store new memories or to retrieve old ones, poor coordination	Blackouts, cirrhosis of the liver, other organ damage, mental and neurological impairment, psychosis, possibly death
Tranquilizers (e.g., Valium™), barbiturates (e.g., phenobarbital)	Depressant	Reduced anxiety and tension, sedation	Increased dosage needed for effects; impaired motor and sensory functions, impaired permanent storage of new information, withdrawal symptoms; possibly convulsions, coma, death (especially when taken with other drugs)
Opium, heroin morphine	Opiate	Euphoria, relief of pain	Loss of appetite, nausea, constipation, withdrawal symptoms, convulsions, coma, possibly death
LSD, psilocybin, mescaline	Psychedelic	Exhilaration, visions and hallucinations, insightful experiences	Psychosis, paranoia, panic reactions
Marijuana	Mild psychedelic (classification controversial)	Relaxation, euphoria, increased appetite, reduced ability to store new memories, other effects depending on mental set and setting	Throat and lung irritation, lung damage (if smoked), impaired immunity; long-term effects not well established

be a mild stimulant, increasing heart rate and making tastes, sounds, and colours seem more intense. But users often report reactions ranging from mild euphoria to relaxation, or even sleepiness.

In moderate doses, marijuana can interfere with the transfer of information to long-term memory, a characteristic it shares with alcohol. In large doses, it can cause hallucinations, a sense of unreality, and sometimes impaired coordination and reaction times. And heavy, prolonged use of marijuana may increase the risk of lung damage and cancer (Barsky et al., 1998; Zhu et al., 2000). Survey research in Ontario has found that the more frequent the use of marijuana, the greater the prevalence of negative consequences (Cunningham, Bondy, & Walsh, 2000). This is called a *dose-response relationship*.

On the other hand, some studies find that marijuana has medical benefits. It reduces the nausea and vomiting that often accompany chemotherapy treatment for cancer and AIDS; it reduces the physical tremors, loss of appetite, and other symptoms caused by multiple sclerosis; it helps reduce the frequency of seizures in some patients with epilepsy; and it alleviates the retinal swelling caused by glaucoma (Grinspoon & Bakalar, 1993; Zimmer & Morgan, 1997).

The Physiology of Drug Effects

Psychoactive drugs produce their psychological effects primarily by acting on brain neurotransmitters, the substances that carry messages from one nerve cell to another. A drug may increase or decrease the release of neurotransmitters, prevent the reabsorption of excess neurotransmitter molecules by the cells that have released them, or block the effects of a neurotransmitter on a receiving nerve cell (see Chapter 4). Figure 5.3 shows how one drug, cocaine, increases the amount of norepinephrine and dopamine in the brain by blocking the reabsorption of these substances. Cocaine also seems to increase the transmission of serotonin (Rocha et al., 1998).

These biochemical changes affect cognitive and emotional functioning. For example, because of alcohol's effect on parts of the brain involved

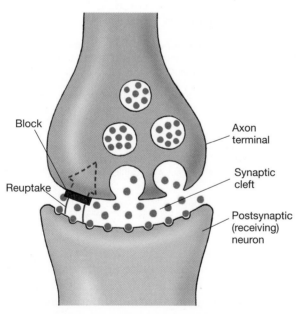

tolerance Increased resistance to a drug's effects accompanying continued use.

withdrawal symptoms Physical and psychological symptoms that occur when someone addicted to a drug stops taking it.

FIGURE 5.3 Cocaine's Effect on the Brain

Cocaine blocks the brain's reabsorption ("reuptake") of the neurotransmitters dopamine and norepinephrine, so levels of these substances rise. The result is overstimulation of certain brain circuits and a brief euphoric high. Then, when the drug wears off, a depletion of dopamine may cause the user to "crash" and become sleepy and depressed.

in judgment, drinkers often are unable to gauge their own competence. Just a couple of drinks can affect perception, response time, coordination, and balance, despite the drinker's own impression of unchanged or even improved performance. Liquor also affects memory, possibly by interfering with the work of serotonin. Information stored before a drinking session remains intact during the session but is retrieved more slowly (Haut et al., 1989). The ability to store new memories for later use also suffers, after the consumption of only two or three drinks (Parker, Birnbaum, & Noble, 1976). Consuming small amounts does not seem to affect *sober* mental performance, but even occasional heavy drinking impairs later abstract thought. In other words, a Saturday-night binge is more dangerous than a daily drink.

As for other recreational drugs, there is no evidence that *light or moderate* use can damage the human brain enough to affect cognitive functioning, but all researchers agree that heavy or frequent use is another matter (see Chapter 11). Research with animals and humans suggests that repeated use of certain drugs, including "designer drugs" (easily synthesized variations of other drugs), can damage the brain and impair intellectual functioning. One study found that heavy users of methamphetamine had damage to dopamine cells and performed more poorly than other people on tests of memory, attention, and movement, even though they had not used the drug for at least 11 months (Volkow et al., 2001). Another study looked at the effects of Ecstasy (3,4 methylenedioxymethamphetamine, or MDMA), a synthetic drug having properties of both a hallucinogen and a stimulant. Compared with nonusers, Ecstasy users showed memory deficits and reduced brain receptors for serotonin. The good news is that a subset of users who had abstained for at least a year did not have lasting damage to their serotonin receptors. The bad news is that these former users were still performing more poorly than nonusers on memory tests (Reneman et al., 2001).

The use of some psychoactive drugs, such as heroin and tranquilizers, can lead to **tolerance**: Over time, more and more of the drug is needed to get the same effect. When habitual heavy users stop taking a drug, they may suffer severe **withdrawal symptoms**, which, depending on the drug, may include nausea, abdominal cramps, sweating, muscle spasms, depression, and sleep problems.

The Psychology of Drug Effects

People often assume that the effects of a drug are automatic, the inevitable result of the drug's chemistry. But reactions to a psychoactive drug involve more than the drug's chemical properties. They also depend on a person's physical condition, experience with the drug, environmental setting, and mental set.

1 *Physical factors include body weight, metabolism, initial state of emotional arousal, and physical tolerance for the drug.* For example, women generally get drunker than men on the same amount of alcohol because women are smaller, on average, and their bodies metabolize alcohol differently (Fuchs et al., 1995). Similarly, many Asians have a genetically determined adverse reaction to even small amounts of alcohol, which can cause severe headaches, facial flushing, and diarrhea (Cloninger, 1990). For individuals, a drug may have one effect after a tiring day and a different one after a rousing quarrel, or the effect may vary with the time of day because of the body's circadian rhythms.

2 *Experience with the drug refers to the number of times a person has used the drug.* Trying a drug—a cigarette, an alcoholic drink, a stimulant—for the first time is often a neutral or unpleasant experience. But reactions typically change once a person has become familiar with the drug's effects.

3 *"Environmental setting" refers to the context in which a person takes the drug.* A person might have one glass of wine at home alone and feel sleepy but have three glasses of wine at a party and feel full of energy. Someone might feel happy and high drinking with good friends but fearful and nervous drinking with strangers. In one study of reactions to alcohol, most of the drinkers became depressed, angry, confused, and unfriendly. Then it dawned on the researchers that anyone might become depressed, angry, confused, and unfriendly if asked to drink bourbon at 9:00 a.m. in a bleak hospital room, which was the setting for the experiment (Warren & Raynes, 1972).

4 *"Mental set" refers to expectations about the drug's effects, as well as reasons for taking the drug.* Some people drink to become more sociable, friendly, or seductive; some drink to try to reduce feelings of anxiety or depression; and some drink to have an excuse for abusiveness or violence. Addicts use drugs to escape from the real world; people living with chronic pain use the same drugs to function in the real world (Portenoy, 1994). The motives for taking a drug greatly influence its effects.

Expectations can sometimes have a more powerful effect than the chemical properties of the drug itself. In several imaginative studies, researchers compared people who were drinking liquor (vodka and tonic) with those who *thought*

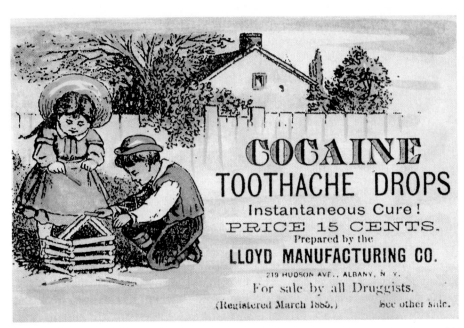

Cultural attitudes toward drugs vary with the times. Before it was banned in 1914, cocaine was widely touted as a cure for everything from toothaches to timidity. It was used in teas, tonics, throat lozenges, and even soft drinks (including, briefly, Coca-Cola™, which derived its name from the coca plant). Similarly, until recent decades, cigarette smoking was promoted as healthy and glamorous.

they were drinking liquor but were actually getting only tonic and lime juice. (Vodka has a subtle taste, and most people could not tell the real and phony drinks apart.) The experimenters found a *"think-drink" effect*: Men behaved more belligerently when they thought they were drinking vodka than when they thought they were drinking plain tonic water, *regardless of the actual content of the drinks*. And both sexes reported feeling sexually aroused when they thought they were drinking vodka, whether they actually received vodka or not (Abrams & Wilson, 1983; Marlatt & Rohsenow, 1980).

Expectations and beliefs about drugs are, in turn, shaped by the culture in which you live. Many people start their day with a cup of coffee because it increases alertness, but when coffee was first introduced in Europe, people protested against it. Women said it suppressed their husbands' sexual performance and made men inconsiderate—and maybe it did! In the nineteenth century, Americans regarded marijuana as a mild sedative with no "mind-altering" properties. They did not expect it to give them a high, and it didn't; it merely put them to sleep (Weil, 1972/1986). Today, motives for using marijuana have changed, and these changes have no doubt affected how people respond to it.

According to one study, patterns of substance use among American secondary school students in the last 30 years have waxed and waned in similar patterns to those of Ontario students. The exceptions are cocaine use, which has been greater in the United States, and LSD use, which has been greater in Ontario (Ivis & Adlaf, 1999). Again, such findings are explained more in terms of the prevailing attitudes of those using the drugs rather than of the availability or properties of the drugs themselves.

None of this means that alcohol and other drugs are merely placebos. Drugs, as we have seen, do have physiological effects, many of them extremely potent. But an understanding of the psychological factors involved in drug use may help us think critically about the reactions individuals have to drugs, and the use of drugs to excuse one's actions.

Quick Quiz

There's no excuse for avoiding this quiz.

See whether you can name the following:

1. An illegal stimulant
2. Two drugs that interfere with the formation of new long-term memories
3. Three types of depressant drugs
4. A legal recreational drug that acts as a depressant on the central nervous system
5. Four factors that influence a person's psychological reactions to a drug

Answers:

1. cocaine; also some amphetamines 2. marijuana and alcohol 3. barbiturates, tranquilizers, and alcohol 4. alcohol 5. the person's physical condition, prior experience with the drug, mental set, and the environmental setting

---

As we have seen in this chapter, fluctuations and changes in consciousness, though interesting in and of themselves, also show us how people's expectations and explanations of their own mental and physical states affect what they do and how they feel. Controversy still exists about some basic issues: the prevalence of SAD and "PMS," the purpose of sleep, the meaning of dreams, the best explanation of hypnosis, the dangers and benefits of drugs. But the scientific scrutiny of biological rhythms, dreams, hypnotic suggestion, and drug-induced states—phenomena once thought outside the bounds of science—can deepen our understanding of the intimate relationship between body and mind.

Psychology In The News *Revisited*

Now let us return to the case of the Da Kine Food and Beverage Shop. Its owner was arrested once again and held in jail. Her supporters called it a sad day for the people, charging that their elected officials had let them down. The Deputy Chief of Police said that the owners of Da Kine were "flaunting their criminal activity and demonstrating their contempt for the laws of Canada," and so the Da Kine was finally shut down. Ironically, the mayor of Vancouver has more recently called for the legalization of marijuana (Mason, 2005).

What is your reaction to this story? Because the consequences of drug *abuse* are so devastating to individuals and to society (see Chapter 11), people often find it difficult to think critically about drug laws and policies. At one extreme, some people cannot accept evidence that their favourite drug— be it coffee, tobacco, alcohol, or marijuana— might have harmful physiological effects. At the other extreme, some cannot accept evidence that their most hated drug—be it alcohol, morphine, marijuana, or the coca leaf—might not be dangerous in all forms or amounts, and might even have some beneficial effects. Both sides often confuse psychological effects with physiological ones, potent drugs with others that have only subtle effects, and light or moderate use with heavy or excessive use.

As we saw earlier, cultural attitudes toward a drug affect people's responses to it, and these attitudes vary with the times. Once a drug is declared illegal, many people assume it is deadly, even though some legal drugs are more dangerous than some illegal ones. Nicotine, which of course is legal, is as addictive as heroin and cocaine, which are illegal. According to the Heart and Stroke Foundation (2001), tobacco use contributes to more than 45 000 deaths in Canada every year, about 25 times the number of deaths from all other forms of legal and illegal drug use combined. Yet most people have a far more negative view of heroin and cocaine than of nicotine.

Emotions have run especially high in debates over marijuana. As we saw, heavy, prolonged use of marijuana poses some physical risks. However, no deaths have ever been attributed to marijuana, and, as we also saw, the drug has some medical benefits. In 1998, when a World Health Organization report concluded that marijuana, used in moderation, was safer than cigarettes and alcohol, United Nations officials suppressed the finding. In 1999, when a scientific panel commissioned by the U.S. government called for scientific trials on marijuana's medical benefits, government officials either ignored or repudiated the recommendation.

Some people are committed to the eradication of all drugs that are illegal, and others think that all drugs should be decriminalized. Others would legalize marijuana for recreational and medicinal use but ban tobacco and most "hard drugs." Still others think that instead of punishing or incarcerating people who use drugs, society would be better off regulating where drugs are used (never at work, for example), providing treatment for addicts, and educating people about the benefits and hazards of drug use—the current approach to cigarette smoking.

As you assess your own views about drugs, keep in mind what this chapter has reported about the universal human longing to experience altered states of consciousness. Human beings everywhere, throughout history, have sought ways to improve their moods and mental states when their biological rhythms temporarily ebb. Where, then, given this information, do you stand in the drug debate? Which psychoactive drugs, if any, should be prohibited? Can we create mental sets and environmental settings that promote safe recreational use of some drugs, minimize the likelihood of drug abuse, and permit the medicinal use of beneficial drugs? What do you think?

Taking Psychology With You   How to Get a Good Night's Sleep

You hop into bed, turn out the lights, close your eyes, and wait for slumber. An hour later, you're still waiting. Finally you drop off, but at 3:00 a.m., to your chagrin, you're awake again. By the time the rooster crows, you have put in a hard day's night.

Insomnia affects most people at one time or another, and many people most of the time. It's no wonder that sleeping pills are a multi-million-dollar business. Yet most over-the-counter pills are of little use for inducing sleep, and some prescription drugs can actually make matters worse. Barbiturates greatly suppress REM sleep, a result that eventually causes wakefulness, and they also suppress Stages 3 and 4, the deeper stages of sleep. Efforts to treat insomnia with melatonin supplements have had mixed results, and their long-term safety is not yet known. Most physicians prescribe sleeping remedies for only short periods of time. Sleep research suggests some better alternatives:

- **Be sure you actually have a sleep problem.** Many people only *think* they sleep poorly. They overestimate how long it takes them to doze off and underestimate how much sleep they are getting. When they are observed in the laboratory, they usually fall asleep in less than 30 minutes and are awake only for very short periods during the night (Bonnet, 1990; Carskadon, Mitler, & Dement, 1974). The real test for diagnosing a sleep deficit is how you feel during the day. Do you doze off without intending to? Do you feel drowsy at meetings or in class? If you function well with less sleep than most people get, you probably shouldn't worry, since worrying itself can cause insomnia.

- **Get a correct diagnosis of the sleep problem.** Do you suffer from sleep apnea (see p. 151)? Do you have a physical disorder that is interfering with sleep? Do you live in a noisy place? (Try earplugs!) Are you fighting your personal biological rhythms by going to bed too early or too late? Do you go to bed early one night and late another? It's better to go to bed at about the same time every night and get up at the same time every morning.

- **Avoid excessive use of alcohol or other drugs.** Many drugs interfere with sleep. For instance, coffee, tea, cola, "energy drinks," and chocolate all contain caffeine, which is a stimulant; alcohol suppresses REM sleep; and tranquilizers such as Valium™ and Librium™ reduce Stage 4 sleep.

- **Don't associate the bedroom with wakefulness.** When environmental cues are repeatedly associated with some behaviour, they can come to trigger the behaviour. If you don't want your bedroom to trigger wakefulness, avoid reading, studying, and watching TV there. Also avoid lying awake for hours waiting for sleep; your frustration will cause arousal that can be associated with the bedroom. If you can't sleep, get up and do something else, preferably something dull and relaxing, in another room. When you feel drowsy, try sleeping again.

- **Take care of your health.** As your grandmother may have told you, good health habits are important for good sleep. Nutrition is one area to watch. The amino acid tryptophan promotes the onset of sleep, and other dietary elements may also influence alertness and relaxation. Exercise during the day also enhances sleep, but it should be avoided right before bedtime because in the short term it heightens alertness.

Finally, when insomnia is related to anxiety and worry, it makes sense to get to the source of your problems. Woody Allen once said, "The lamb and the lion shall lie down together, but the lamb will not be very sleepy." Like a lamb trying to sleep with a lion, you cannot expect to sleep well with stress hormones pouring through your bloodstream and worries crowding your mind. In an evolutionary sense, sleeplessness is an adaptive response to danger and threat. When your anxieties decrease, so may your sleepless nights.

SUMMARY

BIOLOGICAL RHYTHMS: THE TIDES OF EXPERIENCE

- *Consciousness* is the awareness of oneself and the environment. Changing states of consciousness are often associated with *biological rhythms*—periodic fluctuations in physiological functioning. These rhythms are typically synchronized to external cues, but many are also *endogenous*, generated from within. *Circadian* fluctuations occur about once a day; other rhythms occur less or more frequently than that.

- When people live in isolation from all time cues, they tend to live a day that is slightly longer than 24 hours. Circadian rhythms are governed by a biological "clock" in the *suprachiasmatic nucleus (SCN)* of the hypothalamus. The SCN regulates, and in turn is affected by, the hormone *melatonin*, which is responsive to changes in light and dark, and which increases during the dark hours. When a person's normal routine changes, the person may experience *internal desynchronization*, in which the usual circadian rhythms are thrown out of phase with one another. The result may be fatigue, mental inefficiency, and an increased risk of accidents.

- Folklore holds that moods follow a long-term biological rhythm. Some people do show a recurrence of depression every winter, in a pattern that has been labelled *seasonal affective disorder (SAD)*, but serious seasonal depression is rare. The causes of SAD are not yet clear, and it has been difficult to rule out placebo effects in the most common treatment, phototherapy. However, recent research suggests that light treatments can be effective.

- Another long-term rhythm is the menstrual cycle, during which various hormones rise and fall. Well-controlled, double-blind studies on "PMS" do not support claims that emotional symptoms are reliably and universally tied to the menstrual cycle. Overall, women and men do not differ in the emotional symptoms they report or in the number of mood swings they experience over the course of a month. High levels of testosterone have been linked to various behaviours and moods, but no one has suggested that they constitute a psychological syndrome. Expectations and learning affect how we interpret bodily and emotional changes.

THE RHYTHMS OF SLEEP

- Sleep, which recurs on a circadian rhythm, is necessary not only for bodily restoration but also for normal mental functioning. Many people get less than the optimal amount of sleep. Some suffer from insomnia, *sleep apnea*, or *narcolepsy*.

- During sleep, periods of *rapid eye movement*, or *REM*, alternate with non-REM sleep in approximately a 90-minute rhythm. *Non-REM sleep* is divided into four stages on the basis of characteristic brainwave patterns. During REM sleep, the brain is active, and there are other signs of arousal, yet most of the skeletal muscles are limp; vivid dreams are reported most often during REM sleep.

EXPLORING THE DREAM WORLD

- Dreams are often recalled as illogical and bizarre. Some people say they have *lucid dreams*, in which they know they are dreaming. Researchers disagree about whether the eye movements of REM sleep are related to events and actions in dreams.

- The psychoanalytic explanation of dreams is that they allow us to gratify forbidden or unrealistic wishes and desires that have been forced into the unconscious part of the mind. In dreams, according to Freud, thoughts and objects are disguised as symbolic images.

- Another approach holds that dreams express current concerns or help us solve current problems by working through emotional issues, especially during times of crisis. Findings on recurrent dreams, gender differences in dreams, and the dreams of divorced people support this *problem-focused explanation*.

- A third view holds that dreams are the by-product of *mental housekeeping*. According to this information-processing approach, dreams are merely random snippets from an ongoing process during which the brain scans and sorts through new data, or unneeded synaptic associations in the brain are weakened. REM sleep has also been associated with the consolidation of memories, during which the synaptic changes associated with a recently stored memory become durable and stable.

- The *activation-synthesis theory* of dreaming holds that dreams occur when the cortex tries to make sense of spontaneous neural firing initiated in the pons. The dream is the resulting interpretation—the synthesis of the signals with existing knowledge and memories. In this view, dreams do not disguise unconscious wishes, but they can reveal a person's perceptions, conflicts, and concerns.

- All of the current theories of dreams have some support, and all have weaknesses. Most psychologists today accept the notion that dreams are more than incoherent ramblings of the mind, but many psychologists quarrel with specific psychoanalytic interpretations. Some psychologists doubt that people can solve problems during sleep. The mental-housekeeping approach seems to tell us more about REM sleep than about dreams per se. And the activation-synthesis theory does not seem to explain coherent, storylike dreams or non-REM dreams.

THE RIDDLE OF HYPNOSIS

- *Hypnosis* is a procedure in which the practitioner suggests changes in the sensations, perceptions, thoughts, feelings, or behaviour of the subject, and the subject tries to comply. Although hypnosis has been used successfully for many medical and psychological purposes, it does not produce special abilities. Hypnosis can sometimes improve memory for facts about real events, but it also results in confusion between facts and vividly imagined possibilities. Therefore, "hypnotically refreshed" accounts are often full of errors and pseudomemories.

- A leading explanation of hypnosis and its effects is that hypnosis involves *dissociation*, a split in consciousness. In one version of this approach, the split is between a part of consciousness that is hypnotized and a *hidden observer* that watches but does not participate. Dissociation theories are consistent with modern models of the brain.

- Another leading approach, the *sociocognitive explanation*, regards hypnosis as a product of normal social and cognitive processes. In this view, hypnosis is a form of role playing in which the hypnotized person uses active cognitive strategies, including imagination, to comply with the hypnotist's suggestions. The role is so engrossing that the person interprets it as real. Sociocognitive processes can account for the apparent age and past-life "regressions" of people under hypnosis and their reports of alien abductions.

CONSCIOUSNESS-ALTERING DRUGS

- In all cultures, people have found ways to produce *altered states of consciousness*. For example, *psychoactive drugs* alter cognition and emotion by acting on neurotransmitters in the brain. Most psychoactive drugs are classified as *stimulants, depressants, opiates,* or *psychedelics,* depending on their central-nervous-system effects and their impact on behaviour and mood. However, some common drugs, such as marijuana, fall outside these categories.

- When used frequently and in large amounts, some drugs damage neurons in the brain and have a negative effect on learning and memory. However, certain drugs, such as alcohol and marijuana, have some health benefits at moderate doses. The use of some psychoactive drugs leads to *tolerance,* in which increasing dosages are needed for the same effect, and *withdrawal symptoms* if an addict tries to quit.

- Reactions to a psychoactive drug are influenced not only by its chemical properties but also by the user's physical condition, prior experience with the drug, environmental setting, and *mental set*—the person's expectations and motives for taking the drug. Expectations can be even more powerful than the drug itself, as shown by the *"think-drink" effect.* Expectations and beliefs about drugs are in turn affected by a person's culture.

PSYCHOLOGY IN THE NEWS, REVISITED

- In the debate over drug policies, people often find it difficult to distinguish drug use from drug abuse and to separate issues of a drug's legality or illegality from the drug's potential harms and dangers.

KEY TERMS

consciousness   143

biological rhythm   144

endogenous   144

circadian rhythm   144

suprachiasmatic nucleus (SCN)   144

melatonin   145

internal desynchronization   145

seasonal affective disorder (SAD)   147

narcolepsy   151

sleep apnea   151

rapid eye movement (REM) sleep   152

lucid dream   154

activation-synthesis theory   156

hypnosis   159

dissociation   161

psychoactive drug   163

stimulants   164

opiates   164

psychedelic drugs   164

depressants   164

tolerance   166

withdrawal symptoms   166

LOOKING BACK

- Why do you feel "out of sync" when you fly across time zones or change shifts at work? (pp. 145–146)
- If you feel sad in the winter, do you have SAD? (p. 147)
- Does "PMS" cause most women to feel depressed or irritable before their periods? (p. 148)
- Why do we sleep? (pp. 150–151)
- What happens when we go too long without enough sleep? (p. 151)
- Why are you likely to be dreaming when the alarm goes off in the morning? (p. 153)
- Why did Freud call dreams the "royal road to the unconscious"? (pp. 154–155)
- How might your dreams be related to your current problems and concerns? (p. 155)
- How does a disruption of REM sleep affect memory? (p. 156)
- Could dreams be caused by meaningless brain-stem signals? (pp. 156–157)
- Can a hypnotist force you to do things against your will? (p. 159)
- Can hypnosis help you remember the past more accurately? (p. 160)
- What are the legitimate uses of hypnosis in psychology and medicine? (p. 160)
- Are hypnotized persons merely faking or play-acting? (pp. 161–162)
- In its physiological effects, is alcohol a downer or an upper? (p. 164)
- How do recreational drugs affect the brain? (p. 166)
- Why can a glass of wine make you feel tired at one time but sociable and pepped up at another? (p. 167)

Psychology In The News

2004 A RECORD YEAR FOR UFO SIGHTINGS IN CANADA

OTTAWA, ON, June 18, 2005. According to the website *UFO Today*, Canada set a new national record for UFO sightings in 2004. That year brought 882 UFO sightings in Canada, breaking the previous record of 673 set in 2003.

In Nova Scotia, three people spotted a collection of lights in the east, one of them red and bobbing up and down. In Quebec, a couple saw a bright red light that was moving too slowly to be an aircraft; it then plunged to the ground. And two people in Alberta sat and watched as a collection of four lights hovered above them.

For some reason, the Prairies was a hive of activity for UFO sightings in 2004, with 61 reports in Alberta by the end of July, compared to only 76 on the Prairies the entire year before. Manitoba had another 50 by July.

When asked to explain this increase in sightings, Chris Rutkowski of Ufology Research of Manitoba attributed it to people's increased awareness of space missions to more far-reaching targets such as Mars and Saturn.

Are these alien spacecraft? Many people who viewed these odd objects in the skies above Santos, Brazil, were convinced they were seeing UFOs.

6 Sensation and Perception

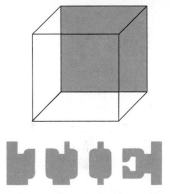

W̲e have all heard stories about UFOs and "flying saucers." Some of us scoff at them; others take them seriously. Why are these accounts so common? Are UFO sightings reported only by people who are silly or gullible, or do smart, savvy people also see alien aircraft? If such sightings are illusions, then why are those who report them so confident that what they saw was real? And why is one report often followed by several others in the same location: because there really are a lot of UFOs in the area or because of the power of suggestion?

In this chapter, we will try to answer these questions by exploring how our sense organs take in information from the environment and how the brain uses this information to construct a model of the world—a model that is not always accurate. We will focus on two closely connected sets of processes that enable us to know what is happening both inside our bodies and in the world beyond our own skins.

The first process, **sensation**, is the detection of physical energy emitted or reflected by physical objects. The cells that do the detecting are located in the sense organs—the eyes, ears, tongue, nose, skin, and internal body tissues. Sensory processes produce an immediate awareness of sound, colour, form, and other building blocks of consciousness.

But to make sense of the world conveyed to us through our senses, we also need **perception**, a set of mental operations that organize sensory signals into meaningful patterns. Our sense of vision produces a two-dimensional image on the back of the eye, but we perceive the world in three dimensions. Our sense of hearing brings us the sound of a C, an E, and a G played simultaneously on the piano, but we *perceive* a C major chord.

Sensation and perception are the foundation of learning, thinking, and acting, and findings on these topics can often be put to practical use—for example, in the design of hearing aids and industrial robots, and in the training of flight controllers, astronauts, and other people who must make crucial decisions based on what they sense and perceive. An understanding of sensation and perception can also help us think more critically about our own experiences. As you read this chapter, ask yourself why people sometimes perceive things that are not there and, conversely, why they sometimes miss things that *are* there—looking without seeing, listening without hearing.

If you stare at the cube, the surface on the outside and front will suddenly be on the inside and back or vice versa, because your brain can interpret the sensory image in two different ways. The purple and white drawing below the cube can also be perceived in two ways. Can you see the letters that form in the white space?

6.1

perception The process by which the brain organizes and interprets sensory information.

sensation The detection of physical energy emitted or reflected by physical objects.

WHAT'S AHEAD

- What kind of "code" in the nervous system helps explain why a pinprick and a kiss feel different?
- Why does your dog hear a "silent" doggie whistle when you can't?
- What kind of bias can influence whether you think you hear the phone ringing when you're in the shower?
- What happens when people are deprived of all external sensory stimulation?

doctrine of specific nerve energies The principle that different sensory modalities exist because signals received by the sense organs stimulate different nerve pathways leading to different areas of the brain.

synesthesia A rare condition in which stimulation of one sense also evokes a sensation in another.

sense receptors Specialized cells that convert physical energy in the environment or the body to electrical energy that can be transmitted as nerve impulses to the brain.

OUR SENSATIONAL SENSES

At some point, you probably learned that there are five senses, corresponding to five sense organs: vision (eyes), hearing (ears), taste (tongue), touch (skin), and smell (nose). Actually, there are more than five senses, though scientists disagree about the exact number. The skin, which is the organ of touch or pressure, also senses heat, cold, and pain, not to mention itching and tickling. The ear, which is the organ of hearing, also contains receptors that account for a sense of balance. The skeletal muscles contain receptors responsible for a sense of bodily movement.

All of our senses evolved to help us survive. Even pain, which causes so much human misery, is an indispensable part of our evolutionary heritage, for it alerts us to illness and injury. But sensory experiences contribute immeasurably to our lives even when they are not helping us stay alive. They entertain us, amuse us, soothe us, inspire us. If we really pay attention to our senses, said poet William Wordsworth, we can "see into the life of things" and hear "the still, sad music of humanity."

The Riddle of Separate Sensations

Sensation begins with the **sense receptors**, cells located in the sense organs. When these receptors detect an appropriate stimulus—light, mechanical pressure, or chemical molecules—they convert the physical energy of the stimulus into electrical impulses that travel along nerves to the brain. Sense receptors are like military scouts who scan the terrain for signs of activity. These scouts cannot make many decisions on their own. They must transmit what they learn to field officers—sensory neurons in the peripheral nervous system (see Chapter 4). The field officers in turn must report to generals at a command centre—the cells of the brain. The generals are responsible for analyzing the reports, combining information brought in by different scouts, and deciding what it all means.

The "field officers" in the sensory system—the sensory nerves—all use exactly the same form of communication, a neural impulse. It is as if they must all send their messages on a bongo drum and can only go "boom." How, then, are we able to experience so many different kinds of sensations? The answer is that the nervous system *encodes* the messages. One kind of code, which is *anatomical*, was first described in 1826 by the German physiologist Johannes Müller (1801–1858), in his **doctrine of specific nerve energies**. According to this doctrine, different sensory modalities (such as vision and hearing) exist because signals received by the sense organs stimulate different nerve pathways leading to different areas of the brain. Signals from the eye cause impulses to travel along the optic nerve to the visual cortex. Signals from the ear cause impulses to travel along the auditory nerve to the auditory cortex. Light and sound waves produce different sensations because of these anatomical differences.

The doctrine of specific nerve energies implies that what we know about the world ultimately reduces to what we know about the state of our own nervous system. Therefore, if sound waves could stimulate nerves that end in the visual part of the brain, we would "see" sound. In fact, a similar sort of crossover does occur in a rare condition called **synesthesia**, in which the stimulation of one sense also evokes a sensation in another. The person may say that the colour purple smells like a rose, the aroma of cinnamon feels like velvet, or the sound of a note on a clarinet tastes like cherries (Cytowic, 2002; Martino & Marks, 2001). Researchers at the University of Waterloo have even worked with a person who sees colours whenever she sees, hears, or thinks about numbers (Smilek, Dixon, Cudahy, & Merikle, 2002). Synesthetes may have unusually direct connections between different sensory areas of the brain, such as those that handle vision and hearing, or an unusual number of connections between these areas (Nunn et al., 2002).

Synesthesia, however, is the exception, not the rule; for most of us, the senses remain separate. Anatomical encoding alone does not completely explain why this is so, nor does it explain variations of experience *within* a particular sense—the sight of pink versus red, the sound of a piccolo versus the sound of a tuba, or the feel of a pinprick versus the feel of a kiss. An additional kind of code is therefore necessary. This second kind of code has been called *functional*.

Functional codes rely on the fact that sensory receptors and neurons fire, or are inhibited from firing, only in the presence of specific sorts of stimuli. At any particular time, then, some cells in the nervous system are firing, and some are not. Information about *which* cells are firing, *how many* cells are firing, the *rate* at which cells are firing, and the *patterning* of each cell's firing constitutes a functional code. You might think of such a code as the neurological equivalent of the Morse code, but much more complicated. Functional encoding may occur all along a sensory route, starting in the sense organs and ending in the brain.

Measuring the Senses

Just how sensitive are our senses? The answer comes from the field of *psychophysics*, which is concerned with how the physical properties of stimuli are related to our psychological experience of them. Drawing on principles from both physics and psychology, psychophysicists have studied how the strength or intensity of a stimulus affects the strength of sensation in an observer.

Absolute Thresholds One way to find out how sensitive the senses are is to show people a series of signals that vary in intensity and ask them to say which signals they can detect. The smallest amount of energy that a person can detect reliably is known as the **absolute threshold**. The word *absolute* is a bit misleading, though, because people detect borderline signals on some occasions and miss them on others. "Reliable" detection is said to occur when a person can detect a signal 50 percent of the time.

If you were having your absolute threshold for brightness measured, you might be asked to sit in a dark room and look at a wall or screen. You would then be shown flashes of light, varying in brightness, one flash at a time. Your task would be to say whether you noticed a flash. Some flashes you would never see. Some you would always see. And sometimes you would miss seeing a flash, even though you had noticed one of equal brightness on other trials. Such errors seem to occur in part because of random firing of cells in the nervous system, which produces fluctuating background "noise," something like the background noise in a radio transmission.

By studying absolute thresholds, psychologists have found that our senses are very sharp indeed. If you have normal sensory abilities, you can see a candle flame on a clear, dark night from 50 kilometres away. You can hear a ticking watch in a perfectly quiet room from 10 metres away. You can taste a teaspoon of sugar diluted in 10 litres of water, smell a drop of perfume diffused through a three-room apartment, and feel the wing of a bee falling on your cheek from a height of 1 centimetre (Galanter, 1962).

Yet despite these impressive sensory skills, our senses are tuned in to only a narrow band of physical energies. For example, we are visually sensitive to only a tiny fraction of all electromagnetic energy; we do not see radio waves or microwaves (see Figure 6.1). Other species can pick up signals that we cannot. Dogs can detect high-frequency sound waves that are beyond our range, as you know if you have ever called your pooch with a

absolute threshold The smallest quantity of physical energy that can be reliably detected by an observer.

Different species sense the world differently. The flower on the left was photographed in normal light. The view on the right, photographed under ultraviolet light, is what a butterfly might see, because butterflies have ultraviolet receptors. The hundreds of tiny bright spots are nectar sources.

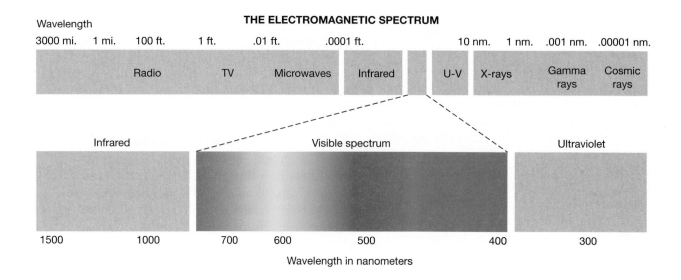

FIGURE 6.1 Visible Spectrum of Electromagnetic Energy

Our visual system detects only a small fraction of the electromagnetic energy around us.

"silent" doggie whistle. Bats and porpoises can hear sounds two octaves beyond our range, and bees can see ultraviolet light, which merely gives human beings a sunburn.

Difference Thresholds Psychologists also study sensory sensitivity by having people compare two stimuli and judge whether they are the same or different. For example, a person might be asked to compare the weight of two blocks, the brightness of two lights, or the saltiness of two liquids. The smallest difference in stimulation that a person can detect reliably (again, half of the time) is called the **difference threshold**, or *just noticeable difference (jnd)*. When you compare two stimuli, A and B, the difference threshold will depend on the intensity or size of A. The larger or more intense A is, the greater the change must be before you can detect a difference. If you are comparing the weights of two pebbles, you might be able to detect a difference of only a fraction of an ounce, but you would not be able to detect such a subtle difference if you were comparing two massive boulders.

In everyday life, we may sometimes think we can detect a difference between stimuli when we cannot. Years ago, as a class project, undergraduate students at Williams College offered tasters three glasses of cola, two of one leading brand and one of the other (or vice versa), and asked them which drink they liked most and least. Each taster was given three trials. Most of the tasters were inconsistent in their preferences, indicating that they had trouble telling the two brands apart (Solomon, 1979), even though most of the students had believed before the experiment that they could distinguish among colas.

Signal-Detection Theory Despite their usefulness, the procedures we have described have a serious limitation. Measurements for any given individual may be affected by the person's general tendency, when uncertain, to respond, "Yes, I noticed a signal (or a difference)" or, "No, I didn't notice anything." Some people are habitual yea-sayers, willing to gamble that the signal was really there. Others are habitual naysayers, cautious and conservative. In addition, alertness, motives, and expectations can influence how a person responds on any given occasion. If you are in the shower and you are expecting an important call, you may think you heard the telephone ring when it didn't. In laboratory studies, when observers want to impress the experimenter, they may lean toward a positive response.

Fortunately, these problems of *response bias* are not insurmountable. According to **signal-detection theory**, an observer's response in a

---

difference threshold The smallest difference in stimulation that can be reliably detected by an observer when two stimuli are compared; also called *just noticeable difference (jnd)*.

signal-detection theory A psychophysical theory that divides the detection of a sensory signal into a sensory process and a decision process.

Get Involved   Now You See It, Now You Don't

Sensation depends on change and contrast in the environment. Hold your hand over one eye and stare at the dot in the middle of the circle on the right. You should have no trouble maintaining an image of the circle. However, if you do the same with the circle on the left, the image will fade. The gradual change from light to dark does not provide enough contrast to keep your visual receptors firing at a steady rate. The circle reappears only if you close and reopen your eye or shift your gaze to the *x*.

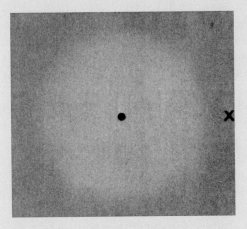 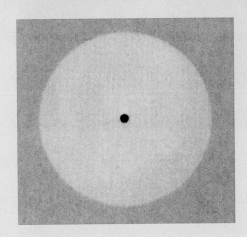

detection task can be divided into a *sensory process*, which depends on the intensity of the stimulus, and a *decision process*, which is influenced by the observer's response bias. Methods are available for separating these two components. For example, the researcher can include some trials in which no stimulus is present and others in which a weak stimulus is present. Under these conditions, four kinds of responses are possible: The person (1) detects a signal that was present (a "hit"), (2) says the signal was there when it was not (a "false alarm"), (3) fails to detect the signal when it was present (a "miss"), or (4) correctly says the signal was absent when it was absent (a "correct rejection").

Yea-sayers will have more hits than naysayers, but they will also have more false alarms because they are too quick to say, "Yup, it was there." Naysayers will have more correct rejections than yea-sayers, but they will also have more misses, because they are too quick to say, "Nope, nothing was there." This information can be fed into a mathematical formula that yields separate estimates of a person's response bias and sensory capacity. The individual's true sensitivity to a signal of any particular intensity can then be predicted.

The old method of measuring thresholds assumed that a person's ability to detect a stimu-lus depended solely on the stimulus. Signal-detection theory assumes that there is no single "threshold," because at any given moment, a person's sensitivity to a stimulus depends on a decision that he or she actively makes. Researchers at Dalhousie University, for example, have found that children with attention deficit/hyperactivity disorder (ADHD) are more likely than other children to commit false alarm and miss errors (Losier, McGrath, & Klein, 1996). This isn't surprising, given that this disorder is defined in terms of short attention span and difficulty staying physically settled in one place for very long. Signal-detection methods have many real-world applications, from screening applicants for jobs requiring keen hearing to training air-traffic controllers, whose decisions about the presence or absence of a blip on a radar screen may mean the difference between life and death.

Sensory Adaptation

Variety, they say, is the spice of life. It is also the essence of sensation, for our senses are designed to respond to change and contrast in the environment. When a stimulus is unchanging or repetitious, sensation often fades or disappears. Receptors or nerve cells higher up in the sensory system get "tired" and fire less frequently. The

The effects of sensory deprivation depend on the circumstances. Being isolated against your will can be terrifying, but many people have found an hour alone in a "flotation tank" to be pleasantly relaxing.

sensory adaptation The reduction or disappearance of sensory responsiveness that occurs when stimulation is unchanging or repetitious.

resulting decline in sensory responsiveness is called **sensory adaptation**. Such adaptation is usually useful because it spares us from having to respond to unimportant information; for example, most of the time you have no need to feel your watch sitting on your wrist. Sometimes, however, adaptation can be hazardous, as when you no longer smell a gas leak that you noticed when you first entered the kitchen.

We never completely adapt to extremely intense stimuli—a terrible toothache, the odour of ammonia, the heat of the desert sun. And we rarely adapt completely to visual stimuli, whether they are weak or intense. Eye movements, voluntary and involuntary, cause the position of an object's image on the back of the eye to keep changing, so that visual receptors located there don't have a chance to "fatigue." But in the laboratory, researchers can stabilize the image of a simple pattern, such as a line, at a particular point on the back of a person's eye. They use an ingenious device consisting of a tiny projector mounted on a contact lens. Although the eyeball moves, the image of the object stays focused on the same receptors. In minutes, the image begins to disappear.

What would happen if our senses adapted to *most* incoming stimuli? Would we sense nothing, or would the brain substitute its own images for the sensory experiences no longer available by way of the sense organs? In early studies of **sensory deprivation** conducted at McGill University, researchers studied this question by isolating male

sensory deprivation The absence of normal levels of sensory stimulation.

volunteers from all patterned sight and sound. Vision was restricted by a translucent visor, hearing by a U-shaped pillow and by background noise from an air conditioner and fan, and touch by cotton gloves and cardboard cuffs. The volunteers took brief breaks to eat and use the bathroom, but otherwise they lay in bed, doing nothing. The results were dramatic. Within a few hours, many of the men felt edgy. Some were so disoriented that they quit the study the first day. Those who stayed longer became confused, restless, and grouchy. Many reported bizarre visions, such as a squadron of marching squirrels or a procession of marching eyeglasses. Few were willing to remain in the study for more than two or three days (Heron, 1957).

However, according to research conducted at the University of British Columbia, the notion that sensory deprivation is unpleasant or even dangerous turned out to be an oversimplification (Suedfeld, 1975). In many of the studies, the experimental procedures themselves probably aroused anxiety: Participants were told about "panic buttons" and were asked to sign "release from legal liability" forms. Later research, using better methods, showed that hallucinations are less dramatic and less disorienting than was thought at first. In fact, many people enjoy time-limited periods of deprivation, and some perceptual and intellectual abilities actually improve. The response to sensory deprivation depends on your expectations and interpretations of what is happening. Reduced sensation can be scary if you are locked in a room for an indefinite period, but relaxing if you have retreated to that room voluntarily for a little time out—at, say, a luxury spa or a monastery.

Thinking Critically About Sensory Deprivation

Still, it is clear that the human brain requires a minimum amount of sensory stimulation in order to function normally. This need may help explain why people who live alone often keep the radio or television set running continuously and why prolonged solitary confinement is used as a form of punishment or even torture.

Sensory Overload

If too little stimulation can be bad for you, so can too much, because it can lead to fatigue and mental confusion. If you have ever felt exhausted, nervous, and headachy after a day crammed with hectic activities and deadlines, you know firsthand about sensory overload.

When people find themselves in a state of overload, they often cope by blocking out unimportant sights and sounds and focusing only on those they find interesting or useful. Psychologists have dubbed this the "cocktail party phenomenon" because at a cocktail party, a person typically focuses on just one conversation, ignoring other voices, the clink of ice cubes, music, and bursts of laughter across the room. The competing sounds all enter the nervous system, enabling the person to pick up anything important—such as the person's own name, spoken by someone several metres away. Unimportant sounds, though, are not fully processed by the brain.

The capacity for **selective attention** protects us in daily life from being overwhelmed by all the sensory signals bombarding our receptors. The brain is not forced to respond to everything the sense receptors send its way. The "generals" in the brain can choose which "field officers" get past the command centre's gates. Those that do not seem to have anything important to say are turned back.

selective attention The focusing of attention on selected aspects of the environment and the blocking out of other aspects.

Quick Quiz

If you are not overloaded, try answering these questions.

1. Even on the clearest night, some stars cannot be seen by the naked eye because they are below the viewer's _____ threshold.
2. If you jump into a cold lake but moments later the water no longer seems so cold, sensory _____ has occurred.
3. If you are immobilized in a hospital bed, with no one to talk to and no TV or radio, and you feel edgy and disoriented, you may be suffering the effects of _____.
4. During a break from your job as a server in a restaurant, you decide to read. For 20 minutes, you are so engrossed that you fail to notice the clattering of dishes or orders being called out to the cook. This is an example of _____.
5. In real-life detection tasks, is it better to be a naysayer or a yea-sayer?

Answers:

1. absolute 2. adaptation 3. sensory deprivation 4. selective attention
5. Neither; it depends on the consequences of a "miss" or a "false alarm" and the probability of an event occurring. You might want to be a yea-sayer if on your way out the door, you think you hear the phone ringing, and you are expecting a call about a job interview. You might want to be a naysayer if on your way out the door, you think you hear the phone ringing, and you are already late for a job interview.

WHAT'S AHEAD

- How does the eye differ from a camera?
- Why can we describe a colour as bluish green but not as reddish green?
- If you were blind in one eye, why might you misjudge the distance of a painting on the wall but not of buildings a block away?
- As a friend approaches, her image on your retina grows larger; why do you continue to see her as the same size?
- Why are perceptual illusions valuable to psychologists?

VISION

Vision is the most frequently studied of all the senses, and with good reason. More information about the external world comes to us through our eyes than through any other sense organ. (Perhaps that is why people say "I see what you mean" instead of "I hear what you mean.") Because we are most active in the daytime, we have been "wired" by evolution to take advantage of the sun's illumination. Animals that are active at night tend to rely more heavily on hearing.

What We See

The stimulus for vision is light; even cats, raccoons, and other creatures famous for their ability to get around in the dark need some light to see. Visible light comes from the sun and other stars and from light bulbs, and it is also reflected off objects. Light travels in the form of waves, and the characteristics of these waves affect three *psychological* aspects of our visual world: hue, brightness, and saturation.

1 **Hue**, the dimension of visual experience specified by colour names, is related to the *wavelength* of light—that is, to the distance between the crests of a light wave. Shorter waves tend to be seen as violet and blue, and longer ones as orange and red. (We say "tend to" because other factors also affect colour perception, as we will see later.) The sun produces white light, a mixture of all the visible wavelengths. Sometimes drops of moisture in the air act like a prism: They separate the sun's white light into the colours of the visible spectrum, and we are treated to a rainbow.

2 **Brightness** is the dimension of visual experience related to the amount, or *intensity*, of the light an object emits or reflects. Intensity corresponds to the amplitude (maximum height) of the wave. Generally speaking, the more light an object reflects, the brighter it appears. However, brightness is also affected by wavelength: Yellows appear brighter than reds and blues when physical intensities are actually equal.

3 **Saturation** (colourfulness) is the dimension of visual experience related to the *complexity* of light—that is, to how wide or narrow the range of wavelengths is. When light contains only a single wavelength, it is said to be "pure," and the resulting colour is said to be completely saturated.

At the other extreme is white light, which lacks any colour and is completely unsaturated. In nature, pure light is extremely rare. Usually, we sense a mixture of wavelengths, and we see colours that are more dull and more pale than are completely saturated ones.

An Eye on the World

Light enters the visual system through the eye, a wonderfully complex and delicate structure. As you read this section, examine Figure 6.2. Notice that the front part of the eye is covered by the transparent *cornea*. The cornea protects the eye and bends incoming light rays toward a *lens* located behind it. A camera lens focuses incoming light by moving closer to or farther from the shutter opening. However, the lens of the eye works by subtly changing its shape, becoming more or less curved to focus light from objects that are close by or far away. The amount of light that gets into the eye is controlled by muscles in the *iris*, the part of the eye that gives it colour. The iris surrounds the round opening, or *pupil*, of the eye. When you enter a dim room, the pupil widens, or dilates, to let more light in. When you emerge into bright sunlight, the pupil contracts to allow less light in. You can see these changes by watching your eyes in a mirror as you change the lighting.

The visual receptors are located in the back of the eye, or **retina**. In a developing embryo, the retina forms from tissue that projects out from the brain, not from tissue destined to form other parts of the eye; thus, the retina is actually an extension of the brain. As Figure 6.3 shows, when the lens of the eye focuses light on the retina, the

hue The dimension of visual experience specified by colour names and related to the wavelength of light.

brightness Lightness or luminance; the dimension of visual experience related to the amount (or intensity) of light emitted from or reflected by an object.

saturation Vividness or purity of colour; the dimension of visual experience related to the complexity of light waves.

retina Neural tissue lining the back of the eyeball's interior; this tissue contains the receptors for vision.

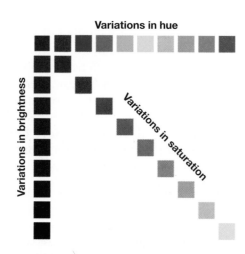

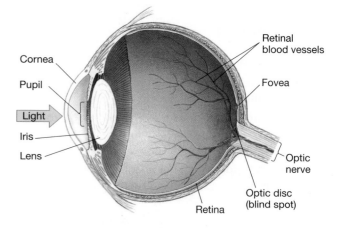

FIGURE 6.2 Major Structures of the Eye

Light passes through the pupil and lens and is focused on the retina at the back of the eye. The point of sharpest vision is at the fovea.

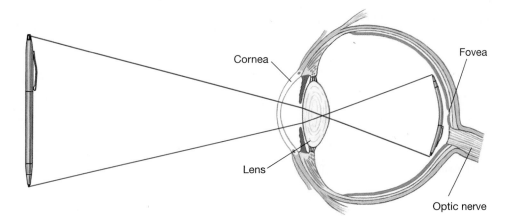

FIGURE 6.3 The Retinal Image

When we look at an object, the light pattern on the retina is upside down. René Descartes (1596–1650) was probably the first person to demonstrate this fact. He cut a piece from the back of an ox's eye and replaced the piece with paper. When he held the eye up to the light, he saw an upside-down image of the room on the paper!

result is an upside-down image (which can actually be seen with an instrument used by eye specialists). Light from the top of the visual field stimulates light-sensitive receptor cells in the bottom part of the retina, and vice versa. The brain interprets this upside-down pattern of stimulation as something that is right side up.

About 120 to 125 million receptors in the retina are long and narrow and are called **rods**. Another 7 or 8 million receptors are cone-shaped and are called, appropriately enough, **cones**. The centre of the retina, or *fovea*, where vision is sharpest, contains only cones, clustered densely together. From the centre to the periphery, the ratio of rods to cones increases, and the outer edges contain virtually no cones.

Rods are more sensitive to light than cones are. They enable us to see in dim light and at night. (Cats see well in dim light in part because they have a high proportion of rods.) Because rods occupy the outer edges of the retina, they also handle peripheral (side) vision. That is why you can sometimes see a star from the corner of your eye even though it is invisible to you when you gaze straight at it. But rods cannot distinguish different wavelengths of light and therefore are not sensitive to colour, which is why it is often hard to distinguish colours clearly in dim light. The cones, on the other hand, are differentially sensitive to specific wavelengths of light and allow us to see colours. But they need much more light than rods do to respond, so they don't help us much when we are trying to recognize our friend in a darkened movie theatre based on his red coat. (These differences are summarized in Table 6.1.)

We have all noticed that it takes some time for our eyes to adjust fully to dim illumination. This process of **dark adaptation** involves chemical changes in the rods and cones. The cones adapt quickly, within 10 minutes or so, but they never become very sensitive to the dim illumination. The rods adapt more slowly, taking 20 minutes or longer, but are ultimately much more sensitive. After the first phase of adaptation, you can see better but not well; after the second phase, your vision is as good as it will ever get.

Rods and cones are connected by synapses to *bipolar neurons*, which in turn communicate with neurons called **ganglion cells** (see Figure 6.4). The axons of the ganglion cells converge to form the *optic nerve*, which carries information out through the back of the eye and on to the brain. Where the optic nerve leaves the eye, at the *optic disk*, there are no rods or cones. The absence of receptors produces a blind spot in the field of vision. Normally, we are unaware of the blind spot because (1) the image projected on the spot is hitting a different, "nonblind" spot in the other eye; (2) our eyes move so fast that we can pick up the complete image; and (3) the brain fills in the gap. You can find your blind spot by following the instructions in the "Get Involved" exercise on page 185.

Why the Visual System Is Not a Camera

Although the eye is often compared with a camera, the visual system, unlike a camera, is not a passive recorder of the external world. Instead of simply registering spots of light and dark, as in a photograph, neurons in the visual system build up a picture of the world by detecting its meaningful features.

Ganglion cells and neurons in the thalamus of the brain respond to simple features in the environment, such as spots of light and dark. But in mammals, special **feature-detector cells** in the visual cortex respond to more complex features.

rods Visual receptors that respond to dim light.

ganglion cells Neurons, in the retina of the eye, which gather information from receptor cells (by way of intermediate bipolar neurons); their axons make up the optic nerve.

cones Visual receptors involved in colour vision.

dark adaptation A process by which visual receptors become maximally sensitive to dim light.

feature-detector cells Cells in the visual cortex that are sensitive to specific features of the environment.

TABLE 6.1 Differences between Rods and Cones

	Rods	Cones
How many?	120–125 million	7–8 million
Where most concentrated?	Periphery of retina	Centre (fovea) of retina
How sensitive?	High sensitivity	Low sensitivity
Sensitive to colour?	No	Yes

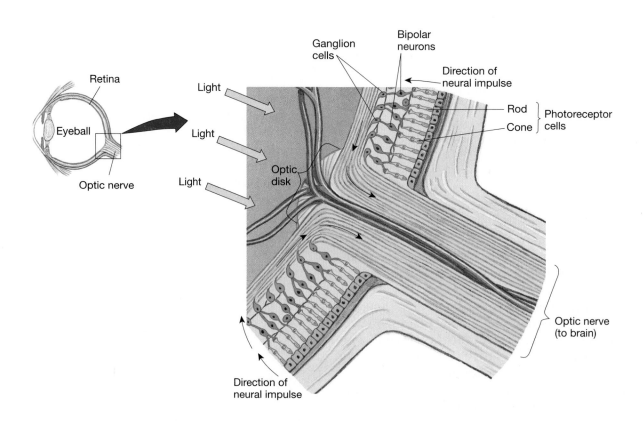

FIGURE 6.4 The Structures of the Retina

For clarity, all cells in this drawing are greatly exaggerated in size. To reach the receptors for vision (the rods and cones), light must pass through the ganglion cells and bipolar neurons as well as the blood vessels that nourish them (not shown). Normally, we do not see the shadow cast by this network of cells and blood vessels because the shadow always falls on the same place on the retina, and such stabilized images are not sensed. But when an eye doctor shines a moving light into your eye, the treelike shadow of the blood vessels falls on different regions of the retina and you may see it—a rather eerie experience.

This fact was first demonstrated by David Hubel and Torsten Wiesel (1962, 1968), who painstakingly recorded impulses from individual cells in the brains of cats and monkeys. (In 1981, they received a Nobel Prize for their work.) Hubel and Wiesel found that different neurons were sensitive to different patterns projected on a screen in front of an animal's eyes. Most cells responded maximally to moving or stationary lines that were oriented in a particular direction and located in a particular part of the visual field. One type of cell might fire most rapidly in response to a horizontal line in the lower right part of the visual field, another to a diagonal line at an angle in the upper left part of the visual field. In the real world, such features make up the boundaries and edges of objects.

Get Involved   Find Your Blind Spot

A blind spot exists where the optic nerve leaves the back of your eye. Find the blind spot in your left eye by closing your right eye and looking at the magician. Then slowly move the book toward and away from yourself. The rabbit should disappear when the book is between 20 and 30 centimetres from your eye.

Since this pioneering work was done, scientists have found that other cells in the visual system have far more complex kinds of specialties. For example, in primates, the visual cortex contains cells that respond maximally to bull's-eyes, spirals, or concentric circles (Gallant, Braun, & Van Essen, 1993). Even more intriguing, some cells in the temporal lobe respond maximally to faces (Kanwisher, 2000; Ó Scalaidhe, Wilson, & Goldman-Rakic, 1997; Young & Yamane, 1992). Some scientists have concluded that evolution has equipped us with a special "face module" in the brain. Researchers at the Rotman Research Institute in Toronto have indicated that the existence of face modules could help explain why a person with brain damage may continue to recognize faces even after losing the ability to recognize other objects. In one case described by Morris Moscovitch at the University of Toronto, a man could recognize a face made up of vegetables, fruits, and flowers like the one in the painting on the next page, but he could not recognize the vegetables (Moscovitch, Winocur, & Behrmann, 1997). Face modules would also help explain why infants show a strong preference for looking at faces (see Chapter 3).

A preference for deciphering faces makes evolutionary sense because it would have ensured our ancestors' ability to distinguish friend from foe. Nevertheless, the existence of such modules remains controversial among neuroscientists (Cohen & Tong, 2001). Some think a preference for faces is really a preference for curved lines, or for eye contact. And it turns out that some of the brain cells that supposedly make up the face module respond to other things, too, depending on a person's experiences and interests. In one fascinating study (Gauthier et al., 2000), cells in the "face module" fired when car buffs examined pictures of classic cars but not when they looked

Cases of brain damage support the idea that particular systems of brain cells are highly specialized. One man's injury left him unable to identify ordinary objects, which he said often looked like "blobs." Yet he had no trouble with faces, even when they were upside down or incomplete. When shown this painting, he could easily see the face, but he could not see the vegetables, fruits, and flowers comprising it (Moscovitch, Winocur, & Behrmann, 1997).

The Trichromatic Theory The **trichromatic theory** (also known as the *Young–Helmholtz theory*) applies to the first level of processing, which occurs in the retina of the eye. The retina contains three basic types of cones. One type responds maximally to blue (or more precisely, to a range of wavelengths near the short end of the spectrum, which give rise to the experience of blue), another to green, and a third to red. The hundreds of colours we see result from the combined activity of these three types of cones.

Total colour-blindness is usually due to a genetic variation that causes cones of the retina to be absent or malfunctional. The visual world then consists of black, white, and shades of gray. Many species of animals are totally colour-blind, but the condition is extremely rare in human beings. Most "colour-blind" people are actually colour *deficient*. Usually, the person is unable to distinguish red and green; the world is painted in shades of blue, yellow, brown, and gray. In rarer instances, a person may be blind to blue and yellow and may see only reds, greens, and grays. Colour deficiency is found in about eight percent of white men, five percent of Asian men, and three percent of indigenous men and black men (Sekuler & Blake, 1994). Because of the way the condition is inherited, it is rare in women.

at pictures of exotic birds, and the exact opposite was true for birdwatchers. Cars, of course, do not have faces!

Even if face or other specialized modules do exist, the brain cannot possibly contain a special area for every conceivable object. In general, the brain's job is to take fragmentary information about lines, angles, shapes, motion, brightness, texture, and patterns, and figure out that a chair is a chair, and that it is next to the dining-room table. The perception of any given object probably depends on the activation of many cells in far-flung parts of the brain and on the overall pattern and rhythm of their activity (Bower, 1998).

How We See Colours

For 300 years, scientists have been trying to figure out why we see the world in living colour. We now know that different processes explain different stages of colour vision.

The Opponent-Process Theory The **opponent-process theory** applies to the second stage of colour processing, which occurs in ganglion cells in the retina and in neurons in the thalamus and visual cortex of the brain. These cells, known as *opponent-process cells*, either respond to short wavelengths but are inhibited from firing by long wavelengths, or vice versa (DeValois & DeValois, 1975). Some opponent-process cells respond in opposite fashion to red and green; that is, they fire in response to one and turn off in response to the other. Others respond in opposite fashion to blue and yellow. (A third system responds in opposite fashion to white and black and thus yields information about brightness.) The net result is a colour code that is passed along to the higher visual centres. Because this code treats red and green—and also blue and yellow—as antagonistic, we can describe a colour as bluish green or yellowish green but not as reddish green or yellowish blue.

Get Involved   A Change of Heart

Opponent-process cells that switch on or off in response to green send an opposite message—"red"—when the green is removed, producing a negative afterimage. Stare at the black dot in the middle of this heart for at least 20 seconds. Then shift your gaze to a white piece of paper or a white wall. Do you get a "change of heart"? You should see an image of a red or pinkish heart, and you might see a blue border as well.

Opponent-process cells that are *inhibited* by a particular colour seem to produce a burst of firing when the colour is removed, just as they would if the opposing colour were present. Similarly, cells that *fire* in response to a colour stop firing when the colour is removed, just as they would if the opposing colour were present. These facts explain why we are susceptible to *negative afterimages* when we stare at a particular hue—why we see, for instance, red after staring at green (see the "Get Involved" exercise). A sort of neural rebound effect occurs: The cells that switch on or off to signal the presence of "green" send the opposite signal ("red") when the green is removed—and vice versa.

Constructing the Visual World

We do not see a retinal image; that image is merely grist for the mill of the mind, which actively interprets the image and constructs the world from the often fragmentary data of the senses. In the brain, sensory signals that give rise to vision, hearing, taste, smell, and touch are combined from moment to moment to produce a unified model of the world. This is the process of *perception*.

Form Perception To make sense of the world, we must know where one thing ends and another begins. In vision, we must separate the teacher from the lectern; in hearing, we must separate the piano solo from the orchestral accompaniment; and in taste, we must separate the marshmallow from the hot chocolate. This process of dividing up the world occurs so rapidly and effortlessly that we take it completely for granted—until we must make out objects in a heavy fog or words in the rapid-fire conversation of someone speaking a foreign language.

The *Gestalt psychologists*, who belonged to a movement that began in Germany and that was influential in the 1920s and 1930s, were among the first to study how people organize the world visually into meaningful units and patterns. In German, *Gestalt* means "form" or "configuration." The Gestalt psychologists' motto was "The whole is more than the sum of its parts." They observed that when we perceive something, properties emerge from the configuration as a whole that are not found in any particular component. When you watch a movie, for example, the motion you "see" is nowhere in the film, which consists of separate static frames projected at 24 frames per second.

One thing the Gestalt psychologists noted was that people always organize the visual field into *figure* and *ground*. The figure stands out from the rest of the environment (see Figure 6.5). Some things stand out as figure by virtue of their intensity or size; it is hard to ignore the blinding flash of a camera or a tidal wave approaching your piece of beach. The lower part of a scene tends to be

6.3

FIGURE 6.5 Figure and Ground

Do you see the goblins or the angels? The woodcut *Heaven and Hell* by M. C. Escher shows both, depending on whether you see the black or white sections as figure or ground.

seen as figure, the upper part as background (Vecera, Vogel, & Woodman, 2002). Unique objects also stand out, such as a banana in a bowl of oranges. Moving objects in an otherwise still environment, such as a shooting star, will usually be seen as figure. Indeed, it is hard to ignore a sudden change of any kind in the environment because our brains are geared to respond to change and contrast. However, selective attention—the ability to concentrate on some stimuli and to filter out others—gives us some control over what we perceive as figure and ground.

Here are some other **Gestalt principles** that describe how the visual system groups sensory building blocks into perceptual units:

Gestalt principles Principles that describe the brain's organization of sensory information into meaningful units and patterns.

1 *Proximity.* Things that are near each other tend to be grouped together. Thus you perceive the dots on the left as two groups of dots, not as eight separate, unrelated ones. Similarly, you may be more likely to perceive the pattern on the right as vertical columns of dots rather than horizontal rows:

2 *Closure.* The brain tends to fill in gaps in order to perceive complete forms. This is fortunate because we often need to decipher less-than-perfect images. The following figures are easily perceived as a triangle, a face, and the letter *e*, even though none of the figures is complete:

3 *Similarity.* Things that are alike in some way (for example, in colour, shape, or size) tend to be perceived as belonging together. In the figure on the left, you see the circles as forming an *X*. In the one on the right, you see horizontal rows rather than vertical columns because the horizontally aligned stars are either all red or all outlined in red:

4 *Continuity.* Lines and patterns tend to be perceived as continuing in time or space. You perceive the figure on the left as a single line partially covered by an oval rather than as two separate lines touching an oval. In the figure on the right, you see two lines, one curved and one straight, instead of two curved and two straight lines, touching at one focal point:

Consumer products are sometimes designed with little thought for visual principles such as those formulated by the Gestalt psychologists—which is why it can be a major challenge to find the pause button on your VCR's remote control or change from AM to FM on your car radio (Bjork, 2000; Norman, 1988). Good design requires, among other things, that crucial distinctions be visually obvious. For instance, knobs and switches with different functions should differ in colour, texture, or shape, and they should stand out as "figure." How would you use this information to redesign some of the products that you use?

Depth and Distance Perception Ordinarily we need to know not only what something is, but also where it is. Touch gives us this information directly, but vision does not, so we must infer an object's location by estimating its distance or depth.

To perform this remarkable feat, we rely in part on **binocular cues**—cues that require the use of two eyes. One such cue is **convergence**, the turning of the eyes inward, which occurs when they focus on a nearby object. The closer the object, the greater the convergence, as you know if you have ever tried to "cross" your eyes by looking at your own nose. As the angle of convergence changes, the corresponding muscular changes provide information to the brain about distance.

The two eyes also receive slightly different retinal images of the same object. You can prove this by holding a finger about 30 centimetres in front of your face and looking at it with only one eye at a time. Its position will appear to shift when you change eyes. Now hold up two fingers, one closer to your nose than the other. Notice that the amount of space between the two fingers appears to change when you switch eyes. The slight difference in lateral (sideways) separation between two objects as seen by the left eye and the right eye is called **retinal disparity**. Because retinal disparity increases as the distance between two objects increases, the brain can use it to infer depth and calculate distance.

Binocular cues help us estimate distances up to about 15 metres. For objects farther away, we use only **monocular cues**, cues that do not depend on using both eyes. One such cue is *interposition:* When an object is interposed between the viewer and a second object, partly blocking the view of the second object, the first object is perceived as being closer. Another monocular cue is *linear perspective:* When two lines known to be parallel appear to be coming together or converging, they imply the existence of depth. For example, if you are standing between railroad tracks, they appear to converge in the distance. These and other monocular cues are illustrated on page 190.

Visual Constancies: When Seeing Is Believing

Your perceptual world would be a confusing place without another important perceptual skill. Lighting conditions, viewing angles, and the distances of stationary objects are all continually changing as we move about, yet we rarely confuse these changes with changes in the objects themselves. This ability to perceive objects as stable or unchanging even though the sensory patterns they produce are constantly shifting is called **perceptual constancy**. The best-studied constancies are visual, and they include the following:

1 *Shape constancy.* We continue to perceive objects as having a constant shape even though the shape of the retinal image produced by an object changes when our point of view changes. If you hold a Frisbee directly in front of your face, its image on the retina will be round. When you set the Frisbee on a table, its image becomes elliptical, yet you continue to identify the Frisbee as round.

2 *Location constancy.* We perceive stationary objects as remaining in the same place even though the retinal image moves about as we move our eyes, heads, and bodies. As you drive along the highway, telephone poles and trees fly by—on your retina. But you know that these objects do not move on their own, and you also know that your body is moving, so you perceive the poles and trees as staying put.

3 *Size constancy.* We see an object as having a constant size even when its retinal image becomes smaller or larger. A friend approaching on the street does not seem to be growing; a car pulling away from the curb does not seem to be shrinking.

perceptual constancy The accurate perception of objects as stable or unchanged despite changes in the sensory patterns they produce.

binocular cues Visual cues to depth or distance requiring two eyes.

convergence The turning inward of the eyes, which occurs when they focus on a nearby object.

retinal disparity The slight difference in lateral separation between two objects as seen by the left eye and the right eye.

monocular cues Visual cues to depth or distance that can be used by one eye alone.

OneKey 6.5

OneKey 6.6

BIZARRO By DAN PIRARO

When size constancy fails.

MONOCULAR CUES TO DEPTH

Most cues to depth do not depend on having two eyes. Some monocular (one-eyed) cues are shown here.

Motion Parallax

When an observer is moving, objects appear to move at different speeds and in different directions. The closer an object, the faster it seems to move; and close objects appear to move backward, whereas distant ones seem to move forward.

Interposition

An object that partly blocks or obscures another one must be in front of the other one and is therefore seen as closer.

Light and Shadow

Both of these attributes give objects the appearance of three dimensions.

Relative Clarity

Because of particles in the air—from dust, fog, or smog—distant objects tend to look hazier, duller, or less detailed.

Texture Gradients

Distant parts of a uniform surface appear denser; that is, its elements seem spaced more closely together.

Relative Size

The smaller an object's image on the retina, the farther away the object appears.

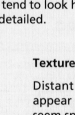

Linear Perspective

Parallel lines will appear to be converging in the distance; the greater the apparent convergence, the greater the perceived distance. This cue is often exaggerated by artists to convey an impression of depth.

Size constancy depends in part on familiarity with objects. You know that people and cars don't change size from moment to moment. It also depends on the apparent distance of an object. An object that is close produces a larger retinal image than the same object farther away, and the brain takes this into account. For example, when you move your hand toward your face, your brain registers the fact that the hand is getting closer, and you correctly perceive its unchanging size despite the growing size of its retinal image. There is, then, an intimate relationship between perceived size and perceived distance.

4   *Brightness constancy.* We see objects as having a relatively constant brightness even though the amount of light they reflect changes as the overall level of illumination changes. Snow remains white even on a cloudy day. We are not fooled because the brain registers the total illumination in the scene, and we automatically take this information into account.

5   *Colour constancy.* We see an object as maintaining its hue despite the fact that the wavelength of light reaching our eyes from the object may change as the illumination changes. For example, outdoor light is "bluer" than indoor light, and objects outdoors therefore reflect more "blue" light than those indoors. Conversely, indoor light from incandescent lamps is rich in long wavelengths and is therefore "yellower." Yet objects usually look the same colour in both places: An apple looks red whether you look at it in your kitchen or outside on the patio. Part of the explanation involves sensory

adaptation, which we discussed earlier. Outdoors, we quickly adapt to short-wavelength (bluish) light, and indoors, we adapt to long-wavelength light. As a result, our visual responses are similar in the two situations. Also, when computing the colour of a particular object, the brain takes into account *all* the wavelengths in the visual field immediately around the object. If an apple is bathed in bluish light, so, usually, is everything else around it. The increase in blue light reflected by the apple is cancelled in the visual cortex by the increase in blue light reflected by the apple's surroundings, so the apple continues to look red.

Visual Illusions: When Seeing Is Misleading

Perceptual constancies allow us to make sense of the world. Occasionally, however, we can be fooled, and the result is a *perceptual illusion.* For psychologists, illusions are valuable because they are systematic errors that provide us with hints about the perceptual strategies of the mind.

Although illusions can occur in any sensory modality, visual illusions have been the best studied. Visual illusions sometimes occur when the strategies that normally lead to accurate perception are overextended to situations where they don't apply. Compare the lengths of the two vertical lines in Figure 6.6. If you are like most people, you perceive the line on the right as slightly longer than the one on the left. Yet they are exactly the same length. (Go ahead, measure them; everyone does.) This is the Müller–Lyer illusion, named after the German sociologist who first described it in 1889.

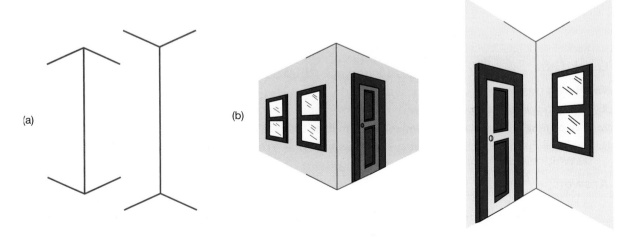

FIGURE 6.6 The Müller–Lyer Illusion

The two lines in (a) are exactly the same length. We are probably fooled into perceiving them as different because the brain interprets the one with the outward-facing branches as farther away, as if it were the far corner of a room (b, left), and the one with the inward-facing branches as closer, as if it were the near edge of a building (b, right).

One explanation for the Müller–Lyer illusion is that the branches on the lines serve as perspective cues that normally suggest depth (Gregory, 1963). The line on the left is like the near edge of a building; the one on the right is like the far corner of a room (see part *b* of the figure). Although the two lines produce retinal images of the same size, the one with the outward-facing branches suggests greater distance. We are fooled into perceiving it as longer because we automatically apply a rule about the relationship between size and distance that is normally useful: When two objects produce the same size retinal image and one is farther away, the farther one is larger. The problem, in this case, is that there is no actual difference in the distance of the two lines, so the rule is inappropriate.

Some illusions are simply a matter of physics. Thus, a chopstick in a half-filled glass of water looks bent because water and air refract light differently. Other illusions occur due to misleading messages from the sense organs, as in sensory adaptation. Still others, like the Müller–Lyer illusion, seem to occur because the brain misinterprets sensory information. Figure 6.7 shows some other startling illusions.

In everyday life, most illusions are harmless or entertaining. But sometimes illusions can lead to industrial and automobile accidents. For example, because large objects often appear to move more slowly than small ones, drivers sometimes underestimate the speed of onrushing trains at railroad crossings and think they can "beat" the train, with tragic results.

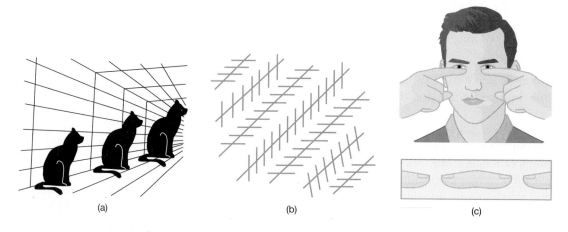

(a)   (b)   (c)

FIGURE 6.7 Fooling the Eye

Although perception is usually accurate, we can be fooled. In (a), the cats as drawn are all the same size; in (b), the diagonal lines are all parallel. To see the illusion depicted in (c), hold your index fingers 10 to 20 centimetres in front of your eyes as shown, and focus straight ahead. Do you see a floating "fingertip frankfurter"? Can you make it shrink or expand?

Quick Quiz

This quiz is no illusion.

1. How can two Gestalt principles help explain why you can make out the Big Dipper on a starry night?
2. *True or false?*: Binocular cues help us locate objects that are very far away.
3. Hold one hand about 30 centimetres from your face and the other one about 15 centimetres away. (a) Which hand will cast the smaller retinal image? (b) Why don't you perceive that hand as smaller?

Answers:

1. Proximity of certain stars encourages you to see them as clustered together to form a pattern; closure allows you to "fill in the gaps" and see the contours of a "dipper."
2. false
3. a. The hand that is 30 centimetres away will cast a smaller retinal image.
   b. Your brain takes the differences in distance into account in estimating size; also, you know how large your hands are. The result is size constancy.

WHAT'S AHEAD

- Why does a note played on a flute sound different from the same note played on an oboe?
- If you habitually listen to loud music through headphones, what kind of hearing impairment are you risking?
- To locate the source of a sound, why does it sometimes help to turn or tilt your head?

HEARING

Like vision, the sense of hearing, or *audition*, provides a vital link with the world around us. Because social relationships rely so heavily on hearing, when people lose their hearing they sometimes come to feel socially isolated. That is why many hearing-impaired people feel strongly about teaching deaf children American Sign Language (ASL) or other gestural languages, which allow them to communicate with and forge close relationships with other signers.

What We Hear

The stimulus for sound is a wave of pressure created when an object vibrates (or when compressed air is released, as in a pipe organ). The vibration (or release of air) causes molecules in a transmitting substance to move together and apart. This movement produces variations in pressure that radiate in all directions. The transmitting substance is usually air, but sound waves can also travel through water and solids, as you know if you have ever put your ear to the wall to hear voices in the next room.

As with vision, *physical* characteristics of the stimulus—in this case, a sound wave—are related in a predictable way to *psychological* aspects of our auditory experience:

1 **Loudness** is the dimension of auditory experience related to the *intensity* of a wave's pressure. Intensity corresponds to the amplitude, or maximum height, of the wave. The more energy contained in the wave, the higher it is at its peak. Perceived loudness is also affected by how high or low a sound is. If low and high sounds produce waves with equal amplitudes, the low sound may seem quieter.

Sound intensity is measured in units called *decibels* (dB). A decibel is one-tenth of a *bel*, a unit named for Alexander Graham Bell, the inventor of the telephone. The average absolute threshold of hearing in human beings is zero decibels. The sound of a humming refrigerator is 50 dB; shop tools average 90 dB; and a jet plane at 15 metres is 140 dB. Decibels are not equally distant, as inches on a ruler are. A 60-decibel sound (such as that of a sewing machine) is not 50 percent louder than a 40-decibel sound (such as that of a whisper); it is 100 times louder.

2 **Pitch** is the dimension of auditory experience related to the frequency of the sound wave and, to some extent, its intensity. *Frequency* refers to how rapidly the air (or other medium) vibrates—that is, the number of times per second the wave cycles through a peak and a low point. One cycle per second is known as 1 *hertz* (Hz). The healthy ear of a young person normally detects frequencies in the range of 16 Hz (the lowest note on a pipe organ) to 20 000 Hz (the scraping of a grasshopper's legs).

3 **Timbre** is the distinguishing quality of a sound. It is the dimension of auditory experience related to the *complexity* of the sound wave—to the relative breadth of the range of frequencies that make up the wave. A pure tone consists of only one frequency but, in nature, pure tones are extremely rare. Usually what we hear is a complex wave consisting of several subwaves with different frequencies. A particular combination of frequencies results in a particular timbre. Timbre is what makes a note played on a flute, which produces relatively pure tones, sound entirely different from the same note played on an oboe, which produces very complex sounds.

When many frequencies are present but are not in harmony, we hear noise. When all the frequencies of the sound spectrum occur, they produce a hissing sound called *white noise*. Just as white light includes all wavelengths of the visible light spectrum, so white noise includes all frequencies of the audible sound spectrum. People sometimes use white-noise machines to mask other sounds when they are trying to sleep.

An Ear on the World

When we look at an ear, we see only its external entrance. The ear actually has an outer, a middle, and an inner section. The soft, funnel-shaped outer ear is well designed to collect sound waves, but hearing would still be quite good without it. The essential parts of the ear are hidden from view, inside the head.

A sound wave passes into the outer ear and through a two-centimetre canal to strike an oval-shaped membrane called the *eardrum*

pitch The dimension of auditory experience related to the frequency of a pressure wave; it is related to the height or depth of a tone.

timbre The distinguishing quality of a sound; the dimension of auditory experience related to the complexity of the pressure wave.

loudness The dimension of auditory experience related to the intensity of a pressure wave.

6.8

OneKey
6.9

organ of Corti [CORE-tee]
A structure in the cochlea containing hair cells that serve as the receptors for hearing.

cochlea [KOCK-lee-uh] A snail-shaped, fluid-filled organ in the inner ear, containing the organ of Corti, where the receptors for hearing are located.

(see Figure 6.8). The eardrum is so sensitive that it can respond to the movement of a single molecule! A sound wave causes it to vibrate with the same frequency and amplitude as the wave itself. This vibration is passed along to three tiny bones in the middle ear, the smallest bones in the human body. These bones, known informally as the "hammer," the "anvil," and the "stirrup," move one after the other, which has the effect of intensifying the force of the vibration. The innermost bone, the stirrup, pushes on a membrane that opens into the inner ear.

The actual organ of hearing is the **organ of Corti**, a chamber inside the **cochlea**, a snail-shaped structure within the inner ear. This organ plays the same role in hearing that the retina plays in vision. It contains the all-important receptor cells, which in this case look like bristles and are called *hair cells*, or *cilia*. Brief exposure to extremely loud noises, or sustained exposure to more moderate ones (heavy city traffic, factory noise, a noisy restaurant), can injure these fragile cells. They

flop over, like broken blades of grass, and if the damage reaches a critical point, hearing loss occurs. In modern societies, with their rock concerts (120 dB in front of the speakers), deafening bars, and millions of automobiles, snowmobiles, power saws, leaf blowers, jackhammers, and sound systems (often played at full blast and listened to through headphones), such damage is common. Many college students already have impaired hearing because of harm to the cilia.

The hair cells of the cochlea are embedded in the rubbery *basilar membrane*, which stretches across the interior of the cochlea. When pressure reaches the cochlea, it causes wavelike motions in fluid within the cochlea's interior. These waves of fluid push on the basilar membrane, causing it to move in a wavelike fashion, too. Just above the hair cells is yet another membrane. As the hair cells rise and fall, their tips brush against it, and they bend. This causes the hair cells to initiate a signal that is passed along to the *auditory nerve*, which then carries the message to the brain. The

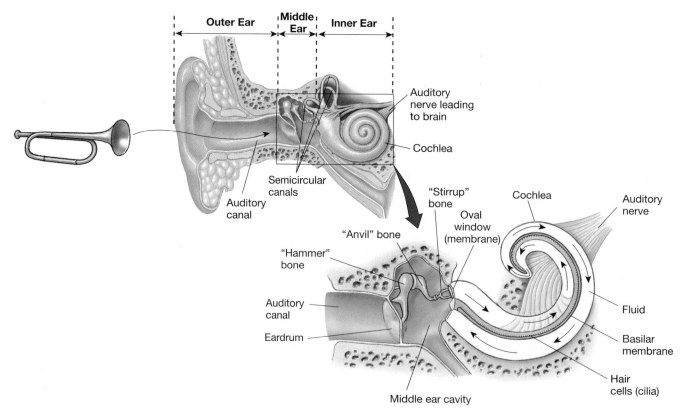

FIGURE 6.8 Major Structures of the Ear

Sound waves collected by the outer ear are channelled down the auditory canal, causing the eardrum to vibrate. These vibrations are then passed along to the tiny bones of the middle ear. Movement of these bones intensifies the force of the vibrations and funnels them to a small membrane separating the middle and inner ear. The receptor cells for hearing (hair cells), located in the organ of Corti within the snail-shaped cochlea, initiate nerve impulses that travel along the auditory nerve to the brain.

particular pattern of hair-cell movement is affected by the manner in which the basilar membrane moves. This pattern determines which neurons fire and how rapidly they fire, and the resulting code in turn determines the sort of sound we hear. For example, we discriminate high-pitched sounds largely on the basis of where activity occurs along the basilar membrane; activity at different sites leads to different neural codes. We discriminate low-pitched sounds largely on the basis of the frequency of the basilar membrane's vibration; again, different frequencies lead to different neural codes.

Could anyone ever imagine such a complex and odd arrangement of bristles, fluids, and snail shells if it did not already exist?

Constructing the Auditory World

Just as we do not see a retinal image, so we do not hear a chorus of brushlike tufts bending and swaying in the dark recesses of the cochlea. Just as we do not see a jumbled collection of lines and colours, so we do not hear a chaotic collection of disconnected pitches and timbres. Instead, we use our perceptual powers to organize patterns of sound and to construct a meaningful auditory world.

For example, in class, your psychology instructor hopes you will perceive his or her voice as "figure" and the hum of a passing airplane, cheers from the athletic field, or distant sounds of a construction crew as "ground." Whether these hopes are realized will depend, of course, on where you choose to direct your attention. Other Gestalt principles also seem to apply to hearing. The *proximity* of notes in a melody tells you which notes go together to form phrases; *continuity* helps you follow a melody on one violin when another violin is playing a different melody; *similarity* in timbre and pitch helps you pick out the soprano voices in a chorus and hear them as a unit; *closure* helps you understand a cellphone caller's words even when interference makes some of the individual sounds unintelligible.

Besides needing to organize sounds, we also need to know where they are coming from. We can estimate the *distance* of a sound's source by using loudness as a cue. For example, we know that a train sounds louder when it is 20 metres away than when it is a kilometre off. To locate the *direction* a sound is coming from, we depend in part on the fact that we have two ears. A sound arriving from the right reaches the right ear a fraction of a second sooner than it reaches the left ear, and vice versa. The sound may also provide a bit more energy to the right ear (depending on its frequency) because it has to get around the head to reach the left ear. It is hard to localize sounds that are coming from directly behind you or from directly above your head because such sounds reach both ears at the same time. When you turn or cock your head, you are actively trying to overcome this problem. Many animals do not have to do this because the lucky things can move their ears independently of their heads.

Quick Quiz

How well can you localize the answers to these questions?

1. Which psychological dimensions of hearing correspond to the intensity, frequency, and complexity of the sound wave?
2. Fred has a nasal voice and Ted has a gravelly voice. Which psychological dimension of hearing describes the difference?
3. An extremely loud or sustained noise can permanently damage the _____ of the ear.
4. During a lecture, a classmate draws your attention to a buzzing fluorescent light that you have not previously noticed. What will happen to your perception of figure and ground?

Answers:

1. loudness, pitch, timbre
2. timbre
3. hair cells (cilia)
4. The buzzing sound will become figure and the lecturer's voice will become ground, at least momentarily.

WHAT'S AHEAD

- Why do saccharin and caffeine taste bitter to some people but not to others?
- Why do you have trouble tasting your food when you have a cold?
- Why do people often continue to "feel" limbs that have been amputated?

OTHER SENSES

Psychologists have been particularly interested in vision and audition because of the importance of these senses to human survival. However, research on the other senses is growing dramatically, as awareness of how they contribute to our lives increases and as new ways are found to study them.

Taste: Savoury Sensations

Taste, or *gustation*, occurs because chemicals stimulate thousands of receptors in the mouth. These receptors are located primarily on the tongue, but some are also found in the throat, inside the cheeks, and on the roof of the mouth. If you look at your tongue in a mirror, you will notice many tiny bumps; they are called **papillae** (from the Latin for "pimples"), and they come in several forms. In all but one of these forms, the sides of each papilla are lined with **taste buds**, which up close look a little like segmented oranges (see Figure 6.9). Because of genetic differences, human tongues can have as few as 500 or as many as 10 000 taste buds (Miller & Reedy, 1990).

The taste buds are commonly referred to, mistakenly, as the receptors for taste. The actual receptor cells, however, are *inside* the buds, 15 to 50 to a bud. These cells send tiny fibres out through an opening in the bud; the receptor sites are on these fibres. The receptor cells are replaced by new cells about every 10 days. However, after age 40 or so, the total number of taste buds (and therefore receptors) declines.

Traditionally, researchers have considered four tastes to be basic: *salty, sour, bitter*, and *sweet*, each produced by a different type of chemical. Many researchers now also include a fifth taste, *umami* (from the Japanese for "delicious"), which is the taste of monosodium glutamate (MSG). Umami is found in many protein-rich foods, but its inclusion remains somewhat controversial. (We know when something is bitter or salty, but no one ever says, "Yum, this steak sure has a great umami taste.") The basic tastes are part of our evolutionary heritage: Bitterness and sourness help us identify foods that are rancid or poisonous; sweetness helps us identify foods that are healthful or rich in calories; salt is necessary for all bodily functions; and umami (if it is basic) can help us identify protein-rich foods.

The basic tastes can be perceived at any spot on the tongue that has receptors, and differences among the areas are small. Interestingly, the centre of the tongue contains no taste buds, and so it cannot produce any sort of taste sensation. But, as in the case of the eye's blind spot, you will not usually notice the lack of sensation because the brain fills in the gap.

When you bite into an egg or a piece of bread or an orange, its unique flavour is composed of some combination of the four or five basic tastes, but the physiological details are still hazy. It has even been difficult to find the receptors for the basic tastes, although recently researchers have proposed candidates for the receptors that process bitter, sweet, and umami (Chaudhari, Landin, & Roper, 2000; Huang et al., 1999; Max et al., 2001; Montmayeur et al., 2001; Zhang et al., 2003).

papillae [pa-PILL-ee] Knoblike elevations on the tongue, containing the taste buds. (Singular: *papilla*.)

taste buds Nests of taste-receptor cells.

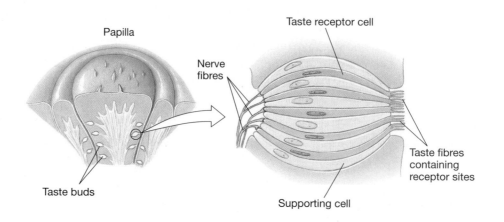

FIGURE 6.9 Taste Receptors

The illustration on the left shows taste buds lining the sides of a papilla on the tongue's surface. The illustration on the right shows an enlarged view of a single taste bud.

Papilla

Taste receptor cell

Nerve fibres

Taste fibres containing receptor sites

Taste buds

Supporting cell

Everyone knows that people live in somewhat different "taste worlds" (Bartoshuk, 1998). Some people love broccoli and others hate it. Some people can eat chili peppers that are burning hot, and others cannot tolerate the mildest jalapeño. One reason for these differences is genetic. About 25 percent of people are by nature *supertasters* who find saccharin, caffeine, broccoli, and many other substances to be unpleasantly bitter. (Women are overrepresented in this group.) "Tasters," in contrast, detect less bitterness, and "nontasters" detect none at all. Supertasters also perceive sweet tastes as sweeter and salty tastes as saltier than other people do, and they feel more "burn" from foods such as ginger, pepper, and hot chilies (Bartoshuk et al., 1998; Lucchina et al., 1998). Supertasters, it seems, have more taste buds, and certain papillae on their tongues are smaller, are more densely packed, and look different from those of non-tasters (Reedy et al., 1993).

Other taste preferences are a matter of culture and learning. Many North Americans who enjoy raw oysters, raw smoked salmon, and raw herring are nevertheless put off by other forms of raw seafood that are popular in Japan, such as sea urchin and octopus. And within a given culture, some people will greedily gobble up a dish that makes others turn green. Some of these learned taste preferences probably begin in the womb or during breast-feeding. A baby whose mother drank carrot juice while pregnant or nursing is likely to be more enthusiastic about eating porridge mixed with carrot juice than porridge mixed with water, whereas babies without this exposure show no such preference (Mennella, Jagnow, & Beauchamp, 2001).

The attractiveness of a food can also be affected by its colour, temperature, and texture. As Goldilocks found out, a bowl of cold porridge is not nearly as delicious as one that is properly heated. And any peanut butter fan will tell you that chunky and smooth peanut butters just don't taste the same. Even more important for taste is a food's odour. Subtle flavours such as chocolate and vanilla would have little taste if we could not smell them (see Figure 6.10). Smell's influence on flavour explains why you have trouble tasting your food when you have a stuffy nose. Most people who chronically have trouble tasting things have a problem with smell, not taste.

Smell: The Sense of Scents

The great author and educator Helen Keller, who became blind and deaf as a toddler, once called

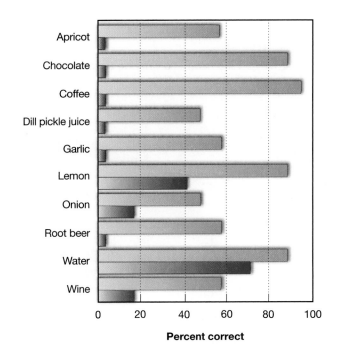

FIGURE 6.10 Taste Test

The orange bars show the percentages of people who could identify a substance dropped on the tongue when they were able to smell it. The blue bars show the percentages who could identify a substance when they were prevented from smelling it (Mozell et al., 1969).

smell "the fallen angel of the senses." Yet our sense of smell, or *olfaction*, although seemingly crude when compared to a bloodhound's, is actually quite good, and is far more useful than most people realize.

The receptors for smell are specialized neurons embedded in a tiny patch of mucous membrane in the upper part of the nasal passage, just beneath the eyes (see Figure 6.11). Millions of receptors in each nasal cavity respond to chemical molecules in the air. When you inhale, you pull these molecules into the nasal cavity, but they can also enter from the mouth, wafting up the throat like smoke up a chimney. These molecules trigger responses in the receptors, and these responses combine to yield the yeasty smell of freshly baked bread or the spicy fragrance of a eucalyptus tree. Signals from the receptors are carried to the brain's olfactory bulb by the *olfactory nerve*, which is made up of the receptors' axons. From the olfactory bulb, they travel to a higher region of the brain.

Figuring out the neural code for smell has been a real challenge. Of the 10 000 or so smells we detect (rotten, burned, musky, fruity, spicy, flowery, resinous, putrid . . .), none seems to be more basic than any other. Moreover, as many as

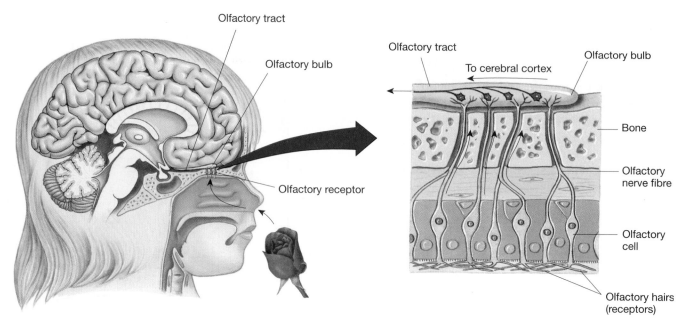

FIGURE 6.11 Receptors for Smell

Airborne chemical molecules (vapours) enter the nose and circulate through the nasal cavity, where the smell receptors are located. The receptors' axons make up the olfactory nerve, which carries signals to the brain. When you sniff, you draw more vapours into the nose and speed their circulation. Vapours can also reach the nasal cavity through the mouth by way of a passageway from the throat.

a thousand kinds of receptors exist, each kind responding to a part of an odour molecule's structure (Axel, 1995; Buck & Axel, 1991). But researchers are making progress; they have discovered that distinct odours activate unique combinations of receptor types, and they have succeeded in identifying some of those combinations (Malnic et al., 1999).

Although smell is less vital for human survival than for the survival of other animals, it is still important. We sniff out danger by smelling smoke, food spoilage, or poison gases. Thus, a deficit in the sense of smell is nothing to turn up your nose at. Such a loss can come about because of infection, disease, injury, or smoking. A person who has smoked 2 packs of cigarettes a day for 10 years must abstain from cigarettes for 10 more years before the sense of smell returns to normal (Frye, Schwartz, & Doty, 1990).

Human odour preferences, like taste preferences, vary. In some societies, people use rancid fat as a hair pomade, but anyone in North America who did so would quickly have a social problem. Within a particular culture, context and experience are all-important. The very same chemicals that contribute to unpleasant body odours and bad breath also contribute to the pleasant bouquet and flavour of cheese.

Smell has not only evolutionary but also cultural significance. These pilgrims in Japan are purifying themselves with holy incense for good luck and health.

Senses of the Skin

The skin's usefulness is more than just skin deep. Besides protecting our innards, our two square yards of skin help us identify objects and establish intimacy with others. By providing a boundary between ourselves and everything else, the skin also gives us a sense of ourselves as distinct from the environment.

The basic skin senses include *touch* (or pressure), *warmth*, *cold*, and *pain*. Within these four types are variations such as itch, tickle, and painful burning. Although certain spots on the skin are especially sensitive to the four basic skin sensations, for many years scientists had difficulty finding distinct receptors for these sensations, except in the case of pressure. A few years ago, however, Swedish researchers found a new kind of nerve fibre that seems to be responsible for at least some types of itching (Schmelz et al., 1997). And more recently, scientists identified a possible cold receptor (McKemy, Neuhausser, & Julius, 2002; Peier et al., 2002).

Perhaps specialized fibres will also be discovered for other skin sensations. In the meantime, many aspects of touch continue to baffle science—for example, why gently touching adjacent pressure spots in rapid succession produces tickle; and why the simultaneous stimulation of warm and cold spots produces not a lukewarm sensation but the sensation of heat. Decoding the messages of the skin senses will eventually tell us how we are able to distinguish sandpaper from velvet and glue from grease.

The Mystery of Pain

Pain, which is not only a skin sense but also an internal sense, has come under special scrutiny. Pain differs from other senses in an important way: When the stimulus producing it is removed, the sensation may continue—sometimes for years. Chronic pain disrupts lives, puts stress on the body, and causes depression and despair. (For ways of coping with pain, see "Taking Psychology With You.")

The Gate-Control Theory of Pain For many years, a leading explanation of pain has been the **gate-control theory**, which was first proposed by McGill University psychologist Ronald Melzack and British physiologist Patrick Wall (1965). According to this theory, pain impulses must get past a "gate" in the spinal cord. The gate is not an actual structure, but rather a pattern of neural activity that either blocks pain messages coming from the skin, muscles, and internal organs or lets those signals through. Normally, the gate is kept shut, either by impulses coming into the spinal cord from large fibres that respond to pressure and other kinds of stimulation or by signals coming down from the brain itself. But when body tissue is injured, the large fibres are damaged and smaller fibres open the gate, allowing pain messages to reach the brain unchecked.

Because the gate-control theory emphasizes the role of the brain in controlling the gate, it correctly predicts that thoughts and feelings can influence our reactions to pain. Researchers at Dalhousie University have shown that, when we dwell on our pain, focusing on it and talking about it constantly instead of acting in spite of it, we often intensify our experience of it (Sullivan, Tripp, & Santor, 1998). Conversely, when we are distracted from our pain, we may not feel it as we usually would—which is why we hear, from time to time, of athletes who are able to finish a performance despite sprained ankles or even broken bones. The gate-control theory also correctly predicts that mild pressure, or other kinds of stimulation, can interfere with severe or protracted pain by closing the spinal gate. When we vigorously rub a banged elbow or apply ice packs, heat, or stimulating ointments to injuries, we are applying this principle.

Updating the Gate-Control Theory The gate-control theory has been extremely useful, but it

gate-control theory The theory that the experience of pain depends in part on whether pain impulses get past a neurological "gate" in the spinal cord and thus reach the brain.

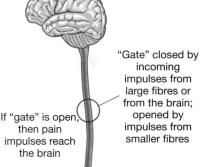

"Gate" closed by incoming impulses from large fibres or from the brain; opened by impulses from smaller fibres

If "gate" is open, then pain impulses reach the brain

does not completely explain the many instances of severe, chronic pain that occur without any sign of injury or disease. In the strange phenomenon of *phantom pain*, for instance, a person continues to feel pain that seemingly comes from an amputated limb or from an organ that has been surgically removed. An amputee may feel the same aching, burning, or sharp pain from sores, calf cramps, throbbing toes, or even ingrown toenails that he or she endured before the surgery. Even when the spinal cord has been completely severed, amputees often continue to report phantom pain from areas below the break. There are no nerve impulses for the spinal cord gate to block or let through. So why is there pain?

These puzzles have led Ronald Melzack (1992, 1993) to revise the gate-control theory. The brain, he says, not only responds to incoming signals from sensory nerves but also is capable of *generating* pain (and other sensations) entirely on its own. An extensive matrix (network) of neurons in the brain gives us a sense of our own bodies and body parts. When this matrix produces abnormal patterns of activity, the result is pain. Such abnormal patterns can occur not only because of input from peripheral nerves, but also as a result of memories, emotions, expectations, or signals from various brain centres. In the case of phantom pain, the abnormal patterns may arise because of a lack of sensory stimulation, or because of the person's efforts to move a nonexistent limb. Evidence from research at the University of Toronto showing that brain areas associated with a missing limb continue to function in its absence is consistent with this view (Davis et al., 1998).

At present, however, no general theory completely explains pain, which has turned out to be extremely complicated, both physiologically and psychologically. Different kinds of pain (from a pinprick, or a bruise, or a stomach ulcer) involve different chemical changes and changes in the activity of neurons at the site of injury or disease, and also in the spinal cord and brain. Genetic differences in the production of painkilling endorphins affect people's perception of pain; a blow experienced as crushing to one person may seem much milder to another (Zubieta et al., 2003). Pain is also affected by cultural beliefs about whether it is appropriate to notice symptoms and

express distress, and by psychological factors, such as stress and a focus on oneself. It can rise and fall in epidemics, as national outbreaks of back pain, whiplash, and repetitive motion injuries illustrate (Gawande, 1998). The people who suffer during such epidemics are not faking it, and their pain is not "just in their heads." But it may be in their brains.

The Environment Within

We usually think of our senses as pipelines to the "outside" world, but two senses keep us informed about the movements of our own bodies. **Kinesthesis** tells us where our body parts are located and lets us know when they move. This information is provided by pain and pressure receptors located in the muscles, joints, and tendons (tissues that connect muscles to bones). Without kinesthesis, you could not touch your finger to your nose with your eyes shut. In fact, you would have trouble with any voluntary movement. Think of how hard walking is when your leg has "fallen asleep" or how clumsy chewing is when a dentist has numbed your jaw.

Equilibrium, or the sense of balance, gives us information about our bodies as a whole. Along with vision and touch, it lets us know whether we are standing upright or on our heads and tells

kinesthesis [KIN-es-THEE-sis] The sense of body position and movement of body parts; also called *kinesthesia*.

equilibrium The sense of balance.

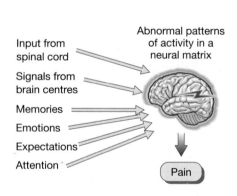

Input from spinal cord
Signals from brain centres
Memories
Emotions
Expectations
Attention
Abnormal patterns of activity in a neural matrix
Pain

Dancers, divers, and gymnasts turn their kinesthetic talents into artistry.

us when we are falling or rotating. Equilibrium relies primarily on three **semicircular canals** in the inner ear (see Figure 6.8 on page 194). These thin tubes are filled with fluid that moves and presses on hair-like receptors whenever the head rotates. The receptors initiate messages that travel through a part of the auditory nerve not involved in hearing.

Normally, kinesthesis and equilibrium work together to give us a sense of our own physical reality, something we take utterly for granted but should not. Oliver Sacks (1985) told the heartbreaking story of Christina, a young British woman who suffered irreversible damage to her kinesthetic nerve fibres because of a mysterious inflammation. At first, Christina was as floppy as a rag doll; she could not sit up, walk, or stand. Then,

slowly, she learned to do these things, relying on visual cues and sheer willpower. But her movements remained unnatural; she had to grasp a fork with painful force or she would drop it. More important, despite her remaining sensitivity to light touch on the skin, she could no longer experience herself as physically embodied: "It's like something's been scooped right out of me, right at the centre. . . ."

With equilibrium, we come, as it were, to the end of our senses. Every second, millions of sensory signals reach the brain, which combines and integrates them to produce a model of reality from moment to moment. How does it know how to do this? Are our perceptual abilities inborn, or must we learn them? We turn next to this issue.

semicircular canals Sense organs in the inner ear, which contribute to equilibrium by responding to rotation of the head.

Quick Quiz

Can you make sense of the following sensory problems?

1. April always has trouble tasting foods, especially those with subtle flavours. What is the most likely explanation of her difficulty?
2. May has chronic shoulder pain. How might the gate-control theory and its revision explain her pain?
3. June, a rock musician, does not hear as well as she used to. What is a likely explanation?

Answers:

1. an impaired sense of smell, possibly due to disease, illness, or cigarette smoking
2. Nerve fibres that normally close the pain "gate" may have been damaged, or a matrix of cells in the brain may be producing abnormal activity.
3. Hearing impairment has many causes, but in June's case, we might suspect that prolonged exposure to loud music has damaged the hair cells of her cochlea.

WHAT'S AHEAD

- Do babies see the world the way adults do?
- What psychological motives could cause people to "see" the face of a religious figure on a brick wall?

PERCEPTUAL POWERS: ORIGINS AND INFLUENCES

What happens when babies first open their eyes? Do they see the same sights, hear the same sounds, smell the same smells, taste the same tastes as an adult does? Are their strategies for organizing the world wired into their brains from the beginning? Or is an infant's world, as William James once suggested, only a "blooming, buzzing confusion,"

waiting to be organized by experience and learning? The truth lies somewhere between these two extremes.

Inborn Abilities

In human beings, most basic sensory abilities, and many perceptual skills, are inborn or develop quite early. Infants can distinguish salty from sweet and can discriminate among odours. They can distinguish a human voice from other sounds. They will startle at a loud noise and turn their heads toward its source, showing that they perceive sound as being localized in space. Many visual skills, too, are present at birth or develop shortly afterward. For example, human infants discriminate sizes and colours very early, possibly even right away. They can distinguish contrasts, shadows, and complex patterns after only a few weeks. And depth perception develops during the first few months.

Testing an infant's perception of depth requires considerable ingenuity. One clever procedure that was used for decades was to place infants on a device called a *visual cliff* (Gibson & Walk, 1960). The "cliff" is a pane of glass covering a shallow surface and a deep one (see Figure 6.12). Both surfaces are covered by a checkerboard pattern. The infant is placed on a board in the middle, and the child's mother tries to lure the baby across either the shallow or the deep side. Babies as young as six months of age will crawl across the shallow side but will refuse to crawl out over the "cliff." Their hesitation shows that they have depth perception.

Of course, by six months of age, a baby has had quite a bit of experience with the world. But infants younger than six months can also be tested on the visual cliff, even though they are unable to crawl. At only two months of age, babies show a drop in heart rate when placed on the deep side of the cliff, but no change when they are placed on the shallow side. A slowed heart rate is usually a sign of increased attention. Thus, although these infants may not be frightened the way an older infant would be, it seems they can perceive the difference between the "shallow" and the "deep" sides of the cliff (Banks & Salapatek, 1984).

Critical Periods

Although many perceptual abilities are inborn, experience also plays a vital role. If an infant misses out on certain experiences during a crucial window of time—a *critical period*—perception will be impaired. Innate abilities will not survive because cells in the nervous system will deteriorate, change, or fail to form appropriate neural pathways.

One way to study critical periods is to see what happens when the usual perceptual experiences of early life fail to take place. To do so, researchers often study animals whose sensory and perceptual systems are similar to our own. For example, like human beings, cats are born with the ability to detect horizontal and vertical lines and other spatial orientations; at birth, kittens' brains are equipped with the same kinds of feature-detector cells that adult cats have. But if they are deprived of normal visual experience, these cells deteriorate or change, and perception suffers (Crair, Gillespie, & Stryker, 1998; Hirsch & Spinelli, 1970).

In one famous study, kittens were exposed to either vertical or horizontal black and white stripes. Special collars kept them from seeing anything else, even their own bodies. After several months, the kittens exposed only to vertical stripes seemed blind to all horizontal contours; they bumped into horizontal obstacles, and they ran to play with a bar that an experimenter held vertically but not to

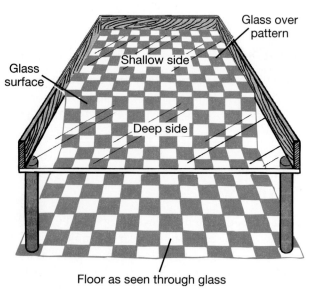

FIGURE 6.12 A Cliff-Hanger

Infants as young as six months usually hesitate to crawl past the apparent edge of a visual cliff, which suggests that they are able to perceive depth.

a bar held horizontally. In contrast, those exposed only to horizontal stripes bumped into vertical obstacles and ran to play with horizontal bars but not vertical ones (Blakemore & Cooper, 1970).

Critical periods for sensory development also seem to exist in human beings. When adults who have been blind from infancy have their vision restored, they may see, but often they do not see well. Their depth perception may be poor, causing them to trip constantly, and they cannot always make sense of what they see. To identify objects, they may have to touch or smell them. But if an infant's congenital blindness is corrected early—during a critical period during the first nine months or so—the prognosis is good. In one study at Toronto's Hospital for Sick Children, improvement started to occur after as little as one hour of visual experience (Maurer et al., 1999).

Similar findings apply to hearing. When adults who were born deaf, or who lost their hearing before learning to speak, receive cochlear implants (devices that stimulate the auditory nerve and allow auditory signals to travel to the brain), they tend to find sounds confusing. In fact, they sometimes ask to have the implants removed. But cochlear implants are more successful in children and in adults who became deaf late in life (Rauschecker, 1999). Young children presumably have not yet passed through the critical period for the processing of sounds, and adults have already had years of auditory experience.

In sum, our perceptual powers are both "wired in" and dependent on experience. Because neurological connections in infants' brains and sensory systems are not completely formed, their senses are far less acute than an adult's. It takes time and experience for their sensory abilities to develop fully. But an infant's world is clearly not the blooming, buzzing confusion that William James took it to be.

Psychological and Cultural Influences on Perception

The fact that some perceptual processes appear to be innate does not mean that all people perceive the world in the same way. Because we care about what we see, hear, taste, smell, and feel, psychological factors can influence what we perceive and how we perceive it. Here are a few of these factors:

1 *Needs.* When we need something, have an interest in it, or want it, we are especially likely to perceive it. For example, hungry individuals

are faster than others at seeing words related to hunger when the words are flashed briefly on a screen (Wispé & Drambarean, 1953).

2 *Beliefs.* What we hold to be true about the world can affect our interpretation of ambiguous sensory signals. When the World Trade Center was attacked, many people thought they saw the face of the devil (or some said Osama bin Laden) in the smoke billowing from the towers. Images that remind people of a crucified Jesus have been reported on walls, dishes, and plates of spaghetti, causing great excitement among those who believe that divine messages can be found on everyday objects—until other explanations emerge. In Riverview, New Brunswick, people claimed to see the image of the Virgin Mary on a billboard advertising pizza. And in Cape Breton, hundreds claimed to have seen Mary's face on a brick wall outside a Tim Hortons doughnut shop. These sightings tend to be explained by peeling paint and shadows.

3 *Emotions.* Emotions can also influence our interpretation of sensory information. A small child afraid of the dark may see a ghost instead of a robe hanging on the door, or a monster instead of a beloved doll. Pain, in particular, is affected by emotion. Soldiers who are seriously wounded often deny being in much pain, even though they are alert and are not in shock. Their relief at being alive may offset the anxiety and fear that contribute so much to pain (although distraction and the body's own pain-fighting mechanisms may also be involved). Conversely, negative emotions such as anger, fear, sadness, or depression can prolong and intensify a person's pain (Fernandez & Turk, 1992; Fields, 1991).

4 *Expectations.* Previous experiences often affect how we perceive the world (Lachman, 1996). The tendency to perceive what you expect is called a **perceptual set**. Perceptual sets can come in handy; they help us fill in words in sentences, for example, when we haven't really heard every one. But perceptaul sets can also cause misperceptions.

People often see what they expect or need to see. If you saw this famous image of smoke billowing from the World Trade Center, did you notice a "face" in it? Whose?

perceptual set A habitual way of perceiving, based on expectations.

In Center Harbor, Maine, local legend has it that veteran newscaster Walter Cronkite was sailing into port one day when he heard a small crowd on shore shouting, "Hello, Walter . . . Hello, Walter." Pleased, he waved and took a bow. Only when he ran aground did he realize what they had really been shouting: "Shallow water . . . shallow water!"

By the way, the previous paragraph has a misspelled word. Did you catch it? If not, probably it was because you expected all the words in this book to be spelled correctly.

Our needs, emotions, expectations, and beliefs are all affected, in turn, by the culture we live in. Different cultures give people practice with different environments. In a classic study done in the 1960s, researchers found that members of some African tribes were much less likely to be fooled by the Müller–Lyer illusion and other geometric illusions than were Westerners. In the West, the researchers observed, people live in a "carpentered" world, full of rectangular structures built with the aid of straightedges and carpenter's squares. Westerners are also used to interpreting two-dimensional photographs and perspective drawings as representations of a three-dimensional world. Therefore, they interpret the kinds of angles used in the Müller–Lyer illusion as right angles extended in space—just the sort of habit that would increase susceptibility to the illusion. The rural Africans in the study, living in a less carpentered environment and in round huts, seemed more likely to take the lines in the figures literally, as two-dimensional, which could explain why they were less susceptible to the illusion (Segall, Campbell, & Herskovits, 1966; Segall et al., 1999).

Culture also affects perception by shaping our stereotypes, directing our attention, and telling us what is important to notice and what is not. Westerners, for example, tend to focus mostly on the figure when viewing a scene, and much less on the ground. East Asians, in contrast, tend to pay attention to the overall context of the scene because of a cultural inclination to see the world holistically (Nisbett, 2003). When Japanese and Americans were shown underwater scenes containing fish that were larger and moving faster than other objects in the scene, they reported the same number of details about the fish, but the Japanese reported more details about everything else in the background (Masuda & Nisbett, 2001). One of the researchers, Richard Nisbett, commented, "If it ain't moving, it doesn't exist for an American" (quoted in Shea, 2001).

Quick Quiz

Direct your perceptual attention now to this quiz.

1. Animal studies suggest that newborns and infants (a) have few perceptual abilities, (b) need visual experiences during a critical period for vision to develop normally, (c) see as well as adults.

2. On the visual cliff, six-month-old babies (a) go right across because they cannot detect depth, (b) cross even though they are afraid, (c) will not cross because they can detect depth, (d) cry or get bored.

3. "Have a nice . . . " says Dewey, but then he gets distracted and doesn't finish the thought. Yet Clarence is sure he heard Dewey wish him a nice day. Why?

Answers:

1. b   2. c   3. perceptual set due to expectations

WHAT'S AHEAD

- Can "subliminal perception" tapes help you lose weight or reduce your stress?
- Why are most psychologists skeptical about ESP?

PUZZLES OF PERCEPTION

We come, finally, to two intriguing questions about perception that have captured the public's imagination for years. First, can we perceive what is happening in the world without being conscious of doing so? Second, can we pick up signals from the world or from other people without using our usual sensory channels at all?

Subliminal Perception

As we saw earlier in our discussion of the "cocktail party phenomenon," even when people are oblivious to speech sounds, they are processing and recognizing those sounds at some level. But these sounds are above people's absolute thresholds. Is it also possible to perceive and respond to messages that are *below* the absolute threshold—too quiet to be consciously heard, or too brief or dim to be consciously seen?

Perceiving without Awareness First, a simple visual stimulus *can* affect your behaviour even when you are unaware that you saw it. For example, people subliminally exposed to a face tended to prefer that face over one they did not "see" in this way (Bornstein, Leone, & Galley, 1987). In some studies, researchers have flashed words subliminally in a person's visual field while the person focuses on the middle of a screen. When the words are related to some personality trait, such as honesty, people are more likely later on to judge someone they read about as having that trait. They have been "primed" to evaluate the person in a certain way (Bargh, 1999). Similarly, researchers at the University of Waterloo found that colour words presented to participants without their awareness affected the subsequent speed with which the participants named a colour patch (Cheesman & Merikle, 1986).

Findings such as these have convinced many psychologists that people often know more than they know they know. In fact, unconscious processing appears to occur not only in perception, but also in memory, thinking, and decision making, as we will see in Chapters 7 and 8. However, even in the laboratory, where researchers have considerable control, the phenomenon can be hard to demonstrate. The strongest evidence comes from studies using simple stimuli (faces or single words, such as *bread*), rather than complex stimuli such as sentences ("Eat whole-wheat bread, not white bread").

Perception versus Persuasion If subliminal priming can affect judgments and preferences, can it be used to manipulate people's attitudes and behaviour? Subliminal persuasion techniques were a hot topic back in the 1950s, when an advertising executive claimed to have increased popcorn and Coke sales at a theatre by secretly flashing the words EAT POPCORN and DRINK COKE on the movie screen. The claim turned out to be a hoax, devised to save the man's struggling advertising company. Ever since, scientists have been skeptical, and the few attempts to demonstrate subliminal persuasion have been disappointing.

Here is an area, however, where the critical-thinking guideline "tolerate uncertainty" seems to apply. Three Canadian psychologists have suggested that previous efforts at subliminal persuasion left out an important ingredient: the person's motivation to pursue a particular goal. Instead of trying to prime a message like "Drink Coke," these researchers used priming to create a state of thirst, using the words *thirst* and *dry*. Later, when given a chance to drink, the primed participants did in fact drink more than controls did—as long as they were already moderately thirsty. Primed participants also found an ad for a thirst-quenching sports drink to be more persuasive than controls did—again, as long as they were already thirsty (Strahan, Spencer, & Zanna, 2002).

Does this mean that advertisers can seduce us into buying soft drinks or voting for political candidates by slipping subliminal slogans and images into television and magazine ads? An advertising firm that created campaign ads for the federal Liberal party in the 2004 election was accused of using subliminal messages when a gun shown in one of the ads fired in just one-thirtieth of a

> **Thinking Critically About Subliminal Persuasion**

Zits

Reprinted with permission of King Features Syndicate.

second—too brief for most people to perceive consciously. Not surprisingly, the ad company vehemently denied the charge that this was a subliminal warning against the Conservatives' stance on gun legislation. Given the many negative findings on subliminal persuasion, and the subtlety of the effects that do occur, we think there's little cause for worry about subliminal manipulation. But the Canadian research will no doubt renew the debate and lead to further research.

As for those subliminal tapes that promise to help you lose weight, stop smoking, relieve stress, read faster, boost your motivation, lower your cholesterol, stop biting your nails, overcome jet lag, or stop taking drugs—all without any effort on your part—here we can be more definite. In study after study, placebo tapes—tapes that do not contain the messages that participants think they do—are shown to be just as "effective" as subliminal tapes (Eich & Hyman, 1992; Merikle & Skanes, 1992; Moore, 1992, 1995). In one typical study, people listened to tapes labelled "memory" or "self-esteem," but some heard tapes that were incorrectly labelled. About half of the participants showed improvement in the area specified by the label, *whether it was correct or not*; the improvement was due to expectations alone (Greenwald et al., 1991). So if you want to improve yourself or your life, you'll have to do it the old-fashioned way: by working at it.

Extrasensory Perception: Reality or Illusion?

Eyes, ears, mouth, nose, skin—we rely on these organs for our experience of the external world. Some people, however, claim they can send and receive messages about the world without relying on the usual sensory channels, by using *extrasensory perception (ESP)*. Reported ESP experiences involve things like telepathy, the direct communication of messages from one mind to another without the usual sensory signals, and precognition, the perception of an event that has not yet happened.

Most ESP claims challenge everything we currently know to be true about the way the world and the universe operate. A lot of people are ready to accept these claims. Should they?

Much of the "evidence" for extrasensory perception comes from anecdotal accounts. But people are not always reliable reporters of their own experiences. They often embellish and exaggerate, or recall only part of what happened. They also tend to forget incidents that don't fit

their beliefs, such as "premonitions" of events that fail to occur. Many ESP experiences could merely be unusual coincidences that are memorable because they are dramatic. What passes for telepathy or precognition could also be based on what a person knows or deduces through ordinary means. If Joanne's father has had two heart attacks, her premonition that her father will die shortly (followed, in fact, by her father's death) may not be so impressive.

The scientific way to establish a phenomenon is to produce it under controlled conditions. Extrasensory perception has been studied extensively by researchers in the field of **parapsychology**. But ESP studies have often been poorly designed, with inadequate precautions against fraud and improper statistical analysis. After an exhaustive review, the National Research Council concluded that there was "no scientific justification . . . for the existence of parapsychological phenomena" (Druckman & Swets, 1988). Other researchers have found rational explanations for various "psychic" phenomena. Michael Persinger and his colleagues at the University of Waterloo, for example, have presented evidence that these perceptions are related to signs of temporal lobe epilepsy (Persinger & Makarec, 1987). People who report having "psychic" experiences, then, also tend to show signs of epilepsy!

The issue has not gone away, however. Many people *really, really* want to believe that ESP exists.

parapsychology The study of purported psychic phenomena such as ESP and mental telepathy.

"What do you mean you didn't know that we were having a pop quiz today?"

James Randi, a famous magician who is dedicated to educating the public about psychic deception, has for years offered a million dollars to anyone who can demonstrate ESP or other paranormal powers under close observation. Many have taken up the challenge; no one has succeeded. The most recent contender is Natalia Lulova, a 12-year-old Russian immigrant who says that she can psychically "see" colours and objects presented to her when she is blindfolded. The trouble is, Natalia can perform only in the presence of her teacher, a New York cab driver, using a blindfold that he provides. Moreover, she only "sees" objects that are below rather than at eye level, and she tilts her head while "seeing," leaving the distinct impression that she's peeking. When she put on a

blindfold provided by Randi, her "powers" left her. Natalia hasn't given up, but we think Randi's money is safe.

The history of research on psychic phenomena has been one of initial enthusiasm because of apparently positive results (Dalton et al., 1996; Bem & Honorton, 1994), followed by disappointment when the results cannot be replicated (Milton & Wiseman, 1999, 2001). The thousands of studies done since the 1940s have failed to make a convincing case for ESP. One researcher who tried for 30 years to establish the reality of psychic phenomena finally gave up in defeat. "I found no psychic phenomena," she wrote, "only wishful thinking, self-deception, experimental error, and even an occasional fraud. I became a skeptic" (Blackmore, 2001).

Quick Quiz

ESP won't help you answer these questions.

1. Based on current evidence, which of these subliminal efforts to get you to drink a soda is most likely to be successful? (a) flashing subliminal DRINK COKE messages as you watch a film, (b) having you listen to subliminal messages saying "You are getting thirsty" while you're sleeping, (c) subliminally exposing you to words associated with thirst

2. What human perceptual processes might explain why so many people interpret unexplained sensations as evidence of ESP, telepathy, or other psychic phenomena?

Answers:

1. c   2. psychological and cultural factors, such as perceptual sets, needs, emotions, wishes, and beliefs

Psychology In The News *Revisited*

The great Greek philosopher Plato once said that "knowledge is nothing but perception." But simple perception is not always the best path to knowledge. As we have seen throughout this chapter, we do not passively register the world "out there"; we mentally construct it. If we are critical thinkers, therefore, we will be aware of how our beliefs and assumptions shape our perceptions.

This means that we should maintain a healthy skepticism when people report seeing spaceships and aliens, even if these reports come

in bunches, as we saw in the story at the beginning of this chapter. Some people, as we have noted, are habitual yea-sayers who, because of their expectations, are quick to think they saw something that wasn't there. All of us, even those of us who are not usually gullible, have needs and beliefs that can fool us into seeing things that we want to see. And all of us occasionally read meanings into sensory experiences that are not inherent in the experience itself. Who has not seen nonexistent water on a hot highway, or felt a nonexistent insect on the skin after merely thinking about bugs?

Many forces conspire to encourage epidemics of UFO sightings. Some come from the popular media, which generate a lot of money by promoting movies, TV shows, and talk-show accounts about extraterrestrials—and which usually portray skeptics as nerds or narrow-minded debunkers. Other forces are inherent in human psychology, including the fallibility of memory and the power of suggestion after an initial report of a sighting. And some reasons for UFO sightings can be traced to normal distortions of perception: When you are looking up at the sky, where there are few points of reference, it is difficult to judge how far away or how big an object is.

Whenever impartial investigators have looked into UFO reports, they have found that what people really saw were weather balloons, rocket launchings, swamp gas, military aircraft, or (in the vast majority of cases) ordinary celestial bodies, such as planets and meteors. The strange objects in the photo accompanying our news story, which look so much like flying saucers, are really lenticular (lens-shaped) clouds.

None of this means that the only real world is the mundane one we see in everyday life. Because our sense organs evolved for particular purposes, our sensory windows on the world are partly shuttered. But we can use reason, ingenuity, and science to pry open those shutters. Ordinary perception tells us that the sun circles the earth, but the great astronomer Copernicus was able to figure out nearly five centuries ago that the opposite is true. Ordinary perception will never let us see ultraviolet and infrared rays directly, but we know they are there, and we can measure them. If science can enable us to overturn the everyday evidence of our senses, who knows what surprises science has in store for us?

Taking Psychology With You   Living with Pain

Temporary pain is an unpleasant but necessary part of life, a warning of disease or injury. Chronic pain is another matter, a serious problem in itself. Back injuries, arthritis, migraine headaches, serious illnesses such as cancer—all can cause unrelieved misery to pain sufferers and their families. Chronic pain can also impair the immune system, putting patients at risk of further complications from their illnesses (Page et al., 1993).

At one time, the only way to combat pain was with drugs or surgery, which were not always effective. Today, we know that pain is affected by attitudes, actions, emotions, and circumstances, and that treatment must take these influences into account. Even social roles can influence a person's response to pain. For example, although women tend to report greater pain than men do, a real-world study of people who were in pain for more than six months found that men suffered more psychological distress than women did, possibly because the male role made it hard for them to admit their pain (Snow et al., 1986).

Many pain-treatment programs encourage patients to manage their pain themselves instead of relying entirely on health care professionals. Usually, these programs combine several strategies:

- **Painkilling medication.** Doctors often worry that patients will become addicted to painkillers or will develop a tolerance to the drugs. The physicians will therefore give a minimal dose and wait until the patient is once again in agony before giving more. This approach is based on outdated notions about addiction. In reality, people who take painkillers to control their pain rarely become addicted. The method now recommended by experts (although doctors and hospitals do not always follow the advice) is to give pain sufferers a continuous dose of painkiller in whatever amount is necessary to keep them pain-free, and to allow them to do this for themselves when they leave the hospital. This strategy leads to reduced dosages rather than larger ones and rarely leads to drug dependence (Hill et al., 1990; Portenoy, 1994).

- **Involvement by family and friends.** When a person is in pain, friends and relatives understandably tend to sympathize and to excuse the sufferer from regular responsibilities. The sufferer takes to bed, avoids physical activity, and focuses on the pain. But focusing on pain tends to increase it, and inactivity can lead to shortened muscles, muscle spasms, and fatigue. So sympathy and attention can backfire and may actually prolong the suffering (Flor, Kerns, & Turk, 1987). One recent study found that the mere presence of a concerned and attentive spouse can increase the brain's response to pain and make the suffering worse (Flor et al., 2002). Similarly, researchers at the University of British Columbia have shown that mothers' reactions to their children's pain can significantly influence their children's experience (Chambers, Craig, & Bennett, 2002). For this reason, many pain experts now encourage family members to reward activity, distraction, and wellness instead of simply offering sympathy. This approach, however, must be used carefully, preferably under the direction of a medical or mental-health professional, because a patient's complaints about pain are an important diagnostic tool for the physician.

- **Self-management.** Patients can learn to identify how, when, and where their pain occurs. This knowledge helps them determine whether the pain is being maintained by external events or is most intense at a certain time of day, and tells them what they might need to do to reduce their pain. Just having a sense of control can have a powerful pain-reducing effect (Cioffi & Holloway, 1993).

- **Relaxation, hypnosis, and acupuncture.** A blue-ribbon panel of experts concluded that relaxation techniques, such as meditating or focusing on reducing tension in specific muscle groups, can help reduce chronic pain from a variety of medical conditions; and hypnosis can reduce pain due to cancer and may help in other conditions as well (NIH Technology Assessment Panel, 1996). Some studies find that acupuncture also helps to reduce some kinds of pain (Holden, 1997), but the best-designed studies have not found such an effect, so many experts remain skeptical.

- **Cognitive behavioural therapy.** When pain is chronic, we may begin to define ourselves in terms of our misery ("I am an ill, suffering person"), which can add to our distress and make the management of our pain more difficult (Pincus & Morley, 2001). Cognitive-behavioural therapy teaches people to recognize the connections among thoughts, feelings, and pain; substitute adaptive thoughts for negative ones; increase feelings of control; and use distraction, relabelling of sensations, and imagery to alleviate suffering (see Chapter 12).

For further information, you can contact pain clinics or services in teaching hospitals and medical schools. There are many reputable clinics around the country, some specializing in specific disorders, such as migraines or back injuries. But take care: There are also many untested therapies and quack practitioners who only prey on people's pain.

SUMMARY

- *Sensation* is the detection and direct experience of physical energy as a result of environmental or internal events. *Perception* is the process by which sensory impulses are organized and interpreted.

OUR SENSATIONAL SENSES

- Sensation begins with the *sense receptors*, which convert the energy of a stimulus into electrical impulses that travel along nerves to the brain. Separate sensations can be accounted for by *anatomical codes* (as set forth by the *doctrine of specific nerve energies*) and *functional codes* in the nervous system. In a rare condition called *synesthesia*, sensation in one modality evokes a sensation in another modality, but these experiences are the exception, not the rule.

- Psychologists specializing in *psychophysics* have studied sensory sensitivity by measuring *absolute* and *difference thresholds. Signal-detection theory*, however, holds that responses in a detection task consist of both a sensory process and a decision process and will vary with the person's motivation, alertness, and expectations.

- Our senses are designed to respond to change and contrast in the environment. When stimulation is unchanging, *sensory adaptation* occurs. Too little stimulation can cause *sensory deprivation.* Too much stimulation can cause sensory overload, which is why we exercise *selective attention.*

VISION

- Vision is affected by the wavelength, intensity, and complexity of light, which produce the psychological dimensions of visual experience—*hue, brightness*, and *saturation.* The visual receptors—*rods* and *cones*—located in the *retina* of the eye send signals (via other cells) to the *ganglion cells* and ultimately to the *optic nerve*, which carries visual information to the brain. Rods are responsible for vision in dim light; cones are responsible for colour vision. *Dark adaptation* occurs in two stages.

- Specific aspects of the visual world, such as lines at various orientations, are detected by *feature-detector cells* in the visual areas of the brain. Some of these cells respond maximally to complex patterns, and even faces. In general, however, the brain takes in fragmentary information about lines, angles, shapes, motion, brightness, texture, and other features of what we see and comes up with a unified view of the world.

- The *trichromatic* and *opponent-process* theories of colour vision apply to different stages of processing. In the first stage, three types of cones in the retina respond selectively to different wavelengths of light. In the second, opponent-process cells in the retina and the thalamus respond in opposite fashion to short and long wavelengths of light.

- Perception involves the active construction of a model of the world from moment to moment. The *Gestalt principles* (e.g., *figure and ground*, *proximity*, *closure*, *similarity*, and *continuity*) describe visual strategies used by the brain to perceive forms.

- We localize objects in visual space by using both *binocular* and *monocular cues* to depth. Binocular cues include *convergence* and *retinal disparity*. Monocular cues include *interposition, linear perspective*, and other cues. *Perceptual constancies* allow us to perceive objects as stable despite changes in the sensory patterns they produce. *Perceptual illusions* occur when sensory cues are misleading or when we misinterpret cues.

HEARING

- Hearing (*audition*) is affected by the intensity, frequency, and complexity of pressure waves in the air or other transmitting substance, corresponding to the experience of *loudness, pitch*, and *timbre* of the sound. The receptors for hearing are *hair cells* (*cilia*) embedded in the *basilar membrane,* located in the *organ of Corti* in the interior of the *cochlea*. These receptors pass signals along to the auditory nerve. The sounds we hear are determined by patterns of hair-cell movement, which produce different neural codes. When we localize sounds, we use as cues subtle differences in how pressure waves reach each of our ears.

OTHER SENSES

- Taste (*gustation*) is a chemical sense. Elevations on the tongue, called *papillae*, contain many *taste buds*, which in turn contain the taste receptors. There are four basic tastes—salty, sour, bitter, and sweet—and possibly a fifth, *umami*, although its inclusion is somewhat controversial. Responses to a particular taste depend in part on genetic differences among individuals; for example, some people are "supertasters." Taste preferences are also affected by culture and learning, and by the texture, temperature, and smell of food.

- Smell (*olfaction*) is also a chemical sense. No basic odours have been identified, and up to a thousand different receptor types exist. But researchers have discovered that distinct odours activate unique combinations of receptor types, and they have started to identify those combinations. Cultural and individual differences also affect people's responses to particular odours.

- The skin senses include touch (pressure), warmth, cold, and pain, and variations such as itch and tickle. Except in the case of pressure, it has been difficult to identify specialized receptors for these senses, but researchers have reported a receptor for one kind of itching and a possible receptor for cold.

- Pain is both a skin sense and an internal sense. According to the *gate-control theory*, the experience of pain depends on whether neural impulses get past a "gate" in the spinal cord and reach the brain. According to a revised version of this theory, a matrix of neurons in the brain can generate pain even in the absence of signals from sensory neurons, which may explain the puzzling phenomenon of *phantom pain*. No one theory, however, completely explains the many varieties of pain.

- *Kinesthesis* tells us where our body parts are located, and *equilibrium* tells us the orientation of the body as a whole. Together, these two senses provide us with a feeling of physical embodiment.

PERCEPTUAL POWERS: ORIGINS AND INFLUENCES

- Many fundamental perceptual skills are inborn or acquired shortly after birth. By using the *visual cliff*, for example, psychologists have learned that babies have depth perception by the age of 6 months and probably even earlier. However, without certain experiences during *critical periods* early in life, cells in the nervous system deteriorate or change, or fail to form appropriate neural pathways, and perception is impaired.

- Psychological influences on perception include needs, beliefs, emotions, and expectations (which produce *perceptual sets*). These influences are affected by culture, which gives people practice with certain kinds of experiences and influences what they attend to. Because psychological factors affect the way we construct the perceptual world, the evidence of our senses is not always reliable.

PUZZLES OF PERCEPTION

- In the laboratory, simple visual subliminal messages can "prime" certain behaviours, judgments, and motivational states, such as thirst. However, there is no evidence that complex behaviours can be altered by "subliminal perception" tapes or similar subliminal techniques.

- *Extrasensory perception (ESP)* refers to paranormal abilities such as telepathy and precognition. Years of research have failed to produce convincing evidence for ESP.

PSYCHOLOGY IN THE NEWS, REVISITED

- Human perception does not merely capture objective reality but also reflects our needs, biases, and beliefs. Thus our eyes and our ears (and especially our brains) can play tricks on us, as the frequent "sightings" of UFOs illustrate.

KEY TERMS

LOOKING BACK

- What kind of "code" in the nervous system helps explain why a pinprick and a kiss feel different? (p. 177)
- Why does your dog hear a "silent" doggie whistle when you can't? (p. 178)
- What kind of bias can influence whether you think you hear the phone ringing when you're in the shower? (p. 178)
- What happens when people are deprived of all external sensory stimulation? (p. 180)
- How does the eye differ from a camera? (p. 183)
- Why can we describe a colour as bluish green but not as reddish green? (p. 186)
- If you were blind in one eye, why might you misjudge the distance of a painting on the wall but not of buildings a block away? (p. 189)
- As a friend approaches, her image on your retina grows larger; why do you continue to see her as the same size? (pp. 189, 191)
- Why are perceptual illusions valuable to psychologists? (p. 191)
- Why does a note played on a flute sound different from the same note played on an oboe? (p. 193)
- If you habitually listen to loud music through headphones, what kind of hearing impairment are you risking? (p. 194)
- To locate the source of a sound, why does it sometimes help to turn or tilt your head? (p. 195)
- Why do saccharin and caffeine taste bitter to some people but not to others? (p. 197)
- Why do you have trouble tasting your food when you have a cold? (p. 197)
- Why do people often continue to "feel" limbs that have been amputated? (p. 200)
- Do babies see the world the way adults do? (p. 203)
- What psychological motives could cause people to "see" the face of a religious figure on a brick wall? (p. 203)
- Can "subliminal perception" tapes help you lose weight or reduce your stress? (p. 206)
- Why are most psychologists skeptical about ESP? (pp. 206–207)

Psychology In The News

MAN–MACHINE CHESS MATCH A DRAW

NEW YORK, February 8, 2003. A disappointed crowd booed last night after Russian chess master Garry Kasparov agreed to a draw in the final game of a six-match series against Deep Junior, the world champion of chess-playing computers. The series, broadcast live on ESPN2 and the Internet, and watched by millions of anxious chess fans around the world, ended in a 3–3 tie.

Kasparov, regarded by many as the greatest chess player in history, has gone up against a computer before. In 1997 he was trounced by a 6-foot-5-inch, 1.4-ton IBM machine named Deep Blue.

In that contest, the computer took two games, Kasparov won one, and the other three were a draw. Before the match, Kasparov had boasted that he was "defending human superiority in a purely intellectual field [that] defines human beings." In an interview posted on an IBM website, however, he acknowledged that in many ways it was more difficult to play against the computer than against a human opponent. "It never tires, never makes tactical mistakes from which you can profit. You have to be on full guard every move of the game, which means it is more exhausting. It never gives you a break." Deep Blue, Kasparov had admitted, was "stronger than all but a handful of top human players."

Kasparov believed it was important to win the match "to find out whether intuition and experience can outweigh the superior calculation powers of the computer."

If he won, he said, he would know that "at least for the time being the human brain still has the edge." After his defeat, he was less than gracious, accusing IBM of secretly providing the computer with help from grandmasters hidden behind a screen. Chess fans immediately posted dire messages on the Internet. "It's over for mankind," sulked one writer. "This is the moment in which human beings begin to take to the sidelines," wrote another. Deep Blue had no comment, but IBM's stock jumped $5 a share.

Kasparov's latest digital adversary, Deep Junior, boasts four 1.9-GHz Pentium processors and three gigabytes of memory. The computer seems to have earned Kasparov's respect; after the match, he admiringly called Deep Junior's chess program the best in the world.

Chess master Garry Kasparov ponders his next move against his mechanical opponent, Deep Junior, in the first of a six-match series. The man at the computer moves pieces on the board when the machine tells him to.

7 Thinking and Intelligence

At one time, the idea of a machine beating a man at his own game seemed ludicrous, but that's no longer true. Do the achievements of Deep Blue and Deep Junior mean that human beings aren't as clever as they think? Are today's superfast, versatile computers more intelligent than we are? Are we really on the threshold of an era in which human beings will "take to the sidelines"? To answer these questions, we first need to have a clear understanding of what *human* thinking and intelligence are.

Each day, in the course of ordinary living, we all make plans, draw inferences, analyze relationships, and organize and reorganize our mental world. Descartes' famous declaration "I think, therefore I am" could just as well have been reversed: "I am, therefore I think." Our powers of thought and intelligence inspired our forebears to give our species the immodest name *Homo sapiens*, Latin for "wise or rational man." Certainly the human mind, which has managed to come up with poker, penicillin, and pantyhose, is a miraculous thing.

But the human mind has also managed to come up with traffic jams, email spam, and war. To better understand why the same species that figured out how to get to the moon is also capable of breathtaking bumbling here on earth, we will examine in this chapter the ways that people reason, solve problems, and grow in intelligence, as well as some of their mental shortcomings. As you read, ask yourself: Could a machine ever do this?

WHAT'S AHEAD

- When you think of a bird, why are you more likely to recall a robin than a penguin?
- How are visual images like images on a computer screen?
- What is happening mentally when you mistakenly take your geography notes to your psychology class?

THOUGHT: USING WHAT WE KNOW

Think for a moment about what *thinking* does for you. It frees you from the confines of the immediate present: You can think about a trip taken three years ago, a party planned for next Saturday, or the War of 1812. It carries you beyond the boundaries of reality: You can imagine unicorns and utopias, Martians and magic. Because you think, you do not need to grope your way blindly through your problems but, with some effort and knowledge, can solve them intelligently and creatively.

To explain such abilities, many cognitive psychologists liken the human mind to an information processor, somewhat analogous to a computer but far more complex. Information-processing approaches capture the fact that the brain does not passively record information but actively alters and organizes it. When we take action, we physically manipulate the environment; when we think, we *mentally* manipulate internal representations of objects, activities, and situations.

The Elements of Cognition

One type of mental representation is the **concept**, a mental category that groups objects, relations, activities, abstractions, or qualities having common properties. The instances of a concept are seen as roughly similar. For example, *golden retriever, cocker spaniel*, and *border collie* are instances of the concept *dog*, and *anger, joy*, and *sadness* are instances of the concept *emotion*. Concepts simplify and summarize information about the world so that it is manageable, so that we can make decisions quickly and efficiently. You may never have seen a *basenji* or eaten *escargots*, but if you know that the first is an instance of *dog* and the second an instance of *food*, you will know, roughly, how to respond (unless you do not like to eat snails, which is what escargots are).

The qualities associated with a concept do not necessarily apply to every instance: Some apples are not red; some dogs do not bark; some birds do not fly. But all the instances of a concept do share a "family resemblance." When we need to decide whether something belongs to a concept, we are likely to compare it to a **prototype**, a representative or most commonplace example of the concept (Rosch, 1973). For instance, which dog is doggier—a golden retriever or a chihuahua? Which fruit is more fruitlike—an apple or a pineapple? Which activity is more representative of sports— football or weightlifting? Most people within a culture can easily tell you which instances of a concept are most representative, or *prototypical*.

Concepts are the building blocks of thought, but they would be of limited use if we merely stacked them up mentally. We must also represent their relationships to one another. One way we accomplish this may be by storing and using **propositions**, units of meaning that are made up of concepts and that express a unitary idea. A proposition can express nearly any sort of

prototype An especially representative example of a concept.

proposition A unit of meaning that is made up of concepts and expresses a single idea.

concept A mental category that groups objects, relations, activities, abstractions, or qualities having common properties.

Some instances of a concept are more representative, or prototypical, than others. For example, Hayden Christensen clearly qualifies as a "bachelor," an unmarried man (at least, as of 2005). But is a Pope a bachelor? What about Harrison Ford, who is divorced and has not remarried but lives with actress Calista Flockhart?

knowledge ("Hortense raises border collies") or belief ("Border collies are smart"). Propositions, in turn, are linked together in complicated networks of knowledge, associations, beliefs, and expectations. These networks, which psychologists call **cognitive schemas**, serve as mental models of aspects of the world. For example, gender schemas represent a person's beliefs and expectations about what it means to be male or female (see Chapter 3). People also have schemas about cultures, occupations, animals, geographical locations, and many other features of the social and natural environment.

Mental images—especially visual images, pictures in the mind's eye—are also important in thinking and in the construction of cognitive schemas. Although no one can directly "see" another person's visual images, psychologists are able to study them indirectly. One method is to measure how long it takes people to rotate an image in their imaginations, scan from one point to another in an image, or read off some detail from an image. The results suggest that visual images are much like images on a computer screen: We can manipulate them, they occur in a mental "space" of a fixed size, and small ones contain less detail than larger ones (Kosslyn, 1980; Shepard & Metzler, 1971).

Most people also report auditory images (for instance, a song, slogan, or poem you can hear in your "mind's ear"), and many report images in other sensory modalities as well—touch, taste, smell, or pain. Some even report kinesthetic images, feelings in the muscles and joints. Athletes often imagine themselves performing a skill, such as diving or sprinting, and this visual and kinesthetic rehearsal seems to improve actual performance (Druckman & Swets, 1988). Mental practice of this sort activates most of the brain circuits involved in the activity itself (Stephan et al., 1995).

Here, then, is a visual summary of the elements of cognition:

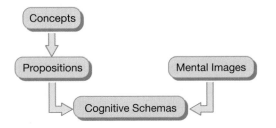

How Conscious Is Thought?

When we think about thinking, we usually have in mind those mental activities that are carried out in a deliberate way with a conscious goal in mind, such as solving a problem, drawing up plans, or making a decision. However, not all mental processing is conscious.

Subconscious and Nonconscious Thinking Some of our cognitive processes lie outside of awareness but can be brought into consciousness with a little effort when necessary. These **subconscious processes** allow us to handle more information and to perform more complex tasks than if we depended entirely on conscious, deliberate thought, and they enable us to perform more than one task simultaneously (Kahneman & Treisman, 1984).

Consider all the automatic routines performed "without thinking," though they might once have required careful, conscious attention: knitting, typing, driving a car, decoding the letters in a word in order to read it. Because of the capacity for automatic processing, people can, with proper training, even learn to perform simultaneously such complex tasks as reading and taking dictation (Hirst, Neisser, & Spelke, 1978). In ordinary life, however, it can be risky to depend on automatic routines when multitasking. For example, your risk of a car accident increases significantly when you talk on your cellphone while driving, even if you use a hands-free phone (Strayer & Johnston, 2001). Functional MRI scans show that when a person does two tasks at once, the amount

Some well-learned skills do not require much conscious thought and can be performed while doing other things. But multitasking can also get you into trouble. It's not a good idea to talk on your cellphone, eat, and drive all at the same time.

cognitive schema An integrated mental network of knowledge, beliefs, and expectations concerning a particular topic or aspect of the world.

subconscious processes Mental processes occurring outside of conscious awareness but accessible to consciousness when necessary.

mental image A mental representation that mirrors or resembles the thing it represents; mental images can occur in many and perhaps all sensory modalities.

of brain activity devoted to each task decreases (Just et al., 2001). Remember this when you try to watch TV and write a term paper at the same time!

Unconscious processes remain outside of awareness. You have no doubt had the odd experience of having a solution to a problem pop into your mind after you have given up trying to find one. With sudden insight, you see how to solve an equation, assemble a cabinet, or finish a puzzle, without quite knowing how you managed to find the solution. Similarly, people will often say they rely on intuition—hunches and gut feelings—rather than conscious reasoning to make decisions.

Insight and intuition probably involve two stages of mental processing (Bowers et al., 1990). In the first stage, clues in the problem automatically activate certain memories or knowledge, and you begin to see a pattern or structure in the problem, although you cannot yet say what it is. This unconscious process guides you toward a hunch or a hypothesis. Then, in the second stage, your thinking becomes conscious, and you become aware of a possible solution. This stage may feel like a sudden revelation ("Aha, I've got it!"), but considerable unconscious mental work has already occurred.

Sometimes people solve problems without experiencing the second stage at all. For example, some people discover the best strategy for winning a card game without being able to consciously identify what they are doing (Bechara et al., 1997). Psychologists call this phenomenon **implicit learning**: You learn a rule or an adaptive behaviour, either with or without a conscious intention to do so, but you don't know how you learned it, and you can't state exactly what it is you have learned (Lieberman, 2000; Stadler & Frensch, 1998).

Mindlessness Usually, of course, much of our thinking is conscious—but we may not be thinking very *hard*. We may act, speak, and make decisions out of habit, without stopping to analyze what we are doing or why we are doing it. This sort of *mindlessness*—mental inflexibility, inertia, and obliviousness to the present context—keeps people from recognizing when a change in the situation requires a change in behaviour.

In one classic study of mindlessness, a researcher approached people as they were about to use a photocopier and made one of three requests: "Excuse me, may I use the Xerox machine," "Excuse me, may I use the Xerox

machine, because I have to make copies," or "Excuse me, may I use the Xerox machine, because I'm in a rush." Normally, people will let someone go before them only if the person has a legitimate reason for doing so, as in the third request. In this study, however, people also complied when the reason sounded like an authentic explanation but was actually meaningless ("because I have to make copies"). They heard the form of the request, but they did not hear its content, and they mindlessly stepped aside (Langer, Blank, & Chanowitz, 1978).

The mindless processing of information has benefits: If we stopped to think twice about everything we did, we would never get anything done ("I'm reaching for my toothbrush; now I'm putting toothpaste on it; now I'm brushing my upper-right molars"). But mindlessness can also lead to errors and mishaps, ranging from the trivial (putting the butter in the dishwasher or locking yourself out of your apartment) to the serious (driving carelessly while on "automatic pilot").

Jerome Kagan (1989) has argued that fully conscious awareness is needed only when we must make a deliberate choice, when events happen that can't be handled automatically, and when unexpected moods and feelings arise. "Consciousness," he says, "can be likened to the staff of a fire department. Most of the time, it is quietly playing pinochle in the back room; it performs [only] when the

Advertisers sometimes count on mindlessness in consumers.

unconscious processes
Mental processes occurring outside of and not available to conscious awareness.

implicit learning Learning that occurs when you acquire knowledge about something without being aware of how you did so and without being able to state exactly what it is you have learned.

alarm sounds." That may be so, but most of us would probably benefit if our mental firefighters paid a little more attention to their jobs. Cognitive psychologists have, therefore, devoted a great deal of study to mindful, conscious thought, decision making, and the capacity to reason.

Quick Quiz

Stay conscious while taking this quiz.

1. Stuffing your mouth with cotton candy, licking a lollipop, and chewing on a piece of beef jerky are all instances of the _____ *eating*.

2. Which example of the concept *chair* is prototypical: high chair, rocking chair, or dining-room chair?

3. In addition to concepts and images, _____, which express a unitary idea, have been suggested as a basic form of mental representation.

4. Peter's mental representation of Thanksgiving includes associations (e.g., with turkeys), attitudes ("It's a time to be with relatives"), and expectations ("I'm going to gain weight from all that food"). They are all part of his _____ for the holiday.

5. Zelda discovers that she has mistakenly dialed her boyfriend's number instead of her mother's. Her error can be attributed to _____.

Answers:

1. concept   2. A plain, straight-backed dining-room chair will be prototypical for most people.   3. propositions   4. cognitive schema   5. mindlessness

---

WHAT'S AHEAD

- Mentally speaking, why is making a cake, well, a piece of cake?
- Why can't logic solve all of our problems?
- What kind of reasoning do juries need to be good at?
- When people say that all opinions and claims are equally valid, what error are they making?

REASONING RATIONALLY

Reasoning is purposeful mental activity that involves operating on information in order to reach conclusions. Unlike impulsive or unconscious responding, reasoning requires us to draw specific inferences from observations, facts, or assumptions.

Formal Reasoning: Algorithms and Logic

In *formal reasoning problems*—the kind you might find, say, on an intelligence test or a college entrance exam—the information needed for drawing a conclusion or reaching a solution is specified clearly, and there is a single right (or best) answer.

In some formal problems and well-defined tasks, all you have to do is apply an **algorithm**, a set of procedures guaranteed to produce a solution even if you do not know how it works. To solve a problem in long division, you apply a series of operations that you learned in elementary school. To make a cake, you apply an algorithm called a recipe.

For other formal problems, the rules of formal logic are crucial tools to have in your mental toolbox. These tools include (among others) the processes of deductive and inductive reasoning. In **deductive reasoning**, a conclusion *necessarily* follows from a set of observations or propositions (*premises*):

DEDUCTIVE REASONING

For example, if the premises "All human beings are mortal" and "I am a human being" are true, then the conclusion "I am mortal" must also be true. In contrast, in **inductive reasoning**, a conclusion *probably* follows from certain propositions or premises, but it could conceivably be false:

---

algorithm A problem-solving strategy guaranteed to produce a solution even if the user does not know how it works.

reasoning The drawing of conclusions or inferences from observations, facts, or assumptions.

deductive reasoning A form of reasoning in which a conclusion follows necessarily from certain premises; if the premises are true, the conclusion must be true.

inductive reasoning A form of reasoning in which the premises provide support for a conclusion, but it is still possible for the conclusion to be false.

INDUCTIVE REASONING

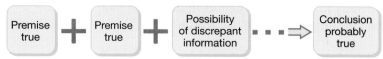

For example, if your premises are "I had a delicious meal at Joe's Restaurant on Monday," "I had a delicious meal there again on Tuesday," and "I had another delicious meal there on Wednesday," you might reasonably reach the conclusion that "Joe's Restaurant consistently serves good food." But those meals could have been a fluke: Maybe the regular chef was on vacation and the meals were prepared by a visiting chef.

Informal Reasoning: Heuristics and Dialectical Thinking

Useful as they are, algorithms and logical reasoning cannot solve all of life's problems. In *informal reasoning problems*, there may be no clearly correct solution (Galotti, 1989). Many approaches, viewpoints, or possible solutions may compete, and you may have to decide which one is most reasonable. Of course, you can engage in this form of reasoning only if you are willing to consider more than one approach or viewpoint. Researchers in Toronto have found that the number of counterarguments a person could generate was positively correlated with years of university education (Toplak & Stanovich, 2003).

Further, the information at your disposal may be incomplete, or people may disagree on what the premises should be. Your position on the controversial issue of abortion, for example, will depend on your premises about when meaningful human life begins, what rights an embryo has, and what rights a woman has to control her own body. People on opposing sides of this issue even disagree on how the premises should be phrased because they have different emotional reactions to terms such as "rights," "meaningful life," and "control over one's body."

The differences between formal and informal reasoning problems are summarized in Table 7.1. These two types of problems typically call for different approaches. Whereas formal problems can often be solved with an algorithm, informal problems often call for a **heuristic**—a rule of thumb that suggests a course of action without guaranteeing an optimal solution. Anyone who has ever played chess or a card game such as hearts is familiar with heuristics ("Get rid of high cards first"). In these games, working out all the possible sequences of moves would be impossible. Heuristics are also useful to an investor trying to predict the stock market ("Buy bonds when interest rates are falling"), a doctor trying to determine the best treatment for a patient ("Use drug X as a first course of action"), and a student trying to decide whether to take a particular course ("Ask friends how they liked the instructor"). All are faced with incomplete information on which to base a decision and may therefore resort to rules of thumb that have proven effective in the past.

heuristic A rule of thumb that suggests a course of action or guides problem solving but does not guarantee an optimal solution.

TABLE 7.1 Two Kinds of Reasoning

In formal reasoning, we apply rules of logic to solve well-specified problems. In informal, everyday reasoning, we must solve problems that are less clearly defined. Here are some differences between the two modes of thought:

Formal	Informal
All premises are supplied.	Some premises are implicit and some are not supplied at all.
There is typically one correct answer.	There are typically several possible answers that vary in quality.
Established methods often exist for solving the problem.	Established procedures of inference that apply to the problem rarely exist.
You usually know when the problem is solved.	It is often unclear whether the current solution is good enough.
The problem is often of limited real-world interest.	The problem typically has personal relevance.
Problems are solved for their own sake.	Problems are often solved as a means of achieving other goals.

Source: Adapted from Galotti, 1989.

In thinking about real-life problems, a person must also be able to use **dialectical reasoning**, the process of comparing and evaluating opposing points of view in order to resolve differences. Philosopher Richard Paul (1984) has described dialectical reasoning as movement "up and back between contradictory lines of reasoning, using each to critically cross-examine the other":

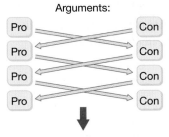

DIALECTICAL REASONING
Arguments:

Most reasonable conclusion based on evidence and logic

Dialectical reasoning is what juries are supposed to do to arrive at a verdict: consider arguments for and against the defendant's guilt, point and counterpoint. It is also what voters are supposed to do when thinking about whether the government should raise taxes or lower them, or about the best way to improve public education.

Reflective Judgment

Many adults clearly have trouble thinking dialectically—they take one position, and that's that. To find out precisely how people reason and justify their conclusions, Karen Kitchener and Patricia King interviewed adolescents and adults of all ages and occupations, asking them where they stood on issues such as nuclear power, the safety of food additives, and the objectivity of the news media. Kitchener and King did not care how much people knew about these issues, or even how they felt about them; they just wanted to know how their respondents had reached their conclusions. More specifically, they wanted to know whether people use *reflective judgment* in thinking about everyday problems (King & Kitchener, 1994; Kitchener & King, 1990). Reflective judgment is basically what we have called critical thinking: the ability to evaluate and integrate evidence, relate that evidence to a theory or opinion, and reach a conclusion that can be defended as reasonable or plausible, while standing ready to reassess that conclusion in the face of new information.

The researchers began by providing their interviewees with statements that described opposing viewpoints on various topics. Then the interviewer asked, What do you think about these statements? How did you come to hold that point of view? On what do your base your position? Can you ever know for sure that your position is correct? Why do you suppose disagreement exists about this issue?

Based on the responses, King and Kitchener were able to identify seven cognitive stages on the road to reflective thought, some occurring in childhood and others unfolding throughout adolescence and adulthood. At each stage, people make different kinds of assumptions about how things are known and use different ways of justifying or defending their beliefs. Each stage builds on the skills of the prior one and lays a foundation for successive ones.

We will not be concerned here with the details of these stages, but only with their broad outlines. In general, people in the two early, *pre-reflective stages* assume that a correct answer always exists and that it can be obtained directly through the senses ("I know what I've seen") or from authorities ("They said so on the news"; "That's what I was brought up to believe"):

PRE-REFLECTIVE JUDGMENT

"I was brought up to believe . . ."
"I just know what I know."

dialectical reasoning A process in which opposing facts or ideas are weighed and compared, with a view to determining the best solution or to resolving differences.

If authorities don't yet have the truth, pre-reflective thinkers tend to reach conclusions on the basis of what "feels right" at the moment. They do not distinguish between knowledge and belief, or between belief and evidence, and they don't see any reason for justifying a belief (King & Kitchener, 1994):

Interviewer: Can you ever know for sure that your position [on evolution] is correct?

Respondent: Well, some people believe that we evolved from apes and that's the way they want to believe. But I would never believe that way and nobody could talk me out of the way I believe because I believe the way that it's told in the Bible.

During the three *quasi-reflective stages*, people recognize that some things cannot be known with absolute certainty, but they are not sure how to deal with these situations. They realize that judgments should be supported by reasons, but they pay attention only to evidence that fits what they already believe. They know that there are alternative viewpoints, but they seem to think that because knowledge is uncertain, any judgment about the evidence is purely subjective. Quasi-reflective thinkers will defend a position by saying, "Well, you have your opinion and I have mine," as if all opinions are created equal:

Here is the response of a college student who uses quasi-reflective reasoning:

QUASI-REFLECTIVE JUDGMENT

"Knowledge is purely subjective."
"We all have a right to our opinion."

Interviewer: Can you say you will ever know for sure that chemicals [in foods] are safe?

Student: No, I don't think so.

Interviewer: Can you tell me why you'll never know for sure?

Student: Because they test them in little animals, and they haven't really tested them in humans, as far as I know. And I don't think anything is for sure.

Interviewer: When people differ about matters such as this, is it the case that one opinion is right and one is wrong?

Student: No. I think it just depends on how you feel personally because people make their decisions based upon how they feel and what research they've seen. So what one person thinks is right, another person might think is wrong. . . . If I feel that chemicals cause cancer and you feel that food is unsafe without it, your opinion might be right to you and my opinion is right to me.

In the last two stages, a person becomes capable of reflective judgment. He or she understands that although some things can never be known with certainty, some judgments are more valid than others because of their coherence, their fit with the evidence, their usefulness, and so on. People at these stages are willing to consider evidence from a variety of sources and to reason dialectically. At the very highest stage, they are able to defend their conclusions as representing the most complete, plausible, or compelling understanding of an issue, based on currently available evidence:

REFLECTIVE JUDGMENT

"Based on the evidence, I believe . . ."
"Here are the reasons for my conclusions . . ."

This interview with a graduate student illustrates reflective thinking:

Interviewer: Can you ever say you know for sure that your point of view on chemical additives is correct?

Student: No, I don't think so [but] I think that we can usually be reasonably certain, given the information we have now, and considering our methodologies.

Interviewer: Is there anything else that contributes to not being able to be sure?

Student: Yes. . . . It might be that the research wasn't conducted rigorously enough. In other words, we might have flaws in our data or sample, things like that.

Interviewer: How then would you identify the "better opinion"?

Student: One that takes as many factors as possible into consideration. I mean one that uses the higher percentage of the data that we have, and perhaps that uses the methodology that has been most reliable.

Interviewer: And how do you come to a conclusion about what the evidence suggests?

Student: I think you have to take a look at the different opinions and studies that are offered by different groups. Maybe some studies offered by the chemical industry, some studies by the government, some private studies . . . . You wouldn't trust, for instance, a study funded by the tobacco industry that proved that cigarette smoking is not harmful . . . you have to try to interpret people's motives and that makes it a more complex soup to try to strain out.

Most people do not show evidence of reflective judgment until their middle or late twenties, if at all. And most undergraduates, regardless of age, tend to score at only Stage 3 during their first year of college. But here's the good news: When students get support for thinking reflectively and have opportunities to practise it, their reasoning tends to become more complex, sophisticated, and well grounded (Kitchener et al., 1993). Moreover, higher education gradually moves people closer to reflective judgment. By their senior year, students typically score at Stage 4; most graduate students score at Stage 4 or 5; and many advanced doctoral students perform consistently at Stage 6 (King & Kitchener, 1994). Longitudinal studies show that these differences do not occur only because lower-level thinkers are more likely to drop out of school along the way.

The gradual development of thinking skills among undergraduates, said one writer (Kroll, 1992), represents an abandonment of "ignorant certainty" in favour of "intelligent confusion." It may not seem so, but this is a big step forward! You can see why, in this book, we emphasize thinking about and evaluating psychological findings, and not just memorizing them.

Talk radio does not exactly encourage reflective judgment!

Quick Quiz

Reflect on the answers to these questions.

1. Most of the holiday gifts Mervin bought this year cost more than they did last year, so he concludes that inflation is increasing. Is he using inductive, deductive, or dialectical reasoning?
2. Yvonne is arguing with Henrietta about whether real estate is a better investment than stocks. "You can't convince me," says Yvonne. "I just know I'm right." Yvonne needs training in _____ reasoning.
3. Seymour thinks the media have a liberal political bias, and Selena thinks they are too conservative. "Well," says Seymour, "I have my truth and you have yours. It's purely subjective." Which of King and Kitchener's levels of thinking describes Seymour's statement?
4. What kind of evidence might resolve the issue that Seymour and Selena are arguing about?

Answers:

1. inductive 2. dialectical 3. quasi-reflective 4. Researchers might have raters watch a random sample of TV news shows and measure the amount of time devoted to conservative and liberal viewpoints. Or raters could read a random sample of newspaper editorials from all over the country and evaluate the editorials as liberal or conservative in outlook. Perhaps you can think of other strategies. However, subjective ratings of entire TV programs or newspapers might not be informative because people often perceive only what they want or expect to perceive.

WHAT'S AHEAD

- Why do people worry about dying in an airplane crash but ignore dangers that are far more likely?

- How might your physician's choice of words about alternative treatments for your illness affect which one you choose?

- When Monday-morning coaches say they knew all along who would win last Saturday's game on *Hockey Night in Canada*, what bias might they be showing?

- Why will a terrible initiation rite make you more loyal to the group that initiated you?

Many of us overestimate the chances of suffering a shark attack. One reason is the availability heuristic: Shark attacks are very rare, but they are dramatic and easy to visualize and recall.

BARRIERS TO REASONING RATIONALLY

Although most people have the capacity to think logically, reason dialectically, and make judgments reflectively, it is abundantly clear that they don't always do so. One obstacle is the need to be right; if your self-esteem depends on winning every argument, you will find it hard to listen with an open mind to competing views. Another obstacle is plain old mental laziness. Many social critics think such laziness is on the rise because television is replacing reading. Reading requires you to be mindful and to follow extended arguments; it gives you the opportunity to examine connections between statements and to spot contradictions. In contrast, television often provides sound bites instead of fully developed arguments, encouraging viewers to form quick, impulsive opinions instead of carefully considered ones.

Human thought processes are also tripped up by many predictable biases and errors. Psychologists have studied dozens of these cognitive pitfalls; here we describe just a few of them.

Exaggerating the Improbable

One common bias is the inclination to exaggerate the probability of rare events—a bias that helps to explain why so many people enter lotteries and why they buy disaster insurance.

People are especially likely to exaggerate the likelihood of a rare event if its consequences are catastrophic. One reason is the **availability heuristic**, the tendency to judge the probability of an event by how easy it is to think of examples or instances (Tversky & Kahneman, 1973). Catastrophes and shocking accidents stand out in our minds and are therefore more "available"

mentally than are other kinds of negative events. This is why people estimate deaths from accidents and disease to be equally frequent, even though 16 times as many people die each year from disease as from accidents (Lichtenstein et al., 1978). The availability heuristic also explains why so many people became terrified of flying after the events of September 11, 2001, even though driving a car remained far riskier (Sivak & Flannagan, 2003). It can even account for such non-catastrophic phenomena as how we read names on a list: Researchers at Bishop's University found that people overestimated the number of names they had seen on a list when the names were famous or familiar (McKelvie, 1997).

Because of the availability heuristic, people will irrationally ignore dangers that are hard to visualize, such as death from cigarette smoking or a rise in skin cancer rates due to depletion of the earth's ozone layer. Parents are often more frightened about unlikely threats to their children, such as being kidnapped by a stranger or dying from a routine immunization shot (both are horrible, but both are extremely rare), than they are about more common problems, such as depression, delinquency, and poor grades, or more common dangers, such as auto accidents or accidental drownings.

Avoiding Loss

In general, people try to avoid or minimize risks and losses when they make decisions. So when a choice is framed in terms of the risk of losing something, they will respond more cautiously than when the same choice is framed in terms of gain.

availability heuristic The tendency to judge the probability of a type of event by how easy it is to think of examples or instances.

They will choose a ticket that has a 10 percent chance of winning a raffle, rather than one that has a 90 percent chance of losing. Or they will rate a condom as effective when they are told it has a 95 percent success rate in protecting against the AIDS virus, but not when they are told it has a 5 percent failure rate—which is exactly the same thing (Linville, Fischer, & Fischhoff, 1992).

Here's another example. Suppose you had to choose between two health programs to combat a disease expected to kill 600 people. Which would you prefer: a program that would definitely save 200 people, or one with a one-third probability of saving all 600 people and a two-thirds probability of saving none? (Problem 1 in Figure 7.1 illustrates this choice.) When asked this question, most people, including physicians, say they prefer the first program. In other words, they reject the riskier though potentially more rewarding solution in favour of a sure gain. However, people *will* take a risk if they think it will result in *avoidance of loss*. Suppose now that you have to choose between a program in which 400 people will definitely die and a program in which there is a one-third probability of nobody dying and a two-thirds probability that all 600 will die. If you think about it, you will see that the alternatives are exactly the same as in the first problem; they are merely worded differently (see Problem 2 in Figure 7.1). Yet this time, most people choose the second solution. They reject risk when they think of the outcome in terms of lives saved but accept risk when they think of the outcome in terms of lives lost (Tversky & Kahneman, 1981).

Few of us will have to face a decision involving hundreds of lives, but we may have to choose between different medical treatments for ourselves or a relative. Our decision may be affected by whether the doctor frames the choice in terms of chances of surviving or chances of dying.

Biases Due to Mental Sets

Another barrier to rational thinking is the development of a **mental set**, a tendency to try to solve new problems by using the same heuristics, strategies, and rules that worked in the past on similar problems. Mental sets make human learning and problem solving efficient; because of them, we do not have to keep reinventing the wheel. But mental sets are not helpful when a problem calls for fresh insights and methods. They cause us to cling rigidly to the same old assumptions, hypotheses, and strategies, blinding us to better or more rapid

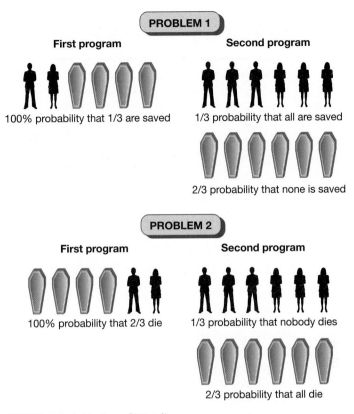

FIGURE 7.1 A Matter of Wording

The decisions we make depend on how the alternatives are framed. When asked to choose between the two programs in Problem 1, which are described in terms of lives saved, most people choose the first program. When asked to choose between the programs in Problem 2, which are described in terms of lives lost, most people choose the second program. Yet the alternatives in the two problems, though worded differently, are actually identical.

solutions. (For an illustration of this point, try the "Get Involved" exercise on the next page.)

One general mental set is the tendency to find patterns in events. This tendency is adaptive because it helps us understand and exert some control over what happens in our lives. But it also leads us to see meaningful patterns even when they don't exist. For example, many people with arthritis think that their symptoms follow a pattern dictated by the weather. They suffer more, they say, when the barometric pressure changes or when it's damp or humid outside. Yet when researchers followed 18 arthritis patients for 15 months, no association whatsoever emerged between weather conditions and the patients' self-reported pain levels, their ability to function in daily life, or a doctor's evaluation of their joint tenderness (Redelmeier & Tversky, 1996). Did the patients say, "Oh, thank you for pointing out that my belief was unfounded! How incredibly interesting"? No, they adamantly refused to believe the results.

mental set A tendency to solve problems using procedures that worked previously on similar problems.

Get Involved   Connect the Dots

Copy the following figure, and see whether you can connect the dots by using no more than four straight lines, without lifting your pencil or pen. A line must pass through each point. Can you do it?

Most people have difficulty with this problem because they have a mental set to interpret the arrangement of dots as a square. Once having done so, they then assume that they can't extend a line beyond the "boundaries" of the square. Now that you know this, you might try again if you haven't yet solved the puzzle. Some possible solutions are given on page 249.

The Hindsight Bias

7.3

Would you have predicted, beforehand, that one dead cow found to have mad cow disease would cripple Canada's beef industry? When people learn the outcome of an event or the answer to a question, they are often sure that they "knew it all along." Armed with the wisdom of hindsight, they see the outcome that actually occurred as inevitable, and they overestimate their ability to have predicted what happened. Compared with judgments made *before* an event takes place, their judgments about their ability to have predicted the event in advance are inflated (Fischhoff, 1975; Hawkins & Hastie, 1990). This **hindsight bias** shows up in political assessments ("I always knew my candidate would win"), medical judgments ("I could have told you that mole was cancerous"), and popular trends ("The first time I heard her sing, I knew Shania Twain was going to be a star").

hindsight bias The tendency to overestimate one's ability to have predicted an event once the outcome is known; the "I knew it all along" phenomenon.

confirmation bias The tendency to look for or pay attention to only the information that confirms one's own belief.

Like mental sets, the hindsight bias can be adaptive. When we try to make sense of the past, we focus on explaining just one outcome, the one that occurred, because explaining outcomes that did not take place can be a waste of time. Then, in light of current knowledge, we reconstruct and misremember our previous judgment (Hoffrage, Hertwig, & Gigerenzer, 2000). But as Scott Hawkins and Reid Hastie (1990) wrote, "Hindsight biases represent the dark side of successful learning and judgment." They are the dark side because when we are sure we knew something "all along," we are also less willing to find out what we need to know in order to make accurate predictions in the future. In medical conferences, for example, when doctors are told the post-mortem findings for

a patient who died, they tend to think the case was easier to diagnose than it actually was ("I would have known it was a brain tumour"), and so they learn less from the case than they should (Dawson et al., 1988).

Perhaps you feel that we're not telling you anything new because you have always known about the hindsight bias. But then, you may just have a hindsight bias about the hindsight bias!

The Confirmation Bias

When people want to make the most accurate judgment possible, they usually try to consider all of the relevant information. But when they are thinking about issues they already feel strongly about, they tend to give in to the **confirmation bias**, paying attention only to evidence that confirms their belief and finding fault with evidence or arguments that point in a different direction (Edwards & Smith, 1996; Kunda, 1990; Nickerson, 1998). You rarely hear someone say, "Oh, thank you for explaining to me why my lifelong philosophy of child raising (or politics, or investing) is wrong. I'm so grateful for the facts!" Like the participants in the arthritis study, the person usually says, "Oh, buzz off, and take your cockamamie ideas with you."

Once you start looking for it, you will see the confirmation bias everywhere. Police officers who are convinced of a suspect's guilt, for example, are likely to take anything the suspect says or does as evidence that confirms it, including the suspect's claims of innocence. It also affects people who experience high levels of anxiety. Researchers at Dalhousie University have found that these people pay more attention to stimuli that are considered psychologically threatening (Stewart et al., 1998). Similarly, researchers at the University of Manitoba have found that people who are prone to panic are more likely to attend to stimuli that imply physical threat than are those who are not prone (Asmundson et al., 1992). Thus, they *confirm* their anxiety and panic.

The confirmation bias can also affect how you react to what you are learning in school. When students read about scientific findings that dispute one of their own cherished beliefs or that challenge the wisdom of their own actions, they tend to acknowledge but minimize the strengths of the research. In contrast, when a study supports their view, they will acknowledge any flaws (such as a small sample or a reliance on self-reports) but will give these flaws less weight than they otherwise would (Sherman & Kunda, 1989). In thinking critically, people often apply a double standard: They think most critically about results they dislike.

Get Involved Confirming the Confirmation Bias

Suppose someone deals out four cards, each with a letter on one side and a number on the other. You can see only one side of each card:

Your job is to find out whether the following rule is true: "If a card has a vowel on one side, then it has an even number on the other side." Which two cards do you need to turn over to find out?

The vast majority of people say they would turn over the E and the 6, but they are wrong. You do need to turn over the E (a vowel), because if the number on the other side is even, it confirms the rule, and if it's odd, the rule is false. However, the card with the 6 tells you nothing. The rule does not say that a card with an even number must always have a vowel on the other side. So it doesn't matter whether the 6 has a vowel or a consonant on the other side. The card you do need to turn over is the 7, because if it has a vowel on the other side, that fact disconfirms the rule.

People do poorly on this problem because they are biased to look for confirming evidence and because they ignore the possibility of disconfirming evidence. Don't feel bad if you missed it; most judges, lawyers, and people with doctorates do, too.

The Need for Cognitive Consistency

The confirmation bias enables us to avoid evidence that contradicts our beliefs. But what happens when disconfirming evidence finally smacks us in the face, and we cannot ignore or discount it any longer? For example, as the twentieth century rolled to an end, predictions of doomsday—the end of the world—escalated. Similar predictions have been made throughout history. When these predictions fail, why do we rarely hear believers say, "Boy, what a fool I was"?

According to the theory of **cognitive dissonance**, people will resolve such conflicts in predictable, though not always obvious, ways (Festinger, 1957). *Dissonance*, the opposite of consistency (*consonance*), is a state of tension that occurs when you simultaneously hold either two cognitions (beliefs, thoughts, attitudes) that are psychologically inconsistent or a belief that is incongruent with your behaviour. This tension is uncomfortable, so you will be motivated to reduce it. You may do this by rejecting or modifying one of those inconsistent beliefs, changing your behaviour, denying the evidence, or rationalizing:

COGNITIVE DISSONANCE

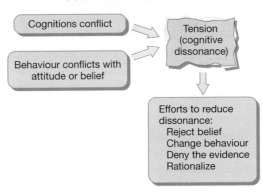

cognitive dissonance A state of tension that occurs when a person simultaneously holds two cognitions that are psychologically inconsistent, or when a person's belief is incongruent with his or her behaviour.

postdecision dissonance In the theory of cognitive dissonance, tension that occurs when you believe you may have made a bad decision.

Many years ago, in a famous field study, Leon Festinger and two associates explored people's reactions to failed prophecies by infiltrating a group of people who thought the world would end on December 21 (Festinger, Riecken, & Schachter, 1956). The group's leader, whom the researchers called Marian Keech, promised that the faithful would be picked up by a flying saucer and whisked to safety at midnight on December 20. Many of her followers quit their jobs and spent all their savings, waiting for the end. What would they do or say, Festinger and his colleagues wondered, to reduce the dissonance between "The world is still muddling along on the 21st" and "I predicted the end of the world and sold off all my worldly possessions"?

The researchers predicted that believers who had made no public commitment to the prophecy, who awaited the end of the world by themselves at home, would simply lose their faith. But those who had acted on their conviction by selling their property and waiting with Keech for the spaceship would be in a state of dissonance. They would have to *increase* their religious belief to avoid the intolerable realization that they had behaved foolishly and others knew it. That is just what happened. At 4:45 a.m., long past the appointed hour of the saucer's arrival, the leader had a new vision. The world had been spared, she said, because of the impressive faith of her little band.

Cognitive-dissonance theory predicts that in more ordinary situations, too, people will resist or rationalize information that conflicts with their existing ideas. For example, if you are a cigarette smoker, your behaviour is dissonant with your awareness that smoking causes illness. You might try to reduce the dissonance by trying to quit, by rejecting the evidence that smoking is bad, by persuading yourself that you will quit later ("after these exams"), by emphasizing the benefits of smoking ("A cigarette helps me relax"), or by deciding that you don't want a long life anyhow ("It will be shorter, but sweeter").

You are particularly likely to try to reduce dissonance under three conditions (Aronson, 2004):

1 *When you need to justify a choice or decision that you made freely.* All car dealers know about "buyer's remorse": The second that people buy a car, they worry that they made the wrong decision or spent too much—a phenomenon called **postdecision dissonance**. You may try to resolve this dissonance by deciding that the car you chose (or the toaster, or house, or spouse) is really, truly the best in the world. However, if someone else made your decision for you, you will not feel much dissonance if it proves misguided. There is no dissonance between "My mom forced me to go to university" and "I hate studying."

2 *When you need to justify behaviour that conflicts with your view of yourself.* If you have a concept of yourself as honest, cheating will put you in a state of dissonance. To avoid feeling like a hypocrite, you will try to reduce the dissonance by justifying your behaviour ("Everyone else does it"; "I had to do it to get into med school and learn to save lives"). If you see yourself as a kind person and you harm someone, you may reduce your dissonance by blaming the person you have victimized (see Chapter 10) or by finding other self-justifying excuses.

3 *When you need to justify the effort put into a decision or choice.* The harder you work to reach a goal, or the more you suffer for it, the more you will try to convince yourself that you value the goal, even if the goal is not so great after all

The more effort you put into reaching a goal, the more likely you are to value it—hence the value we associate with an Olympic gold medal. Canadian Olympic gold medalist Kyle Shewfelt trains daily at the University of Calgary.

(Aronson & Mills, 1959). This explains why harsh initiation rites, whether in social clubs or the military, turn new recruits into loyal members. You might think that people would hate a group that made them suffer. But the cognition "I went through a lot of awful stuff to join this group" is dissonant with the cognition "only to find that I hate the group." Therefore, people must decide either that the initiation rites were not so bad or that they really like the group. This mental re-evaluation is called the **justification of effort**, and it is one of the most common methods of reducing dissonance.

Cognitive-dissonance theory has its limitations. Some people are secure enough to own up to their mistakes instead of rationalizing them. Some people do not have a strong need for consistency, and are therefore less subject than others to feeling cognitive dissonance (Cialdini, Trost, & Newsom, 1995). And in some cultures, such as those of East Asia, contradictions and inconsistencies are seen as inevitable in human life, and people often do not feel a great need to resolve dissonance in the way Westerners do (Choi & Nisbett, 2000; Peng & Nisbett, 1999).

Overcoming Our Cognitive Biases

The fact that our decisions and judgments, and the feelings of regret or pleasure that follow, are not always rational has enormous implications for the legal system, business, medicine, government—in fact, for all areas of life. But before you despair about the human ability to think clearly and rationally, we should tell you that the situation is not hopeless. For one thing, people are not equally irrational in all situations. When they are doing things they have some expertise in, or making decisions that have serious consequences, cognitive biases often diminish (Smith & Kida, 1991).

Further, once we understand a bias, we may be able to reduce or eliminate it. For example, as we saw, doctors are vulnerable to the hindsight bias if they already know what caused a patient's death. But Hal Arkes and his colleagues (1988) were able to reduce a similar bias in neuropsychologists. The psychologists were given a case study and were asked to state one reason that each of three possible diagnoses—alcohol withdrawal, Alzheimer's disease, and brain damage—might have been applicable. This procedure forced the psychologists to consider all the evidence, not just evidence that supported the correct diagnosis. The hindsight bias evaporated when the psychologists realized that the correct diagnosis had not been so obvious at the time the patient was being treated.

Some people, of course, seem to think more clearly than others all the time; we call them "intelligent." But just what is intelligence, and how can we measure and improve it? We take up that question next.

justification of effort The tendency of individuals to increase their liking for something that they have worked hard or suffered to attain; a common form of dissonance reduction.

Quick Quiz

In hindsight, will you say this quiz was easy?

1. In 2003, a person who flew from Hong Kong to Toronto was diagnosed with Severe Acute Respiratory Syndrome (SARS) and subsequently died from the disease. Many people became afraid to get on an airplane, and among those who did, the wearing of surgical masks increased exponentially—even though there were no documented cases of SARS being transmitted between passengers on an airplane. What bias explains this reaction?

2. Stu meets a young woman at the student cafeteria. They hit it off and eventually get married. Says Stu, "I knew that day, when I headed for the cafeteria, that something special was about to happen." What cognitive bias is affecting Stu's thinking, charmingly romantic though it is?

3. In a classic study of cognitive dissonance, students did some boring, repetitive tasks and then had to tell another student, who was waiting to participate in the study, that the work was interesting and fun (Festinger & Carlsmith, 1959). Half the students were offered $20 for telling this lie and the others only $1. Which students do you think decided later that the tasks had been fun after all? Why?

Answers:

1. the availability heuristic
2. the hindsight bias
3. The students who received only $1 were more likely to say the tasks had been fun. They were in a state of dissonance because "The task was as dull as dishwater," is dissonant with "I said I enjoyed it—and for a mere dollar, at that." Those who got $20 could rationalize that the large sum (which really was large in the 1950s) justified the lie.

psychometrics The measurement of mental abilities, traits, and processes.

WHAT'S AHEAD

- How did the original purpose of intelligence testing change when IQ tests came to North America?
- Is it possible to design intelligence tests that are not influenced by culture?
- Why do some psychologists oppose traditional intelligence testing?
- What kind of intelligence allows you to master the unspoken rules for academic success?
- What is "EQ," and why is it as important as IQ?

INTELLIGENCE

Intelligent people disagree on just what intelligence is. Some equate it with the ability to reason abstractly, others with the ability to learn and profit from experience in daily life. Some emphasize the ability to think rationally, others the ability to act purposefully. All of these qualities are probably part of what most people mean by **intelligence**, but theorists weigh them differently.

One of the longest-running debates in psychology is whether an overall quality called "intelligence" even exists. A typical intelligence test asks you to do several things: provide a specific bit of information, notice similarities between objects, solve arithmetic problems, define words, fill in the missing parts of incomplete pictures, arrange pictures in a logical order, arrange blocks to resemble a design, assemble puzzles, use a coding scheme, or judge what behaviour would be appropriate in a particular situation. Researchers use a statistical method called **factor analysis** to try to identify which basic abilities underlie performance on the various items. As we saw in Chapter 2, this procedure identifies clusters of correlated items that seem to be measuring some common trait, ability, or aptitude (called the factor). Most scientists believe that a general ability, or **g factor**, underlies the specific abilities and talents measured by intelligence tests (Jensen, 1998; Spearman, 1927; Wechsler, 1955). But others dispute the existence of a g factor on the grounds that a person can excel in some tasks yet do poorly in others (Gould, 1994; Guilford, 1988). Disagreements over how to define intelligence have led some writers to argue that intelligence is "whatever intelligence tests measure."

intelligence An inferred characteristic of an individual, usually defined as the ability to profit from experience, acquire knowledge, think abstractly, act purposefully, or adapt to changes in the environment.

factor analysis A statistical method for analyzing the intercorrelations among various measures or test scores; clusters of measures or scores that are highly correlated are assumed to measure the same underlying trait, ability, or aptitude (the factor).

mental age (MA) A measure of mental development expressed in terms of the average mental ability at a given age.

g factor A general ability assumed by many theorists to underlie specific mental abilities and talents.

intelligence quotient (IQ) A measure of intelligence now derived from norms provided for standardized intelligence tests.

Measuring Intelligence: The Psychometric Approach

The traditional approach to intelligence, the **psychometric** approach, focuses on how well people perform on standardized aptitude tests. The tests you take in your courses are called *achievement tests* because they are designed to measure skills and knowledge that you have already learned. *Aptitude tests*, in contrast, are designed to measure the ability to acquire skills or knowledge in the future. Vocational aptitude tests can help you decide whether you will do better as a mechanic or a musician, and IQ tests do a pretty good job of predicting school performance. But all mental tests are in some sense achievement tests because they assume past learning or experience with particular objects, words, or situations. The difference between achievement tests and aptitude tests is one of degree and intended use.

The Invention of IQ Tests The first widely used intelligence test was devised in 1904, when the French Ministry of Education asked psychologist Alfred Binet (1857–1911) to find a way to identify children who were slow learners so they could be given remedial work. The ministry was reluctant to let teachers identify such children, because the teachers might have prejudices about poor children or might assume that shy or disruptive children were mentally impaired. They wanted a more objective approach.

Wrestling with the problem, Binet had a great insight: In the classroom, the responses of "dull" children resembled those of ordinary children of younger ages. Bright children, on the other hand, responded like children of older ages. The thing to measure, then, was a child's **mental age (MA)**, or level of intellectual development relative to other children's. Then instruction could be tailored to the child's capabilities.

The test devised by Binet and his colleague, Theodosius Simon, measured memory, vocabulary, and perceptual discrimination. Items ranged from those that most young children could do easily to those that only older children could handle, as determined by the testing of large numbers of children. A scoring system developed later by others used a formula in which the child's mental age was divided by the child's chronological age to yield an **intelligence quotient**, or **IQ** (a quotient is the result of division). Thus a child of 8 who scored like an average 10-year-old would have a mental age of 10 and an IQ of 125 (10 divided by 8, times 100). All average children, regardless of age, would have an IQ of 100 because mental age and chronological age would be the same.

This method of figuring IQ had serious flaws, however. At one age, scores might cluster tightly around the average, whereas at another age they might be more dispersed. As a result, the score necessary to be in the top 10 or 20 or 30 percent of your age group varied, depending on your age. Also, the IQ formula did not make much sense for adults: A 50-year-old who scores like a 30-year-old does not have low intelligence! Today, therefore, intelligence tests are scored differently. The average is usually set arbitrarily at 100, and tests are constructed so that about two-thirds of all people score between 85 and 115. Individual scores are computed from tables based on established norms. These scores are still informally referred to as "IQs," and they still reflect how a person compares with other people, either children of a particular age or adults in general. At all ages, the distribution of scores approximates a normal (bell-shaped) curve, with scores near the average (mean) more common than very high or very low scores (see Figure 7.2).

In the United States, Stanford psychologist Lewis Terman revised Binet's test and established

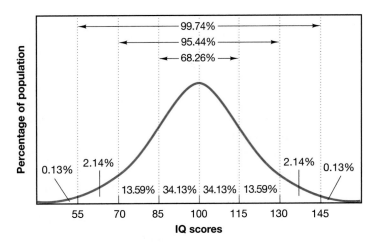

FIGURE 7.2 Expected Distribution of IQ Scores

In a large population, IQ scores tend to be distributed on a normal (bell-shaped) curve. On most tests, about 68 percent of all people will score between 85 and 115; about 95 percent will score between 70 and 130; and about 99.7 percent will score between 55 and 145. In any actual sample, however, the distribution will depart somewhat from the theoretical ideal.

norms for American children. His version, the *Stanford-Binet Intelligence Scale*, was first published in 1916 and has been updated several times since. (For some sample items, see Table 7.2.) Two decades later, David Wechsler designed another test expressly for adults, which became the *Wechsler Adult Intelligence Scale (WAIS)*. It was followed by the *Wechsler Intelligence Scale for Children (WISC)*.

TABLE 7.2 Sample Items from the Stanford-Binet Intelligence Test, Form L-M

The older the test-taker is, the more the test requires in the way of verbal comprehension and fluency.

Age	Task
4	Fills in the missing word when asked, "Brother is a boy; sister is a _____." Answers correctly when asked, "Why do we have houses?"
9	Answers correctly when examiner says, "In an old graveyard in Spain they have discovered a small skull which they believe to be that of Christopher Columbus when he was about 10 years old. What is foolish about that? Examiner presents folded paper; child draws how it will look unfolded.
12	Completes "The streams are dry . . . there has been little rain." Tells what is foolish about statements such as "Bill Jones's feet are so big that he has to put his trousers on over his head."
Adult	Can describe the difference between misery and poverty, character and reputation, laziness and idleness. Explains how to measure 3 pints of water with a 5-pint and a 2-pint can.

Source: From Lewis M. Terman and Maud A. Merrill, *Stanford-Binet Intelligence Scale* (1972 norms ed.). Boston: Houghton Mifflin, 1973. (Currently published by the Riverside Publishing Company.) Items are copyright 1916 by Lewis M. Terman, 1937 by Lewis M. Terman and Maud A. Merrill, © 1960, 1973 by the Riverside Publishing Company. Reproduced or adapted by permission of the publisher.

Although the Wechsler tests produce a general IQ score, they also provide specific scores for different kinds of ability. Verbal items test a person's vocabulary, arithmetic abilities, immediate memory span, ability to recognize similarities (e.g., "How are books and movies alike?"), and general knowledge and comprehension (e.g., "Who was Pierre Elliott Trudeau?" "Why do people who want a divorce have to go to court?"). "Performance" items test a range of nonverbal skills (see Figure 7.3).

In the 1980s, Canadian psychologists queried the relevance of questions about American presidents when testing Canadian children (Violato, 1986). As a result, Canadian norms were established, including, for example, the use of metric measurements. Since then, studies have found that Canadian and American scores on the WISC are comparable (Saklofske, 2003).

Binet had emphasized that his test merely *sampled* intelligence and did not measure everything covered by that term. A test score, he said, could be useful, along with other information, for predicting school performance, but it should not be confused with intelligence itself. The tests were designed to be given to children individually, so that the test-giver could see whether a child was ill or nervous, had poor vision, or was unmotivated. The purpose was to identify children with learning problems, not to rank all children.

But when intelligence testing was brought from France to the United States, its original purpose got lost at sea. In North America, IQ tests became widely used not to bring slow learners up to the average, but to categorize people in school and in the armed services according to their presumed "natural ability." The testers overlooked the fact that people did not all share the same background and experience (Gould, 1996).

Can IQ Tests Be "Culture-Free"? Intelligence tests developed between World War I and the 1960s for use in schools favoured city children over rural ones, middle-class children over poor ones, and white children over nonwhite children. One item asked whether the Emperor Concerto was written by Beethoven, Mozart, Bach, Brahms, or Mahler. (The answer is Beethoven.) Critics complained that the tests did not measure the kinds of knowledge and skills that are intelligent in a minority neighbourhood or some rural settings. They feared that, because teachers thought IQ scores revealed the limits of a child's potential, low-scoring children might not get the educational attention or encouragement they needed.

Thinking Critically About Culture and Intelligence Testing

Test-makers responded by trying to construct tests that were *culture-free*. Such tests were usually nonverbal; in some, instructions were even pantomimed. They also tried to design tests that were *culture-fair*: Instead of trying to eliminate the influence of culture, they attempted to include items that incorporated knowledge and skills common to many different cultures. But both approaches were less successful than originally hoped.

One reason for the disappointing results was that cultures differ in the problem-solving strategies they emphasize (Serpell, 1994). In the West, white, middle-class children typically learn to classify things by category—to say that an apple and a peach are similar because they are both fruits, and that a saw and a rake are similar because they are both tools. But children who are not trained in middle-class ways of sorting things may classify objects according to their sensory qualities or functions. They may say that an apple and a peach are similar because they both taste good. We think that's a charming and innovative answer, but it is one that testers interpret as less intelligent (Miller-

Picture arrangement
(Arrange the panels to make a meaningful story)

Object assembly
(Put together a jigsaw puzzle)

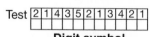

Code

Test

Digit symbol
(Using the key at the top, fill in the appropriate symbol beneath each number)

Picture completion
(Supply the missing feature)

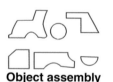

Block design
(Copy the design shown, using another set of blocks)

FIGURE 7.3 Performance Tasks on the Wechsler Tests

Nonverbal items such as these are particularly useful for measuring the abilities of those who have poor hearing, are not fluent in the tester's language, have limited education, or resist doing classroom-type problems. A large gap between a person's verbal score and performance score on a Wechsler test sometimes indicates a specific learning problem. (Object assembly, digit symbol, and picture completion adapted from Cronbach, 1990.)

Jones, 1989). In Canada, similar concerns have been raised about misinterpreting the test responses of First Nations children (Darou, 1992) and Inuit people (Wilgosh, 1991).

It is also difficult to eliminate the influence of culture because cultural values and experiences affect a person's attitude toward exams, comfort in the settings required for testing, motivation, rapport with the test-giver, competitiveness, and experience in solving problems independently rather than with others (Anastasi & Urbina, 1997; López, 1995). For example, cultural stereotypes that portray women or members of particular ethnic, age, or socioeconomic groups as unintelligent can actually depress the performance of people in these groups on IQ and other mental-abilities tests. You might think that a woman would say, "So sexists think women are dumb at math? I'll show them" or that an African-American would say, "So racists believe that blacks aren't as smart as whites? Just give me that exam." But often that is not what happens.

On the contrary, such individuals commonly feel a burden of doubt about their abilities that Claude Steele (1992, 1997) has labelled **stereotype threat**. The threat occurs when people believe that if they do not do well, they will confirm the stereotypes about their group. Their anxiety may then worsen their performance. Or they may cope by "disidentifying" with the test, saying to themselves, in effect, "The outcome of this test has no bearing on how I feel about myself" (Major et al., 1998). As a result, they may not be motivated to do well. Stereotype threat has been shown to affect the test performance of visible minorities, low-income people, women, and elderly people. For instance, Canadian researchers have found that women who were told that a test exhibited strong sex differences in favour of men tended to perform more poorly than women who were told gender-neutral information about it (for example, Spencer, Steele, & Quinn, 1999; Spencer, Steele, & Quinn, 2002; Walsh, Hickey, & Duffy, 1999). Researchers at Queen's University have shown that stereotype threat can even have a detrimental effect on athletes when a particular group becomes dominant in a sport, in this case, long distance runners from East Africa (Baker & Horton, 2003). In short, many members of these groups perform better on tests when they are not feeling self-conscious about themselves as members of negatively stereotyped categories (Aronson & Salinas, 1997; Brown & Josephs, 1999; Croizen & Claire, 1998; Levy, 1996; Steele & Aronson, 1995; Quinn & Spencer, 2001).

An intelligence test is useful only if it is used intelligently. Testing by the army during World War I often occurred under noisy, crowded, and confusing conditions, and many items were culturally loaded. Nevertheless, many people concluded from the results that a high proportion of army recruits were "morons."

Beyond the IQ Test In theory, it should be possible to reduce the impact of cultural bias and stereotype threat by establishing norms that are not based on white urban test-takers or by throwing out test items on which such individuals get higher scores than others. A similar strategy was actually used years ago to eliminate sex differences in IQ (Samelson, 1979). On early tests, girls scored higher than boys at every age. No one was willing to conclude that males were intellectually inferior, so in the 1937 revision of the Stanford-Binet test, Lewis Terman simply deleted the items on which boys had done poorly. Poof! No sex differences.

But few people seem willing to do for cultural differences what Terman did for sex differences, and the reason reveals a dilemma at the heart of intelligence testing. Intelligence and other mental-abilities tests put some groups of children at a disadvantage, yet they also measure skills and knowledge useful in the classroom. How can educators recognize and accept cultural differences and, at the same time, require students to demonstrate mastery of the skills, knowledge, and attitudes that will help them succeed in school and in the larger society?

Today, many schools have discontinued group IQ tests and give the tests only to individual students who may benefit from special education

stereotype threat A burden of doubt a person feels about his or her performance, due to negative stereotypes about his or her group's abilities.

(or gifted-student) programs—Binet's original goal. Test scores are just one part of a general evaluation of the child. But charges of cultural bias continue to be levelled at IQ tests and other standardized aptitude tests, such as the Scholastic Aptitude Test (SAT), given in the U.S., and the Graduate Record Examination (GRE), given in both the U.S. and Canada. Critics also point out that such tests tell us nothing about *how* a person goes about answering questions and solving problems. Nor do they explain why people with low scores often behave intelligently in real life—making smart consumer decisions, winning at the racetrack, and making wise personal choices (Ceci, 1996). Some researchers, therefore, have rejected the psychometric approach to the study and measurement of intelligence and mental abilities altogether, in favour of a cognitive approach.

Dissecting Intelligence: The Cognitive Approach

Cognitive psychologists, thinking critically, have questioned prevailing assumptions about the very meaning of intelligence and the best way to measure it. In contrast to the psychometric approach, which is concerned with how many answers a person gets right on a test, the *cognitive approach* examines many kinds of intelligence and emphasizes the strategies people use when thinking about a problem and arriving at a solution.

Thinking Critically About What It Means to Be Smart

The Triarchic Theory One well-known cognitive theory is Robert Sternberg's **triarchic theory of intelligence** (1988, 1995) (*triarchic* means "three-part"). It distinguishes three aspects of intelligence:

1 *Componential intelligence* refers to the information-processing strategies you use when you are thinking intelligently about a problem. These mental "components" include recognizing the problem, selecting a strategy for solving it, mastering and carrying out the strategy, and evaluating the result. This is the type of intelligence generally tapped by IQ tests.

Some of these operations require not only analytic skills but also **metacognition**, the knowledge or awareness of your own cognitive processes and the ability to monitor and control those processes. Metacognitive skills help you learn. Students who are weak in metacognition fail to notice when a passage in a textbook is difficult, and they do not always realize that they haven't

understood what they've been reading. As a result, they spend too little time on difficult material and too much time on material they already know (Nelson & Leonesio, 1988). In contrast, students who are strong in metacognition check their comprehension by restating what they have read, backtracking when necessary, and questioning what they are reading, so they learn better (Bereiter & Bird, 1985).

But it works in the other direction, too: The kind of intelligence that enhances academic performance can also help you develop metacognitive skills. Students with poor academic skills typically don't recognize the gaps in their learning; they think they're doing fine (Dunning et al., 2003). In one study, students who were in only the 12th percentile on a test of logical reasoning guessed that they had scored in the 62nd percentile and thought that their overall skills in logic put them in the 65th percentile. They were blissfully ignorant not only of logical reasoning but also of their own ignorance (Kruger & Dunning, 1999). In contrast, people with strong academic skills tend to be more realistic, and often they even slightly underestimate their abilities. As Thomas Jefferson said, "He who knows best knows how little he knows."

2 *Experiential intelligence* refers to your creativity in transferring skills to new situations. People with experiential intelligence cope well with novelty and learn quickly to make new tasks automatic; those who are lacking in this area perform well only under a narrow set of circumstances. For example, a student may do well in school, where assignments have specific due dates and feedback is immediate, but be less successful after graduation if her job requires her to set her own deadlines and her employer doesn't tell her how she is doing.

3 *Contextual intelligence* refers to the practical application of intelligence, which requires you to take into account the different contexts in which you find yourself. If you are strong in contextual intelligence, you know when to adapt to the environment (you are in a dangerous neighbourhood, so you become more vigilant). You know when to change environments (you had planned to be a teacher but discover that you dislike working with kids, so you switch to accounting). And you know when to fix the situation (your marriage is rocky, so you and your spouse go for counselling).

Contextual intelligence allows you to acquire **tacit knowledge**—practical, action-oriented

triarchic theory of intelligence A theory of intelligence that emphasizes information-processing strategies, the ability to transfer skills to new situations, and the practical application of intelligence.

metacognition The knowledge or awareness of one's own cognitive processes.

tacit knowledge Strategies for success that are not explicitly taught but that instead must be inferred.

strategies for achieving your goals that are not formally taught but must instead be inferred by observing others (Sternberg et al., 1995). In studies of college professors, business managers, and salespeople, tacit knowledge is a strong predictor of effectiveness on the job (Sternberg et al., 2000). In college students, tacit knowledge about how to be a good student actually predicts academic success as well as college entrance exams do (Sternberg & Wagner, 1989).

Domains of Intelligence Other psychologists, too, are expanding our understanding of what it means to be intelligent. They point out that someone who is intelligent in one area, or domain, is not necessarily intelligent in all others. A Nobel Prize winner in physics may be a nitwit when it comes to making up a budget; a biologist who is cautious and careful in his own field may uncritically accept nonscientific claims about human psychology (Ceci, 1996; Shermer, 1997).

Howard Gardner (1983, 1995) has proposed that the domains of intelligence be expanded to include musical aptitude, kinesthetic intelligence (the bodily grace and physical self-awareness of athletes and dancers), and the capacity for insight into oneself, others, or the natural world. These abilities, Gardner argues, are relatively independent and may even have separate neural structures. People with brain damage often lose intelligence in one domain without losing their competence in the others. Some people with autism and mental retardation may also have *savant syndrome* (*savant* means "learned" in French). This means they have exceptional abilities in one area, such as music, art, or rapid mathematical computation, despite poor functioning in all others.

Two of Gardner's domains, understanding yourself and understanding others, overlap with what some psychologists call **emotional intelligence**: the ability to identify your own and other people's emotions accurately, express your emotions clearly, and regulate emotions in yourself and others (Goleman, 1995; Mayer & Salovey, 1997). People with high emotional intelligence—popularly known as "EQ"—use their emotions to motivate themselves, to spur creative thinking, and to deal empathically with others. People who are low in emotional intelligence are often unable to identify their own emotions; they may insist that they're not depressed when a relationship ends, for example, but meanwhile they start drinking too much, become irritable, and stop going out with friends. They express emotions inappropriately, such as by acting violently or impulsively when they are angry or worried. And they misread nonverbal signals from others; they will give a long-winded account of all their problems even when the listener is obviously bored.

Studies of brain-damaged adults suggest a biological basis for emotional intelligence. Neuroscientist Antonio Damasio (1994) has studied patients with prefrontal-lobe damage that makes them incapable of experiencing strong feelings. Although they score in the normal range on conventional mental tests, these patients persistently make "dumb," irrational decisions in their lives because they cannot assign values to different options based on their own emotional reactions and cannot read emotional cues from others. As we will see again in Chapter 13, feeling and thinking are not always incompatible, as many people assume; in fact, one requires the other.

Thinking Critically about Intelligence(s) Not everyone is enthusiastic about the proliferation of new "intelligences." Some argue that emotional intelligence is not a special cognitive ability but a

emotional intelligence The ability to identify your own and other people's emotions accurately, express your emotions clearly, and regulate emotions in yourself and others.

Some theorists who argue for an expanded definition of intelligence would say that Shania Twain has musical intelligence, a surveyor has spatial intelligence, and a compassionate friend has emotional intelligence.

People with emotional intelligence are skilled at reading nonverbal emotional cues. Which of these boys do you think feels the most confident and relaxed, which one is shyest, and which feels most anxious? What cues are you using to answer?

very concept of intelligence loses all meaning. What is to prevent someone from adding "handicraft intelligence" or "financial intelligence" or "farming intelligence"?

Broadening the notion of intelligence, however, has been extremely useful, for several reasons. It has forced us to go beyond "g" and think more critically about what we mean by intelligence. It has inspired a promising new type of mental testing, in which the test-giver provides ongoing feedback to the test-taker so that the person can learn from the experience and improve his or her performance (Grigorenko & Sternberg, 1998). It has led to a focus on teaching children practical strategies for improving their reading, writing, homework, and test-taking skills. For example, children are being taught to manage their time so they don't procrastinate, and to study differently for multiple-choice exams than for essay exams (Sternberg et al., 1995). Most important, new approaches to intelligence encourage us to overcome the mental set of assuming that the only kind of intelligence necessary for a successful life is the kind captured by IQ tests.

collection of personality traits, such as empathy and extroversion, and that nothing is gained by giving EQ its own popular label (Davies, Stankov, & Roberts, 1998). Others maintain that abilities such as Gardner's musical and kinesthetic intelligences are better thought of as talents, or else the

Quick Quiz

What's your Quiz Quotient (QQ)?

1. In a sense, all mental tests are (aptitude/achievement) tests.
2. Hilda, who is 66, is about to take an IQ test, but she is worried because she knows that older people are often assumed to have diminished mental abilities. Hilda is being affected by _____.
3. What goals do cognitive theories of intelligence have that psychometric theories do not?
4. Logan understands the material in his statistics class, but on tests, he spends the entire period on the most difficult problems and never even gets to the problems he can solve easily. According to the triarchic theory of intelligence, which aspect of intelligence does he need to improve?
5. Tracy does not have an unusually high IQ, but at work she was quickly promoted because she knows how to set priorities, communicate with management, and make others feel valued. Tracy has _____ knowledge about how to succeed on the job.
6. What is wrong with defining intelligence as "whatever intelligence tests measure"?

Answers:

1. achievement
2. stereotype threat
3. to understand people's strategies for solving problems and to use this information to improve mental performance
4. componential intelligence (which includes metacognition)
5. tacit
6. This definition implies that a low score must be entirely the scorer's fault rather than the test's. But the test-taker may be intelligent in domains that the test fails to measure, and the test may be measuring traits other than intelligence.

WHAT'S AHEAD

- To what extent is intelligence heritable?
- What error do many people make when arguing that one group is genetically smarter than another?
- How does the environment nurture or thwart mental ability?
- How do drive and determination influence intellectual success?

THE ORIGINS OF INTELLIGENCE

"Intelligence," as we have seen, can mean many things. But however we define or measure it, clearly some people think and behave more intelligently than others. What accounts for these differences?

Genes and Intelligence

Behavioural geneticists approach this question by doing heritability studies, focusing mainly on the kind of intelligence measured by IQ tests. In Chapter 2, we saw that **heritability** is the proportion of the total variance in a trait within a group that is attributable to genetic variation within the group. This proportion can have a maximum value of 1.0 (which means that the trait is completely heritable). It is usually estimated by doing twin and adoption studies. (You might review pages 52 to 54 if you need to refresh your memory for these procedures.)

Genes and Individual Differences Behavioural-genetic studies show that the kind of intelligence that produces high IQ scores is highly heritable. For children and adolescents, heritability estimates average around .50; that is, about half of the variance in IQ scores is explainable by genetic differences (Chipuer, Rovine, & Plomin, 1990; Devlin, Daniels, & Roeder, 1997; Plomin, 1989). For adults, who are no longer being affected by environmental influences such as schooling, the estimates are even higher—in the .60 to .80 range (Bouchard, 1995; McClearn et al., 1997; McGue et al., 1993).

In studies of twins, the scores of identical twins are always much more highly correlated than those of fraternal twins, a difference that reflects the influence of genes. In fact, the scores of identical twins reared apart are more highly correlated than those of fraternal twins reared together, as you can see in Figure 7.4. In adoption studies, the

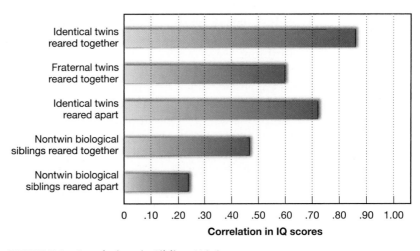

FIGURE 7.4   Correlations in Siblings' IQ Scores

The IQ scores of identical twins are highly correlated, even when they are reared apart. The data in this graph are based on average correlations across many studies (Bouchard & McGue, 1981).

scores of adopted children are more highly correlated with those of their birth parents than with those of their biologically unrelated adoptive parents: The higher the birth parents' scores, the higher the child's score is likely to be. As adopted children grow into adolescence, the correlation between their IQ scores and those of their biologically unrelated family members diminishes, and in adulthood the correlation falls to *zero* (Bouchard, 1997b; Scarr, 1993; Scarr & Weinberg, 1994).

Researchers are now looking for genes that might influence performance on IQ and other mental tests, and they have identified some possible candidates (Chorney et al., 1998; Fisher et al., 1999; Hill et al., 1999; Plomin & Crabbe, 2000). But behavioural-genetic findings do not mean that genes determine IQ. In Chapter 2, we saw that if heredity accounts for only part of why people differ on some trait, then the environment (and random errors in measurement) must account for the rest. Remember, too, that a highly heritable trait can nonetheless be modifiable by the environment.

The Question of Group Differences If genes influence individual differences in intelligence, do they also help account for differences between groups, as many people assume? This issue has tremendous political and social importance, so we are going to look at it closely.

Most of the focus has been on black–white differences, because African-American children score, on average, some 10 to 15 points lower on IQ tests than do white children. (We are talking about averages; the distributions of scores for black children and white children overlap considerably.)

heritability A statistical estimate of the proportion of the total variance in some trait that is attributable to genetic differences among individuals within a group.

A few psychologists have proposed a genetic explanation of this difference (Jensen, 1969, 1981; Rushton, 1988). As you can imagine, this topic is not merely "academic." Racists have used theories of genetic differences between groups to justify their own hatreds, and politicians have used them to argue for cuts in programs that would benefit blacks, other minorities, and poor children. Some researchers themselves have concluded that there is little point in spending money on programs that try to raise the IQs of low-scoring children, of whatever race (Herrnstein & Murray, 1994).

Genetic explanations, however, have a fatal flaw: They use heritability estimates based mainly on white samples to estimate the role of heredity in *group* differences, a procedure that is not valid. This problem sounds pretty technical, but it is not really too difficult to understand, so stay with us.

Thinking Critically About Group Differences in IQ

Consider, first, not people but tomatoes. (Figure 7.5 will help you visualize the following "thought experiment.") Suppose you have a bag of tomato seeds that vary genetically; all things being equal, some will produce tomatoes that are puny and tasteless, and some will produce tomatoes that are plump and delicious. Now you take a bunch of these seeds in your left hand and another bunch from the same bag in your right hand. Though one seed differs genetically from another, there is no average difference between the seeds in your left hand and those in your right. You plant the left hand's seeds in pot A, with some soil that you have doctored with nitrogen and other nutrients, and you plant the right hand's seeds in pot B,

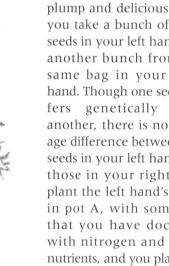

FIGURE 7.5 The Tomato Plant Experiment

In the hypothetical experiment described in the text, even if the differences among plants within each pot were due entirely to genetics, the average difference between pots could be environmental. The same general principle applies to individual and group differences among human beings.

with soil from which you have extracted nutrients. You sing to pot A and put it in the sun; you ignore pot B and leave it in a dark corner.

When the tomato plants grow, they will vary *within* each pot in terms of height, the number of tomatoes produced, and the size of the tomatoes, purely because of genetic differences. But there will also be an average difference between the plants in pot A and those in pot B: The plants in

pot A will be healthier and bear more tomatoes. This difference *between* pots is due entirely to the different soils and the care that has been given to the plants—even though the heritability of the *within*-pot differences is 100 percent (Lewontin, 1970, 2001).

The principle is the same for people as it is for tomatoes. Although intellectual differences *within* groups are at least partly genetic, that does not mean that differences *between* groups are genetic. People in Canada do not grow up, on average, in the same "pots" (environments). Because of a long legacy of racial hostility and discrimination, Aboriginal children, as well as other children of ethnic minorities, often receive far fewer nutrients—literally, in terms of food, and figuratively, in terms of education, encouragement by society, and intellectual opportunities. And as we have seen, negative stereotypes about ethnic groups may cause members of these groups to doubt their own abilities, become anxious and self-conscious, and perform more poorly than they otherwise would on tests.

To complicate matters, doing good research on the origins of racial differences in IQ is extremely difficult, given that racism affects the lives of even affluent, successful members of minority groups (Cose, 1994; Parker, 1997; Staples, 1994). However, the few studies that have overcome past methodological problems fail to reveal any genetic differences between groups in whatever it is that IQ tests measure.

An intelligent reading of the research on intelligence, therefore, does not direct us to conclude that differences among cultural, ethnic, or national groups are permanent, genetically determined, or signs of any group's innate superiority. On the contrary, the research suggests that we should make sure that all children grow up in the best possible soil, with room for the smartest and the slowest to find a place in the sun.

The Environment and Intelligence

By now you may be wondering what kinds of experiences hinder intellectual development and what kinds of environmental "nutrients" promote it. Here are some of the influences associated with reduced mental ability:

- *Poor prenatal care.* If a pregnant woman is malnourished, contracts infections, takes certain drugs, smokes, drinks alcohol, or is exposed to environmental pollutants, the fetus is at risk of having learning disabilities and a lower IQ.

- *Malnutrition.* The average IQ gap between severely malnourished and well-nourished children can be as high as 20 points (Stoch & Smythe, 1963; Winick, Meyer, & Harris, 1975).

- *Exposure to toxins.* Lead, for example, can damage the nervous system, producing attention problems, lower IQ scores, and poor school achievement (Needleman et al., 1996). Many children in North America are exposed to dangerous levels of lead from dust, contaminated soil, old lead-based paint, and old lead pipes; the concentration of lead in black children's blood is 50 percent higher than in white children's (Lanphear et al., 2002).

- *Stressful family circumstances.* Factors that predict reduced intellectual competence include, for example, having a father who does not live with the family, a mother with a history of mental illness, parents with limited work skills, and a history of stressful events in early life (Sameroff et al., 1987). On average, each risk factor reduces a child's IQ score by 4 points. Children with seven risk factors score more than *30 points lower* than those with no risk factors.

In contrast, a healthy and stimulating environment can raise mental performance (Guralnick, 1997; Ramey & Ramey, 1998). In one longitudinal study called the Abecedarian Project, inner-city children who got lots of mental enrichment at home and in child care or school, starting in infancy, had much better school achievement than did children in a control group (Campbell & Ramey, 1995). In general, children's mental abilities improve when parents talk to their children about many topics and describe things accurately and fully, encourage them to think things through, read to them, and expect them to do well.

Perhaps the best evidence for the importance of environmental influences on intelligence is the fact that IQ scores in developed countries have been climbing steadily for at least three generations (Flynn, 1987, 1999) (see Figure 7.6). Recently, a similar increase was documented in Kenya, a developing country: Rural children ages 6 to 8 scored about 11 points higher in 1998 than their peers did in 1984—the fastest rise in a group's average IQ scores ever reported (Daley et al., 2003). Genes cannot possibly have changed fast enough to account for these findings. Most cognitive psychologists attribute the increases to improvements in education, the increased avail-

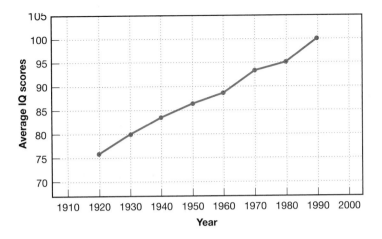

FIGURE 7.6 Climbing IQ Scores

Raw scores on IQ tests have been rising in developed countries for many decades, at a rate much too steep to be accounted for by genetic changes. Because test norms are periodically readjusted to set the average score at 100, most people are unaware of the increase. On this graph, average scores are calibrated according to 1989 norms. As you can see, performance was much lower in 1918 than in 1989. (Adapted from Horgan, 1995.)

ability of jobs requiring abstract thought, and better nutrition and health (Neisser, 1998).

We see, then, that although heredity may provide the range of a child's intellectual potential—a Homer Simpson can never become an Einstein—many other factors affect where in that range the child will fall.

Motivation and Intellectual Success

Even with a high IQ, emotional intelligence, genetic advantages, talent, and practical know-how, you still might get nowhere at all. Talent, unlike cream, does not inevitably rise to the top; success also depends on drive and determination.

Consider a finding from one of the longest-running psychological studies ever conducted. In 1921, researchers began following more than 1500 people with childhood IQ scores in the top one percent of the distribution. As boys and girls, these people were nicknamed "Termites," after Lewis Terman, who originally directed the research. The Termites started out bright, physically healthy, sociable, and well adjusted. As

Parents can play a vital role in their children's intellectual development by reading to them, asking them questions, and providing books and games that arouse their curiosity.

they entered adulthood, most became successful in the traditional ways of the times: men in careers and women as homemakers (Sears & Barbee, 1977; Terman & Oden, 1959). However, some gifted men failed to live up to their early promise, dropping out of school or drifting into low-level work. When the researchers compared the 100 most successful men with the 100 least successful, they found that motivation made the difference. The successful men were ambitious, were socially active, had many interests, and were encouraged by their parents. The least successful men drifted casually through life. There was no average difference in IQ between the two groups.

Motivation to work hard at intellectual tasks depends in turn on your attitudes about intelligence and achievement. For many years, Harold Stevenson and his colleagues have been studying such attitudes in Asia and North America. Since 1980 they have been comparing large samples of grade-school children, parents, and teachers (Stevenson & Stigler, 1992). In 1990, Stevenson, along with Chuansheng Chen and Shin-ying Lee (1993), revisited the original schools to collect new data on fifth-graders, and they also retested many of the children who had been in the 1980 study and who were now in the eleventh grade. Their results have much to teach us about the cultivation of intellect.

In 1980, the Asian children far outperformed the North American children on a broad battery of mathematical tests. On computations and word problems, there was virtually no overlap between schools, with the lowest-scoring Beijing schools doing better than the highest-scoring North American schools. By 1990, the gap between the Asian and the North American children had grown even greater. Only 4 percent of the Chinese children and 10 percent of the Japanese children had math scores as low as those of the *average* North American child. These differences could not be accounted for by educational resources: The Chinese schools had worse facilities and larger classes than the North American ones and, on average, the Chinese parents were poorer and less educated than the North American parents. Nor did it have anything to do with intellectual ability in general; the North American children were just as knowledgeable and capable as the Asian children on tests of general information.

But this research found that Asians and North Americans are worlds apart in their attitudes, expectations, and efforts:

- *Beliefs about intelligence.* North American parents, teachers, and children are far more likely than Asians to believe that mathematical ability is innate (see Figure 7.7). North Americans tend to think that if you "have it," you don't have to work hard, and if you don't have it, there's no point in trying.

- *Standards.* North American parents have far lower standards for their children's performance; they are satisfied with scores barely above average on a 100-point test. In contrast, Chinese and Japanese parents are happy only with very high scores.

- *Values.* North American students do not value education as much as Asian students do, and they are more complacent about mediocre work. When asked what they would wish for if a wizard could give them anything they wanted, more than 60 percent of the Chinese fifth-graders named something related to their education. Can you guess what the North American children wanted? A majority said money or possessions.

When it comes to intellect, then, it's not just what you've got that counts but what you do with it. Complacency, fatalism, or low standards can prevent people from recognizing what they don't know and can reduce their efforts to learn.

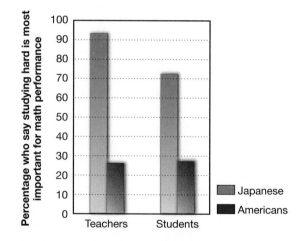

FIGURE 7.7 What's the Secret of Math Success?
Japanese school teachers and students are much more likely than their North American counterparts to believe that the secret to doing well in math is working hard. North Americans tend to think that you either have mathematical intelligence or you don't.

WHAT'S AHEAD

- Why do some researchers think that animals can think?

- People love to talk to their pets—but can their pets learn to talk back?

ANIMAL MINDS

A green heron swipes some bread from a picnicker's table and scatters the crumbs on a nearby stream. When a minnow rises to the bait, the heron strikes, swallowing its prey before you can say "hook, line, and sinker." A sea otter, floating calmly on its back, bangs a mussel shell against a stone that is resting on its stomach. When the shell cracks apart, the otter devours the tasty morsel inside, tucks the stone under its little arm, and dives for another shell, which it will open in the same way.

Incidents such as these have convinced some biologists, psychologists, and ethologists that we are not the only animals with cognitive abilities— that "dumb beasts" aren't so dumb after all. (Ethology is the study of animal behaviour, especially in natural environments.) Researchers at the University of British Columbia likely concluded this when they discovered that scavenging birds regularly showed up at humans' lunch locations in advance of the actual humans and their lunches (Wilkie et al., 1996). Many best-selling books have

described the amazingly humanlike emotions and "thoughts" of animals. But how humanlike are they?

How smart is this otter?

Animal Intelligence

In the 1920s, Wolfgang Köhler (1925) put chimpanzees in situations in which some tempting bananas were just out of reach and watched to see what the apes would do. Most did nothing, but a few turned out to be quite clever. If the bananas were outside the cage, the animal might pull them in with a stick. If they were hanging overhead, and there were boxes in the cage, the chimpanzee might pile up the boxes and climb on

In an early study of animal intelligence, Sultan, a talented chimpanzee studied by Wolfgang Köhler, was able to figure out how to reach a cluster of bananas by stacking some boxes and climbing on top of them.

top of them to reach the fruit. Often the solution came after the animal had been sitting quietly for a while. It appeared as though the chimp had been thinking about the problem and was struck by a sudden insight.

Most learning theorists felt that this seemingly impressive behaviour could be accounted for perfectly well by standard behavioural principles, without resorting to mental explanations (see Chapter 9). Because of their influence, for years any scientist who claimed that animals could think was likely to get laughed at, or worse. Today, however, the study of animal intelligence is enjoying a resurgence, especially in the interdisciplinary field of **cognitive ethology**. Cognitive ethologists argue that some animals can anticipate future events, make plans and choices, and coordinate their activities with those of their comrades—that they are, indeed, capable of thought (Griffin, 1992).

When we think about animal cognition, we must be careful, because even complex behaviour can be genetically prewired and automatic. Researchers at the Vancouver Aquarium and elsewhere, for instance, have discovered that the harbour seal, which is a mammal, can distinguish between the underwater sounds of whales that eat mammals and whales that eat fish (Deecke, Slater, & Ford, 2002). And the assassin bug of South America catches termites by gluing nest material on its back as camouflage, but it is hard to imagine how the bug's tiny dab of brain tissue could enable it to plan this strategy consciously. Moreover, an animal could be aware of its environment and know some things without knowing that it knows and without being able to think about its own thoughts as human beings do—in short, without having metacognition (Budiansky, 1998; Hauser, 2000).

Yet explanations of animal behaviour that leave out any sort of consciousness at all and that attribute animals' actions entirely to instinct do not seem to account for some of the amazing things that animals can do. Like the otter that uses a stone to crack mussel shells, many animals are capable of using objects in the natural environment as rudimentary tools. For example, chimpanzee mothers occasionally show their young how to use stone tools to open hard nuts (Boesch, 1991).

In the laboratory, too, nonhuman primates have accomplished some surprising things. In one study, chimpanzees compared two pairs of food wells containing chocolate chips. One pair might contain, say, five chips and three chips, the other four chips and three chips. Allowed to choose which pair they wanted, the chimps almost always chose the one with the higher total, showing some sort of summing ability (Rumbaugh, Savage-Rumbaugh, & Pate, 1988). In another study, two rhesus monkeys (Rosencrantz and Macduff) learned to order groups of up to four symbols

cognitive ethology The study of cognitive processes in nonhuman animals.

according to the number of symbols in each group (e.g., one square, two trees, three ovals, four flowers). Later, when presented with pairs of symbol groups containing up to nine symbols, they were able to point to the group with more symbols, without any further training (Brannon & Terrace, 1998). This is not exactly algebra, but it does suggest that monkeys have a rudimentary sense of number.

Some researchers (though not all) believe that the great apes—chimpanzees, gorillas, and orangutans—have an understanding of how their own minds and the minds of others work (de Waal, 2001; Suddendorf & Whiten, 2001). When looking in a mirror, these animals may try to find marks on their bodies that are not directly visible, suggesting self-recognition. Chimpanzees console other chimps who are in distress, use deceptive tactics when competing for food, and point to draw attention to objects; these abilities all imply an ability to grasp what is going on in another individual's mind.

Animals and Language

A primary ingredient of human cognition is *language*, the ability to combine elements that are themselves meaningless into an infinite number of utterances that convey meaning. As we saw in Chapter 3, language allows us to express and comprehend an infinite number of novel utterances, created on the spot. We seem to be the only species that evolved to do this naturally. Other primates use a variety of grunts and screeches to warn each other of danger, to attract attention, and to express emotions, but the sounds are not combined to produce original sentences (at least, as far as we

can tell). Bongo may make a certain sound when he finds food, but he cannot say, "The bananas in the next grove are a lot riper than the ones we ate last week and sure beat our usual diet of termites."

Perhaps, however, some animals could acquire language if they got a little help from their human friends. Dozens of researchers have tried to provide chimpanzees and other apes with just such help. Because the vocal tract of an ape does not permit speech, most researchers have tried innovative approaches that rely on gestures or visual symbols. In one project, chimpanzees learned to use as words various geometric plastic shapes arranged on a magnetic board (Premack & Premack, 1983). In another, they learned to punch symbols on a computer-monitored keyboard (Rumbaugh, 1977). In other projects, chimps and a gorilla named Koko mastered hundreds of signs from American Sign Language (ASL) (Fouts & Rigby, 1977; Gardner & Gardner, 1969; Patterson & Linden, 1981). The animals in these studies learned to follow instructions, answer questions, and make requests. They also seemed to be using their newfound skills to apologize for being disobedient, scold their trainers, lie when they were naughty, and even talk to themselves. Most important, they combined individual signs or symbols into longer utterances that they had never seen before.

Because these animals were lovable and the findings were appealing, it was easy for emotional reasoning to prevail over critical thinking. But soon skeptics and some of the researchers themselves began to point out serious problems (Seidenberg & Petitto, 1979; Terrace, 1985). In their desire to talk to the animals and because of their affection for their primate friends, researchers had not always been objective. They had overinterpreted the animals' utterances, and often unwittingly gave nonverbal cues that might have enabled the apes to respond correctly. Further, the animals appeared to be stringing signs and symbols together in no particular order, instead of using grammatical rules to produce novel utterances; "Me eat banana" seemed to be no different from "Banana eat me."

These problems still plague some projects, but today, most researchers have taken the criticisms to heart and have greatly improved their procedures. They have shown that, with careful training, chimps can indeed learn to use symbols to refer to objects. Some animals have even used

Thinking Critically About Apes and Language

"It's always 'Sit,' 'Stay,' 'Heel'—never 'Think,' 'Innovate,' 'Be yourself.'"

Kanzi, a bonobo with the most advanced linguistic skills yet acquired by a nonhuman primate, answers questions and makes requests by punching symbols on a specially designed computer keyboard. He also understands short English sentences. Kanzi is shown here with researcher Sue Savage-Rumbaugh.

signs spontaneously to converse with each other, suggesting that they are not merely imitating or trying to get a reward (Van Cantfort & Rimpau, 1982).

Bonobos (a type of ape) are especially adept at language. One bonobo named Kanzi has learned to understand English words, short sentences, and keyboard symbols, *without formal training* (Savage-Rumbaugh & Lewin, 1994; Savage-Rumbaugh, Shanker, & Taylor, 1998). Kanzi responds correctly to commands such as "Put the key in the refrigerator" and "Go get the ball that is outdoors" even when he has never heard the words combined in that particular way before. He picked up language as children do—by observing others using it, and through normal social interaction. He has also learned, with training, to manipulate keyboard symbols to request favourite foods or activities (games, TV, visits to friends) and to announce his intentions.

You do not even have to be a primate to acquire some aspects of language. Dolphins have learned to understand the difference between requests such as "To left Frisbee, right surfboard take" and "To right surfboard, left Frisbee take," communicated in an artificial gestural language (Herman, Kuczaj, & Holder, 1993). And since the late 1970s, Irene Pepperberg (2000) has been working with an African gray parrot named Alex, teaching him to count, classify, and compare objects by vocalizing English words. Alex is no birdbrain, even though his brain is the size of a walnut; he shows evidence of both linguistic and cognitive ability. When he is shown up to six items and is asked how many there are, he responds with spoken (squawked?) English phrases, such as "two cork(s)" or "four key(s)." He can even

respond correctly to questions about items specified on two or three dimensions, as in "How many blue key(s)?" or "What matter [material] is orange and three-cornered?" Alex also makes requests ("Want pasta") and answers simple questions about objects ("What colour [is this]?" "Which is bigger?"). When he is presented with a blue cork and a blue key and is asked, "What's the same?" he will correctly respond, "Colour." He actually scores slightly better with new objects than with familiar ones, suggesting that he is not merely "parroting" a set of stock phrases. In informal "conversations," Alex tells Pepperberg, "I love you," "I'm sorry," and "Calm down."

Alex is one clever bird—but how clever? His abilities raise intriguing questions about the intelligence of animals and their capacity for specific aspects of language.

Thinking about the Thinking of Animals

These results on animal language and cognition are impressive, but scientists are still divided over just what they mean. Do the animals have true language? Are they "thinking," in human terms? How intelligent are they?

On one side are those who worry about *anthropomorphism*, the tendency to falsely attribute human qualities to nonhuman beings. They tell the story of Clever Hans, a "wonder horse" at the beginning of the twentieth century, who was said to possess mathematical and other abilities (Spitz, 1997). Clever Hans would answer math questions by stamping his hoof the appropriate number of times and respond to other questions by tapping in an established code. But a little careful experimentation by a psychologist, Oskar Pfungst (1911/1965), revealed that when Hans was prevented from seeing his questioners, or when they did not know the answers themselves, his "powers" left him. It seems that questioners were staring at the animal's feet and leaning forward expectantly after stating the problem, then lifting their eyes and relaxing as soon as he completed the right number of taps. Clever Hans was indeed clever, but not at math or other human skills. He was merely responding to nonverbal signals that people were inadvertently providing. (Perhaps he had a high EQ.)

Clever Hans in action.

On the other side are those who warn against *anthropodenial*, the tendency to think, mistakenly, that human beings have nothing in common with other animals, who are, after all, our evolutionary cousins (de Waal, 1997, 2001; Fouts, 1997). The need to see our own species as unique, they say, may keep us from recognizing that other species, too, have cognitive abilities, even if not as intricate as our own.

The outcome of this debate is bound to have an effect on how we view ourselves and our place among other species. Perhaps, as cognitive ethologist Marc Hauser (2000) suggests, we can find a way to study and respect animal minds and emotions without assuming sentimentally that they are just like ours.

Quick Quiz

Regrettably, your pet beagle can't help you answer these questions.

1. Which of the following abilities have primates demonstrated, either in the natural environment or the laboratory? (a) the use of objects as simple tools; (b) the summing of quantities; (c) the use of symbols to make requests; (d) an understanding of short English sentences
2. Barnaby thinks that his pet snake Curly is harbouring angry thoughts about him because Curly has been standoffish and won't curl around his neck anymore. What error is Barnaby making?

Answers:

1. all of them
2. anthropomorphism

Psychology In The News *Revisited*

We human beings have always thought of ourselves as the smartest species around, and for good reason. We have an astounding ability to adapt to change, solve problems in novel ways, invent endless new gizmos, and use language to create everything from puns to poetry. Yet, as this chapter has shown, we are not always as wise in our thinking as we might think, and we may not even be the only animal capable of thought. As if that weren't bad enough, now some people are saying, as in our opening story, that machines are gaining on us in the mental-abilities department—a frequent theme in movies such as *The Matrix* series. Will computers and robots eventually be able to make crucial decisions for us on how to improve public education, manage a baseball team, or schedule the fall TV lineup?

That's hardly likely. Consider the chess-playing accomplishments of Deep Blue and Deep Junior—or, more accurately, the accomplishments of the human programmers who wrote the machines' software. Although the computers' feats are impressive—they can analyze millions of moves per second—real intelligence is more than the capacity to perform computations with lightning speed. As we have seen, it involves the ability to deal with informal reasoning problems, reason dialectically and reflectively, devise mental shortcuts, read emotions, and acquire tacit knowledge. Intelligence also involves mental efficiency: Human beings are intelligent not because they can consider millions of chess positions a second, but because they don't have to! A chess-playing computer's raw calculating power disguises its ineffi-

ciency; it wins by rejecting the same moves millions of times (McCarthy, 1997).

From time to time, a researcher will predict that computers and computerized robots will soon be as smart as we are. But most experts disagree. One robot inventor, when asked whether self-reproducing robots could figure out how to become a doomsday machine and threaten the world, as in the movie *The Terminator*, said that such a prospect is "as far off as a fax machine is from a Star Trek transporter" (quoted in Chang, 2000). Others point out that robots lack the most important requirement for ruling the universe—a mind of their own. They also lack the feelings and emotional skills that give us "emotional intelligence" and make our decisions wiser.

Robots and computers, of course, are not the least bit troubled by their lack of cleverness, inasmuch as they lack a mind to be troubled. As computer scientist David Gelernter (1997) wrote after Deep Blue's victory, "How can an object that wants nothing, fears nothing, enjoys nothing, needs nothing, and cares about nothing have a mind?" Because machines are mindless, they also lack a trait that distinguishes human beings not only from computers but also from other species: We try to understand our own misunderstandings. We want to know what we don't know; we are motivated to overcome our mental shortcomings. Our uniquely human capacity for self-examination is probably the best reason to remain optimistic about our cognitive abilities.

Taking Psychology With You   Becoming More Creative

Take a few moments to answer these items from the Remote Associates Test. Your task is to come up with a fourth word that is associated with each item in a set of three words (Mednick, 1962). For example, an appropriate answer for the set *news–clip–wall* is *paper*. Got the idea? Now try these (the answers are given on page 248):

(1) piggy–green–lash;

(2) surprise–political–favour;

(3) mark–shelf–telephone;

(4) stick–maker–tennis;

(5) cream–cottage–cloth.

Associating elements in new ways by finding a common connection among them is an important component of creativity. People who are uncreative rely on *convergent thinking*, following a particular set of steps that they think will converge on one correct solution. Once they have solved a problem, they tend to develop a mental set and approach future problems in the same way.

Creative people, in contrast, exercise *divergent thinking*; instead of stubbornly sticking to one tried-and-true path, they explore some side alleys and generate several possible solutions. They come up with new hypotheses, imagine other interpretations, and look for connections that may not be immediately obvious. As a result, they are able to use familiar concepts in unexpected ways. Creative thinking can be found in the auto mechanic who invents a new tool, the mother who designs and makes her children's clothes, or the office manager who devises a clever way to streamline work flow (Richards, 1991).

A high IQ does not guarantee creativity. Personality characteristics seem more important, especially these three (Helson, Roberts, & Agronick, 1995; MacKinnon, 1968; McCrae, 1987; Schank, 1988):

- **Nonconformity.** Creative individuals are not overly concerned about what others think of them. They are willing to risk ridicule by proposing ideas that may initially appear foolish or off the mark. Geneticist Barbara McClintock's research was ignored or belittled by many for nearly 30 years. But she was sure she could show how genes move around and produce sudden changes in heredity. In 1983,

when McClintock won the Nobel Prize, the judges called her work the second greatest genetic discovery of our time, after the discovery of the structure of DNA.

- **Curiosity.** Creative people are open to new experiences; they notice when reality contradicts expectations, and they are curious about the reason. For example, Wilhelm Roentgen (1845–1923), a German physicist, was studying cathode rays when he noticed a strange glow on one of his screens. Other people had seen the glow, but they ignored it because it didn't jibe with their understanding of cathode rays. Roentgen studied the glow, found it to be a new kind of radiation, and thus discovered X-rays (Briggs, 1984).

- **Persistence.** After that imaginary light bulb goes on over your head, you still have to work hard to make the illumination last. Or as Thomas Edison, who invented the real light bulb, reportedly put it, "Genius is one-tenth inspiration and nine-tenths perspiration." No invention or work of art springs forth full-blown from a person's head. There are many false starts and painful revisions along the way.

In addition to traits that foster creativity, there are *circumstances* that do so. Creativity flourishes when schools and employers encourage intrinsic motivation and not just extrinsic rewards such as gold stars or money (see Chapters 9 and 14). As Robert Frost once said, "One should never write a poem to pay a gas bill." Intrinsic motives include a sense of accomplishment, intellectual fulfillment, the satisfaction of curiosity, and the sheer love of the activity.

Creativity also increases when people have control over how to perform a task or solve a problem; are evaluated unobtrusively, instead of being constantly observed and judged; and work independently (Amabile, 1983). Organizations encourage creativity when they let people take risks, give them plenty of time to think about problems, and welcome innovation.

In sum, if you hope to become more creative, there are two things you can do. One is to cultivate the personal qualities that lead to creativity. The other is to seek out the kinds of situations that permit you to express those qualities.

SUMMARY

THOUGHT: USING WHAT WE KNOW

- *Thinking* is the mental manipulation of information. Our mental representations simplify and summarize information from the environment.

- A *concept* is a mental category that groups objects, relations, activities, abstractions, or qualities that share certain properties. *Prototypical* instances of a concept are more representative than others. *Propositions* are made up of concepts and express a unitary idea. They may be linked together to form *cognitive schemas*, which serve as mental models of aspects of the world. *Mental images* also play a role in thinking.

- Not all mental processing is conscious. *Subconscious processes* lie outside of awareness but can be brought into consciousness when necessary. *Nonconscious processes* remain outside of awareness but nonetheless affect behaviour and are involved in what we call "intuition" and "insight" and in *implicit learning*. Conscious processing may be carried out in a mindless fashion if we overlook changes in context that call for a change in behaviour.

REASONING RATIONALLY

- *Reasoning* is purposeful mental activity that involves drawing inferences and conclusions from observations or propositions (*premises*).

- *Formal reasoning problems* can often be solved by applying an *algorithm*, a set of procedures that are guaranteed to produce a solution, or by using logical processes, such as *deductive* and *inductive reasoning*.

- *Informal reasoning problems* often have no clearly correct solution. Disagreement may exist about basic premises, information may be incomplete, and many viewpoints may compete. Such problems may call for the application of *heuristics*, rules of thumb that suggest a course of action without guaranteeing an optimal solution. They may also require *dialectical reasoning* about opposing points of view.

- Studies of *reflective judgment* show that many people have trouble thinking dialectically. People in the *pre-reflective* stages do not distinguish between knowledge and belief, or between belief and evidence. Those in the *quasi-reflective* stages think that because knowledge is sometimes uncertain, any judgment about the evidence is purely subjective. Those who think *reflectively* understand that although some things cannot be known with certainty, some judgments are more valid than others because of their coherence, usefulness, fit with the evidence, and so on. Higher education moves people gradually closer to reflective judgment.

BARRIERS TO REASONING RATIONALLY

- The need to be right is an obstacle to rational thinking, as is mental laziness, which many commentators think is encouraged by increased television watching.

- The ability to reason clearly and rationally is also affected by many cognitive biases. People tend to exaggerate the likelihood of improbable events, in part because of the *availability heuristic*; to be swayed in their choices by the desire to *avoid loss*; to be mentally rigid, forming *mental sets* and seeing patterns where none exists; to overestimate their ability to have made accurate predictions (the *hindsight bias*); and to attend mostly to evidence that confirms what they want to believe (the *confirmation bias*).

- The theory of *cognitive dissonance* holds that people are motivated to reduce the tension that exists when two cognitions conflict—by rejecting or changing a belief, changing their behaviour, or rationalizing. People are especially likely to do so when they need to justify a decision (i.e., reduce *postdecision dissonance*), when their actions violate their self-concept, or when they have put hard work into an activity (the *justification of effort*).

- People are not always rational, but once we understand a bias, we may be able to reduce or eliminate it.

INTELLIGENCE

- *Intelligence* is hard to define. Some theorists believe that a general ability (*g factor*) underlies the many specific abilities tapped by intelligence tests, whereas others do not.

- The traditional approach to intelligence, the *psychometric approach*, focuses on how well people perform on standardized aptitude tests. The *intelligence quotient*, or *IQ*, represents how a person has done on an intelligence test, compared to other people. Alfred Binet designed the first widely used intelligence test for the purpose of identifying children who could benefit from remedial work. But in the United

States, people assumed that intelligence tests revealed "natural ability," and they used the tests to categorize people in school and in the armed services.

- IQ tests have been criticized for being biased in favour of white, middle-class people. However, efforts to construct *culture-free* and *culture-fair tests* have been disappointing. Culture affects nearly everything to do with taking a test, from attitudes to problem-solving strategies. Negative stereotypes about a person's ethnicity, gender, or age may cause the person to suffer *stereotype threat*, a burden of doubt about his or her own abilities, which can lead to anxiety or "disidentification" with the test.

- Many schools now use IQ tests only with individual students being evaluated for special programs. But critics still worry about cultural biases and point out that the tests do not tell how a person arrives at an answer or solves a problem.

- In contrast to the psychometric approach, *cognitive approaches* to intelligence emphasize several kinds of intelligence and the strategies people use to solve problems. Sternberg's *triarchic theory of intelligence* proposes three aspects of intelligence: *componential* (including *metacognition*), *experiential*, and *contextual*. Contextual intelligence allows you to acquire *tacit knowledge*, practical strategies that are important for success but are not explicitly taught.

- Intelligence in one domain does not necessarily imply intelligence in another. Howard Gardner proposes that there are actually several "intelligences" besides those usually considered, including musical and kinesthetic intelligence, and the capacity to understand the natural world, yourself, or others. The latter two overlap with what many psychologists call *emotional intelligence*, which is associated with personal, academic, and occupational success.

THE ORIGINS OF INTELLIGENCE

- Behavioural-genetic studies estimate the heritability of intelligence (as measured by IQ tests) to be high: about .50 for children and adolescents and .60 to .80 for adults. But these results do not mean that genes determine intelligence, or that group differences in intelligence are genetic. It is not valid to draw conclusions about ethnic differences in intelligence from estimates based on differences within a group. The available evidence fails to support genetic explanations of these differences.

- Environmental factors such as poor prenatal care, malnutrition, exposure to toxins, and stressful family circumstances are associated with lower performance on mental tests; and a healthy and stimulating environment can improve performance.

- Intellectual achievement also depends on motivation and attitudes. Cross-cultural research shows that beliefs about the origins of mental abilities, parental standards, and attitudes toward education can help account for differences in academic performance.

ANIMAL MINDS

- Some researchers, especially those in the field of *cognitive ethology*, argue that nonhuman animals have greater cognitive abilities than is usually thought. Some animals can use objects as rudimentary tools. Chimpanzees have learned to use numerals to label quantities of items and symbols to refer to objects. Great apes sometimes do things that suggest they have some understanding of how their own minds and the minds of others work, though not all researchers agree.

- In several projects using visual symbol systems or American Sign Language (ASL), primates have acquired linguistic skills. Some animals (even some nonprimates) seem able to use simple grammatical ordering rules to convey or comprehend meaning. However, scientists are still divided as to how to interpret these findings, with some worrying about *anthropomorphism* and others about *anthropodenial*.

KEY TERMS

prototype   214

proposition   214

concept   214

cognitive schema   215

subconscious processes   215

mental image   215

unconscious processes   216

implicit learning   216

algorithm   217

reasoning   217

deductive reasoning   217

inductive reasoning   217

LOOKING BACK

- When you think of a bird, why are you more likely to recall a robin than a penguin? (p. 214)
- How are visual images like images on a computer screen? (p. 215)
- What is happening mentally when you mistakenly take your geography notes to your psychology class? (p. 216)
- Mentally speaking, why is making a cake, well, a piece of cake? (p. 217)
- Why can't logic solve all of our problems? (p. 218)
- What kind of reasoning do juries need to be good at? (p. 219)
- When people say that all opinions and claims are equally valid, what error are they making? (p. 220)
- Why do people worry about dying in an airplane crash but ignore dangers that are far more likely? (p. 222)
- How might your physician's choice of words about alternative treatments for your illness affect which one you choose? (p. 223)
- When Monday-morning coaches say they knew all along who would win last Saturday's game on *Hockey Night in Canada,* what bias might they be showing? (p. 224)
- Why will a terrible initiation rite make you more loyal to the group that initiated you? (pp. 226–227)
- How did the original purpose of intelligence testing change when IQ tests came to North America? (p. 230)
- Is it possible to design intelligence tests that are not influenced by culture? (pp. 230–231)
- Why do some psychologists oppose traditional intelligence testing? (p. 231)
- What kind of intelligence allows you to master the unspoken rules for academic success? (p. 232)
- What is "EQ," and why is it as important as IQ? (p. 233)
- To what extent is intelligence heritable? (p. 235)
- What error do many people make when arguing that one group is genetically smarter than another? (pp. 235–236)
- How does the environment nurture or thwart mental ability? (pp. 236–237)
- How do drive and determination influence intellectual success? (pp. 237–238)
- Why do some researchers think that animals can think? (pp. 239–241)
- People love to talk to their pets—but can their pets learn to talk back? (pp. 241–242)

Answers to the Remote Associates Test on page 245:

back, party, book, match, cheese

Some solutions to the nine-dot problem in the "Get Involved" exercise on page 224 (from Adams, 1986):

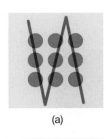

(a)

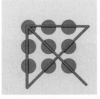

(b)

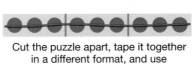

Cut the puzzle apart, tape it together in a different format, and use one line.

(c)

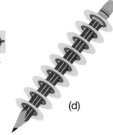

(d)

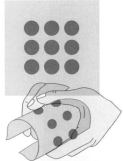

Roll up the puzzle and draw a spiral through the dots.

(e)

1 Line 0 Folds

Lay the paper on the surface of the Earth. Circumnavigate the globe twice + a few centimetres, displacing a little each time so as to pass through the next row on each circuit as you "Go West, young man."

(f)

~ 2 Lines* 0 Folds

*Statistical

Draw dots as large as possible. Wad paper into a ball. Stab with pencil. Open up and see if you did it. If not, try again. "Nobody loses: play until you win."

(g)

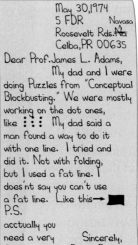

May 30,1974
5 FDR   Navasa
Roosevelt Rds.Na
Ceiba,PR 00635
Dear Prof.James L. Adams,
       My dad and I were
doing Puzzles from "Conceptual
Blockbusting." We were mostly
working on the dot ones,
like ⦂⦂⦂ My dad said a
man found a way to do it
with one line. I tried and
did it. Not with folding,
but I used a fat line. I
does'nt say you can't use
a fat line. Like this→ ◀
P.S.
acctually you
need a very   Sincerely,
fat writing   Becky Buechel
apparatice.   age:10

(h)

Psychology In The News

MAN SPENDS FOUR YEARS IN PRISON FOR A CRIME HE DID NOT COMMIT

WINNIPEG, MB, March 8, 2003. Barbara Stoppel was a 16-year-old girl who worked in a Winnipeg doughnut shop. On the night of December 23, 1981, she was attacked and strangled. Three months later, Thomas Sophonow was arrested for her murder. He was convicted and sent to prison, all the while claiming his innocence.

During four years in prison, Sophonow engaged in numerous appeals and separate trials. Then, in 1985, the Manitoba Court of Appeal ruled that the prosecution was flawed and that evidence presented was unreliable.

Thomas Sophonow's wrongful conviction relied on eyewitness testimony. He was picked out of a live lineup by four witnesses, one of whom even later asked a police officer if he'd picked the right man. The surprising thing is that, although this witness was not absolutely certain he had made a positive identification during either the live or photo lineup, he became more certain as time passed that he had identified the right man. He held this view even after Sophonow was proven innocent.

A retired Supreme Court Justice was asked to chair the inquiry into the case. He said that the photo lineup was "startlingly unfair" because Sophonow's photo was placed in such a way that it stood out from the others. He also concluded that "there is no doubt that mistaken eyewitness identification played a very significant role in the wrongful conviction of Thomas Sophonow." The Supreme Court ordered him acquitted.

Thomas Sophonow spent four years in a Manitoba prison for a crime he did not commit.

8 Memory

Courts of law rely heavily on the testimony of eyewitnesses to determine the truth. However, the case of Thomas Sophonow reminds us that a witness's account is not always reliable. In the absence of corroborating evidence, should a witness's certainty that he is accurate in his identification be sufficient for establishing guilt? Much is at stake in our efforts to answer these questions: getting justice for murder victims as well as avoiding the false conviction of men who are innocent.

Sophonow's story did not end in 1985. At the conclusion of this chapter we will tell you how he fared in later years. Meanwhile, as you read, ask yourself: When should we trust our memories and when should we be cautious about doing so? We all forget a great deal, of course: We watch the evening news and half an hour later can't recall the main story; we enjoy a meal and quickly forget what we ate. Do we also "remember" things that never happened? Are memory malfunctions the exception to the rule, or are they commonplace? If memory is not always reliable, how can any of us hope to know the story of our own lives?

And what are the implications for the legal system, which relies so much on the memories of witnesses and crime victims?

WHAT'S AHEAD

- What's wrong with thinking of memory as a mental video camera?
- Why do "flashbulb" memories of surprising or shocking events sometimes have less wattage than we think?
- If you have a strong emotional reaction to a remembered event, does that mean your memory is accurate?

RECONSTRUCTING THE PAST

Memory refers to the capacity to retain and retrieve information, and also to the structures that account for this capacity. Human beings are capable of astonishing feats of memory. Most of us can easily remember the tune of our national anthem, how

OneKey
8.1

to use an automated teller machine, the most embarrassing experience we ever had, zillions of details about our favourite sports or films, and hundreds of thousands of other bits of information.

Memory confers competence; without it we would be as helpless as newborns, unable to carry out even the most trivial of our daily tasks. Memory also gives us a sense of personal identity; each of us is the sum of our recollections, which is why we feel so threatened when others challenge our memories. Individuals and cultures alike rely on a remembered history for a sense of coherence and meaning; memory gives us our past and guides our future.

The Manufacture of Memory

In ancient times, philosophers compared memory to a soft wax tablet that would preserve anything that chanced to make an imprint on it. Then, with the advent of the printing press, they began to think of memory as a gigantic library, storing specific events and facts for later retrieval. Today, in the audiovisual age, many people compare memory to a tape recorder or a video camera, automatically recording every moment of their lives.

Popular and appealing though this belief about memory is, however, it is utterly wrong. Not everything that happens to us or impinges on our senses is tucked away for later use. Memory is selective. If it were not, our minds would be cluttered with mental junk—the temperature at noon on Thursday, the price of turnips two years ago, a phone number needed only once. Moreover, recovering a memory is not at all like replaying a videotape of an event; it is more like watching a few unconnected frames and then figuring out what the rest of the scene must have been like.

One of the first scientists to make this point was the British psychologist Sir Frederic Bartlett (1932). Bartlett asked people to read lengthy, unfamiliar stories from other cultures and then tell the stories back to him. As the volunteers tried to recall the stories, they made interesting errors: They often eliminated or changed details that did not make sense to them, and they added other details to make the stories coherent, sometimes even adding a moral. Memory, Bartlett concluded, must therefore be largely a *reconstructive process*. We may reproduce some kinds of simple information by rote, said Bartlett, but when we remember complex information, we typically alter it in ways that help us make sense of the material, based on what we already know or think we

source amnesia The inability to distinguish what you originally experienced from what you heard or were told about an event later.

know. Since Bartlett's time, hundreds of studies have found this to be true for everything from stories to conversations to personal experiences (Schacter, 1996, 2001).

In reconstructing their memories, people often draw on many sources. Suppose someone asks you to describe one of your early birthday parties. You may have some direct recollection of the event, but you may also incorporate information from family stories, photographs, or home videos, and even from accounts of other people's birthdays and reenactments of birthdays on television. You take all these bits and pieces and build one integrated account. Later, you may not be able to separate your original experience from what you added after the fact—a phenomenon called **source amnesia**, or *source misattribution*.

A dramatic instance of reconstruction once occurred in Canada with the sad case of H. M., whom we described briefly in Chapter 4. Ever since 1953, when much of H. M.'s hippocampus and the adjacent cortex were surgically removed, he has been unable to form lasting memories for new events, facts, songs, stories, or faces, and so he does not remember much of anything that has happened since his operation (Hilts, 1995; Ogden & Corkin, 1991). To cope with his devastating condition, H. M. has sometimes resorted to reconstructions. On one occasion, after eating a chocolate Valentine's Day heart, H. M. stuck the shiny red wrapping in his shirt pocket. Two hours later, while searching for his handkerchief, he pulled out the paper and looked at it in puzzlement. When a researcher asked why he had the paper in his pocket, he replied, "Well, it could

If these children remember this birthday party later in life, their constructions may include information picked up from family photographs, videos, and stories. Because of source amnesia, they will probably be unable to distinguish their actual memories from information they obtained from elsewhere.

have been wrapped around a big chocolate heart. It must be Valentine's Day!" But a short time later, when she asked him to take out the paper again and say why he had it in his pocket, he replied, "Well, it might have been wrapped around a big chocolate rabbit. It must be Easter!"

Sadly, H. M. *had* to reconstruct the past; his damaged brain could not recall it in any other way. But those of us with normal memory abilities also reconstruct, far more often than we realize.

The Fading Flashbulb

Of course, some unusual, shocking, or tragic events, such as earthquakes or accidents, do hold a special place in memory, especially when we were personally involved. Such events seem frozen in time, with all the details intact. Years ago, Roger Brown and James Kulik (1977) labelled these vivid recollections of emotional events *flashbulb* memories because that term captures the surprise, illumination, and seemingly photographic detail that characterize them. They speculated that the capacity for flashbulb memories may have evolved because such memories had survival value. Remembering the details of a surprising or dangerous experience could have helped our ancestors avoid similar situations.

Despite their intensity, however, even flashbulb memories are not always complete or accurate records of the past. People usually remember the *gist* of a startling, emotional event they experienced or witnessed—say, a violent shoot-out or the assassination of an admired politician—but errors creep into the details (McNally, 2003b). For example, people who saw the 1986 explosion of the space shuttle *Challenger* often swear that they know exactly where they were and what they were doing when the tragedy occurred. On the morning after the explosion, college students reported how they had heard the news. Three years later, when they again recalled how they learned of it, not one student was entirely correct and a third of the students were *completely wrong*, although they felt confident that they were remembering accurately (Neisser & Harsch, 1992). Similarly, 32 months after the announcement of the not-guilty verdict in the controversial trial of O. J. Simpson for the murder of his wife and her friend, only 29 percent of college students' recollections remained accurate, and more than 40 percent contained major distortions (Schmolck, Buffalo, & Squire, 2000). Similar results have been

Thinking Critically About "Flashbulb" Memories

Do you recall where you were and what you were doing on September 11, 2001, when you learned of the attack on the World Trade Center? You probably have a "flashbulb" memory of that event. But even vivid flashbulb memories are not always complete or accurate, and they often change over time.

found for people's flashbulb memories of the destruction of the World Trade Center on September 11, 2001. Students at the University of Toronto were asked to recall details associated with that event one week after and again six months after 9/11. Students who reported a high emotional involvement were more likely to accurately remember event details, but were worse at remembering details about what they were doing when the event occurred (Smith, Bibi, & Sheard, 2003).

Even with flashbulb memories, then, facts tend to get mixed with a little fiction. The conclusion is inescapable: Remembering is an active process, one that involves not only dredging up stored information but also putting two and two together to reconstruct the past. And sometimes we put two and two together and get five.

The Conditions of Confabulation

Because memory is reconstructive, it is subject to **confabulation**—confusing an event that happened to someone else with one that happened to you, or coming to believe that you remember something that never really happened. Such confabulations are especially likely to occur under four circumstances (Garry, Manning, & Loftus, 1996; Hyman & Pentland, 1996; Johnson, 1995):

1   *You have thought about the imagined event many times.* Suppose that at family gatherings you keep

confabulation Confusion of an event that happened to someone else with one that happened to you, or a belief that you remember something when it never actually happened.

hearing about the time that Uncle Sam scared everyone at a New Year's party by pounding a hammer into the wall with such force that the wall collapsed. The story is so colourful that you can practically see Uncle Sam in your mind's eye. The more you think about this event, the more likely you are to believe that you were actually there, even if you were sound asleep in another house. This process has been called "imagination inflation," because your own active imagination inflates your belief that the event really occurred (Garry & Loftus, 2000).

2 *The image of the event contains a lot of details.* Ordinarily, we can distinguish an imagined event from a real one by the amount of detail we recall; real events tend to produce more details. However, the longer you think about an imagined event, the more details you are likely to add—what Sam was wearing, the fact that he'd had too much to drink, the crumbling plaster, people standing around in party hats—and these details may in turn persuade you that the event really happened and that you have a direct memory of it.

3 *The event is easy to imagine.* If forming an image of an event takes little effort (as does visualizing a man pounding a wall with a hammer), then we tend to think that our memory is real. In contrast, when we must make an effort to form an image— for example, of being in a place we have never seen or doing something that is utterly foreign to us—our cognitive efforts apparently serve as a cue that the event did not really take place, or that we were not there when it did.

4 *You focus on your emotional reactions to the event rather than on what actually happened.* Emotional reactions to an imagined event can resemble those that would have occurred in response to a real event, and so they can mislead us. This means that your feelings about an event, no matter how strongly you hold them, are no guarantee that the event really happened. Consider again our Sam story, which happens to be true. A woman we know believed for years that she had been present in the room as an 11-year-old child when her uncle destroyed the wall. Because the story was so vivid and upsetting to her, she felt angry at him for what she thought was his mean and violent behaviour, and she assumed that she must have been angry at the time as well. Then, as an adult, she learned that she was not at the party at all but had merely heard about it repeatedly over the years; and that Sam had not pounded the wall in anger, but as a joke—to inform the assembled guests that he and his wife were about to remodel their home. Nevertheless, our friend's family has had a hard time convincing her that her "memory" of this event is entirely wrong, and they are not sure she believes them yet.

As the Sam story illustrates, and as laboratory research verifies, false memories can be as stable over time as true ones (Brainerd, Reyna, & Brandse, 1995; Poole, 1995; Roediger & McDermott, 1995). And people can believe them just as passionately. There's no getting around it: Memory is reconstructive.

Quick Quiz

Can you reconstruct what you have read so far in order to answer these questions?

1. Memory is like (a) a wax tablet, (b) a giant file cabinet, (c) a video camera, (d) none of these.
2. *True or false?*: Because they are so vivid, flashbulb memories do not become distorted over time.
3. Which of the following confabulated "memories" might people be most inclined to accept as having really happened to them, and why? (a) being lost in a shopping centre at the age of 5, (b) taking a class in astrophysics, (c) visiting a monastery in Tibet as a child, (d) being bullied by another kid in the fourth grade

Answers:

1. d
2. false
3. a and d because they are common events that are easy to imagine in vivid detail. It would be harder to induce someone to believe that he or she had studied astrophysics or visited Tibet, because these are rare events that take effort and knowledge to imagine.

NEVER FORGETS   SOMETIMES FORGETS   ALWAYS FORGETS

WHAT'S AHEAD

- Can your memories of an event be affected by the way someone questions you about them?
- Can children's testimony about sexual abuse be trusted?

MEMORY AND THE POWER OF SUGGESTION

The reconstructive nature of memory helps the mind work efficiently. Instead of cramming our brains with infinite details, we can store the essentials of an experience, and then use our knowledge of the world to figure out the specifics when we need them. But precisely because memory is reconstructive, it is also vulnerable to suggestion—to ideas implanted in our minds after the event, which then become associated with it. This fact raises thorny problems in legal cases that involve eyewitness testimony or people's memories of what happened, when, and to whom.

The Eyewitness on Trial

Without the accounts of eyewitnesses, many guilty people would go free. But because memory is reconstructive, eyewitness testimony is not always reliable, even when the witness is certain about the accuracy of his or her report. As a result, some convictions based on such testimony turn out to be tragic mistakes.

Eyewitnesses are especially likely to make mistaken identifications when the suspect's ethnicity differs from their own. When people say of another group, "They all look alike to me," unfortunately, they are often telling the truth. Because of unfamiliarity with or prejudice toward other ethnic groups, the eyewitness may focus solely on the ethnicity of the person they see committing a crime ("He's black"; "He's white"; "He's an Arab") and ignore the distinctive features that would later make identification more accurate (Levin, 2000). The witness may also rely on ethnic stereotypes to reconstruct what happened (Chance & Goldstein, 1995; Sherman & Bessenoff, 1999).

In a program of research spanning three decades, Elizabeth Loftus and her colleagues have shown that the memories of eyewitnesses are also influenced by the way in which questions are put to the witness and by suggestive comments made during an interrogation or interview. In one classic study, the researchers showed how even subtle changes in the wording of questions can lead a witness to give different answers. People first viewed short films depicting car collisions. Afterward, the researchers asked some of them, "About how fast were the cars going when they hit each other?" Other viewers were asked the same question, but with the verb changed to *smashed, collided, bumped,* or *contacted.* Estimates of how fast the cars were going varied, depending on which word was used. *Smashed* produced the highest average speed estimates (40.8 mph), followed by *collided* (39.3 mph), *bumped* (38.1 mph), *hit* (34.0 mph), and *contacted* (31.8 mph) (Loftus & Palmer, 1974).

In a similar study, the researchers asked some participants, "Did you see a broken headlight?" but asked others, "Did you see the broken headlight?" (Loftus & Zanni, 1975). The question with *the* presupposes a broken headlight and merely asks whether the witness saw it, whereas the question with *a* makes no such presupposition. People who received questions with *the* were far more likely to report having seen something that had not really appeared in the film than were those who received questions with *a*. If a tiny word like *the* can lead people to "remember" what they never saw, you can imagine how the leading questions of police detectives and lawyers might influence a witness's recall.

Misleading information from other sources, too, can profoundly alter what witnesses report. Consider what happened when students were shown the face of a young man who had straight hair, then heard a description of the face supposedly written by another witness—a description that wrongly said the man had light, curly hair (see Figure 8.1). When the students reconstructed

FIGURE 8.1 The Influence of Misleading Information

In a study described in the text, students saw the face of a young man with straight hair, and then had to reconstruct it from memory. On the left is one student's reconstruction in the absence of misleading information about the man's hair. On the right is another person's reconstruction of the same face after exposure to misleading information that mentioned light, curly hair (Loftus & Greene, 1980).

the face using a kit of facial features, a third of their reconstructions contained the misleading detail, whereas only five percent contained it when curly hair was not mentioned (Loftus & Greene, 1980).

Leading questions, suggestive comments, and misleading information affect people's memories not only for events they have witnessed but for their own experiences as well. Researchers have been able to induce people to "recall" complicated events from early in life that never actually happened at all, such as getting lost in a shopping mall, being hospitalized for a high fever, being harassed by a bully, or spilling punch all over the mother of the bride at a wedding (Hyman & Pentland, 1996; Loftus & Pickrell, 1995; Mazzoni et al., 1999). Researchers at the University of Victoria have shown that people are more likely to have such false recollections of events that never happened if the questions about the event are accompanied by photographs that could plausibly have been related to the pseudomemory (Lindsay et al., 2004). In one such study, when people were shown a phoney Disneyland ad featuring Bugs Bunny, about a third later recalled having met a Bugs character at Disneyland (Braun, Ellis, & Loftus, 2002). Some even claimed to remember shaking hands with the character or seeing him in a parade. But these "memories" were impossible, because Bugs Bunny is a Warner

Bros. creation and would definitely be rabbit non grata at Disneyland!

Children's Testimony

The power of suggestion can affect anyone, but many people are especially concerned about its impact on children being questioned about possible sexual abuse. For many decades, most adults believed that children's memories could not be trusted, because young children confuse fantasy with reality and are easily influenced by adults. Then, as the issue of child abuse came to public attention in the 1970s and 1980s, some people began to argue that no child would ever lie about or misremember such a traumatic experience.

Resolving this debate became critical as accusations of child abuse in daycare centres increased across the country. In 1992, for example, a case of abuse in an unlicensed daycare in Martensville, Saskatchewan, was highly publicized. The RCMP arrested nine people, including two of the daycare's owners and several police officers. In all, more than 100 charges of sexual and physical abuse were laid. What sparked the investigation was a parent's noticing a diaper rash on her child. None of the children had complained of abuse, and no parent had actually witnessed any. But during the investigation a police officer repeatedly questioned the children at the daycare, using suggestive techniques in order to obtain testimonies of abuse. Rumours of child mutilation, satanic cults, and other ritualistic abuse spread quickly through the community. Were these people really guilty of unspeakable acts, or had the children been persuaded to make up fanciful stories?

After reviewing the research on this issue, Stephen Ceci from Cornell and Maggie Bruck from McGill University (1995) concluded that both extreme positions—"children always lie" and "children never lie"—are wrong. Ceci and Bruck found that most young children *do* recollect accurately most of what they have observed or experienced. On the other hand, many children *will* say that something happened when it did not. Like adults, they can be influenced by leading questions and suggestions from the person interviewing them. Therefore, instead of asking, "Are children suggestible?" or "Are children's memories accurate?" Ceci and Bruck (1995) proposed asking a more useful question: "Under what conditions are children apt to be suggestible?"

Thinking Critically About Children's Testimony

After two decades of investigation, Bruck has concluded that the clear answer is this: When the interviewer strongly believes the child has been molested, and then uses suggestive techniques to get the child to "reveal" it (Bruck, 2003). Interviewers who are biased in this way fail to think critically; they seek only confirming evidence and ignore discrepant evidence and other explanations for a child's behaviour (Bruck, 2003). They do not accept a child's denial of having been molested; they assume the child is merely "in denial." They use techniques that encourage imagination inflation ("Let's pretend it happened"), which blur reality and fantasy in the child's mind. They pressure or encourage the child to say that certain terrible things happened, they badger the child with repeated questions, they claim that "everyone else" said it happened, or they use bribes and threats (Poole & Lamb, 1998).

One team of researchers analyzed the transcripts of interrogations of children in a case at the McMartin Preschool similar to the Martensville one, and then applied the same suggestive techniques in an experiment with preschool children (Garven et al., 1998). A young man visited the children at their school, read them a story, and handed out treats. The man did nothing aggressive, inappropriate, or surprising. A week later the experimenter questioned the children about the man's visit. She asked children in one group leading questions (Did he shove the teacher? Did he throw a crayon at a kid who was talking?). She asked a second group the same questions, but also used influence techniques used by interrogators in the McMartin and other daycare cases: for example, telling the children what "other kids" had supposedly said, expressing disappointment if answers were negative, and praising children for making allegations.

In the first group, children said "yes, it happened" to about 15 percent of the false allegations about the man's visit. This finding alone refutes the notion that children never lie, misremember, or make things up. In the second group, the three-year-olds, on average, said yes to over 80 percent of the false allegations suggested to them, and the four- to six-year-olds said yes to about half of the allegations (see Figure 8.2). Note that the interviews in this study lasted only 5 to 10 minutes, whereas in actual investigations, interviewers often question children repeatedly over many weeks.

Some people argue that children cannot be induced to report real-life traumatic experiences that never actually happened to them, but that is not so. When schoolchildren were asked for their recollections of an actual sniper incident at their school, many who had been absent from school on

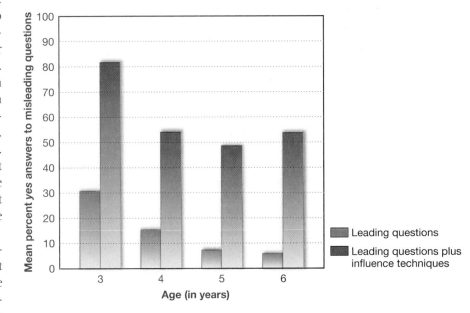

FIGURE 8.2 Social Pressure and Children's False Allegations

When researchers asked preschoolers whether a previous visitor had shoved the teacher, thrown a crayon at a child, or done other aggressive things that had not actually occurred, many said that yes, he had. But when the researchers used influence techniques taken from actual child abuse investigations, *most* of the children said yes (Garven et al., 1998).

that day reported memories of hearing shots, seeing someone lying on the ground, and other details they could not possibly have experienced directly. Apparently, they had been influenced by the accounts of the children who had been there (Pynoos & Nader, 1989).

Research on this important subject has also revealed how children can be interviewed to *reduce* the chances of false reporting. For example, if the interviewer says, "Tell me the reason you came to talk to me today," and nothing more, most actual victims will disclose what happened to them (Bruck, 2003). But here too it is crucial for interviewers to be unbiased and keep an open

mind, so that they do not misunderstand young children's use of words in their replies (one little girl thought her "private parts" were her elbows!) or very young children's habit of drifting from topic to topic (Poole & Lamb, 1998).

In sum, children, like adults, can be accurate in what they report; and, also like adults, they can distort, forget, fantasize, and be misled. As research shows, their memory processes are only human. And the Martensville case? Of the nine people charged, only two were convicted of abuse—and these convictions were later overturned.

Quick Quiz

Now see if your memory processes are accurate.

1. *True or false?*: Mistaken identifications are more likely when a suspect's ethnicity differs from that of the eyewitness, even when the witness feels certain about being accurate.

2. Research suggests that the best way to encourage truthful testimony by children is to (a) reassure them that their friends have had the same experience, (b) reward them for telling you that something happened, (c) scold them if you believe they are lying, (d) avoid leading questions.

3. In psychotherapy, hundreds of people have claimed to recall long-buried memories of having taken part in satanic rituals involving animal and human torture and sacrifice. Yet investigators have been unable to confirm any of these reports (Goodman et al., 1995). Based on what you have learned so far, how might you explain such "memories"?

Answers:

1. true
2. d
3. Therapists who uncritically assume that satanic cults are widespread may ask leading questions and otherwise influence their patients. Patients who are susceptible to their therapists' interpretations may then confabulate and "remember" experiences that did not happen, borrowing details from fictionalized accounts or from other troubling experiences in their lives (Ofshe & Watters, 1994). The result may be source amnesia and the patient's mistaken conviction that the memory is real.

WHAT'S AHEAD

- In general, which is easier: a multiple-choice question or a short-answer essay question?
- Can you know something without knowing that you know it?
- Why is the computer often used as a metaphor for the mind?

IN PURSUIT OF MEMORY

Now that we have seen how memory *doesn't* work—namely, like a tape recorder, an infallible fil-

ing system, or a journal written in indelible ink—we turn to studies of how it *does* work. The ability to remember is not an absolute talent; it depends on the type of performance being called for. If you have a preference for multiple-choice, essay, or true-false exams, you already know this.

Measuring Memory

Conscious, intentional recollection of an event or an item of information is called **explicit memory**. It is usually measured using one of two methods. The first method tests for **recall**, the ability to retrieve and reproduce information encountered

explicit memory Conscious, intentional recollection of an event or of an item of information.

recall The ability to retrieve and reproduce from memory previously encountered material.

earlier. Essay and fill-in-the-blank exams and memory games such as Trivial Pursuit™ or *Jeopardy* require recall. The second method tests for **recognition**, the ability to identify information you have previously observed, read, or heard. The information is given to you, and all you have to do is say whether it is old or new, or perhaps correct or incorrect, or pick it out of a set of alternatives. The task, in other words, is to compare the information you are given with the information stored in your memory. True-false and multiple-choice tests call for recognition.

Recognition tests can be tricky, especially when false items closely resemble correct ones. Under most circumstances, however, recognition is easier than recall. Recognition for visual images is particularly impressive. If you show people 2500 slides of faces and places, and later you ask them to identify which ones they saw out of a larger set, they

will be able to accurately identify more than 90 percent of the original slides (Haber, 1970).

The superiority of recognition over recall was once demonstrated in a study of people's memories of their high-school classmates (Bahrick, Bahrick, & Wittlinger, 1975). The participants, ages 17 to 74, first wrote down the names of as many classmates as they could remember. Recall was poor; even when prompted with yearbook pictures, the youngest people failed to name almost a third of their classmates, and the oldest failed to name most of them. Recognition, however, was far better. When asked to look at a series of cards, each of which contained a set of five photographs, and to say which picture in each set showed a former classmate, recent graduates were right 90 percent of the time—and so were people who had graduated 35 years earlier. The ability to recognize names was nearly as impressive.

recognition The ability to identify previously encountered material.

8.2

Get Involved   Recalling Rudolph's Friends

You can try this test of recall if you are familiar with the poem "'Twas the Night Before Christmas" or the song "Rudolph the Red-Nosed Reindeer." Rudolph had eight reindeer friends; name as many of them as you can. After you have done your best, turn to the "Get Involved" exercise on page 260 for a recognition test on the same information.

Sometimes, information encountered in the past affects our thoughts and actions even though we do not consciously or intentionally remember it—a phenomenon that UBC psychologist Peter Graf and others call **implicit memory** (Graf & Schacter, 1985; Schacter, Chiu, & Ochsner, 1993). To get at this subtle sort of knowledge, researchers must rely on indirect methods, instead of the direct ones used to measure explicit memory. One common method, **priming**, asks you to read or listen to some information and then tests you later to see whether the information affects your performance on another type of task.

Another method of measuring implicit memory, the **relearning method**, or *savings method*, was devised by Hermann Ebbinghaus (1885/1913)

PRIMING

Exposure to information   Influences   Responses to *different* task

over a century ago. The relearning method requires you to relearn information or a task that you have learned earlier. If you master it more quickly the second time around, you must be remembering something from the first experience.

Suppose that you had to read a list of words, some of which began with the letters *def* (such as *define*, *defend*, or *deform*). Later you might be asked

implicit memory Unconscious retention in memory, as evidenced by the effect of a previous experience or previously encountered information on current thoughts or actions.

priming A method for measuring implicit memory in which a person reads or listens to information and is later tested to see whether the information affects performance on another type of task.

relearning method A method for measuring retention that compares the time required to relearn material with the time used to learn the material initially.

to complete word stems (such as *def-*) with the first word that comes to mind. Even if you could not recognize or recall the original words very well, you would be more likely to complete the word fragments with words from the list than you would be if you had not seen the list. In this procedure, the original words "prime" certain responses on the word-completion task (that is, make them more available), showing that people can retain more knowledge about the past than they realize. They know more than they know that they know (Richardson-Klavehn & Bjork, 1988; Roediger, 1990).

Models of Memory

Although people usually refer to memory as a single faculty, as in "I must be losing my memory" or "He has a memory like an elephant's," the term *memory* actually covers a complex collection of abilities and processes. If video or movie cameras are not accurate metaphors for capturing these diverse components of memory, then what metaphor would be better?

As we saw in Chapter 7, many cognitive psychologists liken the mind to an information processor, along the lines of a computer, though more complex. They have constructed *information-processing models* of cognitive processes, liberally borrowing computer-programming terms such as *input, output, accessing,* and *information retrieval.* When you type something on your computer's keyboard, the machine encodes the information into an electronic language, stores it on a disk, and retrieves it when you need to use it. Similarly, in information-processing models of memory, we *encode* information (convert it to a form that the brain can process and use), *store* the information (retain it over time), and *retrieve* the information (recover it for use). In storage, the information may be represented as

concepts, propositions, images, or *cognitive schemas,* mental networks of knowledge, beliefs, and expectations concerning particular topics or aspects of the world. (If you can't retrieve these terms, see Chapter 7.)

In most information-processing models, storage takes place in three interacting memory systems. *A sensory register* retains incoming sensory information for a second or two, until it can be processed further. *Short-term memory (STM)* holds a limited amount of information for a brief period of time, perhaps up to 30 seconds or so, unless a conscious effort is made to keep it there longer. *Long-term memory (LTM)* accounts for longer storage—from a few minutes to decades (Atkinson & Shiffrin, 1968, 1971). Information can pass from the sensory register into short-term memory, and in either direction between short-term and long-term memory, as illustrated in Figure 8.3.

This model, which is often informally called the *"three-box model,"* has dominated research on memory since the late 1960s. However, critics of the three-box model note that the human brain does not operate like your average computer. Most computers process instructions and data sequentially, so the three-box model has emphasized sequential operations; but the human brain performs many operations simultaneously, in parallel. It recognizes patterns all at once rather than as a sequence of information bits, and it perceives new information, produces speech, and searches memory all at the same time. It can do this because millions of neurons are active at once, and each neuron communicates with thousands of others, which in turn communicate with millions more.

Because of these differences between human beings and machines, some cognitive scientists prefer a **parallel distributed processing (PDP)**, or *connectionist,* model. Instead of representing

parallel distributed processing (PDP) model A model of memory in which knowledge is represented as connections among thousands of interacting processing units, distributed in a vast network and all operating in parallel.

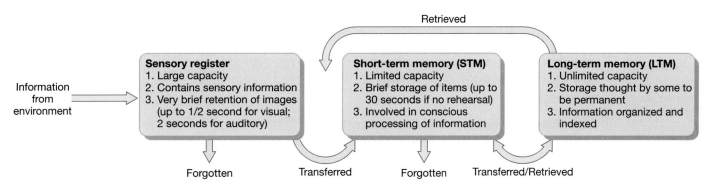

FIGURE 8.3 Three Memory Systems

In the "three-box model" of memory, information that does not transfer out of sensory memory or short-term memory is assumed to be forgotten forever. Once in long-term memory, information can be retrieved for use in analyzing incoming sensory information or performing mental operations in short-term memory.

information as flowing from one system to another, a PDP model represents the contents of memory as connections among a huge number of interacting processing units, distributed in a vast network and all operating in parallel—just like the neurons of the brain (McClelland, 1994; Rumelhart, McClelland, & the PDP Research Group, 1986). As information enters the system, the ability of these units to excite or inhibit each other is constantly adjusted to reflect new knowledge.

Memory researchers are still arguing about which model of memory is most useful. In this chapter, we emphasize the three-box model, but keep in mind that the computer metaphor that inspired it could one day be as outdated as the metaphor of memory as a camera.

Quick Quiz

How well have you encoded and stored what you just learned?

1. Alberta solved a crossword puzzle a few days ago. She no longer recalls the words in the puzzle, but while playing a game of Scrabble, she unconsciously tends to form words that were in the puzzle, showing that she has _____ memories of some of the words.

2. The three basic memory processes are _____, storage, and _____.

3. Do the preceding two questions ask for recall, recognition, or relearning? (And what about this question?)

4. One objection to traditional information-processing theories of memory is that, unlike most computers, the brain performs many independent operations _____.

Answers:

4. simultaneously, or in parallel
3. The first two questions both measure recall; the third question measures recognition.
1. implicit   2. encoding, retrieval

WHAT'S AHEAD

- Why is short-term memory like a leaky bucket?
- When a word is on the tip of your tongue, what errors are you likely to make in recalling it?
- What's the difference between "knowing how" and "knowing that"?

THE THREE-BOX MODEL OF MEMORY

The information-processing model of three sepa-rate memory systems—sensory, short-term, and long-term—remains a leading approach because it offers a convenient way to organize the major findings on memory, does a good job of accounting

8.3

for these findings, and is consistent with the biological facts about memory described in Chapter 4. Let us now peer into each of the "boxes."

The Sensory Register: Fleeting Impressions

In the three-box model, all incoming sensory information must make a brief stop in the **sensory register**, the entryway of memory. The sensory register includes a number of separate subsystems, as many as there are senses. Visual images remain in a visual subsystem for a maximum of half a second. Auditory images remain in an auditory subsystem for a slightly longer time—by most estimates, up to two seconds or so.

sensory register A memory system that accurately but very briefly registers sensory information before the information fades or moves into short-term memory.

Get Involved   Your Sensory Register at Work

In a dark room or closet, swing a flashlight rapidly in a circle. You will see an unbroken circle of light instead of a series of separate points. The reason: The successive images remain briefly in the visual subsystem of the sensory register.

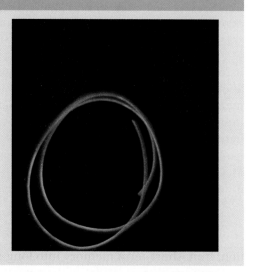

The sensory register acts as a holding bin, retaining information in a highly accurate form until we can select items for attention from the stream of stimuli bombarding our senses. It gives us a brief time to decide whether information is extraneous or important; not everything detected by our senses warrants our attention.

Information that does not quickly go on to short-term memory vanishes forever, like a message written in disappearing ink. That is why people who see an array of 12 letters for just a fraction of a second can report only 4 or 5 of them; by the time they answer, their sensory memories are already fading (Sperling, 1960). The fleeting nature of incoming sensations is actually beneficial; it prevents multiple sensory images—"double exposures"—that might interfere with the accurate perception and encoding of information.

Short-Term Memory: Memory's Scratch Pad

Like the sensory register, **short-term memory (STM)** retains information only temporarily—for up to about 30 seconds by most estimates, although some researchers think that the maximum interval may extend to a few minutes for certain tasks. In short-term memory, the material is no longer an exact sensory image but an encoding of one, such as a word or a phrase. This material either transfers into long-term memory or decays and is lost forever.

Individuals with brain injury, such as H. M., demonstrate the importance of transferring new information from short-term memory into long-term memory. H. M., you will recall, can store information on a short-term basis; he can hold a conversation and he appears to be fine when you first meet him. He also retains implicit memories. However, for the most part, H. M. and other patients like him cannot retain explicit information about new facts and events for longer than a few minutes. Their terrible memory deficits involve a problem in transferring explicit memories from short-term storage into long-term storage. With a great deal of repetition and drill, they can learn some new visual information, retain it in long-term memory, and recall it normally (McKee &

short-term memory (STM) In the three-box model of memory, a limited-capacity memory system involved in the retention of information for brief periods; it is also used to hold information retrieved from long-term memory for temporary use.

Squire, 1992). But usually information does not get into long-term memory in the first place.

Besides retaining new information for brief periods while we are learning it, short-term memory holds information that has been retrieved from long-term memory for temporary use, providing the mental equivalent of a scratch pad while we solve particular problems. Because of the active nature of this process, many psychologists now refer to **working memory**, which includes (a) short-term memory plus (b) the mental processes that control the retrieval of information from long-term memory and interpret that information appropriately depending on the task you are doing (Baddeley, 1992). When you do an arithmetic problem, your working memory contains the numbers and the instructions for doing the necessary operations, and it also carries out those operations and retains the intermediate results from each step. The ability to bring information from long-term memory into working memory is not disrupted in patients like H. M. They can do arithmetic, converse, relate events that predate their injury, and do anything else that requires retrieval of information from long-term into short-term memory. Their problem is with the flow of information in the other direction, from short-term memory into long-term.

People such as H. M. fall at the extreme end of a continuum of forgetfulness, but even those of us with normal memories know from personal experience how frustratingly brief short-term retention can be. We look up a telephone number, are distracted for a moment, and find that the number has vanished from our minds. We meet someone at a gathering and two minutes later find ourselves groping unsuccessfully for the person's name. Is it any wonder that short-term memory has been called a "leaky bucket"?

According to most memory models, if the bucket did not leak it would quickly overflow, because at any given moment short-term memory can hold only so many items. Years ago, George Miller (1956) estimated its capacity to be "the magical number 7 plus or minus 2." Five-digit zip codes and seven-digit telephone numbers fall conveniently in this range; 16-digit credit card numbers do not. Some researchers have questioned whether Miller's magical number is so magical after all; estimates of STM's capacity have ranged from 2 items to 20, with one recent estimate putting the "magical number" at around 4 (Cowan, 2001). Everyone agrees, however, that the number of items that short-term memory can handle at any one time is small.

If this is so, then how do we remember the beginning of a spoken sentence until the speaker reaches the end? After all, most sentences are longer than just a few words. According to most information-processing models of memory, we overcome this problem by grouping small bits of information into larger units, or **chunks**. The real capacity of STM, it turns out, is not a few bits of information but a few chunks. A chunk may be a word, a phrase, a sentence, or even a visual image, and it depends on previous experience. For most Canadians, the acronym RCMP is one chunk, not four, and the date 1867 is one chunk, not four. In contrast, the number 9214 is four chunks and IBF is three—unless your address is 9214 or your initials are IBF. To take a more visual example: If you are unfamiliar with basketball and look at a court full of players, you probably won't be able to remember their positions when you look away. But if you are a fan of the game, you may see a single chunk of information—say, a full-court press—and be able to retain it. Thus, some information is more "chunkable" because of experience. Consistent with this idea, studies at the University of Manitoba have shown that pronounceable chunks are easier to learn and recall than random collections of letters (McMurray & Duffy, 1972), which is what some people's names look like to those who have no experience with that nationality.

chunk A meaningful unit of information; it may be composed of smaller units.

working memory Short-term memory plus the mental processes that control retrieval of information from long-term memory and interpret that information appropriately for a given task.

If you do not play chess, you probably will not be able to recall the positions of these chess pieces after looking away. But experienced chess players can remember the position of every piece after glancing only briefly at the board. They are able to "chunk" the pieces into a few standard configurations, instead of trying to memorize where each piece is located.

Even chunking cannot keep short-term memory from eventually filling up. Fortunately, much of the information we take in during the day is needed for only a few moments. If you are multiplying two numbers, you need to remember them only until you have the answer. If you are talking to someone, you need to keep the person's words in mind only until you have understood them. But some incoming information is needed for longer periods and must be transferred to long-term memory. Items that are particularly meaningful, have an emotional impact, or relate to something already in long-term memory may enter long-term storage easily, with only a brief stay in STM. The destiny of other items depends on how soon new information displaces them in short-term memory. Material in short-term memory is easily displaced unless we do something to keep it there, as we will discuss shortly.

Long-Term Memory: Final Destination

The third box in the three-box model of memory is **long-term memory (LTM)**. The capacity of long-term memory seems to have no practical limits. The vast amount of information stored there enables us to learn, get around in the environment, and build a sense of identity and a personal history.

Organization in Long-Term Memory Because long-term memory contains so much information, it must be organized in some way, so that we can find the particular items we're looking for. One way to organize words (or the concepts they represent) is by the *semantic categories* to which they belong. *Chair*, for example, belongs to the category *furniture*. In a study done many years ago, people had to memorize 60 words that came from four semantic categories: animals, vegetables, names, and professions. The words were presented in random order, but when people were allowed to recall the items in any order they wished, they tended to recall them in clusters corresponding to the four categories (Bousfield, 1953). This finding has been replicated many times.

Evidence on the storage of information by semantic category also comes from cases of people with brain damage. In one such case, a patient called M. D. appeared to have made a complete recovery after suffering several strokes, with one odd exception: He had trouble remembering the names of fruits and vegetables (see illustration on p. 186 of Chapter 6). M. D. could easily name a picture of an abacus or a sphinx, but he drew a

blank when he saw a picture of an apple or a carrot. He could sort pictures of animals, vehicles, and other objects into their appropriate categories but did poorly with pictures of fruits and vegetables. On the other hand, when M. D. was *given* the names of fruits and vegetables, he immediately pointed to the corresponding pictures (Hart, Berndt, & Caramazza, 1985). Apparently, M. D. still had information stored about fruits and vegetables, but his brain damage prevented him from using their names to get to the information when he needed it, unless the names were provided by someone else. This evidence suggests that information about a particular concept (such as *orange*) is linked in some way to information about the concept's semantic category (such as *fruit*).

Moreover, M. D. demonstrates another fascinating semantic category impairment—a problem with biological categories but not nonbiological ones. Researchers at McGill found the same pattern in people with Alzheimer's type dementia (Whatmough et al., 2003). Other Montreal researchers have suggested that memory categories might be organized around living and nonliving concepts (Gold et al., 2003).

Indeed, many models of long-term memory represent its contents as a vast network of interrelated concepts and propositions (Anderson, 1990; Collins & Loftus, 1975). In these models, a small part of a conceptual network for animals might look something like the one in Figure 8.4. The

Culture affects the encoding, storage, and retrieval of information in long-term memory. Navajo healers, who use stylized, symbolic sand paintings in their rituals, must be able to commit to memory dozens of intricate visual designs because no exact copies are made and the paintings are destroyed after each ceremony.

long-term memory (LTM) In the three-box model of memory, the memory system involved in the long-term storage of information.

8.6

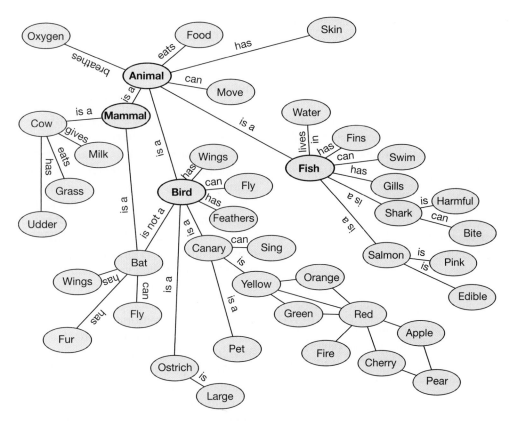

FIGURE 8.4 Part of a Conceptual Grid in Long-Term Memory

Many models of memory represent the contents of long-term semantic memory as an immense network or grid of concepts and the relationships among them. This illustration shows part of a hypothetical grid for *animals*.

way people use these networks, however, depends on experience and education. For example, in rural Liberia, the more schooling children have, the more likely they are to use semantic categories in recalling lists of objects (Cole & Scribner, 1974). This makes sense, because in school, children must memorize a lot of information in a short time, and semantic groupings can help. Unschooled children, having less need to memorize lists, do not cluster items and do not remember them as well as schooled children do. But this does not mean that unschooled children have poor memories. When the task is meaningful to them—say, recalling objects that were in a story or a village scene—they remember extremely well (Mistry & Rogoff, 1994).

We organize information in long-term memory not only by semantic groupings but also in terms of the way words sound or look. Have you ever tried to recall some word that was on the "tip of your tongue"? Nearly everyone experiences such *tip-of-the-tongue (TOT) states*, especially when trying to recall the names of acquaintances or famous persons, the names of objects and places, or the titles of movies or books (Burke et al., 1991). TOT states are reported even by users of sign language, who call them tip-of-the-finger states!

One way to study this frustrating experience is to have people record tip-of-the-tongue episodes in daily diaries. Another is to give people the definitions of uncommon words and ask them to supply the words. When a word is on the tip of the tongue, people tend to come up with words that are similar in meaning to the right one before they finally recall it. For example, for "patronage bestowed on a relative, in business or politics" a person might say "favouritism" rather than the correct response, "nepotism." But verbal information in long-term memory also seems to be indexed by sound and form, and it is retrievable on that basis. Incorrect guesses often have the correct number of syllables, the correct stress pattern, the correct first letter, or the correct prefix or suffix (Brown & McNeill, 1966). For example, for the target word *sampan* (an Asian boat), a person might say "Siam" or "sarong."

semantic memories Memories of general knowledge, including facts, rules, concepts, and propositions.

episodic memories Memories of personally experienced events and the contexts in which they occurred.

procedural memories Memories for the performance of actions or skills ("knowing how").

declarative memories Memories of facts, rules, concepts, and events ("knowing that"); they include semantic and episodic memories.

Information in long-term memory may also be organized by its familiarity, relevance, or association with other information. The method used in any given instance probably depends on the nature of the memory; you would no doubt store information about the major cities of Europe differently from information about your first date. For instance, when Daniel Yarmey (1973) at the University of Guelph showed students 50 pictures of famous people, the students searched systematically through their memory for the people's names using such categories as first letters, professions, where they were last seen, and so on. To understand the organization of long-term memory, then, we must know what kinds of information can be stored there.

The Contents of Long-Term Memory Most theories of memory distinguish skills or habits ("knowing how") from abstract or representational knowledge ("knowing that"). **Procedural memories** are memories of knowing how to do something—for example, knowing how to comb your hair, use a pencil, solve a jigsaw puzzle, knit a sweater, or swim. Many researchers consider procedural memories to be implicit, because once skills and habits are well learned, they do not require much conscious processing. **Declarative memories**, on the other hand, are memories of knowing that something is true, as in knowing that Ottawa is the capital of Canada; they are usually assumed to be explicit.

When he was at the University of Toronto, Endel Tulving showed that declarative memories, in turn, come in two varieties: semantic memories and episodic memories (Tulving, 1985). **Semantic memories** are internal representations of the world, independent of any particular context. They include facts, rules, concepts, and propositions—items of general knowledge. On the basis of your semantic memory of the concept *cat*, you can describe a cat as a small, furry mammal that typically spends its time eating, sleeping, prowling, and staring into space, even though a cat may not be present when you give this description, and you probably won't know how or when you first learned it. **Episodic memories** are internal representations of personally experienced events. When you remember how your cat once surprised you in the middle of the night by pouncing on your face as you slept, you are retrieving an episodic memory.

In this way, episodic memory allows for self-awareness. Think of how you would answer the question "Who are you?" You might mention your nationality (remembering where you were born), your hobbies (remembering that you played the guitar yesterday), and so on. In other words, your sense of who you are is created by remembering what has happened to you—the contents of your episodic memory. Tulving presents a case study of a person who, following a motorcycle accident, lost episodic but not semantic memory. As a result, he lost the ability to know who he was (Tulving, 2001). Figure 8.5 summarizes these kinds of memories.

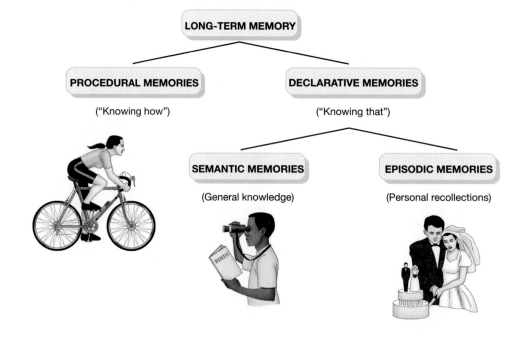

FIGURE 8.5 Types of Long-Term Memories

This diagram summarizes the distinctions among long-term memories. Can you come up with other examples of each memory type?

As we saw in Chapter 4, with sufficient practice, patients such as H. M., who cannot form new declarative memories because of damage to the hippocampus, can acquire new procedural memories; they can learn to solve a puzzle, read mirror-reversed words, or play tennis—even though they do not remember the training sessions in which they learned these skills. Apparently the parts of the brain involved in acquiring procedural memories have remained intact. Conversely, studies at Brock and Simon Fraser universities have discovered that students with learning disabilities may not only have difficulty recalling some everyday declarative memories but also procedural memories for such things as using the library (McNamara & Wong, 2003).

From Short-Term to Long-Term Memory: A Riddle The three-box model of memory is often invoked to explain an interesting phenomenon called the **serial-position effect**. If you are shown a list of items and are then asked immediately to recall them, your retention of any particular item will depend on its position in the list (Glanzer & Cunitz, 1966). Recall will be best for items at the beginning of the list (the **primacy effect**) and at the end of the list (the **recency effect**). When retention of all the items is plotted, the result is a U-shaped curve, as shown in Figure 8.6. A serial-position effect occurs when you are introduced to a lot of people at a party and find you can recall the names of the first few people you met and the last, but almost no one in between. In a fascinating application of the serial-position effect, researchers at the University of Alberta discovered that children who got lost when retracing a route (coming home, for example) did so in the middle of the route and not at the beginning or end (Cornell et al., 1996). This increased police officers' abilities to locate children who had become lost finding their way to a destination. They looked first in the middle of the route!

According to the three-box model, the first few items on a list are remembered well because

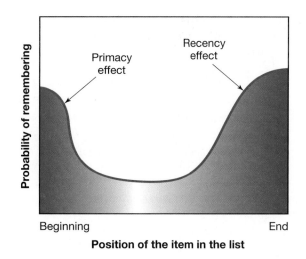

FIGURE 8.6 The Serial-Position Effect
When people try to recall a list of similar items immediately after learning it, they tend to remember the first and last items best and the ones in the middle worst.

short-term memory was relatively "empty" when they entered, so these items did not have to compete with others to make it into long-term memory. They were thoroughly processed, so they remain memorable. The last few items are remembered for a different reason: At the time of recall, they are still sitting in short-term memory. The items in the middle of a list, however, are not so well retained because by the time they get into short-term memory, it is already crowded. As a result, many of these items drop out of short-term memory before they can be stored in long-term memory.

This explanation makes sense except for one thing: Under some conditions, the last items on a list are well remembered even when the test is delayed past the time when short-term memory has presumably been "emptied" and filled with other information (Greene, 1986). In other words, the recency effect occurs even when, according to the three-box model, it should not. At present, then, the serial-position curve remains something of a puzzle.

serial-position effect The tendency for recall of the first and last items on a list to surpass recall of items in the middle of the list.

primacy effect The tendency to remember items at the beginning of a list more easily than other items in the list.

recency effect The tendency to remember items at the end of a list more easily than other items in the list.

Quick Quiz

Find out whether the findings just discussed have transferred from your short-term memory to your long-term memory.

1. The _____ holds images for a fraction of a second.

2. For most people, the abbreviation *P.E.I.* consists of _____ informational chunk(s).

3. Suppose you must memorize a long list of words that includes the following: *desk, pig, gold, dog, chair, silver, table, rooster, bed, copper,* and *horse.* If you can recall the words in any order you wish, how are you likely to group them in recall? Why?

4. When you rollerblade, are you relying on episodic, procedural, or semantic memory? How about when you recall the months of the year? Or when you remember falling while rollerblading on an icy January day?

5. If a child is trying to memorize the alphabet, which sequence should present the greatest difficulty: *abcdefg, klmnopq,* or *tuvwxyz*? Why?

Answers:

1. sensory register 2. one
3. Desk, chair, table, and bed would probably form one cluster; pig, dog, rooster, and horse a second; and gold, silver, and copper a third. Concepts tend to be organized in long-term memory in terms of semantic categories, such as furniture, animals, and metals.
4. procedural; semantic; episodic
5. klmnopq, because of the serial-position effect

WHAT'S AHEAD

- What's wrong with trying to memorize in a rote fashion when you're studying—and what's a better strategy?

- Memory tricks are fun, but are they always useful?

HOW WE REMEMBER

Once we understand how memory works, we can use that understanding to encode and store infor-

Encoding classroom material for later recall usually takes a deliberate effort. Which of these students do you think will remember the material best?

mation so that it "sticks" and will be there when we need it. What are the best strategies to use?

Effective Encoding

Our memories, as we have seen, are not exact replicas of experience. Sensory information is summarized and encoded—for example, as words or images—almost as soon as it is detected. When you hear a lecture, you may hang on every word (we hope you do), but you do not memorize those words verbatim. You extract the main points and encode them.

To remember information well, you have to encode it accurately in the first place. With some kinds of information, accurate encoding takes place automatically, without effort. Think about where you usually sit in your psychology class. When were you last there? You can probably provide this information easily, even though you never made a deliberate effort to encode it. But many kinds of information require *effortful encoding*—the plot of a novel, the procedures for assembling a cabinet, the arguments for and against a proposed law. To retain such information, you might have to select the main points, label concepts, or associate the information with personal experiences or with material you already know.

NICE TRY, BUT "MID-TERM MEMORY LOSS" ISN'T RECOGNIZED BY THE MEDICAL COMMUNITY!

Unfortunately, the only reason for mid-term memory loss is not studying enough—or in the right way.

Unfortunately, people sometimes count on automatic encoding when effortful encoding is needed. For example, some students wrongly assume that they can encode the material in a textbook as effortlessly as they encode where they sit in the classroom. Or they assume that the ability to remember and perform well on tests is innate and that effort will not make any difference. As a result, they wind up in trouble at test time. Experienced students know that most of the information in a university course requires effortful encoding and sometimes hard work.

Rehearsal

An important technique for keeping information in short-term memory and increasing the chances of long-term retention is *rehearsal*, the review or practice of material while you are learning it. When people are prevented from rehearsing, the contents of their short-term memories quickly fade.

In an early study of this phenomenon, people had to memorize meaningless groups of letters. Immediately afterward, they had to start counting backward by threes from an arbitrary number; this counting prevented them from rehearsing the letter groups. Within only 18 seconds, the subjects forgot most of the items. But when they did not have to count backward, their performance was much better, probably because they were rehearsing the items to themselves (Peterson & Peterson, 1959). You are taking advantage of rehearsal when you look up a telephone number and then repeat it over and over in order to keep it in short-term memory until you no longer need it. And when you can't remember a phone number because you have always used speed dial to call it, you are learning what happens when you *don't* rehearse!

A poignant demonstration of the power of rehearsal once occurred during a session with H. M. (Ogden & Corkin, 1991). The experimenter gave H. M. five digits to repeat and remember, but then she was unexpectedly called away. When she returned after more than an hour, H. M. was able to repeat the five digits correctly. He had been rehearsing them the entire time.

Short-term memory holds many kinds of information, including visual information and abstract meanings. But most people—or at least most hearing people—seem to favour speech for encoding and rehearsing the contents of short-term memory. The speech may be spoken aloud or to oneself. When people make errors on short-term memory tests that use letters or words, they often confuse items that sound the same or similar, such as *d* and *t*, or *bear* and *bare*. These errors suggest that they have been rehearsing verbally.

Some strategies for rehearsing are more effective than others. **Maintenance rehearsal** involves merely the rote repetition of the material. This kind of rehearsal is fine for keeping information in STM, but it will not always lead to long-term retention. A better strategy if you want to remember for the long haul is **elaborative rehearsal**, also called *elaboration of encoding* (Cermak & Craik, 1979; Craik & Tulving, 1975). Elaboration involves associating new items of information with material that has already been stored or with other new facts. It can also involve analyzing the physical, sensory, or semantic features of an item.

Suppose that you are studying the hypothalamus, discussed in Chapter 4. Simply memorizing the definition of the hypothalamus in a rote manner is unlikely to help much. But if you can elaborate the concept of the hypothalamus, you are more likely to remember it. For example, knowing that *hypo* means "under" tells you its location—under the thalamus. Knowing that it is part of the limbic system should provide you with a clue that it is probably involved in survival drives

maintenance rehearsal Rote repetition of material in order to maintain its availability in memory.

elaborative rehearsal Association of new information with already stored knowledge and analysis of the new information to make it memorable.

and emotion. Many students try to pare down what they're learning to the bare essentials, but in fact, knowing more details about something makes it more memorable; that's what elaboration means.

Researchers at the University of Toronto discovered that a related strategy for prolonging retention is **deep processing**, or the processing of meaning (Craik & Lockhart, 1972). If you process only the physical or sensory features of a stimulus, such as how the word *hypothalamus* is spelled and how it sounds, your processing will be shallow even if it is elaborated. If you recognize patterns and assign labels to objects or events ("The *hypothalamus is below the thalamus*"), your processing will be somewhat deeper. If you fully analyze the meaning of what you are trying to remember (for example, by encoding the functions and importance of the hypothalamus), your processing will be deeper yet.

Shallow processing is sometimes useful: When you memorize a poem, for instance, you will want to pay attention to (and elaborately encode) the sounds of the words and the patterns of rhythm in the poem, and not just the poem's meaning. Usually, however, deep processing is more effective. That is why, if you try to memorize information that has little or no meaning for you, the information may not stick.

Mnemonics

In addition to using elaborative rehearsal and deep processing, people who want to give their powers of memory a boost sometimes use **mnemonics** [neh-MON-iks], formal strategies and tricks for encoding, storing, and retaining information. (Mnemosyne, pronounced neh-MOZ-eh-nee, was the ancient Greek goddess of memory. Can you remember her?) Some mnemonics take the form of easily memorized rhymes (e.g., "Thirty days hath September/April, June, and November . . ."). Others use formulas (e.g., "**E**very **g**ood **b**oy **d**oes **f**ine" for remembering which notes are on the lines of the treble clef in musical notation). Still others use visual images or word associations.

The best mnemonics force you to encode material actively and thoroughly. They may also reduce the amount of information by chunking it, which is why, in ads, many companies use words for their phone numbers instead of

unmemorable numbers ("Dial GET RICH"). Advertisers also take advantage of mnemonics to increase the likelihood that we will remember brand names. At the University of Manitoba, Malcolm Smith and Mark Phillips (2001) showed that radio ads featuring rhyming mnemonics were more likely to be recalled and recognized even seven days later, regardless of the age of the listener. Many mnemonics make the material meaningful and thus easier to store and retrieve, say, by having you weave unrelated facts and words into a coherent story (Bower & Clark, 1969). If you needed to remember the parts of the digestive system for a physiology course, you could construct a narrative about what happens to a piece of food from the moment it enters a person's mouth, then repeat the narrative aloud to yourself or to a study partner.

Some stage performers with amazing recall rely on more complicated mnemonics. We are not going to spend time on them here because, for ordinary memory tasks, such tricks are often no more effective than rote rehearsal, and sometimes they are actually worse (Wang, Thomas, & Ouellette, 1992). Most memory researchers do not use such mnemonics themselves (Hébert, 2001). After all, why bother to memorize a grocery list using a fancy mnemonic when you can write down what you need to buy? Not surprisingly, the fastest route to a good memory is to follow the principles suggested by the findings in this section and by the research reviewed in "Taking Psychology With You."

deep processing In the encoding of information, the processing of meaning rather than simply the physical or sensory features of a stimulus.

mnemonics [neh-MON-iks] Strategies and tricks for improving memory, such as the use of a verse or a formula.

OneKey 8.7

"YOU SIMPLY ASSOCIATE EACH NUMBER WITH A WORD, SUCH AS 'TABLE' AND 3,476,029."

Quick Quiz

Perhaps mnemosyne will help you answer this question.

Camille is furious with her history professor. "I read the chapter three times, but I still failed the exam," she fumes. "The test must have been unfair." What's wrong with Camille's reasoning, and what are some other possible explanations for her poor performance, based on principles of critical thinking and what you have learned so far about memory?

Answer:

Camille is reasoning emotionally and is not examining the assumptions underlying her explanations. Perhaps she relied on automatic rather than effortful encoding, used maintenance instead of elaborative rehearsal, and used shallow instead of deep processing when she studied. She may also have tried to encode everything, instead of being selective.

WHAT'S AHEAD

- How might new information "erase" old memories?
- What theory explains why you keep dialing an old area code instead of the new one?
- Why is it easier to recall experiences from elementary school if you see pictures of your classmates?
- Why are many researchers skeptical about claims of "repressed" and "recovered" memories?

WHY WE FORGET

Have you ever, in the heat of some deliriously happy moment, said to yourself, "I'll never forget this, never, *never*, NEVER"? Do you find that you can more clearly remember saying those words than the deliriously happy moment itself? Sometimes you encode an event, you rehearse it, you analyze its meaning, you tuck it away in long-term storage—and still you forget it. Is it any wonder that most of us have wished, at one time or another, for a "photographic memory"?

Actually, having a perfect memory is not the blessing that you might suppose. The Russian psychologist Alexander Luria (1968) once told of a journalist, S., who could reproduce giant grids of numbers both forward and backward, even after the passage of many years. S. also remembered the exact circumstances under which he had originally learned the material. To accomplish his astonishing feats, he used mnemonics, especially the formation of visual images. But you should not envy him, for he had a serious problem: He could not forget even when he wanted to. Along with the diamonds of experience, he

Thinking Critically About Having a Perfect Memory

kept dredging up the pebbles. Images he had formed in order to remember kept creeping into consciousness, distracting him and interfering with his ability to concentrate. At times he even had trouble holding a conversation because the other person's words would set off a jumble of associations. In fact, Luria called him "rather dull-witted." Eventually, S. took to supporting himself by travelling from place to place, demonstrating his mnemonic abilities for audiences.

Paradoxically, then, forgetting is adaptive. We need to forget if we wish to remember efficiently (Bjork, Bjork, & Anderson, 1998). Forgetting also contributes to our survival, our happiness, and our very sanity. Think back; would you really want to recall every angry argument, every embarrassing episode, every painful moment in your life? Could it be that self-confidence and optimism depend on locking some follies and grievances in a back drawer of memory?

Nonetheless, most of us forget more than we wish to, and we would like to know why. In the early days of psychology, in an effort to measure pure memory loss independent of personal experience, Hermann Ebbinghaus (1885/1913) memorized long lists of nonsense syllables, such as *bok*, *waf*, or *ged*, and then tested his retention over a period of several weeks. Most of his forgetting occurred soon after the initial learning and then levelled off (see Figure 8.7a). Ebbinghaus's method of studying memory was adopted by generations of psychologists, even though it did not tell them much about the kinds of memories that people care about most.

A century later, Marigold Linton decided to find out how people forget real events rather than nonsense syllables. Like Ebbinghaus, she used herself as a subject, but she charted the curve of

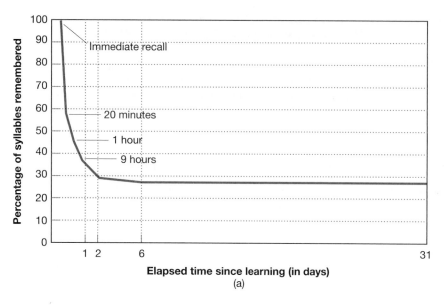

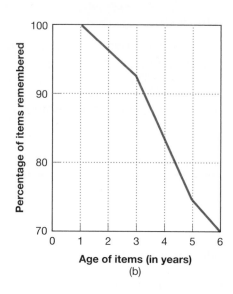

FIGURE 8.7 Two Kinds of Forgetting Curves

When Hermann Ebbinghaus tested his own memory for nonsense syllables, forgetting was rapid at first and then tapered off (a). In contrast, when Marigold Linton tested her own memory for personal events over a period of several years, her retention was excellent at first, but then it fell off at a gradual but steady rate (b).

forgetting over years rather than days. Every day for 12 years she recorded on a 4- × 6-inch card two or more things that had happened to her that day. Eventually, she accumulated a catalogue of thousands of discrete events, both trivial ("I have dinner at the Canton Kitchen: delicious lobster dish") and significant ("I land at Orly Airport in Paris"). Once a month, she took a random sampling of all the cards accumulated to that point, noted whether she could remember the events on them, and tried to date the events. Linton (1978) later told how she had expected the kind of rapid forgetting reported by Ebbinghaus. Instead, as you can see in Figure 8.7b, she found that long-term forgetting was slower and proceeded at a much more constant pace, as details gradually dropped out of her memories.

Of course, some memories, especially those that mark important transitions, are more memorable than others. But why did Marigold Linton, like the rest of us, forget so many details? Psychologists have proposed five mechanisms to account for forgetting: decay, replacement of old memories by new ones, interference, cue-dependent forgetting, and psychological amnesia brought on by repression.

Decay

One commonsense view, the **decay theory**, holds that memory traces fade with time if they are not "accessed" now and then. We have already seen

that decay occurs in the sensory register almost immediately and that it occurs in short-term memory as well unless we keep rehearsing the material. However, the mere passage of time does not account so well for forgetting in long-term memory. People commonly forget things that happened only yesterday while remembering events from many years ago. Indeed, some memories, both procedural and declarative, can last a lifetime. If

decay theory The theory that information in memory eventually disappears if it is not accessed; it applies more to short-term than to long-term memory.

Motor skills, which are stored as procedural memories, can last a lifetime; they never decay. But other kinds of memories can fade, sometimes quickly. Several theories explain why this is so.

you learned to swim as a child, you will still know how to swim at age 30, even if you have not been in a pool or lake for 22 years. We are also happy to report that some school lessons have great staying power. In one study, people did well on a Spanish test some 50 years after taking Spanish in high school, even though most had hardly used Spanish at all in the intervening years (Bahrick, 1984). Decay alone, although it may play some role, cannot entirely explain lapses in long-term memory.

Replacement

Another theory holds that new information entering memory can wipe out old information, just as re-recording on an audiotape or videotape will obliterate the original material. In one study supporting this view, researchers showed people slides of a traffic accident and used leading questions to get them to think that they had seen a stop sign when they had really seen a yield sign, or vice versa (see Figure 8.8). People in a control group who were not misled in this way were able to identify the sign they had actually seen. Later, all

the participants were told the purpose of the study and were asked to guess whether they had been misled. Almost all of those who had been misled continued to insist that they had really, truly seen the sign whose existence had been planted in their minds (Loftus, 1980; Loftus, Miller, & Burns, 1978). The researchers interpreted these findings to mean that the subjects had not just been trying to please them, and that people's original perceptions had in fact been "erased" by the misleading information.

Interference

A third theory holds that forgetting occurs because similar items of information interfere with one another in either storage or retrieval; the information may get into memory and stay there, but it becomes confused with other information. Such interference, which occurs in both short- and long-term memory, is especially common when you have to recall isolated facts—names, addresses, personal identification numbers, area codes, and the like.

Suppose you are at a party and you meet someone named Julie. A little later you meet someone named Judy. You go on to talk to other people, and after an hour, you again bump into Julie, but by mistake you call her Judy. The second name has interfered with the first. This type of interference, in which new information interferes with the ability to remember old information, is called **retroactive interference**:

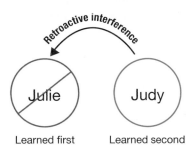

Learned first   Learned second

Retroactive interference is illustrated by the story of an absent-minded professor of ichthyology (the study of fish) who complained that whenever he learned the name of a new student, he forgot the name of a fish. But whereas with replacement, the new memory erases the old and makes it irretrievable, in retroactive interference, loss of the old memory is sometimes just temporary. With a little concentration, that professor could probably recall his new students and his old fish.

Because new information is constantly entering memory, we are all vulnerable to the effects of retroactive interference—or at least most of us

retroactive interference Forgetting that occurs when recently learned material interferes with the ability to remember similar material stored previously.

FIGURE 8.8 The Stop Sign Study

When people who saw a car in front of a yield sign (left) were later asked if they had seen "the stop sign" (a misleading question), many said they had. Similarly, when those shown a stop sign were asked if they had seen "the yield sign," many said yes. These false memories persisted even after the researchers revealed their use of misleading questions, suggesting that the misleading information had erased the participants' original mental representations of the signs (Loftus, 1980; Loftus, Miller, & Burns, 1978).

are. H. M. is an exception; his memories of childhood and adolescence are unusually detailed, clear, and unchanging. H. M. can remember actors who were famous when he was a child, the films they were in, and who their costars were. He also knows the names of friends from the second grade. Presumably, these early declarative memories were not subject to interference from memories acquired since the operation because H. M. has not acquired any new memories.

Interference also works in the opposite direction. Old information (such as the French you learned in high school) may interfere with the ability to remember new information (such as the Spanish you are trying to learn now). This type of interference is called **proactive interference.**

cue-dependent forgetting The inability to retrieve information stored in memory because of insufficient cues for recall.

proactive interference Forgetting that occurs when previously stored material interferes with the ability to remember similar, more recently learned material.

Proactive interference

Julie → Ju~~d~~y

Learned first   Learned second

Over a period of weeks, months, and years, proactive interference may cause more forgetting than retroactive interference does, because we have stored up so much information that can potentially interfere with anything new.

Cue-Dependent Forgetting

state-dependent memory The tendency to remember something when the rememberer is in the same physical or mental state as during the original learning or experience.

Often, when we need to remember, we rely on *retrieval cues*: items of information that can help

us find the specific information we're looking for. For example, if you are trying to remember the last name of an actor, it might help to know the person's first name or the name of a recent movie the actor starred in.

When we lack retrieval cues, we may feel as if we are lost among the stacks in the mind's library. In long-term memory, this type of memory failure, called **cue-dependent forgetting**, may be the most common type of all. Willem Wagenaar (1986), who, like Marigold Linton, recorded critical details about events in his life, found that within a year, he had forgotten 20 percent of those details, and after five years, he had forgotten 60 percent. However, when he gathered cues from witnesses about 10 events that he thought he had forgotten, he was able to recall something about all 10, which suggests that some of his forgetting was cue dependent.

Cues that were present when you learned a new fact or experienced an event are apt to be especially useful later as retrieval aids. That may explain why remembering is often easier when you are in the same physical environment as you were when an event occurred: Cues in the present context match those from the past. Ordinarily, this overlap helps us remember the past more accurately. But it may also account for the eerie phenomenon of *déjà vu*, the false sense we've all had of having been in exactly the same situation before as we're in now (*déjà vu* means "already seen" in French).

Your mental or physical state may also act as a retrieval cue, evoking a **state-dependent memory**. For example, if you are intoxicated when something happens, you may remember it better when you once again have had a few drinks

Charlie Chaplin's film *City Lights* provides a classic illustration of state-dependent memory. After Charlie saves the life of a drunken millionaire, the two spend the rest of the evening in boisterous merrymaking. But the next day, after sobering up, the millionaire fails to recognize Charlie and gives him the cold shoulder. Then, once again, the millionaire gets drunk—and once again he greets Charlie as a pal.

than when you are sober. (This is not an endorsement of drunkenness! Your memory will be best if you are sober during both encoding and recall.) Likewise, if your emotional arousal is especially high or low at the time of an event, you may remember that event best when you are once again in the same emotional state. When victims of violent crimes have trouble recalling details of the experience, it may be in part because they are far less emotionally aroused than they were at the time of the crime (Clark, Milberg, & Erber, 1987). (It may also be because they were too upset or distracted during the event to encode it well.)

You may also be better able to retrieve a memory when your current mood matches the kind of material you are trying to remember. You are likely to remember happy events better when you are feeling happy than when you are sad (Mayer, McCormick, & Strong, 1995). Similarly, you are likely to remember unhappy events better and remember more of them when you are feeling unhappy, which in turn creates a vicious cycle. The more unhappy memories you recall, the more depressed you feel, and the more depressed you feel, the more unhappy memories you recall . . . so you stay stuck in your depression and make it even worse (Lyubomirsky, Caldwell, & Nolen-Hoeksema, 1998). You can break out of this trap by deliberately focusing on memories of happy events instead of unpleasant ones.

The Repression Controversy

A final theory of forgetting is concerned with **amnesia**, the loss of memory for important personal information, a loss that is often painful for the person with amnesia. Amnesia most commonly results from organic conditions such as brain disease or head injury and is usually temporary. In *psychogenic amnesia*, however, the causes of forgetting are psychological, such as a need to escape feelings of embarrassment, guilt, shame, disappointment, or emotional shock. Psychogenic amnesia begins immediately after the precipitating event, involves massive memory loss and loss of personal identity, and usually ends suddenly, after just a few weeks. Despite its frequent portrayal in films and novels, in real life it is actually quite rare (McNally, 2003b).

Psychologists generally accept the notion of psychogenic amnesia. *Traumatic amnesia*, however, is far more controversial. Traumatic amnesia allegedly involves the forgetting of specific traumatic events, sometimes for many years, and does not involve a loss of identity. Traumatic memory is said to be immune to the usual processes of distortion and confabulation; when the memory returns, it supposedly does so with perfect accuracy. The notion of traumatic amnesia originated with the psychoanalytic theory of Sigmund Freud, who argued that the mind defends itself from unwelcome and upsetting memories through the mechanism of **repression**—the involuntary pushing of threatening or upsetting information into the unconscious (see Chapter 2).

Most memory researchers reject the notion that a special unconscious mechanism called "repression" explains either psychogenic or traumatic amnesia. Richard McNally (2003b) reviewed the experimental and clinical evidence carefully and concluded, "The notion that the mind protects itself by repressing or dissociating memories of trauma, rendering them inaccessible to awareness, is a piece of psychiatric folklore devoid of convincing empirical support." The problem for most people who have suffered disturbing experiences is not that they cannot remember, but that they cannot forget: The memories keep intruding. No one has ever "repressed" the memory of being in a concentration camp, being in combat, or being the victim of an earthquake or a terrorist attack. And details of even these horrible experiences are subject to distortion and fading over time, as are all memories.

amnesia (organic) The loss of memory for important personal information. It usually has an organic cause, but in rare cases is psychogenic (psychological in origin).

repression In psychoanalytic theory, the involuntary pushing of threatening or upsetting information into the unconscious.

Thinking Critically About Repression and "Traumatic Amnesia"

Popular ideas about memory have been influenced by the psychodynamic idea that painful memories can be locked away in the unconscious with all the details intact, waiting to be recovered—a notion that modern research has disputed.

Further, "repression" is hard to identify or to distinguish from normal forms of forgetting. People who "forget" disturbing experiences could be intentionally keeping themselves from retrieving their painful memories by distracting themselves when a memory is awakened or by focusing on positive memories. Perhaps, understandably, they are not rehearsing unhappy memories, so the memories become more likely to fade. Perhaps they are simply avoiding the retrieval cues that would evoke the memories. A reluctance to think about an upsetting experience or disclose it to anyone is not the same as an *inability* to remember it (McNally, 2003b).

The debate over traumatic amnesia and repression erupted into the public arena in the 1990s, when claims of recovered memories of sexual abuse began to occur. Many women and some men came to believe, during psychotherapy, that they could recall long-buried—"repressed"—memories of sexual victimization. Criminal charges were lodged against the alleged perpetrators, usually fathers or other relatives. In one typical case, a woman named Laura B. sued her father, claiming he had molested her from the ages of 5 to 23 and had even raped her just days before her wedding. Laura B. said she had repressed all of these experiences and had no recollection of them until her memories emerged during therapy.

For therapists who accept the notion of repression, such claims are entirely believable (Brown,

Scheflin, & Whitfield, 1999; J. Herman, 1992; Pope, 1996). But researchers at the University of Victoria and elsewhere argue that, although real abuse certainly occurs, many false memories of victimization have been encouraged by naive therapists who are unaware of the power of suggestion and the dangers of confabulation (Lindsay & Read, 1994; Loftus & Ketcham, 1994; McNally, 2003b; Schacter, 2001). Only rarely have "recovered" memories been corroborated by objective evidence, so it is difficult and often impossible to determine their accuracy.

For these reasons, many courts, too, have become skeptical of accusations based solely on "repressed" and "recovered" memories. In the case of Laura B., the judge wrote that her recovered memories would not be admissible as evidence because "the phenomenon of memory repression, and the process of therapy used in these cases to recover the memories, have not gained general acceptance in the field of psychology; and are not scientifically reliable" (*State of New Hampshire v. Joel Hungerford*, May 23, 1995). The challenges associated with assessing claims of "historical abuse" are even greater in Canada, where there is no limit on how far back in time a person can go to cite the alleged abuse (Porter et al., 2003).

How, then, should we respond to an individual's claim to have repressed and later recovered memories of abuse? Given current research on memory, we should be skeptical if the person says that, thanks to therapy, he or she now has memories from the first year or two of life. (As we will see in the next section, this is not possible.) We should be skeptical if, over time, the person's memories become more and more implausible—for instance, if the person says that sexual abuse continued day and night for 15 years without ever being remembered and without anyone else in the household noticing anything amiss. And we should hear alarm bells go off if a therapist used suggestive techniques, such as hypnosis, dream analysis, "age regression," guided imagery, and leading questions to "help" a patient recall the alleged abuse, because these techniques increase confabulation (Loftus, 1996; also see Chapter 12). In contrast, a person's recollections are more likely to be trustworthy if there is corroborating evidence from medical records or from the recollections of other family members, and if the person spontaneously recalled the event without pressure from others or the use of suggestive techniques in therapy.

Quick Quiz

If you have not repressed what you just learned, try these questions.

1. After reading Tom Robbins' novel *Even Cowgirls Get the Blues* years ago, Wilma became a fan of the author. Later, she developed a crush on actor/director Tim Robbins, but every time she tried to recall his name she called him "Tom." Why?

2. When a man at his twentieth high-school reunion sees his old friends, he recalls incidents he thought were long forgotten. Why?

3. What mechanisms other than repression could account for a person's psychogenic amnesia?

Answers:

1. proactive interference
2. The sight of his friends provides retrieval cues for the incidents.
3. The person could be intentionally avoiding the memory by using distraction or focusing on positive experiences; failure to rehearse the memory may be causing it to fade; or the person may be avoiding retrieval cues that would evoke the memory.

WHAT'S AHEAD

- Why are the first few years of life a mental blank?
- Why have human beings been called the "story-telling animal"?

AUTOBIOGRAPHICAL MEMORIES

For most of us, our autobiographical memories are by far the most fascinating. We use them to entertain ("Did I ever tell you about the time . . . ?"); we modify them—some people even publish them—to create an image of ourselves; we analyze them to learn more about who we are.

Childhood Amnesia: The Missing Years

A curious aspect of autobiographical memory is that most adults cannot recall any events from earlier than the third or fourth year of life. A few people apparently can recall momentous experiences that occurred when they were as young as two years old, such as the birth of a sibling, but not earlier ones (Newcombe et al., 2000; Usher & Neisser, 1993). As adults, we cannot remember being fed in infancy by our parents, taking our first steps, or uttering our first halting sentences. We are victims of **childhood amnesia** (sometimes called *infantile amnesia*).

There is something disturbing about childhood amnesia—so disturbing that some people adamantly deny it, claiming to remember events from the second or even the first year of life. But like other false memories, these are merely reconstructions based on photographs, family stories, and imagination. The "remembered" event may not even have taken place. Swiss psychologist Jean Piaget (1952) once reported a memory of nearly being kidnapped at the age of two. Piaget remembered sitting in his pram, watching his nurse as she bravely defended him from the kidnapper. He remembered the scratches she received on her face. He remembered a police officer with a short cloak and white baton who finally chased the kidnapper away. But when Piaget was 15, his nurse wrote to his parents confessing that she had made up the entire story. Piaget noted, "I therefore must have heard, as a child, the account of this story . . . and projected it into the past in the form of a visual memory, which was a memory of a memory, but false."

Of course, we all retain procedural memories from the toddler stage, when we first learned to use a fork, drink from a cup, and pull a wagon. We also retain semantic memories acquired early in life: the rules of counting, the names of people and things, knowledge about objects in the world, words and meanings. Further, toddlers who are only one to two years old can often remember past experiences, and some four-year-olds can remember experiences that occurred before age two and a half (Bauer & Dow, 1994; McDonough & Mandler, 1994). What young children do not do well is encode and retain their early episodic

> Thinking Critically About "Memories" from Infancy

childhood (infantile) amnesia The inability to remember events and experiences that occurred during the first two or three years of life.

This infant, who is learning to kick to make a mobile move, may remember the trick a week later—an example of procedural memory. However, when she is older she will not remember the experience itself. Like the rest of us, she will fall victim to childhood amnesia.

memories—memories of particular events—and carry them into later childhood or adulthood.

Freud thought that childhood amnesia was another case of repression, but memory researchers today think that repression has nothing to do with it. Biological psychologists believe that childhood amnesia occurs because brain areas involved in the formation or storage of events, and other areas involved in working memory and decision making (such as the prefrontal cortex), are not well developed until a few years after birth (McKee & Squire, 1993; Newcombe et al., 2000). Cognitive psychologists have proposed other explanations, which include the following:

1 *Lack of a sense of self.* In one view, we cannot have an autobiographical memory of ourselves until we have a self to remember. Indeed, autobiographical memories do not begin until the emergence of a self-concept and, according to researchers at Memorial and Lakehead universities,

this occurs at somewhat different ages for different children, but not before the age of two (Howe, Courage, & Peterson, 1994).

2 *Impoverished encoding.* Preschoolers encode experiences far less elaborately than adults. Young children have not yet mastered the social conventions for reporting events; they do not know what is important and interesting to others. Instead, they tend to rely on adults' questions to provide retrieval cues ("Where did we go for breakfast?" "Who did you go trick-or-treating with?"). This dependency on adults may prevent them from building up a stable core of remembered material that will be available when they are older (Fivush & Hamond, 1991).

3 *A focus on the routine.* Preschoolers tend to focus on the routine, familiar aspects of an experience, such as eating lunch or playing with toys, rather than the distinctive aspects that will provide retrieval cues and make an event memorable in the long run (Fivush & Hamond, 1991).

4 *Children's ways of thinking about the world.* The cognitive schemas used by preschoolers are very different from those used by older children and adults. Only after acquiring language and starting school do children learn to think like adults. Their new, adultlike schemas do not contain the information and cues necessary for recalling earlier experiences, so memories of those experiences are lost (Howe & Courage, 1993).

Whatever the explanation for childhood amnesia, our first memories, even when they are not accurate, may provide useful insights into our personalities, current concerns, ambitions, and attitudes toward life (Kihlstrom & Harackiewicz, 1982). What are *your* first memories?

Memory and Narrative: The Stories of Our Lives

The communications researcher George Gerbner once observed that our species is unique because we are the only animal that tells stories—and lives by the stories we tell. This view of human beings as the "story-telling animal" has had a huge impact

Get Involved   Analyze a Childhood Memory

Write down as much as you can about an incident from your childhood that stands out in your memory. Now ask a friend or family member who was present at the time to write a description of the same event. Do your accounts differ? If so, why? Did you choose a happy memory or a bleak one? What does this exercise tell you about the nature of memory—and about your own personality or present concerns?

in cognitive psychology. The *narratives* we compose to simplify and make sense of our lives have a profound influence on our plans, memories, love affairs, hatreds, ambitions, and dreams.

Thus we say, "I am this way because, as a small child, this happened to me, and then my parents. . . ." We say, "Let me tell you the story of how we fell in love." We say, "When you hear what happened, you'll understand why I felt entitled to take such coldhearted revenge." These stories are not necessarily fiction, as in the child's meaning of "tell me a story." Rather, they are attempts to provide a unifying theme that organizes and gives meaning to the events of our lives. But because these narratives rely heavily on memory, and because memories are reconstructed and are constantly shifting in response to present needs, beliefs, and experiences, our stories are also, to some degree, works of interpretation and imagination. Adult memories thus reveal as much about the present as they do about the past.

Once we have formulated a story's central theme ("My parents opposed my plans," "My lover was domineering"), that theme may then serve as a cognitive schema that guides what we remember and what we forget (Mather, Shafir, & Johnson, 2000). The story's theme may also influence our judgments of events and people in the present. If you have a fight with your lover, for example, the central theme in your story about the fight might be negative ("He was a jerk") or neutral ("It was a mutual misunderstanding"). This theme may bias you to blame or forgive your partner long after you have forgotten what the conflict was all about or who said what (McGregor & Holmes, 1999). You can see that the "spin" you give a story is critical, so be careful about the stories you tell!

As we have seen throughout this chapter, many details about events, even those landmarks we are sure we remember clearly, are probably distorted, forgotten, or added after the fact. By now, you should not be surprised that memory can be as fickle as it can be accurate. As cognitive psychologists have shown repeatedly, we are not merely actors in our personal life dramas; we also write the scripts.

Psychology In The News *Revisited*

At the start of this chapter, we promised to tell you what happened in the life of Thomas Sophonow, wrongfully convicted of the 1981 murder of 16-year-old Barbara Stoppel on the strength of eyewitness testimony.

In 1985, Sophonow was released from prison after serving four years for a crime he did not commit. However, he was not actually cleared of the crime until 2000, when Winnipeg police announced that DNA evidence from the crime scene did not match Sophonow's and that they had a new suspect. Even then, his life did not return to normal. Living in British Columbia after being cleared of Stoppel's murder, Sophonow had his house firebombed. He was also harassed at work, finding one day that a co-worker had pinned the word "Murderer" on his coveralls. That was his last day of work.

Fortunately for Thomas Sophonow, he doesn't have to work for a living anymore. In 2003, at the age of 49, he received a settlement of $2.6 million from the Manitoba government in compensation for the ordeal he suffered as a result of his wrongful conviction. Today, he lives with his wife and children in British Columbia in a large 100-year-old house that he spends his time renovating. He also helps others who have been wrongfully convicted.

How would you feel if your eyewitness testimony resulted in the conviction of an innocent person? Would you be able to admit your mistake, or would you, as at least one witness did in the Sophonow case, cling more resolutely than ever to the accuracy of your memory? Sophonow learned from personal experience what you have learned from this chapter: that eyewitnesses can and do make mistakes, that even memories for shocking or traumatic experiences are vulnerable to distortion and influence by others, and that our confidence in our memories is not a reliable guide to their accuracy.

The Sophonow case is far from unique. Other well-publicized cases in Canada include Guy Paul Morin, David Milgaard, and Donald Marshall Jr., and these are just a few examples. In the United States, it's estimated that as many as 200 000 people, 10 percent of America's prison population, may be innocent of the crimes for which they were convicted. The situation in Canada may well be similar. When psychological scientists examined 40 cases in which wrongful conviction had been established beyond doubt, they found that 90 percent of these cases had involved a false identification by one or more eyewitnesses (Wells et al., 1998).

Obviously, not all eyewitness testimony is erroneous, and such testimony certainly needs to be heard and taken into account. But the potential for errors in identification makes it extremely important to gather evidence carefully, ensure adequate legal representation for defendants, conduct police interviews using proper procedures, and obtain a DNA analysis whenever possible.

The most important lesson to be learned from the research in this chapter is that human memory has both tremendous strengths and tremendous weaknesses. Because our deepest sense of ourselves relies on our memories, this is a difficult truth to accept. If we can do so, we will be able to respect the great power of memory and at the same time retain humility about our capacity for error, confabulation, and self-deception.

Taking Psychology With You   How to Remember What You Study

Someday in the near future, a "memory pill" may be available to perk up our memories. For the time being, however, those of us who hope to improve our memories must rely on mental strategies. Some simple mnemonics can be useful, but, as we have seen, complicated ones are often more bother than they're worth. A better approach is to follow some general guidelines based on the principles in this chapter:

- **Pay attention!** It seems obvious, but often we fail to remember because we never encoded the information in the first place. For example, which of these is the real Lincoln penny?

Most North Americans have trouble recognizing a real penny because they have never attended to the details of a penny's design (Nickerson & Adams, 1979). We are not advising you to do so, unless you happen to be a coin collector or a counterfeiting expert. Just keep in mind that when you do have something to remember, such as the material in this book, you will do better if you encode it well. (The real penny, by the way, is the left one in the bottom row.)

- **Encode information in more than one way.** The more elaborate the encoding of information, the more memorable it will be. Use your imagination! For instance, in addition to remembering a telephone number by the sound of the individual digits, you might note the spatial pattern they make as you punch them in on the telephone.

- **Add meaning.** The more meaningful the material, the more likely it is to link up with information already in long-term memory. Meaningfulness also reduces the number of chunks of information you have to learn. Common ways of adding meaning include making up a story about the material (fitting the material into a cognitive schema), thinking of examples, and forming visual images. (Some people find that the more unusual the image, the better.) If your licence plate happens to be 236MPL, you might think of 236 maples. If you are trying to remember the concept of procedural memory from this chapter, you might make the concept meaningful by thinking of an example from your own life, such as your ability to ride a mountain bike, and then imagine a *P* (for "procedural") superimposed on an image of yourself on your bike.

- **Take your time.** Leisurely learning, spread out over several sessions, usually produces better results than harried cramming (although *reviewing* material just before a test can be helpful). In terms of hours spent, "distributed" (spaced) learning sessions are more efficient than "massed" ones; in other words, three separate one-hour study sessions may result in more retention than one session of three hours.

- **Take time out.** If possible, minimize interference by using study breaks for rest or recreation. Sleep is the ultimate way to reduce interference. In a classic study, students who slept for eight hours after learning lists of nonsense syllables retained them better than students who went about their usual business (Jenkins & Dallenbach, 1924). Sleep is not always possible, of course, but periodic mental relaxation usually is.

- **Overlearn.** You can't remember something you never learned well in the first place. Overlearning—studying information even after you think you know it—is one of the best ways to ensure that you'll remember it.

- **Monitor your learning.** Test yourself frequently, rehearse thoroughly, and review periodically to see how you are doing. Don't just evaluate your learning immediately after reading the material, though—because the information is still in short-term memory, you are likely to feel a false sense of confidence about your ability to recall it later. If you delay making a judgment for at least a few minutes, your evaluation will probably be more accurate (Nelson & Dunlosky, 1991).

Whatever strategies you use, you will find that active learning produces more comprehension and better retention than does passive reading or listening. The mind does not gobble up information automatically; you must make the material digestible. Even then, you should not expect to remember everything you read or hear. Nor should you want to. Piling up facts without distinguishing the important from the trivial is just confusing. Popular books and tapes that promise a "perfect" "photographic" memory, or "instant recall" of everything you learn, fly in the face of what psychologists know about how the mind operates. Our advice: Forget them.

SUMMARY

RECONSTRUCTING THE PAST

- Unlike a tape recorder or video camera, human memory is highly selective and is *reconstructive:* People add, delete, and change elements in ways that help them make sense of information and events. They often have *source amnesia*, the inability to distinguish information stored during an event from information added later. Even *flashbulb memories*, emotionally powerful memories that seem particularly vivid, are often embellished or distorted and tend to become less accurate over time.

- Because memory is reconstructive, it is subject to *confabulation*, the confusion of imagined events with actual ones. Confabulation is more likely when people have thought about the imagined event many times ("imagination inflation"), the image of the event contains many details, the event is easy to imagine, and the focus of attention is on emotional reactions to the event.

MEMORY AND THE POWER OF SUGGESTION

- The reconstructive nature of memory makes memory vulnerable to suggestion. Eyewitness testimony is especially vulnerable to error when the suspect's ethnicity differs from that of the witness, when leading questions are put to a witness, or when a witness is given misleading information.

- Children, like adults, often remember the essential aspects of an event accurately. However, like adults, they can also be suggestible, especially in response to biased interviewing by adults—for example, when they are asked questions that blur the line between fantasy and reality, when they are asked leading questions, when they are threatened or bribed to give the "correct" answer, or when they are pressured to conform to what they believe other children have said.

IN PURSUIT OF MEMORY

- The ability to remember depends in part on the type of performance called for. In tests of *explicit memory* (conscious recollection), *recognition* is usually better than *recall*. In tests of *implicit memory*, which is measured by indirect methods such as *priming* and the *relearning method*, past experiences may affect current thoughts or actions even when these experiences are not consciously and intentionally remembered.

- In *information-processing models*, memory involves the *encoding*, *storage*, and *retrieval* of information. In the *three-box model*, there are three interacting systems: the sensory register, short-term memory, and long-term memory. Some cognitive scientists prefer a *parallel distributed processing (PDP)* or *connectionist* model, which represents knowledge as connections among numerous interacting processing units, distributed in a vast network and all operating in parallel. But the three-box model continues to offer a convenient way to organize the major findings on memory.

THE THREE-BOX MODEL OF MEMORY

- In the three-box model, incoming sensory information makes a brief stop in the *sensory register*, which momentarily retains it in the form of sensory images.

- *Short-term memory (STM)* retains new information for up to 30 seconds by most estimates (unless rehearsal takes place). *Working memory* consists of STM and the mental processes that control the retrieval of information from long-term memory and interpret that information appropriately depending on the task you are doing. The capacity of STM is extremely limited but can be extended if information is organized into larger units by *chunking*. Items that are meaningful, have an emotional impact, or link up to something already in long-term memory may enter long-term storage easily, with only a brief stay in STM.

- *Long-term memory (LTM)* contains an enormous amount of information, which must be organized to make it manageable. For example, words (or the concepts they represent) seem to be organized by semantic categories. Many models of LTM represent its contents as a network of interrelated concepts. The way people use these networks depends on experience and education. Research on *tip-of-the-tongue (TOT)* states shows that words are also indexed in LTM in terms of sound and form.

- *Procedural memories* ("knowing how") are memories for how to perform specific actions; *declarative memories* ("knowing that") are memories for abstract or representational knowledge. Declarative memories include *semantic memories* (general knowledge) and *episodic memories* (memories for personally experienced events).

- The three-box model is often invoked to explain the *serial-position effect* in memory, but, although it can explain the *primacy effect*, it cannot explain why a *recency effect* sometimes occurs even when the model predicts it should not.

HOW WE REMEMBER

- To remember your material well, we must encode it accurately in the first place. Some kinds of information, such as material in a university or college course, require effortful, as opposed to automatic, encoding. Rehearsal of information keeps it in short-term memory and increases the chances of long-term retention. *Elaborative rehearsal* is more likely to result in transfer to long-term memory than is *maintenance rehearsal*, and *deep processing* is usually more effective than *shallow processing*.

- *Mnemonics* can also enhance retention by promoting elaborative encoding and making material meaningful, but for ordinary memory tasks, complex memory tricks are often ineffective or even counterproductive.

WHY WE FORGET

- Forgetting can occur for several reasons. Information in sensory and short-term memory appears to *decay* if it does not receive further processing. New information may "erase" old information in long-term memory. *Proactive* and *retroactive interference* may take place. *Cue-dependent forgetting* may occur when *retrieval cues* are inadequate. The most effective retrieval cues are those that were present at the time of the initial experience. A person's mood or physical state may also act as a retrieval cue, evoking a *state-dependent memory*.

- *Amnesia*, the forgetting of personal information, usually occurs for organic reasons, such as disease or injury to the brain; *psychogenic amnesia*, amnesia that has psychological causes, is rare. *Traumatic amnesia*, which allegedly involves the forgetting of specific traumatic events, sometimes for many years, is highly controversial, as is *repression*, the psychodynamic explanation of traumatic amnesia. Because these concepts lack sufficient empirical support, psychological scientists are skeptical about their validity and about the accuracy of "recovered memories." Critics argue that many therapists, unaware of the power of suggestion and the dangers of confabulation, have encouraged false memories of victimization.

AUTOBIOGRAPHICAL MEMORIES

- Most people cannot recall any events from earlier than the third or fourth year. The reason for such *childhood amnesia* may be partly biological. Cognitive explanations include the lack of a sense of self until the age of two or three, young children's impoverished encoding of their experiences, their focus on routine rather than distinctive aspects of an experience, and their immature cognitive schemas.

- A person's *narrative* "life story" organizes the events of his or her life and gives them meaning. Narratives change as people build up a store of episodic memories, and life stories are, to some degree, works of interpretation and imagination. The central themes of our stories can guide recall and influence our judgments of people and events.

PSYCHOLOGY IN THE NEWS, REVISITED

- Across the country, as DNA evidence has exonerated people falsely convicted of rape, murder, and other crimes, people are becoming more aware of the limitations of eyewitness testimony and the fallibility of memory.

KEY TERMS

LOOKING BACK

- What's wrong with thinking of memory as a mental video camera? (p. 252)
- Why do "flashbulb" memories of surprising or shocking events sometimes have less wattage than we think? (p. 253)
- If you have a strong emotional reaction to a remembered event, does that mean your memory is accurate? (p. 254)
- Can your memories of an event be affected by the way someone questions you about them? (pp. 255–256)
- Can children's testimony about sexual abuse be trusted? (pp. 257–258)
- In general, which is easier: a multiple-choice question or a short-answer essay question? (p. 259)
- Can you know something without knowing that you know it? (p. 259)
- Why is the computer often used as a metaphor for the mind? (p. 260)
- Why is short-term memory like a leaky bucket? (p. 263)
- When a word is on the tip of your tongue, what errors are you likely to make in recalling it? (p. 265)
- What's the difference between "knowing how" and "knowing that"? (p. 266)
- What's wrong with trying to memorize in a rote fashion when you're studying—and what's a better strategy? (pp. 269–270)
- Memory tricks are fun, but are they always useful? (p. 270)
- How might new information "erase" old memories? (p. 273)
- What theory explains why you keep dialing an old area code instead of the new one? (p. 273)
- Why is it easier to recall experiences from elementary school if you see pictures of your classmates? (p. 274)
- Why are many researchers skeptical about claims of "repressed" and "recovered" memories? (pp. 275–276)
- Why are the first few years of life a mental blank? (p. 278)
- Why have human beings been called the "story-telling animal"? (pp. 278–279)

Answers to the "Get Involved" exercises on pages 259 and 260:
Rudolph's eight friends were Dasher, Dancer, Prancer, Vixen, Comet, Cupid, Donder, and Blitzen.

Psychology In The News

A DIVIDED SUPREME COURT OF CANADA UPHOLDS THE "SPANKING LAW"

OTTAWA, ON, January 31, 2004. The top court in the land has decreed that, under certain circumstances, spanking is okay. The decision divided the Supreme Court, which upheld the current law by a vote of 6 to 3. Spanking is allowable for children who are over the age of two and who are not yet teenagers.

The decision was met with mixed views, to say the least. Michael Martens from Focus on the Family said, "Parents can breathe a sigh of relief today that they will not be criminalized for lovingly disciplining their children."

Other groups, such as the Canadian Foundation for Children, Youth, and the Law, presented a very different opinion. A lawyer representing that group said, "To the extent that they [the judges] are relying on the social science evidence, the evidence is that it's never okay to hit a child, even on the government side. That's the irony of this."

Those who work with families engaging in child abuse argue that so-called corporal punishment of any kind is often the first step toward physical abuse. They cite cases of parents whose physical punishments escalated to become clear cases of abuse. Others claim that "willful" children need to know that parents who love them very much may still use physical deterrents to behaviour that might be dangerous or otherwise inappropriate.

The Supreme Court judges themselves disagreed over the ruling. Some said that it improved the situation by placing clear limits on the use of physical punishment by spelling out who could use it (not teachers, for example) and on whom it could be used (not children under the age of two or in their teens, and not children with disabilities). The three dissenting judges were equally as clear in their disagreement with the ruling. Justice Marie Deschamps said the ruling "perpetuates the notion of children as property rather than human beings and sends the message that their bodily integrity and physical security is to be sacrificed to the will of their parents, however misguided."

In another part of the world, British parliament was less divided when they faced this issue, voting 424 to 75 to reject a ban on spanking. By contrast, Sweden, Norway, Finland, Denmark, and Austria have all outlawed physical punishment of children.

Child Welfare League of Canada member Peter Dudding expresses his disagreement with Supreme Court ruling upholding the spanking law (left). Michael Martens voices his approval of the law (right).

9 Learning

If you had been on the Supreme Court making the decision about spanking, how would you have voted? Do you think such physical punishment as spanking or slapping is abusive or is sometimes a necessary parenting strategy?

The debate over how to discipline unruly children has been with us for a long time. At the core of this debate is a general question: What are the best ways to get people to behave well and to discourage them from behaving badly? It may surprise you to know that this issue is a central one for researchers who study learning. To psychologists, **learning** refers not just to the skills acquired in school, but to *any* relatively permanent change in behaviour that occurs because of experience. Experience is the greatest teacher, providing the essential link between the past and the future and enabling a person (or animal) to adapt to changing circumstances. The particular experiences an individual has—both pleasant and unpleasant— affect how the person is likely to act in the future.

Research on learning has been heavily influenced by **behaviourism**, the school of psychology that accounts for behaviour in terms of observable acts and events, without reference to mental entities, such as "mind" or "will" (see Chapter 1). Behaviourists focus on a basic kind of learning called **conditioning**, which involves associations between environmental stimuli and responses. In fact, behaviourism is sometimes referred to informally as stimulus–response ("S–R") psychology.

Behaviourists have shown that two types of conditioning—*classical conditioning* and *operant conditioning*—can explain much of human behaviour. But other approaches, known as *social–cognitive learning theories*, hold that omitting mental processes from explanations of human learning is like omitting passion from descriptions of sex: You may explain the form, but you miss the substance. To social-cognitive theorists, learning is not so much a change in behaviour as a change in knowledge that has the potential for affecting behaviour.

As you read about the principles of conditioning and learning in this chapter, ask yourself what they can teach us about the use of punishment to control unwanted behaviour. Are

conditioning A basic kind of learning that involves associations between environmental stimuli and the organism's responses.

learning A relatively permanent change in behaviour (behavioural potential) due to experience.

behaviourism An approach to psychology that emphasizes the study of observable behaviour and the role of the environment as a determinant of behaviour.

parents who spank their children doing the right thing, or are there better methods of discipline available? How can we most effectively modify other people's behaviour—and our own?

WHAT'S AHEAD

- Why would a dog salivate when it sees a light bulb or hears a buzzer, even though it can't eat these things?
- How can classical conditioning help explain prejudice?
- If you have learned to fear collies, why might you also be scared of sheepdogs?

CLASSICAL CONDITIONING

At the start of the twentieth century, the great Russian physiologist Ivan Pavlov (1849–1936) was studying salivation in dogs, as part of a research program on digestion. His work would shortly win him the Nobel Prize in Physiology or Medicine. One of Pavlov's procedures was to make a surgical opening in a dog's cheek and insert a tube that conducted saliva away from the animal's salivary gland so that the saliva could be measured. To stimulate the reflexive flow of saliva, Pavlov placed meat powder or other food in the dog's mouth. This procedure was later refined by others (see Figure 9.1).

Pavlov was a truly dedicated scientific observer. Many years later, as he lay dying, he even dictated his sensations for posterity! And he instilled in his students the same passion for detail. During his salivation studies, one of these students noticed something that most people would have overlooked or dismissed as trivial. After a dog had been brought to the laboratory a number of times, it would start to salivate *before* the food was placed in its mouth. The sight or smell of the food, the dish in which the food was kept, even the sight of the person who delivered the food each day or the sound of the person's footsteps were enough to start the dog's mouth watering. This new salivary response clearly was not inborn, so it had to have been acquired through experience.

At first, Pavlov treated the dog's drooling as merely an annoying secretion. But he quickly realized that his student had stumbled onto an important phenomenon, one that Pavlov came to believe was the basis of all learning in human beings and other animals (Pavlov, 1927). He called that phenomenon a "conditional" reflex—conditional because it depended on environmental conditions. Later, an error in the translation of his writings transformed "conditional" into "conditioned," the word most commonly used today.

Pavlov soon dropped what he had been doing and turned to the study of conditioned reflexes, to which he devoted the last three decades of his life. Why were his dogs salivating in response to things other than food?

New Reflexes from Old

At first, Pavlov speculated about what his dogs might be thinking and feeling to make them drool

FIGURE 9.1 A Modification of Pavlov's Method

In the apparatus on the right, which was based on Ivan Pavlov's techniques, saliva from a dog's cheek flowed down a tube and was measured by the movement of a needle on a revolving drum. In the photo on the left, Pavlov is in the centre, flanked by his students and a canine subject.

before getting their food. Was the doggy equivalent of "Oh boy, this means chow time" going through their minds? Eventually, however, he decided that such speculation was pointless (Todes, 1997). Instead, he focused on the environment in which the conditioned reflex arose.

The original salivary reflex, according to Pavlov, consisted of an **unconditioned stimulus (US)**, food, and an **unconditioned response (UR)**, salivation. By an unconditioned stimulus, Pavlov meant an event or thing that elicits a response automatically or reflexively. By an unconditioned response, he meant the response that is automatically produced:

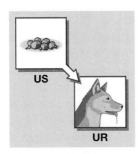

Learning occurs, said Pavlov, when a neutral stimulus is regularly paired with an unconditioned stimulus:

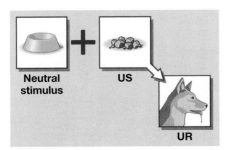

The neutral stimulus then becomes a **conditioned stimulus (CS)**, which elicits a learned or **conditioned response (CR)**, which is usually similar to the original, unlearned one. In Pavlov's laboratory, the sight of the food dish, which had not previously elicited salivation, became a CS for salivation:

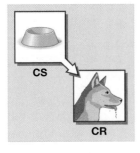

The procedure by which a neutral stimulus becomes a conditioned stimulus eventually became known as **classical conditioning**, also called *Pavlovian* or *respondent conditioning*. Pavlov and his students went on to show that all sorts of things can become conditioned stimuli for salivation if they are paired with food: the ticking of a metronome, the musical tone of a bell or a tuning fork, the vibrating sound of a buzzer, a touch on the leg, a triangle drawn on a large card, even a pinprick or an electric shock. And since Pavlov's day, many automatic, involuntary responses besides salivation have been classically conditioned—for example, heartbeat, stomach secretions, blood pressure, reflexive movements, blinking, and muscle contractions. The optimal interval between the presentation of the neutral stimulus and the presentation of the US depends on the kind of response involved; in the laboratory, the interval is often less than a second.

Principles of Classical Conditioning

Classical conditioning occurs in all species, from worms to *Homo sapiens*. Let's look more closely at some important features of this process: extinction, higher-order conditioning, and stimulus generalization and discrimination.

Extinction Conditioned responses do not necessarily last forever. If, after conditioning, the conditioned stimulus is repeatedly presented without the unconditioned stimulus, the conditioned response eventually disappears, and **extinction** is said to have occurred (see Figure 9.2). Suppose that you train your dog Milo to salivate to the sound of a bell, but then you ring the bell every five minutes and do not follow it with food. Milo will salivate less and less to the bell and will soon stop salivating to the bell altogether; salivation will have been extinguished. However, if you come back the next day and ring the bell, Milo may salivate again for a few trials. The reappearance of the response, which is called **spontaneous recovery**, explains why completely eliminating a conditioned response usually requires more than one extinction session.

Higher-Order Conditioning Sometimes a neutral stimulus can become a conditioned stimulus by being paired with an already established CS, a procedure known as **higher-order conditioning**. Say Milo has learned to salivate to the sight of a food dish. Now you flash a bright light before you present the dish. With repeated pairings of

classical conditioning The process by which a previously neutral stimulus acquires the capacity to elicit a response through association with a stimulus that already elicits a similar or related response.

unconditioned stimulus (US) The classical-conditioning term for a stimulus that elicits a reflexive response in the absence of learning.

unconditioned response (UR) The classical-conditioning term for a reflexive response elicited by a stimulus in the absence of learning.

extinction The weakening and eventual disappearance of a learned response; in classical conditioning, it occurs when the conditioned stimulus is no longer paired with the unconditioned stimulus.

conditioned stimulus (CS) The classical-conditioning term for an initially neutral stimulus that comes to elicit a conditioned response after being associated with an unconditioned stimulus.

conditioned response (CR) The classical-conditioning term for a response that is elicited by a conditioned stimulus; it occurs after the conditioned stimulus is associated with an unconditioned stimulus.

spontaneous recovery The reappearance of a learned response after its apparent extinction.

higher-order conditioning In classical conditioning, a procedure in which a neutral stimulus becomes a conditioned stimulus through association with an already established conditioned stimulus.

FIGURE 9.2 Acquisition and Extinction of a Salivary Response

A neutral stimulus that is consistently followed by an unconditioned stimulus for salivation will become a conditioned stimulus for salivation (left). But when this conditioned stimulus is then repeatedly presented without the unconditioned stimulus, the conditioned salivary response will weaken and eventually disappear (right); it has been extinguished.

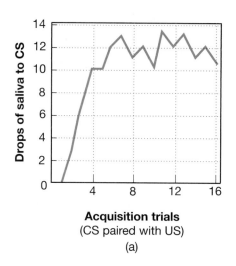

Acquisition trials
(CS paired with US)
(a)

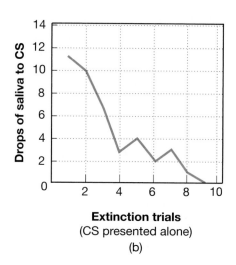

Extinction trials
(CS presented alone)
(b)

the light and the dish, Milo may learn to salivate to the light. The procedure for higher-order conditioning is illustrated in Figure 9.3.

Higher-order conditioning may explain why some words trigger emotional responses in us—why they can inflame us to anger or evoke warm, sentimental feelings. When words are paired with objects or other words that already elicit some emotional response, they, too, may come to elicit that response (Chance, 1999; Staats & Staats, 1957). For example, a child may learn a positive response to the word *birthday* because of its association with gifts and attention. Conversely, the child may learn a negative response to ethnic or national labels, such as *Swede*, *Pole*, or *Jew*, if those words are paired with words that the child has already learned are disagreeable, such as *dumb* or *dirty*. Higher-order conditioning, in other words, may contribute to the formation of prejudices.

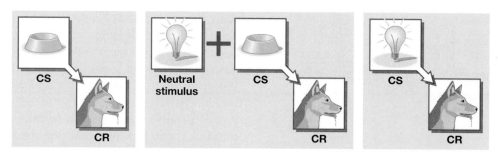

FIGURE 9.3 Higher-Order Conditioning

In this illustration of higher-order conditioning, the food dish is a previously conditioned stimulus for salivation (left). When the light, a neutral stimulus, is paired with the dish (centre), the light, too, becomes a conditioned stimulus for salivation (right).

Get Involved   Conditioning an Eye-Blink Response

Try out your behavioural skills by conditioning an eye-blink response in a willing friend, using classical-conditioning procedures. You will need a drinking straw and something to make a ringing sound—a spoon tapped on a water glass works well. Tell your friend that you are going to blow in his or her eye through the straw, but don't say why. Immediately before each puff of air, make the ringing sound. Repeat this procedure 10 times. Then make the ringing sound while holding the straw up to the person's eye, but don't puff. Your friend will probably blink anyway and may continue to do so for one or two more repetitions of the sound before the response extinguishes. Can you identify the US, the UR, the CS, and the CR in this exercise?

Stimulus Generalization and Discrimination

After a stimulus becomes a conditioned stimulus for some response, other similar stimuli may produce a similar reaction—a phenomenon known as **stimulus generalization**. For example, if you condition your patient pooch Milo to salivate to middle C on the piano, Milo may also salivate to D, which is one tone above C, even though you did not pair D with food. Stimulus generalization is described nicely by an old English proverb: "He who hath been bitten by a snake fears a rope."

The mirror image of stimulus generalization is **stimulus discrimination**, in which *different* responses are made to stimuli that resemble the conditioned stimulus in some way. Suppose that you have conditioned Milo to salivate to middle C on the piano by repeatedly pairing the sound with food. Now you play middle C on a guitar, without following it by food (but you continue to follow C on the piano by food). Eventually, Milo will learn to salivate to a C on the piano and not to salivate to the same note on the guitar; that is, he will discriminate between the two sounds. If you keep at this long enough, you could train Milo to be a pretty discriminating drooler!

What Is Actually Learned in Classical Conditioning?

For classical conditioning to be most effective, the stimulus to be conditioned should *precede* the unconditioned stimulus rather than follow it or occur simultaneously with it. This makes sense, because in classical conditioning, the conditioned stimulus becomes a *signal* for the unconditioned stimulus. Classical conditioning is in fact an evolutionary adaptation, one that enables the organism to anticipate and prepare for a biologically important event that is about to happen. In Pavlov's studies, for instance, a bell, buzzer, or other stimulus was a signal that meat was coming, and the dog's salivation was preparation for digesting food.

Today, therefore, many psychologists contend that what an animal or person actually learns in classical conditioning is not merely an association between two paired stimuli that occur close together in time, but rather *information* conveyed by one stimulus about another: for example, "If a tone sounds, food is likely to follow" (Davey, 1992). This view is supported by the research of Robert Rescorla (1988), who showed, in a series of imaginative studies, that the mere pairing of an unconditioned stimulus and a neutral stimulus is not enough to produce learning. To become a conditioned stimulus, the neutral stimulus must reliably signal, or predict, the unconditioned stimulus. If food occurs just as often without a preceding tone as with it, the tone is unlikely to become a conditioned stimulus for salivation—because the tone does not provide any information about the likelihood of getting food.

In everyday life, too, a potential CS may sometimes predict an unconditioned stimulus and sometimes not, so conditioning is less certain than when the CS and US always occur together in the laboratory. A friend of ours, behaviourist Paul Chance, gave us this example: Suppose you work in an office where you are allowed to receive routine calls only from other employees; you may take outside calls only in emergencies. One day, there are three emergencies: Your lover calls to jilt you, the police call to report that your new car was stolen, and your landlord calls to tell you that a broken water pipe has flooded your apartment. If these were the only calls you got, the next time you heard the phone ring (the CS) you might freak out (the CR). But if they occurred randomly among 50 routine business calls, the phone's ringing would probably not upset you (any more than it already has!) because it would not necessarily signal another disaster.

Rescorla (1988) concluded that "Pavlovian conditioning is not a stupid process by which the organism willy-nilly forms associations between any two stimuli that happen to co-occur. Rather, the organism is better seen as an information seeker using logical and perceptual relations among events, along with its own preconceptions, to form a sophisticated representation of its world." Not all learning theorists agree with this conclusion; an orthodox behaviourist would say that it is silly to talk about the preconceptions of a rat. The important point, however, is that concepts such as "information seeking," "preconceptions," and "representations of the world" open the door to a more cognitive view of classical conditioning.

stimulus generalization After conditioning, the tendency to respond to a stimulus that resembles one involved in the original conditioning; in classical conditioning, it occurs when a stimulus that resembles the CS elicits the CR.

stimulus discrimination The tendency to respond differently to two or more similar stimuli; in classical conditioning, it occurs when a stimulus similar to the CS fails to evoke the CR.

Quick Quiz

Classical-conditioning terms can be hard to learn, so be sure to take this quiz before going on.

A. Name the unconditioned stimulus, unconditioned response, conditioned stimulus, and conditioned response in these two situations:

1. Five-year-old Samantha is watching a storm from her window. A huge bolt of lightning is followed by a tremendous thunderclap, and Samantha jumps at the noise. This happens several more times. There is a brief lull and then another lightning bolt. Samantha jumps in response to the bolt.

2. Gregory's mouth waters whenever he eats anything with lemon in it. One day, while reading an ad that shows a big glass of lemonade, Gregory notices his mouth watering.

B. In the view of many learning theorists, pairing a neutral and an unconditioned stimulus is not enough to produce learning; the neutral stimulus must _____ the unconditioned stimulus.

Answers:

B. signal or predict

2. US = the taste of lemon; UR = salivation elicited by the taste of lemon; CS = the picture of a glass of lemonade; CR = salivation elicited by the picture.

1. US = the thunderclap; UR = jumping elicited by the noise; CS = the sight of the lightning; CR = jumping elicited by the lightning.

A.

WHAT'S AHEAD

- Why do advertisers often include pleasant music and gorgeous scenery in ads for their products?
- How would a classical-conditioning theorist explain your irrational fear of heights or mice?
- If you eat licorice and then go on an amusement park ride that nauseates you, how might your taste for licorice change?
- How can sitting in a doctor's office make you feel sick?

CLASSICAL CONDITIONING IN REAL LIFE

If a dog can learn to salivate to the ringing of a bell, so can you. In fact, you probably have learned to salivate to the sound of a lunch bell, not to mention the phrase *hot fudge sundae*, "mouthwatering" pictures of food in magazines, the sight of a server in a restaurant, and a voice calling out "Dinner's ready!" But the role of classical conditioning goes far beyond the learning of simple reflexive responses; conditioning affects us every day in many ways.

One of the first psychologists to recognize the real-life implications of Pavlovian theory was John B. Watson, who founded American behaviourism and enthusiastically promoted Pavlov's ideas.

Watson believed that the whole rich array of human emotion and behaviour could be accounted for by conditioning principles. For example, he thought that you learned to love another person when that person was paired with stroking and cuddling. Watson turned out to be wrong about love, which is a lot more complicated than he thought (see Chapter 14). But he was right about the power of classical conditioning to affect our emotions, preferences, and tastes.

Learning to Like

Classical conditioning plays a big role in our emotional responses to objects, events, and places. It can explain why sentimental feelings sweep over us when we see a school mascot, a national flag, or the logo of the Olympic Games: These objects have been associated in the past with positive feelings.

Many advertising techniques for getting us to like clients' products are also based on the principles first demonstrated by Pavlov, whether ad executives realize it or not. In one study, students at the University of British Columbia looked at slides of either a beige pen or a blue pen. During the presentation, half the students heard a song from a recent musical film, and half heard a selection of traditional music from India. (The experimenter made the reasonable assumption that the show tune would be more appealing to the young

Canadians participating in the study.) Later the students were allowed to choose one of the pens. Almost three-fourths of those who heard the popular music chose a pen that was the same colour as the one they had seen in the slides. An equal number of those who heard the Indian music chose a pen that differed in colour from the one they had seen (Gorn, 1982).

In classical-conditioning terms, the music in this study was an unconditioned stimulus for internal responses associated with pleasure or displeasure, and the pens became conditioned stimuli for similar responses. You can see why television commercials often pair products with music, attractive people, or other appealing sounds and images.

Learning to Fear

Positive emotions are not the only ones that can be classically conditioned; so can dislikes and negative emotions such as fear. A person can learn to fear just about anything if it is paired with something that elicits pain, surprise, or embarrassment. Human beings, however, are biologically primed to be especially susceptible to certain kinds of acquired fears. It is far easier to establish a conditioned fear of spiders, snakes, and heights than of butterflies, flowers, and toasters (Öhman & Mineka, 2001). The former can be dangerous to your health, so in the process of evolution, human beings acquired a tendency to learn quickly to be wary of them.

When fear of an object or situation becomes irrational and interferes with normal activities, it qualifies as a *phobia*. To demonstrate how a phobia might be learned, John Watson and Rosalie Rayner (1920) deliberately established a rat phobia in an 11-month-old boy named Albert. The details of the study are a little hazy, and for ethical

reasons, no psychologist today would do such a thing to a child. Nevertheless, the study remains a classic, and its main conclusion, that fears can be conditioned, is still well accepted.

"Little Albert" was a placid child who rarely cried. When Watson and Rayner gave him a furry white rat to play with (a live one, not a toy), Albert showed no fear; in fact, he was delighted. However, like most children, Albert was afraid of loud noises. When the researchers made a loud noise by striking a steel bar with a hammer, he would jump and fall sideways onto the mattress he was sitting on. The noise made by the hammer was an unconditioned stimulus for the unconditioned response of fear.

Having established that Albert liked rats, Watson and Rayner set about teaching him to fear them. Again they offered him a rat, but this time, as Albert reached for it, one of the researchers struck the steel bar. Startled, Albert fell onto the mattress. The researchers repeated this procedure several times. Albert began to whimper and tremble. Finally, the rat was offered alone, without the noise. Albert fell over, cried, and crawled away as fast as he could; the rat had become a conditioned stimulus for fear (see Figure 9.4). Tests done a few days later showed that Albert's fear had generalized to other hairy or furry objects, including white rabbits, cotton wool, a Santa Claus mask, and even John Watson's hair.

Unfortunately, Watson and Rayner lost access to Little Albert, so they were unable to reverse the conditioning. However, Watson and Mary Cover Jones did reverse another child's conditioned fear—one that was, as Watson put it, "home-grown" rather than psychologist-induced (Jones, 1924). A three-year-old named Peter was deathly afraid of rabbits. Watson and Jones eliminated this fear with a method called **counterconditioning**, in which a conditioned stimulus

counterconditioning In classical conditioning, the process of pairing a conditioned stimulus with a stimulus that elicits a response that is incompatible with an unwanted conditioned response.

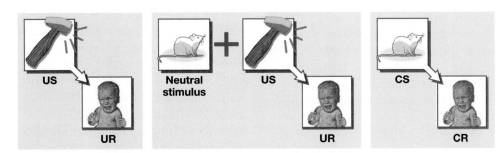

FIGURE 9.4 The Creation of a Fear

In the Little Albert study, noise from a hammer striking a steel bar was an unconditioned stimulus for fear (left). When a white rat, a neutral stimulus, was paired with the noise (centre), the rat then became a conditioned stimulus for fear (right).

is paired with some other stimulus that elicits a response incompatible with the unwanted response. In this case, the rabbit (the CS) was paired with a snack of milk and crackers, and the snack produced pleasant feelings incompatible with the conditioned response of fear. At first, the researchers kept the rabbit some distance from Peter, so that his fear would remain at a low level. Otherwise, Peter might have learned to fear milk and crackers! But gradually, over several days, they brought the rabbit closer and closer. Eventually Peter learned to like rabbits; he was even able to sit with the rabbit in his lap, playing with it with one hand while he ate with the other. A variation of this procedure, called *systematic desensitization*, was later devised for treating phobias in adults (see Chapter 12).

Accounting for Taste

Classical conditioning can also explain how we learn to like and dislike many foods and odours. In the laboratory, researchers have taught animals to dislike foods or odours by pairing them with drugs that cause nausea or other unpleasant symptoms. One researcher trained slugs to associate the smell of carrots, which slugs normally like, with a bitter-tasting chemical that they detest. Soon the slugs were avoiding the smell of carrots. The researcher then demonstrated higher-order conditioning by pairing the smell of carrots with the smell of potato. Sure enough, the slugs began to avoid the smell of potato as well (Sahley, Rudy, & Gelperin, 1981).

Many people have learned to dislike a food after eating it and then falling ill, even when the food wasn't the reason for the sickness. The food, previously a neutral stimulus, becomes a conditioned stimulus for nausea or for other symptoms produced by the illness. Psychologist Martin Seligman once told how he himself was conditioned to hate béarnaise sauce. One night, shortly after he and his wife ate a delicious filet mignon with béarnaise sauce, he came down with a gastrointestinal illness. Naturally, he felt wretched. His misery had nothing to do with the béarnaise sauce, of course, yet the next time he tried it, he found he disliked the taste (Seligman & Hager, 1972).

Notice that unlike conditioning in the laboratory, Seligman's aversion to the sauce occurred after only one pairing of the sauce with illness and with a considerable delay between the conditioned and unconditioned stimuli. Moreover, Seligman's wife did not become a conditioned

Whether we say "yum" or "yuck" to a food may depend on a past experience involving classical conditioning.

stimulus for nausea, and neither did his dinner plate or the server, even though they, too, had been paired with illness. Why? In earlier work with rats, John Garcia and Robert Koelling (1966) had provided the answer: the existence of a greater biological readiness to associate sickness with taste than with sights or sounds. Later work established the same principle for many species, including human beings. Like the tendency to acquire certain fears, this biological tendency probably evolved through natural selection because it enhanced survival: Eating bad food is more likely to be followed by illness and death than are seeing particular sights or hearing particular sounds.

Reacting to Medical Treatments

Because of classical conditioning, medical treatments can create unexpected misery or relief from symptoms, for reasons that are entirely unrelated to the treatment itself.

For example, unpleasant reactions to a treatment can generalize to a wide range of other stimuli. This is a particular problem for cancer patients. The nausea and vomiting resulting from chemotherapy often generalize to the place where the therapy takes place, the waiting room, the sound of a nurse's voice, or the smell of rubbing alcohol. The drug treatment is an unconditioned stimulus for nausea and vomiting, and through association, the other, previously neutral, stimuli become conditioned stimuli for these responses. Even *mental images* of the sights and smells of the clinic may become conditioned stimuli for nausea (Dadds et al., 1997; Redd et al., 1993).

Some cancer patients also acquire a classically conditioned anxiety response to anything associated with their chemotherapy. In one study, patients who drank a particular lemon-lime drink before their therapy sessions developed an anxiety response to that drink—an example of higher-order conditioning. They continued to feel anxious even when the drink was offered in their homes rather than at the clinic (Jacobsen et al., 1995). Even newborn infants can develop conditioned responses in anticipation of painful procedures. Babies born to diabetic mothers may be subjected to repeated heel lancing in the first 24 to 36 hours of life to monitor blood glucose. Researchers in Toronto and Halifax have shown that babies who go through this procedure show more intense pain responses to routine blood tests, which require a needle in the back of the hand, than do babies who have not had the repeated heel lancing procedure (Taddio et al., 2002).

On the other hand, patients may have *reduced* pain and anxiety when they take placebos—pills and injections that have no active ingredients, or treatments that have no direct physical effect on the problem (see Chapter 1). Placebos can be amazingly powerful, especially when they take the form of a large pill, a pill with a brand name, or an injection (Benedetti & Levi-Montalcini, 2001). Why do placebos work? Cognitive psychologists emphasize the role of expectations. Behaviourists, however, would say that the doctor's white coat, the room in the doctor's office or medical clinic, and pills and injections all become conditioned stimuli for relief from symptoms,

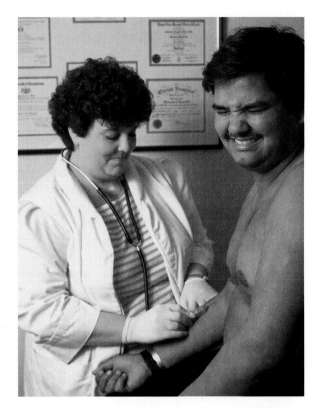

The anxiety that many people feel about having blood drawn can generalize to the nurse, the room, the sight of needles. . . .

because these stimuli have been associated in the past with *real* drugs (Ader, 1997, 2000). The real drugs are the unconditioned stimuli, the relief they bring is the unconditioned response, and the placebos (conditioned stimuli) acquire the ability to elicit similar reactions (conditioned responses).

Quick Quiz

We hope you have not acquired a classically conditioned fear of quizzes. See whether you can supply the correct term to describe the outcome in each of these situations.

1. After a child learns to fear spiders, he also responds with fear to ants, beetles, and other crawling bugs.
2. A toddler is afraid of the bath, so her father puts just a little water in the tub and gives the child a lollipop to suck on while she is being washed. Soon, the little girl loses her fear of the bath.
3. A factory worker's mouth waters whenever a noontime bell signals the beginning of his lunch break. One day, the bell goes haywire and rings every half hour. By the end of the day, the worker has stopped salivating to the bell.

Answers:

1. stimulus generalization   2. counterconditioning   3. extinction

WHAT'S AHEAD

- What do praising a child and quitting your nagging have in common?
- How can operant principles account for superstitious rituals?
- What is the best way to discourage a friend from interrupting you while you're studying?
- How do trainers teach guide dogs to perform the amazing services they do for their owners?

OPERANT CONDITIONING

At the end of the nineteenth century, in the first known scientific study of anger, G. Stanley Hall (1899) asked people to describe angry episodes they had experienced or observed. One person told of a three-year-old girl who broke out in furious, seemingly uncontrollable sobs when she was punished by being kept home from a ride. In the middle of her tantrum, the child suddenly stopped crying and asked her nanny in a perfectly calm voice if her father was in. Told no, she immediately resumed her sobbing.

Children, of course, cry for many valid reasons—pain, discomfort, fear, illness, fatigue—and these cries deserve an adult's sympathy and attention. The child in Hall's study, however, was crying for a different reason. She had learned from prior experience that an outburst of sobbing would bring her attention and possibly the ride she wanted. Her behaviour, though some might call it "naughty," was perfectly understandable because, in the past, crying had paid off. The child's tantrum illustrates one of the most basic laws of learning: *Behaviour becomes more likely or less likely depending on its consequences.*

An emphasis on environmental consequences is at the heart of **operant conditioning** (also called *instrumental conditioning*), the second type of conditioning studied by behaviourists. In classical conditioning, it does not matter whether an animal's or person's behaviour has consequences; in Pavlov's procedure, for example, the dog got food whether it salivated or not. But in operant conditioning, the organism's response (the little girl's sobbing, for example) *operates* or produces effects on the environment. These effects, in turn, influence whether the response will occur again.

Classical and operant conditioning also tend to differ in the types of responses they involve. In classical conditioning, the response is typically

operant conditioning The process by which a response becomes more likely to occur or less so, depending on its consequences.

the neighborhood Jerry Van Amerongen

STAY OUT

An instantaneous learning experience.

Reprinted with special permission of King Features Syndicate.

reflexive, an automatic reaction to something happening in the environment, such as the sight of food or the sound of a bell. Generally, responses in operant conditioning are complex and are not reflexive—for instance, riding a bicycle, writing a letter, climbing a mountain . . . or throwing a tantrum.

The Birth of Radical Behaviourism

Operant conditioning has been studied since the start of the twentieth century, although it was not called that until later. Edward Thorndike (1898), then a young doctoral candidate, set the stage by observing cats as they tried to escape from a "puzzle box" to reach a scrap of fish that was just outside the box. At first, the cat would scratch, bite, or swat at parts of the cage in an unorganized way. Then, after a few minutes, it would chance on the successful response (loosening a bolt, pulling a string, or hitting a button) and rush out to get the reward. Placed in the box again, the cat now took a little less time to escape, and after several trials, the animal immediately made the correct response. According to Thorndike, the correct response had been "stamped in" by its satisfying result, getting the food. In contrast, annoying or unsatisfying results "stamped out" behaviour. Behaviour, said Thorndike, is controlled by its consequences.

This general principle was elaborated and extended to more complex forms of behaviour by B. F. (Burrhus Frederic) Skinner (1904–1990). Skinner called his approach "radical behaviourism" to distinguish it from the behaviourism of John Watson, who emphasized classical conditioning. Skinner argued that to understand behaviour we should focus on the external causes of an action and the action's consequences. He avoided terms that Thorndike used, such as "satisfying" and "annoying," which reflect assumptions about what an organism feels and wants. To explain behaviour, he said, we should look outside the individual, not inside.

The Consequences of Behaviour

In Skinner's analysis, which has inspired an immense body of research, a response ("operant") can lead to one of three types of consequences.

1 *A neutral consequence neither increases nor decreases the probability that the response will recur.* If a door handle squeaks each time you turn it, but you ignore the sound and it has no effect on your likelihood of opening the door in the future, the squeak is considered a neutral consequence. We will not be concerned further with neutral consequences.

2 **Reinforcement** *strengthens the response or makes it more likely to recur.* When your dog begs for food at the table, and you give her the lamb chop off your plate, her begging is likely to increase:

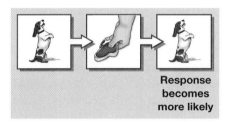

Response becomes more likely

Reinforcers are roughly equivalent to rewards, and many psychologists use *reward* and *reinforcer* as approximate synonyms. However, strict behaviourists avoid the word *reward* because it implies that something has been earned that results in happiness or satisfaction. To a behaviourist, a stimulus is a reinforcer if it strengthens the preceding behaviour, whether or not the organism experiences pleasure or a positive emotion. Conversely, no matter how pleasurable a stimulus is, it is not a reinforcer if it does not increase the likelihood of a response. It's great to get a paycheque, but if you get paid regardless of the effort you put into your work, the money will not reinforce "hardwork behaviour."

3 **Punishment** *weakens the response or makes it less likely to recur.* Any aversive (unpleasant) stimulus or event may be a punisher. If your dog begs for food from the table and you sternly say "No," her begging is likely to decrease—as long as you don't then feel guilty and give her the lamb chop anyway:

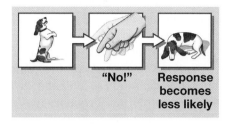

"No!" Response becomes less likely

Parents, employers, and governments resort to reinforcers and punishers all the time—to get kids to behave well, employees to work hard, and constituents to pay taxes—but they do not always use them effectively. For example, they may wait too long to deliver the reinforcer or punisher. In general, the sooner a reinforcer or punisher follows a response, the greater its effect; you are likely to respond more reliably when you do not have to wait ages for a paycheque, a smile, or a grade. When there is a delay, other responses occur in the interval, and the connection between the desired or undesired response and the consequence may not be made.

Primary and Secondary Reinforcers and Punishers Food, water, light stroking of the skin, and a comfortable air temperature are naturally reinforcing because they satisfy biological needs. They are therefore known as **primary reinforcers**. Similarly, pain and extreme heat or cold are inherently punishing and are therefore known as **primary punishers**. Primary reinforcers and punishers can be very powerful, but they also have some drawbacks, both in real life and in research. For one thing, a primary reinforcer may be ineffective if an animal or person is not in a deprived state; a glass of water is not much of a reward if you just drank three glasses. Also, for obvious ethical reasons, psychologists cannot go around using primary punishers (say, hitting their subjects) or taking away primary reinforcers (say, starving their subjects).

Fortunately, behaviour can be controlled just as effectively by **secondary reinforcers** and **secondary punishers**, which are learned. Money, praise, applause, good grades, awards, and gold stars are common secondary reinforcers. Criticism, demerits, catcalls, scolding, fines, and bad grades are common secondary punishers. Most behaviourists believe that secondary reinforcers and punishers acquire their ability to influence

reinforcement The process by which a stimulus or event strengthens or increases the probability of the response that it follows.

primary reinforcer A stimulus that is inherently reinforcing, typically satisfying a physiological need; an example is food.

primary punisher A stimulus that is inherently punishing; an example is electric shock.

secondary reinforcer A stimulus that has acquired reinforcing properties through association with other reinforcers.

secondary punisher A stimulus that has acquired punishing properties through association with other punishers.

punishment The process by which a stimulus or event weakens or reduces the probability of the response that it follows.

behaviour by being paired with primary reinforcers and punishers. (If that reminds you of classical conditioning, reinforce your excellent thinking with a pat on the head! Indeed, secondary reinforcers and punishers are often called *conditioned* reinforcers and punishers.) One secondary reinforcer, money, has considerable power over most people's behaviour because it can be exchanged for primary reinforcers such as food and shelter. It is also associated with other secondary reinforcers, such as praise and respect.

positive reinforcement A reinforcement procedure in which a response is followed by the presentation of, or increase in intensity of, a reinforcing stimulus; as a result, the response becomes stronger or more likely to occur.

negative reinforcement A reinforcement procedure in which a response is followed by the removal, delay, or decrease in intensity of an unpleasant stimulus; as a result, the response becomes stronger or more likely to occur.

Positive and Negative Reinforcers and Punishers

In our example of the begging dog, something pleasant (getting the lamb chop) followed the dog's begging response, so the response increased. Similarly, if a good grade follows your studying, your efforts to study are likely to continue or increase. This kind of process, in which a pleasant consequence makes a response more likely, is known as **positive reinforcement**. But there is another type of reinforcement, **negative reinforcement**, which involves the *removal* of something *unpleasant*. For example, if someone nags you all the time to study, but stops nagging when you comply, your studying is likely to increase—because you will then avoid the nagging:

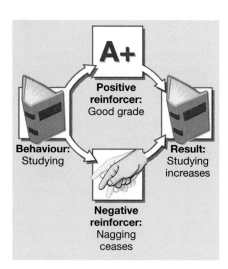

The positive–negative distinction can also be applied to punishment: Something unpleasant may occur following some behaviour (positive punishment), or something *pleasant* may be *removed* (negative punishment). For example, if your friends tease you for being an egghead (positive punishment) or if studying makes you lose time with your friends (negative punishment), you may stop studying:

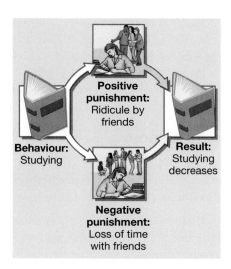

The distinction between positive and negative reinforcement and punishment has been a source of confusion and frustration for generations of students, turning many strong minds to mush. You will master these terms more quickly if you understand that "positive" and "negative" have nothing to do with "good" or "bad." They refer to procedures—giving something or taking something away.

In the case of reinforcement, think of a positive reinforcer as something that is added or obtained (you might picture a plus sign), and a negative reinforcer as avoidance of, or escape from, something unpleasant (you might picture a minus sign). *In either case, a response becomes more likely.* Do you recall what happened when Little Albert learned to fear rats through a process of classical conditioning? After he acquired this fear, crawling away was negatively reinforced by escape from the now-fearsome rodent. The negative reinforcement that results from escaping or avoiding something you perceive as unpleasant explains why so many fears are long-lasting. When you avoid a feared object or situation, you also cut off all opportunities for extinguishing your fear.

Understandably, people often confuse negative reinforcement with positive punishment, because both involve an unpleasant stimulus. With punishment, though, you are subjected to the unpleasant stimulus, and with negative reinforcement, the unpleasant stimulus is taken away. To keep these terms straight, remember that punishment—whether positive or negative—*decreases* the likelihood of a response, whereas reinforcement—whether positive or negative—*increases* it. In real life, punishment and negative reinforcement often go hand in hand. If you use a choke collar on your dog to teach it to heel, a yank on the collar punishes the act of walking ahead of you, but release of the collar negatively reinforces the act of staying by your side.

You can positively reinforce your studying of this material by taking a snack break. As you master the material, a decrease in your anxiety will negatively reinforce studying. But we hope you won't punish your efforts by telling yourself "I'll never get it" or "It's too hard"!

Quick Quiz

What kind of consequence will follow if you can't answer these questions?

1. A child nags her father for a cookie; he keeps refusing, but finally, unable to stand the nagging any longer, he hands over the cookie. For him, the ending of the child's pleas is a _____. For the child, the cookie is a _____.

2. An able-bodied driver is careful not to park in a handicapped space anymore after paying a large fine for doing so. The loss of money is a _____.

3. Identify which of the following are commonly used as secondary reinforcers: quarters spilling from a slot machine, a winner's blue ribbon, a piece of candy, an A on an exam, frequent-flyer miles.

4. During late-afternoon "happy hours," bars and restaurants sell drinks at reduced prices, and appetizers are often free. What undesirable behaviour may be rewarded by this practice?

Answers:

1. negative reinforcer; positive reinforcer
2. punisher—or more precisely, a negative punisher (because something desirable, money, was taken away)
3. All items except the candy are secondary reinforcers (the candy is a primary reinforcer).
4. One possible answer: The reduced prices, free appetizers, and cheerful atmosphere all reinforce heavy alcohol consumption just before the commuter rush hour, thus possibly contributing to binge drinking and drunk driving.

Principles of Operant Conditioning

Thousands of operant-conditioning studies have been done, many using animals. A favourite experimental tool is the *Skinner box*, a cage equipped with a device that delivers food or water when an animal makes a desired response (see Figure 9.5). In the original version, a machine connected to the cage recorded each response and produced a graph on a piece of paper, showing the cumulative number of responses across time; nowadays, computers are used.

Early in his career, Skinner (1938) used the Skinner box for a classic demonstration of operant conditioning. A rat that had previously learned to eat from the food-releasing device was placed in the box. Because no food was present, the animal

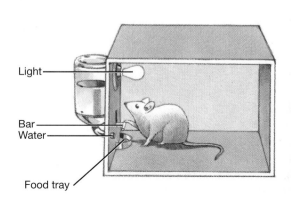

FIGURE 9.5 The Skinner Box

When a rat in a Skinner box presses a bar, a food pellet or drop of water is automatically released. The photo shows Skinner at work on one of the boxes.

proceeded to do typical ratlike things, scurrying about the box, sniffing here and there, and randomly touching parts of the floor and walls. Quite by accident, it happened to press a lever mounted on one wall, and immediately, a pellet of tasty rat food fell into the food dish. The rat continued its movements and again happened to press the bar, causing another pellet to fall into the dish. With additional repetitions of bar pressing followed by food, the animal began to behave less randomly and to press the bar more consistently. Eventually, Skinner had the rat pressing the bar as fast as it could. Since then, behavioural researchers have used the Skinner box and similar devices to discover many important techniques and applications of operant conditioning.

Extinction In operant conditioning, as in classical, **extinction** is a procedure that causes a previously learned response to stop. In operant conditioning, extinction takes place when the reinforcer that maintained the response is removed or is no longer available. At first, there may be a spurt of responding, but then the responses gradually taper off and eventually cease. Suppose you put a coin in a vending machine and get nothing back. You may throw in another coin, or perhaps even two, but then you will probably stop trying. The next day, you may put in yet another coin, an example of *spontaneous recovery*. Eventually, however, you will give up on that machine. Your response will have been extinguished.

Stimulus Generalization and Discrimination In operant conditioning, as in classical, **stimulus generalization** may occur. That is, responses may generalize to stimuli that were not present during the original learning situation but that resemble the original stimuli. For example, a pigeon that has been trained to peck at a picture of a circle may also peck at a slightly oval figure. But if you wanted to train the bird to discriminate between the two shapes, you would present both the circle and the oval, giving reinforcers whenever the bird pecked at the circle and withholding reinforcers when it pecked at the oval. Eventually, **stimulus discrimination** would occur.

Sometimes an animal or human being learns to respond to a stimulus only when some other stimulus, called a **discriminative stimulus**, is present. The discriminative stim-

ulus signals whether a response, if made, will pay off. In a Skinner box containing a pigeon, a light may serve as a discriminative stimulus for pecking at a circle. When the light is on, pecking brings a reward; when it is off, pecking is futile. Human behaviour is controlled by many discriminative stimuli, both verbal ("Store hours are 9 to 5") and nonverbal (traffic lights, doorbells, the ring of a telephone, other people's facial expressions). We all learn to respond correctly to these stimuli in order to get through the day efficiently and get along with others.

Learning on Schedule When a response is first acquired, learning is usually most rapid if the response is reinforced each time it occurs; this procedure is called **continuous reinforcement**. However, once a response has become reliable, it will be more resistant to extinction if it is rewarded on an **intermittent (partial) schedule of reinforcement**, which involves reinforcing only some responses, not all of them. Skinner (1956) happened on this fact when he ran short of food pellets for his rats and was forced to deliver reinforcers less often. Not all scientific discoveries are planned!

Intermittent reinforcement helps explain why people often get attached to "lucky" hats, charms, and rituals. A batter pulls his earlobe, gets a home run, and from then on always pulls his earlobe as he steps up to the plate. A student takes an exam with a purple pen and gets an A, and from then on will not take an exam without a purple pen. Such rituals persist because sometimes they are followed, purely coincidentally, by a reinforcer—a hit, a good grade—and so they became resistant to extinction.

Skinner (1948/1976) once demonstrated this phenomenon by creating eight "superstitious" pigeons in his laboratory. He rigged the pigeons'

Thinking Critically About Superstitions

continuous reinforcement
A reinforcement schedule in which a particular response is always reinforced.

extinction The weakening and eventual disappearance of a learned response; in operant conditioning, it occurs when a response is no longer followed by a reinforcer.

intermittent (partial) schedule of reinforcement A reinforcement schedule in which a particular response is sometimes, but not always, reinforced.

stimulus generalization In operant conditioning, the tendency for a response that has been reinforced (or punished) in the presence of one stimulus to occur (or be suppressed) in the presence of other, similar stimuli.

stimulus discrimination In operant conditioning, the tendency of a response to occur in the presence of one stimulus but not in the presence of other, similar stimuli that differ from it on some dimension.

discriminative stimulus A stimulus that signals when a particular response is likely to be followed by a certain type of consequence.

"Maybe you're right, maybe it won't ward off evil spirits, but maybe it will, and these days who wants to take a chance?"

cages so that food was delivered every 15 seconds, even if the bird didn't lift a feather. Pigeons are often in motion, so when the food came, each animal was likely to be doing something. That something was then reinforced by delivery of the food. The behaviour, of course, was reinforced entirely by chance, but it still became more likely to occur, and thus to be reinforced again. Within a short time, six of the pigeons were practising some sort of consistent ritual—turning in counterclockwise circles, bobbing the head up and down, or swinging their heads to and fro. None of these activities had the least effect on the delivery of the reinforcer; the birds were behaving "superstitiously." It was as if they thought their movements were responsible for bringing the food.

Get Involved The Well-Behaved Pet

If you have a pet, you can use operant-conditioning principles to teach your animal something you'd like it to do. Choose something simple. One student we know taught her cat to willingly enter the garage for the night by feeding the animal a special treat there each evening at the same time. Soon the cat was "asking" to get into the garage at bedtime! Another student taught her pastured horse to come to her and submit willingly to the halter by rewarding the animal's occasional approach with a carrot. Soon the horse was approaching regularly and could be put on an intermittent schedule of reinforcement. Be creative, and see whether you can make your pet better behaved or more co-operative in some way.

Many kinds of intermittent schedules have been studied. Some deliver a reinforcer only after a certain number of responses have occurred; others do so only if a response is made after a certain amount of time has passed since the last reinforcer. The number of responses that must occur or the amount of time that must pass may be fixed (e.g., three responses or five seconds) or may vary around some average. These patterns of reinforcement affect the rate, form, and timing of behaviour. The details are beyond the scope of this book, but here's an example. Suppose your sweetheart sends you 10 email messages each day, playfully spacing them at unpredictable intervals, although they come on average every hour or so. You will probably check your email regularly, at a low but steady rate. But if your sweetheart sends you just one email every day, at around dinnertime, you'll probably start checking around 5:00 p.m., keep doing so until the message arrives (your reward), and then stop looking at all until the next evening.

Now listen up, because here comes one of the most useful things to know about operant conditioning: If you want a response to persist after it has been learned, you should reinforce it *intermittently*, not continuously. If you are continuously giving Harry, your hamster, a treat for pushing a ball with his nose, and then you suddenly stop the reinforcement, Harry will soon stop pushing that ball. Because the change in reinforcement is large, from continuous to none at all, Harry will easily discern the change. But if you have been reinforcing Harry's behaviour only every so often, the change will not be so dramatic, and your hungry hamster will keep responding for quite a while. Pigeons, rats, and people on intermittent schedules of reinforcement have responded in the laboratory thousands of times without reinforcement before throwing in the towel, especially when the timing of the reinforcer varies. Animals will sometimes work so hard for an unpredictable, infrequent bit of food that the energy they expend is greater than that gained from the reward; theoretically, they could actually work themselves to death!

It follows that if you want to get rid of a response—your own or someone else's—you should be careful *not* to reinforce it intermittently. If you are going to extinguish undesirable behaviour by ignoring it—a child's tantrums, a friend's midnight phone calls, a parent's unasked-for advice—you must be absolutely consistent in withholding reinforcement (your attention). Otherwise, the other person will learn that if he or she keeps up the screaming, calling, or advice-giving long enough, it will eventually be rewarded. One of the most common errors people make, from a behavioural point of view, is to reward intermittently the very responses that they would like to eliminate.

Shaping For a response to be reinforced, it must first occur. But suppose you want to train Harry the hamster to pick up a marble, a child to use a fork properly, or a friend to play terrific tennis.

Behavioural techniques such as shaping have many useful applications. Monkeys have been trained to assist their paralyzed owners by opening doors, helping with feeding, and turning the pages of books. Miniature "guide horses" help blind people navigate the streets of the city. Note the cool protective sneakers!

shaping An operant-conditioning procedure in which successive approximations of a desired response are reinforced.

successive approximations In the procedure of shaping, behaviours that are ordered in terms of increasing similarity or closeness to the desired response.

instinctive drift During operant learning, the tendency for an organism to revert to instinctive behaviour.

Such behaviours, and most others in everyday life, have almost no probability of appearing spontaneously. You could grow old and gray waiting for them to occur so that you could reinforce them. The operant solution to this dilemma is a procedure called **shaping**.

In shaping, you start by reinforcing a tendency in the right direction, and then you gradually require responses that are more and more similar to the final, desired response. The responses that you reinforce on the way to the final one are called **successive approximations**. In the case of Harry and the marble, you might deliver a food pellet if the hamster merely turned toward the marble. Once this response was well established, you might then reward Harry for taking a step toward the marble. After that, you could reward him for approaching the marble, then for touching the marble, then for putting both paws on the marble, and finally for holding it. With the achievement of each approximation, the next one would become more likely, making it available for reinforcement.

Using shaping and other techniques, Skinner was able to train pigeons to play ping-pong with their beaks and to "bowl" in a miniature alley, complete with a wooden ball and tiny bowling pins. (Skinner had a great sense of humour.) Animal trainers routinely use shaping to teach dogs to act as the "eyes" of the blind and to act as the "limbs" of people with spinal cord injuries; these talented companions learn to turn on light switches, open refrigerator doors, and reach for boxes on shelves.

Biological Limits on Learning All principles of operant conditioning, like those of classical conditioning, are limited by an animal's genetic dispositions and physical characteristics; if you try to use shaping to teach a fish to dance the samba, you're going to get pretty frustrated (and wear out the fish). Operant-conditioning procedures always work best when they capitalize on inborn tendencies.

Years ago, two psychologists who became animal trainers, Keller and Marian Breland (1961), learned what happens when you ignore biological constraints on learning. They found that their animals were having trouble learning tasks that should have been easy. For example, a pig was supposed to drop large wooden coins into a box. Instead, the pig would drop the coin, push at it with its snout, throw it in the air, and push at it some more. This odd behaviour actually delayed delivery of the reinforcer (food, which is *very* reinforcing to a pig), so it was hard to explain in terms of operant principles. The Brelands finally realized that the pig's rooting instinct—using its snout to uncover and dig up edible roots—was keeping it from learning the task. They called such a reversion to instinctive behaviour **instinctive drift**.

In human beings, too, operant learning is affected by genetics, biology, and the evolutionary history of our species. As we saw in Chapter 3, human children are biologically disposed to learn language without much effort, and they may be disposed to learn some arithmetic operations, as well (Geary, 1995). Further, as we saw in Chapter 2, temperaments and other inborn dispositions may set limits on how a person responds to reinforcers and punishers. It will be easier to shape belly-dancing behaviour if a person is temperamentally disposed to be outgoing and extroverted than if the person is by nature shy.

Skinner: The Man and the Myth

Because of his groundbreaking work on operant conditioning, B. F. Skinner is one of the best known of American psychologists—and also one of the most misunderstood. For example, many people (even some psychologists) think that Skinner denied the existence of human consciousness and the value of studying it. In reality, Skinner (1972, 1990) maintained that we can study private, internal events—what we call perceptions, emotions, and thoughts—by observing our own sensory responses, the verbal reports of others, and the conditions under which such events occur. But he insisted that thoughts and feelings cannot *explain* behaviour; these components of consciousness, he said, are themselves simply behaviours that occur because of reinforcement and punishment.

Skinner aroused strong passions in both his supporters and his detractors. Perhaps the issue that most provoked and angered people was his insistence that free will is an illusion. Human beings, he said, just like other animals, are shaped by their environments and their genetic heritage. Skinner therefore refused to credit personal traits (such as curiosity) or mental events (such as intentions and motives) for anyone's accomplishments, including his own. He regarded himself not as a "self" but as a "repertoire of behaviours" resulting from an environment that encouraged looking, searching, and investigating (Bjork, 1993). (When asked once how he could stand being misunderstood so often, he said he only needed to be understood three or four times a year—his own intermittent schedule of reinforcement.)

Because Skinner thought that the environment could and should be manipulated to solve people's behavioural problems and improve the world, some critics have portrayed him as cold-blooded. But Skinner, who was a kind and mild-mannered man, felt that it would be unethical not to try to improve human behaviour by applying behavioural principles. He practised what he preached, proposing many ways to advance society and reduce human suffering. At the height of public criticism of Skinner, in 1972, the American Humanist Association recognized his efforts on behalf of humanity by honouring him with its Humanist of the Year Award.

Quick Quiz

Can you apply the principles of operant conditioning to your own quiz-taking behaviour? In each of the following situations, choose the best alternative, and give your reason for choosing it.

1. You want your two-year-old to ask for water with a word instead of a grunt. Should you give him water when he says "wa-wa" or wait until his pronunciation improves?

2. Your roommate keeps interrupting your studying even though you have asked her to stop. Should you ignore her completely or occasionally respond for the sake of good manners?

3. Your father, who rarely calls you, has finally left you a message on your voice mail. Should you reply quickly or wait a while so he will know how it feels to be ignored?

Answers:

1. You should reinforce "wa-wa," an approximation of water, because complex behaviours need to be shaped.

2. From a behavioural view, you should ignore her completely because intermittent reinforcement (attention) could cause her interruptions to persist.

3. If you want to encourage communication, you should reply quickly because immediate reinforcement is more effective than delayed reinforcement.

WHAT'S AHEAD

- Why do efforts to "crack down" on wrongdoers often go awry?
- What's the best way to discourage a child from throwing tantrums?
- Why does paying children for good grades sometimes backfire?

OPERANT CONDITIONING IN REAL LIFE

Operant principles can clear up many mysteries about why people behave as they do, and why, in spite of all the well-meaning motivational seminars they attend or resolutions they make, they have trouble changing when they want to. If life at work and at home remains full of the same old reinforcers, punishers, and discriminative stimuli (a grumpy boss, an unresponsive spouse, a refrigerator stocked with fattening goodies), any new responses that have been acquired may fail to generalize.

To help people change unwanted, dangerous, or self-defeating habits, behaviourists have carried operant principles out of the laboratory and into the wider world of the classroom, athletic field, prison, mental hospital, nursing home, rehabilitation ward, child-care centre, factory, and office. The use of operant techniques (and classical ones) in such real-world settings is called **behaviour modification** (also known as *applied behavioural analysis*).

Behaviour modification has had some enormous successes (Kazdin, 2001). Behaviourists have taught parents how to toilet-train their children in only a few sessions (Azrin & Foxx, 1974). They have taught brain-damaged patients to control inappropriate behaviour, focus their attention, and improve their

behaviour modification The application of conditioning techniques to teach new responses or to reduce or eliminate problematic behaviour.

Why do so many people ignore warnings and threats of punishment?

language abilities (McGlynn, 1990). They have developed the most effective programs available for helping autistic children improve their social, language, and academic skills (Green, 1996b). And they have helped ordinary folk eliminate unwanted habits, such as smoking and nail biting, or acquire wanted ones, such as practising the piano or studying.

Yet when people try to apply the principles of conditioning to commonplace problems, their efforts sometimes miss the mark. They may not have a good grasp of the principles you have been learning about in this chapter; for example, they may delay the reinforcer too long, or reinforce unwanted behaviour intermittently. Further, both punishment and reinforcement have their pitfalls, as we are about to see.

The Pros and Cons of Punishment

In a novel called *Walden Two* (1948/1976), Skinner imagined a utopia in which reinforcers were used so wisely that undesirable behaviour was rare. Unfortunately, we do not live in a utopia; bad habits and antisocial acts abound.

An obvious approach to getting rid of them might seem to be punishment. Nearly all Western countries—including Canada, as outlined in the opening news story—have banned physical punishment of schoolchildren by principals and teachers. Still, punishment is used frequently in our society. In their relationships, for example, people punish one another frequently, by yelling, scolding, and sulking. The question is this: Does all this punishment work?

When Punishment Works Sometimes punishment is unquestionably effective. Some severely autistic children have been known to chew their own fingers to the bone, stick objects in their eyes, or tear out their hair. If you ignore such behaviour, the children will seriously injure themselves. If you respond with concern and affection, you may unwittingly reward the behaviour. But immediately punishing the self-destructive behaviour eliminates it (Lovaas, 1977; Lovaas, Schreibman, & Koegel, 1974). Mild punishers, such as a spray of water in the face, or even a firm "No!", are often just as effective as strong ones, such as a slap.

Punishment can also deter some young criminals from repeating their offences. A study of the criminal records of all Danish men born between 1944 and 1947 (nearly 29 000 men) examined

Thinking Critically About Punishment

repeat arrests (recidivism) through age 26 (Brennan & Mednick, 1994). After any given arrest, punishment reduced rates of subsequent arrests for both minor and serious crimes, though recidivism still remained fairly high. Contrary to the researchers' expectations, however, the severity of punishment made no difference: Fines and probation were about as effective as jail time. What mattered most was the *consistency* of the punishment. This is understandable: When punishment is inconsistent—when lawbreakers sometimes get away with their crimes—their behaviour is intermittently reinforced and therefore becomes resistant to extinction.

Punishment can also influence driving behaviour. For example, when photo radar was placed on a section of highway on Vancouver Island, people slowed down, not only in the section with the radar, but on other parts of the highway as well. In other words, people generalized their learning to other locations (Chen, Meckle, & Wilson, 2002). The average speed of vehicles decreased by only three percent, however. But given that photo radar catches all speeders, why was there not a greater effect? It may have something to do with the nature of punishment: whereas the effect is immediate when police officers themselves catch speeders, when photo radar is used the ticket arrives weeks later—and punishment has been found to be most effective when delivered immediately (Estes, 1944).

In sum, these results show that punishment can reduce some crime rates, but they also show why harsh sentencing laws and simplistic efforts to "crack down" on wrongdoers often fail or even backfire. Moreover, in some contexts, "harsh" is a relative concept. Researchers at the University of Windsor, for instance, have shown that street youths develop a certain immunity to legal sanctions against street crimes such as theft, prostitution, and possession of narcotics. These legal consequences pale in comparison with more immediate and intense problems of the street such as poverty and addiction (Baron & Kennedy, 1998).

When Punishment Fails What about punishment that occurs every day, in families, schools, and workplaces? Laboratory and field studies find that it, too, often fails, for several reasons:

1 *People often administer punishment inappropriately or mindlessly.* They swing in a blind rage or shout things they don't mean, applying punishment so broadly that it covers all sorts of irrelevant things the target might have done.

2 *The recipient of punishment often responds with anxiety, fear, or rage.* Through a process of classical conditioning, these emotional side effects may then generalize to the entire situation in which the punishment occurs—the place, the person delivering the punishment, and the circumstances. These negative emotional reactions can create more problems than the punishment solves. A teenager who has been severely punished may strike back or run away. A spouse who is constantly abused will feel bitter and resentful and is likely to retaliate with small acts of hostility. Being physically punished in childhood is a risk factor for depression, aggression, low self-esteem, and many other problems (Barrish, 1996; Gershoff, 2002; Straus & Kantor, 1994).

3 *The effectiveness of punishment is often temporary, depending heavily on the presence of the punishing person or circumstances.* All of us can probably remember some transgressions of childhood that we never dared commit when our parents were around—but that we promptly resumed as soon as they were gone. All we learned was not to get caught.

4 *Most misbehaviour is hard to punish immediately.* Punishment, like reward, works best if it quickly follows a response. But outside the laboratory, rapid punishment is often hard to achieve, and during the delay, the behaviour may be reinforced many times. For example, if you punish your dog when you get home for getting into the doggie treats and eating them all up, the punishment will not do any good because you are too late: Your pet's misbehaviour has already been reinforced by all those delicious treats.

5 *Punishment conveys little information.* If it immediately follows the misbehaviour, punishment may tell the recipient what not to do. But it does not communicate what the person (or animal) *should* do. For example, spanking a toddler for messing in her pants will not teach her to use the potty chair, and scolding a student for learning slowly will not teach him to learn more quickly.

6 *An action intended to punish may instead be reinforcing because it brings attention.* Indeed, in some cases, angry attention may be just what the offender is after. If a mother yells at a child who is throwing a tantrum, the very act of yelling may give him what he wants—a reaction from her. In the schoolroom, teachers who scold children in front of other students, thus putting them in the limelight, often unwittingly reward the very misbehaviour they are trying to eliminate.

Many harried parents resort to physical punishment without being aware of its many negative consequences for themselves and their children. Based on your reading of this chapter, what alternatives does this mother have?

Because of these drawbacks, most psychologists believe that punishment, especially severe punishment, is a poor way to eliminate unwanted behaviour in most situations. When punishment must be used, these guidelines should be kept in mind: (1) It should not involve physical abuse—for example, parents can use "time-outs" and loss of privileges (negative punishers) instead of hitting; (2) it should be accompanied by information about what kind of behaviour would be appropriate; and (3) it should be followed, whenever possible, by the reinforcement of desirable behaviour.

Fortunately, a good alternative to punishment exists: extinction of the responses you want to discourage. Of course, the simplest form of extinction—ignoring the behaviour—is often hard to carry out. It is not easy to ignore a child nagging for a cookie before dinner, a roommate interrupting your concentration, or a dog barking its lungs out. And, as we saw in the example of self-destructive autistic children, ignoring the behaviour is not always appropriate. A teacher cannot ignore a child who is hitting a playmate. The dog owner who ignores Fido's backyard barking may soon hear "barking" of another sort from the neighbours. A parent whose child is a video-game addict cannot ignore the behaviour, because playing video games is rewarding to the child. One solution: Combine extinction of undesirable acts with reinforcement of alternative ones. For example, the parent of a video-game addict might ignore the child's pleas for "just one more game" and at the same time praise the child for doing something else that is incompatible with video-game playing, such as reading or playing basketball.

The Problems with Reward

So far, we have been praising the virtues of reinforcement. But like punishers, rewards do not always work as expected. Let's look at two complications that arise when people try to use them.

Misuse of Rewards Suppose you are a fourth-grade teacher, and a student has just turned in a paper full of grammatical and punctuation errors. This child has little self-confidence and is easily discouraged. What should you do? Many people think the answer is to give the paper a high mark anyway, in order to bolster the child's self-esteem. Indeed, teachers everywhere are handing out lavish praise, happy-face stickers, and high grades in hopes that students' academic performance will improve as they learn to "feel good about themselves."

The problem, from a behavioural point of view, is that to be effective, rewards must be tied to the behaviour you are trying to increase. When rewards are dispensed indiscriminately, just to be kind, they become meaningless because they no longer reinforce desired behaviour; the result is minimal effort and mediocre work. Real self-esteem emerges from effort, persistence, and the gradual acquisition of skills, and is nurtured by a teacher's genuine appreciation of the content of the child's work (Damon, 1995). In the case of the child who turned in a poorly written paper, the teacher could praise its strengths but should also give feedback on the paper's weaknesses and show the child how to correct them.

Thinking Critically About Rewards

CARTOONISTS & WRITERS SYNDICATE http://CartoonWeb.com

I CAN'T ACTUALLY 'READ' IT—BUT I'M TOLD IT MAKES SPECIFIC REFERENCE TO MY OUTSTANDING ACHIEVEMENT IN 'SELF-ESTEEM STUDIES'...

GABLE
THE GLOBE AND MAIL
Toronto
CANADA

Why Rewards Can Backfire A little girl we know came home from school one day in a huff after her teacher announced that good work would be rewarded with play money that could later be exchanged for privileges. "Doesn't she think I can learn without being bribed?" the child asked her mother indignantly.

This child's reaction illustrates another problem in the use of reinforcers. Most of our examples of operant conditioning have involved **extrinsic reinforcers**, which come from an outside source and are not inherently related to the activity being reinforced. Money, praise, gold stars, applause, hugs, and thumbs-up signs are all extrinsic reinforcers. But people (and probably some other animals, too) also work for **intrinsic reinforcers**, such as enjoyment of the task and the satisfaction of accomplishment. As psychologists have applied operant conditioning in real-world settings, they have found that extrinsic reinforcement sometimes becomes too much of a good thing: If you focus on it exclusively, it can kill the pleasure of doing something for its own sake.

intrinsic reinforcers Reinforcers that are inherently related to the activity being reinforced, such as enjoyment of the task and the satisfaction of accomplishment.

extrinsic reinforcers Reinforcers that are not inherently related to the activity being reinforced, such as money, prizes, and praise.

Get Involved   What's Reinforcing Your Behaviour?

For each activity that you do, indicate whether the reinforcers are extrinsic or intrinsic.

Activity	Mostly extrinsic	Mostly intrinsic	About equally extrinsic and intrinsic
Studying	_____	_____	_____
Housework	_____	_____	_____
Worship	_____	_____	_____
Grooming	_____	_____	_____
Job	_____	_____	_____
Dating	_____	_____	_____
Attending class	_____	_____	_____
Reading unrelated to school	_____	_____	_____
Sports	_____	_____	_____
Cooking	_____	_____	_____

Is there an area of your life in which you'd like intrinsic reinforcement to play a larger role? What can you do to make that happen?

Consider what happened when psychologists gave nursery-school children the chance to draw with felt-tipped pens (Lepper, Greene, & Nisbett, 1973). The children already liked this activity and readily took it up during free play. First, the researchers recorded how long each child spontaneously played with the pens. Then they told some of the children that if they would draw with felt-tipped pens for a man who had come "to see what kinds of pictures boys and girls like to draw with Magic Markers," they would get a prize, a "Good Player Award" complete with gold seal and red ribbon. After drawing for six minutes, each child got the award, as promised. Other children did not expect a reward and were not given one.

A week later, the researchers again observed the children's free play. Those children who had expected and received a reward were spending much less time with the pens than they had before the start of the experiment. In contrast, children who were not given an award continued to show as much interest in playing with the pens as they had initially, as you can see in Figure 9.6. Similar results have occurred in other studies when children have been offered a reward for playing with a toy or at an activity they already enjoy (Deci, Koestner, & Ryan, 1999).

Why should extrinsic rewards undermine the pleasure of doing something for its own sake? One possibility is that when we are paid for an activity, we interpret it as work. It is as if we say to ourselves, "I'm doing this because I'm being paid for it. Since I'm being paid, it must be something I wouldn't do if I didn't have to." When the

"That is the correct answer, Billy, but I'm afraid you don't win anything for it."

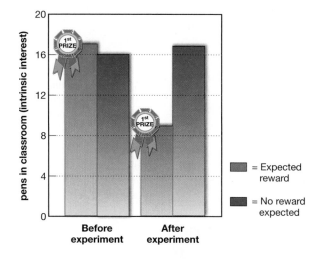

FIGURE 9.6 Turning Play into Work

Extrinsic rewards can sometimes reduce the intrinsic pleasure of an activity. When preschoolers were promised a prize for drawing with felt-tipped pens, the behaviour temporarily increased. But after the children got their prizes, they spent less time with the pens than they had before the study began.

reward is withdrawn, we refuse to "work" any longer. Or perhaps, because we regard extrinsic rewards as controlling, they reduce our sense of autonomy and choice ("I guess I should just do what I'm told to do—and *only* what I'm told to do") (Deci & Ryan, 1987). A third, more behavioural, explanation is that extrinsic reinforcement sometimes raises the rate of responding above some optimal, enjoyable level. Then the activity really does become work.

However, extrinsic rewards do not always weaken the impact of intrinsic ones. If you get money, a high grade, or a trophy for doing a task well, rather than for just doing it, your intrinsic motivation is not likely to decline (Eisenberger & Cameron, 1996, 1998). If you have always been crazy about reading or playing the banjo, you will probably keep reading or playing even when you are not getting a grade or applause for doing so (Mawhinney, 1990). In such cases, you will probably attribute your continued involvement in the activity to your own intrinsic interests and motivation rather than to the reward.

So, what is the take-home message about extrinsic rewards? First, sometimes they are necessary: Few people would trudge off to work every morning if they never got paid; and in the classroom, teachers may need to offer incentives to unmotivated students. Second, extrinsic rewards should be used sparingly, so that intrinsic pleasure in an activity can blossom. As one mother wrote in *Newsweek*, children need to discover for themselves "the joy of music from songs, the power of mathematics from counting and all of human wisdom from reading" (Skreslet, 1987). And finally, educators and employers can avoid the trap of either–or thinking by recognizing that most people do their best when they get tangible rewards *and* when they have interesting, challenging, and varied kinds of work to do.

Effective behaviour modification, as you can see, is not only a science but an art. In "Taking Psychology With You," we offer additional guidelines for mastering that art.

Quick Quiz

Is the art of mastering quizzes intrinsically reinforcing yet?

A. According to behavioural principles, what is happening in the following scenarios?

1. An adolescent whose parents have hit him for minor transgressions since he was small runs away from home.

2. A young woman whose parents paid her to clean her room while she was growing up is a slob when she moves to her own apartment.

3. Two parents scold their young daughter every time they catch her sucking her thumb. The thumb sucking continues anyway.

B. In a fee-for-service system of health care, doctors are paid for each visit by a patient or for each service performed; the longer the visit, the higher the fee. In contrast, some physicians in Canada are paid a salary that does not vary depending upon the number of patients treated. Given what you know about operant conditioning, what are the advantages and disadvantages of each system?

Answers:

A.

1. The physical punishment was painful, and through a process of classical conditioning, the situation in which it occurred also became unpleasant. Because escape from an unpleasant stimulus is negatively reinforcing, the boy ran away.

2. Extrinsic reinforcers are no longer available, and room-cleaning behaviour has been extinguished. Also, extrinsic rewards may have displaced the intrinsic satisfaction of having a tidy room.

3. Punishment has failed, possibly because it rewards thumb sucking with attention or because thumb sucking still brings the child pleasure whenever the parents are not around.

B. In a fee-for-service system, the doctor is likely to provide the attention and tests that ill patients need. However, this system also rewards doctors for unnecessary tests and patient visits, contributing to the explosion in health care costs. In a salary system, doctors may spend more time with a given patient, since their income does not depend upon how many patients they see in a given day.

WHAT'S AHEAD

- Can you learn something without any obvious reinforcement?
- Why do two people often learn different lessons from exactly the same experience?
- Does watching violence on TV make people more aggressive?

LEARNING AND THE MIND

For half a century, behaviourism was the dominant force in North American psychology. Behaviourists liked to compare the mind to an engineer's hypothetical "black box," a device whose workings must be inferred because they cannot be observed directly. To them, the box's contents did not further the understanding of behaviour; it was enough to know that pushing a button on the lid would produce a predictable response. But even as early as the 1930s, some psychologists argued that behaviourism could not account for the complexities of human behaviour. Even a few behaviourists could not resist trying to peek into that black box.

Latent Learning

One behaviourist, Edward Tolman (1938), committed virtual heresy at the time by noting that his laboratory rats, when pausing at turning points in a maze, seemed to be *deciding* which way to go. Moreover, the animals sometimes seemed to be learning even without any reinforcement. What, he wondered, was going on in their little rat brains that might account for this puzzle?

In a classic experiment, Tolman and C. H. Honzik (1930) placed three groups of rats in mazes and observed the rats' behaviour each day for more than two weeks. The rats in Group 1 always found food at the end of the maze and quickly learned to find it without going down blind alleys. The rats in Group 2 were never provided with a food reward and, as you would expect, followed no particular route. Group 3 was the interesting group. These rats were not provided with a food reward for 10 days, and seemed to wander aimlessly, but on the eleventh day they were given food at the end of the maze, and then quickly learned to run to the end of the maze. By the next day, they were doing as well as Group 1, which had been rewarded from the beginning (see Figure 9.7).

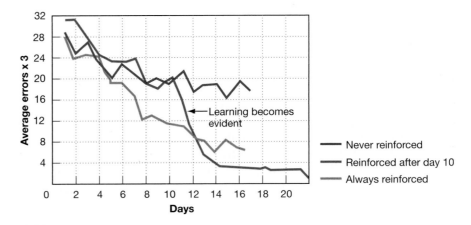

FIGURE 9.7 Latent Learning

In a classic experiment, rats that always found food in a maze made fewer and fewer errors in reaching the food (green curve). Rats that never found food showed little improvement (blue curve). Rats in a third group got no food for 10 days, and then were given food on the eleventh (red curve). These animals showed rapid improvement from then on, quickly equalling the performance of the rats that had received food from the start. This result suggests that learning involves cognitive changes that can occur in the absence of reinforcement and that may not be acted on until a reinforcer becomes available (Tolman & Honzik, 1930).

Group 3 had demonstrated **latent learning**, learning that is not immediately expressed in performance. A great deal of human learning also remains latent until circumstances allow or require it to be expressed. A driver finds her way to Fourth and Kumquat Streets using a new route she has never used before. A little boy observes a parent setting the table or tightening a screw but does not act on this learning for years; then he finds he knows how to do these things, even though he has never done them before.

Latent learning not only occurs without any obvious reinforcer; it also raises questions about what, exactly, is learned during learning. In the Tolman and Honzik study, the rats that did not get any food until the eleventh day seemed to have acquired a mental representation of the maze. They had been learning the whole time; they simply had no reason to act on that learning until they began to find food. Similarly, the driver taking a new route can do so because she already knows how the city is laid out.

What seems to be acquired in latent learning, therefore, is not a specific response, but knowledge about responses and their consequences. We learn how the world is organized, which paths lead to which places, and which actions can produce which payoffs. This knowledge permits us to be creative and flexible in reaching our goals.

latent learning A form of learning that is not immediately expressed in an overt response; it occurs without obvious reinforcement.

OneKey
9.5

Social–Cognitive Learning Theories

observational learning A process in which an individual learns new responses by observing the behaviour of another (a model) rather than through direct experience; sometimes called *vicarious conditioning*.

The black box was pried open further in the 1940s, when two social scientists proposed a major modification of radical behaviourism, which they called *social-learning theory* (Dollard & Miller, 1950). Most human learning, they argued, is acquired by observing other people in a social context, rather than through standard conditioning procedures. By the 1960s and 1970s, social-learning theory was in full bloom, and a new element had been added: the human capacity for higher-level cognitive processes. Its proponents agreed with behaviourists that human beings, along with the rat and the rabbit, are subject to the laws of operant and classical conditioning. But they added that human beings, unlike the rat and the rabbit, are full of attitudes, beliefs, and expectations that affect the way they acquire information, make decisions, reason, and solve problems.

These mental processes affect what individuals will do at any given moment and also, more generally, the personality traits they develop (see Chapter 2). People differ in their attitudes, expectations, and perceptions, and can therefore live through the same event yet come away with entirely different lessons from it (Bandura, 2001). All siblings know this. One may regard being grounded by their father as evidence of his all-around meanness, and another may see the same behaviour as evidence of his care and concern for his children.

Because of this emphasis on mental processes, one leading theorist, Walter Mischel, has called his approach *cognitive social-learning theory* (Mischel, 1973; Mischel & Shoda, 1995); another, Albert Bandura, calls his *social-cognitive theory* (Bandura, 1986). We will use the more widely accepted term **social-cognitive theory** to include all modern social-learning approaches. These approaches share an emphasis on the importance of beliefs, perceptions, and observations of others' behaviour in determining what we learn and how we behave.

social-cognitive theories Theories that emphasize how behaviour is learned and maintained through observation and imitation of others, positive consequences, and cognitive processes such as plans, expectations, and beliefs.

Learning by Observing Late one night, a friend who lives in a rural area was awakened by a loud clattering and banging. Her whole family raced outside to find the source of the commotion. A raccoon had knocked over a "raccoon-proof" garbage can and seemed to be demonstrating to an assembly of other raccoons how to open it: If you jump up and down on the can's side, the lid will pop off.

According to our friend, the observing raccoons learned from this episode how to open stubborn garbage cans, and the observing humans learned how smart raccoons can be. In short, they all benefited from **observational learning**: learning by watching what others do and what happens to them for doing it.

Behaviourists have always acknowledged the importance of observational learning, which they call *vicarious conditioning*, and have tried to explain it in stimulus-response terms. But social-cognitive theorists believe that in human beings, observational learning cannot be fully understood without taking into account the thought processes of the learner (Meltzoff & Gopnik, 1993). These theorists emphasize the knowledge that results when a person sees a *model*—another person—behaving in certain ways and experiencing the consequences (Bandura, 1977).

None of us would last long without observational learning. We would have to learn to avoid oncoming cars by walking into traffic and suffering the consequences, or learn to swim by jumping into a deep pool and flailing around. Learning would be not only dangerous but also inefficient. Parents and teachers would be busy 24 hours a day shaping children's behaviour. Bosses would have to stand over their employees' desks, rewarding every little link in the complex behavioural chains we call typing, report writing, and accounting.

Like father, like daughter. Parents can be powerful role models.

Many years ago, Albert Bandura and his colleagues showed just how important observational learning is, especially for children who are learning the rules of social behaviour (Bandura, Ross, & Ross, 1963). The researchers had nursery-school children watch a short film of two men, Rocky and Johnny, playing with toys. (Apparently the children did not think this behaviour on the part of adults was the least bit odd.) In the film, Johnny refuses to share his toys, and Rocky responds by clobbering him. Rocky's aggressive actions are rewarded because he winds up with all the toys. Poor Johnny sits dejectedly in the corner, while Rocky marches off in triumph with a sack full of his loot and a hobbyhorse under his arm.

After viewing the film, each child was left alone for 20 minutes in a playroom full of toys, including some of the items shown in the film. Watching through a one-way mirror, the researchers found that the children were much more aggressive in their play than a control group that had not seen the film. Some children imitated Rocky almost exactly. At the end of the session, one little girl even asked the experimenter for a sack!

Of course, children imitate positive activities, too. Matt Groening, the creator of the cartoon *The Simpsons*, decided it would be funny if the Simpsons' eight-year-old daughter Lisa played the baritone sax. Sure enough, across the country, little girls began imitating her. Cynthia Sikes, a saxophone teacher in New York, told *The New York Times* (January 14, 1996): "When the show started, I got an influx of girls coming up to me saying, 'I want to play the saxophone because Lisa Simpson plays the saxophone.'"

The Case of Media Violence These findings on latent learning, the role of perceptions in learning, and observational learning are relevant to an ongoing debate: Does media violence make people behave more aggressively? Every time a child or teenager commits a shocking murder or assault, there is a public outcry over the countless acts of violence that children see on television, in films, and in video games. Politicians and parents blame the media, and the media claim to be blameless. What does the evidence show?

First, since Bandura's early research, hundreds of other experimental studies of children, teenagers, and adults have corroborated his findings, convincing many psychologists that observing aggression does increase aggressiveness (APA Commission on Violence and Youth, 1993;

Thinking Critically About Violence

Bushman & Anderson, 2001; Eron, 1995). Meta-analysis shows that the greater the exposure to violence in movies and on television, the stronger the likelihood of a person's behaving aggressively, even after controlling for social class, intelligence, and other factors (Anderson & Bushman, 2001). Moreover, when grade-school children cut back on the time they spend watching TV or playing video games (which are often violent), their aggressiveness declines (Robinson et al., 2001).

But media violence does not cause all viewers, or even most viewers, to become aggressive, and some psychologists believe that the relationship between media violence and real violence is not strong enough to worry about (Freedman, 1988). Interestingly, although the number of violent video games increased throughout the 1990s, overall rates of teenage violence actually declined. Children watch many different programs and movies, and have many models to observe besides those they see in the media, including parents and peers. Further, cause and effect work in the opposite direction as well: Children and adults who are habitually aggressive like to watch violent shows, and are more affected by them than are less aggressive people. After watching violent films, they feel angrier than nonaggressive people do, and are more likely to behave aggressively toward others (Bushman, 1995).

In the social-cognitive view, both conclusions about the relationship of media violence to violent

Does playing violent video games make children more aggressive? The answer is more complicated than yes or no.

behaviour have merit. Repeated acts of aggression in the media *do* model behaviour that some people will imitate. On the other hand, our perceptions and interpretations of what we are watching, along with personality traits such as aggressiveness and sociability, intervene between what we see, what we learn, and how we respond. One person may learn from seeing people being blown away in a film that violence is cool and masculine; another may conclude that violence is ugly and stupid.

What should individuals or society do, if anything, about media violence? Even if only a small percentage of viewers become more aggressive, that fact can have huge social consequences because the total audiences for TV, movies, and video games are immense (Bushman & Anderson, 2001). But censorship, which some people think is the answer, brings its own set of problems: Should we ban *Hamlet?* Cartoons? Jackie Chan martial-arts films? Although Canada has a policy that bans gratuitous or glamorized violence before 9 p.m., many of the shows we see are from the United States, and American stations can't be forced to follow Canadian rules. Similarly, even if a "V-chip" (invented by Tim Collings at Simon Fraser University) is installed in your TV to block parts of violent programs, Canadian cable companies are prevented from making changes to the American shows they buy. So, as you can see, the psychological facts do not automatically give us answers about media violence and the aggression that media images inspire in some viewers.

Quick Quiz

If only *The Matrix* movies had scenes of students taking quizzes!

1. A friend asks you to meet her at a new restaurant across town; you have never been there, but you find your way anyway because you have experienced _____ learning.

2. To a social-cognitive theorist, the fact that we can learn without being reinforced for any obvious responses shows that we do not learn specific responses but rather _____.

3. After watching her teenaged sister put on some lipstick, a little girl takes a lipstick and applies it to her own lips. She has acquired this behaviour through a process of _____.

4. The families of victims shot at a high school by two fellow students claimed in a lawsuit against several video-game manufacturers that the tragedy would not have happened had the killers not had access to violent games. How would you evaluate this claim?

Answers:

1. latent
2. knowledge about responses and their consequences
3. observational learning
4. Although a link has been established between media violence and aggressiveness, it is not a strong one, and it is impossible to prove cause and effect in any given case. Violence has many different causes; for example, some teenagers kill because they have been taunted and rejected by their classmates. Further, a person's response to media violence is influenced by his or her perceptions and attitudes.

Psychology In The News *Revisited*

How can the behavioural and social–cognitive learning principles covered in this chapter help us think about the Supreme Court decision on spanking, described in our opening story?

Findings on learning certainly do not rule out all use of punishment, whether by parents or others. As we saw, punishment is sometimes effective; for example, it deters some young criminals from repeating their offences. And some psychologists argue that the occasional, moderate use of punishment in the home—even spanking—has no long-term detrimental outcomes for most middle-class children, so long as it occurs in an otherwise loving context and as a quick action of last resort when a child is misbehaving (Baumrind, Larzelere, & Cowan, 2002).

But as a routine method of parental discipline, punishment often backfires or makes matters worse. For example, teenagers who have been routinely punished may become more rebellious, or they may even run away. And routine or severe punishment can have long-term negative psychological consequences. When parents insult, humiliate, or ridicule a child, the results are especially devastating.

When children or adults behave badly, punishing them conveys little information about how they might solve their problems constructively. Moreover, the punishment may create a climate of fear, tension, and anger, especially if severe penalties are imposed for minor infractions. Human beings, as we have seen, bring their minds to their experiences, and if they perceive their punishment as being unfair, inequitable, or overly harsh, their bad behaviour is unlikely to change.

Effective parenting requires a host of skills. In the language of learning theory, these include knowing how to properly apply rewards and punishers—with consistency, careful timing, and reinforcement of "successive approximations" toward the desired behaviour. Mild punishers are often as effective as harsh ones, and when punishment is used, it should be combined with reinforcement of good behaviour. (Moreover, the effectiveness of induction—appealing to the child's own resources, abilities, sense of responsibility, and feelings for others—is outlined in Chapter 3.)

For more tips about applying learning principles in your own life, read the "Taking Psychology With You" feature below. By using the techniques derived from learning theory, we can all learn to fashion healthier environments for ourselves, our families, and our fellow human beings—so long as we exercise those techniques with patience, care, and good judgment.

Taking Psychology With You   Shape Up!

Operant conditioning can seem deceptively simple—a few rewards here, a bit of shaping there, and you're done. In practice, though, behaviour modification can be full of unwanted surprises, even in the hands of experts. Here are a few things to keep in mind if you want to modify someone's behaviour:

- **Accentuate the positive.** Most people notice bad behaviour more than good and therefore miss opportunities to use reinforcers. Parents, for example, often scold a child for bedwetting but fail to give praise for dry sheets in the morning; or they punish a child for poor grades but fail to reward studying.

- **Reinforce small improvements.** A common error is to withhold reinforcement until behaviour is perfect (which may be never). Has your child's grade in math improved from a D to a C? Has your favourite date, who is usually an awful cook, managed to serve up a half-decent omelet? Has your messy roommate left some dirty dishes in the sink but vacuumed the rug? It's probably time for a reinforcer. On the other hand, you don't want to overdo praise or give it insincerely. Gushing about every tiny step in the right direction will cause your praise to lose its value, and soon nothing less than a standing ovation will do.

- **Find the right reinforcers.** You may have to experiment a bit to find which reinforcers a person (or animal) actually wants. Try varying the reinforcers; the same ones used again and again can get boring. Reinforcers, by the way, do not have to be things. You can also use valued activities, such as going out to dinner, to reinforce other behaviour.

- **Always examine what you are reinforcing.** It is easy to reinforce undesirable behaviour just by responding to it. Suppose someone is always yelling at you at the slightest provocation. If you respond to the yelling at all, whether by crying, apologizing, or yelling back, you are likely to reinforce it. An alternative might be to explain in a calm voice that you will henceforth not respond to complaints unless they are communicated without yelling—and then, if the yelling continues, walk away. When the person does speak civilly, you can reward this behaviour with your attention and goodwill.

- **Analyze the reasons for a person's undesirable behaviour before responding to it.** A child screaming in a supermarket may be saying, "I'm going out of my head with boredom. Help!" A lover who sulks may be saying, "I'm not sure you really care about me; I'm frightened." Once you understand the purpose of someone's behaviour, you may be more effective in dealing with it.

These guidelines apply to your own behaviour, as well. Assume, for example, that you want to get yourself to study more. Here are some behavioural strategies for increasing the time you spend with your books:

- **Analyze the situation.** Are there circumstances that keep you from studying, such as a friend who is always pressuring you to go out or a rock band that practises next door? If so, you need to change the discriminative stimuli in your environment during study periods. Try to find a comfortable, cheerful, quiet, well-lit place. Not only will you concentrate better, but you may also have positive emotional responses to the environment, which may generalize to the activity of studying.

- **Set realistic goals.** Goals should be demanding but achievable. If a goal is too vague, as in "I'm going to work harder," you won't know what behavioural changes are necessary to reach it or how to recognize when you have done so (what does "harder" mean?). If your goal is focused, as in "I am going to study two hours every evening instead of one," or "I will read 25 pages instead of 15," you have specified both a course of action and a goal you can achieve (and reward).

- **Keep records.** Chart your progress in some way, perhaps by making a graph. This will keep you honest, and the progress you see on the graph will serve as a secondary reinforcer.

- **Don't punish yourself.** If you did not study enough last week, don't brood about it or berate yourself with self-defeating thoughts, such as "I'll never be a good student" or "I'm a failure." Think about the coming week instead.

Above all, be patient. Shaping behaviour is a creative skill that takes time to learn. Like Rome, new habits cannot be built in a day.

SUMMARY

- Research on *learning* has been heavily influenced by *behaviourism*, which accounts for behaviour in terms of observable events, without reference to mental entities such as "mind" or "will." Behaviourists have focused on two types of *conditioning:* classical and operant.

CLASSICAL CONDITIONING

- *Classical conditioning* was first studied by Russian physiologist Ivan Pavlov. In this type of learning, when a neutral stimulus is paired with an *unconditioned stimulus (US)* that elicits a reflexive *unconditioned response (UR)*, the neutral stimulus comes to elicit a similar or related response. The neutral stimulus is then called a *conditioned stimulus (CS)*, and the response it elicits is a *conditioned response (CR)*. Nearly any kind of involuntary response can become a CR.

- In *extinction*, the conditioned stimulus is repeatedly presented without the unconditioned stimulus, and the conditioned response eventually disappears—although later it may reappear (*spontaneous recovery*). In *higher-order conditioning*, a neutral stimulus becomes a conditioned stimulus by being paired with an already established conditioned stimulus. In *stimulus generalization*, after a stimulus becomes a conditioned stimulus for some response, other similar stimuli may produce the same reaction. In *stimulus discrimination*, different responses are made to stimuli that resemble the conditioned stimulus in some way.

- Many theorists believe that what an animal or person learns in classical conditioning is not just an association between the unconditioned and the conditioned stimulus, but information conveyed by one stimulus about another. Indeed, classical conditioning appears to be an evolutionary adaptation that allows an organism to prepare for a biologically important event. Considerable evidence exists that a neutral stimulus does not become a CS unless it reliably signals or predicts the US.

CLASSICAL CONDITIONING IN REAL LIFE

- Classical conditioning may account for positive emotional responses to particular objects and events, fears and phobias, the acquisition of likes and dislikes, and reactions to medical treatments and placebos. John Watson showed how fears may be learned and then may be unlearned through a process of *counterconditioning*. Human beings (and many other species) are biologically primed to acquire some adaptive responses easily, such as conditioned taste aversions and certain fears.

OPERANT CONDITIONING

- In *operant conditioning*, behaviour becomes more likely to occur or less so, depending on its consequences. Responses are generally not reflexive and are more complex than in classical conditioning. Research in this area is closely associated with B. F. Skinner, who called his approach "radical behaviourism."

- In the Skinnerian analysis, *reinforcement* strengthens or increases the probability of a response. *Punishment* weakens or decreases the probability of a response. Immediate consequences usually have a greater effect on a response than do delayed consequences.

- Reinforcers are called *primary* when they are naturally reinforcing (e.g., because they satisfy a biological need) and *secondary* when they have acquired their ability to strengthen a response through association with other reinforcers. A similar distinction is made for punishers.

- Reinforcement and punishment may be either positive or negative, depending on whether the consequence involves a stimulus that is presented or one that is removed or avoided. In *positive reinforcement*, something pleasant follows a response; in *negative reinforcement*, something unpleasant is removed following a response. In *positive punishment*, something unpleasant follows the response; in *negative punishment*, something pleasant is removed.

- Using the Skinner box and similar devices, behaviourists have shown that *extinction, stimulus generalization*, and *stimulus discrimination* occur in operant as well as in classical conditioning. A *discriminative stimulus* signals that a response is likely to be followed by a certain type of consequence.

- The pattern of responding in operant conditioning depends in part on the *schedule of reinforcement*. *Continuous reinforcement* leads to the most rapid learning. However, *intermittent (partial) reinforcement* makes a response more resistant to extinction (and therefore helps account for the persistence of superstitious rituals). One of the most common errors people make is to reward intermittently the responses they would like to eliminate.

- *Shaping* is used to train behaviours with a low probability of occurring spontaneously. Reinforcers are given for *successive approximations* to the desired response, until the desired response is achieved.

- Biology places limits on what an animal or person can learn through operant conditioning. For example, animals sometimes have trouble learning a task because of *instinctive drift*.

OPERANT CONDITIONING IN REAL LIFE

- *Behaviour modification*, the application of conditioning principles, has been used successfully in many settings, but punishment and reinforcement both have their pitfalls.

- Punishment, when used properly, can discourage undesirable behaviour, including criminal behaviour. But it is frequently misused and may have unintended consequences. It is often administered inappropriately because of the emotion of the moment; it may produce rage and fear; its effects are often only temporary; it is hard to administer immediately; it conveys little information about the kind of behaviour that is desired; and it may provide attention that is rewarding. Extinction of undesirable behaviour, combined with reinforcement of desired behaviour, is generally preferable to the use of punishment.

- Reinforcers can also be misused. Rewards that are given out indiscriminately, as in efforts to raise children's self-esteem, do not reinforce desirable behaviour. An exclusive reliance on *extrinsic reinforcement* can sometimes undermine the power of *intrinsic reinforcement*. But money and praise do not usually interfere with intrinsic pleasure when a person is rewarded for doing well rather than for merely participating in an activity, or when a person is already highly interested in the activity.

LEARNING AND THE MIND

- In the 1930s, Edward Tolman studied *latent learning*, in which no obvious reinforcer is present during learning and a response is not expressed until later on, when reinforcement does become available. What seems to be acquired in latent learning is not a specific response, but knowledge about responses and their consequences.

- The 1960s and 1970s saw the increased influence of *social-cognitive theories* of learning, which focus on *observational learning*, in which the learner imitates a model, and on the role played by beliefs, interpretations of events, and other cognitions.

- Social-cognitive theorists argue that because people differ in their perceptions and beliefs, they may learn different lessons from the same event or situation. For example, some people become more aggressive after observing violent images, but most people do not. Moreover, cause and effect also work in the opposite direction: Aggressive individuals are drawn to and are more affected by violent media images than are nonaggressive individuals.

PSYCHOLOGY IN THE NEWS, REVISITED

- Behavioural and social–cognitive learning theories help us understand when punishment might be constructive and appropriate, and also when it backfires, causing resentment and rebellion in the recipient. Learning techniques can be enormously helpful for individuals and institutions, but they must be applied wisely and carefully.

KEY TERMS

conditioning 285

learning 285

behaviourism 285

classical conditioning 287

unconditioned stimulus (US) 287

unconditioned response (UR) 287

extinction (in classical conditioning) 287

LOOKING BACK

- Why would a dog salivate when it sees a light bulb or hears a buzzer, even though it can't eat these things? (p. 287)
- How can classical conditioning help explain prejudice? (p. 288)
- If you have learned to fear collies, why might you also be scared of sheepdogs? (p. 289)
- Why do advertisers often include pleasant music and gorgeous scenery in ads for their products? (p. 291)
- How would a classical-conditioning theorist explain your irrational fear of heights or mice? (p. 291)
- If you eat licorice and then go on an amusement park ride that nauseates you, how might your taste for licorice change? (p. 292)
- How can sitting in a doctor's office make you feel sick? (p. 292)
- What do praising a child and quitting your nagging have in common? (p. 296)
- How can operant principles account for superstitious rituals? (pp. 298–299)
- What is the best way to discourage a friend from interrupting you while you're studying? (p. 299)
- How do trainers teach guide dogs to perform the amazing services they do for their owners? (p. 300)
- Why do efforts to "crack down" on wrongdoers often go awry? (pp. 302–303)
- What's the best way to discourage a child from throwing tantrums? (p. 304)
- Why does paying children for good grades sometimes backfire? (pp. 304–305)
- Can you learn something without any obvious reinforcement? (p. 307)
- Why do two people often learn different lessons from exactly the same experience? (p. 308)
- Does watching violence on TV make people more aggressive? (pp. 309–310)

Psychology In The News

ANTI-WAR PROTESTS MOUNTED IN CITIES ACROSS CANADA

MONTREAL, PQ, March 2003. People across Canada took to the streets to voice their protest against the United States' war against Iraq. From St. John's to Victoria thousands of protesters marched, carrying anti-war banners and chanting "No to war, yes to peace." In some cities, American flags were burned.

The largest turnout was in Montreal, where tens of thousands rallied in front of the U.S. consulate, burning the American flag and chanting that U.S. President George W. Bush was a terrorist. In Toronto, four arrests were made when a small number of protesters lobbed objects at the police who were guarding the U.S. consulate.

Demonstrations in the United States were considerably more tense. In midtown Manhattan,

215 people were arrested in an antiwar "die-in" as they chanted "No business as usual." Hecklers called the protesters "traitors" and "freaks" and yelled "Get a job!" at students in the crowd. The protesters called those who disagreed with them "idiots" and tried to drown them out with chants of "Peace is patriotic."

Anti-war protesters gather in front of the U.S. consulate in Toronto to voice their opposition to the U.S. war in Iraq.

10 Behaviour in Social and Cultural Context

"Why war?" is surely one of the most important questions humanity faces. What are the psychological, economic, and cultural motives behind war? How are attitudes toward war formed, and how and when do they change? Why do some people dissent from the majority opinion, and why are others uncomfortable and angry with dissenters? Why, in the midst of so much violence and cruelty in the world, are there also countless examples of kindness, sacrifice, and heroism?

Researchers in the fields of *social psychology* and *cultural psychology* address these questions, and many other puzzles of human behaviour, by examining the influence of the social and cultural environment on the actions of individuals and groups. *Social* psychologists study how social roles, attitudes, relationships, and groups influence people to do things they would not necessarily do on their own—to act bravely, mindlessly, aggressively, or even cruelly. *Cultural* psychologists study the broader influence of culture and ethnicity on roles and relationships in society.

In this book, we have included discussions of social and cultural influences on child-rearing practices, moral development, test performance, love and attachment, the communication of emotion, and many other areas of life. In this chapter, we will focus on the basic social and cultural forces that affect behaviour and make human beings less independent than they might think. As you read, ask yourself where your own opinions about the U.S. war against Iraq came from: The Canadian or American government's argument? Your friends and family? Television? Religious leaders? Information gained by reading about the issues? How did you feel when you encountered someone—personally, or in the news—whose opinions differed from your own?

WHAT'S AHEAD

- How do social rules regulate behaviour—and what is likely to happen when you violate them?
- Do you have to be mean or disturbed to inflict pain on someone just because an authority tells you to?
- How can ordinary college students be transformed into sadistic prison guards?
- How can people be "entrapped" into violating their moral principles?

ROLES AND RULES

"We are all fragile creatures entwined in a cobweb of social constraints," social psychologist Stanley Milgram once said. The constraints he referred to are social **norms**, rules about how we are supposed to act, enforced by threats of punishment if we violate them and promises of reward if we follow them. Norms are the conventions of everyday life that make interactions with other people predictable and orderly; like a cobweb, they are often as invisible as they are strong. Every society has norms for just about everything in human experience: for conducting courtships, for raising children, for making decisions, for behaviour in public places. Some norms are enshrined in law, such as "A person may not beat up another person, except in self-defence." Some are unspoken cultural understandings, such as "A man may beat up another man who insults his masculinity." And some are unspoken regulations that people learn to follow unconsciously, such as "You may not sing at the top of your lungs on a public bus."

In every society, people also fill a variety of social **roles**, positions that are regulated by norms about how people in those positions should behave. Gender roles define the proper behaviour for a man and a woman. Occupational roles determine the correct behaviour for a manager and an employee, a professor and a student. Family roles set tasks for parent and child, husband and wife. Certain aspects of every role must be carried out or there will be penalties—emotional, financial, or professional. As a student, for instance, you know just what you have to do to pass your psychology course (or you should by now!).

When you violate a role requirement, intentionally or unintentionally, you will tend to feel uncomfortable—or other people will try to make you feel uncomfortable. For instance, in tradi-

norms (social) Rules that regulate social life, including explicit laws and implicit cultural conventions.

role A given social position that is governed by a set of norms for proper behaviour.

Many roles in modern life require us to give up our individuality. If one of these members of the British Coldstream Guards suddenly broke into a dance, his career would be brief—and the dazzling effect of the parade would be ruined. But when does adherence to a role go too far?

tional families, it is part of the woman's role to take care of relationships—send gifts to relatives, write thank-you notes, organize parties, remember an aunt's birthday, and so forth. If a woman does not do these things when she is expected to, her friends and relatives will probably criticize her (di Leonardo, 1987). And traditional male norms have required a man to be strong, reject qualities associated with women (such as emotional "weakness" and crying), keep his problems to himself, and retaliate aggressively if threatened (Fischer et al., 1998). When men violate these norms, for example by revealing their fears and worries, they may be regarded by both sexes as being "too feminine" and poorly adjusted (Kimmel, 1995). Indeed, researchers at Concordia have shown that children as young as two years of age expect people to behave according to gender-based roles. Photos showing adults engaging in gender-inconsistent behaviours (e.g., men putting on lipstick) drew the children's attention more than did gender-consistent photos (Serbin, Poulin-Dubois, & Eichstedt, 2002). Of course, role requirements can change, as they have for both sexes in Western cultures. Nowadays male politicians and athletes even cry in public, a "feminine" act that not long ago would have cost them their careers.

Naturally, people bring their own personalities and interests to the roles they play. Just as two actors will play the same part differently although they are reading from the same script, you will have your own "reading" of how to play the role of student, friend, parent, or employer. Nonetheless, the requirements of a social role are strong—so strong that they may even cause you to behave in ways that shatter your fundamental sense of the kind of person you are. We turn now to two classic studies that illuminate the power of social roles in our lives.

The Obedience Study

In the early 1960s, Stanley Milgram (1963, 1974) designed a study that would become world-famous. Milgram wanted to know how many people would obey an authority figure when directly ordered to violate their own ethical standards. Participants in the study, however, thought they were part of an experiment on the effects of punishment on learning. Each was assigned, apparently at random, to the role of "teacher." Another person, introduced as a fellow volunteer, was the "learner." Whenever the learner, seated in an adjoining room, made an error in reciting a list of word pairs he was supposed to have memorized, the teacher had to give him an electric shock by depressing a lever on a machine (see Figure 10.1). With each error, the voltage (marked from 0 to 450) was to be increased by another 15 volts. The shock levels on the machine were labelled from SLIGHT SHOCK to DANGER—SEVERE SHOCK and, finally, ominously, XXX. In reality, the learners were confederates of Milgram and did not receive any shocks, but none of the teachers ever realized this during the study. The actor-victims played their parts convincingly: As the study continued, they shouted in pain and pleaded to be released, all according to a prearranged script.

Before doing this study, Milgram asked a number of psychiatrists, students, and middle-class adults how many people they thought would "go all the way" to XXX on orders from the researcher. The psychiatrists predicted that most people would refuse to go beyond 150 volts, when the learner first demanded to be freed, and that only one person in a thousand, someone who was disturbed and sadistic, would administer the highest voltage. The nonprofessionals agreed with this prediction, and all of them said that they personally would disobey early in the procedure.

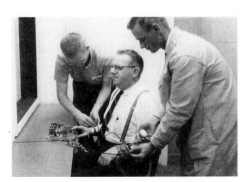

FIGURE 10.1 The Milgram Obedience Experiment

On the left is Milgram's original shock machine; in 1963, it looked pretty ominous. On the right, the "learner" is being strapped into his chair by the experimenter and the "teacher."

That is not, however, the way the results turned out. Every single person administered some shock to the learner, and about two-thirds of the participants, of all ages and from all walks of life, obeyed to the fullest extent. Many protested to the experimenter, but they backed down when he calmly asserted, "The experiment requires that you continue." They obeyed no matter how much the victim shouted for them to stop and no matter how painful the shocks seemed to be. They obeyed even when they themselves were anguished about the pain they believed they were causing. As Milgram (1974) noted, participants would "sweat, tremble, stutter, bite their lips, groan, and dig their fingernails into their flesh"—but still they obeyed.

More than 1000 people at several American universities eventually went through replications of the Milgram study. Most of them, men and women equally, inflicted what they thought were dangerous amounts of shock to another person. Researchers in other countries have also found high percentages of obedience, ranging to more than 90 percent in Spain and the Netherlands (Meeus & Raaijmakers, 1995; Smith & Bond, 1994).

Milgram and his team subsequently set up several variations of the study to determine the circumstances under which people might disobey the experimenter. They found that virtually nothing the victim did or said changed the likelihood of compliance—even when the victim said he had a heart condition, screamed in agony, or stopped responding entirely, as if he had collapsed. However, people *were* more likely to disobey under the following conditions:

- *When the experimenter left the room.* Many people then subverted authority by giving low levels of shock but reporting that they had followed orders.

- *When the victim was right there in the room,* and the teacher had to administer the shock directly to the victim's body.

- *When two experimenters issued conflicting demands* to continue the experiment or to stop at once. In this case, no one kept inflicting shock.

- *When the person ordering them to continue was an ordinary man,* apparently another volunteer, instead of the authoritative experimenter.

- *When the subject worked with peers who refused to go further.* Seeing someone else rebel gave subjects the courage to disobey.

Obedience, Milgram concluded, was more a function of the *situation* than of the particular personalities of the participants. "The key to [their] behaviour," Milgram (1974) summarized, "lies not in pent-up anger or aggression but in the nature of their relationship to authority. They have given themselves to the authority; they see themselves as instruments for the execution of his wishes; once so defined, they are unable to break free."

The Milgram study has had its critics. Some consider it unethical because people were kept in the dark about what was really happening until the session was over (of course, telling them in advance would have invalidated the study) and because many suffered emotional pain (Milgram countered that they would not have felt pain if they had simply disobeyed instructions). Others question the conclusion that personality traits always have less influence on behaviour than the demands of the situation; certain traits, such as hostility and rigidity, do increase obedience to authority in real life (Blass, 1993, 2000).

Some psychologists also object to the parallel Milgram drew between the behaviour of the study's participants and the brutality of the Nazis and others who have committed acts of barbarism in the name of duty (Berkowitz, 1999; Darley, 1995). The people in Milgram's study obeyed only when the experimenter was hovering right there, and many of them felt enormous discomfort and conflict. In contrast, most Nazis acted without direct supervision by authorities, without external pressure, and without feelings of anguish.

Nevertheless, this famous and compelling study has had a tremendous influence on public awareness of the dangers of uncritical obedience. As John Darley (1995) observed, "Milgram shows us the beginning of a path by means of which ordinary people, in the grip of social forces, become the origins of atrocities in the real world."

The Prison Study

Another study that became world-famous is known as the Stanford Prison Study. Its designers, Philip Zimbardo and Craig Haney, wanted to know what would happen if ordinary college students were randomly assigned to the roles of prisoners and guards (Haney, Banks, & Zimbardo, 1973). And so they set up a serious-looking "prison" in the basement of a Stanford building, complete with individual cells, different uniforms for prisoners and guards (including night sticks for the guards), and so forth. The students agreed to live there for two weeks.

The results were dramatic. Within a short time, the prisoners became distressed, helpless, and panicky. They developed emotional symptoms and physical ailments. Some became apathetic; others became rebellious. Within an equally short time, the guards began to enjoy their new power. Some tried to be nice, helping the prisoners and doing little favours for them. Some were "tough but fair," holding strictly to "the rules." But about a third became tyrannical. They almost always chose to be harsh and abusive, even when the prisoners were not resisting in any way. The researchers, who had not expected such a speedy and alarming transformation of healthy students, ended this study after only six days.

Generations of students and the general public have seen compelling clips from the videos made at the time. To the researchers, their study demonstrated the power of roles: The guards' aggression, they said, was entirely a result of wearing a guard's uniform and having the power of the guard's role (Haney, Banks, & Zimbardo, 1973; Haney & Zimbardo, 1998). Recently, however, critics have argued that the prison study is really another example of obedience to authority and of how willingly some people obey instructions—in this case, from Zimbardo himself (Haslam & Reicher, 2003). Consider the briefing that Zimbardo provided to the "guards" at the beginning of the study:

> You can create in the prisoners feelings of boredom, a sense of fear to some degree, you can create a notion of arbitrariness that their life is totally controlled by us, by the system, you, me, and they'll have no privacy. . . . We're going to take away their individuality in various ways. In general what all this leads to is a sense of powerlessness. That is, in this situation we'll have all the power and they'll have none (The Stanford Prison Study video, quoted in Haslam & Reicher, 2003).

These are pretty powerful suggestions to the guards about how they would be permitted to behave, and they convey Zimbardo's personal encouragement (*we'll* have all the power), so it is not surprising that some took Zimbardo at his word and behaved quite brutally. Still, in real prisons, guards do have the kind of power that was given to these students. In any case, the study remains a

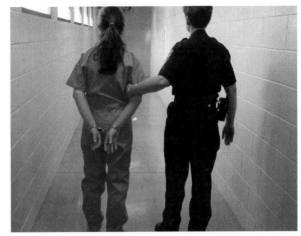

Prisoners and guards quickly learn their respective roles, which usually have more influence on their behaviour than their personalities do.

powerful demonstration of how the *social situation*—whether the role itself or obedience to authority—affects behaviour, causing people to behave in ways they might not otherwise choose to.

Why People Obey

Of course, obedience to authority or to the norms of a situation is not always harmful or bad. A certain amount of routine compliance with rules is necessary in any group, and obedience to authority has many benefits for individuals and society. A nation could not operate if all its citizens ignored traffic signals, cheated on their taxes, dumped garbage wherever they chose, or assaulted each other. An organization could not function if its members came to work only when they felt like it. But obedience also has a darker aspect. Throughout history, the plea "I was only following orders" has been offered to excuse actions carried out on behalf of orders that were foolish, destructive, or illegal. The writer C. P. Snow once observed that "more hideous crimes have been committed in the name of obedience than in the name of rebellion."

Most people follow orders because of the obvious consequences of disobedience: They can be suspended from school, fired from their jobs, or arrested. They may also obey because of what they hope to gain: being liked, getting certain advantages or promotions from the authority, or learning from the authority's greater knowledge or experience. Primarily, though, people obey because they are deeply convinced of the authority's legitimacy. They obey not in hopes of gaining some tangible benefit, but because they like and respect the authority and value the relationship (Tyler, 1997).

But what about all those obedient people in Milgram's study who felt they were doing wrong and who wished they were free, but who could not untangle themselves from the "cobweb of social constraints?" Why do people obey when it is not in their interests, or when obedience requires them to ignore their own values or even commit a crime? How do they become morally disengaged from the consequences of their actions? Researchers looking at the social context of behaviour draw our attention to several factors that cause people to obey when they would rather not (Bandura, 1999; Gourevich, 1998; Kelman & Hamilton, 1989; Staub, 1999):

1 *Allocating responsibility to the authority.* One common way that people justify their behaviour is to hand over responsibility to the authority, thereby absolving themselves of accountability for their own actions. In Milgram's study, many who administered the highest levels of shock adopted the attitude "It's his problem; I'm just following orders." In contrast, individuals who refused to give high levels of shock took responsibility for their own actions and refused to grant the authority legitimacy. "One of the things I think is very cowardly," said a 32-year-old engineer, "is to try to shove the responsibility onto someone else. See, if I now turned around and said, 'It's your fault . . . it's not mine,' I would call that cowardly" (Milgram, 1974).

2 *Routinizing the task.* When people define their actions in terms of routine duties and roles, their behaviour starts to feel normal, just a job to be done. Becoming absorbed in busywork distracts them from raising doubts or ethical questions, and it fosters an uncritical, mindless attention to details that obscures the larger picture. In the Milgram study, some people became so fixated on the "learning task" that they shut out any moral concerns about the learner's demands to be let out. Routinization is typically the mechanism by which governments enlist citizens to aid and abet programs of genocide. Nazi bureaucrats kept meticulous records of every victim, and in Cambodia in the 1970s the Khmer Rouge recorded the names and histories of the millions of victims they tortured and killed. "I am not a violent man," said Sous Thy, one of the clerks who recorded these names, to a reporter from *The New York Times.* "I was just making lists."

3 *Wanting to be polite.* Good manners protect people's feelings and make relationships and civilization possible. But once people are caught in what they perceive to be legitimate roles and are obeying a legitimate authority, good manners ensnare them into further obedience. They do not want to rock the boat, appear to doubt the experts, or be rude, because they know they will be disliked for doing so (Collins & Brief, 1995).

Most people learn the language of manners ("please," "thank you," "I'm sorry for missing your birthday"), but they literally lack the words to justify disobedience and rudeness toward an authority they respect. In the Milgram study, many people could not find the words to justify walking out, so they stayed. One woman kept apologizing to

Routinization enables people to commit or collaborate in atrocities. During the Cambodian genocide of 1975–1979, 1.7 million people lost their lives under the ruthless regime of Pol Pot. More than 16 000 political prisoners were tortured and killed at one infamous prison. Authorities kept meticulous records and photos of each victim in order to make their barbarous activities seem mundane and normal. This man, Ing Pech, one of only seven survivors, was spared because he had skills useful to his captors. He now runs a museum at the prison.

the experimenter, trying not to offend him with her worries for the victim: "Do I go right to the end, sir? I hope there's nothing wrong with him there." (She did go right to the end.) A man repeatedly protested and questioned the experimenter, but he too obeyed, even when the victim had apparently collapsed in pain. "He thinks he is killing someone," Milgram (1974) commented, "yet he uses the language of the tea table."

4 *Becoming entrapped.* **Entrapment** is a process in which individuals escalate their commitment to a course of action in order to justify their investment in it (Brockner & Rubin, 1985). The first steps of entrapment pose no difficult choices, but one step leads to another, and before you realize it, you have become committed to a course of action that poses problems. In Milgram's study, once subjects had given a 15-volt shock, they had committed themselves to the experiment. The next level was "only" 30 volts. Because each increment was small, before they knew it most people were administering what they believed were dangerously strong shocks. At that point, it was difficult to explain a sudden decision to quit. Participants who questioned the procedure early were less likely to become entrapped and more likely to eventually disobey (Modigliani & Rochat, 1995).

Individuals and nations alike are vulnerable to the sneaky process of entrapment. You start dating someone you like moderately; before you know it, you have been together so long that you can't break up, although you don't want to become committed, either. Government leaders start a war they think will end quickly. Years later, the nation has lost so many soldiers and so much money that the leaders believe they cannot retreat without losing face.

A chilling study of entrapment was conducted with 25 men who had served in the Greek military police during the authoritarian regime that ended in 1974 (Haritos-Fatouros, 1988). A psychologist interviewed the men, identifying the steps used in training them to use torture in questioning prisoners. First the men were ordered to stand guard outside the interrogation and torture cells. Then they stood guard inside the detention rooms, where they observed the torture of prisoners. Then they "helped" beat up prisoners. Once they had obediently followed these orders and became actively involved, the torturers found their actions easier to carry out. The principle of entrapment in training torturers is not a practice only of "bad" people in enemy cultures. In a book appropriately called *Unspeakable Acts, Ordinary People,* John Conroy (2000) documented cases of torture by Chicago police officers against prisoners; by the British Army against IRA suspects in Northern Ireland; and by Israeli soldiers against Palestinians.

As Milgram would have predicted, even torturers see themselves as otherwise "good guys" who are just "doing their jobs." This is a difficult concept for people who divide the world into "good guys" versus "bad guys" and cannot imagine that good guys might do cruel things. Yet in everyday life, as in the Milgram study, people often set out on a path that is morally ambiguous, only to find that they have travelled a long way toward violating their own principles. From Greece's torturers to the Khmer Rouge's dutiful clerks, from Milgram's well-meaning volunteers to all of us in our everyday lives, people face the difficult task of drawing a line beyond which they will not go. For many, the demands of the role defeat the inner voice of conscience.

entrapment A gradual process in which individuals escalate their commitment to a course of action to justify their investment of time, money, or effort.

Quick Quiz

Step into your role of student to answer these questions.

1. About what proportion of the people in Milgram's obedience study administered the highest level of shock? (a) two-thirds, (b) one-half, (c) one-third, (d) one-tenth
2. Which of the following actions by the "learner" reduced the likelihood of being shocked by the "teacher" in Milgram's study? (a) protesting noisily, (b) screaming in pain, (c) complaining of having a heart ailment, (d) nothing he did made a difference
3. A friend of yours, who is moving, asks you to bring over a few boxes. Since you are there anyway, he asks you to fill them with books. Before you know it, you have packed up his entire kitchen, living room, and bedroom. What social-psychological process is at work here?

Answers:

1. a   2. d   3. entrapment

WHAT'S AHEAD

- What is one of the most common mistakes people make when explaining the behaviour of others?
- Why do so many people blame victims of tragedy or crime for having brought their misfortunes on themselves?
- What is the "Big Lie," and why does it work so well?
- What is the difference between ordinary techniques of persuasion and the coercive techniques used by cults?

SOCIAL INFLUENCES ON BELIEFS

Social psychologists are interested not only in what people do in social situations, but also in what goes on in their heads while they're doing it. Researchers in the area of **social cognition** examine how people's perceptions of themselves and others affect their relationships and how the social environment influences thought, memory, perception, and beliefs. We will consider two important topics in this area: explanations about behaviour and the formation of attitudes.

social cognition An area in social psychology concerned with social influences on thought, memory, perception, and beliefs.

OneKey
10.3

Attributions

People read detective stories to find out *who* did the dirty deed, but in real life we also want to know *why* people do things—was it because of a terrible childhood, a mental illness, possession by a demon, or what? According to **attribution theory**, the explanations we make about our behaviour and the behaviour of others generally fall into two categories. When we make a *situational attribution*, we are identifying the cause of an action as something in the situation or environment: "Joe stole the money because his family is starving." When we make a *dispositional attribution*, we are identifying the cause of an action as something in the person, such as a trait or a motive: "Joe stole the money because he is a born thief."

When people are trying to find reasons for someone else's behaviour, they reveal a common bias: They tend to overestimate personality traits and underestimate the influence of the situation (Forgas, 1998; Nisbett & Ross, 1980). In terms of attribution theory, they tend to ignore situational attributions in favour of dispositional ones. This tendency has been called the **fundamental attribution error** (Jones, 1990; Van Boven, Kamada, & Gilovich, 1999). Were the hundreds of people

attribution theory The theory that people are motivated to explain their own and other people's behaviour by attributing causes of that behaviour to a situation or a disposition.

fundamental attribution error The tendency, in explaining other people's behaviour, to overestimate personality factors and underestimate the influence of the situation.

who obeyed Milgram's experimenters sadistic by nature? Were the student guards in the prison study sadistic and the prisoners cowardly? Those who think so are committing the fundamental attribution error.

The impulse to explain other people's behaviour in terms of their personalities is so strong that we do it even when we know that the other person was *required* to behave in a certain way (Yzerbyt et al., 2001). People are especially likely to overlook situational attributions when they are in a good mood and not inclined to think about other people's motives critically, or when they are distracted and preoccupied and don't have time to stop and ask themselves, "Why, exactly, *is* Aurelia behaving like such a dim-wit today?" (Forgas, 1998). Instead, they leap to the easiest attribution, which is dispositional: It's all because of her dim personality. They are less likely to wonder if Aurelia has recently joined a group of friends who are encouraging dim-witted behaviour, or is under unusual pressure that is making her act "out of character."

Attributions

"Why is Aurelia behaving like a dim-wit?"

Situational

"She's under pressure."

Dispositional

"She's self-involved and clueless."

(may lead to)

Fundamental Attribution Error

Ignoring influence of situation on behaviour and emphasizing personality traits alone

The fundamental attribution error is especially prevalent in Western nations, where middle-class people tend to believe that individuals are responsible for their own actions. In countries such as India, where everyone is embedded in caste and family networks, and in Japan, China, Korea, and Hong Kong, where people are more group oriented than in the West, people are more likely to be aware of situational constraints on behaviour (Choi et al., 2003; Choi, Nisbett, & Norenzayan, 1999; Miyamoto & Kitayama, 2002). Thus, if someone is behaving oddly, makes a mistake, or plays badly in a soccer match, a person from India

Children learn the value of self-serving attributions at an early age.

or China, unlike a Westerner, is more likely to make a situational attribution of the person's behaviour ("He's under pressure") than a dispositional one ("He's incompetent") (Menon et al., 1999).

Westerners do not always prefer dispositional attributions, however. When it comes to explaining their *own* behaviour, they often reveal a **self-serving bias**: They tend to choose attributions that are favourable to them, taking credit for their good actions (a dispositional attribution) but letting the situation account for their failures, embarrassing mistakes, or harmful actions (Campbell & Sedikides, 1999). For instance, most North Americans, when angry, will say, "I am furious for good reason—this situation is intolerable." They are less likely to say, "I am furious because I am an ill-tempered grinch." On the other hand, if they do something admirable, such as donating to charity, they are likely to attribute their motives to a personal disposition ("I'm so generous") instead of the situation ("That guy on the phone pressured me into it").

According to the **just-world hypothesis**, attributions are also affected by the need to believe that the world is fair and that justice prevails, and particularly that good people are rewarded and bad guys punished. Melvin Lerner, at the University of Waterloo, has shown that this belief helps people make sense out of senseless events and feel safe in the presence of threatening events (Lerner, 1980). Unfortunately, it also leads to a dispositional attribution called *blaming the victim*. If a friend is fired, a woman is raped, or an unarmed man is shot by a police officer (as happened in the tragic case of Dudley George in Ontario in 1995), it is reassuring to think that they all must have done something to deserve what happened or to provoke it: The friend wasn't doing his work,

the woman was dressed too "provocatively," the man shouldn't have been protesting in a provincial park. Interestingly, cross-national research has shown that Canadians score higher on measures of just-world beliefs than do Europeans (Loo, 1998; MacLean & Chown, 1988); in a comparison of social science students in Britain and Canada, for example, the Canadian students were more likely to blame elderly people who were experiencing poor health or financial difficulties. Blaming the victim is virtually universal, however, when people are ordered to harm others or find themselves entrapped into harming others (Bandura, 1999). In the Milgram study, some "teachers" made comments such as, "[The learner] was so stupid and stubborn he deserved to get shocked" (Milgram, 1974).

An extreme example of blaming the victim occurred in the aftermath of the World Trade Center attack on 9/11, when the Rev. Jerry Falwell said that America deserved the 3000 deaths and brought this harsh punishment upon itself because God was displeased with the country's godless, secular ways. Falwell's remarks angered many people, but they showed how powerful is the desire to find a reason for something inexplicably horrible—and how desperately eager many people are to preserve their faith in a just world.

Of course, sometimes dispositional (personality) attributions *do* explain a person's behaviour. The point to remember is that attributions, whether they are accurate or not, have tremendously important consequences. Here's an example that will apply to your own relationships. Happy couples tend to attribute their partners' occasional lapses to something in the situation ("Poor Horace is under a lot of stress") and the partners' positive actions to stable, internal dispositions ("Horace has the sweetest nature"). But

self-serving bias The tendency, in explaining one's own behaviour, to take credit for one's good actions and rationalize one's mistakes.

just-world hypothesis The notion that many people need to believe that the world is fair and that justice is served, that bad people are punished and good people rewarded.

unhappy couples do just the reverse. They attribute lapses to their partners' personalities ("Henry is a hopeless mama's boy") and good behaviour to the situation ("Yeah, he gave me a present, but only because his mother told him to"). These attributional habits, which can change over time, are strongly related to satisfaction or dissatisfaction with the partner (Karney & Bradbury, 2000). The attributions you make about your partner, your parents, and your friends will make a big difference in how you get along with them—and how long you will put up with their failings.

Quick Quiz

To what do you attribute your success in answering these questions?

1. What kind of attribution is being made in each case, situational or dispositional? (a) A man says, "My wife has sure become a grouchy person." (b) The same man says, "I'm grouchy because I've had a bad day at the office." (c) A woman reads about high unemployment in poor communities and says, "Well, if those people weren't so lazy, they would find work."

2. What principles of attribution theory are suggested by the items in the preceding question?

Answers:

1. a. dispositional   b. situational   c. dispositional
2. Item a illustrates the fundamental attribution error; b, the self-serving bias; and c, blaming the victim, possibly because of the just-world hypothesis.

Attitudes

People hold attitudes about all sorts of things—politics, people, food, children, movies, sports heroes, you name it. An *attitude* is a belief about people, groups, ideas, or activities. Some attitudes are *explicit*: We are aware of them; they shape our conscious decisions and actions; and they can be measured on self-report questionnaires. Others are *implicit*: We are unaware of them; they may influence our behaviour in ways we do not recognize; and they are measured in various indirect ways, as we will see later in discussing the attitudes involved in prejudice (Wilson, Lindsey, & Schooler, 2000).

Implicit and explicit attitudes often do not have the same causes or consequences—in fact, they often are not even strongly related to each other (Rudman, 2004). Explicit attitudes reflect recent experiences and conscious beliefs. But implicit attitudes largely stem from past, forgotten events, when you formed your emotional associations toward an activity, event, or group of people. As you can imagine, they can therefore be very resistant to change.

Shifting Opinions versus Bedrock Beliefs On most topics, like movies and sports, people easily accept the fact that attitudes range from casual opinions to passionate convictions. If your best friend is neutral about baseball whereas you are an insanely devoted fan, your friendship will probably survive. But when the subject involves beliefs that give meaning and purpose to a person's life—most notably, politics and religion—it's another ball game, so to speak. For example, some people regard the traditions of their religion as sacred sources of guidance, which are to be taken literally and which offer the only possible route to salvation. Others regard the precepts of their religion as general guides that are open to interpretation; they accept some rituals and beliefs, but not all of them. Still others find religious beliefs and rituals to be of little personal relevance, or actively rebel against them. Research conducted at the University of Manitoba indicates that the number of people falling in this last category is on the rise in Western countries, though more so in Europe than North America (Altemeyer, 2004).

Perhaps the one religious attitude that causes the most controversy and bitterness around the world is the one toward religious diversity itself—whether accepting or intolerant. Some people of all religions accept a world of differing religious views and practices, and believe that church and state should be separate. But for many conservatives and fundamentalists (in any religion), religion and politics are inseparable, and they believe that one religion should prevail (Jost et al., 2003). You can see, then, why the irreconcilable attitudes of religious tolerance and intolerance cause continuing conflict and, in extreme cases, can be used to justify war and terrorism, as is happening across the Middle East.

Some convictions are thus deeply ingrained and difficult to change, especially if they are emotionally based implicit ones. Other attitudes, however, are more flexible, depending on the groups you belong to, the experiences you have, your economic circumstances, and many other social and environmental influences.

One such influence is your *generational identity*, the characteristic attitudes and values that result from being a certain age at a certain moment in history. Each generation shares many of the same experiences, such as financial busts or booms, increases or decreases in rates of violence, job and marital opportunities (or the lack of them), technological breakthroughs, war or peace. The ages between 16 and 24 appear to be critical for the formation of a generational identity. The social and political events that occur during these years make deeper impressions and exert more lasting influence than those that happen later in life (Inglehart, 1990; Schuman & Scott, 1989). In both Canada and the United States, key generational events were the Depression in the 1930s, the postwar baby boom, and the civil rights and women's movements of the 1960s and 1970s. Canada, of course, has experienced its own unique generational events, including Newfoundland's becoming a province in 1949, the development of medicare in the 1950s and 1960s, the adoption of a national flag in 1965, the FLQ crisis in 1972, and the collapse of the Meech Lake Accord in 1990. All of these have helped shape the identity of Canadians. Finally, the attacks in 2001 on New York and Washington, which shattered the sense of safety and security that most North Americans had felt, might well shape the generational identity of young Canadians and Americans.

Of course, attitudes change as a result of new information and experience. But they also change because of a psychological need for consistency. In Chapter 7, we discussed **cognitive dissonance**, the uncomfortable feeling that occurs when two attitudes, or an attitude and behaviour, are in conflict (are dissonant). To resolve this dissonance, one of those attitudes has to change. For example, if a politician or celebrity you admire does something stupid, immoral, or illegal, you can restore consistency by lowering your opinion of the person. Or you can decide that the person's behaviour wasn't so stupid or immoral after all . . . and besides, everyone else does it, too.

Most people think that their attitudes are based on thinking, a result of reasoned conclusions and decisions. Sometimes, of course, that's true! But some attitudes are a result of not thinking at all. Instead, they are a result of social influence—efforts by others to get us to change our minds by using subtle manipulation and sometimes outright coercion.

Friendly Persuasion All around you, every day, advertisers, politicians, and friends are trying to influence your attitudes. One weapon they use is the drip, drip, drip of a repeated idea. Repeated exposure even to a nonsense syllable such as *zug* is enough to make a person feel more positive toward it (Zajonc, 1968). The attitude-boosting **familiarity effect** of merely seeing the same thing repeatedly is a robust phenomenon. It has been demonstrated across cultures, across species, and across states of consciousness—it works even for stimuli you aren't aware of seeing (Monahan, Murphy, & Zajonc, 2000).

The effectiveness of familiarity has long been known to politicians and advertisers: Repeat something often enough, even the basest lie, and eventually the public will believe it. Hitler's propaganda minister, Joseph Goebbels, called this technique the "Big Lie." Its formal name is the **validity effect**.

In a series of experiments, Hal Arkes and his associates demonstrated how the validity effect operates (Arkes, 1993; Arkes, Boehm, & Xu, 1991). In a typical study, people read a list of statements, such as "Mercury has a higher boiling point than copper" or "Over 400 Hollywood films were produced in 1948." They had to rate each statement for its validity, on a scale of 1 (definitely false) to 7 (definitely true). A week or two later, they again rated the validity of some of these statements and also rated others that they had not seen previously. The result: Mere repetition increased the perception that the familiar statements were true. The same effect also occurred for other kinds of statements, including unverifiable opinions (e.g., "At least 75 percent of all politicians are basically dishonest"), opinions that subjects initially felt were true, and even opinions they initially felt were false. "Note that no attempt has been made to persuade," said Arkes (1993). "No supporting arguments are offered.

familiarity effect The tendency of people to feel more positive toward a person, item, product or other stimulus that they have seen often.

validity effect The tendency of people to believe that a statement is true or valid simply because it has been repeated many times.

cognitive dissonance A state of tension that occurs when a person simultaneously holds two cognitions that are psychologically inconsistent, or when a person's belief is incongruent with his or her behaviour.

The more familiar things are, the more we tend to like them. The Oreo name on this cereal takes advantage of the familiarity effect: Oreo cookies have been advertised since 1912.

We just have subjects rate the statements. Mere repetition seems to increase rated validity. This is scary."

Another effective technique for influencing people's attitudes is to have arguments presented by someone who is considered admirable, knowledgeable, or beautiful; this is why advertisements are full of sports heroes, experts, and models (Cialdini, 2001; Pratkanis & Aronson, 2001). Persuaders may also try to link their message with a nice, warm, fuzzy feeling. In one early study, students who were given peanuts and Pepsi™ while listening to a speaker's point of view were more likely to be convinced by it than were students who listened to the same words without the pleasant munchies and soft drinks (Janis, Kaye, & Kirschner, 1965). This finding has been replicated many times, perhaps explaining why so much business is conducted over lunch, and so many courtships over dinner! Similarly, researchers at Concordia have found that humour helps make a potentially threatening message more persuasive by reducing the fear associated with the message (Conway & Dubé, 2002).

In sum, here are three good ways to influence attitudes:

Fear tactics to get people to quit doing risky things usually backfire. But perhaps this campaign to persuade men to quit smoking will be the exception!

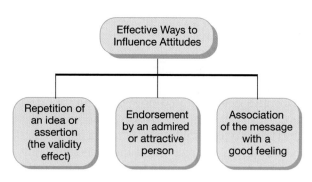

On the other hand, one of the most common ways of trying to get people to change their attitudes and behaviour—by scaring them to death—is actually one of the least effective. Fear tactics are often used to try to persuade people to quit smoking, drive only when sober, use condoms, check for signs of cancer, and, nowadays, prepare for terrorist attacks. But the use of fear can backfire. It often scares people so much that they become defensive or feel hopeless and hence ignore the message ("That will never happen to me, and if it does, there isn't anything I can do about it"). Fear tactics can be effective, however, when the message also provides specific information about how to avoid the danger and when people feel able to take advantage of this information (Aronson, 2004).

Coercive Persuasion Every few years the news reports the shocking deaths, through suicide or self-defence, of members of a formerly unknown cult. From 1994 to 1997, for example, more than 70 members of the Order of the Solar Temple, including more than 30 men, women, and children in Quebec, either committed mass suicide or murder-suicide. Cult leaders Luc Jouret and Joseph de Mambro persuaded their followers that by committing suicide they would be reborn on the star Sirius and avoid the imminent destruction of the earth.

Were these people mentally ill? Had they all been "brainwashed"? "Brainwashing" implies that a person has had a sudden change of mind without being aware of what is happening; it sounds mysterious and strange. In fact, the methods of persuasion involved are neither mysterious nor unusual, but they are indeed *coercive*—that is, designed to suppress an individual's ability to reason, think critically, and make choices in his or her own best interests. Studies of religious, political, and other cults have identified some of the key processes of coercive persuasion (Galanter, 1989; Ofshe & Watters, 1994; Singer, Temerlin, & Langone, 1990; Zimbardo & Leippe, 1991):

Thinking Critically About "Brainwashing"

1 *The person is put under physical or emotional stress.* The individual may not be allowed to eat, sleep, or exercise; may be isolated in a dark room with no stimulation or food; or may be induced into a trancelike state through repetitive chanting or fatigue.

2 *The person's problems are reduced to one simple explanation, which is repeatedly emphasized.* There are as many simplistic explanations as there are cults, but here are two real examples: Are you afraid or unhappy? It all stems from the pain of being born. Are you struggling financially? It's your fault for not fervently wanting to be rich. Members may also be taught to simplify their problems by blaming a particular enemy: Jews, the government, nonbelievers . . .

3 *The leader offers unconditional love, acceptance, and attention.* The new recruit may be given a "love bath" from the group—constant praise and affection. Euphoria and well-being are intense because they typically follow exhaustion and fatigue. In exchange, the leader demands everyone's adoration and obedience.

4 *A new identity based on the group is created.* The recruit is told that he or she is part of the chosen, the elite, or the saved. To foster this new identity, many cults require their members to wear special clothes, eat special diets, or assume a new name.

5 *The person is subjected to entrapment.* At first, the new member agrees only to do small things, but gradually the demands increase: for example, to spend a weekend with the group, then another weekend, then take weekly seminars, then advanced courses, then to contribute money, and so on. No leader ever says to a new recruit at the outset, "If you follow me, you will eventually give up your marriage, home, children, and perhaps your life"; but by the end, that is just what many do.

6 *The person's access to information is severely controlled.* As soon as a person is a committed believer or follower, the group limits the person's choices, denigrates critical thinking, makes fun of doubts, and insists that any private distress is due to lack of belief in the group. Total conformity is demanded. The person may be physically isolated from the outside world and thus from antidotes to the leader's ideas. In many groups, members are required to break all ties with their parents, who are the strongest link to the members' former world and thus the greatest threat to the leader's control.

These members of the Aum Shinrikyo ("Supreme Truth") sect in Japan, wearing masks of their leader's face, take the uniformity of cult identity to an extreme. The group's founder instructed his devotees to place a nerve gas in a Japanese subway, which killed ten and sickened thousands of other passengers. One former member said of the sect, "Their strategy is to wear you down and take control of your mind. They promise you heaven, but they make you live in hell."

Some people may be more vulnerable than others to coercive influence, but these techniques are powerful enough to overwhelm even mentally healthy and well-educated individuals. For example, research on contemporary suicide bombers in the Middle East—including Mohamed Atta, one of the 19 hijackers who destroyed the World Trade Center—shows that they had no psychopathology and were often quite educated and affluent. Like other revolutionaries, the people who become suicide bombers are idealistic and angry about perceived injustices. But they take extreme measures because they have become entrapped in closed groups led by charismatic leaders. They are separated from their families, are indoctrinated and trained for 18 months or more, and eventually become emotionally bonded to the group and the leader (Atran, 2003). One expert on suicide bombers observed that the first line of defence against them is for communities to learn "how to minimize the receptivity of *mostly ordinary people* to recruiting organizations" (Atran, 2003; our emphasis).

A key step in increasing people's resistance to coercive persuasion, therefore, is to dispel their illusion of invulnerability to these tactics (Sagarin et al., 2002). Another is to teach people how to articulate and defend their own positions and think critically. These skills prepare people to resist propaganda and make them less vulnerable to manipulation by others (Tormala & Petty, 2002).

Quick Quiz

Now, how can we persuade you to take this quiz without coercing you?

1. Candidate Carson spends $3 million to make sure his name is seen and heard frequently, and to repeat unverified charges that his opponent is a thief. What psychological processes is he relying on to win?

2. A friend urges you to join a "life-renewal" group called "The Feeling Life." Your friend has been spending increasing amounts of time with her fellow Feelies, and you have some doubts about them. What questions would you want to have answered before joining up?

Answers:

1. the familiarity effect and the validity effect

2. A few things to consider: Is there an autocratic leader who tolerates no dissent or criticism, while rationalizing this practice as a benefit for members? ("Doubt and disbelief are signs that your feeling side is being repressed.") Have long-standing members given up their friends, families, interests, and ambitions for this group? Does the leader offer simple but unrealistic promises to repair your life and all that troubles you? Are members required to make extreme sacrifices by donating large amounts of time and money?

WHAT'S AHEAD

- Why do people in groups often go along with the majority even when the majority is dead wrong?

- How can "groupthink" lead to bad, even catastrophic, decisions?

- In an emergency, are you more likely to get help when there are lots of strangers in the area or only a few?

- What enables some people to be nonconformists, take risks to help others, or blow the whistle on wrongdoers?

INDIVIDUALS IN GROUPS

Even when a group is not at all coercive, something happens to us when we join a bunch of other people. We act differently than we would on our own, regardless of whether the group has convened to solve problems and make decisions, has gathered to have fun, consists of anonymous bystanders or anonymous members of an Internet chat room, or is just a loose collection of individuals hanging out in a bar. The decisions we make and the actions we take, in groups, may depend less on our personal desires than on the structure and dynamics of the group itself.

Conformity

One thing people in groups do is conform, taking action or adopting attitudes as a result of real or imagined group pressure.

Suppose that you are required to appear at a psychology laboratory for an experiment on perception. You join seven other students seated in a

room. You are shown a 10-inch line and asked which of three other lines is identical to it:

Test line   A   B   C

The correct answer, line A, is obvious, so you are amused when the first person in the group chooses line B. "Bad eyesight," you say to yourself. "He's off by two whole inches!" The second person also chooses line B. "What a dope," you think. But by the time the fifth person has chosen line B, you are beginning to doubt yourself. The sixth and seventh students also choose line B, and now you are worried about *your* eyesight. The experimenter looks at you. "Your turn," he says. Do you follow the evidence of your own eyes or the collective judgment of the group?

This was the design for a series of famous studies of conformity conducted by Solomon Asch (1952, 1965). The seven "nearsighted" students were actually Asch's confederates. Asch wanted to know what people would do when a group unanimously contradicted an obvious fact. He found that when people made the line comparisons on their own, they were almost always accurate. But in the group, only 20 percent of the students remained completely independent on every trial, and often they apologized for not agreeing with the others. One-third conformed to the group's incorrect decision more than half the time, and the rest conformed at least some of the time. Whether they conformed or not, the students often felt uncertain of their decision. As one participant later said, "I felt disturbed, puzzled, separated, like an outcast from the rest."

Asch's experiment has been replicated many times and in many countries over the years. In North America, conformity has declined since the 1950s, when Asch first did his work, suggesting that conformity reflects social norms, which can change over time (Bond & Smith, 1996). Conformity varies with cultural norms, too. People in individualist cultures, such as many in Canada, value individual rights and place the "self" above duty to others. They are somewhat less conformist than people in collectivist cultures, who consider social harmony to be more important than individual rights (see Chapter 2).

Regardless of culture, however, everyone conforms under some circumstances and for similar reasons. Some do so because they identify with group members and want to be like them. Some want to be liked. Some believe the group has knowledge that is superior to their own. And some conform out of pure self-interest, to keep their jobs, win promotions, or win votes. Also, it is not so easy to be a nonconformist! Group members are often uncomfortable with deviants and will try to persuade them to conform. If pleasant persuasion fails, the group may punish, isolate, or reject the nonconformist (Moscovici, 1985).

Like obedience, conformity has both its positive and its negative sides. Society runs more smoothly when people know how to behave in a given situation and when they share the same attitudes and manners. Conformity in dress, preferences, and ideas confers a sense of being "in sync" with friends and colleagues. But conformity can also suppress critical thinking and creativity. In a group, many people will deny their private beliefs, agree with silly notions, and even repudiate their own values.

Groupthink

Close, friendly groups usually work well together. But they face the problem of getting the best ideas and efforts from their members while avoiding an extreme form of conformity called **groupthink**, the tendency to think alike and suppress dissent. According to Irving Janis (1982, 1989), groupthink occurs when a group's need for total agreement overwhelms its need to make the wisest decision. The symptoms of groupthink include the following:

- *An illusion of invulnerability.* The group believes it can do no wrong and is 100 percent correct in its decisions.

- *Self-censorship.* Dissenters decide to keep quiet rather than make trouble, offend their friends, or risk being ridiculed.

- *Pressure on dissenters to conform.* The leader teases or humiliates dissenters or otherwise pressures them to go along.

- *An illusion of unanimity.* By discouraging dissent, leaders and group members create an illusion of consensus; they may even explicitly order suspected dissenters to keep quiet.

groupthink In close-knit groups, the tendency for all members to think alike for the sake of harmony and to suppress disagreement.

Sometimes people like to conform to feel part of the group . . . and sometimes they like to assert their individuality.

Janis (1982) examined the records of historical military decisions and identified key features of groups that are vulnerable to groupthink: Their members feel that they are part of a tightly connected team; they are isolated from other viewpoints; they feel under pressure from outside forces; and they have a strong, directive leader. Do you notice the similarities between these features and those of coercive persuasion?

Throughout history, groupthink has led to disastrous decisions in military and civilian life. In 1992, for example, the group that created the Charlottetown Accord, which proposed significant changes to Canada's constitution, made some clear mistakes in their judgments of Canadians' attitudes toward those changes. Groupthink could help explain why this group did not obtain accurate estimates of people's support for such changes as declaring a distinct status for Quebec and creating a new and more powerful Senate. Mistakes were also made regarding the number of changes that were put before the Canadian people all at once. Such judgments may stem from a government's illusion of invulnerability. And in 1986, NASA officials insulated themselves from the dissenting objections of engineers who warned them that the space shuttle *Challenger* was unsafe; NASA launched it anyway, and it exploded shortly after takeoff. Tragically, NASA appears not to have learned from this disaster. When an expert panel warned in 2002 that the space shuttles still had many safety problems, NASA removed five of the panel's nine members and two of its consultants. Early in 2003, the *Columbia* exploded upon re-entry, killing its entire crew.

Cohesion alone does not inevitably cause groupthink. A main factor in determining whether a group will fall victim to groupthink has to do with *group norms*: the standards or rules about appropriate behaviour and thought governing members of the group (Postmes, Spears, & Cihangir, 2001). Some groups demand consensus; they want all members to dress, think, and behave the same way. Others, even cohesive ones, not only tolerate but value innovative and dissenting views, and set norms that call for independent thinking and action. Groupthink can therefore be counteracted by creating conditions that explicitly encourage and reward the expression of doubt and dissent and by basing decisions on majority rule instead of unanimity (Kameda & Sugimori, 1993).

The Anonymous Crowd

Suppose you were in trouble on a city street or in another public place—say, being mugged or having a sudden appendicitis attack. Do you think you would be more likely to get help if (a) one other person was passing by, (b) several other people were in the area, or (c) dozens of people were in the area? Most people would choose the third answer, but that is not how human beings operate. On the contrary, the more people there are around you, the *less* likely it is that one of them will come to your aid. Why?

The answer has to do with a group process called the **diffusion of responsibility**, in which responsibility for an outcome is diffused, or spread, among many people, reducing each individual's personal sense of responsibility. One result is *bystander apathy*: In crowds, when someone is in trouble, individuals often fail to take action or call for help because they assume that someone else will do so (Darley & Latané, 1968). For example, in an American case that became famous many years ago, a woman named Kitty Genovese was repeatedly stabbed to death on the street as dozens of her neighbours listened and watched—without calling for help. Similar tragedies have been documented in Canada. In a Vancouver suburb, 30 people watched three men beat and shoot to death a high-school student (Tanner, 2003). People are most likely to come to a stranger's aid if they are the only ones around to help, because responsibility cannot be diffused.

In work groups, the diffusion of responsibility sometimes takes the form of *social loafing*: Each member of a team slows down, letting others work harder (Karau & Williams, 1993; Latané, Williams, & Harkins, 1979). Social loafing occurs when individual group members are not accountable for the work they do; when people feel that working

diffusion of responsibility In groups, the tendency of members to avoid taking action because they assume that others will.

"...AND WE ARE FIRMLY OPPOSED TO ANY FORM OF GROUPTHINK."

"RIGHT, J.B.!" "Right, J.B.!" "Right, J.B.!" "Right, J.B.!" "RIGHT, J.B.!"

harder would only duplicate their colleagues' efforts; when workers feel that others are getting a "free ride"; or when the work itself is uninteresting (Shepperd, 1995). When the challenge of the job is increased or when each member of the group has a different, important job to do, the sense of individual responsibility rises and social loafing declines (Harkins & Szymanski, 1989; Williams & Karau, 1991).

The most extreme instances of the diffusion of responsibility occur in large, anonymous mobs or crowds—whether they are cheerful ones, such as sports spectators, or angry ones, such as rioters. In crowds like these, people often lose all awareness of their individuality and seem to "hand themselves over" to the mood and actions of the crowd, a state called **deindividuation** (Festinger, Pepitone, & Newcomb, 1952). Celebrations can even turn into riots, as evidenced in the 2001 Canada Day riot in Edmonton, in which rioters smashed store windows and clashed with police. You are more likely to feel deindividuated in a large city, where no one recognizes you, than in a small town, where it is hard to hide. (You are also more likely to feel deindividuated in large classes, where you might—mistakenly!—think you are invisible to the teacher.) Sometimes organizations actively promote the deindividuation of their members in order to enhance conformity and allegiance to the group. This is an important function of uniforms or masks, which eliminate each member's distinctive identity.

Deindividuation has long been considered a prime reason for mob violence. According to this explanation, because deindividuated people in crowds "forget themselves" and do not feel accountable for their actions, they are more likely to violate social norms and laws than they would be on their own: breaking store windows, looting, getting into fights, or rioting at a sports event. But deindividuation does not always make people more combative. Sometimes it makes them more friendly; think of all the chatty, anonymous people on buses and planes who reveal things to their seatmates they would never tell anyone they knew.

What really seems to be happening when people are in large crowds or anonymous situations is not that they become "mindless" or "uninhibited." Rather, they become more likely to conform to the norms of the *specific situation* (Postmes & Spears, 1998). For example, when students who were protesting free trade went on wild sprees during the Summit of the Americas and broke local laws of Quebec City, they did so not because their "aggressiveness" had been released but because they were conforming to the group norms of their fellow protesters. Crowd norms can also foster helpfulness, as evidenced by the Newfoundlanders who opened their homes to stranded air travellers in the aftermath of the 9/11 attacks.

Two classic experiments illustrate the power of the situation to influence what deindividuated people will do. In one, women who wore Ku Klux

deindividuation In groups or crowds, the loss of awareness of one's own individuality.

People in crowds, feeling anonymous, often seem to "forget themselves" and do destructive things they would never do on their own—if that is the norm for the crowd in that situation. This crowd became destructive after the Vancouver Canucks lost in the seventh game of the Stanley Cup Finals to the New York Rangers in 1994.

Wearing a uniform or disguise increases deindividuation and provides a cue for behaviour. The women shown here wearing Ku Klux Klan-like disguises behaved more aggressively than did individuated women (Zimbardo, 1970).

Klan-like disguises that completely covered their faces and bodies (see photo) delivered twice as much apparent electric shock to another woman as did women who not only were undisguised but also wore large name tags (Zimbardo, 1970). In a second experiment, women who were wearing nurses' uniforms gave *less* shock than did women in regular dress (Johnson & Downing, 1979). Evidently, the KKK disguises were a signal to behave aggressively; the nurses' uniforms were a signal to behave in a nurturing manner.

Quick Quiz

On your own, take responsibility for identifying which phenomenon discussed in the previous section is illustrated in each of the following situations.

1. The prime minister's closest advisers are afraid to disagree with his views on fiscal policy.
2. You are at a costume party wearing a silly gorilla suit. When you see a chance to play a practical joke on the host, you do it.
3. Walking down a busy street, you see that fire has broken out in a store window. "Someone must already have called the fire department," you say.

Answers:

1. groupthink   2. deindividuation   3. diffusion of responsibility (causing bystander apathy)

Disobedience and Dissent

We have seen how roles, norms, and pressures to obey authority and conform to one's group can cause people to behave in ways they might not otherwise do. Yet throughout history men and women have disobeyed orders they believed to be wrong and have gone against prevailing cultural beliefs; their actions have changed the course of history. Until 1929, for instance, the federal government defined those who could vote in Canada as "A male person, including an Indian, excluding a Mongolian or Chinese. . . . No woman, idiot, lunatic or criminal shall vote." Nellie McClung pioneered the women's suffrage movement by battling Canadian laws and government to have women declared "persons" under the law and thus gain the right to vote. Similarly, Aboriginals in Canada have fought for their right to self-government in ways that have included dissent and disobedience of discriminatory laws.

Dissent and *altruism*, the willingness to take selfless or dangerous action on behalf of others, are in part a matter of personal convictions and conscience. However, just as there are situational reasons for obedience and conformity, so are there external influences on a person's decision to state an unpopular opinion, choose conscience over conformity, or help a stranger in trouble. Here are some of the situational factors involved in deciding to "rock the boat" or behave courageously:

1 *You perceive the need for intervention or help.* It may seem obvious, but before you can take independent action, you must realize that such action is necessary. Sometimes people willfully blind themselves to wrongdoing to justify their own inaction ("I'm just minding my business"; "I have no idea what they're doing over there at that concentration camp"). But blindness to the need for action also occurs when a situation imposes too many demands on people's attention. For example, residents of densely populated and fast-paced cities cannot stop to offer help to everyone who seems to need it; they would never do anything else (Levine et al., 1994).

2 *The situation increases the likelihood that you will take responsibility.* When you are in a large crowd of observers or in a large organization, it is easy to avoid action because of the diffusion of responsibility. Conversely, when you are in an environment that rewards independent thinking and dissent and discourages social loafing, you may behave accordingly. The decision to take responsibility also depends on the risk involved. It is easier to be a whistleblower or to protest a company policy when you know you can find another job, but what if jobs in your field are scarce and you have a family to support? People are less likely to take an independent action if situational risks are high.

Dr. Nancy Olivieri knew that she faced potentially severe personal and professional consequences for blowing the whistle on the dangers of a new drug, deferiprone, intended for the treatment of a genetic blood disorder. The dangers of remaining silent, however, were greater.

Some cultures place a higher value on helping strangers than other cultures do. In Brazil and other Latin American countries, for example, it is important to be *simpático*, a good-natured, kind person who goes out of his or her way to help others. In studies of strangers' helpfulness to one another across 23 cities in different countries, cultural norms were more important than population density in predicting levels of helpfulness. Pedestrians in busy Copenhagen and Vienna, for example, were kinder to strangers than were passersby in slow-paced Kuala Lumpur—or busy New York (Levine, 2003).

3 *The cost–benefit ratio supports your decision to get involved.* The cost of helping or protesting might be embarrassment and wasted time or, more seriously, lost income, loss of friends, and even physical danger. The cost of not helping or remaining silent might be guilt, blame from others, loss of honour, or the injury or death of others. A study at the University of Alberta, for example, showed that personal cost—such as time commitment and the possibility that helping others might affect one's ranking in class—was an important factor for students in deciding whether or not to help another student who had missed a class and needed notes (Bell et al., 1995). And the whistleblowers at NASA profoundly understood the costs of not voicing their concerns about the safety of the space shuttles, and decided to speak up—though some were marginalized or ignored for doing so.

4 *You have an ally.* In Asch's conformity experiment, the presence of one other person who gave the correct answer was enough to overcome agreement with the majority. In Milgram's experiment, the presence of a peer who disobeyed the experimenter's instruction to shock the learner sharply increased the number of people who also disobeyed. One dissenting member of a group may be viewed as a troublemaker and two dissenting members as a conspiracy, but several are a coalition. An ally reassures a person of the rightness of the protest, and that their combined efforts may eventually persuade the majority (Wood et al., 1994).

5 *You become entrapped.* Once having taken the initial step of getting involved, most people will increase their commitment. In one study, nearly 9000 U.S. federal employees were asked whether they had observed wrongdoing at work, whether they had told anyone about it, and what happened if they had told. Nearly half of the sample had observed some serious cases of wrongdoing, such as stealing federal funds, accepting bribes, or creating a situation that was dangerous to public safety. Of that half, 72 percent had done nothing at all, but the other 28 percent had reported the problem to their immediate supervisors. Once they had taken that step, a majority of the whistle-blowers eventually took the matter to higher authorities (Graham, 1986).

As you can see, certain social and cultural factors make altruism, disobedience, and dissent more likely to occur, just as other factors suppress them. In the case of Rosa Parks, for example, consider what else, besides her undeniable personal courage, supported her act of civil disobedience that fateful day in 1955 when she refused to give up her seat on the bus to a white man. She certainly perceived the injustice of the situation. She knew she would have allies in the newly awakening civil rights movement, which had been galvanized by a U.S. Supreme Court decision outlawing school segregation and by the recent horrible lynching of a teenaged black boy named Emmett Till. She weighed the costs and benefits, and decided that freedom was worth the price. Once she had been arrested, she was entrapped; there was no going back. In short, the times and the social circumstances enabled her historic decision—and its consequences.

WHAT'S AHEAD

- In what different ways do people balance their ethnic identity and their membership in the larger culture?

- What is an effective antidote to "us–them" thinking?

- How do stereotypes benefit us, and how do they distort reality?

US VERSUS THEM: GROUP IDENTITY

Each of us develops a personal identity that is based on our particular traits and unique life history. But we also develop **social identities** based on the groups we belong to, including our national, religious, political, and occupational groups (Brewer & Gardner, 1996; Tajfel & Turner, 1986). Social identities are important because they give us a sense of place and position in the world. Without them, most of us would feel like loose marbles rolling around in an unconnected universe. It feels good to be part of an "us," but does that mean that we must automatically feel superior to "them"?

Ethnic Identity

In multicultural societies such as Canada's, different social identities sometimes collide. In particular, people often face the dilemma of balancing an **ethnic identity**, a close identification with a religious or ethnic group, and **acculturation**, identification with the dominant culture (Cross, 1971; Phinney, 1996; Spencer & Dornbusch, 1990).

   According to John Berry at Queen's University, there are four ways of balancing ethnic identity and acculturation, depending on whether ethnic identity is strong or weak and whether identifi-

cation with the larger culture is strong or weak (Berry, 1994; Phinney, 1990). People who are *bicultural* have strong ties both to their ethnicity and to the larger culture: They say, "I am proud of my ethnic heritage, but I identify just as much with my country." They can alternate easily between their culture of origin and the majority culture, slipping into the customs and language of each as circumstances dictate. People who choose *assimilation* have weak feelings of ethnicity but a strong sense of acculturation: Their attitude, for example, might be "I'm a Canadian, period." *Ethnic separatists* have a strong sense of ethnic identity but weak feelings of acculturation: They may say, "My ethnicity comes first; if I join the mainstream, I'm betraying my origins and selling out." And some people feel *marginal*, connected to neither their ethnicity nor the dominant culture: They may not want to identify with any ethnic or national group, or feel that they don't belong anywhere.

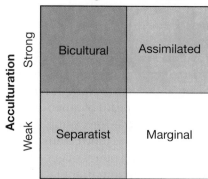

A person's degree of acculturation may change throughout life in response to experiences and societal events. For example, many immigrants

social identity The part of a person's self-concept that is based on his or her identification with a nation, ethnic group, gender, or other social affiliation.

ethnic identity A person's identification with a racial, religious, or ethnic group.

acculturation The process by which members of minority groups come to identify with and feel part of the mainstream culture.

arrive in North America with every intention of becoming "true" Canadians or Americans. If they encounter discrimination or setbacks, however, they may decide that acculturation is harder than they anticipated or that ethnic separatism offers greater solace. In any case, acculturation is rarely a complete accommodation to mainstream culture. Research at UBC and elsewhere has shown that many individuals pick and choose among the values, food, traditions, and customs of the mainstream culture, while also keeping aspects of their heritage that are important to their self-identity (Chun, Organista, & Marin, 2002; Ryder, Alden, & Paulhus, 2000).

It is a sign of our multiethnic times that many people are now refusing to be pigeonholed into any single ethnic category. In the 2001 Canadian census, over 11 million people, or 38 percent of the population, reported multiple ethnic origins (Statistics Canada). Indeed, some observers are now writing that North America is moving toward a "post-ethnic" stage, in which young people are becoming less likely to define themselves by their ethnic identity than by their youth identity—a hip-hopper, a *roquero* (rocker), a pop-culture fan, and so forth. On the streets, in the marketplace, and in intimate relationships, many of the old ethnic rules and divisions are breaking down.

Ethnocentrism

Nonetheless, having an ethnic or national identity is still important to most people. Unfortunately, it often leads to **ethnocentrism**, the belief that your own culture or ethnic group is superior to all others. Ethnocentrism is universal, probably because it aids survival by increasing people's attachment to their own group and willingness to work on its behalf. It is even embedded in some languages: The Chinese word for China means "the centre of the world," and both the Inuit and the Navajo call themselves simply "The People."

Ethnocentrism rests on a fundamental social identity: us. As soon as people have created a category called "us," however, they invariably perceive everybody else as "not-us." This in-group solidarity can be manufactured in a minute in the laboratory, as Henri Tajfel and his colleagues (1971) demonstrated in an experiment with British schoolboys. Tajfel showed the boys slides with varying numbers of dots on them and asked the boys to guess how many dots there were. The boys were arbitrarily told that they were "overestimators" or "underestimators" and were then asked to work on another task. In this phase, they had a chance to give points to other boys identified as overestimators or underestimators. Although each boy worked alone in his cubicle, almost every one assigned far more points to boys he thought were like him, whether an overestimator or an underestimator. As the boys emerged from their rooms, they were asked, "Which were you?"— and the answers received a mix of cheers and boos from the others.

Us–them social identities are strengthened when two groups compete with each other. Years ago, Muzafer Sherif and his colleagues used a natural setting, a Boy Scout camp called Robbers Cave, to demonstrate the effects of competition on hostility and conflict between groups (Sherif, 1958; Sherif et al., 1961). Sherif randomly assigned

ethnocentrism The belief that one's own ethnic group, nation, or religion is superior to all others.

Ethnic identities are changing these days, as bicultural (and increasingly multiethnic) North Americans blend aspects of mainstream culture with their own traditions. But many like to celebrate the traditions of their ethnic heritage, as shown by these photos of Chinese-Canadian children, Ukrainian teens, and Young Canadian Aboriginals.

11- and 12-year-old boys to two groups, the Eagles and the Rattlers. To build a sense of in-group identity and team spirit, he had each group work together on projects such as making a rope bridge and building a diving board. Sherif then put the Eagles and Rattlers in competition for prizes. During fierce games of football, baseball, and tug-of-war, the boys whipped up a competitive fever that soon spilled off of the playing fields. They began to raid each other's cabins, call each other names, and start fist fights. No one dared to have a friend from the rival group. Before long, the Rattlers and the Eagles were as hostile toward each other as any two gangs fighting for turf or any two nations fighting for dominance. Their hostility continued even when they were just sitting around together watching movies.

Then Sherif decided to try to undo the hostility he had created and make peace between the Eagles and Rattlers. He and his associates set up a series of predicaments in which both groups needed to work together to reach a desired goal—pooling their resources to get a movie they all wanted to see, for example, or pulling a staff truck up a hill on a camping trip. This policy of *interdependence* in reaching mutual goals was highly successful in reducing the boys' "ethnocentrism," competitiveness, and hostility; the boys eventually made friends with their former enemies (see Figure 10.2). Interdependence has a similar effect in adult groups (Gaertner et al., 1990). The reason, it seems, is that co-operation causes people to think of themselves as members of one big group instead of two opposed groups, "us" and "them."

stereotype A summary impression of a group, in which a person believes that all members of the group share a common trait or traits (positive, negative, or neutral).

Stereotypes

You can probably think of a million ways that your friends and family members differ—Jeff is stodgy, Ruth is bossy, Farah is outgoing. But if you have never met a person from Turkey or Tibet, you are likely to stereotype Turks and Tibetans. A **stereotype** is a summary impression of a group of people in which all members of the group are viewed as sharing a common trait or traits. Stereotypes may be negative, positive, or

neutral. There are stereotypes of people who drive Jeeps or BMWs, of men who wear earrings and of women who wear business suits, of engineering students and art students, of feminists and fraternity men. They can be maintained in a number of ways, such as through the jokes we tell. For example, research at Lakehead University has shown that stereotypes of the elderly, such as impotency and unattractiveness, are common to many jokes (Bowd, 2003).

Stereotypes aren't necessarily bad. They are, as some psychologists have called them, useful "tools in the mental toolbox"—energy-saving devices that allow us to make efficient decisions (Macrae, Milne, & Bodenhausen, 1994). They help us quickly process new information and retrieve memories. They allow us to organize experience, make sense of differences among individuals and groups, and predict how people will behave.

However, although stereotypes reflect real differences among people, they also distort that reality in three ways (Judd et al., 1995). First, *they exaggerate differences between groups*, making the stereotyped group seem odd, unfamiliar, or dangerous, not like "us." Second, *they produce selective perception*; people tend to see only the evidence that fits the stereotype and reject any perceptions that do not fit. Third, *they underestimate differences within other groups*. Stereotypes create the impression that all members of other groups are the same.

Some stereotypes stem from a person's cultural values. Many North Americans, for example, have strongly negative stereotypes about fat

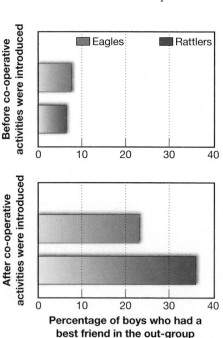

FIGURE 10.2 The Experiment at Robbers Cave

In this study, competitive games fostered hostility between the Rattlers and the Eagles. Very few boys had a best friend from the other group (top graph). But after the boys had to co-operate to solve various problems, the percentage who made friends across "enemy lines" shot up (bottom graph) (Sherif et al., 1961).

Which woman is the chemical engineer and which is the assistant? The Western stereotype holds that women are not engineers in the first place, but if they are, they are Western. Actually, the engineer at this refinery is the Kuwaiti woman on the left.

people because of a cultural ideology that individuals are responsible for what happens to them and for how they look.

Cultural values can affect how people evaluate a particular action (Taylor & Porter, 1994). Chinese students in Hong Kong, where communalism and respect for elders are valued, think that a student who comes late to class or argues with a parent about grades is being selfish and disrespectful of adults. But Australian students, who value individualism, think that the same behaviour is perfectly appropriate (Forgas & Bond, 1985). You can see how the Chinese might form negative stereotypes of "disrespectful" Australians, and how the Australians might form negative stereotypes of the "spineless" Chinese. And it is a small step from negative stereotypes to prejudice.

Quick Quiz

Do you have a positive or a negative stereotype of quizzes?

1. Frank, an African-Canadian college student, finds himself caught between two philosophies on his campus. One holds that blacks should remain fully integrated in mainstream culture. The other holds that blacks should immerse themselves in the history, values, and contributions of African culture. The first group values _____ whereas the second emphasizes _____.
2. John knows and likes the South Asian minority in his town, but he privately believes that Anglo culture is superior to all others. His belief is evidence of his _____.
3. What strategy does the Robbers Cave study suggest for reducing "us–them" thinking and hostility between groups?

Answers:

1. acculturation, ethnic identity   2. ethnocentrism   3. interdependence in reaching mutual goals

---

WHAT'S AHEAD

- Is prejudice more likely to be a *cause* of war or a *result* of it?
- If you believe that women are naturally better than men, are you "sexist"?
- Why isn't mere contact between cultural groups enough to reduce prejudice between them? What does work?

GROUP CONFLICT AND PREJUDICE

A *prejudice* consists of a negative stereotype and a strong, unreasonable dislike or hatred of a group. Prejudices often remain immune to evidence. In his classic book *The Nature of Prejudice*, Gordon Allport (1954/1979) described the responses characteristic of a prejudiced person when confronted with evidence contradicting his or her beliefs:

Mr. X: The trouble with Jews is that they only take care of their own group.

Mr. Y: But the record of the Community Chest campaign shows that they give more generously, in proportion to their numbers, to the general charities of the community, than do non-Jews.

Mr. X: That shows they are always trying to buy favour and intrude into Christian affairs. They think of nothing but money; that is why there are so many Jewish bankers.

Mr. Y: But a recent study shows that the percentage of Jews in the banking business is negligible, far smaller than the percentage of non-Jews.

Mr. X: That's just it; they don't go in for respectable business; they are only in the movie business or run night clubs.

Notice that Mr. X doesn't even try to respond to Mr. Y's evidence; he just moves along to another reason for his dislike of Jews. That is the slippery nature of prejudice.

The Origins of Prejudice

Prejudice is universal because it has so many sources and functions: psychological, social, cultural, and economic.

1 *Psychological functions.* Prejudice often serves to ward off feelings of doubt and fear. Thus, a straight person who has doubts or anxieties about his own sexuality may develop a hatred of gay people. Prejudice also allows people to use the target group as a scapegoat: "Those people are the

OneKey
10.6

source of all my troubles." For example, researchers at UBC have posited that prejudices against people with physical disabilities can stem from a deep-rooted need to avoid disease (Park, Faulkner, & Schaller, 2003). And, as research from many nations has confirmed, prejudice is a tonic for low self-esteem: People puff up their own feelings of low self-worth by disliking or hating groups they see as inferior (Islam & Hewstone, 1993; Stephan et al., 1994; Tajfel & Turner, 1986). Prejudice toward a scapegoat may also be a way for people to displace feelings of anger and cope with feelings of powerlessness. In the aftermath of the attacks on the World Trade Center and the Pentagon, some white Americans took out their anger on fellow Americans who happened to be

Arab, Sikh, Pakistani, Hindu, or Afghan. Two men in Chicago beat up an Arab-American taxi driver, yelling, "This is what you get, you mass murderer!"

2 *Social and cultural functions.* Not all prejudices have deep-seated psychological roots. Some are acquired through groupthink and other social pressures to conform to the views of friends, relatives, or associates. Some may be passed along mindlessly from one generation to another, as when parents communicate to their children, "We don't associate with people like that." And some unconscious (implicit) prejudices are acquired from advertising, TV shows, and news reports that contain derogatory images and stereotypes of certain groups.

Get Involved   Probing Your Prejudices

Are you prejudiced? No? Is there any group of people you tend to regard in a negative light because of their gender, ethnicity, sexual orientation, nationality, religion, physical appearance, or political views? Write down your deepest thoughts and feelings about this group. Take as long as you want, and do not censor yourself or say what you think you ought to say. Now reread what you have written. Which of the many sources of prejudice discussed in the text might be contributing to your views? Do you feel that your attitudes toward the group are legitimate, or are you uncomfortable about having them?

Prejudice also serves cultural purposes, bonding people to their own ethnic or national group and its ways. Indeed, this may be a major evolutionary reason for its universality and persistence (Fishbein, 1996). In this respect, prejudice is the flip side of ethnocentrism; it is not only that *we* are good and kind, but also that *they* are bad or evil. By disliking "them," we feel closer to others who are like "us."

3 *Economic functions.* Prejudice makes official forms of discrimination seem legitimate, by justifying the majority group's dominance, status, or greater wealth (Sidanius, Pratto, & Bobo, 1996). Historically, for example, white men in positions of power have justified their exclusion of women, blacks, and other minorities from the workplace and politics by claiming those minorities were inferior, irrational, and incompetent (Gould, 1996). But any majority group—of any ethnicity, gender, or nationality—that discriminates against a minority will call upon prejudice to legitimize its actions (Islam & Hewstone, 1993).

Although it is widely believed that prejudice is a primary cause of conflict between groups,

prejudice is actually more often a *result* of conflict. When any two groups are in direct competition for jobs, or when people are worried about their incomes and the stability of their communities, prejudice between them increases (Doty, Peterson, & Winter, 1991).

Consider the rise and fall of attitudes toward Chinese immigrants in the United States in the nineteenth century, as reported in newspapers of the time (Aronson, 2004). When the Chinese were working in the gold mines and potentially taking jobs from white labourers, whites described them as depraved, vicious, and bloodthirsty. Just a decade later, when the Chinese began working on the transcontinental railroad—doing difficult and dangerous jobs that few white men wanted—prejudice against them declined. Whites described them as hardworking, industrious, and law-abiding. Then, after the railroad was finished and the Chinese had to compete with Civil War veterans for scarce jobs, white attitudes changed again. Whites now considered the Chinese to be "criminal," "crafty," "conniving," and "stupid." (The white newspapers did not report the attitudes of the Chinese.)

The ultimate competition between groups, of course, is war. When two nations are at war, prejudice against the enemy allows each side to continue feeling righteous about its cause. Drawing on the principles of persuasion and influence described earlier (such as the validity effect), along with propaganda images that demonize and dehumanize the enemy, each side tries to convince its citizens that the enemy is less than human and thus deserves to be killed (Keen, 1986). Fomenting prejudice against the perceived enemy—calling them vermin, rats, mad dogs, heathens, baby killers, or monsters—legitimizes the attackers' motives for war. In this respect, the U.S.-led war against Iraq in the spring of 2003 was extremely unusual because it was posed as a war against Saddam Hussein and his regime but not against the Iraqi people. Accordingly, there were few of the kinds of anti-Arab cartoons that appeared in the aftermath of 9/11 (see example below).

Defining and Measuring Prejudice

Prejudice is a weasel—hard to grasp and hold onto. One problem is that not all prejudiced people are prejudiced in the same way or to the same extent. Suppose that Raymond wishes to be tolerant and open-minded, but he grew up in a small homogeneous community and feels uncomfortable with members of other cultural and religious groups. Should we put Raymond in the same category as Rupert, an outspoken bigot who actively discriminates against others? Do good intentions count? What if

Thinking Critically About Defining and Measuring Prejudice

Raymond knows nothing about Muslims and mindlessly blurts out a remark that reveals his ignorance? Is that prejudice or just thoughtlessness? These questions complicate the measurement of prejudice.

Similar complexities occur in defining "sexism." In research with 15 000 men and women in 19 nations, psychologists found that "hostile sexism," which reflects active dislike of women, is different from "benevolent sexism," in which superficially positive attitudes put women on a pedestal but nonetheless reinforce women's subordination. The latter type of sexism is affectionate but patronizing, conveying the attitude that women are so wonderful, good, kind, and moral that they should stay at home, away from the rough-and-tumble (and power and income) of public life (Glick et al., 2000). In all 19 countries studied, men had significantly higher hostile sexism scores than women did, but in about half the countries, women endorsed benevolent sexism as much as men did.

The researchers believe that benevolent sexism is "a particularly insidious form of prejudice" because, lacking a tone of hostility to women, it doesn't seem to men like it is a "prejudice," and also because women "may find its sweet allure difficult to resist" (Glick & Fiske, 2001). Both forms of sexism—whether you think women are "too good" for equality or "not good enough"—legitimize gender discrimination. (And, by the way, what about women who are prejudiced against men? Is that a form of "sexism"?)

Perhaps the greatest barrier to measuring prejudice today is that most people know they should

In times of war, people in every country stereotype "them" (the enemy) as aggressors who are less than human—often as "vermin," dogs, or pigs. After 9/11, anti-American demonstrators in Jakarta portrayed George W. Bush as a rabid dog, and an American cartoonist lumped all Muslim nations into a "barrel of vermin."

not have any (Cunningham, Preacher, & Banaji, 2001). If you ask people directly about their prejudices, most will say, in effect, "Me, prejudiced? Not at all!" Indeed, on surveys in Canada and the United States, the numbers of people who admit to believing that blacks are inferior to whites or women inferior to men have dropped sharply in the last 20 years (Plant & Devine, 1998; Dovidio, 2001).

This change, however, may simply reflect a growing awareness that it isn't cool to admit prejudice, rather than a real decline in prejudiced feelings. When white students fill out a prejudice questionnaire in the presence of a black experimenter, their prejudice scores are lower than when the experimenter is white (Fazio et al., 1995). In the presence of the black researcher, apparently, the students mask their true feelings. Similarly, in studies of job discrimination, most whites do not discriminate against black job candidates who have strong qualifications, but they are far more likely to choose *average* white candidates over *average* black ones (Dovidio & Gaertner, 2000). This finding suggests that, although old-fashioned discrimination may be gone, it lives on in a subtler form.

The Many Targets of Prejudice

Prejudice has a long and universal history. Why do new prejudices keep emerging, others fade away, and some old ones persist?

Some prejudices rise and fall with events. Many Japanese-Canadians were forcibly relocated to internment camps during the Second World War as anti-Japanese sentiment ran high, but this prejudice has almost vanished. In contrast, some hatreds, notably homophobia and anti-Semitism, reflect people's deeper anxieties and are therefore more persistent.

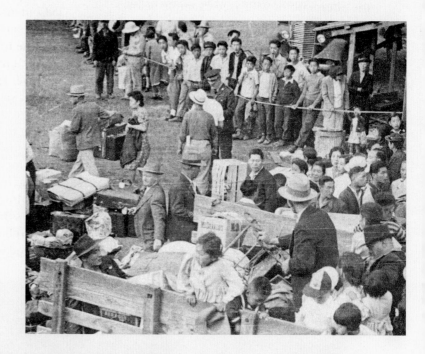

One reason that prejudice lives on, as Gordon Allport (1954/1979) observed years ago, is that "defeated intellectually, prejudice lingers emotionally." That is, people may lose their *explicit* prejudice toward a group but retain an *implicit*, unconscious prejudice or negative emotional feeling (Rudman, 2004). Implicit attitudes and prejudices are assumed to be automatic and unintentional, and hence a truer measure of a person's "real" feelings (Cunningham, Preacher, & Banaji, 2001). Researchers have developed four different ways to measure implicit prejudices:

1 *Measures of symbolic racism.* Some researchers believe that prejudice against blacks lurks behind a mask of *symbolic racism*, in which whites disguise their animosity toward black individuals by claiming they are concerned only about social issues such as "reverse discrimination" or "hard-core criminals" (Jones, 1997). Instead of asking respondents about feelings of prejudice toward blacks in general, therefore, researchers probe for hostile feelings that might lie beneath surface attitudes. The same people who will not admit to disliking Aboriginals, for example, might agree that

In-groups often justify their status and economic privileges by the denigration or exclusion of anyone who is different—Aboriginal peoples by whites, women by men. During times of economic recession, many people regard recent immigrants as competitors, and want them to "go home". Groups such as the Ku Klux Klan epitomize this ugly side of the in-group concept.

"Aboriginals are getting too demanding in their push for self-determination" (Brauer, Wasel, & Niedenthal, 2000).

2 *Measures of behaviour rather than attitudes.* Some investigators observe how people unconsciously behave when they are with a possible object of prejudice. Some individuals sit farther away than they normally would, display negative facial expressions, or show other nonverbal signs of discomfort (Fazio et al., 1995; Guglielmi, 1999).

Another behavioural approach is to observe what allegedly unprejudiced people do when they are angered or stressed (Jones, 1991; Sinclair & Kunda, 1999). In one experiment, Canadian students thought they were giving shocks to other students in a study of biofeedback. Anglophones initially showed less aggression toward francophones than toward other anglophones. But as soon as the anglophone students were angered by overhearing derogatory remarks about themselves, they showed more aggression toward francophones than toward other anglophones (Meindl & Lerner, 1985). The same pattern appears in studies of how whites behave toward blacks (Rogers & Prentice-Dunn, 1981), straights toward homosexuals, and non-Jewish students toward Jews (Fein & Spencer, 1997).

These findings imply that people are willing to control negative feelings toward targets of prejudice under normal conditions. But as soon as they are angry or frustrated, or get a jolt to their self-esteem, their real prejudice reveals itself.

3 *Measures of physiological responses to the target group.* Joining forces with physiological psychologists, some social psychologists are studying how social forces get "inside" us biologically (Amodio, Harmon-Jones, & Devine, 2003; Cacioppo et al., 2000). In the case of prejudice—or, more neutrally, emotional reactivity to groups other than one's own—they have found, for example, that when blacks and whites see pictures of each other, activity in the amygdala (the brain structure associated with fear and other negative emotions) is elevated. It is not elevated when they see pictures of members of their own group (Hart et al., 2000).

4 *Measures of unconscious associations with the target group.* A fourth way of measuring implicit prejudices taps people's associations between a stimulus and unconscious feelings of pleasantness or unpleasantness (Cunningham, Preacher, & Banaji, 2001; Dovidio, 2001). Using this method, researchers have found that many people who describe themselves as unprejudiced nonetheless have unconscious negative associations with certain groups. For example, it takes white students longer to respond to associations between black faces and positive words (e.g., *triumph, honest*) or to associations between white faces and negative words (e.g., *devil, failure*) than it does to respond to black faces and negative words or white faces and positive words. This test has also been used to identify apparently unconscious prejudices against women, the elderly, and Asians (Greenwald, McGhee, & Schwartz, 1998). The researchers have established that these results are not due merely to unfamiliarity with other groups.

Findings on implicit prejudice suggest that efforts to reduce prejudice by appealing to moral or intellectual arguments are not enough. They must also touch people's deeper insecurities, fears, or negative associations with a group. One study of white students who took a diversity education course found that the students' prejudices toward blacks, both implicit and explicit, had declined by the end of the term, but for different reasons. Their explicit prejudices had been reduced because of a greater understanding of racial issues and a wish to overcome their own biases. But their implicit prejudices were reduced only when they lost their fear of blacks, made black friends in the course, and felt respect and affection for the black professor who taught it (Rudman, 2004).

As you can see, defining and measuring prejudice are not easy tasks. They involve distinguishing explicit attitudes from unconscious ones, active hostility from simple discomfort, what people say from what they feel, and what people feel from how they actually behave.

Reducing Conflict and Prejudice

Just as social psychologists investigate the situations that increase prejudice and animosity toward other groups, they have also examined the conditions that might reduce them. Of course, given the many sources and functions of prejudice, no *one* method will work in all situations. But social psychologists have identified four external conditions that must be met before conflict and prejudice between groups can be lessened (Dovidio, Gaertner, & Validzic, 1998; Pettigrew, 1998; Slavin & Cooper, 1999; Staub, 1999; Stephan, 1999; Wittig & Grant-Thompson, 1998):

1 *Both sides must have equal legal status, economic opportunities, and power.* This requirement is the spur behind efforts to change laws that permit discrimination. Women would never have gotten the right to vote, attend college, or do "men's work" without persistent challenges to the laws that permitted gender discrimination. But changing the law is not enough if two groups remain in competition for jobs or if one group retains power and dominance over the other.

2 *Authorities and community institutions must endorse egalitarian norms and thereby provide moral support and legitimacy for both sides.* Society must establish norms of equality and support them in the actions of its officials—teachers, employers, the judicial system, government officials, and the police. Where segregation is official government policy or an unofficial but established practice, conflict and prejudice not only will continue but also will seem "normal" and justified.

3 *Both sides must have opportunities to work and socialize together, formally and informally.* According to the *contact hypothesis*, prejudice declines when people have the chance to get used to one another's rules, food, music, customs, and attitudes, thereby discovering their shared interests and shared humanity. Stereotypes are shattered once people realize that "those people" aren't, in fact, "all alike."

The contact hypothesis has been supported by many studies in the laboratory and in the real world: studies of newly integrated housing projects in the American South during the 1950s and 1960s; relationships between German and immigrant Turkish children in German schools; young people's attitudes toward the elderly; healthy people's attitudes toward the mentally ill; nondisabled children's attitudes toward the disabled; and straight people's prejudices toward gay men and lesbians (Fishbein, 1996; Herek & Capitanio, 1996; Pettigrew, 1997; Wilner, Walkley, & Cook, 1955).

4 *Both sides must co-operate, working together for a common goal.* As we saw, co-operation often reduces us–them thinking and prejudice by creating an encompassing social identity ("We're all in this together")—the Eagles and Rattlers solu-

Tensions between groups often subside when people work together on a common goal. Here, volunteers from Habitat for Humanity, a group that constructs housing for low-income people, build a new home in the Watts area of Los Angeles.

tion. For example, to reduce the intergroup tension and competition that exist in many schools, Elliot Aronson and his colleagues have developed the "jigsaw" method of building co-operation. Students from different ethnic groups work together on a task that is broken up like a jigsaw puzzle; each person needs to co-operate with the others to put the assignment together. Students in such classes—from elementary school through college—tend to do better, like their classmates better, and become less stereotyped in their thinking than students in traditional classrooms (Aronson, 2000; Aronson & Patnoe, 1997; Slavin & Cooper, 1999).

Each of these four approaches to creating greater harmony between groups is important, but none is sufficient on its own. Clearly, contact between two groups is not enough; at many multiethnic high schools, ethnic groups often form cliques and gangs, fighting other cliques and defending their own ways. Likewise, co-operation in working for a common goal may not work when members of a group have unequal status or believe the teacher or employer is playing favourites. Perhaps one reason that group conflicts and prejudice are so persistent is that all four conditions for reducing them are rarely met at the same time.

Quick Quiz

Try to overcome your prejudice against quizzes by taking this one.

1. What are four important conditions required for reducing prejudice and conflict between groups?

2. Surveys find that large percentages of ethnic minorities hold negative stereotypes of one another and resent other minorities almost as much as they resent whites. What are some reasons that people who have themselves been victims of stereotyping and prejudice would hold the same attitudes toward others?

Answers:

1. Both sides must have equal status and power; have the moral, legal, and economic support of authorities; have opportunities to socialize formally and informally; and co-operate for a common goal.

2. ethnocentrism; low self-esteem; conformity with relatives and friends who share these prejudices; parental lessons and messages conveyed by the media; and economic competition for jobs and resources

Psychology In The News *Revisited*

After reading this chapter, perhaps you can begin to see why, in our opening story, emotions ran so high regarding the war in Iraq. Any state of conflict with another group or nation enhances ethnocentrism, the feeling that "we" are the best and "we" are right. And it produces us–them thinking: not only between one nation and another, but between people who take different positions, such as pro-war and anti-war groups ("You are all traitors!" "You are all idiots!").

Regardless of whether you originally supported or opposed the war, consider some of the social-psychological findings of relevance. Before the war began, most Canadians and Americans had voiced reservations about it. But in building its case for invasion, the U.S. government took advantage of the validity effect—for example, by issuing frequent statements equating Iraq with Al Qaeda and with the production of nuclear bombs. Over half of the American population came to believe these allegations, although there was never any evidence of such a link. (There was, of course, plenty of evidence of Saddam Hussein's cruelty to his people.) After the war started, however, most Americans put aside their private doubts and united in support of what they perceived as a common goal. They may also have had a need

to reduce cognitive dissonance: "The war is wrong" is certainly inconsistent with "My country would never do the wrong thing."

In the weeks following the invasion of Iraq, Americans who took a dissenting position toward the war were often made to feel uncomfortable and isolated, and were pressured to conform. In most areas of the country, opponents were in the minority, as in the case of the Dixie Chicks, whose lead singer had publicly criticized President Bush and in so doing enraged the group's conservative southern fans. In some places, however, including many college campuses, *supporters* of the war were the ones in the minority. A Columbia University sophomore who plans to become a Marine officer told *The New York Times* (April 2, 2003), "Because there's so few of us, I think it's very hard at times to feel that you can be vocal about what you're doing. . . . People too often pigeonhole each other."

She was exactly right, of course. As we saw, pigeonholing is just what people do when they have stereotypes and prejudices: They fail to see the humanity and variation among their opponents.

The Nazis, of course, systematically exterminated millions of Jews, Gypsies, homosexuals, disabled people, and anyone else not of

Thinking Critically About "Evil" Cultures

the "pure" Aryan "race." But Canadians and Americans slaughtered native peoples in North America, Turks slaughtered Armenians, the Khmer Rouge slaughtered millions of fellow Cambodians, the Spanish conquistadors slaughtered native peoples in Mexico and South America, Idi Amin waged a reign of terror against his own people in Uganda, the Japanese slaughtered Koreans and Chinese, Iraqis slaughtered Kurds, despotic political regimes in Argentina and Chile killed thousands of dissidents and rebels, the Hutu in Rwanda murdered thousands of Tutsi, and in the former Yugoslavia, Bosnian Serbs massacred thousands of Bosnian Muslims in the name of "ethnic cleansing."

Many people assume that such outbreaks of horrifying violence are a result of inner aggressive drives, the sheer evil of a murderer like Hitler (or Stalin, Idi Amin, Saddam Hussein, and countless other dictators), or "age-old tribal hatreds." In fact, policies of genocide against a perceived outside enemy are almost always generated by governments that feel weakened and vulnerable (Smith, 1998). Governments then rely on the social-psychological processes discussed in this chapter—including obedience to authority, conformity, rationalization, the validity effect, groupthink, deindividuation, stereotyping, and prejudice—to carry out their policies.

That is why, from the standpoint of social and cultural psychology, all human beings, like all cultures, contain the potential for good *and* bad. The philosopher Hannah Arendt (1963) covered the trial of Adolf Eichmann, a Nazi officer who supervised the deportation and death of millions of Jews. Arendt used the phrase *the banality of evil* to describe how it was possible for Eichmann and other ordinary people in Nazi Germany to commit the atrocities they did. (*Banal* means "commonplace" or "unoriginal.") The compelling evidence for the banality of evil is, perhaps, the hardest lesson in psychology.

The research discussed in this chapter suggests that ethnocentrism and prejudice will always be with us, as long as differences exist among groups. But it can also help us formulate realistic yet nonviolent ways of living in a diverse world. (The conditions for reducing conflict [page 344] are a good place to start.) By identifying the conditions that create the banality of evil, perhaps we can create others that foster the "banality of virtue"—everyday acts of kindness, selflessness, and generosity.

These paintings done by children in wartime poignantly illustrate their fears and hopes. Can understanding the principles of social psychology help us create a world in which conflicts and differences, though inevitable, need not lead to violence and war?

Taking Psychology With You   Travels Across the Cultural Divide

A French salesman worked for a company that was bought by Americans. When the new American manager ordered him to step up his sales within the next three months, the employee quit in a huff, taking his customers with him. Why? In France, it takes years to develop customers; in family-owned businesses, relationships with customers may span generations. The American wanted instant results, as Americans often do, but the French salesman knew this was impossible and quit. The American view was "He wasn't up to the job; he's lazy and disloyal, so he stole my customers." The French view was "There is no point in explaining anything to a person who is so stupid as to think you can acquire loyal customers in three months" (Hall & Hall, 1987).

Both men were committing the fundamental attribution error: assuming that the other person's behaviour was due to personality rather than the situation—in this case, a situation governed by cultural rules. Many corporations now realize that such rules are not trivial and that success in a global economy depends on understanding them. You, too, can benefit from the psychological research on cultures, whether you plan to do business abroad, intend to visit as a tourist, or just want to get along better in your own society.

- **Be sure you understand the other culture's rules, manners, and customs.** If you find yourself getting angry over something a person from another culture is doing, try to find out whether your expectations and perceptions of that person's behaviour are appropriate. For example, Koreans typically do not shake hands when greeting strangers, whereas most North Americans and Europeans do. People who shake hands as a gesture of friendship and courtesy are likely to feel insulted if another person refuses to do the same, unless they understand this cultural difference.

   Or suppose that you are shopping in the Middle East or Latin America, where bargaining on a price is the usual practice. If you are not used to bargaining, the experience is likely to be exasperating—you will not know whether you got taken or got a great deal. On the other hand, if you are from a bargaining culture, you will feel just as exasperated if a seller offers you a flat price. "Where's the fun in this?" you'll say. "The whole human transaction of shopping is gone!"

- **When in Rome, do as the Romans do—as much as possible.** Most of the things you really need to know about a culture are not to be found in guidebooks. To learn the unspoken

rules of a culture, look, listen, and observe. What is the pace of life like? Do people regard brash individuality and loud speech as admirable or embarrassing? When customers enter a shop, do they greet and chat with the shopkeeper or ignore the person as they browse?

   Remember, though, that even when you know the rules, you may find it difficult to carry them out. In the Middle East, two men will look directly at one another as they talk, but such direct gazes would be deeply uncomfortable to most Japanese and a sign of insult or confrontation to some African-Americans (Keating, 1994). Knowing this fact about gaze rules can help people accept the reality of different customs, but most of us will still feel uncomfortable trying to change our own ways.

- **Avoid stereotyping.** Try not to let your awareness of general cultural differences cause you to overlook individual variations within cultures. During a dreary Boston winter, Roger Brown (1986) went to the Bahamas for a vacation. To his surprise, he found the people he met unfriendly, rude, and sullen. As a social psychologist, he came up with a situational attribution for their behaviour: He decided that the reason was that Bahamians had to deal with spoiled, demanding foreigners. He tried out this hypothesis on a cab driver. The cab driver looked at Brown in amazement, smiled cheerfully, and told him that Bahamians don't mind tourists, just *unsmiling* tourists.

   And then Brown realized what had been going on. "Not tourists generally, but this tourist, myself, was the cause," he wrote. "Confronted with my unrelaxed wintry Boston face, they had assumed I had no interest in them and had responded non-committally, inexpressively. I had created the Bahamian national character. Everywhere I took my face it sprang into being. So I began smiling a lot, and the Bahamians changed their national character. In fact, they lost any national character and differentiated into individuals."

   Wise travellers can use their knowledge of cultural differences to expand their understanding of human behaviour, while avoiding the trap of stereotyping. Sociocultural research teaches us to appreciate the many cultural rules that govern people's behaviour, values, and attitudes. Yet we should not forget Roger Brown's lesson that every human being is an individual—one who not only reflects his or her culture, but also shares the common concerns of all humanity.

SUMMARY

- Social and cultural psychologists emphasize environmental influences on behaviour. *Social psychologists* study how social roles, attitudes, relationships, and groups influence individuals; *cultural psychologists* study the influence of culture on human behaviour.

ROLES AND RULES

- Two classic studies illustrate the power of *norms* and *roles* to affect individual actions. In Milgram's obedience study, most people in the role of "teacher" inflicted what they thought was extreme shock on another person because of the authority of the experimenter. In Zimbardo's prison study, college students quickly fell into the role of "prisoner" or "guard."

- Obedience to authority contributes to the smooth running of society, but obedience can also lead to actions that are deadly, foolish, or illegal. People obey orders because they can be punished if they do not, out of respect for the authority, and to gain advantages. Even when they would rather not obey, they may do so because they hand over responsibility for their actions to the authority; because their role is *routinized* into duties that are performed mindlessly; because they are embarrassed to violate the rules of good manners and lack the words to protest; or because they have been *entrapped*.

SOCIAL INFLUENCES ON BELIEFS

- Researchers in the area of *social cognition* study how people's relationships and social environment affect their beliefs and perceptions. According to *attribution theory*, people are motivated to search for causes to which they can attribute their own and other people's behaviour. Their attributions may be *situational* or *dispositional*. The *fundamental attribution error* occurs when people overestimate personality traits as a cause of behaviour and underestimate the influence of the situation. A *self-serving bias* allows people to excuse their own mistakes by blaming the situation yet taking credit for their good deeds. According to the *just-world hypothesis*, most people need to believe that the world is fair and that people

get what they deserve. To preserve this belief, they may blame victims of abuse or injustice for provoking or deserving it, instead of blaming the perpetrators.

- People hold many *attitudes* about people, things, and ideas. Attitudes may be *explicit* (conscious) or *implicit* (unconscious). Some are fairly ingrained and difficult to change; others are subject to social influences and are more changeable. One important external influence on attitudes is the shared experiences of a person's age group, which create a *generational identity*. Attitudes may change as an effort to reduce *cognitive dissonance*.

- One powerful way to influence attitudes is through the *familiarity effect* and the *validity effect*: Simply exposing people repeatedly to a name or product makes them like it more, and repeating a statement over and over again makes it seem more believable. Other techniques of attitude change include associating a product or message with someone who is famous, attractive, or expert, and linking the product with good feelings. Fear tactics tend to backfire.

- Tactics of *coercive persuasion* include putting a person under extreme stress; defining problems simplistically; offering the appearance of unconditional love and acceptance in exchange for unquestioning loyalty; creating a new identity for the person; using entrapment; and controlling access to outside information. Even ordinary people without any psychopathology can be vulnerable to these techniques.

INDIVIDUALS IN GROUPS

- In groups, individuals often behave differently than they would on their own. Conformity has many benefits; it permits the smooth running of society and allows people to feel in harmony with others like them. As the famous Asch experiment showed, most people will conform to the judgments of others even when the others are plain wrong. People in collectivist cultures value conformity and the sense of group harmony it creates more than do people in individualist cultures. But everyone conforms under some conditions.

- Most people conform to social pressure because they identify with a group, trust the group's judgment or knowledge, hope for personal gain, or wish to be liked. But they also may conform mindlessly and self-destructively, violating their own preferences and values because "everyone else is doing it."

- Groups that are strongly cohesive, are isolated from other views, are under outside pressure, and have strong leaders are vulnerable to groupthink, the tendency of group members to think alike, censor themselves, actively suppress disagreement, and feel that their decisions are invulnerable. Groupthink often produces faulty decisions because group members fail to seek disconfirming evidence for their ideas. However, groups can be structured to counteract groupthink.

- *Diffusion of responsibility* in a group can lead to inaction on the part of individuals, such as *bystander apathy* or, in work groups, *social loafing*. The diffusion of responsibility is likely to occur under conditions that promote *deindividuation*, the loss of awareness of one's individuality. Deindividuation increases when people feel anonymous, as in a large group or crowd, or when they are wearing masks or uniforms. In some situations, crowd norms lead deindividuated people to behave aggressively, but in others, crowd norms foster helpfulness.

- The willingness to speak up for an unpopular opinion, blow the whistle on illegal practices, or help a stranger in trouble and perform other acts of *altruism* is partly a matter of personal belief and conscience. But several situational factors are also important: The person perceives that help is needed; the situation increases the likelihood that the person will take responsibility; the person decides that the cost of not doing anything is greater than the cost of getting involved; the person has an ally; and the person becomes entrapped in a commitment to help or dissent.

US VERSUS THEM: GROUP IDENTITY

- People develop *social identities* based on their group affiliations, including nationality, ethnicity, gender, and other social memberships. Social identities provide a feeling of place and connection in the world.

- In culturally diverse societies, many people face the problem of balancing their *ethnic identity* with *acculturation* into the larger society. Depending on whether ethnic identity and acculturation are strong or weak, a person may become *bicultural*, choose *assimilation*, become an *ethnic separatist*, or feel *marginal*.

- *Ethnocentrism*, the belief that one's own ethnic group or nation is superior to all others, promotes "us–them" thinking. One effective strategy for reducing us–them thinking and hostility between groups is co-operation, when both sides must work together to reach a common goal.

- *Stereotypes* help people rapidly process new information, organize experience, and predict how others will behave. But they distort reality by (1) exaggerating differences between groups, (2) underestimating the differences within groups, and (3) producing selective perception.

GROUP CONFLICT AND PREJUDICE

- A *prejudice* is an unreasonable negative feeling toward a category of people. Prejudice has psychological, social-cultural, and economic functions. Psychologically, it wards off feelings of anxiety and doubt; provides a simple explanation of complex problems; and bolsters self-esteem when a person feels threatened. But other causes of prejudice are social: People acquire prejudices through conformity and groupthink, parental lessons, and media images. Prejudice has the cultural purpose of bonding people to their social groups and nations. Prejudice also serves to justify a majority group's economic interests and dominance, and even to legitimize war. During times of economic insecurity and competition for jobs, prejudice rises significantly.

- Prejudice is a challenge to define and measure. For example, "hostile sexism" is different from "benevolent sexism," though both legitimize gender discrimination. People often disagree on whether racism and other prejudices are declining or have merely taken new forms. Because many people are unwilling to admit their prejudices openly, some researchers measure *symbolic racism* (prejudice disguised in opinions about race-related social issues); people's actual behaviour toward a target group when they are stressed or insulted; people's physiological responses; or people's unconscious, *implicit* prejudice as revealed in emotional associations to a target group.

- Four external conditions are required for reducing prejudice and conflict between groups: Both sides must have equal legal status, economic standing, and power; both sides must have the legal and moral support of authorities and cultural institutions; both sides must have opportunities to work and socialize together (the *contact hypothesis*); and both sides must work together for a common goal.

PSYCHOLOGY IN THE NEWS, REVISITED

- Although many people believe that only bad or evil people do bad deeds, the principles of social and cultural psychology show that under certain conditions, good people are often induced to do bad things too. All individuals are affected by the rules and norms of their cultures. And everyone is influenced to one degree or another by the social processes of obedience and conformity, persuasion, bystander apathy, groupthink, deindividuation, ethnocentrism, stereotyping, and prejudice.

KEY TERMS

LOOKING BACK

- How do social rules regulate behaviour—and what is likely to happen when you violate them? (p. 318)
- Do you have to be mean or disturbed to inflict pain on someone just because an authority tells you to? (p. 320)
- How can ordinary college students be transformed into sadistic prison guards? (pp. 320–321)
- How can people be "entrapped" into violating their moral principles? (p. 323)
- What is one of the most common mistakes people make when explaining the behaviour of others? (p. 324)
- Why do so many people blame victims of tragedy or crime for having brought their misfortunes on themselves? (p. 325)
- What is the "Big Lie," and why does it work so well? (p. 327)
- What is the difference between ordinary techniques of persuasion and the coercive techniques used by cults? (pp. 328–329)
- Why do people in groups often go along with the majority even when the majority is dead wrong? (pp. 330–331)
- How can "groupthink" lead to bad, even catastrophic, decisions? (pp. 331–332)
- In an emergency, are you more likely to get help when there are lots of strangers in the area or only a few? (p. 332)
- What enables some people to be nonconformists, take risks to help others, or blow the whistle on wrongdoers? (pp. 334–335)
- In what different ways do people balance their ethnic identity and their membership in the larger culture? (p. 336)
- What is an effective antidote to "us–them" thinking? (p. 338)
- How do stereotypes benefit us, and how do they distort reality? (pp. 338–339)
- Is prejudice more likely to be a *cause* of war or a *result* of it? (p. 340)
- If you believe that women are naturally better than men, are you "sexist"? (p. 341)
- Why isn't mere contact between cultural groups enough to reduce prejudice between them? What does work? (pp. 344–345)

Psychology In The News

MAN WHO MURDERS HIS SIX CHILDREN JUDGED MENTALLY FIT

VANCOUVER ISLAND, BC, October 3, 2003. Can a man who drugs his six children with codeine, then murders them, be considered sane? What if, after doing this, he sets his house on fire and tries to kill himself by cutting his throat in front of his wife?

Jay Handel, 46, did exactly these things on March 11, 2002. During the subsequent trial, he slit his wrists in the courtroom. The defence claimed that he should not be held responsible for his actions by reason of mental disorder. Specifically, the court received expert testimony indicating that Handel had a narcissistic personality, believing that he was the focus of all things that happened in his life and that everything revolved around him.

The judge and jury, however, decided that Handel did understand the difference between right and wrong when he murdered his children, and that his actions were planned and deliberate. The Crown acknowledged that Handel could have been suffering from psychological problems, but not to the extent that he did not know what he was doing when he murdered his children.

Yet Jay Handel's life was fraught with trouble. His father had hanged himself, and other members of his family had psychiatric problems. Handel's wife testified that he was constantly angry and would often berate her.

On March 10, she told him she was leaving him. He then said, "Don't worry about the kids, they're safe from you." Chilling words, as it turned out.

Jay Handel murdered his six children (pictured above), set his house on fire, and tried to kill himself by slitting his throat. Can a man who does these things be considered sane?

11 Psychological Disorders

Was Jay Handel "crazy"? We all have our own ideas about what a disturbed individual is like, from watching films and TV shows and from observing people on the streets whose behaviour is clearly not normal. They talk or shout to themselves, they wear odd garments or layers of clothing even in hot weather, they confide to any willing listener that the government is following them. When people think of "mental illness," they usually think of people who behave in bizarre ways like these. Would you place Handel's acts of violence in this list?

In truth, most psychological problems are far less dramatic than the public's impression of them, and far more common than Handel's story. Some people go through episodes of complete inability to function, yet get along fine between those episodes. Many people function adequately every day, yet suffer constant melancholy, always feeling below par. Some cannot control their worries or tempers.

In this chapter, you will learn about the many psychological problems that cause people unhappiness and anguish. You will learn about the severe disorders that really do make people unable to control their behaviour. But you will also learn why diagnosing mental problems is not the same as diagnosing medical problems such as diabetes or appendicitis. You will also see why psychologists and psychiatrists often find it difficult to agree on a diagnosis.

One of the most common worries that people have is "Am I normal?" It is normal to fear being abnormal—especially when you are reading about psychological problems! But it is also normal to have problems. All of us on occasion have difficulties that seem too much to handle. As you read about each disorder, therefore, ask yourself how you would pinpoint when "normal" problems shade into "abnormal" ones on the spectrum of human behaviour. And as you read, consider an even tougher question: What is the relationship between psychological disorders and personal responsibility?

When does "abnormal" behaviour indicate mental illness? The answer depends partly on culture and context. The beautiful facial painting on this Samburu tribesman is perfectly normal in his culture, but a Calgary businessman who did the same thing would raise concerns.

mental disorder Any behaviour or emotional state that causes a person great suffering, is self-destructive, seriously impairs the person's ability to work or get along with others, or endangers others or the community.

WHAT'S AHEAD

- What are three approaches to defining mental disorder?
- Why is the standard guide to the diagnosis of mental disorders controversial?
- Why were slaves who tried to escape once considered to be mentally ill?
- How reliable are "projective" tests like the popular Rorschach Inkblot Test?

DEFINING AND DIAGNOSING DISORDER

Many people confuse abnormal behaviour—behaviour that deviates from the norm—with mental disorder, but the two are not the same. A person may behave in ways that are statistically rare (collecting ceramic pigs, being a genius at math, committing murder) without having a mental disorder. Conversely, some mental disorders, such as depression and anxiety, are extremely common.

In our opening news story, we saw that someone could be mentally troubled, even disordered, but still be aware of the consequences of his actions—and therefore be held legally responsible for them. If the frequency of a behaviour is not a guide, nor is awareness of consequences, how then should we define "mental disorder"?

Dilemmas of Definition

One problem with trying to define "mental disorder" is that the definition depends on whether we are taking society's point of view, the view of people who are affected by the troubled individual, or the perspective of the troubled individuals themselves.

1 *Mental disorder as a violation of cultural standards.* One approach to defining mental disorder emphasizes the roles and rules of the culture. Every society sets up standards for its members to follow, and those who break the most important rules are usually considered deviant or disturbed. However, many of these rules are specific to a particular time or group. For example, it is not uncommon for bereaved people to have momentary visions of a deceased relative or to "hear" the person's voice. But in most of North America, these hallucinations are considered abnormal, and

people who have them often fear they might be "crazy." In contrast, the Chinese, the Hopi, and members of many other cultures regard such visions as perfectly normal.

2 *Mental disorder as emotional distress.* A second approach identifies mental disorder in terms of a person's own suffering—as from depression, anxiety, incapacitating fears, or problems with drugs. In this definition, a behaviour that is unendurable or upsetting for one person, such as lack of interest in sex, may be acceptable and normal for another. But it does not cover the behaviour of people who are clearly disturbed and dangerous to others, yet are not troubled about their actions.

3 *Mental disorder as behaviour that is self-destructive or harmful to others.* A third approach emphasizes the negative consequences of a person's behaviour. Some behaviour is harmful to the individual sufferer—such as the behaviour of a woman who is so afraid of crowds that she cannot leave her house, a man who drinks so much that he cannot keep a job, and a student who is so anxious that he cannot take exams. In other cases, the individual may report feeling fine and deny that anything is wrong, yet behave in ways that are disruptive, dangerous, or out of touch with reality—as when a child sets fires, a compulsive gambler loses the family savings, or a woman hears voices telling her to stalk a celebrity.

In this chapter, we define **mental disorder** broadly, as any behaviour or emotional state that causes a person great suffering; is self-destructive; seriously impairs the person's ability to work or get along with others; or endangers others or the community. By this definition, many people will have some mental-health problem in the course of their lives, or their loved ones will.

Dilemmas of Diagnosis

Even armed with a general definition of mental disorder, psychologists have found that classifying mental disorders into distinct categories is not an easy task. In this section we will examine why this is so.

Classifying Disorders: The DSM The standard reference manual used to diagnose all mental disorders is the *Diagnostic and Statistical Manual of Mental Disorders* (DSM), published by the American Psychiatric Association (APA) (1994, 2000). The DSM's primary aim is *descriptive*: to provide clear diagnostic categories so that clinicians and researchers can agree on which disorders they are talking about and can then study and treat these disorders. For a list of the DSM's major categories, see Table 11.1.

The DSM lists the symptoms of each disorder and, wherever possible, gives information about the typical age of onset, predisposing factors, course of the disorder, prevalence of the disorder, sex ratio of those affected, and cultural issues that might affect diagnosis. When clinicians make a diagnosis, the DSM encourages them to take into account many factors, such as the client's personality traits, medical conditions, stresses at work and at home, and the duration and severity of the problem.

The DSM has had an extraordinary impact worldwide. Virtually all textbooks in psychiatry and psychology base their discussions of mental disor-

ders on the DSM. Lawyers and judges often refer to the manual's list of mental disorders, even though the DSM warns that its categories "may not be wholly relevant to legal judgments." With each new edition of the manual, the number of mental disorders has grown (see Figure 11.1). The first edition, in 1952, was only 86 pages long and contained about 100 diagnoses. The DSM-IV, published in 1994 and revised slightly in 2000, is 900 pages long and contains nearly 400 diagnoses (Houts, 2002).

What is the reason for this explosion of "mental disorders"? Supporters of the new categories answer that it is important to distinguish disorders precisely in order to treat them properly. Critics point to an economic reason: Insurance companies require clinicians to assign their clients an appropriate DSM code number for the diagnosed disorder, which puts pressure on

TABLE 11.1 Major Diagnostic Categories in the DSM-IV

Disorders usually first diagnosed in infancy, childhood, or adolescence include mental retardation, attention deficit disorders (such as hyperactivity or an inability to concentrate), and developmental problems.

Delirium, dementia, amnesia, and other cognitive disorders are those resulting from brain damage, degenerative diseases such as syphilis or Alzheimer's, toxic substances, or drugs.

Substance-related disorders are problems associated with excessive use of or withdrawal from alcohol, amphetamines, caffeine, cocaine, hallucinogens, nicotine, opiates, or other drugs.

Schizophrenia and other psychotic disorders are disorders characterized by delusions, hallucinations, and severe disturbances in thinking and emotion.

Mood disorders include major depression, bipolar disorder (manic depression), and dysthymia (chronic depressed mood).

Anxiety disorders include generalized anxiety disorder, phobias, panic attacks with or without agoraphobia, posttraumatic stress disorder, and obsessive thoughts or compulsive rituals.

Eating disorders include anorexia nervosa (self-starvation because of an irrational fear of being or becoming fat) and bulimia nervosa (episodes of binge eating and vomiting).

Somatoform disorders involve physical symptoms (e.g., paralysis, heart palpitations, fatigue) for which no organic cause can be found. This category includes hypochondria (an extreme preoccupation with health and the unfounded conviction that one is ill) and conversion disorder (in which a physical symptom, such as a paralyzed arm or blindness, serves a psychological function, perhaps by preventing a person from dealing with a psychologically difficult situation).

Dissociative disorders include dissociative amnesia (in which important events cannot be remembered after a traumatic event) and dissociative identity disorder, characterized by the presence of two or more distinct identities or personalities.

Sexual and gender identity disorders include problems of sexual (gender) identity, such as transsexualism (wanting to be the other sex), problems of sexual performance (such as premature ejaculation or lack of orgasm), and paraphilias (needing unusual or bizarre imagery or acts for sexual arousal).

Impulse control disorders involve an inability to resist an impulse to perform some act that is harmful to the individual or to others, such as pathological gambling, stealing (kleptomania), setting fires (pyromania), or having violent rages.

Personality disorders are inflexible and maladaptive patterns that cause distress to the individual or impair the ability to function; they include paranoid, narcissistic, and antisocial personality disorders.

Additional conditions that may be a focus of clinical attention include "problems in living" such as bereavement, academic difficulties, spiritual problems, and acculturation problems.

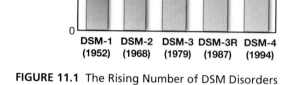

FIGURE 11.1 The Rising Number of DSM Disorders

Mental disorders in the DSM have increased nearly fourfold since the first edition (Houts, 2002).

compilers of the manual to add more diagnoses so that physicians and psychologists will be compensated. This reason pertains more to the United States than Canada, however, since health care in the United States is privatized to a much greater extent than it is in this country.

Problems with the DSM Because of the DSM's powerful influence, critics maintain that it is important to be aware of its limitations and some inherent problems in the very effort to classify and label mental disorders:

Thinking Critically About Diagnosing Disorders

1 *The danger of overdiagnosis.* "If you give a small boy a hammer," wrote Abraham Kaplan (1967), "it will turn out that everything he runs into needs pounding." Likewise, say critics, if you give mental-health professionals a diagnostic label, it will turn out that everyone they run into has the symptoms of the new disorder.

Consider "attention deficit/hyperactivity disorder" (ADHD), a label given to children (and adults) who are impulsive, restless, and easily frustrated and who have trouble concentrating. Since ADHD was added to the DSM, it has become the fastest-growing disorder in North America, where it is diagnosed at least 10 times as often as it is in Europe. In Canada, the prevalence of this disorder in 1989 was 9 percent in boys and 3.3 percent in girls (Szatmari, Offord, & Boyle, 1989). More recent studies indicate a wide variation in the

prevalence of symptoms associated with ADHD, showing that between 9 and 23 percent of boys between the ages of 2 and 11 display hyperactive or impulsive behaviours (Statistics Canada, 2004). It may be a true disorder in some cases, but some psychologists fear that parents, teachers, and mental-health professionals are overusing this diagnosis, especially with boys, who make up 80 to 90 percent of all ADHD cases. The critics argue that normal boyish behaviour—being rambunctious, refusing to nap, being playful, not listening to teachers in school—is being turned into an illness (Panksepp, 1998).

2 *The power of diagnostic labels.* Being given a diagnosis reassures people who are seeking an explanation for their emotional symptoms or problems ("Whew! So *that's* what I've got!"). But it can also create a self-fulfilling prophecy: The client tries to conform to the assigned diagnosis, and the clinician interprets everything the client does as confirmation of the diagnosis (Maddux, 1996).

Moreover, once a person has been given a diagnosis, other people begin to see that person primarily in terms of the label; it sticks like lint. For example, when a rebellious, disobedient teenager is diagnosed as having "oppositional defiant disorder," people tend to see him as a person with a permanent, official disorder; something is wrong with his personality. They therefore overlook other possible explanations of his actions: Maybe he is defiant because he has been mistreated or because his parents never listen to him. And once he is labelled, observers tend to ignore changes in his behaviour and occasions when he is not defiant.

3 *The confusion of serious mental disorders with normal problems.* The DSM is not called "The Diagnostic and Statistical Manual of Mental Disorders and a Whole Bunch of Everyday Problems." Yet each edition adds more everyday problems. The latest includes "disorder of written expression" (having trouble writing clearly), "mathematics disorder" (not doing well in math), "religious or spiritual problem," and "caffeine-induced sleep disorder" (which at least is easy to cure; just switch to decaf). Some critics fear that by lumping together such ordinary difficulties with true mental illnesses, such as schizophrenia, the DSM implies that everyday problems are comparable to disorders—and equally likely to require treatment (Houts, 2002). Moreover, a study in Canada, the United States, and the Netherlands

NEWLY DISCOVERED LEARNING DISABILITIES

GO-CARTITIS
Instead of focussing on topic at hand, kid fantasizes about go-carts.

DOODLER'S SYNDROME
Child insists on drawing, thus completely shutting out teacher's voice.

What is a divisor? SALLY?

Critics say the DSM turns many normal behaviours into "disorders" or "disabilities."

disorders in the DSM are just as affected by contemporary prejudices and values. Today you don't have a disorder if you want to have sex "too often" (once called, in women, "nymphomania"), but you do if you do not want to have sex often "enough" (hypoactive sexual desire disorder) (Groneman, 2000). Emotional problems allegedly associated with menstruation remain in the DSM, but behavioural problems associated with testosterone have never even been considered for inclusion. In short, critics maintain, many diagnoses still depend on a cultural consensus about what constitutes normal behaviour, as well as what constitutes a mental disorder.

concluded that diagnostic accuracy is hampered by the DSM's many dimensions and ambiguous symptoms (Hartman et al., 2001).

4 *The illusion of objectivity and universality.* Finally, some psychologists argue that the whole enterprise of the DSM is a vain attempt to impose a veneer of science on an inherently subjective process (Kutchins & Kirk, 1997; Maddux, 1993; Tiefer, 1995). Many decisions about what to include as a disorder, say these critics, are based not on empirical evidence but on group consensus. The problem is that group consensus often reflects prevailing attitudes and prejudices rather than objective evidence.

It is easy to identify prejudices in past notions of mental problems. In the early years of the nineteenth century, a physician named Samuel Cartwright argued that many slaves were suffering from *drapetomania*, an urge to escape from slavery (Kutchins & Kirk, 1997; Landrine, 1988). (He coined the term from *drapetes*, the Latin word for "runaway slave," and *mania*, meaning "mad" or "crazy.") Thus doctors could assure slave owners that a mental illness, not the intolerable condition of slavery, made slaves seek freedom. Today, of course, "drapetomania" seems foolish and cruel.

Over the years, psychiatrists have quite properly rejected many other "disorders" that reflected cultural prejudices and lacked empirical validation, such as lack of vaginal orgasm, childhood masturbation disorder, and homosexuality (Wakefield, 1992). But critics argue that many

Advantages of the DSM Defenders of the DSM agree that the boundaries between "normality" and "mental disorder" are fuzzy and often difficult to determine. And they recognize that many psychological symptoms fall along a continuum, ranging from mild to severe. However, they point out that new studies are improving empirical sup-

Harriet Tubman (on the left) poses with some of those she helped to escape from slavery on the "underground railroad." Slaveholders welcomed the idea that Tubman and others who insisted on their freedom had a "mental disorder" called "drapetomania."

port for many of the DSM's categories (Beutler & Malik, 2002; Widiger & Clark, 2000).

Defenders argue, further, that when the manual is used correctly and diagnoses are made with valid objective tests, the DSM improves the reliability of diagnosis (Wittchen et al., 1995). The DSM's categories help clinicians distinguish among disorders that might share certain symptoms (such as irritability or delusions) in order to select the most appropriate treatment (Kessler et al., 1994).

Moreover, the DSM-IV included, for the first time, a list of *culture-bound syndromes*, disorders that are specific to particular cultural contexts. All students will surely sympathize with the West African disorder of "brain fag," mental exhaustion due to excessive studying! Other culture-bound syndromes include *amok* in Malaysia, brooding followed by a violent outburst; *shin-byung* in Korea, a syndrome of anxiety and bodily complaints accompanied by feelings of being possessed by ancestral spirits; *taijin-kyofu-sho* in Japan, an intense fear that one is offending or embarrassing others; and *ataque de nervios* throughout Latin America, an episode of uncontrollable shouting, crying, trembling, and verbal or physical aggression. The DSM acknowledges that these syndromes rarely overlap with DSM diagnostic categories, yet can cause great mental suffering in the cultures in which they occur. At the same time, DSM defenders argue, some disorders are universal, although they may take different forms. All over the world, from the Inuit of Nunavut to the Yoruba of Nigeria, some individuals have delusions, are severely depressed, suffer panic attacks, or cannot control their behaviour. In every culture, such people are considered to have mental illnesses (Butcher, Lim, & Nezami, 1998; Kleinman, 1988).

Dilemmas of Measurement

Clinical psychologists and psychiatrists usually make a diagnosis by interviewing a patient and observing the person's behaviour when he or she arrives at the office, hospital, or clinic (Luhrmann, 2000). But many also use psychological tests to help them decide on a diagnosis. Such tests are also commonly used in schools (e.g., to determine whether a child has a learning disorder or emotional problem) and in court settings (e.g., to try to determine which parent should have custody in a divorce case).

Projective Tests **Projective tests** are based on psychodynamic assumptions (see Chapter 2); that

is, they are designed to reveal unconscious motives, feelings, and conflicts. These tests consist of ambiguous pictures, sentences, or stories that the test taker interprets or completes. A child or adult may be asked to draw a person, a house, or some other object, or to finish a sentence (such as "My father . . ." or "Women are . . ."). The assumption behind all projective tests is that the person's unconscious thoughts and feelings will be "projected" onto the test and revealed in the person's responses.

Projective tests can help clinicians establish rapport with their clients and encourage clients to open up about anxieties and conflicts they may be ashamed to discuss. But the evidence is overwhelming that they are too unreliable to be used, as they often currently are, for assessing personality traits or diagnosing mental disorders (Dawes, 1994; Lilienfeld, 1999). Different clinicians often interpret the same person's scores differently; they may be projecting their own beliefs and assumptions when they decide what a specific response means. The tests also have low validity, failing to measure what they are supposed to measure. One reason is that responses to a projective test are significantly affected by sleepiness, hunger, drugs, worry, verbal ability, the clinician's instructions, the clinician's own personality (friendly and warm, or cool and remote), and other events occurring that day (Anastasi, 1988; Lilienfeld, Wood, & Garb, 2000).

One of the most popular projectives is the **Rorschach Inkblot Test**, which was devised by Swiss psychiatrist Hermann Rorschach in 1921. It consists of 10 cards with symmetrical abstract

Thinking Critically About Projective Tests

Rorschach Inkblot Test A projective personality test that requires respondents to interpret abstract, symmetrical inkblots.

projective tests Psychological tests used to infer a person's motives, conflicts, and unconscious dynamics on the basis of the person's interpretations of ambiguous stimuli.

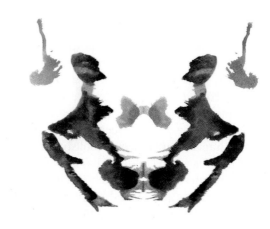

What do you see in this Rorschach inkblot?

patterns, originally formed by spilling ink on paper and folding the paper in half. The test-taker reports what he or she sees in the inkblots, and the clinician interprets the answers according to the symbolic meanings emphasized by psychodynamic theories. One kind of response, for instance, might be interpreted as evidence of a person's dependency.

Although the Rorschach is widely used among clinicians, efforts to confirm its reliability and validity have repeatedly failed (Wood et al., 2003). The Rorschach does not reliably diagnose depression, posttraumatic stress reactions, personality disorders, serious mental disorders, or evidence of sexual abuse. In recent years, a scoring method called the Comprehensive System has become popular (Exner, 1993). But this method, too, has significant problems with reliability and validity. Claims of the system's success often come from Rorschach workshops where clinicians are taught how to use the test, which is hardly an impartial way of assessing it (Wood et al., 2003).

Many psychotherapists use projective tests with children, to help those who have suffered traumatic experiences express feelings they cannot reveal verbally. But during the 1980s, some therapists began using projective methods for another purpose: to determine *whether* a child had been sexually abused. They claimed they could identify a child who had been abused by observing how the child played with "anatomically detailed" dolls (dolls with realistic genitals)—and that is how many of them testified in hundreds of court cases (Ceci & Bruck, 1995).

Unfortunately, these therapists did not test their beliefs by using a fundamental scientific procedure: comparison with a control group (see Chapter 1). They had not asked, "How do *nonabused* children play with these dolls?" When psychological scientists conducted controlled research to answer this question, they found that large percentages of nonabused children are also fascinated with the doll's genitals. They will poke at them, grab them, insert sticks into a female doll's vagina, and do other things that alarm adults! The important conclusion was that therapists cannot reliably diagnose sexual abuse on the basis of children's doll play (Bruck et al., 1995; Koocher et al., 1995; Lilienfeld, Wood, & Garb, 2000; Poole & Lamb, 1998). You can see how someone who did not realize the unreliability of projective tests might end up making inferences about a child's behaviour that were dangerously wrong.

Objective Tests Many clinicians also use **objective tests (inventories)**. As we discussed in Chapter 2, these are standardized questionnaires that ask about the test-taker's behaviour and feelings. Some inventories, such as the Beck Depression Inventory, the Spielberger State-Trait Anger Inventory, and the Taylor Manifest Anxiety Scale, assess specific emotional problems. The most widely used objective test for assessing disorders, the **Minnesota Multiphasic Personality Inventory (MMPI)**, is organized into 10 categories, or *scales*, covering such problems as depression, paranoia, schizophrenia, and introversion.

Inventories are generally more reliable and more valid than either projective methods or subjective clinical judgments (Dawes, 1994; Meyer et al., 2001). But inventories also have some problems. In spite of recent revisions of the MMPI, one continuing problem is that it often fails to take into account differences among cultural, regional, and socioeconomic groups. Also, while the MMPI and other objective tests have good validity when used to diagnose many mental disorders, they have a high rate of false positives; that is, they sometimes label a person's responses as evidence of mental disorder when no abnormality actually exists (Guthrie & Mobley, 1994). And finally, objective tests such as the MMPI are often inappropriately used in business, industry, legal settings, and schools by persons who are not well trained in testing (or in psychology).

We turn now to a closer examination of some of the disorders described in the DSM. Of course we cannot cover all of them in one chapter, so we have singled out several that illustrate the range of psychological problems that afflict humanity.

objective tests (inventories) Standardized objective questionnaires requiring written responses; they typically include scales on which people are asked to rate themselves.

Minnesota Multiphasic Personality Inventory (MMPI) A widely used objective personality test.

For years, many therapists used anatomically detailed dolls as a projective test to determine whether a child had been sexually abused, but this practice has not been supported by empirical evidence.

WHAT'S AHEAD

- What is the difference between ordinary anxiety and an anxiety disorder?

- Why is the most disabling of all phobias known as the "fear of fear"?

- When is checking the stove before leaving home a sign of caution, and when does it signal a disorder?

generalized anxiety disorder A continuous state of anxiety marked by feelings of worry and dread, apprehension, difficulties in concentration, and signs of motor tension.

OneKey
11.2

ANXIETY DISORDERS

Anyone who is waiting for important news, or living in a situation that is unpredictable and uncontrollable, quite sensibly feels *anxiety*, a general state of apprehension or psychological tension. And anyone who is in a dangerous and unfamiliar situation, such as making a first parachute jump or facing an annoyed hippopotamus, quite sensibly feels flat-out fear. In the short run, these emotions are adaptive because they energize us to cope with danger. They ensure that we don't make that first jump without knowing how to operate the parachute, and that we get away from that hippo as fast as we can.

But sometimes fear and anxiety become detached from any actual danger, or these feelings continue even when danger and uncertainty are past. The result may be *chronic anxiety*, marked by long-lasting feelings of apprehension and doom; *panic attacks*, short-lived but intense feelings of spontaneous anxiety; *phobias*, excessive fears of specific things or situations; or *obsessive-compulsive disorder*, in which repeated thoughts and rituals are used to ward off anxious feelings.

Anxiety and Panic

The chief characteristic of **generalized anxiety disorder** is continuous, uncontrollable anxiety— a feeling of foreboding and dread—that occurs on a majority of days during a six-month period and that is not brought on by physical causes such as disease, drugs, or drinking too much coffee. Symptoms include restlessness or feeling keyed up, difficulty concentrating, irritability, muscle tension and jitteriness, disturbed sleep, and unwanted, intrusive worries.

Some people suffer from generalized anxiety disorder without having lived through any specific anxiety-producing event. They may have a physiological tendency to experience anxiety symptoms—sweaty palms, a racing heart, shortness of breath—when they are in unfamiliar, challenging, or uncontrollable situations. Other chronically anxious people may have a history, starting in childhood, of being unable to control or predict their environments (Barlow, 2000). Whatever the origins of their anxiety, people with generalized anxiety disorder have mental habits that foster their worries and keep their anxiety bubbling along; they perceive everything as an opportunity for disaster (McNally, 1996; Riskind et al., 2000). This helps explain why generalized anxiety disorder tends to be costly for our health-care system. A study in Quebec found that 34 percent of those with anxiety disorders reported using medical or mental-health services 10 or more times in the previous year (McCusker et al., 1997). In Ontario, a study of over 9000 people showed that more than 12 percent had anxiety disorders, and 86 percent of those with the disorders had visited their doctors for problems related to anxiety (Parikh, Lin, & Lesage, 1997).

Posttraumatic Stress Disorder Stress symptoms, including insomnia, agitation, and jumpiness, are entirely normal in the immediate aftermath of any crisis or trauma, such as war, rape, torture, natural disasters, sudden bereavement, or terrorist attacks. But if the symptoms persist for one month or longer and begin to impair a person's functioning, the sufferer may have **posttraumatic stress disorder (PTSD)**. Typical symptoms of PTSD include reliving the trauma in recurrent, intrusive thoughts; a sense of detachment from others and a loss of interest in familiar activities; and increased physiological arousal, reflected in insomnia, irritability, and impaired concentration. These symptoms may recur for months, years, or even decades (Breslau et al., 1998; Kessler et al., 1995).

Most people who live through a traumatic experience eventually recover. One major national survey of Americans found that about 60 percent had experienced a traumatic event, but only 8 percent of the men and 20 percent of the women developed PTSD (Kessler et al., 1995). Some experts predicted an epidemic of PTSD after 9/11, but it never materialized. Even after the Oklahoma City terrorist bombing in 1995, only a third of the survivors, all of whom were injured, developed PTSD (North et al., 1999).

Why, if most people recover, do a minority continue to have PTSD symptoms for years? People who develop long-lasting PTSD have often had a prior family history of psychological problems and other traumatic experiences, and poor emotional adjustment to them (Ozer et al., 2003). Many seem to lack the psychological and neurological resources to deal with their difficult experiences; a post-9/11 study of people in Saskatchewan, for example, found that those with probable panic disorder prior to 9/11 suffered significantly more adverse psychological effects following the attacks (Asmundson et al., 2004). They are also more likely than more resilient people to have the personality trait of neuroticism (negative emotionality, described in Chapter 2); to have lower-than-average intelligence, which may impair their ability to cope cognitively with trauma; and to have a relatively smaller hippocampus (McNally, 2003a).

Couldn't these factors be a result of PTSD rather than a cause? At first, it seemed so. Researchers believed that severe trauma caused neuron damage or loss in the hippocampus, producing PTSD symptoms—impaired memory, recurrent fears, and so forth. But this hypothesis has been refuted. One team used MRIs to measure hippocampal size in identical twins, only one of whom in each pair had been in combat in Vietnam. If trauma affects the hippocampus, then the size of the hippocampus should have been different in the veterans who developed PTSD compared to their identical twins. But this was not what the researchers found. Two things were necessary for a vet to develop chronic PTSD: serving in combat *and* having a smaller hippocampus than normal (Gilbertson et al., 2002). Twins who had the smaller hippocampus but no military service did not develop PTSD, and neither did the twins who *did* experience combat but who had normal-sized hippocampi. PTSD, therefore, seems to be a result of impaired neurological and cognitive functioning that existed before the trauma took place (McNally, 2003a).

Panic Disorder Another kind of anxiety disorder is **panic disorder**, in which a person has recurring

This grief-stricken soldier has just learned that the body bag on the flight with him contains the remains of a close friend who was killed in action. Understandably, soldiers like him suffer post-traumatic stress symptoms. But why do most people eventually recover, whereas others have PTSD for many years?

attacks of intense fear or panic, often with feelings of impending doom or death. These panic attacks may last from a few minutes to (more rarely) several hours. Symptoms include trembling and shaking, dizziness, chest pain or discomfort, rapid heart rate, feelings of unreality, hot and cold flashes, sweating, and, as a result of all these physical reactions, a fear of dying, going crazy, or losing control. Many sufferers fear they are having a heart attack.

Although panic attacks seem to occur out of nowhere, they in fact usually occur in the aftermath of stress, prolonged emotion, specific worries, or frightening experiences (Beck, 1988; McNally, 1998). For example, a friend of ours was on a plane that was a target of a bomb threat while airborne at 33 000 feet. He coped beautifully at the time, but two weeks later, seemingly out of nowhere, he had a panic attack.

Such delayed attacks after life-threatening scares are common. The essential difference between people who develop panic disorder and those who do not lies in *how they interpret their bodily reactions* (Barlow, 2000; McNally, 1998). Healthy people who have occasional panic attacks see them correctly as a result of a passing crisis or period of stress, comparable to another person's migraines. But people who develop panic disorder regard the attack as a sign of illness or impending death, and they begin to live their lives in restrictive ways, trying to avoid future attacks. It is this self-imposed restriction that makes this disorder so difficult for its sufferers (and their families).

People who have panic disorder are found throughout the world, but culture influences the particular symptoms they experience (Barlow, Chorpita, & Turovsky, 1996). Feelings of choking or being smothered, numbness, and fear of dying are most common in Latin America and southern Europe; fear of public places is most common in northern Europe and America; and a fear of going crazy is more common in the Americas than in Europe. In Greenland, some fishermen suffer from "kayak-angst"—a sudden attack of dizziness and fear that occurs while they are fishing in small, one-person kayaks (Amering & Katschnig, 1990).

Fears and Phobias

Are you afraid of bugs, snakes, or dogs? Are you vaguely uncomfortable with them or so afraid that you can't stand to be around one? A **phobia** is an exaggerated fear of a specific situation, activity, or thing. Some common phobias—such as fear of

phobia An exaggerated, unrealistic fear of a specific situation, activity, or object.

THE FAR SIDE® BY GARY LARSON

© 1985 FarWorks, Inc. All Rights Reserved/Dist. by Creators Syndicate

The Far Side® by Gary Larson © 1985 FarWorks, Inc. All Rights Reserved. Used with permission.

Luposlipaphobia: The fear of being pursued by timber wolves around a kitchen table while wearing socks on a newly waxed floor.

snakes, insects, heights (acrophobia), or enclosed spaces (claustrophobia)—may have evolved in human beings because these fears were adaptive for the species (Öhman & Mineka, 2003). Other, more idiosyncratic phobias, such as fear of cats or the colour purple (porphyrophobia), may be acquired through classical conditioning, as we saw in Chapter 9. Still other phobias, such as fear of dirt and germs (mysophobia) or of the number 13 (triskaidekaphobia), may reflect personality differences or cultural traditions. Whatever its source, a phobia is truly frightening and often incapacitating for its sufferer. It is not just a tendency to say "ugh" at tarantulas or skip the snake display at the zoo.

People who have a *social phobia* become extremely anxious in situations in which they will be observed by others—eating in a restaurant, speaking in front of a group or crowd, having to perform for others. They worry that they will do or say something that will be excruciatingly humiliating or embarrassing. Again, these phobias are more severe forms of the occasional shyness and social anxiety that everyone experiences. For people with a social phobia, the mere thought of going out on a date is scary enough to cause sweating, trembling, nausea, and an overwhelming feeling of inadequacy. So they don't go, increasing their fear and isolation.

Get Involved What Scares You?

Everyone fears something. Stop for a moment to think about what you fear most. Heights? Snakes? Speaking in public? Ask yourself these questions: (1) How long have you feared this thing or situation? (2) How would you respond if you could not avoid this thing or situation? (3) How much would you be willing to rearrange your life to avoid this feared thing or situation? After considering these questions, would you regard your fear as a full-blown phobia? What are your criteria for deciding?

By far the most disabling fear disorder is **agoraphobia**. In ancient Greece, the *agora* was the social, political, business, and religious centre of town, the public meeting place away from home. The fundamental fear in agoraphobia is of being trapped in a crowded public place, where escape might be difficult or where help might be unavailable if the person has a panic attack. Individuals with agoraphobia report many specific fears—of being in a crowded movie theatre, driving in traffic or tunnels, or going to parties—but the underlying fear is of being away from a safe place, usually home, or a safe person, usually a parent or spouse.

Agoraphobia usually begins with a panic attack that seems to have no reason (McNally, 1998). The attack is so unexpected and scary that the agoraphobic-to-be begins to avoid situations that he or she thinks may provoke another one. A woman we know had a panic attack while driving on a freeway. This was a perfectly normal posttraumatic response to the suicide of her husband a few weeks earlier. But thereafter she avoided freeways—as if the freeway, and not the suicide, had caused the attack. Because so many of the actions associated with agoraphobia arise as a mistaken effort to avoid a panic attack, psychologists regard agoraphobia as a "fear of fear" rather than a fear of places.

Obsessions and Compulsions

Obsessive-compulsive disorder (OCD) is characterized by recurrent, persistent, unwished-for thoughts or images (*obsessions*) or by repetitive, ritualized, stereotyped behaviours that the person feels must be carried out to avoid disaster (*compulsions*). Of course, many people have trivial compulsions and practise superstitious rituals. Hockey players are famous for them—have you noticed, for example, how many players don't shave during the playoffs? Obsessions and compulsions become a disorder when they become uncontrollable and interfere with a person's life.

People who have obsessive thoughts often find them frightening or repugnant—thoughts of killing a child, of becoming contaminated by a handshake, or of having unknowingly hurt someone in a traffic accident. Obsessive thoughts take many forms, but they are alike in reflecting impaired ways of reasoning and processing information.

People who suffer from compulsions likewise feel they have no control over them. The most common compulsions are hand washing, counting, touching, and checking. A woman *must* check the furnace, lights, locks, oven, and fireplace three times before she can sleep; or a man *must* wash his hands and face precisely eight times before he leaves the house. Most sufferers do not enjoy such rituals and realize that the behaviour is senseless. But if they try to forgo the ritual, they feel mounting anxiety that is relieved only by giving in to it. For one young man with OCD, stairs became a treadmill he could not get off: "At first I'd walk up and down the stairs only three or four times," he recalled. "Later I had to run up and down 63 times in 45 minutes. If I failed, I had to start all over again from the beginning" (quoted in King, 1989).

Some cases of obsessive-compulsive disorder may involve a brain abnormality, because several

agoraphobia A set of phobias, often set off by a panic attack, involving the basic fear of being away from a safe place or person.

obsessive-compulsive disorder (OCD) An anxiety disorder in which a person feels trapped in repetitive, persistent thoughts (*obsessions*) and repetitive, ritualized behaviours (*compulsions*) designed to reduce anxiety.

In the apartment of a woman with OCD, nearly every inch is covered with stuff—junk mail, wrapping paper, broken electric toothbrushes, empty Kleenex boxes, and clothes. The woman becomes extremely anxious at even the thought of throwing anything out. She keeps only one spot uncluttered: the half of the bed she sleeps on.

parts of the brain are hyperactive in people with OCD (Schwartz et al., 1996). Normally, once danger is past or a person realizes that there is no cause for fear, the brain's alarm signal turns off.

In people with OCD, however, false alarms keep clanging and the emotional networks keeping sending out mistaken "fear!" messages. The sufferer feels in a constant state of danger and tries repeatedly to reduce the resulting anxiety.

Quick Quiz

We hope you don't feel anxious about matching each term on the left with its description on the right.

1. social phobia
2. generalized anxiety disorder
3. posttraumatic stress disorder
4. agoraphobia
5. compulsion
6. obsession

a. need to perform a ritual
b. fear of fear; fear of being trapped with no way of escape
c. continuing sense of doom and worry
d. repeated, unwanted thoughts
e. fear of meeting new people
f. anxiety following a severe shock

Answers:

1.e 2.c 3.f 4.b 5.a 6.d

WHAT'S AHEAD

- How can you tell whether you have major depression or just the blues?
- What are the "poles" in bipolar disorder?
- How do some people think themselves into depression?

MOOD DISORDERS

In the DSM, *mood disorders* include disturbances in mood ranging from extreme depression to extreme mania. Of course, most people feel sad from time to time, and also joyful. And most people, at some time in their lives, will know the wild grief that accompanies tragedy and bereavement. These normal feelings, however, are a far cry from the clinical disorders described by the DSM.

Depression

Anxiety, painful though it is, is at least a sign that a person is engaged in the future: It reflects the belief that something bad will happen. But depressed people feel burned out about the future: They are sure that nothing good will ever happen. Some people go through life with constant but low-grade unhappiness; they can do what they need to but nearly always report their mood as sad or "down in the dumps." Others suffer from **major depression**, a serious mood disorder that involves emotional, behavioural, cognitive, and physical changes severe enough to disrupt a person's ordinary functioning. The writer William Styron, who fought and recovered from major depression, used the beginning of Dante's classic poem *The Divine Comedy* to convey his suffering:

> In the middle of the journey of our life I found myself in a dark wood. For I had lost the right path.

"For those who have dwelt in depression's dark wood," wrote Styron in *Darkness Visible*, "and known its inexplicable agony, the return from the abyss is not unlike the ascent of the poet, trudging upward and upward out of hell's black depths and at last emerging into what he saw as 'the shining world.'"

People with major depression feel despairing and hopeless. They may think often of death or suicide. They lose interest or pleasure in their usual activities. They feel unable to get up and do things; it takes an enormous effort even to get dressed. Their thinking patterns feed their bleak moods. They exaggerate minor failings, ignore or discount positive events, and interpret any little thing that goes wrong as evidence that nothing will ever go right. Emotionally healthy people who are sad or grieving do not see themselves as completely worthless and unlovable. But depressed people interpret losses as signs of personal failure and conclude that they will never be happy again.

major depression A mood disorder involving disturbances in emotion (excessive sadness), behaviour (loss of interest in one's usual activities), cognition (thoughts of hopelessness), and body function (fatigue and loss of appetite).

Even people who are rich, successful, and adored by millions can suffer from major depression. The suicide of Nirvana's lead singer, Kurt Cobain, shocked and saddened his many fans.

Depression is accompanied by physical changes as well. The depressed person may overeat or stop eating, have difficulty falling asleep or sleeping through the night, have trouble concentrating, and feel tired all the time. Some sufferers have other physical reactions, such as headaches or inexplicable pain.

Major depression occurs at least twice as often among women as among men, all over the world (Nolen-Hoeksema, 2002). However, because women are more likely to talk about their feelings than men and more likely to seek help, depression in males may be underdiagnosed. Men who are depressed often try to mask the feeling by withdrawing, drinking heavily or abusing other drugs, or behaving violently (Canetto, 1992; Kessler et al., 1994).

Bipolar Disorder

At the opposite pole from depression is *mania*, an abnormally high state of exhilaration. You might think it's impossible to feel too good, but mania is not the normal joy of being in love or winning the Pulitzer Prize. Instead of feeling fatigued and listless, the manic person is excessively "wired."

Instead of feeling hopeless and powerless, the person feels powerful and is full of plans—but these plans are usually based on delusional ideas, as in thinking that he or she has solved the world's problems. People in a state of mania often get into terrible trouble, going on extravagant spending sprees, making impulsive and bad decisions, or having risky sexual adventures.

When people experience at least one episode of mania alternating with episodes of depression, they are said to have **bipolar disorder** (formerly called *manic-depressive disorder*). This is a much rarer problem than depression and distinctly different. Although more women than men suffer from depression, bipolar disorder occurs equally in both sexes. The great humorist Mark Twain had bipolar disorder, which he described as "periodical and sudden changes of mood . . . from deep melancholy to half-insane tempests and cyclones." Other writers, artists, musicians, and scientists have suffered from this disorder too (Jamison, 1992). During the "highs" many of these artists create their best work, but the price of the "lows" is disastrous relationships, bankruptcy, and sometimes suicide (Barondes, 1998).

Psychological explanations of bipolar disorder have not been supported. Therefore, most researchers believe that it results primarily from genetic or other biological abnormalities, although the precise genes and mechanisms are still unknown. In contrast, depression may have several origins, as we are about to see.

Theories of Depression

Psychologists have investigated four contributing factors to major depression: genetic factors, life experiences, problems with close attachments, and cognitive habits. Few researchers think that any one of these factors alone produces chronic depression. Most researchers now emphasize a **vulnerability-stress model** of depression, in which a person's vulnerabilities (in genetic predispositions, personality traits, or habits of thinking) *interact* with stressful events (such as sexual victimization, violence, or loss of a close relationship) to produce any given case of depression (Hankin & Abramson, 2001). Let's consider the evidence for each contributing factor.

1 *Biological factors.* Studies of adopted children and twins support the notion that major depression is a moderately heritable disorder (Bierut et al., 1999; Kendler et al., 1993). A University of

bipolar disorder A mood disorder in which episodes of both depression and mania (excessive euphoria) occur.

vulnerability-stress models Approaches that emphasize how individual vulnerabilities (e.g., in genes or personality traits) interact with external stresses or circumstances to produce mental disorders.

Is there any doubt what emotion this painting conveys? The artist Jacob Lawrence has captured the body language of depression in the posture, downcast eyes, sombre mood, and drooping heads and shoulders of his figures.

Source: Jacob Lawrence (1917–2000), Depression, 1950. Tempera on paper, 22 × 30 1/2 in. (55.9 × 77.5 cm). Collection of Whitney Museum of American Art, New York. Gift of David M. Solinger. 66.98. Photo © 2000: Whitney Museum of American Art, New York. Photo by Geoffery Clements. Artwork © Gwendolyn Knight Lawrence. Courtesy of Jacob and Gwendolyn Lawrence Foundation.

British Columbia study with twins, for example, has shown that physiology-based symptoms, such as loss of appetite and sex drive, are more heritable than emotion-based symptoms, such as tearfulness (Jang et al., 2004). Psychologists are hunting for the genes that might be involved, although it is unlikely that a single gene directly "causes" severe depression. As in the case of posttraumatic stress disorder, a genetic predisposition must interact with stressful events to create the disorder.

Psychologists have recently identified a gene (called 5-HTT) that comes in two forms: a long form that apparently helps protect people from depression, and a short form that makes them more vulnerable to it (Caspi et al., 2003). In a study of 847 New Zealanders who were followed from birth to age 26, the researchers found that 43 percent of those who possessed two copies of the short form of this gene (one from each parent) became severely depressed in the aftermath of major stress (such as the loss of a job, disabling injuries, a death in the family, or abuse suffered in childhood). Yet only 17 percent of those with two copies of the long form of this gene became depressed, *even when they suffered the same stresses.* And people who inherited one long form of the gene from one parent and a short form from the other fell in between in their susceptibility to depression (33 percent).

Genes may exert their effects on depression by affecting levels of serotonin and other neurotransmitters in the brain. Genes may also affect production of the stress hormone cortisol, which, at high levels, can damage cells in the hippocampus and amygdala (Sapolsky, 2000; Sheline, 2000). In depressed patients, the system that regulates reactions to stress is in overdrive; it doesn't shut down when it should, and it keeps overproducing cortisol (Plotsky, Owens, & Nemeroff, 1998).

Nonetheless, genes cannot account for all cases of depression; after all, even among the New Zealanders with the greatest genetic vulnerability, more than half did not become depressed. Nor do genes seem to account for the sex difference in depression rates: In the New Zealand study, women were no more likely than men to have the short form of the 5-HTT gene.

2 *Life experiences and circumstances.* Another line of investigation emphasizes the experiences and social circumstances that may lead to stress and depression in vulnerable individuals. One such risk factor is a history of separations and losses, both past and present, and of insecure attachments (Weissman, Markowitz, & Klerman, 2000). A study at l'Université de Montréal, for example, found that depression in parents was associated with poor parenting skills and problem-solving ability, which in turn create environments that increase the likelihood of psychological problems in their children (Ellenbogen & Hodgins, 2004). Another risk factor is violence: Inner-city adolescents of both sexes who are exposed to high rates of violence report higher levels of depression and more attempts to commit suicide than those who are not subjected to constant violence in their lives or communities (Mazza & Reynolds, 1999).

Psychologists investigating reasons for the sex difference in depression rates have ruled out genetic and hormonal explanations (Nolen-Hoeksema, 2002). Many now believe that women are more likely than men to suffer from depression in part because of the sexes' different roles, status, and experiences. That is, men are more likely than women to be both married and working fulltime, a combination of roles that is strongly associated with mental health and low rates of depression (Brown, 1993). Women have less satisfying work and family lives than men do, they are more likely to live in poverty, and they are more likely to endure discrimination and sexual abuse—all of which increase the likelihood of depression (Belle & Doucet, 2003; Klonoff,

Landrine, & Campbell, 2000; Weiss, Longhurst, & Mazure, 1999). Motherhood is an additional risk factor: The more children a woman has, the more likely she is to become depressed, especially if she is unemployed (McGrath et al., 1990).

3 *Cognitive habits.* Depression involves specific, negative ways of thinking about one's situation (Beck, 1991). Typically, depressed people believe that their situation is *permanent* ("Nothing good will ever happen to me") and *uncontrollable* ("I'm depressed because I'm ugly and horrible and I can't do anything about it"). Expecting nothing to get better, they do nothing to improve their lives and therefore remain unhappy.

Where do these beliefs come from? In the 1970s, the theory of *learned helplessness* held that people become depressed when their efforts to avoid pain or to control the environment consistently fail (Seligman, 1975). However, a fatal flaw with this theory was that not all depressed people have actually failed in their lives, and, as just noted, even living in painful or difficult situations does not make everyone depressed. The real problem for depressed people is not that they are *helpless* but that they feel *hopeless* and pessimistic, believing that nothing good will ever happen to them and that they are powerless to change the future (Abramson, Metalsky, & Alloy, 1989; Seligman, 1991). In a study of university students who were unhappy because they got worse grades than they expected, depression persisted only in those who had pessimistic explanations ("I'm stupid and always will be") *and* low self-esteem, resulting in hopelessness (Metalsky et al., 1993).

Another cognitive bad habit strongly associated with depression is *rumination*—brooding about everything that is wrong in your life, sitting alone thinking about how unmotivated you feel, and worrying that no one loves you. People who ruminate endlessly this way tend to have longer and more intense periods of depression than do those who are able to distract themselves, look outward, and seek solutions. Beginning in adolescence, women are more likely than men to develop a ruminating, introspective style, rehearsing the reasons for their unhappiness. This tendency contributes both to longer-lasting depressions in women and to the sex difference in reported rates (Nolen-Hoeksema, 2002). People with ruminating cognitive styles that foster hopelessness are at greater risk of developing full-blown, major depression than are people who think positively (Chorpita & Barlow, 1998).

These factors combine in different ways to produce any given case of depression.

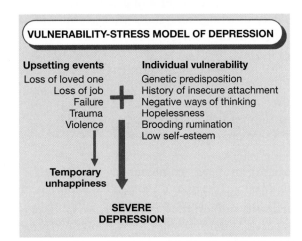

Quick Quiz

Don't let another quiz make you vulnerable to depression!

1. Vulnerability-stress theories attribute depression to an interaction between _____ and _____.

2. Biological researchers find that depressed people have unusually high levels of the stress hormone _____.

3. Depressed people tend to believe that the reasons for their unhappiness are (a) controllable, (b) temporary, (c) out of their hands, (d) caused by the situation.

4. A news headline announces that a gene has been identified as the cause of depression. Does this mean that everyone with the gene will become depressed? How should critical thinkers interpret this research?

Answers:

1. individual vulnerabilities in genetics or personality traits; stressful events   2. cortisol   3. c   4. No, it means that people with the gene are *more* likely to become depressed if they also undergo severely stressful experiences. Critical thinkers would also want to make sure the research is replicated, and they would realize that not all kinds of depression might be influenced by genetics.

By understanding the causes of depression as an interaction among an individual's genetics, ways of thinking, and experiences, we can see why the same precipitating event affects two people entirely differently: why one is able to roll with the punches of life and another is knocked flat.

WHAT'S AHEAD

- When does being self-centred become a disorder?
- What do a charming but heartless tycoon and a remorseless killer have in common?
- Why are some people seemingly incapable of feeling guilt and shame?

PERSONALITY DISORDERS

personality disorders Rigid personality patterns that cause personal distress or an inability to get along with others.

Personality disorders stem from personality traits that cause a person to feel great distress or to have an inability to get along with others. The DSM-IV describes such a disorder as "an enduring pattern of inner experience and behaviour that deviates markedly from the expectations of the individual's culture [and] is pervasive and inflexible." Personality disorders are thus not caused by medical conditions, stress, or situations that temporarily induce a person to behave in ways that are out of character.

Problem Personalities

paranoid personality disorder A disorder characterized by unreasonable, excessive suspiciousness and mistrust, and irrational feelings of being persecuted by others.

Personality disorders come in many varieties. One, **paranoid personality disorder**, involves pervasive, unfounded suspiciousness and mistrust of other people; irrational jealousy; secretiveness; and doubt about the loyalty of others. People with paranoid personalities have delusions of being persecuted by everyone from their closest relatives to government agencies, and their beliefs are immune to disconfirming evidence.

narcissistic personality disorder A disorder characterized by an exaggerated sense of self-importance and self-absorption.

Narcissistic personality disorder involves an exaggerated sense of self-importance and self-absorption. The word *narcissism* gets its name from the Greek myth of Narcissus, a beautiful young man who fell in love with his own image. Narcissistic individuals are preoccupied with fantasies of their own importance, power, and brilliance. They demand constant attention and admiration and feel entitled to special favours, without, however, being willing to reciprocate.

antisocial personality disorder (APD) A disorder characterized by antisocial behaviour such as lying, stealing, manipulating others, and sometimes violence; and a lack of guilt, shame, and empathy.

Given this description, do you know a narcissist or two? Of course you do—and that is the

Narcissus fell in love with his own image, and now he has a personality disorder named after him—just what a narcissist would expect!

problem. It is hard to know where value judgments end (say, about someone's selfishness) and a clear disorder begins (Maddux & Mundell, 1997). Cultures differ too in how they draw the line. American society often encourages people to pursue dreams of unlimited success, physical beauty, and ideal love, but such dreams might be considered signs of serious disturbance in a more group-oriented society.

Antisocial Personality Disorder

Throughout history, societies have recognized and feared the few members in their midst who lack all human connection to anyone else—who can cheat, con, and kill without flinching. In the 1830s these individuals were said to be afflicted with "moral insanity," and in the twentieth century they came to be called "psychopaths" or "sociopaths." The DSM, in an effort to avoid such emotionally charged labels, now refers to **antisocial personality disorder (APD)**. APD occurs in only about three percent of all males and less than one percent of all females. UBC psychologist Robert Hare has estimated that APD may account for more than half of all serious crimes committed in North America (Hare, 1993).

Symptoms of APD According to the DSM, people diagnosed with APD must meet at least three of seven criteria: (1) They repeatedly break the law;

(2) they are deceitful, using aliases and lies to con others; (3) they are impulsive and unable to plan ahead; (4) they repeatedly get into physical fights or assaults; (5) they show reckless disregard for their own safety or that of others; (6) they are irresponsible, failing to meet obligations to others; and (7) they lack remorse for actions that harm others. They must also have had a *history* of these behavioural problems since childhood. In people with APD, as one researcher found, remorselessness and rule breaking start early and take different forms at different ages: "biting and hitting at age 4, shoplifting and truancy at age 10, selling drugs and stealing cars at age 16, robbery and rape at age 22, and fraud and child abuse at age 30" (Moffitt, 1993).

However, not all violent people have APD; otherwise healthy people may commit crimes, even murder, for many motives. Nor are all psychopaths violent. Some are sadistic, able to kill a pet, a child, or a random adult without a twinge of regret, but others direct their energies into con games or career advancement, abusing other people emotionally or economically rather than physically (Robins, Tipp, & Przybeck, 1991). The common quality of people with APD is that they completely lack conscience and empathy. If caught in a lie or a crime, they may seem sincerely sorry and promise to make amends, but it is all an act.

Causes of APD Something certainly seems to be amiss in the emotional wiring of psychopaths—the wiring that allows all primates to feel connected to others of their kind. When that wiring goes awry, even some chimpanzees behave in ways that are comparable to the actions of human psychopaths! They use deception and manipulate others to get their way, they are unmoved by the suffering of others of their kind, they are aggressive, and they are fearless (Lilienfeld, 1999). Researchers have proposed several possible physiological causes of this disorder.

1 *Abnormalities in the central nervous system.* Antisocial individuals do not respond physiologically to the threat of punishment the way other people do; this may be why they can behave fearlessly in situations that would scare others to death. Normally, when a person is anticipating danger, pain, or punishment, the electrical conductance of the skin changes, a classically conditioned response that indicates anxiety or fear. But people with APD are slow to develop such responses, which suggests that they are unable to

feel the anxiety necessary for learning that their actions will have unpleasant consequences (see Figure 11.2). Their inability to feel emotional arousal—empathy, guilt, fear of punishment, and anxiety under stress—suggests some aberration in the central nervous system (Hare, 1965, 1996; Lykken, 1995; Raine et al., 2000). This abnormality distinguishes violent, antisocial teenagers who become career criminals from those who outgrow adolescent antisocial behaviour. Boys who, at age 15, have unusually low levels of physiological arousal are more likely to become criminal offenders by age 24. But antisocial adolescents who have normal levels and whose responses can be classically conditioned do not usually get involved in a life of crime as adults (Raine & Liu, 1998).

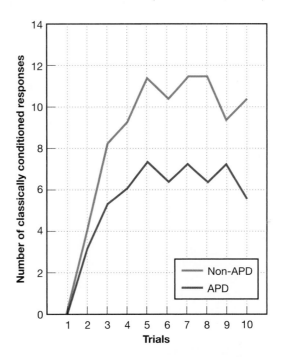

FIGURE 11.2 Emotions and Antisocial Personality Disorder

In several experiments, people with antisocial personality disorder (APD) were less likely than others to develop classically conditioned responses to anticipated danger, pain, or shock—responses that indicate normal anxiety (Hare, 1965). This deficit may be related to the ability of people with APD to act without remorse or regard for the consequences.

2 *Genetically influenced problems with impulse control.* People who are antisocial, hyperactive, or impulsive may share a common inherited disorder involving an inability to control responses to frustration and provocation (Luengo et al., 1994; Raine, 1996). The biological children of parents with antisocial personality disorder, substance-abuse problems, or disorders involving an inability to control impulsive behaviour are at greater-than-normal risk of developing these disorders themselves, even when these children are reared by others (Nigg & Goldsmith, 1994).

3 *Brain damage.* Another, more significant, cause of antisocial personality disorder may be brain damage resulting from physical neglect, accidents, battering, or injury. Psychopaths arrested for vicious crimes are more likely than nonviolent criminals and noncriminals to have been severely battered as children (Lewis, 1992; Milner & McCanne, 1991; Raine et al., 2001).

One area of special interest to those studying APD is the prefrontal cortex, which, as we saw in Chapter 4, is responsible for planning and impulse control. One PET-scan study found that cold-blooded "predatory" murderers had less brain activity in this area than did men who murdered in the heat of passion or controls who had not murdered anybody (Raine et al., 1998). And in-depth analyses of two young adults whose prefrontal cortex was damaged in infancy—one was run over by a car when she was 15 months old, and the other had a brain tumour removed—showed that both grew up to be compulsive liars, thieves, and heartless rule breakers. They could not hold jobs or plan for the future, could not distinguish right from wrong, and lacked empathy (Anderson et al., 1999).

Keep in mind, however, that not all psychopaths have injured brains, and that biological abnormalities alone are rarely enough to produce a psychopathic personality. As with depression and many other disorders, an individual's own genetic or other biological vulnerability must be combined with experiences or stressors. According to the vulnerability-stress model, more than one factor is necessary for the disorder to emerge.

For example, in a longitudinal study of boys who had been physically abused in childhood, those who had a deficiency in a crucial gene later had far more arrests for violent crimes than did abused boys who had a normal gene (Caspi et al., 2002). Although only 12 percent of the abused boys had this genetic deficiency, they accounted for nearly half of all later convictions for violent crimes. However, boys who had the deficient gene but who were not maltreated did not grow up to be violent. Another combination of factors that increase the risk of APD is damage to the prefrontal cortex plus rejection by the mother and institutionalization during the first year (Raine, Brennan, & Mednick, 1994).

In sum, most individuals with APD develop the disorder when a biological vulnerability is combined with physical abuse, parental neglect or rejection, environmental stresses, or living in a subculture that rewards ruthlessness and hard-heartedness.

Some people with APD are sadistic and violent. Gary L. Ridgway (left), the deadliest convicted serial killer in U.S. history, strangled 48 women, placing their bodies in "clusters" around the country. He did this because, he said coolly, he wanted to keep track of them. "I killed so many women, I have a hard time keeping them straight," he told the court. But other people with APD use charm and elaborate scams to deceive and defraud. Babyfaced Christopher Rocancourt (right, wearing tie), shown with actor Mickey O'Rourke, conned celebrities and others into giving him money and doing him favours (some illegal) by adopting countless false identities, such as movie producer, cat burglar, diamond smuggler, or financier. After he was finally arrested on charges of passport counterfeiting, he persuaded authorities to free him on bond—and promptly jumped bail.

Quick Quiz

There is (as yet) no diagnosis of Test-Avoidance Personality Disorder, so take this quiz!

A. Can you diagnose each of the following disorders?

1. Ann can barely get out of bed in the morning. She feels that life is hopeless and despairs of ever feeling good about herself.

2. Connie constantly feels a sense of impending doom; for days her heart has been beating rapidly, and she can't relax.

3. Damon is totally absorbed in his own feelings and wishes.

4. Edna believes that everyone is out to get her and no one can be trusted.

B. What are three possible biological contributions to APD?

C. Suppose you read about an unusually brutal assault committed by a gang member during a robbery. Should you assume that he has an antisocial personality disorder? Why or why not?

Answers:

A. 1. major depression   2. generalized anxiety disorder   3. narcissistic personality disorder   4. paranoid personality disorder

B. central nervous system abnormalities, genetically influenced problems with impulse control, and brain damage

C. Behaving antisocially or even violently is not the same thing as having antisocial personality disorder. Many factors could have contributed to the gang member's act of violence, including conformity to the demands and norms of his fellow gang members, or his perceptions of danger during the robbery.

WHAT'S AHEAD

- In what ways might genes contribute to alcoholism?
- Why is alcoholism more common in Ireland than in Italy?
- Why don't policies of abstinence from alcohol reduce problem drinking?
- If you take morphine to control chronic pain, does that mean you will become addicted to it?

DRUG ABUSE AND ADDICTION

Most people who use drugs (legal, illegal, or prescription) use them in moderation; but some people depend too much on them, and others abuse drugs even at the cost of their own health. The DSM-IV defines *substance abuse* as "a maladaptive pattern of substance use leading to clinically significant impairment or distress." Symptoms of such impairment include failure to hold a job, care for children, or complete schoolwork; use of the drug in hazardous situations (e.g., while driving a car or operating machinery); and frequent conflicts with others about use of the drug or as a result of using the drug.

In Chapter 5, we described the major psychoactive drugs and their effects. In this section, focusing on the example of alcoholism, we will consider the two dominant approaches to understanding addiction and drug abuse—the biological model and the learning model—and then see how they might be reconciled.

Biology and Addiction

Are addicts people who refuse to exert free will and moral responsibility, or are they suffering from a disease over which they have no control? Do they belong in prison or in treatment?

The *biological model* holds that addiction, whether to alcohol or any other drug, is due primarily to a person's biochemistry, metabolism, and genetic predisposition. Most of the genetic evidence comes from twin and family studies of alcoholism. These studies show that although genes are involved, it is too simple to say, as some people do, that "genes cause alcoholism." Evidence of an inherited vulnerability to alcohol is stronger for men than for women, but even this link depends on the *kind* of alcoholism (Cloninger, 1990; Goodwin et al., 1994; McGue, 1999; Schuckit & Smith, 1996). There is a heritable component in males for the kind of alcoholism that begins in adolescence and is linked to impulsivity, antisocial behaviour, and criminality (Bohman et al., 1987; McGue, 1999). But for male alcoholics who begin drinking heavily in adulthood, genetic factors are only weakly involved, if at all.

For a while, researchers thought they had found an "alcoholism gene" that affected brain

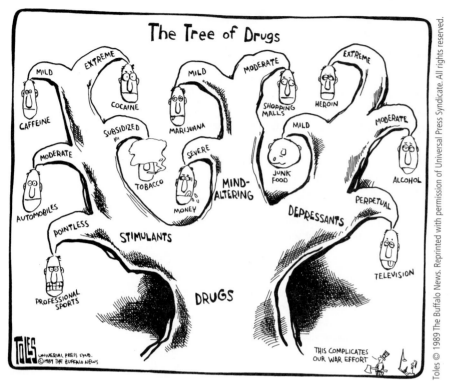

By poking fun at the things people do to make themselves feel better, this cartoon reminds us that many "addictions" are not biochemical.

of becoming alcoholic within the decade. This was true regardless of their initial drinking habits or family history (Schuckit, 1998; Schuckit & Smith, 1996). Some people may inherit not only a general susceptibility to substance abuse but also a vulnerability to specific drugs—heroin, alcohol, cocaine, or nicotine (Tsuang et al., 2001). As with so many other disorders, however, tracking down the genes involved has been difficult.

The usual way of looking at the relationship between biological factors and addiction is to assume that the former cause the latter. However, there is strong evidence that the relationship also works the other way: *Addictions result from the abuse of drugs* (Robinson, 2003). Heavy drinking alters brain function, reduces the level of painkilling endorphins, produces nerve damage, shrinks the cerebral cortex, and damages the liver. Heavy use of alcohol, cocaine, heroin, methamphetamine, or other drugs also reduces the number of receptors for dopamine (Volkow et al., 2001). (See Figure 11.3.) These changes then create addiction: a craving for more of the drug. Thus drug abuse, which begins as a voluntary action, can turn into drug addiction, a compulsive behaviour that the addict finds almost impossible to control.

receptors for dopamine, a neurotransmitter involved in the sensation of pleasure. This hypothesis has not been well supported (Plomin & McGuffin, 2003). Actually, the strongest evidence to date is not that genes are involved with alcoholism but with protection *against* alcoholism. There is a genetic factor that causes low activity of an enzyme that is important in the metabolism of alcohol. People who lack this enzyme respond to alcohol with unpleasant symptoms, such as flushing and nausea. This genetic protection is common among Asians but rare among Europeans, which may be one reason that rates of alcoholism are much lower in Asian than in Caucasian populations (Heath et al., 2003). On the other hand, Aboriginals often have the same genetic protection that Asians do, yet they have much higher rates of alcoholism.

Within populations, genes might contribute to traits or temperaments (such as impulsivity) that predispose a person to become alcoholic. Genes may also affect how much a person needs to drink before feeling high. In an ongoing longitudinal study of 450 young men (half of whom had alcoholic fathers and half of whom did not), the men who, at age 20, had to drink more than others to feel any reaction were at increased risk

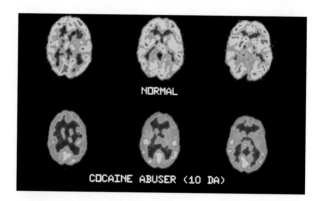

FIGURE 11.3 The Addicted Brain

PET-scan studies show that the brains of cocaine addicts have fewer receptors for dopamine, a neurotransmitter involved in pleasurable sensations. (The more yellow and red in the brain image, the more receptors there are.) The brains of people addicted to methamphetamine, alcohol, and even food show a similar pattern (Volkow et al., 2001).

Learning, Culture, and Addiction

The *learning model* examines the role of the environment, learning, and culture in encouraging or discouraging drug abuse and addiction. Four major findings underscore the importance of understanding social, psychological, and cultural factors:

1 *Addiction patterns vary according to cultural practices and the social environment.* Alcoholism is much more likely to occur in societies that forbid children to drink but condone drunkenness in adults (as in Ireland) than in societies that teach children how to drink responsibly and moderately but condemn adult drunkenness (as in Italy, Greece, and France). In cultures with low rates of alcoholism (except for those committed to a religious rule that forbids use of all psychoactive drugs), adults demonstrate correct drinking habits to their children, gradually introducing them to alcohol in safe family settings. Alcohol is not used as a rite of passage into adulthood, nor is it associated with masculinity and power (Peele & Brodsky, 1991; Vaillant, 1983). Abstainers are not sneered at, and drunkenness is not considered charming, comical, or manly; it is considered stupid or obnoxious. Even within Canada drinking patterns differ, suggesting that even regional culture can affect alcohol consumption. For example, in Alberta there is more abstinence but also more heavy drinking than in Quebec (Andrews & Layne, 1985; Health and Welfare Canada, 1989), a finding supported by the fact that accident-related visits to hospital emergency rooms in Alberta are more likely to be alcohol-related than are similar emergency room visits in Quebec (Cherpitel, Giesbrecht, & Macdonald, 1999).

Within a particular country, addiction rates can rise or fall rapidly in response to cultural changes. In colonial America, the average person actually drank two to three times the amount of liquor consumed today, yet alcoholism was not a serious problem. Drinking was a universally accepted social activity; families drank and ate together. Alcohol was believed to produce pleasant feelings and relaxation, and Puritan ministers endorsed its use (Critchlow, 1986). Then, between 1790 and 1830, when the American frontier was expanding, drinking came to symbolize masculine independence and toughness. The saloon became the place for drinking away from home. As people stopped drinking in moderation, with their families, alcoholism rates shot up—as the learning model would predict.

2 *Policies of total abstinence tend to increase rates of addiction rather than reduce them.* The temperance movement of the early twentieth century held that drinking inevitably leads to drunkenness, and drunkenness to crime. The solution it won for the Prohibition years (1920 to 1933) was national absti-

Alcoholism rates vary with cultural practices. They are lowest in cultures in which people drink moderately with meals and children learn the rules of social drinking from their families, as at this Jewish family's Passover seder.

nence in the United States (in Canada, alcohol was legal throughout most of this period). But this victory backfired: Again in accordance with the learning model, Prohibition reduced rates of drinking overall, but it *increased* rates of alcoholism among those who did drink in the United States. Because people were denied the opportunity to learn to drink moderately, they drank excessively when given the chance (McCord, 1989). And of course, when a substance is forbidden, it becomes more attractive to some people. In the Netherlands, where marijuana is not illegal, 28 percent of tenth-graders have tried it—compared with 41 percent in the United States, where marijuana is absolutely prohibited (*Time*, March 5, 2001).

3 *Not all addicts have withdrawal symptoms when they stop taking a drug.* When heavy users of a drug stop taking it, they often suffer such unpleasant symptoms as nausea, abdominal cramps, depression, and sleep problems, depending on the drug. But these symptoms are far from universal. During the Vietnam War, nearly 30 percent of American soldiers were taking heroin in doses far stronger than those available on the streets of U.S. cities. These men believed themselves to be addicted, and experts predicted a drug-withdrawal disaster among the returning veterans. It never materialized; over 90 percent of the men simply gave up the drug, without significant withdrawal pain, when they came home to new circumstances (Robins, Davis, & Goodwin, 1974). Similarly, the majority of people who are addicted to cigarettes, tranquilizers, or painkillers are able to stop taking these drugs without outside help and without severe withdrawal symptoms (Prochaska, Norcross, & DiClemente, 1994). The reason this finding is surprising to many is that, by definition, people who can quit without help aren't entering programs to help them quit, so they are invisible to the medical world. But they have been identified in random-sample community surveys.

4 *Addiction does not depend on properties of the drug alone but also on the reasons for taking it.* Addicts use drugs to escape from the real world, but people living with chronic pain use some of the same drugs, including morphine and other opiates, in order to function in the real world—and they do not inevitably become addicted (Portenoy, 1994). In a study of 100 hospital patients who had been given strong doses of narcotics for post-operative pain, 99 had no withdrawal symptoms upon leaving the hospital (Zinberg, 1974). And of 10 000 burn patients who received narcotics as part of their hospital care, not one became an addict (Perry & Heidrich, 1982).

In the case of alcohol, most people drink simply to be sociable, to conform to the group they are with, or to relax when they are stressed, and these people are unlikely to become addicted. The problem occurs when people drink to disguise or suppress their anxiety or depression, or when they drink alone to drown their sorrows and forget their worries (Cooper et al., 1995; Mohr et al., 2001). College and university students who feel alienated and uninvolved with their studies are more likely than their happier peers to go binge

The Rastafarian church in Jamaica regards marijuana as a "wisdom weed," and even young children smoke it as part of their religious tradition. Under such circumstances, its use does not lead to addiction or "harder" drugs.

drinking, with the conscious intention of getting drunk (Flacks & Thomas, 1998). In many cases, then, the decision to start abusing drugs depends more on the individual's motives than on the chemical properties of the drug itself.

Debating the Causes of Addiction

The biological and learning models both contribute to our understanding of drug use and addiction. Yet among many researchers and public-health professionals, these views are quite polarized. What we have here is a case of either–or thinking on a national scale, with passions running high because of the implications for the treatment of alcoholics and other addicts.

The argument is most heated in the debate over whether former alcoholics can learn to drink moderately without becoming intoxicated and dependent again on alcohol. Those who advocate the disease model say there is no such thing as a former alcoholic; once an addict has even a single drink, he or she will not be able to stop. In this view, problem drinkers who learn to cut back to social-drinking levels were never true alcoholics in the first place. Those who champion the learning model, on the other hand, argue that some problem drinkers can learn to drink moderately if they learn safe-drinking skills, acquire other ways of coping with stress, and avoid friends and situations that pressure them to drink excessively (Marlatt, 1996; Marlatt et al., 1998; Vaillant, 1983).

Thinking Critically About Theories of Addiction

How can we assess these two positions critically? Can we locate common ground between them? Because alcoholism and problem drinking occur for many reasons, neither model offers the only solution. Many alcoholics cannot learn to drink moderately, especially if they have been drinking heavily for many years—by which time, as we saw earlier, physiological changes in their brains and bodies may have turned them from drug abusers into drug addicts. On the other hand, total-abstinence groups like Alcoholics Anonymous are ineffective for many people. According to its own surveys and those done independently, one-third to one-half of all people who join AA drop out. Many of these dropouts benefit from programs such as Rational Recovery, Moderation Management, and DrinkWise, which teach people how to drink moderately and keep their drinking under control (Fletcher, 2001; Marlatt, 1996; Peele & Brodsky, 1991; Rosenberg, 1993).

So instead of asking, "Can addicts and problem drinkers learn to drink moderately?" we should ask, "What are the factors that make it more likely that someone can learn to control problem drinking?" Problem drinkers who are most likely to become moderate drinkers have a history of less severe dependence on the drug. They lead more stable lives and have jobs and families. In contrast, those who are at greater risk of drug abuse or alcoholism have these risk factors:

- The person has a physiological vulnerability to a drug, or has been using a drug long enough to damage or change the brain;

- The person believes that he or she has no control over the drug;

- The person lives in a culture or a social group that promotes and rewards binge drinking and discourages moderate drug use;

- The person comes to rely on a drug as a way of avoiding problems, suppressing anger or fear, or coping with stress;

- The person's peer group drinks heavily or uses other drugs excessively.

Get Involved   Test Your Motives for Drinking

If you drink, why do you do so? Check all of the motives that apply to you:

____ to relax	____ to be sociable
____ to escape from worries	____ to cope with depression
____ to enhance a good meal	____ to get drunk and lose control
____ to conform to peers	____ to rebel against authority
____ to express anger or other uncomfortable feelings	____ to relieve boredom
	____ other (specify)

Do your reasons promote abuse or responsible use? How do you respond physically to alcohol? What have you learned about drinking from your family, your friends, and cultural messages? What do your answers tell you about your own vulnerability to addiction?

Quick Quiz

If you are addicted to passing exams, answer these questions.

1. What is the most reasonable conclusion about the role of genes in alcoholism? (a) Without a key gene, a person cannot become alcoholic; (b) the presence of a key gene will almost always cause a person to become alcoholic; (c) genes may increase a person's vulnerability to some kinds of alcoholism.

2. Which cultural practice is associated with *low* rates of alcoholism? (a) gradual introduction to drinking in family settings, (b) infrequent binge drinking, (c) drinking as a rite of passage into adulthood, (d) policies of prohibition

3. Many college and university students drink to get drunk, and often binge when drinking. To reduce this problem, some schools have instituted "zero-tolerance" programs, permitting no alcohol at all. Others are trying "social norming," replacing norms that encourage binge drinking with norms that endorse moderate drinking. According to the research described in this section, which policies are more likely to work? Why or why not?

Answers:

1. c 2. a 3. Abstinence policies are much less likely to be effective than social-norming policies. Zero-tolerance programs do not address the reasons that students binge, do not affect the student culture that fosters binge drinking, and do not teach students how to drink moderately.

WHAT'S AHEAD

- Why are many clinicians and researchers skeptical about multiple personality disorder?
- Why did the number of "multiple personality" cases jump from a handful to many thousands in only a decade?

DISSOCIATIVE IDENTITY DISORDER

In this section we will examine one of the most controversial diagnoses ever to arise in psychiatry and psychology: **dissociative identity disorder**, formerly and still popularly called *multiple personality disorder* (MPD). This disorder describes the apparent emergence, within one person, of two or more distinct identities, each with its own name, memories, preferences, and personality traits.

dissociative identity disorder A controversial disorder marked by the apparent appearance within one person of two or more distinct personalities, each with its own name and traits; commonly known as *multiple personality disorder* (MPD).

The MPD Controversy Cases of multiple personality portrayed on TV, in popular books, and in films based on real cases, such as *The Three Faces of Eve* and *Sybil*, have captivated the public for years. Among mental-health professionals, however, two competing views of MPD exist. On one side are those who think that MPD is common but often unrecognized or misdiagnosed. They believe the disorder originates in childhood as a means of coping with unspeakable horrors, such as torture (Gleaves, 1996; Kluft, 1993). Consistent with this notion, research in Winnipeg has found that people who suffered childhood abuse in addition to adult trauma were more likely to be diagnosed with MPD (Pearson, 1997). In this view, the trauma produces a mental "splitting" (*dissociation*): One personality emerges to handle everyday experiences, another to cope with the bad ones. MPD patients are frequently described as having lived for years with several personalities of which they were unaware, until hypnosis revealed them.

On the other side are those who believe that most cases of MPD are unwittingly generated by clinicians themselves, during their interactions with vulnerable clients who have other kinds of psychological problems (Ofshe & Watters, 1994). They point out that before 1980, only a handful of MPD cases had ever been diagnosed anywhere in the world; yet since 1980, *tens of thousands* of cases have been reported. Skeptics think such numbers are suspicious, a sign that the disorder is being wildly overdiagnosed by its proponents. Clinicians who deeply believe in

Thinking Critically About "Multiple Personality Disorder"

Popular books and films about multiple personality spawned countless imitators like *Lizzie*—and thousands of reported cases. According to critics, most of this increase was a result of unwitting therapist influence and sensational stories in the media.

the prevalence of MPD may even be creating the disorder in their clients through suggestive (and unreliable) techniques like hypnosis, and also through the power of suggestion, sometimes bordering on coercion (Acocella, 1999; McHugh, 1993; Merskey, 1995; Rieber, 1999; Spanos, 1996).

You can see this pressure at work in the comments of psychiatrist Richard Kluft (1987), who wrote that efforts to determine the presence of MPD—that is, to get the person to reveal a "dissociated" personality—may require "between 2 and 4 hours of continuous interviewing. Interviewees must be prevented from taking breaks to regain composure. . . . In one recent case of singular difficulty, the first sign of dissociation was noted in the 6th hour, and a definitive spontaneous switching of personalities occurred in the 8th hour." Mercy! After eight hours of "continuous interviewing" without a single break, how many of us wouldn't do what the interviewer wanted?

Clinicians who conduct such interrogations argue that they are merely *permitting* other personalities to reveal themselves. However, in numerous malpractice cases across the country, courts have ruled, on the basis of the testimony of scientific experts in psychiatry and psychology, that it is more likely that these clinicians were actively creating personalities through suggestion and sometimes outright intimidation (Loftus, 1996).

The Sociocognitive Explanation No one disputes that some troubled, highly imaginative individuals can produce many different "personalities" when asked. But the *sociocognitive explanation* of MPD holds that this phenomenon is simply an extreme form of the ability we all have to present different aspects of our personalities to others (Spanos, 1996). In this view, the diagnosis of MPD provides a culturally acceptable way for some troubled people to make sense of their problems (Hacking, 1995; Kenny, 1986; Showalter, 1997). It allows them to account for sexual or criminal behaviour that they now regret or find intolerably embarrassing; they can claim their "other personality did it." In turn, therapists who are looking for MPD reward such patients with attention and praise for revealing more and more personalities (Rieber, 1999).

The story of the rise and fall of MPD offers an important lesson in critical thinking, because unskeptical media coverage of sensational MPD cases played a major role in fostering the rise of MPD diagnoses. When Canadian psychiatrist Harold Merskey (1992) reviewed the published cases of MPD, including Sybil's, he was unable to find a single one in which a patient developed MPD without being influenced by the therapist's suggestions or reports about the disorder in books and the media. MPD also became a lucrative business, benefiting hospitals that opened MPD clinics, therapists who had a new disorder to treat, and psychiatrists and patients who wrote best-selling books.

Of course, there have been legitimate examples of this rare disorder. But even the authors of *The Three Faces of Eve* became alarmed by the media hype and proliferation of questionable cases. Thirty years later, they reported that of the hundreds of possible MPD cases that had been referred to them in the intervening years, they thought only one was a genuine multiple personality (Thigpen & Cleckley, 1984). Each case, therefore, must be examined on its own merits. But the story of MPD teaches us to think critically about disorders that become trendy—to consider other explanations, to examine assumptions and biases, and to demand good evidence.

Quick Quiz

Any one of your personalities may answer this question.

In August 2003, Donna Walker was arrested for trying to convince an Indiana couple that she was their long-missing daughter. She claimed that her "bad girl" personality (Allison) was responsible for this deception and also for her long history of perpetrating hoaxes on police, friends, and the media. Her "good girl" personality (Donna), she said, was a victim of childhood sexual abuse who spent years working as an FBI informant. (She did, according to the FBI, although some of her reports for them were fabricated.) One agent reported that Walker has as many as seven personalities who come and go. As a critical thinker, what questions would you want to ask about Walker and her multiple-personality defence?

Answer:

Some possible questions to ask: Is there corroborating evidence for Walker's claims that she was molested as a child? (She said she was abused from ages 4 to 13 by a family member and then by the minister of her church, and that she was sent to a psychiatric hospital at 13.) How much of the rest of her life story can be independently corroborated? Did Walker claim to have "other personalities" only when she was in a jam with the law or was there evidence of MPD throughout her life? Could she have another mental disorder, such as schizophrenia or antisocial personality disorder?

WHAT'S AHEAD

- What's the difference between schizophrenia and a "split personality"?
- Is schizophrenia partly heritable?
- Could schizophrenia begin in the womb?

SCHIZOPHRENIA

To be schizophrenic is best summed up in a repeating dream that I have had since childhood. In this dream I am lying on a beautiful sunlit beach but my body is in pieces. . . . I realize that the tide is coming in and that I am unable to gather the parts of my dismembered body together to run away. . . . This to me is what schizophrenia feels like; being fragmented in one's personality and constantly afraid that the tide of illness will completely cover me. (Quoted in Rollin, 1980)

In 1911, Swiss psychiatrist Eugen Bleuler coined the term **schizophrenia** to describe cases in which the personality loses its unity. Contrary

11.4

schizophrenia A psychotic disorder or group of disorders marked by positive symptoms (e.g., delusions, hallucinations, disorganized and incoherent speech, and inappropriate behaviour) and negative symptoms (e.g., emotional flatness and loss of motivation).

to popular belief, people with schizophrenia do *not* have a "split" or "multiple" personality. As this haunting quotation illustrates, schizophrenia is a fragmented condition in which words are split from meaning, actions from motives, perceptions from reality. It is an example of a **psychosis**, a mental condition that involves distorted perceptions of reality and an inability to function in most aspects of life.

psychosis An extreme mental disturbance involving distorted perceptions and irrational behaviour; it may have psychological or organic causes.

Symptoms of Schizophrenia

Schizophrenia is the cancer of mental illness: elusive, complex, and varying in form. In general, schizophrenia produces two kinds of symptoms. *Active* or *positive symptoms* involve an exaggeration or distortion of normal thinking processes and behaviour. These symptoms are called "positive" because they are *additions* to normal behaviour; healthy people do not believe that their brains are receiving Martian signals. In contrast, *negative symptoms* involve the *loss* or absence of normal traits and abilities, such as the ability to speak fluently or take care of oneself.

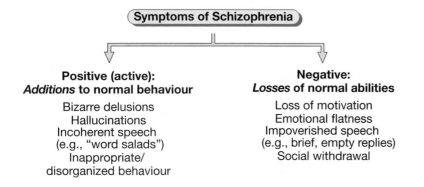

Symptoms of Schizophrenia

Positive (active):
Additions to normal behaviour
Bizarre delusions
Hallucinations
Incoherent speech
(e.g., "word salads")
Inappropriate/
disorganized behaviour

Negative:
Losses of normal abilities
Loss of motivation
Emotional flatness
Impoverished speech
(e.g., brief, empty replies)
Social withdrawal

The most common active symptoms include the following:

1 *Bizarre delusions,* such as the belief that dogs are extraterrestrials disguised as pets. Some people with schizophrenia have delusions of identity, believing that they are Moses, Jesus, or another famous person. Some have paranoid delusions, taking innocent events—a stranger's cough, a helicopter overhead—as evidence that everyone is plotting against them. They often report that their thoughts have been inserted into their heads by someone controlling them or are being broadcast on television. And some people have delusional obsessions. A woman named Margaret Mary Ray believed with all her heart that late-night talk-show host David Letterman was in love with her.

She stalked him day and night for a decade, writing him letters and repeatedly breaking into his house. (Eventually, she committed suicide.)

2 *Hallucinations.* Hallucinations are false sensory experiences that feel intensely real. Some are visual (e.g., seeing a strange face in the mirror) or tactile (e.g., feeling insects crawling over the body). But by far the most common hallucination among people with schizophrenia is hearing voices; it is virtually a hallmark of the disease. Some sufferers of schizophrenia are so tormented by these voices that they commit suicide to escape them. One man described how he heard as many as 50 voices cursing him, urging him to steal other people's brain cells, or ordering him to kill himself. Once he picked up a ringing telephone and heard them screaming, "You're guilty!" over and over. They yelled "as loud as humans with megaphones," he told a reporter. "It was utter despair. I felt scared. They were always around" (Goode, 2003).

3 *Disorganized, incoherent speech,* consisting of an illogical jumble of ideas and symbols, linked by meaningless rhyming words or by remote associations called *word salads.* A patient of Bleuler's wrote, "Olive oil is an Arabian liquor-sauce which the Afghans, Moors and Moslems use in ostrich farming. The Indian plantain tree is the whiskey of the Parsees and Arabs. Barley, rice and sugar cane called artichoke, grow remarkably well in India. The Brahmins live as castes in Baluchistan. The Circassians occupy Manchuria and China. China is the Eldorado of the Pawnees" (Bleuler, 1911/1950).

4 *Grossly disorganized and inappropriate behaviour,* which may range from childlike silliness to unpredictable and violent agitation. The person may wear three overcoats and gloves on a hot day, start collecting garbage, or hoard scraps of food.

In contrast to these positive symptoms, negative symptoms include loss of motivation; poverty of speech (making only brief, empty replies in conversation, because of diminished thought rather than an unwillingness to speak); and, most notably, emotional flatness—unresponsive facial expressions, poor eye contact, and diminished emotionality. Some people with schizophrenia completely withdraw into a private world, sitting for hours without moving, in a condition called *catatonic stupor.* (Catatonic states may also produce frenzied, purposeless behaviour that goes on for hours.) These negative symptoms may appear months before active ones do, and they often persist even when the active symptoms are in remission.

Schizophrenia typically emerges in late adolescence or early adulthood. In some people, the symptoms appear suddenly. In others, the onset is more gradual; negative symptoms slowly emerge, and friends and family report a slow change in personality. The person may stop working or bathing, become isolated and withdrawn, and start behaving in peculiar ways. The more breakdowns and relapses the person has had, the poorer the chances for complete recovery. Yet, as we will see in the next chapter, many sufferers learn to control the symptoms, often with the help of antipsychotic medication (Torrey, 2001). Significant numbers completely recover (Harding, Zubin, & Strauss, 1992).

The mystery of schizophrenia is that we could go on listing symptoms and variations all day and never finish. Some people with schizophrenia are almost completely impaired in all spheres; others do extremely well in certain areas. Still others have normal moments of lucidity in otherwise withdrawn lives. One adolescent crouched in a rigid catatonic posture in front of a television for the month of October; later, he was able to report on all the highlights of the World Series he had seen. A middle-aged man, hospitalized for 20 years, believing he was a prophet of God and

that monsters were coming out of the walls, was able to interrupt his ranting to play a good game of chess (Wender & Klein, 1981).

Theories of Schizophrenia

Any disorder that has so many variations and symptoms will pose many problems for those trying to find its origins. Early psychodynamic and learning theories, which held that schizophrenia results from being raised by an erratic, cold, rejecting mother or from living in an unpredictable environment, have not been supported. Most researchers now believe that schizophrenia is caused by genetic problems that produce subtle abnormalities in the brain. As usual, however, genes must interact with certain stressors in the environment during prenatal development, birth, and adolescence. Here is some evidence on the contributing factors:

1 *Genetic predispositions.* A person has a much greater risk of developing schizophrenia if an identical twin develops the disorder, even if the twins are reared apart (Gottesman, 1991, 1994). Children with one schizophrenic parent have a lifetime risk of 12 percent, and children with two schizophrenic parents have a lifetime risk of 35–46 percent, compared to a risk in the general population of only 1–2 percent (Goldstein, 1987). (See Figure 11.4.) In a Finnish study of identical

When people with schizophrenia are asked to draw pictures, their drawings are often distorted, lack colour, include words, and reveal flat emotion. One patient was asked to copy a picture of flowers from a magazine (top right). The initial result is shown on the left. The drawing in the centre shows improvement, and the drawing on the right shows how much the patient progressed after several months of treatment.

FIGURE 11.4 Genetic Vulnerability to Schizophrenia

This graph, based on combined data from 40 European twin and adoption studies, shows that the closer the genetic relationship to a person with schizophrenia, the higher the risk of developing the disorder. (Based on Gottesman, 1991.)

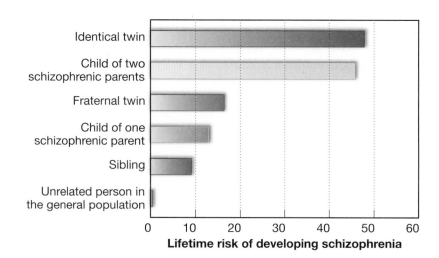

Lifetime risk of developing schizophrenia

twins, fully 83 percent of the variation in the risk of becoming schizophrenic was due to combined genetic factors, and only 17 percent to unique environmental factors (Cannon et al., 1998). Researchers all over the world are trying to track down genes that might be involved in specific symptoms, such as hallucinations, sensitivity to sounds, and cognitive impairments. But to date, no genes have been reliably identified (Plomin & McGuffin, 2003).

2 *Structural brain abnormalities.* Most individuals with schizophrenia have abnormalities in the brain, including a decrease in the volume of the temporal lobe or hippocampus, reduced numbers of neurons in the prefrontal cortex, or enlargement of the *ventricles*, spaces in the brain that are filled with cerebrospinal fluid (see Figure 11.5) (Akbarian et al., 1996; Heinrichs, 1993; Zorrilla et al., 1997). Schizophrenics are also more likely than healthy individuals to have abnormalities in the thalamus, the traffic-control centre that filters sensations and focuses attention (Andreasen et al., 1994; Gur et al., 1998). Investigators are also looking for abnormalities in the auditory cortex and Broca's and Wernicke's areas, all involved in speech perception and processing. Such abnormalities might explain the nightmare of voice hallucinations.

3 *Neurotransmitter abnormalities.* Abnormalities in several neurotransmitters, including serotonin, glutamate, and dopamine, have been associated with schizophrenia (Sawa & Snyder, 2002).

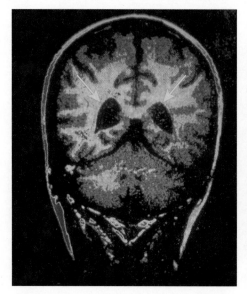 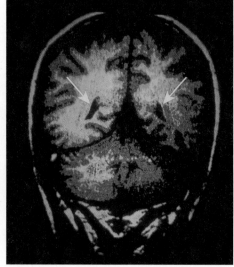

FIGURE 11.5 Schizophrenia and the Brain

MRI scans show that a person with schizophrenia (left) is more likely than a healthy person (right) to have enlarged ventricles, or spaces, in the brain (see arrows) (Andreasen et al., 1994).

However, similar neurotransmitter abnormalities are also found in many other mental disorders, such as depression and alcoholism, making it difficult to know whether these abnormalities play a specific role in schizophrenia.

4 *Prenatal problems or birth complications.* Damage to the fetal brain significantly increases the likelihood of schizophrenia (and of other mental disorders). Such damage may occur if the mother suffers from malnutrition (Susser et al., 1996), if she gets an infectious virus during prenatal development (Mednick, Huttunen, & Machón, 1994), or if there are complications during birth that injure the baby's brain or deprive it of oxygen (Cannon et al., 2000; Rosso et al., 2000).

5 *Adolescent abnormalities in brain development.* The last factor contributing to schizophrenia occurs in adolescence, when the brain undergoes a natural pruning away of synapses in the brain. Normally, this pruning helps make the brain more efficient in handling the new challenges of adulthood. But it appears that schizophrenic brains aggressively prune away too many synapses,

which may explain why the first full-blown schizophrenic episode typically occurs in adolescence or early adulthood. The reason for the excessive pruning is not yet known, but it may involve genetic dispositions, fetal brain damage, or stressful life experiences (McGlashan & Hoffman, 2000).

Thus the developmental pathway of schizophrenia looks like something of a relay. It seems to start with a genetic predisposition, which must combine with prenatal risk factors or birth complications that affect brain development. The resulting vulnerability then awaits events in adolescence—synaptic pruning within the brain or external stressors—that serve as a trigger for the disease (Conklin & Iacono, 2002). This model explains why one identical twin may develop schizophrenia but not the other: Both may have the genetic susceptibility, but only one was exposed to other risk factors in the womb, birth complications, or stressful life events (Cannon et al., 2000). These factors may combine in different ways as well, explaining why some schizophrenics recover and others do not. The riddle of schizophrenia is likely to be several riddles, all waiting to be solved.

Quick Quiz

The following quiz is not a hallucination.

1. A patient with schizophrenia hears voices in her head when no one is around. Is this an example of a positive symptom or a negative one?
2. *True or false?*: Most people with schizophrenia have a schizophrenic parent.

Answers:

1. positive 2. false

Psychology In The News *Revisited*

We have come to the end of a long walk along the spectrum of psychological problems—from those that are normal conditions of life, such as occasional anxiety or "caffeine-induced sleep disorder," to mental disorders that are severely disabling, such as schizophrenia. What does the case of Jay Handel, who murdered his six children, burned down his house, and twice attempted suicide, teach us?

One lesson is that mental disorders, unlike physical illnesses, remain difficult to use as explanations for violent or unusual behaviour. Even though the defence in Jay Handel's case claimed that a narcissistic personality meant that Handel could not see that what he was doing was wrong, the Crown argued that Handel's personality disorder could not explain away his actions. Furthermore, there are still no genetic tests or other biological measurements that allow a clinician to reliably diagnose schizophrenia, depression, and most other disorders. Until there are, diagnosing mental disorder will remain an art as well as a science, one subject to the biases and judgment errors of those doing the classifying (Luhrmann, 2000).

Handel's story raises the important social question of how a civilized society should handle individuals who commit crimes and then claim that a mental disorder was to blame. For example, romance writer Janet Dailey, accused of plagiarizing whole passages from another writer's work, said she was suffering from "a psychological problem that I never even suspected I had."

Do you find this excuse convincing, or do you think it's an effort to avoid responsibility for illegal actions? Now consider a more serious example, the tragic story of Andrea Yates, a Texas woman who killed her five young children in a state of extreme despair. She had suffered from clinical depression and psychotic episodes for years and in her blackest depressions became mute and catatonic. She tried to kill herself twice. Her father, two brothers, and a sister had suffered different degrees of mental illness, including depression. Yates was overwhelmed by the burden of raising and homeschooling all of her children with no help from her husband, who reportedly permitted her two hours a week of personal time. Although she suffered a postpartum psychotic episode after the birth of their fourth child and a clinical psychologist warned her against having another, her husband refused to consider birth control, although not for religious reasons. "We want as many as nature will allow," he said (Yardley, 2001). Yates was eventually sentenced to life in prison.

Do Jay Handel and Andrea Yates deserve our condemnation for their horrible acts of murder, or our pity? Unquestionably, many people do suffer from mental disorders that make it difficult or even impossible for them to control their behaviour. How can we distinguish impairments that legitimately reduce a person's responsibility for his or her actions from unjustified excuses or faking?

Thinking Critically About Mental Disorders and Responsibility

When thinking about the relationship of mental disorder to personal responsibility, we face a dilemma. The law recognizes, rightly, that people who are mentally incompetent, delusional, or disturbed should not be judged by the same standards as mentally healthy individuals. At the same time, society has an obligation to protect its citizens from harm and to reject easy excuses for violations of the law. To balance these two positions, we need to find ways to ensure that people who commit crimes or behave reprehensibly face the consequences of their behaviour. We also must ensure that people who are suffering from psychological problems have the compassionate support of society in their search for help. After all, psychological problems of one kind or another are problems that all of us will have at some time in our lives.

Taking Psychology With You   When a Friend Is Suicidal

Suicide can be frightening to those who find themselves fantasizing about it, and it is devastating to the family and friends of those who go through with it. In Canada, suicide is a relatively rare cause of death. Every year about 4000 people commit suicide, whereas cancer, for example, claims almost 60 000 lives per year (Malenfant, 2004). And in the last 20 years, the rate of suicide has gradually declined (Statistics Canada, 2005).

Women are more likely than men to attempt suicide, primarily as a cry for help, whereas men are more likely to succeed. But this gender difference depends on culture and circumstances. In Finland, more males than females attempt suicide; and in Canada and the United States, men in prison have high rates of attempted suicide (Canetto & Sakinofsky, 1998). Moreover, men's efforts to commit suicide are not always as obvious as those of women: Some men provoke confrontations with the police, hoping to be shot; some intentionally kill themselves in car accidents; and men are more likely than women to destroy themselves with drugs.

Because of the many widespread myths about suicide, it is important to become informed and know what to do in a crisis:

- **Take all suicide threats seriously.** Some people assume they can't do anything when a friend talks about committing suicide. "He'll just do it at another place, another time," they think. In fact, most suicides occur during an acute crisis. Once the person gets through the crisis, the desire to die fades.

Others believe that if a friend is *talking* about committing suicide, he or she won't really *do* it. This belief also is false. Few people commit suicide without signalling their intentions. Most are ambivalent: "I want to kill myself, but I don't want to be dead—at least not forever." Most suicidal people want relief from the terrible pain of feeling that nobody cares and that life is not worth living (Baumeister, 1990). Getting these thoughts and fears out in the open is an important first step.

- **Know the danger signs.** A person is at risk of trying to commit suicide if he or she has tried to do it before; has become withdrawn and listless; has a history of depression; reveals specific plans for carrying out the suicide or gives away cherished possessions; expresses no concern about religious prohibitions or the impact on family members; and has access to a lethal method, such as a gun (Garland & Zigler, 1994).

- **Get involved: Ask questions, and get help.** If you believe a friend is suicidal, do not be afraid to ask, "Are you thinking of suicide?" This question does not "put the idea" in anyone's mind. If your friend is contemplating the action, he or she will probably be relieved to talk about it, which in turn will reduce feelings of isolation and despair. Don't try to talk your friend out of it by debating whether suicide is right or wrong, and don't put on phony cheerfulness. If your friend's words scare you, say so. By allowing your friend to unburden his or her grief, you help the person get through the immediate crisis.

- **Do not leave your friend alone.** If necessary, get the person to a clinic or a hospital emergency room, or call a local suicide hotline or the Canadian nationwide referral hotline, 1-800-448-3000. Don't worry about doing the wrong thing. In an emergency, the worst thing you can do is nothing at all.

In her haunting book *Night Falls Fast: Understanding Suicide*, Kay Jamison (1999), a psychologist who suffers from bipolar disorder, explored this difficult subject from the standpoint both of a mental-health professional and of a person who has "been there." In describing the aftermath of her own suicide attempt, she wrote: "I do know . . . that I should have been dead but was not—and that I was fortunate enough to be given another chance at life, which many others were not."

SUMMARY

DEFINING AND DIAGNOSING DISORDER

- When defining *mental disorder*, mental-health professionals emphasize the violation of cultural standards, the emotional suffering caused by the behaviour, and whether the behaviour is harmful to others or society.

- The *Diagnostic and Statistical Manual of Mental Disorders* (DSM), which is used throughout the world, is designed to provide objective criteria and categories for diagnosing mental disorders. Critics argue that the diagnosis of mental disorders, unlike those of medical diseases, is inherently a subjective process that can never be entirely objective. They believe the DSM fosters overdiagnosis, overlooks the influence of diagnostic labels on clients and therapists, confuses serious mental disorders with everyday problems in living, and creates an illusion of objectivity and universality.

- Supporters of the DSM believe that when the DSM criteria are used correctly and when empirically validated objective tests are used, reliability in diagnosis improves. The DSM now lists many *culture-bound syndromes*. But many disorders, including depression and schizophrenia, are found all over the world.

- In diagnosing psychological disorders, clinicians often use *projective tests* such as the Rorschach Inkblot Test or, with children, the use of anatomically detailed dolls. These methods have low reliability and validity, creating problems when they are used in the legal arena or in diagnosing disorders. In general, *objective tests (inventories)*, such as the *MMPI*, are more reliable and valid than projective ones.

ANXIETY DISORDERS

- *Generalized anxiety disorder* involves continuous, chronic anxiety, with signs of nervousness, worry, and irritability. When anxiety results from exposure to uncontrollable or unpredictable danger, it can lead to *posttraumatic stress disorder*, which involves mentally reliving the trauma, emotional detachment, and increased physiological arousal. *Panic disorder* involves sudden, intense attacks of profound fear. Panic attacks are common in the aftermath of stress or frightening experiences; those who go on to develop a disorder tend to interpret the attacks as a sign of impending disaster.

- *Phobias* are unrealistic fears of specific situations, activities, or things. Common *social phobias* include fears of speaking in public, using public restrooms, or being observed by others. *Agoraphobia*, the fear of being away from a safe place or person, is the most disabling phobia. It often begins with a panic attack, which the person tries to avoid in the future by staying close to "safe" places or people.

- *Obsessive-compulsive disorder (OCD)* involves recurrent, unwished-for thoughts or images (obsessions) and repetitive, ritualized behaviours (compulsions) that a person feels unable to control. Parts of the brain involved in fear and responses to threat are more active than normal in people with OCD.

MOOD DISORDERS

- Symptoms of *major depression* include distorted thinking patterns, low self-esteem, physical ailments such as fatigue and loss of appetite, and prolonged grief and despair. Women are twice as likely as men to suffer from major depression, but depression in men may be underdiagnosed. In *bipolar disorder*, a person experiences episodes of both depression and *mania* (excessive euphoria). It is equally common in both sexes.

- *Vulnerability-stress models* of depression look at interactions between individual vulnerabilities and stressful experiences. Some people have a genetic predisposition to become depressed when they undergo severe stress, and others may be genetically protected. Genes may affect levels of serotonin and the stress hormone cortisol. Life experiences that increase the risk of depression include problems with work and family life, poverty, discrimination, sexual abuse, and violence. Cognitive habits also play an important role: believing that the origin of one's unhappiness is permanent and uncontrollable; feeling hopeless and pessimistic; and brooding or ruminating about one's problems.

PERSONALITY DISORDERS

- *Personality disorders* are characterized by rigid, self-destructive traits that cause distress or an inability to get along with others. They include, among others, *paranoid, narcissistic,* and *antisocial personality disorders*.

- A person with antisocial personality disorder lacks empathy and remorse, is unafraid of punishment, is impulsive and lacks self-control, and has a life history of behavioural problems. The disorder may stem from abnormalities in the central nervous system, genetically influenced problems with impulse control, or brain damage (for example, to the prefrontal cortex). These biological vulnerabilities often interact with stressful or violent environments to produce the disorder.

DRUG ABUSE AND ADDICTION

- The effects of drugs depend on whether they are used moderately or are abused. Signs of *substance abuse* include impaired ability to work or get along with others, use of the drug in hazardous situations, recurrent arrests for drug use, and conflicts with others caused by drug use.

- According to the *biological model* of addiction, some people have a biological vulnerability to alcoholism and other addictions, due to genetic factors that affect their metabolism, biochemistry, or personality traits. But heavy drug abuse also changes the brain in ways that make addiction more likely.

- Advocates of the *learning model* of addiction point out that addiction patterns vary according to culture, learning, and accepted practice; that many people can stop taking drugs without experiencing withdrawal symptoms; that drug abuse depends on the reasons for taking a drug; and that abuse increases when people are not taught moderate use.

- Although the biological and learning models are polarized on many issues, the evidence suggests that addiction and abuse result from an interaction between biological and psychological vulnerability and a person's culture, learning history, motives for taking a drug, and situation.

DISSOCIATIVE IDENTITY DISORDER

- In *dissociative identity disorder* (commonly called *multiple personality disorder*, or MPD), two or more distinct personalities and identities appear to split off (*dissociate*) within one person. Considerable controversy surrounds the validity and nature of MPD. Some clinicians think it is common, often goes undiagnosed, and originates in childhood trauma. Others offer a *sociocognitive* explanation. They argue that most cases result from pressure and suggestion by clinicians who believe in the disorder, interacting with vulnerable patients who find MPD a plausible explanation for their problems. Media coverage of sensational alleged cases of

MPD was a major contribution to the rise in the number of cases after 1980.

SCHIZOPHRENIA

- *Schizophrenia* is a psychotic disorder involving *positive* or *active* symptoms (including delusions, hallucinations, disorganized speech called *word salads*, and inappropriate behaviour) and *negative symptoms* (including loss of motivation, poverty of speech, emotional flatness, and *catatonic stupor*). Cases of schizophrenia vary in severity, duration, and prognosis.
- Schizophrenia appears to involve genetic predispositions that lead to structural brain abnormalities, such as enlarged ventricles and neurotransmitter abnormalities. However, genetic predispositions must interact with certain stressors in the environment during prenatal development (such as the mother's malnutrition or a prenatal viral infection), birth complications, and excessive pruning of synapses during adolescence.

PSYCHOLOGY IN THE NEWS, REVISITED

- The diagnosis of mental disorders raises important questions for issues of personal responsibility in the law and everyday life. When people claim to have a mental disorder, psychologists and others must struggle to decide whether the claim is an excuse for illegal or destructive actions, or whether these individuals truly have a disorder that reduces their ability to control their behaviour.

KEY TERMS

mental disorder   354
projective tests   358
Rorschach Inkblot Test   358
objective tests (inventories)   359
Minnesota Multiphasic Personality Inventory (MMPI)   359
generalized anxiety disorder   360

posttraumatic stress disorder (PTSD)   361
panic disorder   361
phobia   362
agoraphobia   363
obsessive-compulsive disorder (OCD)   363
major depression   364
bipolar disorder   365
vulnerability-stress models   365

personality disorders   368
paranoid personality disorder   368
narcissistic personality disorder   368
antisocial personality disorder (APD)   368
dissociative identity disorder   376
schizophrenia   377
psychosis   378

LOOKING BACK

- What are three approaches to defining mental disorder? (p. 354)
- Why is the standard guide to the diagnosis of mental disorders so controversial? (pp. 356–357)
- Why were slaves who tried to escape once considered to be mentally ill? (p. 357)
- How reliable are "projective" tests like the popular Rorschach Inkblot Test? (p. 359)
- What is the difference between ordinary anxiety and an anxiety disorder? (p. 360)
- Why is the most disabling of all phobias known as the "fear of fear"? (p. 363)
- When is checking the stove before leaving home a sign of caution, and when does it signal a disorder? (p. 363)
- How can you tell whether you have major depression or just the blues? (p. 364)
- What are the "poles" in bipolar disorder? (p. 365)
- How do some people think themselves into depression? (pp. 365–367)
- When does being self-centred become a disorder? (p. 368)
- What do a charming but heartless tycoon and a remorseless killer have in common? (p. 369)
- Why are some people seemingly incapable of feeling guilt and shame? (pp. 369–370)
- In what ways might genes contribute to alcoholism? (p. 372)
- Why is alcoholism more common in Ireland than in Italy? (p. 373)
- Why don't policies of abstinence from alcohol reduce problem drinking? (p. 373)
- If you take morphine to control chronic pain, does that mean you will become addicted to it? (p. 374)
- Why are many clinicians and researchers skeptical about multiple personality disorder? (p. 376)
- Why did the number of "multiple personality" cases jump from a handful to many thousands in only a decade? (p. 376)
- What's the difference between schizophrenia and a "split personality"? (pp. 377–378)
- Is schizophrenia partly heritable? (p. 379)
- Could schizophrenia begin in the womb? (p. 381)

Psychology In The News

EX–SCHOOLTEACHER FINALLY CLEARED OF SEXUAL ABUSE CHARGES

RICHMOND, BC, 1998. It took three gruelling trials and five and a half years, but Michael Kliman was finally found not guilty of a sexual abuse charge that became a nightmare for him. The accusers were two women who had recovered memories of abuse they alleged to have occurred over 20 years ago, when they were students in Kliman's grade six class. Some of these memories were recovered during psychotherapy.

However, the accusations were implausible, given that Kliman taught in an open area classroom with another teacher, and that in order to have committed the abuse he would have had to leave the room at least six times per week for periods of 15 or 20 minutes at a time. The other teacher could not recall Kliman being out of the room that often. As well, some of the alleged abuse was supposed to have taken place in areas where witnesses would have been likely, but witnesses were not found.

Still, Michael Kliman had to go to court three times. The first time, he was convicted. The second resulted in a hung jury. The third was tried before a judge alone and Kliman was found not guilty.

Some of the memories of the alleged abuse surfaced when one of the women was undergoing therapy for an eating disorder and other symptoms. In the sessions, she was encouraged to regress to childhood and to examine old school photographs. The therapy is based, in part, on the assumption that there is a possible connection between eating disorders and child sexual abuse. "Healing," therefore, involves identifying the perpetrator of this abuse and dealing with that at a conscious level. The therapy is very controversial, however, as many psychologists believe it has the potential to create false memories rather than uncover repressed ones.

Allegations of sexual abuse rocked the typically peaceful community of Richmond, B.C. Michael Kliman, a middle school teacher, was found not guilty in 1998, after a series of trials lasting five and a half years. His accusers allegedly recovered memories of the abuse during psychotherapy.

12 Approaches to Treatment and Therapy

BIOLOGICAL TREATMENTS FOR MENTAL DISORDERS

KINDS OF PSYCHOTHERAPY

EVALUATING PSYCHOTHERAPY

PSYCHOLOGY IN THE NEWS, REVISITED

TAKING PSYCHOLOGY WITH YOU: HOW TO EVALUATE SELF-HELP GROUPS AND BOOKS

Were the techniques used by the woman's therapist standard practice in psychotherapy? How is a layperson supposed to tell the difference between good therapy and bad? When does psychotherapy help people with their problems and when does it do emotional damage—to themselves or others not even engaging in the therapy? These questions are especially pressing today, when new kinds of therapies keep emerging, all claiming successful cures.

Most people get through the normal problems of life with the healing help of time and friends. Some people, however, develop one or more of the disorders described in the previous chapter, such as depression, panic attacks, obsessive-compulsive disorder, phobias, posttraumatic stress disorder, or schizophrenia. What kind of therapy might help them? People have plenty of ordinary difficulties too, from marital conflict to coping with the loss of a loved one. What kind of therapy might help them?

In this chapter, we will evaluate two major approaches to treatment. *Biological treatments* include drugs or direct intervention in brain function; they are primarily prescribed by psychiatrists or other physicians in a hospital or on an outpatient basis. *Psychotherapy* covers an array of psychological approaches, including psychodynamic therapies, cognitive and behavioural therapies, family therapy, and humanist therapies.

Each of these approaches can successfully handle some problems but not others. Each can help some people but not others. And in some cases, the misuse of medication or of therapeutic techniques can be harmful. At the end of this chapter we will tell you what happened to Michael Kliman. As you read, see whether you can come up with some things you would want to know when evaluating any form of therapy.

antipsychotic drugs Drugs used primarily in the treatment of schizophrenia and other psychotic disorders.

WHAT'S AHEAD

- What kinds of drugs are used to treat psychological disorders?
- Can mental disorders be cured by brain surgery?
- Why is "shock therapy" hailed by some clinicians but condemned by others?

BIOLOGICAL TREATMENTS FOR MENTAL DISORDERS

For hundreds of years, people have tried to find the origins of mental illness, attributing the causes at various times to evil spirits, pressure in the skull, disease, or bad environments. The contemporary mental-health world continues to alternate between viewing mental disorders as diseases that can be treated medically and as emotional problems that must be treated psychologically (Luhrmann, 2000). Today, biological explanations and treatments are on the rise. This is partly because of evidence that some disorders have a genetic component or involve a biochemical or neurological abnormality (see Chapter 11), and partly because economic and social forces are fostering biomedical solutions.

The Question of Drugs

The most commonly used biological treatment is medication. Because drugs are so widely prescribed these days, both for severe disorders such as schizophrenia and for more common problems such as anxiety and depression, consumers need to understand what these drugs are, how they can best be used, and their limitations.

Drugs Commonly Prescribed for Mental Disorders The main classes of drugs used in the treatment of mental disorders are these:

1 **Antipsychotic drugs**, also called *neuroleptics*—older ones such as Thorazine™ and Haldol™ and newer, second-generation ones such as Clozaril™ and Risperdal™—are used primarily in the treatment of schizophrenia and other psychoses, though increasingly they are being used for nonpsychotic disorders such as impulse control problems and bipolar disorder. Research at the Universities of Toronto and British Columbia has also shown some benefits of using antipsychotic medication to treat severe depression (Kennedy & Lam, 2003). Many antipsychotic drugs block or reduce the sensitivity of brain receptors that respond to dopamine. Some also increase levels of serotonin, a neurotransmitter that inhibits dopamine activity.

Antipsychotic drugs can reduce agitation, delusions, and hallucinations, and they can shorten schizophrenic episodes. However, they offer little relief from other symptoms, such as jumbled thoughts, difficulty concentrating, emotional flatness, or inability to interact with others (see Chapter 11). Although antipsychotic medication allows many people to be released from hospitals, these individuals cannot always care for themselves, and they often fail to keep taking their medication because of unpleasant side effects, such as uncontrollable tremors (Luhrmann, 2000; Masand, 2000). Even the newer drugs have side

These photos show the effects of antipsychotic drugs on the symptoms of a young man with schizophrenia. In the photo on the left, he was unmedicated; in the photo on the right, he had taken medication. However, these drugs do not help all people with psychotic disorders.

effects and risks. For example, researchers at Laval University have identified patients who experience significant weight gain and an increased risk of diabetes while taking antipsychotic medication (Chagnon et al., 2004).

2   Antidepressant drugs are used primarily in the treatment of depression, anxiety, phobias, and obsessive-compulsive disorder. In Canada, the use of these drugs more than doubled between 1994 and 2001, and during the same period the number of people taking more than one kind of antidepressant tripled (Patten & Beck, 2004). *Monoamine oxidase inhibitors (MAOIs)*, such as Nardil™, elevate the level of norepinephrine and serotonin in the brain by blocking or inhibiting an enzyme that deactivates these neurotransmitters. *Tricyclic antidepressants*, such as Elavil™, boost norepinephrine and serotonin levels by preventing the normal reabsorption, or "reuptake," of these substances by the cells that have released them. *Selective serotonin reuptake inhibitors (SSRIs)*, such as Prozac™, work on the same principle as the tricyclics but specifically target serotonin.

Antidepressants are nonaddictive, but they can produce some unpleasant physical reactions, including dry mouth, headaches, constipation, nausea, restlessness, gastrointestinal problems, weight gain, and, in as many as one-third of all patients, decreased sexual desire and blocked or delayed orgasm (Hollon, Thase, & Markowitz, 2002). MAOIs interact with foods containing a chemical found in cheese and beer, so dietary restrictions may be required. Researchers at Queen's University have also found that some people being treated for bipolar disorder experience manic episodes when they are withdrawn from antidepressant therapy (Ali & Milev, 2003).

Some investigators are studying herbs like St. John's wort. A meta-analysis of clinical studies found that St. John's wort was more effective than a placebo for milder forms of depression (Kim, Streltzer, & Goebert, 1999), but the efficacy of this herb remains in dispute.

3   Tranquilizers, such as Valium™ and Xanax™, increase the activity of the neurotransmitter gamma-aminobutyric acid (GABA). Although they were developed to treat people with mild anxiety, they are often overprescribed by general physicians for patients who complain of more serious mood disorders. Tranquilizers may help people with panic disorder and individuals who are having an acute anxiety attack (Ballenger

"Before Prozac, she loathed company."

et al., 1988), but they are not considered the treatment of choice over a long period of time. Symptoms almost always return if the medication is stopped, and a significant percentage of people who take tranquilizers overuse them and develop problems with withdrawal and tolerance (i.e., they need larger and larger doses).

4   A special category of drug, a salt called **lithium carbonate**, often helps people who suffer from bipolar disorder (depression alternating with euphoria) (Keck & McElroy, 1998). It may produce its effects by moderating levels of norepinephrine or by protecting brain cells from being overstimulated by another neurotransmitter, glutamate (Nonaka, Hough, & Chuang, 1998). Lithium must be given in exactly the right dose, and bloodstream levels of the drug must be carefully monitored, because too little will not help and too much is toxic—sometimes even fatal. Unfortunately, in some people, lithium produces short-term side effects (tremors) and long-term problems (kidney damage). A study in Quebec also found that, owing to lithium's effect on memory and reaction time, elderly patients taking the drug are twice as likely to get in a car accident while driving (Etminan et al., 2004). Newer drugs for people with bipolar disorder include Tegretol™, Depakote™, and some of the newer antipsychotics (Bowden et al., 2000; McElroy & Keck, 2000).

For a review of these drugs and their uses, see Table 12.1.

Some Cautions about Drug Treatments Without question, drugs have rescued some people from

antidepressant drugs Drugs used primarily in the treatment of mood disorders, especially depression and anxiety.

lithium carbonate A drug frequently given to people suffering from bipolar disorder.

tranquilizers Drugs commonly but often inappropriately prescribed for patients who complain of unhappiness, anxiety, or worry.

TABLE 12.1 Drugs Used in the Treatment of Psychological Disorders

	Antipsychotics (neuroleptics)	Antidepressants	Tranquilizers	Lithium Carbonate
Example	Thorazine Haldol Clozaril Risperdal	Prozac (SSRI) Nardil (MAOI) Elavil (tricyclic) Paxil (SSRI)	Valium Xanax	
Primarily used for	Schizophrenia Other psychoses Impulsive anger Bipolar disorder	Depression Anxiety disorders Panic disorder Obsessive-compulsive disorder	Mood disorders Panic disorder	Bipolar disorder

Thinking Critically About Drug Treatments

emotional despair, suicide, obsessive-compulsive disorder, and panic attacks. They have enabled severely depressed or mentally disturbed people to function and respond to psychotherapy. Yet many psychiatrists and drug companies are trumpeting the benefits of medication without informing the public of its limitations, so a few words of caution are in order.

1 *The placebo effect.* New drugs, like new psychotherapies, often promise quick and effective cures, as was the case with the arrival of Clozaril, Xanax, and Prozac. But the **placebo effect** (see Chapter 1) ensures that many people will respond positively to a new drug just because of the enthusiasm surrounding it and their own expectations that the drug will make them feel better. After a while, when placebo effects decline, many drugs turn out to be neither as effective as promised nor as widely applicable. This has happened repeatedly with each new generation of tranquilizers and each new "miracle" antipsychotic drug and antidepressant, including Prozac (Greenberg et al., 1994; Moncrieff, 2001).

In fact, some investigators believe that most of the effectiveness of antidepressants is due to a placebo effect (Kirsch & Saperstein, 1998). Even researchers who quarrel with that strong conclusion acknowledge that the drugs are less effective than commonly believed. For example, overall, only about half of all depressed patients respond positively to any given antidepressant medication, and of them, only about 40 percent are actually responding to the specific biological effects of the drugs (Hollon, Thase, & Markowitz, 2002).

2 *High dropout and relapse rates.* A person may have short-term success with antipsychotic or antidepressant drugs. However, in part because of

placebo effect The apparent success of a medication or treatment that is due to the patient's expectations or hopes rather than to the drug or treatment itself.

these drugs' unpleasant side effects, one-half to two-thirds of people eventually stop taking them (Glenmullen, 2000). When they do, they are quite likely to relapse, especially if they have not learned how to cope with their problems (Antonuccio et al., 1999). Moreover, a study at the University of Calgary found that only 41 percent of people newly diagnosed with psychoses were taking their medication properly, and 39 percent weren't taking it at all (Coldham, Addington, & Addington, 2002). On a more optimistic note, a study at the University of Toronto indicated that fewer people are dropping off medication regimens when taking newer generations of antipsychotic drugs (Awad & Voruganti, 2004).

3 *Dosage problems.* The challenge with drugs is to find the *therapeutic window,* the amount that is enough but not too much. This problem is compounded by the fact that the same dose of a drug may be metabolized differently in men and women, old people and young people, and different ethnic groups (Willie et al., 1995). When psychiatrist Keh-Ming Lin moved from Taiwan to the United States, he was amazed to learn that the dosage of antipsychotic drugs given to American patients with schizophrenia was often 10 times higher than the dose for Chinese patients. In subsequent studies, Lin and his colleagues confirmed that Asian patients require significantly lower doses of the medication for optimal treatment (Lin, Poland, & Chien, 1990). Similarly, black people suffering from depression or bipolar disorder seem to need lower dosages of tricyclic antidepressants and lithium than do other ethnic groups (Strickland et al., 1991, 1995). Ethnic groups may differ in the dosages they can tolerate because of variations in metabolic rates, amount of body fat, the number or type of drug receptors in the brain, or cultural practices such as smoking cigarettes and eating certain foods. Obviously, it is important to get the dosage correct. Research in Ontario has revealed that about four percent of people over the age of 66 who are taking lithium end up being hospitalized for dose-related problems, and that this number increases significantly when these patients are taking other medications common to this age group (Juurlink et al., 2004).

4   *Long-term risks.* Antipsychotic drugs can have dangerous, even fatal, consequences if taken for many years. Antidepressants, in contrast, are assumed to be quite safe, but the effects of taking them indefinitely are still unknown (Glenmullen, 2000; Valenstein, 1998). In 2003, the SSRI Paxil™ was linked to an increased risk of suicide attempts in young people, causing Health Canada to issue a stronger warning regarding the potential relationship between the use of SSRI drugs and the risk of self-harm. The general public and even many physicians do not realize that new drugs are often tested on only a few hundred people for only a few weeks or months, even when the drug is one that patients might take for years. For example, Clozapine™ was tested in controlled trials that lasted only six weeks (*FDA Drug Bulletin*, 1990), and none of the other second-generation antipsychotic drugs have been used long enough to determine their long-term risks (Gupta et al., 1999). In fact, the Health Canada website describes an association between Clozapine use and cardiovascular problems, some surfacing in the first month of usage (Health Canada, 2002). Ritalin™ is increasingly given to many children diagnosed with attention deficit/hyperactivity disorder, but no studies have examined the drug's effect on children who take it for longer than 14 months (National Institutes of Health consensus report, November 19, 1998). Many physicians and the public, feeling reassured if a drug is effective in the short run, overlook the possibility of long-term dangers.

These cautions are the reason that it is important to think critically about the popularity of an exclusively biological approach to mental disorders. Many doctors prescribe drugs routinely, often without accompanying psychotherapy for the person's problems. This overprescription is partly a result of financially overburdened health care systems. The cost of a single patient visit for a prescription is far less than the cost of 10 visits for psychotherapy.

Overprescription is also a result of advertising by drug companies, especially in the United

"I think the dosage needs adjusting. I'm not nearly as happy as the people in the ads."

States. In 1997 the Food and Drug Administration (FDA) permitted pharmaceutical companies to advertise directly to consumers, a practice still forbidden in Canada and Europe. (Of course, many of these advertisements are seen by Canadians watching American television or reading American magazines.) Most consumers do not realize that once a drug is approved by the FDA (or Health Canada), doctors are permitted to prescribe it for different conditions and for populations other than those on which it was originally tested. That is why antidepressants are now being marketed for "social phobias"; why Prozac, when its patent expired, was renamed Sarafem™ and marketed to women for "Premenstrual Dysphoric Disorder"; why Ritalin, widely given to school-aged children, is now being prescribed for two- and three-year-olds; why Paxil, until recently, was prescribed for children and teenagers, although studies had found that it was no more effective for young people than placebos were; and why antipsychotics such as Risperdal are being used for nonpsychotic disorders such as impulsive aggression. Most worrisome for the future of impartial research, most of the researchers who are studying the effectiveness of medication have strong financial ties to the pharmaceutical industry, in the form of consulting fees, funding for studies, stock investments, and patents (Angell, 2000; Bodenheimer, 2000).

The overprescription of drugs for mood disorders in North America also occurs because of a common but mistaken assumption: that if a disorder appears to have biological origins or involve biochemical abnormalities, then biological treatments must be most appropriate. But, in fact, changing your behaviour and thoughts—through psychotherapy or other new experiences—can also change the way your brain functions. This point was dramatically illustrated in two PET-scan studies of people with obsessive-compulsive disorder. Among those who were taking Prozac, the metabolism of glucose in the brain improved, suggesting that the drug was having a beneficial effect. But exactly the *same* brain changes occurred in people who were getting cognitive-behavioural therapy and no medication (see Figure 12.1) (Baxter et al., 1992; Schwartz et al., 1996). And, unlike antidepressants, cognitive-behavioural therapy also restores depressed people's brainwave patterns during sleep to normal (Thase et al., 1998).

In sum, consumers must think critically about the benefits and limitations of medication for psychological problems. Drugs for mental disorders are neither totally miraculous nor totally worthless. Their effectiveness depends on why the individual is taking them, how severe the problem is, and whether the person learns how to function better and cope with the problem.

Direct Brain Intervention

For most of human history, a person suffering from mental illness often got a rather extreme form of "help." A well-meaning tribal healer or, later, a doctor would try to release the "psychic pressures" believed to be causing the symptoms by drilling holes in the victim's skull. (It didn't work.) However, the basic impulse—trying to cure mental illness by intervening directly in the brain—has continued.

One effort is through **psychosurgery**, surgery designed to destroy selected areas of the brain thought to be responsible for emotional disorders or disturbed behaviour. The most famous form of modern psychosurgery was invented in 1935, when a Portuguese neurologist, Antonio Egas Moniz, drilled two holes into the skull of a mental patient and used a specially designed instrument to cut or crush nerve fibres running from the prefrontal lobes to other areas. This operation, called a *prefrontal lobotomy*, was supposed to reduce the patient's emotional symptoms without impairing intellectual ability. The procedure—which, incredibly, was never assessed or validated scientifically—was performed on tens of thousands of people. Thousands of lobotomies were also performed in Canada during the same time period (Simmons, 1987). Tragically, these lobotomies left many patients apathetic, withdrawn, and unable to care for themselves (Valenstein, 1986). Yet Moniz won a Nobel Prize for his work.

Today, psychosurgery is rare, but some neurosurgeons are still operating on the brains of severely depressed, anxious, or obsessive-compulsive patients whose symptoms have not responded to drugs or psychotherapy (Marino & Cosgrove, 1997). However, reports of success are anecdotal, based largely on the physician's subjective impressions. No randomized controlled trials have been conducted on these forms of psychosurgery (Vertosick, 1997).

Another controversial procedure is **electroconvulsive therapy (ECT)**, or "shock therapy," which is used for the treatment of severe depression, although no one knows how or why it works. An electrode is placed on one or both sides of the head, and a brief current is turned on. The current triggers a seizure that typically lasts one minute, causing the body to convulse. Today, unlike in the past, patients are given muscle relaxants and anaesthesia, so they sleep through the procedure and their convulsions are minimized. Research at UBC has shown that ECT yielded good short-term results for over 85 percent of people who were given the treatment for major depressive disorder (Lam et al., 1999). However, ECT is *ineffective* with other disorders, such as schizophrenia or alcoholism, though it is occasionally misused for these conditions.

ECT's supporters cite research showing that when ECT is used properly, it is safe and causes no long-term cognitive impairment, significant memory loss, or detectable brain damage (Abrams, 1997; Fink, 1999). Critics counter that ECT is often used improperly and that it can in fact damage the brain. Both sides agree that relapse rates are

electroconvulsive therapy (ECT) A procedure used in cases of prolonged and severe major depression, in which a brief brain seizure is induced.

psychosurgery Any surgical procedure that destroys selected areas of the brain believed to be involved in emotional disorders or violent, impulsive behaviour.

FIGURE 12.1 Psychotherapy and the Brain

These PET scans show the brain of a person with obsessive-compulsive disorder before and after behaviour therapy. Before therapy, the glucose metabolic rates in the right caudate nucleus (rCd) were elevated. After therapy, this area calmed down, becoming less active, just as it did with medication (Schwartz et al., 1996).

high even when ECT is temporarily successful (Hollon, Thase, & Markowitz, 2002).

Researchers are now looking for other, milder ways to electrically stimulate the brains of severely depressed individuals. One method, *transcranial magnetic stimulation (TMS)*, involves the use of a pulsing magnetic coil held to a person's skull at the left prefrontal cortex. The patient is awake, and the procedure does not cause memory loss, seizures, or other side effects (Little et al., 2000; Wasserman & Lisanby, 2001). Compared to control patients who get a sham treatment without the stimulation, depressed patients given TMS treatments every day for two to four weeks are more likely to improve (George, 1998). This method is promising and safer than ECT, but no one yet really knows why it works or whether it will hold up in further research.

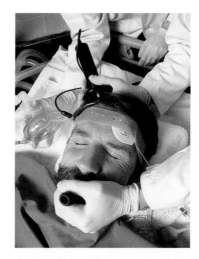

On the left, a man receives electroconvulsive therapy (ECT), which has been used successfully to treat suicidal depression. Supporters and critics continue to disagree about its potential for misuse or harm. On the right, researcher Anna Docherty demonstrates transcranial magnetic stimulation (TMS), a newer and milder method that is being used to treat not only depression but also the auditory hallucinations of schizophrenia.

Quick Quiz

No amount of electric shock will stimulate test-taking ability.

A. Match these treatments with the problems for which they are typically used.

1. antipsychotic drugs
2. antidepressant drugs
3. lithium carbonate
4. electroconvulsive therapy

a. suicidal depression
b. bipolar disorder
c. schizophrenia
d. depression and anxiety
e. obsessive-compulsive disorder

B. Give four reasons that the public should be cautious about claims that drugs for psychological disorders are miracle cures.

C. Jezebel has had occasional episodes of depression that seem to be getting worse. Her physician prescribes an antidepressant. Before taking it, what questions should Jezebel ask herself, and the doctor?

Answers:

A.
1. c
2. d, e
3. b
4. a

B. Placebo effects are common; dropout and relapse rates are high; appropriate dosages can be difficult to determine and can vary by sex, age, and ethnicity; and some drugs have unknown or long-term risks.

C. Has the physician prescribed the drug casually, without taking her full medical and psychological history? Has the physician considered all possible reasons for her depression? Would psychotherapy be appropriate, either with or without medication? Does the medication have any unpleasant side effects or long-term risks? Will the doctor continue to monitor her reactions to the drug on a regular basis?

psychodynamic therapies Psychotherapies that share the goal of exploring the unconscious dynamics of personality, although they differ from Freudian analysis in various ways.

transference In psychodynamic therapies, a critical process in which the client transfers unconscious emotions or reactions, such as emotional feelings about his or her parents, onto the therapist.

psychoanalysis A theory of personality and a "depth" method of psychotherapy developed by Sigmund Freud; it emphasizes unconscious motives and conflicts.

free association In psychodynamic therapies, the process of saying freely whatever comes to mind in connection with dreams, memories, fantasies, or conflicts.

WHAT'S AHEAD

- Why are psychodynamic therapies called "depth" therapies?
- How do cognitive therapists help people get rid of self-defeating thoughts?
- Why do humanist therapists focus on the "here and now" instead of the "why and how"?
- Why do family therapists prefer to treat families rather than individuals?

KINDS OF PSYCHOTHERAPY

All good psychotherapists want to help clients think about their lives in new ways and find solutions to the problems that plague them. In this section we will consider the major schools of psychotherapy. To illustrate the philosophy and methods of each one, we will focus on a fictional fellow named Murray. Murray is a smart guy whose problem is all too familiar to many students: He procrastinates. He just can't seem to settle down and write his term papers. He keeps getting incompletes, and before long the incompletes turn to Fs. Why does Murray procrastinate, manufacturing his own misery? What kind of therapy might help him?

Psychodynamic Therapy

Sigmund Freud was the father of the "talking cure," as one of his patients called it. In his method of **psychoanalysis**, patients talk not about their immediate problems, but about their dreams and memories of childhood. Freud believed that intensive analysis of these dreams and memories would give patients insight into the unconscious reasons for their symptoms and unhappiness. With insight and emotional release, the person's symptoms would disappear.

In orthodox psychoanalysis, which is rarely practised today, the client meets with the therapist as often as several times a week, for a period of years. The client lies on a sofa, with the analyst sitting out of view, and says whatever comes to mind without censoring, a technique called **free association**. (The popular image of therapy in cartoons and movies still often includes a person lying on a couch.) The analyst listens to the client's free associations and dreams, but rarely comments. There is no rush to solve the problem that brought the client into therapy. In fact, a person may come in complaining of a symptom such as anxiety or

headaches, and the therapist may not get around to that symptom for months or even years. The analyst views the symptom as only the tip of the mental iceberg.

Freud's psychoanalytic method has evolved into many different forms of **psychodynamic therapy**, which share the goal of exploring the unconscious dynamics of personality, such as defences and conflicts (see Chapter 2). Proponents of these therapies often refer to them as "depth" therapies because the goal is to delve into the deep, unconscious processes believed to be the source of the patient's problems, rather than to concentrate on "superficial" symptoms and conscious beliefs.

A major element of all psychodynamic therapies, from Freudian to present forms, is **transference**, the client's transfer (displacement) of emotional elements of his or her inner life—usually feelings about the parents—outward onto the analyst. Have you ever found yourself responding to a new acquaintance with unusually quick affection or dislike, and later realized it was because the person reminded you of a relative that you loved or loathed? That experience is similar to transference. In therapy, a woman who failed to resolve her oedipal love for her father might believe she has fallen in love with the analyst. A man who is unconsciously angry at his mother for rejecting him might become furious with his analyst for going on vacation. Through analysis of transference in the therapy setting, psychodynamic therapists believe that clients can see their emotional conflicts in action, and can thereby work through and resolve them.

"HAVE A COUPLE OF DREAMS, AND CALL ME IN THE MORNING."

One popular modern psychodynamic approach is based on *object-relations theory* (see Chapter 2). Object-relations therapists argue that unconscious expectations and habits, established in early relations with important family members, reproduce themselves in adult relationships. As two such analysts put it, "Experiences with our mother, father, siblings, and others form powerful impressions, like engravings on some inner wall of our psyche, which become the standards against which all other relationships are measured" (Dym & Glenn, 1993).

Today, most psychodynamic therapists reject the orthodox psychoanalytic approach, while retaining the key goals of examining transference, probing for unconscious motives that stem from childhood experiences, and breaking through the client's unconscious defences (Schafer, 1992; Westen, 1998). They sit facing the client, they participate more actively, and they are more goal-directed than traditional analysts. Many practise time-limited therapy, consisting of 15, 20, or 25 sessions. Without delving into the client's entire history, the therapist listens to the client's problems and formulates the main issue (Groves, 1996). The rest of the therapy focuses on the person's self-defeating habits and recurring problems. For example, our friend Murray might gain the insight that he procrastinates as a way of expressing anger toward his parents. He might realize that he is angry because they insist that he study for a career he dislikes. Ideally, Murray will come to this insight by himself. If the analyst suggests it, Murray might feel too defensive to accept it.

Behaviour and Cognitive Therapy

Unlike psychodynamic therapists, psychologists who practise behaviour therapy or cognitive therapy would not worry much about Murray's past, his parents, or his unconscious anxieties. Psychologists who practise behaviour therapy would get right to the problem: What are the reinforcers in Murray's environment that are maintaining his behaviour? "Mur," they would say, "forget about insight. You have lousy study habits." Psychologists who practise cognitive therapy would focus on helping Murray understand how his beliefs about studying, writing papers, and success are woefully unrealistic. Often, these two approaches are combined.

Behavioural Techniques **Behaviour therapy** is based on techniques derived from the behavioural

Many popular TV shows and movies, such as *The Sopranos* and *Analyze This* (with Robert De Niro as a mobster patient and Billy Crystal as his psychoanalyst), feature psychodynamic therapists. This is one reason that many people mistakenly think that all therapies are psychodynamic.

principles of classical and operant conditioning that we discussed in Chapter 9. (You may want to review those principles before going on.) Here are some of these methods (Kazdin, 2001; Martin & Pear, 1999):

1 **Systematic desensitization**. Systematic desensitization is a step-by-step process of desensitizing a client to a feared object or experience. It is based on the classical-conditioning procedure of *counterconditioning,* in which a stimulus (such as a dog) for an unwanted response (such as fear) is paired with some other stimulus or situation that elicits a response incompatible with the undesirable one (see Chapter 9). In this case, the incompatible response is usually relaxation. The client learns to relax deeply while imagining or looking at a sequence of feared stimuli, arranged in a hierarchy ranging from the least frightening to the most frightening. The hierarchy itself is provided by the client. The sequence for a person who is terrified of spiders might be to read the classic children's story *Charlotte's Web*, then look at pictures of small, cute spiders, then pictures of tarantulas, then move on to observing a real spider, and so

systematic desensitization In behaviour therapy, a step-by-step process of desensitizing a client to a feared object or experience; it is based on the classical-conditioning procedure of counterconditioning.

12.4

behaviour therapy A form of therapy that applies principles of classical and operant conditioning to help people change self-defeating or problematic behaviours.

In this "virtual reality" version of systematic desensitization, people with spider phobias are gradually exposed to computerized but extremely lifelike images of spiders in a realistic, three-dimensional environment.

graduated exposure In behaviour therapy, a method in which a person suffering from an anxiety disorder, such as a phobia or panic attacks, is taken directly into the feared situation until the anxiety subsides.

skills training In behaviour therapy, an effort to teach the client skills that he or she may lack, as well as new constructive behaviours to replace self-defeating ones.

behavioural self-monitoring In behaviour therapy, a method of keeping careful data on the frequency and consequences of the behaviour to be changed.

on. At each step the person must become relaxed and comfortable before going on. Eventually, the fear responses are extinguished.

2   Graduated exposure. When people are afraid of some situation, object, or upsetting memory, they usually do everything they can to avoid confronting or thinking of it. Naturally, this only makes the fear worse. Exposure treatments are aimed at reversing this tendency. For example, a person who is trying to avoid thinking of a traumatic event might be asked to imagine the event over and over, until it no longer evokes the same degree of panic. Likewise, a person suffering from agoraphobia might be taken into the very situation that he or she fears most—a department store, say, or a subway—and would remain there, with the therapist, until the panic and anxiety declined. Notice how different this approach is from the psychodynamic one, in which the goal is to uncover the presumably unconscious reason that the agoraphobic feels afraid of going out.

3   Behavioural self-monitoring. Before people can change their behaviour, they have to identify the reinforcers (rewarding consequences) that are

supporting their unwanted habits: attention from others, temporary relief from tension or unhappiness, or tangible rewards such as money or a good meal. One way to do this is for the client to keep a record of the behaviour that he or she wishes to change. For example, a man who wants to curb his overeating may not be aware of how much he eats throughout the day to relieve tension; a behavioural record might show that he eats more junk food than he realized in the late afternoon. A mother complains that her child "always" has temper tantrums; a behavioural record will show when, where, and with whom they occur. Once the unwanted behaviour is identified, along with the reinforcers that have been maintaining it, a treatment program can be designed to change it. For instance, the man might find other ways to reduce stress and make sure that he is nowhere near junk food in the late afternoon. The mother can learn to respond to her child's tantrum not with her attention (or a cookie to buy silence), but with a time-out: banishing the child to a corner where no positive reinforcers are available.

4   Skills training. It is not enough to tell someone "Don't be shy" if the person does not know how to make small talk with others, or "Don't yell" if the person does not know how to express feelings calmly. Therefore, some behaviour therapists teach the skills a client might lack, by modelling these skills and also by asking the client to practise them in a role-playing situation. A shy person, for example, might learn how to converse in social settings by focusing on other people rather than on his or her own insecurity. Countless skills-training programs have been designed for parents who don't know how to discipline children, for people who don't know how to manage anger, and for many other behavioural problems. Modelling and role-playing techniques have also been effective in teaching people with schizophrenia how to behave appropriately in social situations (Marder et al., 1996).

Get Involved   Cure Your Fears

In Chapter 11, a "Get Involved" exercise asked you to identify your greatest fear. Now see whether systematic desensitization procedures will help you conquer it. Write down a list of situations that evoke your fear, starting with one that produces little anxiety (e.g., seeing a photo of a tiny brown spider) and ending with the most frightening one possible (e.g., looking at live tarantulas at the pet store). Then find a quiet room where you will have no distractions or interruptions, sit in a comfortable reclining chair, and relax all the muscles of your body. Breathe slowly and deeply. Imagine the first, easiest scene, remaining as relaxed as possible. Do this until you can confront the image without becoming the least bit anxious. When that happens, go on to the next scene in your hierarchy. Do not try this all at once; space out your sessions over time. Does it work?

A behaviourist would treat Murray's procrastination in several ways. Murray might not know how he actually spends his time when he is avoiding his studies. Afraid that he hasn't time to do everything, he does nothing. Keeping a behavioural diary would let Murray know exactly how he spends his time, and how much time he should realistically allot to a project. Instead of having a vague, impossibly huge goal, such as "I'm going to reorganize my life," Murray would establish specific small goals, such as reading the two books necessary for an English paper and writing one page of an assignment. If Murray does not know how to write clearly, however, even writing one page might feel overwhelming; he might also need some skills training, such as a basic composition class. Most of all, the therapist would encourage Murray to change the reinforcers that are maintaining his "procrastination behaviour"—perhaps the immediate gratification of partying with friends, or temporary distraction from his fear of failure—and replace them with reinforcers for getting the work done.

Cognitive Techniques Of course, people's thoughts and motivations can influence their behaviour. **Cognitive therapy** helps clients identify the beliefs and expectations that might be unnecessarily prolonging their anger, fear, depression, conflicts, and other problems (Persons, Davidson, & Tompkins, 2001). Clients examine the evidence for their beliefs—say, that everyone is mean and selfish, that ambition is hopeless, or that love is doomed. They learn to consider other explanations of the behaviour of people who annoy them: Perhaps their father's strict discipline was intended not to control but to protect them. Researchers in Quebec, for example, have reported on the successful treatment of older adults with generalized anxiety disorder (Ladouceur et al., 2004). The therapists helped these adults change their beliefs in ways that reduced their tendency to worry—for instance, to become more tolerant of uncertainty (rather than worrying about the unknown) and to focus on problem solving (rather than on the emotions of worry). By requiring people to identify their assumptions and biases, examine the evidence, and consider other interpretations, cognitive therapy, as you can see, teaches critical thinking!

One of the best-known contemporary schools of cognitive therapy is Albert Ellis's **rational emotive behaviour therapy (REBT)** (Ellis, 1993; Ellis & Blau, 1998). In this approach, which reflects Ellis's own no-nonsense, get-on-with-it attitude, the therapist uses rational arguments to directly challenge a client's unrealistic beliefs or expectations. Ellis has pointed out that people who are emotionally upset often *overgeneralize*: They decide that one annoying act by someone means that person is totally bad in every way, or that a normal mistake they made is evidence that they are rotten to the core. Many people also *catastrophize*, transforming a small problem into a disaster: "I failed this test, and now I'll flunk out of school, and no one will ever like me, and even my cat will hate me, and I'll never get a job . . ." The therapist challenges these thoughts directly, showing the client why they are irrational and misguided.

Another leading form of cognitive therapy, devised by Aaron Beck (1976, 1991), avoids direct challenges to the client's beliefs. Beck pioneered in the application of cognitive therapy for depression. As we saw in Chapter 11, depression often arises from specific, pessimistic thoughts—for example, that the sources of your misery are permanent and that nothing good will ever happen to you again. For Beck, these beliefs are not "irrational"; rather, they are unproductive or based on misinformation. A therapist using Beck's approach would encourage you to test your beliefs against the evidence. If you say, "But I *know* he's out to get me," the therapist might say, "Oh, yes? How do you know? Did he tell you, or are you reading his mind?"

rational emotive behaviour therapy (REBT) A form of cognitive therapy devised by Albert Ellis, designed to challenge the client's unrealistic or irrational thoughts.

cognitive therapy A form of therapy designed to identify and change irrational, unproductive ways of thinking and hence to reduce negative emotions and their behavioural consequences.

Get Involved   Mind over Mood

See whether cognitive-therapy techniques can help you control your moods. Think of a time recently when you felt a particularly strong emotion, such as depression, anger, or anxiety. On a piece of paper, record (1) the situation—who was there, what happened, and when; (2) the intensity of your feeling at the time, from weak to strong; and (3) the thoughts that were going through your mind (e.g., "She never cares about what I want to do"; "I hate being angry"; "He's going to leave me").

Now examine your thoughts. What is the worst thing that can happen if those thoughts are true? Are your thoughts accurate or are you "mind-reading" the other person's intentions and motives? Is there another way to think about this situation or the other person's behaviour? If you practise this exercise repeatedly, you may learn how your thoughts affect your moods—and find out that you have more control over your feelings than you realized (from Greenberger & Padesky, 1995).

A cognitive therapist might treat Murray's procrastination by having Murray write down his thoughts about work, read the thoughts as if someone else had said them, and then write a rational response to each one. This technique would encourage Murray to examine the validity of his assumptions and beliefs. Many procrastinators are perfectionists; if they cannot do something perfectly, they will not do it at all. Unable to accept their limitations, they set impossible standards and catastrophize:

Negative Thought	**Rational Response**
If I don't get an A+ on paper, my life will be ruined.	My life will be a lot worse if I keep getting incompletes. It's better to get a B or even a C than to do nothing at all.
My professor is going to think I'm an idiot when he reads this. I'll feel humiliated by his criticism.	He hasn't accused me of being an idiot yet. If he makes some criticisms, I can learn from them and do better next time.

Strict behaviourists consider thoughts to be "behaviours" that are modifiable by learning principles; they do not regard thoughts as causes of behaviour. But most psychologists believe that thoughts and behaviour influence each other, which is why **cognitive-behavioural therapy** is more common than either cognitive therapy or behaviour therapy alone.

Humanist and Existential Therapy

Humanist therapy, like its parent philosophy *humanism*, starts from the assumption that people seek self-actualization and self-fulfillment. The humanist therapist generally does not dig into past conflicts, but aims instead to help clients feel better about themselves and free themselves from self-imposed limits. Humanist therapists want to know how clients subjectively perceive their own situations, so they can help them develop the will and confidence to bring about change. That is why they explore what is going on "here and now," not the issues of "why and how."

In **client-centred (nondirective) therapy**, developed by Carl Rogers, the therapist's role is to listen to the client's needs in an accepting, nonjudgmental way and offer what Rogers called *unconditional positive regard* (see Chapter 2). Whatever the client's specific complaint is, the goal is to build the client's self-esteem and sense of acceptance, and help the client find a more productive way of seeing his or her problems. Thus a

Client-centred therapy emphasizes the importance of the therapist's warmth and empathy.

Rogerian might assume that Murray's procrastination masks his low self-regard, and that Murray is out of touch with his real feelings and wishes. Perhaps he is not passing his courses because he is trying to please his parents by majoring in pre-law, when he would secretly rather become an artist.

Rogers (1951, 1961) believed that effective therapists must be warm and genuine in expressing their feelings and must respect their clients' feelings, too. For Rogers, *empathy*, the therapist's ability to understand and accept what the client says, is the crucial ingredient of successful therapy. The therapist shows a basic level of empathy by listening carefully and being able to restate accurately the client's remarks: "You tell me that you feel frustrated, Murray, because no matter how hard you try, you don't succeed." But the therapist shows advanced empathy by understanding the *meaning* of the client's remarks: "Working that hard without results must really make you unhappy and maybe make you feel a bit sorry for yourself." The client, according to Rogers, will eventually internalize the therapist's support and become more self-accepting.

Existential therapy helps clients explore the meaning of existence and face with courage the great questions of life, such as death, freedom, alienation from oneself and others, loneliness, and meaninglessness. Existential therapists, like humanist therapists, believe that our lives are not inevitably determined by our pasts or our circumstances—that we have the power to choose our own destinies. As Irvin Yalom (1989) explained, "The crucial first step in therapy is the patient's assumption of responsibility for his or her life predicament. As long as one believes that

---

cognitive-behavioural therapy A form of therapy designed to affect thinking and behaviour, acknowledging both as being important contributors to mental health.

humanist therapy A form of psychotherapy based on the philosophy of humanism, which emphasizes people's free will to change, not past conflicts.

existential therapy A form of therapy designed to help clients explore the meaning of existence and face the great questions of life, such as death, freedom, alienation, and loneliness.

client-centred (nondirective) therapy A humanist approach to therapy devised by Carl Rogers, which emphasizes the therapist's empathy with the client and the use of unconditional positive regard.

one's problems are caused by some force or agency outside oneself, there is no leverage in therapy."

Yalom argues that the goal of therapy is to help clients cope with the inescapable realities of life and death and the struggle for meaning. However grim our experiences may be, he believes, "they contain the seeds of wisdom and redemption." Perhaps the most remarkable example of a man able to find seeds of wisdom in a barren landscape was Victor Frankl (1905–1997), who developed a form of existential therapy after surviving a Nazi concentration camp. In that pit of horror, Frankl (1955) observed, some people maintained their sanity because they were able to find meaning in the experience, shattering though it was.

Some observers believe that, ultimately, all therapies are existential. In different ways, therapy helps people determine what is important to them, what values guide them, and what changes they will have the courage to make. An existential therapist might help Murray think about the significance of his procrastination, what his ultimate goals in life are, and how he might find the strength to carry out his ambitions.

Family and Couples Therapy

Murray's situation is getting worse. His father has begun to call him Tomorrow Man, which upsets his mother, and his younger brother, the math major, has been calculating how much tuition money Murray's incompletes are costing. His older sister Isabel, the biochemist who never had an incomplete in her life, now proposes that all of them go to a family therapist. "Murray's not the only one in this family with complaints," she says.

Family therapists would maintain that Murray's problem developed in the context of his family, that it is sustained by the dynamics of his family, and that any change he makes will affect all members of his family (McDaniel, Lusterman, & Philpot, 2001). One leading family therapist, Salvador Minuchin (1984), compared the family to a kaleidoscope, a changing pattern of mosaics in which the pattern is larger than any one piece. In this view, efforts to isolate and treat one member of the family without the others are doomed. Only if all family members reveal their differing perceptions of each other can mistakes and misperceptions be identified. A teenager, for instance, may see his mother as crabby and nagging when actually she is tired and worried. A parent may see a child as rebellious when in fact the child is lonely and desperate for attention.

Family members are usually unaware of how they influence one another. By observing the entire family, the family therapist hopes to discover tensions and imbalances in power and communication. For example, in some families a child may have a chronic illness or a psychological disorder, such as anorexia, that affects the workings of the whole family. One parent may become over-involved with the sick child while the other parent

Family therapist Alan Entin (1992) uses photographs to help people identify themes and problems in their family histories. When one woman was asked to talk about a photo of her parents (left), she began to cry; she felt that it revealed her father's alienation from her and the rest of his family. Does the picture on the right convey a happy cohesive family to you, or a divided one? Shortly after it was taken, the couple divorced; the father took custody of the children . . . and the mother kept the dog.

retreats, and each may start blaming the other. The child, in turn, may cling to the illness or disorder as a way of expressing anger, keeping the parents together, getting the parents' attention, or asserting control (Luepnitz, 1988).

Some family therapists look for patterns of behaviour across generations (Carter & McGoldrick, 1988; Kerr & Bowen, 1988). The therapist and client may create a family tree showing psychologically significant events across as many generations as possible (McGoldrick, Gerson, & Shellenberger, 1999). This method may reveal historical patterns, as you can see in Figure 12.2.

Even when it is not possible to treat the whole family, some therapists will treat individuals in a **family-systems perspective**, which recognizes that people's behaviour in a family is as interconnected as that of two dancers (Bowen, 1978; Lerner, 1989). Clients learn that if they change in any way, even for the better, their families may protest noisily, or may send subtle messages that read, "Change back!" Why? Because when one family member changes, each of the others must change too. As the saying goes, it takes two to tango, and if one dancer stops, so must the other. But most people do not like change. They are comfortable with old patterns and habits, even those that cause them trouble. They want to keep dancing the same old dance, even if their feet hurt.

When a couple is arguing frequently about issues that never seem to get resolved, they may benefit from *couples therapy*, which is designed to help couples understand and resolve the inevitable conflicts that occur in all relationships. Couples therapists generally insist on seeing both partners, so that they will hear both sides of the story. They cut through the blaming and attacking ("She never listens to me!" "He never does anything!") and focus on helping the couple resolve, or learn to live with, their differences (Christensen & Jacobson, 2000).

Family and couples therapists may use psychodynamic, behavioural, cognitive, or humanist approaches in their work; what they have in common is a focus on the family or couple. In Murray's case, a family therapist would observe how Murray's procrastination fits his family dynamics. Perhaps it allows Murray to get his

family-systems perspective An approach to doing therapy with individuals or families by emphasizing how each family member forms part of a larger, interacting system.

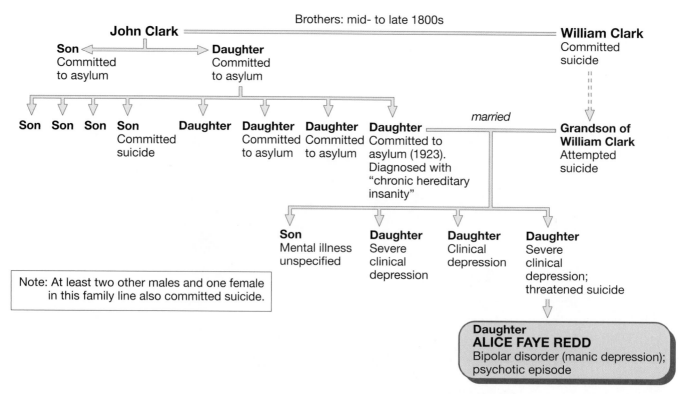

FIGURE 12.2 One Family's History of Mental Illness

Family trees of mental disorders can reveal patterns across generations. Alice Faye Redd was convicted of defrauding elderly investors of $10 million, money she then lost in lavish spending and extravagant investment schemes. Prosecution and defence psychiatrists agreed that she suffered from bipolar disorder. Alice Redd's daughter constructed this multi-generation family record of depression and suicide in an effort to have her mother committed for treatment, but the court sentenced Redd to 15 years in prison.

father's attention and his mother's sympathy. Perhaps it keeps Murray from facing his greatest fear: that if he does finish his work, it will not measure up to his father's high standards. The therapist will not only help Murray change his work habits, but also help his family deal with a changed Murray.

Psychotherapy in Practice

The kinds of psychotherapy that we have discussed are all quite different in theory, and so are their techniques (see Table 12.2). Yet in practice, many psychotherapists take an *integrative approach,* drawing on methods and ideas from various schools and avoiding strong allegiances to any one theory. This flexibility enables them to treat clients with whatever methods work best.

All successful therapies, regardless of approach, share a key element: They are able to motivate the client into wanting to change, and they replace a client's pessimistic or unrealistic story—the "story" each of us develops over time to explain our lives and problems—with one that is more hopeful or attainable (Freedman & Combs, 1996; Howard, 1991; Schafer, 1992). Some therapists explicitly focus on helping clients change their life stories and their own role in them. For example, David Epston worked with an immigrant woman named Marisa, who had been abused and rejected all her life. "To tell a story about your life turns it into a history," he told her, "one that can be left behind, and makes it easier for you to create a future of your own design" (quoted in O'Hanlon, 1994). Marisa came to see that she could tell a new story about her experiences. Instead of seeing the tragedies that had befallen her as evidence that she was a worthless victim, as she always had, she now saw the same events as evidence of her strength and endurance. "My life has a future now," she told him. "It will never be the same again."

TABLE 12.2 The Major Schools of Therapy Compared

	Primary Goal	Methods
Psychodynamic		
Psychoanalytic	Insight into unconscious motives and feelings	Probing unconscious motives through dream analysis, free association, transference
Modern Psychodynamic	Same	Analyst more active and directive; therapy briefer
Cognitive-Behavioural		
Behavioural	Modification of self-defeating behaviours	Systematic desensitization, exposure (flooding), behaviour records, skills training
Cognitive	Modification of irrational or unvalidated beliefs	Challenging unwarranted beliefs, catastrophizing, and mind reading, or prompting client to test beliefs against evidence
Humanist and Existential		
Humanist	Insight; self-acceptance and self-fulfillment; new, optimistic perceptions of self and world	Providing a nonjudgmental setting in which to discuss life issues; use of empathy and unconditional positive regard by therapist
Existential	Finding meaning in life and accepting inevitable losses	Varies with therapist; philosophic discussions about meaning of life, client's goals, finding courage
Family and Couples		
Family	Modification of family patterns	May use any or all of the above methods to change family patterns that perpetuate problems
Couples	Resolution of conflicts, breaking out of destructive habits	May use any or all of the above methods to help the couple communicate better and resolve conflicts

Quick Quiz

Don't be a procrastinator like our friend Murray; take this quiz now. Match each method or concept with the therapy associated with it.

1. transference
2. systematic desensitization
3. facing the fear of death
4. reappraisal of thoughts
5. unconditional positive regard
6. exposure to feared situation
7. avoidance of "catastrophizing"
8. analysis of generational patterns

a. cognitive therapy
b. psychodynamic therapy
c. humanist therapy
d. behaviour therapy
e. family therapy
f. existential therapy

Answers:

1. b 2. d 3. f 4. a 5. c 6. d 7. a 8. e

WHAT'S AHEAD

- What is the "scientist–practitioner gap" and why has it been widening?
- What is the "therapeutic alliance" and why does it matter?
- What sorts of people make the best therapists and the best clients?
- Which form of psychotherapy is most likely to help if you are anxious or depressed?
- Under what conditions can psychotherapy be harmful?

EVALUATING PSYCHOTHERAPY

Poor Murray! He is getting a little baffled by all these therapies. He wants to make a choice soon— no sense in procrastinating about that, too! Is there any scientific evidence, he wonders, that might help him decide which therapy will be best for him?

The Scientist–Practitioner Gap

Many psychotherapists believe that trying to evaluate psychotherapy using standard empirical methods is an exercise in futility: Numbers and graphs cannot possibly capture the complex exchange that takes place between a therapist and a client (Beutler, 2000; Edelson, 1994). Psychotherapy, they say, is an art that you acquire from clinical experience; it is not a science.

Thinking Critically About Research and Psychotherapy

Scientific psychologists agree that research has little to say about the existential aims of therapy, such as helping people come to terms with illness and death or helping them choose which values to live by. But scientists are concerned that when therapists fail to keep up with empirical findings in the field—findings on the most beneficial methods, on ineffective or potentially harmful techniques, and on topics relevant to their practice, such as memory, hypnosis, and child development—their clients may suffer.

Over the years, the breach between scientists and therapists has widened, creating what is commonly called the *scientist–practitioner gap*. One reason for the growing split has been the rise of professional schools that are unconnected to academic psychology departments and that train students solely to do therapy (Dawes, 1994). Graduates of these schools sometimes know little about research methods or even about different therapy techniques.

The scientist–practitioner gap has also widened because of the proliferation of new therapies trying to get a foothold in a crowded market. Simon Fraser University psychologist Barry Beyerstein has pointed out that some of these therapies are packaged and promoted without any scientific support at all (Beyerstein, 1999). For example, one popular therapy, Neurolinguistic Programming (NLP), claims to match people's learning styles with their "brain types" and thereby enhance their communication skills. The U.S. National Research Council concluded that there is no credible evidence for NLP's claims or methods (Druckman & Swets, 1988).

Other therapies re-package established techniques, using a new name and terminology. For example, Eye Movement Desensitization and Reprocessing (EMDR) is built on the tried-and-true behavioural techniques of desensitization and exposure for treating anxiety (Lohr, Tolin, & Lilienfeld, 1998). EMDR's founder, Francine Shapiro (1995), added eye-movement exercises: Clients move their eyes from side to side, following the therapist's moving finger, while concentrating on the memory to be desensitized. Thousands of therapists have been trained to do EMDR, and they have claimed success in treating everything from posttraumatic stress disorder and panic attacks to eating disorders and sexual dysfunction. But there is no evidence from controlled studies that EMDR is any better than standard exposure treatments (Goldstein et al., 2000; Lohr et al., 1999; Taylor et al., 2003).

Because of the proliferation of questionable therapies, and because of rising health costs, psychotherapists are increasingly being called on to provide empirical assessments of therapy (Davison, 2000). Which therapies are most effective, which therapies are best for which disorders, and which therapies are ineffective or potentially harmful? Hundreds of studies have been conducted to answer these questions. And York University psychologist David Rennie has suggested that such studies should consider both quantitative and qualitative data: Numbers can be convenient and persuasive, but the narratives of those receiving psychotherapy often tell equally important stories about a therapy's effectiveness (Rennie, 1994).

The Therapeutic Alliance

Psychotherapy is, first and foremost, a relationship. As with all relationships, its success depends on the qualities that each person brings to the encounter. Successful therapy also depends on

the bond the therapist and client establish between them, called the **therapeutic alliance**. When both parties respect and understand each other and agree on the goals of treatment, the client is more likely to improve.

Qualities of the Participants   Clients who are most likely to do well in therapy are, not surprisingly, those who are motivated to improve and solve their problems (Orlinsky & Howard, 1994). They tend to have support from their families and a habit of dealing actively with problems instead of avoiding them. For example, these attributes are predictive of therapeutic success for men who have a history of abusing their spouses, as shown by research at l'Université de Montréal (Brodeur, Brochu, & Lemire, 2001). In contrast, people who are temperamentally negative and bitter are more resistant to therapy and less likely to benefit from it (Kopta et al., 1994). The personality of the therapist affects the outcome of therapy, too, particularly the qualities that Carl Rogers praised: empathy, warmth, and genuineness. The most successful therapists make their clients feel respected, accepted, and understood (Orlinsky & Howard, 1994).

Culture and the Therapeutic Connection   Many therapists and clients establish a successful therapeutic alliance in spite of being from different backgrounds. But sometimes cultural differences cause misunderstandings that result from ignorance or prejudice (Comas-Díaz & Greene, 1994; Sue, 1998). Cultural norms, as well as a lifetime of marginalization, may keep some Canadian Aboriginals from revealing feelings that they believe a white therapist would not understand or accept. However, group therapy has been a popular approach with Aboriginal clients, in part because the practice is more similar to traditional healing practices in these groups. But when the groups feature a composition that mirrors Euro-Canadian society, they can be problematic for treating relatively traditional Aboriginals (Waldram & Wong, 1995).

More and more psychotherapists are becoming "sensitized to the issues" caused by cultural differences (Sue, 1998). For example, Latino and Asian clients are likely to react to a formal interview with a therapist with relative passivity and deference, leading some therapists to misdiagnose this normal cultural behaviour as a shyness problem. Latinos may respond to catastrophic stress with an *ataque de nervios*, a nervous attack of

therapeutic alliance The bond of confidence and mutual understanding established between therapist and client, which allows them to work together to solve the client's problems.

Some psychotherapists fit their approach to the client's cultural background. For example, at UBC, Charles Chen has shown that rational-emotive therapy can be successful with Chinese clients, given its focus on cognition over emotion. However, Chen has found that some REBT techniques, such as confrontation and exercises that arouse shame, are difficult to use effectively with Chinese clients (Chen, 1995).

randomized controlled trials Research designed to determine the effectiveness of a new medication or form of therapy, in which people with a given problem or disorder are randomly assigned to one or more treatment groups or to a control group.

screaming, swooning, and agitation. Clinicians need to determine when this episode is a culturally influenced response and when it might be a sign of panic disorder (Costantino & Malgady, 1996).

Being aware of cultural differences, however, does not mean that the therapist should stereotype clients (Sue, 1998). Some Asians, after all, do have problems with excessive shyness, and some Latinos do have emotional disorders. It does mean that therapists must ensure that their clients find them to be trustworthy and effective; and it means that clients must be aware of their own prejudices, too.

When Therapy Helps

By now, Murray is really motivated to change. He has just read a study showing that procrastinators not only get worse grades than other students do, but also have more stress and illness during the semester (Tice & Baumeister, 1997). It is time to select a therapeutic approach. But how?

Problems of Assessing Therapy In studying the effectiveness of specific therapies, researchers must face a common problem: No matter what kind of therapy is involved, clients are motivated to tell you it worked. "Dr. Blitznik is a genius!" they will exclaim. "I would *never* have taken that job (or moved to Toronto, or found my true love) if it hadn't been for Dr. Blitznik! I was cured in a week!" Every kind of therapy ever devised produces enthusiastic testimonials from people who feel it saved their lives.

The problem with testimonials is that none of us can be our own control group. How do people know they wouldn't have taken the job, moved to Toronto, or found true love anyway—maybe even sooner—if Dr. Blitznik had not kept them in treatment? Second, Dr. Blitznik's success could be due to the *placebo effect* (which we discussed earlier in this chapter in the context of new medications): The client's anticipation of success and the buzz about Dr. B's fabulous new method might be the active ingredients, rather than Dr. B's therapy itself (Davison, 2000). And third, notice that you never hear testimonials from the people who dropped out, who weren't helped, or who actually got worse.

So researchers cannot be satisfied with testimonials, no matter how glowing. They know that thanks to the *justification of effort* effect (see Chapter 7), people who have put time, money, and effort into something will tell you it was worth it. No one wants to say, "Yeah, I saw Dr. Blitznik for five years, and boy, was it ever a waste of time."

To guard against these problems, clinical researchers conduct **randomized controlled trials**, in which people with a given problem or disorder are randomly assigned to one or more treatment groups or to a control group. Sometimes the results have been surprising, even shocking. For example, in the aftermath of natural and human-made disasters, such as earthquakes or terrorist attacks, trauma specialists often rush to the scene to treat survivors for symptoms of trauma. Yet independent assessments of these interventions find that most people benefit just as much by simply talking with friends and other survivors. Sometimes the intervention *slows* recovery, by preventing victims from drawing on their own wellsprings of resilience. And sometimes the intervention actually *harms* people because of the scientifically unsupported techniques the therapists use, such as having survivors keep ventilating their emotions without also learning good methods of coping (Gist & Lubin, 1999).

You can see, then, why the careful assessment of psychotherapeutic claims and methods is so important. We turn now to the evidence showing the benefits of psychotherapy, and which therapies work best.

What Works? There have been a number of important efforts to review the overall effectiveness of different therapeutic approaches for different disorders (e.g., Chambless et al., 1998; Chambless & Ollendick, 2001; Hollon, Thase, & Markowitz,

2002). For many problems and most emotional disorders, cognitive and behaviour therapies have emerged as the methods of choice. These therapies are particularly effective for the following problems:

- *Depression.* Cognitive therapy's greatest success has been in the treatment of mood disorders, especially depression. It is often as effective as antidepressants, and people in cognitive therapy are less likely than those on drugs to relapse when the treatment is over. The reason may be that the lessons learned in cognitive therapy last a long time after treatment (Antonuccio et al., 1999; Hollon, Thase, & Markowitz, 2002; McNally, 1994; Seligman et al., 1999; Whisman, 1993).

- *Anxiety disorders.* Exposure techniques are more effective than any other treatment for post-traumatic stress disorder, agoraphobia, and specific phobias, such as fear of dogs or of public speaking. And cognitive-behavioural therapy is often more effective than medication for panic disorder, generalized anxiety disorder, and obsessive-compulsive disorder (Kozak, Liebowitz, & Foa, 2000; Schwartz et al., 1996).

- *Anger and impulsive violence.* Cognitive therapy is often successful in reducing chronic anger, abusiveness, and hostility, and it also teaches people how to express anger more calmly and constructively (Deffenbacher et al., 1996, 1998; Kassinove, 1995).

- *Health problems.* Cognitive and behaviour therapies are highly successful in helping people cope with pain, chronic fatigue syndrome, headaches, and irritable bowel syndrome; quit smoking or overcome other addictions; recover from eating disorders such as bulimia and binge eating; improve their sleeping patterns; and manage other health problems (Butler et al., 1991; Skinner, 1990; Stepanski & Perlis, 2000; Wilson & Fairburn, 1993).

- *Childhood and adolescent behaviour problems.* Behaviour therapy is the most effective treatment for behaviour problems that range from bedwetting to defiant rebelliousness, and even for problems that have biological origins, such as autism (Green, 1996a; Weisz et al., 1995).

In addition, young adults with schizophrenia are greatly helped by family intervention therapies that teach parents behavioural skills for dealing with their troubled children, and that educate

IN THE BLEACHERS By Steve Moore

Batters overcoming ***bonkinogginophobia,***
a fear of the ball.

the family about how to cope with the illness constructively (Chambless et al., 1998; Goldstein & Miklowitz, 1995). Nine studies found that over a two-year period, only 30 percent of the schizophrenic patients in such family intervention treatments relapsed, compared to 65 percent of those whose families were not involved. Family therapy, especially when designed to be culturally sensitive to the family's culture of origin, has also been shown to be effective for delinquent, aggressive adolescents (Dudley-Grant, 2001).

However, no single type of therapy can help everyone. Recall that depression has different origins and comes in different degrees of intensity, so the same intervention—whether a medication or a form of psychotherapy—will not benefit all sufferers (Parker, Parker, & Eyers, 2003). Cognitive-behavioural therapy is designed for specific, identifiable problems, but some people may not be motivated to do the "homework" that this therapy requires. Others may seek therapy for less clearly defined difficulties, wishing to introspect about their feelings and lives, find solace and courage, or explore moral issues. And some people are too deeply troubled by personality disorders or psychoses to respond well to any kind of psychotherapy.

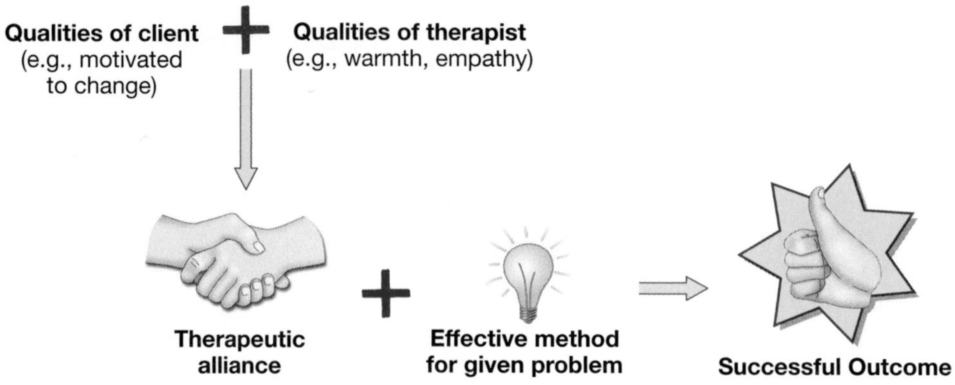

FIGURE 12.3 The Ingredients of Successful Therapy

Some problems, and some clients, are immune to any single kind of therapy but may respond to *combined* methods. For example, people who have severe, recurrent depressions often do better on a combination of antidepressants and psychotherapy than with either method alone (Hollon, Thase, & Markowitz, 2002; Keller et al., 2000). A leading treatment for sex offenders combines cognitive therapy, behavioural techniques, sex education, group therapy, and social-skills training (Abel et al., 1988; Kaplan, Morales, & Becker, 1993).

In sum, the factors contributing to successful therapy are the qualities of the participants, the strength of the therapeutic alliance, and the specific methods of the therapy (see Figure 12.3).

When Therapy Harms

Every treatment and intervention, including aspirin, carries risks, and so does psychotherapy. But the risks to clients increase when any of the following occurs:

Thinking Critically About the Risks of Therapy

1 *Sexual intimacies or other unethical behaviour on the part of the therapist.* The ethical guidelines of the Canadian Psychological Association (CPA) prohibit therapists from having any sexual intimacies with their clients, or violating other professional boundaries. Occasionally, some therapists behave like cult leaders, persuading their clients that their mental health depends on staying in therapy and severing their connections to their "toxic" families (Mithers, 1994; Watters & Ofshe, 1999). Such "psychotherapy cults" are created by the therapist's use of techniques that foster the client's dependency and isolation, prevent the client from terminating therapy, and reduce the client's ability to think critically (see Chapter 10).

2 *Prejudice or cultural ignorance on the part of the therapist.* Some therapists may be prejudiced against some clients because of the client's gender, culture, religion, or sexual orientation. A therapist may try to induce a client to conform to the therapist's standards and values, even if they are not appropriate to the client or in the client's best interest (Brodsky, 1982; López, 1989). For example, for many years gay men and lesbians who entered therapy were told that homosexuality was a mental illness that could be cured. Some of the so-called treatments were harsh, such as electric shock for "inappropriate" arousal. Other kinds of "reparative" therapies that supposedly turn gay men and lesbians into heterosexuals still surface from time to time. They are often promoted in campaigns by conservative Christians who believe that homosexuality is a sin, with testimonials from alleged converts. But there is no reliable empirical evidence from scientifically designed studies supporting these claims, and both the American Psychological Association and the American Psychiatric Association have gone on record opposing reparative therapies on ethical and scientific grounds.

3 *The use of empirically unsupported, potentially dangerous techniques.* In Chapter 8 we saw that memory does not work like a video camera or tape recorder; memories are not "buried" in the brain, awaiting magic methods to root them out. Yet many therapists claim that they can help clients accurately retrieve painful old memories. They use various unreliable methods to do so, including hypnosis, sodium amytal (a barbiturate misleadingly called "truth serum"), guided imagery, and dream analysis. These techniques all enhance the client's suggestibility (Mazzoni, Loftus, & Kirsch, 2001). For example, when a therapist tells a client that his or her dreams are memories of something that really happened, suggestible clients begin to confuse their dreams with reality (Mazzoni et al., 1999).

Many research psychologists are greatly concerned that a significant minority of registered, licensed psychotherapists—between one-fourth and one-third of them—have used one or more of these inappropriate techniques specifically to help clients "retrieve" memories of sexual abuse, as you can see in Figure 12.4 (Poole et al., 1995), and as described in the news story that begins this chapter. Research in Canada and the United States finds that the percentages of those using the techniques have not declined appreciably in recent years (Katz, 2001; Polusny & Follette, 1996; Nunez, Poole, & Memon, 2002).

4 *Inappropriate or coercive influence, which can create new problems for the client.* In a healthy therapeutic alliance, therapists and clients come to agree on an explanation for the client's problems. Of course, the therapist will influence this explanation, according to his or her training and philosophy. Some therapists, however, cross the line. They so zealously believe in the prevalence of certain disorders that they actually induce the client to produce the symptoms they are looking for (McHugh, 1993; McNally, 2003a; Merskey, 1995; Watters & Ofshe, 1999). Therapist influence, and sometimes downright coercion, is a likely reason for the huge numbers of people who were diagnosed with multiple personality disorder in the 1980s and 1990s (see Chapter 11).

To avoid these risks and benefit from what effective psychotherapy has to offer, people looking for a therapy that can help them must become educated consumers.

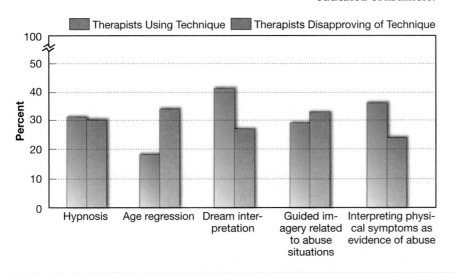

FIGURE 12.4 Psychotherapists' Attitudes Toward Suggestive Techniques

Although suggestive techniques can produce false memories, between one-fourth and one-third of licensed clinical psychologists use these methods regularly "to help clients recall memories of sexual abuse." About the same percentages disapprove of using such techniques. (The rest neither use the methods nor disapprove of them.) The percentages are from two combined random samples of American clinical psychologists with Ph.D.s (Poole et al., 1995). The numbers have not changed appreciably in recent years.

Quick Quiz

Find out if you are an educated consumer of psychotherapy by taking this quiz.

1. Which of the following is the most important predictor of successful therapy? (a) how long it lasts, (b) the insight it provides the client, (c) the bond between therapist and client, (d) whether the therapist and client are matched according to gender

2. In general, which type of psychotherapy is most effective for anxiety and depression?

3. What are four possible sources of harm in psychotherapy?

4. Ferdie is spending too much time playing softball and not enough time studying, so he signs up for "sportaholic therapy" (ST). The therapist tells him the cure is to quit softball cold turkey and tap his temples three times whenever he feels the urge to play. After a few months, Ferdie announces that ST isn't helping and he's going to quit. The therapist gives him testimonials of other clients who swear by ST, adding that Ferdie's doubts are actually a sign that the therapy is working. What are some problems with this argument? (Bonus: What kind of therapy might help Ferdie manage his time better?)

Answers:

1. c 2. cognitive-behavioural 3. unethical behaviour, prejudice or biased treatment, inappropriate or coercive influence, and the use of empirically unsupported techniques 4. The therapist has violated the principle of falsifiability (see Chapter 1). If Ferdie is helped by the treatment, that shows it works; if he is not helped, that still shows it works and Ferdie is simply "in denial" about its benefits. Also, Ferdie is not hearing testimonials from people who have dropped out of ST and were not helped by it. (Bonus: A good behavioural time-management program might help, so Ferdie can play softball and get other things done, too.)

Psychology In The News *Revisited*

Now that we have reviewed the major kinds of psychotherapy, along with their successes and risks, let's return to the issues raised by the sexual abuse case brought against Michael Kliman on the basis of recovered memories. Kliman, who was by then a retired elementary school vice-principal, was cleared of all charges.

It must be noted that the two women who pressed charges against Michael Kliman had significant and undeniable problems, including anorexia and borderline personality disorder, for which therapy could well have been prescribed. They deserved the best therapeutic interventions clinical psychology could provide. As it turned out, however, regression therapy was far from the best for the woman who received it. It did her no good, and it nearly ruined another person's life.

How can you, as a potential consumer of psychological services, distinguish between techniques that are beneficial and techniques that can harm? As a critical thinker, what questions should you ask about the therapist and the therapist's approach?

The first step is to make sure you are dealing with a reputable individual with appropriate credentials and training. As we saw in Chapter 1, to become a licensed psychologist, a person must have an advanced degree and a period of supervised training. However, the word *psychotherapist* is unregulated; anyone can set up any kind of program and call it "therapy." In Canada and the United States, people can be credentialed as "experts" in various techniques and therapies simply by attending a weekend seminar or a training program lasting a week or two.

Second, it is important to ask whether a therapist practises one of the empirically supported methods described in this chapter, and whether the basic assumptions of the therapist are likewise validated by empirical research. There is nothing especially new about regression therapy. Some would say it is based on long-held principles derived from psychotherapy and Freudian analysis. These therapies are founded on the assumption that we repress troubling thoughts, and that it is therapeutic to bring these thoughts to consciousness where they can be dealt with openly and constructively. But can the same be applied to regression into childhood? We cannot be sure that someone is bringing accurate memories to consciousness when he or she is "taken back" to early years.

Besides choosing a therapist carefully, consumers need to be realistic about what they expect of psychotherapy. In the hands of an empathic and knowledgeable practitioner, psychotherapy can help you make decisions and clarify your values and goals. It can teach you new skills and new ways of thinking. It can help you get along better with your family and break out of destructive family patterns. It can get you through bad times when no one seems to care or to understand what you are feeling. It can teach you how to manage depression, anxiety, and anger.

However, despite its many benefits, psychotherapy cannot transform you into someone you're not. It cannot turn an introvert into an extrovert. It cannot cure an emotional disorder overnight. It cannot provide a life without problems. And it is not intended to substitute for experience—for work that is satisfying, relationships that are sustaining, and activities that are enjoyable.

Taking Psychology With You   How to Evaluate Self-Help Groups and Books

Not all psychological problems require the aid of a professional. Nowadays, thousands of programs and books are designed to help people help themselves. More than 2000 self-help books are published every year, and an estimated 7 to 15 million adults belong to self-help groups. Do these books and groups help?

Self-help groups are available (online and in person) for alcoholics, relatives of alcoholics, people suffering from depression, anorexia, or schizophrenia, women with breast cancer, parents of murdered children, diabetics, rape victims, stepparents, relatives of patients with Alzheimer's disease, and people with just about any other concern you can think of (Davison, Pennebaker, & Dickerson, 2000). Members say that the primary benefits are the awareness that they are not alone, encouragement when they are feeling down, and help in feeling better about themselves.

Self-help groups offer understanding, empathy, and solutions to shared problems. Such groups can be reassuring and supportive in ways that family, friends, and psychotherapists sometimes may not be (Dunkel-Schetter, 1984). For example, people with disabilities face unique challenges that involve coping not only with physical problems but also with the condescension, hostility, and prejudice of many nondisabled people (Linton, 1998). Other disabled people, who share these challenges, can offer the right kind of empathy and useful advice. Similarly, research in Ontario and elsewhere has shown the many benefits that support groups provide for women with breast cancer (Gray, 1997) and men with prostate cancer (Poole et al., 2001).

Self-help groups do not provide psychotherapy, and they are not designed to help people with serious psychological difficulties. They are not regulated by law or by professional standards, and they vary widely in their philosophies and methods. Some are accepting and tolerant, offering support and spiritual guidance. Others are confrontational and coercive, and members who disagree with the premises of the group may be made to feel deviant, crazy, or "in denial." If you choose to become part of a support group, be sure it falls in the first category.

As for self-help books, there is one for every problem, from how to toilet-train your children to how to find happiness in seven steps. When self-help books propose a specific, well-supported program for the reader to follow, they can actually be as effective as treatment administered by a therapist—*if* the reader follows through with the program (Christensen & Jacobson, 1994). Unfortunately, most books do not do this. After serving as chair of the APA's Task Force on Self-Help Therapies, Gerald Rosen (1981) concluded, "Psychologists have published untested materials, advanced exaggerated claims, and accepted the use of misleading titles that encourage unrealistic expectations regarding outcome." That was written more than 20 years ago, and the situation is worse today. The information in this chapter suggests some guidelines for evaluating a self-help book:

Formal and informal support groups provide a setting for sharing concerns and exchanging constructive advice, as these men with AIDS are doing.

- **The authors should be qualified,** which means that they have conducted good research or are thoroughly versed in the field. Personal accounts by people who have survived difficulties can be helpful and inspirational, of course, but an author's own experience is not grounds for generalizing to everyone.

- **The book's advice should be based on sound scientific theory,** not on the author's pseudoscientific theories, armchair observations, or political views. This criterion rules out, among other kinds of books, most of the love manuals in which the author's own lovelorn stories or tales of woe with the other sex become the basis of an entire philosophy of love, marriage, and happiness. *Men Are from Mars, Women Are from Venus*, by John Gray (whose "Ph.D." was from a mail-order, unaccredited college), is based on pure stereotyping; *Why Marriages Succeed or Fail*, by John Gottman (whose Ph.D. in psychology is from a prestigious university), is based on years of experimental research.

- **The book should not promise the impossible.** This lets out books that promise you perfect sex, total love, or high self-esteem in 30 days. It also lets out books or tapes that promote techniques whose effectiveness has been disconfirmed by research, such as dream analysis or "subliminal" messages.

- **The advice should be organized in a systematic program,** step by step, not as a vague pep talk to "take charge of your life" or "find love in your heart"; and the reader should be told how to evaluate his or her progress.

Some books do meet these criteria. One is *Changing for Good* (Prochaska, Norcross, & DiClemente, 1994), which describes the ingredients of effective change that apply to people in and out of therapy. But as long as people yearn for a magic bullet to cure their problems, quick-fix solutions will find a ready audience.

SUMMARY

BIOLOGICAL TREATMENTS FOR MENTAL DISORDERS

- Over the centuries, people trying to understand and treat psychological disorders have alternated between biological and psychological explanations. Today, biological treatments are on the rise because of research findings on the genetic and biological causes of some disorders, and because of economic and social factors.

- The medications most commonly prescribed for mental disorders include *antipsychotic drugs*, used in treating schizophrenia and other psychotic disorders; *antidepressants*, used in treating depression, anxiety disorders, and obsessive-compulsive disorder; *tranquilizers*, often prescribed for emotional problems; and *lithium carbonate*, a salt used to treat bipolar disorder.

- Drawbacks of drug treatment include the *placebo effect*; high dropout and relapse rates among people who take medications without also learning how to cope with their problems; the difficulty of finding the correct dose (the *therapeutic window*) for each individual, compounded by the fact that a person's ethnicity, sex, and age can influence a drug's effectiveness; and the long-term risks of medication, known and unknown. Medication can be helpful and can even save lives, but in an age when commercial interests are heavily invested in promoting drugs for psychological problems, the public is largely unaware of drugs' limitations. Medication should not be prescribed mindlessly and routinely, especially when non-drug therapies can work as well as drugs for many mood and behavioural problems.

- When drugs or psychotherapy have failed to help seriously disturbed people, some psychiatrists have intervened directly in the brain. *Psychosurgery*, which destroys selected areas of the brain thought to be responsible for a mental disorder, is rarely done today. *Electroconvulsive therapy (ECT)*, in which a brief current is sent through the brain, has been used successfully to treat suicidal depression. However, controversy exists about its effects on the brain and the appropriateness of its use. A newer method, *transcranial magnetic stimulation*, is showing promise in treating severe depression.

KINDS OF PSYCHOTHERAPY

- *Psychodynamic ("depth") therapies* include Freudian *psychoanalysis* and its modern variations, such as approaches based on *object-relations theory*. These therapies explore unconscious dynamics by using *free association* and focusing on the process of *transference*.

- *Behaviour and cognitive therapies* draw on principles of learning and cognition. Behaviour therapists use such methods as *systematic desensitization*, based on *counterconditioning*; *graduated exposure*; *behavioural self-monitoring*; and *skills training*. Cognitive therapists aim to change the irrational thoughts involved in negative emotions and self-defeating actions. Albert Ellis's *rational emotive behaviour therapy (REBT)* and Aaron Beck's form of cognitive therapy are two leading approaches.

- *Humanist therapy* attempts to help people feel better about themselves by focusing on here-and-now issues and on the human capacity for self-fulfillment and self-actualization. Carl Rogers's *client-centred (nondirective) therapy* emphasizes the importance of the therapist's empathy and ability to provide *unconditional positive regard*. *Existential therapy* helps people cope with philosophical dilemmas, such as the meaning of life and the fear of death.

- *Family therapies* share the view that individual problems develop in the context of the whole family network. They tend to share a *family-systems perspective*, understanding that any one person's behaviour in the family affects everyone else, sometimes across generations. In *couples therapy*, the therapist sees both partners in a relationship to help them resolve ongoing quarrels and disputes.

- In practice, most therapists are *integrative*, drawing on many methods and ideas. Whatever their approach, successful therapies share the goal of helping people form more adaptive "life stories."

EVALUATING PSYCHOTHERAPY

- A *scientist–practitioner gap* has developed because of the different assumptions held by researchers and many clinicians regarding the value of empirical research for doing psychotherapy and for assessing its effectiveness. The gap has led to a proliferation of scientifically unsupported psychotherapies.

- Successful therapy requires a *therapeutic alliance* between the therapist and the client, so that they understand each other and can work together. The clients who benefit most from psychotherapy are motivated to solve their problems—hostile, negative individuals are more resistant to treatment. For their part, good therapists are empathic and constructive. When therapist and client are of different ethnicities, both must try to avoid prejudice, misunderstanding, and stereotyping. The therapist must also distinguish normal cultural patterns from mental disorders.

• In assessing the effectiveness of psychotherapy, researchers must control for the placebo effect and the *justification of effort* effect. They rely on *randomized controlled trials* to determine which therapies are empirically supported.

• Some therapies are demonstrably better than others for specific problems. Behaviour therapy and cognitive-behavioural therapy are the most effective for depression, anxiety disorders, anger problems, certain health problems and eating disorders, and childhood and adolescent behaviour problems. Family therapies are helpful for young adults with schizophre-

nia and for aggressive adolescents. Some problems and populations, such as people with severe depression or sex offenders, may respond best to combined therapeutic approaches.

• In some cases, therapy is harmful. The therapist may behave unethically; be prejudiced against a client; inadvertently create disorders through undue influence or suggestion; or use empirically unsupported and potentially harmful techniques, such as unreliable methods of "recovering" memories of abuse.

PSYCHOLOGY IN THE NEWS, REVISITED

• Because of the growing number of unlicensed psychotherapists and the rise of new therapies whose methods and assumptions have little or no empirical validation, consumers need to choose a therapist carefully, select the kind of therapy best suited for their problem, and be realistic about what they expect of psychotherapy.

KEY TERMS

antipsychotic drugs 388
antidepressant drugs 389
lithium carbonate 389
tranquilizers 389
placebo effect 390
electroconvulsive therapy (ECT) 392
psychosurgery 392
psychodynamic therapies 394

transference 394
psychoanalysis 394
free association 394
systematic desensitization 395
behaviour therapy 395
graduated exposure 396
skills training 396
behavioural self-monitoring 396
rational emotive behaviour therapy (REBT) 397

cognitive therapy 397
cognitive-behavioural therapy 398
humanist therapy 398
existential therapy 398
client-centred (nondirective) therapy 398
family-systems perspective 400
therapeutic alliance 403
randomized controlled trials 404

LOOKING BACK

• What kinds of drugs are used to treat psychological disorders? (pp. 388–389)
• Can mental disorders be cured by brain surgery? (p. 392)
• Why is "shock therapy" hailed by some clinicians but condemned by others? (pp. 392–393)
• Why are psychodynamic therapies called "depth" therapies? (p. 394)
• How do cognitive therapists help people get rid of self-defeating thoughts? (pp. 397–398)
• Why do humanist therapists focus on the "here and now" instead of the "why and how"? (p. 398)
• Why do family therapists prefer to treat families rather than individuals? (p. 399)
• What is the "scientist–practitioner gap" and why has it been widening? (p. 402)
• What is the "therapeutic alliance" and why does it matter? (p. 403)
• What sorts of people make the best therapists and the best clients? (p. 403)
• Which form of psychotherapy is most likely to help if you are anxious or depressed? (p. 405)
• Under what conditions can psychotherapy be harmful? (pp. 406–407)

Psychology In The News

MAN WHO STABS HIS WIFE 47 TIMES GETS FIVE-AND-A-HALF-YEAR SENTENCE

BURNABY, BC, 1999. In 1994, Bert Stone stabbed his wife 47 times and then put her body in the tool box in the back of his pickup truck. Shortly thereafter he left Canada for Mexico, leaving a note saying "Sorry, but she just wouldn't stop yelling at me." The Stones had been married for 10 months.

Remarkably, Bert Stone was given a sentence of less than six years for the crime. The defence was that Stone's offence had been a "crime of passion" and that he had been provoked by relentless nagging and arguing. His defence contained testimony describing a marriage fraught with stress and negative emotion— arguing, insults, and raised voices.

The Canadian Criminal Code defines a crime of provocation as "a wrongful act or insult that is of such a nature as to be sufficient to deprive any ordinary person of the power of self control."

Stone's sentence was met with public outcry, especially from organizations advocating for victims of domestic abuse. Eventually, the duration of Stone's sentence was appealed to the BC Supreme Court, though it was not overturned. His claim that living with his wife was sufficiently stressful to help explain his decision to kill her has held up to appeal.

A display at the Vancouver Art Gallery serves as a reminder of women killed by domestic violence in British Columbia. Bert Stone, of Burnaby, B.C., stabbed his wife to death in 1994, but received a sentence of less than six years for his crime.

13 Emotion, Stress, and Health

Almost everyone can understand Bert Stone's feelings. Most of us will, at some time, learn first-hand how intense the emotions of anger and frustration can be. In those moments, we want to indulge ourselves in the furious, if fleeting, impulse for retaliation.

Fortunately, most people do not act on their furious impulses, or at least they act on them in nonviolent ways. Why do some people seem to yield to their emotions, apparently losing control of them, whereas others are able to stop rage and other unpleasant feelings from turning into violent or self-destructive actions?

In this chapter we will explore this question, and others, as we examine the physiology and psychology of emotions and stress. Prolonged negative emotions such as anger can certainly be stressful, and stress can certainly produce negative emotions. But both of these processes are shaped by how we interpret the events that happen to us, by the demands of the situation we are in, and by the rules of our culture. As you read, see whether you can think of some explanations for Bert Stone's behaviour other than "he couldn't

help it." And see whether you can come up with some ideas for reducing unpleasant emotions and stressful experiences in your own life.

WHAT'S AHEAD

- Which facial expressions of emotion do most people recognize the world over?
- Which little structure in the brain sees to it that you cross the street fast when a truck is headed toward you?
- Which two hormones can make you "too excited to eat"?
- In a competition, who is likely to be happier, the third-place winner or the second-place winner?
- Why can't an infant feel shame or guilt?

THE NATURE OF EMOTION

People often curse their emotions, wishing to be freed from anger, jealousy, shame, guilt, and grief. Yet imagine a life without emotions. You would be unmoved by the magic of music. You would never

Thinking Critically About "Irrational" Emotions

care about losing someone you love, not only because you would not know sadness but also because you would not know love. You would never laugh because nothing would strike you as funny. And you would be a social klutz because you would not be able to know what other people were feeling.

Because emotions can get us into trouble, for centuries emotion was regarded as the opposite of thinking, and an inferior opposite at that. The heart (emotion) was said to be part of our "irrational" mammalian heritage, in contrast to our "rational" human capacity for thought and logic. Today, psychologists avoid such either–or thinking.

As we have seen in other chapters, normal thought processes involve many "irrational" biases, such as the confirmation bias, the hindsight bias, the self-serving bias, and biases in the construction of memories. Conversely, emotions are not always irrational, even when they are uncomfortable. Emotions bind people together, motivate them to achieve their goals, and help them make decisions and plans (Damasio, 1994; Oatley, 1990). When you are faced with a decision between two appealing and justifiable career alternatives, for example, your sense of which one "feels right" emotionally may help you make the better choice. Disgust, which is pretty disgusting, probably evolved as a mechanism that protects infants and adults from eating tainted or poisonous food. Even embarrassment, so painful to the individual, serves important functions: It appeases others when you feel you have made a fool of yourself, broken a moral rule, or violated a social norm (Keltner & Anderson, 2000).

In defining **emotion**, psychologists focus on three major components: *physiological* changes in the face, brain, and body, *cognitive* processes such as interpretations of events, and *cultural* influences that shape the experience and expression of emotion. If we compare human emotions to a tree, the biological capacity for emotion is the trunk and root system; thoughts and explanations create the many branches; and culture is the gardener that shapes the tree and prunes it, cutting off some limbs and cultivating others. Let's begin with the trunk.

Emotion and the Body

Research on the physiological aspects of emotion suggests that people everywhere are born with certain basic or **primary emotions**, which typically include fear, anger, sadness, happiness, sur-

prise, disgust, and contempt. These emotions have distinctive neural pathways in the brain, as discovered by researchers at l'Université de Montréal (Pelletier et al., 2003). They also have distinctive physiological patterns and corresponding facial expressions, and the situations that evoke them are the same all over the world: Everywhere, sadness follows perception of loss, fear follows perception of threat and bodily harm, anger follows perception of insult or injustice, and so forth (Scherer, 1997). In contrast, **secondary emotions** include all the variations and blends of emotion that vary from one culture to another and develop gradually with increasing cognitive maturity.

Researchers in the physiological tradition are studying the biological aspects of emotions: facial expressions, brain regions and circuits, and the autonomic nervous system.

The Face of Emotion The most obvious place to look for emotion is on the face, where emotions are often visibly expressed. In 1872, Charles Darwin argued that human facial expressions— the smile, the frown, the grimace, the glare—are as "wired in" as the wing flutter of a frightened bird, the purr of a contented cat, and the snarl of a threatened wolf. Such expressions evolved, he said, because they allowed our forebears to tell at a glance the difference between a friendly stranger and a hostile one.

Modern psychologists have supported Darwin's idea by showing that certain emotional displays are recognized the world over (see Figure 13.1). Paul Ekman and his colleagues have gathered abundant evidence for the universality of seven basic facial expressions of emotion—expressions that correspond to the list of emotions usually identified as primary: anger, happiness, fear, surprise, disgust, sadness, and contempt (Ekman, 2003; Ekman & Heider, 1988; Ekman et al., 1987). In every culture they have studied—in Brazil, Chile, Estonia, Germany, Greece, Hong Kong, Italy, Japan, New Guinea, Scotland, Sumatra, Turkey, Canada, and the United States—a large majority of people recognize the emotional expressions portrayed by those in other cultures. Even most members of isolated tribes that have never watched a movie or read *People* magazine, such as the Foré of New Guinea or the Minangkabau of West Sumatra, can recognize the emotions expressed in pictures of people who are entirely foreign to them, and we can recognize theirs.

Ekman and his associates developed a special coding system to analyze and identify each of the

secondary emotions Emotions that are specific to certain cultures.

emotion A state of arousal involving facial and bodily changes, brain activation, cognitive appraisals, subjective feelings, and tendencies toward action.

primary emotions Emotions that are considered to be universal and biologically based; they generally include fear, anger, sadness, happiness, surprise, disgust, and contempt.

FIGURE 13.1 Some Universal Expressions

Can you tell what feelings are being conveyed here? Most people around the world can readily identify expressions of surprise, disgust, happiness, sadness, anger, fear, and contempt—no matter what the age, culture, sex, or historical era of the person conveying the emotion.

nearly 80 muscles of the face, as well as the combinations of muscles associated with various emotions (Ekman, 2003). When people try to hide their feelings and "put on" an emotion, they generally use different groups of muscles than they do for authentic ones. For example, when people try to pretend that they feel sad, only 15 percent manage to get the eyebrows, eyelids, and forehead wrinkle exactly right, mimicking the way true grief is expressed spontaneously. Authentic smiles last only two seconds; false smiles may last ten seconds or more (Ekman, Friesen, & O'Sullivan, 1988).

The Functions of Facial Expressions Interestingly, facial expressions not only can reflect our internal feelings; they also may *influence* our internal feelings. In the process of **facial feedback**, the facial muscles send messages to the brain about the basic emotion being expressed: A smile tells us that we're happy, a frown that we're angry or

perplexed (Izard, 1990). When people are told to smile and look pleased or happy, their positive feelings increase; when they are told to look angry, displeased, or disgusted, positive feelings decrease (Kleinke, Peterson, & Rutledge, 1998).

Facial feedback affects emotional states even when people are not specifically asked to imitate an emotion, but just to alter their facial muscles. For example, when people are told to contract the facial muscles involved in smiling (though not actually instructed to smile) and are then shown cartoons, they find the cartoons funnier than if they are contracting their muscles in a way that is incompatible with smiling (Strack, Martin, & Stepper, 1988). And when they are asked to contort their facial muscles into patterns associated with anger, that is often the emotion they feel. As one young man put it, "When my jaw was clenched and my brows down, I tried not to be angry but it just fit the position" (Laird, 1974). If

facial feedback The process by which the facial muscles send messages to the brain about the basic emotion being expressed.

GREAT MOMS IN HISTORY.

IT WON'T KILL YOU TO SMILE A LITTLE, MONA!

Great moms have always understood the importance of facial feedback.

you put on an "angry" face, your heart rate will rise faster than if you put on a "happy" face (Levenson, Ekman, & Friesen, 1990). (The next time you are feeling sad or afraid, try purposely smiling, even if no one is around. Keep smiling. Does facial feedback work for you?)

As Darwin suggested, facial expressions also probably evolved to help us communicate our emotional states to others and provoke a response from them—"Come help me!" "Get away!" (Fridlund, 1994). Indeed, researchers at UBC have found that facial expressions convey these social messages as universally as they convey emotions (Yik & Russell, 1999). This signalling function begins in infancy. A baby's expressions of misery, angry frustration, or disgust are apparent to most parents, who respond by soothing an uncomfortable baby, feeding a grumpy one, or removing unappealing food from a disgusted one (Izard, 1994b; Stenberg & Campos, 1990). And an infant's smile of joy usually melts the heart of the weariest parent, provoking a happy cuddle. Obviously a baby's facial expressions have survival value! Babies seem primed to respond to adults' expressions, too. Tiny newborns will suck longer on a pacifier if it produces a happy face than if it produces a face with a neutral or negative expression (Walker-Andrews, 1997). (If you become or are already a parent, remember this.)

Starting at the end of their first year, babies begin to alter their own behaviour in reaction to their parents' facial expressions of emotion, and this ability, too, has survival value. Do you recall the visual-cliff studies described in Chapter 6? These studies were originally designed to test for depth perception, which emerges early in infancy. But in one experiment, one-year-old babies were put on a more ambiguous visual cliff that did not drop off sharply and thus did not automatically evoke fear, as the original cliff did. In this case, the babies' behaviour depended on the mother's expression: 74 percent crossed the cliff when their mothers put on a happy, reassuring expression, but not a single infant crossed when the mother showed an expression of fear (Sorce et al., 1985). If you have ever watched a toddler take a tumble

and then look at his or her parent before deciding whether to cry or to forget it, you will understand the influence of parental facial expressions, and why they have such survival value for babies. An infant needs to be able to read the parent's facial signals of alarm or safety because young children do not yet have the experience necessary for judging danger.

Finally, facial expressions of emotion can generate emotions in others, which is why moods can literally be contagious. When people see pictures of facial expressions of emotion or other nonverbal emotional signals, their own facial muscles subtly mimic the ones they are observing. This unconscious process often activates a similar emotional state in themselves (Dimberg, Thunberg, & Elmehed, 2000; Neumann & Strack, 2000). Have you ever been in a cheerful mood, had lunch with a depressed friend, and come away feeling vaguely depressed yourself? Have you ever stopped to have a chat with a friend who was nervous about an upcoming exam, and ended up feeling edgy yourself? That's *mood contagion* at work.

Facial expressions, then, are important clues to a person's emotions, but they are only part of the emotional picture. People can feel sad, anxious, or angry without letting it show. And, of course, people often use facial expressions to lie about their feelings as well as to express them. In Shakespeare's play *Henry VI*, the villain who will become the evil King Richard III says,

> Why, I can smile, and murder while I smile; And cry content to that which grieves my heart; And wet my cheeks with artificial tears, And frame my face to all occasions.

Facial expressions do not always convey the emotion being felt. A posed, social smile from politicians like Paul Martin or Stephen Harper may have nothing to do with true feelings of happiness.

Emotion and the Brain Another line of research seeks to identify parts of the brain that are involved in specific emotions or that are responsible for different aspects of emotional experience: recognizing another person's emotion, feeling an emotion, expressing an emotion, and acting on an emotion. For example, people who have a stroke that affects two areas involved in disgust are often unable to feel disgusted! One young man with stroke damage in these regions could recognize all of the basic facial expressions except for disgust, and he had little or no emotional response to images and ideas that would be disgusting to most people, such as feces-shaped chocolate (Calder et al., 2000). (Are you making a disgusted expression as you read that? He couldn't.)

Most emotions motivate a response of some sort: to embrace or approach the person who instills joy in you, attack a person who makes you angry, withdraw from a scene that disgusts you, or flee from a person or situation that frightens you (Brehm, 1999). The prefrontal regions of the brain are involved in these impulses to approach or withdraw. Regions of the *left* prefrontal cortex appear to be specialized for the motivation to approach others (as with happiness, a positive emotion, and anger, a negative one). People with damage to this area often lose the capacity for joy

(Davidson & Henriques, 2000; Heller & Nitschke, 1997). In contrast, regions of the *right* prefrontal region are specialized for withdrawal or escape (as in disgust, depression, and fear) (Davidson, Jackson, & Kalin, 2000; Harmon-Jones & Allen, 1998; Harmon-Jones et al., 2002). People with damage to the right prefrontal cortex may feel excessively manic and euphoric, with little emotional balance.

The *amygdala*, a small structure in the brain's limbic system, plays a key role in emotion, especially anger and fear. The amygdala is responsible for evaluating sensory information, quickly determining its emotional importance, and making the initial decision to approach or withdraw from a person or situation (Adolphs, 2001; LeDoux, 1996). The amygdala quickly assesses danger or threat, which is a good thing, because otherwise you could be standing in the street asking, "Is it wise to cross now, while that very large truck is coming toward me?" The amygdala's initial response may then be overridden by a more accurate appraisal from the cortex. This is why you jump with fear when you suddenly feel a hand on your back in a dark alley, and why your fear evaporates when the cortex registers that the hand belongs to a friend whose lousy idea of humour is to scare you in a dark alley.

Get Involved Turn on Your Right Hemisphere

These faces have expressions of happiness on one side and sadness on the other. Look at the nose of each face; which face looks happier? Which face looks sadder?

(a)

(b)

You are likely to see face b as the happier one and face a as the sadder one. The likely reason is that in most people the left side of a picture is processed by the right side of the brain, where recognition of emotional expression primarily occurs (see Chapter 4; Oatley & Jenkins, 1996).

If either the amygdala or critical areas of the cortex are damaged, abnormalities result in the ability to process fear. People with damage in

the amygdala often have difficulty recognizing fear in others (Adolphs, 2001; Damasio, 1994). One such woman could accurately *display* fear and

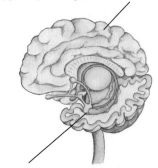

2. The cerebral cortex generates a more complete picture; it can override signals sent by the amygdala ("It's only Mike in a down coat").

1. The amygdala scrutinizes information for its emotional importance ("It's a bear! Be afraid! Run!").

other emotions herself, but she could not *perceive* or recognize expressions of fear in others (Anderson & Phelps, 2000). In contrast, people with damage to areas of the cortex often lose the capacity to put aside their fear when the emotion is no longer necessary. The result can be constant, irrational feelings of impending doom and anxiety, and obsessive thoughts of danger—as is the case in obsessive-compulsive disorder, discussed in Chapter 11.

The Energy of Emotion When the amygdala and prefrontal cortex signal "Danger! Get outta here!" you need to be able to move fast. The next stage of the emotional relay is the release of hormones, which produce the energy of emotion. When you are under stress or experience an intense emotion, the sympathetic division of the autonomic nervous system spurs the adrenal glands to send out two hormones, *epinephrine* and *norepinephrine* (see

Intense but short-lived "road rage" results in part from physiological arousal caused by the stress of driving. That's why passengers rarely feel as furious as the driver does.

Chapter 4). These chemical messengers produce a state of arousal and alertness. The pupils dilate, widening to allow in more light; the heart beats faster; breathing speeds up; and blood sugar rises, providing the body with more energy to act. Digestion slows down, so that blood flow can be diverted from the stomach and intestines to the muscles and surface of the skin. (This is why, when you are excited, scared, furious, or wildly in love, you may not want to eat.) The ultimate purpose of all these physiological changes is to prepare the body to respond quickly to danger or threat, excitement or opportunity (Frijda, 1988; Lang, 1995).

The adrenal glands produce epinephrine and norepinephrine in response to many challenges in the environment. These hormones will surge if you are laughing at a comedian, playing a video game, worrying about an exam, cheering at a sports event, reacting to an insult, or driving on a hot day in terrible traffic. Epinephrine in particular provides the energy of an emotion—that familiar tingle of excitement. At high levels, it can create the sensation of being "seized" or "flooded" by an emotion that is out of your control. In a sense, you *are* out of control, because people cannot consciously alter their heart rate, blood pressure, and digestive tract. However, you can learn to control your *actions* when you are under the sway of an emotion. And no emotion, no matter how urgent or compelling, lasts forever. As arousal subsides, anger may pale into annoyance, ecstasy into contentment, fear into suspicion, past emotional whirlwinds into calm breezes.

Although epinephrine and norepinephrine are released during many emotional states, emotions also differ from one another physiologically: Fear, disgust, anger, sadness, surprise, and happiness are associated with different patterns of brain activity and autonomic nervous system activity, as measured by heart rate, electrical conductivity of the skin, and finger temperature (Damasio et al., 2000; Levenson, 1992). These distinctive patterns may explain why people all over the world use similar terms to describe basic (primary) emotions, saying they feel "hot and bothered" when they are angry, feel "cold and clammy" when they are afraid, and have a "lump in the throat" when they are sad. These metaphors capture what is going on in their bodies (Oatley & Duncan, 1994).

In sum, the physiology of emotion involves characteristic facial expressions; activity in specific parts of the brain, notably the amygdala and regions of the prefrontal cortex; and sympathetic nervous system activity that prepares the body for action. But these physical changes cannot explain why, of two students about to take an exam, one feels psyched up and the other feels overwhelmed by anxiety. And hormones alone won't tell you whether you are thrilled or frightened, sick or just in love.

Quick Quiz

We hope that a little surge of hormonal energy will help you answer these questions.

1. A three-year-old sees her dad dressed as a gorilla and runs away in fear. What brain structure is probably involved in her emotional reaction?
2. Ana Maria is watching an old Laurel and Hardy film, which makes her chuckle and makes her want to see more funny movies. Which side of her prefrontal cortex is likely to be most active?
3. Casey is watching *Hatchet Murders in the Dorm: Sequel XVII.* What hormones cause his heart to pound and his palms to sweat when the murderer is stalking an unsuspecting victim?

Answers:

1. the amygdala   2. the left   3. epinephrine and norepinephrine

---

Emotion and the Mind

Two friends of ours returned from a mountain-climbing trip to Nepal. One said, "I was ecstatic! The crystal-clear skies, the millions of stars, the friendly people, the majestic mountains, the harmony of the universe!" The other said, "I was miserable! The bedbugs and fleas, the lack of toilets, the yak-butter tea, the awful food, the unforgiving mountains!"

Same trip, two different reactions to it. Why? In the first century C.E., the Stoic philosophers suggested an answer: People do not become angry or sad or ecstatic because of actual events, but because of their explanations of those events. Modern psychologists have verified the Stoics' ideas experimentally and are identifying the cognitive processes involved in emotions.

Many years ago, Stanley Schachter and Jerome Singer (1962) argued that the experience of emotion depends on two factors: *physiological arousal* and a *cognitive interpretation* of that arousal. Your body may be churning away in high gear, but unless you can interpret, explain, and label those changes, you will not feel a true emotion. This idea spurred other investigators to study how emotions are created or influenced by beliefs, perceptions of the situation, expectations, and *attributions*—the explanations that people make of their own and other people's behaviour (see

Chapter 10). Human beings, after all, are the only species that can say, "The more I thought about it, the madder I got." In fact, we often do think ourselves into an emotional state—in this case, anger—and by implication, we can think ourselves out of it.

Psychologists have studied the role of cognitions in all kinds of emotions, from joy to sadness. For example, imagine that you get an A on your psychology mid-term; how will you feel? Or perhaps you get a D on that mid-term; how will you feel then? Most people assume that success brings happiness and failure brings unhappiness, but the emotions you feel will depend more on how you *explain* your grade than on what you actually get. Do you attribute your grade to your own efforts (or lack of them) or to the teacher, fate, or luck? In a series of experiments, students who believed they did well because of their own efforts tended to feel proud, competent, and satisfied. Those who believed they did well because of a lucky fluke or chance tended to feel gratitude, surprise, or guilt ("I don't deserve this"). Those who believed their failures were their own fault tended to feel regretful, guilty, or resigned. And those who blamed others tended to feel angry (Weiner, 1986).

Here is a more surprising example of how thoughts affect emotions. Of two Olympic contenders—one who wins a second-place silver medal and one who wins a third-place bronze

Surprisingly, third place winners tend to be happier about their performance than those who come in second. Certainly, Olympic fencing bronze medalist Jean-Michel Henry of France (left) looks happier than silver medalist Pavel Kolobkov of the Unified Team (right). (Eric Srecki, centre, won the gold for France.)

medal—who will feel happier? Won't it be the silver medalist? Nope. In a study of athletes' reactions to placing second and third in the 1992 Olympics and the 1994 Empire State Games, the bronze medalists were happier than the silver medalists (Medvec, Madey, & Gilovich, 1995). Apparently, the athletes were comparing their performance to "what might have been." The second-place winners, comparing themselves to the gold medalists, were unhappy that they didn't get the gold. But the third-place winners, comparing themselves to those who did worse than they, were happy that they earned a medal at all!

Cognitions and physiology are inextricably linked in the experience of emotion. Thoughts affect emotions, and emotional states influence thoughts. For example, blaming others for your woes can make you feel angry, and brooding and ruminating on your problems and worries can make you anxious or depressed (Mor & Winquist, 2002). But once you are angry or unhappy you may be more inclined to think the worst of other people's motives (Lerner, Goldberg, & Tetlock, 1998).

Some emotions require only minimal or primitive cognitions. A conditioned sentimental response to a patriotic symbol or a warm fuzzy feeling toward a familiar souvenir involves simple,

unconscious reactions (Izard, 1994a; Murphy, Monahan, & Zajonc, 1995). An infant's primitive emotions do not have much mental sophistication: "Hey, I'm mad because no one is feeding me!"

As a child's cerebral cortex matures, however, cognitions, and therefore emotions, become more cognitively complex: "Hey, I'm mad because this situation is entirely wrong-headed and unfair!" Some emotions depend entirely on the maturation of higher cognitive capacities. Shame and guilt, for example, do not occur until a child is two or three years old, because these *self-conscious* emotions require the emergence of a sense of self and the ability to perceive that you have behaved badly or let another person down (Baumeister, Stillwell, & Heatherton, 1994; Tangney et al., 1996).

Today, almost all theories of emotion hold that attributions, beliefs, and the meanings people give to events are essential to the creation of most emotions. But where do these attributions, beliefs, and meanings come from? When people decide that it is shameful for a man to dance on a table with a lampshade on his head, or for a woman to walk down a street with her arms and legs uncovered, where do their ideas about shame originate? If you are a person who loudly curses others when you are angry, where did you learn that cursing is acceptable? To answer these questions, we turn to the third major aspect of emotional experience: the role of culture.

Children need to have a sense of self before they can feel the "moral emotions" of shame, guilt, or remorse.

Get Involved Examing Your Emotions after an Exam

After your next psychology test, write down the reasons you think you got the grade you did. Do you attribute the grade to your own efforts, or perhaps a lack of effort? If you did not do as well as you hoped, do you blame yourself or the teacher? If you did do well, do you take credit, or do you think your success was a lucky fluke? How are these explanations related to your feelings about your grade?

Quick Quiz

How are your thoughts affecting your feelings about this quiz?

1. What are the two factors in Schachter and Singer's view of emotion?
2. Dara and Dinah get B's on their psychology mid-term, but Dara is ecstatic and proud, and Dinah is furious. What expectations and attributions are probably affecting their emotional reactions?
3. At a party, you see a stranger flirting with your date. You are flooded with jealousy. What cognitions might be causing this emotion? *Be specific.* What alternative thoughts might reduce your jealous feelings?

Answers:

1. physiological arousal and a cognitive interpretation of that arousal
2. Dara was probably expecting a lower grade and is attributing her B to her own efforts; Dinah was probably expecting a higher grade and is attributing her B to the instructor's unfairness, bad luck, or other external reasons.
3. Possible thoughts causing jealousy are "My date finds other people more attractive," "That person is trying to steal my date," or "My date's behaviour is humiliating me." But you could be saying, "It's a compliment to me that other people find my date attractive" or "It pleases me that my date is getting such deserved attention."

WHAT'S AHEAD

- Do Germans, Japanese, and Canadians always mean the same thing when they smile at others?
- Why do people show sadness at funerals even when they are not feeling sad?
- Are women really more "emotional" than men?

EMOTION AND CULTURE

A young wife leaves her house one morning to draw water from the local well as her husband watches from the porch. On her way back from the well, a male stranger stops her and asks for some water. She gives him a cupful and then invites him home to dinner. He accepts. The husband, wife, and guest have a pleasant meal together. The husband, in a gesture of hospitality, invites the guest to spend the night—with his wife. The guest accepts. In the morning, the husband leaves early to bring home breakfast. When he returns, he finds his wife again in bed with the visitor.

At what point in this story will the husband feel angry? The answer depends on his culture (Hupka, 1981, 1991). A North American husband would feel rather angry at a wife who had an extramarital affair, and a wife would feel rather angry at being offered to a guest as if she were a lamb chop. But these reactions are not universal. A Pawnee husband of the nineteenth century would be enraged at any man who dared ask his wife for water. An Ammassalik Inuit husband finds it perfectly honourable to offer his wife to a stranger, but only once; he would be angry to find his wife and the guest having a second encounter. And a century ago, a Toda husband in India would not be angry at all because the Todas allowed both husband and wife to take lovers. Both spouses might feel angry, though, if one of them had a *sneaky* affair, without announcing it publicly.

People in most cultures feel angry in response to insult and the violation of social rules. But, as this story shows, they often disagree about what an insult is or what the correct rule should be. In this section, we will explore how culture influences the emotions we feel and the ways in which we express them.

The Varieties of Emotion

Are some emotions specific to particular cultures and not found elsewhere? What does it mean, for example, that some languages have words for subtle emotional states that other languages lack (Mesquita & Frijda, 1992)? The Germans have *schadenfreude*, a feeling of joy at another's misfortune. The Japanese speak of *hagaii*, helpless anguish tinged with frustration. And Tahitians have *mehameha*, a trembling sensation that Tahitians feel when ordinary categories of perception are suspended—at twilight, in the brush, watching fires glow without heat. In the West, an event that cannot be identified is usually greeted with fear. Yet *mehameha* does not describe what Westerners call fear or terror (Levy, 1984).

Do these interesting linguistic differences mean that Germans are more likely than others actually to feel *schadenfreude*, the Japanese to feel *hagaii*, and the Tahitians to feel *mehameha*? Or are they just more willing to give these subtle emotions a single name? Certainly many non-German Westerners feel something like *schadenfreude* at the downfall or humiliation of their political opponents who once defeated them or ex-lovers who once jilted them!

Many psychologists would say that all human beings are capable of feeling the primary, hardwired emotions—the ones that have distinctive physiological hallmarks in the brain, face, and nervous system. But individuals might indeed differ in their abilities to experience secondary emotions, including variations such as *schadenfreude*, *hagaii*, or *mehameha*.

The difference between primary emotions and more complex cultural variations is reflected in language, all over the world. In Chapter 7, we noted that a *prototype* is a typical representative of a class of things. People everywhere consider the primary emotions to be prototypical examples of the concept *emotion*: For example, most people will say that "anger" and "sadness" are more representative of an emotion than "irritability" and "nostalgia" are. Prototypical emotions are reflected in the emotion words that young children learn first:

happy, sad, mad, and *scared.* Interestingly, studies at Brock University with three-year-olds have found that girls at that age are more likely than boys to have an understanding of emotions that goes beyond these prototypes. This was also true for children with better general verbal ability (Bosacki & Moore, 2004). As children develop, they begin to draw emotional distinctions that are less prototypical and more specific to their language and culture, such as *ecstatic, depressed, hostile,* or *anxious* (Hupka, Lenton, & Hutchison, 1999; Russell & Fehr, 1994; Shaver, Wu, & Schwartz, 1992). In this way, they come to experience the nuances of emotional feeling that their cultures emphasize.

Cultural psychologists don't think much of the primary–secondary distinction because, for them, there is *no* aspect of any emotion that is not deeply influenced by culture. Anger may be universal, but the way it is experienced and felt will vary from culture to culture—whether it feels good or bad, useful or destructive. Culture even affects which emotions are defined as basic or "primary." Anger is regarded as a primary emotion by individualistic Western psychologists; but in collectivist cultures, described in Chapter 2, shame and loss of face are more central emotions (Kitayama & Markus, 1994). And on the tiny Micronesian atoll of Ifaluk, everyone would say that *fago* is the most fundamental emotion. *Fago*, translated as "compassion/love/sadness," reflects the sad feeling one has when a loved one is absent or in need, and the pleasurable sense of compassion in being able to care and help (Lutz, 1988).

Thinking Critically About "Basic" Emotions

This father is clearly proud of his family, but pride is not on most lists of primary emotions—although it is probably a universal emotional feeling. Should it be considered a "primary" emotion or a variation of happiness?

What, then, would theories of primary emotions look like from a non-Western perspective? They might start with shame and *fago*, which are just blips on the radar screen of Western emotion research. And they might also include empathy, pride, envy, greed, and love, which are felt by human beings everywhere yet are omitted from most lists of "universals" because they don't seem to have corresponding facial expressions (Zajonc, 2003).

Both sides in this debate agree that cultures determine much of what people feel emotional *about*. As we saw, disgust is universal, but the *content* of what produces disgust changes as an infant matures, and it varies across cultures. People in some cultures learn to become disgusted by bugs (which other people find beautiful or tasty), unfamiliar sexual practices, dirt, death, "contamination" by a handshake with a stranger, or particular foods (e.g., meat if they are vegetarian, or pork if they are Muslims or Orthodox Jews). Most people feel disgust when their culture's moral rules are broken (Rozin, Lowery, & Ebert, 1994).

Communicating Emotions

Suppose that someone who was dear to you died. Would you cry, and if so, would you do it alone or in public? Would you wail and tear your clothes, or try to keep your feelings to yourself? Your answer will depend in part on your culture's **display rules** for emotion (Ekman et al., 1987; Gross, 1998). In some cultures, grief is expressed by weeping; in others, by tearless resignation; and

in still others by dance, drink, and song. Once you feel an emotion, how you express it is rarely a matter of "I say what I feel." You may be obliged to disguise what you feel. You may wish you could feel what you say.

Even the smile, which seems a straightforward signal of friendliness, has many meanings and uses that are not universal. Americans smile more frequently than Germans, not because Americans are inherently friendlier but because they differ in their notions of when a smile is appropriate. After a German–American business meeting, Americans often complain that the Germans were cold and aloof, and the Germans often complain that the Americans were excessively cheerful, hiding their real feelings under the mask of a smile (Hall & Hall, 1990). The Japanese smile even more than Americans, to disguise embarrassment, anger, or other negative emotions whose public display is considered rude and incorrect. Americans also seem to be more expressive than Canadians. When York University's Peter Waxer studied the behaviour of audience members in Canadian and American TV game shows, he found that American women were more expressive with their hands than were Canadian women, and that American men smiled more than did Canadian men (Waxer, 1985).

Display rules also govern *body language*, nonverbal signals of body movement, posture, gesture, and gaze (Birdwhistell, 1970). Most aspects of body language are specific to particular languages and cultures, which makes even the simplest gesture subject to misunderstanding and

display rules Social and cultural rules that regulate when, how, and where a person may express (or suppress) emotions.

Around the world, the cultural rules for expressing emotions (or suppressing them) differ. The display rule for a formal Japanese wedding portrait is "no direct expressions of emotion"—but not every member of this family has learned that rule yet.

offence. The sign of the University of Texas football team, the Longhorns, is to extend the index finger and the pinkie. Be careful where you make this gesture! In Italy and other parts of Europe, it means you're saying a man's wife has been unfaithful to him—a serious insult.

When people are talking to each other, a mismatch of body languages will make their conversation feel "out of sync"; they may feel as confused and emotionally upset as if they had had a verbal misunderstanding. In contrast, when people's gestures and body language are in synchrony, they will feel greater rapport and emotional harmony (see Figure 13.2). The ability to synchronize body language is crucial to smooth interaction between people (Anderson, Keltner, & John, 2003; Bernieri et al., 1996; Hatfield, Cacioppo, & Rapson, 1994). When people feel uncomfortable with someone from another culture, the reason may simply be that their body languages are out of sync.

Display rules tell us not only what to do when we *are* feeling an emotion, but also how and when to show an emotion we do *not* feel. Most people are expected to demonstrate sadness at funerals, happiness at weddings, and affection toward relatives. What if we don't actually feel sad, happy, or affectionate? Acting out an emotion we do not really feel because we believe it is socially appropriate is called **emotion work**. It is part of our efforts to regulate our emotions when we are with others (Gross, 1998). Sometimes emotion work is a job requirement: Flight attendants, waiters, and customer-service representatives must "put on a happy face" to convey cheerfulness, even if they are privately angry about a rude or drunken

emotion work Expression of an emotion, often because of a role requirement, that a person does not really feel.

customer. And bill collectors must put on a stern face to convey threat, even if they feel sorry for the person they are collecting money from (Hochschild, 1983).

Gender and Emotion

"Women are too emotional," men often complain. "Men are too uptight," women often reply. This is one of the oldest gender stereotypes (Plant et al., 2000). But what does "too emotional" mean? We need to define our terms and examine our assumptions.

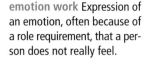
Thinking Critically About Gender Differences in Emotionality

Although women are more likely than men to suffer from the mood disorder of severe depression (see Chapter 11), there is little evidence that one sex feels any of the everyday emotions more often than the other, whether the emotion is anger, worry, embarrassment, anxiety, love, or grief (Fischer et al., 1993; Kring & Gordon, 1998; Oatley & Duncan, 1994). The major difference between the sexes has less to do with whether they *feel* emotions than with how and when their emotions are *expressed*. The expression of emotions is profoundly affected by gender roles, the requirements of the situation, and culture.

In North America, gender roles encourage women to be more emotionally expressive than men. Women smile more than men do, gaze at their listeners more, have more emotionally expressive faces, use more expressive hand and body movements, and touch other people more (DePaulo, 1992; Kring & Gordon, 1998). Women also smile more than men to pacify others, convey deference to someone of higher status, or smooth

FIGURE 13.2 The Contagion of Emotion

These volunteers, videotaped in a study of conversational synchrony, are obviously "in sync" with one another, even though they have just met. The degree to which two people's gestures and expressions are synchronized affects the rapport they feel with one another. Such synchrony can also create a "contagion" of moods (Bernieri et al., 1991).

"It's truly remarkable, Louis, thirty-seven years next Tuesday and never a cross word between us."

over conflicts (LaFrance, Hecht, & Paluck, 2003; Shields, 2002). In fact, women who don't smile when others expect them to are often disliked, even if they are actually smiling as often as men would.

Women also talk about their emotions more than men do. They are far more likely to cry, and to acknowledge emotions that reveal vulnerability and weakness, such as "hurt feelings," fear, sadness, loneliness, shame, and guilt (Grossman & Wood, 1993; Timmers, Fischer, & Manstead, 1998). In contrast, most North American men express only one emotion more freely than women: anger toward strangers, especially other men. Otherwise, men are expected to control and mask negative feelings. When they are worried or afraid, they are more likely than women to use vague terms, saying that they feel moody, frustrated, or "on edge" (Fehr et al., 1999; Smith & Reise, 1998).

However, the influence of a particular situation often overrides gender rules (LaFrance, Hecht, & Paluck, 2003; Snodgrass, 1992). You won't find many gender differences in emotional expressiveness at a hockey game or the World Series—everyone gets to cheer and boo! Another important situational constraint on emotional expression is the status of the participants. A man is as likely as a woman to control his temper when the target of anger is someone with higher status or power; few people, no matter how angry, will readily sound off at a professor, police officer, or employer. And the sexes do similar "emotion work" when the situation or job requires it. A male flight attendant has to smile as much with passengers as a female one does, and a female FBI agent has to be as emotionally strong and controlled as a male agent does.

Moreover, North American gender differences are by no means universal. Italian, French, Spanish, and Middle Eastern men can have entire conversations using highly expressive hand gestures and facial expressions, and you won't find sex differences in nonverbal expressiveness in their cultures. In contrast, in Asian cultures, both sexes are taught to control emotional expression (Matsumoto, 1996; Mesquita & Frijda, 1992). Cultures also determine which emotions men and women express most freely. Israeli and Italian men are more likely than women to mask feelings of sadness, but British, Spanish, Swiss, and German men are more likely than their female counterparts to *express* this emotion (Wallbott, Ricci-Bitti, & Bänninger-Huber, 1986).

In sum, the answer to "Which sex is more emotional?" is this: sometimes men, sometimes women, and sometimes neither, depending on the circumstances and their culture.

The emotion "tree," as we have seen, can take many shapes, depending on physiology, cognitive processes, and cultural rules. Next we will see how these three factors can help us understand those difficult situations in which stress and negative emotions threaten to overwhelm us and even to make us ill.

Both sexes feel emotionally attached to friends, but often they express their affections differently. From childhood on, girls tend to prefer "face to face" friendships, based on shared feelings; boys tend to prefer "side by side" friendships, based on shared activities.

WHAT'S AHEAD

- Why are you more likely to get a cold when you're "stressed out"?
- Which stressors pose the greatest hazard to your health?
- Why do optimists tend to live longer than pessimists?
- When is a sense of control good for you, and when is it not?

general adaptation syndrome According to Hans Selye, a series of physiological responses to stressors that occur in three phases: alarm, resistance, and exhaustion.

Do you see work as a bottomless pit of obligations or as a tidy stack of achievements? The answer affects how "stressed" you are.

THE NATURE OF STRESS

No life is entirely free of stress. We are all vulnerable to *stressors*—conflicts that annoy us, pressures that fatigue us, and tragedies and losses that temporarily shatter our lives. The question that most fascinates everyone is whether these events are linked to illness, and whether, by controlling our emotional reactions to events, we can improve our health and well-being.

Stress and the Body

The modern era of stress research began in 1956, when the Canadian physician Hans Selye (1907–1982) published *The Stress of Life*. Environmental stressors such as heat, cold, pain, toxins, and danger, Selye wrote, disrupt the body's equilibrium. The body then mobilizes its resources to fight off these stressors and restore normal functioning.

Selye's Theory Selye described the body's response to external stressors of all kinds as a **general adaptation syndrome**, physiological reactions that occur in three phases:

1 *The alarm phase,* in which the body mobilizes the sympathetic nervous system to meet the immediate threat—from taking a test you haven't studied for to running from a rabid dog. As we saw earlier, the release of adrenal hormones, epinephrine and norepinephrine, occurs with any intense emotion and produces a boost in energy, tense muscles, reduced sensitivity to pain, the shutting down of digestion (so that blood will flow more efficiently to the brain, muscles, and skin), and a rise in blood pressure. Decades earlier, psychologist Walter Cannon (1929) called this reaction the "fight or flight" response, a term still popularly used.

Stress hormones elevated

Blood flow increases

Heart rate speeds up

Digestion slows

Muscles tense

2   *The resistance phase,* in which your body attempts to resist or cope with a persistent stressor that cannot be avoided. During this phase, the physiological responses of the alarm phase continue, but these very responses make the body more vulnerable to *other* stressors. For example, when your body has mobilized to fight off the flu, you may find you are more easily annoyed by minor frustrations. In most cases, the body will eventually adapt to the stressor and return to normal.

3   *The exhaustion phase,* in which persistent stress depletes the body of energy and therefore increases vulnerability to physical problems and eventually illness. The same reactions that allow the body to respond effectively in the alarm and resistance phases are unhealthy as long-range responses. Tense muscles can cause headache and neck pain. Increased blood pressure can become chronic hypertension. If normal digestive processes are interrupted or shut down for too long, digestive disorders may result.

Selye did not believe that people should aim for a stress-free life. Some stress, he said, is positive and productive, even if it also requires the body to produce short-term energy: competing in an athletic event, falling in love, working hard on a project you enjoy. And some negative stress is simply unavoidable; it's called life!

Current Approaches   Many of Selye's ideas about the general adaptation syndrome proved to be correct. Some were particularly insightful, such as his observation that the same biological changes that are adaptive in the short run, because they permit the body to respond quickly to danger, can become hazardous in the long run. Modern researchers are learning exactly how this happens.

When you are under stress, your brain's hypothalamus sends messages to the endocrine glands along two major pathways. One, as Selye observed, activates the sympathetic division of the autonomic nervous system for "fight or flight." In addition, we now know, the hypothalamus releases chemical messengers that spur the adrenal cortex to secrete *cortisol* and other hormones that elevate blood sugar and protect the body's tissues from inflammation in case of injury (McEwen, 1998). The result is increased energy, which is crucial for short-term responses to stress. But if cortisol and other stress hormones stay high too long, they can be harmful, contributing to hypertension, other physical disorders, and possibly emotional problems.

Selye thought that all stressors affect the body in roughly the same ways, but we now know that different stressors may evoke somewhat different responses. Also, people vary widely in their responses to a stressor, depending on their learning history, gender, pre-existing medical conditions, and genetic predispositions for high blood pressure, obesity, diabetes, or other problems (McEwen, 2000; Taylor et al., 2000b). For example, most people

Alas, the same stress hormones that help in the short run can have unwanted long-term consequences.

The immune system consists of fighter cells that look more fantastical than any alien creature Hollywood could design. This one is about to engulf and destroy a cigarette-shaped parasite that causes a tropical disease.

react to the stress of public speaking with a temporary increase in cortisol. With time and practice, they adapt and calm down, and cortisol declines. However, a small percentage of people do not adapt; in fact, their cortisol levels continue to increase (Kirschbaum, Prussner, & Stone, 1995).

Of the many bodily systems affected by stress, one of the most intensively studied has been the immune system, which enables the body to fight disease and infection. The white blood cells of the immune system are designed to recognize foreign substances (*antigens*), such as flu viruses, bacteria, and tumour cells, and then destroy or deactivate them. When an antigen invades the body, the immune system deploys different kinds of white blood cells as weapons, depending on the nature of the enemy. Prolonged stress can suppress some or many of these white blood cells. In one study of medical students who had the herpes virus, herpes outbreaks were more likely to occur when the students were feeling lonely or were under pressure from exams. Loneliness and tension apparently suppressed the immune system's capabilities, permitting the existing herpes virus to erupt (Glaser et al., 1985).

Stressors Affecting the Body Some kinds of stressors are especially likely to affect the immune system, thereby increasing the risk of illness or poor health:

1 *Noise.* Loud noise becomes stressful (apart from what it does to your hearing) when it goes on day in and day out without relief. Children who live or go to school near noisy airports have higher blood pressure and higher levels of stress hormones, are more distractible, and have more learning and attention difficulties than do children in quieter environments (Cohen et al., 1980; Evans, Bullinger, & Hygge, 1998). In adults, constant loud noise contributes to cardiovascular problems, irritability, fatigue, and aggressiveness, probably because of overstimulation of the sympathetic nervous system (Staples, 1996).

2 *Bereavement and loss.* In the two years following bereavement, widowed people, especially men, are more susceptible to illness and their mortality rate is higher than would otherwise be expected (Stroebe, Stroebe, & Schut, 2001). Bereaved and divorced people may be vulnerable in part because, feeling unhappy, they don't sleep well, stop eating properly, smoke more, and take more drugs. But broken attachments also seem to affect the body at a cellular level, producing cardiovascular changes, fewer white blood cells, and other abnormal responses of the immune system (Stroebe et al., 1996).

3 *Work-related problems.* Because work is central in most people's lives, the effects of unemployment or of a chronically stressful work environment can be more severe than other kinds of stressors. A Swedish study found that people who reported a history of severe workplace problems over a decade had 5.5 times the risk of developing colon or rectal cancers, even when diet and other factors linked to these malignancies were taken into account (Courtney et al., 1993).

Work-related stress can also increase a person's vulnerability to a more mundane illness—the common cold. Heroic volunteers in the war against winter colds were given either ordinary nose drops or nose drops containing a cold virus. Everyone was then quarantined for five days. The people most likely to get a cold's miserable symptoms were those who had been underemployed or unemployed for at least a month (see Figure 13.3). The longer the work problems had lasted, the greater the likelihood of illness (Cohen et al., 1998).

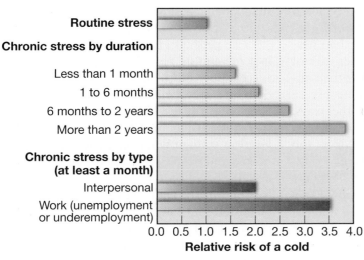

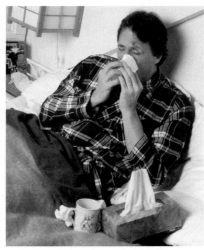

FIGURE 13.3 Stress and the Common Cold

Chronic stress lasting a month or more boosts the risk of catching a cold. The risk is increased among people undergoing problems with their friends or loved ones, and is highest among people who are out of work (Cohen et al., 1998).

4 *Poverty and powerlessness.* People at the lower rungs of the socioeconomic ladder have worse health and higher mortality rates for almost every disease and medical condition than do those at the top (Gallo & Matthews, 2003). In Canada, poverty disproportionately affects single-parent families (especially those headed by women), families on social assistance, and urban Aboriginal families (Anand et al., 2001; McIntyre et al., 2000). Children may be the most vulnerable to the chronic stress associated with poverty. In 1996, one in five children (under the age of 18) in Canada lived in poverty, a 28 percent increase over the 1989 poverty rate (Canadian Council on Social Development, 2001; Health Canada, 1999; McClelland, 2001).

Before you try to persuade your instructors that the stress of chronic studying is bad for your health, consider this mystery: None of the chronic stressors we just discussed leads in a direct, simple way to illness or affects everyone in the same way. Some people exposed to a flu virus are sick all winter; others don't even get the sniffles. Some people in high-pressure careers wind up with heart disease; others work just as hard but remain healthy. Why?

Some people have particular physiological vulnerabilities to stress. But stress, like emotion, is also greatly affected by how people think about their experiences and what they do when they feel upset.

Stress and the Mind

Some people manufacture their own misery. Send them to a beach for a week to escape the pressures of civilization, and they take along a suitcase full of worries and irritations. Others stay serene in the midst of chaos and conflict; they seem to carry along their own inner tranquilizer. These two kinds of people are distinguished by how they explain events and by the degree of control they feel they have over what happens to them.

Optimism and Pessimism When something bad happens to you, what is your first reaction? Do you tell yourself that you will somehow come through it okay, or do you gloomily mutter, "More proof that if something can go wrong for me, it will"?

These responses to bad events reflect *optimistic* and *pessimistic explanatory styles*, and as far as health is concerned, optimism—the general expectation that, overall, things will go well in spite of the occasional setback—is a lot better for you (Carver & Scheier, 1999; Peterson, 2000). Pessimists don't expect that anything will ever go right, and that attitude is associated with lower achievement, more illness, and slower recovery from setbacks.

If you are a pessimist, you will probably protest that optimism is just a *result*, not a cause, of good health or good fortune; it's easy to think positively when you feel good! But optimism actually seems to produce good health and even prolong life, whereas the "catastrophizing" style of pessimists is associated with untimely death (Maruta et al., 2000; Peterson et al., 1998).

Optimists may have better health than pessimists in part because they take better care of themselves when they get sick, whether their ailment is a simple cold or a life-threatening disease like AIDS. And they also cope better in other ways, which we will be discussing shortly. Pessimists often do self-destructive things: They drink too much, smoke, fail to wear seat belts, drive too fast, and refuse to take medication for illness. This may be why pessimists, especially men, are more likely than optimists to die untimely deaths as a result of accidents or violence (Peterson et al., 1998). But optimism is also directly associated with better immune function, such as a rise in the white blood cells that fight infection (Räikkönen et al., 1999; Segerstrom et al., 1998).

Pessimists, naturally, accuse optimists of being unrealistic. Yet health and well-being often depend on having some "positive illusions" about yourself and your circumstances (Taylor et al., 2000a). Positive illusions are not the same as denial. Optimists do not deny their problems or avoid facing bad news. On the contrary, they are more likely than pessimists to be active problem solvers, get support from friends, and seek information that can help them (Aspinwall & Taylor, 1997; Brissette, Scheier, & Carver, 2002). They do not give up at the first sign of a setback or escape into wishful thinking. They keep their senses of humour, plan for the future, and reinterpret the

locus of control A general expectation about whether the results of your actions are under your own control (internal locus) or beyond your control (external locus).

situation in a positive light (Aspinwall & Brunhart, 1996; Chang, 1998).

Can pessimists be "cured" of their gloomy outlook? Optimists, naturally, think so! One program successfully "inoculated" elementary-school children against becoming pessimistic and depressed in adolescence by teaching them optimistic explanatory styles (Gillham et al., 1995). Another intervention studied what happened when healthy people and people with a neuromuscular disease either focused on their burdens or counted their blessings. Those who focused on what they had to be grateful for had higher well-being and fewer physical symptoms (Emmons & McCullough, 2003). Another method worked for psychologist Rachel Hare-Mustin, whose mother cured her budding childhood pessimism with humour. "Nobody likes me," Rachel lamented. "Don't say that," her mother said. "Everybody hasn't met you yet."

The Sense of Control Optimism is related to another important cognitive ingredient in health: having an internal locus of control (Chang, 1998; Marshall et al., 1994). **Locus of control** refers to your general expectation about whether you can control the things that happen to you (Rotter, 1990). People who have an *internal locus of control* ("internals") tend to believe that they are responsible for what happens to them. Those who have an *external locus of control* ("externals") tend to believe that their lives are controlled by luck, fate, or other people. Having an internal locus of control is associated with good health, academic achievement, political activism, and emotional well-being (Lang & Heckhausen, 2001; Strickland, 1989).

Most people can tolerate all kinds of stressors if they feel able to predict or control them. The crowd you choose to join for a football game is not as stressful as the crowd you cannot escape on a busy street; the music you choose to play at ear-splitting volume is not as stressful as the rotten music you are forced to listen to when you are put on hold on the phone. People who have the greatest control over their work pace and activities—that is, executives and managers—have fewer illnesses and stress symptoms than do employees who have little control, who feel trapped doing repetitive tasks, and who have a low chance of promotion (Karasek & Theorell, 1990). The greatest threat to health and well-being occurs when you feel caught in a situation you cannot escape, one that goes on without a foreseeable end. Conversely, feelings of control can reduce or even eliminate the link between stressors

and illness that we described earlier. People who have an internal locus of control are better able than externals to resist infection by cold viruses and even the health-impairing effects of poverty and discrimination (Cohen, Tyrrell, & Smith, 1993; Krieger & Sidney, 1996; Lachman & Weaver, 1998).

Feeling in control affects the immune system, which may be why it helps to speed up recovery from surgery and some diseases (Shapiro, Schwartz, & Astin, 1996; E. Skinner, 1996). As with optimism, feeling in control makes people more likely to take action to improve their health when necessary. In a group of patients recovering from heart attacks, for example, those who believed the heart attack occurred because they smoked, didn't exercise, or had a stressful job were more likely to change their bad habits and recover more quickly. In contrast, those who thought their illness was due to bad luck or fate—factors outside their control—were less likely to generate plans for recovery and more likely to resume their old unhealthy habits (Affleck et al., 1987; Ewart, 1995).

The Limits of Control Overall, then, a sense of control is a good thing. But the question must always be asked: control over what? It is surely not beneficial for people to believe they can control absolutely every aspect of their lives; some things, such as death, taxes, or being a random victim of a crime, are out of anyone's control. Health and well-being are not enhanced by self-blame ("Whatever goes wrong with my health is my fault") or the belief that all disease can be prevented by doing the right thing ("If I just take vitamins and work out daily, I'll never get sick").

Thinking Critically About the Benefits of "Control"

Eastern and Western cultures tend to hold different attitudes about the ability to and desirability of controlling one's own life. In general, Western cultures celebrate **primary control**, in which people try to influence events by trying to exert control over them: If you are in a bad situation, you are supposed to change it, fix it, or fight it. The Eastern approach emphasizes **secondary control**, in which people try to accommodate to a bad situation by changing their own aspirations or desires: If you have a problem, you are supposed to live with it or act in spite of it (Azuma, 1984; Rothbaum, Weisz, & Snyder, 1982). North American and Japanese horror films illustrate this difference. In North American horror films, the goal is to exorcise the demon, de-haunt the house, exterminate the ghost, and defeat the evil spirits. In Japanese horror films, the ghosts and demons are scary, but usually they are . . . just there. The humans have to learn to live with them.

People who are ill or under stress can reap the benefits of both Western and Eastern forms of control by avoiding either–or thinking: for example, by taking responsibility for future actions while not blaming themselves unduly for past ones. Among women who are recovering from sexual assault or coping with cancer, for example, adjustment is related to a woman's belief that she is not to blame for being raped or for getting sick but that she *is* in charge of taking care of herself from now on (Frazier, 2003; Taylor, Lichtman, & Wood, 1984). "I felt that I had lost control of my body somehow," said one cancer survivor, "and the way for me to get back some control was to find out as much as I could." This way of

primary control An effort to modify reality by changing other people, the situation, or events; a "fighting back" philosophy.

secondary control An effort to accept reality by changing your own attitudes, goals, or emotions; a "learn to live with it" philosophy.

Who has more "stress"—corporate managers in highly competitive jobs or assembly-line workers in routine and predictable jobs? Research finds that people who are bossed suffer more from job stress than their bosses do, especially if the employees cannot control many aspects of their work (Karasek & Theorell, 1990).

thinking allows a person to avoid guilt and self-blame while retaining a sense of self-efficacy—the belief that you are basically in charge of your own life and can take steps to get better. Many problems require us to decide what we can change and to accept what we cannot; perhaps the secret of healthy control lies in knowing the difference.

Quick Quiz

We hope these questions are not sources of stress for you.

1. Steve is unexpectedly called on in class to discuss a question. He hasn't the faintest idea of the answer, and he feels his heart start to pound and his palms to sweat. According to Selye, Steve is in the _____ phase of his stress response.

2. Maria has worked as a file clerk for 17 years, in a job that is closely supervised and boring. Her boss must make many rapid-fire decisions every day and is always complaining of the pressures of responsibility. Which of them probably has the more stressful job? (a) Maria, (b) the boss, (c) both equally, (d) neither job is stressful. (Bonus: Why?)

3. "I'll never find anyone else to love because I'm not good-looking; that one romance was a fluke" illustrates a(n) _____ explanatory style.

4. On television, a self-described health expert explains that "no one gets sick if they don't want to be sick," because we can all control our bodies. As a critical thinker, how should you assess this claim?

Answers:

1. alarm
2. a, because Maria has less control than her boss does over every aspect of her work
3. pessimistic
4. Skeptically. First, you would want to define your terms: What does "control" mean, and what kind of control is the supposed expert referring to? People can control some things, such as how much they exercise and whether they smoke, and they can control some aspects of treatment once they become ill; but they cannot control everything that happens to them. Second, you would examine the assumption that control is always a good thing; the belief that we have total control over our lives could lead to depression and unwarranted self-blame when illness strikes.

WHAT'S AHEAD

- Why are people who are chronically angry and mistrustful their own worst enemy?
- Which disease is depression most clearly linked to?
- Can revealing your unresolved emotions help your health?

STRESS AND EMOTION

Perhaps you have heard people say things like "She was so depressed, it's no wonder she got cancer" or "He's always so angry, he's going to give himself a heart attack one day." Are negative emotions—especially anger and depression—hazardous to health?

There is good evidence that once a person already has a virus or medical condition, or is living in a chronically stressful situation, negative emotions can indeed increase the risk of illness and affect the course of recovery. Feeling anxious, helpless, and depressed, for example, can delay the healing of wounds after surgery, whereas feeling hopeful can significantly speed healing (Kiecolt-Glaser et al., 1998). People who become depressed after a heart attack are significantly more likely to die from cardiac causes in the succeeding year, even controlling for severity of the disease and other risk factors (Frasure-Smith et al., 1999). And a major factor that increases the risk of illness for people living in poverty, along with having an external locus of control, is chronic anger and other negative emotions (Gallo & Matthews, 2003).

But can negative emotions, all on their own, cause illness?

Hostility and Depression

One of the first modern efforts to link emotions and illness was research in the 1970s on the "Type A personality," a set of qualities thought to be associated with heart disease (Friedman &

Rosenman, 1974). Type A people are ambitious, have a sense of time urgency, are irritable, respond physiologically to threat and challenge very quickly, and are impatient with anyone who gets in their way. Type B people are calmer and less intense. It seemed logical that Type A's would be at greater risk of heart trouble than Type B's.

It turned out, however, that being highly reactive to stress and challenge is not in itself a risk factor in heart disease; Type A people often enjoy, indeed thrive on having, a difficult workload (Krantz & Manuck, 1984). The next round of research uncovered what it was about the behaviour of some Type A's that *is* dangerous to health: hostility. By "hostility" we do not mean the irritability or anger that everyone feels on occasion. The toxic kind is *cynical* or *antagonistic hostility*, which characterizes people who are mistrustful of others and ready to provoke mean, furious arguments (Marshall et al., 1994; T. Miller et al., 1996).

In a study of male physicians who had been interviewed as medical students 25 years earlier, those who were chronically angry and resentful were five times as likely as nonhostile men to get heart disease, even when other risk factors, such as smoking and a poor diet, were taken into account (Ewart & Kolodner, 1994; Williams, Barefoot, & Shekelle, 1985; see Figure 13.4). These findings have been repeated in other large-scale studies, with blacks and whites, and with women as well as men (Williams et al., 2000). Proneness to anger is a significant risk factor, all on its own, for impairments of the immune system, elevated blood pressure, and heart disease.

Can depression also lead to illness? Several large-scale studies have found that people who

FIGURE 13.4 Hostility and Heart Disease

Anger is more hazardous to health than a heavy workload. Men who had the highest hostility scores as young medical students were the most likely to have coronary heart disease 25 years later (Williams, Barefoot, & Shekelle, 1985).

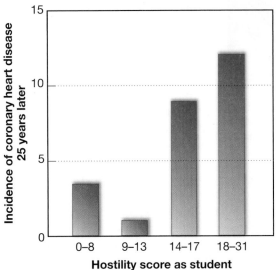

are clinically depressed are at considerably greater risk of heart attack, cardiovascular disease, and early death than nondepressed people are. This finding, too, has held up even after controlling for high blood pressure, smoking, obesity, amount of exercise, and family history of heart disease (Ford et al., 1998; Schulz et al., 2000). Other research, however, has failed to find a link between depression and heart disease or between depression and other causes of death, such as cancer or AIDS (Wulsin, Vaillant, & Wells, 1999).

All we can say at present, therefore, is that chronic depression seems to be a significant risk factor for heart disease, though probably not in a direct way. Depressed people may simply fail to take care of themselves, reducing the body's ability to recover (Schulz et al., 2000).

Emotional Inhibition and Expression

You might assume by now that the safest thing to do when you feel angry, depressed, or worried

A classic Type A personality.

Everyone has secrets and private moments of sad reflection. But when you feel sad or fearful for too long, keeping your feelings to yourself may increase your stress.

is to try to suppress the feeling. But anyone who has tried to banish an unwelcome thought, bitter memory, or pangs of longing for an ex-lover knows how hard it can be to do this. When you are trying to avoid a thought, you are in fact processing the thought more frequently—rehearsing it. That is why, when you are obsessed with someone you were once romantically involved with, trying not to think of the person actually prolongs your emotional responsiveness to him or her (Wegner & Gold, 1995).

Most people try to suppress their feelings some of the time, but some people, "suppressors," do so almost all of the time; they have a personality trait called *emotional inhibition* (Basic Behavioral Science Task Force, 1996). Suppressors tend to deny feelings of anxiety, anger, or fear and pretend that everything is fine. Yet when they are in stressful or emotion-producing situations, their physiological responses, such as heart rate and blood pressure, rise sharply. Suppressors are at greater risk of becoming ill than people who can acknowledge their fears (Cohen & Herbert, 1996). Why?

One answer is that the prolonged inhibition of thoughts and emotions requires physical effort that is stressful to the body. The inability or unwillingness to confide important events also seems to affect the immune system. People who are able to express matters of great emotional importance show elevated levels of disease-fighting white blood cells, whereas people who suppress such feelings tend to have decreased levels (Petrie, Booth, & Pennebaker, 1998).

The Benefits of Confession Given the findings on the harmful effects of *feeling* negative emotions and also of *suppressing* them, what is a person supposed to do with them? Occasional feelings of anger, anxiety, and sadness are, of course, inevitable. It is only when people hold on to them too long, rehearsing them and brooding about them, that they can become harmful.

One way to let them go comes from research on the benefits of confession: divulging private thoughts and feelings that make you ashamed or depressed (Pennebaker, 1997). The cause of such feelings can be transitions that are normal but stressful, such as starting college, or painful secrets. A group of college students were asked to write about either a personal, traumatic experience or a neutral topic for 20 minutes a day for four days. Those who were asked to reveal their "deepest thoughts and feelings" about a traumatic event all had something to talk about. Many told stories of sexual coercion, physical beatings, humiliation, or parental abandonment. Yet most had never discussed these experiences with anyone. The researchers collected data on the students' physical symptoms, white blood cell counts, emotions, and visits to the health centre. On every measure, the students who wrote about traumatic experiences were better off than those who did not (Pennebaker, Kiecolt-Glaser, & Glaser, 1988).

Get Involved   True Confessions

To see whether the research on the benefits of confession will benefit you, take a moment to jot down your "deepest thoughts and feelings" about being in college, your past, a secret, your future . . . anything you have never told anyone. Do this again tomorrow, and again for a few days in a row. Write down your feelings after writing, too. Are you upset, troubled, sad, or relieved? Does your account change over time? Research suggests that if you do this exercise now, you may have fewer colds, headaches, and trips to the doctor next year (Pennebaker, Colder, & Sharp, 1990).

Of course, confession can make you feel worse if you reveal your secrets to a confidant who is judgmental, is unable to help, or betrays your confidence (Kelly, 1999). Moreover, confession's benefits occur only when the revelation produces insight and understanding, thereby ending the stressful repetition of obsessive thoughts and unresolved feelings (Kennedy-Moore & Watson, 2001; Lepore, Ragan, & Jones, 2000). One young woman, who had been molested at the age of 9 by a boy a year older, at first wrote about her feelings of embarrassment and guilt. By the third day, she was writing about how angry she felt at the boy. By the last day, she had begun to see the whole event differently; he was a child too, after all. When the study was over, she said, "Before, when I thought about it, I'd lie to myself. . . . Now, I don't feel like I even have to think about it because I got it off my chest. I finally admitted that it happened."

The Benefits of Letting Grievances Go Another important way of letting go of negative emotions is to give up the thoughts that produce grudges and replace them with a different perspective. In recent years, there has been a surge of research not only on anger but on anger's antidote: forgiveness. When people rehearse their grievances and hold unforgiving grudges, their blood pressure, heart rate, and skin conductance rise (see Figure 13.5). Forgiving thoughts (as in the example above—"he was a child too") reduce these signs of physiological arousal and restore feelings of control (Witvliet, Ludwig, & Vander Laan, 2001). Forgiveness, like confession when it works, helps people see events in a new light. It promotes empathy, the ability to see the situation from another person's perspective. It strengthens and repairs relationships (Karremans et al., 2003). Forgiveness does *not* mean that the offended person denies, ignores, or excuses the offence, which might be serious. It does mean that the victim is able, finally, to come to terms with the injustice and let go of obsessive feelings of hurt, rage, and vengefulness. As the Chinese proverb says, "He who pursues revenge should dig two graves."

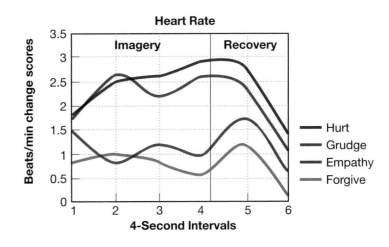

FIGURE 13.5 Heartfelt Forgiveness

Participants in this study were asked to think of someone who they felt had offended or hurt them. Then they were asked to imagine unforgiving reactions (rehearsing the hurt and harbouring a grudge) and forgiving reactions (feeling empathy, forgiving). People's heart rates increased much more sharply, and took longer to return to normal, when their thoughts were unforgiving (Witvliet, Ludwig, & Vander Laan, 2001).

In sum, health psychology suggests a middle path between "keeping your cool" and "getting hot and bothered": learning to identify, express, and deal with negative emotions, without ruminating on them and letting them erode your relationships (Richards & Gross, 2000). If anger, anxiety, and sadness are getting the better of you, try the optimist's solution, and focus on the reasons in your life for positive emotions such as love, gratitude, and joy (Fredrickson et al., 2003).

Quick Quiz

You'll reduce stress if you can answer these fons.

1. Which aspect of Type A behaviour is most hazardous to the heart? (a) working hard, (b) being in a hurry, (c) cynical hostility, (d) high physical reactivity to work, (e) general grumpiness
2. Alexa has many worries about being in college, but she is afraid to tell anyone. What might be the healthiest solution for her? (a) trying not to think about her problems, (b) writing down her feelings in a diary, (c) talking frequently to strangers who won't judge her, (d) expressing her fears whenever she feels them

Answers:

1. c   2. b

WHAT'S AHEAD

- When you're feeling overwhelmed, what are some ways to calm yourself?
- Why is it important to move beyond the emotions caused by a problem and deal with the problem itself?
- How can you learn to rethink your problems?
- When do friends reduce your stress, and when do they just make matters worse?

EMOTIONS, STRESS, AND HEALTH: HOW TO COPE

We have noted that most people who are under stress, even those living in difficult situations, do not become ill. In addition to feeling optimistic and in control, and not wallowing around in negative emotions, how do they manage to cope? The word *cope* implies that people are behaving in ways that barely help them keep their heads above water ("How are you doing?" "Oh, I'm coping"). But some people cope in ways that not only help them *survive* adversity but help them *thrive*, by learning from their experiences and coming out stronger because of them (see Figure 13.6).

Cooling Off

The most immediate way to cope with the physiological tension of stress and negative emotions is to calm down: to take time out and reduce the body's physical arousal through meditation or relaxation. For example, *progressive relaxation* training—learning to alternately tense and relax the muscles, from toes to head, and to meditate by clearing your mind—lowers blood pressure, stress hormones, and feelings of anger or anxiety, and improves immune function (Scheufele, 2000).

Another effective buffer between stressors and illness is exercise. People who are physically fit have fewer health problems than people who are less fit even when they are under the same pressures. They also show lower physiological arousal to stressors (see Figure 13.7). The more that people exercise, the less anxious, depressed, and irritable they are, and the fewer colds and other illnesses they have (Hendrix et al., 1991; Vita et al., 1998).

Perhaps you can think of other ways to cool off when you're hot and bothered. Many people respond beneficially to the soothing touch of

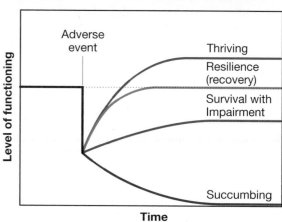

FIGURE 13.6 Succumbing, Surviving, or Thriving

People may respond to adversity by giving up, surviving with some impairment, recovering fully, or thriving—learning from the experience and coming out stronger because of it (Carver, 1998)!

massage (Field, 2001). Others listen to music, write in a journal, or bake bread. Such activities give the body a chance to recover from the "alarm phase" of its stress response and from the intensity of negative emotions. But you can't always jog away from your problems. Relaxation is not going to change the fact that you may lose your job, your best friend has betrayed a confidence, or you need a serious operation. Sometimes other coping strategies are necessary.

Solving the Problem

A woman we know, whom we will call Nancy, was struck by tragedy when she was 22. She and her new husband were driving home when a car ran out of control and crashed into them. When Nancy awoke in a hospital room, she learned that her husband had been killed and that she herself had permanent spinal injury and would never walk again. For many months, Nancy reacted with rage and despair. "Get it out of your system," her friends said. "You need to get in touch with your feelings." "But I know I'm miserable," Nancy lamented. "What do I *do*?"

The advice Nancy's friends gave her and her reply illustrate the difference between *emotion-focused* and *problem-focused coping* (Lazarus, 2000; Lazarus & Folkman, 1984). Emotion-focused coping concentrates on the emotions the problem has caused, whether anger, anxiety, or grief. For a period of time after any tragedy or disaster, it is normal to give in to these emotions and feel overwhelmed by them. In this stage, people often need to talk obsessively about the event in order to come to terms with it, make sense of it, and decide what to do about it (Lepore, Ragan, & Jones, 2000).

Eventually, though, most people become ready to concentrate on solving the problem itself. The specific steps in problem-focused coping depend on the nature of the problem: whether it is a pressing but one-time decision; a continuing difficulty, such as living with a disability; or an anticipated event, such as having an operation. Once the problem is identified, the coper can learn as much as possible about it from professionals, friends, books, and others in the same predicament (Clarke & Evans, 1998). Becoming informed increases the feeling of control and can speed recovery (Doering

et al., 2000). In Nancy's case, she learned more about her medical condition and prognosis, how other accident victims had coped, and the occupations that were possible for her (which was most of them). Nancy stayed in school, remarried, got a Ph.D. in psychology, and now does research and counselling with disabled people.

Rethinking the Problem

Some problems cannot be solved; these are the tragedies that occur out of the blue and the unavoidable facts of life, such as an inability to have children. Even when you cannot fix a problem, however, you can change the way you think about it. Here are four effective cognitive coping methods.

1 *Reappraising the situation.* Although you may not be able to get rid of a stressor (that nasty neighbour is unlikely to move; you cannot undo the fact that you lost your job or have a chronic illness), you can choose to think about it differently—a process called *reappraisal*. As we saw earlier in discussing emotion, confession, and forgiveness, the way you think about a situation or provocation affects the emotions you feel about it. Reappraisal can turn anger into sympathy, worry into determination, and feelings of loss into feelings of opportunity (Folkman & Moskowitz, 2000). Maybe that job you lost was pretty dismal but you were too afraid to look for another; now you can.

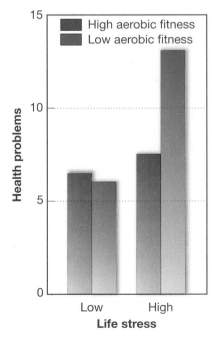

FIGURE 13.7 Fitness and Health

Among people under low stress, aerobically fit individuals had about the same number of health problems as those who were less fit. But among people under high stress, fit individuals had fewer health problems (Roth & Holmes, 1985).

The ultimate example of rethinking your problems.

2 *Learning from the experience.* Most victims of traumatic events and life-threatening illnesses report that the experience made them stronger, more resilient, even better human beings (McFarland & Alvaro, 2000). The ability to find meaning and benefits even in the worst adversity seems crucial to psychological recovery. It even slows the course of serious diseases. In a longitudinal study of men with HIV who had been recently bereaved, those who "tried not to think about it" showed sharper declines in immune function and were more likely to die during the follow-up period than were men who found meaning and purpose in the loss. The latter said they had acquired greater appreciation of the loved one, a perception of life as being fragile and precious, or other benefits. "I would say that his death lit up my faith," said one man (Taylor et al., 2000a).

3 *Making social comparisons.* In a difficult situation, successful copers often compare themselves to others who are (they feel) less fortunate. Even if they have fatal diseases, they find someone who is worse off (Taylor & Lobel, 1989; Wood, Michela, & Giordano, 2000). One AIDS sufferer said in an interview, "I made a list of all the other diseases I would rather not have than AIDS. Lou Gehrig's disease, being in a wheelchair; rheumatoid arthritis, when you are in knots and in terrible pain." Another said: "I really have an advantage in a sense over other people. . . . I have the opportunity to look at my life, to make changes, and to deeply appreciate the time that I have" (Reed, 1990).

Sometimes successful copers also compare themselves to those who are doing *better* than they are (Collins, 1996). They might say, "He and I have the same kinds of family problems; how come he's doing so much better in school than I am? What does he know that I don't?" Such comparisons are beneficial when they provide a person with information about ways of coping, managing an illness, or improving a stressful situation (Suls, Martin, & Wheeler, 2002).

4 *Cultivating a sense of humour.* Unfortunately, we now have to report some research that makes us very grumpy. In earlier editions of this book we reported studies that suggested that humour is not only fun, but healthy: that it hastens recovery from illness and even prolongs life.

Well, darn, science marches on, and sometimes it makes us give up our favourite notions. University of Western Ontario's Rod Martin (2001), who has been studying humour for more than 20 years and has long believed in its benefits, did a meta-analysis of all research on the effects of humour and laughter on immune function, pain, blood pressure, longevity, and symptoms of illness. To his surprise (and dismay), he found that overall, having a good sense of humour or watching funny movies won't help anyone live longer, avoid the flu, or recover from injury faster. On the other hand, Martin found, during times of stress, humour is a better way of coping than fuming and stomping around the house, especially if it is the kind of humour that allows you to see the ridiculous aspects of the problem and gain a sense of distance from it or control over it. (Sarcastic, hostile humour just tends to make matters worse.)

Drawing on Social Support

A final way to deal with negative emotions and stress is to reach out to others. Your health depends not only on what is going on in your body and mind but also on what is going on in your relationships: what you take from them, and what you give to them.

When Friends Help You Cope . . . Think of all the ways in which family members, friends, neighbours, and co-workers can help you. They can offer concern and affection. They can help you evaluate problems and plan a course of action. They can offer resources and services such as lending you money or a car, or taking notes in class for you when you are sick. Most of all, they are sources of attachment and connection, which everyone needs throughout life.

But friends are not only nice to have; they also improve your health. Remember the study we described earlier, showing that stress increases your risk of getting a cold? Well, having a lot of friends and social contacts reduces that risk. In a group of nearly 300 volunteers exposed to a flu virus, those with the most friends were the least likely to get sick (Cohen et al., 1997). Social support is especially important for people who have stressful jobs that require high cardiovascular responsiveness day after day, such as firefighters. Having social support helps the heart rate and stress hormones return to normal more quickly after a stressful episode (Roy, Steptoe, & Kirschbaum, 1998).

People who live in a network of close connections even live longer than those who do not. In studies that followed thousands of adults for 10 years, people who had many friends, connections, or memberships in church and other groups lived longer, on average, than those who had few. The importance of having social networks was unrelated to physical health at the time the studies began, to socioeconomic status, and to risk factors like smoking (Berkman & Syme, 1979; House, Landis, & Umberson, 1988).

. . . And Coping with Friends Of course, sometimes other people *aren't* helpful. Sometimes they themselves are the source of unhappiness, stress, and anger.

In close relationships, the same person who is a source of support can also become a source of stress, especially if the two parties are arguing all the time. Being in an unhappy, bitter, uncommunicative marriage can significantly impair health. It makes the partners depressed and angry, affects their diet and other health habits, and also directly influences the cardiovascular, endocrine, and immune systems (Kiecolt-Glaser & Newton, 2001). Married couples who argue in a hostile fashion—criticizing, interrupting, or insulting the other person, and becoming angry and defensive—show significant elevations of stress hormones and poorer immune function afterward. Couples who argue in a positive fashion—trying to find common ground, compromising, listening to each other's concerns, and using humour to defuse tension—do not show these impairments (Kiecolt-Glaser et al., 1993; Malarkey et al., 1994). As one student of ours observed, "This study gives new meaning to the accusation 'You make me sick!'" It also suggests that learning to argue fairly and constructively may have physical as well as psychological benefits.

In addition to being sources of conflict, friends and relatives may be unsupportive in times of trouble simply out of ignorance or awkwardness. They may abandon you or say something stupid and hurtful. Sometimes they

actively block your efforts to change bad health habits—say, to cut down on binge drinking or smoking—by making fun of you or pressuring you to conform to what "everyone" does. And sometimes, because they have never been in the same situation and don't know what to do to help, they offer the wrong kind of support. For example, they may try to cheer you up, saying, "Everything will be fine," rather than let you talk about your fears or find solutions (Bolger et al., 1996). That is why support groups of people experiencing the same illness (such as breast cancer or AIDS), problem (such as a parent's alcoholism), or tragedy (such as the death of a child) are often more helpful than friends who haven't "been there."

Finally, we should not forget the benefits of *giving* support, rather than always being on the receiving end. Julius Segal (1986), a psychologist who worked with Holocaust survivors, hostages, refugees, and other survivors of catastrophe, wrote that a key element in their recovery was compassion for others, or "healing through helping." People who frequently help their friends and family with practical and emotional support also live longer than self-oriented nonhelpers (Brown et al., 2003). Why? The ability to look outside yourself is related to all of the successful coping mechanisms we have discussed. It encourages you to solve problems instead of blaming others or just venting your emotions, helps you reappraise the situation by seeing it from another person's perspective, fosters forgiveness, and allows you to gain perspective on your own problems. "Healing through helping" thus helps you live with situations that are facts of life.

Friends can be our greatest source of warmth, support, and fun . . . and also sources of exasperation, anger, and misery.

Quick Quiz

Can you cope with these questions?

1. You accidentally broke your glasses. Which response is an example of cognitive reappraisal? (a) "I am such a stupid clumsy idiot!" (b) "I never do anything right." (c) "What a shame, but I've been wanting new frames anyway." (d) "I'll forget about it in aerobics class."

2. Finding out what your legal and financial resources are when you have been victimized by a crime is an example of (a) problem-focused coping, (b) emotion-focused coping, (c) distraction, (d) reappraisal.

3. "This class drives me crazy, but I'm better off than my friends who aren't in college" is an example of (a) distraction, (b) social comparison, (c) denial, (d) empathy.

4. Your roommate has turned your room into a garbage dump, filled with rotten leftover food and unwashed clothes. Assuming that you don't like living with rotting food and dirty clothes, what coping strategies described in this section might help you?

Answers:

1. c 2. a 3. b 4. You might solve the problem by finding a compromise (e.g., clean the room together). You could reappraise the seriousness of the problem ("I only have to live with this person until the end of the term.") or compare your roommate to others ("at least mine is generous and friendly."). You might try to find the humour in being so mismatched. And you might mobilize some social support—offer your friends a pizza dinner if they help you clean up.

Psychology In The News *Revisited*

Let us return now to the case of Bert Stone, who claimed that his wife's nagging was so stressful that it drove him to kill her. Remember that they had been married for less than a year, and that he stabbed her not once, but 47 times. Stone was given a less than six-year sentence after the court accepted the argument that the nagging and yelling had been too much for him to cope with.

This chapter described the connections between emotion, cognition, and stress. When we are feeling extreme emotions or when major stressors require the body to cope with threat, fear, or danger, the body whirls into action to give us the energy to respond. Just about everyone, for example, has experienced the intense anger and frustration that can arise as a result of ongoing quarrels with a partner.

But, as we also saw, biology does not give us the whole picture. It is equally important to understand the role of perceptions, beliefs, and expectations in generating emotions and stress. Stone blamed his wife for her relentless nag-

ging, and rage was the resulting emotion. But what if he had been able to interpret her behaviour another way—say, as evidence of her own unhappiness and frustration? Perhaps then he might have reacted to their arguments with other emotions, such as sadness that their relationship was falling apart. What if he had focused not on the reasons for his anger, but on the reasons for his sadness—say, at how painful it is to accept that a marriage is failing? Perhaps then his dominant feelings would have been sorrow and regret.

This chapter also examined the importance of having a sense of control over events, noting the helplessness and panic that can ensue when people lose their feelings of control. Westerners, particularly, tend to have a philosophy of fighting back against unwelcome events rather than of accepting disappointments and losses.

Finally, we saw that there are better ways of coping than murdering the person causing your anger and stress! These include rethinking the problem, learning from it, comparing oneself to others less fortunate, helping others, and finding a good, strong support group. Bert Stone might not have been able to control his anger at his wife. But if he had had better ways of managing his distress, he could have controlled her behaviour. He could have sought marriage counselling, or he could have simply walked away, for example. (In "Taking Psychology With You," we offer further suggestions for handling anger.)

Keep in mind, though, that successful coping does not mean eliminating all sources of stress or all difficult emotions. It does not mean constant happiness or a life without pain and frustration. The healthy person faces problems, deals with them, and gets beyond them, but the problems are necessary if the person is to acquire coping skills that endure. To wish for a life without stress, or a life without emotion, would be like wishing for a life without friends. The result might be calm, but it would be joyless and ultimately hazardous to your health. The stresses and passions of life—the daily hassles, the emotional ups and downs, and the occasional tragedies—force us to grow, and to grow up.

Taking Psychology With You   The Dilemma of Anger—"Let It Out" or "Bottle It Up"?

What do you do when you feel angry? Do you tend to brood and sulk, collecting your righteous complaints like acorns for the winter, or do you erupt, hurling your wrath upon anyone or anything at hand? Do you discuss your feelings when you have calmed down? Does "letting anger out" get rid of it for you, or does it only make it more intense? The answers are crucial for how you get along with your family, neighbours, employers, and strangers.

Chronic feelings of anger and an inability to control anger can be as emotionally devastating and unhealthy as chronic problems with depression or anxiety. In contrast to much pop-psych advice, research shows that expressing anger does not always get it "out of your system"; often people feel worse after an angry confrontation, both physically and mentally (Bushman, Baumeister, & Stack, 1999; Tavris, 1989). When people talk incessantly about their anger or act on that feeling, they tend to rehearse their grievances and pump up their blood pressure. Conversely, when people learn to control their tempers and express anger constructively, they usually feel better, not worse; calmer, not angrier (Deffenbacher et al., 1998).

When people are feeling angry, they have a choice of doing any number of things. They can write letters, play the piano, jog, try to solve the problem that is causing their anger, abuse their friends or family, hit a punching bag, or yell. If a particular action soothes their feelings or gets the desired response from others, they are likely to acquire a habit. Soon that habit feels "natural," as if it could never be changed; indeed, many people justify their violent tempers by saying, "I couldn't help myself." But they can. If you have learned an abusive or aggressive habit, the research in this chapter offers practical suggestions for relearning constructive ways of managing anger:

- **Don't sound off in the heat of anger; let bodily arousal cool down.** Whether your arousal comes from background stresses such as heat, crowds, or loud noise or from conflict with another person, take time to relax. Time allows you to decide whether you are really angry or just tired and tense. This is the reason for the sage old advice to count to 10, count to 100, or sleep on it. Other cooling-off strategies include taking a time-out in the middle of an argument, meditating or relaxing, and calming yourself with a distracting activity.

- **Don't take it personally.** If you feel that you have been insulted, check your perception for its accuracy. Could there be another reason for the behaviour you find offensive? People who are quick to feel anger tend to interpret other people's actions as intentional offences. People who are slow to anger tend to give others the benefit of the doubt, and they are not as focused on their own injured pride. Empathy ("Poor guy, he's feeling rotten") is usually incompatible with anger, so practise seeing the situation from the other person's perspective. And be sure you understand another person's nonverbal communication before you decide that you have been insulted! In Stockton, California, a driver used a hand signal to alert a car behind him at a stoplight that the other driver's headlights were off. The driver of the second car interpreted this gesture as a sign of disrespect, shot at the first car—and killed a passenger. Perhaps this is why the Canadian Automobile Association recommends that drivers avoid gesturing when driving, pointing out that even friendly gestures can be misinterpreted.

- **If you decide that expressing anger is appropriate, be sure you use the right verbal and nonverbal language to make yourself understood.** Because cultures (and families) have different display rules, be sure the recipient of your anger understands what you are feeling and what complaint you are trying to convey. If your way of expressing anger is to sulk, expecting everyone else to read your mind, you are not communicating clearly.

- **Think carefully about how to express anger so that you will get the results you want.** What do you want your anger to accomplish? Do you just want to make the other person feel bad, or do you want the other person to understand your concerns and make amends? Shouting "You moron! How *could* you be so stupid!" might accomplish the former goal, but it's not likely to get the person to apologize, let alone to change his or her behaviour.

If your goal is to improve a bad situation or achieve justice, then learning how to express anger so the other person will listen is essential. People who have been the targets of injustice have learned that outbursts of anger may draw society's attention to a problem, but real change requires sustained political effort, challenges to unfair laws, and the use of tactics that persuade rather than alienate the opposition.

Of course, if you just want to blow off steam, go right ahead; but you risk becoming a hothead!

SUMMARY

THE NATURE OF EMOTION

- Thoughts and emotions are not "opposite"; each influences the other. Both processes can be rational or irrational, and both are necessary for making plans and wise decisions. The experience of *emotion* involves physiological changes in the face, brain, and autonomic nervous system; cognitive processes; and cultural norms and regulations. *Primary emotions* are thought to be universal, whereas *secondary emotions* are specific to cultures.

- Some basic facial expressions—anger, fear, sadness, happiness, disgust, surprise, contempt—are widely recognized across cultures. They probably evolved to foster communication with others, enhance survival, and signal our intentions to others. As studies of *facial feedback* show, expressions also help us to identify our own emotional states. Facial expressions can also generate emotions in others through unconscious mimicry, which can create *mood contagion*. However, because people can and do disguise their emotions, their expressions do not always communicate accurately.

- Many aspects of emotion are associated with specific parts of the brain. The *amygdala* is responsible for initially evaluating the emotional importance of incoming sensory information, and is especially involved in fear. The *cerebral cortex* provides the cognitive ability to override this initial appraisal. Emotions generally involve the motivation to approach or withdraw; regions of the *left* prefrontal cortex appear to be specialized for the motivation to approach others (as with happiness and anger), whereas regions of the *right* prefrontal region are specialized for withdrawal or escape (as with disgust and fear).

- During the experience of any emotion, *epinephrine* and *norepinephrine* produce a state of physiological arousal to prepare the body for an output of energy. But different emotions are also associated with different patterns of autonomic nervous system activity.

- Schachter and Singer's theory of emotion held that emotions result from arousal *and* the labelling or interpretation of that arousal. Research spurred by this theory has investigated the cognitive processes involved in different emotions, such as the *attributions* people make about others' behaviour and the way people interpret and evaluate events.

- Some emotions involve simple, unconscious reactions, such as a conditioned response to an emotional symbol. Others, such as shame and guilt, require complex cognitive capacities. As children mature, their cognitions and therefore their emotions become more complex.

EMOTION AND CULTURE

- Physiological researchers believe that all human beings share the ability to experience primary emotions, whereas secondary emotions may be culture-specific—a view supported by research on emotion *prototypes*. But cultural psychologists believe that culture affects every aspect of emotional experience, including which emotions are considered basic and what people feel emotional about.

- Culture strongly influences the *display rules* that regulate how and whether people express their emotions. The ability to synchronize moods through *body language* is important for rapport and smooth interactions. *Emotion work* is the effort a person makes to display an emotion he or she does not feel but feels obliged to convey.

- Women and men are equally likely to feel all emotions, from love to anger, although gender rules shape differences in emotional expression. On average, in North America, women are more verbally and nonverbally expressive than men except for anger at strangers. But the situation can override gender rules; both sexes are less expressive to a person of higher status than they, both sexes will do the "emotion work" their job requires, and some situations foster expressiveness in everybody. Gender differences also vary across cultures.

THE NATURE OF STRESS

- Hans Selye argued that environmental stressors such as heat, pain, and danger produce a *general adaptation syndrome*, in which the body responds in three stages: *alarm, resistance*, and *exhaustion*. If a stressor persists, it may overwhelm the body's ability to cope, and fatigue or illness may result. Studies of the immune system have confirmed that stress can suppress the activity of disease-fighting white blood cells and make illness more likely.

- Modern research has supported and added to Selye's work. When a person is under stress, the hypothalamus sends messages to the endocrine glands along two major pathways. One activates the sympathetic division of the autonomic nervous system. In the other, the hypothalamus releases chemical messengers that spur production of *cortisol* and other hormones that increase energy. Excess levels of cortisol can become harmful in the long run. Responses to stress differ across individuals, depending on the type of stressor and the individual's own genetic predispositions.

- Several chronic stressors increase the risk of illness: constant, uncontrollable noise; bereavement and loss; unemployment and work-related problems; and poverty and powerlessness. However, most people who experience these stressors do not become ill. Health psychologists study the psychological, social, and biological factors that explain why only some people get sick.

- Two important psychological factors that affect health are having an *optimistic explanatory style* (in contrast to a *pessimistic* one) and having an *internal locus of control*. Optimism and control improve immune function and also increase a person's ability to tolerate pain, live with ongoing problems, and recover from illness. Health and well-being may depend on the right combination of *primary control,* trying to change the stressful situation, and *secondary control,* learning to accept and accommodate to the stressful situation. Cultures differ in the kind of control they emphasize and value.

STRESS AND EMOTION

- Researchers have sought links between emotions and illness. Having a competitive, impatient *Type A personality* is not itself related to heart disease, but *cynical or antagonistic hostility*, which is often part of the Type A pattern, is. Chronic depression also seems to be a risk factor in causing heart disease, but its link to other illnesses remains unclear.

- People who are emotionally inhibited are at greater risk of illness than people who acknowledge and cope with negative emotions. The effort to suppress worries, secrets, and memories of upsetting experiences can paradoxically lead to obsessively ruminating on these thoughts and become stressful to the body.

- Two ways of letting go of negative emotions include revealing them on paper or to others, if this produces new insight and understanding; and forgiveness, letting go of grudges.

EMOTIONS, STRESS, AND HEALTH: HOW TO COPE

- One way to cope with stress and negative emotions is to reduce their physical effects, for example through relaxation and exercise. Another is to focus on solving the problem (*problem-focused coping*) rather than on ventilating the emotions caused by the problem (*emotion-focused coping*). A third is to rethink the problem, which involves *reappraisal*, learning from the experience; comparing oneself to others; and seeing humour in the situation.

- *Social support* is essential in maintaining physical health and emotional well-being; it even prolongs life and speeds recovery from illness. However, friends and family can also be sources of stress. In close relationships, couples who fight in a hostile and negative way show impaired immune function. *Giving* support to others—"healing through helping"—is also associated with health and hastens recovery from traumatic experiences.

PSYCHOLOGY IN THE NEWS, REVISITED

- We may not always be able to control the physiological arousal produced by stress or intense emotions, but we generally are able to decide how to behave when we are upset. Coping with stress does not mean trying to live without pain or problems. It means learning how to live with them.

KEY TERMS

LOOKING BACK

- Which facial expressions of emotion do most people recognize the world over? (p. 414)
- Which little structure in the brain sees to it that you cross the street fast when a truck is headed toward you? (p. 417)
- Which two hormones can make you "too excited to eat"? (p. 418)
- In a competition, who is likely to be happier, the third-place winner or the second-place winner? (p. 420)
- Why can't an infant feel shame or guilt? (p. 420)
- Do Germans, Japanese, and Canadians always mean the same thing when they smile at others? (p. 423)
- Why do people show sadness at funerals even when they are not feeling sad? (p. 424)
- Are women really more "emotional" than men? (pp. 424–425)
- Why are you more likely to get a cold when you're "stressed out"? (p. 428)
- Which stressors pose the greatest hazard to your health? (pp. 428–429)
- Why do optimists tend to live longer than pessimists? (pp. 429–430)
- When is a sense of control good for you, and when is it not? (pp. 430–431)
- Why are people who are chronically angry and mistrustful their own worst enemy? (p. 433)
- Which disease is depression most clearly linked to? (p. 433)
- Can revealing your unresolved emotions help your health? (p. 434)
- When you're feeling overwhelmed, what are some ways to calm yourself? (p. 436)
- Why is it important to move beyond the emotions caused by a problem and deal with the problem itself? (p. 437)
- How can you learn to rethink your problems? (pp. 437–438)
- When do friends reduce your stress, and when do they just make matters worse? (pp. 438–439)

Psychology In The News

INTERNET DATING SERVICE ATTRACTS OVER A MILLION PEOPLE

TORONTO, ON, May 31, 2003. The dating company Lavalife started out as a telephone service, but it wasn't until it moved to the Internet that it became huge. Now, over 250 000 people in the Toronto area alone use the service. They represent only one-quarter of the over one million users, composed of equal numbers of men and women. Female users are particularly complimentary about the service, pointing out that it gives them much more control and choice compared to conventional ways of meeting people, such as in bars or through friends. The website features categories such as Dating, Relationships, and Intimate Encounters, so people know one another's intentions from the start. Lavalife attributes much of its success to its very aggressive advertising campaign, targeting young urbanites in centres such as Toronto.

FUGITIVE RAPIST CAPTURED IN MEXICO

PUNTA DE MITAS, MEXICO, June 22, 2003. Andrew Luster, 39, the wealthy great-grandson of cosmetics magnate Max Factor, was captured today in this small fishing village on the coast of Mexico. Luster had fled during his trial on charges of raping three women after drugging them with the date-rape drug "Liquid X" (GHB), a powerful sedative that can induce coma. He then videotaped himself having sex with the women after they passed out. He was convicted in absentia and sentenced to 124 years in prison. Luster, who eluded capture for five months, was finally nabbed by a bounty hunter. He will begin serving his sentence immediately.

DYING TO BE THIN

TORONTO, ON, April 3, 2002. A Health Canada Task Force on the Treatment of Obesity discovered that there had been at least three deaths in Canada for which coroners' juries cited dieting as a causal factor. One of the big concerns is so-called "yo-yo dieting" in which weight loss and weight gain follow one another in rapid cycles. Another concern is diets that feature dangerously low calorie intake.

The Task Force has concluded that diets providing less that 1200 calories

Jennifer Rosenthal needed a liver transplant after she took usnic acid to "stay in shape."

per day based on regular food may be insufficient in their provision of vitamins, minerals, and nutrients. Such diets require careful supplementation in order to be safe. According to the Task Force, diets of under 900 calories per day should be followed only under medical supervision by a doctor with special training in the treatment of obesity.

The Task Force provides good advice regarding diets that restrict what we ingest. Other dieting approaches that are at least as worrisome feature substances that claim to accelerate weight loss. One such substance is usnic acid. Jennifer Rosenthal, a 28-year-old woman from Long Beach, California, decided to try usnic acid to "stay in shape," although she was not overweight, because the

Hip and clever online dating ads are pervasive in Toronto restaurants and bars.

label on the bottle said the chemical would make her body burn calories "at an accelerated rate." Rosenthal took the pills for 17 days. A month later she suffered complete liver failure and went into a coma. If she had not received an emergency liver transplant, she would have died. Usnic acid has now been implicated in liver disease or death in numerous cases.

NASH WINS NBA MVP AWARD

PHOENIX, AZ, March 2005. Steve Nash, from Victoria, BC, is a major reason why the NBA's Phoenix Suns are near the top of the league's overall standings. Nash, who has always been an excellent passer of the basketball, leads the entire league in assists per game, and is also one of the league's top shooters. At six feet three inches, Nash is relatively short by NBA standards. The NBA all-star relies on great quickness, ball-handling ability, and fitness to dominate on the court. All this takes incredible dedication to a training regimen that includes hours of work on such things as core fitness, balance, and fundamental skills.

Soaring above the giants, Victoria's Steve Nash drives to the basket.

14 The Major Motives of Life: Love, Sex, Food, and Work

THE SOCIAL ANIMAL: MOTIVES FOR LOVE

THE EROTIC ANIMAL: MOTIVES FOR SEX

THE HUNGRY ANIMAL: MOTIVES TO EAT

THE COMPETENT ANIMAL: MOTIVES TO ACHIEVE

MOTIVES, VALUES, AND WELL-BEING

PSYCHOLOGY IN THE NEWS, REVISITED

TAKING PSYCHOLOGY WITH YOU: WHAT MOTIVATES YOU?

Why would so many people take their chances and date someone they've met online? Why would attractive, wealthy men like Andrew Luster resort to sexual coercion and rape? Why do so many people struggle to lose weight, even subjecting themselves to the risks of drugs and surgery, and why do so many dieters fail? And what motivates people like Steve Nash to pursue their dreams with such dedication?

The word *motivation*, like the word *emotion*, comes from the Latin root meaning "to move," and the psychology of motivation is indeed the study of what moves us, and why we do what we do. To psychologists, **motivation** refers to an inferred process within a person or animal that causes the organism to move toward a goal or away from an unpleasant situation. The goal may be to get married or avoid marriage. The goal may be to eat or avoid eating. The goal may be to satisfy a biological need, as in eating a sandwich to reduce hunger, or to fulfill a psychological ambition, such as being the first person to row across the Atlantic in a dinghy. But whereas the things that motivate, say, a rabbit are pretty basic (keep eating, keep running from danger, keep multiplying), human motivation is more complex, because people are conscious creatures who think and plan ahead, set goals for themselves, and plot strategies to reach those goals.

In this chapter, we will examine four central areas of human motivation: love, sex, food, and achievement. We will see how happiness and well-being are affected by the kinds of goals we set for ourselves, and by whether we are spurred to reach those goals because of **intrinsic motivation**, enjoyment of an activity for its own sake, or **extrinsic motivation**, pursuit of a goal for external rewards.

As you read, see whether this information helps you understand the enduring appeal of romantic love, the reasons for Andrew Luster's cruel rapes, the desperate risks some people take to lose weight, and the determination of Steve Nash to become a star.

motivation An inferred process within a person or animal that causes movement either toward a goal or away from an unpleasant situation.

need for affiliation The motive to associate with other people, as by seeking friends, companionship, or love.

intrinsic motivation The desire to do something for its own sake and for the internal pleasure it provides.

extrinsic motivation The desire to do something for the sake of external rewards, such as money or fame.

WHAT'S AHEAD

- When someone says "I love you," can you be sure what the person means?
- Do men and women differ in their ability to love?
- How are your beliefs about love affected by your income?

THE SOCIAL ANIMAL: MOTIVES FOR LOVE

Everybody needs somebody. One of the deepest and most universal of human motives is the **need for affiliation**, the need to be with others, make friends, co-operate, love. Human survival depends on the infant's ability to form attachments (see Chapter 3), on parents' devotion to their children, and on adults' ability to have close partners and friends. While the need for attachment and companionship is universal, however, love—that most intense of attachments—takes various forms and has many meanings. Psychologists want to know not only why we love, but whom we love and how we love.

The Psychology of Love

Do you have a favourite love story? Is it a romantic one, where the couple falls madly in love at first sight and, after a few silly misunderstandings, lives happily ever after, without a single quarrel or miserable moment? Or is it a practical one, where parents choose a perfect partner for their child, and the couple becomes close and loving after spending years together?

Many romantics believe there is only "one true love" awaiting them. Considering that there

JUMP START reprinted by permission of United Feature Syndicate, Inc.

are nearly 6 billion people on the planet, the odds of finding said person are a bit daunting! What if you're in Winnipeg or Dubai and your true love is in Dubrovnik or St. John's? You could wander for years and never cross paths.

Fortunately, evolution has made it possible to form deep and lasting attachments without travelling the world. In fact, the first major predictor of whom we love is plain *proximity*: the people who are nearest to you are most likely to be dearest to you, too. We usually choose our friends and lovers from the set of people who live closest to us, or who study or work near us. (If there aren't any immediate local candidates, today's love-seekers can use the Internet, but proximity remains a highly desirable attribute; dating sites can filter out anyone who is geographically undesirable.) And although romantics also believe that "opposites attract," the fact is that we tend to choose friends and loved ones who are most like us. *Similarity*—in looks, attitudes, beliefs, values, personality, and interests—is the second key predictor of whom we love (Berscheid & Reis, 1998).

The Ingredients of Love Once you have found a possible partner, *how* do you love? The oldest answer distinguishes *passionate ("romantic") love*, characterized by a turmoil of intense emotions and sexual passion, from *companionate love*, characterized by affection and trust (Hatfield & Rapson, 1996). Passionate love is the stuff of crushes, infatuations, "love at first sight," and the early stage of love affairs. It may burn out completely or subside into companionate love.

Robert Sternberg (1997) has added a third element in his *triangular theory*, which holds that the three ingredients of love are *passion* (euphoria and sexual excitement), *intimacy* (feeling close to and understood by the loved one), and *commitment* (long-term loyalty). People combine these elements in every possible way, producing different kinds of love. For example, romantic love is intimacy and passion, without commitment; companionate love is intimacy and commitment, without passion; empty love is commitment, but without intimacy or passion; friendship is intimacy alone; and infatuation is passion alone. In Sternberg's view, ideal love integrates all three elements: passion, closeness, and the security that comes from commitment.

When people are asked to define the key ingredients of love, most agree that love is a mix of passion, intimacy, and commitment (Aron &

Westbay, 1996; Lemieux & Hale, 2000). However, in most relationships, romantic passion subsides over the years and intimacy increases. Intimacy is based on deep knowledge of the other person, which accumulates gradually and thus needs time to produce a maximum degree of closeness; but passion is based on emotion, which is generated by novelty and change. That is why passion is usually highest at the beginning of a relationship, when two people begin to disclose things about themselves to each other, and lowest when knowledge of the other person's beliefs and habits is at its maximum—when it seems that there is nothing left to learn about the beloved. And the negative correlation between passion and intimacy explains why passion is often reawakened when a couple is separated or unexpected crises occur (Baumeister & Bratslavsky, 1999). A study in Canada and Germany, however, found that intimacy is significantly more predictive of relationship quality than is passion (Hassebrauck & Fehr, 2002).

As this happy couple illustrates, like attracts like—and love can outlast initial romantic passion.

The critical-thinking guideline "define your terms" may never be more important than in matters of love. The way we define "real" love deeply affects our satisfaction with relationships, and even whether our relationships last. After all, if you believe that the only real love is romantic love, that love is *defined* by sexual passion and hot emotion, then you may decide you are "out of love" when the initial phase of attraction fades, as it eventually must—and you will be repeatedly disappointed (Solomon, 1994).

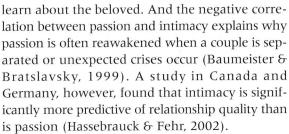

Thinking Critically About Love

The Attachment Theory of Love Some people seem secure in their love relationships, whereas others are always fretting and worrying about them. According to Phillip Shaver and Cindy Hazan (1993), adults, just like infants, can be *secure*, *avoidant*, or *anxious–ambivalent* in their attachments (see Chapter 3). Securely attached lovers are, well, secure: They are rarely jealous or worried about being abandoned. Anxious or ambivalent lovers are always agitated about their relationships; they want to be close but worry that their partners will leave them. Other people often describe them as "clingy," which may be why they

"My preference is for someone who's afraid of closeness, like me."
An avoidant lover in action.

are more likely than secure lovers to suffer from unrequited love (Aron, Aron, & Allen, 1998). Avoidant people distrust and avoid intimate attachments. Not surprisingly, secure attachment is associated with greater marital satisfaction, as discovered in a study at l'Université du Québec (Lussier, Sabourin, & Turgeon, 1997).

Where do these differences come from? In the *attachment theory of love*, people acquire their attachment styles in large part from how their parents cared for them. As children, they form internal "working models" of relationships: Can I trust others? Am I worthy of being loved? Will my beloved leave me? If a child's parents were cold and rejecting and provided little or no contact comfort, that is how the child learns to expect other relationships to be. If children form secure attachments to trusted parents, they become more trusting of others, expecting to form other secure attachments with friends and lovers in adulthood (Levy, Blatt, & Shaver, 1998).

The distribution of the three basic styles of attachment among adults is in fact very similar to that found for infants: about 64 percent secure, 25 percent avoidant, and 11 percent anxious or ambivalent. Further, the kinds of relationships that people have as adults are strongly related to their reports of how their parents treated them (Mickelson, Kessler, & Shaver, 1997). Securely attached adults report having had warm, close relationships with their parents. Although they recognize their parents' flaws, they describe their parents as having been more loving and kind than

insecurely attached people do. Anxious–ambivalent people report feeling more ambivalence toward their parents, especially their mothers, and also describe their parents ambivalently—as having been both harsh and kind.

People with an avoidant attachment style describe their parents in almost entirely negative terms (Levy, Blatt, & Shaver, 1998). Avoidant individuals are most likely to report having had cold, rejecting parents, extended periods of separation from their mothers, or childhood environments that prevented them from making close ties with others (Feeney & Noller, 1990; Hazan & Shaver, 1994; Klohnen & Bera, 1998). The avoidant style is particularly resistant to change, because people who are busy avoiding one another never learn to trust someone long enough to become securely attached. However, even avoidant or anxiously attached people can have successful, stable relationships if they find securely attached partners who will put up with their insecurities (Kirkpatrick & Davis, 1994; Koski & Shaver, 1997).

Keep in mind, though, that a person's own temperament may help account for the consistency of attachment styles from childhood to adulthood, as well as for the "working models" of relationships that are formed during childhood. Certainly some parents are cold, punitive, and rejecting. But a temperamentally fearful and avoidant child may reject even a kind parent's efforts to console and cuddle, and that child may therefore come to believe that all relationships are untrustworthy.

Gender, Culture, and Love Which of the sexes is more romantic? Which truly understands "true" love? Which falls in love but won't commit? Pop-psych books are full of answers, along with advice for dealing with all those love-challenged heartbreakers who love you and leave you. But all stereotypes oversimplify. Research at the University of Winnipeg and elsewhere has shown that neither sex loves more than the other in terms of "love at first sight," passionate love, or companionate love over the long haul (Dion & Dion, 1993; Fehr, 2001, 1993; Hatfield & Rapson, 1996). Men and women are equally likely to suffer the heart-crushing torments of unrequited love. Both sexes suffer mightily when a love relationship ends—assuming they did not want it to.

However, women and men do differ, on average, in how they *express* love. Males in many cultures learn early that revelations of emotion can be construed as evidence of vulnerability and weakness, which are considered unmasculine (see Chapter 13). Thus, men in such cultures often develop ways of expressing love that differ from women's. In contemporary Western society, many women express feelings of love in words, whereas many men express these feelings in actions—doing things for the partner, supporting the family financially, or just sharing the same activity, such as watching TV or a football game (Baumeister & Bratslavsky, 1999; Cancian, 1987; Swain, 1989). Similarly, many women tend to define "intimacy" as shared revelations of feelings, but many men define intimacy as just hanging out together.

Get Involved   What Is Your Love Attachment Style?

Which of the following three statements best describes how you typically feel in your romantic relationships?

Secure style: I find it relatively easy to get close to others and am comfortable depending on them and having them depend on me. I don't often worry about being abandoned or about someone getting too close.

Avoidant style: I am somewhat uncomfortable being close; I find it difficult to trust others completely or allow myself to depend on them. Love partners often want me to be more intimate than I feel comfortable being.

Anxious–ambivalent style: I find that others are reluctant to get as close as I would like. I often worry that my partner doesn't really love me or won't stay with me. I want to merge completely with another person, and this desire sometimes scares people away.

If you are currently in a dating relationship—and have the nerve!—ask your partner how he or she would reply. Do you have the same attachment styles? (Adapted from Hazan & Shaver, 1987.)

These gender differences in ways of expressing the universal motives of love and intimacy do not just pop up from nowhere; they reflect social, economic, and cultural forces. For example, for many years, Western men were more romantic than women in their choice of partner, and women in turn were far more pragmatic than men. One reason was that a woman did not just marry a man; she married a standard of living. Therefore she could not afford to marry someone "unsuitable" or waste her time in a relationship that was "not going anywhere," even if she loved the guy. She married, in short, for extrinsic reasons rather than intrinsic ones. In contrast, a man could afford to be sentimental in his choice of partner. In the 1960s, two-thirds of a sample of university men said they would not marry someone they did not love, but only one-fourth of the women ruled out the possibility (Kephart, 1967).

As women entered the workforce and as two incomes became necessary in most families, however, the gender difference in romantic love waned, and so did economic reasons for marriage—all over the world. Nowadays, in every developed nation, only tiny numbers of women and men would consider marrying someone they did not love, even if the person had all the "right" qualities. Pragmatic reasons for marriage, with romantic love being a remote luxury, persist only in economically underdeveloped countries, such as India and Pakistan, and in other cultures in which the extended family still controls female sexuality and the terms of marriage (Hatfield & Rapson, 1996). Even in these countries the tight rules over marriage choices are loosening, as films such as India's *Monsoon Wedding* illustrate.

Marriage for financial security is still the only option for many women from impoverished nations—like this bride, whose husband chose her from a mail-order catalogue.

Quick Quiz

Are you passionately committed to quizzes yet?

1. According to Sternberg's triangular theory of love, the three major ingredients of love are _____.

2. Tiffany is wildly in love with Timothy, and he with her, but she can't stop worrying about him and doubting his love. She wants to be with him constantly, but when she feels jealous she pushes him away. According to the attachment theory of love, which style of attachment does Tiffany have?

3. *True or false?*: Until recently, most men in Western societies were more likely than women to marry for love.

Answers:

1. passion, intimacy, commitment
2. anxious–ambivalent
3. true

WHAT'S AHEAD

- Is one kind of orgasm better or healthier for women than another?
- What part of the anatomy do psychologists think is the "sexiest sex organ"?
- How do the sexual rules for heterosexual couples foster misunderstandings?
- Can psychological theories about smothering mothers or absent fathers explain why some men are gay?

THE EROTIC ANIMAL: MOTIVES FOR SEX

Most people believe that sex is a biological drive, merely a matter of doing what comes naturally. It is certainly true that in most other species, sexual behaviour is genetically programmed. Without instruction, a male stickleback fish knows exactly what to do with a female stickleback, and a whooping crane knows when to whoop. But as sex researcher Leonore Tiefer (2004) observes, for human beings "sex is not a natural act." For one thing, the activities that one culture considers "natural"—say, mouth-to-mouth kissing or oral sex—are often considered "unnatural" in another culture or historical time. For another, people have to learn from experience and culture what they are supposed to do with their sexual desires and how they are expected to behave. Human sexuality is a blend of biological, psychological, and cultural factors.

Desire and sensuality are lifelong pleasures.

The Biology of Desire

Biological researchers have contributed to our understanding of sexual motivation by sweeping away the cobwebs of superstition and ignorance about how the body works.

Hormones and Sexual Response One biological factor that seems to promote sexual desire in both sexes is the hormone testosterone. Its role has been documented in studies of men who have been given synthetic hormones that suppress the production of testosterone, of men and women who have abnormally low testosterone levels, and of women who have kept diaries of their sexual activity while also having their hormone levels periodically measured (Bradford & Pawlak, 1993; Carani et al., 1992; Dabbs, 2000; Sherwin, 1998b).

These findings have led pharmaceutical companies and some physicians to promote testosterone treatments for women and men who complain of low sexual desire. But there are significant problems with this apparent solution. One is that there is no consensus on how much sexual activity is "not enough," or on the difference between "low" and "deficient" levels of testosterone. The symptoms of "androgen deficiency" (low libido, fatigue, lack of well-being) are also those of depression and marital problems. And the side effects range from unpleasant to harmful (International Consensus Conference, 2002).

Moreover, hormones and behaviour travel a two-way street: Testosterone does contribute to sexual arousal, but sexual activity also produces higher levels of testosterone (Sapolsky, 1997). That is why sex offenders who are chemically castrated when they take a medication that suppresses production of testosterone do not always lose their sexual desires.

Arousal and Orgasm Physiological research has dispelled a lot of nonsense written about female sexuality, such as the once-common notions that normal or "good" women don't have orgasms, or that mature women should have the "right kind" of orgasm (Ehrenreich, 1978).

The first modern attack on these beliefs came from Alfred Kinsey and his associates (Kinsey, Pomeroy, & Martin, 1948; Kinsey et al. 1953), in their pioneering books on male and female

sexuality. Kinsey's team surveyed thousands of Americans about their sexual attitudes and behaviour, and also reviewed the existing research on sexual physiology. In *Sexual Behavior in the Human Female*, they observed that "males would be better prepared to understand females, and females to understand males, if they realized that they are alike in their basic anatomy and physiology." For example, the penis and the clitoris develop from the same embryonic tissues; they differ in size, of course, but not in sensitivity.

The idea that men and women are sexually similar in any way was extremely shocking in 1953. At that time many people believed that women were not as sexually motivated as men, and that women cared more about affection than sexual satisfaction—notions soundly refuted by Kinsey's interviews. Kinsey did believe, however, that women overall have a "lesser sexual capacity" than men, reflected in women's lower frequency of masturbation and orgasm. Although he acknowledged that many women are taught to avoid, dislike, or feel ambivalent about sex, he tended to attribute this gender difference to biology.

The next wave of sex research began in the 1960s with the laboratory research of physician William Masters and his associate Virginia Johnson (1966). In studies of physiological changes during sexual arousal and orgasm, Masters and Johnson confirmed that male and female orgasms are

The "Kinsey Report" on women, officially titled Sexual Behavior in the Human Female, was not exactly greeted with praise and acceptance—or with clear thinking.

indeed remarkably similar and that all orgasms are physiologically the same, regardless of the source of stimulation. But Masters and Johnson disagreed with Kinsey's assertion that women have a lesser sexual capacity than men. On the contrary, they argued, women's capacity for sexual response "infinitely surpasses that of men" because a woman, unlike most men, is able to have repeated orgasms until exhaustion or a ringing telephone makes her stop.

However, just as Kinsey might have underestimated women's sexual capacity, Masters and Johnson might have overestimated it. Their research was limited by the selection of a sample consisting only of men and women who were easily orgasmic, and they did not investigate how people's physiological responses might vary according to their age, experience, and culture (Tiefer, 2004). Thus, in their eagerness to show that the physiology of arousal and orgasm were the same in both sexes, Masters and Johnson tended to overlook individual differences (Irvine, 1990).

Since Masters and Johnson's studies, sex researchers have learned much more about individual variation in sexual physiology and responsiveness (Ellison, 2000; Tiefer, 2004; Zilbergeld, 1992). They have learned that people's *physiological* responses do not always correlate with their *subjective* experience of desire and arousal (Irvine, 1990). Thus, vaginal lubrication is not always a sign of arousal; it can also be a response to nervousness, excitement, disgust, or fear. Similarly, a man's erection is not always due to sexual stimulation; it can also be a response to fear, anger, disgust, or other emotions.

The question of whether men and women are alike or different in some underlying, biologically based "sex drive" continues to provoke lively debate. Some physiological researchers believe that the hormones and brain circuits involved in sexual behaviour differ for men and women (Tolman & Diamond, 2001). They maintain that for men, the "wiring" for sex overlaps with that for dominance and aggression, which is why sex and aggression are more likely to be linked in men than women. Research at Brock University, however, has shown that the link between sex and aggression differs from one man to another and is a matter of conscious decisions that are predicted by personality factors and intelligence (Bogaert, 2001). For women, the circuits for sexuality and nurturance seem to overlap, contributing to women's greater likelihood of associating sex with the emotional relationship in which it occurs.

Others argue that although women on average are certainly as capable as men of *sexual pleasure*, men, testosterone-infused creatures that they are, have a greater *sex drive* than women do. Proponents of this view point out that every kind of sexual behaviour—including masturbation, erotic fantasies, and orgasm—universally occurs at a higher rate among men than women, even when men are forbidden by cultural or religious rules to engage in sex at all; for example, Catholic priests have more of these sexual experiences than Catholic nuns do (Baumeister, Catanese, & Vohs, 2001; Dabbs, 2000; Oliver & Hyde, 1993; Peplau, 2002).

Many social psychologists, however, maintain that most gender differences in sexual behaviour reflect women's and men's different roles and experiences in life, and have little or nothing to do with biologically based drives or brain circuits (Eagly & Wood, 1999). Studies of men at the Clarke Institute of Psychiatry in Toronto, for example, have shown that male sexual arousal can be affected by classical conditioning. Pairing pictures of females with videotapes of arousing sexual interactions increased males' sexual arousal when the photo was shown by itself at a later time (Lalumière & Quinsey, 1998). Women's sexuality is also influenced by learning, and as long as large numbers of women are taught to fear, dislike, or avoid sex, social psychologists say, it is impossible to know what women's "sexual drive" might really be like. A middle view is that men's sexual behaviour is more biologically influenced ("driven") than is women's, whereas women's sexual desires and responsiveness are more affected by circumstances, the specific relationship, and cultural norms (Baumeister, 2000; Peplau et al., 2000).

Evolution and Sex Biological approaches to sexuality have had a boost in recent years from evolutionary psychologists, who believe that sex differences in courtship and mating practices evolved in response to species' survival needs

"It's a guy thing."

This Kenyan man has 40 wives and 349 children (all of whom, apparently, come to visit). Although he is unusual, in societies around the world it is more common for men to have many wives than for women to have many husbands. Evolutionary psychologists think the reason is that men have evolved to sow as many wild oats as they can, whereas women have evolved to be happy with just a few grains.

(Buss, 1994). In this view, it is evolutionarily adaptive for males to compete with other males for access to young and fertile females, and to try to win and then inseminate as many females as possible. The more females a male mates with, the more genes he can pass along. The human record in this regard was achieved by a man who fathered 899 children (Daly & Wilson, 1983). (What else he did with his time is not known.)

In contrast, according to evolutionary psychologists, females need to shop for the best genetic deal, because they can conceive and bear only a limited number of offspring. Having such a large biological investment in each pregnancy, they can't afford to make mistakes. Besides, mating with a lot of different males would produce no more offspring than staying with just one. So, in the evolutionary view, females try to attach themselves to dominant males, who have resources and status and are likely to have "superior" genes.

In human beings and other species, according to proponents of this view, the result of these two opposite sexual strategies is that males generally want sex more often than females do; males are often fickle and promiscuous, whereas females are usually devoted and faithful; males are drawn to sexual novelty, whereas females want stability and security; males will sometimes resort to sexual coercion and rape; males are relatively undiscriminating in their choice of partners, whereas females are cautious and choosy; and males are competitive and concerned about dominance, whereas females are less so.

In human beings, some of these sex differences do appear to be universal, or at least very common. In one massive international project, scientists studied many thousands of people in cultures all across the globe (Buss, 1994; Schmitt, 2003). Around the world, men are more interested in the youth and beauty of their sexual partners, presumably because youth is associated with fertility. They are more sexually jealous and possessive, presumably because males can never be 100 percent sure that their children are really theirs genetically. They are quicker to have sex with partners they don't know well, and more inclined toward promiscuity, presumably so that their sperm will be distributed as widely as possible. Women, in contrast, tend to emphasize the financial resources or prospects of a potential mate, his status, and his willingness to commit to a relationship (Bailey et al., 1994; Buss, 1996; Buunk et al., 1996; Mealey, 2000; Sprecher, Sullivan, & Hatfield, 1994).

One problem with this evolutionary view is that it is an after-the-fact explanation of a stereotype; the actual behaviour of human beings and other animals often contradicts the image of the sexually promiscuous male and the coy and choosy female (Barash & Lipton, 2001; Birkhead, 2001; Fausto-Sterling, 1997; Hrdy, 1994). In species after species—birds, fish, and mammals, including human beings—females are sexually ardent and often have many male partners. The female's sexual behaviour does not seem to depend only on

Thinking Critically About Evolutionary Theories of Sex

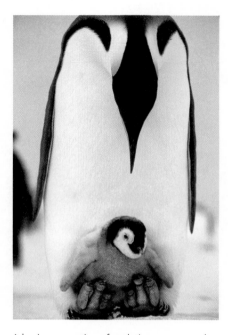

A basic assumption of evolutionary approaches to sexuality is that females across species have greater involvement in child rearing than males do. But there are many exceptions. Female emperor penguins, for example, take off every winter, leaving behind males like this doting dad to care for the kids.

the goal of being fertilized by the male: Females have sex when they are not ovulating and even when they are already pregnant! And in many species, from penguins to primates, males do not just mate and run. They stick around, feeding the infants, carrying them, and protecting them against predators (Hrdy, 1988; Snowdon, 1997; Taub, 1984).

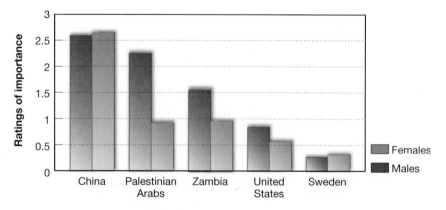

FIGURE 14.1 Attitudes Toward Chastity

In many places, men care more about a partner's chastity than women do, as evolutionary psychologists would predict. But culture has a powerful effect on these attitudes, as this graph shows. Notice that in China, both partners prefer a partner who has not yet had intercourse, whereas in Sweden, chastity is a nonissue. (From Buss, 1995.)

These findings have sent evolutionary theorists scurrying to figure out the evolutionary benefits of female promiscuity and male nurturance. Perhaps, in some species, females need sperm from several males in order to ensure conception by the healthiest sperm (Baker, 1996). Or perhaps females have multiple partners in order to increase the number of males who will support the female's offspring. This motive is quite explicit among the Barí people of Venezuela. A man who impregnates a woman is considered the child's primary father. But if she takes a lover during her pregnancy (an approved practice), he is considered a secondary father, and he is expected to supply mother and baby with extra food (Beckerman et al., 1998). Thus, sexual behaviour can be influenced by its potential to result in a *parental investment* by either partner. In Canada (and around the world), both men and women become more particular in their relationship choices when parental investment becomes a greater possibility (Woodward & Richards, 2005).

Critics, however, argue that all evolutionary explanations, whether of female fidelity or promiscuity, are inadequate when applied to human beings, because human sexual behaviour is so amazingly varied and changeable. Cultures range from those in which women have many children to those in which they have very few; from those in which men are intimately involved in child rearing to those in which they do nothing at all; from those in which women may have many lovers to those in which women may be killed if they have sex outside of marriage (Hatfield & Rapson, 1996). In many places, the chastity of a potential mate is much more important to men than to women; but elsewhere it is important to both sexes—or to neither one (see Figure 14.1).

Finally, an important critique of evolutionary theories of sexuality is that what people say on a questionnaire may not have anything to do with their actual choices! Plenty of women don't date or marry rich men, nor do all men date or marry stereotypically beautiful women. Many happily find partners who are plain, financially challenged, or merely average Joes and Janes. As we saw in our discussion of love, most people choose partners based on their proximity and similarity. Actually, this makes good evolutionary sense, because our prehistoric ancestors, unlike undergraduates filling out questionnaires about their ideal mate, did not have 5000 fellow students to choose from. They lived in small bands, so if they were lucky they might get to choose between Urp and Ork, and that was about it. They could not hold out for some knockout or rich guy down the road (Hazan & Diamond, 2000).

This evidence, say the critics, argues against a universal, genetically determined sexual strategy. What evolution *has* bestowed on us, they say, is an amazingly flexible brain. Biology influences sexual behaviour but does not control it, as we shall see next.

The Psychology of Desire

Psychologists are fond of observing that the sexiest sex organ is the brain, where perceptions begin. People's values, fantasies, and beliefs profoundly affect their sexual desire and behaviour. That is why a touch on the knee by an exciting new date feels terrifically sexy, but the same touch by a creepy stranger on a bus feels disgusting. It is why a worried thought can kill sexual arousal in a second, and why a fantasy can be more erotic than reality.

The Many Motives for Sex To most people, the primary motives for sex are pretty obvious: to enjoy the pleasure of it, to express love and intimacy, or to make babies. But there are other motives too, not all of them so positive. Studies of several hundred university students and more than 1500 older adults identified six factors underlying the many reasons that people give for having sex (Cooper, Shapiro, & Powers, 1998):

- *Enhancement*—the emotional satisfaction or physical pleasure of sex.
- *Intimacy*—emotional closeness with the partner.
- *Coping*—dealing with negative emotions and disappointments.
- *Self-affirmation*—reassurance that one is attractive or desirable.
- *Partner approval*—the desire to please or appease one's partner, perhaps to avoid the partner's anger or rejection.
- *Peer approval*—the wish to impress one's friends, be part of the group, and conform to what "everyone else" seems to be doing.

In this research, men and women did not differ in their motives for intimacy, but men were much more likely to have had sex for all the other motives, especially peer approval. The older that people were, the more likely they were to have sex for intimacy and for self-enhancement (pleasure), and the less likely they were to have sex for peer or partner approval.

Perhaps you can think of other motives for sex, too: spiritual transcendence, money, duty, power over the partner, submission to the partner, rebellion . . . People's motives for having sex affect many aspects of their sexual behaviour,

The many motivations for sex range from sex for profit to sex for fun.

including whether they engage in sex in the first place, whether they enjoy it, whether they have unprotected or otherwise risky sex, and whether they have few or many partners (Browning et al., 2000). Extrinsic motives, such as having sex for purposes of coping and gaining approval, are most strongly associated with risky sexual behaviour, including having many partners and not using birth control (Cooper, Shapiro, & Powers, 1998).

Many studies of university students find that significant numbers of women *and* men are having sex for motives other than pleasure or intimacy (Impett & Peplau, 2002). In one study, university students in dating relationships kept a daily diary of their sexual experiences. Fifty percent of the women and 26 percent of the men reported consenting to unwanted sexual activity during that time (O'Sullivan & Allgeier, 1998). Men may do so because of peer pressure, inexperience, a desire for popularity, or a fear of seeming homosexual or "unmasculine." Women may do so because they do not want to lose the relationship; because they feel obligated, once the partner has spent time and money on them; or because the partner makes them feel guilty.

Sexual Coercion and Rape One of the most persistent differences in the sexual experiences of women and men has to do with their perceptions of, and experiences with, sexual coercion. In Canada, surveys show that between 16 percent (Rodgers, 1994) and 35 percent (Kelly & DeKeseredy, 1993) of women have experienced at least one physical assault during a date with a male. No fewer than 45 percent of women in one survey reported having been sexually abused since leaving high school (Kelly & DeKeseredy, 1993). And nearly one-fourth of American women between the ages of 18 and 59 reported in a survey that a man—usually a husband or boyfriend—

had forced them to do something sexually that they did not want to do (Laumann et al., 1994). But only about 3 percent of the men said they had ever forced a woman into a sexual act. Obviously, what many women regard as coercion is not always seen as coercive by men.

What motivates some men to rape? There appear to be several different motivations:

- *Peer approval.* University men who have physically coerced their dates into having sex have often been pressured by male friends to prove their masculinity by "scoring" (Kanin, 1985).

- *Anger, revenge, or a desire to dominate or humiliate the victim.* This motive is apparent among soldiers who rape captive women during war, and then often kill them (Olujic, 1998). Similarly, the rape of women in the Canadian military (Nicol, 1998) could be viewed in terms of the rapists' motives to humiliate the women and get women to leave the military. Aggressive motives also occur in the rape of men by other men, usually by anal penetration (King & Woollett, 1997). This form of rape typically occurs in youth gangs, where the intention is to humiliate rival gang members, and in prison, where again the motive is to conquer and degrade the victim.

- *Having the personality traits of narcissism, insecurity, defensiveness, or hostility toward women.* Sexually aggressive males often are narcissistic, are unable to empathize with women, and feel entitled to have sexual relations with whatever woman they choose. They misperceive women's behaviour in social situations, equate feelings of power with sexuality, and blame women for "provoking" them (Bushman et al., 2003; Drieschner & Lange, 1999; Malamuth et al., 1995; Zurbriggen, 2000).

- *Contempt for the victim and a sadistic pleasure in inflicting pain* (Knight, Prentky, & Cerce, 1994). A minority of rapists are men who are primarily motivated to injure or murder their victims.

You can see that the answer to the question "Why do people have sex?" is not obvious, and is by no means a simple matter of "doing what's natural." In addition to the intrinsic motives of intimacy, pleasure, procreation, and love, extrinsic motives include intimidation, dominance, insecurity, appeasing the partner, approval from peers,

This ad, which is directed at men, emphasizes the importance of respect and communication in sexual relationships. Do you think it is effective? Why or why not?

and the wish to prove oneself a real man or a desirable woman.

The Culture of Desire

Think about kissing. Westerners like to think about kissing, and to do it, too. But if you think kissing is natural, try to remember your first serious kiss and all you had to learn about noses, breathing, and the position of teeth and tongue. The sexual kiss is so complicated that some cultures have never even gotten around to it. They think that kissing another person's mouth—the very place that food enters!—is disgusting (Tiefer, 2004). Others have elevated the sexual kiss to high art; why do you suppose one version is called "French" kissing?

As the kiss illustrates, having the physical equipment to perform a sexual act is not all there is to sexual motivation. People have to learn, from cultural norms, peers, and parental lessons, what is supposed to turn them on (or off), which parts of the body and what activities are erotic (or repulsive), and even how to have sexual relations (Laumann & Gagnon, 1995).

The range of cultural variations in sexuality is remarkable. To men in cultures where women are required to cover up completely in public, the sight of a woman's ankle—let alone her entire leg—is highly arousing; to Western men today, an ankle doesn't do it. In some cultures, oral sex is regarded as a bizarre sexual deviation; in others, it is not only considered normal but also supremely desirable. In some cultures, sex is seen as something joyful and beautiful, an art to be cultivated as one might cultivate the skill of gourmet cook-

Kissing is a learned skill—one that some people start practising earlier than others.

ing. In others, it is considered ugly and dirty, something to be "gotten through" as quickly as possible. However, people living in Canada and the United States who are from areas of the world considered to be very conservative, such as the Middle East and Asia, are becoming more liberal in their attitudes (Leiblum, Wioegel, & Brickle, 2003).

Sexual Scripts How do cultures transmit their rules and requirements about sex to their members? During childhood and adolescence, people learn their culture's *gender roles*—collections of rules that determine the proper attitudes and behaviour for men and women, sexual and otherwise (see Chapter 10). Just as an actor in the role of Hamlet needs a script to learn his part, a person following a gender role needs a **sexual script** that instructs men and women on how to behave in sexual situations (Gagnon & Simon,

sexual scripts Sets of implicit rules that specify proper sexual behaviour for a person in a given situation, varying with the person's age, culture, and gender.

These teenagers are following the sexual scripts for their gender—the boys, by ogling and making sexual remarks about girls to impress their peers, and the girls, by preening and wearing makeup to look good for boys.

1973; Laumann & Gagnon, 1995). If you are a teenage girl, are you supposed to be sexually adventurous and assertive, or sexually modest and passive? How about if you are a teenage boy? What if you are an older woman or an older man? The answers differ from culture to culture, as members act in accordance with the sexual scripts for their gender and age.

In many parts of the world, boys acquire their attitudes about sex in a competitive atmosphere where the goal is to impress other males, and they talk and joke about masturbation and other sexual experiences with their friends. While boys are learning to value physical sex, girls are learning to value relationships and to make themselves attractive. Many learn that their role is to be sexually desirable (which is good), but not to indulge in their own sexual pleasures (which would be bad)—unless they are following the sexual scripts of the characters in *Sex and the City*! The different scripts for heterosexual couples can create conflicting motives for sexuality and misreadings of one another's behaviour. Is she dressing that way to look sexy or to tell me she wants sex? Is he really interested in me or just in hooking up for tonight?

Gay men and lesbians follow sexual scripts, too. But they tend to be more flexible than heterosexuals in establishing rules for their relationships, because neither partner is following a traditional gender role (Peplau & Spalding, 2000; Rose, Zand, & Cini, 1993).

Culture, Gender, and Sex

Where do sexual scripts and gender differences come from? As we saw earlier, evolutionary psychologists think that evolutionary processes such as natural selection best account for gender differences in sexuality: why men often pressure women for sex, why women tend to reject casual sex, and why women "give in" and men "make a move" when they do not really want to (Buss, 1994; Gangestad & Simpson, 2000; Oliver & Hyde, 1993).

But social and cultural psychologists believe that gender roles reflect a culture's economic and social arrangements. When those arrangements change, so do people's attitudes and behaviour. Whenever women have needed marriage to ensure their social and financial security, they have regarded sex as a bargaining chip, an asset to be rationed rather than an activity to be enjoyed for its own sake (Hatfield & Rapson, 1996). A woman with no economic resources of her own cannot afford to casually seek sexual pleasure if that means risking an unwanted pregnancy, the security of marriage, her reputation in society, her physical safety, or, in some cultures, her very life. When women become self-supporting and able to control their own fertility, however, they are more likely to want sex for pleasure rather than as a means to another goal.

Get Involved   Is the Double Standard Still Alive?

Think of all the words you know to describe a sexually active woman, and then think of words for a sexually active man. Is one list longer than the other? Are the two lists equally negative or positive in their connotations? What does this exercise tell you about the survival of the double standard and your culture's sexual scripts?

The Riddle of Sexual Orientation

Why do most people become heterosexual, some homosexual, and others bisexual? Many psychological explanations for homosexuality have been proposed over the years, but none of them has been supported. Homosexuality is not a result of having a "smothering mother," an absent father, or emotional problems. It is not caused by same-sex sexual play in childhood or adolescence, which is actually quite common (Lamb, 2002). It is not caused by "seduction" by an older adult (Rind, Tromovich, & Bauserman, 1998). It is not caused

by parental practices or role models. Most gay men recall that they rejected the typical "boy" role and boys' toys and games from a very early age, in spite of enormous pressures from their parents and peers to conform to the traditional male role (Bailey & Zucker, 1995). Conversely, the overwhelming majority of children of gay parents do not become gay, as a learning model would predict, although they are more likely than the children of straight parents to be open-minded about homosexuality and gender roles (Bailey et al., 1995; Patterson, 1992, 1995).

Many researchers, therefore, have been turning to biological explanations of sexual orientation. The evidence to date, however, is inconclusive. In the early 1990s, a few studies of gay men reported associations between sexual orientation and specific areas of the brain (Allen & Gorski, 1992; LeVay, 1991). These studies got lots of press, but they have not been replicated (Byne, 1995). Researchers have also examined the role of prenatal exposure to androgens (Bailey & Pillard, 1995; Gladue, 1994). Female babies accidentally exposed in the womb to masculinizing hormones—androgens or other chemicals—are more likely than other girls to become bisexual or lesbian, and to prefer "boys' toys" and activities (Collaer & Hines, 1995; Meyer-Bahlburg et al., 1995). However, most "androgenized" girls do not become lesbians, and most lesbians were not exposed to atypical prenatal hormones (Peplau et al., 2000).

Sexual orientation does seem to be moderately heritable, particularly in men (Bailey & Pillard, 1995; Bailey, Dunn, & Martin, 2000; Whitam, Diamond, & Martin, 1993). But the vast majority of gay men and lesbians do not have a close gay relative, and their siblings, including twins, are overwhelmingly likely to be heterosexual (Peplau et al., 2000).

So we are left with a real puzzle. One problem with trying to find "the" origin of sexual orientation is that sexual identity and behaviour take many different forms. Some people are equally attracted to men and women, and some are heterosexual in behaviour but have homosexual fantasies (Baumrind, 1995; Byne, 1995). Some gay men are "feminine" in interests and manner, but many are not; some lesbians are "butch," i.e., "masculine," in interests and manner, but many other lesbians are not (Singh et al., 1999). Some lesbians do have an exclusively same-sex orientation their whole lives, but most seem to have more fluid sexual orientations: They have sex with the person they fall in love with, male or female (Diamond, 2003; Peplau et al., 2000). In some cultures, teenage boys go through a homosexual phase that they do not define as homosexual and that does not affect their future relations with women (Herdt, 1984). In Lesotho, in South Africa, women have intimate relations with other women, including passionate kissing and oral sex, but they do not define these acts as sexual, as they do when a man is the partner (Kendall, 1999).

Genetics cannot account for the diversity of such customs nor for the diversity of experience

Gay marriage is now legal In Canada, but people in gay relationships still confront many people's negative attitudes toward homosexuality. Psychologists are working to understand why the issue of legalizing gay and lesbian marriage evokes so much anger and controversy.

among homosexuals. At present, therefore, we will have to tolerate uncertainty about the origins of sexual orientation. Perhaps the routes to homosexual orientation differ on average for males and females and also differ for individuals.

Thinking Critically About Findings on Homosexuality

Now, how are you reacting to these findings? Your responses are probably affected by your feelings about homosexuality. Many gay men and lesbians welcome biological research on the grounds that it supports what they have been saying all along: Sexual orientation is not a matter of choice, but a fact of nature. Others fear that people who are prejudiced against homosexuals will use this research to argue that gay people have a biological "defect" that should be eradicated or "corrected." But people who are hostile to homosexuals can use any theory, biological or psychological, to justify their wish to eliminate homosexuality. They have often used learning theories to argue, mistakenly, that "if it's learned, it can be unlearned," and thus to subject gay men, and even "unboyish" boys as young as three years old, to harsh and punitive forms of behaviour modification (Burke, 1996).

Research on sexuality can thus be used for many contradictory purposes and political goals, depending on the values and attitudes of the culture in which such findings emerge. As long as a society is uncomfortable about homosexuality, preconceptions and prejudice are likely to cloud its reactions to anything that psychologists learn about it.

WHAT'S AHEAD

- Is overweight usually a result of psychological problems?
- What theory explains why it's so hard for heavy people to lose weight—and just as hard for thin people to gain it?
- Why are people all over the world getting fatter?
- Why are so many competent professional women determined to be very thin?

THE HUNGRY ANIMAL: MOTIVES TO EAT

Many people spend a lot of time and energy thinking about their bodies and wanting to "fix" them. They long to be thin, or thinner, struggling unsuccessfully their whole lives to shed pounds. Others think that fat is just fine. How much do genes, psychology, and environment affect our motivation to eat or not to eat?

The Genetics of Weight

set point The genetically influenced weight range for an individual, maintained by biological mechanisms that regulate food intake, fat reserves, and metabolism.

At one time, most psychologists thought that being overweight was a sign of emotional disturbance. If you were fat, it was because you hated your mother, feared intimacy, or were trying to fill an emotional hole in your psyche by loading up on rich desserts. The evidence for psychological theories of overweight, however, came mainly from self-reports and from flawed studies that lacked control groups or objective measures of how much people were actually eating (Allison & Heshka, 1993). When researchers did controlled experiments, they learned that fat people, on average, are no more and no less emotionally disturbed than average-weight people (Stunkard, 1980).

Even more surprising, studies showed that *heaviness is not always caused by overeating.* Many heavy people do eat large quantities of food, but so do some thin people. Many thin people eat very little, but so do some obese people. In one study that carefully monitored everything that subjects were eating, two 260-pound women maintained their weights while consuming only 1000 calories a day (Wooley, Wooley, & Dyrenforth, 1979). In another study, which had volunteers gorge themselves for months, it was as hard for slender people to gain weight as it is for most heavy people to lose weight. The minute the study was over, the slender people lost weight as fast as dieters gained it back (Sims, 1974).

The leading explanation for such findings has been that a biological mechanism keeps your body weight at a genetically influenced **set point**—the weight you stay at when you are not trying to gain or lose (Lissner et al., 1991). The set point can vary about 10 percent in either direction. For example, a woman with a set point of 150 pounds might weigh anywhere from 135 to 165. But if her weight dips below 135 or goes above 165, her body will produce either an insatiable urge to eat or a loss of appetite, to bring its fat levels back into line.

Set-point research has focused on how the body regulates appetite, eating, and weight gain and loss. Everyone has a genetically programmed *basal metabolism rate*, the rate at which the body burns calories for energy, and a fixed number of fat cells, which store fat for energy and thus can change in size. A complex interaction of metabolism, fat cells, and hormones keeps people at the weight their bodies are designed to be, much as a thermostat keeps a house at a preset temperature. When a heavy person diets, the body's metabolism slows down to conserve energy and fat reserves. When a thin person overeats, metabolism speeds up, burning energy. In one study, in which 16 slender volunteers ate 1000 extra calories every day for eight weeks, their metabolisms sped up to burn the excess calories. They became like hummingbirds, in constant movement: fidgeting, pacing, changing their positions frequently while seated, and so on (Levine, Eberhardt, & Jensen, 1999).

Set-point theory predicts that the heritability of weight and body fat should be high, and indeed it is: In twin and adoption studies, heritability estimates fall between .40 and .70 (Comuzzie & Allison, 1998). Pairs of adult identical twins who grow up in different families are just as similar in body weight and shape as twins raised together. The early family environment has almost *no effect at all* on body shape, weight gain, or percentage of fat in the body (Stunkard et al., 1990). When identical twins gain weight, they usually gain it in the same place: Some pairs store extra pounds around their waists, others on their hips and thighs (Bouchard et al., 1990).

Genes are also involved in some types of obesity. In a study of 171 Pima Indians in Arizona, two-thirds of the women and half of the men became obese over time, and the slower their metabolisms, the greater the weight gain. After adding anywhere from 20 to 45 pounds, however, the Pimas stopped gaining weight. Their metabolism rates rose, and their weights stabilized at the new, higher level (Ravussin et al., 1988). Many Pimas apparently have a set point for plumpness.

A few years ago, a team of researchers isolated a genetic variation that causes mice to become obese (Zhang et al., 1994). The usual form of the gene, called "obese," or *ob* for short, causes fat cells to secrete a protein, which the researchers named *leptin* (from the Greek *leptos*, "slender"). Leptin travels through the blood to the brain's hypothalamus, which is involved in the regulation of appetite. Injecting leptin into mice reduces the animals' appetites, speeds up their metabolisms, and makes them more active; as a result, the animals shed weight (Halaas et al., 1995).

Body weight and shape are strongly affected by genetic factors. The Pimas of the American Southwest gain weight easily but lose it slowly, whereas the Bororo nomads of Nigeria can eat a lot of food yet remain slender.

Both of these mice have a mutation in the ob gene, which usually makes mice chubby, like the one on the left. But when leptin is injected daily, the mice eat less and burn more calories, becoming slim, like his friendly pal. Unfortunately, leptin injections do not have the same results in most human beings..

The story of leptin is, however, a good cautionary tale for consumers. When the effects of leptin were discovered in mice and the presence of leptin was discovered in humans, one pharmaceutical company thought it had a surefire obesity drug at hand: Take leptin, lose weight! It seemed to be too good to be true, and, alas, it was. The role of leptin in human obesity is more complicated than it is in mice. For most obese people, leptin does not play a major role, and taking more of it does not produce much weight loss (Comuzzie & Allison, 1998).

Researchers have also discovered a gene that modulates production of a protein that apparently converts excess calories into heat rather than fat. Possession of this gene may be the reason that slim people stay slim even when they overeat (Arsenijevic et al., 2000).

But be cautious about the enthusiasm that always accompanies such findings. Critical thinkers should be wary of oversimplified claims that a gene or a hormone "determines" anything, or that its discovery is "a major breakthrough." Dozens of genes and body chemicals are involved in appetite, metabolism rates, and weight regulation. Moreover, these elements often conflict. You have receptors in your nose and mouth that might keep urging you to eat more ("The food is right there! It's good! Eat!"), receptors in your gut telling you to quit ("You've had enough already!"), and leptins and other chemicals telling you that you have stored enough fat or not enough. One hormone makes you hungry and eager to eat more, and another turns off your appetite after a meal,

Thinking Critically About Weight-Loss "Breakthroughs"

making you eat less (Travis, 2002). That is why no single gene or chemical is the key to obesity—or the cure.

The complexity of the mechanisms governing appetite and weight also helps explain why "appetite-suppressing" drugs fail in the long run. A drug that affects one part of the eating–weight gain interaction might have an unintended influence on another.

Culture, Psychology, and Weight

Despite the obvious involvement of genes in weight and body shape, they cannot explain the recent increase in rates of overweight and extreme obesity (Pinel, Assanand, & Lehman, 2000). If most people have normal set points, why are so many people everywhere getting fatter? In 2001, approximately 16 percent of Canadians over the age of 40 were obese (Canadian Community Health Survey, 2000/01). It has even been found that recent immigrants to Canada are more likely to become overweight or obese the longer they have lived in Canada (Cairney & Ostbye, 1999). In July 2001, the United Nations, so used to dealing with problems of starvation and malnutrition, announced that "Obesity is the dominant unmet global health issue," especially in the United States, Canada, Great Britain, Japan, Australia, and even coastal China and Southeast Asia.

The Environment and Obesity Genes have not changed in the last decades, but the environment certainly has. The leading environmental culprits causing the worldwide weight-gain epidemic are (1) the increased abundance of low-cost, varied, high-calorie foods; (2) the habit of eating high-calorie food on the run rather than in leisurely meals; (3) the rise in "energy-saving" devices, such as remote controls; (4) the speed and convenience of driving rather than walking or biking; and (5) the preference for watching television and videos rather than doing anything active (Hill & Peters, 1998; Robinson, 1999).

Most human beings are predisposed to gain weight when rich food is abundant because, in the past, starvation was all too often a real possibility. Therefore, a tendency to store calories in the form of fat provided a definite survival advantage. Unfortunately, evolution did not design a comparable mechanism to prevent people without hummingbird metabolisms from gaining excess weight when food is easily available, tasty, rich, varied, and cheap. That, of course, is precisely the situation today, surrounded as we are by 3/4-pound burgers, fries, chips, tacos, candy bars, and pizzas (Pinel, Assanand, & Lehman, 2000). Moreover, in North America, food and drink portions have doubled and even tripled in size from what they were only a generation ago (Critser, 2002). When people from other cultures move to the United States, they often put on pounds because of the change in dietary habits. For example, many Mexican-Americans born in the United States are fatter than those who were born in Mexico. One reason is that in Mexico, poor people eat corn tortillas, which are cheap; and their diet overall is lower in fat and higher in fibre than that of their relatives in the north. But Mexican-Americans born in the United States tend to eat flour tortillas, which are often made with lard and are thus much higher in calories, and they eat other high-calorie foods because of acculturation to American ways. As a result, they have higher obesity rates than their kin in Mexico (Sundquist & Winkleby, 2000).

Another nongenetic influence on weight is exercise, which boosts the body's metabolic rate and may lower its set point. Among Canada's youth, unsurprisingly, those who are overweight and obese spend significantly less time exercising and more time watching television than those who are not overweight (Janssen et al., 2004). When obese women are put on severely restricted diets, their metabolic rates drop sharply, as set-point theory would predict. But when obese women are put on a diet combined with moderate physical activity—daily walking—they lose weight, and their metabolic rates rise almost to previous levels (Wadden et al., 1990). Exercise even promotes weight loss in people who are genetically susceptible to obesity, like the Pima Indians. Pimas who live in Mexico are more physically active than Pimas who live in Arizona, and their weight is therefore significantly lower (Esparza et al., 2000).

Cultural Attitudes Eating habits and activity levels, in turn, are shaped by a culture's customs and standards of what the ideal body should look like: fat, thin, muscular, soft. In many places around the world, especially in those where famine and crop failures are common, fat is taken as a sign of health, affluence in men, and sexual desirability in women (Stearns, 1997). Among the Calabari of Nigeria, brides are put in special "fattening huts" where they do nothing but eat, so as to become plump enough to please their husbands. And at the Hangandi festival in Niger, the fattest woman wins the beauty contest.

Interviews with young women born in the Philippines and living in British Columbia revealed clear differences between Filipino and Canadian beliefs about body, food, and health. While native-born Canadians value thinness, Filipino beliefs favour fatness and eating to maximize resistance to illness. Over time, however, the women interviewed said that they had come to accept the Canadian beliefs (Farrales & Chapman, 1999). And while Canadian women tend to overestimate the fatness of their abdomen, hips, thighs, and legs, women from India focus more on their face, neck, shoulders, and chest, thus demonstrating differences in how ideal body shape is construed in the two countries (Gupta et al., 2001).

Ironically, while people of all ethnicities and social classes have been getting fatter, the cultural ideal for white women in Canada, the United States, and Europe has been getting thinner. The ideal of the voluptuously curvy woman, big-breasted and big-hipped, was popular before World War I and after World War II. But in the flapper era of the 1920s and again starting in the 1960s, big breasts and hips became unfashionable. Today the North American female ideal is an odd combination: big breasts but no hips. The cultural ideal for men has changed, too. Until relatively recently, most heavily muscled men were labourers and farmers, so being physically strong and muscular was a sign of being working class. In the past decade, pressures have increased for middle-class men to be "buff" and strong (Bordo, 2000).

Why did these changes occur? One explanation is that white men and women associate overweight, in either sex, with softness, laziness, and weakness (Crandall & Martinez, 1996). And they associate the curvy, big-breasted female body with femininity, nurturance, and motherhood. Hence big breasts are fashionable in eras that celebrate women's role as mothers—such as after World War II, when women were encouraged to give up their wartime jobs and have many children (Stearns, 1997). However, among many whites, femininity is also associated, alas, with incompetence. Thus, whenever women have entered traditionally male spheres of education and work, as they did in the 1920s and again since the 1970s, professionally ambitious women have tried to look boyishly thin and muscular in order to avoid appearing "soft," feminine, and dumb (Silverstein

Should a woman be voluptuous and curvy or slim as a reed? Should a man be thin and unmuscled or strong and buff? Genes and evolution cannot explain cultural changes in attitudes toward the ideal body. During the 1950s, actresses like Jayne Mansfield (left) embodied the post-war ideal: curvy, buxom, and "womanly." Today, many women struggle to look like Calista Flockhart (second from left): skinny, angular, and boyish. Men, too, have been caught up in body-image changes. The soft and scrawny hippie ideal of the 1960s (second from right) is a far cry from today's muscular, macho ideal (right).

& Perlick, 1995; Silverstein, Peterson, & Perdue, 1986). Today's big-breasted but otherwise skinny female ideal may reflect cultural ambivalence about whether women's proper role is domestic or professional. As for men, having a strong, muscular body is now a sign of affluence rather than poverty. It means a man has the money and time to join a gym and work out.

Weight and Health: Biology versus Culture

What happens when your genetic disposition clashes with your culture's notions of the ideal body? The battle between biology and culture can cause physical and emotional problems, because being extremely overweight or starving to be underweight can both be harmful.

Cultures that regard overweight as a sign of health and sexiness are obviously more accepting of people who are heavy. But obesity is now a serious health problem of epidemic proportions. When combined with a lack of aerobic fitness, it is a leading risk factor in diabetes, high blood pressure, heart disease, stroke, cancer, infertility, sleep apnea, and many other disorders. In Canada, diabetes is three times more prevalent among Aboriginal peoples (Health Canada, 2002), primarily as a result of

diet, which has changed quite dramatically for this population over the last two generations.

Efforts to match a cultural standard of excessive thinness can also pose serious risks to health. Evolution has programmed women for a reserve of fat necessary for the onset of menstruation, healthy childbearing, nursing, and, after menopause, the production and storage of estrogen. In cultures that think women should be very thin, many women become obsessed with weight and are continually dieting, forever fighting their bodies' need for a certain amount of fat. A significant minority of women develop serious eating disorders that reflect an irrational terror of being "too fat" (Walsh & Devlin, 1998). In **bulimia**, the person binges (eats vast quantities of rich food) and then purges by inducing vomiting or using laxatives. In **anorexia nervosa**, the person eats hardly anything and therefore becomes dangerously thin; anorexics have severely distorted body images, thinking they are fat even when they are emaciated. Although many sufferers of these disorders recover, others damage their health permanently or, in the case of anorexia, die of heart or kidney failure or osteoporosis.

Bulimia and anorexia are far more common in women than in men. But eating disorders and body-image distortions among boys and men are

bulimia An eating disorder characterized by episodes of bingeing and purging.

anorexia (nervosa) An eating disorder characterized by fear of being fat, a distorted body image, radically reduced consumption of food, and emaciation.

increasing, though they take different forms (Bordo, 2000). Just as anorexic women see their gaunt bodies as being too fat, men with the comparable delusion, which one group of researchers calls an "Adonis complex," see their muscular bodies as being too puny. So they abuse steroids and exercise or pump iron compulsively (Pope, Phillips, & Olivardia, 2000).

Genes may play a role in the development of eating disorders, just as they do in obesity, body weight, and shape (Allison & Faith, 1997). However, genetic dispositions clearly interact with cultural pressures and with a person's psychological conflicts. Ballerinas, models, actresses, and jockeys are under enormous professional pressure to be thin; fashion models weigh 25 percent less than the average American woman (Brumberg, 2000). Women who have eating disorders have internalized this unrealistic standard, and tend to be depressed, perfectionistic, and more self-critical than are healthy eaters (Lehman & Rodin, 1989; Stice, 2002; Walsh & Devlin, 1998). And research in Canada and elsewhere has shown that the mothers of those with eating disorders were more likely to be perfectionists themselves and to be concerned with weight and shape (Woodside et al., 2002).

But why are many men becoming as vulnerable as women to media images of nearly impossible body shapes, devouring magazines that promise "Perfect Abs in 10 Days!" and spending billions on cosmetic surgery? One explanation is that, in an era of growing equality and challenges to traditional masculinity, men want to look strong and "manly" to distinguish themselves from "soft" women (Pope, Phillips, & Olivardia, 2000). A Canadian study, for example, showed that low self-esteem based on appearance and high levels of vanity predicted a higher drive for muscularity in males (Morrison et al., 2004). Another explanation is that commercial interests know a vulnerable audience when they see one—and they also know how to create one.

In sum, within a given environment, genes interact with cultural rules, psychological needs, and individual habits in order to shape, in this case quite literally, who we are.

Anorexics cannot see the difference between being fashionably thin and being dangerously skeletal. This anorexic woman died.

Quick Quiz

Is all this information about eating making you hungry for knowledge?

1. *True or false?*: Emotional problems explain why fat people are heavy.

2. Falling and rising levels of leptin help the brain regulate appetite and _____ and play a role in maintaining a person's genetically influenced _____.

3. Rising rates of obesity can best be explained by (a) genetic changes over the past few decades, (b) a lack of willpower, (c) an abundance of high-calorie food and sedentary lifestyles, (d) the increase in eating disorders.

4. Bill, who is thin, reads in the newspaper that genes set the range of body weight and shape. "Oh, good," he exclaims, "now I can eat all the junk food I want; I was born to be skinny." What's wrong with Bill's conclusion?

Answers:

1. false   2. metabolism, set point   3. c   4. Bill is right to recognize that there may be limits to how heavy he can become. But he may also be oversimplifying and jumping to conclusions. Many people who have a set point for leanness will gain considerable weight on fatty foods and excess calories, especially if they don't exercise. Also, rich junk food is unhealthy for reasons that have nothing to do with becoming overweight.

WHAT'S AHEAD

- Why is "doing your best" an ineffective goal to set for yourself?

- When you are learning a new skill, which should you concentrate on: mastering it or performing it well in front of others?

- Which aspects of a job are more important than money in increasing your work satisfaction and involvement?

- How is the *desire* to achieve affected by the *opportunity* to achieve?

need for achievement A learned motive to meet personal standards of success and excellence in a chosen area.

Thematic Apperception Test (TAT) A projective test that asks respondents to interpret a series of drawings showing scenes of people; usually scored for unconscious personality traits and motives, such as the need for achievement, power, or affiliation.

THE COMPETENT ANIMAL: MOTIVES TO ACHIEVE

Almost every adult works. But "work" does not only mean paid employment. Students work at studying. Homemakers work, often more hours than do salaried employees, at running a household. Artists, poets, and actors work, even if they are paid erratically (or not at all). Most people are motivated to work in order to meet the basic needs for food and shelter. Yet survival alone does not explain why some people want to do their work well and others just want to get it done. And it does not explain why some people work merely to make a living and put their passions for achievement into unpaid activities—learning to become an accomplished trail rider or travelling to Madagascar to add a rare helmet vanga to their list of birds sighted. What keeps everybody doing what they do?

Psychologists, particularly those in the field of *industrial/organizational psychology*, have measured the psychological qualities that spur achievement and success and also the environmental conditions that influence productivity and satisfaction. Their findings apply not only to understanding why people thrive or wilt at their jobs, but also to understanding people's aspirations and achievements in general.

The Effects of Motivation on Work

In the early 1950s, David McClelland and his associates (1953) speculated that some people have a **need for achievement** that motivates them as much as hunger motivates people to eat. To measure the strength of this motive, McClelland used a variation of the **Thematic Apperception Test (TAT)**, which requires the test-taker to make up a story about a set of ambiguous pictures, such as

The Many Motives of Accomplishment

Learning from Nobel Prize Winners

To Inspire Others

Shirin Ebadi

Iran

Nobel Prize for Peace 2003 "It is hoped that being selected for the Nobel Peace Prize for 2003 will be a source of inspiration for women everywhere."

To Pursue Moral Ends

Lester Pearson

Canada

Nobel Prize for Peace 1975 "A gap has developed between our technological and material advances and our moral development. We must close this gap."

To Achieve Justice for All

Desmond Tutu

South Africa

Nobel Prize for Peace 1984 "In a world of beauty and plenty, millions suffer in poverty, poor health, and danger because of racism and political policy."

To Protect Our World

Wangari Maathai

Kenya

Nobel Prize for Peace 2004 "There is much to protect in this world—the environment, democracy, human rights."

a young man sitting at a desk. (The TAT is one of many *projective tests*, which are based on the assumption that a person will project unconscious motives and feelings onto an ambiguous stimulus; see Chapter 11.) The strength of the achievement motive, said McClelland (1961), is captured in the fantasies the test-taker reveals. "In fantasy anything is at least symbolically possible," he explained. "A person may rise to great heights, sink to great depths, kill his grandmother, or take off for the South Sea Islands on a pogo stick."

Needless to say, people with high achievement motivation do not fantasize about taking off for the South Seas or sinking to great depths. They tell stories about working hard, inventing a cure for cancer, and clobbering the opposition with their wit and brilliance. High scorers are more likely to start their own businesses. They set high personal standards, and they like challenges (McClelland, 1987).

The TAT is one of the few projective tests that have modest empirical support for the measurement of achievement motivation. But it does not have strong test–retest reliability, meaning that people's responses are easily influenced by what is going on at that moment in their lives rather than by some "inner drive" to succeed. Some people might tell stories of achieving against all odds not because they are determined to do so, but because they are idly daydreaming about entering the Tour de France or just saw the movie *Against All Odds*. Also, it isn't clear that the TAT tells researchers anything they would not learn by just *asking* people about their ambitions (Lilienfeld, Wood, & Garb, 2000). But the method launched many investigations into the question of why some people seem to have a drive to "make it," no matter what, and others just drift along.

The Importance of Goals Today the predominant approach to understanding achievement motivation emphasizes goals rather than inner drives: What you accomplish depends on the goals you set for yourself and the reasons you pursue them (Barron & Harackiewicz, 2001; Locke & Latham, 2002). Not just any old goals will promote achievement, though. A goal is most likely to improve your motivation and performance when three conditions are met (Cooper, Shapiro, & Powers, 1998; Higgins, 1998):

- *The goal is specific.* Defining a goal as "doing your best" is as ineffective as having no goals at all. You need to be specific about what you are going to do and when you are going to do it: "I will write four pages of this paper today."

To Live Healthy and Sustainable Lives

Michael Smith

Canada

Nobel Prize for Chemistry 1993 "Humans are destroying other species at an alarming rate. We must learn to control our demands on a planet with finite resources."

To Learn from Others

Robert A. Mundell

Canada

Nobel Prize for Economics 1999 "We owe much to the valuable mentors in our lives—the providers of wise advice and priceless education."

To Alleviate Suffering

Marie Curie

France

Nobel Prize for Physics 1903, Chemistry 1911 "The discoveries of science can and must be used to alleviate suffering and make the world a better place for all."

To Give to Humankind

William Golding

United Kingdom

Nobel Prize for Literature 1983 "For the good of humankind, world leaders do not need to politicize and manoeuvre. They need to give."

approach goals Goals framed in terms of desired outcomes or experiences, such as learning to scuba dive.

avoidance goals Goals framed in terms of avoiding unpleasant experiences, such as trying not to look foolish in public.

- *The goal is challenging but achievable.* You are apt to work harder for tough but realistic goals, which make you feel gratified when you reach them, than for either easy goals that pose no challenge or impossible goals that can never be attained.

- *The goal is framed in terms of getting what you want rather than avoiding what you do not want.* **Approach goals** are positive experiences that you seek directly, such as "learning to scuba dive" or "trying to get a better grade." **Avoidance goals** involve the effort to avoid unpleasant experiences, such as "trying not to make a fool of myself" or "trying to avoid being dependent."

People who frame their goals in specific, achievable approach terms (e.g., "I'm going to lose weight by jogging three times a week") feel better about themselves, feel more competent, are more optimistic and less depressed, and even have fewer colds and other physical symptoms than people who frame the same goals in avoidance terms (e.g., "I'm going to lose weight by staying away from rich foods"). Can you guess why? Framing goals in a positive way allows you to focus on what you can actively, concretely do to accomplish them, instead of focusing on what you have to give up (Coats, Janoff-Bulman, & Alpert, 1996; Elliot & Sheldon, 1998).

Defining your goals is only the first step on the road to success; next you need to know what to do when you hit a pothole. Some people give up when a goal becomes difficult or they are faced with a setback, whereas others become even more determined to succeed. Talent or ambition alone does not predict who will push on and who will give up. The crucial factor is whether a person's main motivation is to perform well in front of others or to learn the task for the satisfaction of it.

performance goals Goals framed in terms of performing well in front of others, being judged favourably, and avoiding criticism.

mastery (learning) goals Goals framed in terms of increasing one's competence and skills.

People who are motivated by **performance goals** are concerned primarily with doing well, being judged favourably, and avoiding criticism (Dweck, 1992; Dweck & Sorich, 1999). When such people are focused on how well they are performing and then do poorly, they often decide the fault is theirs, and they stop trying to improve. Because their goal is to demonstrate their abilities, they set themselves up for grief when they temporarily fail—as all of us must if we are to learn anything new. In contrast, those who are motivated by **mastery (learning) goals** are concerned with increasing their competence and skills.

Therefore, they regard failure as a source of useful information that will help them improve. Failure and criticism do not discourage them because they know that learning takes time.

Mastery goals are powerful intrinsic motivators (Elliot & McGregor, 2001). Students who are in school primarily to master new areas of knowledge choose more challenging projects, persist in the face of difficulty, use deeper and more elaborate study strategies, and *enjoy* learning more than do students who are there only to get a degree and a "meal ticket." However, for ambitious individuals who already have high achievement motivation—those determined to become great athletes, scientists, or musicians—performance and mastery goals work hand in hand. Focusing on specific ways of improving their performance raises their intrinsic motivation and satisfaction (Barron & Harackiewicz, 2001).

Children acquire performance or mastery goals early, from the actions adults praise them for and from what they observe in their environments. Many parents believe in the importance of praising their child's intelligence and ability when the child does well ("Wow, Katie, are you smart!"). Yet, surprisingly, such praise can backfire (see Chapter 9). Praise can be a good thing, but its effects depend on what children are praised *for* and how children interpret the praise (Henderlong & Lepper, 2002).

In several studies, children who were praised for their intelligence and ability later cared more about performance goals and less about learning goals than did children praised for their *efforts* (see Figure 14.2). After these "smart" children failed a problem-solving game, they tended to give up on subsequent ones, enjoyed them less, and lied to other kids about how well they had done. And they actually performed less well than children who had been praised for their efforts (Mueller & Dweck, 1998). The reason seems to be that most North American children regard intelligence and ability as fixed traits that you can't do anything about. Therefore, if you fail, you might as well give up. But effort is subject to improvement; you can always try again, and that is the key to mastery. As one learning-oriented child said, "Mistakes are our friends" (Dweck & Sorich, 1999).

Expectations and Self-Efficacy How hard you work for something also depends on your expectations. If you are fairly certain of success, you will work harder to reach your goal than if you are fairly certain of failure.

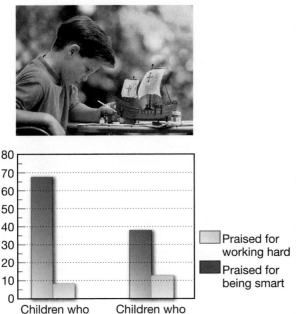

FIGURE 14.2 Mastery and Motivation

Children praised for being smart rather than for working hard tend to lose the pleasure of learning. Nearly 70 percent of fifth grade students who were praised for intelligence later chose performance goals (doing "problems that aren't too hard, so I don't get many wrong") rather than learning goals (doing "problems that I'll learn a lot from, even if I won't look so smart")—compared to fewer than 10 percent of children who were praised for their efforts (Mueller & Dweck, 1998). They also lied more about how they did.

A classic experiment showed how quickly experience affects these expectations. Young women were asked to solve 15 anagram puzzles. Before working on each one, they had to estimate their chances of solving it. Half of the women started off with very easy anagrams, but half began with insoluble ones. Sure enough, those who started with the easy ones increased their estimates of success on later ones. Those who began with the impossible ones decided they would all be impossible. These expectations, in turn, affected the young women's ability to actually solve the last 10 anagrams, which were the same for everyone. The higher the expectation of success, the more anagrams the women solved (Feather, 1966). Once acquired, therefore, expectations can create a **self-fulfilling prophecy** (Merton, 1948): Your expectations make you behave in ways that make the expectation come true. You expect to succeed, so you work hard—and succeed. Or you expect to fail, so you don't do much work, and as a result you do poorly.

But where do expectations come from? One source is your level of confidence in your abilities. Do you feel able to handle challenges? Albert Bandura calls this feeling **self-efficacy**. No one is born with self-efficacy; you acquire it, through experience in mastering new skills, overcoming obstacles, and learning from occasional failures. Self-efficacy also comes from having successful role models who teach you that your ambitions are possible, and from having people around to give you constructive feedback and encouragement (Bandura, 1997, 2001).

People who have a strong sense of self-efficacy are quick to cope with problems, rather than stewing and brooding about them. Studies in North America, Europe, and Russia find that self-efficacy has a positive effect on just about every aspect of people's lives: how well they do on a task, how persistently they pursue their goals, the kind of career choices they make, their ability to solve complex problems, their motivation to work for political and social goals, their health habits, and even their chances of recovery from a heart attack (Bandura et al., 2001; Ewart, 1995; Maddux, 1995; Stajkovic & Luthans, 1998).

The Effects of Work on Motivation

Imagine that you live in a town that has one famous company, Boopsie's Biscuits & Buns. Everyone in the town is grateful for the 3B company and goes to work there with high hopes. Soon, however, an odd thing starts happening to many employees. They complain of fatigue and irritability. They are taking lots of sick leave. Productivity declines. What's going on at Boopsie's Biscuits & Buns? Is everybody suffering from sheer laziness?

Most people would answer that something is the matter with those employees. However, many psychologists have criticized the idea that achievement depends entirely on personality traits and motives to succeed. This notion, they say, leads to the incorrect inference that people who don't "make it" have only themselves to blame (Morrison & Von Glinow, 1990). Some people undoubtedly do lack motivation, but accomplishment does not depend on internal motives alone. We also need to ask: How does the work we do, and the conditions under which we do it, nurture or crush our motivation to succeed?

Working Conditions Several aspects of the work environment are known to increase job

self-efficacy A person's belief that he or she is capable of producing desired results, such as mastering new skills and reaching goals.

self-fulfilling prophecy An expectation that is fulfilled because of the tendency of the person holding it to act in ways that bring it about.

Like employees, students can have poor working conditions that affect their motivation. They may have to study in crowded quarters or may have small siblings who interrupt and distract them.

involvement, motivation, and satisfaction (S. Brown, 1996; Judge et al., 2001; Kohn & Schooler, 1983):

- The work feels meaningful and important to employees.

- Employees have control over many aspects of their work, such as setting their own hours and making decisions.

- Tasks are varied rather than repetitive.

- The company maintains clear and consistent rules.

- Employees have supportive relationships with their superiors and co-workers.

- Employees receive useful feedback about their work, so they know what they have accomplished and what they need to do to improve.

- The company offers opportunities for its employees to learn and advance.

Companies that foster these conditions tend to have more productive and satisfied employees. Workers tend to become more creative in their thinking and feel better about themselves and their work than they do if they feel stuck in routine, boring jobs that give them no flexibility or control over their daily tasks (Karasek & Theorell, 1990; Locke & Latham, 1990). Conversely, when people with high achievement motivation are put in situations that frustrate their desire and ability to succeed, they become dissatisfied and stressed out, and their achievement motive declines (Jenkins, 1994).

Did you notice anything missing from that list of beneficial working conditions? Where is money, supposedly the great motivator? Actually, work motivation is related not to the amount of money you get, but to how and when you get it. The strongest motivator is *incentive pay*, bonuses that are given upon completion of a goal rather than as an automatic raise (Locke et al., 1981). Incentive pay increases people's feelings of competence and accomplishment ("I got this raise because I deserved it"). This doesn't mean that people should accept low pay so they will like their jobs better, or that they should never demand cost-of-living raises!

Opportunities to Achieve Another important working condition that affects achievement is having the opportunity to achieve. When someone does not do well at work, others are apt to say it is the individual's own fault because he or she lacks the internal drive to "make it." But what the person may really lack is a fair chance to make it, and this is especially true for those who have been subjected to systematic discrimination, such as women and ethnic minorities. At one time, for example, women were said to be less successful than men in the workplace because women had an internalized "fear of success." Yet this apparent internal "motive" vanished as opportunities for women improved and sex discrimination was made illegal.

Similarly, when the proportion of men and women in an occupation changes, so do people's motivations to work in that field (Kanter, 1977/1993). Many occupations are still highly segregated by gender; there are few male secretaries or female auto mechanics. As a result, many people form gender stereotypes about the requirements of such careers: "Female" jobs require kindness and nurturance, "male" jobs require strength and smarts. Accordingly, female engineers working in the oil industry in Alberta have achieved success by conforming to primarily masculine symbols that one author has called the "frontier myth" and the "romanticized cowboy hero" (Miller, 2004). But these stereotypes stifle many people's aspirations to enter a nontraditional career at all (Cejka & Eagly, 1999). As gender segregation breaks down, however, people's motivations change. When law and bartending were almost entirely male professions, and nursing and child care almost entirely female, few women aspired to become lawyers or bartenders and few men to become nurses. Now that it isn't odd to see a female lawyer or bartender or, increasingly, a male nurse or daycare worker, people's motivation to enter these fields has changed rapidly.

Thinking Critically About Why People Achieve—or Don't

Once in a career, people may become more motivated to advance up the ladder or less so, depending on how many rungs they are permitted to climb. Men *and* women who work in jobs with no prospect of promotion tend to play down the importance of achievement, fantasize about quitting, and emphasize the social benefits of their jobs instead of the intellectual or financial benefits (Kanter, 1977/1993). Women and members of minority groups often encounter a "glass ceiling," a barrier to promotion that is so subtle as to be transparent, yet strong enough to prevent advancement. Researchers can determine that a company has a glass ceiling when a woman or minority person's educational level, work experience, and professional accomplishments do not predict advancement as they do for white men (Graham, 1994; Valian, 1998).

As you can see, work motivation and satisfaction depend on the right fit between qualities of the individual and conditions of the work. The illustration below summarizes the factors within individuals and in their environments that promote or inhibit intrinsic motivation.

WHAT'S AHEAD

- Does more money produce more happiness?
- What kind of conflict do you have when you want to study for a big exam but you also want to go out partying?
- Do you have to satisfy basic needs for security and belonging before you can become "self-actualized"?

MOTIVES, VALUES, AND WELL-BEING

Throughout this chapter we have been looking at the central concerns of human life: love, sex, food, and work. In these domains and many others, a key conclusion emerges: People who are motivated by the intrinsic satisfaction of an activity are happier and more satisfied than those motivated solely by extrinsic rewards (Deci & Ryan, 1985; Kasser & Ryan, 2001).

We saw, too, how intrinsic motivation will rise or fall depending on the goals we choose and the reasons we pursue them. Goals, in turn, are determined by the values we place on what is important in life: freedom, religion, beauty, equality, wealth, fame, wisdom, serenity, salvation, sexual passion, the desire to improve the world, or anything else. Psychology cannot tell us which values or goals to choose; individuals, cultures, and religions emphasize different ones—such as serenity or salvation, wisdom or wealth. But research does illuminate the psychological *consequences* of our choices.

For example, although North American culture puts a high value on accumulating wealth, the pursuit of material things for their own sake has some dark consequences. According to studies conducted in both America (an affluent nation) and Russia (a struggling nation), people who are primarily motivated to get rich have poorer psychological adjustment and lower well-being than do people whose primary values are self-acceptance, affiliation with others, or wanting to make the world a better place (Kasser & Ryan, 1996; Ryan et al., 1999). This is especially true when the reasons for striving for money are, again, extrinsic (e.g., you do it to impress others) rather than intrinsic (e.g., you do it so you can afford to do the volunteer work you love) (Carver & Baird, 1998; Srivastava, Locke, & Bartol, 2001).

Whichever values and goals you choose, if they are in conflict, the discrepancy can produce emotional stress and unhappiness. Two motives conflict when the satisfaction of one leads to the inability to act on the other—that is, when you want to have your cake and eat it, too. Researchers have identified three kinds of motivational conflicts (Lewin, 1948):

1 *Approach–approach conflicts* occur when you are equally attracted to two or more possible activities or goals. For example, you would like to be a veterinarian *and* a rock singer; you would like to go out Tuesday night with friends *and* study like mad for an exam Wednesday.

2 *Avoidance–avoidance conflicts* require you to choose between the lesser of two evils because you dislike both alternatives. Novice parachute jumpers, for example, must choose between the fear of jumping and the fear of losing face if they don't jump.

3 *Approach–avoidance conflicts* occur when a single activity or goal has both a positive and a negative aspect. You might find skiing to be fun, but it is expensive. You might want to pursue a degree in women's studies, but your parents want you to major in something that they think is more career-oriented, like business or computer science.

Conflicts like these are inevitable, part of the price and pleasure of living. But if conflicts remain unresolved, they can take an emotional toll. In students, high levels of conflict and ambivalence about goals and values are associated with anxiety, depression, headaches and other symptoms, and more visits to the health centre (Emmons & King, 1988). In contrast, students who are "true to themselves," who strive for goals that are consistent with the qualities they value most, are healthier and have a greater sense of meaning and purpose in life than do those who are pursuing goals discrepant with their core values (McGregor & Little, 1998; Sheldon & Houser-Marko, 2001).

Are some psychological goals more important to our well-being than others? The humanist psychologist Abraham Maslow (1970) thought so.

THE FAR SIDE® BY GARY LARSON

The Far Side® by Gary Larson © 1985 FarWorks, Inc. All Rights Reserved. Used with permission.

© 1985 FarWorks, Inc All Rights Reserved/Dist. by Creators Syndicate

"C'mon, c'mon—it's either one or the other."

A classic avoidance–avoidance conflict.

Maslow envisioned people's motives as forming a pyramid, a *hierarchy of needs*. At the bottom level of the pyramid were basic survival needs for food, sleep, and water; at the next level were security needs, for shelter and safety; at the third level were social needs, for belonging and affection; at the fourth level were esteem needs, for self-respect and the respect of others; and at the top were needs for self-actualization and "self-transcendence." Maslow argued that your needs must be met at each level before you can even think of the matters posed by the level above it. You can't worry about achievement if you are hungry, cold, and poor. You can't become self-actualized if you haven't satisfied your needs for self-esteem and love. Human beings behave badly, he argued, only when their lower needs are frustrated.

This theory, which seemed logical and was so optimistic about human progress, became immensely popular. "Motivational experts" still often refer to it, using colourful pictures of Maslow's pyramid. But the theory, which was based mostly on Maslow's observations and intuitions, has had little empirical support (Sheldon et al., 2001; Smither, 1998). Can you think of some reasons this would be so? One is that people may have *simultaneous* needs for comfort and safety *and* for attachments, self-esteem, and competence. Another is that individuals who have met their "lower" needs do not inevitably seek "higher" ones, nor is it the case that people behave badly only when their lower needs are frustrated. Higher needs may even supersede lower ones. History is full of examples of people who would rather die of torture or starvation than sacrifice their convictions; or who would rather explore, risk, or create than be safe and secure at home.

Recently, a different way of thinking about universal psychological needs has been developed by researchers who studied large samples of students in the United States and South Korea (Sheldon et al., 2001). Although students aren't actually typical of all human beings on the planet, the findings are provocative and support many of the points of this chapter. The top four psychological needs turned out to be *autonomy* (feeling that you are making choices based on your "true interests and values"), *competence* (feeling able to master challenges), *relatedness* (feeling close to others who are important to you), and *self-esteem* (having self-respect). Other needs were of lesser importance, including pleasure, self-actualization (which was at the top of Maslow's list), popularity, and, at the bottom, once again . . . money and luxury.

In sum, psychological well-being depends on finding activities and choosing goals that are intrinsically satisfying; on being able to resolve conflicts between competing goals; and on feeling that we have the freedom to choose which goals we want to pursue.

Quick Quiz

Do you wish to approach or avoid this quiz?

1. A Pakistani student says she desperately wants an education and a career as a pharmacist, but she also does not want to be disobedient to her parents, who have arranged a marriage for her back home. Which kind of conflict does she have?

2. Maslow's popular hierarchy of needs has several flaws. What are they?

3. Letitia just got her law degree. She wanted to work in environmental law, but a corporate firm specializing in real-estate contracts has offered her a job and an enormous salary that seem too good to refuse. Why should she think carefully and critically in making a decision?

Answers:

1. approach–avoidance

2. It was not based on extensive empirical research; it has not been well supported by research; the needs he proposed can be simultaneous rather than hierarchical; "higher" needs often supersede "lower" ones.

3. Because taking a job primarily for its extrinsic benefits might suppress her intrinsic satisfaction in the work; because people motivated solely to acquire money often have poorer psychological adjustment and a lower sense of well-being than others; and because while money provides material benefits, psychological needs are also important, such as autonomy, competence, self-esteem, and connection to others.

Psychology In The News *Revisited*

Understanding the biological, psychological, and cultural influences on motivation can help us understand the stories that opened this chapter and other stories that make the news every day.

Over a million people use the online Lavalife service to find intimate relationship and romance, and new subscribers are joining every day. In terms of motivation, passionate romance must matter a great deal to many of these people or the service would never have flourished as it has. But as we saw, passionate romance is only one element of love. It characterizes the early stage of love affairs, when the lovers still don't know much about each other, and it often creates unrealistic expectations that can lead to disappointment. If a relationship is to last, the lovers must also pass the tests of intimacy and commitment.

Our second news item, about the rape conviction of Andrew Luster, illustrates the darker motivations of sexuality. As we saw, the motives for sex among men who rape have less to do with physical pleasure than with hostility toward women, peer pressure to prove their masculinity, narcissism, and a cultural script that endorses (or tolerates) promiscuous, impersonal sex for men. The fact that Luster had to drug his victims into a stupor in order to have sex with them suggests also a deep fear of women who are sexually assertive.

The news item about the risks of diet drugs reveals the problems that arise when people seek miracle cures for their weight problems. Jennifer Rosenthal's near death from usnic acid came right on the heels of the death of Steve Bechler, a 23-year-old pitcher for the Baltimore Orioles, who collapsed and died during a spring-training workout. His death was linked to ephedra, another substance widely promoted for weight loss—one that has caused strokes, seizures, heart disorders, and psychotic break-downs. Unfortunately, Jennifer Rosenthal never thought to ask whether usnic acid had been tested on humans or studied for its effectiveness, risks, and side effects. She did not ask whether it had been approved by the FDA. "I didn't think about that kind of stuff," she told a reporter from *The New York Times* (Grady, 2003). "Not very smart."

Indeed, not very smart—and her story is an object lesson in why consumers should call upon their own good critical-thinking skills to assess claims of "miracle pills." As we saw in this chapter, the mechanisms that govern weight gain and loss, appetite, eating, and hunger are enormously complex and interrelated, involving genetics, hormones, exercise, portion sizes, social pressures, and culture. No wonder so many people yearn for an oversimplified solution, one that does not require them to change their eating or exercise habits.

Finally, the story of Steve Nash shows the importance of intrinsic motivation, setting challenging but achievable goals, and persisting in the pursuit of one's dreams despite being smaller than other players and growing up in a part of the world not noted for its professional basketball players. Nash's training regimen is extensive, as is his dedication to it.

Abraham Maslow may have been wrong about a universal hierarchy of motives, but perhaps each of us develops our own hierarchy as we grow from childhood to old age. For some people, the needs for love, security, or safety will dominate. For others, the need for achievement or power will rule. Some of us will wrestle with conflicting motives; for others, one consuming ambition will hold sway over all others. The motives and goals that inspire us, and the choices we make in their pursuit, are what give our lives passion, colour, and meaning. Choose wisely.

Taking Psychology With You   What Motivates You?

At the end of the first chapter of this book, we discussed not only what psychology can do for you but also what it cannot. As we hope this final chapter has shown, psychology can teach us a great deal about the many motives of human life: the meanings of love, the mysteries of sex, the dilemmas we create for ourselves about eating and weight, and the conditions that enhance or suppress the pursuit of achievement. Psychology cannot tell us which motives, goals, and values to choose in the first place: love, wealth, security, passion, freedom, fame, the desire to improve the world, or anything else. However, it can tell us how best to achieve the goals that are important to us, and how to ensure that those goals are intrinsically satisfying.

Think for a moment about your own values and goals, for now and for the future. Would you like to improve your love life? Enjoy school more? Lose weight? Become a better tennis player? If the theories and findings in this chapter—indeed, in this book—are to be of long-lasting personal value to you, they must jump off the printed page and into your daily life. And so, in this final "Taking Psychology With You," let's apply the lessons of motivational research to your own life.

- **Seek activities that are intrinsically pleasurable, even if they don't "pay off."** If you really, really want to study Swahili or Swedish even though these languages are not in your pre-law requirements, try to find a way to do it. If you are not enjoying your major or your job, consider finding a career that would be more intrinsically pleasurable; or at least make sure you have other projects and activities that you do enjoy for their own sake. The overriding conclusion of this chapter is that people feel happier and are healthier when they feel intrinsically motivated in their work and family lives, rather than motivated only by external rewards or obligations.

- **Focus on learning goals rather than on performance goals.** In general, you will be better able to cope with setbacks if your goal is to learn rather than to show off how good you are. Regard failure as a chance to learn rather than as a sign of incompetence. The more you are able to focus on improvement, the better your performance will be—in any activity, from cooking to studying to learning to play an instrument to making friends.

- **Assess your working conditions.** Remember that everyone has "working conditions," whether you are a student, a self-employed writer, or a homemaker. If your motivation and well-being are starting to wilt, check out your environment. Are you getting support from others? Do you have opportunities to develop ideas and vary your routine, or are you expected to toe the line and do the same thing day after day? Do you perceive institutional barriers that might limit your advancement in your chosen field, and are your perceptions accurate?

- **Take steps to resolve motivational conflicts.** Many students in an approach–avoidance conflict tend to think a great deal about their conflicts but not do anything to resolve them. A student in one study, for instance, remained unhappily stuck between his goal of achieving independence and his desire to be cared for by his parents (Emmons & King, 1988). The reconciliation of conflicts like these is important for your well-being.

Most of all, think critically about the goals you have chosen for yourself: Are they what you want to do, or what someone else wants you to do? Do they reflect your values? In a commencement address some years ago, Mario Cuomo, the former governor of New York, had these words of wisdom for the graduating students: "When you've parked the second car in the garage, and installed the hot tub, and skied in Colorado, and windsurfed in the Caribbean, when you've had your first love affair and your second and your third, the question will remain: Where does the dream end for me?"

SUMMARY

- *Motivation* refers to an inferred process within a person or animal that causes that organism to move toward a goal—to satisfy a biological need or achieve a psychological ambition—or away from an unpleasant situation. Motivation may be *intrinsic*, for the inherent pleasure of an activity, or *extrinsic*, for external rewards.

THE SOCIAL ANIMAL: MOTIVES FOR LOVE

- All human beings have a *need for affiliation*—for connection, attachment, and love. Two strong predictors of whom people will love are *proximity* and *similarity*. But love itself takes various forms and has different meanings. Traditionally, *passionate ("romantic") love* has been distinguished from *companionate love*. According to the *triangular theory of love*, love consists of different combinations of passion, intimacy, and commitment. *Attachment theory* views adults' love relationships, like those of infants, as being secure, avoidant, or anxious–ambivalent.

- Men and women are equally likely to feel love and need attachment, but they differ, on average, in how they express feelings of love and how they define intimacy. In Western societies, women often express love in words, whereas men express it in actions. But as women have entered the workforce in large numbers and pragmatic reasons for marriage have faded, the two sexes have become more alike in endorsing romantic love as a requirement for marriage.

THE EROTIC ANIMAL: MOTIVES FOR SEX

- Biological research finds that testosterone influences sexual desire in both sexes, although hormones do not "cause" sexual behaviour in a simple, direct way. The Kinsey surveys of male and female sexuality and the laboratory research of Masters and Johnson showed that physiologically, there is no "right" kind of orgasm for women to have, and that both sexes are capable of sexual arousal and response.

- Some researchers believe that men have a higher frequency of many sexual behaviours, on average, because they have a stronger "sex drive" than women do. Others believe that gender differences in sexual motivation and behaviour are a result of differences in roles, cultural norms, and opportunity. A compromise view is that male sexuality is more biologically influenced than is women's, whereas female sexuality is more governed by circumstances, relationships, and cultural norms.

- Evolutionary psychologists argue that men and women have evolved different sexual strategies and behaviour in response to survival problems faced in the distant past. In this view, it has been adaptive for males to be promiscuous, to be attracted to young partners, and to want sexual novelty, and for females to be monogamous, to be choosy about partners, and to prefer security to novelty. Critics counter that human sexual behaviour is too varied and flexible to fit a single evolutionary explanation. Moreover, our ancestors probably did not have a wide range of partners to choose from; what may have evolved is mate selection based on proximity and similarity.

- Psychological, social, and cultural approaches to sexual motivation emphasize the ways that values, beliefs, and fantasies affect sexual desire and response. Men and women have sex to satisfy many different psychological motives, including pleasure, intimacy, coping, self-affirmation, the partner's approval, or peer approval. Extrinsic motives for sex, such as peer approval, are associated with riskier sexual behaviour than intrinsic motives are. Both sexes may agree to intercourse for nonsexual motives: Men sometimes feel obligated to "make a move" to prove their masculinity, and women sometimes feel obliged to "give in" to preserve the relationship. People's motives for consenting to unwanted sex vary, depending on their own feelings of security and commitment in the relationship.

- A major gender difference in sexual experience has to do with rape and perceptions of sexual coercion: What many women regard as coercion is not always seen as such by men. Men who rape do so for diverse reasons, including peer pressure; anger, revenge, or a desire to humiliate the victim; narcissism and hostility toward women; and sometimes sadism.

- Cultures differ widely in determining what parts of the body people learn are erotic, which sexual acts are considered erotic or repulsive, and whether sex itself is good or bad. Cultures transmit these ideas through *gender roles* and *sexual scripts*, which specify appropriate sexual behaviour given a person's gender, age, and sexual orientation.

- As in the case of love, gender differences (and growing similarities) in sexuality are strongly affected by cultural and economic factors. As gender roles become more alike, so has the sexual behaviour of men and women.

- The origins of sexual orientation are still unknown. Traditional psychological explanations have not been supported. Genetic and hormonal factors may be involved, although the evidence is inconclusive. Biology, culture, learning, and circumstance probably interact in complex ways to produce a given person's orientation. Research on this issue is sensitive because people often confuse scientific questions about the origins of homosexuality with their own emotional feelings about the topic.

THE HUNGRY ANIMAL: MOTIVES TO EAT

- Overweight and obesity are not simply a result of failed willpower, emotional disturbance, or overeating. Hunger, weight, and eating are regulated by a set of bodily mechanisms, such as *basal metabolism rate* and number of fat cells, that keep people close to their genetically influenced *set point*. Genes influence body shape, extent of weight gain, and percentage of fat in the body. Genes also account for certain types of obesity; the *ob* gene regulates *leptin*, which enables the *hypothalamus* to regulate appetite and metabolism.

- Set-point theory alone cannot explain why rates of overweight and obesity are rising all over the world, among all social classes, ethnicities, and ages. The reasons reflect the interaction of an evolved genetic disposition to gain weight when rich food is plentiful, and an environment that provides cheap, varied, high-calorie food and rewards sedentary lifestyles. Eating habits and activity levels are also affected by cultural standards of what the ideal body should look like—heavy or thin, soft or muscular.

- When genetic predispositions clash with culture, physical and mental problems can result. In cultures that foster overeating and regard overweight as a sign of attractiveness and health, obesity is acceptable, but obesity is associated with a greatly elevated risk of many diseases and disabilities. In cultures that foster unrealistically thin bodies, eating disorders increase, especially *bulimia* and *anorexia*. These disorders are far more common in women than in men, but as pressures on men to have muscular bodies have increased, body-image problems in men are increasing too.

THE COMPETENT ANIMAL: MOTIVES TO ACHIEVE

- The study of the *need for achievement* began with research using the *Thematic Apperception Test (TAT)*. People who are motivated by a high need for achievement set high but realistic standards for success and excellence. The TAT has empirical problems, but it launched the study of the factors that motivate achievement.

- People achieve more when they have specific, focused goals; when they set high but achievable goals for themselves; and when they have *approach goals* (seeking a positive outcome) rather than *avoidance goals* (avoiding an unpleasant outcome). The motivation to achieve depends not only on ability, but also on whether people set *mastery (learning) goals*, in which the focus is on learning the task well, or *performance goals*, in which the focus is on performing well for others. *Mastery (learning) goals* lead to persistence in the face of failures and setbacks; *performance goals* often lead to giving up. People's expectations can create *self-fulfilling prophecies* of success or failure. These expectations stem from one's level of *self-efficacy*.

- Work motivation also depends on circumstances of the job itself. Working conditions that promote motivation and satisfaction are those that provide workers with a sense of meaningfulness, control, variation in tasks, clear rules, supportive relationships, feedback, and opportunities for advancement and learning. *Incentive pay* is more effective than predictable raises in elevating work motivation. One factor in the motivation to enter a career is its gender ratio. A person's motivation to achieve also depends on the person's having the opportunity to be promoted.

MOTIVES, VALUES, AND WELL-BEING

• Satisfaction and well-being increase when people enjoy the *intrinsic satisfaction* of an activity and when their goals and values are in harmony. In an *approach–approach conflict*, a person is equally attracted to two goals. In an *avoidance–avoidance conflict*, a person is equally repelled by two goals. An *approach–avoidance* conflict is the most difficult to resolve, because the person is both attracted to and repelled by the same goal. Prolonged conflict can lead to physical symptoms and reduced well-being.

• Abraham Maslow believed that human motives could be ranked along a *hierarchy of needs*, from basic biological needs for survival to higher psychological needs for self-actualization. This popular theory has not been well supported empirically. A more recent approach suggests that people have four major psychological needs, for autonomy, competence, relatedness, and self-esteem.

KEY TERMS

motivation   448

need for affiliation   448

intrinsic motivation   448

extrinsic motivation   448

sexual scripts   459

set point   462

bulimia   466

anorexia (nervosa)   466

need for achievement   468

Thematic Apperception Test (TAT)   468

approach goals   470

avoidance goals   470

performance goals   470

mastery (learning) goals   470

self-efficacy   471

self-fulfilling prophecy   471

LOOKING BACK

- When someone says "I love you," can you be sure what the person means? (p. 449)
- Do men and women differ in their ability to love? (p. 450)
- How are your beliefs about love affected by your income? (p. 451)
- Is one kind of orgasm better or healthier for women than another? (p. 453)
- What part of the anatomy do psychologists think is the "sexiest sex organ"? (p. 457)
- How do the sexual rules for heterosexual couples foster misunderstandings? (p. 460)
- Can psychological theories about smothering mothers or absent fathers explain why some men are gay? (p. 460)
- Is overweight usually a result of psychological problems? (p. 462)
- What theory explains why it's so hard for heavy people to lose weight—and just as hard for thin people to gain it? (p. 462)
- Why are people all over the world getting fatter? (p. 464)
- Why are so many competent professional women determined to be very thin? (p. 465)
- Why is "doing your best" an ineffective goal to set for yourself? (pp. 469–470)
- When you are learning a new skill, which should you concentrate on: mastering it or performing it well in front of others? (p. 470)
- Which aspects of a job are more important than money in increasing your work satisfaction and involvement? (pp. 471–472)
- How is the *desire* to achieve affected by the *opportunity* to achieve? (pp. 472–473)
- Does more money produce more happiness? (p. 474)
- What kind of conflict do you have when you want to study for a big exam but you also want to go out partying? (p. 474)
- Do you have to satisfy basic needs for security and belonging before you can become "self-actualized"? (p. 475)

APPENDIX: STATISTICAL METHODS

Nineteenth-century English statesman Benjamin Disraeli reportedly once named three forms of dishonesty: "lies, damned lies, and statistics." It is certainly true that people can lie with the help of statistics. It happens all the time: Advertisers, politicians, and others with some claim to make either use numbers inappropriately or ignore certain critical ones. (When hearing that "four out of five doctors surveyed" recommended some product, have you ever wondered just how many doctors were surveyed and whether they were representative of all doctors?) People also use numbers to convey a false impression of certainty and objectivity when the true state of affairs is uncertainty or ignorance. But it is people, not statistics, that lie. When statistics are used correctly, they neither confuse nor mislead. On the contrary, they expose unwarranted conclusions, promote clarity and precision, and protect us from our own biases and blind spots.

If statistics are useful anywhere, it is in the study of human behaviour. If human beings were all alike, and psychologists could specify all the influences on behaviour, there would be no need for statistics. But any time we measure human behaviour, we are going to wind up with different observations or scores for different individuals. Statistics can help us spot trends amid the diversity.

This appendix will introduce you to some basic statistical calculations used in psychology. Reading the appendix will not make you into a statistician, but it will acquaint you with some ways of organizing and assessing research data. If you suffer from a "math phobia," relax: You do not need to know much math to understand this material. However, you should have read Chapter 1, which discussed the rationale for using statistics and described various research methods. You may want to review the basic terms and concepts covered in that chapter. Be sure that you can define *hypothesis, sample, correlation, independent variable, dependent variable, random assignment, experimental group, control group, descriptive statistics, inferential statistics* and *test of statistical significance*. (Correlation coefficients, which are described in some detail in Chapter 1, will not be covered here.)

To read the tables in this appendix, you will also need to know the following symbols:

N = the total number of observations or scores in a set

X = an observation or score

Σ = the Greek capital letter sigma, read as "the sum of"

$\sqrt{}$ = the square root of

(*Note:* Boldfaced terms in this appendix are defined in the glossary at the end of the book.)

ORGANIZING DATA

Before we can discuss statistics, we need some numbers. Imagine that you are a psychologist and that you are interested in that most pleasing of human qualities, a sense of humour. You suspect that a well-developed funny bone can protect people from the negative emotional effects of stress. You already know that in the months following a stressful event, people who score high on sense-of-humour tests tend to feel less tense and moody than more sobersided individuals do. You realize, though, that this correlational evidence does not prove cause and effect. Perhaps people with a healthy sense of humour have other traits, such as flexibility or creativity, that act as the true stress buffers. To find out whether humour itself really softens the impact of stress, you do an experiment.

First, you randomly assign subjects to two groups, an experimental group and a control group. To keep our calculations simple, let's assume there are only 15 people per group. Each person individually views a silent film that most North Americans find fairly stressful, one showing Australian aboriginal boys undergoing a puberty rite involving genital mutilation. Subjects in the experimental group are instructed to make up a humorous monologue while watching the film. Those in the control group are told to make up a straightforward narrative. After the film, each person answers a mood questionnaire that measures current feelings of tension, depression, aggressiveness, and anxiety. A person's overall score on the questionnaire can range from 1 (no mood disturbance) to 7 (strong mood disturbance). This procedure provides you with 15 "mood disturbance" scores for each group. Have people who tried to be humorous reported less disturbance than those who did not?

Constructing a Frequency Distribution

Your first step might be to organize and condense the "raw data" (the obtained scores) by constructing a **frequency distribution** for each group. A frequency distribution shows how often each possible score actually occurred. To construct one, you first order all the possible scores from highest to lowest. (Our mood

TABLE A.1   Some Hypothetical Raw Data

These scores are for the hypothetical humour-and-stress study described in the text.

Experimental group

4,5,4,4,3,6,5,2,4,3,5,4,4,3,4

Control group

6,4,7,6,6,4,6,7,7,5,5,5,7,6,6

TABLE A.2   Two Frequency Distributions

The scores are from Table A.1.

| | Experimental Group | | | Control Group | | |
Mood Disturbance Score	Tally	Frequency		Mood Disturbance Score	Tally	Frequency
7		0		7	////	4
6	/	1		6	𝈫𝈫 /	6
5	///	3		5	///	3
4	𝈫𝈫 //	7		4	//	2
3	///	3		3		0
2	/	1		2		0
1		1		1		0
		N = 15				N = 15

disturbance scores will be ordered from 7 to 1.) Then you tally how often each score was actually obtained. Table A.1 gives some hypothetical raw data for the two groups, and Table A.2 shows the two frequency distributions based on these data. From these distributions you can see that the two groups differed. In the experimental group, the extreme scores of 7 and 1 did not occur at all, and the most common score was the middle one, 4. In the control group, a score of 7 occurred four times, the most common score was 6, and no one obtained a score lower than 4.

Because our mood scores have only seven possible values, our frequency distributions are quite manageable. Suppose, though, that your questionnaire had yielded scores that could range from 1 to 50. A frequency distribution with 50 entries would be cumbersome and might not reveal trends in the data clearly. A solution would be to construct a *grouped frequency distribution* by grouping adjacent scores into equalsized *classes* or *intervals*. Each interval could cover, say, five scores (1–5, 6–10, 11–15, and so forth). Then you could tally the frequencies within each *interval*. This procedure would reduce the number of entries in each distribution from 50 to only 10, making the overall results much easier to grasp. However, information would be lost. For example, there would be no way of knowing how many people had a score of 43 versus 44.

Graphing the Data

As everyone knows, a picture is worth a thousand words. The most common statistical picture is a **graph,** a drawing that depicts numerical relationships. Graphs appear at several points in this book, and are routinely used by psychologists to convey their findings to others. From graphs, we can get a general impression of what the data are like, note the relative frequencies of different scores, and see which score was most frequent.

In a graph constructed from a frequency distribution, the possible score values are shown along a hori-

zontal line (the *x-axis* of the graph) and frequencies along a vertical line (the *y-axis*), or vice versa. To construct a **histogram,** or **bar graph,** from our mood scores, we draw rectangles (bars) above each score, indicating the number of times it occurred by the rectangle's height (see Figure A.1).

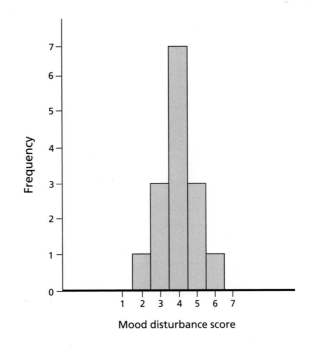

FIGURE A.1   A Histogram

This graph depicts the distribution of mood disturbance scores shown on the left side of Table A.2.

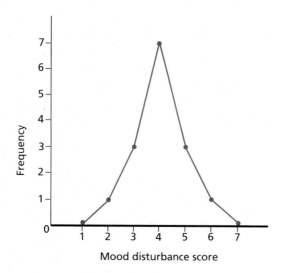

FIGURE A.2 A Frequency Polygon

This graph depicts the same data as Figure A.1.

A slightly different kind of "picture" is provided by a **frequency polygon,** or **line graph.** In a frequency polygon, the frequency of each score is indicated by a dot placed directly over the score on the horizontal axis, at the appropriate height on the vertical axis. The dots for the various scores are then joined together by straight lines, as in Figure A.2. When necessary an "extra" score, with a frequency of zero, can be added at each end of the horizontal axis, so that the polygon will rest on this axis instead of floating above it.

A word of caution about graphs: They may either exaggerate or mask differences in the data, depending on which units are used on the vertical axis. The two graphs in Figure A.3, although they look quite different, actually depict the same data. Always read the units on the axes of a graph; otherwise, the shape of a histogram or frequency polygon may be misleading

DESCRIBING DATA

Having organized your data, you are now ready to summarize and describe them. As you will recall from Chapter 1, procedures for doing so are known as *descriptive statistics.* In the following discussion, the word *score* will stand for any numerical observation.

Measuring Central Tendency

Your first step in describing your data might be to compute a **measure of central tendency** for each group. Measures of central tendency characterize an entire set of data in terms of a single representative number.

The Mean. The most popular measure of central tendency is the arithmetic mean, usually called simply the **mean**. It is often expressed by the symbol *M*. Most people are thinking of the mean when they say "average." We run across means all the time: in grade point averages, temperature averages, and batting averages. The mean is valuable to the psychologist because it takes all the data into account and it can be used in further statistical analyses. To compute the mean, you simply add up a set of scores and divide the total by the number of scores in the set. Recall that in mathematical notation, Σ means "the sum of," X stands for the individual scores, and N represents the total number of scores in a set. Thus the formula for calculating the mean is:

$$M = \frac{\Sigma X}{N}$$

Table A.3 shows how to compute the mean for our experimental group. Test your ability to perform this calculation by computing the mean for the control group yourself. (You can find the answer, along with other control group statistics, on page 482) Later, we will describe how a psychologist would compare the two means statistically to see if there is a significant difference between them.

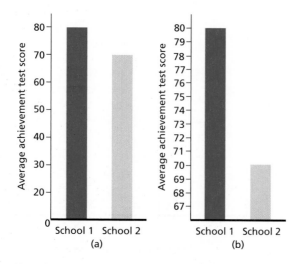

FIGURE A.3 Same Data, Different Impressions

These two graphs depict the same data, but have different units on the vertical axis.

The Median. Despite its usefulness, sometimes the mean can be misleading, as we noted in Chapter 1. Suppose you piled some children on a seesaw in such a

TABLE A.3 Calculating a Mean and a Median

The scores are from the left side of Table A.1.

Mean (M)

$$M = \frac{4+5+4+4+3+6+5+2+4+3+5+4+4+3+4}{15}$$

$$= \frac{60}{15}$$

$$= 4$$

Median

Scores, in order: 2, 3, 3, 3, 4, 4, 4, $\boxed{4,}$ 4, 4, 4, 5, 5, 5, 6

↑
Median

---

way that it was perfectly balanced, and then a 200-pound adult came and sat on one end. The centre of gravity would quickly shift toward the adult. In the same way, one extremely high score can dramatically raise the mean (and one extremely low score can dramatically lower it). In real life, this can be a serious problem. For example, in the calculation of a town's mean income, one millionaire would offset hundreds of poor people. The mean income would be a misleading indication of the town's actual wealth.

When extreme scores occur, a more representative measure of central tendency is the **median,** or midpoint in a set of scores or observations ordered from highest to lowest. In any set of scores, the same *number* of scores falls above the median as below it. The median is not affected by extreme scores. If you were calculating the *median* income of that same town, the one millionaire would offset only one poor person.

When the number of scores in the set is odd, calculating the median is a simple matter of counting in from the ends to the middle. However, if the number of scores is even, there will be two middle scores. The simplest solution is to find the mean of those two scores and use that number as the median. (When the data are from a grouped frequency distribution, a more complicated procedure is required, one beyond the scope of this appendix.) In our experimental group, the median score is 4 (see Table A.3). What is it for the control group?

The Mode. A third measure of central tendency is the **mode**, the score that occurs most often. In our experimental group, the modal score is 4. In our control group, it is 6. In some distributions, all scores occur with equal frequency, and there is no mode. In others,

two or more scores "tie" for the distinction of being most frequent. Modes are used less often than other measures of central tendency. They do not tell us anything about the other scores in the distribution; they often are not very "central"; and they tend to fluctuate from one random sample of a population to another more than either the median or the mean.

Measuring Variability

A measure of central tendency may or may not be highly representative of other scores in a distribution. To understand our results, we also need a **measure of variability** that will tell us whether our scores are clustered closely around the mean or widely scattered.

The Range. The simplest measure of variability is the **range**, which is found by subtracting the lowest score from the highest one. For our hypothetical set of mood disturbance scores, the range in the experimental group is 4 and in the control group it is 3. Unfortunately, though, simplicity is not always a virtue. The range gives us some information about variability but ignores all scores other than the highest and lowest ones.

The Standard Deviation. A more sophisticated measure of variability is the **standard deviation (SD)**. This statistic takes every score in the distribution into account. Loosely speaking, it gives us an idea of how much, on the average, scores in a distribution differ from the mean. If the scores were all the same, the standard deviation would be zero. The higher the standard deviation, the more variability there is among scores.

To compute the standard deviation, we must find out how much each individual score deviates from the mean. To do so we simply subtract the mean from each score. This gives us a set of *deviation scores.* Deviation scores for numbers above the mean will be positive, those for numbers below the mean will be negative, and the positive scores will exactly balance the negative ones. In other words, the sum of the deviation scores will be zero. That is a problem, since the next step in our calculation is to add. The solution is to *square* all the deviation scores (that is, to multiply each score by itself). This step gets rid of negative values. Then we can compute the average of the *squared* deviation scores by adding them up and dividing the sum by the number of scores (N). Finally, we take the square root of the result, which takes us from squared units of measurement back to the same units that were used originally (in this case, mood disturbance levels).

The calculations just described are expressed by the following formula:

$$SD = \sqrt{\frac{\Sigma(X-M)^2}{N}}$$

Table A.4 shows the calculations for computing the standard deviation for our experimental group. Try your hand at computing the standard deviation for the control group.

Remember, a large standard deviation signifies that scores are widely scattered, and that therefore the mean is not terribly typical of the entire population. A small standard deviation tells us that most scores are clustered near the mean, and that therefore the mean is representative. Suppose two classes took a psychology exam, and both classes had the same mean score, 75 out of a possible 100. From the means alone, you might conclude that the classes were similar in performance. But if Class A had a standard deviation of 3 and Class B had a standard deviation of 9, you would know that there was much more variability in performance in Class B. This information could be useful to an instructor in planning lectures and making assignments.

Transforming Scores

Sometimes researchers do not wish to work directly with raw scores. If, for example, the raw scores are tiny fractions, researchers may prefer numbers that are more manageable. Or they may want to work with scores that reveal where a person stands relative to others. In such cases, raw scores can be transformed to other kinds of scores.

Percentile Scores.   One common transformation converts each raw score to a **percentile score** (also called a *centile rank*). A percentile score gives the percentage of people who scored at or below a given raw score. Suppose you learn that you have scored 37 on a psychology exam. In the absence of any other information, you may not know whether to celebrate or cry. But if you are told that 37 is equivalent to a percentile score of 90, you know that you can be pretty proud of yourself; you have scored as high as, or higher than, 90 percent of those who have taken the test. On the other hand, if you are told that 37 is equivalent to a percentile score of 50, you have scored only at the median—only as high as, or higher than, half of the other students. The highest possible percentile rank is 99, or more precisely, 99.99, because you can never do better than 100 percent of a group when you are a member of the group. (Can you say what the lowest possible percentile score is? The answer is on page 482.) Standardized tests such as those described in previous chapters often come with tables that allow for the easy conversion of any raw score to the appropriate percentile score, based on data from a larger number of people who have already taken the test.

Percentile scores are easy to understand and easy to calculate. However, they also have a drawback: They merely rank people and do *not* tell us how far apart people are in terms of raw scores. Suppose you scored in the 50th percentile on an exam, June scored in the 45th, Tricia scored in the 20th, and Sean scored in the 15th. The difference between you and June may seem identical to that between Tricia and Sean (five percentiles). But in terms of *raw* scores you and June are probably more alike than Tricia and Sean, because exam scores usually cluster closely together around the midpoint of the distribution and are farther apart at the extremes. Because percentile scores do not preserve the spatial relationships in the original distribution of scores, they are inappropriate for computing many kinds of statistics. For example, they cannot be used to calculate means.

TABLE A.4   Calculating a Standard Deviation

Scores (X)	Deviation scores (X − M)	Squared deviation scores (X − M)²
6	2	4
5	1	1
5	1	1
5	1	1
4	0	0
4	0	0
4	0	0
4	0	0
4	0	0
4	0	0
4	0	0
3	−1	1
3	−1	1
3	−1	1
2	−2	4
	0	14

$$SD = \sqrt{\frac{\Sigma(X-M)^2}{N}} = \sqrt{\frac{14}{15}} = \sqrt{.93} = .97$$

Note: When data from a sample are used to estimate the standard deviation of the population from which the sample was drawn, division is by N −1 instead of N, for reasons that will not concern us here.

Z-scores. Another common transformation of raw scores is to **z-scores**, or **standard scores.** A z-score tells you how far a given raw score is above or below the mean, using the standard deviation as the unit of measurement. To compute a z-score, you subtract the mean of the distribution from the raw score and divide by the standard deviation:

$$z = \frac{X - M}{SD}$$

Unlike percentile scores, z-scores preserve the relative spacing of the original raw scores. The mean itself always corresponds to a z-score of zero, since it cannot deviate from itself. All scores above the mean have positive z-scores and all scores below the mean have negative ones. When the raw scores form a certain pattern called a *normal distribution* (to be described shortly), a z-score tells you how high or low the corresponding raw score was, relative to the other scores. If your exam score of 37 is equivalent to a z-score of +1.0, you have scored 1 standard deviation above the mean. Assuming a roughly normal distribution, that's pretty good, because in a normal distribution only about 16 percent of all scores fall at or above 1 standard deviation above the mean. But if your 37 is equivalent to a z-score of −1.0, you have scored 1 standard deviation below the mean—a poor score.

Z-scores are sometimes used to compare people's performance on different tests or measures. Say that Elsa earns a score of 64 on her first psychology test and Manuel, who is taking psychology from a different instructor, earns a 62 on his first test. In Elsa's class, the mean score is 50 and the standard deviation is 7, so Elsa's z-score is (64 − 50)/7 = 2.0. In Manuel's class, the mean is also 50, but the standard deviation is 6. Therefore, his z-score is also 2.0 [(62 − 50)/6]. Compared to their respective classmates, Elsa and Manuel did equally well. *But be careful:* This does *not* imply that they are equally able students. Perhaps Elsa's instructor has a reputation for giving easy tests and Manuel's for giving hard ones, so Manuel's instructor has attracted a more industrious group of students. In that case, Manuel faces stiffer competition than Elsa does, and even though he and Elsa have the same z-score, Manuel's performance may be more impressive.

You can see that comparing z-scores from different people or different tests must be done with caution. Standardized tests, such as IQ tests and various personality tests, use z-scores derived from a large sample of people assumed to be representative of the general population taking the tests. When two tests are standardized for similar populations, it is safe to compare z-scores on them. But z-scores derived from special samples, such as students in different psychology classes, may not be comparable.

Curves

In addition to knowing how spread out our scores are, we need to know the *pattern* of their distribution. At this point we come to a rather curious phenomenon. When researchers make a very large number of observations, many of the physical and psychological variables they study have a distribution that approximates a pattern called a **normal distribution.** (We say "approximates" because a *perfect* normal distribution is a theoretical construct and is not actually found in nature.) Plotted in a frequency polygon, a normal distribution has a symmetrical, bell-shaped form known as a **normal curve** (see Figure A.4).

A normal curve has several interesting and convenient properties. The right side is the exact mirror image of the left. The mean, median, and mode all have the same value and are at the exact centre of the curve, at the top of the "bell." Most observations or scores cluster around the centre of the curve, with far fewer out at the ends, or "tails," of the curve. Most important, as Figure A.4 shows, when standard deviations (or z-scores) are used on the horizontal axis of the curve, the percentage of scores falling between the mean and any given point on the horizontal axis is always the same. For example, 68.26 percent of the scores will fall between plus and minus 1 standard deviation from the mean; 95.44 percent of the scores will fall between plus and minus 2 standard deviations from the mean; and 99.74 percent of the scores will fall between plus and minus 3 standard deviations from the mean. These percentages hold for any normal curve, no matter what the size of the standard deviation. Tables are available showing the percentages of scores in a normal distribution that lie between the mean and various points (as expressed by z-scores).

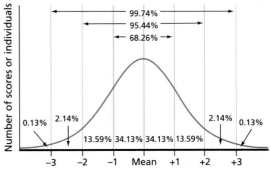

FIGURE A.4   A Normal Curve

When standard deviations (or z-scores) are used along the horizontal axis of a normal curve, certain fixed percentages of scores fall between the mean and any given point. As you can see, most scores fall in the middle range (between +1 and −1 standard deviations from the mean).

The normal curve makes life easier for psychologists when they want to compare individuals on some trait or performance. For example, since IQ scores from a population form a roughly normal curve, the mean and standard deviation of a test are all the information you need in order to know how many people score above or below a particular score. On a test with a mean of 100 and a standard deviation of 15, about 68.26 percent of the population scores between 85 and 115—1 standard deviation below and 1 standard deviation above the mean (see Chapter 6).

Not all types of observations, however, are distributed normally. Some curves are lopsided, or *skewed*, with scores clustering at one end or the other of the horizontal axis (see Figure A.5). When the "tail" of the curve is longer on the right than on the left, the curve is said to be positively, or right, skewed. When the opposite is true, the curve is said to be negatively, or left, skewed. In experiments, reaction times typically form a right-skewed distribution. For example, if people must press a button whenever they hear some signal, most will react quite quickly; but a few will take an unusually long time, causing the right "tail" of the curve to be stretched out.

Knowing the shape of a distribution can be extremely valuable. Paleontologist Stephen Jay Gould (1985) has told how such information helped him cope with the news that he had a rare and serious form of cancer. Being a researcher, he immediately headed for the library to learn all he could about his disease. The first thing he found was that it was incurable, with a median mortality of only eight months after discovery. Most people might have assumed that a "median mortality of eight months" means "I will probably be dead in eight months." But Gould realized that although half of all patients died within eight months, the other half survived longer than that.

Since his disease had been diagnosed in its early stages, he was getting top-notch medical treatment, and he had a strong will to live, Gould figured he could reasonably expect to be in the half of the distribution that survived beyond eight months. Even more cheering, the distribution of deaths from the disease was right-skewed: The cases to the left of the median of eight months could only extend to zero months, but those to the right could stretch out for years. Gould saw no reason why he should not expect to be in the tip of that right-hand tail.

For Stephen Jay Gould, statistics, properly interpreted, were "profoundly nurturant and life-giving." They offered him hope and inspired him to fight his disease. Gould remained professionally active for 20 more years. When he died in 2002, it was from an unrelated type of cancer.

ANSWERS:

Control group statistics:

$$\text{Mean} = \frac{\Sigma X}{N} = \frac{87}{15} = 5.8$$

$$\text{Median} = 6$$

$$\text{Standard Deviation} = \sqrt{\frac{\Sigma(X - M)^2}{N}} = \sqrt{\frac{14.4}{15}}$$
$$= \sqrt{.96} = .98$$

Lowest possible percentile score: 1 (or, more precisely, .01)

DRAWING INFERENCES

Once data are organized and summarized, the next step is to ask whether they differ from what might have been expected purely by chance (see Chapter 1). A researcher needs to know whether it is safe to infer that the results from a particular sample of people are valid for the entire population from which the sample was drawn. **Inferential statistics** provide this information. They are used in both experimental and correlational studies.

The Null Versus the Alternative Hypothesis

In an experiment, the scientist must assess the possibility that his or her experimental manipulations

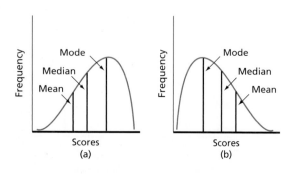

FIGURE A.5 Skewed Curves

Curve (a) is skewed negatively, to the left. Curve (b) is skewed positively, to the right. The direction of a curve's skewness is determined by the position of the long tail, not by the position of the bulge. In a skewed curve, the mean, median, and mode fall at different points.

will have no effect on the subjects' behaviour. The statement expressing this possibility is called the **null hypothesis.** In our stress-and-humour study, the null hypothesis states that making up a funny commentary will not relieve stress any more than making up a straightforward narrative will. In other words, it predicts that the difference between the means of the two groups will not deviate significantly from zero. Any obtained difference will be due solely to chance fluctuations. In contrast, the **alternative hypothesis** (also called the experimental or research hypothesis) states that on the average the experimental group will have lower mood disturbance scores than the control group.

The null hypothesis and the alternative hypothesis cannot both be true. Our goal is to reject the null hypothesis. If our results turn out to be consistent with the null hypothesis, we will not be able to do so. If the data are inconsistent with the null hypothesis, we will be able to reject it with some degree of confidence. Unless we study the entire population, though, we will never be able to say that the alternative hypothesis has been proven. No matter how impressive our results are, there will always be some degree of uncertainty about the inferences we draw from them. Since we cannot prove the alternative hypothesis, we must be satisfied with showing that the null hypothesis is unreasonable.

Students are often surprised to learn that in traditional hypothesis testing it is the null hypothesis, not the alternative hypothesis, that is tested. After all, it is the alternative hypothesis that is actually of interest. But this procedure does make sense. The null hypothesis can be stated precisely and tested directly. In the case of our fictitious study, the null hypothesis predicts that the difference between the two means will be zero. The alternative hypothesis does not permit a precise prediction because we don't know how much the two means might differ (if, in fact, they do differ). Therefore, it cannot be tested directly.

Testing Hypotheses

Many computations are available for testing the null hypothesis. The choice depends on the design of the study, the size of the sample, and other factors. We will not cover any specific tests here. Our purpose is simply to introduce you to the kind of *reasoning* that underlies hypothesis testing. With that in mind, let us return once again to our data. For each of our two groups we have calculated a mean and a standard deviation. Now we want to compare the two sets of data to see if they differ enough for us to reject the null hypothesis. We wish to be reasonably certain that our observed differences did not occur entirely by chance.

What does it mean to be "reasonably certain"? How different from zero must our result be to be taken seriously? Imagine, for a moment, that we had infinite resources and could somehow repeat our experiment, each time using a new pair of groups, until we had "run" the entire population through the study. It can be shown mathematically that if only chance were operating, our various experimental results would form a normal distribution. This theoretical distribution is called "the sampling distribution of the difference between means," but since that is quite a mouthful, we will simply call it the *sampling distribution* for short. If the null hypothesis were true, the mean of the sampling distribution would be zero. That is, on the average, we would find no difference between the two groups. Often, though, because of chance influences or *random error,* we would get a result that deviated to one degree or another from zero. On rare occasions, the result would deviate a great deal from zero.

We cannot test the entire population, though. All we have are data from a single sample. We would like to know whether the difference between means that we actually obtained would be close to the mean of the theoretical sampling distribution (if we *could* test the entire population) or far away from it, out in one of the "tails" of the curve. Was our result highly likely to occur on the basis of chance alone or highly unlikely?

Before we can answer that question, we must have some precise way to measure distance from the mean of the sampling distribution. We must know exactly how far from the mean our obtained result must be to be considered "far away." If only we knew the standard deviation of the sampling distribution, we could use it as our unit of measurement. We don't know it, but fortunately, we can use the standard deviation of our *sample* to estimate it. (We will not go into the reasons that this is so.)

Now we are in business. We can look at the mean difference between our two groups and figure out how far it is (in terms of standard deviations) from the mean of the sampling distribution. As mentioned earlier, one of the convenient things about a normal distribution is that a certain fixed percentage of all observations falls between the mean of the distribution and any given point above or below the mean. These percentages are available from tables. Therefore, if we know the "distance" of our obtained result from the mean of the theoretical sampling distribution, we automatically know how likely our result is to have occurred strictly by chance.

To give a specific example, if it turns out that our obtained result is 2 standard deviations above the mean of the theoretical sampling distribution, we know that the probability of its having occurred by chance is less than 2.3 percent. If our result is 3 standard deviations above the mean of the sampling distribution, the probability of its having occurred by

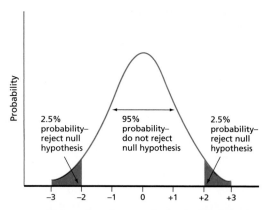

FIGURE A.6   Statistical Significance

This curve represents the theoretical sampling distribution discussed in the text. The curve is what we would expect by chance if we did our hypothetical stress-and-humour study many times, testing the entire population. If we used the conventional significance level of .05, we would regard our obtained result as significant only if the probability of getting a result that far from zero by chance (in either direction) totalled 5 percent or less. As shown, the result must fall far out in one of the tails of the sampling distribution. Otherwise, we cannot reject the null hypothesis.

chance is less than .13 percent—less than 1 in 800. In either case, we might well suspect that our result did not occur entirely by chance after all. We would call the result **statistically significant.** (Psychologists usually consider any highly unlikely result to be of interest, no matter which direction it takes. In other words, the result may be in either "tail" of the sampling distribution.)

To summarize: Statistical significance means that if only chance were operating, our result would be highly improbable, so we are fairly safe in concluding that more than chance was operating—namely, the influence of our independent variable. We can reject the null hypothesis, and open the champagne. As we noted in Chapter 1, psychologists usually accept a

finding as statistically significant if the likelihood of its occurring by chance is 5 percent or less (see Figure A.6). This cutoff point gives the researcher a reasonable chance of confirming reliable results as well as reasonable protection against accepting unreliable ones.

Some cautions are in order, though. As noted in Chapter 1, conventional tests of statistical significance have drawn serious criticisms in recent years. Statistically significant results are not always psychologically interesting or important. Further, statistical significance is related to the size of the sample. A large sample increases the likelihood of reliable results. But there is a trade-off: The larger the sample, the more probable it is that a small result having no practical importance will reach statistical significance. On the other hand, with the sample sizes typically used in psychological research, there is a good chance of falsely concluding that an experimental effect has *not* occurred when one actually has (Hunter, 1997). For these reasons, it is always useful to know how much of the total variability in scores was accounted for by the independent variable (the **effect size**). (The computations are not discussed here.) If only 3 percent of the variance was accounted for, then 97 percent was due either to chance factors or to systematic influences of which the researcher was unaware. Because human behaviour is affected by so many factors, the amount of variability accounted for by a single psychological variable is often modest. But sometimes the effect size is considerable even when the results don't quite reach significance.

Oh, yes, about those humour findings: Our fictitious study is similar to two somewhat more complex ones done by Herbert M. Lefcourt and Rod A. Martin (1986). Women who tried to be funny reported less mood disturbance than women who merely produced a straightforward narrative. They also grimaced and fidgeted less during the film, suggesting that they really did feel less stress. The results were not statistically significant for men. Other findings, however, suggest that humour can shield both sexes from stress (see Chapter 12). *The moral:* When gravity gets you down, try a little levity.

SUMMARY

- When used correctly, statistics expose unwarranted conclusions, promote precision, and help researchers spot trends amid diversity.
- Often, the first step in data analysis is to organize and condense data in a *frequency distribution,* a tally showing how often each possible score (or interval of scores) occurred. Such information can also be depicted in a *histogram* (bar graph) or a *frequency polygon* (line graph).

- Descriptive statistics summarize and describe the data. *Central tendency* is measured by the *mean, median,* or, less frequently, the *mode.* Since a measure of central tendency may or may not be highly representative of other scores in a distribution, it is also important to analyze variability. A large *standard deviation* means that scores are widely scattered about the mean; a small one means that most scores are clustered near the mean.

- Raw scores can be transformed into other kinds of scores. *Percentile scores* indicate the percentage of people who scored at or below a given raw score. *Z-scores (standard scores)* indicate how far a given raw score is above or below the mean of the distribution.

- Many variables have a distribution approximating a *normal distribution,* depicted as a *normal curve.* The normal curve has a convenient property: When standard deviations are used as the units on the horizontal axis, the percentage of scores falling between any two points on the horizontal axis is always the same. Not all types of observations are distributed normally, however. Some distributions are *skewed* to the left or right.

- Inferential statistics can be used to test the *null hypothesis* and to tell a researcher whether a result differed significantly from what might have been expected purely by chance. Basically, hypothesis testing involves estimating where the obtained result would have fallen in a theoretical *sampling distribution* based on studies of the entire population in question. If the result would have been far out in one of the "tails" of the distribution, it is considered statistically significant. A statistically significant result may or may not be psychologically interesting, important, or informative so many researchers also compute the *effect size.*

KEY TERMS

frequency distribution   482

graph   483

histogram/bar graph   483

frequency polygon/line graph   484

measure of central tendency   484

mean   484

median   485

mode   485

range   485

standard deviation   485

percentile score   486

z-score (standard score)   487

normal distribution   487

normal curve   487

inferential statistics   488

null hypothesis   489

alternative hypothesis   489

statistically significant   490

effect size   490

GLOSSARY

absolute threshold The smallest quantity of physical energy that can be reliably detected by an observer.

accommodation In Piaget's theory, the process of modifying existing cognitive schemas in response to experience and new information.

acculturation The process by which members of minority groups come to identify with and feel part of the mainstream culture.

activation-synthesis theory The theory that dreaming results from the cortical synthesis and interpretation of neural signals triggered by activity in the lower part of the brain.

adrenal hormones Hormones that are produced by the adrenal glands and that are involved in emotion and stress.

agoraphobia A set of phobias, often set off by a panic attack, involving the basic fear of being away from a safe place or person.

algorithm A problem-solving strategy guaranteed to produce a solution even if the user does not know how it works.

amnesia (organic) The loss of memory for important personal information. It usually has an organic cause, but in rare cases is psychogenic (psychological in origin).

amygdala [uh-MIG-dul-uh] A brain structure involved in the arousal and regulation of emotion and the initial emotional response to sensory information.

anorexia (nervosa) An eating disorder characterized by fear of being fat, a distorted body image, radically reduced consumption of food, and emaciation.

antidepressant drugs Drugs used primarily in the treatment of mood disorders, especially depression and anxiety.

antipsychotic drugs Drugs used primarily in the treatment of schizophrenia and other psychotic disorders.

antisocial personality disorder (APD) A disorder characterized by antisocial behaviour such as lying, stealing, manipulating others, and sometimes violence; and a lack of guilt, shame, and empathy.

applied psychology The study of psychological issues that have direct practical significance; also, the application of psychological findings.

approach goals Goals framed in terms of desired outcomes or experiences, such as learning to scuba dive.

archetypes [AR-ki-types] Universal, symbolic images that appear in myths, art, stories, and dreams; to Jungians, they reflect the collective unconscious.

arithmetic mean An average that is calculated by adding up a set of quantities and dividing the sum by the total number of quantities in the set.

assimilation In Piaget's theory, the process of absorbing new information into existing cognitive schemas.

attribution theory The theory that people are motivated to explain their own and other people's behaviour by attributing causes of that behaviour to a situation or a disposition.

autonomic nervous system The subdivision of the peripheral nervous system that regulates the internal organs and glands.

availability heuristic The tendency to judge the probability of a type of event by how easy it is to think of examples or instances.

avoidance goals Goals framed in terms of avoiding unpleasant experiences, such as trying not to look foolish in public.

axon A neuron's extending fibre that conducts impulses away from the cell body and transmits them to other neurons or to muscle or gland cells.

basic psychology The study of psychological issues in order to seek knowledge for its own sake rather than for its practical application.

behaviour modification The application of conditioning techniques to teach new responses or to reduce or eliminate problematic behaviour.

behaviour therapy A form of therapy that applies principles of classical and operant conditioning to help people change self-defeating or problematic behaviours.

behavioural geneticists Scientists who study an interdisciplinary field of study concerned with the genetic bases of individual differences in behaviour and personality.

behavioural self-monitoring In behaviour therapy, a method of keeping careful data on the frequency and consequences of the behaviour to be changed.

behaviourism An approach to psychology that emphasizes the study of observable behaviour and the role of the environment as a determinant of behaviour.

binocular cues Visual cues to depth or distance requiring two eyes.

biological perspective A psychological approach that emphasizes bodily events and changes associated with actions, feelings, and thoughts.

biological rhythm A periodic, more or less regular fluctuation in a biological system; it may or may not have psychological implications.

bipolar disorder A mood disorder in which episodes of both depression and mania (excessive euphoria) occur.

brain stem The part of the brain at the top of the spinal cord, consisting of the medulla and the pons.

brightness Lightness or luminance; the dimension of visual experience related to the amount (or intensity) of light emitted from or reflected by an object.

bulimia An eating disorder characterized by episodes of bingeing and purging.

case study A detailed description of a particular individual being studied or treated.

cell body The part of the neuron that keeps it alive and determines whether it will fire.

central nervous system (CNS) The portion of the nervous system consisting of the brain and spinal cord.

cerebellum A brain structure that regulates movement and balance, and that is involved in some kinds of higher cognitive tasks.

cerebral cortex A collection of several thin layers of cells covering the cerebrum; it is largely responsible for higher mental functions. *Cortex* is Latin for "bark" or "rind."

cerebral hemispheres The two halves of the cerebrum.

cerebrum [suh-REE-brum] The largest brain structure, consisting of the upper part of the brain; it is in charge of most sensory, motor, and cognitive processes. From the Latin for "brain."

childhood (infantile) amnesia The inability to remember events and experiences that occurred during the first two or three years of life.

chunk A meaningful unit of information; it may be composed of smaller units.

circadian [sur-CAY-dee-un] rhythm A biological rhythm with a period (from peak to peak or trough to trough) of about 24 hours; from the Latin *circa*, "about," and *dies*, "a day."

classical conditioning The process by which a previously neutral stimulus acquires the capacity to elicit a response through association with a stimulus that already elicits a similar or related response.

client-centred (nondirective) therapy A humanist approach to therapy devised by Carl Rogers, which emphasizes the therapist's empathy with the client and the use of unconditional positive regard.

cochlea [KOCK-lee-uh] A snail-shaped, fluid-filled organ in the inner ear, containing the organ of Corti, where the receptors for hearing are located.

coefficient of correlation A measure of correlation that ranges in value from −1.00 to +1.00.

cognitive-behavioural therapy A form of therapy designed to affect thinking and behaviour, acknowledging both as being important contributors to mental health.

cognitive dissonance A state of tension that occurs when a person simultaneously holds two cognitions that are psychologically inconsistent, or when a person's belief is incongruent with his or her behaviour.

cognitive ethology The study of cognitive processes in non-human animals.

cognitive perspective A psychological approach that emphasizes mental processes in perception, memory, language, problem solving, and other areas of behaviour.

cognitive schema An integrated mental network of knowledge, beliefs, and expectations concerning a particular topic or aspect of the world.

cognitive therapy A form of therapy designed to identify and change irrational, unproductive ways of thinking and hence to reduce negative emotions and their behavioural consequences.

collective unconscious In Jungian theory, the universal memories and experiences of humankind, represented in the symbols, stories, and images (archetypes) that occur across all cultures.

collectivist cultures Cultures in which the self is regarded as embedded in relationships, and harmony with one's group is prized above individual goals and wishes.

concept A mental category that groups objects, relations, activities, abstractions, or qualities having common properties.

conditioned response (CR) The classical-conditioning term for a response that is elicited by a conditioned stimulus; it occurs after the conditioned stimulus is associated with an unconditioned stimulus.

conditioned stimulus (CS) The classical-conditioning term for an initially neutral stimulus that comes to elicit a conditioned response after being associated with an unconditioned stimulus.

conditioning A basic kind of learning that involves associations between environmental stimuli and the organism's responses.

cones Visual receptors involved in colour vision.

confabulation Confusion of an event that happened to someone else with one that happened to you, or a belief that you remember something when it never actually happened.

confirmation bias The tendency to look for or pay attention to only the information that confirms one's own belief.

consciousness Awareness of oneself and the environment.

conservation The understanding that the physical properties of objects—such as the number of items in a cluster or the amount of liquid in a glass—can remain the same even when their form or appearance changes.

contact comfort In primates, the innate pleasure derived from close physical contact; it is the basis of an infant's first attachment.

continuous reinforcement A reinforcement schedule in which a particular response is always reinforced.

control condition In an experiment, a comparison condition in which subjects are not exposed to the same treatment of the independent variable as are those in the experimental condition.

convergence The turning inward of the eyes, which occurs when they focus on a nearby object.

corpus callosum [CORE-pus ca-LOW-suhm] The bundle of nerve fibres connecting the two cerebral hemispheres.

correlation A measure of how strongly two variables are related to each other.

correlational study A descriptive study that looks for a consistent relationship between two phenomena.

counterconditioning In classical conditioning, the process of pairing a conditioned stimulus with a stimulus that elicits a response that is incompatible with an unwanted conditioned response.

critical thinking The ability and willingness to assess claims and make objective judgments on the basis of well-supported reasoning and evidence, rather than emotion and anecdote.

cross-sectional study A study in which individuals of different ages are compared at a given time.

crystallized intelligence Cognitive skills and specific knowledge of information acquired over a lifetime; it is heavily dependent on education and tends to remain stable over the lifetime.

cue-dependent forgetting The inability to retrieve information stored in memory because of insufficient cues for recall.

culture A program of shared rules that govern the behaviour of members of a community or society, and a set of values, beliefs, and attitudes shared by most members of that community.

dark adaptation A process by which visual receptors become maximally sensitive to dim light.

decay theory The theory that information in memory eventually disappears if it is not accessed; it applies more to short-term than to long-term memory.

declarative memories Memories of facts, rules, concepts, and events ("knowing that"); they include semantic and episodic memories.

deductive reasoning A form of reasoning in which a conclusion follows necessarily from certain premises; if the premises are true, the conclusion must be true.

deep processing In the encoding of information, the processing of meaning rather than simply the physical or sensory features of a stimulus.

defence mechanisms Methods used by the ego to prevent unconscious anxiety or threatening thoughts from entering consciousness.

deindividuation social identity The part of a person's self-concept that is based on his or her identification with a nation, ethnic group, gender, or other social affiliation.

dendrites A neuron's branches that receive information from other neurons and transmit it toward the cell body.

dependent variable A variable that an experimenter predicts will be affected by manipulations of the independent variable.

depressants Drugs that slow down activity in the central nervous system.

descriptive methods Methods that yield descriptions of behaviour but not necessarily causal explanations.

descriptive statistics Statistics that organize and summarize research data.

dialectical reasoning A process in which opposing facts or ideas are weighed and compared, with a view to determining the best solution or to resolving differences.

difference threshold The smallest difference in stimulation that can be reliably detected by an observer when two stimuli are compared; also called *just noticeable difference (jnd)*.

diffusion of responsibility In groups, the tendency of members to avoid taking action because they assume that others will.

discriminative stimulus A stimulus that signals when a particular response is likely to be followed by a certain type of consequence.

display rules Social and cultural rules that regulate when, how, and where a person may express (or suppress) emotions.

dissociation A split in consciousness in which one part of the mind operates independently of others.

dissociative identity disorder A controversial disorder marked by the apparent appearance within one person of two or more distinct personalities, each with its own name and traits; commonly known as *multiple personality disorder* (MPD).

doctrine of specific nerve energies The principle that different sensory modalities exist because signals received by the sense organs stimulate different nerve pathways leading to different areas of the brain.

double-blind study An experiment in which neither the participants nor the individuals running the study know which participants are in the control group and which are in the experimental group until after the results are tallied.

ego In psychoanalysis, the part of personality that represents reason, good sense, and rational self-control.

egocentric thinking Seeing the world from only your own point of view; the inability to take another person's perspective.

elaborative rehearsal Association of new information with already stored knowledge and analysis of the new information to make it memorable.

electroconvulsive therapy (ECT) A procedure used in cases of prolonged and severe major depression, in which a brief brain seizure is induced.

electroencephalogram (EEG) A recording of neural activity detected by electrodes.

emotion A state of arousal involving facial and bodily changes, brain activation, cognitive appraisals, subjective feelings, and tendencies toward action.

emotion work Expression of an emotion, often because of a role requirement, that a person does not really feel.

emotional intelligence The ability to identify your own and other people's emotions accurately, express your emotions clearly, and regulate emotions in yourself and others.

empirical Relying on or derived from observation, experimentation, and measurement.

endocrine glands Internal organs that produce hormones and release them into the bloodstream.

endogenous Generated from within rather than by external cues.

endorphins [en-DOR-fins] Chemical substances in the nervous system that are similar in structure and action to opiates; they are involved in pain reduction, pleasure, and memory, and are known technically as *endogenous opioid peptides.*

entrapment A gradual process in which individuals escalate their commitment to a course of action to justify their investment of time, money, or effort.

episodic memories Memories of personally experienced events and the contexts in which they occurred.

equilibrium The sense of balance.

ethnic identity A person's identification with a racial, religious, or ethnic group.

ethnocentrism The belief that one's own ethnic group, nation, or religion is superior to all others.

evolutionary psychology A field of psychology emphasizing evolutionary mechanisms that may help explain human commonalities in cognition, development, emotion, social practices, and other areas of behaviour.

existential therapy A form of therapy designed to help clients explore the meaning of existence and face the great questions of life, such as death, freedom, alienation, and loneliness.

existentialism A philosophic approach that emphasizes the inevitable dilemmas and challenges of human existence.

experiment A controlled test of a hypothesis in which the researcher manipulates one variable to discover its effect on another.

experimenter effects Unintended changes in subjects' behaviour due to cues inadvertently given by the experimenter.

explicit memory Conscious, intentional recollection of an event or of an item of information.

extinction The weakening and eventual disappearance of a learned response; in classical conditioning, it occurs when the conditioned stimulus is no longer paired with the unconditioned stimulus.

extrinsic motivation The desire to do something for the sake of external rewards, such as money or fame.

extrinsic reinforcers Reinforcers that are not inherently related to the activity being reinforced, such as money, prizes, and praise.

facial feedback The process by which the facial muscles send messages to the brain about the basic emotion being expressed.

factor analysis A statistical method for analyzing the intercorrelations among various measures or test scores; clusters of measures or scores that are highly correlated are assumed to measure the same underlying trait, ability, or aptitude (the factor).

familiarity effect The tendency of people to feel more positive toward a person, item, product or other stimulus that they have seen often.

family-systems perspective An approach to doing therapy with individuals or families by emphasizing how each family member forms part of a larger, interacting system.

feature-detector cells Cells in the visual cortex that are sensitive to specific features of the environment.

field research Descriptive or experimental research conducted in a natural setting outside the laboratory.

fluid intelligence The capacity for deductive reasoning and the ability to use new information to solve problems; it is relatively independent of education and tends to decline in old age.

free association In psychodynamic therapies, the process of saying freely whatever comes to mind in connection with dreams, memories, fantasies, or conflicts.

frontal lobes Lobes at the front of the brain's cerebral cortex; they contain areas involved in short-term memory, higher-order thinking, initiative, social judgment, and (in the left lobe, typically) speech production.

functionalism An early psychological approach that emphasized the function or purpose of behaviour and consciousness.

fundamental attribution error The tendency, in explaining other people's behaviour, to overestimate personality factors and underestimate the influence of the situation.

g factor A general ability assumed by many theorists to underlie specific mental abilities and talents.

ganglion cells Neurons, in the retina of the eye, which gather information from receptor cells (by way of intermediate bipolar neurons); their axons make up the optic nerve.

gate-control theory The theory that the experience of pain depends in part on whether pain impulses get past a neurological "gate" in the spinal cord and thus reach the brain.

gender identity The fundamental sense of being male or female; it is independent of whether the person conforms to the social and cultural rules of gender.

gender schema A cognitive schema (mental network) of knowledge, beliefs, metaphors, and expectations about what it means to be male or female.

gender typing The process by which children learn the abilities, interests, personality traits, and behaviours associated with being masculine or feminine in their culture.

general adaptation syndrome According to Hans Selye, a series of physiological responses to stressors that occur in three phases: alarm, resistance, and exhaustion.

generalized anxiety disorder A continuous state of anxiety marked by feelings of worry and dread, apprehension, difficulties in concentration, and signs of motor tension.

genes The functional units of heredity; they are composed of DNA and specify the structure of proteins.

Gestalt principles Principles that describe the brain's organization of sensory information into meaningful units and patterns.

glia [GLY-uh or GLEE-uh] Cells that support, nurture, and insulate neurons; remove debris when neurons die; and modify neuronal functioning.

graduated exposure In behaviour therapy, a method in which a person suffering from an anxiety disorder, such as a phobia or panic attacks, is taken directly into the feared situation until the anxiety subsides.

groupthink In close-knit groups, the tendency for all members to think alike for the sake of harmony and to suppress disagreement.

heritability A statistical estimate of the proportion of the total variance in some trait that is attributable to genetic differences among individuals within a group.

heuristic A rule of thumb that suggests a course of action or guides problem solving but does not guarantee an optimal solution.

higher-order conditioning In classical conditioning, a procedure in which a neutral stimulus becomes a conditioned stimulus through association with an already established conditioned stimulus.

hindsight bias The tendency to overestimate one's ability to have predicted an event once the outcome is known; the "I knew it all along" phenomenon.

hippocampus A brain structure involved in the storage of new information in memory.

hormones Chemical substances, secreted by organs called glands, that affect the functioning of other organs.

hue The dimension of visual experience specified by colour names and related to the wavelength of light.

humanist psychology A psychological approach that emphasizes free will, personal growth, resilience, and the achievement of human potential.

humanist therapy A form of psychotherapy based on the philosophy of humanism, which emphasizes people's free will to change, not past conflicts.

hypnosis A procedure in which the practitioner suggests changes in the sensations, perceptions, thoughts, feelings, or behaviour of the subject.

hypothalamus A brain structure involved in emotions and drives vital to survival, such as hunger, thirst, emotion, sex, and reproduction; it regulates the autonomic nervous system.

hypothesis A statement that attempts to predict or to account for a set of phenomena; scientific hypotheses specify relationships among events or variables and are empirically tested.

id In psychoanalysis, the part of personality containing inherited psychic energy, particularly sexual and aggressive instincts.

implicit learning Learning that occurs when you acquire knowledge about something without being aware of how you did so and without being able to state exactly what it is you have learned.

implicit memory Unconscious retention in memory, as evidenced by the effect of a previous experience or previously encountered information on current thoughts or actions.

independent variable A variable that an experimenter manipulates.

individualist cultures Cultures in which the self is regarded as autonomous, and individual goals and wishes are prized above duty and relations with others.

induction A method of child rearing in which the parent appeals to the child's own resources, abilities, sense of responsibility, and feelings for others in correcting misbehaviour.

inductive reasoning A form of reasoning in which the premises provide support for a conclusion, but it is still possible for the conclusion to be false.

inferential statistics Statistical procedures that allow researchers to draw inferences about how statistically meaningful a study's results are.

instinctive drift During operant learning, the tendency for an organism to revert to instinctive behaviour.

intelligence quotient (IQ) A measure of intelligence now derived from norms provided for standardized intelligence tests.

intelligence An inferred characteristic of an individual, usually defined as the ability to profit from experience, acquire knowledge, think abstractly, act purposefully, or adapt to changes in the environment.

intermittent (partial) schedule of reinforcement A reinforcement schedule in which a particular response is sometimes, but not always, reinforced.

internal desynchronization A state in which biological rhythms are not in phase (synchronized) with one another.

intrinsic motivation The desire to do something for its own sake and for the internal pleasure it provides.

intrinsic reinforcers Reinforcers that are inherently related to the activity being reinforced, such as enjoyment of the task and the satisfaction of accomplishment.

just-world hypothesis The notion that many people need to believe that the world is fair and that justice is served, that bad people are punished and good people rewarded.

justification of effort The tendency of individuals to increase their liking for something that they have worked hard or suffered to attain; a common form of dissonance reduction.

kinesthesis [KIN-es-THEE-sis] The sense of body position and movement of body parts; also called *kinesthesia*.

language acquisition device According to many psycholinguists, an innate mental module that allows young children to develop language if they are exposed to an adequate sampling of conversation.

latent learning A form of learning that is not immediately expressed in an overt response; it occurs without obvious reinforcement.

lateralization Specialization of the two cerebral hemispheres for particular operations.

learning perspective A psychological approach that emphasizes how the environment and experience affect a person's or animal's actions; it includes *behaviourism* and *social–cognitive learning theories*.

learning A relatively permanent change in behaviour (behavioural potential) due to experience.

libido [li-BEE-do] In psychoanalysis, the psychic energy that fuels the life or sexual instincts of the id.

limbic system A group of brain areas involved in emotional reactions and motivated behaviour.

lithium carbonate A drug frequently given to people suffering from bipolar disorder.

localization of function Specialization of particular brain areas for particular functions.

locus of control A general expectation about whether the results of your actions are under your own control (internal locus) or beyond your control (external locus).

long-term memory (LTM) In the three-box model of memory, the memory system involved in the long-term storage of information.

longitudinal study A study in which individuals are followed and periodically reassessed over a period of time.

loudness The dimension of auditory experience related to the intensity of a pressure wave.

lucid dream A dream in which the dreamer is aware of dreaming.

maintenance rehearsal Rote repetition of material in order to maintain its availability in memory.

major depression A mood disorder involving disturbances in emotion (excessive sadness), behaviour (loss of interest in one's usual activities), cognition (thoughts of hopelessness), and body function (fatigue and loss of appetite).

mastery (learning) goals Goals framed in terms of increasing one's competence and skills.

medulla [muh-DUL-uh] A structure in the brain stem responsible for certain automatic functions, such as breathing and heart rate.

melatonin [mel-a-TOE-nin] A hormone, secreted by the pineal gland, that is involved in the regulation of daily biological rhythms.

menarche [men-ARR-kee] The onset of menstruation.

menopause The cessation of menstruation and of the production of ova; it is usually a gradual process lasting up to several years.

mental age (MA) A measure of mental development expressed in terms of the average mental ability at a given age.

mental disorder Any behaviour or emotional state that causes a person great suffering, is self-destructive, seriously impairs the person's ability to work or get along with others, or endangers others or the community.

mental image A mental representation that mirrors or resembles the thing it represents; mental images can occur in many and perhaps all sensory modalities.

mental set A tendency to solve problems using procedures that worked previously on similar problems.

meta-analysis A procedure for combining and analyzing data from many studies; it determines how much of the variance in scores across all studies can be explained by a particular variable.

metacognition The knowledge or awareness of one's own cognitive processes.

Minnesota Multiphasic Personality Inventory (MMPI) A widely used objective personality test.

mnemonics [neh-MON-iks] Strategies and tricks for improving memory, such as the use of a verse or a formula.

monocular cues Visual cues to depth or distance that can be used by one eye alone.

motivation An inferred process within a person or animal that causes movement either toward a goal or away from an unpleasant situation.

MRI (magnetic resonance imaging) A method for studying body and brain tissue, using magnetic fields and special radio receivers.

myelin sheath [MY-uh-lin] A fatty insulation that surrounds the axon of some neurons.

narcissistic personality disorder A disorder characterized by an exaggerated sense of self-importance and self-absorption.

narcolepsy A sleep disorder involving sudden and unpredictable daytime attacks of sleepiness or actual sleep.

need for achievement A learned motive to meet personal standards of success and excellence in a chosen area.

need for affiliation The motive to associate with other people, as by seeking friends, companionship, or love.

negative correlation An association between increases in one variable and decreases in another.

negative reinforcement A reinforcement procedure in which a response is followed by the removal, delay, or decrease in intensity of an unpleasant stimulus; as a result, the response becomes stronger or more likely to occur.

nerve A bundle of nerve fibres (axons and sometimes dendrites) in the peripheral nervous system.

neuron A cell that conducts electrochemical signals; the basic unit of the nervous system; also called a *nerve cell*.

neurotransmitter A chemical substance that is released by a transmitting neuron at the synapse and that alters the activity of a receiving neuron.

nonshared environment Unique aspects of a person's environment and experience that are not shared with family members.

norms (social) Rules that regulate social life, including explicit laws and implicit cultural conventions.

norms In test construction, established standards of performance.

object-relations school A psychodynamic approach that emphasizes the importance of the infant's first two years of life and the baby's formative relationships, especially with the mother.

objective tests (inventories) Standardized questionnaires requiring written responses; they typically include scales on which people are asked to rate themselves.

observational learning A process in which an individual learns new responses by observing the behaviour of another (a model) rather than through direct experience; sometimes called *vicarious conditioning*.

observational study A study in which the researcher carefully and systematically observes and records behaviour without interfering with the behaviour; it may involve either naturalistic or laboratory observation.

obsessive-compulsive disorder (OCD) An anxiety disorder in which a person feels trapped in repetitive, persistent thoughts (*obsessions*) and repetitive, ritualized behaviours (*compulsions*) designed to reduce anxiety.

occipital [ahk-SIP-uh-tuhl] lobes Lobes at the lower back part of the brain's cerebral cortex; they contain areas that receive visual information.

Oedipus complex In psychoanalysis, a conflict occurring in the phallic (oedipal) stage, in which a child desires the parent of the other sex and views the same-sex parent as a rival.

object permanence The understanding, which develops throughout the first year, that an object continues to exist even when you cannot see it or touch it.

operant conditioning The process by which a response becomes more likely to occur or less so, depending on its consequences.

operational definition A precise definition of a term in a hypothesis; specifies the operations for observing and measuring the process or phenomenon being defined.

opiates Drugs derived from the opium poppy that relieve pain and commonly produce euphoria.

opponent-process theory A theory of colour perception that assumes that the visual system treats pairs of colours as opposing or antagonistic.

organ of Corti [CORE-tee] A structure in the cochlea containing hair cells that serve as the receptors for hearing.

panic disorder An anxiety disorder in which a person experiences recurring panic attacks, periods of intense fear, and feelings of impending doom or death, accompanied by physiological symptoms such as rapid heart rate and dizziness.

papillae [pa-PILL-ee] Knob-like elevations on the tongue, containing the taste buds. (Singular: *papilla*.)

parallel distributed processing (PDP) Model A model of memory in which knowledge is represented as connections among thousands of interacting processing units, distributed in a vast network and all operating in parallel.

paranoid personality disorder A disorder characterized by unreasonable, excessive suspiciousness and mistrust, and irrational feelings of being persecuted by others.

parapsychology The study of purported psychic phenomena such as ESP and mental telepathy.

parasympathetic nervous system The subdivision of the autonomic nervous system that operates during relaxed states and that conserves energy.

parietal [puh-RYE-uh-tuhl] lobes Lobes at the top of the brain's cerebral cortex; they contain areas that receive information on pressure, pain, touch, and temperature.

perception The process by which the brain organizes and interprets sensory information.

perceptual constancy The accurate perception of objects as stable or unchanged despite changes in the sensory patterns they produce.

perceptual set A habitual way of perceiving, based on expectations.

performance goals Goals framed in terms of performing well in front of others, being judged favourably, and avoiding criticism.

peripheral nervous system (PNS) All portions of the nervous system outside the brain and spinal cord; it includes sensory and motor nerves.

personality A distinctive and relatively stable pattern of behaviour, mannerisms, thoughts, motives, and emotions that characterizes an individual.

personality disorders Rigid personality patterns that cause personal distress or an inability to get along with others.

PET (positron-emission tomography) scan A method for analyzing biochemical activity in the brain, using injections of a glucose-like substance containing a radioactive element.

phobia An exaggerated, unrealistic fear of a specific situation, activity, or object.

pitch The dimension of auditory experience related to the frequency of a pressure wave; it is related to the height or depth of a tone.

pituitary gland [pi-TOO-i-terry] A small endocrine gland at the base of the brain that releases many hormones and regulates other endocrine glands.

placebo An inactive substance or fake treatment used as a control in an experiment.

placebo effect The apparent success of a medication or treatment that is due to the patient's expectations or hopes rather than to the drug or treatment itself.

pons A structure in the brain stem involved in, among other things, sleeping, waking, and dreaming.

positive correlation An association between increases in one variable and increases in another, or between decreases in one and decreases in another.

positive reinforcement A reinforcement procedure in which a response is followed by the presentation of, or increase in intensity of, a reinforcing stimulus; as a result, the response becomes stronger or more likely to occur.

postdecision dissonance In the theory of cognitive dissonance, tension that occurs when you believe you may have made a bad decision.

posttraumatic stress disorder (PTSD) An anxiety disorder in which a person who has experienced a traumatic or life-threatening event has symptoms such as psychic numbing, reliving of the trauma, and increased physiological arousal.

power assertion A method of child rearing in which the parent uses punishment and authority to correct the child's misbehaviour.

primacy effect The tendency to remember items at the beginning of a list more easily than other items in the list.

primary control An effort to modify reality by changing other people, the situation, or events; a "fighting back" philosophy.

primary emotions Emotions that are considered to be universal and biologically based; they generally include fear, anger, sadness, happiness, surprise, disgust, and contempt.

primary punisher A stimulus that is inherently punishing; an example is electric shock.

primary reinforcer A stimulus that is inherently reinforcing, typically satisfying a physiological need; an example is food.

priming A method for measuring implicit memory in which a person reads or listens to information and is later tested to see whether the information affects performance on another type of task.

principle of falsifiability The principle that a scientific theory must make predictions that are specific enough to expose the theory to the possibility of disconfirmation.

proactive interference Forgetting that occurs when previously stored material interferes with the ability to remember similar, more recently learned material.

procedural memories Memories for the performance of actions or skills ("knowing how").

projective tests Psychological tests used to infer a person's motives, conflicts, and unconscious dynamics on the basis of the person's interpretations of ambiguous stimuli.

proposition A unit of meaning that is made up of concepts and expresses a single idea.

prototype An especially representative example of a concept.

psychedelic drugs Consciousness-altering drugs that produce hallucinations, change thought processes, or disrupt the normal perception of time and space.

psychoactive drug A drug capable of influencing perception, mood, thinking, memory, or behaviour.

psychoanalysis psychodynamic theories Theories that explain behaviour and personality in terms of unconscious dynamics within the individual.

psychoanalysis A theory of personality and a "depth" method of psychotherapy developed by Sigmund Freud; it emphasizes unconscious motives and conflicts.

psychodynamic perspective A psychological approach that emphasizes unconscious dynamics within the individual, such as inner forces, conflicts, or the movement of instinctual energy.

psychodynamic therapies Psychotherapies that share the goal of exploring the unconscious dynamics of personality, although they differ from Freudian analysis in various ways.

psychological tests Procedures used to measure and evaluate personality traits, emotional states, aptitudes, interests, abilities, and values.

psychology The discipline concerned with behaviour and mental processes and how they are affected by an organism's physical state, mental state, and external environment; often represented by Ψ, the Greek letter psi (usually pronounced "sy").

psychometrics The measurement of mental abilities, traits, and processes.

psychosis An extreme mental disturbance involving distorted perceptions and irrational behaviour; it may have psychological or organic causes.

psychosurgery Any surgical procedure that destroys selected areas of the brain believed to be involved in emotional disorders or violent, impulsive behaviour.

puberty The age at which a person becomes capable of sexual reproduction.

punishment The process by which a stimulus or event weakens or reduces the probability of the response that it follows.

random assignment A procedure for assigning people to experimental and control groups in which each individual has the same probability as any other of being assigned to a given group.

randomized controlled trials Research designed to determine the effectiveness of a new medication or form of therapy, in which people with a given problem or disorder are randomly assigned to one or more treatment groups or to a control group.

rapid eye movement (REM) sleep Sleep periods characterized by eye movement, loss of muscle tone, and dreaming.

rational emotive behaviour therapy (REBT) A form of cognitive therapy devised by Albert Ellis, designed to challenge the client's unrealistic or irrational thoughts.

reasoning The drawing of conclusions or inferences from observations, facts, or assumptions.

recall The ability to retrieve and reproduce from memory previously encountered material.

recency effect The tendency to remember items at the end of a list more easily than other items in the list.

reciprocal (mutual) determinism In social–cognitive theories, the two-way interaction between aspects of the environment and aspects of the individual in the shaping of personality traits.

recognition The ability to identify previously encountered material.

reinforcement The process by which a stimulus or event strengthens or increases the probability of the response that it follows.

relearning method A method for measuring retention that compares the time required to relearn material with the time used to learn the material initially.

reliability In test construction, the consistency of test scores from one time and place to another.

representative sample A group of individuals, selected from a population for study, which matches that population in important characteristics such as age and sex.

repression In psychoanalytic theory, the involuntary pushing of threatening or upsetting information into the unconscious.

reticular activating system (RAS) A dense network of neurons found in the core of the brain stem; it arouses the cortex and screens incoming information.

retina Neural tissue lining the back of the eyeball's interior; this tissue contains the receptors for vision.

retinal disparity The slight difference in lateral separation between two objects as seen by the left eye and the right eye.

retroactive interference Forgetting that occurs when recently learned material interferes with the ability to remember similar material stored previously.

rods Visual receptors that respond to dim light.

role A given social position that is governed by a set of norms for proper behaviour.

Rorschach Inkblot Test A projective personality test that requires respondents to interpret abstract, symmetrical inkblots.

saturation Vividness or purity of colour; the dimension of visual experience related to the complexity of light waves.

schizophrenia A psychotic disorder or group of disorders marked by positive symptoms (e.g., delusions, hallucinations, disorganized and incoherent speech, and inappropriate behaviour) and negative symptoms (e.g., emotional flatness and loss of motivation).

seasonal affective disorder (SAD) A controversial disorder in which a person experiences depression during the winter and an improvement of mood in the spring.

secondary control An effort to accept reality by changing your own attitudes, goals, or emotions; a "learn to live with it" philosophy.

secondary emotions Emotions that are specific to certain cultures.

secondary punisher A stimulus that has acquired punishing properties through association with other punishers.

secondary reinforcer A stimulus that has acquired reinforcing properties through association with other reinforcers.

selective attention The focusing of attention on selected aspects of the environment and the blocking out of other aspects.

self-efficacy A person's belief that he or she is capable of producing desired results, such as mastering new skills and reaching goals.

self-fulfilling prophecy An expectation that is fulfilled because of the tendency of the person holding it to act in ways that bring it about.

self-serving bias The tendency, in explaining one's own behaviour, to take credit for one's good actions and rationalize one's mistakes.

semantic memories Memories of general knowledge, including facts, rules, concepts, and propositions.

semicircular canals Sense organs in the inner ear, which contribute to equilibrium by responding to rotation of the head.

sensation The detection of physical energy emitted or reflected by physical objects.

sense receptors Specialized cells that convert physical energy in the environment or the body to electrical energy that can be transmitted as nerve impulses to the brain.

sensory adaptation The reduction or disappearance of sensory responsiveness that occurs when stimulation is unchanging or repetitious.

sensory deprivation The absence of normal levels of sensory stimulation.

sensory register A memory system that accurately but very briefly registers sensory information before the information fades or moves into short-term memory.

separation anxiety The distress that most children develop, at about six to eight months of age, when their primary caregivers temporarily leave them with others.

serial-position effect The tendency for recall of the first and last items on a list to surpass recall of items in the middle of the list.

set point The genetically influenced weight range for an individual, maintained by biological mechanisms that regulate food intake, fat reserves, and metabolism.

sex hormones Hormones that regulate the development and functioning of reproductive organs and that stimulate the development of male and female sexual characteristics; they include androgens, estrogens, and progesterone.

sexual scripts Sets of implicit rules that specify proper sexual behaviour for a person in a given situation, varying with the person's age, culture, and gender.

shaping An operant-conditioning procedure in which successive approximations of a desired response are reinforced.

short-term memory (STM) In the three-box model of memory, a limited-capacity memory system involved in the retention of information for brief periods; it is also used to hold information retrieved from long-term memory for temporary use.

signal-detection theory A psychophysical theory that divides the detection of a sensory signal into a sensory process and a decision process.

significance tests Statistical tests that assess how likely it is that a study's results occurred merely by chance.

single-blind study An experiment in which subjects do not know whether they are in an experimental or a control group.

skills training In behaviour therapy, an effort to teach the client skills that he or she may lack, as well as new constructive behaviours to replace self-defeating ones.

sleep apnea A disorder in which breathing briefly stops during sleep, causing the person to choke and gasp, and momentarily awaken.

social cognition An area in social psychology concerned with social influences on thought, memory, perception, and beliefs.

social–cognitive learning theory A major contemporary learning view of personality, which holds that personality traits result from a person's learning history and his or her expectations, beliefs, perceptions of events, and other cognitions.

social–cognitive theories Theories that emphasize how behaviour is learned and maintained through observation and imitation of others, positive consequences, and cognitive processes such as plans, expectations, and beliefs.

socialization The process by which children learn the behaviours, attitudes, and expectations required of them by their society or culture.

sociocultural perspective A psychological approach that emphasizes social and cultural influences on behaviour.

somatic nervous system The subdivision of the peripheral nervous system that connects to sensory receptors and to skeletal muscles; sometimes called the *skeletal nervous system.*

source amnesia The inability to distinguish what you originally experienced from what you heard or were told about an event later.

spinal cord A collection of neurons and supportive tissue running from the base of the brain down the centre of the back, protected by a column of bones (the spinal column).

spinal reflexes Automatic behaviours produced by the spinal cord without brain involvement.

spontaneous recovery The reappearance of a learned response after its apparent extinction.

standard deviation A commonly used measure of variability that indicates the average difference between scores and their mean.

standardize In test construction, to develop uniform procedures for giving and scoring a test.

state-dependent memory The tendency to remember something when the rememberer is in the same physical or mental state as during the original learning or experience.

stem cells Immature cells that renew themselves and have the potential to develop into mature cells; given encouraging environments, stem cells from early embryos can develop into any cell type.

stereotype A summary impression of a group, in which a person believes that all members of the group share a common trait or traits (positive, negative, or neutral).

stereotype threat A burden of doubt a person feels about his or her performance, due to negative stereotypes about his or her group's abilities.

stimulants Drugs that speed up activity in the central nervous system.

stimulus discrimination The tendency to respond differently to two or more similar stimuli; in classical conditioning, it occurs when a stimulus similar to the CS fails to evoke the CR.

stimulus generalization After conditioning, the tendency to respond to a stimulus that resembles one involved in the original conditioning; in classical conditioning, it occurs when a stimulus that resembles the CS elicits the CR.

subconscious processes Mental processes occurring outside of conscious awareness but accessible to consciousness when necessary.

successive approximations In the procedure of shaping, behaviours that are ordered in terms of increasing similarity or closeness to the desired response.

superego In psychoanalysis, the part of personality that represents conscience, morality, and social standards.

suprachiasmatic [soo-pruh-kie-az-MAT-ick] nucleus (SCN) An area of the brain containing a biological clock that governs circadian rhythms.

surveys Questionnaires and interviews that ask people directly about their experiences, attitudes, or opinions.

sympathetic nervous system The subdivision of the autonomic nervous system that mobilizes bodily resources and increases the output of energy during emotion and stress.

synapse action potential A brief change in electrical voltage that occurs when a neuron is stimulated; it serves to produce an electrical impulse.

synesthesia A rare condition in which stimulation of one sense also evokes a sensation in another.

systematic desensitization In behaviour therapy, a step-by-step process of desensitizing a client to a feared object or experience; it is based on the classical-conditioning procedure of counter-conditioning.

tacit knowledge Strategies for success that are not explicitly taught but that instead must be inferred.

taste buds Nests of taste-receptor cells.

telegraphic speech A child's first word combinations, which omit (as a telegram did) unnecessary words.

temperaments Physiological dispositions to respond to the environment in certain ways; they are present in infancy and are assumed to be innate.

temporal lobes Lobes at the sides of the brain's cerebral cortex; they contain areas involved in hearing, memory, perception, emotion, and (in the left lobe, typically) language comprehension.

thalamus A brain structure that relays sensory messages to the cerebral cortex.

Thematic Apperception Test (TAT) A projective test that asks respondents to interpret a series of drawings showing scenes of people; usually scored for unconscious personality traits and motives, such as the need for achievement, power, or affiliation.

theory An organized system of assumptions and principles that purports to explain a specified set of phenomena and their interrelationships.

therapeutic alliance The bond of confidence and mutual understanding established between therapist and client, which allows them to work together to solve the client's problems.

timbre The distinguishing quality of a sound; the dimension of auditory experience related to the complexity of the pressure wave.

tolerance Increased resistance to a drug's effects accompanying continued use.

trait A characteristic of an individual, describing a habitual way of behaving, thinking, or feeling.

tranquilizers Drugs commonly but often inappropriately prescribed for patients who complain of unhappiness, anxiety, or worry.

transference In psychodynamic therapies, a critical process in which the client transfers unconscious emotions or reactions, such as emotional feelings about his or her parents, onto the therapist.

triarchic theory of intelligence A theory of intelligence that emphasizes information-processing strategies, the ability to transfer skills to new situations, and the practical application of intelligence.

trichromatic theory A theory of colour perception that proposes three mechanisms in the visual system, each sensitive to a certain range of wavelengths; their interaction is assumed to produce all the different experiences of hue. Also known as the Young–Helmholtz theory.

unconditional positive regard To Carl Rogers, love or support given to another person with no conditions attached.

unconditioned response (UR) The classical-conditioning term for a reflexive response elicited by a stimulus in the absence of learning.

unconditioned stimulus (US) The classical-conditioning term for a stimulus that elicits a reflexive response in the absence of learning.

unconscious processes Mental processes occurring outside of and not available to conscious awareness.

validity effect The tendency of people to believe that a statement is true or valid simply because it has been repeated many times.

validity The ability of a test to measure what it was designed to measure.

variables Characteristics of behaviour or experience that can be measured or described by a numerical scale; variables are manipulated and assessed in scientific studies.

volunteer bias A shortcoming of findings derived from a sample of volunteers instead of a representative sample; the volunteers may differ from those who did not volunteer.

vulnerability-stress models Approaches that emphasize how individual vulnerabilities (e.g., in genes or personality traits) interact with external stresses or circumstances to produce mental disorders.

withdrawal symptoms Physical and psychological symptoms that occur when someone addicted to a drug stops taking it.

working memory Short-term memory plus the mental processes that control retrieval of information from long-term memory and interpret that information appropriately for a given task.

BIBLIOGRAPHY

Blue type indicates Canadian research or a researcher associated with a Canadian university.

Abel, E. L. (1995). An update on incidence of FAS: FAS is not an equal opportunity birth defect. *Neurotoxicology and Teratology, 17*(4), 437–443.

Abel, Gene G.; Mittelman, Mary; Becker, Judith V.; et al. (1988). Predicting child molesters' respons to treatment. *Annals of the New York Academy of Sciences, 528,* 223–234.

Abrams, David B., & Wilson, G. Terence (1983). Alcohol, sexual arousal, and self-control. *Journal of Personality and Social Psychology, 45,* 188–198.

Abrams, R. (1997). *Electroconvulsive therapy* (3rd ed.). Oxford, England: Oxford University Press.

Abramson, Lyn Y.; Metalsky, Gerald I.; & Alloy, Lauren B. (1989). Hopelessness depression: A theory-based subtype of depression. *Psychological Review, 96,* 358–372.

Ackerman, S.; Zuroff, D. C.; & Moskowitz, D. S. (2000). Generativity in midlife and young adults: Links to agency, communion, and subjective well-being. *International Journal of Aging and Human Development, 50*(1), 17–41.

Acocella, Joan (1999). *Creating hysteria: Women and multiple personality disorder.* San Francisco: Jossey-Bass.

Adams, J. L. (1986). *The care and feeding of ideas.* London: Penguin.

Ader, Robert (1997). The role of conditioning. In A. Harrington (Ed.), *The placebo effect: An interdisciplinary exploration.* Cambridge, MA: Harvard University Press.

Ader, Robert (2000). True or false: The placebo effect as seen in drug studies is definitive proof that the mind can bring about clinically relevant changes in the body: The placebo effect: If it's all in your head, does that mean you only think you feel better? *Advances in Mind-Body Medicine, 16,* 7–11.

Adolphs, Ralph (2001). Emotion, social cognition, and the human brain. Invited address presented at the annual meeting of the American Psychological Society, Toronto.

Affleck, Glenn; Tennen, Howard; Croog, Sydney; & Levine, Sol (1987). Causal attribution, perceived control, and recovery from a heart attack. *Journal of Social and Clinical Psychology, 5,* 339–355.

Ainsworth, Mary D. S. (1973). The development of infant–mother attachment. In B. M. Caldwell & H. N. Ricciuti (Eds.), *Review of child development research* (Vol. 3). Chicago: University of Chicago Press.

Ainsworth, Mary D. S. (1979). Infant–mother attachment. *American Psychologist, 34,* 932–937.

Akbarian, Schahram; Kim, J. J.; Potkin, Steven G.; et al. (1996). Maldistribution of interstitial neurons in prefrontal white matter of the brains of schizophrenic patients. *Archives of General Psychiatry, 53,* 425–436.

Ali, S., & Milev, R. (2003). Switch to mania upon discontinuation of antidepressants in patients with mood disorders: A review of the literature. *Canadian Journal of Psychiatry, 48*(4), 258–264.

Allen, Laura S., & Gorski, Robert A. (1992). Sexual orientation and the size of the anterior commissure in the human brain. *Proceedings of the National Academy of Sciences, 89,* 7199–7202.

Allison, David B., & Faith, Myles S. (1997). Issues in mapping genes for eating disorders. *Psychopharmacology Bulletin, 33,* 359–368.

Allison, David B., & Heshka, Stanley (1993). Emotion and eating in obesity? A critical analysis. *International Journal of Eating Disorders, 13,* 289–295.

Allport, Gordon W. (1937). *Personality: A psychological interpretation.* New York: Holt, Rinehart and Winston.

Allport, Gordon W. (1954/1979). *The nature of prejudice.* Reading, MA: Addison-Wesley.

Allport, Gordon W. (1961). *Pattern and growth in personality.* New York: Holt, Rinehart and Winston.

Altemeyer, B. (2004). The decline of organized religion in Western civilization. *International Journal for the Psychology of Religion, 14*(2), 77–89.

Amabile, Teresa M. (1983). *The social psychology of creativity.* New York: Springer-Verlag.

Ambert, A. M. (1997). *Parents, children, and adolescents: Interactive relationships and development in context.* New York: Hawthorne Press.

American Psychiatric Association (1994). *The diagnostic and statistical manual of mental disorders* (4th ed.). Washington, DC: American Psychiatric Association.

American Psychiatric Association (2000). *The diagnostic and statistical manual of mental disorders, IV-TR.* Washington, DC: American Psychiatric Association.

Amering, Michaela, & Katschnig, Heinz (1990). Panic attacks and panic disorder in cross-cultural perspective. *Psychiatric Annals, 20,* 511–516.

Amodio, David M.; Harmon-Jones, Eddie; & Devine, Patricia G. (2003). Individual differences in the activation and control of affective race bias as assessed by startle eye-blink response and self-report. *Journal of Personality and Social Psychology, 84,* 738–753.

Anand, S. S.; Yusuf, S.; Jacobs, R.; Davis, A. D.; Yi, Q.; Gerstein, H.; Montague, P. A.; & Lonn, E. (2001). Risk factors, atherosclerosis, and cardiovascular disease among Aboriginal people in Canada: The study of health assessment and risk evaluation in Aboriginal peoples (SHARE-AP), *Lancet, 358* (9288), 1147–1153.

Anastasi, Anne (1988). *Psychological testing* (6th ed.). New York: Macmillan.

Anastasi, Anne, & Urbina, Susan (1997). *Psychological testing* (7th ed.). Upper Saddle River, NJ: Prentice Hall.

Anderson, Adam K., & Phelps, Elizabeth A. (2000). Expression without recognition: Contributions of the human amygdala to emotional communication. *Psychological Science, 11,* 106–111.

Anderson, Amanda (in press). *The way we argue now: A study in the cultures of theory.* Princeton: Princeton University Press.

Anderson, Cameron; Keltner, Dacher; & John, Oliver P. (2003). Emotional convergence between people over time. *Journal of Personality and Social Psychology, 84,* 1054–1068.

Anderson, Craig A., & Bushman, Brad J. (2001). Effects of violent video games on aggressive behavior, aggressive cognition, aggressive affect, physiological arousal, and prosocial behavior: A meta-analytic review of the scientific literature. *Psychological Science, 12,* 353–359.

Anderson, John R. (1990). *The adaptive nature of thought.* Hillsdale, NJ: Erlbaum.

Anderson, S. W.; Bechara, A.; Damasio, H.; Tranel, D.; & Damasio, A. R. (1999). Impairment of social and moral behavior related to early damage in human prefrontal cortex. *Nature Neuroscience, 2,* 1032–1037.

Andreasen, Nancy C.; Arndt, Stephan; Swayze, Victor, II; et al. (1994). Thalamic abnormalities in schizophrenia visualized through magnetic resonance image averaging. *Science, 266,* 294–298.

Andrews, F. K., & Layne, N. (1985). Drinking patterns in Canada: Variations in drinking frequencies and demographic characteristics of current drinkers. *Canadian Journal of Addiction, 76,* 38–42.

Angell, Marcia (2000, May 18). Is academic medicine for sale? [Editorial] *New England Journal of Medicine, 342,* 1516–1518.

Antonova, Irina; Arancio, Ottavio; Trillat, Anne-Cecile; et al. (2001). Rapid increase in clusters of presynaptic proteins at onset of long-lasting potentiation. *Science, 294,* 1547–1550.

Antonuccio, David O.; Danton, William G.; & DeNelsky, Garland Y.; et al. (1999). Raising questions about antidepressants. *Psychotherapy and Psychosomatics, 68,* 3–14.

APA Commission on Violence and Youth (1993). *Violence and youth: Psychology's response.* Washington, DC: American Psychological Association.

Arendt, Hannah (1963). *Eichmann in Jerusalem: A report on the banality of evil.* New York: Viking.

Arkes, Hal R. (1993). Some practical judgment and decision-making research. In N. J. Castellan, Jr., et al. (Eds.), *Individual and group decision making: Current issues.* Hillsdale, NJ: Erlbaum.

Arkes, Hal R.; Boehm, Lawrence E.; & Xu, Gang (1991). The determinants of judged validity. *Journal of Experimental Social Psychology, 27,* 576–605.

Arkes, Hal R.; Faust, David; Guilmette, Thomas J.; & Hart, Kathleen (1988). Eliminating the hindsight bias. *Journal of Applied Psychology, 73,* 305–307.

Arnett, Jeffrey J. (1999). Adolescent storm and stress, reconsidered. *American Psychologist, 54,* 317–326.

Arnett, Jeffrey J. (2000). Emerging adulthood: A theory of development from the late teens through the twenties. *American Psychologist, 55,* 469–480.

Aron, Arthur, & Westbay, Lori (1996). Dimensions of the prototype of love. *Journal of Personality and Social Psychology, 70,* 535–551.

Aron, Arthur; Aron, Elaine N.; & Allen, Joselyn (1998). Motivations for unreciprocated love. *Personality and Social Psychology Bulletin, 24,* 787–796.

Aronson, Elliot (2004). *The social animal* (9th ed.). New York: Worth.

Aronson, Elliot, & Mills, Judson (1959). The effect of severity of initiation on liking for a group. *Journal of Abnormal and Social Psychology, 59,* 177–181.

Aronson, Elliot, & Patnoe, S. (1997). *The jigsaw classroom: Building cooperation in the classroom.* New York: Longman.

Aronson, Joshua, & Salinas, Moises F. (1997). *Stereotype threat, attribution ambiguity, and Latino underperformance.* Unpublished manuscript, University of Texas, Austin.

Arsenijevic, D.; Onuma, H.; Pecqueur, C.; et al. (2000, December 26). Disruption of the uncoupling protein-2 gene in mice reveals a role in immunity and reactive oxygen species production. *Nature Genetics, 4,* 387–388.

Asch, Solomon E. (1952). *Social psychology.* Englewood Cliffs, NJ: Prentice-Hall.

Asch, Solomon E. (1965). Effects of group pressure upon the modification and distortion of judgments. In H. Proshansky & B. Seidenberg (Eds.), *Basic studies in social psychology.* New York: Holt, Rinehart and Winston.

Aserinsky, Eugene, & Kleitman, Nathaniel (1955). Two types of ocular motility occurring in sleep. *Journal of Applied Physiology, 8,* 1–10.

Asmundson, G. J. G.; Carleton, R. N.; Wright, K. D.; & Taylor, S. (2004). Psychological sequelae of remote exposure to the September 11th terrorist attacks in Canadians with and without panic. *Cognitive Behavior Therapy, 33*(2), 51–59.

Asmundson, G. J.; Sandler, L. S.; Wilson, K. G.; & Walker, J. R. (1992). Selective attention toward physical threat in patients with panic disorder. *Journal of Anxiety Disorders, 6*(4), 295–303.

Aspinwall, Lisa G., & Brunhart, Susanne M. (1996). Distinguishing optimism from denial: Optimistic beliefs predict attention to health threats. *Personality and Social Psychology Bulletin, 22,* 993–1003.

Aspinwall, Lisa G., & Taylor, Shelley E. (1997). A stitch in time: Self-regulation and proactive coping. *Psychological Bulletin, 121,* 417–436.

Atkinson, Richard C., & Shiffrin, Richard M. (1968). Human memory: A proposed system and its control processes. In K. W. Spence & J. T. Spence (Eds.), *The psychology of learning and motivation: Vol. 2. Advances in research and theory.* New York: Academic Press.

Atkinson, Richard C., & Shiffrin, Richard M. (1971, August). The control of short-term memory. *Scientific American, 225*(2), 82–90.

Atran, Scott (2003, March 7). Genesis of Suicide Terrorism. *Science, 299,* 1534–1539.

AuBuchon, Peter G., & Calhoun, Karen S. (1985). Menstrual cycle symptomatology: The role of social expectancy and experimental demand characteristics. *Psychosomatic Medicine, 47,* 35–45.

Awad, A. G., & Voruganti, L. N. P. (2004). New antipsychotics, compliance, quality of life and subjective tolerability: Are patients better off? *Canadian Journal of Psychiatry, 49*(5), 297–302.

Axel, Richard (1995, October). The molecular logic of smell. *Scientific American,* 154–159.

Azrin, Nathan H., & Foxx, Richard M. (1974). *Toilet training in less than a day.* New York: Simon & Schuster.

Azuma, Hiroshi (1984). Secondary control as a heterogeneous category. *American Psychologist, 39,* 970–971.

Baddeley, Alan D. (1992). Working memory. *Science, 255,* 556–559.

Bahrick, Harry P. (1984). Semantic memory content in permastore: Fifty years of memory for Spanish learned in school. *Journal of Experimental Psychology: General, 113,* 1–29.

Bahrick, Harry P.; Bahrick, Phyllis O.; & Wittlinger, Roy P. (1975). Fifty years of memory for names and faces: A cross-sectional approach. *Journal of Experimental Psychology: General, 104,* 54–75.

Bailey, J. Michael, & Pillard, Richard C. (1995). Genetics of human sexual orientation. *Annual Review of Sex Research, 6,* 126–150.

Bailey, J. Michael, & Zucker, Kenneth J. (1995). Childhood sex-typed behavior and sexual orientation: A conceptual analysis and quantitative review. *Developmental Psychology, 31,* 43–55.

Bailey, J. Michael; Bobrow, David; Wolfe, Marilyn; & Mikach, Sarah (1995). Sexual orientation of adult sons of gay fathers. *Developmental Psychology, 31,* 124–129.

Bailey, J. Michael; Dunne, Michael P.; & Martin, Nicholas G. (2000). Genetic and environmental influences on sexual orientation and its correlates in an Australian twin sample. *Journal of Personality and Social Psychology, 78,* 524–536.

Bailey, J. Michael; Gaulin, Steven; Agyei, Yvonne; & Gladue, Brian A. (1994). Effects of gender and sexual orientation on evolutionarily relevant aspects of human mating psychology. *Journal of Personality and Social Psychology, 66,* 1081–1093.

Baillargeon, Renée (1994). How do infants learn about the physical world? *Current Directions in Psychological Science, 5,* 133–140.

Baillargeon, Renée (1999). Young infants' expectations about hidden objects: A reply to three challenges. *Developmental Science, 2*, 115–163.

Baker, J., & Horton, S. (2003). East African running dominance revisited: A role for stereotype threat? *British Journal of Sports Medicine, 37*(6), 553–555.

Baker, Mark C. (2001). *The atoms of language: The mind's hidden rules of grammar.* New York: Basic Books.

Baker, Robert A. (1992). *Hidden memories: Voices and visions from within.* Buffalo, NY: Prometheus.

Baker, Robin (1996). *The sperm wars: The science of sex.* New York: Basic Books.

Bakermans-Kranenburg, Marian J.; van IJzendoorn, Marinus H.; & Juffer, Femmie (2003). Less is more: Meta-analyses of sensitivity and attachment interventions in early childhood. *Psychological Bulletin, 129*, 195–215.

Ball, K.; Berch, D. B.; Helmers, K. F.; et al. (2002, November 13). Effects of cognitive training interventions with older adults: A randomized controlled trial. *Journal of the American Medical Association, 288*, 2271–2281.

Ballenger, James C.; Burrows, Graham D.; DuPont, Robert L.; et al. (1988). Alprazolam in panic disorder and agoraphobia: Results from a multicenter trial. *Archives of General Psychiatry, 45*, 413–421.

Baltes, Paul B., & Graf, Peter (1996). Psychological aspects of aging: Facts and frontiers. In D. Magnusson (Ed.), *The lifespan development of individuals.* Cambridge, England: Cambridge University Press.

Bandura, Albert (1977). *Social learning theory.* Englewood Cliffs, NJ: Prentice-Hall.

Bandura, Albert (1986). *Social foundations of thought and action: A social cognitive theory.* Englewood Cliffs, NJ: Prentice-Hall.

Bandura, Albert (1997). *Self-efficacy: The exercise of control.* New York: Freeman.

Bandura, Albert (1999). Moral disengagement in the perpetration of inhumanities. *Personality and Social Psychology Review, 3*, 193–209.

Bandura, Albert (2001). Social cognitive theory: An agentic perspective. *Annual Review of Psychology, 52*, 1–26. Palo Alto, CA: Annual Reviews.

Bandura, Albert; Caprara, Gian Vittorio; Barbaranelli, Claudio; Pastorelli, Concetta; & Regalia, Camillo (2001). Sociocognitive self-regulatory mechanisms governing transgressive behavior. *Journal of Personality and Social Psychology, 80*, 125–135.

Bandura, Albert; Ross, Dorothea; & Ross, Sheila A. (1963). Vicarious reinforcement and imitative learning. *Journal of Abnormal and Social Psychology, 67*, 601–607.

Banks, Martin S. (with Philip Salapatek) (1984). Infant visual perception. In P. Mussen (series ed.), M. M. Haith & J. J. Campos (vol. eds.), *Handbook of child psychology: Vol. II. Infancy and developmental psychobiology* (4th ed.). New York: Wiley.

Barash, David P., & Lipton, Judith Eve (2001). *The myth of monogamy: Fidelity and infidelity in animals and people.* New York: W. H. Freeman.

Barber, Theodore X. (1979). Suggested ("hypnotic") behavior: The trance paradigm versus an alternative paradigm. In E. Fromm & R. E. Shor (Eds.), *Hypnosis: Developments in research and new perspectives* (2nd ed.). New York: Aldine.

Barbuto, J. E. (1997). A critique of the Myers-Briggs Type Indicator and its operationalization of Carl Jung's psychological types. *Psychological Reports, 80*, 611–625.

Bargh, John A. (1999, January 29). The most powerful manipulative messages are hiding in plain sight. *The Chronicle of Higher Education*, B6.

Barinaga, Marcia (1992). Challenging the "no new neurons" dogma. *Science, 255*, 1646.

Barlow, David H. (2000). Unraveling the mysteries of anxiety and its disorders from the perspective of emotion theory. *American Psychologist, 55*, 1247–1263.

Barlow, David H.; Chorpita, Bruce F.; & Turovsky, Julia (1996). Fear, panic, anxiety, and disorders of emotion. In D. A. Hope et al. (Eds.), *Nebraska Symposium on Motivation, 1995: Perspectives on anxiety, panic, and fear.* Lincoln, NE: University of Nebraska Press.

Baron, S. W., & Kennedy, L. W. (1998). Deterrence and homeless male street youths. *Canadian Journal of Criminology, 40*(1), 27–60.

Barondes, Samuel H. (1998). *Mood genes: Hunting for origins of mania and depression.* New York: W. H. Freeman.

Barrish, Barbara M. (1996). The relationship of remembered parental physical punishment to adolescent self-concept. *Dissertation Abstracts International, Section B, 57*, 2171.

Barron, Kenneth S., & Harackiewicz, Judith M. (2001). Achievement goals and optimal motivation: Testing multiple goal models. *Journal of Personality and Social Psychology, 80*, 706–722.

Barsky, S. H.; Roth, M. D.; Kleerup, E. C.; Simmons, M.; & Tashkin, D. P. (1998). Histopathologic and molecular alterations in bronchial epithelium in habitual smokers of marijuana, cocaine, and/or tobacco. *Journal of the National Cancer Institute, 90*, 1198–1205.

Bartlett, Frederic C. (1932). *Remembering.* Cambridge, England: Cambridge University Press.

Bartoshuk, Linda M. (1998). Born to burn: Genetic variation in taste. Paper presented at the annual meeting of the American Psychological Association, San Francisco.

Bartoshuk, Linda M.; Duffy, V. B.; Lucchina, L. A.; et al. (1998). PROP (6-n-propylthiouracil) supertasters and the saltiness of NaCl. *Annals of the New York Academy of Sciences, 855*, 793–796.

Bashore, Theodore R.; Ridderinkhof, K. Richard; & van der Molen, Maurits W. (1997). The decline of cognitive processing speed in old age. *Current Directions in Psychological Science, 6*, 163–169.

Basic Behavioral Science Task Force of the National Advisory Mental Health Council (1996). Basic behavioral science research for mental health: Vulnerability and resilience. *American Psychologist, 51*, 22–28.

Bassetti, C.; Vella, S.; Donati, F.; et al. (2000). SPECT during sleepwalking. *Lancet, 356*, 484–485.

Basson, R.; McInnis, R.; Smith, M.; Hodgson, G.; & koppiker, N. (2002). Efficacy and safety of sildenafil citrate in women with sexual dysfunction associated with female sexual arousal disorder. *Journal of Women's Health and Gender Based Medicine, 11*, 339–349.

Bauer, Patricia J., & Dow, Gina Annunziato (1994). Episodic memory in 16- and 20-month-old children: Specifics are generalized but not forgotten. *Developmental Psychology, 30*, 403–417.

Baumeister, Roy F. (1990). Suicide as escape from self. *Psychological Review, 97*, 90–113.

Baumeister, Roy F. (2000). Gender differences in erotic plasticity: The female sex drive as socially flexible and responsive. *Psychological Bulletin, 126*, 347–374.

Baumeister, Roy F., & Bratslavsky, Ellen (1999). Passion, intimacy, and time: Passionate love as a function of change in intimacy. *Personality and Social Psychology Review, 3*, 49–67.

Baumeister, Roy F.; Catanese, Kathleen R.; & Vohs, Kathleen D. (2001). Is there a gender difference in strength of sex drive? Theoretical views, conceptual distinctions, and a review of relevant evidence. *Personality and Social Psychology Review, 5,* 242–273.

Baumeister, Roy F.; Dale, Karen; & Sommer, Kristin L. (1998). Freudian defense mechanisms and empirical findings in modern social psychology: Reaction formation, projection, displacement, undoing, isolation, sublimation, and denial. *Journal of Personality, 66,* 1081–1124.

Baumeister, Roy F.; Stillwell, Arlene M.; & Heatherton, Todd F. (1994). Guilt: An interpersonal approach. *Psychological Bulletin, 115,* 243–267.

Baumrind, Diana (1989). Rearing competent children. In W. Damon (Ed.), *Child development today and tomorrow.* San Francisco: Jossey-Bass.

Baumrind, Diana (1991). Parenting styles and adolescent development. In R. Lerner, A. C. Petersen, & J. Brooks-Gunn (Eds.), *The encyclopedia of adolescence.* New York: Garland.

Baumrind, Diana (1995). Commentary on sexual orientation: Research and social policy implications. *Developmental Psychology, 31,* 130–136.

Baumrind, Diana; Larzelere, Robert E.; & Cowan, Philip (2002). Ordinary physical punishment—Is it harmful? Commentary on Gershoff's Review. *Psychological Bulletin, 128*(4), 580–589.

Baxter, Lewis R.; Schwartz, Jeffrey M.; Bergman, Kenneth S.; et al. (1992). Caudate glucose metabolic rate changes with both drug and behavior therapy for obsessive-compulsive disorder. *Archives of General Psychiatry, 49,* 681–689.

Bechara, Antoine; Dermas, Hanna; Tranel, Daniel; & Damasio, Antonio R. (1997). Deciding advantageously before knowing the advantageous strategy. *Science, 275,* 1293–1294.

Beck, Aaron T. (1976). *Cognitive therapy and the emotional disorders.* New York: International Universities Press.

Beck, Aaron T. (1988). Cognitive approaches to panic disorder: Theory and therapy. In S. Rachman & J. D. Maser (Eds.), *Panic: Psychological perspectives.* Hillsdale, NJ: Erlbaum.

Beck, Aaron T. (1991). Cognitive therapy: A 30-year retrospective. *American Psychologist, 46,* 368–375.

Beckerman, Stephen; Lizarralde, Roberto; Ballew, Carol; et al. (1998). The Barí partible paternity project: Preliminary results. *Current Anthropology, 39,* 164–167.

Beer, Jeremy M.; Arnold, Richard D.; & Loehlin, John C. (1998). Genetic and environmental influences on MMPI factor scales: Joint model fitting to twin and adoption data. *Journal of Personality and Social Psychology, 74,* 818–827.

Bekenstein, Jonathan W., & Lothman, Eric W. (1993). Dormancy of inhibitory interneurons in a model of temporal lobe epilepsy. *Science, 259,* 97–100.

Bell, J.; Grekul, J.; Lamba, N.; Minas, C.; & Harrell, A. W. (1995). The impact of cost on student helping behavior. *Journal of Social Psychology. 135*(1), 49–56.

Belle, Deborah, & Doucet, Joanne (2003). Poverty, inequality, and discrimination as sources of depression among U.S. women. *Psychology of Women Quarterly, 27,* 101–113.

Belsky, Jay; Hsieh, Kuang-Hua; & Crnic, Keith (1996). Infant positive and negative emotionality: One dimension or two? *Developmental Psychology, 32,* 289–298.

Bem, Daryl J., & Honorton, Charles (1994). Does psi exist? Replicable evidence for an anomalous process of information transfer. *Psychological Bulletin, 115,* 4–18.

Bem, Sandra L. (1993). *The lenses of gender.* New Haven, CT: Yale University Press.

Benedetti, Fabrizio, & Levi-Montalcini, Rita (2001). Opioid and non-opioid mechanisms of placebo analgesia. Paper presented at the annual meeting of the American Psychological Society, Toronto.

Benjamin, Ludy T., Jr. (1998). Why Gorgeous George, and not Wilhelm Wundt, was the founder of psychology: A history of popular psychology in America. Invited address presented at the National Institute on the Teaching of Psychology, St. Petersburg Beach.

Bereiter, Carl, & Bird, Marlene (1985). Use of thinking aloud in identification and teaching of reading comprehension strategies. *Cognition and Instruction, 2,* 131–156.

Berenbaum, Sheri A.; Duck, S.C.; & Bryk, K. (2000). Behavioural effects of prenatal versus postnatal androgen excess in children with 12-hydroxylase-deficient congenital adrenal hyperplasia. *Journal of Clinical Endocrinology & Metabolism, 85,* 727–753.

Berenbaum, Sheri A., & Snyder, Elizabeth (1995). Early hormonal influences on childhood sex-typed activity and playmate preferences: Implications for the development of sexual orientation. *Developmental Psychology, 31,* 31–42.

Berger, F.; Gage, F. H.; & Vijayaraghavan, S. (1998). Nicotinic receptor-induced apoptotic cell death of hippocampal progenitor cells. *Journal of Neuroscience, 18,* 6871–6881.

Berkman, Lisa F., & Syme, S. Leonard (1979). Social networks, host resistance, and mortality: A nine-year follow-up study of Alameda County residents. *American Journal of Epidemiology, 109,* 186–204.

Berkowitz, Leonard (1999). Evil is more than banal: Situationism and the concept of evil. *Personality and Social Psychology Review, 3,* 246–253.

Berkowitz, Marvin W., & Grych, John H. (2000). Early character development and education. *Early Education & Development, 11,* 55–72.

Bernhardt, Paul C; Dabbs, James M., Jr.; Fielden, Julie A.; & Lutter, Candice D. (1998). Testosterone changes during vicarious experiences of winning and losing among fans at sporting events. *Physiology & Behavior, 65,* 59–62.

Bernieri, Frank J.; Davis, Janet M.; Rosenthal, Robert; & Knee, C. Raymond (1991). *Interactional synchrony and the social affordance of rapport: A validation study.* Unpublished manuscript, Oregon State University, Corvallis.

Bernieri, Frank J.; Gillis, John S.; Davis, Janet M.; & Grahe, Jon E. (1996). Dyad rapport and the accuracy of its judgment across situations: A lens model analysis. *Journal of Personality and Social Psychology, 71,* 110–129.

Berry, John W. (1994). Acculturative stress. In W. J. Lonner & R. S. Malpass (Eds.), *Psychology and culture.* Needham Heights, MA: Allyn & Bacon.

Berscheid, Ellen, & Reis, Harry T. (1998). Attraction and close relationships. In D. T. Gilbert, S. T. Fiske, & G. Lindzey (Eds.), *The handbook of social psychology, Vol. 2* (4th ed.). New York: McGraw-Hill.

Beutler, Larry E. (2000). David and Goliath: When empirical and clinical standards of practice meet. *American Psychologist, 55,* 997–1007.

Beutler, Larry E., & Malik, Mary L. (Eds.) (2002). *Rethinking the DSM: A psychological perspective.* Washington, DC: American Psychological Association.

Beyerstein, Barry L. (1996). Graphology. In G. Stein (Ed.), *The encyclopedia of the paranormal.* Amherst, NY: Prometheus Books.

Beyerstein, Barry L. (1999). Fringe psychotherapies: The public at risk. In W. Sampson (Ed.), *A Guide to Alternative Medicine.* London: Gordon and Breech.

Bierut, Laura Jean; Heath, Andrew C.; Bucholz, Kathleen K.; et al. (1999). Major depressive disorder in a community-based twin sample: Are there different genetic contributions for men and women? *Archives of General Psychiatry, 56,* 557–563.

Birdwhistell, Ray L. (1970). *Kinesics and context: Essays on body motion communication*. Philadelphia: University of Pennsylvania Press.

Birkhead, Tim (2001). *Promiscuity: An evolutionary history of sperm competition*. Cambridge, MA: Harvard University Press.

Bishop, Katherine M., & Wahlsten, Douglas (1997). Sex differences in the human corpus callosum: Myth or reality? *Neuroscience and Biobehavioral Reviews, 21,* 581–601.

Bjork, Daniel W. (1993). *B. F. Skinner: A life*. New York: Basic Books.

Bjork, Elizabeth L.; Bjork, Robert A.; & Anderson, M. C. (1998). Varieties of goal-directed forgetting. In J. M. Golding & C. M. MacLoed (Eds.), *Intentional forgetting*. Mahway, NJ: Erlbaum.

Bjork, Robert A. (October, 2000). Human factors 101: How about just trying things out? *APS Observer, 13,* 3, 30.

Blackmore, Susan (2001, March/April). Giving up the ghosts: End of a personal quest. *Skeptical Inquirer, 25.*

Blagrove, Mark (1996). Problems with the cognitive psychological modeling of dreaming. *Journal of Mind and Behavior, 17,* 99–134.

Blakemore, Colin, & Cooper, Grahame F. (1970). Development of the brain depends on the visual environment. *Nature, 228,* 477–478.

Blass, Thomas (1993). What we know about obedience: Distillations from 30 years of research on the Milgram paradigm. Paper presented at the annual meeting of the American Psychological Association, Toronto.

Blass, Thomas (Ed.) (2000). *Obedience to authority: Current perspectives on the Milgram paradigm*. Mahwah, NJ: Erlbaum.

Bleuler, Eugen (1911/1950). *Dementia praecox or the group of schizophrenias*. New York: International Universities Press.

Bliss, T. V., & Collingridge, G. L. (1993). A synaptic model of memory: Long-term potentiation in the hippocampus. *Nature, 361* (6407), 31–39.

Blum, Deborah (1997). *Sex on the brain: The biological differences between men and women*. New York: Viking.

Blum, Deborah (2002). *Love at Goon Park: Harry Harlow and the science of affection*. Cambridge, MA: Perseus Books.

Bodenheimer, Thomas (2000, May 18). Uneasy alliance—clinical investigators and the pharmaceutical industry [Health policy report]. *New England Journal of Medicine, 342,* 1539–1544.

Boesch, Cristophe (1991). Teaching among wild chimpanzees. *Animal Behavior, 41,* 530–532.

Bogaert, A. F. (2001). Personality, individual differences, and preferences for the sexual media. *Archives of Sexual Behavior, 30*(1), 29–53.

Bohannon, John N., & Stanowicz, Laura (1988). The issue of negative evidence: Adult responses to children's language errors. *Developmental Psychology, 24,* 684–689.

Bohman, Michael; Cloninger, R.; Sigvardsson, S.; & von Knorring, Anne-Liis (1987). The genetics of alcoholisms and related disorders. *Journal of Psychiatric Research, 21,* 447–452.

Boivin, D.B., & James, F. O. (2002). Phase-dependent effect of room light exposure in a 5-h advance of the sleep-wake cycle: Implications for jet lag. *Journal of Biological Rhythms, 17*(3), 266–276.

Bolger, Niall; Foster, Mark; Vinokur, Amiram D.; & Ng, Rosanna (1996). Close relationships and adjustment to a life crisis: The case of breast cancer. *Journal of Personality and Social Psychology, 70,* 283–294.

Bond, Rod, & Smith, Peter B. (1996). Culture and conformity: A meta-analysis of studies using Asch's (1952b, 1956) line judgment task. *Psychological Bulletin, 119,* 111–137.

Bonnet, Michael H. (1990). The perception of sleep onset in insomniacs and normal sleepers. In R. R. Bootzin, J. F. Kihlstrom, & D. L. Schacter (Eds.), *Sleep and cognition*. Washington, DC: American Psychological Association.

Bordo, Susan (2000). *The male body*. New York: Farrar, Straus and Giroux.

Borkenau, Peter; Riemann, Rainer; Angleitner, Alois; & Spinath, Frank N. (2001). Genetic and environmental influences on observed personality: Evidence from the German observational study of adult twins. *Journal of Personality and Social Psychology, 80,* 655–668.

Bornstein, Robert F.; Leone, Dean R.; & Galley, Donna J. (1987). The generalizability of subliminal mere exposure effects: Influence of stimuli perceived without awareness on social behavior. *Journal of Personality and Social Psychology, 53,* 1070–1079.

Bosacki, S. L., & Moore, C. (2004). Preschoolers' understanding of simple and complex emotions: Links with gender and language. *Sex Roles, 50*(9–10), 659–675.

Bosworth, Hayden B., & Schaie, K. Warner (1999). Survival effects in cognitive function, cognitive style, and sociodemographic variables in the Seattle Longitudinal Study. *Experimental Aging Research, 25,* 121–139.

Bouchard, Claude; Tremblay, A.; Despres, J. P.; et al. (1990, May 24). The response to long-term overfeeding in identical twins. *New England Journal of Medicine, 322,* 1477–1482.

Bouchard, Thomas J., Jr. (1995). Nature's twice-told tale: Identical twins reared apart—what they tell us about human individuality. Paper presented at the annual meeting of the Western Psychological Association, Los Angeles.

Bouchard, Thomas J., Jr. (1997a). The genetics of personality. In K. Blum & E. P. Noble (Eds.), *Handbook of psychiatric genetics*. Boca Raton, FL: CRC Press.

Bouchard, Thomas J., Jr. (1997b). IQ similarity in twins reared apart: Findings and responses to critics. In R. J. Sternberg & E. Grigorenko (Eds.), *Intelligence: Heredity and environment*. New York: Cambridge University Press.

Bouchard, Thomas J., Jr., & McGue, Matthew (1981). Familial studies of intelligence: A review. *Science, 212,* 1055–1058.

Bousfield, W. A. (1953). The occurrence of clustering in the recall of randomly arranged associates. *Journal of General Psychology, 49,* 229–240.

Bowd, A. (2003). Stereotypes of elderly persons in narrative jokes. *Research on Aging, 25*(1), 22–35.

Bowden, Charles L.; Calabrese, Joseph R.; McElroy, Susan L.; et al. (2000). A randomized, placebo-controlled 12-month trial or divalproex and lithium in treatment of outpatients with bipolar I disorder. *Archives of General Psychiatry, 57,* 481–489.

Bowen, Murray (1978). *Family therapy in clinical practice*. New York: Jason Aronson.

Bower, Bruce (1998, February 21). All fired up: Perception may dance to the beat of collective neuronal rhythms. *Science news, 153,* 120–121.

Bower, Gordon H., & Clark, M. C. (1969). Narrative stories as mediators of serial learning. *Psychonomic Science, 14,* 181–182.

Bowers, Kenneth S.; Regehr, Glenn; Balthazard, Claude; & Parker, Kevin (1990). Intuition in the context of discovery. *Cognitive Psychology, 22,* 72–110.

Bowlby, John (1982). *Attachment and loss. Vol. 1. Attachment* (Rev. ed.). New York: Basic Books.

Bradford, John M., & Pawlak, Anne (1993). Effects of cyproterone acetate on sexual arousal patterns of pedophiles. *Archives of Sexual Behavior, 22,* 629–641.

Brainerd, C. J.; Reyna, V. F.; & Brandse, E. (1995). Are children's false memories more persistent than their true memories? *Psychological Science, 6,* 359–364.

Brannon, Elizabeth M., & Terrace, Herbert S. (1998). Ordering of the numerosities 1 to 9 by monkeys. *Science, 282,* 746–749.

Brauer, Markus; Wasel, Wolfgang; & Niedenthal, Paula (2000). Implicit and explicit components of prejudice. *Review of General Psychology, 4,* 79–101.

Braun, Kathryn A.; Ellis, Rhiannon; & Loftus, Elizabeth F. (2002). Make my memory: How advertising can change our memories of the past. *Psychology & Marketing, 19,* 1–23.

Braungert, J. M.; Plomin, Robert; DeFries, J. C.; & Fulker, D. W. (1992). Genetic influence on tester-rated infant temperament as assessed by Bayley's Infant Behavior Record: Nonadoptive and adoptive siblings and twins. *Developmental Psychology, 28,* 40–47.

Brazelton, Timony R.; Rossi, Fabio M.; Keshet, Gilmor I.; & Blau, Helen M. (2000). From marrow to brain: expression of neuronal phenotypes in adult mice. *Science, 290,* 1775–1779.

Brehm, Jack W. (1999). The intensity of emotion. *Personality and Social Psychology Review, 3,* 2–22.

Breland, Keller, & Breland, Marian (1961). The misbehavior of organisms. *American Psychologist, 16,* 681–684.

Brennan, Patricia A., & Mednick, Sarnoff A. (1994). Learning theory approach to the deterrence of criminal recidivism. *Journal of Abnormal Psychology, 103,* 430–440.

Breslau, Naomi; Kessler, Ronald C.; Chilcoat, Howard D.; et al. (1998). Trauma and posttraumatic stress disorder in the community: The 1996 Detroit area survey of trauma. *Archives of General Psychiatry, 55,* 626–632.

Brewer, Marilynn B., & Gardner, Wendi (1996). Who is this "we"? Levels of collective identity and self representations. *Journal of Personality and Social Psychology, 71,* 83–93.

Briggs, John (1984, December). The genius mind. *Science Digest, 92*(12), 74–77, 102–103.

Brissette, Ian; Scheier, Michael F.; & Carver, Charles S. (2002). The role of optimism in social network development, coping, and psychological adjustment during a life transition. *Journal of Personality and Social Psychology, 82,* 102–111.

Brockner, Joel, & Rubin, Jeffrey Z. (1985). *Entrapment in escalating conflicts: A social psychological analysis.* New York: Springer-Verlag.

Brodeur, N.; Brochu, S.; & Lemire, G. (2001). Dropout and completion of treatment among spouse abusers. *Violence and Victims, 16*(2), 127–143.

Brodsky, Annette M. (1982). Sex, race, and class issues in psychotherapy research. In J. H. Harvey & M. M. Parks (Eds.), *Psychotherapy research and behavior change: Vol. 1. The APA Master Lecture Series.* Washington, DC: American Psychological Association.

Bronfenbrenner, Urie (1995). Developmental ecology through space and time: A future perspective. In P. Moen, G. H. Elder, Jr., et al. (Eds.), *Examining lives in context: Perspectives on the ecology of human development.* Washington, DC: American Psychological Association.

Brooks-Gunn, J. (1986). Differentiating premenstrual symptoms and syndromes. *Psychosomatic Medicine, 48,* 385–387.

Brown, D.; Scheflin, A. W.; & Whitfield, C. L. (1999). Recovered memories: The current weight of the evidence in science and in the courts. *Journal of Psychiatry and Law, 27,* 5–156.

Brown, George W. (1993). Life events and affective disorder: Replications and limitations. *Psychosomatic Medicine, 55,* 248–259.

Brown, Roger (1986). *Social psychology* (2nd ed.). New York: Free Press.

Brown, Roger; Cazden, Courtney; & Bellugi, Ursula (1969). The child's grammar from I to III. In J. P. Hill (Ed.), *Minnesota Symposium on Child Psychology* (Vol. 2). Minneapolis: University of Minnesota Press.

Brown, Roger, & Kulik, James (1977). Flashbulb memories. *Cognition, 5,* 73–99.

Brown, Roger, & McNeill, David (1966). The "tip of the tongue" phenomenon. *Journal of Verbal Learning and Verbal Behavior, 5,* 325–337.

Brown, Ryan P., & Josephs, Robert A. (1999). A burden of proof: Stereotype relevance and gender differences in math performance. *Journal of Personality and Social Psychology, 76,* 246–257.

Brown, Stephanie L.; Nesse, Randolph M.; Vinokur, Amiram D.; & Smith, Dylan M. (2003). Providing social support may be more beneficial than receiving it: Results from a prospective study of mortality. *Psychological Science, 14,* 320–327.

Brown, Steven P. (1996). A meta-analysis and review of organizational research on job involvement. *Psychological Bulletin, 120,* 235–255.

Browning, James R.; Hatfield, Elaine; Kessler, Debra; & Levine, Tim (2000). Sexual motives, gender, and sexual behavior. *Archives of Sexual Behavior, 29,* 135–153.

Bruck, Maggie (2003). Effects of suggestion on the reliability and credibility of children's reports. Invited address at the annual meeting of the American Psychological Society, Atlanta.

Bruck, Maggie; Ceci, Stephen J.; Francoeur, E.; & Renick, A. (1995). Anatomically detailed dolls do not facilitate preschoolers' reports of a pediatric examination involving genital touching. *Journal of Experimental Psychology: Applied, 1,* 95–109.

Bruer, John T. (1999). *The myth of the first three years.* New York: Free Press.

Brumberg, Joan J. (2000). *Fasting girls: The history of anorexia nervosa.* New York: Vintage.

Buck, Linda, & Axel, Richard (1991). A novel multigene family may encode odorant receptors: A molecular basis for odor recognition. *Cell, 65,* 175–187.

Budiansky, Stephen (1998). *If a lion could talk: Animal intelligence and the evolution of consciousness.* New York: Free Press.

Bukowski, William M. (2001). Friendship and the worlds of childhood. In D. W. Nangle & C. A. Erdley (Eds.), The role of friendship in psychological adjustment. *New directions for child and adolescent development, No. 91.* San Francisco, CA: Jossey-Bass.

Burke, Deborah M.; MacKay, Donald G.; Worthley, Joanna S.; & Wade, Elizabeth (1991). On the tip of the tongue: What causes word finding failures in young and older adults? *Journal of Memory and Language, 30,* 237–246.

Burke, Phyllis (1996). *Gender shock.* New York: Basic Books.

Bursik, Krisanne (1998). Moving beyond gender differences: Gender role comparisons of manifest dream content. *Sex Roles, 38,* 203–214.

Bushman, Brad J. (1995). Moderating role of trait aggressiveness in the effects of violent media on aggression. *Journal of Personality and Social Psychology, 69,* 950–960.

Bushman, Brad J., & Anderson, Craig A. (2001). Media violence and the American public: Scientific facts versus media misinformation. *American Psychologist, 56,* 477–489.

Bushman, Brad J.; Baumeister, Roy; & Stack, Angela D. (1999). Catharsis, aggression, and persuasive influence: Self-fulfilling or self-defeating prophecies? *Journal of Personality and Social Psychology, 76,* 367–376.

Bushman, Brad; Bonacci, Angelica M.; van Dijk, Mirjam; & Baumeister, Roy F. (2003). Narcissism, sexual refusal, and aggression: Testing a narcissistic reactance model of sexual coercion. *Journal of Personality and Social Psychology, 84,* 1027–1040.

Buss, David M. (1994). *The evolution of desire: Strategies of human mating.* New York: Basic Books.

Buss, David M. (1995). Evolutionary psychology: A new paradigm for psychological science. *Psychological Inquiry, 6,* 1–30.

Buss, David M. (1996). Sexual conflict: Can evolutionary and feminist perspectives converge? In D. M. Buss & N. Malamuth (Eds.), *Sex, power, conflict: Evolutionary and feminist perspectives.* New York: Oxford University Press.

Bussey, Kay, & Bandura, Albert (1992). Self-regulatory mechanisms governing gender development. *Child Development, 63,* 1236–1250.

Bussey, Kay, & Bandura, Albert (1999). Social-cognitive theory of gender development and differentiation. *Psychological Review, 106,* 676–713.

Butcher, James N.; Lim, Jeeyoung; & Nezami, Elahe (1998). Objective study of abnormal personality in cross-cultural settings: The MMPI-2. *Journal of Cross-Cultural Psychology, 29,* 189–211.

Butler, S.; Chalder, T.; Ron, M.; et al. (1991). Cognitive behaviour therapy in chronic fatigue syndrome. *Journal of Neurology, Neurosurgery & Psychiatry, 54,* 153–158.

Buunk, Bram; Angleitner, Alois; Oubaid, Viktor; & Buss, David M. (1996). Sex differences in jealousy in evolutionary and cultural perspective: Tests from the Netherlands, Germany, and the United States. *Psychological Science, 7,* 359–363.

Byne, William (1993). Sexual orientation and brain structure: Adding up the evidence. Paper presented at the annual meeting of the International Academy of Sex Research, Pacific Grove, CA.

Byne, William (1995). Science and belief: Psychobiological research on sexual orientation. *Journal of Homosexuality, 28,* 303–344.

Cacioppo, J. T.; Berntson, G. G.; Sheridan, J. F.; & McClintock, M. K. (2000). Multilevel integrative analyses of human behavior: Social neuroscience and the complementing nature of social and biological approaches. *Psychological Bulletin, 126,* 829–843.

Cahill, Larry; Haier, Richard J.; White, N. S.; et al. (2001). Sex-related differences in amygdala activity during emotionally influenced memory storage. *Neurobiology of Learning and Memory, 75,* 1–9.

Cahill, Larry; Prins, Bruce; Weber, Michael; & McGaugh, James L. (1994). ß-adrenergic activation and memory for emotional events. *Nature, 371,* 702–704.

Cairney, J., & Ostbye, T. (1999). Time since immigration and excess body weight. *Canadian Journal of Public Health-Revue Canadienne de Santé Publique, 90,* 120–124.

Calder, A. J.; Keane, J.; Manes, F.; Antoun, N.; & Young, A. W. (2000). Impaired recognition and experience of disgust following brain injury. *Nature Neuroscience, 3,* 1077–1078.

Campbell, Frances A., & Ramey, Craig T. (1995). Cognitive and school outcomes for high risk students at middle adolescence: Positive effects of early intervention. *American Educational Research Journal, 32,* 743–772.

Campbell, Jennifer; Trapnell, Paul D.; Heine, Steven J.; et al. (1996). Self-concept clarity: Measurement, personality correlates, and cultural boundaries. *Journal of Personality and Social Psychology, 70,* 141–156.

Campbell, Joseph (1949/1968). *The hero with 1,000 faces* (2nd ed.). Princeton, NJ: Princeton University Press.

Campbell, W. Keith, & Sedikides, Constantine (1999). Self-threat magnifies the self-serving bias: A meta-analytic integration. *Review of General Psychology, 3,* 23–43.

Canadian Community Health Survey (2000/01). Ottawa, Canada.

Canadian Council on Social Development (2001). *Highlights: The progress of Canada's children 2001.* Ottawa: Author. Retrieved June 3, 2003, from http://www.ccsd.ca/pubs/2001/pcc2001/hl.htm

Canadian Psychological Association (2000). *Canadian Code of Ethics for Psychologists: Third Edition, 2000.* Retrieved February 15, 2005, from http://www.cpa.ca/ethics2000.html

Canadian Psychological Association (2005). *Provincial/Territorial Licensing Requirements for Psychologists 2005.* Retrieved February 15, 2005, from http://www.cpa.ca/licensing.html

Cancian, Francesca M. (1987). *Love in America: Gender and self-development.* Cambridge, England: Cambridge University Press.

Canetto, Silvia S. (1992). Suicide attempts and substance abuse: Similarities and differences. *Journal of Psychology, 125,* 605–620.

Canetto, Silvia S., & Sakinofsky, Isaac (1998). The gender paradox in suicide. *Suicide and Life-Threatening Behavior, 28,* 1–23.

Cannon, Tyrone D.; Huttunen, Matti O.; Loennqvist, Jouko; et al. (2000). The inheritance of neuropsychological dysfunction in twins discordant for schizophrenia. *American Journal of Human Genetics, 67,* 369–382.

Cannon, Tyrone D.; Kaprio, Jaakko; Loennqvist, Jouko; Huttunen, Matti O.; & Koskenvuo, Markku (1998). The genetic epidemiology of schizophrenia in a Finnish twin cohort: A population-based modeling study. *Archives of General Psychiatry, 55,* 67–74.

Cannon, Walter B. (1929). *Bodily changes in pain, hunger, fear and rage* (2nd ed.). New York: Appleton.

Carani, C.; Bancroft, J.; Granata, A.; et al. (1992). Testosterone and erectile function, nocturnal penile tumescence and rigidity, and erectile response to visual erotic stimuli in hypogonadal and eugonadal men. *Psychoneuroendocrinology, 17,* 647–654.

Carskadon, Mary A.; Mitler, Merrill M.; & Dement, William C. (1974). A comparison of insomniacs and normals: Total sleep time and sleep latency. *Sleep Research, 3,* 130 [Abstract].

Carstensen, Laura L.; Pasupathi, Monisha; Mayr, Ulrich; & Nesselroade, John R. (2000). Emotional experience in everyday life across the adult life span. *Journal of Personality and Social Psychology, 79,* 644–655.

Carter, Betty, & McGoldrick, Monica (Eds.) (1988). *The changing family life cycle: A framework for family therapy* (2nd ed.). New York: Gardner Press.

Cartwright, Rosalind D. (1990). A network model of dreams. In R. R. Bootzin, J. F. Kihlstrom, & D. L. Schacter (Eds.), *Sleep and cognition.* Washington, DC: American Psychological Association.

Cartwright, Rosalind D. (1996). Dreams and adaptations to divorce. In D. Barrett (Ed.), *Trauma and dreams.* Cambridge: Harvard University Press.

Cartwright, Rosalind D.; Young, Michael A.; Mercer, Patricia; & Bears, Michael (1998). Role of REM sleep and dream variables in the prediction of remission from depression. *Psychiatry Research, 80,* 249–255.

Carver, Charles S. (1998). Resilience and thriving: Issues, models, and linkages. *Journal of Social Issues, 54,* 245–266.

Carver, Charles S., & Baird, Eryn (1998). The American dream revisited: Is it *what* you want or *why* you want it that matters? *Psychological Science, 9,* 289–292.

Carver, Charles S., & Scheier, Michael F. (1999). Optimism. In C. R. Snyder (Ed.), *Coping: The psychology of what works*. New York: Oxford University Press.

Caspi, Avshalom (2000). The child is father of the man: Personality continuities from childhood to adulthood. *Journal of Personality and Social Psychology, 78*, 158–172.

Caspi, Avshalom; McClay, Joseph; Moffitt, Terrie E.; et al. (2002, August 2). Role of genotype in the cycle of violence in maltreated children. *Science, 297*, 851–857.

Caspi, Avshalom, & Moffitt, Terrie E. (1991). Individual differences are accentuated during periods of social change: The sample case of girls at puberty. *Journal of Personality and Social Psychology, 61*, 157–168.

Caspi, Avshalom; Sugden, Karen; Moffitt, Terrie E.; et al. (2003). Influence of life stress on depression: Moderation by a polymorphism in the 5-HTT gene. *Science, 301*, 386–389.

Cattell, Raymond B. (1965). *The scientific analysis of personality*. Baltimore, MD: Penguin.

Cattell, Raymond B. (1973). *Personality and mood by questionnaire*. San Francisco: Jossey-Bass.

Ceci, Stephen J. (1996). *On intelligence: A bioecological treatise on intellectual development*. Cambridge, MA: Harvard University Press.

Ceci, Stephen J., & Bruck, Maggie (1995). *Jeopardy in the courtroom: A scientific analysis of children's testimony*. Washington, DC: American Psychological Association.

Cejka, Mary Ann, & Eagly, Alice H. (1999). Gender-stereotypic images of occupations correspond to the sex segregation of employment. *Personality and Social Psychology Bulletin, 25*, 413–423.

Cermak, Laird S., & Craik, Fergus I. M. (Eds.) (1979). *Levels of processing in human memory*. Hillsdale, NJ: Erlbaum.

Cervone, Daniel, & Shoda, Yuichi (1999). Beyong traits in the study of personality coherence. *Current Directions in Psychological Science, 8*, 27–32.

Chagnon, Y. C.; Mérette, C.; Bouchard, R. H.; Émond, C.; Roy, M. A.; & Maziade, M. (2004). A genome wide linkage study of obesity as secondary effect of antipsychotics in multigenerational families of eastern Quebec affected by psychoses. *Molecular Psychiatry, 9*(12), 1067–1074.

Chambers, C. T.; Craig, K. D.; & Bennett, S. M. (2002). The impact of maternal behaviour on children's pain experiences. An experimental analysis. *Journal of Pediatric Psychology, 27*(3), 293–301.

Chambless, Dianne L., and the Task Force on Psychological Interventions (1998). Update on empirically validated therapies II. *The Clinical Psychologist, 51*, 3–16.

Chambless, Dianne L., & Ollendick, T. H. (2001). Empirically supported psychological interventions: Controversies and evidence. *Annual Review of Psychology, 52*, 685–716.

Chance, June E., & Goldstein, Alvin G. (1995). The other-race effect in eyewitness identification. In S. L. Sporer, G. Koehnken, & R. S. Malpass (Eds.), *Psychological issues in eyewitness identification*. Hillsdale, NJ: Erlbaum.

Chance, Paul (1999). *Learning and behavior* (4th ed.). Pacific Grove: Brooks/Cole.

Chandra, R. K. (2001). Effect of vitamin and trace-element supplementation on cognitive function in elderly subjects. *Nutrition, 17*, 709–712.

Chang, Edward C. (1998). Dispositional optimism and primary and secondary appraisal of a stressor. *Journal of Personality and Social Psychology, 74*, 1109–1120.

Chang, Kenneth (2000, September 12). Can robots rule the world? Not yet. *New York Times, Science section, B1*.

Charles, Susan T.; Reynolds, Chandra A.; & Gatz, Margaret (2001). Age-related differences and change in positive and negative affect over 23 years. *Journal of Personality and Social Psychology, 80*, 136–151.

Chaudhari, Nirupa; Landin, A. M.; & Roper, S. D. (2000). A metabotropic glutamate receptor variant functions as a taste receptor. *Nature Neuroscience, 3*, 113–119

Chaves, J. F. (1989). Hypnotic control of clinical pain. In N. P. Spanos & J. F. Chaves (Eds.), *Hypnosis: The cognitive-behavioral perspective*. Buffalo, NY: Prometheus Books.

Cheesman, J., & Merikle, P. M. (1986). Distinguishing conscious from unconscious perceptual processes. *Canadian Journal of Psychology, 40*(4), 343–367.

Chehab, Farid F.; Mounzih, K.; Lu, R.; & Lim, M. E. (1997, January 3). Early onset of reproductive function in normal female mice treated with leptin. *Science, 275*, 88–90.

Chen, C. P. (1995). Counseling applications of RET in a Chinese cultural context. *Journal of Rational-Emotive and Cognitive Behavior Therapy, 13*(2), 117–129.

Chen, G.; Meckle, W.; & Wilson, J. (2002). Speed and safety effect of photo radar enforcement on a highway corridor in British Columbia. *Accident Analysis and Prevention, 34*(2), 129–138.

Cherpitel, C. J.; Giesbrecht, N.; & Macdonald, S. (1999). Alcohol and injury: A comparison of emergency room populations in two Canadian provinces. *American Journal of Drug and Alcohol Abuse, 25*(4), 743–759.

Chipperfield, J. G.; Perry, R. P.; & Weiner, B. (2003). Discrete emotions in later life. *Journals of Gerontology: Series B: Psychological Sciences & Social Sciences, 58B*(1), 23–34.

Chipuer, Heather M.; Rovine, Michael J.; & Plomin, Robert (1990). LISREL modeling: Genetic and environmental influences on IQ revisited. *Intelligence, 14*, 11–29.

Choi, Incheol; Dalal, Reeshad; Kim-Prieto, Chu; & Park, Hyekyung (2003).Culture and judgment of causal relevance. *Journal of Personality and Social Psychology, 84*, 46–59.

Choi, Incheol, & Nisbett, Richard (2000). Cultural psychology of surprise: Holistic theories and recognition of contradiction. *Journal of Personality and Social Psychology, 79*, 890–905.

Choi, Incheol; Nisbett, Richard E.; & Norenzayan, Ara (1999). Causal attribution across cultures: Variation and universality. *Psychological Bulletin, 125*, 47–63.

Chomsky, Noam (1957). *Syntactic structures*. The Hague, Netherlands: Mouton.

Chomsky, Noam (1980). Initial states and steady states. In M. Piatelli-Palmerini (Ed.), *Language and learning: The debate between Jean Piaget and Noam Chomsky*. Cambridge, MA: Harvard University Press.

Chorney, M. J.; Chorney, K.; Seese, N.; et al. (1998). A quantitative trait locus associated with cognitive ability in children. *Psychological Science, 9*, 159–166.

Chorpita, Bruce F., & Barlow, David H. (1998). The development of anxiety: The role of control in the early environment. *Psychological Bulletin, 124*, 3–21.

Chrisler, Joan C. (2000). PMS as a culture-bound syndrome. In J. C. Chrisler, C. Golden, & P. D. Rozee (Eds.), *Lectures on the psychology of women* (2nd ed.). New York: McGraw-Hill.

Christensen, Andrew, & Jacobson, Neil S. (1994). Who (or what) can do psychotherapy: The status and challenge of nonprofessional therapies. *Psychological Science, 5*, 8–14.

Christensen, Andrew, & Jacobson, Neil S. (2000) *Reconcilable differences*. New York: Guilford.

Christensen, Larry, & Burrows, Ross (1990). Dietary treatment of depression. *Behavior Therapy, 21*, 183–194.

Chun, Kevin M.; Organista, Pamela B.; & Marin, Gerardo (Eds.) (2002). *Acculturation: Advances in theory, measurement, and applied research*. Washington, DC: American Psychological Association.

Church, A. Timothy, & Lonner, Walter J. (1998). The cross-cultural perspective in the study of personality: Rationale and current research. *Journal of Cross-Cultural Psychology, 29,* 32–62.

Cialdini, Robert B. (2001). *Influence: Science and practice* (4th ed.). Boston: Allyn & Bacon.

Cialdini, Robert B.; Trost, Melanie R.; & Newsom, Jason T. (1995). Preference for consistency: The development of a valid measure and the discovery of surprising behavioral implications. *Journal of Personality and Social Psychology, 69,* 318–328.

Cinque, Guglielmo (1999). *Adverbs and functional heads: A cross-linguistic approach*. New York: Oxford University Press.

Cioffi, Delia, & Holloway, James (1993). Delayed costs of suppressed pain. *Journal of Personality and Social Psychology, 64,* 274–282.

Cioffi, Frank (1998). *Freud and the question of pseudoscience*. Chicago, IL: Open Court.

Claes, M. (1998). Adolescents' closeness with parents, siblings, and friends in three countries: Canada, Belgium, and Italy. *Journal of Youth & Adolescence, 27*(2), 165–184.

Clark, Margaret S.; Milberg, Sandra; & Erber, Ralph (1987). Arousal state dependent memory: Evidence and some implications for understanding social judgments and social behavior. In K. Fiedler & J. P. Forgas (Eds.), *Affect, cognition and social behavior*. Toronto, Canada: Hogrefe.

Clarke, Peter, & Evans, Susan H. (1998). *Surviving modern medicine*. Rutgers, NJ: Rutgers University Press.

Cloninger, C. Robert (1990). *The genetics and biology of alcoholism*. Cold Springs Harbor, ME: Cold Springs Harbor Press.

Clopton, Nancy A., & Sorell, Gwendolyn T. (1993). Gender differences in moral reasoning: Stable or situational? *Psychology of Women Quarterly, 17,* 85–101.

Coats, Erik J.; Janoff-Bulman, Ronnie; & Alpert, Nancy (1996). Approach versus avoidance goals: Differences in self-evaluation and well-being. *Personality and Social Psychology Bulletin, 22,* 1057–1067.

Cohen, David B. (1999). *Stranger in the nest: Do parents really shape their child's personality, intelligence, or character?* New York: Wiley.

Cohen, Jonathan D., & Tong, Frank (2001). The face of controversy. *Science, 293,* 2405–2407.

Cohen, Sheldon; Doyle, W. J.; Skoner, D. P.; et al. (1997). Social ties and susceptibility to the common cold. *Journal of the American Medical Association, 277,* 1940–1944.

Cohen, Sheldon; Evans, Gary W.; Krantz, David S.; & Stokols, Daniel (1980). Physiological, motivational, and cognitive effects of aircraft noise on children. *American Psychologist, 35,* 231–243.

Cohen, Sheldon; Frank, Ellen; Doyle, William J.; et al. (1998). Types of stressors that increase susceptibility to the common cold in healthy adults. *Health Psychology, 17,* 214–223.

Cohen, Sheldon, & Herbert, Tracy B. (1996). Health psychology: psychological factors and physical disease from the perspective of human psychoneuroimmunology. *Annual Review of Psychology, 47,* 113–142.

Cohen, Sheldon; Tyrrell, David A.; & Smith, Andrew P. (1993). Negative life events, perceived stress, negative affect, and susceptibility to the common cold. *Journal of Personality and Social Psychology, 64,* 131–140.

Cohn, Lawrence D. (1991). Sex differences in the course of personality development: A meta-analysis. *Psychological Bulletin, 109,* 252–266.

Colcombe, Stanley, & Kramer, Arthur F. (2003). Fitness effects on the cognitive function of older adults: A meta-analytic study. *Psychological Science, 14,* 125–130.

Coldham, E. L.; Addington, J.; & Addington, D. (2002). Medication adherence of individuals with a first episode of psychosis. *Acta Psychiatrica Scandinavica, 106*(4), 286–290.

Cole, Michael, & Scribner, Sylvia (1974). *Culture and thought*. New York: Wiley.

Collaer, Marcia L., & Hines, Melissa (1995). Human behavioral sex differences: A role for gonadal hormones during early development? *Psychological Bulletin, 118,* 55–107.

Collings, P. (2001). "If you got everything, it's good enough": Perspectives on successful aging in a Canadian Inuit community. *Journal of Cross-Cultural Gerontology, 16*(2), 127–155.

Collins, Allan M., & Loftus, Elizabeth F. (1975). A spreading-activation theory of semantic processing. *Psychological Review, 82,* 407–428.

Collins, Barry E., & Brief, Diana E. (1995). Using person-perception vignette methodologies to uncover the symbolic meanings of teacher behaviors in the Milgram paradigm. *Journal of Social Issues, 51,* 89–106.

Collins, W. Andrew; Maccoby, Eleanor E.; Steinberg, Laurence; Hetherington, E. Mavis; & Bornstein, Marc H. (2000). Contemporary research on parenting: The case of nature and nurture. *American Psychologist, 55,* 218–232.

Comas-Díaz, Lillian, & Greene, Beverly (1994). *Women of color: Integrating ethnic and gender identities in psychotherapy*. New York: Guilford.

Comuzzie, Anthony G., & Allison, David B. (1998). The search for human obesity genes. *Science, 280,* 1374–1377.

Conklin, Heather M., & Iacono, William G. (2002). Schizophrenia: A neurodevelopmental perspective. *Current Directions in Psychological Science, 11,* 33–37.

Conroy, John (2000). *Unspeakable acts, ordinary people: The dynamics of torture*. New York: Knopf.

Conway, M., & Dubé, L. (2002). Humor in persuasion on threatening topics: Effectiveness is a function of audience sex role orientation. *Personality and Social Psychology Bulletin, 28*(7), 863–873.

Cooper, M. Lynne; Frone, Michael R.; Russell, Marcia; & Mudar, Pamela (1995). Drinking to regulate positive and negative emotions: A motivational model of alcohol use. *Journal of Personality and Social Psychology, 69,* 990–1005.

Cooper, M. Lynne; Shapiro, Cheryl M.; & Powers, Anne M. (1998). Motivations for sex and risky sexual behavior among adolescents and young adults: A functional perspective. *Journal of Personality and Social Psychology, 75,* 1528–1558.

Coren, Stanley (1996). Daylight saving time and traffic accidents. *New England Journal of Medicine, 334,* 924.

Corkin, Suzanne (1984). Lasting consequences of bilateral medial temporal lobectomy: Clinical course and experimental findings in H. M. *Seminars in Neurology, 4,* 249–259.

Corkin, Suzanne; Amaral, David G.; Gonzalez, R. Gilberto; et al. (1997). H. M.'s medial temporal lobe lesion: Findings from magnetic resonance imaging. *Journal of Neuroscience, 17,* 3964–3979.

Cornell, E. H.; Heth, C. D.; Kneubuhler, Y.; & Sehgal, S. (1996). Serial position effects in children's route reversal errors: Implications for police search operations. *Applied Cognitive Psychology, 10*(4), 301–326.

Cose, Ellis (1994). *The rage of a privileged class*. New York: HarperCollins.

Costa, Paul T., Jr.; McCrae, Robert R.; Martin, Thomas A.; et al. (1999). Personality development from adolescence through adulthood: Further cross-cultural comparisons of age differences. In V. J. Molfese & d. Molfese (Eds.), *Temperament and personality development across the life span*. Hillsdale, NJ: Erlbaum.

Costantino, Giuseppe, & Malgady, Robert G. (1996). Culturally sensitive treatment: Cuento and hero/heroine modeling therapies for Hispanic children and adolescents. In E. D. Hibbs & P. S. Jensen (Eds.), *Psychosocial treatments for child and adolescent disorders: Empirically based strategies for clinical practice*. Washington, DC: American Psychological Association.

Council, J. R.; Kirsch, Irving; & Grant, D. L. (1996). Imagination, expectancy and hypnotic responding. In R. G. Kunzendorf, N. K. Spanos, & B. J. Wallace (Eds.), *Hypnosis and imagination*. Amityville, NY: Baywood.

Courage, Mary L., & Howe, Mark L. (2002). From infant to child: The dynamics of cognitive change in the second year of life. *Psychological Bulletin, 128,* 250–277.

Courtney, J. G.; Longnecker, M. P.; Theorell, T.; & Gerhardsson de Verdier, M. (1993). Stressful life events and the risk of colorectal cancer. *Epidemiology, 4,* 407–414.

Cowan, Nelson (2001). The magical number 4 in short-term memory: A reconsideration of mental storage capacity. *Behavioral and Brain Sciences, 24,* 87–185.

Cowen, Emory L.; Wyman, Peter A.; Work, William C.; & Parker, Gayle R. (1990). The Rochester Child Resilience Project (RCRP): Overview and summary of first year findings. *Development and Psychopathology, 2,* 193–212.

Craik, Fergus I. M., & Lockhart, Robert (1972). Levels of processing: A framework for memory research. *Journal of Verbal Learning and Verbal Behavior, 11,* 671–684.

Craik, Fergus I. M., & Tulving, Endel (1975). Depth of processing and the retention of words in episodic memory. *Journal of Experimental Psychology: General, 104,* 268–294.

Crair, Michael C.; Gillespie, Deda C.; & Stryker, Michael P. (1998). The role of visual experience in the development of columns in cat visual cortex. *Science, 279,* 566–570.

Cramer, Phebe (2000). Defense mechanisms in psychology today: Further processes for adaptation. *American Psychologist, 55,* 637–646.

Crandall, Christian S., & Martinez, Rebecca (1996). Culture, ideology, and antifat attitudes. *Personality and Social Psychology Bulletin, 22,* 1165–1176.

Crews, Frederick (Ed.) (1998). *Unauthorized Freud: Doubters confront a legend*. New York: Viking.

Crick, Francis, & Mitchison, Graeme (1995). REM sleep and neural nets. *Behavioural Brain Research, 69,* 147–155.

Critchlow, Barbara (1986). The powers of John Barleycorn: Beliefs about the effects of alcohol on social behavior. *American Psychologist, 41,* 751–764.

Critser, Greg (2002). *Supersize*. New York: Houghton-Mifflin.

Croizen, Jean-Claude, & Claire, Theresa (1998). Extending the concept of stereotype threat to social class: The intellectual underperformance of students from low socioeconomic backgrounds. *Personality and Social Psychology Bulletin, 24,* 588–594.

Cronbach, Lee (1990). *Essentials of psychological testing* (5th ed.). New York: Harper & Row.

Cross, William E. (1971). The Negro-to-Black conversion experience: Toward a psychology of Black liberation. *Black World, 20,* 13–27.

Csikszentmihalyi, Mihaly, & Larson, Reed (1984). *Being adolescent: Conflict and growth in the teenage years*. New York: Basic Books.

Cunningham, J. A.; Bondy, S. J.; & Walsh, G. W. (2000). The risks of cannabis use: Evidence of a dose-response relationship. *Drug and Alcohol Review, 19*(2), 137–142.

Cunningham, William A.; Preacher, Kristopher J.; & Banaji, Mahzarin R. (2001). Implicit attitude measures: Consistency, stability, and convergent validity. *Psychological Science, 12,* 163–170.

Cytowic, Richard E. (2002). *Synesthesia: Union of the senses*. Cambridge, MA: MIT Press.

Czeisler, Charles A.; Duffy, Jeanne F.; Shanahan, Theresa L.; et al. (1999). Stability, precision, and near-24-hour period of the human circadian pacemaker. *Science, 284,* 2177–2181.

Dabbs, James M., Jr. (2000). *Heroes, rogues, and lovers: Testosterone and behavior*. New York: McGraw-Hill.

Dabbs, James M., Jr.; Alford, Elizabeth Carriere; & Fielden, Julie A. (1998). Trial lawyers and testosterone: Blue-collar talent in a white-collar world. *Journal of Applied Social Psychology, 28,* 84–94.

Dabbs, James M., Jr.; Carr, Timothy S.; Frady, Robert L.; & Riad, Jasmin K. (1995). Testosterone, crime, and misbehavior among 692 male prison inmates. *Personality and Individual Differences, 18,* 627–633.

Dabbs, James M., Jr.; Hargrove, Marian F.; & Heusel, Colleen (1996). Testosterone differences among college fraternities: Well-behaved vs. rambunctious. *Personality and Individual Differences, 20,* 157–161.

Dabbs, James M., Jr.; Strong, Rebecca; & Milun, Rhonda (1997). Exploring the mind of testosterone: A beeper study. *Journal of Research in Personality, 31,* 577–587.

Dadds, Mark R.; Bovbjerg, Dana H.; Redd, William H.; & Cutmore, Tim R. H. (1997). Imagery in human classical conditioning. *Psychological Bulletin, 122,* 89–103.

Daley, Tamara C.; Whaley, Shannon E.; Sigman, Marian D.; et al (2003). IQ on the rise: The Flynn Effect in rural Kenyan children. *Psychological Science, 14,* 215–219.

Dalton, K. S.; Morris, D. L.; Delanoy, D. I.; et al. (1996). Security measures in an automated ganzfeld system. *Journal of Parapsychology, 60,* 129–147.

Daly, Martin, & Wilson, Margo (1983). *Sex, evolution, and behavior* (2nd ed.). Belmont, CA: Wadsworth.

Damasio, Antonio R. (1994). *Descartes' error: Emotion, reason, and the human brain*. New York: Grosset/Putnam.

Damasio, A. R.; Grabowski, T. J.; Bechara, A.; et al. (2000). Subcortical and cortical brain activity during the feeling of self-generated emotions. *Nature Neuroscience, 3,* 1049–1056.

Damasio, Hanna; Grabowski, Thomas J.; Frank, Randall; et al. (1994). The return of Phineas Gage: Clues about the brain from the skull of a famous patient. *Science, 264,* 1102–1105.

Damasio, Hanna; Grabowski, Thomas J.; Tranel, Daniel; et al. (1996). A neural basis for lexical retrieval. *Nature, 380,* 499–505.

Damon, William (1995). *Greater expectations*. New York: Free Press.

Darley, John M. (1995). Constructive and destructive obedience: A taxonomy of principal agent relationships. In A. G. Miller, B. E. Collins, & D. E. Brief (Eds.), Perspectives on obedience to authority: The legacy of the Milgram experiments. *Journal of Social Issues, 51*(3), 125–154.

Darley, John M., & Latané, Bibb (1968). Bystander intervention in emergencies: Diffusion of responsibility. *Journal of Personality and Social Psychology, 8,* 377–383.

Darou, W. G. (1992.) Native Canadians and intelligence testing. *Canadian Journal of Counselling, 26*(2), 96–99.

Dasen, Pierre R. (1994). Culture and cognitive development from a Piagetian perspective. In W. J. Lonner & R. S. Malpass

(Eds.), *Psychology and culture*. Needham Heights, MA: Allyn & Bacon.

Daum, Irene, & Schugens, Markus M. (1996). On the cerebellum and classical conditioning. *Psychological Science, 5,* 58–61.

Davey, Graham C. (1992). Classical conditioning and the acquisition of human fears and phobias: A review and synthesis of the literature. *Advances in Behaviour Research and Therapy, 14,* 29–66.

Davidson, Richard J.; Abercrombie, H.; Nitschke, J. B.; & Putnam, K. (1999). Regional brain function, emotion, and disorders of emotion. *Current Opinion in Neurobiology, 9,* 228–234.

Davidson, Richard J., & Henriques, Jeffrey B. (2000). Regional brain function in sadness and depression. In J. Borod (Ed.), *The neuropsychology of emotion*. New York: Oxford University Press.

Davidson, Richard J.; Jackson, Daren C.; & Kalin, Ned H. (2000). Emotion, plasticity, context, and regulation: Perspectives from affective neuroscience. *Psychological Bulletin, 126,* 890–909.

Davies, Michael J.; Baer, David J.; Judd, Joseph T; et al. (2002). Effects of moderate alcohol intake on fasting insulin and glucose concentrations and insulin sensitivity in postmenopausal women: A randomized controlled trial. *Journal of the American Medical Association, 287,* 2559–2562.

Davies, Michaela; Stankov, Lazar; & Roberts, Richard D. (1998). Emotional intelligence: In search of an elusive construct. *Journal of Personality and Social Psychology, 75,* 989–1015.

Davis, B. E.; Moon, R. Y.; Sachs, H. C.; & Ottolini, M. C. (1998). Effects of sleep position on infant motor development. *Pediatrics, 102,* 1135–1140.

Davison, Gerald C. (2000). Stepped care: Doing more with less? *Journal of Consulting and Clinical Psychology, 68,* 580–585.

Davison, Kathryn P.; Pennebaker, James W.; & Dickerson, Sally S. (2000). Who talks? The social psychology of illness support groups. *American Psychologist, 55,* 205–217.

Dawes, Robyn M. (1994). *House of cards: Psychology and psychotherapy built on myth*. New York: Free Press.

Dawson, Neal V.; Arkes, Hal R.; Siciliano, C.; et al. (1988). Hindsight bias: An impediment to accurate probability estimation in clinicopathologic conferences. *Medical Decision Making, 8*(4), 259–264.

de Lacoste-Utamsing, Christine, & Holloway, Ralph L. (1982). Sexual dimorphism in the human corpus callosum. *Science, 216,* 1431–1432.

De Robertis, Michael M., & Delaney, Paul A. (2000). A second survey of the attitudes of university students to astrology and astronomy. *Journal of the Royal Astronomical Society of Canada, 94,* 112–122.

de Waal, Frans (1997, July). Are we in anthropodenial? *Discover,* 50–53.

de Waal, Frans (2001). *The ape and the sushi master: Cultural reflections by a primatologist*. New York: Basic Books.

De Wolff, Marianne, & van IJzendoorn, Marinus H. (1997). Sensitivity and attachment: A meta-analysis on parental antecedents of infant attachment. *Child Development, 68,* 571–591.

Dean, Geoffrey (1992). The bottom line: Effect size. In B. Beyerstein & D. Beyerstein (Eds.), *The write stuff: Evaluations of graphology—The study of handwriting analysis*. Buffalo, NY: Prometheus Books.

Deaux, Kay (1985). Sex and gender. *Annual Review of Psychology, 36,* 49–81.

Deci, Edward L.; Koestner, Richard; & Ryan, Richard M. (1999). A meta-analytic review of experiments examining the effects of extrinsic rewards on intrinsic motivation. *Psychological Bulletin, 125,* 627–668.

Deci, Edward L., & Ryan, Richard M. (1985). *Intrinsic motivation and self-determination of human behavior*. New York: Plenum.

Deeke, V. B.; Slater, P. J. B.; & Ford, J. K. B. (2002). Selective habituation shapes acoustic predatory recognition in harbour seals. *Nature, 420*(6912), 171–173.

Deffenbacher, Jerry L.; Dahlen, Eric R.; Lynch, Rebekah S.; et al. (1998). Application of Beck's cognitive therapy to general anger reduction. Paper presented at the annual meeting of the American Psychological Association, San Francisco.

Deffenbacher, Jerry L.; Oetting, Eugene R.; Lynch, Rebekah S.; & Morris, Chad D. (1996). The expression of anger and its consequences. *Behaviour Research and Therapy, 34,* 575–590.

Dement, William (1978). *Some must watch while some must sleep*. New York: Norton.

Dement, William (1992). *The sleepwatchers*. Stanford, CA: Stanford Alumni Association.

Dennett, Daniel C. (1991). *Consciousness explained*. Boston: Little, Brown.

DePaulo, Bella M. (1992). Nonverbal behavior and self-presentation. *Psychological Bulletin, 111,* 203–243.

DeValois, Russell L., & DeValois, Karen K. (1975). Neural coding of color. In E. C. Carterette & M. P. Friedman (Eds.), *Handbook of perception* (Vol. 5). New York: Academic Press.

Devlin, B.; Daniels, Michael; & Roeder, Kathryn (1997). The heritability of IQ. *Nature, 388,* 468–471.

di Leonardo, Micaela (1987). The female world of cards and holidays: Women, families, and the work of kinship. *Signs, 12,* 1–20.

Diamond, Lisa M. (2003). Was it a phase? Young women's relinquishment of lesbian/bisexual identities over a 5-year period. *Journal of Personality and Social Psychology, 84,* 352–364.

Diamond, Marian C. (1993, Winter–Spring). An optimistic view of the aging brain. *Generations, 17,* 31–33.

Dien, Dora S. (1982). A Chinese perspective on Kohlberg's theory of moral development. *Developmental Review, 2,* 331–341.

Digman, John M. (1996). The curious history of the five-factor model. In J. S. Wiggins (Ed.), *The five-factor model of personality: Theoritical perspectives*. New York: Guilford Press.

Digman, John M., & Shmelyov, Alexander G. (1996). The structure of temperament and personality in Russian children. *Journal of Personality and Social Psychology, 71,* 341–351.

Dimberg, Ulf; Thunberg, Monika; & Elmehed, Kurt (2000). Unconscious facial reactions to emotional facial expressions. *Psychological Science, 11,* 86–89.

Dinges, David F.; Whitehouse, Wayne G.; Orne, Emily C.; Powell, John W.; Orne, Martin T.; & Erdelyi, Matthew H. (1992). Evaluating hypnotic memory enhancement (hypermnesia and reminiscence) using multitrial forced recall. *Journal of Experimental Psychology: Learning, Memory, and Cognition, 18,* 1139–1147.

Dion, Kenneth L., & Dion, Karen K. (1993). Gender and ethnocultural comparisons in styles of love. *Psychology of Women Quarterly, 17,* 463–474.

Doering, Charles H.; Brodie, H. K. H.; Kraemer, H. C.; Becker, H. B.; & Hamburg, D. A. (1974). Plasma testosterone levels and psychologic measures in men over a 2-month period. In R. C. Friedman, R. M. Richard, & R. L. Vande Wiele (Eds.), *Sex differences in behavior*. New York: Wiley.

Doering, Stephan; Katzlberger, Florian; Rumpold, Gerhard; et al. (2000). Videotape preparation of patients before hip replacement surgery reduces stress. *Psychosomatic Medicine, 62,* 365–373.

Dollard, John, & Miller, Neal E. (1950). *Personality and psychotherapy: An analysis in terms of learning, thinking, and culture.* New York: McGraw-Hill.

Dolnick, Edward (1990, July). What dreams are (really) made of. *The Atlantic Monthly, 226,* 41–45, 48–53, 56–58, 60–61.

Domhoff, G. William (1996). *Finding meaning in dreams: A quantitative approach.* New York: Plenum.

Doty, Richard M.; Peterson, Bill E.; & Winter, David G. (1991). Threat and authoritarianism in the United States, 1978–1987. *Journal of Personality and Social Psychology, 61,* 629–640.

Dovidio, John F. (2001). On the nature of contemporary prejudice: The third wave. *Journal of Social Issues, 57*(4), 829–849.

Dovidio, John F., & Gaertner, Samuel L. (2000). Aversive racism and selection decisions: 1989 and 1999. *Psychological Science, 11,* 315–319.

Dovidio, John F.; Gaertner, Samuel L.; & Validzic, Ana (1998). Intergroup bias: Status, differentiation, and a common in-group identity. *Journal of Personality and Social Psychology, 75,* 109–120.

Drevets, W. C. (2000). Neuroimaging studies of mood disorders. *Biological Psychiatry, 48,* 813–829.

Drieschner, K., & Lange, A. (1999). A review of cognitive factors in the etiology of rape: Theories, empirical studies, and implications. *Clinical Psychology Review, 19,* 57–77.

Druckman, Daniel, & Swets, John A. (Eds.) (1988). *Enhancing human performance: Issues, theories, and techniques.* Washington, DC: National Academy Press.

Dudley-Grant, G. Rita (2001). Eastern Caribbean family psychology with conduct-disordered adolescents from the Virgin Islands. *American Psychologist, 56,* 47–57.

Duncan, Paula D.; Ritter, Philip L.; Dornbusch, Sanford M.; et al. (1985). The effects of pubertal timing on body image, school behavior, and deviance. *Journal of Youth and Adolescence, 14,* 227–235.

Dunkel-Schetter, Christine (1984). Social support and cancer: Findings based on patient interviews and their implications. *Journal of Social Issues, 40*(4), 77–98.

Dunning, David; Johnson, Kerri; Ehrlinger, Joyce; & Kruger, Justin (2003). Why people fail to recognize their own incompetence. *Current Directions in Psychological Science, 12,* 83–87.

Durrant, J. E. (1994). Sparing the rod: Manitobans' attitudes toward the abolition of physical discipline and implications for policy change. *Canada's Mental Health, 41*(4), 2–6.

Dweck, Carol S. (1992). The study of goals in psychology. *Psychological Science, 3,* 165–167.

Dweck, Carol S., & Sorich, Lisa A. (1999). Mastery-oriented thinking. In C. R. Snyder (Ed.), *Coping: The psychology of what works.* New York: Oxford University Press.

Dym, Barry, & Glenn, Michael L. (1993). *Couples: Exploring and understanding the cycles of intimate relationships.* New York: HarperCollins.

Eagly, Alice H., & Wood, Wendy (1999). The origins of sex differences in human behavior: Evolved dispositions versus social roles. *American Psychologist, 54,* 408–423.

Eastman, Charmane I.; Young, Michael A.; Fogg, Louis F.; et al. (1998). Bright light treatment of winter depression: A placebo-controlled trial. *Archives of General Psychiatry, 55,* 883–889.

Ebbinghaus, Hermann M. (1885/1913). *Memory: A contribution to experimental psychology* (H. A. Ruger & C. E. Bussenius, trans.). New York: Teachers College Press, Columbia University.

Eccles, Jacquelynne S.; Midgley, Carol; Wigfield, Allan; et al. (1993). Development during adolescence: The impact of stage- environment fit on young adolescents' experiences in schools and in families. *American Psychologist, 48,* 90–101.

Eckensberger, Lutz H. (1994). Moral development and its measurement across cultures. In W. J. Lonner & R. Malpass (Eds.), *Psychology and culture.* Needham Heights, MA: Allyn & Bacon.

Edelson, Marshall (1994). Can psychotherapy research answer this psychotherapist's questions? In P. F. Talley, H. H. Strupp, & S. F. Butler (Eds.), *Psychotherapy research and practice: Bridging the gap.* New York: Basic Books.

Edwards, Kari, & Smith, Edward E. (1996). A disconfirmation bias in the evaluation of arguments. *Journal of Personality and Social Psychology, 71,* 5–24.

Efran, Jay S.; Greene, Mitchell A.; & Gordon, Don E. (1998, March/April). Lessons of the new genetics: Finding the right fit for our clients. *Family Therapy Networker, 22,* 26–41.

Ehrenreich, Barbara (1978). *For her own good: 150 years of the experts' advice to women.* New York: Doubleday.

Ehrenreich, Barbara (2001, June 4). What are they probing for? [Essay.] *Time,* p. 86.

Eich, E., & Hyman, R. (1992). Subliminal self-help. In D. Druckman & R. A. Bjork (Eds.), *In the mind's eye: Enhancing human performance.* Washington, DC: National Academy Press.

Eisenberg, Nancy (1995). Prosocial development: A multi-faceted model. In W. M. Kurtines & J. L. Gewirtz (Eds.), *Moral development: An introduction.* Boston: Allyn & Bacon.

Eisenberg, Nancy; Guthrie, Ivanna K.; Cumberland, Amanda; et al. (2002). Prosocial development in early adulthood: A longitudinal study. *Journal of Personality and Social Psychology, 82,* 993–1006.

Eisenberger, Robert, & Cameron, Judy (1996). Detrimental effects of reward: Reality or myth? *American Psychologist, 51,* 1153–1166.

Eisenberger, Robert, & Cameron, Judy (1998). Reward, intrinsic interest, and creativity: New findings. [Comment.] *American Psychologist, 53,* 676–679.

Ekman, Paul (2003). *Emotions revealed.* New York: Times Books.

Ekman, Paul, & Heider, Karl G. (1988). The universality of a contempt expression: A replication. *Motivation and Emotion, 12,* 303–308.

Ekman, Paul; Friesen, Wallace V.; & O'Sullivan, Maureen (1988). Smiles when lying. *Journal of Personality and Social Psychology, 54,* 414–420.

Ekman, Paul; Friesen, Wallace V.; O'Sullivan, Maureen; et al. (1987). Universals and cultural differences in the judgments of facial expression of emotion. *Journal of Personality and Social Psychology, 53,* 712–717.

Elgar, F. J.; Knight, J.; Worrall, G. J.; & Sherman, G. (2003). Attachment characteristics and behavioural problems in rural and urban juvenile delinquents. *Child Psychiatry & Human Development, 34*(1), 35–48.

Ellenbogen, M. A., & Hodgins, S. (2004). The impact of high neuroticism in parents on children's psychosocial functioning in a population at high risk for major affective disorder: A family-environmental pathway of intergenerational risk. *Development and Psychopathology, 16*(1), 113–136.

Elliot, Andrew J., & McGregor, Holly A. (2001). A 2 X 2 achievement goal framework. *Journal of Personality and Social Psychology, 80,* 501–519.

Elliot, Andrew J., & Sheldon, Kennon M. (1998). Avoidance personal goals and the personality-illness relationship. *Journal of Personality and Social Psychology, 75,* 1282–1299.

Ellis, Albert (1993). Changing rational-emotive therapy (RET) to rational emotive behavior therapy (REBT). *Behavior Therapist, 16,* 257–258.

Ellis, Albert, & Blau, S. (1998). Rational emotive behavior therapy. *Directions in Clinical and Counseling Psychology, 8,* 41–56.

Ellison, Carol R. (2000). *Women's sexualities.* Oakland, CA: New Harbinger.

Emery, Robert E., & Laumann-Billings, Lisa (1998). An overview of the nature, causes, and consequences of abusive family relationships. *American Psychologist, 53,* 121–135.

Emmons, Robert A., & King, Laura A. (1988). Conflict among personal strivings: Immediate and long-term implications for psychological and physical well-being. *Journal of Personality and Social Psychology, 54,* 1040–1048.

Emmons, Robert A., & McCullough, Michael E. (2003). Counting blessings versus burdens: An experimental investigation of gratitude and subjective well-being in daily life. *Journal of Personality and Social Psychology, 84,* 377–389.

Englander-Golden, Paula; Whitmore, Mary R.; & Dienstbier, Richard A. (1978). Menstrual cycle as focus of study and self-reports of moods and behavior. *Motivation and Emotion, 2,* 75–86.

Entin, Alan D. (1992). Family photographs: Visual icons and emotional history. Paper presented at the annual meeting of the American Psychological Association, Washington, DC.

Ericksen, Julia A., & Steffen, Sally A. (1999). *Kiss and tell: Surveying sex in the twentieth century.* Cambridge, MA: Harvard University Press.

Erikson, Erik H. (1950/1963). *Childhood and society* (2nd ed.). New York: Norton.

Erikson, Erik H. (1982). *The life cycle completed.* New York: Norton.

Eriksson, P. S.; Perfilieva, E; Bjork-Eriksson, T.; et al. (1998). Neurogenesis in the adult human hippocampus. *Nature Medicine, 4,* 1313–1317.

Eron, Leonard D. (1995). Media violence: How it affects kids and what can be done about it. Invited address presented at the annual meeting of the American Psychological Association, New York.

Ervin-Tripp, Susan (1964). Imitation and structural change in children's language. In E. H. Lenneberg (Ed.), *New directions in the study of language.* Cambridge, MA: MIT Press.

Escera, Carles; Cilveti, Robert; & Grau, Carles (1992). Ultradian rhythms in cognitive operations: Evidence from the P300 component of the event-related potentials. *Medical Science Research, 20,* 137–138.

Esparza, J.; Fox, C.; Harper, I. T.; et al. (2000, January 24). Daily energy expenditure in Mexican and USA Pima Indians: Low physical activity as a possible cause of obesity. *International Journal of Obesity and Related Metabolic Disorders, 1,* 55–59.

Estes, W. K. (1944). An experimental study of punishment, *Psychological Monographs, 57*(263), 5.

Etminan, M.; Hemmelgarn, B.; Delaney, J. A. C.; & Suissa, S. (2004). The use of lithium and the risk of injurious motor vehicle crash in elderly adults: Case-control study nested within a cohort. *British Medical Journal, 328*(7439), 558–559.

Evans, Christopher (1984). *Landscapes of the night* (edited and completed by Peter Evans). New York: Viking.

Evans, Gary W.; Bullinger, Monika; & Hygge, Staffan (1998). Chronic noise exposure and physiological response: A prospective study of children living under environmental stress. *Psychological Science, 9,* 75–77.

Ewart, Craig K. (1995). Self-efficacy and recovery from heart attack. In J. E. Maddux (Ed.), *Self-efficacy, adaptation, and adjustment: Theory, research, and application.* New York: Plenum.

Ewart, Craig K., & Kolodner, Kenneth B. (1994). Negative affect, gender, and expressive style predict elevated ambulatory blood pressure in adolescents. *Journal of Personality and Social Psychology, 66,* 596–605.

Exner, John E. (1993). *The Rorschach: A comprehensive system: Vol. 1. Basic foundations* (3rd ed.). New York: Wiley.

Eyer, Diane E. (1992). *Mother-infant bonding: A scientific fiction.* New Haven, CT: Yale University Press.

Fagot, Beverly I. (1993, June). Gender role development in early childhood: Environmental input, internal construction. Invited address presented at the annual meeting of the International Academy of Sex Research, Monterey, CA.

Fagot, Beverly I.; Hagan, R.; Leinbach, Mary D.; & Kronsberg, S. (1985). Differential reactions to assertive and communicative acts of toddler boys and girls. *Child Development, 56,* 1499–1505.

Fagot, Beverly I., & Leinbach, Mary D. (1993). Gender-role development in young children: From discrimination to labeling. *Developmental Review, 13,* 205–224.

Falk, Ruma & Greenbaum, Charles W. (1995). Significance tests die hard. The amazing persistence of probalistic misconception. *Theory & Psychology, 5*(1), 75–98.

Farrales, L. L., & Chapman, G. E. (1999). Filipino women living in Canada: Constructing meanings of body, food, and health. *Health Care for Women International, 20*(2), 179–194.

Fast, D. K.; Conry, J.; & Loock, C. A. (1999). Identifying fetal alcohol syndrome among youth in the criminal justice system. *Journal of Developmental & Behavioral Pediatrics, 20*(5), 370–372.

Fausto-Sterling, Anne (1997). Beyond difference: A biologist's perspective. *Journal of Social Issues, 53,* 233–258.

Fazio, Russell H.; Jackson, Joni R.; Dunton, Bridget C.; & Williams, Carol J. (1995). Variability in automatic activation as an unobtrusive measure of racial attitudes: A bona fide pipeline? *Journal of Personality and Social Psychology, 69,* 1013–1027.

FDA Drug Bulletin (1990, April). Two new psychiatric drugs. *20*(1), 9.

Feather, N. T. (1966). Effects of prior success and failure on expectations of success and subsequent performance. *Journal of Personality and Social Psychology, 3,* 287–298.

Fee, E. J., & Shaw, K. (1998). Pitch modifications in Mi'kmaq child-directed speech. *Proceedings of the 29th Annual Child Language Research Forum.* Clarke, E.V. (Ed.), Chicago: Center for the Study of Language and Information, 47–54.

Feeney, Judith A., & Noller, Patricia (1990). Attachment style as a predictor of adult romantic relationships. *Journal of Personality and Social Psychology, 58,* 281–291.

Fehr, Beverley (1993). How do I love thee . . . Let me consult my prototype. In S. Duck (Ed.), *Individuals in Relationships* (Vol. 1). Newbury Park, CA: Sage.

Fehr, Beverley; Baldwin, Mark; Collins, Lois; et al. (1999). Anger in close relationships: An interpersonal script analysis. *Personality and Social Psychology Bulletin, 25,* 299–312.

Fein, Steven, & Spencer, Steven J. (1997). Prejudice as self-image maintenance: Affirming the self through derogating others. *Journal of Personality and Social Psychology, 73,* 31–44.

Feingold, Alan (1988). Cognitive gender differences are disappearing. *American Psychologist, 43,* 95–103.

Fernald, Anne, & Mazzie, Claudia (1991). Prosody and focus in speech to infants and adults. *Developmental Psychology, 27,* 209–221.

Fernandez, Ephrem, & Turk, Dennis C. (1992). Sensory and affective components of pain: Separation and synthesis. *Psychological Bulletin, 112,* 205–217.

Festinger, Leon (1957). *A theory of cognitive dissonance.* Evanston, IL: Row, Peterson.

Festinger, Leon, & Carlsmith, J. M. (1959). Cognitive consequences of forced compliance. *Journal of Abnormal and Social Psychology, 58,* 203–210.

Festinger, Leon; Pepitone, Albert; & Newcomb, Theodore (1952). Some consequences of deindividuation in a group. *Journal of Abnormal and Social Psychology, 47,* 382–389.

Festinger, Leon; Riecken, Henry W.; & Schachter, Stanley (1956). *When prophecy fails.* Minneapolis: University of Minnesota Press.

Field, Tiffany M. (2001). Massage therapy facilitates weight gain in preterm infants. *Current Directions in Psychological Science, 10,* 51–54.

Fields, Howard (1991). Depression and pain: A neurobiological model. *Neuropsychiatry, Neuropsychology, and Behavioral Neurology, 4,* 83–92.

Fiez, J. A. (1996). Cerebellar contributions to cognition. *Neuron, 16,* 13–15.

Fink, Max (1999). *Electroshock: Restoring the mind.* New York: Oxford University Press.

Fischer, Ann R.; Tokar, David M.; Good, Glenn E.; & Snell, Andrea F. (1998). More on the structure of male role norms. *Psychology of Women Quarterly, 22,* 135–155.

Fischer, Pamela C.; Smith, Randy J.; Leonard, Elizabeth; et al. (1993). Sex differences on affective dimensions: Continuing examination. *Journal of Counseling and Development, 71,* 440–443.

Fischhoff, Baruch (1975). Hindsight is not equal to foresight: The effect of outcome knowledge on judgment under uncertainty. *Journal of Experimental Psychology: Human Perception and Performance, 1,* 288–299.

Fishbein, Harold D. (1996). *Peer prejudice and discrimination.* Boulder, CO: Westview Press.

Fisher, P. J.; Turic, D.; McGuffin, P.; et al. (1999). DNA pooling identifies QTLs for general cognitive ability in children on chromosome 4. *Human Molecular Genetics, 8,* 915–922.

Fisher, S., & Greenberg, R. (1996). *Freud scientifically appraised.* New York: John Wiley.

Fivush, Robyn, & Hamond, Nina R. (1991). Autobiographical memory across the school years: Toward reconceptualizing childhood amnesia. In Flacks, Richard, & Thomas, Scott L. (1998, November 27). Among affluent students, a culture of disengagement. *Chronicle of Higher Education,* A48.

Flacks, Richard, & Thomas, Scott L. (1998, November 27). Among affluent students, a culture of disengagement. *Chronicle of Higher Education,* A48.

Flavell, John H. (1999). Cognitive development: Children's knowledge about the mind. *Annual Review of Psychology, 50,* 21–45.

Fleeson, William (2001). Toward a structure- and process-integrated view of personality: Traits as density distributions of states. *Journal of Personality and Social Psychology, 80,* 1011–1027.

Fletcher, Anne M. (2001). *Sober for good.* New York: Houghton-Mifflin.

Flor, Herta; Kerns, Robert D.; & Turk, Dennis C. (1987). The role of spouse reinforcement, perceived pain, and activity levels of chronic pain patients. *Journal of Psychosomatic Research, 31,* 251–259.

Flor, Herta; Lutzenberger, Werner; Knost, B.; et al. (2002). *Spouse pressure alters brain response to pain.* Poster presented at the annual meeting of the Society for Neuroscience, Orlando.

Flynn, James R. (1987). Massive IQ gains in 14 nations: What IQ tests really measure. *Psychological Bulletin, 95,* 29–51.

Flynn, James R. (1999). Searching for justice: the discovery of IQ gains over time. *American Psychologist, 54,* 5–20.

Folkman, Susan, & Moskowitz, Judith T. (2000). Positive affect and the other side of coping. *American Psychologist, 55,* 647–654.

Ford, D. E.; Mead, L. A.; Chang, P. P.; et al. (1998). Depression is a risk factor for coronary artery disease in men: the precursors study. *Archives of Internal Medicine, 158,* 1422–1426.

Forgas, Joseph P. (1998). On being happy and mistaken: Mood effects on the fundamental attribution error. *Journal of Personality and Social Psychology, 75,* 318–331.

Forgas, Joseph P., & Bond, Michael H. (1985). Cultural influences on the perception of interaction episodes. *Personality and Social Psychology Bulletin, 11,* 75–88.

Fortin, S.; Godbout, L.; & Braun, C. M. J. (2003). Cognitive structure of executive deficits in frontally lesioned head trauma patients performing activities of daily living. *Cortex, 39*(2), 273–291.

Foulkes, D. (1962). Dream reports from different states of sleep. *Journal of Abnormal and Social Psychology, 65,* 14–25.

Fouts, Roger S. (with Stephen T. Mills) (1997). *Next of kin: What chimpanzees have taught me about who we are.* New York: Morrow.

Fouts, Roger S., & Rigby, Randall L. (1977). Man-chimpanzee communication. In T. A. Seboek (Ed.), *How animals communicate.* Bloomington: University of Indiana Press.

Frankl, Victor E. (1955). *The doctor and the soul: An introduction to logotherapy.* New York: Knopf.

Frasure-Smith, Nancy; Lesperance, F.; Juneau, M.; Talajic, M.; & Bourassa, M. G. (1999). Gender, depression, and one-year prognosis after myocardial infarction. *Psychosomatic Medicine, 61,* 26–37.

Frazier, Patricia A. (2003). Perceived control and distress following sexual assault: A longitudinal test of a new model. *Journal of Personality and Social Psychology, 84,* 1257–1269.

Fredrickson, Barbara L. (2001). The role of positive emotions in positive psychology. *American Psychologist, 56,* 218–226.

Fredrickson, Barbara L.; Tugade, Michele M.; Waugh, Christian E.; & Larkin, Gregory R. (2003). What good are positive emotions in crises? *Journal of Personality and Social Psychology, 84,* 365–376.

Freedman, Hill, & Combs, Gene (1996). *Narrative therapy.* New York: Norton.

Freedman, Jonathan L. (1988). Television violence and aggression: What the evidence shows. In S. Oskamp (Ed.), *Television as a social issue (Applied Social Psychology Annual,* Vol. 8). Newbury Park, CA: Sage.

Freud, Anna (1967). *Ego and the mechanisms of defence* (The writings of Anna Freud, Vol. 2) (rev. ed.). New York: International Universities Press.

Freud, Sigmund (1900/1953). The interpretation of dreams. In J. Strachey (Ed.), *The standard edition of the complete psychological works of Sigmund Freud* (Vols. 4 and 5). London: Hogarth Press.

Freud, Sigmund (1905). Three essays on the theory of sexuality. In J. Strachey (Ed.), *Standard edition* (Vol. 7).

Freud, Sigmund (1920/1960). *A general introduction to psychoanalysis* (Joan Riviere, trans.). New York: Washington Square Press.

Freud, Sigmund (1923/1962). *The ego and the id* (Joan Riviere, trans.). New York: Norton.

Freud, Sigmund (1961). *Letters of Sigmund Freud, 1873–1939.* Edited by Ernst L. Freud. London: Hogarth Press.

Fridlund, Alan J. (1994). *Human facial expression: An evolutionary view.* San Diego: Academic Press.

Friedman, Meyer, & Rosenman, Ray (1974). *Type A behavior and your heart.* New York: Knopf.

Friedrich, William; Fisher, Jennifer; Broughton, Daniel; et al. (1998). Normative sexual behavior in children: A contemporary sample. *Pediatrics, 101,* 1–8. See also http://www.pediatrics.org/cgi/content/full/101/4/e9.

Frijda, Nico H. (1988). The laws of emotion. *American Psychologist, 43,* 349–358.

Frome, Pamela M., & Eccles, Jacquelynne S. (1998). Parents' influence on children's achievement-related perceptions. *Journal of Personality and Social Psychology, 74,* 435–452.

Frye, Richard E.; Schwartz, B. S.; & Doty, Richard L. (1990). Dose-related effects of cigarette smoking on olfactory function. *Journal of the American Medical Association, 263,* 1233–1236.

Fuchs, C. S.; Stampfer, M. J.; Colditz, G. A.; et al. (1995, May 11). Alcohol consumption and mortality among women. *New England Journal of Medicine, 332,* 1245–1250.

Gaertner, Samuel L.; Mann, Jeffrey A.; Dovidio, John F.; et al. (1990). How does cooperation reduce intergroup bias? *Journal of Personality and Social Psychology, 59,* 692–704.

Gage, Fred H.; Kempermann, G.; Palmer, T. D.; et al. (1998). Multipotent progenitor cells in the adult dentate gyrus. *Journal of Neurobiology, 36,* 249–266.

Gagnon, John, & Simon, William (1973). *Sexual conduct: The social sources of human sexuality.* Chicago: Aldine.

Galanter, Eugene (1962). Contemporary psychophysics. In R. Brown, E. Galanter, H. Hess, & G. Mandler (Eds.), *New directions in psychology.* New York: Holt, Rinehart and Winston.

Galanter, Marc (1989). *Cults: Faith, healing, and coercion.* New York: Oxford University Press.

Gallant, Jack L.; Braun, Jochen; & Van Essen, David C. (1993). Selectivity for polar, hyperbolic, and Cartesian gratings in macaque visual cortex. *Science, 259,* 100–103.

Gallant, Sheryle J.; Hamilton, Jean A.; Popiel, Debra A.; et al. (1991). Daily moods and symptoms: Effects of awareness of study focus, gender, menstrual-cycle phase, and day of the week. *Health Psychology, 10,* 180–189.

Gallo, Linda C., & Matthews, Karen A. (2003). Understanding the association between socioeconomic status and physical health: Do negative emotions play a role? *Psychological Bulletin, 129,* 10–51.

Gallo, Vittorio, & Chittajallu, Ramesh (2001). Unwrapping glial cells from the synapse: What lies inside? *Science, 292,* 872–873.

Galotti, Kathleen (1989). Approaches to studying formal and everyday reasoning. *Psychological Bulletin, 105,* 331–351.

Gangestad, Steven W., & Simpson, Jeffry A. (2000). The evolution of human mating: Trade-offs and strategic pluralism. *Behavioral and Brain Sciences, 23,* 1–72.

Gao, Jia-Hong; Parsons, Lawrence M.; Bower, James M.; et al. (1996). Cerebellum implicated in sensory acquisition and discrimination rather than motor control. *Science, 272,* 545–547.

Garbarino, James, & Bedard, Claire (2001). *Parents under siege.* New York: The Free Press.

Garcia, John, & Koelling, Robert A. (1966). Relation of cue to consequence in avoidance learning. *Psychonomic Science, 4,* 23–124.

Gardner, Howard (1983). *Frames of mind: The theory of multiple intelligences.* New York: Basic Books.

Gardner, Howard (1995). Perennial antinomies and perpetual redrawings: Is there progress in the study of mind? In R. L. Solso & D. W. Massar (Eds.), *The science of the mind: 2001 and beyond.* New York: Oxford University Press.

Gardner, R. Allen, & Gardner, Beatrice T. (1969). Teaching sign language to a chimpanzee. *Science, 165,* 664–672.

Garland, Ann F., & Zigler, Edward (1994). Adolescent suicide prevention: Current research and social policy implications. *American Psychologist, 48,* 169–182.

Garmezy, Norman (1991). Resilience and vulnerability to adverse developmental outcomes associated with poverty. *American Behavioral Scientist, 34,* 416–430.

Garry, Maryanne, & Loftus, Elizabeth F. (2000). Imagination inflation is not a statistical artifact. Paper presented at the annual meeting of the American Psychological & Law Society, New Orleans.

Garry, Maryanne; Manning, Charles G.; & Loftus, Elizabeth F. (1996). Imagination inflation: Imagining a childhood event inflates confidence that it occurred. *Psychonomic Bulletin & Review, 3,* 208–214.

Garven, Sena; Wood, James M.; Malpass, Roy S.; & Shaw, John S., III (1998). More than suggestion: The effect of interviewing techniques from the McMartin Preschool case. *Journal of Applied Psychology, 83,* 347–359.

Gauthier, Irene; Skudlarksi, P.; Gore, J. C.; & Anderson, A. W. (2000). Expertise for cars and birds recruits brain areas involved in face recognition. *Nature Neuroscience, 3,* 191–197.

Gawande, Atul (1998, September 21). The pain perplex. *The New Yorker,* 86, 88, 90, 92–94.

Gay, Peter (1988). *Freud: A life for our time.* New York: Norton.

Gazzaniga, Michael S. (1967). The split brain in man. *Scientific American, 217*(2), 24–29.

Gazzaniga, Michael S. (1983). Right hemisphere language following brain bisection: A 20-year perspective. *American Psychologist, 38,* 525–537.

Gazzaniga, Michael S. (1985). *The social brain: Discovering the networks of the mind.* New York: Basic Books.

Gazzaniga, Michael S. (1988). *Mind matters.* Boston: Houghton Mifflin.

Gazzaniga, Michael S. (1998). *The mind's past.* Berkeley, CA: University of California Press.

Geary, David C. (1995). Reflections of evolution and culture in children's cognition: Implications for mathematical development and instruction. *American Psychologist, 50,* 24–37.

Gelernter, David (1997, May 19). How hard is chess? *Time,* 72–73.

George, C. F. P. (2001). Reduction in motor vehicle collisions following treatment of sleep apnoea with nasal CPAP. *Thorax, 56,* 508–512.

George, Mark S. (1998). Why would you ever want to?: Toward understanding the antidepressant effect of prefrontal rTMS. *Human Psychopharmacology Clinical & Experimental, 13,* 307–313.

Gershoff, Elizabeth T. (2002). Corporal punishment by parents and associated child behaviors and experiences: A meta-analytic and theoretical review. *Psychological Bulletin, 128*(4), 539–579.

Gibson, Eleanor, & Walk, Richard (1960). The "visual cliff." *Scientific American, 202,* 80–92.

Gilbertson, Mark W.; Shenton, Martha E.; Ciszewski, Aleksandra; et al. (2002). Smaller hippocampal volume predicts pathologic vulnerability to psychological trauma. *Nature Neuroscience, 5,* 1242–1247.

Gillham, Jane E.; Reivich, Karen J.; Jaycox, Lisa H.; & Seligman, Martin E. P. (1995). Prevention of depressive symptoms in schoolchildren: A two-year follow-up. *Psychological Science, 6,* 343–351.

Gilligan, Carol (1982). *In a different voice.* Cambridge, MA: Harvard University Press.

Gilmore, David D. (1990). *Manhood in the making: Cultural concepts of masculinity*. New Haven CT: Yale University Press.

Gist, Richard, & Lubin, Bernard (Eds.) (1999). *Response to disaster: Psychosocial, community, and ecological approaches*. Philadelphia, PA: Brunner/Mazel (Taylor & Francis).

Gladue, Brian A. (1994). The biopsychology of sexual orientation. *Current Directions in Psychological Science, 3*, 150–154.

Glanzer, Murray, & Cunitz, Anita R. (1966). Two storage mechanisms in free recall. *Journal of Verbal Learning and Verbal Behavior, 5*, 351–360.

Glaser, R.; Kiecolt-Glaser, J. K.; Speicher, C. E.; & Holliday, J. E. (1985). Stress, loneliness, and changes in herpesvirus latency. *Journal of Behavioral Medicine, 8*, 249–260.

Glassner, Barry (2001, October 26). The fate of false fears. *Chronicle of Higher Education*, B16–18.

Gleaves, David H. (1996). The sociocognitive model of dissociative identity disorder: A reexamination of the evidence. *Psychological Bulletin, 120*, 42–59.

Glenmullen, Joseph (2000). *Prozac backlash: Overcoming the dangers of Prozac, Zoloft, Paxil, and other antidepressants with safe, effective alternatives*. New York: Simon & Schuster.

Glick, Peter, & Fiske, Susan T. (2001). An ambivalent alliance: Hostile and benevolent sexism as complementary justifications for gender inequality. *American Psychologist, 56*, 109–118.

Glick, Peter; Fiske, Susan T.; Mladinic, Antonio; et al. (2000). Beyond prejudice as simple antipathy: Hostile and benevolent sexism across cultures. *Journal of Personality and Social Psychology, 79*, 763–775.

Gold, D.; Beauregard, M.; Lecours, A. R.; & Chertkow, H. (2003). Semantic category differences in cross-forming priming. *Journal of the International Neuropsychological Society, 9*(5), 796–805.

Goldin-Meadow, S., & Mylander, C. (1998). Spontaneous sign systems created by deaf children in two cultures. *Nature, 391*, 279–281.

Goldman-Rakic, Patricia S. (1996). Opening the mind through neurobiology. Invited address at the annual meeting of the American Psychological Association, Toronto, Canada.

Goldstein, Alan J.; de Beurs, Edwin; Chambless, Dianne L.; & Wilson, Kimberly A. (2000). EMDR for panic disorder with agoraphobia: Comparison with waiting list and credible attention-placebo control conditions. *Journal of Consulting and Clinical Psychology, 68*, 947–956.

Goldstein, Michael J. (1987). Psychosocial issues. *Schizophrenia Bulletin, 13*(1), 157–171.

Goldstein, Michael, & Miklowitz, David (1995). The effectiveness of psychoeducational family therapy in the treatment of schizophrenic disorders. *Journal of Marital and Family Therapy, 21*, 361–376.

Goleman, Daniel (1995). *Emotional intelligence*. New York: Bantam.

Golub, Sharon (1992). *Periods: From menarche to menopause*. Newbury Park, CA: Sage.

Goode, Erica (2003, May 6). Experts see mind's voices in new light. *The New York Times*, Science Times, D1, D4.

Goodman, Gail S.; Qin, Jianjian; Bottoms, Bette L.; & Shaver, Phillip R. (1995). *Characteristics and sources of allegations of ritualistic child abuse*. Final report to the National Center on Child Abuse and Neglect, Washington, DC. [Executive summary and complete report available from NCCAN, 1-800-394-3366.]

Goodwin, Donald W.; Knop, Joachim; Jensen, Per; et al. (1994). Thirty-year follow-up of men at high risk for alcoholism. In T. F. Babor & V. M. Hesselbrock (Eds.), *Types of alcoholics: Evidence from clinical, experimental, and genetic research*. New York: New York Academy of Sciences.

Goodwyn, Susan, & Acredolo, Linda (1998). Encouraging symbolic gestures: A new perspective on the relationship between gesture and speech. In J. Iverson & S. Goldin-Meadow (Eds.), *The nature and functions of gesture in children's communication*. San Francisco: Jossey-Bass.

Gopnik, Alison; Meltzoff, Andrew N.; & Kuhl, Patricia K. (1999). *The scientist in the crib*. New York: Morrow.

Gopnik, Myrna; Choi, Sooja; & Baumberger, Therese (1996). Cross-linguistic differences in early semantic and cognitive development. *Cognitive Development, 11*, 197–227.

Gorn, Gerald J. (1982). The effects of music in advertising on choice behavior: A classical conditioning approach. *Journal of Marketing, 46*, 94–101.

Gottesman, Irving I. (1991). *Schizophrenia genesis: The origins of madness*. New York: Freeman.

Gottesman, Irving I. (1994). Perils and pleasures of genetic psychopathology. Distinguished Scientist Award address presented at the annual meeting of the American Psychological Association, Los Angeles.

Gould, Elizabeth; Beylin, A; Tanapat, Patima; et al. (1999). Learning enhances adult neurogenesis in the hippocampal formation. *Nature Neuroscience, 2*, 260–265.

Gould, Elizabeth; Reeves, Alison J.; Graziano, Michael S. A.; & Gross, Charles G. (1999). Neurogenesis in the neocortex of adult primates. *Science, 286*, 548–552.

Gould, Elizabeth; Tanapat, Patima; McEwen, Bruce S.; et al. (1998). Proliferation of granule cell precursors in the dentate gyrus of adult monkeys is diminished by stress. *Proceedings of the National Academy of Science, 95*, 3168–3171.

Gould, Stephen Jay (1994, November 28). Curveball. [Review of The Bell Curve, by Richard J. Herrnstein and Charles Murray.] *The New Yorker*, 139–149.

Gould, Stephen Jay (1996). *The mismeasure of man* (rev. ed.). New York: Norton.

Gourevich, Philip (1998). *We wish to inform you that tomorrow we will be killed with our families: Stories from Rwanda*. New York: Farrar, Straus & Giroux.

Grady, Denise (2003, March 4). Seeking to fight fat, she lost her liver. *The New York Times*, Science Section, 1, 6.

Graf, Peter, & Schacter, Daniel A. (1985). Implicit and explicit memory for new associations in normal and amnesic subjects. *Journal of Experimental Psychology: Learning, Memory, and Cognition, 11*, 501–518.

Graham, Jill W. (1986). Principled organizational dissent: A theoretical essay. *Research in Organizational Behavior, 8*, 1–52.

Graham, Sandra (1994). Motivation in African Americans. *Review of Educational Research, 64*, 55–117.

Gray, R. (1997). A qualitative study of breast cancer self-help groups. *Psycho-Oncology, 6*(4), 279–289.

Green, Gina (1996a). Behavioral treatment of autistic persons: A review of research from 1980 to the present. *Research in Developmental Disabilities, 17*, 433–465.

Green, Gina (1996b). Early behavioral intervention for autism: What does research tell us? In C. Maurice, G. Green, & S. C. Luce (Eds.), *Behavioral Intervention for Young Children with Autism*. Austin, TX: PRO-ED.

Greenberger, Dennis, & Padesky, Christine A. (1995). *Mind over mood: A cognitive therapy treatment manual for clients*. New York: Guilford.

Greenfield, Patricia (1976). Cross-cultural research and Piagetian theory: Paradox and progress. In K. F. Riegel & J. A. Meacham (Eds.), *The developing individual in a changing world: Vol. 1. Historical and cultural issues*. The Hague, Netherlands: Mouton.

Greenough, William T., & Anderson, Brenda J. (1991). Cerebellar synaptic plasticity: Relation to learning vs neural activity. *Annals of the New York Academy of Sciences, 627*, 231–247.

Greenough, William T., & Black, James E. (1992). Induction of brain structure by experience: Substrates for cognitive development. In M. Gunnar & C. A. Nelson (Eds.), *Behavioral developmental neuroscience: Vol. 24. Minnesota Symposia on Child Psychology*. Hillsdale, NJ: Erlbaum.

Greenough, William T.; Cohen, N. J.; & Juraska, J. M. (1999). New neurons in old brains: Learning to survive? *Nature Neuroscience, 2*, 203–205.

Greenwald, Anthony G.; McGhee, Debbie E.; & Schwartz, Jordan L. K. (1998). Measuring individual differences in implicit cognition: The Implicit Association Test. *Journal of Personality and Social Psychology, 74*, 1464–1480.

Greenwald, Anthony G.; Spangenberg, Eric R.; Pratkanis, Anthony R.; & Eskenazi, Jay (1991). Double-blind tests of subliminal self-help audiotapes. *Psychological Science, 2*, 119–122.

Gregory, Richard L. (1963). Distortion of visual space as inappropriate constancy scaling. *Nature, 199*, 678–679.

Griffin, Donald R. (1992). *Animal minds*. Chicago: University of Chicago Press.

Grigorenko, Elena L., & Sternberg, Robert J. (1998). Dynamic testing. *Psychological Bulletin, 124*, 75–111.

Grinspoon, Lester, & Bakalar, James B. (1993). *Marihuana, the forbidden medicine*. New Haven, CT: Yale University Press.

Groneman, Carol (2000). *Nymphomania: A history*. New York: Norton.

Gross, C. G. (2000). Neurogenesis in the adult brain: death of a dogma. *Nature Review of Neuroscience, 1*, 67–73.

Gross, James J. (1998). The emerging field of emotion regulation: An integrative review. *Review of General Psychology, 2*, 271–299.

Grossman, Michele, & Wood, Wendy (1993). Sex differences in intensity of emotional experience: A social role interpretation. *Journal of Personality and Social Psychology, 65*, 1010–1022.

Groves, James E. (Ed.) (1996). *Essential papers on short-term dynamic therapy*. New York: New York University Press.

Guglielmi, R. Sergio (1999). Psychophysiological assessment of prejudice: Past research, current status, and future directions. *Personality and Social Psychology Review, 3*, 123–157.

Guilford, J. P. (1988). Some changes in the structure-of-intellect model. *Educational and Psychological Measurement, 48*, 1–4.

Gupta, M. A.; Chaturvedi, S. K.; Chandarana, P. C.; & Johnson, A. M. (2001). Weight-related body image concerns among 18-24-year-old women in Canada and India: An empirical comparative study. *Journal of Psychosomatic Research, 50*(4), 193–198.

Gupta, S.; Mosnik, D.; Black, D. W.; et al. (1999). Tardive dyskinesia: Review of treatments past, present, and future. *Annals of Clinical Psychiatry, 11*, 257–266.

Gur, R. C.; Turetsky, B. I.; Matsui, M.; et al. (1999). Sex differences in brain gray and white matter in healthy young adults: correlations with cognitive performance. *Journal of Neuroscience, 19*, 4065–4072.

Gur, R. E.; Maany, V.; Mozley, P. D.; et al. (1998). Subcortical MRI volumes in neuroleptic-naive and treated patients with schizophrenia. *American Journal of Psychiatry, 155*, 1711–1717.

Guralnick, M. J. (Ed.) (1997). *The effectiveness of early intervention*. Baltimore: Brookes.

Guthrie, Paul C., & Mobley, Brenda D. (1994). A comparison of the differential diagnostic efficiency of three personality disorder inventories. *Journal of Clinical Psychology, 50*, 656–665.

Haber, Ralph N. (1970, May). How we remember what we see. *Scientific American, 222*, 104–112.

Hacking, Ian (1995). *Rewriting the soul: Multiple personality and the sciences of memory*. Princeton: Princeton University Press.

Haimov, I., & Lavie, P. (1996). Melatonin—A soporific hormone. *Current Directions in Psychological Science, 5*, 106–111.

Halaas, Jeffrey L.; Gajiwala, Ketan S.; Maffei, Margherita; et al. (1995). Weight-reducing effects of the plasma protein encoded by the obese gene. *Science, 269*, 543–546.

Hall, C. S.; Domhoff, G. W.; Thick, K. A.; & Weesner, K. E. (1982). The dreams of college men and women in 1950 and 1980: A comparison of dream content and sex differences. *Sleep, 5*, 188–194.

Hall, Edward T. (1959). *The silent language*. Garden City, NY: Doubleday.

Hall, Edward T. (1976). *Beyond culture*. New York: Anchor.

Hall, Edward T. (1983). *The dance of life: The other dimension of time*. Garden City, NY: Anchor Press/Doubleday.

Hall, Edward T., & Hall, Mildred R. (1987). *Hidden differences: Doing business with the Japanese*. Garden City, NY: Anchor Press/Doubleday.

Hall, Edward T., & Hall, Mildred R. (1990). *Understanding cultural differences*. Yarmouth, ME: Intercultural Press.

Hall, G. S. (1899). A study of anger. *American Journal of Psychology, 10*, 516–591.

Halliday, G. (1993). Examination dreams. *Perceptual and Motor Skills, 77*, 489–490.

Halpern, Diane F. (1995). *Sex differences in cognitive abilities*. Mahwah, NJ: Lawrence Erlbaum Associates, Inc.

Haney, Craig; Banks, Curtis; & Zimbardo, Philip (1973). Interpersonal dynamics in a simulated prison. *International Journal of Criminology and Penology, 1*, 69–97.

Haney, Craig, & Zimbardo, Philip (1998). The past and future of U.S. prison policy: Twenty-five years after the Stanford Prison Experiment. *American Psychologist, 53*, 709–727.

Hankin, Benjamin L., & Abramson, Lyn Y. (2001). Development of gender differences in depression: An elaborated cognitive vulnerability-transactional stress theory. *Psychological Bulletin, 127*, 773–796.

Hardie, Elizabeth A. (1997). PMS in the workplace: Dispelling the myth of cyclic function. *Journal of Occupational and Organizational Psychology, 70*, 97–102.

Harding, Courtenay M.; Zubin, Joseph; & Strauss, John S. (1992). Chronicity in schizophrenia: Revisited. *British Journal of Psychiatry, 161*(Suppl. 18), 27–37.

Hare, Robert D. (1965). Temporal gradient of fear arousal in psychopaths. *Journal of Abnormal Psychology, 70*, 442–445.

Hare, Robert D. (1993). *Without conscience: The disturbing world of the psychopaths among us*. New York: Pocket Books.

Hare, Robert D. (1996). Psychopathy: A clinical construct whose time has come. *Criminal Justice and Behavior, 23*, 24–54.

Haritos-Fatouros, Mika (1988). The official torturer: A learning model for obedience to the authority of violence. *Journal of Applied Social Psychology, 18*, 1107–1120.

Harkins, Stephen G., & Szymanski, Kate (1989). Social loafing and group evaluation. *Journal of Personality and Social Psychology, 56*, 934–941.

Harley, B.; Hart, D.; & Lapkin, S. (1986). The effects of early bilingual schooling on first language skills. *Applied Psycholinguistics, 7*(4), 295–321.

Harlow, Harry F. (1958). The nature of love. *American Psychologist, 13*, 673–685.

Harlow, Harry F., & Harlow, Margaret K. (1966). Learning to love. *American Scientist, 54*, 244–272.

Harmon-Jones, Eddie; Abramson, Lyn Y.; Sigelman, Jonathan; et al. (2002). Proneness to hypomania/mania symptoms or depression symptoms and asymmetrical frontal cortical responses to an anger-evoking event. *Journal of Personality and Social Psychology, 82,* 610–618.

Harmon-Jones, Eddie, & Allen, John J. B. (1998). Anger and frontal brain activity: EEG asymmetry consistent with approach motivation despite negative affective valence. *Journal of Personality and Social Psychology, 74,* 1310–1316.

Harris, Judith R. (1998). *The nurture assumption.* New York: The Free Press.

Hart, A. J.; Whalen, P. J.; Shin, L. M.; et al. (2000). Differential response in the human amygdala to racial outgroup vs. ingroup face stimuli. *NeuroReport, 11,* 2351–2355.

Hart, John, Jr.; Berndt, Rita S.; & Caramazza, Alfonso (1985, August 1). Category-specific naming deficit following cerebral infarction. *Nature, 316,* 339–340.

Hartman, C.; Hox, J.; Mellenbergh, G. J.; et al. (2001). DSM-IV internal construct validity: When a taxonomy meets data. *Journal of Child Psychology and Psychiatry, 42*(6), 817–836.

Hartup, William (1999). Peer experience and its developmental significance. In M. Bennett (Ed.), *Developmental Psychology: Achievements and prospects.* Philadelphia, PA: Psychology Press.

Haslam, S. Alexander, & Reicher, Stephen (2003, Spring). Beyond Stanford: Questioning a role-based explanation of tyranny. *Society for Experimental Social Psychology Dialogue, 18,* 22–25.

Hassebrauck, M., & Fehr, B. (2002). Dimensions of relationship quality. *Personal Relationships. 9*(3), 253–270.

Hatfield, Elaine; Cacioppo, John T.; & Rapson, Richard L. (1994). *Emotional contagion.* New York: Cambridge University Press.

Hatfield, Elaine, & Rapson, Richard L. (1996). *Love and sex: Cross-cultural perspectives.* Boston: Allyn & Bacon.

Hauser, Marc (2000). *Wild minds: What animals really think.* New York: Holt.

Haut, Jennifer S.; Beckwith, Bill E.; Petros, Thomas V.; & Russell, Sue (1989). Gender differences in retrieval from long-term memory following acute intoxication with ethanol. *Physiology and Behavior, 45,* 1161–1165.

Hawkins, Scott A., & Hastie, Reid (1990). Hindsight: Biased judgments of past events after the outcomes are known. *Psychological Bulletin, 107,* 311–327.

Hayman, Ronald (2001). *A life of Jung.* New York: W. W. Norton.

Hazan, Cindy, & Diamond, Lisa M. (2000). The place of attachment in human mating. *Review of General Psychology, 4,* 186–204.

Hazan, Cindy, & Shaver, Phillip R. (1994). Attachment as an organizational framework for research on close relationships. *Psychological Inquiry, 5,* 1–22.

Health and Welfare Canada, National Alcohol and Other Drugs Survey (1989). *Highlights Report* (M. Eliany, N. Giesbrecht, M. Nelson, et al., Eds.), Minister of Supply and Services Canada, Ottawa, 1990.

Health Canada (1999). *Canadian injury data. Mortality 1997 and hospitalizations 1996–97.* Ottawa: Bureau of Reproductive and Child Health, Laboratory for Disease Control, Health Protection Branch, Department of National Health and Welfare.

Health Canada (2002, January 14). *Association of CLOZARIL (clozapine) with cardiovascular toxicity.* Health Products and Food Branch, Ottawa, Canada.

Health Canada (2002). *Diabetes among Aboriginal (First Nations, Inuit and Métis) People in Canada: The evidence.* Retrieved March 27, 2005, from http://www.hc-sc.gc.ca/fnihb-dgspni/fnihb/cp/adi/publications/the_evidence.htm#Referencs.

HealthOntario.com (2005). *Sleep apnea.* Retrieved July 10, 2005, from http://www.healthyontario.com/english/channel_condition_detail.asp?disease_id=201&dowhat=accept_disclaimer.

Heart and Stroke Foundation (2001). *Smoking.* Retrieved July 10, 2005, from http://ww2.heartandstroke.ca/Page.asp?PageID=33&ArticleID=622&Src=living&From=SubCategory.

Heath, A. C.; Madden, P. A. F.; Bucholz, K. K.; et al. (2003). Genetic and genotype x environment interaction effects on risk of dependence on alcohol, tobacco, and other drugs: new research. In R. Plomin et al. (Eds.), *Behavioral genetics in the postgenomic era.* Washington, DC: APA Books.

Hebb, D. O. (1949). *The organization of behavior.* New York: Wiley-Interscience.

Hébert, Richard (2001, September). Code overload: Doing a number on memory. *APS Observer, 14,* 1, 7–11.

Heinrichs, R. Walter (1993). Schizophrenia and the brain: Conditions for a neuropsychology of madness. *American Psychologist, 48,* 221–233.

Heller, W., & Nitschke, J.B. (1997). Regional brain activity in emotion: A framework for understanding cognition in depression. *Cognition Emotion II,* 637–661.

Helson, Ravenna, & McCabe, Laurel (1993). The social clock project in middle age. In B. F. Turner & L. E. Troll (Eds.), *Women growing older.* Newbury Park, CA: Sage.

Helson, Ravenna; Roberts, Brent; & Agronick, Gail (1995). Enduringness and change in creative personality and the prediction of occupational creativity. *Journal of Personality and Social Psychology, 6,* 1173–1183.

Helson, Ravenna, & Srivastava, Sanjay (2001). Three paths of adult development: Conservers, seekers, and achievers. *Journal of Personality and Social Psychology, 80,* 995–1010.

Henderlong, Jennifer, & Lepper, Mark (2002). The effects of praise on children's intrinsic motivation: A review and synthesis. *Psychological Bulletin, 128,* 774–795.

Hendrix, William H.; Steel, Robert P.; Leap, Terry L.; & Summers, Timothy P. (1991). Development of a stress-related health promotion model: Antecedents and organizational effectiveness outcomes. *Journal of Social Behavior and Personality, 6,* 141–162.

Herdt, Gilbert (1984). *Ritualized homosexuality in Melanesia.* Berkeley: University of California Press.

Herek, G.M. & Capitano, J.P. (1996). "Some of my best friends": Intergroup contact, concealable stigma, and heterosexuals' attitudes toward gay men and lesbians. *Personality and Social Psychology Bulletin, 22,* 412–424.

Herman, John H. (1992). Transmutative and reproductive properties of dreams: Evidence for cortical modulation of brain-stem generators. In J. Antrobus & M. Bertini (Eds.), *The neuropsychology of dreaming.* Hillsdale, NJ: Erlbaum.

Herman, Louis M.; Kuczaj, Stan A.; & Holder, Mark D. (1993). Responses to anomalous gestural sequences by a language-trained dolphin: Evidence for processing of semantic relations and syntactic information. *Journal of Experimental Psychology: General, 122,* 184–194.

Herman-Giddens, M. E.; Slora, E. J.; Wasserman, R. C.; et al. (1997). Secondary sexual characteristics and menses in young girls seen in office practice: A study from the Pediatric Research in Office Settings network, *Pediatrics, 99*(4), 505–512.

Heron, Woodburn (1957). The pathology of boredom. *Scientific American, 196*(1), 52–56.

Herrnstein, Richard J., & Murray, Charles (1994). *The bell curve: Intelligence and class structure in American life.* New York: Free Press.

Hetherington, E. Mavis, & Kelly, John (2002). *For better or for worse: divorce reconsidered.* New York: W. W. Norton & Company, Inc.

Higgins, E. Tory (1998). Promotion and prevention: Regulatory focus as a motivational principle. *Advances in Experimental Social Psychology, 30,* 1–46.

Hilgard, Ernest R. (1977). *Divided consciousness: Multiple controls in human thought and action.* New York: Wiley-Interscience.

Hilgard, Ernest R. (1986). *Divided consciousness: Multiple controls in human thought and action* (2nd ed.). New York: Wiley.

Hill, Harlan F.; Chapman, C. Richard; Kornell, Judy A.; et al. (1990). Self-administration of morphine in bone marrow transplant patients reduces drug requirement. *Pain, 40,* 121–129.

Hill, James O., & Peters, John C. (1998). Environmental contributions to the obesity epidemic. *Science, 280,* 1371–1374.

Hill, L.; Craig, I. W.; Ball, D. M.; et al. (1999). DNA pooling and dense marker maps: A systematic search for genes for cognitive ability. *NeuroReport, 10,* 843–848.

Hilts, Philip J. (1995). *Memory's ghost: The strange tale of Mr. M. and the nature of memory.* New York: Simon & Schuster.

Hirsch, Helmut V. B., & Spinelli, D. N. (1970). Visual experience modifies distribution of horizontally and vertically oriented receptive fields in cats. *Science, 168,* 869–871.

Hirst, William; Neisser, Ulric; & Spelke, Elizabeth (1978, January). Divided attention. *Human Nature, 1,* 54–61.

Hobson, J. Allan (1988). *The dreaming brain.* New York: Basic Books.

Hobson, J. Allan (1990). Activation, input source, and modulation: A neurocognitive model of the state of the brain mind. In R. R. Bootzin, J. F. Kihlstrom, & D. L. Schacter (Eds.), *Sleep and cognition.* Washington, DC: American Psychological Association.

Hobson, J. Allan; Pace-Schott, Edward F.; & Stickgold, Robert (2000). Dreaming and the brain: Toward a cognitive neuroscience of conscious states. *Behavioral and Brain Sciences, 23,* 793–842, 904–1018, 1083–1121.

Hochschild, Arlie (1983). *The managed heart.* Berkeley: University of California Press.

Hodges, Ernest V. E., & Perry, David G. (1999). Personal and interpersonal antecedents and consequences of victimization by peers. *Journal of Personality and Social Psychology, 76,* 677–685.

Hoffman, Martin L. (1990). Empathy and justice motivation. *Motivation and Emotion, 14,* 151–172.

Hoffman, Martin L. (1994). Discipline and internalization. *Developmental Psychology, 30,* 26–28.

Hoffrage, Ulrich; Hertwig, Ralph; & Gigerenzer, Gerd (2000). Hindsight bias: A by-product of knowledge updating? *Journal of Experimental Psychology: Learning, Memory, & Cognition, 26,* 566–581.

Hofstede, Geert, & Bond, Michael H. (1988). The Confucius connection: From cultural roots to economic growth. *Organizational Dynamics,* 5–21.

Holden, Constance (1997). Thumbs up for acupuncture. [News report.] *Science, 278,* 1231.

Holden, George W., & Miller, Pamela C. (1999). Enduring and different: A meta-analysis of the similarity in parents' child rearing. *Psychological Bulletin, 125,* 223–254.

Hollon, Steven D.; Thase, Michael E.; & Markowitz, John C. (2002). Treatment and prevention of depression. *Psychological Science in the Public Interest, 3,* 39–77.

Holowka, S.; Brosseau-Lapre, F.; & Petitto, L. A. (2002). Semantic and conceptual knowledge underlying bilingual babies' first signs and words. *Language Learning, 52(2),* 205–262.

Hooker, Evelyn (1957). The adjustment of the male overt homosexual. *Journal of Projective Techniques, 21,* 18–31.

Horgan, John (1995, November). Get smart, take a test: A long-term rise in IQ scores baffles intelligence experts. *Scientific American, 273,* 12, 14.

Horney, Karen (1926/1973). The flight from womanhood. *The International Journal of Psycho-Analysis, 7,* 324–339. Reprinted in J. B. Miller (Ed.), *Psychoanalysis and women.* New York; Brunner/Mazel, 1973.

Hotz, Robert Lee (2000, November 29). Women use more of brain when listening, study says. *Los Angeles Times,* A1, A18–19.

House, James S.; Landis, Karl R.; & Umberson, Debra (1988, July 19). Social relationships and health. *Science, 241,* 540–545.

Houts, Arthur C. (2002). Discovery, invention, and the expansion of the modern Diagnostic and Statistical Manuals of Mental Disorders. In L. E. Beutler & M. L. Malik (Eds.), *Rethinking the DSM: A psychological perspective.* Washington, DC: American Psychological Association.

Howard, George S. (1991). Culture tales: A narrative approach to thinking, cross-cultural psychology, and psychotherapy. *American Psychologist, 46,* 187–197.

Howe, Mark L., & Courage, Mary L. (1993). On resolving the enigma of infantile amnesia. *Psychological Bulletin, 113,* 305–326.

Howe, Mark L.; Courage, Mary L.; & Peterson, Carole (1994). How can I remember when "I" wasn't there? Long-term retention of traumatic experiences and emergence of the cognitive self. *Consciousness and Cognition, 3,* 327–355.

Hrdy, Sarah B. (1988). Empathy, polyandry, and the myth of the coy female. In R. Bleier (Ed.), *Feminist approaches to science.* New York: Pergamon.

Hrdy, Sarah B. (1994). What do women want? In T. A. Bass (Ed.), *Reinventing the future: Conversations with the world's leading scientists.* Reading, MA: Addison-Wesley.

Hrdy, Sarah B. (1999). *Mother nature.* New York: Pantheon.

Huang, L.; Shanker, Y. G.; Dubauskaite, J.; et al. (1999). Ggamma13 colocalizes with gustducin in taste receptor cells and mediates IP3 responses to bitter denatonium. *Nature Neuroscience, 2,* 1055–1062.

Hubel, David H., & Wiesel, Torsten N. (1962). Receptive fields, binocular interaction and functional architecture in the cat's visual cortex. *Journal of Physiology (London), 160,* 106–154.

Hubel, David H., & Wiesel, Torsten N. (1968). Receptive fields and functional architecture of monkey striate cortex. *Journal of Physiology (London), 195,* 215–243.

Hulbert, Ann (2003). *Raising America: Experts, parents and a century of advice about children.* New York: Knopf.

Hultsch, David F.; Hertzog, Christopher; Small, Brent J.; & Dixon, Roger A. (1999). Use it or lose it: Engaged lifestyle as a buffer of cognitive decline in aging? *Psychology and Aging, 14,* 245–263.

Hunter, John E. (1997). Needed: A ban on the significance test. *Psychological Science, 8,* 3–7.

Hupka, Ralph B. (1981). Cultural determinants of jealousy. *Alternative Lifestyles, 4,* 310–356.

Hupka, Ralph B. (1991). The motive for the arousal of romantic jealousy. In P. Salovey (Ed.), *The psychology of jealousy and envy.* New York: Guilford Press.

Hupka, Ralph B.; Lenton, Alison P.; & Hutchison, Keith A. (1999). Universal development of emotion categories in natural language. *Journal of Personality and Social Psychology, 77,* 247–278.

Hur, Yoon-Mi; Bouchard, Thomas J., Jr.; & Lykken, David T. (1998). Genetic and environmental influence on morningness-eveningness. *Personality and Individual Differences, 25,* 917–925.

Hyde, Janet S. (2000). A gendered brain? [Review of Sex and cognition, by Doreen Kimura.] *Journal of Sex Research, 37,* 191.

Hyde, Janet S.; Fennema, Elizabeth; & Lamon, Susan J. (1990). Gender differences in mathematics performance: A meta-analysis. *Psychological Bulletin, 107,* 139–155.

Hyde, Janet S., & Linn, Marcia C. (1988). Gender differences in verbal ability: A meta-analysis. *Psychological Bulletin, 104,* 53–69

Hyman, Ira E., Jr., & Pentland, Joel (1996). The role of mental imagery in the creation of false childhood memories. *Journal of Memory and Language, 35,* 101–117.

Ikonomidou, Chrysanthy; Bittigau, Petra; Ishimaru, Masahiko J.; et al. (2000, February 11). Ethanol-induced apoptotic neurodegeneration and fetal alcohol syndrome. *Science, 287,* 1056–1060.

Impett, Emily A., & Peplau, Letitia Anne (2002). Why some women consent to unwanted sex with a dating partner: Insights from attachment theory. *Psychology of Women Quarterly, 26,* 360–370.

Inglehart, Ronald (1990). *Culture shift in advanced industrial society.* Princeton, NJ: Princeton University Press.

Inglis, James, & Lawson, J. S. (1981). Sex differences in the effects of unilateral brain damage on intelligence. *Science, 212,* 693–695.

Ingram, J. L.; Stodgell, C. J.; Hyman, S. l.; et al. (2000). Discovery of allelic variants of HOXA1 and HOXB1: genetic susceptibility to autism spectrum disorders. *Teratology, 62,* 693–695.

International Consensus Conference (2002, June). *Female Androgen Deficiency Syndrome: Definition, Diagnosis, and Classification: International Consensus Conference,* Princeton, NY. http://www.med-scape.com/viewprogram/302

Irvine, Janice M. (1990). *Disorders of desire: Sex and gender in modern American sexology.* Philadelphia: Temple University Press.

Islam, Mir Rabiul, & Hewstone, Miles (1993). Intergroup attributions and affective consequences in majority and minority groups. *Journal of Personality and Social Psychology, 64,* 936–950.

Ivis, F. J., & Adlaf, E. M. (1999). A comparison of trends in drug use among students in the USA and Ontario, Canada: 1975–1997. *Drugs: Education, Prevention and Policy, 6*(1), 17–27.

Izard, Carroll E. (1990). Facial expressions and the regulation of emotions. *Journal of Personality and Social Psychology, 58,* 487–498.

Izard, Carroll E. (1994a). Four systems for emotion activation: Cognitive and noncognitive processes. *Psychological Review, 100,* 68–90.

Izard, Carroll E. (1994b). Innate and universal facial expressions: Evidence from developmental and cross-cultural research. *Psychological Bulletin, 115,* 288–299.

Jacobsen, Paul B; Bovbjerg, Dana H.; Schwartz, Marc D.; et al. (1995). Conditioned emotional distress in women receiving chemotherapy for breast cancer. *Journal of Consulting & Clinical Psychology, 63,* 108–114.

Jaffee, Sara, & Hyde, Janet S. (2000). Gender differences in moral orientation: A meta-analysis. *Psychological Bulletin, 126,* 703–726.

James, Jacquelyn B., & Lewkowicz, Corinne J. (1997). Themes of power and affiliation across time. In M. E. Lachman & J. B. James (Eds.), *Multiple paths of midlife development.* Chicago: University of Chicago Press.

James, William (1890/1950). *Principles of psychology* (Vol. 1). New York: Dover.

James, William (1902/1936). *The varieties of religious experience.* New York: Modern Library.

Jamison, Kay (1992). *Touched with fire: Manic depressive illness and the artistic temperament.* New York: Free Press.

Jamison, Kay (1999). *Night falls fast: Understanding suicide.* New York: Knopf.

Jancke, Lutz; Schlaug, Gottfried; & Steinmetz, Helmuth (1997). Hand skill asymmetry in professional musicians. *Brain and Cognition, 34,* 424–432.

Jang, K. L.; Livesley, W. J.; Taylor, S.; & Stein, M. B. (2004). Heritability of individual depressive symptoms. *Journal of Affective Disorders, 80*(2–3), 125–133.

Jang, K. L.; Livesley, W. J.; & Vernon, P. A. (1996). Heritability of the Big Five personality dimensions and their facets: A twin study. *Journal of Personality, 81,* 295–304.

Jang, Kerry L.; McRae, Robert R.; Angleitner, Alois; et al. (1998). Heritability of facet-level traits in a cross-cultural twin sample: Support for a hierarchical model of personality. *Journal of Personality and Social Psychology, 74,* 1556–1565.

Janis, Irving L. (1982). *Groupthink: Psychological studies of policy decisions and fiascoes* (2nd ed.). Boston: Houghton Mifflin.

Janis, Irving L. (1989). *Crucial decisions: Leadership in policy-making and crisis management.* New York: Free Press.

Janis, Irving L.; Kaye, Donald; & Kirschner, Paul (1965). Facilitating effects of "eating-while-reading" on responsiveness to persuasive communications. *Journal of Personality and Social Psychology, 1,* 181–186.

Janssen, I.; Katzmarzyk, P. T.; Boyce, W. F.; et al. (2004). Overweight and obesity in Canadian adolescents and their associations with dietary and physical activity patterns. *Journal of Adolescent Health, 35*(5), 360–367.

Jenkins, J. M., & Rasbash, J. (2003). The role of the shared family context in differential parenting. *Developmental Psychology, 39*(1), 99–113.

Jenkins, John G., & Dallenbach, Karl M. (1924). Obliviscence during sleep and waking. *American Journal of Psychology, 35,* 605–612.

Jenkins, Sharon Rae (1994). Need for power and women's careers over 14 years: Structural power, job satisfaction, and motive change. *Journal of Personality and Social Psychology, 66,* 155–165.

Jensen, Arthur R. (1969). How much can we boost IQ and scholastic achievement? *Harvard Educational Review, 39,* 1–123.

Jensen, Arthur R. (1981). *Straight talk about mental tests.* New York: Free Press.

Jensen, Arthur R. (1998). *The g factor: The science of mental ability.* Westport, CT: Praeger/Greenwood.

Johnson, Marcia K. (1995). The relation between memory and reality. Paper presented at the annual meeting of the American Psychological Association, New York.

Johnson, Mark H.; Dziurawiec, Suzanne; Ellis, Hadyn; & Morton, John (1991). Newborns' preferential tracking of face-like stimuli and its subsequent decline. *Cognition, 40,* 1–19.

Johnson, Robert, & Downing, Leslie (1979). Deindividuation and valence of cues: Effects of prosocial and antisocial behavior. *Journal of Personality and Social Psychology, 37,* 1532–1538.

Jones, Edward E. (1990). *Interpersonal perception.* New York: Macmillan.

Jones, James M. (1991). Psychological models of race: What have they been and what should they be? In J. D. Goodchilds (Ed.), *Psychological perspectives on human diversity in America.* Washington, DC: American Psychological Association.

Jones, James M. (1997). *Prejudice and racism* (2nd ed.). New York: McGraw-Hill.

Jones, Mary Cover (1924). A laboratory study of fear: The case of Peter. *Pedagogical Seminary, 31,* 308–315.

Jost, John T.; Glaser, Jack; Kruglanski, Arie W.; & Sulloway, Frank J. (2003). Political conservatism as motivated social cognition. *Psychological Bulletin, 129,* 339–375.

Judd, Charles M.; Park, Bernadette; Ryan, Carey S.; et al. (1995). Stereotypes and ethnocentrism: Diverging interethnic perceptions of African American and white American youth. *Journal of Personality and Social Psychology, 69,* 460–481.

Judge, Timothy A.; Thoresen, Carl J.; Bono, Joyce E.; & Patton, Gregory K. (2001). The job satisfaction-job performance relationship: A qualitative and quantitative review. *Psychological Bulletin, 127,* 376–407.

Juurlink, D. N.; Mamdani, M. M.; Kopp, A.; et al. (2004). Drug-induced lithium toxicity in the elderly: A population-based study. *Journal of the American Geriatric Society, 52*(5), 794–798.

Jusczyk, Peter W. (2002). How infants adapt speech-processing capacities to native-language structure. *Current Directions in Psychological Science, 11,* 15–18.

Jusczyk, Peter W.; Houston, D.; & Newsome, M. (1999). The beginnings of word segmentation in English-learning infants. *Cognitive Psychology, 39,* 159–207.

Just, Marcel A.; Carpenter, Patricia A.; Keller, T. A.; et al. (2001). Interdependence of nonoverlapping cortical systems in dual cognitive tasks. *NeuroImage, 14,* 417–426.

Kagan, Jerome (1989). *Unstable ideas: Temperament, cognition, and self.* Cambridge, MA: Harvard University Press.

Kagan, Jerome (1993). The meanings of morality. *Psychological Science, 4,* 353, 357–360.

Kagan, Jerome (1994). *Galen's prophecy: Temperament in human nature.* New York: Basic Books.

Kagan, Jerome (1997). Temperament and the reactions to unfamiliarity. *Child Development, 68,* 139–143.

Kagan, Jerome (1998a). How we become what we are. Paper presented at the annual meeting of the Family Therapy Network Symposium, Washington, DC.

Kagan, Jerome (1998b). *Three seductive ideas.* Cambridge, MA: Harvard University Press.

Kahneman, Daniel, & Treisman, Anne (1984). Changing views of attention and automaticity. In R. Parasuraman, D. R. Davies, & J. Beatty (Eds.), *Varieties of attention.* New York: Academic Press.

Kameda, Tatsuya, & Sugimori, Shinkichi (1993). Psychological entrapment in group decision making: An assigned decision rule and a groupthink phenomenon. *Journal of Personality and Social Psychology, 65,* 282–292.

Kanin, Eugene J. (1985). Date rapists: Differential sexual socialization and relative deprivation. *Archives of Sexual Behavior, 14,* 219–231.

Kanter, Rosabeth M. (1977/1993). *Men and women of the corporation.* New York: Basic Books.

Kanwisher, Nancy (2000). Domain specificity in face perception. *Nature Neuroscience, 3,* 759.

Kaplan, Abraham (1967). A philosophical discussion of normality. *Archives of General Psychiatry, 17,* 325–330.

Kaplan, Meg S.; Morales, Miguel; & Becker, Judith V. (1993). The impact of verbal satiation of adolescent sex offenders: A preliminary report. *Journal of Child Sexual Abuse, 2,* 81–88.

Karasek, Robert, & Theorell, Tores (1990). *Healthy work: Stress, productivity, and the reconstruction of working life.* New York: Basic Books.

Karau, Steven J., & Williams, Kipling D. (1993). Social loafing: A meta-analytic review and theoretical integration. *Journal of Personality and Social Psychology, 65,* 681–706.

Karney, Benjamin, & Bradbury, Thomas N. (2000). Attributions in marriage: State or trait? A growth curve analysis. *Journal of Personality and Social Psychology, 78,* 295–309.

Karni, Avi; Tanne, David; Rubenstein, Barton S.; Askenasy, Jean J. M.; & Sagi, Dov (1994). Dependence on REM sleep of overnight improvement of a perceptual skill. *Science, 265,* 679–682.

Karraker, Katherine H.; Vogel, Dena A.; & Lake, Margaret A. (1995). Parents' gender-stereotyped perceptions of newborns: The eye of the beholder revisited. *Sex Roles, 33,* 687–701.

Karremans, Johan C.; Van Lange, Paul A. M.; Ouwerkerk, Jaap W.; & Kluwer, Esther S. (2003). When forgiving enhances psychological well-being: The role of interpersonal commitment. *Journal of Personality and Social Psychology, 84,* 1011–1026.

Kashima, Yoshihisa; Yamaguchi, Susumu; Kim, Uichol; et al. (1995). Culture, gender, and self: A perspective from individualism-collectivism research. *Journal of Personality and Social Psychology, 69,* 925–937.

Kasser, Tim, & Ryan, Richard M. (1996). Further examining the American dream: Correlates of financial success as a central life aspiration. *Personality and Social Psychology Bulletin, 22,* 280–287.

Kasser, Tim, & Ryan, Richard M. (2001). Be careful what you wish for: Optimal functioning and the relative attainment of intrinsic and extrinsic goals. In P. Schmuck & K. M. Sheldon (Eds.), *Life goals and well-being.* Lengerich, Germany: Pabst Science Publishers.

Kassinove, Howard (Ed.) (1995). *Anger disorders: Definition, diagnosis, treatment.* Washington, DC: Taylor & Francis.

Katigbak, M.S.; Church, A.T.; Guanzon-Lapena, M.A.; Carlota, A.J.; & del Pilar, G.H. (2002). Are indigenous personality dimensions culture specific?: Phillippine inventories and the five factor model. *Journal of Personality and Social Psychology, 82,* 89–101.

Katz, Phyllis A., & Ksansnak, Keith R. (1994). Developmental aspects of gender role flexibility and traditionality in middle childhood and adolescence. *Developmental Psychology, 30,* 272–282.

Katz, Zender (2001). Canadian psychologists' education, trauma history, and the recovery of memories of childhood sexual abuse. (Doctoral Dissertation, Simon Fraser University, 2001.) *Dissertations Abstracts International, 61,* 3848.

Kaufman, Joan, & Zigler, Edward (1987). Do abused children become abusive parents? *American Journal of Orthopsychiatry, 57,* 186–192.

Kazdin, Alan E. (2001). *Behavior modification in applied settings* (6th ed.). Belmont, CA: Wadsworth.

Keating, Caroline F. (1994). World without words: Messages from face and body. In W. J. Lonner & R. Malpass (Eds.), *Psychology and culture.* Needham Heights, MA: Allyn & Bacon.

Keck, Paul E., Jr., & McElroy, Susan L. (1998). Pharmacological treatment of bipolar disorders. In P. E. Nathan & J. M. Gorman (Eds.), *A guide to treatments that work.* New York: Oxford University Press.

Keen, Sam (1986). *Faces of the enemy: Reflections of the hostile imagination.* San Francisco: Harper & Row.

Keller, Martin B.; McCullough, James P.; Klein, Daniel N.; et al. (2000, May 18). A comparison of nefazodone, the cognitive behavioral-analysis system of psychotherapy, and their combination for the treatment of chronic depression. *New England Journal of Medicine, 342,* 1462–1470.

Kelly, Anita E. (1999). Revealing personal secrets. *Current Directions in Psychological Science, 8,* 105–109.

Kelly, K., & DeKeseredy, W. (1993). The incidence and prevalence of woman abuse in Canadian university and college dating relationships. *Journal of Human Justice, 4*(2), 25–52.

Kelman, Herbert C., & Hamilton, V. Lee (1989). *Crimes of obedience: Toward a social psychology of authority and responsibility.* New Haven, CT: Yale University Press.

Keltner, Dacher, & Anderson, Cameron (2000). Saving face for Darwin: The functions and uses of embarrassment. *Current Directions in Psychological Science, 9,* 187–192.

Kempermann, G.; Brandon, E. P.; & Gage, F. H. (1998). Environmental stimulation of 120/SvJ mice causes increased cell proliferation and neurogenesis in the adult dentate gyrus. *Current Biology, 8,* 939–942.

Kendall [no first name] (1999). Women in Lesotho and the (Western) construction of homophobia. In E. Blackwood & S. E. Wieringa (Eds.), *Female desires: Same-sex relations and transgender practices across cultures.* New York: Columbia University Press.

Kendler, Kenneth S.; Pedersen, Nancy; Johnson, Lars; Neale, Michael C.; & Mathie, A. (1993). A Swedish pilot twin study of affective illness, including hospital and population-ascertained subsamples. *Archives of General Psychiatry, 50,* 699–706.

Kennedy, S. H., & Lam, R. W. (2003). Enhancing outcomes in the management of treatment resistant depression: A focus on atypical antipsychotics. *Bipolar Disorders, 5*(Suppl. 2), 36–47.

Kennedy-Moore, Eileen, & Watson, Jeanne C. (2001). How and when does emotional expression help? *Review of General Psychology, 5,* 187–212.

Kenny, Michael G. (1986). *The passion of Ansel Bourne: Multiple personality in American culture.* Washington, DC: Smithsonian Press.

Kephart, William M. (1967). Some correlates of romantic love. *Journal of Marriage and the Family, 29,* 470–474.

Kerr, Michael E., & Bowen, Murray (1988). *Family evaluation: An approach based on Bowen theory.* New York: Norton.

Kessler, Ronald C.; McGonagle, Katherine A.; Zhao, Shanyang; et al. (1994). Lifetime and 12-month prevalence of DSM-III-R psychiatric disorders in the United States: Results from the National Comorbidity Survey. *Archives of General Psychiatry, 51,* 8–19.

Kessler, Ronald C.; Sonnega, A.; Bromet, E.; et al. (1995). Posttraumatic stress disorder in the National Comorbidity Survey. *Archives of General Psychiatry, 52,* 1048–1060.

Kiecolt-Glaser, Janice K.; Malarkey, William B.; Chee, MaryAnn; et al. (1993). Negative behavior during marital conflict is associated with immunological down-regulation. *Psychosomatic Medicine, 55,* 395–409.

Kiecolt-Glaser, Janice K., & Newton, Tamara L. (2001). Marriage and health: His and hers. *Psychological Bulletin, 127,* 472–503.

Kiecolt-Glaser, Janice K.; Page, Gayle G.; Marucha, Phillip T.; et al. (1998). Psychological influences on surgical recovery: Perspectives from psychoneuroimmunology. *American Psychologist, 53,* 1209–1218.

Kihlstrom, John F. (1994). Hypnosis, delayed recall, and the principles of memory. *International Journal of Clinical and Experimental Hypnosis, 40,* 337–345.

Kihlstrom, John F. (1995). From a subject's point of view: The experiment as conversation and collaboration between investigator and subject. Invited address presented at the annual meeting of the American Psychological Society, New York.

Kihlstrom, John F. (1998). Dissociations and dissociation theory in hypnosis: Comment on Kirsch and Lynn (1998). *Psychological Bulletin, 123,* 186–191.

Kihlstrom, John F., & Harackiewicz, Judith M. (1982). The earliest recollection: A new survey. *Journal of Personality, 50,* 134–148.

Kim, Hannah L.; Streltzer, Jon; & Goebert, Deborah (1999). St. John's wort for depression: A meta-analysis of well-defined clinical trials. *Journal of Nervous and Mental Diseases, 187,* 532–538.

Kimmel, Michael (1995). *Manhood in America: A cultural history.* New York: Free Press.

King, M., & Woollett, E. (1997). Sexually assaulted males: 115 men consulting a counseling service. *Archives of Sexual Behavior, 26,* 579–588.

King, Pamela (1989, October). The chemistry of doubt. *Psychology Today, 58,* 60.

King, Patricia M., & Kitchener, Karen S. (1994). *Developing reflective judgment: Understanding and promoting intellectual growth and critical thinking in adolescents and adults.* San Francisco: Jossey Bass.

Kinsey, Alfred C.; Pomeroy, Wardell B.; & Martin, Clyde E. (1948). *Sexual behavior in the human male.* Philadelphia: Saunders.

Kinsey, Alfred C.; Pomeroy, Wardell B.; Martin, Clyde E.; & Gebhard, Paul H. (1953). *Sexual behavior in the human female.* Philadelphia: Saunders.

Kirkpatrick, Lee A., & Davis, Keith A. (1994). Attachment style, gender, and relationship stability: A longitudinal analysis. *Journal of Personality and Social Psychology, 66,* 502–512.

Kirsch, Irving (1997). Response expectancy theory and application: A decennial review. *Applied and Preventive Psychology, 6,* 69–70.

Kirsch, Irving, & Lynn, Steven J. (1995). The altered state of hypnosis: Changes in the theoretical landscape. *American Psychologist, 50,* 846–858.

Kirsch, Irving, & Lynn, Steven J. (1998). Dissociation theories of hypnosis. *Psychological Bulletin, 123,* 100–113.

Kirsch, Irving; Montgomery, G.; & Sapirstein, G. (1995). Hypnosis as an adjunct to cognitive behavioral psychotherapy: A meta-analysis. *Journal of Consulting and Clinical Psychology, 63,* 214–220.

Kirsch, Irving, & Sapirstein, Guy (1998). Listening to Prozac but hearing placebo: A meta-analysis of antidepressant medication. *Prevention & Treatment, 1,* Article 0002a, posted electronically June 26, 1998 on the Website of the American Psychological Association.

Kirsch, Irving; Silva, Christopher E.; Carone, James E.; Johnston, J. Dennis; & Simon, B. (1989). The surreptitious observation design: An experimental paradigm for distinguishing artifact from essence in hypnosis. *Journal of Abnormal Psychology, 98,* 132–136.

Kirschbaum, C.; Prussner, J. C.; & Stone, A. A. (1995). Persistent high cortisol responses to repeated psychological stress in a subpopulation of healthy men. *Psychosomatic Medicine, 57,* 468–474.

Kitayama, Shinobu, & Markus, Hazel R. (1994). Introduction to cultural psychology and emotion research. In S. Kitayama & H. R. Markus (Eds.), *Emotion and culture: Empirical studies of mutual influence.* Washington, DC: American Psychological Association.

Kitchener, Karen S., & King, Patricia M. (1990). The Reflective Judgment Model: Ten years of research. In M. L. Commons (Ed.), *Models and methods in the study of adolescent and adult thought: Vol. 2. Adult development.* Westport, CT: Greenwood Press.

Kitchener, Karen S.; Lynch, Cindy L.; Fischer, Kurt W.; & Wood, Phillip K. (1993). Developmental range of reflective judgment: The effect of contextual support and practice on developmental stage. *Developmental Psychology, 29,* 893–906.

Klein, Raymond, & Armitage, Roseanne (1979). Rhythms in human performance: 1 1/2-hour oscillations in cognitive style. *Science, 204,* 1326–1328.

Klein, Stanley B., & Kihlstrom, John F. (1998). On bridging the gap between social-personality psychology and neuropsychology. *Personality and Social Psychology Review, 2,* 228–242.

Kleinke, Chris L.; Peterson, Thomas R.; & Rutledge, Thomas R. (1998). Effects of self-generated facial expressions on mood. *Journal of Personality and Social Psychology, 74,* 272–279.

Kleinman, Arthur (1988). *Rethinking psychiatry: From cultural category to personal experience.* New York: Free Press.

Klima, Edward S., & Bellugi, Ursula (1966). Syntactic regularities in the speech of children. In J. Lyons & R. J. Wales (Eds.), *Psycholinguistics papers.* Edinburgh, Scotland: Edinburgh University Press.

Klimoski, R. (1992). Graphology and personal selection. In B. Beyerstein & D. Beyerstein (Eds.), *The write stuff: Evaluations of graphology—The study of handwriting analysis.* Buffalo, NY: Prometheus Books.

Klohnen, Eva C., & Bera, Stephan (1998). Behavioral and experiential patterns of avoidantly and securely attached women across adulthood: A 31-year longitudinal perspective. *Journal of Personality and Social Psychology, 74,* 211–223.

Klonoff, Elizabeth A.; Landrine, Hope; & Campbell, Robin (2000). Sexist discrimination may account for well-known gender differences in psychiatric symptoms. *Psychology of Women Quarterly, 24,* 93–99.

Kluft, Richard P. (1987). The simulation and dissimulation of multiple personality disorder. *American Journal of Clinical Hypnosis, 30,* 104–118.

Kluft, Richard P. (1993). Multiple personality disorders. In D. Spiegel (Ed.), *Dissociative disorders: A clinical review.* Lutherville, MD: Sidran.

Knight, Raymond A.; Prentky, Robert A.; & Cerce, David D. (1994). The development, reliability, and validity of an inventory for the multidimensional assessment of sex and aggression. *Criminal Justice and Behavior, 21,* 72–94.

Kochanska, Grazyna (2002). Mutually responsive orientation between mothers and their young children: A context for the early development of conscience. *Current Directions in Psychological Science, 11,* 191–195.

Kolb, B.; Gibb, R.; & Gorny, G. (2000). Cortical plasticity and the development of behavior after early frontal cortical injury. *Developmental Neuropsychology, 18*(3), 423–444.

Kolb, Bryan, & Whishaw, Ian Q. (1998). Brain plasticity and behavior. *Annual Review of Psychology, 49,* 43–64.

Kohlberg, Lawrence (1964). Development of moral character and moral ideology. In M. Hoffman & L. W. Hoffman (Eds.), *Review of child development research.* New York: Russell Sage Foundation.

Kohlberg, Lawrence (1984). *Essays on moral development: Vol. 2. The psychology of moral development: The nature and validity of moral stages.* San Francisco: Harper & Row.

Köhler, Wolfgang (1925). *The mentality of apes.* New York: Harcourt, Brace.

Kohn, Melvin, & Schooler, Carmi (1983). *Work and personality: An inquiry into the impact of social stratification.* Norwood, NJ: Ablex.

Koocher, Gerald P.; Goodman, Gail S.; White, C. Sue; et al. (1995). Psychological science and the use of anatomically detailed dolls in child sexual-abuse assessments. *Psychological Bulletin, 118,* 199–222.

Kopta, Stephen M.; Howard, Kenneth I.; Lowry, Jenny L.; & Beutler, Larry E. (1994). Patterns of symptomatic recovery in psychotherapy. *Journal of Consulting and Clinical Psychology, 62,* 1009–1016.

Koski, Lilah R., & Shaver, Phillip R. (1997). Attachment and relationship satisfaction across the lifespan. In R. J. Sternberg & M. Hojjat (Eds.), *Satisfaction in close relationships.* New York: Guilford.

Kosslyn, Stephen M. (1980). *Image and mind.* Cambridge, MA: Harvard University Press.

Koulack, D. (1997). Recognition memory, circadian rhythms, and sleep. *Perceptual and Motor Skills, 85*(1), 99–104.

Kozak, Michael J.; Liebowitz, Michael R.; & Foa, Edna B. (2000). Cognitive-behavior therapy and pharmacotherapy for OCD: The NIMH-sponsored collaborative study. In W. K. Goodman, M. Rudorfer, & J. Maser (Eds.), *Treatment challenges in obsessive compulsive disorder.* Mahwah, NJ: Erlbaum.

Kramer, Arthur F., & Willis, Sherry L. (2002). Enhancing the cognitive vitality of older adults. *Current Directions in Psychological Science, 11,* 173–177.

Krantz, David S., & Manuck, Stephen B. (1984). Acute psychophysiologic reactivity and risk of cardiovascular disease: A review and methodological critique. *Psychological Bulletin, 96,* 435–464.

Krieger, Nancy, & Sidney, S. (1996). Racial discrimination and blood pressure: The CARDIA study of young black and white adults. *American Journal of Public Health, 86,* 1370–1378.

Kring, Ann M., & Gordon, Albert H. (1998). Sex differences in emotion: Expression, experience, and physiology. *Journal of Personality and Social Psychology, 74,* 686–703.

Kripke, Daniel F. (1974). Ultradian rhythms in sleep and wakefulness. In E. D. Weitzman (Ed.), *Advances in sleep research* (Vol. 1). Flushing, NY: Spectrum.

Kroll, Barry M. (1992). *Teaching hearts and minds: College students reflect on the Vietnam War in literature.* Carbondale: Southern Illinois University Press.

Krueger, Robert E. (2000). Phenotypic, genetic, and non-shared environmental parallels in the structure of personality: A view from the Multidimensional Personality Questionnaire. *Journal of Personality and Social Psychology, 79,* 1057–1067.

Krueger, Robert F.; Hicks, Brian M.; & McGue, Matt (2001). Altruism and antisocial behavior: Independent tendencies, unique personality correlates, distinct etiologies. *Psychological Science, 12,* 397–402.

Kruger, Justin, & Dunning, David (1999). Unskilled and unaware of it: How difficulties in recognizing one's own incompetence lead to inflated self-assessments. *Journal of Personality and Social Psychology, 77,* 1121–1134.

Krupa, David J.; Thompson, Judith K.; & Thompson, Richard F. (1993). Localization of a memory trace in the mammalian brain. *Science, 260,* 989–991.

Kuhl, Patricia K.; Andruski, Jean E.; Chistovich, Inna A.; et al. (1997, August 1). Cross-language analysis of phonetic units in language addressed to infants. *Science, 277,* 684–686.

Kuhl, Patricia K.; Williams, Karen A.; Lacerda, Francisco; et al. (1992, January 31). Linguistic experience alters phonetic perception in infants by 6 months of age. *Science, 255,* 606–608.

Kunda, Ziva (1990). The case for motivated reasoning. *Psychological Bulletin, 108,* 480–498.

Kutchins, Herb, & Kirk, Stuart A. (1997). *Making us crazy: DSM. The psychiatric bible and the creation of mental disorders.* New York: Free Press.

Kwak, K., & Berry, J. W. (2001). Generational differences in acculturation among Asian families in Canada: A comparison of Vietnamese, Korean, and East-Indian groups. *International Journal of Psychology, 36*(3), 152–162.

LaBerge, Stephen (1986). *Lucid dreaming.* New York: Ballantine Books.

LaBerge, Stephen, & Levitan, Lynne (1995). Validity established of DreamLight cues for eliciting lucid dreaming. *Dreaming: Journal of the Association for the Study of Dreams, 5,* 159–168.

Lachman, Margie E., & Weaver, Suzanne L. (1998). The sense of control as a moderator of social class differences in health and well-being. *Journal of Personality and Social Psychology, 74,* 763–773.

Lachman, Sheldon J. (1996). Processes in perception: Psychological transformations of highly structured stimulus material. *Perceptual and Motor Skills, 83,* 411–418.

Ladouceur, R.; Léger, E.; Dugas, M.; & Freeston, M. H. (2004). Cognitive-behavioral treatment of generalized anxiety disorder (GAD) for older adults. *International Psychogeriatrics, 16*(2), 195–207.

LaFrance, Marianne; Hecht, Marvin A.; & Paluck, Elizabeth L. (2003). The contingent smile: A meta-analysis of sex differences in smiling. *Psychological Bulletin, 129,* 305–334.

Laird, James D. (1974). Self-attribution of emotion: The effects of expressive behavior on the quality of emotional experience. *Journal of Personality and Social Psychology, 29,* 475–486.

Lakoff, Robin T., & Coyne, James C. (1993). *Father knows best: The use and abuse of power in Freud's case of "Dora."* New York: Teachers College Press.

Lalumière, M. L., & Quinsey, V. L. (1998). Pavlovian conditioning of sexual interests in human males. *Archives of Sexual Behavior, 27,* 241–252.

Lamb, Sharon (2002). *The secret lives of girls.* New York: The Free Press.

Lam, R. (1998). Seasonal affective disorder: Diagnosis and management. *Primary Care Psychiatry, 4,* 63–74.

Lam, R. W.; Bartley, S.; Yatham, L. N.; et al. (1999). Clinical predictors of short-term outcome in electroconvulsive therapy. *Canadian Journal of Psychiatry, 44*(2), 158–163.

Landrine, Hope (1988). Revising the framework of abnormal psychology. In P. Bronstein & K. Quina (Eds.), *Teaching a psychology of people.* Washington, DC: American Psychological Association.

Lang, Frieder R., & Heckhausen, Jutta (2001). Perceived control over development and subjective well-being: Differential benefits across adulthood. *Journal of Personality and Social Psychology, 81,* 509–523.

Lang, Peter (1995). The emotion probe: Studies of motivation and attention. *American Psychologist, 50,* 372–385.

Langer, Ellen J. (1983). *The psychology of control.* Beverly Hills, CA: Sage.

Langer, Ellen J.; Blank, Arthur; & Chanowitz, Benzion (1978). The mindlessness of ostensibly thoughtful action: The role of placebic information in interpersonal interaction. *Journal of Personality and Social Psychology, 36,* 635–642.

Lanphear, B. P.; Hornung, R.; Ho, M.; et al. (2002). Environmental lead exposure during early childhood. *Journal of Pediatrics, 140,* 49–47.

Latané, Bibb; Williams, Kipling; & Harkins, Stephen (1979). Many hands make light the work: The causes and consequences of social loafing. *Journal of Personality and Social Psychology, 37,* 822–832.

Laumann, Edward O., & Gagnon John H. (1995). A sociological perspective on sexual action. In R. G. Parker & J. H. Gagnon (Eds.), *Conceiving sexuality: Approaches to sex research in a postmodern world.* New York: Routledge.

Laumann, Edward O.; Gagnon, John H.; Michael, Robert T.; & Michaels, Stuart (1994). *The social organization of sexuality.* Chicago: University of Chicago Press.

Laurence, J. R., & Perry, C. (1988). *Hypnosis, will, and memory: A psycho-legal history.* New York: Guilford Press.

Laursen, Brett, & Collins, W. Andrew (1994). Interpersonal conflict during adolescence. *Psychological Bulletin, 115,* 197–209.

Lavie, Peretz (1976). Ultradian rhythms in the perception of two apparent motions. *Chronobiologia, 3,* 21–218.

Lazarus, Richard S. (2000). Toward better research on stress and coping. *American Psychologist, 55,* 665–673.

Lazarus, Richard S., & Folkman, Susan (1984). *Stress, appraisal, and coping.* New York: Springer.

LeDoux, Joseph E. (1996). *The emotional brain.* New York: Simon & Schuster.

Lefton, L. A.; Boyes, M. C.; & Ogden, N. A. (2000). *Psychology.* Scarborough, ON: Prentice-Hall Canada, Inc.

Lehman, Adam K., & Rodin, Judith (1989). Styles of self-nurturance and disordered eating. *Journal of Consulting and Clinical Psychology, 57,* 117–122.

Leiblum, S.; Wiegel, M.; & Brickle, F. (2003). Sexual attitudes of US and Canadian medical students: The role of ethnicity, gender, religion and acculturation. *Sexual and Relationship Therapy, 18*(4), 473–491.

Lemieux, Robert, & Hale, Jerold L. (2000). Intimacy, passion, and commitment among married individuals: Further testing of the Triangular Theory of Love. *Psychological Reports, 87,* 941–948.

Lepore, Stephen J.; Ragan, Jennifer D.; & Jones, Scott (2000). Talking facilitates cognitive-emotional processes of adaptation to an acute stressor. *Journal of Personality and Social Psychology, 78,* 499–508.

Lepowsky, Maria (1994). *Fruit of motherland: Gender in an egalitarian society.* New York: Columbia University Press.

Lepper, Mark R.; Greene, David; & Nisbett, Richard E. (1973). Undermining children's intrinsic interest with extrinsic rewards. *Journal of Personality and Social Psychology, 28,* 129–137.

Leproult, Rachel; Copinschi, Georges; Buxton, Orfeu; & Van Cauter, Eve (1997). Sleep loss results in an elevation of cortisol levels the next evening. *Sleep, 20,* 865–870.

Leproult, Rachel; Van Reeth, Olivier; Byrne, Maria M.; et al. (1997). Sleepiness, performance, and neuroendocrine function during sleep deprivation: Effects of exposure to bright light or exercise. *Journal of Biological Rhythms, 12,* 245–258.

Lerner, Harriet G. (1989). *The dance of intimacy.* New York: Harper & Row.

Lerner, Jennifer S.; Goldberg, Julie H.; & Tetlock, Philip E. (1998). Sober second thought: The effects of accountability, anger, and authoritarianism on attributions of responsibility. *Personality and Social Psychology Bulletin, 24,* 563–574.

Lerner, Melvin J. (1980). *The belief in a just world: A fundamental delusion.* New York: Plenum.

Lester, Barry M.; LaGasse, Linda L.; & Seifer, Ronald (1998, October 23). Cocaine exposure and children: The meaning of subtle effects. *Science, 282,* 633–634.

LeVay, Simon (1991). A difference in hypothalamic structure between heterosexual and homosexual men. *Science, 253,* 1034–1037.

Levenson, Robert W. (1992). Autonomic nervous system differences among emotions. *Psychological Science, 3,* 23–27.

Levenson, Robert W.; Ekman, Paul; & Friesen Wallace V. (1990). Voluntary facial action generates emotion-specific automatic nervous system activity. *Psychophysiology, 27,* 363–384.

Levin, Daniel T. (2000). Race as a visual feature: Using visual search and perceptual discrimination tasks to understand face categories and the cross-race recognition deficit. *Journal of Experimental Psychology: General, 129,* 559–574.

Levine, James A.; Eberhardt, Norman L.; & Jensen, Michael D. (1999, January 8). Role of nonexercise activity thermogenesis in resistance to fat gain in humans. *Science, 283,* 212–214.

Levine, Robert V. (2003, May/June). The kindness of strangers. *American Scientist, 91,* 227–233.

Levine, Robert V.; Martinez, Todd S.; Brase, Gary; & Sorenson, Kerry (1994). Helping in 36 U.S. cities. *Journal of Personality and Social Psychology, 67,* 69–82.

Levy, Becca. (1996). Improving memory in old age through implicit self-stereotyping. *Journal of Personality and Social Psychology, 71,* 1092–1107.

Levy, David A. (1997). *Tools of critical thinking: Metathoughts for psychology.* Boston: Allyn & Bacon.

Levy, Jerre; Trevarthen, Colwyn; & Sperry, Roger W. (1972). Perception of bilateral chimeric figures following hemispheric deconnection. *Brain, 95,* 61–78.

Levy, Kenneth N.; Blatt, Sidney J.; & Shaver, Phillip R. (1998). Attachment styles are parental representations. *Journal of Personality and Social Psychology, 74,* 407–419.

Levy, Robert I. (1984). The emotions in comparative perspective. In K. R. Scherer & P. Ekman (Eds.), *Approaches to emotion.* Hillsdale, NJ: Erlbaum.

Lewin, Kurt (1948). *Resolving social conflicts.* New York: Harper.

Lewis, Dorothy O. (1992). From abuse to violence: Psychophysiological consequences of maltreatment. *Journal of the American Academy of Child and Adolescent Psychiatry, 31,* 383–391.

Lewis, Michael (1997). *Altering fate: Why the past does not predict the future.* New York: Guilford Press.

Lewontin, Richard C. (1970). Race and intelligence. *Bulletin of the Atomic Scientists, 26*(3), 2–8.

Lewontin, Richard C. (2001, March 5). Genomania: A disorder of modern biology and medicine. Invited address at the University of California, Los Angeles.

Lewy, Alfred J.; Ahmed, Saeeduddin; Jackson, Jeanne L.; & Sack, Robert L. (1992). Melatonin shifts human circadian rhythms according to a phase response curve. *Chronobiology International, 9,* 380–392.

Lichtenstein, Sarah; Slovic, Paul; Fischhoff, Baruch; et al. (1978). Judged frequency of lethal events. *Journal of Experimental Psychology: Human Learning and Memory, 4,* 551–578.

Lickona, Thomas (1983). *Raising good children.* New York: Bantam.

Lieberman, Matthew (2000). Intuition: A social cognitive neuroscience approach. *Psychological Bulletin, 126,* 109–137.

Liepert, J.; Bauder, H.; Miltner, W. H.; et al. (2000). Treatment-induced cortical reorganization after stroke in humans. *Stroke, 31,* 1210–1216.

Lilienfeld, Scott O. (1999, September/October). Projective measures of personality and psychopathology: How well do they work? *Skeptical Inquirer,* 32–39.

Lilienfeld, Scott O.; Wood, James M.; & Garb, Howard N. (2000). The scientific status of projective techniques. *Psychological Science in the Public Interest, 1,* 27–66.

Lin, Keh-Ming; Poland, Russell E.; & Chien, C. P. (1990). Ethnicity and psychopharmacology: Recent findings and future research directions. In E. Sorel (Ed.), *Family, culture, and psychobiology.* New York: Legas.

Lindsay, D. S.; Hagen, L.; Read, J. D.; et al. (2004). True photographs and false memories. *Psychological Science, 15*(3), 149–154.

Lindsay, D. Stephen, & Read, J. D. (1994). Psychotherapy and memories of childhood sexual abuse: A cognitive perspective. *Applied Cognitive Psychology, 8,* 281–338.

Linton, Marigold (1978). Real-world memory after six years: An in vivo study of very long-term memory. In M. M. Gruneberg, P. E. Morris, & R. N. Sykes (Eds.), *Practical aspects of memory.* London: Academic Press.

Linton, Simi (1998). *Claiming disability: Knowledge and identity.* New York: New York University Press.

Linville, P. W.; Fischer, G. W.; & Fischhoff, B. (1992). AIDS risk perceptions and decision biases. In J. B. Pryor & G. D. Reeder (Eds.), *The social psychology of HIV infection.* Hillsdale, NJ: Erlbaum.

Lissner, L.; Odell, P. M.; D'Agostino, R. B.; et al. (1991, June 27). Variability of body weight and health outcomes in the Framingham population. *New England Journal of Medicine, 324,* 1839–1844.

Litman, L. C. (2005). *Clinical Psychopharmacology and Related Medical Training and Board Certification for Psychologists: Questions & Answers.* Retrieved February 15, 2005, from http://www.cpa.ca/Pharmpsych/Litman1.pdf

Little, John T.; Kimbrell, Tim A.; Wassermann, Eric M.; et al. (2000). Cognitive effects of 1- and 20-hertz repetitive transcranial magnetic stimulation in depression: Preliminary report. *Neuropsychiatry, Neuropsychology, & Behavioral Neurology, 13,* 119–124.

Locher, R.; Suter, P. M.; & Vetter, W. (1998). Ethanol suppresses smooth muscle cell proliferation in the postprandial state: a new antiatherosclerotic mechanism of ethanol? *American Journal of Clinical Nutrition, 67,* 338–341.

Locke, Edwin A., & Latham, Gary P. (1990). Work motivation and satisfaction: Light at the end of the tunnel. *Psychological Science, 1,* 240–246.

Locke, Edwin A., & Latham, Gary P. (2002). Building a practically useful theory of goal setting and task motivation. *American Psychologist, 57,* 705–717.

Locke, Edwin A.; Shaw, Karyll; Saari, Lise; & Latham, Gary (1981). Goal-setting and task performance: 1969–1980. *Psychological Bulletin, 90,* 125–152.

Loehlin, John C. (1992). *Genes and environment in personality development.* Newbury Park CA: Sage.

Loehlin, John C.; Horn, J. M.; & Willerman, L. (1996). Heredity, environment, and IQ in the Texas adoption study. In R. J. Sternberg & E. Grigorenko (Eds.), *Intelligence: Heredity and Environment.* New York: Cambridge University Press.

Loftus, Elizabeth F. (1980). *Memory.* Reading, MA: Addison-Wesley.

Loftus, Elizabeth F. (1996). Memory distortion and false memory creation. *Bulletin of the American Academy of Psychiatry and the Law, 24,* 281–295.

Loftus, Elizabeth F., & Greene, Edith (1980). Warning: Even memory for faces may be contagious. *Law and Human Behavior, 4,* 323–334.

Loftus, Elizabeth F., & Ketcham, Katherine (1994). *The myth of repressed memory.* New York: St. Martin's Press.

Loftus, Elizabeth F.; Miller, David G.; & Burns, Helen J. (1978). Semantic integration of verbal information into a visual memory. *Journal of Experimental Psychology: Human Learning and Memory, 4,* 19–31.

Loftus, Elizabeth F., & Palmer, John C. (1974). Reconstruction of automobile destruction: An example of the interaction between language and memory. *Journal of Verbal Learning and Verbal Behavior, 13,* 585–589.

Loftus, Elizabeth F., & Pickrell, Jacqueline E. (1995). The formation of false memories. *Psychiatric Annals, 25,* 720–725.

Loftus, Elizabeth F., & Zanni, Guido (1975). Eyewitness testimony: The influence of the wording of a question. *Bulletin of the Psychonomic Society, 5,* 86–88.

Lohr, Jeffrey M.; Montgomery, Robert W.; Lilienfeld, Scott O.; & Tolin, David F. (1999). Pseudoscience and the commercial promotion of trauma treatments. In R. Gist & B. Lubin (Eds.), *Response to disaster: Psychosocial, community, and ecological approaches.* Philadelphia, PA: Brunner/Mazel (Taylor & Francis).

Lohr, Jeffrey M.; Tolin, D. F.; & Lilienfeld, Scott O. (1998). Efficacy of Eye Movement Desensitization and Reprocessing: Implications for behavior therapy. *Behavior Therapy, 29,* 123–156.

Lonner, Walter J. (1995). Culture and human diversity. In E. Trickett, R. Watts, & D. Birman (Eds.), *Human diversity: Perspectives on people in context.* San Francisco: Jossey-Bass.

Loo, R. (1998). A psychometric and cross-national examination of a belief in a just world scale. *Journal of Applied Social Psychology, 32*(7), 1396–1406.

Lopez, N. L; Bonenberger, J. L; & Schneider, H. G. (2001). Parental disciplinary history, current levels of empathy, and moral reasoning in young adults. *North American Journal of Psychology, 3,* 193–204.

López, Steven R. (1989). Patient variable biases in clinical judgment: Conceptual overview and methodological considerations. *Psychological Bulletin, 106,* 184–203.

López, Steven R. (1995). Testing ethnic minority children. In B. B. Wolman (Ed.), *The encyclopedia of psychology, psychiatry, and psychoanalysis.* New York: Holt.

Losier, B. J.; McGrath, P. J.; & Klein, R. M. (1996). Error patterns of the Continuous Performance Test in non-medicated and medicated samples of children with and without ADHD: A meta-analytic review. *Journal of Child Psychology and Psychiatry and Allied Disciplines, 37*(8), 971–987.

Lott, Bernice (1997). The personal and social consequences of a gender difference ideology. *Journal of Social Issues, 53,* 279–298.

Lovaas, O. Ivar (1977). *The autistic child: Language development through behavior modification.* New York: Halsted Press.

Lovaas, O. Ivar; Schreibman, Laura; & Koegel, Robert L. (1974). A behavior modification approach to the treatment of autistic children. *Journal of Autism and Childhood Schizophrenia, 4,* 111–129.

Lucchina, L. A.; Curtis, O. F.; Putnam, P.; et al. (1998). Psychophysical measurement of 6-n-propylthiouracil (PROP) taste perception. *Annals of the New York Academy of Sciences, 855,* 816–819.

Luengo, M. A.; Carrillo-de-la-Peña, M. T.; Otero, J. M.; & Romero, E. (1994). A short-term longitudinal study of impulsivity and antisocial behavior. *Journal of Personality and Social Psychology, 66,* 542–548.

Luepnitz, Deborah A. (1988). *The family interpreted: Feminist theory in clinical practice.* New York: Basic Books.

Lugaresi, Elio; Medori, R.; Montagna, P.; et al. (1986, October 16). Fatal familial insomnia and dysautonomia with selective degeneration of thalamic nuclei. *New England Journal of Medicine, 315,* 997–1003.

Luhrmann, T. M. (2000). *Of two minds: the growing disorder in American psychiatry.* New York: Knopf.

Luria, Alexander R. (1968). *The mind of a mnemonist* (L. Soltaroff, trans.). New York: Basic Books.

Luria, Alexander R. (1980). *Higher cortical functions in man* (2nd rev. ed.). New York: Basic Books.

Lussier, Y.; Sabourin, S.; & Turgeon, C. (1997). Coping strategies as moderators of the relationship between attachment and marital adjustment. *Journal of Social and Personal Relationships, 14*(6), 777–791.

Lutz, Catherine (1988). *Unnatural emotions.* Chicago: University of Chicago Press.

Lykken, David T. (1995). *The antisocial personalities.* Hillsdale, NJ: Erlbaum.

Lykken, David T., & Tellegen. Auke (1996). Happiness is a stochastic phenomenon. *Psychological Science, 7,* 186–189.

Lynn, Steven Jay; Rhue, Judith W.; & Weekes, John R. (1990). Hypnotic involuntariness: A social cognitive analysis. *Psychological Review, 97,* 69–184.

Lytton, Hugh, & Romney, David M. (1991). Parents' differential socialization of boys and girls: A meta-analysis. *Psychological Bulletin, 109,* 267–296.

Lyubomirsky, Sonja; Caldwell, Nicole D.; & Nolen-Hoeksema, Susan (1998). Effects of ruminative and distracting responses to depressed mood on retrieval of autobiographical memories. *Journal of Personality and Social Psychology, 75,* 166–177.

Maas, James B. (1998). *Power sleep.* New York: Villard.

MacArthur Foundation Research Network on Successful Midlife Development (1999). Report of latest findings (Orville G. Brim, director; 2145 14th Avenue, Vero Beach, FL 32960).

Maccoby, Eleanor E. (1998). *The two sexes: Growing up apart, coming together.* Cambridge, MA: Belknap Press/Harvard University Press.

Maccoby, Eleanor E. (2002). Gender and group process: A developmental perspective. *Current Directions in Psychological Science, 11,* 54–58.

MacDonald, D. A. (2000). Spirituality: Description, measurement, and relation to the Five Factor Model of personality. *Journal of Personality, 68*(1), 153–197.

MacKinnon, Donald W. (1968). Selecting students with creative potential. In P. Heist (Ed.), *The creative college student: An unmet challenge.* San Francisco: Jossey-Bass.

Maclean, M. J., & Chown, S. M. (1988). Just world beliefs and attitudes toward helping elderly people: A comparison of British and Canadian university students. *International Journal of Aging and Human Development, 26*(4), 249–260.

MacLean, Paul (1993). Cerebral evolution of emotion. In M. Lewis & J. M. Haviland (Eds.), *Handbook of emotions.* New York: Guilford Press.

Macmillan, Malcolm (2000). *An odd kind of fame: Stories of Phineas Gage.* Cambridge: MIT Press, 2000.

Macrae, C. Neil; Milne, Alan B.; & Bodenhausen, Galen V. (1994). Stereotypes as energy-saving devices: A peek inside the cognitive toolbox. *Journal of Personality and Social Psychology, 66,* 37–47.

Maddux, James E. (1993, Summer). The mythology of psychopathology: A social cognitive view of deviance, difference, and disorder. *General Psychologist, 29,* 34–45.

Maddux, James E. (Ed.) (1995). *Self-efficacy, adaptation, and adjustment: Theory, research, and application.* New York: Plenum.

Maddux, James E. (1996). The social-cognitive construction of difference and disorder. In D. F. Barone, J. E. Maddux, & C. R. Snyder (Eds.), *Social cognitive psychology: History and current domains.* New York: Plenum.

Maddux, James E., & Mundell, Clare E. (1997). Disorders of personality. In V. Derlega, B. Winstead, & W. Jones (Eds.), *Personality: Contemporary theory and research* (2nd ed.). Chicago: Nelson-Hall.

Maguire, Eleanor A.; Gadian, David G.; Johnsrude, Ingrid S.; et al. (2000). Navigation-related structural change in the hippocampi of taxi drivers. *Proceedings of the National Academy of Sciences, 97,* 4398–4403.

Major, Brenda; Spencer, Steven; Schmader, Toni; et al. (1998). Coping with negative stereotypes about intellectual performance: The role of psychological disengagement. *Personality and Social Psychology Bulletin, 24,* 34–50.

Maki, Pauline M.; & Resnick, Susan M. (2000). Longitudinal effects of estrogen replacement therapy on PET cerebral blood flow and cognition. *Neurobiology of Aging, 21,* 373–383.

Malamuth, Neil, & Dean, Karol (1990). Attraction to sexual aggression. In A. Parrot & L. Bechhofer (Eds.), *Acquaintance rape: The hidden crime.* Newark, NJ: Wiley.

Malamuth, Neil M.; Linz, Daniel; Heavey, Christopher L.; et al. (1995). Using the confluence model of sexual aggression to predict men's conflict with women: A 10-year follow-up study. *Journal of Personality and Social Psychology, 69,* 353–369.

Malarkey, William B.; Kiecolt-Glasser, Janice K.; Pearl, Dennis; & Glasser, Ronald (1994). Hostile behavior during marital conflict alters pituitary and adrenal hormones. *Psychosomatic Medicine, 56,* 41–51.

Malaspina, Dolores (2001). Paternal factors and schizophrenia risk: De novo mutations and imprinting. *Schizophrenia Bulletin, 27,* 379–393.

Malenfant, E. C. (2004). Suicide in Canada's immigrant population. *Health Reports, 15*(2), 9–17.

Malinosky-Rummell, Robin, & Hansen, David J. (1993). Long-term consequences of childhood physical abuse. *Psychological Bulletin, 114,* 68–79.

Malnic, B.; Hirono, J.; Sato, T.; & Buck, L. B. (1999). Combinatorial receptor codes for odors. *Cell, 96,* 713–723.

Maquet, Pierre (2001). The role of sleep in learning and memory. *Science, 294,* 1048–1052.

Marcus, Gary F. (1999). *The algebraic mind.* Cambridge, MA: MIT Press.

Marcus, Gary F.; Pinker, Steven; Ullman, Michael; et al. (1992). Overregularization in language acquisition. *Monographs of the Society for Research in Child Development, 57* (Serial No. 228), 1–182.

Marcus-Newhall, Amy; Pedersen, William C.; Carlson, Mike; & Miller, Norman (2000). Displaced aggression is alive and well: A meta-analytic review. *Journal of Personality and Social Psychology, 78,* 670–689.

Marder, Stephen R.; Wirshing, William C.; Mintz, Jim; et al. (1996). Two-year outcome of social-skills training and group psychotherapy for outpatients with schizophrenia. *American Journal of Psychiatry, 153,* 1585–1592.

Marino, Raul, Jr., & Cosgrove, G. Rees (1997). Neurosurgical treatment of neuropsychiatric illness. *Psychiatric Clinics of North America, 20,* 933–943.

Markus, Hazel R., & Kitayama, Shinobu (1991). Culture and the self: Implications for cognition, emotion, and motivation. *Psychological Review, 98,* 224–253.

Markus, Rob; Panhuysen, Geert; Tuiten, Adriaan; & Koppeschaar, Hans (2000). Effects of food on cortisol and mood in vulnerable subjects under controllable and uncontrollable stress. *Physiology and Behavior, 70,* 333–342.

Marlatt, G. Alan (1996). Models of relapse and relapse prevention: A commentary. *Experimental and Clinical Psychopharmacology, 4,* 55–60.

Marlatt, G. Alan; Baer, John S.; Kivlahan, Daniel R.; et al. (1998). Screening and brief intervention for high-risk college student drinkers. *Journal of Consulting and Clinical Psychology, 66,* 604–615.

Marlatt, G. Alan, & Rohsenow, Damaris J. (1980). Cognitive processes in alcohol use: Expectancy and the balanced placebo design. In N. K. Mello (Ed.), *Advances in substance abuse* (Vol. 1). Greenwich, CT: JAI Press.

Marshall, Grant N.; Wortman, Camille B.; Vickers, Ross R., Jr.; et al. (1994). The five-factor model of personality as a framework for personality health research. *Journal of Personality and Social Psychology, 67,* 278–286.

Martin, Carol Lynn; Ruble, Diane N.; & Szkrybalo, Joel (2002). Cognitive theories of early gender development. *Psychological Bulletin, 128,* 903–933.

Martin, Garry, & Pear, Joseph (1999). *Behavior modification: What it is and how to do it* (6th ed.). Upper Saddle River, NJ: Prentice Hall.

Martin, Rod A. (2001). Humor, laughter, and physical health: Methodological issues and research findings. *Psychological Bulletin, 127,* 504–519.

Martino, Gail, & Marks, Lawrence E. (2001). Synesthesia: Strong and weak. *Current Directions in Psychological Science, 10,* 61–69.

Maruta, T.; Colligan R. C.; Malinchoc, M.; & Offord, K. P. (2000). Optimists vs. pessimists: Survival rate among medical patients over a 30-year period. *Mayo Clinic Proceedings, 75,* 140–143.

Masand, P. S. (2000). Side effects of antipsychotics in the elderly. *Journal of Clinical Psychiatry, 61*(Suppl. 8), 43–49.

Maslow, Abraham H. (1970). *Motivation and personality* (2nd ed.). New York: Harper & Row.

Maslow, Abraham H. (1971). *The farther reaches of human nature.* New York: Viking.

Mason, G. (2005, June 11). Legalizing pot: the debate can't be left to Beaver. *Globe and Mail,* Page A8.

Masten, Ann S. (2001). Ordinary magic: Resilience processes in development. *American Psychologist, 56,* 227–238.

Masten, Ann S., & Coatsworth, J. Douglas (1998). The development of competence in favorable and unfavorable environments. *American Psychologist, 53,* 205–220.

Masters, William H., & Johnson, Virginia E. (1966). *Human sexual response.* Boston: Little, Brown.

Masuda, Takahiko, & Nisbett, Richard E. (2001). Attending holistically versus analytically: Comparing the context sensitivity of Japanese and Americans. *Journal of Personality and Social Psychology, 81,* 922–934.

Mather, Mara; Shafir, Eldar; & Johnson, Marcia K. (2000). Misremembrance of options past: Source monitoring and choice. *Psychological Science, 11,* 132–138.

Matsumoto, David (1996). *Culture and psychology.* Pacific Grove, CA: Brooks-Cole.

Matthews, Karen A.; Wing, Rena R.; Kuller, Lewis H.; et al. (1990). Influences of natural menopause on psychological characteristics and symptoms of middle-aged healthy women. *Journal of Consulting and Clinical Psychology, 58,* 345–351.

Maurer, Daphne; Lewis, Terri L.; Brent, Henry P.; & Levin, Alex V. (1999). Rapid improvement in the acuity of infants after visual input. *Science, 286,* 108–110.

Mawhinney, T. C. (1990). Decreasing intrinsic "motivation" with extrinsic rewards: Easier said than done. *Journal of Organizational Behavior Management, 11,* 175–191.

Max, M.; Shanker, Y. G.; Huang, L.; et al. (2001). Tas1r3, encoding a new candidate taste receptor, is allelic to the sweet responsiveness locus Sac. *Nature Genetics, 28,* 58–63.

Maxfield, Michael, & Widom, Cathy S. (1996). The cycle of violence. Revisited 6 years later. *Archives of Pediatric and Adolescent Medicine, 150,* 390–395.

Mayberry, Rachel I., & Nicoladis, Elena (2000). Gesture reflects language development: Evidence from bilingual children. *Current Directions in Psychological Science, 9,* 192–196.

Mayer, John D.; McCormick, Laura J.; & Strong, Sara E. (1995). Mood-congruent memory and natural mood: New evidence. *Personality and Social Psychology Bulletin, 21,* 736–746.

Mayer, John D., & Salovey, Peter (1997). What is emotional intelligence? In P. Salovey & D. Sluyter (Eds.), *Emotional development and emotional intelligence: Implications for educators.* New York: Basic Books.

Mazur, Allen, & Lamb, Theodore A. (1980). Testosterone, status, and mood in human males. *Hormones and Behavior, 14,* 236–246.

Mazza, James J., & Reynolds, William M. (1999). Exposure to violence in young inner-city adolescents: Relationships with suicidal ideation, depression, and PTSD symptomatology. *Journal of Abnormal Child Psychology, 27*, 203–213.

Mazzoni, Giuliana A.; Loftus, Elizabeth F.; & Kirsch, Irving (2001). Changing beliefs about implausible autobiographical events: A little plausibility goes a long way. *Journal of Experimental Psychology: Applied, 7*, 51–59.

Mazzoni, Giuliana A.; Loftus, Elizabeth F.; Seitz, Aaron; & Lynn, Steven J. (1999). Changing beliefs and memories through dream interpretation. *Applied Cognitive Psychology, 13*, 125–144.

McCarthy, John (1997). AI as sport [Review of Kasparov versus Deep Blue: Computer chess comes of age, by Monty Newborn]. *Science, 276*, 1518–1519.

McClearn, Gerald E.; Johanson, Boo; Berg, Stig; et al. (1997). Substantial genetic influence on cognitive abilities in twins 80 or more years old. *Science, 176*, 1560–1563.

McClelland, David C. (1961). *The achieving society.* New York: Free Press.

McClelland, David C. (1987). Characteristics of successful entrepreneurs. *Journal of Creative Behavior, 3*, 219–233.

McClelland, David C.; Atkinson, John W.; Clark, Russell A.; & Lowell, Edgar L. (1953). *The achievement motive.* New York: Appleton-Century-Crofts.

McClelland, James L. (1994). The organization of memory: A parallel distributed processing perspective. *Revue Neurologique, 150*, 570–579.

McClelland, S. (2001, September 17). Child poverty. *Maclean's, September 114*(38), 18–23.

McClintock, Martha K., & Herdt, Gilbert (1996). Rethinking puberty: The development of sexual attraction. *Current Directions in Psychological Science, 6*, 178–183.

McCord, Joan (1989). Another time, another drug. Paper presented at conference on Vulnerability to the Transition from Drug Use to Abuse and Dependence, Rockville, MD.

McCord, Joan (1992). The Cambridge-Somerville study: A pioneering longitudinal-experimental study of delinquency prevention. In J. McCord & R. E. Tremblay (Eds.), *Preventing antisocial behavior: Interventions from birth through adolescence.* New York: Guilford Press.

McCrae, Robert R. (1987). Creativity, divergent thinking, and openness to experience. *Journal of Personality and Social Psychology, 52*, 1258–1265.

McCrae, Robert R.; Costa, Paul T., Jr.; Ostendorf, Fritz; et al. (2000). Nature over nurture: Temperament, personality, and life span development. *Journal of Personality and Social Psychology, 78*, 173–186.

McCusker, J.; Boulenger, J. -P.; Boyer, R.; et al. (1997). Use of health services for anxiety disorders: A multisite study in Quebec. *Canadian Journal of Psychiatry, 42*, 730–736.

McDaniel, Susan H.; Lusterman, Don-David; & Philpot, Carol L. (Eds.) (2001). *Casebook for integrating family therapy: An ecosystemic approach.* Washington, DC: American Psychological Association.

McDonough, Laraine, & Mandler, Jean M. (1994). Very long-term recall in infancy. *Memory, 2*, 339–352.

McElroy, Susan L., & Keck, Paul E., Jr. (2000). Pharmacologic agents for the treatment of acute bipolar mania. *Biological Psychiatry, 48*, 539–557.

McEwen, Bruce S. (1983). Gonadal steroid influences on brain development and sexual differentiation. *Reproductive Physiology IV (International Review of Physiology), 27*, 99–145.

McEwen, Bruce S. (1998). Protective and damaging effects of stress mediators. *New England Journal of Medicine, 338*, 171–179.

McEwen, Bruce S. (2000). Allostasis and allostatic load: Implications for neuropsychopharmacology. *Neuropsychopharmacology, 22*, 108–124.

McFarland, Cathy, & Alvaro, Celeste (2000). The impact of motivation on temporal comparisons: Coping with traumatic events by perceiving personal growth. *Journal of Personality and Social Psychology, 79*, 327–343.

McFarlane, Jessica; Martin, Carol L.; & Williams, Tannis M. (1988). Mood fluctuations: Women versus men and menstrual versus other cycles. *Psychology of Women Quarterly, 12*, 201–223.

McFarlane, Jessica M., & Williams, Tannis M. (1994). Placing premenstrual syndrome in perspective. *Psychology of Women Quarterly, 18*, 339–373.

McGaugh, James L. (1990). Significance and remembrance: The role of neuromodulatory systems. *Psychological Science, 1*, 15–25.

McGlashan, Thomas H., & Hoffman, Ralph E. (2000). Schizophrenia as a disorder of developmentally reduced synaptic connectivity. *Archives of General Psychiatry, 57*, 637–648.

McGlone, Jeannette (1978). Sex differences in functional brain asymmetry. *Cortex, 14*, 122–128.

McGlynn, Susan M. (1990). Behavioral approaches to neuropsychological rehabilitation. *Psychological Bulletin, 108*, 420–441.

McGoldrick, Monica; Gerson, Randy; & Shellenberger, Sylvia (1999). *Genograms: Assessment and intervention* (2nd ed.). New York: W. W. Norton.

McGrath, Ellen; Keita, Gwendolyn P.; Strickland, Bonnie; & Russo, Nancy F. (Eds.) (1990). *Women and depression: Risk factors and treatment issues.* Washington, DC: American Psychological Association.

McGregor, Ian, & Holmes, John G. (1999). How storytelling shapes memory and impressions of relationship events over time. *Journal of Personality and Social Psychology, 76*, 403–419.

McGregor, Ian, & Little, Brian R. (1998). Personal projects, happiness, and meaning: On doing well and being yourself. *Journal of Personality and Social Psychology, 74*, 494–512.

McGue, Matt (1999). The behavioral genetics of alcoholism. *Current Directions in Psychological Science, 8*, 109–115.

McGue, Matt; Bouchard, Thomas J., Jr.; Iacono, William G.; & Lykken, David T. (1993). Behavioral genetics of cognitive ability: A life-span perspective. In R. Plomin & G. E. McClearn (Eds.), *Nature, nurture, and psychology.* Washington, DC: American Psychological Association.

McGue, Matt, & Lykken, David T. (1992). Genetic influence on risk of divorce. *Psychological Science, 3*, 368–373.

McHugh, Paul R. (1993, December). Psychotherapy awry. *American Scholar,* 17–30.

McIntyre, L.; Connor, S. K.; & Warren, J. (2000). Child hunger in Canada: Results of the 1994 National Longitudinal Survey of Children and Youth. *Canadian Medical Association Journal, 163*(8), 961–965.

McKee, Richard D., & Squire, Larry R. (1992). Equivalent forgetting rates in long-term memory for diencephalic and medial temporal lobe amnesia. *Journal of Neuroscience, 12*, 3765–3772.

McKee, Richard D., & Squire, Larry R. (1993). On the development of declarative memory. *Journal of Experimental Psychology: Learning, Memory, and Cognition, 19*, 397–404.

McKelvie, S. J. (1997). The availability heuristic: Effects of fame and gender on the estimated frequency of male and female names. *Journal of Social Psychology, 137*(1), 63–78.

McKemy, D. D.; Neuhausser, W. M.; & Julius, D. (2002). Identification of a cold receptor reveals a general role for TRP channels in thermosensation. *Nature, 416*, 52–58.

McKinlay, John B.; McKinlay, Sonja M.; & Brambilla, Donald (1987). The relative contributions of endocrine changes and social circumstances to depression in mid-aged women. *Journal of Health and Social Behavior, 28,* 345–363.

McMurray, D. W., & Duffy, T. M. (1972). Meaningfulness and pronounceability as chunking units in short-term memory. *Journal of Experimental Psychology, 96*(2), 291–296.

McNally, Richard J. (1994). *Panic disorder: A critical analysis.* New York: Guilford.

McNally, Richard J. (1996). Cognitive bias in the anxiety disorders. In D. A. Hope et al. (Eds.), *Nebraska Symposium on Motivation, 1995: Perspectives on anxiety, panic, and fear.* Lincoln, NE: University of Nebraska Press.

McNally, Richard J. (1998). Panic attacks. In *Encyclopedia of mental health* (Vol. 3). New York: Academic Press.

McNally, Richard J. (2003a). Progress and controversy in the study of posttraumatic stress disorder. *Annual Review of Psychology, 54,* 229–252.

McNally, Richard J. (2003b). *Remembering trauma.* Cambridge, MA: Harvard University Press.

McNamara, J. K., & Wong, B. (2003). Memory for everyday information in students with learning disabilities. *Journal of Learning Disabilities, 36*(5), 394–406.

McNeill, David (1966). Developmental psycholinguistics. In F. L. Smith & G. A. Miller (Eds.), *The genesis of language: A psycholinguistic approach.* Cambridge MA: MIT Press.

Mealey, Linda (2000). *Sex differences: Developmental and evolutionary strategies.* San Diego: Academic Press.

Medawar, Peter B. (1982). *Pluto's republic.* Oxford, England: Oxford University Press.

Mednick, Sarnoff A. (1962). The associative basis of the creative process. *Psychological Review, 69,* 220–232.

Mednick, Sarnoff A.; Huttunen, Matti O.; & Machón, Ricardo (1994). Prenatal influenza infections and adult schizophrenia. *Schizophrenia Bulletin, 20,* 263–267.

Medvec, Victoria H.; Madey, Scott F.; & Gilovich, Thomas (1995). When less is more: Counterfactual thinking and satisfaction among Olympic medalists. *Journal of Personality and Social Psychology, 69,* 603–610.

Meeus, Wim H. J., & Raaijmakers, Quinten A. W. (1995). Obedience in modern society: The Utrecht studies. In A. G. Miller, B. E. Collins, & D. E. Brief (Eds.), *Perspectives on obedience to authority: The legacy of the Milgram experiments. Journal of Social Issues, 51*(3), 155–175.

Meindl, James R., & Lerner, Melvin J. (1985). Exacerbation of extreme responses to an out-group. *Journal of Personality and Social Psychology, 47,* 71–84.

Meltzoff, Andrew N., & Gopnik, Alison (1993). The role of imitation in understanding persons and developing a theory of mind. In S. Baron-Cohen, H. Tager-Flusberg, & D. Cohen (Eds.), *Understanding other minds.* New York: Oxford University Press.

Melzack, Ronald (1992, April). Phantom limbs. *Scientific American, 266,* 120–126. [Reprinted in the special issue *Mysteries of the Mind,* 1997.]

Melzack, Ronald (1993). Pain: Past, present and future. *Canadian Journal of Experimental Psychology, 47,* 615–629.

Melzack, Ronald, & Wall, Patrick D. (1965). Pain mechanisms: A new theory. *Science, 13,* 971–979.

Mennella, Julie A.; Jagnow, C. P.; & Beauchamp, Gary K. (2001). Prenatal and postnatal flavor learning by human infants. *Pediatrics, 107,* E88.

Menon, Tanya; Morris, Michael W.; Chiu, Chi-yue; & Hone, Ying-yi (1999). Culture and the construal of agency: Attribution to individual versus group dispositions. *Journal of Personality and Social Psychology, 76,* 701–717.

Merikle, Philip M., & Skanes, Heather E. (1992). Subliminal self-help audiotapes: A search for placebo effects. *Journal of Applied Psychology, 77,* 772–776.

Merskey, Harold (1992). The manufacture of personalities: The production of MPD. *British Journal of Psychiatry, 160,* 327–340.

Merskey, Harold (1995). The manufacture of personalities: The production of multiple personality disorder. In L. M. Cohen, J. N. Berzoff, & M. R. Elin (Eds.), *Dissociative identity disorder: Theoretical and treatment controversies.* Northvale, NJ: Aronson.

Merton, Robert K. (1948). The self-fulfilling prophecy. *Antioch Review, 8,* 193–210.

Mesquita, Batja, & Frijda, Nico H. (1992). Cultural variations in emotions: A review. *Psychological Bulletin, 112,* 179–204.

Metalsky, Gerald I.; Joiner, Thomas E., Jr.; Hardin, Tammy S.; & Abramson, Lyn Y. (1993). Depressive reactions to failure in a naturalistic setting: A test of the hopelessness and self-esteem theories of depression. *Journal of Abnormal Psychology, 102,* 101–109.

Meyer, Gregory J.; Finn, Stephen E.; Eyde, Lorraine D.; et al. (2001). Psychological testing and psychological assessment. *American Psychologist, 56,* 128–165.

Meyer-Bahlburg, Heino F. L.; Ehrhardt, Anke A.; Rosen, Laura R.; et al. (1995). Prenatal estrogens and the development of homosexual orientation. *Developmental Psychology, 31,* 12–21.

Mickelson, Kristin D.; Kessler, Ronald C.; & Shaver, Phillip R. (1997). Adult attachment in a nationally representative sample. *Journal of Personality and Social Psychology, 73,* 1092–1106.

Milgram, Stanley (1963). Behavioral study of obedience. *Journal of Abnormal and Social Psychology, 67,* 371–378.

Milgram, Stanley (1974). *Obedience to authority: An experimental view.* New York: Harper & Row.

Miller, G. E. (2004). Frontier masculinity in the oil industry: The experience of women engineers. *Gender, Work and Organizations, 11*(1), 47–73.

Miller, George A. (1956). The magical number seven, plus or minus two: Some limits on our capacity for processing information. *Psychological Review, 63,* 81–97.

Miller, Gregory E., & Cohen, Sheldon (2001). Psychological interventions and the immune system: A meta-analytic review and critique. *Health Psychology, 20,* 47–63.

Miller, Inglis J., & Reedy, Frank E. (1990). Variations in human taste bud density and taste intensity perception. *Physiology and Behavior, 47,* 1213–1219.

Miller, Neal E. (1978). Biofeedback and visceral learning. *Annual Review of Psychology, 29,* 421–452.

Miller, Todd Q.; Smith, Timothy W.; Turner, Charles W.; et al. (1996). A meta-analytic review of research on hostility and physical health. *Psychological Bulletin, 119,* 322–348.

Miller-Jones, Dalton (1989). Culture and testing. *American Psychologist, 44,* 360–366.

Milner, Brenda (1970). Memory and the temporal regions of the brain. In K. H. Pribram & D. E. Broadbent (Eds.), *Biology of memory.* New York: Academic Press.

Milner, J. S., & McCanne, T. R. (1991). Neuropsychological correlates of physical child abuse. In J. S. Milner (Ed.), *Neuropsychology of aggression.* Norwell, MA: Kluwer Academic.

Milton, Julie, & Wiseman, Richard (1999). Does Psi exist? Lack of replication of an anomalous process of information transfer. *Psychological Bulletin, 125,* 387–391.

Milton, Julie, & Wiseman, Richard (2001). Does psi exist? Reply to Storm and Ertel (2001). *Psychological Bulletin, 127,* 434–438.

Minuchin, Salvador (1984). *Family kaleidoscope*. Cambridge, MA: Harvard University Press.

Mischel, Walter (1973). Toward a cognitive social learning reconceptualization of personality. *Psychological Review, 80,* 252–253.

Mischel, Walter, & Shoda, Yuichi (1995). A cognitive affective system theory of personality: Reconceptualizing situations, dispositions, dynamics, and invariance in personality structure. *Psychological Review, 102,* 246–268.

Mishkin, M.; Suzuki, W. A.; Gadian, D. G.; & Vargha-Khadem, F. (1997). Hierarchical organization of cognitive memory. *Philosophical Transactions of the Royal Society of London, B: Biological Science, 352,* 1461–1467.

Mistry, Jayanthi, & Rogoff, Barbara (1994). Remembering in cultural context. In W. J. Lonner & R. Malpass (Eds.), *Psychology and culture.* Needham Heights, MA: Allyn & Bacon.

Mithers, Carol L. (1994). *Reasonable insanity: A true story of the seventies.* Reading, MA: Addison-Wesley.

Miyamoto, Yuri, & Kitayama, Shinobu (2002). Cultural variation in correspondence bias: The critical role of attitude diagnosticity of socially constrained behavior. *Journal of Personality and Social Psychology, 83,* 1239–1248.

Modigliani, Andre, & Rochat, François (1995). The role of interaction sequences and the timing of resistance in shaping obedience and defiance to authority. In A. G. Miller, B. E. Collins, & D. E. Brief (Eds.), Perspectives on obedience to authority: The legacy of the Milgram experiments. *Journal of Social Issues, 51*(3), 107–125.

Moen, Phyllis (2001). Gender, age and the life course. In R. H. Binstock & L. K. George (Eds.), *Handbook of aging and the social sciences* (5th ed.). San Diego, CA: Academic Press.

Moen, Phyllis, & Wethington, Elaine (1999). Midlife development in a life course context. In S. L. Willis & J. E. Reid (Eds.), *Life in the middle: Psychological and social development in middle age.* San Diego, CA: Academic Press.

Moffitt, Terrie E. (1993). Adolescence-limited and life-course-persistent antisocial behavior: A developmental taxonomy. *Psychological Review, 100,* 674–701.

Mohr, Cynthia; Armeli, Stephen; Tennen, Howard; et al. (2001). Daily interpersonal experiences, context, and alcohol consumption: Crying in your beer and toasting good times. *Journal of Personality and Social Psychology, 80,* 489–500.

Monahan, Jennifer L.; Murphy, Sheila T.; & Zajonc, R. B. (2000). Subliminal mere exposure: Specific, general, and diffuse effects. *Psychological Science, 11,* 462–466.

Moncrieff, Joanna (2001). Are antidepressants overrated? A review of methodological problems in antidepressant trials. *Journal of Nervous and Mental Disease, 189,* 288–295.

Montmayeur, J. P.; Liberies, S. D.; Matsunami, H.; & Buck, L. B. (2001). A candidate taste receptor gene near a sweet taste locus. *Nature Neuroscience, 4,* 492–498.

Moore, Robert Y. (1997). Circadian rhythms: Basic neurobiology and clinical applications. *Annual Review of Medicine, 48,* 253–266.

Moore, Timothy E. (1992, Spring). Subliminal perception: Facts and fallacies. *Skeptical Inquirer, 16,* 273–281.

Moore, Timothy E. (1995). Subliminal self-help auditory tapes: An empirical test of perceptual consequences. *Canadian Journal of Behavioural Science, 27,* 9–20.

Moore, Timothy E., & Pepler, Debra J. (2004). Wounding words: Maternal verbal aggression and children's adjustment. *Journal of Family Violence.*

Mor, Nilly, & Winquist, Jennifer (2002). Self-focused attention and negative affect: A meta-analysis. *Psychological Bulletin, 128,* 638–662.

Morelli, Gilda A.; Rogoff, Barbara; Oppenheim, David; & Goldsmith, Denise (1992). Cultural variation in infants' sleeping arrangements: Questions of independence. *Developmental Psychology, 28,* 604–613.

Morrison, Ann M., & Von Glinow, Mary Ann (1990). Women and minorities in management. *American Psychologist, 45,* 200–208.

Morrison, T. G.; Morrison, M. A.; Hopkins, C.; & Rowan E. T. (2004). Muscle mania: Development of a new scale examining drive for muscularity in Canadian males. *Psychology of Men and Masculinity, 5*(1), 30–39.

Moscovici, Serge (1985). Social influence and conformity. In G. Lindzey & E. Aronson (Eds.), *Handbook of social psychology* (Vol. 2, 3rd ed.). New York: Random House.

Moscovitch, Morris; Winocur, Gordon; & Behrmann, Marlene (1997). What is special about face recognition? Nineteen experiments on a person with visual object agnosia and dyslexia but normal face recognition. *Journal of Cognitive Neuroscience, 9,* 555–604.

Mozell, Maxwell M.; Smith, Bruce P.; Smith, Paul E.; Sullivan, Richard L.; & Swender, Philip (1969). Nasal chemoreception in flavor identification. *Archives of Otolaryngology, 90,* 367–373.

Mroczek, Daniel K., & Kolarz, Christian M. (1998). The effect of age on positive and negative affect: A developmental perspective on happiness. *Journal of Personality and Social Psychology, 75,* 1333–1349.

Mueller, Claudia M., & Dweck, Carol S. (1998). Praise for intelligence can undermine children's motivation and performance. *Journal of Personality and Social Psychology, 75,* 33–52.

Mukamal, Kenneth J.; Conigrove, Katherine M; Mittleman, Murray A.; et al. (2003). Roles of drinking pattern and type of alcohol consumed in coronary heart disease in men. *New England Journal of Medicine, 348,* 109–118.

Müller, Ralph-Axel; Courchesne, Eric; & Allen, Greg (1998). The cerebellum: So much more. [Letter.] *Science, 282,* 879–880.

Murphy, Sheila T.; Monahan, Jennifer L.; & Zajonc, R. B. (1995). Additivity of nonconscious affect: Combined effects of priming and exposure. *Journal of Personality and Social Psychology, 69,* 589–602.

Myers, Ronald E., & Sperry, R. W. (1953). Interocular transfer of a visual form discrimination habit in cats after section of the optic chiasm and corpus callosum. *Anatomical Record, 115,* 351–352.

Nash, Michael R. (1987). What, if anything, is regressed about hypnotic age regression? A review of the empirical literature. *Psychological Bulletin, 102,* 42–52.

Nash, Michael R. (2001, July). The truth and the hype of hypnosis. *Scientific American, 285,* 46–49, 52–55.

Nash, Michael R., & Nadon, Robert (1997). Hypnosis. In D. L. Faigman, D. Kaye, M. J. Saks, & J. Sanders (Eds.), *Modern scientific evidence: The law and science of expert testimony.* St. Paul, MN: West.

National Science Board (2000). *Science and engineering indicators 2000.*

National Science Foundation. Chapter 8: Science and technology: Attitudes and public understanding. Arlington, VA: [A reprint of the relevant section of this chapter can be found in the January/February 2001 issue of *Skeptical Inquirer*, pp. 12–15.]

Needleman, Herbert L.; Riess, Julie A.; Tobin, Michael J.; et al. (1996). Bone lead levels and delinquent behavior. *Journal of the American Medical Association, 275,* 363–369.

Neher, Andrew (1996). Jung's theory of archetypes: A critique. *Journal of Humanistic Psychology, 36,* 61–91.

Neisser, Ulric (Ed.) (1998). *The rising curve: Long-term gains in IQ and related measures.* Washington, DC: American Psychological Association.

Neisser, Ulric, & Harsch, Nicole (1992). Phantom flashbulbs: False recollections of hearing the news about Challenger. In E. Winograd & U. Neisser (Eds.), *Affect and accuracy in recall: Studies of "flashbulb memories."* New York: Cambridge University Press.

Nelson, Thomas O., & Dunlosky, John (1991). When people's judgments of learning (JOLs) are extremely accurate at predicting subsequent recall: The "delayed JOL effect." *Psychological Science, 2,* 267–270.

Nelson, Thomas O., & Leonesio, R. Jacob (1988). Allocation of self-paced study time and the "labor in vain effect." *Journal of Experimental Psychology: Learning, Memory, and Cognition, 14,* 676–686.

Netting, Jessa (2001, April 7). Gray matters: Neurons get top billing, but lesser-known brain cells also star. *Science News, 159,* 222–223.

Neugarten, Bernice (1979). Time, age, and the life cycle. *American Journal of Psychiatry, 136,* 887–894.

Neumann, Roland, & Strack, Fritz (2000). "Mood contagion": The automatic transfer of mood between persons. *Journal of Personality and Social Psychology, 79,* 211–223.

Newcombe, Nora S.; Drummey, Anna B.; Fox, Nathan A.; et al. (2000). Remembering early childhood: How much, how, and why (or why not). *Current Directions in Psychological Science, 9,* 55–58.

Newman, Leonard S., & Baumeister, Roy F. (1996). Toward an explanation of the UFO abduction phenomenon: Hypnotic elaboration, extraterrestrial sadomasochism, and spurious memories. *Psychological Inquiry, 7,* 99–126.

Newman, Lucille F., & Buka, Stephen (1991, Spring). Clipped wings. *American Educator,* 27–33, 42.

NICHD Early Child Care Research Network (1997). The effects of infant-child care on infant-mother attachment security (Results of the NICHD study of early child care). *Child Development, 68,* 860–879.

NICHD Early Child Care Research Network (2002). Child-care structure–process–outcome: Direct and indirect effects of child-care quality on young children's development. *Psychological Science, 13,* 199–206.

Nickerson, Raymond A., & Adams, Marilyn Jager (1979). Long-term memory for a common object. *Cognitive Psychology, 11,* 287–307.

Nickerson, Raymond S. (1998). Confirmation bias: A ubiquitous phenomenon in many guises. *Review of General Psychology, 2,* 175–220.

Nicol, J. (1998). Mystery At Gagetown. *Maclean's, 111*(28), 22.

Nigg, Joel T., & Goldsmith, H. Hill (1994). Genetics of personality disorders: Perspectives from personality and psychopathology research. *Psychological Bulletin, 115,* 346–380.

NIH Technology Assessment Panel on Integration of Behavioral and Relaxation Approaches into the Treatment of Chronic Pain and Insomnia (1996). *Journal of the American Medical Association, 276,* 313–318.

Nisbett, Richard A. (2003). *The geography of thought: How Asians and westerners think differently—and why.* New York: The Free Press.

Nisbett, Richard E., & Ross, Lee (1980). *Human inference: Strategies and shortcomings of social judgment.* Englewood Cliffs, NJ: Prentice-Hall.

Nolen-Hoeksema, Susan (2002). Gender differences in depression. In I. H. Gotlib & C. Hammen (Eds.), *Handbook of depression.* New York: Guilford.

Nonaka, S.; Hough, C. J.; & Chuang, De-Maw (1998, March 3). Chronic lithium treatment robustly protects neurons in the central nervous system against excitotoxicity by inhibiting N-methyl-D-aspartate receptor-mediated calcium influx. *Proceedings of the National Academy of Sciences, 95,* 2642–2647.

Norman, Donald A. (1988). *The psychology of everyday things.* New York: Basic Books.

North, C. S.; Nixon, S. J.; Shariat, S.; et al. (1999). Psychiatric disorders among survivors of the Oklahoma City bombing. *Journal of the American Medical Association, 282,* 755–762.

Nunez, Narina; Poole, Debra A.; & Memon, Amina (2002). Psychology's two cultures revisited: Implications for the integration of science with practice. *Scientific Review of Mental Health Practice, 1.*

Nunn, J. A.; Gregory, L. J.; Brammer, M.; et al. (2002). Functional magnetic resonance imaging of synesthesia: Activation of V4/V8 by spoken words. *Nature Neuroscience, 5,* 371–375.

Ó Scalaidhe, Séamas P.; Wilson, Fraser A. W.; & Goldman-Rakic, Patricia S. (1997). A real segregation of face-processing neurons in prefrontal cortex. *Science, 278,* 1135–1138.

Oatley, Keith (1990). Do emotional states produce irrational thinking? In K. J. Gilhooly, M. T. G. Keane, R. H. Logie, & G. Erdos (Eds.), *Lines of thinking* (Vol. 2). New York: Wiley.

Oatley, Keith, & Duncan, Elaine (1994). The experience of emotions in everyday life. *Cognition and Emotion, 8,* 369–381.

Oatley, Keith, & Jenkins, Jennifer M. (1996). *Understanding emotions.* Cambridge, MA: Blackwell.

Ofshe, Richard J., & Watters, E. (1994). *Making monsters: False memory, psychotherapy, and sexual hysteria.* New York: Scribners.

Ogden, Jenni A., & Corkin, Suzanne (1991). Memories of H. M. In W. C. Abraham, M. C. Corballis, & K. G. White (Eds.), *Memory mechanisms: A tribute to G. V. Goddard.* Hillsdale, NJ: Erlbaum.

O'Hanlon, Bill (1994, November/December). The third wave. *Family Therapy Networker,* 18–29.

Öhman, Arne, & Mineka, Susan (2001). Fears, phobias, and preparedness: Toward an evolved module of fear and fear learning. *Psychological Review, 108,* 483–522.

Öhman, Arne, & Mineka, Susan (2003). The malicious serpent: Snakes as a prototypical stimulus for an evolved module of fear. *Current Directions in Psychological Science, 12,* 5–9.

Okonkwo, Rachel U. N. (1997). Moral development and culture in Kohlberg's theory: A Nigerian (Igbo) evidence. *IFE Psychologia: An International Journal, 5,* 117–128.

Olds, James (1975). Mapping the mind onto the brain. In F. G. Worden, J. P. Swazy, & G. Adelman (Eds.), *The neurosciences: Paths of discovery.* Cambridge, MA: Colonial Press.

Olds, James, & Milner, Peter (1954). Positive reinforcement produced by electrical stimulation of septal area and other regions of the rat brain. *Journal of Comparative and Physiological Psychology, 47,* 419–429.

Oliver, Mary Beth, & Hyde, Janet S. (1993). Gender differences in sexuality: A meta-analysis. *Psychological Bulletin, 114,* 29–51.

Olujic, M. B. (1998). Embodiment of terror: Gendered violence in peacetime and wartime in Croatia and Bosnia-Herzegovina. *Medical Anthropology Quarterly, 12,* 31–50.

O'Rahilly, Ronan, & Müller, Fabiola (2001). *Human embryology and teratology.* New York: Wiley.

Orlinsky, David E., & Howard, Kenneth I. (1994). Unity and diversity among psychotherapies: A comparative perspective. In B. Bongar & L. E. Beutler (Eds.), *Foundations of psychotherapy: Theory, research, and practice*. New York: Oxford University Press.

O'Sullivan, L. F., & Allgeier, Elizabeth R. (1998). Feigning sexual desire: Consenting to unwanted sexual activity in heterosexual dating relationships. *Journal of Sex Research, 35,* 234–243.

Overeem, S.; Mignot, E.; Gert van Dijk, J.; & Lammers, G. J. (2001). Narcolepsy: clinical features, new pathophysiologic insights, and future perspectives. *Journal of Clinical Neurophysiology, 18,* 78–105.

Ozer, Emily J.; Best, Suzanne R.; Lipsey, Tami L.; & Weiss, Daniel S. (2003). Predictors of posttraumatic stress disorder and symptoms in adults: A meta-analysis. *Psychological Bulletin, 129,* 52–73.

Page, Gayle G.; Ben-Eliyahu, Shamgar; Yirmiya, Raz; & Liebeskind, John C. (1993). Morphine attenuates surgery-induced enhancement of metastatic colonization in rats. *Pain, 54,* 21–28.

Palmer, T. D.; Schartz, P. H.; Taupin, P.; et al. (2001). Cell culture. Progenitor cells from human brain after death. *Nature, 411,* 42–43.

Panksepp, Jaak (1998). Attention deficit hyperactivity disorders, psychostimulants, and intolerance of childhood playfulness: A tragedy in the making? *Current Directions in Psychological Science, 7,* 91–98.

Parikh, S. V.; Lin, E.; & Lesage, A. D. (1997). Mental health treatment in Ontario: Selected comparisons between the primary care and specialty sectors. *Canadian Journal of Psychiatry, 42,* 929–934

Park, J. H.; Faulkner, J.; & Schaller, M. (2003). Evolved disease-avoidance processes and contemporary anti-social behavior: Prejudicial attitudes and avoidance of people with physical disabilities. *Journal of Nonverbal Behavior, 27*(2), 65–87.

Park, Robert L. (2000). *Voodoo science: The road from foolishness to fraud.* New York: Oxford University Press.

Parker, Elizabeth S.; Birnbaum, Isabel M.; & Noble, Ernest P. (1976). Alcohol and memory: Storage and state dependency. *Journal of Verbal Learning and Verbal Behavior, 15,* 691–702.

Parker, Gordon; Parker, Kay; & Eyers, Kerrie (2003). Cognitive behavior therapy for depression: Choose horses for courses. *American Journal of Psychiatry, 160,* 825–834.

Parker, Gwendolyn M. (1997). *Trespassing: My sojourn in the halls of privilege.* Boston: Houghton Mifflin.

Parlee, Mary B. (1982). Changes in moods and activation levels during the menstrual cycle in experimentally naive subjects. *Psychology of Women Quarterly, 7,* 119–131.

Parlee, Mary B. (1994). The social construction of premenstrual syndrome: A case study of scientific discourse as cultural contestation. In M. G. Winkler & L. B. Cole (Eds.), *The good body: Asceticism in contemporary culture.* New Haven, CT: Yale University Press.

Patten, S. B., & Beck, C. A. (2004). Major depression and mental health care utilization in Canada: 1994 to 2000. *Canadian Journal of Psychiatry, 49*(5), 303–309.

Patterson, Charlotte J. (1992). Children of lesbian and gay parents. *Child Development, 63,* 1025–1042.

Patterson, Charlotte J. (1995). Sexual orientation and human development: An overview. *Developmental Psychology, 31,* 3–11.

Patterson, Francine, & Linden, Eugene (1981). *The education of Koko.* New York: Holt, Rinehart and Winston.

Patterson, Gerald R.; Forgatch, Marion S.; Yoerger, Karen L.; & Stoolmiller, Mike (1998). Variables that initiate and maintain an early-onset trajectory for juvenile offending. *Development and Psychopathology, 10,* 531–547.

Patterson, Gerald R.; Reid, John; & Dishion, Thomas (1992). *Antisocial boys.* Eugene, OR: Castalia.

Paul, Richard W. (1984, September). Critical thinking: Fundamental to education for a free society. *Educational Leadership,* 4–14.

Paunonen, Sampo V. (2003). Big Five factors or personality and replicated predictions of behavior. *Journal of Personality and Social Psychology, 81,* 524–539.

Paunonen, Sampo V., & Ashton, Michael C. (2001). Big Five factors and facets and the prediction of behavior. *Journal of Personality and Social Psychology, 81,* 524–539.

Pavlov, Ivan P. (1927). *Conditioned reflexes* (G. V. Anrep, Trans.). London: Oxford University Press.

Pearlin, Leonard (1982). Discontinuities in the study of aging. In T. K. Hareven & K. J. Adams (Eds.), *Aging and life course transitions: An interdisciplinary perspective.* New York: Guilford.

Pearson, M. L. (1997). Childhood trauma, adult trauma, and dissociation. *Dissociation: Progress in the Dissociative Disorders, 10*(1), 58–62.

Peele, Stanton, & Brodsky, Archie, with Mary Arnold (1991). *The truth about addiction and recovery.* New York: Simon & Schuster.

Peier, A. M.; Moqrich, A.; Hergarden, A. C.; et al. (2002). A TRP channel that senses cold stimuli and menthol. *Cell, 108,* 705–715.

Pelletier, M.; Bouthillier, A.; Lévesque, J.; et al. (2003). Separate neural circuits for primary emotions? Brain activity during self-induced sadness and happiness in professional actors. *Neuroreport: For Rapid Communication in Neuroscience Research, 14*(8), 1111–1116.

Peng, Kaiping, & Nisbett, Richard E. (1999). Culture, dialectics, and reasoning about contradiction. *American Psychologist, 54,* 741–754.

Pennebaker, James W. (1997). Writing about emotional experiences as a therapeutic process. *Psychological Science, 8,* 162–166.

Pennebaker, James W.; Colder, Michelle; & Sharp, Lisa K. (1990). Accelerating the coping process. *Journal of Personality and Social Psychology, 58,* 528–527.

Pennebaker, James W.; Kiecolt-Glaser, Janice; & Glaser, Ronald (1988). Disclosure of traumas and immune function: Health implications for psychotherapy. *Journal of Consulting and Clinical Psychology, 56,* 239–245.

Peplau, Letitia Anne (2002). Current research on gender and sexuality. Invited Master Lecture presented at the annual meeting of the American Psychological Association, Chicago.

Peplau, Letitia Anne, & Spalding, Leah R. (2000). The close relationships of lesbians, gay men and bisexuals. In C. Hendrick & S. Hendrick (Eds.), *Close relationships: A sourcebook.* Thousand Oaks, CA: Sage.

Peplau, Letitia Anne; Spalding, Leah R.; Conley, Terri D.; & Veniegas, Rosemary C. (2000). The development of sexual orientation in women. *Annual Review of Sex Research, 10,* 70–99.

Pepperberg, Irene (2000). *The Alex studies: Cognitive and communicative abilities of grey parrots.* Cambridge, MA: Harvard University Press.

Perry, Samuel W., & Heidrich, George (1982). Management of pain during debridement: A survey of U.S. burn units. *Pain, 13,* 267–280.

Persinger, M. A., & Makarec, K. (1987). Possible learned detection of exogenous brain frequency electromagnetic fields: A case study. *Perceptual and Motor Skills, 65,* 444–446.

Persons, Jacqueline; Davidson, Joan; & Tompkins, Michael A. (2001). *Essential components of cognitive-behavior therapy for depression.* Washington, DC: American Psychological Association.

Pert, Candace B., & Snyder, Solomon H. (1973). Opiate receptor: Demonstration in nervous tissue. *Science, 179,* 1011–1014.

Peterson, Christopher (2000). The future of optimism. *American Psychologist, 55,* 44–55.

Peterson, Christopher; Seligman, Martin E. P.; Yurko, Karen H.; et al. (1998). Catastrophizing and untimely death. *Psychological Science, 9,* 127–130.

Peterson, Lloyd R., & Peterson, Margaret J. (1959). Short-term retention of individual verbal items. *Journal of Experimental Psychology, 58,* 193–198.

Petrie, Keith J.; Booth, Roger J.; & Pennebaker, James W. (1998). The immunological effects of thought suppression. *Journal of Personality and Social Psychology, 75,* 1264–1272.

Pettigrew, Thomas F. (1998). Intergroup contact theory. *Annual Review of Psychology, 49,* 65–85. Palo Alto, CA: Annual Reviews.

Pfungst, Oskar (1911/1965). *Clever Hans (The horse of Mr. von Osten): A contribution to experimental animal and human psychology.* New York: Holt, Rinehart and Winston.

Phillips, Micheal D.; Lowe, M. J.; Lurito, J. T.; et al. (2001). Temporal lobe activation demonstrates sex-based differences during passive listening. *Radiology, 220,* 202–207.

Phinney, Jean S. (1990). Ethnic identity in adolescents and adults: Review of research. *Psychological Bulletin, 108,* 499–514.

Phinney, Jean S. (1996). When we talk about American ethnic groups, what do we mean? *American Psychologist, 51,* 918–927.

Piaget, Jean (1929/1960). *The child's conception of the world.* Paterson, NJ: Littlefield, Adams.

Piaget, Jean (1932). *The moral judgment of the child.* New York: Macmillan.

Piaget, Jean (1952a). *The origins of intelligence in children.* New York: International Universities Press.

Piaget, Jean (1952b). *Play, dreams, and imitation in childhood.* New York: W. W. Norton.

Piaget, Jean (1984). Piaget's theory. In P. Mussen (series Ed.) & W. Kessen (vol. Ed.), *Handbook of child psychology: Vol. 1. History, theory, and methods* (4th ed.). New York: Wiley.

Pincus, Tamar, & Morley, Stephen (2001). Cognitive-processing bias in chronic pain: A review and integration. *Psychological Bulletin, 127,* 599–617.

Pinel, John P. J.; Assanand, Sunaina; & Lehman, Darrin R. (2000). Hunger, eating, and ill health. *American Psychologist, 55,* 1105–1116.

Pinker, Steven (1994). *The language instinct: How the mind creates language.* New York: Morrow.

Pinker, Steven (1999). *Words and rules: The ingredients of language.* New York: Basic Books. Poulin-Dubois et al., 1998.

Pittenger, David J. (1993). The utility of the Myers-Briggs Type Indicator. *Review of Educational Research, 63,* 467–488.

Plant, E. Ashby, & Devine, Patricia G. (1998). Internal and external motivation to respond without prejudice. *Journal of Personality and Social Psychology, 75,* 811–832.

Plant, E. Ashby; Hyde, Janet S.; Keltner, Dacher; & Devine, Patricia G. (2000). The gender stereotyping of emotions. *Psychology of Women Quarterly, 24,* 81–92.

Plomin, Robert (1989). Environment and genes: Determinants of behavior. *American Psychologist, 44,* 105–111.

Plomin, Robert; Asbury, Kathryn; & Dunn, Judith F. (2001). Why are children in the same family so different? Nonshared environment a decade later. *Canadian Journal of Psychiatry, 46,* 225–233.

Plomin, Robert; Corley, Robin; DeFries, J. C.; & Fulker, D. W. (1990). Individual differences in television viewing in early childhood: Nature as well as nurture. *Psychological Science, 1,* 371–377.

Plomin, Robert, & Crabbe, John (2000). DNA. *Psychological Bulletin, 126,* 806–828.

Plomin, Robert, & DeFries, John C. (1985). *Origins of individual differences in infancy: The Colorado Adoption Project.* New York: Academic Press.

Plomin, Robert; DeFries, John C.; McClearn, Gerald E.; & McGuffin, Peter (2001). *Behavioral genetics* (4th ed.). New York: Worth.

Plomin, Robert, & McGuffin, Peter (2003). Psychopathology in the postgenomic era. *Annual Review of Psychology, 54,* 205–228.

Plotsky, Paul M.; Owens, Michael J.; & Nemeroff, Charles B. (1998). Psychoneuroendocrinology of depression: Hypothalamic-pituitary-adrenal axis. *Psychoneuroendocrinology, 21,* 293–307.

Pollak, Richard (1997). *The creation of Dr. B: A biography of Bruno Bettelheim.* New York: Simon & Schuster.

Polusny, Melissa A., & Follette, Victoria M. (1996). Remembering childhood sexual abuse: A national survey of psychologists' clinical practices, beliefs, and personal experiences. *Professional Psychology: Research and Practice, 27,* 41–52.

Poole, Debra A. (1995). Strolling fuzzy-trace theory through eyewitness testimony (or vice versa). *Learning and Individual Differences, 7,* 87–93.

Poole, Debra A., & Lamb, Michael E. (1998). *Investigative interviews of children.* Washington, DC: American Psychological Association.

Poole, Debra A.; Lindsay, D. Stephen; Memon, Amina; & Bull, Ray (1995). Psychotherapy and the recovery of memories of childhood sexual abuse: U.S. and British practitioners' opinions, practices, and experiences. *Journal of Consulting and Clinical Psychology, 63,* 426–437.

Poole, G. D.; Poon, C.; Achille, M.; et al. (2001). Social support for prostate cancer patients: The effect of support groups. *Journal of Psychosocial Oncology, 19*(2), 1–16.

Pope, Harrison G., Jr.; Phillips, Katharine A.; & Olivardia, Roberto (2000). *The Adonis complex: The secret crisis of male body obsession.* New York: Free Press.

Pope, Kenneth S. (1996). Memory, abuse, and science: Questioning claims about the false memory syndrome epidemic. *American Psychologist, 51,* 957–974.

Portenoy, Russell K. (1994). Opioid therapy for chronic nonmalignant pain: Current status. In H. L. Fields & J. C. Liebeskind (Eds.), *Progress in pain research and management. Pharmacological approaches to the treatment of chronic pain: Vol. 1.* Seattle: International Association for the Study of Pain.

Porter, S.; Campbell, M. A.; Birt, A. R.; & Woodworth, M. T. (2003). "He said, she said": A psychological perspective on historical memory evidence in the courtroom. *Canadian Psychology, 44*(3), 190–206.

Postmes, Tom, & Spears, Russell (1998). Deindividuation and antinormative behavior: A meta-analysis. *Psychological Bulletin, 123,* 238–259.

Postmes, Tom; Spears, Russell; & Cihangir, Sezgin (2001). Quality of decision making and group norms. *Journal of Personality and Social Psychology, 80,* 918–930.

Potter, W. James (1987). Does television viewing hinder academic achievement among adolescents? *Human Communication Research, 14,* 27–46.

Powell, Russel A., & Boer, Douglas P. (1995). Did Freud misinterpret reported memories of sexual abuse as fantasies? *Psychological Reports, 77,* 563–570.

Pratkanis, Anthony, & Aronson, Elliot (2001). *The age of propaganda.* (Rev. ed.). New York: W. H. Freeman.

Premack, David, & Premack, Ann James (1983). *The mind of an ape.* New York: Norton.

Prochaska, James O.; Norcross, John C.; & DiClemente, Carlo C. (1994). *Changing for good.* New York: Morrow.

Pynoos, R. S., & Nader, K. (1989). Children's memory and proximity to violence. *Journal of the American Academy of Child and Adolescent Psychiatry, 28,* 236–241.

Quinn, Diane M., & Spencer, Steven J. (2001). The interference of stereotype threat with women's generation of mathematical problem-solving strategies. *Journal of Social Issues, 57,* 55–71.

Quinn, Paul C. (2002). Category representation in young infants. *Current Directions in Psychological Science, 11,* 66–70.

Radetsky, Peter (1991, April). The brainiest cells alive. *Discover, 12,* 82–85, 88, 90.

Räikkönen, Katri; Matthews, Karen A.; Flory, Janine D.; et al. (1999). Effects of optimism, pessimism, and trait anxiety on ambulatory blood pressure and mood during everyday life. *Journal of Personality and Social Psychology, 76,* 104–113.

Raine, Adrian (1996). Autonomic nervous system factors underlying disinhibited, antisocial, and violent behavior. Biosocial perspectives and treatment implications. *Annals of the New York Academy of Sciences, 794,* 46–59.

Raine, Adrian; Brennan, Patricia; & Mednick, Sarnoff A. (1994). Birth complications combined with early maternal rejection at age one year predispose to violent crime at age 18 years. *Archives of General Psychiatry, 51,* 984–988.

Raine, Adrian; Lencz, Todd; Bihrle, Susan; LaCasse, Lori; & Colletti, Patrick (2000). Reduced prefrontal gray matter volume and reduced autonomic activity in antisocial personality disorder. *Archives of General Psychiatry, 57,* 119–127.

Raine, Adrian, & Liu, Jiang-Hong (1998). Biological predispositions to violence and their implications for biosocial treatment and prevention. *Psychology, Crime & Law, 4,* 107–125.

Raine, Adrian; Meloy, J. R.; Bihrle, S.; et al. (1998). Reduced prefrontal and increased subcortical brain functioning assessed using positron emission tomography in predatory and affective murderers. *Behavioral Science and Law, 16,* 319–332.

Raine, Adrian; Park, Sohee; Lencz, Todd; et al. (2001). Reduced right hemisphere activation in severely abused violent offenders during a working memory task: An fMRI study. *Aggressive Behavior, 27,* 111–129.

Ramey, Craig T., & Ramey, Sharon Landesman (1998). Early intervention and early experience. *American Psychologist, 53,* 109–120.

Rapkin, Andrea J.; Chang, Li C.; & Reading, Anthony E. (1988). Comparison of retrospective and prospective assessment of premenstrual symptoms. *Psychological Reports, 62,* 55–60.

Rapoport, M. (2001). The cerebellum in psychiatric disorders. *International Review of Psychiatry, 13*(4), 295–301.

Rathbun, Constance; DiVirgilio, Letitia; & Waldfogel, Samuel (1958). A restitutive process in children following radical separation from family and culture. *American Journal of Orthopsychiatry, 28,* 408–415.

Rauschecker, Josef P. (1999). Making brain circuits listen. *Science, 285,* 1686–1687.

Ravussin, Eric; Lillioja, Stephen; Knowler, William; et al. (1988). Reduced rate of energy expenditure as a risk factor for body-weight gain. *New England Journal of Medicine, 318,* 467–472.

Redd, W. H.; Dadds, M. R.; Futterman, A. D.; Taylor, K.; & Bovbjerg, D. (1993). Nausea induced by mental images of chemotherapy. *Cancer, 72,* 629–636.

Redelmeier, Donald A., & Tversky, Amos (1996). On the belief that arthritis pain is related to the weather. *Proceedings of the National Academy of Sciences, 93,* 2895–2896.

Reed, Geoffrey M. (1990). Stress, coping, and psychological adaptation in a sample of gay and bisexual men with AIDS. Unpublished doctoral dissertation, University of California, Los Angeles.

Reedy, F. E.; Bartoshuk, L. M.; Miller, I. J.; Duffy, V. B.; Lucchina, L.; & Yanagisawa, K. (1993). Relationships among papillae, taste pores, and 6-n-propylthiouracil (PROP) suprathreshold taste sensitivity. *Chemical Senses, 18,* 618–619.

Reid, R. L. (1991). Premenstrual syndrome. *New England Journal of Medicine, 324,* 1208–1210.

Reneman, Liesbeth; Lavalaye, Jules; Schmand, Ben; et al. (2001). Cortical serotonin transporter density and verbal memory in individuals who stopped using 3,4-methylene-dioxymethamphetamine (MDMA or "ecstasy"). *Archives of General Psychology, 58,* 901–906.

Rennie, D. L. (1994). Human science and counseling psychology: closing the gap between research and practice. *Counselling Psychology Quarterly, 7*(3), 235–250.

Repetti, Rena L.; Taylor, Shelley E.; & Seeman, Teresa E. (2002). Risky families: Family social environments and the mental and physical health of offspring. *Psychological Bulletin, 128,* 330–366.

Rescorla, Robert A. (1988). Pavlovian conditioning: It's not what you think it is. *American Psychologist, 43,* 151–160.

Rest, James; Narváez, Darcia; Bebeau, Muriel J.; & Thoma, Stephen J. (1999). *Postconventional moral thinking: A neo-Kohlbergian approach.* Hillsdale, NJ: Erlbaum.

Restak, Richard (1983, October). Is free will a fraud? *Science Digest, 91*(10), 52–55.

Restak, Richard M. (1994). *The modular brain.* New York: Macmillan.

Reynolds, Brent A., & Weiss, Samuel (1992). Generation of neurons and astrocytes from isolated cells of the adult mammalian central nervous system. *Science, 255,* 1707–1710.

Reynolds, Kristi; Lewis, L. Brian; Nolen, John David L.; et al. (2003). Alcohol consumption and risk of stroke: A meta-analysis. *Journal of the American Medical Association, 289,* 579–588.

Richards, Jane M., & Gross, James J. (2000). Emotion regulation and memory: The cognitive costs of keeping one's cool. *Journal of Personality and Social Psychology, 79,* 410–424.

Richards, Ruth L. (1991). Everyday creativity and the arts. Paper presented at the annual meeting of the American Psychological Association, San Francisco.

Richardson, John T. E. (Ed.) (1992). *Cognition and the menstrual cycle.* New York: Springer-Verlag.

Richardson-Klavehn, Alan, & Bjork, Robert A. (1988). Measures of memory. *Annual Review of Psychology, 39,* 475–543.

Ridley-Johnson, Robyn; Cooper, Harris; & Chance, June (1983). The relation of children's television viewing to school achievement and I.Q. *Journal of Educational Research, 76,* 294–297.

Rieber, Robert W. (1999). Hypnosis, false memory and multiple personality: A trinity of affinity. *History of Psychiatry, 10*(37, Pt. 1), 3–11.

Rind, Bruce, & Tromovitch, Philip (1997). A meta-analytic review of findings from national samples on psychological correlates of child sexual abuse. *Journal of Sex Research, 34,* 237–255.

Rind, Bruce; Tromovitch, Philip; & Bauserman, Robert (1998). A meta-analytic examination of assumed properties of child sexual abuse using college samples. *Psychological Bulletin, 124,* 22–53.

Riskind, John H.; Williams, Nathan L.; Gessner, Theodore L.; et al. (2000). The looming maladaptive style: Anxiety, danger, and schematic processing. *Journal of Personality and Social Psychology, 79,* 837–852.

Roan, Shari (2002, April 29). Late-late motherhood. *The Los Angeles Times,* S1, S6.

Roberts, Brent W.; Caspi, Avshalom; & Moffitt, Terrie E. (2001). The kids are alright: Growth and stability in personality development from adolescence to adulthood. *Journal of Personality and Social Psychology, 81,* 670–683.

Robins, Lee N.; Davis, Darlene H.; & Goodwin, Donald W. (1974). Drug use by U.S. Army enlisted men in Vietnam: A follow-up on their return home. *American Journal of Epidemiology, 99,* 235–249.

Robins, Lee N.; Tipp, Jayson; & Przybeck, Thomas R. (1991). Antisocial personality. In L. N. Robins & D. A. Regier (Eds.), *Psychiatric disorders in America.* New York: Free Press.

Robinson, Terry E. (2003). The psychology and neurobiology of addiction. Invited address presented at the annual meeting of the American Psychological Association, Atlanta.

Robinson, Thomas N. (1999, October 27). Reducing children's television viewing to prevent obesity: A randomized controlled trial. *Journal of the American Medical Association, 282,* 1561–1567.

Robinson, Thomas; Wilde, M. L.; Navracruz, L. C.; et al. (2001). Effects of reducing children's television and video game use on aggressive behavior: a randomized controlled trial. *Archives of Pediatric and Adolescent Medicine, 155,* 13–14.

Rocha, Beatriz A.; Scearce-Levie, Kimberly; Lucas, Jose J.; et al. (1998). Increased vulnerability to cocaine in mice lacking the serotonin-1B receptor. *Nature, 393,* 175–178.

Rodgers, K. (1994). Wife Assault: The Findings of a National Survey. *Juristat: Service Bulletin.* Ottawa: Canadian Centre for Justice Statistics, *14*(9), 3.

Roediger, Henry L. (1990). Implicit memory: Retention without remembering. *American Psychologist, 45,* 1043–1056.

Roediger, Henry L., & McDermott, Kathleen B. (1995). Creating false memories: Remembering words not presented in lists. *Journal of Experimental Psychology: Learning, Memory, & Cognition, 21,* 803–814.

Rogers, Carl (1951). *Client-centered therapy: Its current practice, implications, and theory.* Boston: Houghton Mifflin.

Rogers, Carl (1961). *On becoming a person.* Boston: Houghton Mifflin.

Rogers, Ronald W., & Prentice-Dunn, Steven (1981). Deindividuation and anger-mediated interracial aggression: Unmasking regressive racism. *Journal of Personality and Social Psychology, 41,* 63–73.

Rollin, Henry (Ed.) (1980). *Coping with schizophrenia.* London: Burnett.

Rose, Suzanna; Zand, Debra; & Cini, Marie A. (1993). Lesbian courtship scripts. In E. D. Rothblum & K. A. Brehony (Eds.), *Boston marriages.* Amherst: University of Massachusetts Press.

Rosenberg, Harold (1993). Prediction of controlled drinking by alcoholics and problem drinkers. *Psychological Bulletin, 113,* 129–139.

Rosenthal, Norman E. (1998). *Winter blues: Seasonal affective disorder: What it is and how to overcome it.* New York: Guilford Press.

Rosenthal, Robert (1994). Interpersonal expectancy effects: A 30-year perspective. *Current Directions in Psychological Science, 3,* 179–179.

Rosenzweig, Mark R. (1984). Experience, memory, and the brain. *American Psychologist, 39,* 365–376.

Rosso, Isabelle M.; Cannon, Tyrone D.; Huttunen, Tiia; et al. (2000). Obstetric risk factors for early-onset schizophrenia in a Finnish birth cohort. *American Journal of Psychiatry, 157,* 801–807.

Roth, David L., & Holmes, David S. (1985). Influence of physical fitness in determining the impact of stressful life events on physical and psychologic health. *Psychosomatic Medicine, 47,* 164–173.

Rothbart, Mary K.; Ahadi, Stephan A.; & Evans, David E. (2000). Temperament and personality: Origins and outcomes. *Journal of Personality and Social Psychology, 78,* 122–135.

Rothbaum, Fred; Weisz, John; Pott, Martha; et al. (2000). Attachment and culture: Security in the United States and Japan. *American Psychologist, 55,* 1093–1104.

Rothbaum, Fred M.; Weisz, John R.; & Snyder, Samuel S. (1982). Changing the world and changing the self: A two-process model of perceived control. *Journal of Personality and Social Psychology, 42,* 5–37.

Rotter, Julian B. (1990). Internal versus external control of reinforcement: A case history of a variable. *American Psychologist, 45,* 489–493.

Rowe, John W., & Kahn, Robert L. (1998). *Successful aging.* New York: Pantheon.

Rowe, Walter F. (1993, Winter). Psychic detectives: A critical examination. *Skeptical Inquirer, 17,* 159–165.

Roy, Mark P.; Steptoe, Andrew; & Kirschbaum, Clemens (1998). Life events and social support as moderators of individual differences in cardiovascular and cortisol reactivity. *Journal of Personality and Social Psychology, 75,* 1273–1281.

Rozin, Paul; Lowery, Laura; & Ebert, Rhonda (1994). Varieties of disgust faces and the structure of disgust. *Journal of Personality and Social Psychology, 66,* 870–881.

Rudman, Laurie A. (2004). Sources of implicit attitudes. *Current Directions in Psychological Science, 13*(2), 80–83.

Ruggiero, Vincent R. (1988). *Teaching thinking across the curriculum.* New York: Harper & Rowe.

Rumbaugh, Duane M. (1977). *Language learning by a chimpanzee: The Lana project.* New York: Academic Press.

Rumbaugh, Duane M.; Savage-Rumbaugh, E. Sue; & Pate, James L. (1988). Addendum to "Summation in the chimpanzee (Pan troglodytes)." *Journal of Experimental Psychology: Animal Behavior Processes, 14,* 118–120.

Rumelhart, David E.; McClelland, James L.; & the PDP Research Group (1986). *Parallel distributed processing: Explorations in the microstructure of cognition* (Vols. 1 and 2). Cambridge, MA: MIT Press.

Rushton, J. Philippe (1988). Race differences in behavior: A review and evolutionary analysis. *Personality and Individual Differences, 9,* 1009–1024.

Russell, James A., & Fehr, Beverley (1994). Fuzzy concepts in a fuzzy hierarchy: Varieties of anger. *Journal of Personality and Social Psychology, 67,* 186–205.

Rutter, Michael; Pickles, Andrew; Murray, Robin; & Eaves, Lindon (2001). Testing hypotheses on specific environmental causal effects on behavior. *Psychological Bulletin, 127,* 291–324.

Ryan, Richard M.; Chirkov, Valery I.; Little, Todd D.; et al. (1999). The American dream in Russia: Extrinsic aspirations and well-being in two cultures. *Personality and Social Psychology Bulletin, 25,* 1509–1524.

Ryder, Andrew G.; Alden, Lynn E.; & Paulhus, Delroy L. (2000). Is acculturation unidimensional or bidimensional? A head-to-head comparison in the prediction of personality, self-identity, and adjustment. *Journal of Personality and Social Psychology, 79,* 49–65.

Sack, Robert L., & Lewy, Alfred J. (1997). Melatonin as a chronobiotic: Treatment of circadian desynchrony in night workers and the blind. *Journal of Biological Rhythms, 12,* 595–603.

Sacks, Oliver (1985). *The man who mistook his wife for a hat and other clinical tales.* New York: Simon & Schuster.

Sagan, Eli (1988). *Freud, women, and morality: The psychology of good and evil.* New York: Basic Books.

Sagarin, Brad; Cialdini, Robert B.; Rice, William E.; & Serna, Sherman B. (2002). Dispelling the illusion of invulnerability: The motivations and mechanisms of resistance to persuasion. *Journal of Personality and Social Psychology, 83,* 526–541.

Sahley, Christie L.; Rudy, Jerry W.; & Gelperin, Alan (1981). An analysis of associative learning in a terrestrial mollusk: 1. Higher-order conditioning, blocking, and a transient US preexposure effect. *Journal of Comparative Physiology, 144,* 1–8.

Saklofske, D. H. (2003). Canada. In Georgas, J. (Ed.). *Culture and children's intelligence: Cross-cultural analysis of the WISC-III.* San Diego, CA: Academic Press, 61–75.

Salthouse, Timothy, A. (1998). The what and where of cognitive aging. Address presented at the annual meeting of the American Psychological Association, San Francisco.

Samelson, Franz (1979). Putting psychology on the map: Ideology and intelligence testing. In A. R. Buss (Ed.), *Psychology in social context.* New York: Irvington.

Sameroff, Arnold J.; Seifer, Ronald; Barocas, Ralph; et al. (1987). Intelligence quotient scores of 4-year-old children: Social-environmental risk factors. *Pediatrics, 79,* 343–350.

Sapolsky, Robert M. (1997). *The trouble with testosterone.* New York: Touchstone.

Sapolsky, Robert M. (2000). The possibility of neurotoxicity in the hippocampus in major depression: A primer on neuron death. *Biological Psychiatry, 48,* 755–765.

Sarbin, Theodore R. (1991). Hypnosis: A fifty year perspective. *Contemporary Hypnosis, 8,* 1–15.

Savage-Rumbaugh, Sue, & Lewin, Roger (1994). *Kanzi: The ape at the brink of the human mind.* New York: Wiley.

Savage-Rumbaugh, Sue; Shanker, Stuart; & Taylor, Talbot (1998). *Apes, language and the human mind.* New York: Oxford University Press.

Sawa, Akira, & Snyder, Solomon H. (2002, April 26). Schizophrenia: Diverse approaches to a complex disease. *Science, 296,* 692–694.

Scarr, Sandra (1993). Biological and cultural diversity: The legacy of Darwin for development. *Child Development, 64,* 1333–1353.

Scarr, Sandra, & Weinberg, Robert A. (1994). Educational and occupational achievement of brothers and sisters in adoptive and biologically related families. *Behavioral Genetics, 24,* 301–325.

Schachter, Stanley, & Singer, Jerome E. (1962). Cognitive, social, and physiological determinants of emotional state. *Psychological Review, 69,* 379–399.

Schacter, Daniel L. (1996). *Searching for memory: The brain, the mind, and the past.* New York: Basic Books.

Schacter, Daniel L. (2001). *The seven sins of memory: How the mind forgets and remembers.* Boston: Houghton Mifflin.

Schacter, Daniel L.; Chiu, C.-Y. Peter; & Ochsner, Kevin N. (1993). Implicit memory: A selective review. *Annual Review of Neuroscience, 16,* 159–182.

Schafer, Roy (1992). *Retelling a life: Narration and dialogue in psychoanalysis.* New York: Basic Books.

Schaie, K. Warner (1993). The Seattle longitudinal studies of adult intelligence. *Current Directions in Psychological Science, 2,* 171–175.

Schaie, K. Warner, & Willis, Sherry L. (2002). *Adult development and aging* (5th ed.). Upper Saddle River, NJ: Prentice Hall.

Schaie, K. Warner, & Zuo, Yan-Ling (2001). Family environments and cognitive functioning. In R. J. Sternberg & E. Grigorenko (Eds.), *Cognitive development in context.* Hillsdale, NJ: Erlbaum.

Schank, Roger, with Peter Childers (1988). *The creative attitude.* New York: Macmillan.

Scherer, Klaus R. (1997). The role of culture in emotion-antecedent appraisal. *Journal of Personality and Social Psychology, 73,* 902–922.

Scheufele, Peter M. (2000). Effects of progressive relaxation and classical music on measurements of attention, relaxation, and stress responses. *Journal of Behavioral Medicine, 23,* 207–228.

Schlossberg, Nancy K., & Robinson, Susan P. (1996). *Going to plan B.* New York: Simon & Schuster/Fireside.

Schmelz, M.; Schmidt, R.; Bickel, A.; et al. (1997). Specific C-receptors for itch in human skin. *Journal of Neuroscience, 17,* 8003–8008.

Schmolck, H.; Buffalo, E. A.; & Squire, L. R. (2000). Memory distortions develop over time: Recollections of the O. J. Simpson trial verdict after 15 and 32 months. *Psychological Science, 11,* 39–45.

Schnell, Lisa, & Schwab, Martin E. (1990, January 18). Axonal regeneration in the rat spinal cord produced by an antibody against myelin-associated neurite growth inhibitors. *Nature, 343,* 269–272.

Schuckit, Marc A. (1998). Relationship among genetic, environmental, and psychological variables in predicting alcoholism. Invited address presented at the annual meeting of the American Psychological Association, San Francisco.

Schuckit, Marc A., & Smith, T. L. (1996). An 8-year follow-up of 450 sons of alcoholic and control subjects. *Archives of General Psychiatry, 53,* 202–210.

Schulz, Richard; Beach, S. R.; Ives, D. G.; et al. (2000). Association between depression and mortality in older adults: The Cardiovascular Health Study. *Archives of Internal Medicine, 160,* 1761–1768.

Schuman, Howard, & Scott, Jacqueline (1989). Generations and collective memories. *American Journal of Sociology, 54,* 359–381.

Schwartz, Jeffrey; Stoessel, Paula W.; Baxter, Lewis R.; et al. (1996). Systematic changes in cerebral glucose metabolic rate after successful behavior modification treatment of obsessive-compulsive disorder. *Archives of General Psychiatry, 53,* 109–113.

Sears, Pauline, & Barbee, Ann H. (1977). Career and life satisfactions among Terman's gifted women. In J. C. Stanley, W. C. George, & C. H. Solano (Eds.), *The gifted and the creative: A fifty-year perspective.* Baltimore, MD: Johns Hopkins University Press.

Segal, Julius (1986). *Winning life's toughest battles.* New York: McGraw-Hill.

Segall, Marshall H.; Campbell, Donald T.; & Herskovits, Melville J. (1966). *The influence of culture on visual perception.* Indianapolis: Bobbs-Merrill.

Segall, Marshall H.; Dasan, Pierre R.; Berry, John W.; & Poortinga, Ype H. (1999). *Human behavior in global perspective: An introduction to cross-cultural psychology* (2nd ed.). Boston, MA: Allyn & Bacon.

Segerstrom, Suzanne C.; Taylor, Shelley E.; Kemeny, Margaret E.; & Fahey, John L. (1998). Optimism is associated with mood, coping, and immune change in response to stress. *Journal of Personality and Social Psychology, 74,* 1646–1655.

Seidenberg, Mark S., & Petitto, Laura A. (1979). Signing behavior in apes: A critical review. *Cognition, 7,* 177–215.

Seifer, Ronald; Schiller, Masha; Sameroff, Arnold; et al. (1996). Attachment, maternal sensitivity, and infant temperament during the first year of life. *Developmental Psychology, 32,* 12–25.

Sekuler, Robert, & Blake, Randolph (1994). *Perception* (3rd ed.). New York: Knopf.

Seligman, Martin E. P. (1975). *Helplessness: On depression, development, and death.* San Francisco: Freeman.

Seligman, Martin E. P. (1991). *Learned optimism.* New York: Knopf.

Seligman, Martin E. P., & Csikszentmihalyi, Mihaly (2000). Positive psychology: An introduction. *American Psychologist, 55,* 5–14.

Seligman, Martin E. P., & Hager, Joanne L. (1972, August). Biological boundaries of learning: The sauce-béarnaise syndrome. *Psychology Today,* 59–61, 84–87.

Seligman, Martin E. P.; Schulman, Peter; DeRubeis, Robert J.; & Hollon, Steven D. (1999). The prevention of depression and anxiety. *Prevention & Treatment, 2,* electronic posting December 21, 1999, on the Website of the American Psychological Association.

Selye, Hans (1956). *The stress of life.* New York: McGraw-Hill.

Senghas, Ann, & Coppola, Marie (2001). Children creating language: How Nicaraguan Sign Language acquired a spatial grammar. *Psychological Science, 12,* 323–328.

Serbin, Lisa A.; Poulin-Dubois, D.; Colburne, K. A.; et al. (2001). Gender stereotyping in infancy: Visual preferences for and knowledge of gender-stereotyped toys in the second year. *International Journal of Behavioral Development, 25*(1), 7–15.

Serbin, Lisa A.; Poulin-Dubois, D.; & Eichstedt, J. A. (2002). Infants' response to gender-inconsistent events. *Infancy, 3*(4), 531–542.

Serbin, Lisa A.; Powlishta, Kimberly K.; & Gulko, Judith (1993). The development of sex typing in middle childhood. *Monographs of the Society for Research in Child Development, 58*(2), Serial No. 232, v-74.

Serpell, Robert (1994). The cultural construction of intelligence. In W. J. Lonner & R. S. Malpass (Eds.), *Psychology and culture.* Needham Heights, MA: Allyn & Bacon.

Shapiro, Deane H.; Schwartz, Carolyn E.; & Astin, John A. (1996). Controlling ourselves, controlling our world. *American Psychologist, 51,* 1213–1230.

Shapiro, Francine (1995). *Eye movement desensitization and reprocessing: Basic principles, protocols, and procedures.* New York: Guilford.

Shatz, Marilyn, & Gelman, Rochel (1973). The development of communication skills: Modifications in the speech of young children as a function of the listener. *Monographs of the Society for Research in Child Development, 38.*

Shaver, Phillip R., & Hazan, Cindy (1993). Adult romantic attachment: Theory and evidence. In D. Perlman & W. H. Jones (Eds.), *Advances in personal relationships* (Vol. 4). London: Kingsley.

Shaver, Phillip R.; Wu, Shelley; & Schwartz, Judith C. (1992). Cross-cultural similarities and differences in emotion and its representation: A prototype approach. In M. S. Clark (Ed.), *Review of Personality and Social Psychology* (Vol. 13). Newbury Park, CA: Sage.

Shaw, Daniel S.; Keenan, Kate; & Vondra, Joan I. (1994). Developmental precursors of externalizing behavior: Ages 1 to 3. *Developmental Psychology, 30,* 355–364.

Shea, Chrisopher (2001, September). White man can't contextualize. *Lingua Franca,* 44–47, 49–51.

Sheldon, Kennon M.; Elliot, Andrew J.; Kim, Youngmee; & Kasser, Tim (2001). What is satisfying about satisfying events? Testing 10 candidate psychological needs. *Journal of Personality and Social Psychology, 80,* 325–339.

Sheldon, Kennon M., & Houser-Marko, Linda (2001). Self-concordance, goal attainment, and the pursuit of happiness: Can there be an upward spiral? *Journal of Personality and Social Psychology, 80,* 152–165.

Sheline, Yvette I. (2000). 3D MRI studies of neuroanatomic changes in unipolar major depression: The role of stress and medical comorbidity. *Biological Psychiatry, 48,* 791–800.

Shepard, Roger N., & Metzler, Jacqueline (1971). Mental rotation of three-dimensional objects. *Science, 171,* 701–703.

Shepperd, James A. (1995). Remedying motivation and productivity loss in collective settings. *Current Directions in Psychological Science, 4,* 131–140.

Sherif, Muzafer (1958). Superordinate goals in the reduction of intergroup conflicts. *American Journal of Sociology, 63,* 349–356.

Sherif, Muzafer; Harvey, O. J.; White, B. J.; Hood, William; & Sherif, Carolyn (1961). *Intergroup conflict and cooperation: The Robbers Cave experiment.* Norman: University of Oklahoma Institute of Intergroup Relations.

Sherman, Bonnie R., & Kunda, Ziva (1989). Motivated evaluation of scientific evidence. Paper presented at the annual meeting of the American Psychological Society, Arlington, VA.

Sherman, Jeffrey W., & Bessenoff, Gayle R. (1999). Stereotypes as source-monitoring cues: On the interaction between episodic and semantic memory. *Psychological Science, 10,* 106–110.

Shermer, Michael (1997). *Why people believe weird things: Pseudoscience, superstition, and other confusions of our time.* New York: Freeman.

Sherwin, Barbara B. (1998a). Estrogen and cognitive functioning in women. *Proceedings of the Society for Experimental Biological Medicine, 217,* 17–22.

Sherwin, Barbara B. (1998b). Use of combined estrogen-androgen preparations in the postmenopause: Evidence from clinical studies. *International Journal of Fertility & Women's Medicine, 43,* 98–103.

Shields, Stephanie (2002). *Gender and the social meaning of emotion.* Cambridge, MA: Cambridge University Press.

Shields, Stephanie A. (1975). Functionalism, Darwinism, and the psychology of women: A study in social myth. *American Psychologist, 30,* 739–754.

Showalter, Elaine (1997). *Hystories: Hysterical epidemics and modern culture.* New York: Columbia University Press.

Shweder, Richard A.; Mahapatra, Manamohan; & Miller, Joan G. (1990). Culture and moral development. In J. W. Stigler, R. A. Shweder, & G. Herdt (Eds.), *Cultural psychology: Essays on comparative human development.* Cambridge, England: Cambridge University Press.

Sidanius, Jim; Pratto, Felicia; & Bobo, Lawrence (1996). Racism, conservatism, affirmative action, and intellectual sophistication: A matter of principled conservatism or group dominance? *Journal of Personality and Social Psychology, 70,* 476–490.

Siegel, Alan B. (1991). *Dreams that can change your life.* Los Angeles: Tarcher.

Siegel, Ronald K. (1989). *Intoxication: Life in pursuit of artificial paradise.* New York: Dutton.

Siegler, Robert S. (2001). Cognition, instruction, and the quest for meaning. In S. M. Carver & D. Klahr (Eds.), *Cognition and instruction: Twenty-five years of progress.* Mahwah, NJ: Erlbaum.

Silverstein, Brett, & Perlick, Deborah (1995). *The cost of competence: Why inequality causes depression, eating disorders, and illness in women.* New York: Oxford University Press.

Silverstein, Brett; Peterson, Barbara; & Perdue, Lauren (1986). Some correlates of the thin standard of bodily attractiveness in women. *International Journal of Eating Disorders, 5,* 145–155.

Simmons, H. G. (1987). Psychosurgery and the abuse of psychiatric authority in Ontario. *Journal of Health Politics, Policy, and Law, 12,* 537–550.

Simons, Leon A.; McCallum, John; Friedlander, Yechiel; et al. (2000). Moderate alcohol intake is associated with survival in the elderly: The Dubbo study. *Medical Journal of Australia, 172,* 121–124.

Sims, Ethan A. (1974). Studies in human hyperphagia. In G. Bray & J. Bethune (Eds.), *Treatment and management of obesity.* New York: Harper & Row.

Sinclair, Lisa, & Kunda, Ziva (1999). Reactions to a Black professional: Motivated inhibition and activation of conflicting stereotypes. *Journal of Personality and Social Psychology, 77,* 885–904.

Singer, M.T.; Temerlin, M.K.; & Langone, M.D. (1990). Psychotherapy cults. *Cultic Studies Journal, 7,* 101–125.

Singh, Devendra; Vidaurri, Melody; Zambarano, Robert J.; & Dabbs, James M., Jr. (1999). Lesbian erotic role identification: Behavioral, morphological, and hormonal correlates. *Journal of Personality and Social Psychology, 76,* 1035–1049.

Sivak, Michael, & Flannagan, Michael J. (2003). Flying and driving after the September 11 attacks. *American Scientist, 91,* 6–8.

Skinner, B. F. (1938). *The behavior of organisms: An experimental analysis.* New York: Appleton-Century-Crofts.

Skinner, B. F. (1948/1976). *Walden Two.* New York: Macmillan.

Skinner, B. F. (1956). A case history in the scientific method. *American Psychologist, 11,* 221–233.

Skinner, B. F. (1972). The operational analysis of psychological terms. In B. F. Skinner, *Cumulative record* (3rd ed.). New York: Appleton-Century-Crofts.

Skinner, B. F. (1990). Can psychology be a science of mind? *American Psychologist, 45,* 1206–1210.

Skinner, Ellen A. (1996). A guide to constructs of control. *Journal of Personality and Social Psychology, 71,* 549–570.

Skreslet, Paula (1987, November 30). The prizes of first grade. *Newsweek,* 8.

Slade, Pauline (1984). Premenstrual emotional changes in normal women: Fact or fiction? *Journal of Psychosomatic Research, 28,* 1–7.

Slavin, Robert E., & Cooper, Robert (1999). Improving intergroup relations: Lessons learned from cooperative learning programs. *Journal of Social Issues, 55,* 647–663.

Smilek, D.; Dixon, J. J.; Cudahy, C.; & Merikle, P. M. (2002). Concept-driven color experiences in digit-color synesthesia. *Brain and Cognition, 48*(2–3), 570–573.

Smith, Carlyle (1995). Sleep states and memory processes. *Behavioural Brain Research, 69,* 137–145.

Smith, Carolyn A.; Lizotte, Alan J.; Thornberry, Terence P.; et al. (1997). Resilient youth: Identifying factors that prevent high-risk youth from engaging in delinquency and drug use. In J. Hagan (Ed.), *Delinquency and disrepute in the life course.* Greenwich, CT: JAI Press.

Smith, David N. (1998). The psychocultural roots of genocide: Legitimacy and crisis in Rwanda. *American Psychologist, 53,* 743–753.

Smith, James F., & Kida, Thomas (1991). Heuristics and biases: Expertise and task realism in auditing. *Psychological Bulletin, 109,* 472–489.

Smith, Larissa L., & Reise, Steven P. (1998). Gender differences on negative affectivity: An IRT study of differential item functioning on the Multidimensional Personality Questionnaire Stress Reaction Scale. *Journal of Personality and Social Psychology, 75,* 1350–1362.

Smith, M. C.; Bibi, U.; & Sheard, D. E. (2003). Evidence for the differential impact of time and emotion on personal and event memories for September 11, 2001. *Applied Cognitive Psychology, 17*(9), 1047–1055.

Smith, M. C., & Phillips, M. R., Jr. (2001). Age differences in memory for radio advertisements: The role of mnemonics. *Journal of Business Research, 53*(2), 103–109.

Smith, Peter B., & Bond, Michael H. (1994). *Social psychology across cultures: Analysis and perspectives.* Boston: Allyn & Bacon.

Smither, Robert D. (1998). *The psychology of work and human performance* (3rd ed.). New York: Longman.

Snidman, Nancy; Kagan, Jerome; Riordan, Linda; et al. (1995). Cardiac function and behavioral reactivity during infancy. *Psychophysiology, 32,* 199–207.

Snodgrass, Sara E. (1992). Further effects of role versus gender on interpersonal sensitivity. *Journal of Personality and Social Psychology, 62,* 154–158.

Snow, Barry R; Pinter, Isaac; Gusmorino, Paul; et al. (1986). Sex differences in chronic pain: Incidence and causal mechanisms. Paper presented at the annual meeting of the American Psychological Association, Washington, DC.

Snowdon, Charles T. (1997). The "nature" of sex differences: Myths of male and female. In P. A. Gowaty (Ed.), *Feminism and evolutionary biology.* New York: Chapman and Hall.

Snyder, C. R., & Shenkel, Randee J. (1975, March). The P. T. Barnum effect. *Psychology Today,* 52–54.

Solms, Mark (2000). "The new neuropsychology of sleep: Implications for psychoanalysis": Comment on J. Allan Hobson and Edward Pace-Schott's response. *Neuro-psychoanalysis, 2,* 193–201.

Solomon, Paul R. (1979). Science and television commercials: Adding relevance to the research methodology course. *Teaching of Psychology, 6,* 26–30.

Solomon, Robert C. (1994). *About love.* Lanham, MD: Littlefield Adams.

Somer, Oya, & Goldberg, Lewis R. (1999). The structure of Turkish trait-descriptive adjectives. *Journal of Personality and Social Psychology, 76,* 431–450.

Sommer, Robert (1969). *Personal space: The behavioral basis of design.* Englewood Cliffs, NJ: Prentice-Hall.

Sorce, James F.; Emde, Robert N.; Campos, Joseph; & Klinnert, Mary D. (1985). Maternal emotional signaling: Its effect on the visual cliff behavior of 1-year-olds. *Developmental Psychology, 21,* 195–200.

Spanos, Nicholas P. (1991). A sociocognitive approach to hypnosis. In S. J. Lynn & J. W. Rhue (Eds.), *Theories of hypnosis: Current models and perspectives.* New York: Guilford Press.

Spanos, Nicholas P. (1996). *Multiple identities and false memories: A sociocognitive perspective.* Washington, DC: American Psychological Association.

Spanos, Nicholas P.; Burgess, Cheryl A.; Roncon, Vera; et al. (1993). Surreptitiously observed hypnotic responding in simulators and in skill-trained and untrained high hypnotizables. *Journal of Personality and Social Psychology, 65,* 391–398.

Spanos, Nicholas P.; Menary, Evelyn; Gabora, Natalie J.; et al. (1991). Secondary identity enactments during hypnotic past-life regression: A sociocognitive perspective. *Journal of Personality and Social Psychology, 61,* 308–320.

Spanos, Nicholas P.; Stenstrom, Robert J.; & Johnson, Joseph C. (1988). Hypnosis, placebo, and suggestion in the treatment of warts. *Psychosomatic Medicine, 50,* 245–260.

Spear, Linda P. (2000). Neurobiological changes in adolescence. *Current Directions in Psychological Science, 9,* 111–114.

Spearman, Charles (1927). *The abilities of man.* London: Macmillan.

Spelke, Elizabeth S. (2000). Core knowledge. *American Psychologist, 55,* 1233–1243.

Spence, Janet T. (1985). Gender identity and its implications for concepts of masculinity and femininity. In T. Sonderegger (Ed.), *Nebraska Symposium on Motivation, 1984.* Lincoln, NE: University of Nebraska Press.

Spencer, M. B., & Dornbusch, Sanford M. (1990). Ethnicity. In S. S. Feldman & G. R. Elliott (Eds.), *At the threshold: The developing adolescent.* Cambridge, MA: Harvard University Press.

Spencer, S. J.; Steele, C. M.; & Quinn, D. M. (1999). Stereotype threat and women's math performance. *Journal of Experimental Social Psychology, 35*(1), 4–28.

Spencer, S. J.; Steele, C. M.; & Quinn, D. M. (2002). Stereotype threat and women's math performance. In Forden, Carie (Ed.), *Readings in the psychology of gender: Exploring our differences and commonalities* (pp. 54–68). Needham Heights, MA, US: Allyn & Bacon.

Sperling, George (1960). The information available in brief visual presentations. *Psychological Monographs, 74*(498).

Sperry, Roger W. (1964). The great cerebral commissure. *Scientific American, 210*(1), 42–52.

Sperry, Roger W. (1982). Some effects of disconnecting the cerebral hemispheres. *Science, 217,* 1223–1226.

Spilich, George J.; June, Lorraine; & Renner, Judith (1992). Cigarette smoking and cognitive performance. *British Journal of Addiction, 87,* 113–126.

Spitz, Herman H. (1997). *Nonconscious movements: From mystical messages to facilitated communication.* Mahwah, NJ: Erlbaum.

Sprecher, Susan; Sullivan, Quintin; & Hatfield, Elaine (1994). Mate selection preferences: Gender differences examined in a national sample. *Journal of Personality and Social Psychology, 66,* 1074–1080.

Spring, Bonnie; Chiodo, June; & Bowen, Deborah J. (1987). Carbohydrates, tryptophan, and behavior: A methodological review. *Psychological Bulletin, 102,* 234–256.

Springer, Sally P., & Deutsch, Georg (1998). Left brain, right brain: *Perspectives from cognitive neuroscience.* New York: Freeman.

Squier, Leslie H., & Domhoff, G. William (1998). The presentation of dreaming and dreams in introductory psychology textbooks: A critical examination with suggestions for textbook authors and course instructors. *Dreaming, 8,* 149–168.

Squire, Larry R. (1987). *Memory and the brain.* New York: Oxford University Press.

Squire, Larry R., & Zola-Morgan, Stuart (1991). The medial temporal lobe memory system. *Science, 253,* 1380–1386.

Srivastava, Abhishek; Locke, Edwin A.; & Bartol, Kathryn M. (2001). Money and subjective well-being: It's not the money, it's the motives. *Journal of Personality and Social Psychology, 80,* 959–971.

Staats, Carolyn K., & Staats, Arthur W. (1957). Meaning established by classical conditioning. *Journal of Experimental Psychology, 54,* 74–80.

Stadler, Michael A., & Frensch, Peter A. (1998). *Handbook of implicit learning.* Thousand Oaks, CA: Sage.

Stajkovic, Alexander D., & Luthans, Fred (1998). Self-efficacy and work-related performance: A meta-analysis. *Psychological Bulletin, 124,* 240–261.

Stam, Henderikus J. (1989). From symptom relief to cure: Hypnotic interventions in cancer. In N. P. Spanos & J. F. Chaves (Eds.), *Hypnosis: The cognitive-behavioral perspective.* Buffalo, NY: Prometheus Books.

Stanovich, Keith (1996). *How to think straight about psychology* (4th ed.). New York: HarperCollins.

Staples, Brent (1994). *Parallel time.* New York: Pantheon.

Staples, Susan L. (1996). Human response to environmental noise: Psychological research and public policy. *American Psychologist, 51,* 143–150.

Statistics Canada (1998). *General Social Survey.* Retrieved July 10, 2005, from http://www.statcan.ca/english/survey/household/general/timeuse.htm.

Statistics Canada (2001). *2001 Census of Canada.* Retrieved July 19, 2005, from http://www12.statcan.ca/english/census01/home/index.cfm#2001.

Statistics Canada (2004). *Prevalence of Hyperactivity-Impulsivity and Inattention Among Canadian Children: Findings from the First Data Collection Cycle (1994-1995) of the National Longitudinal Survey of Children and Youth—June 2002.* Retrieved November 29, 2004, from http://www11.sdc.gc.ca/en/cs/sp/arb/publications/research/2002-000170/page10.shtml.

Statistics Canada (2005). *Suicides, and suicide rate, by sex and by age group.* Retrieved July 8, 2005, from http://www40.statcan.ca/l01/cst01/health01.htm.

Stattin, Haken, & Magnusson, David (1990). *Pubertal maturation in female development.* Hillsdale, NJ: Erlbaum.

Staub, Ervin (1999). The roots of evil: Social conditions, culture, personality, and basic human needs. *Personality and Social Psychology Review, 3,* 179–192.

Stearns, Peter N. (1997). *Fat history: Bodies and beauty in the modern West.* New York: New York University Press.

Steele, Claude M. (1992, April). Race and the schooling of Black Americans. *Atlantic Monthly,* 68–78.

Steele, Claude M. (1997). A threat in the air: How stereotypes shape intellectual identity and performance. *American Psychologist, 52,* 613–629.

Steele, Claude M., & Aronson, Joshua (1995). Stereotype threat and the intellectual test performance of African-Americans. *Journal of Personality and Social Psychology, 69,* 797–811.

Steinberg, Laurence D. (1990). Interdependence in the family: Autonomy, conflict and harmony in the parent-adolescent relationship. In S. S. Feldman & G. R. Elliott (Eds.), *At the threshold: The developing adolescent.* Cambridge, MA: Harvard University Press.

Stenberg, Craig R., & Campos, Joseph (1990). The development of anger expressions in infancy. In N. Stein, B. Leventhal, & T. Trabasso (Eds.), *Psychological and biological approaches to emotion.* Hillsdale, NJ: Erlbaum.

Stepanski, Edward, & Perlis, Michael (2000). Behavioral sleep medicine: An emerging subspecialty in health psychology. *Journal of Psychosomatic Research, 49,* 343–347.

Stephan, K. M.; Fink, G. R.; Passingham, R. E.; et al. (1995). Functional anatomy of the mental representation of upper movements in healthy subjects. *Journal of Neurophysiology, 73,* 373–386.

Stephan, Walter G.; Ageyev, Vladimir; Coates-Shrider, Lisa; et al. (1994). On the relationship between stereotypes and prejudice: An international study. *Personality and Social Psychology Bulletin, 20,* 277–284.

Stern, Marilyn, & Karraker, Katherine H. (1989). Sex stereotyping of infants: A review of gender labeling studies. *Sex Roles, 20,* 501–522.

Sternberg, Robert J. (1988). *The triarchic mind: A new theory of human intelligence.* New York: Viking.

Sternberg, Robert J. (1995). *In search of the human mind.* Orlando, FL: Harcourt Brace.

Sternberg, Robert J. (1997). Construct validation of a triangular love scale. *European Journal of Social Psychology, 27,* 313–335.

Sternberg, Robert J.; Forsythe, George B.; Hedlund, Jennifer; et al. (2000). *Practical intelligence in everyday life.* New York: Cambridge University Press.

Sternberg, Robert J., & Wagner, Richard K. (1989). Individual differences in practical knowledge and its acquisition. In P. Ackerman, R. J. Sternberg, & R. Glaser (Eds.), *Individual differences.* New York: Freeman.

Sternberg, Robert J.; Wagner, Richard K.; Williams, Wendy M.; & Horvath, Joseph A. (1995). Testing common sense. *American Psychologist, 50,* 912–927.

Stevenson, H. W.; Chen, C.; & Lee, S-Y. (1993). Mathematics achievement of Chinese, Japanese, and American children: Ten years later. *Science, 259,* 53–58.

Stevenson, Harold W., & Stigler, James W. (1992). *The learning gap.* New York: Summit.

Stewart, Abigail J., & Ostrove, Joan M. (1998). Women's personality in middle age: Gender, history, and midcourse corrections. *American Psychologist, 53,* 1185–1194.

Stewart, Abigail J., & Vandewater, Elizabeth A. (1999). "If I had it to do over again . . .": Midlife review, midcourse corrections, and women's well-being in midlife. *Journal of Personality and Social Psychology, 76,* 270–283.

Stewart, S. H.; Conrod, P. J.; Gignac, M. L.; & Pihl, R. O. (1998). Selective processing biases in anxiety-sensitive men and women. *Cognition & Emotion, 12*(1), 105–133.

Stice, Eric (2002). Risk and maintenance factors for eating pathology: A meta-analytic review. *Psychological Bulletin, 128,* 825–848.

Stoch, M. B., & Smythe, P. M. (1963). Does undernutrition during infancy inhibit brain growth and subsequent intellectual development? *Archives of Diseases in Childhood, 38,* 546–552.

Strack, Fritz; Martin, Leonard L.; & Stepper, Sabine (1988). Inhibiting and facilitating conditions of the human smile: A nonobtrusive test of the facial-feedback hypothesis. *Journal of Social and Personality Psychology, 54,* 768–777.

Strahan, Erin J.; Spencer, Steven J.; & Zanna, Mark P. (2002). Subliminal priming and persuasion: Striking while the iron is hot. *Journal of Experimental Social Psychology 38,* 556–568.

Straus, Murray A., & Kantor, Glenda Kaufman (1994). Corporal punishment of adolescents by parents: A risk factor in the epidemiology of depression, suicide, alcohol abuse, child abuse, and wife beating. *Adolescence, 29,* 543–561.

Strayer, David L., & Johnston, William A. (2001). Driven to distraction: Dual-task studies of simulated driving and conversing on a cellular telephone. *Psychological Science, 12,* 462–466.

Streissguth, Ann P.; Barr, Helen M.; Bookstein, Fred L.; et al. (1999). The long-term neurocognitive consequences of prenatal alcohol exposure: A 14-year study. *Psychological Science, 10,* 186–190.

Strickland, Bonnie R. (1989). Internal–external control expectancies: From contingency to creativity. *American Psychologist, 44,* 1–12.

Strickland, Tony L.; Lin, Keh-Ming; Fu, Paul; et al. (1995). Comparison of lithium ratio between African-American and Caucasian bipolar patients. *Biological Psychiatry, 37,* 325–330.

Strickland, Tony L.; Ranganath, Vijay; Lin, Keh-Ming; et al. (1991). Psychopharmacological considerations in the treatment of black American populations. *Psychopharmacology Bulletin, 27,* 441–448.

Stroebe, Margaret; Stroebe, Wolfgang; & Schut, Henk (2001). Gender differences in adjustment to bereavement: An empirical and theoretical review. *Review of General Psychology, 5,* 62–83.

Stroebe, Wolfgang; Stroebe, Margaret; Abakoumkin, Georgios; & Schut, Henk (1996). The role of loneliness and social support in adjustment to loss: A test of attachment versus stress theory. *Journal of Personality and Social Psychology, 70,* 1241–1249.

Stunkard, Albert J. (Ed.) (1980). *Obesity.* Philadelphia: Saunders.

Stunkard, Albert J.; Harris, J. R.; Pedersen, N. L.; & McClearn, G. E. (1990, May 24). The body-mass index of twins who have been reared apart. *New England Journal of Medicine, 322,* 1483–1487.

Suddendorf, Thomas, & Whiten, Andrew (2001). Mental evolution and development: Evidence for secondary representation in children, great apes, and other animals. *Psychological Bulletin, 127,* 629–650.

Sue, Stanley (1998). In search of cultural competence in psychotherapy and counseling. *American Psychologist, 53,* 440–448.

Suedfeld, Peter (1975). The benefits of boredom: Sensory deprivation reconsidered. *American Scientist, 63*(1), 60–69.

Sullivan, Michael J. L.; Tripp, Dean A.; & Santor, Darcy (1998). Gender differences in pain and pain behaviour: The role of catastrophizing. Paper presented at the annual meeting of the American Psychological Association, San Francisco.

Sulloway, Frank J. (1992). *Freud, biologist of the mind: Beyond the psychoanalytic legend* (Rev. ed.). Cambridge, MA: Harvard University Press.

Suls, Jerry; Martin, René; & Wheeler, Ladd (2002). Social comparison: Why, with whom, and with what effect? *Current Directions in Psychological Science, 11,* 159–163.

Sundquist, J., & Winkleby, M. (2000, June). Country of birth, acculturation status and abdominal obesity in a national sample of Mexican-American women and men. *International Journal of Epidemiology, 29,* 470–477.

Suomi, S.J. (1991). Uptight and laid-back monkeys; Individual differences in response to social challenges. In S.E. Brauth, W.S. Hall, & R.J. Dooling (Eds.), *Plasticity of development* (pp. 27–56). Cambridge, MA: MIT Press.

Super, Charles A., & Harkness, Sara (1994). The developmental niche. In W. J. Lonner & R. Malpass (Eds.), *Psychology and culture.* Needham Heights, MA: Allyn & Bacon.

Susman, Elizabeth J.; Inoff-Germain, Gale; Nottelmann, Editha D.; et al. (1987). Hormones, emotional dispositions, and aggressive attributes in young adolescents. *Child Development, 58,* 1114–1134.

Susser, Ezra; Neugebauer, Richard; Hoek, Hans W.; et al. (1996). Schizophrenia after prenatal famine: Further evidence. *Archives of General Psychiatry, 53,* 25–31.

Swain, Scott (1989). Covert intimacy: Closeness in men's friendships. In B. J. Risman & P. Schwartz (Eds.), *Gender in intimate relationships.* Belmont, CA: Wadsworth.

Szatmari, P.; Offord, D. R.; & Boyle, M. H. (1989). Ontario Child Health Study: Prevalence of attention deficit disorder with hyperactivity. *Journal of Child Psychology and Psychiatry, 30*(2), 219–230.

Taddio, A.; Shah, V.; Gilbert-MacLeod, C.; & Katz, J. (2003). Conditioning and hyperalgesia in newborns exposed to repeated heel lances. *Journal of the American Medical Association, 288*(7), 857–861.

Tafarodi, R. W. (1998). Paradoxical self-esteem and selectivity in the processing of social information. *Journal of Personality and Social Psychology, 74,* 1118–1196.

Tafarodi, R. W.; Lang, J. M.; & Smith, A. J. (1999). Self-esteem and the cultural trade-off: Evidence for the role of individualism-collectivism. *Journal of Cross-Cultural Psychology, 30,* 620–640.

Tafarodi, R. W., & Milne, A. B. (2002). Decomposing global self-esteem. *Journal of Personality, 70,* 443–483.

Tafarodi, R. W.; Tam, J.; & Milne, A. R. (2001). Selective memory and the persistence of paradoxical self-esteem. *Personality and Social Psychology Bulletin, 27,* 1179–1189.

Tajfel, Henri; Billig, M. G.; Bundy, R. P.; & Flament, C. (1971). Social categorization and intergroup behavior. *European Journal of Social Psychology, 1,* 149–178.

Tajfel, Henri, & Turner, John C. (1986). The social identity theory of intergroup behavior. In S. Worchel & W. G. Austin (Eds.), *Psychology of intergroup relations.* Chicago: Nelson-Hall.

Tangney, June P.; Wagner, Patricia E.; Hill-Barlow, Deborah; et al. (1996). Relation of shame and guilt to constructive versus destructive responses to anger across the lifespan. *Journal of Personality and Social Psychology, 70,* 797–809.

Tanner, A. (2003, January 26). Would you have ignored her screams? *The Province* (Vancouver), p. A13.

Taub, David M. (1984). *Primate paternalism.* New York: Van Nostrand Reinhold.

Tavris, Carol (1989). *Anger: The misunderstood emotion* (rev. ed.). New York: Simon & Schuster/Touchstone.

Taylor, Donald M., & Porter, Lana E. (1994). A multicultural view of stereotyping. In W. J. Lonner & R. Malpass (Eds.), *Psychology and culture.* Needham Heights, MA: Allyn & Bacon.

Taylor, Eugene (2001). Positive psychology and humanistic psychology: A reply to Seligman. *Journal of Humanistic Psychology, 41,* 13–29.

Taylor, Shelley E.; Kemeny, Margaret E.; Reed, Geoffrey M.; Bower, Julienne E.; & Gruenewald, Tara L. (2000a). Psychological resources, positive illusions, and health. *American Psychologist, 55,* 99–109.

Taylor, Shelley E.; Klein, Laura C.; Lewis, Brian P.; et al. (2000b). Biobehavioral responses to stress in females: Tend-and-befriend, not fight-or-flight. *Psychological Review, 107,* 411–429.

Taylor, Shelley E.; Lichtman, Rosemary R.; & Wood, Joanne V. (1984). Attributions, beliefs about control, and adjustment to breast cancer. *Journal of Personality and Social Psychology, 46,* 489–502.

Taylor, Shelley E., & Lobel, Marci (1989). Social comparison activity under threat: Downward evaluation and upward contacts. *Psychological Review, 96,* 569–575.

Taylor, Steven; Thordarson, Dana S.; Maxfield, Louise; et al. (2003). Comparative efficacy, speed, and adverse effects of three PTSD treatments: Exposure therapy, EMDR, and relaxation training. *Journal of Consulting and Clinical Psychology, 71,* 330–338.

Terman, Lewis M., & Oden, Melita H. (1959). *Genetic studies of genius: Vol. 5. The gifted group at mid-life.* Stanford, CA: Stanford University Press.

Terman, Michael; Terman, Jiuan Su; & Ross, Donald C. (1998). A controlled trial of timed bright light and negative air ionization for treatment of winter depression. *Archives of General Psychiatry, 55,* 875–882.

Terrace, H. S. (1985). In the beginning was the "name." *American Psychologist, 40,* 1011–1028.

Thase, Michael E.; Fasiczka, Amy L.; Berman, Susan R.; et al. (1998). Electroencephalographic sleep profiles before and after cognitive behavior therapy of depression. *Archives of General Psychiatry, 55,* 138–144.

Thigpen, Corbett H., & Cleckley, Hervey M. (1984). On the incidence of multiple personality disorder: A brief communication. *International Journal of Clinical and Experimental Hypnosis, 32,* 63–66.

Thomassen, R.; van Schaick, H. W.; & Blansjaar, B. A. (1998). Prevalence of dementia over age 100. *Neurology, 50,* 283–286.

Thompson, Clara (1943/1973). Penis envy in women. *Psychiatry, 6,* 123–125. Reprinted in J. B. Miller (Ed.), *Psychoanalysis and women.* New York: Brunner/Mazel, 1973.

Thompson, R., & Zuroff, D. C. (1999). Dependency, self-criticism, and mothers' responses to adolescent sons' autonomy and competence. *Journal of Youth & Adolescence, 28*(3), 365–384.

Thompson, Ross A., & Nelson, Charles A. (2001). Developmental science and the media: Early brain development. *American Psychologist, 56,* 5–15.

Thorndike, Edward L. (1898). Animal intelligence: An experimental study of the associative processes in animals. *Psychological Review Monograph Supplement, 2* (Whole No. 8).

Thorndike, Edward L. (1903). *Educational Psychology.* New York: Columbia University Teachers College.

Thorpe, C. M.; Floresco, S. B.; Carr, J. A. R.; & Wilkie, D. M. (2002). Alterations in time-place learning induced by lesions to the rat medial prefrontal cortex. *Behavioural Processes, 59*(2), 87–100.

Tice, Dianne M., & Baumeister, Roy F. (1997). Longitudinal study of procrastination, performance, stress, and health: The costs and benefits of dawdling. *Psychological Science, 8,* 454–458.

Tiefer, Leonore (2004). *Sex is not a natural act, and other essays* (Rev. ed.). Boulder, CO: Westview.

Timmers, Monique; Fischer, Agneta H.; & Manstead, Antony S. R. (1998). Gender differences in motives for regulating emotions. *Personality and Social Psychology Bulletin, 24,* 974–985.

Todes, Daniel P. (1997). From the machine to the ghost within: Pavlov's transition from digestive physiology to conditional reflexes. *American Psychologist, 52,* 947–955.

Tolman, D. L., & Diamond, Lisa M. (2001). Desegregating sexuality research: Cultural and biological perspectives on gender and desire. *Annual Review of Sex Research, 12,* 33–74.

Tolman, Edward C. (1938). The determiners of behavior at a choice point. *Psychological Review, 45,* 1–35.

Tolman, Edward C., & Honzik, Chase H. (1930). Introduction and removal of reward and maze performance in rats. *University of California Publications in Psychology, 4,* 257–275.

Toma, J. G.; Akhavan, M.; Frenandes, K. J.; et al. (2001). Isolation of multipotent adult stem cells from the dermis of mammalian skin. *Nature Cell Biology, 3,* 778–784.

Tormala, Zakary L., & Petty, Richard E. (2002). What doesn't kill me makes me stronger: The effects of resisting persuasion on attitude certainty. *Journal of Personality and Social Psychology, 83,* 1298–1313.

Tomasello, Michael (2000). Culture and cognitive development. *Current Directions in Psychological Science, 9,* 37–40.

Toplak, M. E., & Stanovich, K. E. (2003). Associations between myside bias on an informal reasoning task and amount of postsecondary education. *Applied Cognitive Psychology, 17*(7), 851–860.

Torrey, E. Fuller (2001). *Surviving schizophrenia* (4th ed.). TK.

Travis, John (2002, February 16). The hunger hormone? *Science News, 161,* 107–108.

Triandis, Harry C. (1995). *Individualism and collectivism.* Boulder, CO: Westview Press.

Triandis, Harry C. (1996). The psychological measurement of cultural syndromes. *American Psychologist, 51,* 407–415.

Tronick, Edward Z.; Morelli, Gilda A.; & Ivey, Paula K. (1992). The Efe forager infant and toddler's pattern of social relationships: Multiple and simultaneous. *Developmental Psychology, 28,* 568–577.

Tsuang, Ming T.; Bar, Jessica L.; Harley, Rebecca M.; Lyons, Michael J. (2001). The Harvard Twin Study of Substance Abuse: What we have learned. *Harvard Review of Psychiatry, 9,* 267–279.

Tulving, E. (2001). Origin of autonoesis in episodic memory. In H. L. Roediger, & J. S. Nairne (Eds.), *Nature of remembering: Essays in honor of Robert G. Crowder* (pp. 17–34). Washington DC: American Psychological Association.

Tulving, Endel (1985). How many memory systems are there? *American Psychologist, 40,* 385–398.

Turiel, Elliot (2002). *The culture of morality.* Cambridge, England: Cambridge University Press.

Turkheimer, Eric (2000). Three laws of behavior genetics and what they mean. *Current Directions in Psychological Science, 9*, 160–164.

Turner, C. F.; Ku, L.; Rogers, S. M.; et al. (1998). Adolescent sexual behaviour, drug use, and violence: Increased reporting with computer survey technology. *Science, 280*, 867–873.

Tversky, Amos, & Kahneman, Daniel (1973). Availability: A heuristic for judging frequency and probability. *Cognitive Psychology, 5*, 207–232.

Tversky, Amos, & Kahneman, Daniel (1981). The framing of decisions and the psychology of choice. *Science, 211*, 453–458.

Tyler, Tom R. (1997). The psychology of legitimacy: A relational perspective on voluntary deference to authorities. *Personality and Social Psychology Review, 1*, 323–345.

Ullian, Erik M.; Sapperstein, Stephanie K.; Christopherson, Karen S.; & Barres, Ben A. (2001). Control of synapse number by glia. *Science, 291*, 657–661.

Usher, JoNell A., & Neisser, Ulric (1993). Childhood amnesia and the beginnings of memory for four early life events. *Journal of Experimental Psychology: General, 122*, 155–165.

Uttal, William R. (2001). *The new phrenology: The limits of localizing cognitive processes in the brain.* Cambridge, MA: MIT Press/Bradford Books.

Vaillant, George E. (1983). *The natural history of alcoholism: Causes, patterns, and paths to recovery.* Cambridge, MA: Harvard University Press.

Vaillant, George E. (Ed.) (1992). *Ego mechanisms of defence.* Washington, DC: American Psychiatric press.

Valenstein, Elliot (1986). *Great and desperate cures: The rise and decline of psychosurgery and other radical treatments for mental illness.* New York: Basic Books.

Valenstein, Elliot (1998). *Blaming the brain: The truth about drugs and mental health.* New York: The Free Press.

Valian, Virginia (1998). *Why so slow? The advancement of women.* Cambridge, MA: MIT Press.

Van Boven, Leaf; Kamada, Akiko; & Gilovich, Thomas (1999). The perceiver as perceived: Everyday intuitions about the correspondence bias. *Journal of Personality and Social Psychology, 77*, 1188–1199.

Van Cantfort, Thomas E., & Rimpau, James B. (1982). Sign language studies with children and chimpanzees. *Sign Language Studies, 34*, 15–72.

Van de Castle, R. (1994). *Our dreaming mind.* New York: Ballantine Books.

van Praag, H.; Kempermann, G.; & Gage, F. H. (1999). Running increases cell proliferation and neurogenesis in the adult mouse dentate gyrus. *Nature Neuroscience, 2*, 266–270.

Vecera, S. P.; Vogel, E. K.; & Woodman, G. F. (2002). Lower region: A new cue for figure-ground segregation. *Journal of Experimental Psychology: General, 131*, 194–205.

Verhaeghen, Paul, & Salthouse, Timothy A. (1997). Meta-analyses of age-cognition relations in adulthood: Estimates of linear and nonlinear age effects and structural models. *Psychological Bulletin, 122*, 231–249.

Vertosick, Frank T. (1997, October). Lobotomy's back. *Discover,* 66–72.

Vila, J., & Beech, H. R. (1980). Premenstrual symptomatology: An interaction hypothesis. *British Journal of Social and Clinical Psychology, 19*, 73–80.

Violato, C. (1986). Canadian versions of the information subtests of the Wechsler tests of intelligence. *Canadian Psychology, 27*(1), 69–74.

Vita, A. J.; Terry, R. B.; Hubert, H. B.; & Fries, J. F. (1998). Aging, health risks, and cumulative disability. *New England Journal of Medicine, 338*, 1035–1041.

Volkow, Nora D.; Chang, Linda; Wang, Gene-Jack; et al. (2001). Association of dopamine transporter reduction with psychomotor impairment in methamphetamine abusers. *American Journal of Psychiatry, 158*, 377–382.

Voyer, Daniel; Voyer, Susan; & Bryden, M. P. (1995). Magnitude of sex differences in spatial abilities: A meta-analysis and consideration of critical variables. *Psychological Bulletin, 117*, 250–270.

Wadden, Thomas A.; Foster, G. D.; Letizia, K. A.; & Mullen, J. L. (1990, August 8). Long-term effects of dieting on resting metabolic rate in obese outpatients. *Journal of the American Medical association, 264*, 707–711.

Wakefield, Jerome C. (1992). Disorder as harmful dysfunction: A conceptual critique of DSM-III-R's definition of mental disorder. *Psychological Review, 99*, 232–247.

Waldram, J. B., & Wong, S. (1995). Group therapy of Aboriginal offenders in a Canadian forensic psychiatric facility. *American Indian and Alaska Native Mental Health Research, 6*(2), 34–56.

Walker, Anne (1994). Mood and well-being in consecutive menstrual cycles: Methodological and theoretical implications. *Psychology of Women Quarterly, 18*, 271–290.

Walker, Elaine F. (2002). Adolescent neurodevelopment and psychopathology. *Current Directions in Psychological Science, 11*, 24–28.

Walker, Lawrence J.; de Vries, Brian; & Trevethan, Shelley D. (1987). Moral stages and moral orientations in real-life and hypothetical dilemmas. *Child Development, 58*, 842–858.

Walker-Andrews, Arlene S. (1997). Infants' perception of expressive behaviors: Differentiation of multimodal information. *Psychological Bulletin, 121*, 437–456.

Wallbott, Harald G.; Ricci-Bitti, Pio; & Bänninger-Huber, Eva (1986). Non-verbal reactions to emotional experiences. In K. R. Scherer, H. G. Wallbott, & A. B. Summerfield (Eds.), *Experiencing emotion: A cross-cultural study.* Cambridge, England: Cambridge University Press.

Waller, Niels G.; Kojetin, Brian A.; Bouchard, Thomas J., Jr.; et al. (1990). Genetic and environmental influences on religious interests, attitudes, and values: A study of twins reared apart and together. *Psychological Science, 1*, 138–142.

Wallerstein, J.; Lewis, J.; & Blakeslee, S. (2000). *The unexpected legacy of divorce: A 25-year landmark study.* New York: H.B. Fenn.

Walsh, B. Timothy, & Devlin, Michael J. (1998). Eating disorders: Progress and problems. *Science, 280*, 1387–1390.

Walsh, M.; Hickey, C.; & Duffy. J. (1999). Influence of item content and stereotype situation on gender differences in mathematical problem solvng. *Sex Roles, 41*(3–4), 219–240.

Wang, Alvin Y.; Thomas, Margaret H.; & Ouellette, Judith A. (1992). The keyword mnemonic and retention of second-language vocabulary words. *Journal of Educational Psychology, 84*, 520–528.

Wark, Gillian R., & Krebs, Dennis (1996). Gender and dilemma differences in real-life moral judgment. *Developmental Psychology, 32*, 220–230.

Warren, Gayle H., & Raynes, Anthony E. (1972). Mood changes during three conditions of alcohol intake. *Quarterly Journal of Studies on Alcohol, 33*, 979–989.

Wasserman, Eric W., & Lisanby, Sarah H. (2001). Therapeutic application of repetitive transcranial magnetic stimulation: A review. *Clinical Neurophysiology, 112*, 1367–1377.

Watson, David; Hubbard, Brock; & Wiese, David (2000). Self-other agreement in personality and affectivity: The role of acquaintanceship, trait visibility, and assumed similarity. *Journal of Personality and Social Psychology, 78*, 546–558.

Watson, John B. (1925). *Behaviorism.* New York: Norton.

Watson, John B., & Rayner, Rosalie (1920). Conditioned emotional reactions. *Journal of Experimental Psychology, 3,* 1–14.

Watters, Ethan, & Ofshe, Richard (1999). *Therapy's delusions.* New York: Scribner.

Waxer, P. H. (1985). Video ethology: Television as a data base for cross-cultural studies in nonverbal displays. *Journal of Nonverbal Behavior, 9*(2), 111–120.

Webb, Wilse B., & Cartwright, Rosalind D. (1978). Sleep and dreams. In M. Rosenzweig & L. Porter (Eds.), *Annual Review of Psychology, 29,* 223–252.

Webster, Richard (1995). *Why Freud was wrong.* New York: Basic Books.

Wechsler, David (1955). *Manual for the Wechsler Adult Intelligence Scale.* New York: Psychological Corporation.

Wegner, Daniel M., & Gold, Daniel B. (1995). Fanning old flames: Emotional and cognitive effects of suppressing thoughts of a past relationship. *Journal of Personality and Social Psychology, 68,* 782–792.

Weil, Andrew T. (1972/1986). *The natural mind: A new way of looking at drugs and the higher consciousness.* Boston: Houghton Mifflin.

Weiner, Bernard (1986). *An attributional theory of motivation and emotion.* New York: Springer-Verlag.

Weiss, Erica; Longhurst, James G.; & Mazure, Carolyn M. (1999). Childhood sexual abuse as a risk factor for depression in women: Psychological and neurological correlates. *American Journal of Psychiatry, 156,* 816–828.

Weissman, Myrna M.; Markowitz, John C.; & Klerman, Gerald L. (2000). *Comprehensive guide to interpersonal psychotherapy.* New York: Basic Books.

Weisz, John R.; Weiss, Bahr; Han, Susan S.; et al. (1995). Effects of psychotherapy with children and adolescents revisited: A meta-analysis of treatment outcome studies. *Psychological Bulletin, 117,* 450–468.

Weitzenhoffer, André M. (1996). Catalepsy tests: What do they tell us? *International Journal of Clinical and Experimental Hypnosis, 44,* 307–323.

Wells, Gary L.; Small, Mark; Penrod, Steven; et al. (1998). Eyewitness identification procedures: Recommendations for lineups and photospreads. *Law and Human Behavior, 22,* 602–647.

Wender, Paul H., & Klein, Donald F. (1981). *Mind, mood, and medicine: A guide to the new biopsychiatry.* New York: Farrar, Straus and Giroux.

Werner, Emmy E. (1989). High-risk children in young adulthood: A longitudinal study from birth to 32 years. *American Journal of Orthopsychiatry, 59,* 72–81.

Werner, Peter; Pitt, D.; & Raine, C. S. (2001). Multiple sclerosis: altered glutamate homeostasis in lesions correlates with aligodendrocyte and axonal damage. *Annals of Neurology, 50,* 169–180.

West, Melissa O., & Prinz, Ronald J. (1987). Parental alcoholism and childhood psychopathology. *Psychological Bulletin, 102,* 204–218.

Westen, Drew (1998). The scientific legacy of Sigmund Freud: Toward a psychodynamically informed psychological science. *Psychological Bulletin, 124,* 333–371.

Westen, Drew, & Shedler, Jonathan (1999). Revising and assessing axis II, Part II: Toward an empirically based and clinically useful classification of personality disorders. *American Journal of Psychiatry, 156,* 273–285.

Wethington, Elaine (2000). Expecting stress: Americans and the "midlife crisis." *Motivation & Emotion, 24,* 85–103.

Whatmough, C.; Chertkow, H.; Murtha, S.; et al. (2003). The semantic category effect increases with worsening anomia in Alzheimer's type dementia. *Brain & Language, 84*(1), 134–147.

Wheeler, David L. (1998, September 11). Neuroscientists take stock of brain-imaging studies. *Chronicle of Higher Education,* A20–A21.

Whisman, M. (1993). Mediators and moderators of change in cognitive therapy of depression. *Psychological Bulletin, 114,* 248–265.

Whitam, Frederick L.; Diamond, Milton; & Martin, James (1993). Homosexual orientation in twins: A report on 61 pairs and 3 triplet sets. *Archives of Sexual Behavior, 22,* 187–206.

Wickelgren, Ingrid (1997). Estrogen stakes claim to cognition. *Science, 276,* 675–678.

Widiger, Thomas, & Clark, Lee Anna (2000). Toward DSM-V and the classification of psychopathology. *Psychological Bulletin, 126,* 946–963.

Wilgosh, L. (1991). Underachievement in culturally different gifted children. *European Journal for High Ability, 2*(2), 166–173.

Wilkie, D. M.; Carr, J. A. R.; Siegenthaler, A.; & Lenger, B. (1996). Field observations of time-place behaviour in scavenging birds. *Behavioural Processes, 38*(1), 77–88.

Williams, Janice E.; Paton, Catherine C.; Siegler, Ilene C.; et al. (2000). Anger proneness predicts coronary heart disease risk. *Circulation, 101,* 2034–2039.

Williams, Kipling D., & Karau, Steven J. (1991). Social loafing and social compensation: The effects of expectations of co-worker performance. *Journal of Personality and Social Psychology, 61,* 570–581.

Williams, Redford B., Jr.; Barefoot, John C.; & Shekelle, Richard B. (1985). The health consequences of hostility. In M. A. Chesney & R. H. Rosenman (Eds.), *Anger and hostility in cardiovascular and behavioral disorders.* New York: Hemisphere.

Willie, Charles V.; Rieker, Patricia P.; Kramer, Bernard M.; & Brown, Bertram S. (Eds.) (1995). *Mental health, racism, and sexism* (Rev. ed.). Pittsburgh: University of Pittsburgh Press.

Wilner, D.M.; Walkley, R.P.; & Cook, S.W. (1955). *Human relations in interacial housing.* Minneapolis: University of Minnesota Press.

Wilson, G. Terence, & Fairburn, Christopher G. (1993). Cognitive treatments for eating disorders. *Journal of Consulting and Clinical Psychology, 61,* 261–269.

Wilson, Matthew A., & Louie, Kenway (2001). Temporally structured replay of awake hippocampal ensemble activity during rapid eye movement sleep. *Neuron, 29,* 145–156.

Wilson, Timothy D.; Lindsey, S.; & Schooler, T. Y. (2000). A model of dual attitudes. *Psychological Review, 107,* 101–126.

Winick, Myron; Meyer, Knarig Katchadurian; & Harris, Ruth C. (1975). Malnutrition and environmental enrichment by early adoption. *Science, 190,* 1173–1175.

Winnicott, D. W. (1957/1990). *Home is where we start from.* New York: Norton.

Wispé, Lauren G., & Drambarean, Nicholas C. (1953). Physiological need, word frequency, and visual duration thresholds. *Journal of Experimental Psychology, 46,* 25–31.

Witelson, Sandra F.; Glazer, I. I.; & Kigar, D. L. (1994). Sex differences in numerical density of neurons in human auditory association cortex. *Society for Neuroscience Abstracts, 30* (Abstr. No. 582.12).

Wittchen, Hans-Ulrich; Kessler, Ronald C.; Zhao, Shanyang; & Abelson, Jamie (1995). Reliability and clinical validity of UM-CIDI DSM-III-R generalized anxiety disorder. *Journal of Psychiatric Research, 29,* 95–110.

Wittig, Michele Andrisin, & Grant-Thompson, Sheila (1998). Practical approaches to resolving intergroup contact: The utility of Allport's conditions for predicting perceptions of improved racial attitudes and beliefs. *Journal of Social Issues, 54*(4), 795–812.

Witvliet, Charlotte vanOyen; Ludwig, Thomas E.; & Vander Laan, Kelly L. (2001). Granting forgiveness or harboring grudges: Implications for emotion, physiology, and health. *Psychological Science, 12,* 117–123.

Wood, James M.; Nezworski, M. Teresa; Lilienfeld, Scott O.; & Garb, Howard N. (2003). *What's wrong with the Rorschach?* San Francisco: Jossey-Bass.

Wood, Joanne V.; Michela, John L.; & Giordano, Caterina (2000). Downward comparison in everyday life: Reconciling self-enhancement models with the mood-cognition priming model. *Journal of Personality and Social Psychology, 79,* 563–579.

Wood, Wendy; Lundgren, Sharon; Ouellette, Judith A.; et al. (1994). Minority influence: A meta-analytic review of social influence processes. *Psychological Bulletin, 115,* 323–345.

Woodside, D. B.; Bulik, C. M.; Halmi, K. A.; et al. (2002). Personality, perfectionism and attitudes towards eating in parents of individuals with eating disorders. *International Journal of Eating Disorders, 31*(3), 290–299.

Woodward, K., & Richards, M. H. (2005). The parental investment model and minimum mate choice criteria in humans. *Behavioral Ecology, 16*(1), 57–61.

Woody, Erik Z., & Bowers, Kenneth S. (1994). A frontal assault on dissociated control. In S. J. Lynn & J. W. Rhue (Eds.), *Dissociation: Clinical, theoretical and research perspectives.* New York: Guilford.

Woody, Erik Z., & Sadler, Pamela (1998). On reintegrating dissociated theories: Comment on Kirsch and Lynn (1998). *Psychological Bulletin, 123,* 192–197.

Wooley, Susan; Wooley, O. Wayne; & Dyrenforth, Susan (1979). Theoretical, practical, and social issues in behavioral treatments of obesity. *Journal of Applied Behavior Analysis, 12,* 3–25.

Wulsin, L. R.; Vaillant, G. E.; & Wells, V. E. (1999). A systematic review of the mortality of depression. *Psychosomatic Medicine, 61,* 6–17.

Wurtman, Richard J. (1982). Nutrients that modify brain function. *Scientific American, 264*(4), 50–59.

Wurtman, Richard J., & Lieberman, Harris R. (Eds.) (1982–1983). Research strategies for assessing the behavioral effects of foods and nutrients. *Journal of Psychiatric Research, 17*(2) [whole issue].

Wygant, Steven A. (1997). Moral reasoning about real-life dilemmas: Paradox in research using the Defining Issues Test. *Personality and Social Psychology Bulletin, 23,* 1022–1033.

Yalom, Irvin D. (1989). *Love's executioner and other tales of psychotherapy.* New York: Basic Books.

Yapko, Michael (1994). *Suggestions of abuse: True and false memories of childhood sexual trauma.* New York: Simon & Schuster.

Yardley, Jim (2001, September 8). Despair plagued mother held in children's deaths. *The New York Times,* A16.

Yarmey, A. D. (1973). I recognize your face but I can't remember your name: Further evidence on the tip of the tongue phenomenon. *Memory & Cognition, 1*(3), 287–290.

Yazigi, R. A.; Odem, R. R.; & Polakoski, K. L. (1991, October 9). Demonstration of specific binding of cocaine to human spermatozoa. *Journal of the American Medical Association, 266*(14), 1956–1959.

Yik, M. S. M., & Russell, J. A. (1999). Interpretation of faces: a cross-cultural study of prediction from Fridlund's theory. *Cognition and Emotion, 13*(1), 93–104.

Young, Malcolm P., & Yamane, Shigeru (1992). Sparse population coding of faces in the inferotemporal cortex. *Science, 256,* 1327–1331.

Yzerbyt, Vincent Y.; Corneille, Olivier; Dumont, Muriel; & Hahn, Kirstin (2001). The dispositional inference strikes back: Situational focus and dispositional suppression in causal attribution. *Journal of Personality and Social Psychology, 81,* 365–376.

Zadra, A. L.; Donderi, D. C.; & Pihl, R. O. (1992). Efficacy of lucid dream induction for lucid and non-lucid dreamers. *Dreaming, 2*(2), 85–97.

Zadra, A. L.; O'Brien, S. A.; & Donderi, D. C. (1998). Dream content, dream recurrence and well-being: A replication with a younger sample. *Imagination, Cognition and Personality, 17*(4), 293–311.

Zahn-Waxler, Carolyn (1996). Environment, biology, and culture: Implications for adolescent development. *Developmental Psychology, 32,* 571–573.

Zajonc, Robert B. (1968). Attitudinal effects of mere exposure. *Journal of Personality and Social Psychology, 9,* Monograph Supplement 2, 1–27.

Zajonc, R. B. (2003). The power of words. Invited address presented to the American Psychological Society, Atlanta.

Zhang, Yiying; Hoon, M. A.; Chandrashekar, J.; et al. (2003). Coding of sweet, bitter, and umami tastes: different receptor cells sharing similar signaling pathways. *Cell, 112,* 293–301.

Zhang, Yiying; Proenca, Ricardo; Maffei, Margherita; et al. (1994). Positional cloning of the mouse obese gene and its human homologue. *Nature, 372*(6505), 425–432.

Zhu, L. X.; Sharma, S.; Stolina, M.; et al. (2000). Delta-9-tetrahydrocannabinol inhibits antitumor immunity by a CB2 receptor-mediated, cytokine-dependent pathway. *Journal of Immunology, 165,* 373–380.

Zilbergeld, Bernie (1992). *The new male sexuality.* New York: Bantam.

Zimbardo, Philip G. (1970). The human choice: Individuation, reason, and order versus deindividuation, impulse, and chaos. In W. J. Arnold & D. Levine (Eds.), *Nebraska Symposium on Motivation, 1969.* Lincoln, NE: University of Nebraska Press.

Zimbardo, Philip G., & Leippe, Michael R. (1991). *The psychology of attitude change and social influence.* New York: McGraw-Hill.

Zimmer, Lynn, & Morgan, John P. (1997). *Marijuana myths, marijuana fact: A review of the scientific evidence.* New York: Lindesmith Center.

Zinberg, Norman (1974). The search for rational approaches to heroin use. In P. G. Bourne (Ed.), *Addiction.* New York: Academic Press.

Zorrilla, L. T.; Cannon, T. D.; Kronenberg, S.; et al. (1997, December 15). Structural brain abnormalities in schizophrenia: A family study. *Biological Psychiatry, 42,* 1080–1086.

Zubieta, Jon-Kar; Heitzeg, M. M.; Smith, Y. R.; et al. (2003). COMT val158met genotype affects mu-opioid neurotransmitter responses to a pain stressor. *Science, 299,* 1240–1243.

Zurbriggen, Eileen L. (2000). Social motives and cognitive power-sex associations: Predictors of aggressive sexual behavior. *Journal of Personality and Social Psychology, 78,* 559–581.

NAME INDEX

SUBJECT INDEX

Abecedarian Project, 237
abnormal behaviour, 354
Aboriginal people
    alcoholism, 372
    and cultural norms, 403
    discrimination, effects of,
        236
    marginalization, 403
    self-government, 334
absolute thresholds, 177
academic/research psychologists,
    10t
accommodation, 81
accomplishment, 469–470
acculturation, 336–337
acetylcholine, 118
achievement motivation
    expectations, 470–471
    goals, 469–470
    opportunities to achieve,
        472–473
    Thematic Apperception Test
        (TAT), 468–472
    work, effects of, 471–473
    working conditions, 471–472
achievement tests, 228
action potential, 116–117
activation-synthesis theory,
    156–157
acupuncture, 209
addiction
    biological perspective,
        371–372
    and the brain, 372f
    causes, 374–375
    cultural practices, 373
    drug abuse, result of, 372
    reasons for taking drugs, 374
    social influences, 373
    total abstinence policies, 373
    withdrawal symptoms, 373
adjustment, 94
adolescence
    abnormalities in brain devel-
        opment, 381
    adjustment, 94
    behaviour problems, and psy-
        chotherapy, 405–406
    brain development, 94
    connection, 95
    cultural influences, 95
    described, 92
    gender differences, 92
    menarche, 93

peer groups, 59
physiology of, 92–94
psychology of, 94–95
puberty, 92, 93
separation, 95
sexual attraction, 93
turmoil, 94–95
adrenal glands, 119, 418
adrenal hormones, 119
adulthood
    ages, 96–97
    current approaches to adult
        development, 97
    early trauma, effect of,
        101–102
    emerging adulthood, 98
    Erikson's stages of develop-
        ment, 96–97
    menopause, 98, 99
    mental functioning changes,
        100f
    middle years of adulthood,
        98–99
    old age, 99–101
    stages, 96–97
    transitions of life, 97–99
agoraphobia, 363
agreeableness, 49
AIDS, 73
alarm phase, 426–427
alcohol
    see also addiction
    "alcoholism gene," 371–372
    as depressant, 164
    moderate social drinking,
        164
    during pregnancy, 73
alertness cycles, 147
algorithm, 217
allies, 335
allocation of responsibility, 322
Allport, Gordon, 48
alpha waves, 152
altered states of consciousness
    classification of drugs,
        163–165
    cultural rituals, 163
    depressants, 164
    opiates, 164
    psychedelic drugs, 164
    stimulants, 164
altruism, 334–335
Alzheimer's disease, 118
ambivalent attachment, 75

American Association of Marriage
    and Family Therapists,
    160
American Humanist Association,
    301
American Psychiatric Association,
    149, 354, 406
American Psychological
    Association, 406
American Sign Language, 241
amnesia
    childhood amnesia, 277–278
    defined, 275
    infantile amnesia, 277–278
    psychogenic amnesia, 275
    source amnesia, 252
    traumatic amnesia, 275–276
amok, 358
amphetamines, 164
amygdala, 125, 417
amyotrophic lateral sclerosis,
    108, 136
anal stage, 42
androgens, 120
anger, 405, 422, 441–442, 458
anima, 44
animals
    anthropodenial, 243
    anthropomorphism, 243
    cognition in, 239–243
    cognitive ethology, 240
    intelligence, 239–241
    and language, 241–242
animus, 44
anonymity, 332–334
anorexia nervosa, 466
antagonism, 49
antagonistic hostility, 433
anthropodenial, 243
anti-war protests, 316, 346–347
antidepressant drugs, 389
antipsychotic drugs, 388–389
antisocial personality disorder
    (APD)
    biological perspective, 370
    brain damage, 370
    causes, 369–370
    defined, 368
    and emotions, 369f
    impulse control problems,
        369
    symptoms, 368–369
anxiety disorders
    agoraphobia, 363

CREDITS

Photos and Cartoons

CHAPTER 8 *Page 250:* CP Photo/Aaron Harris; *p. 252:* (T) Frank Siteman/Stock Boston; *p. 253:* AP/Wide World Photos; *p. 255:* Sidney Harris; *p. 259:* Pearson Education/Modern Curriculum Press/Pearson Learning;*p. 262:* Ed Carlin/The Picture Cube; *p. 263:* Hank DeLespinasse/The Image Bank; *p. 264:* Jerry Jacka Photography; *p. 268:* Tony Freeman/Photo Edit; *p. 269:* © Jennifer K. Berman, Humerus Cartoons Syndicate; *p. 270:* Sidney Harris; *p. 272:* Sidney Harris; *p. 273:* The Image Works; *p. 275:* United Artists/The Kobal Collection; *p. 275:* © Bill Frymire/Masterfile; *p. 278:* Carolyn Rovee-Collier; *p. 280:* AP/Wide World Photos.

CHAPTER 9 *Page 284:* (L & R) CP Photo/Simon Hayter; *p. 292:* Cameramann/The Image Works; *p. 293:* Michael Newman/Photo Edit; *p. 300:* (L) Stephen Ferry/Liaison/Getty Images, (R) Guide Horse Foundation; *p. 302:* Peter Glass/Peter Glass Photography; *p. 304:* (T) D. Young-Wolff/Photo Edit, Brian Gable, Cartoonists & Writers Syndicate/cartoonweb.com; *p. 308:* Adam Woolfitt; *p. 309:* Lon C. Diehl/Photo Edit.

CHAPTER 10 *Page 316:* Vince Talotta/Toronto Star; *p. 318:* Giuliano Colliva/Liaison/Getty Images; *p. 321:* David Frazier/Photo Edit; *p. 322:* David Harvey/National Geographic Image Collection; *p. 327:* Amy Etra/PhotoEdit; *p. 328:* A. Ramey/Photo Edit; *p. 329:* The Sankei Shimbun; *p. 331:* (L) Magnum Photos, Inc., (R) AP/Wide World Photos; *p. 332:* Sidney Harris; *p. 333:* (L) CP Photo/Chuck Stoody, (R) Philip G. Zimbardo, Inc.; *p. 335:* CP Photo/The Toronto Star-Rick Madonik; *p. 337:* (L) Gunter Marx Photography/CORBIS, (M) Joel Gordon/Joel Gordon Photography, (R) CP Photo; *p. 338:* Penny Tweedie/Woodfin Camp & Associates; *p. 341:* (L) AP/Wide World Photos, (R) Copley News Service; *p. 342:* (TL) National Archives and Records Administration, (TR) Tak Toyota/Library and Archives Canada/C-046350, (B) CP Photo/AP Photo/Patrick Gardin; *p. 343:* (TL) Library of Congress, (TR) Glenbow Archives NA-3170-3, (BL) Bettman/CORBIS, (BR) Archives of Ontario/John Boyd/C7-3, 21329; *p. 345:* A. Ramey/Photo Edit; *p. 347:* (L) Dinko/UNICEF, (R) UNICEF.

CHAPTER 11 *Page 352:* CP Photo/MarkAllen; *p. 354:* Art Wolfe/Stone/Getty Images; *p. 357:* (T) Detail from original reprinted by permission. © The New Yorker Collection 2001 Roz Chast from cartoonbank.com. All rights reserved., (B) Sophia Smith Collection, Smith College; *p. 358:* (T) Yoav Levy/Phototake NYC; *p. 359:* Bettmann/CORBIS; *p. 361:* David Turnley/Bettman/CORBIS; *p. 363:* Michael Lutsky/Washington Post Writers Group; *p. 365:* Retna Ltd. USA; *p. 368:* COR-BIS-Bettmann. Hand coloured for Scott Foresman-Addision Wesley Longman by Cheryl Kucharzak; *p. 370:* (L) AP/Wide World Photos (R) Don Camp/Liaison/Getty Images; *p. 373:* Leland Bobbe/Stone/Getty Images; *p. 374:* Matrix International, Inc.; *p. 377:* Photofest/Jagarts; *p. 379:* Al Vercoutere, Malibu, CA.

CHAPTER 12 *Page 386:* Al Harvey/www.slidefarm.com; *p. 388:* AP/Wide World Photos; *p. 393:* (L) Photo Researchers, Inc., (R) George Ruhe/New York Times Pictures; *p. 394:* Sidney Harris; *p. 395:* New York Times Pictures; *p. 396:* Mary Levin/University of Washington Photography; *p. 398:* Michael Newman/Photo Edit; *p. 399:*(L & R) Alan Entin, Ph.D.; *p. 403:* Sidney Harris; *p. 404:* Cindy Charles/Photo Edit; *p. 412:* Michael Schumann/Corbis/SABA Press Photos, Inc.

CHAPTER 13 *Page 412:* CP Photo/Chuck Stoody; *p. 415:* (T from left to R) Barry Lewis-Network/Matrix International, Inc., Erika Stone, Laura Dwight Photography, Eric Gay/AP/Wide World Photos, Reuters/Fred Prouser/Getty Images Inc. - Hulton Archive Photos, AP/Wide World Photos, Sovfoto/Eastfoto; *p. 416:* (T) Heidi S. Mario, (B) CP Photo/Jeff McIntosh; *p. 418:* Dion Ogust/The Image Works; *p. 420:* (T) Duomo Photography Incorporated, (B) Darama/CORBIS; *p. 422:* Stock Boston; *p. 423:* Magnum Photos, Inc.; *p. 429:* (T) © Charles Barsotti from cartoonbank.com. All rights reserved., (BL) Janice Rubin, (BR) Joel Gordon Photography; *p. 426:* R. Wahlstrom/Image Bank/Getty Images; *p. 428:* Juergen Berger, Max-Planck Institute/Science Photo Library/Photo Researchers, Inc.; *p. 431:* (L & R) The Image Works; *p. 434:* Barbara Singer/Photonica; *p. 436:* Amana America, Inc.; *p. 437:* Mary Hancock; *p. 438:* Universal Press Syndicate; *p. 439:* (L) Stone/Getty Images, (R) NBC Photo; *p. 442:* BIZARRO © Dan Piraro. Reprinted with permission of Universal Press Syndicate. All rights reserved.

CHAPTER 14 *Page 446:* (T) Ann Johansson, (B) Dick Loek/Toronto Star; *p. 447:* CP Photo/AP Photo/Mark J. Terrill; *p. 451:* Magnum Photos, Inc.; *p. 452:* Stone/Getty Images; *p. 453:* Kinsey Institute for Research - Sex, Gender and Reproduction; *p. 454:* © The New Yorker Collection 1995 Donald Reilly from cartoonbank.com. All rights reserved.; *p. 455:* Magnum Photos, Inc.; *p. 456:* Stone/Getty Images; *p. 457:* (L) Liaison/Getty Images, (R) Carol Ford/Stone/Getty Images; *p. 458:* Rachel Epstein/Photo Edit; *p. 462:* (T) Les Van/Unicorn Stock Photos, (BL) John Eastcott/Yva Momatiuk/Woodfin Camp & Associates, (BR) Cassy Cohen/Photo Edit; *p. 461:* Jiim Young/Reuters /Landov; *p. 463:* (L) Dennis Stock/Magnum Photos, Inc., (R) Photo Researchers, Inc; *p. 464:* Amgen Inc.; *p. 466:* (L to R) CinemaPhoto/CORBIS, Michael Caulfield/AP/Wide World Photos, Phil McCarten/Photo Edit, Frank Siteman/Stock Boston; *p. 467:* William Thompson/Index Stock Imagery, Inc.; *p. 468:* (L to R) Henghameh Fahimi/AFP/Getty Images, © Bettmann/CORBIS, © Bettmann/CORBIS, Radu Sigheti/Reuters /Landov; *p. 469:* (L to R) © Relke Christopher/CORBIS Sygma, © Beth A. Keiser/CORBIS, AFP/Getty Images, © Bettmann/CORBIS; *p. 472:* Index Stock Imagery, Inc.

Figures and Tables

CHAPTER 1 *Page 15:* Figure 1.1 (T) Jose L. Pelaez/Corbis/Stock Market, (B) Unicorn Stock Photos; *p. 23:* Figure 1.2 adapted from *Understanding Statistics, An Information Introduction For the Behavioral Sciences*, 1st edition by Wright. © 1976. Reprinted with permission of Wadsworth, a division of Thomson Learning. www.thomsonrights.com. Fax 800-730-2215.

CHAPTER 2 *Page 50:* Costa et al., 1999; *p. 60:* Table 2.2 from Harry C. Triandis, "The psychological measurement of cultural syndrome," *American Psychologist, 51,* 407–415, 1996. Copyright © 1996 by the American Psychological Association. Adapted with permission; *pp. 66–67:* from "The P. T. Barnum Effect" by C. R. Snyder, *Psychology Today,* March 1975. Reprinted with permission from Psychology Today Magazine. Copyright © 1975 Sussex Publishers, Inc.

CHAPTER 3 *Page 74:* from Helen Bee, *The Developing Child.* Copyright © 1989 by Harper & Row, Publishers, Inc. Reprinted by permission of Allyn & Bacon; *p. 75:* Figure 3.1 from "More Infants Are Sleeping with Their Parents," by Donald McNeil, Jr. *New York Times,* January 15th, 2003, Harlow Primate Laboratory, University of Wisconsin; *p. 82:* Figure 3.2 Laura Dwight Photography; *p. 83:* Figure 3.3 from Rene Baillargeon, "How do infants learn about the physical world" *Current Directions in Psychological Science, Vol. 5* (1994). Reprinted by permission of Blackwell Publishers; *p. 100:* Figure 3.4 from Rene Baillargeon, "How do infants learn about the physical world," *Current Directions in Psychology, Vol. 5* (1994). Reprinted by permission of Blackwell Publishers.

CHAPTER 4 *Page 116:* Figure 4.6 Orietta Agostoni from *ABC's of the Human Min*d, Reader's Digest, 1990, p. 64; *p. 122:* Figure 4.8 (L) Photo Researchers, Inc., (R) Dr. Michael E. Phelps, Figure 4.9 Howard Sochurek, Inc.; *p. 128:* Figure 4.13 (L) The Francis A. Countway Library of Medicine, (R) Hanna Damasio, M.D.; *p. 134:* Figure 4.16 Michael D. Phillips/Radiology Society of North America.

CHAPTER 5 *Page 149:* Figure 5.1 McFarlane, Martin & Williams, 1988.

CHAPTER 6 *Page 184:* Table 6.1, Reprinted with permission from the American Academy of Otolaryngology–Head and Neck Surgery, Washington, DC.; *p.188:* Figure 6.5 M.C. Escher's "Circle Limit IV." Copyright © 2003 Cordon Art B.V. - Baarn-Holland. All rights reserved; *p. 197:* Figure 6.10 Mozell et al., 1969.

CHAPTER 7 *Page 218:* Table 7.1 from Kathleen Galotti, "Two kinds of reasoning." *Psychological Bulletin, 105,* 331–351, Table 1, p. 335, 1989. Copyright © 1989 by the American Psychological Association. Adapted with permission; *pp. 220–221:* from Patricia King and Karen Kitchener, *Developing Reflexive Judgment: Understanding and Promoting Intellectual Growth and Critical Thinking in Adolescents and Adults.* Copyright © 1994 by Jossey-Bass, Inc., Publishers. Reprinted by permission of John Wiley & Sons, Inc.; *p. 224:* 9-dot problem from *Conceptual Blockbusting: A Guide to Better Ideas* by James L. Adams. Copyright © 1986 by Perseus Books Group. Reproduced with permission of Perseus Books Group in the format textbook via Copyright Clearance Center. Electronic rights by permission of Perseus Books Group; *p. 229:* Table 7.2, Copyright © 1972 by The Riverside Publishing

Company. Reproduced from *Stanford Binet Intelligence Scale, Form L-M,* Manual for 3rd Revision, Part 2, pp. 68–111 by Lewis M. Terman and Maude A. Merrill, with permission of the publisher. All rights reserved; *p. 230:* Figure 7.3 Simulated items similar to those in the Weschler Intelligence Scales for Adults and Children. Copyright 1959, 1955, 1974, 1981, 1991 by The Psychological Corp., a Harcourt Assessment Company. Reproduced by permission. All rights reserved; *p. 235:* Figure 7.4 Bouchard & McGue, 1981; *p. 237:* Figure 7.6 Adapted from J. Horgan, "Get Smart: Take a Test: A Long Term Rise in IQ Scores Baffles Intelligence Experts." *Scientific American,* November, 1995, p. 14. Reprinted by permission of Dimitry Schildlovsky; *p. 245:* from Mednick, Sarnoff. A. (1962). The associative basis of the creative process. *Psychological Review, 69,* 220–232.

CHAPTER 8 *Page 256:* Figure 8.1 from "Serial Position Effect," in "Memory" by Elizabeth Loftus, p. 25. Copyright © 1980 by Addison Wesley Publishing. Reprinted by permission; *p. 257:* Figure 8.2 from Gaven, Sena; Wood, James M.; Malpass, Roy S.; Shaw, John S. III (1998). "More Than Suggestion: The Effect of Interviewing Techniques" from the McMartin Preschool Case. *Journal of Applied Psychology, 83,* pp. 347–359. Copyright © 1998 by the American Psychological Association. Adapted with permission; *p. 272:* Figure 8.7 "I Remember It Well," from "Two Kinds of Forgetting Curves," by M. Linton. *Psychology Today,* Vol. 13:2, July 1979. Reprinted with permission from Psychology Today Magazine. Copyright © 1979 Sussex Publishers, Inc.

CHAPTER 9 *Page 286:* Figure 9.1a The Granger Collection; *p. 288:* Figure 9.2 "Acquisition and Extinction of a Salivary Response" from *Conditioned Reflexes* by I.P. Pavlov. Copyright © 1927. Reprinted by permission of Oxford University Press; *p. 297:* Figure 9.5b Joe McNally Photography; *p. 306:* Figure 9.6 "Intrinsic Motivation: Turning Play into Work," by D. Greene, M.R. Lepper. *Psychology Today,* September 1974. Reprinted with permission from Psychology Today Magazine. Copyright © 1974 Sussex Publishers, Inc.; *p. 307:* Figure 9.7 From "Introduction and Removal of Reward and Maze Performance in Rats," by E.C. Tolman and C.H. Honzik from *Psychology, 4* (1930). University of California Publications.

CHAPTER 10 *Page 319:* Figure 10.1 Alexandra Milgram.

CHAPTER 11 *Page 369:* Figure 11.2 from "Antisocial Personality Disorder," by Robert Hare. *Journal of Psychology, F 1A,* 1985. Reprinted by permission of the Helen Dwight Reid Educational Foundation. Published by Heldref Publications; *p. 372:* Figure 11.3 Brookhaven National Laboratory; *p. 380:* Figure 11.4 based on Gottesman, 1991, Figure 11.5 Howard Sochurek, Inc.

CHAPTER 12 *Page 392:* Figure 12.1 Dr. Jeffrey M. Schwartz.

CHAPTER 13 *Page 417:* from Chimeric faces, figure 5.5, p. 146 in Keith Oatley and Jennifer J. Jenkins, *Understanding Emotions,* 1996. Reproduced by permission of Blackwell Publishers; *p. 424:* Figure 13.2 Frank

J. Bernieri, PhD; *p. 429:* Figure 13.3 "Stress and the Cold" *The New York Times Health*, May 12, 1998. Adapted with permission, (photo) Dion Ogust/The Image Works; *p. 433:* Figure 13.4 Bill Varie/CORBIS; *p. 436:* Figure 13.6 Gina Ferazzi/Los Angeles Times Syndicate; *p. 437:* Figure 13.7 (graph) from "Influence of physical fitness in determining the impact of stressful life events on physical and psychological health," by David L. Roth and Davis S. Holmes. *Psychosomatic Medicine*, 47, pp. 167–173. Reprinted by permission of Lippincott, Williams & Wilkins, (photo) Ken Fisher/Stone/ Getty Images.

CHAPTER 14 *Page 471:* Figure 14.2 (photo) Dan Bosler/Stone/Getty Images, (graph) from Muller, Claudia M. and Dweck, Carol S. (1998). Praise for intelligence can undermine children's motivation and performance. *Journal of Personality and Social Psychology, 75,* 33–52. Copyright © 1998 by the American Psychological Association. Reprinted with permission.